The Oxford Handbook of Traumatic Stress Disorders

OXFORD LIBRARY OF PSYCHOLOGY

Editor in Chief PETER E. NATHAN

The Oxford Handbook of Traumatic Stress Disorders

Edited by

J. Gayle Beck

Denise M. Sloan

OXFORD
UNIVERSITY PRESS

OXFORD
UNIVERSITY PRESS

Oxford University Press, Inc., publishes works that further
Oxford University's objective of excellence in
research, scholarship, and education.

Oxford New York
Auckland Cape Town Dar es Salaam Hong Kong Karachi
Kuala Lumpur Madrid Melbourne Mexico City Nairobi
New Delhi Shanghai Taipei Toronto

With offices in
Argentina Austria Brazil Chile Czech Republic France Greece
Guatemala Hungary Italy Japan Poland Portugal Singapore
South Korea Switzerland Thailand Turkey Ukraine Vietnam

Published by Oxford University Press, Inc.
198 Madison Avenue, New York, New York 10016
www.oup.com

Library of Congress Cataloging-in-Publication Data
The Oxford handbook of traumatic stress disorders / edited by J. Gayle Beck, Denise M. Sloan.
p. cm. — (Oxford Library of psychology)
ISBN-13: 978-0-19-539906-6 (acid-free paper)
ISBN-10: 0-19-539906-4 (acid-free paper)
1. Post-traumatic stress disorder. 2. Post-traumatic stress disorder—Treatment.
I. Beck, J. Gayle. II. Sloan, Denise M.
RC552.P67O94 2012
616.85'21—dc23
2011031287

9 8 7 6 5 4 3 2 1
Printed in the United States of America
on acid-free paper

To Bruce, for 'getting it' (JGB)
To Brian and Colin for their love and support (DMS)
and
To all the trauma survivors who have helped us learn
about traumatic stress disorders (JGB and DMS)

CONTENTS

Oxford Library of Psychology ix

About the Editors xi

Contributors xiii

Table of Contents xix

Chapters 1–532

Index 533

OXFORD LIBRARY OF PSYCHOLOGY

The *Oxford Library of Psychology*, a landmark series of handbooks, is published by Oxford University Press, one of the world's oldest and most highly respected publishers, with a tradition of publishing significant books in psychology. The ambitious goal of the *Oxford Library of Psychology* is nothing less than to span a vibrant, wide-ranging field and, in so doing, to fill a clear market need.

Encompassing a comprehensive set of handbooks, organized hierarchically, the *Library* incorporates volumes at different levels, each designed to meet a distinct need. At one level are a set of handbooks designed broadly to survey the major subfields of psychology; at another are numerous handbooks that cover important current focal research and scholarly areas of psychology in depth and detail. Planned as a reflection of the dynamism of psychology, the *Library* will grow and expand as psychology itself develops, thereby highlighting significant new research that will impact on the field. Adding to its accessibility and ease of use, the *Library* will be published in print and, later on, electronically.

The *Library* surveys psychology's principal subfields with a set of handbooks that capture the current status and future prospects of those major subdisciplines. This initial set includes handbooks of social and personality psychology, clinical psychology, counseling psychology, school psychology, educational psychology, industrial and organizational psychology, cognitive psychology, cognitive neuroscience, methods and measurements, history, neuropsychology, personality assessment, developmental psychology, and more. Each handbook undertakes to review one of psychology's major subdisciplines with breadth, comprehensiveness, and exemplary scholarship. In addition to these broadly-conceived volumes, the *Library* also includes a large number of handbooks designed to explore in depth more specialized areas of scholarship and research, such as stress, health and coping, anxiety and related disorders, cognitive development, or child and adolescent assessment. In contrast to the broad coverage of the subfield handbooks, each of these latter volumes focuses on an especially productive, more highly focused line of scholarship and research. Whether at the broadest or most specific level, however, all of the *Library* handbooks offer synthetic coverage that reviews and evaluates the relevant past and present research and anticipates research in the future. Each handbook in the *Library* includes introductory and concluding chapters written by its editor to provide a roadmap to the handbook's table of contents and to offer informed anticipations of significant future developments in that field.

An undertaking of this scope calls for handbook editors and chapter authors who are established scholars in the areas about which they write. Many of the nation's and world's most productive and best-respected psychologists have agreed to edit *Library* handbooks or write authoritative chapters in their areas of expertise.

For whom has the *Oxford Library of Psychology* been written? Because of its breadth, depth, and accessibility, the *Library* serves a diverse audience, including graduate students in psychology and their faculty mentors, scholars, researchers, and practitioners in psychology and related fields. Each will find in the *Library* the information they seek on the subfield or focal area of psychology in which they work or are interested.

Befitting its commitment to accessibility, each handbook includes a comprehensive index, as well as extensive references to help guide research. And because the *Library* was designed from its inception as an online as well as a print resource, its structure and contents will be readily and rationally searchable online. Further, once the *Library* is released online, the handbooks will be regularly and thoroughly updated.

In summary, the *Oxford Library of Psychology* will grow organically to provide a thoroughly informed perspective on the field of psychology, one that reflects both psychology's dynamism and its increasing interdisciplinarity. Once published electronically, the *Library* is also destined to become a uniquely valuable interactive tool, with extended search and browsing capabilities. As you begin to consult this handbook, we sincerely hope you will share our enthusiasm for the more than 500-year tradition of Oxford University Press for excellence, innovation, and quality, as exemplified by the *Oxford Library of Psychology*.

Peter E. Nathan
Editor-in-Chief
Oxford Library of Psychology

ABOUT THE EDITORS

J. Gayle Beck, Ph.D., joined the Department of Psychology at the University of Memphis in 2008 as the Lillian and Morrie Moss Chair of Excellence. Prior to this position, she served as Professor and Associate Chair at University at Buffalo–SUNY. During her doctoral training at University at Albany–SUNY, she conducted research that helped to reformulate the conceptualization of anxiety and anxiety-based disorders. Following completion of a clinical internship at UMDNJ-Rutgers Medical School, Dr. Beck joined the faculty at the University of Houston, then University at Buffalo, and most recently, University of Memphis. Dr. Beck's current research focus is the mental health consequences of intimate partner violence. She heads the Athena Project at the University of Memphis, a research clinic providing free assessment and treatment services to women who have experienced domestic violence. Dr. Beck is the President of the Society of Clinical Psychology (Division 12) of the American Psychological Association and Past-President of the Association of Behavioral and Cognitive Therapy. Her career has been guided by the belief that empirically-grounded treatments offer the possibility to reduce emotional problems.

Denise M. Sloan, Ph.D., is an Associate Director, Education, Behavioral Science Division, National Center for PTSD, and an Associate Professor of Psychiatry, Boston University School of Medicine. She received her B.A. from the State University of New York at Stony Brook and her M.A. and Ph.D. from Case Western Reserve University. Her research expertise is in psychosocial treatments for PTSD and emotional impairments in depression and anxiety disorders. She has received funding from her work from several organizations, including the National Institute for Mental Health and the Department of Defense. Dr. Sloan is a member of the editorial board for the journals *Behavior Therapy, Psychosomatic Medicine, Journal of Clinical Psychology,* and *Journal for Contemporary Psychotherapy.*

CONTRIBUTORS

Ron Acierno
Department of Psychiatry and Behavioral Sciences
Medical University of South Carolina
Charleston, SC

Ananda B. Amstadter
Department of Psychiatry
Virginia Commonwealth University School of Medicine
Virginia Institute for Psychiatric and Behavioral Genetics

Teresa M. Au
National Center for PTSD
VA Boston Healthcare System
Boston University
Boston, MA

Heather E. Baldwin
Center for Refugee Trauma and Resilience
Children's Hospital Boston
Boston, MA

Tali Manber Ball
Department of Psychiatry
University of California, San Diego
La Jolla, CA

Erin R. Barnett
Executive Division, National Center for Posttraumatic Stress Disorder
VA Medical Center
White River Junction VT
And
Department of Psychiatry
Dartmouth Medical School
Hanover, NH

J. Gayle Beck
Department of Psychology
University of Memphis
Memphis, TN

Aartjan T. F. Beekman
VU University Amsterdam
Amsterdam, The Netherlands

Quinn M. Biggs
Center for the Study of Traumatic Stress
Uniformed Services University of the Health Sciences
Bethesda, MD

Tatyana Biyanova
School of Medicine
Yale University
New Haven, CT

Michelle J. Bovin
Department of Psychology
Temple University
Philadelphia, PA

Naomi Breslau
College of Human Medicine
Michigan State University
East Lansing, MI

Richard A. Bryant
School of Psychology
University of New South Wales
Sydney, Australia

Melissa J. Brymer
Department of Psychiatry and Biobehavioral Sciences
UCLA/Duke University National Center for Child Traumatic Stress
University of California, Los Angeles
Los Angeles, CA

Kathleen M. Chard
Cincinnati VA Medical Center
University of Cincinnati School of Medicine
Cincinnati, OH

Joan M. Cook
Yale School of Medicine
National Center for PTSD
New Haven, CT

Jesse R. Cougle
Department of Psychology
Florida State University
Tallahassee, FL

Esther Deblinger
School of Osteopathic Medicine
University of Medicine and Dentistry of New Jersey
Child Abuse Research Education and Service (CARES) Institute
Newark, NJ

Rachel Dekel
The Louis and Gabi Weisfeld School of Social Work
Bar Ilan University
Ramat-Gan, Israel

Douglas L. Delahanty
Department of Emergency Medicine
Northeastern Ohio Universities College of Medicine (NEOUCOM)
Department of Psychology
Kent State University
Kent, OH

Eileen M. Delaney
National Center for PTSD
VA Boston Healthcare System
Boston, MA

Alexandra De Young
Centre of National Research on Disability and Rehabilitation
School of Medicine
School of Psychology
University of Queensland
Herston, Australia

Belinda Dow
Centre of National Research on Disability and Rehabilitation
School of Medicine
School of Psychology
University of Queensland
Herston, Australia

Boris Drožđek
Psychotrauma Centrum Zuid Nederland/ Reinier van Arkel groep
Hertogenbosch, The Netherlands

Anke Ehlers
Department of Experimental Psychology
University of Oxford
Oxford, UK

Thomas Ehring
Department of Clinical Psychology
University of Amsterdam
Amsterdam, The Netherlands

B. Heidi Ellis
Children's Hospital Boston
Center for Refugee Trauma and Resilience
Boston, MA

Diane L. Elmore
American Psychological Association
Washington, DC

Lisa S. Elwood
School of Psychological Sciences
University of Indianapolis
Indianapolis, IN

Edna B. Foa
Center for the Treatment and Study of Anxiety
University of Pennsylvania
Philadelphia, PA

Steffany J. Fredman
VA National Center for PTSD, Women's Health Sciences Division
Boston University School of Medicine
Boston, MA

Matthew J. Friedman
National Center for PTSD
VA Medical Center
White River Junction, VT

Carol S. Fullerton
Center for the Study of Traumatic Stress
Uniformed Services University of the Health Sciences
Bethesda, MD

Matthew Goldenberg
ASD Workgroup
Center for the Study of Traumatic Stress
Uniformed Services University of the Health Sciences
Bethesda, MD

Christine Gray
ASD Workgroup
Center for the Study of Traumatic Stress
Uniformed Services University of the Health Sciences
Bethesda, MD

Christian Grillon
National Institute of Mental Health
Mood and Anxiety Disorders Program
Bethesda, MD
Jennifer M. Guimond
Center for the Study of Traumatic Stress
Uniformed Services University of the Health Sciences
Bethesda, MD
Jessica L. Hamblen
Executive Division, National Center for Posttraumatic Stress Disorder
VA Medical Center
White River Junction, VT
And
Department of Psychiatry, Dartmouth Medical School
Hanover, NH
Whitney M. Herge
Department of Psychology
University of Miami
Miami, FL
Barbara A. Hermann
Executive Division, National Center for Posttraumatic Stress Disorder
VA Medical Center
White River Junction, VT
And
Department of Psychiatry, Dartmouth Medical School
Hanover, NH
Devon E. Hinton
Massachusetts General Hospital
Harvard Medical School
Department of Psychiatry
Boston, MA
Darren W. Holowka
National Center for PTSD
VA Boston Healthcare System
Boston University School of Medicine
Boston, MA
Lee Hyer
Mercer School of Medicine
Macon, GA
Terence M. Keane
VA Boston Healthcare System
Boston University School of Medicine
Boston, MA
Justin Kenardy
Centre of National Research on Disability and Rehabilitation
School of Medicine
School of Psychology
University of Queensland
Herston, Australia
Dean G. Kilpatrick
National Crime Victims Research and Treatment Center
Medical University of South Carolina
Charleston, SC
Lynda A. King
VA Boston Healthcare System
Boston University School of Medicine
Boston, MA
Birgit Kleim
University of Zurich
Zurich, Switzerland
Annette M. La Greca
Department of Psychology
University of Miami
Miami, FL
Shmuel Lissek
Department of Psychology
University of Minnesota-Twin Cities
Minneapolis, MN
Brett T. Litz
National Center for PTSD
VA Boston Healthcare System
Boston University School of Medicine
Boston, MA
Megan C. Kearns
School of Medicine
Emory University
Atlanta, GA
Karestan C. Koenen
Department of Epidemiology
Columbia University Mailman School of Public Health
Weili Lu
Department of Psychiatric Rehabilitation and Counseling Professions
University of Medicine and Dentistry of New Jersey
Newark, NJ

Alexandra Macdonald
VA National Center for PTSD
Behavioral Science Division
Boston University School of Medicine
Boston, MA
Sonja March
Centre of National Research on Disability and Rehabilitation School of Medicine
University of Queensland
Herston, Australia
Brian P. Marx
National Center for PTSD
VA Boston Healthcare System
Boston University School of Medicine
Boston, MA
James E. McCarroll
ASD Workgroup
Center for the Study of Traumatic Stress Uniformed Services University of the Health Sciences
Bethesda, MD
Mark W. Miller
VA Boston Healthcare System
Boston University School of Medicine
Boston, MA
Candice M. Monson
Ryerson University
Toronto, Canada
And
VA National Center for PTSD, Women's Health Sciences Division
Boston University School of Medicine Boston, MA
Kim T. Mueser
Departments of Psychiatry and Community and Family Medicine
Dartmouth Medical School
Hanover, NH
Nisha Nayak
Center for the Treatment and Study of Anxiety
University of Pennsylvania
Philadelphia, PA
Felicia Neubauer
Child Abuse Research Education and Service (CARES) Institute
School of Osteopathic Medicine
University of Medicine and Dentistry of New Jersey
Newark, NJ
Angela Nickerson
Massachusetts General Hospital
Harvard Medical School,
Boston, MA
Nicole R. Nugent
Department of Psychiatry and Human Behavior
Warren Alpert Medical School of Brown University
Maria L. Pacella
Department of Psychology
Kent State University
Kent, OH
Michelle Pelcovitz
Traumatic Stress Studies Division
Mount Sinai School of Medicine
New York, NY
Anica P. Pless
VA Boston Healthcare System
Boston, MA
Elisabeth Pollio
University of Medicine and Dentistry of NJ
School of Osteopathic Medicine
Child Abuse Research Education and Service (CARES) Institute
Newark, NJ
Mark B. Powers
Center for the Treatment and Study of Anxiety
University of Pennsylvania
Philadelphia, PA
Laura Pratchett
Traumatic Stress Studies Division
James J. Peters VA Medical Center
Bronx, NY
Robert S. Pynoos
UCLA/Duke National Center for Child Traumatic Stress
Department of Psychiatry and Biobehavioral Sciences
University of California, Los Angeles
Los Angeles, CA
Dori Reissman
ASD Workgroup
Center for the Study of Traumatic Stress Uniformed Services University of the Health Sciences
Bethesda, MD

Patricia A. Resick
Women's Health Sciences Division
National Center for PTSD
VA Boston Healthcare System and Boston University School of Medicine
Boston, MA

Heidi Resnick
National Crime Victims Research and Treatment Center
Medical University of South Carolina
Charleston, SC

Barbara Olasov Rothbaum
School of Medicine
Emory University
Atlanta, GA

Sophie Rubin
Department of Psychology
Western Michigan University
Kalamazoo, MI

Josef I. Ruzek
National Center for PTSD
VA Palo Alto Health Care System
Pacific Graduate School of Psychology
Stanford University
Palo Alto, CA

Patcho Santiago
ASD Workgroup
Center for the Study of Traumatic Stress
Uniformed Services University of the Health Sciences
Bethesda, MD

Paula P. Schnurr
Executive Division, National Center for Posttraumatic Stress Disorder,
VA Medical Center
White River Junction, VT
And
Department of Psychiatry, Dartmouth Medical School, Hanover, NH

Jennifer L. Schuster
National Center for PTSD–Women Health Sciences Division
VA Boston Healthcare System
Boston, MA

Caroline Silva
National Center for PTSD
VA Boston Healthcare System
Boston, MA

Denise M. Sloan
National Center for PTSD, VA Boston Healthcare System
Boston University School of Medicine
Boston, MA

C. Richard Spates
Department of Psychology
Western Michigan University
Kalamazoo, MI

Avron Spiro, III
Massachusetts Veterans Epidemiology Research and Information Center
VA Boston Healthcare System
Boston University School of Public Health
Boston, MA

Murray B. Stein
Department of Psychiatry
San Diego State University
San Diego, CA

Alan M. Steinberg
UCLA/Duke National Center for Child Traumatic Stress, Department of Psychiatry and Biobehavioral Sciences, University of California, Los Angeles, CA

Martha Strachan
Department of Psychiatry
Medical University of South Carolina
Charleston, SC

Cortney J. Taylor
Department of Psychology
University of Miami
Miami, FL

Silvana Turkovic
Trauma Consultants Ltd.
Department of Psychology
Cleveland State University
Cleveland, OH

Mary P. Tyler
Center for the Study of Traumatic Stress
Uniformed Services University of the Health Sciences
Bethesda, MD

Monica Uddin
Center for Molecular Medicine and Genetics
Department of Psychiatry & Behavioral Neurosciences
Wayne State University School of Medicine
Detroit, MI

Robert J. Ursano
Center for the Study of Traumatic Stress
Uniformed Services University of the Health Sciences
Bethesda, MD

Willeke H. van Zelst
University Medical Centre Groningen
Groningen, The Netherlands

Patricia J. Watson
UCLA/Duke National Center for Child Traumatic Stress
Department of Psychiatry and Biobehavioral Sciences University of California, Los Angeles
Los Angeles, CA
And
National Center for PTSD,
Department of Psychiatry
Dartmouth Medical School
Hanover, NH

Frank W. Weathers
Department of Psychology
Auburn University
Auburn, AL

John P. Wilson
Department of Psychology
Cleveland State University
Cleveland, OH

Rachel Yehuda
Mount Sinai School of Medicine
Traumatic Stress Studies Division
James J. Peters VA Medical Center
New York, NY

Catherine A. Yeager
Einsenhower General Medical Center
Augusta, GA

CONTENTS

Part One • Introduction

1. Traumatic Stress Disorders: Historical Context and Current Focus 3
   J. Gayle Beck and *Denise M. Sloan*

Part Two • Classification and Phenomenology

2. Defining Traumatic Events: Research Findings and Controversies 11
   Jesse R. Cougle, Dean G. Kilpatrick, and *Heidi Resnick*
3. Classification of Acute Stress Disorder 28
   Maria L. Pacella and *Douglas L. Delahanty*
4. Classification of Posttraumatic Stress Disorder 39
   Tali Manber Ball and *Murray B. Stein*
5. Future of Classification in Posttraumatic Stress Disorder 54
   Terence M. Keane and *Mark W. Miller*

Part Three • Epidemiology and Special Populations

6. The Epidemiology of Acute Stress Disorder and Other Early Responses to Trauma in Adults 69
   Quinn M. Biggs, Jennifer M. Guimond, Carol S. Fullerton, Robert J. Ursano, and *ASD Workgroup (Christine Gray, Matthew Goldenberg, Dori Reissman, James E. McCarroll, Patcho Santiago, Mary P. Tyler)*
7. Epidemiology of Posttraumatic Stress Disorder in Adults 84
   Naomi Breslau
8. Traumatic Stress Disorders in Children and Adolescents 98
   Annette M. La Greca, Cortney J. Taylor, and *Whitney M. Herge*
9. Traumatic Stress in Older Adults 119
   Joan M. Cook, Tatyana Biyanova, and *Diane L. Elmore*
10. Traumatic Stress in Special Populations 128
   Kim T. Mueser and *Weili Lu*

Part Four • Contributions from Theory

11. Genetics and Genomics of Posttraumatic Stress Disorder 143
   Monica Uddin, Ananda B. Amstadter, Nicole R. Nugent, and *Karestan C. Koenen*
12. Biological Contributions to PTSD: Differentiating Normative from Pathological Response 159
   Rachel Yehuda, Laura Pratchett, and *Michelle Pelcovitz*

13. Learning Models of PTSD 175
Shmuel Lissek and *Christian Grillon*
14. Information Processing in Posttraumatic Stress Disorder 191
Anke Ehlers, Thomas Ehring, and *Birgit Kleim*
15. Family Models of Posttraumatic Stress Disorder 219
Candice M. Monson, Steffany J. Fredman, Rachel Dekel, and *Alexandra Macdonald*

Part Five • Assessment
16. Assessing PTSD Symptoms 235
Michelle J. Bovin and *Frank W. Weathers*
17. Assessing Acute Traumatic Stress Symptoms 250
Richard A. Bryant
18. Assessing Trauma-related Symptoms in Children and Adolescents 262
Sonja March, Alexandra De Young, Belinda Dow, and *Justin Kenardy*
19. Psychometric Concerns in the Assessment of Trauma-related Symptoms in Older Adults 282
Willeke H. van Zelst and *Aartjan T. F. Beekman*
20. Assessment of PTSD in Non-Western Cultures: The Need for New Contextual and Complex Perspectives 302
Boris Droždek, John P. Wilson, and *Silvana Turkovic*
21. Assessing PTSD-related Functional Impairment and Quality of Life 315
Darren W. Holowka and *Brian P. Marx*

Part Six • Prevention/Early Intervention
22. Risk and Protective Factors for Traumatic Stress Disorders 333
Lynda A. King, Anica P. Pless, Jennifer L. Schuster, Carrie M. Potter, Crystal L. Park, Avron Spiro, III, and *Daniel W. King*
23. Community-based Early Intervention with Trauma Survivors 347
Josef I. Ruzek
24. Individual Approaches to Prevention and Early Intervention 363
Teresa M. Au, Caroline Silva, Eileen M. Delaney, and *Brett T. Litz*
25. Prevention and Early Intervention Programs for Children and Adolescents 381
Melissa J. Brymer, Alan M. Steinberg, Patricia J. Watson, and *Robert S. Pynoos*
26. Prevention and Early Intervention Programs for Older Adults 393
Martha Strachan, Lisa S. Elwood, Ananda B. Amstadter, and *Ron Acierno*
27. Prevention and Early Intervention Programs for Special Populations 403
Heather E. Baldwin and *B. Heidi Ellis*

Part Seven • Treatment
28. PTSD Treatment Research: An Overview and Evaluation 415
Jessica L. Hamblen, Erin R. Barnett, Barbara A. Hermann, and *Paula P. Schnurr*

29. Empirically Supported Psychological Treatments: Prolonged Exposure 427
Nisha Nayak, Mark B. Powers, and *Edna B. Foa*
30. Empirically Supported Psychological Treatments: Cognitive Processing Therapy 439
Kathleen M. Chard, Jennifer L. Schuster, and *Patricia A. Resick*
31. Empirically Supported Psychological Treatments: EMDR 449
C. Richard Spates and *Sophie Rubin*
32. Promising Psychological Treatments 463
Megan C. Kearns and *Barbara Olasov Rothbaum*
33. Treating Trauma-related Symptoms in Children and Adolescents 473
Esther Deblinger, Elisabeth Pollio, and *Felicia Neubauer*
34. PTSD at Late Life: Context and Treatment 491
Lee Hyer and *Catherine A. Yeager*
35. Treating Trauma-related Symptoms in Special Populations 504
Devon E. Hinton and *Angela Nickerson*
36. Pharmacotherapy for PTSD 513
Matthew J. Friedman

Part Eight • Conclusions/Summary

37. Traumatic Stress Disorders: Looking Back and Moving Forward 527
Denise M. Sloan and *J. Gayle Beck*

Index 533

PART 1

Introduction

Traumatic Stress Disorders: Historical Context and Current Focus

J. Gayle Beck *and* Denise M. Sloan

Abstract

This chapter provides an introduction and overview to this handbook, focusing on the historical context that underlies current issues within the trauma literature. This handbook contains eight parts, focusing on classification and phenomenology, epidemiology and special populations, contributions from theory, assessment, prevention and early intervention, and treatment. The historical underpinnings of each area are delineated, with attention to their linkage with current research.

Key Words: History, trauma, introduction

The experience of traumatic events is an integral part of the human experience. Whether discussed by religious organizations, portrayed in the visual arts, or recounted in fiction, human suffering, at the hands of other men or owing to fate of a natural disaster, is an essential element of the human fabric. Oddly, professional attention to trauma and its sequelae have a considerably shorter history, beginning with observations from surgeons concerning emotional reactions among individuals who were seriously injured in accidents (e.g., Erichsen, 1866; Page, 1883). Throughout the relatively brief history of the psychological study of trauma, a number of themes have consistently emerged. Many of these themes remain as essential elements within our current study of traumatic stress disorders, as summarized within this volume.

In this introductory chapter, we will highlight some of these themes as they have influenced the organization of this handbook. As will be noted throughout this volume, our awareness and conceptualization of mental health problems following trauma has evolved over time, sometimes returning to a previous perspective as a result of advances in empirical knowledge, shifts in cultural awareness, or some combination of these forces. Official recognition, in the form of diagnostic criteria for posttraumatic stress disorder, came in 1980 (American Psychiatric Association [APA], 1980). The introduction of this diagnostic category was surrounded by controversy involving a number of issues, many of which continue as active concerns today. As is detailed throughout this volume, these concerns have been the grist for considerable scientific progress.

As the reader will note, after the introductory part, this volume is subdivided into eight parts, summarizing the current state of knowledge about (1) classification and phenomenology, (2) epidemiology and special populations, (3) contributions from theory, (4) assessment, (5) prevention and early intervention efforts, and (6) treatment of individuals with post-trauma mental health symptoms. Below, we provide some historical context for the organization of this volume and highlight concerns that have captured societal and scientific interest across the years.

What Is Trauma? What Mental Health Conditions Follow Exposure to a Trauma?

In some respects, the concept of a trauma defies adequate definition. Although each of us could indicate whether a given event was or was not a trauma by using our personal working definition, when we as scientists collectively begin to articulate what a trauma is, we are humbled by the task. Each attempt at a definition seems to leave out at least one important element. As the diagnostic criteria for PTSD evolved from *DSM-III* onward, the American Psychiatric Association has worked to refine its working definition of a trauma, beginning with a description that emphasized normative comparison (the "existence of a recognizable stressor that would evoke significant symptoms of distress in almost everyone" [APA, 1980, p. 239]). At present, a trauma is defined within *DSM-IV* (American Psychiatric Association [APA], 1994) as an event that involved "actual or threatened death or serious injury, or a threat to the physical integrity of self or others" (p. 467) and the individual's response was one of fear, helplessness, or horror. Various authors have argued that this definition is unnecessarily restrictive and should be expanded to include a variety of other types of stressful events, including workplace harassment, involvement in a lawsuit, or prolonged financial hardship (e.g., Seides, 2010). Others have argued that this type of definitional expansion represents "conceptual bracket creep" in the definition of a traumatic stressor (McNally & Breslau, 2008) and a change in this direction will result in defining most everyday stressors as traumas. Because posttraumatic stress disorders are singularly characterized by identification of the proximal, causal event (the trauma), our definitional conundrum creates a fundamental fissure in an otherwise tidy conceptualization of these conditions. This issue is examined within many of the chapters in part two, which are devoted to issues involved in classification and phenomenology.

As noted throughout these chapters, we have made considerable progress in trying to decipher when negative emotional reactions following trauma exposure are "normative" and when these reactions are more serious and warrant professional attention. Currently, there is on-going discussion concerning the role of negative emotional states and the trauma experience, which is reflected in several chapters in this part. For example, the working revisions for the PTSD diagnostic criteria suggest that negative emotional states might be better subsumed within an additional symptom cluster (American Psychiatric Association [APA], 2010), rather than as an essential element of the trauma experience. This revision will move subjective experience away from the definition of a trauma and into one of the symptom categories for PTSD. As well, discussion abounds concerning the nature of negative emotions in the trauma experience (e.g., Brewin, Andrews, & Rose, 2000; Lee, Scragg, & Turner, 2001). Historically, there have been varied depictions of posttrauma responses that range from despair to rage to anxiety (e.g., Kardiner, 1941). As such, discussion of the role of negative emotion in posttrauma adaptation represents an issue that has received considerable discussion over the years.

Moreover, current thinking regarding acute stress reactions, with particular focus on acute stress disorder, are subsumed within this part. The chapters contained within this part grapple with a number of longstanding issues within the trauma literature, including efforts to predict who will develop significant mental health problems in the aftermath of trauma exposure, how to best understand the trajectory of negative emotional responses that relate to trauma exposure, why some individuals are naturally resilient to negative mental health outcomes following trauma, and reflections on how a specific cultural context might shift the experience of specific symptoms and their conceptualization.

Keeping Track of Trauma Outcomes

A considerable amount of our early understanding of trauma outcomes is located within military history archives (e.g., Boone & Richardson, 2010; Shephard, 2004). As articulated by Shephard, initial efforts to track negative mental health outcomes following combat were inextricably woven with efforts to identify individual characteristics that were associated with "shell shock" and "war neurosis." Part three of this volume provides overviews of our current research in this domain, focusing on epidemiology of adverse emotional responses to trauma, both in the interval initially following exposure and as more chronic responses. As the reader will note, work in this area has become increasingly sophisticated, as we have developed specialized knowledge domains that focus on children, older adults, and special populations such as individuals with significant mental illness. This work has resulted in some important advances, including careful documentation of the multiple comorbid conditions that are likely to accompany PTSD. As highlighted by several authors in this part, the articulation of diagnostic criteria for PTSD allowed determination of how many individuals in many different types of cohorts actually experience PTSD. The ability to separate

PTSD from related psychiatric conditions and more general distress represents a quantum leap forward in understanding trauma outcomes. This work has also permitted careful documentation of what had been informally observed for decades—namely, that posttrauma symptomatology is associated with significant functional limitations, increased risk of health problems, and reduced quality of life.

Interestingly, this is one arena where increasing sophistication with respect to classification of posttrauma outcomes has resulted in some unintended consequences. For example, with the introduction of acute stress disorder (ASD) in *DSM-IV* (APA, 1994), posttrauma symptoms in the immediate aftermath of an extreme event could be officially diagnosed and treated. However, ASD can only last during the one-month interval following trauma exposure, a time span so brief as to preclude careful epidemiological study. This has resulted in uncertain figures with respect to what normal adjustment looks like during the immediate aftermath of a trauma and how prevalent ASD might be among different sectors of population. On the other end of the continuum, researchers have grappled with "delayed onset" PTSD, wondering whether this really represents true PTSD emerging years after trauma exposure or it is the development of full-syndrome PTSD following an interval of heightened subsyndromal symptoms. Clearly, this is an arena where the more data we collect, the more questions appear to surface. The chapters in part three begin to define many of these questions and the answers that we have to date.

What Causes PTSD?

Throughout art and literature, we have grappled with understanding the cause of mental disorders. At the most basic level, we ask whether emotional disorders are created by genetic and biologic causes ("nature") or by social and environmental forces ("nurture"). Within the trauma literature, a number of conceptual paradigms have evolved, each providing scaffolding for empirical studies designed to help us understand factors that create and maintain PTSD. As articulated in part four, research within the trauma field has benefited from conceptual developments about genetics, biological processes related to extreme stress, learning theory, information processing and other cognitive models, and family processes. Although there is great consensus that there is not just one cause of PTSD, it is enlightening to see the advanced understanding that has evolved within the last three decades in each of these areas.

Importantly, each of these chapters beautifully illustrates the immense progress that we have made in understanding PTSD. As reviewed by Flora (2002), prior to 1979, soldiers who had adverse reactions to combat were felt to be weak of character or to possess a personality flaw. Conversely, those who were seemingly untouched by the horror of war were deemed to be healthy. The field has made tremendous progress, incorporating developments that are grounded in other disciplines (e.g., Sapolsky, Krey, & McEwen, 1984) and grappling with how to account for the diverse range of outcomes that are known as PTSD. Moreover, each of the chapters within this part neatly sets the stage for developing interventions to both prevent and treat PTSD.

Measurement

Assessment of trauma-related symptoms also has matured as a field, as noted in the six chapters contained in part five. Developments in the assessment arena have paralleled the specialization noted when reviewing epidemiology, with particular attention to children, older adults, and specialized populations such as refugees. As well, advances in the assessment domain have included the development of structured interviewer-administered measures, psychophysiological measures, behavioral assessment devices, and instruments devised to be used as quick screeners in a variety of environments. Importantly, concerns about the cultural sensitivity of these assessment tools have become paramount, owing to expansion of research and clinical efforts beyond known cultural boundaries. Although this type of outreach is vital for the field, careful attention to how culture influences the experience and expression of trauma-related mental health problems is essential in these efforts. Notably, PTSD has been documented to occur throughout many countries (e.g., Green et al., 2003), with similarity of symptom profiles and prevalence rates when direct comparison is possible (e.g., North et al. 2005). However, as described by Osterman and de Jong (2007), the development of culturally sensitive assessment devices needs to go beyond simple symptom counts. Ideally, culturally sensitive assessment devices can be anchored to a broader model that explicates how specific aspects of a given culture influence risk and protective factors, as well as reporting styles. This feature of assessment is likely to witness tremendous growth, particularly given the historical significance of this issue.

A second issue traditionally has pervaded the assessment domain, notably concerns about deliberate exaggeration of trauma-related symptomatology and distress in order to obtain gain (e.g., disability compensation, a favorable legal judgment). This issue has received considerable discussion, as highlighted by the vigorous debate in the late 1930s between two noted psychiatrists, Francis Prideaux and Edward Mapother, whose opinions about whether combat soldiers with "shell shock" should receive a disability pension (Shephard, 2004). Importantly, public attitudes have historically gyrated around this issue when discussion of PTSD occurs in the popular media. As noted in several chapters in part five, the field is beginning to accumulate a research base to document the strengths of various approaches to detecting malingering.

The Challenge of Prevention

At first blush, posttrauma problems seem like an ideal arena for the development of prevention and early intervention efforts. Unlike most mental health problems, the putative cause of PTSD and ASD is clear—namely, an identifiable traumatic event. Unfortunately, this apparent simplicity is misleading. The history of trauma is replete with examples of well-intended efforts to stave off the negative effects of combat, natural disaster, and civilian traumas such as serious car accidents, most of which have been ineffective at best. Part six contains six thoughtful chapters that examine the many issues inherent in prevention and early intervention of negative psychological outcomes of trauma. As with other arenas, some degree of specialization has evolved, with uneven progress occurring with respect to prevention efforts for individuals versus communities, for children versus adults versus elders, and for special populations.

Despite this uneven progress, it is within the prevention domain that we can most clearly grasp the extent of progress that has occurred since the scientific study of trauma outcomes first began. Understanding how to devise an effective prevention or early intervention program requires a considerable amount of knowledge, such as knowing who to target, how to identify these individuals, why to target them, and what to do to address potential negative outcomes. Although our science is imperfect within each of these specific arenas, we have many more insights than were available when Grinker, Spiegel, Hanson, and others were attempting to provide early intervention to British combat troops during the early part of World War II (Boone & Richardson, 2010). During this era, considerable energy was devoted to debating whether intensive intervention showed superior outcomes relative to rest and social support. The issue of how to gauge outcomes also surfaced during this era, with additional debate about whether quantifiable change was relevant. Since this time, the field has evolved considerably, with much greater knowledge about the anticipated trajectories of symptomatology following trauma exposure. Moreover, our understanding of risk and resilience factors is considerably more refined, as are our methodology and analytic tools for modeling outcomes. Both prevention and early intervention programs hold considerable promise at present, although scientific developments in this area are proceeding slowly owing to the expense that is inherent in this type of work. As noted within part six, many interesting ideas are beginning to receive attention within this arena. In particular, considerable discussion has occurred about community-level programs, no doubt spurred on by increased awareness of the radiating psychological effects of trauma. The development of advanced technologies offers new, creative possibilities for delivery of these interventions, an option that no one could fathom two decades ago. In many respects, the prevention domain is likely to blossom in the near future, as we finally have the knowledge base upon which to grow.

Treatment of Trauma-related Outcomes

The organization of part seven differs in some respects from other parts of this volume. In particular, contained within this part are three chapters specifically devoted to empirically supported treatments for PTSD, reflecting decades of work designed to assist trauma survivors. Whether fueled by the need to restore functioning to psychologically injured troops during a war effort or recognition of the unfortunate frequency of sexual victimization among women, treatment development traditionally has occupied a central place within the trauma literature. In the years preceding formal introduction of the diagnosis of PTSD, treatment development efforts tended to focus on specific trauma populations, such as combat veterans, battered women, and rape victims. The specific social and cultural demands of each population echo throughout the early treatment literature, as reviewed in many of the chapters in this part. Interestingly, despite divergent theoretical orientations and differing populations of interest, many similar principles of treatment emerged in these publications, including the development of interventions designed to help the trauma survivor face reminders of her trauma and strategies intended to address the oppressive load of negative thoughts about the self and the world. Simultaneously, we have gained considerable understanding about the process of treating PTSD patients, notably the importance of forging a good working alliance, ways to determine if an individual is not ready for exposure-based treatment, and the like (e.g., Foa, Keane, Friedman, & Cohen, 2009). Under the category of treating PTSD, one will find a rich literature that reflects decades of challenging clinical and research efforts. These efforts include work with children and adolescents, with older adults, and with special populations such as refugees.

Taken as a whole, this literature helps the reader see the unity that underlies our conceptual understanding of posttrauma mental health problems. As detailed throughout many chapters in this part, our models of PTSD have evolved sufficiently to articulate clear treatment principles; these in turn have been tested using randomized controlled trials, as well as using qualitative methodological approaches. Although early authors may have suggested that treatment of each type of trauma is fundamentally unique, this argument is difficult to sustain when looking at the treatment literature as it is summarized in this part. In some respects, part seven provides an apt summary for this volume, as it blends well our knowledge of classification, phenomenology, epidemiology, theory, and assessment.

References

American Psychiatric Association. (1980). *Diagnostic and statistical manual of mental disorders* (3rd ed.). Washington, DC: Author.

American Psychiatric Association. (1994). *Diagnostic and statistical manual of mental disorders* (4th ed). Washington, DC: Author.

American Psychiatric Association. (2010). *American Psychiatric Association DSM-5 development.* Retrieved from http://www.dsm5.org.

Boone, K. N., & Richardson, F. C. (2010). War neurosis: A cultural historical and theoretical inquiry. *Journal of Theoretical and Philosophical Psychology, 30,* 109–121.

Brewin, C. R., Andrews, B., & Rose, S. (2000). Fear, helplessness, and horror in posttraumatic stress disorder: Investigating *DSM-IV* criterion A2 in victims of violent crime. *Journal of Traumatic Stress, 13,* 499–509.

Erichsen, J. E. (1866). *On railway and other injuries of the nervous system.* London: Walton & Maberly.

Foa, E. B., Keane, T. M., Friedman, M. J., & Cohen, J. A. (2009). *Effective treatments for PTSD* (2nd ed.). New York: Guilford.

Flora, C. M. (2002). A short history of PTSD from the military perspective. In M. B. Williams and J. F. Sommer, Jr. (Eds.), *Simple and complex posttraumatic stress disorder: Strategies for comprehensive treatment in clinical practice* (pp. 3–8). Binghamton, NY: Haworth.

Green, B. L., Friedman, M., de Jong, J. V. M., Solomon, S. D., Keane, T. M., Fairbank, J. A., & Daniel, Y. (2003). *Trauma interventions in war and peace: Prevention, practice, and policy.* Amsterdam: Kluwer Academic/Plenum Press.

Kardiner, A. (1941). *The traumatic neuroses of war.* New York: Hoeber Press.

Lee, D. A., Scragg, P., & Turner, S. (2001). The role of shame and guilt in traumatic events: A clinical model of shame-based and guilt-based PTSD. *British Journal of Medical Psychology, 74,* 451–466.

McNally, R. J., & Breslau, N. (2008). Does virtual trauma cause posttraumatic stress disorder? *American Psychologist, 63,* 282–283.

North, C. S., Pfefferbaum, B., Narayanan, P., Thielman, S. B., McCoy, G., Dumont, C. E., & Spitznagel, E. K. (2005). Comparison of post-disaster psychiatric disorders after terrorist bombings in Nairobi and Oklahoma City. *British Journal of Psychiatry, 186,* 487–493.

Osterman, J. E., & de Jong, J. V. M. (2007). Cultural issues and trauma. In M. Friedman, T. M. Keane, and P. A. Resick (Eds.), *Handbook of PTSD: Science and practice* (pp. 425–446). New York: Guilford.

Page, H. (1883). *Injuries of the spine and spinal cord without apparent mechanical lesion and nervous shock in their surgical and medico-legal aspects.* London: Churchill.

Sapolsky, R. M., Krey, L. C., & McEwen, B. S. (1984). Stress down-regulates corticosterone receptors in a site-specific manner in the brain. *Endocrinology 114,* 287–292.

Seides, R. (2010). Should the current *DSM-IV-TR* definition for PSTD be expanded to include serial and multiple microtraumas as aetiologies? *Journal of Psychiatric and Mental Health Nursing, 17,* 725–731.

Shephard, B. (2004). Risk factors and PTSD: A historian's perspective. In G. M. Rosen (Ed.), *Posttraumatic stress disorder: Issues and controversies* (pp. 39–61). New York: John Wiley.

PART 2

Classification and Phenomenology

CHAPTER

2

Defining Traumatic Events: Research Findings and Controversies

Jesse R. Cougle, Dean G. Kilpatrick, *and* Heidi Resnick

Abstract

Since the posttraumatic stress disorder (PTSD) diagnosis was introduced in the DSM-III (American Psychiatric Association [APA], 1980) controversy has existed over what constitutes a Criterion A stressor, or a potentially traumatic event. Such definitions have considerable research, clinical, and legal implications. In this chapter, we review the history of Criterion A, conditional risk of PTSD associated with specific stressors, and situational and demographic variables likely to increase risk of PTSD. Significant attention is given to the controversies surrounding Criterion A, as well as limitations of extant research. We conclude with specific recommendations for future inquiry with particular emphasis on the importance of comprehensive assessment of Criterion A stressor exposure and PTSD assessment that captures the effects of exposure to more than one Criterion A stressor.

Key Words: Traumatic events; posttraumatic stress disorder; risk factors; Diagnostic and Statistical Manual; Criterion A; diagnosis

Introduction

Traumatic event exposure is an essential component of posttraumatic stress disorder (PTSD). Controversy has existed over what defines a potentially traumatic event (PTE) ever since the PTSD diagnosis was added to *DSM-III* (APA, 1980). In the *DSM* diagnosis of PTSD, Criterion A, or the stressor criterion, plays a key gatekeeping role because it determines which stressor events can be assessed for PTSD (Kilpatrick, Resnick, & Acierno, 2009; Weathers & Keane, 2007). Thus, stressor events that are included in a given definition of Criterion A are defined as meeting the threshold for PTSD eligibility and become potentially traumatic events (PTEs); events that are not included, by definition, do not meet this eligibility threshold. Therefore, how Criterion A is defined has a potential impact on PTSD caseness and prevalence. This impact on PTSD prevalence and caseness is potential because, as has been described elsewhere (Kilpatrick et al., 2009), the proportion of those *who actually* develop PTSD after exposure to given types of stressor events (i.e., Criterion A vs. others) is an empirical question that is determined by data and not by a *DSM* definition. For an individual being assessed for clinical or forensic purposes, the definition of Criterion A is important because it establishes eligibility to receive a PTSD diagnosis in a clinical case and whether psychological harm in the form of PTSD was either caused or aggravated by a given stressor event in a forensic or compensation case. In summary, how Criterion A is defined is a high-stakes issue because the definition has the potential to impact PTSD prevalence, PTSD caseness, access to treatment for PTSD, and whether PTSD can be diagnosed in forensic or compensation cases.

As has been noted elsewhere (Kilpatrick et al., 2009), the question of how to define Criterion A raises both philosophical and empirical issues. Philosophical and value judgments are involved in deciding what the primary purpose of Criterion A should be. Should it include all stressor events that are capable of producing PTSD or should it include only those events that have a high probability of producing PTSD? Is it important to define Criterion A so that individuals having experienced less than truly terrible events are eligible to be evaluated for the PTSD diagnosis? Does expanding the types of stressor events included in Criterion A undermine efforts to encourage resilience or does doing so make it possible for some individuals who need it to get access to services? None of these questions can be answered by data alone because how they are answered is based more on philosophy and values than on data.

In this chapter, we summarize some of the controversies and research findings regarding this criterion. We also review evidence regarding conditional risk of PTSD associated with different types of PTEs, situational determinants of risk associated with PTEs, and demographic variables likely to increase risk. We conclude with recommendations for future research.

Criterion A: A Brief History

The ongoing controversy regarding Criterion A is reflected in the changing definitions of this criterion in each successive edition of the *DSM*. Table 2.1 provides the current *DSM-IV* and proposed *DSM-5* definitions of Criterion A. In *DSM-III*, a Criterion A potentially traumatic event (PTE) was defined as the "existence of a recognizable stressor that would evoke significant symptoms of distress in almost everyone" (APA, 1980, p. 238). The accompanying text of this criterion described the stressor as evoking "symptoms of distress in most people" (p. 236) and described the experience as outside the range of normal experiences, specifically excluding bereavement, chronic illness, business losses, or marital conflict. By describing the criterion in this manner, PTSD was conceptualized as more a product of discrete events than of a combination of events and individual vulnerabilities. This definition was criticized by many because it is clear that some of the most severe events do not lead to longer term symptoms in most people. Further, we now know that exposure to many PTEs, such as interpersonal violence, accidents, and natural disasters, is quite common and cannot truly be considered outside the range of normal experiences (Kessler, Sonnega, Bromet, Hughes, & Nelson, 1995; Resnick, Kilpatrick, Dansky, Saunders, & Best, 1993).

In the *DSM-III-R* (APA, 1987), the Criterion A definition was restricted somewhat. The description of traumatic events as being "outside the range of usual human experience" and "markedly distressing to almost everyone" (p. 250) was retained, and a more detailed list of qualifying events was provided: "a serious threat to one's life or physical integrity; serious threat or harm to one's children, spouse, or other close relatives and friends; sudden destruction of one's home or community; or seeing another person who has recently been, or is being seriously injured or killed as the result of an accident or physical violence" (p. 247–248). The *DSM-III-R* also emphasized the subjective aspects of traumatic event experience as involving "intense fear, terror, and helplessness" (p. 247). Further, the descriptive text introduced a new class of traumatic events involving indirect exposure, including "learning about a serious threat or harm to a close friend or relative" (p. 248). Some of the same criticisms were made of this revision; in particular, the description of events "outside the range of usual human experience" was criticized on similar grounds as its predecessor (Davidson & Foa, 1991).

With the *DSM-IV* (APA, 1994), Criterion A was split into two parts (see table 2.1 for definitions and relevant accompanying text). The first part states that the individual "experienced, witnessed, or was confronted with an event or events that involved actual or threatened death or serious injury, or the threat to physical integrity of self or others" (APA, 2000, p. 467). The list of qualifying events was also expanded to include "being diagnosed with a life-threatening illness"; "learning about the sudden unexpected death of a family member or a close friend"; and "learning that one's child has a life-threatening disease" (p. 464). Inclusion of these new events has been criticized by some as leading to a "conceptual bracket creep" in the types of events that would qualify as traumatic (McNally, 2003). The additional wording that describes being "confronted" with a distressing event has also been criticized for its vagueness. For example, theoretically it is possible that simply viewing an event on television (e.g., the 9/11 attacks) might be viewed by some as sufficient to constitute "confrontation." Controversy over the broadening definitions of PTEs will be discussed later.

Table 2.1. Criterion A definitions and accompanying text from DSM-IV and proposed revisions for DSM-5

DSM-IV	DSM-5 proposed revisions
The person has been exposed to a traumatic event in which both of the following were present: (1) the person experienced, witnessed, or was confronted with an event or events that involved actual or threatened death or serious injury, or a threat to the physical integrity of self or others. (2) the person's response involved intense fear, helplessness, or horror. Note: In children, this may be expressed instead by disorganized or agitated behavior.	The person was exposed to one or more of the following event(s): death or threatened death, actual or threatened serious injury, or actual or threatened sexual violation, in one or more of the following ways*: 1. Experiencing the event(s) him/herself 2. Witnessing, in person, the event(s) as they occurred to others 3. Learning that the event(s) occurred to a close relative or close friend; in such cases, the actual or threatened death must have been violent or accidental 4. Experiencing repeated or extreme exposure to aversive details of the event(s) (e.g., first responders collecting body parts; police officers repeatedly exposed to details of child abuse); this does not apply to exposure through electronic media, television, movies, or pictures, unless this exposure is work related.
Accompanying text: • ...exposure to an extreme traumatic stressor involving direct personal experience of an event that involves actual or threatened death or serious injury, or other threat to one's physical integrity; or witnessing an event that involves death, injury, or a threat to the physical integrity of another person; or learning about unexpected or violent death, serious harm, or threat of death or injury experienced by a family member or other close associate (Criterion A1). • The person's response to the event must involve intense fear, helplessness, or horror (or in children, the response must involve disorganized or agitated behavior) (Criterion A2). • Traumatic events that are experienced directly include, but are not limited to, military combat, violent personal assault (sexual assault, physical attack, robbery, mugging), being kidnapped, being taken hostage, terrorist attack, torture, incarceration as a prisoner of war or in a concentration camp, natural or manmade disasters, severe automobile accidents, or being diagnosed with a life-threatening illness. For children, sexually traumatic events may include developmentally inappropriate sexual experiences without threatened or actual violence or injury. Witnessed events include, but are not limited to, observing the serious injury or unnatural death of another person due to violent assault, accident, war, or disaster or unexpectedly witnessing a dead body or body parts. Events experienced by others that are learned about include, but are not limited to, violent personal assault, serious accident, or serious injury experienced by a family member or a close friend; learning about the sudden, unexpected death of a family member or a close friend; or learning that one's child has a life-threatening disease.	*Accompanying text*: Not yet available

* For children, inclusion of loss of parent or other attachment figure is being considered.
DSM-IV = Diagnostic and Statistical Manual of Mental Disorders, Fourth Edition (American Psychiatric Association, 1994).
DSM-5 = Diagnostic and Statistical Manual of Mental Disorders, Fifth Edition (proposed revisions, retrieved from: http://www.dsm5.org/ProposedRevisions/Pages/proposedrevision.aspx?rid=165).

The second feature of Criterion A (i.e., A2) in *DSM-IV* states that the individual must respond to the event with "intense fear, helplessness, or horror." The subjective evaluation of the event as traumatic is fundamental to the A2 criterion. Weathers and Keane (2007) provided useful terminology for distinguishing between these features of Criterion A: meeting the A1 criterion qualifies an event as being potentially traumatic, while potentially traumatic events that meet the A2 criterion can be considered traumatic.

Criterion A2 has generated controversy as well. Some have argued that traumatic events are often characterized by other emotions, including guilt, shame, or disgust (Adler, Wright, Bliese, Eckford, & Hoge, 2008; Brewin, Andrews, & Rose, 2000; Roemer, Orsillo, Borkovec, & Litz, 1998). In addition, it appears that A2 has little positive predictive value, though events that do *not* meet A2, rarely result in PTSD (Breslau & Kessler, 2001; Schnurr, Spiro, Vielhauer, Findler, & Hamblen, 2002), confirming that A2 has negative predictive power.

Recommendations for Criterion A1 changes in the PTSD diagnosis range from eliminating it altogether and emphasizing greater specificity in terms of key re-experiencing symptoms related to events that the individual perceived as threatening to physical or psychological well-being (Brewin, Lanius, Novac, Schnyder, & Galea, 2009), to retaining Criterion A and allowing for additional empirical study of which events and/or event characteristics are most likely to increase risk of PTSD following exposure (Kilpatrick et al., 2009). In either case, emphasis on functional impairment criteria was also recommended (Brewin et al., 2009; Kilpatrick et al., 2009). Other recommendations are to retain but narrow the criteria—for example, eliminating events that are indirectly experienced (McNally, 2009).

Preliminary drafts of the proposed revisions for *DSM-5* (see table 2.1) indicate that Criterion A2 will be dropped and further specificity will be added to the definition of qualifying events (APA, 2010). Such events must involve direct exposure—either experiencing or witnessing—or learning of a violent or accidental event occurring to a close relative or friend. Repeated exposure to relevant details (e.g., seeing photographs of injuries or death as part of one's job) may also qualify as a Criterion A event. Exposure to events via media, including television, movies, or pictures, is explicitly excluded from meeting this criterion.

Criterion A Events: Too Broad or Too Narrow?

One aspect of the debate over Criterion A is whether the definition is too broad or too narrow. Critics who argue it is too broad have singled out categories of secondary exposure, including learning about injury, or unexpected or violent death occurring to others, as particularly problematic (McNally, 2003, 2009). This expansion, which occurred in *DSM-III-R* and was made more explicit in *DSM-IV*, is thought by some to have diluted the construct of PTSD by including low-level stressors that are not truly traumatic. This potential problem is thought to lead to significant heterogeneity in PTSD samples. Further, some critics argue that unnecessarily broad definitions of trauma may lead researchers and clinicians to pathologize normal reactions to stressful events. Critics have pointed to research suggesting that PTSD can develop due to inappropriate sexual remarks, killing livestock, and uncomplicated delivery as being particularly egregious examples of "bracket creep" (McNally, 2009). However, much of the research purporting to demonstrate that PTSD develops following exposure to minor events suffers from a host of methodological problems, including failure to assess comprehensively for exposure to other PTEs, lack of evaluation of PTSD relative to such events, and failure to use state-of-the-science PTSD assessment instruments.

Evidence that the *DSM-IV* Criterion A1 definition has led to significant increases in cases of PTSD is mixed. Data from the National Comorbidity Survey-Replication, which assessed PTSD using *DSM-IV* criteria and a longer list of qualifying events, revealed lower prevalence of lifetime PTSD (6.8%; Kessler et al. 2005) than the earlier survey that relied on *DSM-III-R* criteria (7.8%; Kessler et al., 1995). In the *DSM-IV* field trial (Kilpatrick et al., 1998) various definitions of Criterion A were evaluated in a sample that included patients seeking treatment related to a PTE (N = 400), as well as adults in the general population (N = 128). Lifetime histories of high- and low-magnitude events were evaluated, with high-magnitude events meeting Criterion A according to the *DSM-III-R*. The prevalence of PTSD in this sample was not affected by more or less restrictive definitions of Criterion A.

Breslau and Kessler (2001) also examined changes in Criterion A prevalence as well as changes in PTSD prevalence owing to the expanded definition of Criterion A in a sample of 2181 adults. They found the lifetime prevalence of Criterion

A1 exposure to be quite high (89.6%), and they noted a 59.2% increase in the total number of events experienced that was accounted for by the expanded *DSM-IV* definition of A1. Further, the conditional probability of PTSD from *DSM-III* and *DSM-III-R* Criterion A events was greater than that for *DSM-IV* criterion A1 events (11.1% vs. 7.3%). Overall, they noted that 37.8% of all PTSD cases were due to stressors added to the *DSM-IV*, with most of these PTSD cases being due to learning of the unexpected death of a close friend or relative. This investigation had certain limitations, however. First, as they note, "there is no precise way to quantify the impact of the broader range of stressors in DSM-IV versus DSM-III or DSM-III-R because the explicated added stressors in the DSM-IV overlap, in part, with stressors in earlier definitions" (p. 701). They were unable to isolate PTSD cases due to new *DSM-IV* stressors, since the five new stressors they considered, including violent death of a family member, could have also qualified as Criterion A events under *DSM-III* and *DSM-III-R* (Weathers & Keane, 2007). Further, given that they only examined PTSD in relation to most bothersome and a randomly selected event, they were unable to truly ascertain whether overall lifetime PTSD prevalence would be increased by the addition of the new *DSM-IV* Criterion A1 events.

Very recently, investigators examined whether PTSD prevalence would be affected by using a non-restrictive definition of Criterion A and determining PTSD diagnosis based on symptom, duration, and impairment criteria (Kilpatrick et al., 2009). This question was addressed in large household probability samples of U.S. adolescents and Florida adults. Overall, they found that very few cases of PTSD occurred in the absence of Criterion A1 events, thus providing little evidence that bracket creep affects PTSD prevalence.

There is some evidence to suggest that non-Criterion A1 stressors may lead to PTSD or at least significant PTSD symptoms (e.g., Gold, Marx, Soler-Baillo, & Sloan, 2005; Long et al, 2008). Such data have been taken by some to mean that Criterion A1 should be broadened to include other stressors. However, much of the supporting evidence is limited by use of self-report symptom measures and a failure to include assessment of or adequately control for lifetime PTE exposure and/or related prior PTSD. Many relevant studies also failed to include full diagnostic criteria including functional impairment, and assessed PTSD only in reference to subjectively defined "worst" events rather than in reference to index Criterion A and non-Criterion A events occurring across individuals (e.g., first, most recent, randomly selected). Additional exploration of whether some non-Criterion A events are actually more likely to occur in some cases *due to* impaired functioning might be useful. In addition, research to evaluate to what extent prior PTSD or Criterion A event exposure increases risk of symptom report in reference to non-Criterion A events would be helpful.

Must Traumatic Events Be Directly Experienced?

An additional controversy over Criterion A relates to whether traumatic events must be directly experienced. Beginning in *DSM-III-R*, events involving indirect exposure were listed as potentially meeting Criterion A. Among the categories of specific events was "learning about a serious threat or harm to a close friend or relative" (APA, 1987, p. 248). The list of types of indirect exposure was expanded in *DSM-IV*, though each of these types was included, at least implicitly, in the *DSM-III-R*. Epidemiological studies indicate that indirect exposure in the form of unexpected death to a loved one constitutes the most common Criterion A1 event, as well as the most common worst stressful event to which PTSD symptoms are anchored and evaluated (Breslau et al., 1998; Roberts, Gilman, Breslau, Breslau, & Koenen, 2011).

The inclusion of indirect exposure in Criterion A1 is controversial because some argue that this led to substantial increases in the percentage of the population with lifetime event exposure in some studies (e.g., Breslau & Kessler, 2001). These exposure events have also been associated with lower risk of PTSD. For example, Breslau and Kessler (2001) found that events involving learning about harm or unexpected death to others were associated with lower conditional probability of PTSD than events involving direct exposure (7.3% vs. 11.1%).

It should be noted, however, that death of a family member due to criminal or vehicular homicide has been found to be associated with risk of PTSD and levels of distress similar to prevalence among those with direct assault/event exposure (Amick-McMullan, Kilpatrick, & Resnick, 1991; Freedy, Resnick, Kilpatrick, Dansky, & Tidwell, 1994; Zinzow, Rheingold, Hawkins, Saunders, & Kilpatrick, 2009). Thus, failure to separate out such types of events from other "confronted" events limits conclusions that may be drawn related to overall prevalence of secondary exposure to these types of PTE. Critics who are wary of the broadening definitions of trauma are especially concerned about the inclusion of indirect exposure in Criterion A1. Many view the assessment of indirect exposure (learning about harm befalling a family member or close friend) to be sufficiently vague so as to allow for the assignment of a PTSD diagnosis due to various forms of information, including learning about the 9/11 attacks via television (McNally, 2009). However, since such events very likely do not involve harm occurring to a close friend or relative, according to *DSM-IV* criteria, a PTSD diagnosis would not be assigned. Likewise, the fact that these events are defined as capable of producing PTSD does not mean that there is a high probability that they will do so.

Preliminary drafts of the proposed revisions in *DSM-5* have retained indirect exposure as a qualifying event but with some specifications. According to these proposed revisions, PTEs may be learned to have "occurred to a close relative or close friend" and "in such cases the actual or threatened death must have been violent or accidental" (APA, 2010, para. 1). The "violent or accidental" qualifier should exclude those events involving the death of a loved one due to a severe medical condition (e.g., heart attack, life-threatening illness). It remains to be seen whether these revisions will lead to significant reductions in lifetime Criterion A or PTSD prevalence.

Assessment of PTSD in Relation to Which Criterion A1 Event?

PTSD symptoms are generally assessed in relation to specific Criterion A1 stressors; however, it is quite common for individuals to experience multiple PTEs (Kessler et al., 1995). The issue of which Criterion A1 event should be the focus of the PTSD assessment is complex. Clinical and epidemiological assessments of PTSD typically involve the presentation of a list of Criterion A1 events on which individuals are asked to provide history (e.g., Kessler et al., 1995). Among those events respondents endorse, they are asked to focus on the worst or most bothersome event and then PTSD symptoms are assessed in relation to this event.

The "worst event" assessment method is a practical solution to the difficulty imposed by assessing PTSD for people who have experienced multiple PTEs. Evidence suggests that few individuals who fail to meet for PTSD diagnosis in relation to their worst event meet it due to other traumatic events. For example, Breslau, Davis, Peterson, and Schultz (1997) evaluated PTSD in response to both worst event and up to two additional events and found that the events designated as worst accounted for 84% of total lifetime PTSD cases.

This method has certain limitations. Worst events are by definition perceived to be more extreme than the types of same events to which individuals are usually exposed. Generally speaking, a car accident that is considered a worst event will likely be more severe and distressing than a typical car accident, and it will likely carry with it greater risk of PTSD. Indeed, Breslau, Peterson, Poisson, Schultz, and Lucia (2004) found that the risk of PTSD associated with car accidents was 6.5% when it was a worst event, although it was only 2.3% as a randomly selected event. Thus, this method is prone to overstating the conditional risk of PTSD following exposure to different traumatic events.

The "worst event" method also does not take into account the impact of multiple or ongoing PTEs. Traumatic events experienced in the context of combat or domestic violence, in particular, can be quite varied. PTSD in response to the worst lifetime event may remit prior to the onset of a subsequent occurrence of PTSD due to a less distressing related event. Even though respondents may report few past-month PTSD symptoms in response to a "worst" incident, they may still meet diagnostic criteria for current PTSD due to a less bothersome event. Thus, anchoring PTSD symptoms to a worst event that occurred long ago could give a false impression of remission.

Respondents may choose worst events for reasons unrelated to the PTSD symptoms they produced. For example, some may be more likely to choose the unexpected death of a loved one as the worst of many events since this event represents the loss of someone close to them and may have special significance that other Criterion A1 events do not possess. Indeed, researchers have found that the unexpected death of a loved one was overrepresented among worst events identified as such based on its actual prevalence in the sample (Breslau et al., 2004). Some worst events may also be easier to disclose than an event that is actually most distressing to the respondent (e.g., sexual assault).

Another factor that has not been adequately addressed in the context of history of multiple types or incidents of exposure to PTEs is more complex, or *aggregate*, patterns of PTSD symptoms

(Kilpatrick et al., 2009). Specifically, intrusion and avoidance symptoms may occur in reference to multiple traumatic events. Thus, an individual who has experienced several traumatic events during his or her life (e.g., sexual assault as a child, physical assault as an adult, injurious accident as an adult), may have intrusive and/or avoidance symptoms that incorporate any or all of these events. This issue may also be relevant in the context of what might be traditionally categorized as single types of PTEs that comprise multiple event experiences. For example, an individual in military service might experience military sexual trauma, exposure to improvised explosive device attacks, and being under enemy fire or witnessing death or injury of a friend or others. PTSD diagnostic criteria might be considered aggregate in such instances if the person has intrusion and/or avoidance symptoms incorporating several different traumatic events. The reliance on the worst-event method of assessment may miss such cases in which multiple PTE exposure is present. Potential methods for the assessment of PTSD in reference to multiple events will be discussed in the concluding section.

Challenges to Evaluating Conditional Risk of PTSD Due to Different Traumatic Events

Two basic methodologies have been used to determine conditional risk of PTSD associated with different Criterion A events. One method involves structured interviews of large, representative samples that may or may not have been exposed to a number of different Criterion A events (e.g., Kessler et al., 1995). In these studies, lifetime PTE history is generally assessed and lifetime and current PTSD is evaluated in relation to the most bothersome PTE. The second method involves the recruitment of samples that were exposed to specific PTEs, usually very recently, and the evaluation of PTSD in response to these events. Both methods include different challenges, which we will discuss below.

Nationally representative surveys, such as the National Comorbidity Survey (Kessler et al., 1995), are often used to determine prevalence rates of PTE exposure, as well as lifetime and current PTSD diagnoses. These surveys often rely or report on worst-event methods for determining PTSD diagnoses. This method, as already discussed, is problematic in that it tends to overstate the conditional risk of PTSD associated with different events (Breslau et al., 2004). It is also likely to neglect to evaluate the risk associated with stressors of lower magnitude. To address this limitation, certain studies have attempted to also evaluate PTSD anchored to a randomly selected event. This method is thought to provide a more accurate assessment of the true risk of PTSD associated with various events.

Epidemiological studies very rarely capture PTSD in response to recent events. Many cases of lifetime and current PTSD are determined with reference to events that occurred years prior to the assessment. Naturally, certain limitations will arise from relying on such retrospective assessments. For example, prospective research has demonstrated that half of individuals meeting diagnostic criteria for depression at an earlier point in time did not recall their depressive episodes before age 21 (Wells & Horwood, 2004). Those with remitted PTSD should also be less likely to recall experiencing symptoms constituting the PTSD diagnosis, especially if the symptoms remitted many years ago.

A recent analysis by Moffit and colleagues (2010) speaks directly to the problems of ascertaining lifetime psychiatric diagnoses through retrospective cross-sectional methods. These investigators compared prevalence rates of diagnoses in the longitudinal Dunedin New Zealand birth cohort study with rates obtained in two U.S. National Comorbidity Surveys and found that lifetime prevalence rates were approximately doubled when assessed prospectively relative to retrospectively. Further, past-year prevalence rates were comparable across surveys, which suggests that these marked differences are not due to differences in culture or assessment instruments. However, this study did not report on PTSD as a separate category, thus it is difficult to ascertain how PTSD specific prevalence would be affected.

An additional method for determining conditional risk of PTSD involves assessing individuals who are exposed to specific traumatic events. Such investigations typically involve recently exposed samples and different recruitment methods (e.g., emergency rooms) than the kind used in epidemiological studies (e.g., household probability sampling). Since these studies tend to rely on recently exposed samples, they are less vulnerable to the limitations of recall listed above. In addition, since they assess PTSD anchored to specific events, they are not subject to the problems inherent in worst-event assessment methods.

These investigations also have certain limitations, however. First, the assessment point for current PTSD varies widely between studies. For example, recent studies have examined early risk factors for current PTSD at six months posttrauma (Ehring, Ehlers, & Glucksman, 2008; Kleim, Ehlers, & Glucksman, 2007). However, diagnoses occurring at this point are considered chronic PTSD according to *DSM-IV* (APA, 1994). Such study designs do not allow investigators to determine conditional risk of *ever having* PTSD, which only requires one month duration of symptoms. Similar studies have examined the conditional risk of current PTSD using one-year postevent assessments (Irish et al., 2009). In short, these studies assess varying degrees of PTSD *chronicity* rather than *risk*. This complicates efforts to determine conditional risk.

Focused studies examining PTSD due to specific PTE are also limited by the representativeness of individuals typically assessed. For example, the assessment of PTSD due to rape is complicated by the fact that most women do not report such events to authorities and do not present to hospitals following such events (Resnick et al., 1993). Researchers must often rely on advertisements or referrals through support agencies (e.g., Halligan, Michael, Clark, & Ehlers, 2003). In addition, recruitment of assault or accident survivors through hospital emergency rooms is likely to involve more severe types of Criterion A1 events, which may lead to overestimation of the risk of PTSD associated with these events.

Conditional Risk of PTSD Associated with Specific Criterion A1 Events

The risk of PTSD associated with Criterion A1 events varies considerably by event type. Below we review the conditional risk of PTSD associated with different events. Estimates will be reviewed from both large-scale, representative epidemiological studies and recently exposed samples.

Accidents

Studies of accident-related PTSD often recruit participants from patients admitted to the emergency room. Varying prevalence of PTSD following traumatic injury have been found, possibly due to the heterogeneous nature of the injuries for which these samples are admitted. For example, Zatzick and colleagues (2007) found relatively high rates of PTSD (23%) at 12 months postinjury in their large sample, though O'Donnell et al. (2008) found that only 8% met for PTSD in their sample at the 12-month assessment point. Epidemiological studies have found conditional probabilities of PTSD that were quite low for accidents that were worst or only events (6.3% men, 8.8% women; Kessler et al., 1995). Breslau et al. (2004) also found conditional risk of PTSD following car accidents that were low for both worst (6.3%) and randomly selected events (2.3%), though PTSD following "other serious accidents" was more common (worst: 21.6%; randomly selected: 16.8%).

Prospective studies of accident-related PTSD tend to restrict recruitment to individuals who are admitted to the emergency room who also exhibit significant injury. Many studies exclude patients who are admitted with only mild cuts or abrasions (Ehring et al., 2008) or who are admitted to the hospital for less than 24 hours (O'Donnell et al., 2008). These criteria may lead to the inflation of PTSD rates. This range restriction also likely contributes to the inconsistent findings regarding the association between injury severity and PTSD, which will be discussed later.

Interpersonal Violence

Physical and sexual assault are consistently associated with some of the highest probabilities of PTSD. Epidemiological studies have found high conditional probabilities of PTSD due to rape for both men (65%) and women (45.9%; Kessler et al., 1995). The conditional risk of PTSD was also high when rape was a randomly selected event (49%; Breslau et al., 2004). Prospective studies of female rape victims have also found high rates of PTSD, with one study revealing that 65% met criteria at one month posttrauma, while 47% met at three months (Rothbaum, Foa, Riggs, Murdock, & Walsh, 1992).

Lower conditional risk of PTSD has been found for physical assault in some studies. For example, Breslau et al. (1997) found the conditional risk of PTSD due to being "badly beaten up" to be 31.9% when using randomly selected event criteria. Despite the fact that these events are more common in men than women (11.1% vs. 6.9%), the risk of PTSD due to physical assault is much lower in men (1.8% vs. 21.3% for women; Kessler et al., 1995). Event-focused prospective studies typically combine physical and sexual assault victims, though one prospective study of physical assault victims found risk of PTSD to be at 22% at six months postassault (Elklit & Brink, 2004). Riggs, Rothbaum, and Foa (1995) examined the longitudinal course of symptoms following physical assault and found that while 71% of women and 50% of men met symptom (but not duration) criteria for PTSD at the initial assessment (M = 18.68 days postassault), no men and only 21% of women met criteria for PTSD three months later. As noted by Pimlott-Kubiak and Cortina (2003), women may also be exposed to different types of interpersonal aggression and/or different frequencies or differential risk of injuries in association with physical assault. They found that, controlling for patterns of interpersonal aggression experienced, gender differences were not observed in terms of physical or mental health problems within the large National Violence Against Women sample. Such factors related to differential characteristics or patterns of exposure should be studied further when considering gender or other potential additional risk factors for PTSD.

Conditional risk of PTSD associated with childhood sexual and physical abuse has also been studied. For example, using a worst-event method, Kessler et al. (1995) found the risk of lifetime PTSD due to childhood sexual abuse to be 12.2% for men and 26.5% for women, and the risk of PTSD due to childhood physical abuse to be 22.3% for men and 48.5% for women. High prevalence of lifetime PTSD was found among a representative sample of women who had experienced childhood physical assault compared to those who had not experienced childhood physical assault (53.8% vs. 11.2%; Duncan, Saunders, Kilpatrick, Hanson, & Resnick, 1996). Studies of children referred for psychiatric evaluation found higher rates of PTSD among those who were sexually abused (42.3%) compared to those who had suffered nonsexual abuse (8.7%; McLeer, Callaghan, Henry, & Wallen, 1994). Using data from a household probability sample of adolescents ages 12 to 17, Kilpatrick, Saunders, and Smith (2003) found higher prevalence of lifetime PTSD in association with a history of sexual assault compared to no sexual assault among boys (28.2% vs. 5.4%) and girls (29.8% vs. 7.1%). Lifetime PTSD prevalence was also higher among those who reported a history of physical assault or physically abusive punishment compared to those without such history among boys (15.2% vs. 3.1%) and among girls (27.4% vs. 6%). Other data indicate that interpersonal violence events that first occur in childhood may increase later risk of PTSD in adulthood following subsequent stressor exposure (e.g., Binder et al., 2008; Smith, Saunders, & Kilpatrick, 2008).

Combat

Epidemiological studies indicate that combat is the most commonly nominated worst event among men with *DSM-III-R* PTSD (Kessler et al., 1995). Though combat-related exposure is rare among men (6.4% lifetime prevalence), the conditional risk of PTSD associated with worst-event combat is quite high (38.8%; Kessler et al., 1995). Studies focusing on combat veterans have found varying rates of combat-related PTSD, though this has been a source of some controversy. For example, the National Vietnam Veterans Readjustment Study (NVVRS) found that 30.9% of a sample of 1200 veterans had developed PTSD during their lifetimes (Kulka et al., 1988). A reanalysis of a subsample of the NVVRS using extremely rigorous criteria revealed that 18.7% had developed war-related PTSD during their lifetimes (Dohrenwend, Turner, Turse et al., 2006). Recently, approximately 12–20% of Iraq combat veterans were found to have PTSD postdeployment, depending on the criteria used; these rates were higher than the rates found following deployment to Afghanistan (6.2–11.5%; Hoge et al., 2004). Both of these studies found strong dose relationships between duration or frequency of combat exposure and likelihood of developing PTSD.

Natural Disaster

Studies of PTSD following natural disaster are less common than those for interpersonal violence or accidents. However, they are useful in that the occurrence and timing of the Criterion A1 events are objectively verifiable. They also typically involve large populations who have been exposed and who can be followed over time. The assumption is that such exposures are uniformly distributed across samples, though obviously there will be varying degrees of exposure and varying degrees of risk depending on exposure severity.

Epidemiological studies indicate that natural disasters constitute "worst events" for a small minority of individuals reporting lifetime PTSD (5.2% for men, 3.5% for women; Kessler et al., 1995). In addition, the conditional risk of PTSD associated with natural disasters is quite low (3.8% for randomly selected event, 4.1% for worst event; Breslau et al., 2004). Focused studies of specific trauma-exposed populations, such as Florida residents affected by hurricanes, have also found low population-based prevalence rates of disaster-related PTSD (3.6%; Acierno et al., 2007). However, high rates of hurricane-related PTSD (22.5%) were recently reported in a sample of Hurricane Katrina survivors (Galea, Tracy, Norris, & Coffey, 2008).

These higher rates are likely due to the high death toll, severe property damage, and relocation that were unique to Katrina.

Witnessed Violence

Exposure to witnessed violence represents one of the most common types of Criterion A1 events. Data from the National Comorbidity Survey found that 35.6% of men and 14.5% of women witnessed someone being badly injured or killed (Kessler et al., 1995); witnessed violence was also the second most common worst event reported by men with lifetime PTSD (combat being the most common). Conditional risk of PTSD associated with witnessed violence varies, likely due to the variability in severity of exposure. For example, Breslau et al. (2004) found the risk to be 7.3% and 11.4% for randomly selected and worst-event traumas, respectively. However, North, Smith, and Spitznagel (1994) found that 20% of men and 36% of women who had been exposed to a mass shooting spree met diagnostic criteria for PTSD one month later. Seeing someone accidentally injured or killed would likely lead to lower risk of PTSD than witnessed violence involving intentional acts of harm in which the exposed individual may have actually been in serious danger. These characteristics are not typically distinguished in epidemiological studies. However, Kilpatrick et al. (2003) found that witnessed violence increased PTSD risk after controlling for the effects of direct exposure to violence.

Unexpected Death of a Loved One

Though unexpected death of a loved one was arguably considered a Criterion A event in *DSM-III-R*, it was given greater emphasis in *DSM-IV* and was specifically assessed in epidemiological studies using *DSM-IV* criteria (e.g., Kessler et al., 2005). As discussed previously, when Criterion A was broadened to include this event, it led to substantial increases in PTSD cases in one study (Breslau & Kessler, 2001). Unexpected death of a loved one represents the most common specific Criterion A1 in recent epidemiological studies (Breslau et al., 1998; Roberts et al., 2011) and is the event most likely to be identified as "worst" (Breslau et al., 2004). The conditional risk of PTSD associated with such events is in the moderate range for Criterion A1 events, with 14.3% meeting PTSD criteria in the Detroit Area Survey (Breslau et al., 1998). One epidemiological study assessed homicide-related PTSD in family members and friends of victims of criminal homicide and alcohol-related vehicular homicide and found that 23.3% of immediate family survivors experienced PTSD at some point in their lives, while 4.8% met criteria for PTSD in the past six months (Amick-McMullan et al., 1991).

Focused longitudinal studies of individuals who had recently experienced the unexpected death of a loved one are complicated by the difficulties inherent in identifying and enrolling those who may still be experiencing significant grief reactions. A few noteworthy studies have been conducted, however. For example, one investigation examined rates of PTSD among bereaved parents of 12- to 28-year-olds who had suffered violent death (accident, suicide, or homicide) and found that 5% of fathers and 34% of mothers met criteria for PTSD four months after their child's death, while 14% of fathers and 21% of mothers met criteria two years following the event (Murphy et al., 1999). The rates of PTSD at four months were significantly associated with cause of death, with the highest rates among mothers and fathers who had lost their child to homicide (mothers: 60%, fathers: 40%). An additional study of widows and widowers found at two months post-loss that 10% whose spouse had died of chronic illness met diagnostic criteria for PTSD, 9% whose spouse died unexpectedly had PTSD, and 36% of those whose spouses died from accidents or suicides met criteria for PTSD (Zisook, Chentsova-Dutton, & Shuchter, 1998).

Overall, there appears to be greater conditional risk of PTSD associated with violent unexpected deaths than unexpected deaths, broadly considered. These findings have implications for the new Criterion A definition put forward in preliminary revisions of the *DSM-5*. The new Criterion, as mentioned earlier, specifies that the unexpected deaths must be violent or accidental in nature; thus, medically related unexpected deaths would not qualify. This will likely have the effect of reducing the prevalence of exposure to unexpected death of a loved one as well as increasing the conditional risk associated with this event.

Situational Determinants of PTSD Risk

Various features of Criterion A events are associated with increased risk of PTSD. These will be discussed next.

Direct Threat versus Witnessed Threat

Among the situational determinants of risk includes the perception that either the individual or someone else is at risk during the traumatic event. As previously discussed, evidence suggests that events involving direct threat to the individual (e.g., physical assault) are likely to lead to greater PTSD symptoms than those in which the individual witnesses threat, serious injury, or death to someone else (i.e., witnessed violence). However, Alden, Regambal, & Laposa (2008) found that emergency department healthcare workers who experienced direct threat events reported comparable PTSD symptoms to those who experienced witnessed threat events. The direct-threat group reported greater arousal symptoms and work-related consequences, including an unwillingness to take overtime shifts, negative feelings toward the hospital, and job dissatisfaction. Interestingly, the witnessed-threat group appraised their PTSD symptoms more negatively than the direct-threat group, which provides evidence of the role of trauma type in influencing symptom presentation.

Severity of Potentially Tramatic Event

Meta-analytic findings suggest traumatic event severity, including measures of combat exposure among combat veterans and factors such as injury within crime victim samples, is a potent risk factor for PTSD (Brewin, Andrews, & Valentine, 2000). Interestingly, the effect sizes for this risk factor vary according to whether the study design was prospective or retrospective, with retrospective studies yielding greater associations between severity and PTSD risk. Such findings suggest that PTSD diagnosis may negatively bias retrospective recall of traumatic events. However, it is also possible that more severe traumatic events are those that are both most likely to be remembered and to result in PTSD.

There is marked variability in the assessment of PTE severity across studies and PTE types. Civilian PTE severity is typically assessed using more subjective criteria than that used for combat or motor vehicle accidents (Brewin, Andrews, & Valentine, 2000). Studies of motor vehicle accident survivors often use objective measures of injury severity. This perhaps explains why a strong relationship between combat severity and PTSD exists (Brewin, Andrews, & Valentine, 2000), though the relationship between PTE severity and PTSD is less consistently demonstrated for motor vehicle accidents (Taylor & Koch, 1995). This is also evidence for the importance of subjective appraisal of PTEs in determining risk.

Analyses of the role of injury severity in risk of PTSD are often complicated by range restriction. Many individuals who suffer motor vehicle accidents are not injured severely enough to present to emergency rooms and be recruited for risk-factor studies, whereas those who are most severely injured (e.g., in need of life-saving surgery) are often unable to participate in such studies. One recent prospective study examined a large sample of individuals hospitalized for traumatic injuries and found that mild traumatic brain injury, objectively identified, increased risk for PTSD at 3 months and 12 months postinjury (Bryant et al., 2010).

Pain and Ongoing Stressors

Level of pain reported shortly after traumatic injury has been found to increase risk of PTSD (Norman, Stein, Dimsdale, & Hoyt, 2008). More prolonged, chronic pain following traumatic events is also related to PTSD chronicity (Bryant, Marosszeky, Crooks, Baguley, & Gurka, 1999). This has led some to hypothesize a mutual maintenance model in which PTSD and chronic pain are maintained by common or mutually reinforcing factors (e.g., behavioral avoidance, arousal; Sharp & Harvey, 2001).

There is also evidence that stressors resulting from Criterion A1 events increase risk of PTSD. For example, Blanchard and colleagues (1996) found prospective evidence that litigation related to motor vehicle accidents increases risk of PTSD, although it was also true that more serious cases were more likely to result in lawsuits. Additionally, researchers found that hurricane-related financial loss and postdisaster stressors were associated with greater risk of PTSD among survivors of Hurricane Katrina (Galea et al., 2008). The mechanisms by which postdisaster stressors increase risk of PTSD have not been studied extensively, but it is possible that increased risk may be a consequence of increased anxiety or hyperarousal produced by such stressors (i.e., symptom overlap). Postevent stressors might also serve as reminders and lead to more negative perceptions of the event.

Perceived Responsibility for the Trauma

Attributions of responsibility for different traumatic events have been studied in relation to risk for PTSD. For example, Delahanty et al. (1997) found that those who blamed others for their motor vehicle accidents experienced greater PTSD symptoms at 6 months and 12 months postaccident than a control group that experienced minor accidents; individuals who blamed themselves did not differ from the control group in PTSD symptoms at these later assessments. These findings were subsequently replicated by Hickling, Blanchard, Buckley, and Taylor (1999), who found that those who blamed themselves for their motor vehicle accidents recovered more quickly than those who blamed others. Researchers also found that self-blame for traumatic events leading to severe burns was associated with lower risk of acute stress disorder than other-blame in a sample of hospitalized burn victims (Lambert, Difede, & Contrada, 2004). Some research has found self-blame to predict *increased* risk of PTSD (Filipas & Ullman, 2006) or more severe psychological distress (Weaver & Clum, 1995) among sexual assault or abuse survivors, which implicates the importance of considering event type, as well as rationality of attributions when assessing their potential role.

Demographic Risk Factors for PTSD Following Traumatic Event Exposure

Certain demographic variables have also emerged as risk factors for PTSD following traumatic event exposure, though the associations between some of these variables (e.g., age, ethnicity) and increased risk are inconsistent. This literature will be discussed next.

Gender

There is now an abundance of evidence indicating that women are at greater risk of PTSD compared to men. In the National Comorbidity Survey, differences in risk of *DSM-III-R* PTSD were noted among those exposed to trauma, with 20.4% of women meeting PTSD diagnostic criteria compared to 8.4% of men (Kessler et al., 1995). Tolin and Foa's (2006) meta-analysis demonstrated the consistency of this relationship across 25 years of research. Greater conditional risk of PTSD among women is found even when controlling for trauma type. For example, one prospective study found that women had rates of PTSD that were over twice as high as men following a motor vehicle accident (Fullerton et al., 2001). These findings complement epidemiological studies that have found comparable gender differences in the prevalence rates of other anxiety disorders (Kessler et al., 1994). However, as noted earlier, differential characteristics of assault (e.g., physical assault) or different patterns of exposure to a range of events may also account for some observed gender differences in PTSD prevalence (Pimlott-Kubiak & Cortina, 2003) and ongoing research should consider and attempt to control for such factors when evaluating gender differences in PTSD.

Age

There is some evidence to suggest that conditional risk of PTSD declines with older age. For example, Brewin, Andrews, and Valentine's (2000) meta-analysis indicated that younger age at the time of exposure was associated with greater risk of PTSD. Interestingly, they found that younger age only predicted increased risk of PTSD in military samples, though it was not associated with increased risk in civilian samples. Younger age was also more strongly related to increased PTSD risk for men than for women, though this was likely a product of the military study findings, which mostly examined all-male samples.

Ethnicity

There is some evidence implicating a relationship between ethnic minority status and increased risk for PTSD. Meta-analytic findings have demonstrated such a relationship, though it was stronger in military samples than in civilian samples and was present in male but not female samples (Brewin, Andrews, & Valentine, 2000). Race may act as a proxy for other demographic risk factors, including socioeconomic status or exposure severity. Consistent with this explanation, Breslau et al. (1998) found a much higher conditional risk of PTSD among nonwhites compared to whites (14.0% vs. 7.3%), though this difference was made nonsignificant when controlling for other demographic variables. An analysis of the National Vietnam Veterans Readjustment Survey revealed that, compared to whites, elevated rates of PTSD among blacks were accounted for by greater exposure, and higher rates of PTSD among Hispanics were accounted for by a combination of greater exposure, younger age, lesser education, and lower scores on the Armed Forces Qualification Test (Dohrenwend et al., 2008).

Recently published data from the National Epidemiological Survey on Alcohol and Related Conditions (N = 34,653) found the highest prevalence of PTSD among blacks (8.7%) and the lowest among Asians (4.0%), with Hispanics (7.0%) and whites (7.4%) having prevalence rates in the middle (Roberts et al., 2011). Analyses of conditional risk found that blacks were at greater risk of PTSD and Asians were at lower risk of PTSD than whites, after adjusting for gender, age at interview, and trauma characteristics.

Income and Education

Lower socioeconomic status has been linked to increased conditional risk for PTSD (Brewin, Andrews, & Valentine, 2000). This relationship has been demonstrated prospectively in event-focused studies. For example, Irish et al. (2008) found that lower income was modestly predictive of greater PTSD symptoms at six weeks and one year following a motor vehicle accident. Lower education is also associated with increased risk for PTSD. A Vietnam twin registry study revealed that less than high school education at the time of entry into the military was uniquely predictive of combat-related PTSD, even after controlling for other risk factors (Koenen et al., 2002). Lower income may be associated with fewer resources for coping with the trauma, and both lower income and lower educational attainment may be proxies for low intelligence, an established risk factor for PTSD following trauma (Brewin, Andrews, & Valentine, 2000).

Conclusions

We have hoped to discuss many issues of relevance to the topic of what constitutes a traumatic event. These issues have important implications for the assessment of PTSD. Many of the controversies and limitations we mentioned might be resolved as further studies are conducted. Next we list some future areas of research that would be beneficial to address.

Future Directions

1. How Should We Address the Issue of Cumulative Exposure?

The question of how to address cumulative exposure to multiple stressor events—PTEs, traumatic events, and lesser stressors—over a lifetime requires additional attention both conceptually and with respect to measurement. All major epidemiological studies (e.g., Breslau & Kessler, 2001; Kessler et al., 1995; Kilpatrick, Acierno, Resnick, Saunders, & Best, 2000; Kilpatrick et al., 2009; Resnick et al., 1993) have found that many individuals have been exposed to multiple PTEs and traumatic events, but few studies include comprehensive assessment of PTSD in reference to all potential qualifying PTEs as well as other stressors. The PTSD assessment strategy most often used in cases of exposure to multiple events is to assess PTSD with regard to the "worst" event and/or to a randomly selected event. Neither of these approaches permits adequate assessment of potential cumulative exposure to PTEs or of whether cumulative exposure to PTEs may account for PTSD symptoms that may appear to result from exposure to a recent event that is not a PTE. There has been little to no research investigating whether an "aggregate PTSD" due to multiple events differs in important ways from PTSD linked to a specific event. How prevalent is the aggregate type? Is the consideration of this type clinically or empirically useful? Such questions deserve further inquiry.

Criterion A was born in controversy, and it is unlikely that the proposed changes in its definition in the *DSM-5* will resolve this controversy, particularly the arguments about the definition that involve philosophical issues and value judgments. However, some of the questions about Criterion A do lend themselves to empirical investigation. We believe that the most important questions about Criterion A cannot be answered without a new strategy for assessing PTSD that incorporates a way to assess the potential impact of having experienced more than one PTE when that occurs. Here we review key issues related to optimal or improved strategy to assess PTSD in reference to multiple PTE exposure history, as well as a newly developed PTSD assessment measure designed to implement that approach. We then summarize points regarding additional areas of research that are needed.

NEED FOR A PTSD ASSESSMENT STRATEGY THAT ADDRESSES EXPOSURE TO MULTIPLE PTES

When the PTSD diagnosis was first established in 1980, most traumatic stress researchers and clinicians were focused on a single type of PTE (e.g., accidents, child abuse, combat, disasters, or violence against women). Exposure to all such events was considered to be rare, so there was little consideration of the possibility that a substantial number of individuals may have been exposed to more than one PTE throughout their lives. Therefore, if PTE exposure is assumed to be rare and exposure to multiple PTE types and/or multiple exposure to PTEs of the same type are thought to be exceedingly rare, then a PTSD assessment approach that focuses on changes in symptomatology and functioning after exposure to a specific PTE makes a great deal of sense because most people having experienced a PTE will have experienced only one event. However, as noted throughout the chapter, exposure to multiple events is common, making the assessment task more complicated. A range of qualifying

PTEs and other stressor events may occur across the life span, including interpersonal violence events that first occur in childhood and which may moderate risk of PTSD to subsequent events (e.g., Binder et al., 2008; Smith et al., 2008). Getting a more comprehensive picture of whether PTSD develops following specific qualifying or other stressor events and what the trajectory or course of reported symptoms is among those with multiple-event exposure would be helpful in addressing key questions about Criterion A. One approach to accomplishing this would be to use an assessment measure that includes comprehensive evaluation of event exposure history and chronology, and that allows for assessment of PTSD symptom onset or worsening in reference to any referent events. The proposed *DSM-5* criteria for PTSD explicitly state that it is necessary to demonstrate that PTSD symptoms are associated with traumatic events, defined as having begun or worsened after the traumatic event(s) (APA, 2010). This requirement means that it is important for PTSD diagnosis to establish whether each PTSD symptom occurred or got worse after a specific PTE occurred. In cases involving more than one PTE, assessment would appear to require assessing whether PTSD symptoms are associated with (i.e., the symptom began after or was worsened by) each PTE experienced by the individual. There are two potential ways to approach this diagnostic requirement.

The first way is to use a traditional PTSD assessment instrument such as the Clinician-Administered PTSD Schedule (CAPS; Blake et al., 1995) or PTSD Checklist (Weathers, Litz, Herman, Huska, & Keane, 1993) and apply it to every PTE reported by an individual. Given that the proposed PTSD diagnosis for *DSM-5* now has 20 PTSD symptoms, this assessment strategy would be lengthy when applied to multiple PTEs and might prove to be burdensome. Particularly in cases with PTE exposure during childhood and subsequent PTE exposure as an adult, those assessed would have to make difficult, and perhaps impossible, judgments about when a symptom first occurred and whether it worsened after each PTE.

A second approach toward PTSD symptom assessment involves comprehensive assessment of lifetime PTE exposure in conjunction with assessment of PTSD symptoms in reference to any PTE reported. The procedure used in the National Women's Study (NWS) PTSD Module (Kilpatrick, Acierno, Resnick, Saunders, & Best, 1997; Resnick et al., 1993), is one such approach that has been shown to be a reliable and valid measure that yields comparable results to those obtained with structured diagnostic interviews such as the SCID (Kilpatrick et al., 1998).

A PROPOSED METHOD TO ASSESS PSTD IN REFERENCE TO HISTORY OF SINGLE OR MULTIPLE PTE EXPOSURE

We recently modified the NWS PTSD Module and constructed a new self-report PTSD measure, the National Stressful Events Survey (NSES) PTSD Module (Kilpatrick, Resnick, Baber, Guille, & Gros, 2010), that is designed to measure PTSD using the proposed *DSM-5* Criteria. The NSES measure was constructed for use in a large Web survey, but it can also be used in a structured interview format. Specifically, the assessment strategy used has four parts. First, a comprehensive assessment of lifetime exposure to PTEs is conducted. Second, additional descriptive information is obtained about a subset of PTEs experienced—for example, the first, most recent, and worst PTE experienced. Third, individuals with any lifetime PTE exposure are asked whether they have ever had each PTSD symptom at any time during their lives. Fourth, for each lifetime symptom endorsed, a series of follow-up questions are asked. For PTSD symptoms that include direct reference to a PTE (e.g., recurrent distressing dreams that are related to the content of the event; inability to remember an important aspect of the traumatic event), a follow-up question asks the respondent to identify which of any lifetime PTE or PTEs was/were involved in the symptom content. For other PTSD symptoms not directly referencing PTEs (e.g., hypervigilance, problems with concentration), a follow-up question asks if the symptom either happened or got worse after a PTE, and if so, to identify each lifetime PTE that is applicable.

Other follow-ups include obtaining information about symptom recency and about how disturbing the symptom has been during the past month. This approach allows for evaluation of meeting criteria in reference to any lifetime PTE reported. For example, number of intrusion, persistent avoidance, negative alterations in cognitions and mood, alterations in arousal and reactivity symptoms in reference to specific events can be computed and those events associated with meeting necessary criteria for diagnosis may be determined. Additional questions are included to assess functional impairment and duration criteria.

Questions related to PTSD in association with complex history of PTE exposure may be possible to address using this approach. In some cases, individuals with a history of exposure to multiple PTEs may meet full symptom criteria in reference to several events. It may also be possible that an individual may report symptoms in reference to multiple events but not fully meet criteria in reference to any single PTE. The latter pattern might provoke additional needed discussion regarding the issue of "aggregate PTSD" if it was clear, for example, that all necessary criterion symptoms occurred within the same time frame (e.g., past month), but constituted a mix of PTEs as reference events.

2. *What Additional Research Is Needed about Bereavement and PTSD?*

The proposed *DSM-5* definition of Criterion A includes learning about events involving the death of a relative or close friend if the death was violent or accidental. This definition is more restrictive than in *DSM-IV* because it excludes deaths due to natural causes. In addition, proposals have been put forth advocating the inclusion of a prolonged grief (PG) or complicated grief (CG) diagnosis within the *DSM-5*. There is overlap between some of the criteria and symptoms of the proposed PG and CG diagnoses with those of the proposed PTSD diagnosis, but two types of additional research are needed to clarify PTSD as a response to learning about the deaths of loved ones and how PTSD relates to PG and/or CG. First, research is needed that tests the assumption in the *DSM-5* proposed definition that development of PTSD is limited to those who learn about accidental or violent deaths versus learning about deaths occurring due to natural causes. Without information comparing PTSD associated with learning about different types of deaths, it will be difficult to determine whether restricting the types of deaths to accidents or violent deaths is supported by data. Second, research is needed about the degree to which there is overlap between PTSD and the proposed PG or CG diagnoses following bereavement associated with different types of deaths.

3. *How Meaningful Are Recollections of Distant Traumatic Events and Their Associated Sequelae?*

Recent epidemiological evidence suggests that the prevalence of some psychiatric diagnoses doubles if prospective rather than retrospective designs are used (Moffit et al., 2010), although this study did not specifically address PTSD. Much of what we know about the consequences of various traumatic events relies on retrospective studies, and findings from such studies may underestimate the prevalence of exposure to PTEs. Expansive, longitudinal studies that are able to capture the occurrence of a variety of recent traumatic events can address the problems associated with recall failure to some extent and should provide more accurate estimates of lifetime PTSD prevalence. However, given that exposure to some types of PTEs begins early in life and given the high cost of longitudinal research with probability samples, there is still an important role for well-designed retrospective studies.

References

Acierno, R., Ruggiero, K. J., Galea, S., Resnick, H. S., Koenen, K., Roitzsch, J., de Arellano, M., et al. (2007). Psychological sequelae resulting from the 2004 Florida hurricanes: Implications for postdisaster intervention. *American Journal of Public Health, 97*(Suppl. 1), S103–108.

Adler, A. B., Wright, K. M., Bliese, P. D., Eckford, R., & Hoge, C. W. (2008). A2 Diagnostic criterion for combat-related posttraumatic stress disorder, *Journal of Traumatic Stress, 21*, 301–308.

Alden, L. E., Regambal, M. J., & Laposa, J. M. (2008). The effects of direct versus witnessed threat on emergency department healthcare workers: Implications for PTSD Criterion A. *Journal of Anxiety Disorders, 22*, 1337–1346.

American Psychiatric Association. (1980). *Diagnostic and statistical manual of mental disorders* (3rd ed.). Washington, DC: Author.

American Psychiatric Association. (1987). *Diagnostic and statistical manual of mental disorders* (3rd ed., rev.). Washington, DC: Author.

American Psychiatric Association. (1994). *Diagnostic and statistical manual of mental disorders* (4th ed.). Washington, DC: Author.

American Psychiatric Association. (2000). *Diagnostic and statistical manual of mental disorders* (4th ed., text rev.). Washington, DC: Author.

American Psychiatric Association. (2010). *Proposed Revision – APA DSM-5*. Retrieved from: http://www.dsm5.org/ProposedRevisions/Pages/ proposedrevision.aspx?rid=165.

Amick-McMullan, A., Kilpatrick, D. G., & Resnick, H. S. (1991). Homicide as a risk factor for PTSD among surviving family members. *Behavior Modification, 15*, 545–559.

Binder, E. B., Bradley, R. G., Liu, W., Epstein, M. P., Deveau, T. C., Mercer, K. B., et al. (2008). Association of FKBP5 polymorphisms and childhood abuse with risk of posttraumatic stress disorder symptoms in adults. *Journal of the American Medical Association, 299*, 1291–1305.

Blake, D. D., Weathers, F. W., Nagy, L. M., Kaloupek, D. G., Gusman, F. D., Charney, D. S., & Keane, T. M. (1995). The development of a clinician-administered PTSD scale. *Journal of Traumatic Stress, 8*, 75–90.

Blanchard, E. B., Hickling, E. J., Taylor, E., Loos, W. R., Forneris, C. A., & Jaccard, J. (1996). Who develops PTSD from motor vehicle accidents? *Behaviour Research and Therapy, 34*, 1–10.

Breslau, N., Davis, G. C., Peterson, E. L., and Schultz, L. (1997). Psychiatric sequelae of posttraumatic stress disorder in women. *Archives of General Psychiatry, 54*, 81–87.

Breslau, N., & Kessler, R. C. (2001). The stressor criterion in *DSM–IV* posttraumatic stress disorder: An empirical investigation. *Biological Psychiatry, 50*, 699–704.

Breslau, N., Kessler, R. C., Chilcoat, H. D., Schultz, L. R., Davis, G. C., & Andreski, P. (1998). Trauma and posttraumatic stress disorder in the community: The 1996 Detroit area survey of trauma. *Archives of General Psychiatry, 55*, 626–632.

Breslau, N., Peterson, E. L., Poisson, L. M., Schultz, L. R., & Lucia, V. C. (2004). Estimating post-traumatic stress disorder in the community: Lifetime perspective and the impact of typical traumatic events. *Psychological Medicine, 34*, 889–898.

Brewin, C. R., Andrews, B., & Rose, S. (2000). Fear, helplessness, and horror in posttraumatic stress disorder: Investigating DSM-IV criterion A2 in victims of violent crime. *Journal of Traumatic Stress, 13*(3), 499–509.

Brewin, C. R., Andrews, B., & Valentine, J. D. (2000). Meta-analysis of risk factors for posttraumatic stress disorder in trauma-exposed adults. *Journal of Consulting and Clinical Psychology, 68*, 748–766.

Brewin, C.R., Lanius, R.A., Novac, A., Schnyder, U., & Galea, S. (2009). Reformulating PTSD for DSM-V: Life After Criterion A. *Journal of Traumatic Stress, 22*, 366–373.

Bryant, R. A., Marosszeky, J. E., Crooks, J., Baguley, I. J., & Gurka, J. A. (1999). Interaction of posttraumatic stress disorder and chronic pain following traumatic brain injury. *Journal of Head Trauma Rehabilitation, 14*, 588–594.

Bryant, R. A., O'Donnell, M. L., Creamer, M., McFarlane, A. C., Clark, C. R., & Silove, D. (2010). The psychiatric sequelae of traumatic injury. *American Journal of Psychiatry, 167*, 312–320.

Davidson, J. R. T., & Foa, E. B. (1991). Diagnostic issues in PTSD: Considerations for the DSM IV. *Journal of Abnormal Psychology, 100*, 346–355.

Delahanty, D. L., Herberman, H. B., Craig, K. J., Hayward, M. C., Fullerton, C. S., Ursano, R. J., et al. (1997). Acute and chronic distress and posttraumatic stress disorder as a function of responsibility for serious motor vehicle accidents. *Journal of Consulting and Clinical Psychology, 65*, 560–567.

Dohrenwend, B. P., Turner, J. B., Turse, N. A., Adams, B. G., Koenen, K. C., & Marshall, R. (2006). The psychological risks of Vietnam for U.S. veterans: A revisit with new data and methods. *Science, 313*, 979–982.

Duncan, R. D., Saunders, B. E., Kilpatrick, D. G., Hanson, R. F., & Resnick, H. S. (1996). Childhood physical assault as a risk factor for PTSD, depression, and substance abuse: Findings from a national survey. *American Journal of Orthopsychiatry, 66*, 437–448.

Ehring, T., Ehlers, A., & Glucksman, E. (2008). Do cognitive models help in predicting the severity of posttraumatic stress disorder, phobia, and depression after motor vehicle accidents? A prospective longitudinal study. *Journal of Consulting and Clinical Psychology, 76*, 219-230.

Elklit, A., & Brink, O. (2004). Acute stress disorder as a predictor of post-traumatic stress disorder in physical assault victims. *Journal of Interpersonal Violence, 19*, 709–726.

Filipas, H. H., & Ullman, S. E. (2006). Child sexual abuse, coping responses, self-blame, posttraumatic stress disorder, and adult sexual revictimization. *Journal of Interpersonal Violence*, 21, 652–672.

Freedy, J. R., Resnick, H. S., Kilpatrick, D. G., Dansky, B. S., & Tidwell, R. P. (1994). The psychological adjustment of recent crime victims in the criminal justice system. *Journal of Interpersonal Violence, 9*, 450–468.

Fullerton, C. S., Ursano, R. J., Epstein, R. S., Crowley, B., Vance, K., Kao, T. C., Dougall, A., & Baum, A. (2001). Gender differences in posttraumatic stress disorder after motor vehicle accidents. *American Journal of Psychiatry, 158*(9), 1486–1491.

Galea, S., Tracy, M., Norris, F., & Coffey, S. (2008). Financial and social circumstances, the incidence and course of PTSD in Mississippi during the first two years after Hurricane Katrina. *Journal of Traumatic Stress, 21*, 357–368.

Gold, S. D., Marx, B. P., Soler-Baillo, J. M., & Sloan, D. M. (2005). Is life stress more traumatic than traumatic stress? *Journal of Anxiety Disorders, 19*, 687–698.

Halligan, S. L., Michael, T., Clark, D. M., & Ehlers, A. (2003). Posttraumatic stress disorder following assault: The role of cognitive processing, trauma memory, and appraisals. *Journal of Consulting and Clinical Psychology, 71*, 419–431.

Hickling, E. J., Blanchard, E. B., Buckley, T. C., & Taylor, A. E. (1999). Effects of attribution of responsibility for motor vehicle accidents on severity of PTSD symptoms, ways of coping, and recovery over six months. *Journal of Traumatic Stress, 12*, 345–353.

Hoge, C. W., Castro, C. A., Messer, S. C., McGurk, D., Cotting, D. I., & Koffman, R. L. (2004). Combat duty in Iraq and Afghanistan, mental health problems and barriers to care. *New England Journal of Medicine, 351*, 13–22.

Irish, L., Ostrowski, S. A., Fallon, W. F., Spoonster, E., Van Dulmen, M., Sledjeski, E. M., & Delahanty, D. L. (2008). Trauma history characteristics and subsequent PTSD symptoms in motor vehicle accident victims. *Journal of Traumatic Stress, 21*, 77–384.

Kessler, R. C., Berglund, P., Demler, O., Jin, R., Merikangas, K. R., & Walters, E. E. (2005). Lifetime prevalence and age-of-onset distributions of *DSM-IV* disorders in the National Comorbidity Survey Replication. *Archives of General Psychiatry, 62*, 593–602.

Kessler, R. C., McGonagle, K. A., Zhao, S., Nelson, C. B., Hughes, M., Eshleman, S., Wittchen, H.-U. & Kendler, K. S. (1994). Lifetime and 12-month prevalence of DSM-III-R psychiatric disorders in the United States: Results from the National Comorbidity Survey. *Archives of General Psychiatry*, 51, 8–19.

Kessler, R. C., Sonnega, A., Bromet, E., Hughes, M., & Nelson, C. B. (1995). Posttraumatic stress disorder in the National Comorbidity Survey. *Archives of General Psychiatry, 52*, 1048–1060.

Kilpatrick, D. G., Acierno, R., Resnick, H. S., Saunders, B. E., & Best, C. L. (1997). A 2-year longitudinal analysis of the relationship between violent assault and substance use in women. *Journal of Consulting and Clinical Psychology, 65*, 834–847.

Kilpatrick, D. G., Acierno, R. E., Resnick, H. S., Saunders, B. E., & Best, C. L. (2000). Risk factors for adolescent substance abuse and dependence: Data from a national sample. *Journal of Consulting and Clinical Psychology, 68*, 19–30.

Kilpatrick, D. G., Resnick, H. S., & Acierno, R. (2009). Should PTSD Criterion A be retained? *Journal of Traumatic Stress, 22*, 374–383.

Kilpatrick, D. G., Resnick, H. S., Baber, B., Guille, C., & Gros, K. (2010). National Stressful Events Survey PTSD Module. Unpublished instrument.

Kilpatrick, D. G., Resnick, H. S., Freedy, J. R., Pelcovitz, D., Resick, P., Roth, S., et al. (1998). Posttraumatic stress disorder field trial: Evaluation of the PTSD construct-Criteria A through E. In T. Widiger, A. Frances, H. Pincus, R. Ross, M. First, W. Davis, et al. (Eds.), *DSM-IV Sourcebook, Vol. 4* (pp. 803–844). Washington, DC: American Psychiatric Press.

Kilpatrick, D. G., Saunders, B. E., & Smith, D. W. (2003). *Youth Violence: Prevalence and Implications* (Research in Brief NCJ 194972). Washington, DC: National Institute of Justice.

Kleim, B., Ehlers, A., & Glucksman, E. (2007). Early predictors of chronic post-traumatic stress disorder in assault survivors. *Psychological Medicine, 37,* 1457–1468.

Koenen, K. C., Harney, R., Lyons, M. J., Wolfe, J., Simpson, J. C., Goldberg, J., et al. (2002). A twin registry study of familial and individual risk factors for trauma exposure and posttraumatic stress disorder. *Journal of Nervous and Mental Disease, 190,* 209–218.

Kulka, R. A., Schlenger, W. E., Fairbank, I. A., Hough, R. L., Jordan, B. K., Marmar, C. R. and Weiss, D. S. (1988). *Contractual Report of Findings from the National Vietnam Veterans Readjustment Study.* Research Triangle Park, NC: Research Triangle Institute.

Lambert, J., Difede, J., & Contrada, R. (2004). The relationship of attribution of responsibility to acute stress disorder among hospitalized burn patients. *Journal of Nervous and Mental Disease, 192,* 304–312.

Long, M. E., Elhai, J. D., Schweinle, A., Gray, M. J., Grubaugh, A. L., & Frueh, B. C. (2008). Differences in posttraumatic stress disorder diagnostic rates and symptom severity between Criterion A1 and non-Criterion A1 stressors. *Journal of Anxiety Disorders, 22,* 1255–1263.

McLeer, S., Callaghan, M., Henry, D., & Wallen, J. (1994). Psychiatric disorders in sexually abused children. *Journal of the American Academy of Child and Adolescent Psychiatry, 33,* 313–319.

McNally, R. J. (2003). Progress and controversy in the study of posttraumatic stress disorder. *Annual Review of Psychology, 54,* 229–252.

McNally, R. J. (2009). Can we fix PTSD in DSM-V? *Depression and Anxiety, 26,* 597–600.

Moffit, T. E., Caspi, A., Taylor, A., Kokaua, J., Milne, B. J., Polanczyk, G., & Poulton, R. (2010). How common are common mental disorders? Evidence that lifetime prevalence rates are doubled by prospective *versus* retrospective ascertainment. *Psychological Medicine, 40,* 899–909.

Murphy, S. A., Braun,T., Tillery, L., Cain, K. C., Johnson, L. C., & Beaton, R. D. (1999). PTSD among Bereaved parents following the violent deaths of their 12- to 28-year-old children: A longitudinal prospective analysis. *Journal of Traumatic Stress,* 12, 273–291.

Norman, S. B., Stein, M. B., Dimsdale, J. E., & Hoyt, D. B. (2008). Pain in the aftermath of trauma is a risk factor for a post-traumatic stress disorder. *Psychological Medicine, 38,* 533–542.

North, C. S., Smith, E. M., & Spitznagel, E. L. (1994). Post-traumatic stress disorder in survivors of a mass shooting. *American Journal of Psychiatry, 15,* 82–88.

O'Donnell, M. L., Creamer, M. C., Parslow, R., Elliott, P., Holmes, A. C. N., Ellen, S., et al. (2008). A predictive screening index for posttraumatic stress disorder and depression following traumatic injury. *Journal of Consulting and Clinical Psychology, 76*(6), 923–932.

Pimlott-Kubiak, S., & Cortina, L. M. (2003). Gender, victimization, and outcomes: Reconceptualizing risk. *Journal of Consulting and Clinical Psychology, 71,* 528–539.

Resnick, H. S., Kilpatrick, D., Dansky, B., Saunders, B., & Best, C. (1993). Prevalence of civilian trauma and posttraumatic stress disorder in a representative national sample of women. *Journal of Consulting and Clinical Psychology, 61,* 984–991.

Riggs, D., Rothbaum, B. O., & Foa, E. (1995). A prospective examination of symptoms of posttraumatic stress disorder in vicitms of nonsexual assault. *Journal of Interpersonal Violence, 10,* 201–214.

Roberts, A. L., Gilman, S. E., Breslau, J., Breslau, N., & Koenen, K. C. (2011). Race/ethnic differences in exposure to traumatic events, development of post-traumatic stress disorder, and treatment-seeking for post-traumatic stress disorder in the United States. *Psychological Medicine, 41,* 71–83.

Roemer, L., Orsillo, S. M., Borkovec, T. D., & Litz, B. T. (1998). Emotional response at the time of a potentially traumatizing event and PTSD symptomatology: A preliminary retrospective analysis of the DSM-IV criterion A-2. *Journal of Behavior Therapy and Experimental Psychiatry, 29,* 123–130.

Rothbaum, B. O., Foa, E. B., Riggs, D. S., Murdock, T., & Walsh, W. (1992). A prospective evaluation of post-traumatic stress disorder in rape victims. *Journal of Traumatic Stress, 5,* 455–475.

Schnurr, P. P., Spiro, A., Vielhauer, M. J., Findler, M. N., & Hamblen, J. L. (2002). Trauma in the lives of older men: Findings from the normative aging study. *Journal of Clinical Geropsychology, 8,* 175–187.

Sharp, T. J., & Harvey, A. G. (2001). Chronic pain and Posttraumatic Stress Disorder: Mutual maintenance? *Clinical Psychology Review, 21,* 857–877.

Smith, D. W., Saunders, B. E., & Kilpatrick, D. G. (2008). Prevalence and correlates of dating violence in a national sample of adolescents. *Journal of the American Academy of Child and Adolescent Psychiatry, 47,* 755–762.

Taylor, S., & Koch, W. J. (1995). Anxiety disorders due to motor vehicle accidents: Nature and treatment. *Clinical Psychology Review, 15,* 721–738.

Tolin, D. F., & Foa, E. B. (2006). Sex differences in trauma and posttraumatic stress disorder: A quantitative review of 25 years of research. *Psychological Bulletin, 132,* 959–992.

Weaver, T. L., & Clum, G. A. (1995). Psychological distress associated with interpersonal violence: A meta-analysis. *Clinical Psychology Review, 15,* 115–140.

Weathers, F. W., & Keane, T. M. (2007). The Criterion A problem revisited: Controversies and challenges in defining and measuring psychological trauma. *Journal of Traumatic Stress, 20,* 107–121.

Weathers, F., Litz, B., Herman, D., Huska, J., & Keane, T. (1993, October). *The PTSD Checklist (PCL): Reliability, validity, and diagnostic utility.* Paper presented at the Annual Convention of the International Society for Traumatic Stress Studies, San Antonio, TX.

Wells, J. E., & Horwood, L. J. (2004). How accurate is recall of key symptoms of depression? A comparison of recall and longitudinal reports. *Psychological Medicine, 34,* 1001–1011.

Zatzick, D. F., Rivara, F. P., Nathans, A. B., Jurkovich, G. J., Wang, J., Fan, M., Russo, J., Salkever, D. S., & MacKenzie, E. J. (2007). A nationwide US study of post-traumatic stress after hospitalization for physical injury. *Psychological Medicine, 37,* 1469–1480.

Zinzow, H. M., Rheingold, A. A., Hawkins, A. O., Saunders, B. E., & Kilpatrick, D. G. (2009). Losing a loved one to homicide: Prevalence and mental health correlates in a national sample of young adults. *Journal of Traumatic Stress, 22,* 20–27.

Zisook, S., Chentsova-Dutton, Y., & Shuchter, S. R. (1998). PTSD following bereavement. *Annals of Clinical Psychiatry, 10,* 157–163.

CHAPTER

3 Classification of Acute Stress Disorder

Maria L. Pacella *and* Douglas L. Delahanty

Abstract

The diagnosis of acute stress disorder (ASD) was created to identify survivors soon after a trauma who were likely to develop posttraumatic stress disorder (PTSD). Though ASD demonstrates acceptable predictive power, subsequent research has often failed to display high rates of sensitivity or specificity. These qualities, in combination with the large amount of shared diagnostic features between ASD and PTSD, have led researchers to question the utility of the diagnosis. However, other early predictors of PTSD also appear to suffer from similar criticisms of the ASD diagnosis. This chapter will review research examining the predictive utility of ASD in various populations, in the context of other cognitive, biological, and psychosocial predictors of PTSD, and in disorders other than PTSD. Finally, in light of the proposed changes to the ASD diagnosis for the DSM-5, future directions for research into early predictors of PTSD will be discussed.

Key Words: Acute stress disorder, posttraumatic stress disorder, dissociation, peritraumatic dissociation, intervention

Classification of Acute Stress Disorder

Initial posttraumatic stress symptoms are common following a trauma, yet for the majority of trauma survivors these symptoms are transient and do not develop into a consequent psychological disorder in need of psychological intervention. Previous research has estimated that 60% of men and 50% of women will be exposed to at least one traumatic event in their lifetime; however, epidemiological estimates of lifetime rates of posttraumatic stress disorder (PTSD) are relatively low (≈7–8%; Kessler et al., 2005; Kessler, Sonnega, Bromet, Hughes, & Nelson, 1995). Given that only a small percentage of trauma survivors develop posttraumatic stress disorder (PTSD), early identification of those individuals at highest risk of developing PTSD is important for efficient dedication of limited intervention resources.

Diagnostic criteria for PTSD require that symptoms be present for at least one month (*Diagnostic and Statistical Manual of Mental Disorders-IV-TR*; American Psychiatric Association [APA], 2000). Historically, this one-month duration criterion provided a window of time following trauma exposure during which symptomatic survivors were not diagnosable. Recognizing a need to describe and classify acute reactions experienced in the first month posttrauma, and to identify high-risk trauma survivors who were likely to develop PTSD, the diagnosis of acute stress disorder (ASD) was developed and included in the 4th edition of the *DSM* (APA, 1994). Prior to the inclusion of ASD, the only diagnostic option for trauma survivors who experienced severe posttraumatic symptoms within one month posttrauma was nonspecific adjustment disorder, which halted examination of preventive or early interventions for initial PTSD symptoms

(Marshall, Spitzer, & Liebowitz, 1999). The inclusion of ASD in the *DSM-IV* led to a resurgence in research examining early predictors of PTSD and early interventions to reduce/prevent the development of subsequent PTSD in recently traumatized survivors. The current chapter will provide a brief overview of ASD diagnostic criteria, followed by a review of research examining the extent to which ASD serves as a useful precursor diagnosis for PTSD risk. This literature will be reviewed in the context of comparing ASD symptoms to other biological, cognitive, and psychosocial predictors of PTSD. Finally, we will conclude with a brief discussion of cultural considerations of relevance to the ASD diagnosis and future directions in light of proposed changes to the ASD diagnostic criteria for the *DSM-5*.

Acute Stress Disorder

According to the *DSM-IV-TR*, a diagnosis of ASD requires that an individual react with intense fear, helplessness, or horror in response to a traumatic event that involved actual or threatened death or serious injury to one's self or others (Criterion A). Clinically significant social, occupational, or other functional impairment is also required, as is the experience of at least three of the following five dissociative symptoms: a subjective sense of emotional numbing or detachment from oneself or one's surroundings, reduced awareness of oneself or one's surroundings, derealization, depersonalization, and/or an inability to recall certain parts of the trauma (APA, 2000). Additionally, diagnosis with ASD requires endorsement of one symptom from each of the following clusters: re-experiencing (e.g., intrusive thoughts, flashbacks, nightmares), avoidance (e.g., avoid trauma-related thoughts and reminders), and persistent hyper-arousal (e.g., hyper-vigilance, exaggerated startle response, difficulty sleeping). These symptoms and consequent functional disturbances must persist for a minimum of two days and a maximum of four weeks (APA, 2000). If the condition endures for longer than one month, a diagnosis of PTSD should be considered.

Criterion A and the symptoms constituting the re-experiencing, avoidance, and hyper-arousal criteria are identical for ASD and PTSD. However, in addition to the differing time frames, there are other differences between the diagnostic criteria for ASD and PTSD. In order to diagnose PTSD, individuals must report at least one re-experiencing symptom, three avoidance or numbing symptoms, and two hyper-arousal symptoms. In contrast, a diagnosis of ASD requires only one symptom from each of these symptom clusters. The largest difference between the diagnoses of ASD and PTSD is the focus on dissociative symptoms as part of the ASD diagnosis, whereas a PTSD diagnosis lacks the inclusion of a dissociation criterion. Given that PTSD symptoms are relatively common soon after a traumatic event, the decision to require three dissociative symptoms and only one symptom from each of the other clusters was made so as to not negatively label the natural course of early post-traumatic symptoms (Marshall & Garakani, 2002).

The dissociation criterion was initially proposed due to its strong theoretical association with the development of PTSD (Bryant, 2006; Harvey & Bryant, 2002). That is, dissociation has been hypothesized to prevent the incorporation of fragmented, disorganized traumatic memories into existing cognitive schemas (Engelhard, van den Hout, Kindt, Arntz, & Schouten, 2003; Foa & Riggs, 1993), leading to the development of PTSD symptoms. Although initial dissociative responses may be adaptive as they potentially protect the individual from immediate overwhelming emotions (van der Hart, Nijenhuis, Steele, & Brown, 2004), dissociative symptoms may also preclude recovery in the long term by preventing emotional processing of the event (Foa & Hearst-Ikeda, 1996; Horowitz, 1986; Marmar et al., 1994; van der Kolk & van der Hart, 1989).

Despite theoretical support for the focus on dissociation in ASD, at the time when the diagnosis was included in the *DSM-IV*, little empirical evidence was available to justify the dissociative criterion for the ASD diagnosis. It was not until several years after the ASD was included in the *DSM* that a standardized instrument to assess ASD was developed (Bryant, Harvey, Dang, & Sackville, 1998)

The addition of ASD to the *DSM-IV* led to controversy, not only over the focus on dissociation but also over whether ASD represented a distinct disorder from PTSD and whether it uniquely contributed to identifying high-risk trauma survivors. To examine these questions, researchers sought to determine whether the ASD diagnosis could better identify individuals at risk for PTSD than other predictors (including initial PTSD symptoms), and whether the ASD diagnosis could distinguish between high-risk individuals and those displaying normal reactions to a traumatic event.

Are ASD and PTSD Distinct Disorders?

Despite the focus on dissociation in ASD, ASD and PTSD share several diagnostic features, leading researchers to question the extent to which the ASD diagnosis is distinct from the PTSD diagnosis (Marshall et al., 1999). One argument for the distinctive nature of ASD is provided by examining incidence rates of both disorders soon after trauma. Harvey and Bryant (2002) reviewed nine studies that reported rates of PTSD (minus the one-month duration criterion) within one month after a range of traumas including sexual and nonsexual assault, motor vehicle accidents, and victims of war. Rates of PTSD ranged from 8–100%, with more than half of the samples reporting rates of at least 30%. However, rates of ASD following similar types of trauma typically do not exceed 19% (Harvey & Bryant, 2002), suggesting that the diagnoses are capturing different adaptation levels posttrauma. Further, whereas 100% of assault victims met criteria for PTSD within one month of the trauma, only 43% of these victims satisfied ASD criteria (Jaycox, Johnson, & Foa, 1997, as cited in Marshall et al., 1999). In contrast to these findings, results from a study of 138 survivors of violent crime revealed a 95.5% overlap and comparable sensitivity, specificity, and positive and negative predictive power between ASD and early PTSD diagnoses (Brewin, Andrews, & Rose, 2003). However, Brewin and colleagues (2003) not only recognized the need for replication of this finding but also called for more investigation into this topic in a variety of trauma samples. This is especially important given that both ASD and PTSD criteria were based upon self-report assessments. In sum, research into whether PTSD and ASD represent distinct diagnoses has produced equivocal results, and more study is necessary to determine whether ASD is distinct from early PTSD symptoms.

Distinguishing Between ASD and Normal Responses Following Trauma

In the acute aftermath of a traumatic event, most survivors display a range of emotional, cognitive, physical, interpersonal, and psychosomatic responses. These responses include, but are not limited to, the previously mentioned PTSD symptom clusters, as well as agitation, depression, irritability, shock, fear, guilt, anxiety, anger, despair, and withdrawal (Friedman, 2009; Harvey & Bryant, 2002; Marshall et al., 1999; Rothbaum & Foa, 1993; Shalev et al., 1998; 2002). Flynn and Norwood (2004) developed a list of additional common responses following disasters that include physical (fatigue, dizziness, ulcers, heart palpitations), emotional (feeling overwhelmed, anticipating harm to self or others), cognitive (difficulty making decisions, reduced attention span), behavioral (ritualistic behavior, crying), and spiritual (crisis of faith, anger at God, displaced anger) domains.

Initial stress responses are often transient and difficult to define due to their instability (Yitzhaki, Solomon, & Kotler, 1991). However, after a few days posttrauma, responses of individuals who are likely to develop psychological disorders begin to stabilize into a form that resembles the symptoms of both PTSD and depression (Isserlin, Zerach, & Solomon, 2008; Shalev, 2002). For example, intrusions are often experienced universally by trauma victims (Rothbaum & Foa, 1993; Shalev, Schreiber, & Galai, 1993; Soladatos, Paparrigopoulos, Pappa, & Christodoulou, 2006), whereas emotional numbing and avoidance are typically less common (Shalev, 2002). Ironson and colleagues (1997) found that numbing symptoms were the least common cluster experienced (42%), with hyper-arousal symptoms being the most common (70%), followed by intrusions (58%).

Shalev (2002) reported that most survivors experience some PTSD symptoms within a week of the event, and the symptom patterns follow that of a normal distribution, whereas depressive symptoms are not normally distributed. Given that PTSD symptoms are relatively common soon after a traumatic event, the difficult question facing researchers and clinicians alike is what constitutes normal versus pathological responses to trauma. The answer appears to lie mainly with the duration and severity of the symptoms; symptoms are considered to be normal if they dissipate fairly quickly (within a few weeks) and do not interfere with the normal functioning of the individual (Classen, Koopman, & Spiegel, 1993). Moreover, Rothbaum and Davis (2003) reported that a "normal" reaction to a traumatic experience consists of an initial spike of symptoms that steadily declines over time; if the fear fails to extinguish and the symptom levels remain high, this is thought to be a "maladaptive generalized activation of the alarm response" (Schwarz & Perry, 1994, p.313). Symptoms persisting longer than a few weeks or symptoms that interfere with daily functioning are considered pathological. Therefore, symptoms included in the ASD diagnosis are considered to be normal reactions to trauma, but the frequency, intensity, and duration of the symptoms signal possible long-term distress and the potential need for intervention (Koopman, Classen, Cardena, & Spiegel, 1995).

Does ASD Reliability Predict PTSD?

One of the reasons for developing the ASD diagnosis was to have a means by which to identify trauma survivors most likely to develop PTSD. Ideally, the ASD diagnosis should display high predictive power (likelihood that someone with ASD will develop PTSD), high negative predictive power (likelihood that someone without ASD will not develop PTSD), high sensitivity (probability that someone with PTSD had ASD), and high specificity (probability that someone without PTSD did not have ASD). However, research examining the predictive utility of ASD has questioned its ability to identify survivors at high risk for PTSD. Although the majority (e.g., 70–80%) of trauma survivors diagnosed with ASD develop PTSD, approximately 50% of survivors who develop PTSD do not initially meet criteria for ASD (Bryant, 2003b; Bryant, 2006; Bryant, Creamer, O'Donnell, Silove, McFarlane, 2008; Friedman, 2009). The predictive utility of ASD may also differ depending on the type of trauma experienced. In a recent review, Isserlin and colleagues (2008) reported that across four studies, an ASD diagnosis correctly predicted a PTSD diagnosis in 42–78% of participants after a motor vehicle accident (MVA); while, in participants who developed PTSD, 29–73% of them had ASD (poor sensitivity). Sensitivity was better in assault survivors (between 83–89% of individuals diagnosed with PTSD had met ASD criteria); however, the lowest sensitivity and specificity rates were reported following medically related trauma events (e.g., cancer diagnosis, myocardial infarction), with specificity no greater than 34% (Isserlin et al., 2008).

Therefore, an ASD diagnosis appears to demonstrate acceptable predictive power, but unsatisfactory negative predictive power, sensitivity, and specificity. Posited explanations for these less than favorable characteristics of the ASD diagnosis derive largely from the focus on dissociation in the ASD diagnostic criteria (Bryant, 2006, Harvey & Bryant, 2002; Marshall et al., 1999).

ASD Dissociative Symptoms

Researchers have largely concluded that dissociative symptoms (Criterion B) do not add meaningful predictive ability to the ASD diagnosis. Brewin, Andrews, Rose, and Kirk (1999) reported that ASD predicted later PTSD in survivors of violent crime, but that the contribution of dissociation to the prediction was small—only accounting for an additional 2% of variance above the traditional PTSD symptom clusters. The authors concluded that the full diagnosis of ASD was better at predicting PTSD than was any symptom cluster on its own, but that simply using a criterion of three or more re-experiencing or hyper-arousal symptoms would have achieved similar predictive results to those obtained using the full ASD diagnostic criteria. Similarly, results of a study of children and adolescent MVA survivors revealed that the dissociation criterion (assessed 2–4 weeks posttrauma) did not uniquely contribute to PTSD diagnosis six months posttrauma, and that using a criterion of three or more re-experiencing symptoms (or six or more re-experiencing/hyper-arousal symptoms) was as useful at predicting PTSD as was the ASD diagnosis (Dalgeish et al., 2008). However, it is important to note that the latter criteria was not a reliable predictor of PTSD either, as their sensitivities were less than 50%.

In the largest study of the predictive utility of ASD to date, Bryant. Creamer, and colleagues (2008) conducted a longitudinal multi-site investigation designed to clarify mixed findings regarding ASD. Survivors of mixed traumas ($N = 597$) were assessed for ASD in-hospital with the Acute Stress Disorder Interview (ASDI; Bryant et al., 1998), and PTSD was assessed three months later ($n = 507$). Overall, a diagnosis of ASD accurately identified 45% of the participants who developed PTSD, but two-thirds of the participants who did not screen positive for ASD developed PTSD. Generally, dissociative symptoms displayed low sensitivity but high specificity; when dissociative symptoms were removed from the analyses, the sensitivity of the remaining clusters of the ASD diagnosis improved, but specificity and positive predictive power decreased. In contrast, using initial PTSD criteria as a predictor of three-month PTSD resulted in stronger positive predictive power and comparable rates of sensitivity, specificity, and negative predictive power as found with the ASD criteria. These findings led the researchers to conclude that ASD failed to uniquely contribute to the prediction of PTSD above the presence of initial PTSD symptoms. Further, though a mixed-trauma sample was recruited for the study, it was composed mainly of accident and fall victims. The authors suggested that ASD may be more useful in predicting PTSD in more severely traumatized populations (e.g., general assault, survivors of sexual assault; [Gilboa-Schechtman & Foa, 2001]), as dissociative symptoms frequently occur in individuals with complex trauma histories (specifically, survivors of childhood abuse; Foa & Hearst-Ikeda, 1996; Riggs, Dancu, Gershuny, Greenberg, & Foa, 1992).

Although the majority of studies have criticized the inclusion of dissociation symptoms in the ASD diagnosis, eliminating dissociative symptoms does not appear to substantially increase the predictive ability of ASD. In a review of studies reporting on the predictive utility of ASD and ASD minus dissociation symptoms, removal of the dissociation criteria resulted in only a slight increase in predictive value, from 38% to 44% (Isserlin et al., 2008). Similarly, Bryant, Creamer et al. (2008) suggested that the variability of acute symptoms made symptom presentation too complex to have good predictive power and that, although ASD symptoms are not reliable early predictors of PTSD, neither are early PTSD symptoms. In general, it is difficult to rely on early symptoms of PTSD as valid predictors of subsequent PTSD because many trauma survivors recover on their own in the months following trauma (Bryant, 2003a), and initial PTSD symptoms fail to adequately distinguish between those who will recover from initial symptoms and those who will develop PTSD (Shalev, Freedman, Peri, Brandes, & Sahar, 1997). An additional possible explanation for mixed findings regarding the predictive utility of acute trauma responses was provided by a methodological review of traumatic stress disorders (e.g., PTSD, ASD, and depression) following physical injury (O'Donnell, Creamer, Bryant, Schnyder, & Shalev, 2003). The authors proposed that failure to control for current pain levels and analgesia use in hospital may account for unreliable symptom reporting in the acute aftermath of trauma. Alternatively, others have suggested that the relatively poor performance of ASD in predicting PTSD may stem from differences between studies in the timing of follow-up assessments, as ASD was highly predictive of PTSD 7–10 months posttrauma in bystanders of a shooting (Classen, Koopman, Hales, & Spiegel, 1998).

Timing of ASD Assessment

The predictive utility of ASD may also differ depending upon when it is assessed. The diagnostic criteria for ASD state that symptoms must be present for at least two days in order for a trauma survivor to be eligible for the diagnosis. Therefore, an individual may be diagnosed with ASD as soon as three days posttrauma or as late as four weeks posttrauma. Few studies have investigated whether the timing of assessment influences the predictive utility of ASD. Bryant, Creamer, and colleagues (2008) assessed trauma survivors within one month posttrauma and found that the rates of ASD and predictive power remained the same whether participants completed the instrument within 10 days of the trauma or between 10 and 30 days after the trauma. These results are in contrast to the results of a prior study that reported greater predictive accuracy of the Acute Stress Disorders Instrument (ASDI) if it was administered to participants closer to four weeks posttrauma (Murray, Ehlers, & Mayou, 2002). Attempts to determine the extent to which timing of ASD assessment impacted the predictive utility of the diagnosis, while simultaneously distinguishing between peritraumatic and persistent dissociation, would aid greatly in determining the extent to which ASD is a useful predictor of PTSD.

ASD Assessment

Mixed findings regarding the relationship between ASD and PTSD may also stem from differences in the manner in which ASD was assessed. Although ASD was introduced in 1994, it was not until four years later that the ASDI was developed to assess diagnostic levels of ASD (Bryant et al., 1998). Given the lack of an independent standard with which to compare the ASDI, accurate construct validity assessments, especially concurrent validity, were difficult to establish (Bryant, 2003a). Following the development of the ASDI clinical interview, two self-report measures were developed to assess ASD: the Stanford Acute Stress Reaction Questionnaire (SASRQ; Cardena, Koopman, Classen, Waelde, & Spiegel, 2000) which assesses the frequency of each ASD symptom; and the Acute Stress Disorder Scale (ASDS; Bryant, Moulds, & Guthrie, 2000), which is a self-report version of the ASDI. Prior to the development of these scales, ASD was assessed using a combination of PTSD measures and the PDEQ. Variation in measurement of the construct may have lead to inconsistencies in reported prevalence rates and the evaluation of predictive utility. For instance, Broomhall et al. (2009) reported that use of either the ASDS or the ASDI tended to find higher rates of ASD than other combinations of measures as these measures relied on dichotomous data.

Populations for Which ASD May Possess Greater Predictive Power

Though the utility of the ASD diagnosis at identifying trauma survivors at risk for PTSD is questionable, its ability to predict future psychopathology may be greater in certain groups than others. For example, there may be differences in the predictive merit of ASD depending on whether or not the study sample included survivors of mild traumatic brain injury (mTBI). Approximately 81% of mTBI survivors diagnosed with ASD subsequently met PTSD diagnostic criteria (Harvey & Bryant, 1998, 2000), indicating higher predictive power for ASD in survivors with mTBI. These findings may be due to the symptom overlap between mTBI and ASD; specifically, both share a dissociation cluster and postconcussive symptoms (PCS: dizziness, fatigue, irritability, sleep problems, depression; Chen, Johnston, Petrides, & Pitto, 2008). Bryant, Creamer, et al. (2008) reported that the sensitivity and positive predictive power of the ASDI may be greater for individuals who experienced mTBI because a greater proportion of mTBI survivors meet the dissociation requirement of ASD. Further, results from a large-scale multisite study conducted by Broomhall and colleagues (2009) revealed that individuals who experienced mTBI were marginally more likely to develop ASD. Again, these results were due to the symptom overlap of ASD and PCS, as the mTBI survivors scored higher on three of the dissociative symptoms than survivors who did not have mTBI, but not on the re-experiencing cluster (Broomhall et al., 2009). Harvey and Bryant (2000) also reported that increasing the number of symptoms in the re-experiencing, avoidance, and hyperarousal clusters increased the positive predictive power and maintained the negative predictive power for ASD in mTBI survivors. However, any other change to the dissociative requirement resulted in a worsening of negative predictive power.

The extent to which ASD can serve to predict PTSD status may also differ between men and women. Females are more likely to develop PTSD posttrauma and oftentimes report higher levels of PD than males (Bryant & Harvey, 2003; Fullerton et al., 2001). Bryant and Harvey (2003) assessed MVA survivors for ASD within one month of the accident and for PTSD six months post-MVA. Results revealed that the ASD's positive predictive power was higher for females (93%) than for males (57%), most likely due to the fact that females tended to experience higher levels of PD and PTSD than males (Bryant & Harvey, 2003). Consequently, the negative predictive power of ASD was higher for males than for females, in that the lack of ASD in males was more accurately predictive of the absence of PTSD.

Additionally, ASD may have higher predictive utility for other posttraumatic psychological consequences, as research suggests that ASD may be useful in predicting posttraumatic responses beyond PTSD symptoms (Isserlin et al., 2008; Staab, Grieger, Fullerton, & Ursano, 1996). Individuals with ASD have been reported to have a higher risk of depression in a variety of trauma samples including rescue workers, typhoon survivors, and MVA survivors (Fullerton, Ursano, & Wang, 2004; Staab et al., 1996; Wang, Tsay, & Bond, 2005). Blanchard and colleagues (2004) also reported that the ASD symptom severity score predicted depressive symptoms in undergraduate college students in a study examining geographical proximity to the 9/11 attacks. Given the high comorbidity between PTSD and depression, it follows that the two disorders may share similar predictors in the aftermath of a traumatic event (Bromet, Sonnega, Kessler, 1998; O'Donnell, Creamer, & Pattison, 2004).

Summary

Despite the criticisms voiced against the ASD diagnosis, others have pointed out that no other sole indicator, whether cognitive, biological, or psychosocial, accurately predicts PTSD without the same issues of weak sensitivity and specificity (Bryant, Creamer, et al., 2008). Any currently examined early predictor of PTSD, taken on an individual basis, is too weak to identify at-risk trauma survivors for intervention because they do not accurately distinguish between those who naturally recover and those whose symptoms persist (Marshall et al., 1999). Marshall and colleagues (1999) suggested that rather than serving as a means by which to classify trauma survivors as to who will or will not develop PTSD, ASD may simply identify survivors who are likely to develop more severe PTSD symptoms. It is likely that multiple risk factors or interactions between risk factors represent the best indicator of who will develop psychopathology posttrauma, leading to the question of whether additional biological and/or cognitive factors could enhance the predictive power of ASD. Future research is needed to determine whether combining measures (ASD, biological factors, cognitive reactions) will increase the predictive utility of acute responses to trauma, as well as increase accuracy in identifying those in need of intervention.

The need to identify survivors at high risk for PTSD who may benefit from early intervention combined with noted limitations of the existing ASD diagnosis have led to a number of proposed changes to the ASD diagnostic criteria in the *DSM-5* (*http://www.dsm5.org/ProposedRevisions*). Based largely on the literature reviewed above, the *DSM-5* task force members have proposed major revisions to the criteria, including collapsing the different symptom clusters into a single cluster and requiring the endorsement of at least 8 of the proposed 14 symptoms, without requiring any specific number of symptoms from any symptom cluster. These changes eliminate the focus on dissociation and are intended to more precisely represent the variety of early post-traumatic reactions displayed by trauma survivors.

Dissociation Criteria of ASD versus Peritraumatic Dissociation

In examining predictors of PTSD, one of the more contradictory findings concerns the relationship between the dissociative component of ASD and peritraumatic dissociation. Although one of the major criticisms of the ASD diagnosis is its heavy emphasis on dissociative symptoms, recent meta-analyses of acute predictors of PTSD have found that peritraumatic dissociation (PD) is the strongest early predictor of subsequent PTSD (Breh & Seidler, 2007; Lensvelt-Mulders et al., 2008; Ozer, Best, Lipsey, & Weiss, 2003). Time of onset is the only distinguishing factor between PD and the dissociation criteria of ASD: whereas PD requires that dissociative symptoms occur during or immediately after the traumatic event in question (Marmar, Weiss & Metzler, 1997; Marmar et al., 1994), the dissociation criteria of ASD impose no such requirement. This has led to much debate as to the role of dissociation and PD as risk factors for PTSD. Whereas the dissociation criteria of ASD either do not add or add very little to the predictive validity of the diagnosis, meta-analyses have confirmed that PD reliably predicts subsequent PTSD with effect sizes ranging from. 35–.40 (Breh & Seidler, 2007; Lensvelt-Mulders et al., 2008; Ozer, Best, Lipsey, & Weiss, 2003). However, several independent studies have failed to replicate these findings, leading researchers to question whether PD provides a unique contribution to the prediction of PTSD (Brewin et al. 1999; Bryant, 2007; Marmar et al., 1994; Marshall and Schell, 2002; Marx & Sloan, 2005; van der Veldon & Wittmann, 2008).

One possible explanation for differential findings regarding the predictive utility of PD versus ASD, and more specifically the dissociative component of ASD, concerns issues of timing. Whereas PD requires that dissociative symptoms occur during or immediately after the traumatic event (Marmar et al., 1997, 1994), the dissociation criteria of ASD impose no such time constraint. Consequently, in satisfying the dissociation cluster of the ASD diagnosis, it is unclear whether the reported dissociation occurred at the time of the trauma or at any point leading to the time of assessment. In addition, studies examining the predictive utility of dissociation have typically differed in the amount of time passing between trauma experience and the assessment of dissociation. Preliminary research on the construct of *persistent* dissociation has suggested that PD and persistent dissociation may have differential predictive utility (Panasetis & Bryant, 2003). Survivors of either an MVA or nonsexual assault completed an assessment of PD (Peritraumatic Dissociative Experiences Questionnaire: PDEQ; Marmar et al., 1997) twice with different sets of instructions each time. All participants were assessed within one month of the trauma in order to meet the requirements of an ASD diagnosis. The first set of instructions asked trauma survivors to report on dissociation that occurred during the trauma, whereas the second set of instructions asked participants to report on dissociation that occurred at the time of assessment. Results revealed that dissociation at the time of the assessment (e.g., persistent dissociation) was more strongly associated with ASD severity than PD, lending support to the idea that differential predictive utility of the ASD diagnosis may be due to the time posttrauma that symptoms were assessed.

Additional research has suggested that combining measures of PD with measures of ASD may increase the predictive utility of the ASD diagnosis. Birmes et al. (2003) examined the combined predictive utility of PD (as measured with the PDEQ within the first 24 hours of an assault) and acute stress disorder (assessed two weeks posttrauma). Though the sample size was small, results revealed that both PDEQ scores and an ASD diagnosis were unique and independent predictors of PTSD three months posttrauma, and that the combination of peritraumatic dissociation and acute stress symptoms accounted for the largest amount of variance

(32.8%) in PTSD symptoms. In a partial replication of this study, Birmes et al (2005) retrospectively assessed PD, peritraumatic distress, and ASD within 5–10 weeks posttrauma in a sample of survivors of an industrial disaster. PTSD symptoms were assessed six months posttrauma. Results revealed that each predictor contributed a unique amount of variance to the model and together they explained 60% of the variance in PTSD symptoms, supporting the idea that the combination of PD and acute stress symptoms may significantly improve the ability to predict those at highest risk for PTSD.

Cross-cultural Considerations

Given the relatively new development of ASD, the potential refinement of the diagnosis for *DSM-5*, and mixed literature regarding its utility as a measure of likely PTSD risk, very little research has been done examining its cross-cultural validity. However, indirect conclusions may be inferred from reports of cultural differences in PD. Previous research has posited that Hispanics are more likely to experience PD due to their culture of acceptance of beliefs that life events are beyond their control, the tendency to accept and underplay stress, and the lack of resources to deal with traumatic events (Fierros & Smith, 2006; Pole, Best, Metzler, & Marmar, 2005; Reuf, Litz, & Schlenger, 2000). Zatzick, Marmar, Weiss, and Metzler (1994) sought to determine whether retrospectively assessed trauma-linked dissociation varied across Caucasian, Hispanic, and African-American Vietnam war veterans, but found that after controlling for extent/severity of trauma exposure, no race/ethnic differences in dissociation emerged. With the refinement of the ASD diagnosis in the *DSM-5*, future research is necessary to determine the extent to which ASD symptomatology and/or prevalence rates may differ across races/cultures.

Summary and Conclusions

In general, research examining initial reactions following a traumatic event and the extent to which these reactions are associated with longer term psychopathology has not produced any valid predictors of persistent posttraumatic distress. Many variables have been consistently associated with risk for PTSD; however, independently, they account for a small amount of the variance in PTSD symptoms and display relatively poor specificity. The ASD diagnosis also falls to similar criticism. As discussed in this chapter, at the time of the creation of the ASD diagnostic criteria, relatively little empirical evidence existed to inform the content of the symptoms. Perhaps the most disputed component of the ASD diagnosis is the focus on dissociative symptoms. However, the predictive utility of the ASD diagnosis minus the dissociative criteria is not substantially improved. These shortcomings have led to much debate as to whether ASD should be included in the upcoming *DSM-5*, and if included, whether the ASD symptoms and diagnostic criteria should be revised.

There appears to be significant merit to retaining the ASD diagnosis (or a similar diagnosis intended to identify trauma survivors at risk for the development of persistent posttraumatic distress). For instance, research has suggested that intervening with individuals meeting ASD criteria can significantly reduce the development of PTSD. Bryant (2006) demonstrated that cognitive behavioral therapy offered to people with ASD prevented PTSD in 80% of treatment completers. In a second study, Bryant, Mastrodomenica, and colleagues (2008) examined the efficacy of five sessions of either prolonged exposure (PE) or cognitive restructuring, and a wait list control group in the treatment of ASD. Results revealed that PE led to the greatest improvements in PTSD symptoms immediately postintervention (6 weeks) and at the follow-up assessment (6 months posttrauma).

Although evidence exists for the efficacy of early interventions at reducing distress and preventing PTSD in symptomatic individuals (Bryant, 2003a), the issue of identification of high-risk individuals is central to the efficacy of the therapies. This is especially true as research has suggested that immediate psychological interventions applied broadly to trauma survivors (such as critical incident stress debriefing) are at best ineffective and, at worse, may increase PTSD symptoms (Bisson, Jenkins, Alexander, & Bannister, 1997; Mayou, Ehlers, & Hobbs, 2000; McNally, Bryant, & Ehlers, 2003; Raphael &Wilson, 2000). Further, as mentioned earlier, the inability to reliably identify individuals at high risk for the development of PTSD greatly hinders the testing of other novel early interventions. This is because it is difficult to demonstrate the efficacy of interventions at reducing/preventing PTSD when few trauma victims develop the disorder. Therefore, research into the early identification of and intervention with high-risk trauma survivors is hindered without a means by which to predict who is most likely to develop PTSD.

Future Directions

Given the major revision of the ASD criteria proposed for *DSM-5*, opportunities for future research in the area of acute reactions to trauma are enormous. First, it will be necessary to determine whether the ASD diagnosis as proposed will predict subsequent PTSD with both sensitivity and specificity. Further, research is necessary into whether the predictive utility of ASD differs between men and women, children and adults, and across different cultures/ethnicities. As existing predictors of PTSD account for a relatively small amount of variance in subsequent PTSD symptoms/severity, the combining of ASD symptoms with other predictors (PTSD symptoms, panic, cognitive appraisals) may serve to increase the predictive utility of the diagnosis. Finally, research into the development of screening measures to quickly assess ASD symptoms in order to inform those in need of early interventions is greatly needed.

References

American Psychiatric Association. (1994). *Diagnostic and statistical manual of mental disorders* (4th ed.). Washington, DC: Author.

American Psychiatric Association. (2000). *Diagnostic and statistical manual of mental disorders* (4th ed., text rev.). Washington, DC: Author.

American Psychiatric Association. (2010). *Proposed draft revisions to DSM disorders and criteria.* Retrieved from http://www.dsm5.org/ProposedRevisions.

Birmes, P., Brunet, A., Carreras, D., Ducasse, J. L., Charlet, J. P., Lauque, D., & Schmitt, L. (2003). The predictive power of peritraumatic dissociation and acute stress symptoms for stress symptoms: A three-month prospective study. *American Journal of Psychiatry, 160,* 1337–1339.

Birmes, P. J., Brunet, A., Coppin-Calmes, D., Arbus, C., Coppin, D., Charlet, J., & Schmitt, L. (2005). Symptoms of peritraumatic and acute traumatic stress among victims of an industrial disaster. *Psychiatric Services, 56*(1), 93–95.

Bisson, J. I., Jenkins, P. L., Alexander, J., & Bannister, C. (1997). Randomized controlled trial of psychological debriefing for victims of acute burn trauma. *British Journal of Psychiatry, 171,* 78–81.

Blanchard, E. B., Kuhn, E., Rowell, D. L., Hickling, E. J., Wittrick, D., Rogers, R. L., & Steckler, D. C. (2004). Studies of the vicarious traumatization of college students by the September 11th attacks: Effects of proximity, exposure and connectedness. *Behaviour Research and Therapy, 42,* 191–205.

Breh, D. C., & Seidler, G. H. (2007). Is peritraumatic dissociation a risk factor for PTSD? *Journal of Trauma and Dissociation, 8*(1), 53–69.

Brewin, C. R., Andrews, B., & Rose, S. (2003). Diagnostic overlap between acute stress disorder and PTSD in victims of violent crime. *American Journal of Psychiatry, 160,* 783–785.

Brewin, C. R., Andrews, B., Rose, S., & Kirk, M. (1999). Acute stress disorder and posttraumatic stress disorder in victims of violent crime. *American Journal of Psychiatry, 156*(3), 360–366.

Bromet, E., Sonnega, A., & Kessler, R. C. (1998). Risk Factors for DSM-III-R posttraumatic stress disorder findings from the National Comorbidity Survey. *American Journal of Epidemiology, 147*(4), 353–361.

Broomhall, L. G. J., Clark, R. C., McFarlane, A. C., O'Donnell, M., Bryant., R. A., Creamer, M., & Silove, D. (2009). Early stage assessment and course of acute stress disorder after mild traumatic brain injury. *Journal of Nervous and Mental Disease, 197*(3), 178–181.

Bryant, R. A. (2003a). Acute stress disorder: Is it a useful diagnosis? *Clinical Psychologist, 7*(2), 67–79.

Bryant, R. A. (2003b). Early predictors of posttraumatic stress disorder. *Biological Psychiatry, 53,* 789–795.

Bryant, R. A. (2006). Acute stress disorder. *Psychiatry, 5*(7), 238–239.

Bryant, R. A. (2007). Does dissociation further our understanding of PTSD? *Journal of Anxiety Disorders, 21,* 183–191.

Bryant, R. A., Creamer, M., O'Donnell, M.vL., Silove, D., & McFarlane, A.vC. (2008). A multisite study of the capacity of acute stress disorder diagnosis to predict posttraumatic stress disorder. *Journal of Clinical Psychiatry, 69*(6), 923–929.

Bryant, R. A. & Harvey, A. G. (2003). Gender differences in the relationship between acute stress disorder and posttraumatic stress disorder following motor vehicle accidents. *Australian & New Zealand Journal of Psychiatry, 37*(2), 226–229.

Bryant, R. A., Harvey, A. G., Dang, S. T., & Sackville, T. (1998). Assessing acute stress disorder: Psychometric properties of a structured clinical interview. *Psychological Assessment, 10*(3) 215–220.

Bryant, R. A., Mastrodomenica, J., Felmingham, K. L., Hopwood, S., Kenny, L., Kandris, E., & Creamer, M. (2008). Treatment of acute stress disorder: A randomized controlled trial. *Archives of General Psychiatry, 65*(6), 659–667.

Bryant, R. A., Moulds, M. L., & Guthrie, R. M. (2000). Acute Stress Disorder Scale: A self-report measure of acute stress disorder. *Psychological Assessment, 12*(1), 61–68.

Cardena, E., Koopman, C., Classen, C., Waelde, L. C., & Spiegel, D. (2000). Psychometric properties of the Stanford Acute Stress Reaction Questionnaire (SASRQ): A valid and reliable measure of acute stress. *Journal of Traumatic Stress, 13,* 719–734.

Chen, J., Johnston, K. M., Petrides, M., & Pitto, A. (2008). Neural substrates of symptoms of depression following concussion in male athletes with persisting postconcussion symptoms. *Archives of General Psychiatry, 65*(1), 81–89.

Classen, C., Koopman, C., Hales, R., & Spiegel, D. (1998). Acute stress disorder as a predictor of posttraumatic stress symptoms. *American Journal of Psychiatry, 155*(5), 620–624.

Classen, C., Koopman, C., & Spiegel, D. (1993). Trauma and dissociation. *Bulletin of the Menninger Clinic,* 57(2), 178–194.

Dalgeish, T., Mesier-Stedman, R., Kassam-Adams, N., Ehlers, A., Winstron, F., Smith, P., & Yule, W. (2008). Predictive validity of acute stress disorder in children and adolescents. *British Journal of Psychiatry, 192,* 392–393.

Engelhard, I. M., van den Hout, M. A., Kindt, M., Arntz, A., & Schouten, E. (2003). Peritraumatic dissociation and posttraumatic stress after pregnancy loss: A prospective. study. *Behaviour Research and Therapy, 41,* 67–78.

Fierros, M., & Smith, C. (2006). The relevance of Hispanic culture to the treatment of a patient with posttraumatic stress disorder (PTSD). *Psychiatry, 3*(10), 49–55.

Flynn, B. W., & Norwood, A. E. (2004). Defining normal psychological reactions to disaster. *Psychiatric Annals, 34*(8), 597–603.

Foa, E. B., & Hearst-Ikeda, D. (1996). Emotional dissociation in response to trauma: An information processing approach. In L. K. Michelson & W. J. Ray (Eds.), *Handbook of dissociation: Theoretical, empirical, and clinical perspectives* (pp. 207–224). New York: Plenum Press.

Foa, E. B., & Riggs, D. S. (1993). Post-traumatic stress disorder in rape victims. In J. Oldham, M. B. Riba, & A. Tasman (Eds.), *Annual review of psychiatry* (pp. 273–303). Washington, DC: American Psychiatric Association.

Friedman, M. J. (2009). Phenomenology of posttraumatic stress disorder and acute stress disorder. In M. M. Antony & M. B. Stein (Eds.), *The Oxford handbook of anxiety and related disorders* (pp 65- 72). New York: Oxford University Press.

Fullerton, C. S., Ursano, R. J., Epstein, R. S., Cowley, B., Vance, K., Kao, T-C., & Baum, A. (2001). Gender differences in posttraumatic stress disorder after motor vehicle accidents. *American Journal of Psychiatry, 158*, 1486–1491.

Fullerton, C. S., Ursano, R. J., & Wang, L. (2004). Acute stress disorder, posttraumatic stress disorder, and depression in disaster or rescue workers. *American Journal of Psychiatry, 161*, 1371–1376.

Gilboa-Schechtman, E., & Foa, E. B. (2001). Patterns of recovery from trauma: The use of intraindividual analysis. *Journal of abnormal Psychology, 110*, 392–400.

Harvey, A. G., & Bryant, R. A. (1998). The relationship between acute stress disorder and posttraumatic stress disorder: A prospective evaluation of motor vehicle accident survivors. *Journal of Counseling and Clinical Psychology, 66*(3), 507–512.

Harvey, A. G., & Bryant, R. A. (2000). Two-year prospective evaluation of the relationship between acute stress disorder and posttraumatic stress disorder following mild traumatic brain injury. *American Journal of Psychiatry, 157*(4), 626–628.

Harvey, A. G., & Bryant, R. A. (2002). Acute stress disorder: A synthesis and critique. *Psychological Bulletin, 128*(6), 886–902.

Horowitz, M. J. (1986). Stress-response syndromes: A review of posttraumatic and adjustment disorders. *Hospital and Community Psychiatry, 37*, 241–249.

Ironson, G., Wynings, C., Schneiderman, N., Baum, A., Rodriguez, M., Greenwood, D., & Fletcher, M. A. (1997). Posttraumatic stress symptoms, intrusive thoughts, loss, and immune function after Hurricane Andrew. *Psychosomatic Medicine, 59*, 128–141.

Isserlin, L., Zerach, G., & Solomon, Z. (2008). Acute stress responses: A review and synthesis of ASD, ASR, and CSR. *American Journal of Orthopsychiatry, 78*(4), 423–429.

Kessler, R. C., Berglund, P., Demler, O., Jin, R., Merikangas, K. R., & Walters, E. E. (2005). Lifetime prevalence and age-of-onset distributions of DSM-IV Disorders in the National Comorbidity Survey Replication. *Archives of General Psychiatry, 62*, 593–768.

Kessler, R. C., Sonnega, A., Bromet, E., Hughes, M., & Nelson, C. B. (1995). Posttraumatic stress disorder in the National Comorbidity Survey. *Archives of General Psychiatry, 52*, 1048–1060.

Koopman, C., Classen, C., Cardena, E., & Spiegel, D. (1995). When disaster strikes, acute stress disorder may follow. *Journal of Traumatic Stress, 8*(1), 29–45.

Lensvelt-Mulders, G., van der Hart, O., van Ochten, J. M., van Son, M. J. M., Steele, K., & Breeman, L. (2008). Relations among peritraumatic dissociation and posttraumatic stress: A meta-analysis. *Clinical Psychology Review, 28*, 1138–1151.

Marmar, C. R., Weiss, D. S., & Metzler, T. J. (1997). The peritraumatic dissociative experiences questionnaire. In J. P. Wilson and T. M. Keane (Eds.), *Assessing psychological trauma and PTSD* (pp. 412–428). New York: Guilford.

Marmar, C. R, Weiss, D. S., Schlenger, W. E., Fairbank, J. A., Jordan, B. K., Kulka, R. A., & Hough, R. L. (1994). Peritraumatic dissociation and posttraumatic stress in male Vietnam theater veterans. *American Journal of Psychiatry, 151*(6), 902–907.

Marshall, G. N., & Schell, T. L. (2002). Reappraising the link between peritraumatic dissociation and PTSD symptom severity: Evidence from a longitudinal study of community violence survivors. *Journal of Abnormal Psychology, 111*(4), 626–636.

Marshall, R. D., & Garakani, A. (2002). Psychobiology of the acute stress response and its relationship to the psychobiology of post-traumatic stress disorder. *Psychiatric Clinics of North America, 25*, 385–395.

Marshall, R. D., Spitzer, R., & Liebowitz, M. R. (1999). Review and critique of the new DSM-IV diagnosis of acute stress disorder. *American Journal of Psychiatry. 156*(11), 1677–1685.

Marx, B. P., & Sloan, D. M. (2005). Peritraumatic dissociation and experiential avoidance as predictors of posttraumatic stress symptomatology. *Behaviour Research and Therapy, 43*, 549–583.

Mayou, R., Ehlers, A., & Hobbs, M. (2000). Psychological debriefing for road traffic accident victims: Three year follow-up of a randomized controlled trial. *British Journal of Psychiatry, 176*, 589–593.

McNally, R. J., Bryant, R. A., & Ehlers, A. (2003). Does early psychological intervention promote recovery from posttraumatic stress? *Psychological Science, 4*, 45–79.

Murray, J., Ehlers, A., & Mayou, R. A. (2002). Dissociation and posttraumatic stress disorder: Two prospective studies of motor vehicle accident survivors. *British Journal of Psychiatry, 180*, 363–368.

O'Donnell, M. L., Creamer, M., Bryant, R. A., Schnyder, U., & Shalev, A. (2003). Posttraumatic disorders following injury: An empirical and methodological review. *Clinical Psychology Review, 23*, 587–603.

O'Donnell, M. L., Creamer, M., & Pattison, P. (2004). Posttraumatic stress disorder and depression following trauma: Understanding comorbidity. *American Journal of Psychiatry, 161*, 1390–1396.

Ozer, E. J., Best, S. R., Lipsey, T. L., & Weiss, D. S. (2003). Predictors of posttraumatic stress disorder and symptoms in adults: A meta-analysis. *Psychological Bulletin, 129*, 52–73.

Panasetis, P., & Bryant, R. A. (2003). Peritraumatic versus persistent dissociation in acute stress disorder. *Journal of Traumatic Stress, 16*(6), 563–566.

Pole, N., Best, S. R., Metzler, T., & Marmar, C. R. (2005). Why are Hispanics at greater risk for PTSD? *Cultural Diversity and Ethnic Minority Psychology, 11*(2), 144–161.

Raphael, B., & Wilson, J. P. (Eds.). (2000). *Psychological debriefing: Theory, practice and evidence.* Cambridge, England: Cambridge University Press.

Reuf, A., Litz, B., & Schlenger, W. (2000). Hispanic ethnicity and risk for combat-related posttraumatic stress disorder. *Cultural Diversity and Ethnic Minority Psychology, 6*(3), 235–251.

Riggs, D. S., Dancu, C. V., Gershuny, B. S., Greenberg, D., & Foa, E. B. (1992). Anger and post-traumatic stress disorder in female crime victims. *Journal of Traumatic Stress, 5*(4), 613–625.

Rothbaum B. O., & Davis, M. (2003). Applying learning principles to the treatment of post- trauma reactions. *Annals of the New York Academy of Sciences, 1008*, 112–121.

Rothbaum B. O., & Foa, E. B. (1993). Subtypes of posttraumatic stress disorder and duration of Symptoms. In J. R. T. Davidson & E. B. Foa (Eds.), *Posttraumatic stress disorder: DSM IV and beyond* (pp 23–35). Washington, DC: American Psychiatric Press.

Schwartz, E. D., & Perry, B. D. (1994). The post-traumatic response in children and adolescents. *Psychiatric Clinics of North America, 17*(2), 311–326.

Shalev, A. Y. (2002). Acute stress reactions in adults. *Biological Psychiatry, 51*, 532–543.

Shalev A. Y., Freedman S., Peri T., Brandes D., & Sahar T. (1997). Predicting PTSD in trauma survivors: Prospective evaluation of self-report and clinician administered instruments. *British Journal of Psychiatry, 170*, 558–564.

Shalev, A. Y., Freedman, S., Peri, T., Brandes, D., Sahar, T, Orr S. P., & Pitman, R. K. (1998). Prospective study of posttraumatic stress disorder and depression following trauma. *American Journal of Psychiatry, 155*, 630–637.

Shalev, A.Y., Schreiber, S., & Galai, T. (1993). Early psychological responses to traumatic injury. *Journal of Traumatic Stress, 6*(4), 441–450.

Soldatos, C. R., Paparrigopoulos, T. J., Pappa, D. A., & Christodoulou, G. N. (2006). Early post- traumatic stress disorder in relation to acute stress reaction: An ICD-10 study among help seekers following an earthquake. *Psychiatry Research, 143*, 245–253.

Staab, J. P., Grieger, T. A., Fullerton, C. S., & Ursano, R. J. (1996). Acute stress disorder, subsequent posttraumatic stress disorder, and depression after a series of typhoons. *Anxiety, 2*, 219–225.

van der Hart, O., Nijenhuis, E., Steele, K., & Brown, D. (2004). Trauma-related dissociation: Conceptual clarity lost and found. *Australian and New Zealand Journal of Psychiatry, 38*, 906–914.

van der Kolk, B. A., & van der Hart, O. (1989). Pierre Janet and the breakdown of adaptation psychological trauma. *American Journal of Psychiatry, 146*, 1530–1540.

van der Veldon, P. G., & Wittmann, L. (2008). The independent predictive value of peritraumatic dissociation for PTSD symptomology after type I trauma: A systematic review of prospective studies. *Clinical Psychology Review, 28*, 1009–1020.

Wang, C. H., Tsay, S. L., & Bond, E. A. (2005). Posttraumatic stress disorder, depression, anxiety, and quality of life in patients with traffic-related injuries. *Journal of Advanced Nursing, 52*, 22–30.

Yehuda, R. (2002). Posttraumatic stress disorder. *New England Journal of Medicine, 10*(2), 108–114.

Yitzhaki T., Solomon Z., & Kotler M. (1991). The clinical picture of acute combat stress reaction among Israeli soldiers in the 1982 Lebanon war. *Military Medicine, 156*, 193–197.

Zatzick, D. F., Marmar, C. R., Weiss, D. S., & Metzler, T. (1994). Does trauma-linked dissociation vary across ethnic groups? *Journal of Nervous and Mental Diseases, 182*(10), 576–582.

CHAPTER

4 Classification of Posttraumatic Stress Disorder

Tali Manber Ball *and* Murray B. Stein

Abstract

This chapter reviews the current diagnostic criteria of posttraumatic stress disorder (PTSD). Areas of specificity and overlap with major depressive disorder and generalized anxiety disorder are discussed. Despite significant overlap in symptom criteria, clinicians can reliably distinguish between these conditions. The chapter then discusses boundaries of the PTSD diagnosis as it currently stands, specifically focusing on the relationship and comorbidity between PTSD and complicated bereavement, dissociative disorders, personality disorders particularly borderline personality disorder, somatoform disorders, and chronic pain. The proposed syndrome of complex PTSD, designed to capture reactions to prolonged interpersonal trauma, is also described. Finally, issues relating to the cross-cultural validity of PTSD are raised. Topics relevant to the upcoming revision to the Diagnostic and Statistical Manual of Mental Disorders (DSM) are highlighted throughout.

Key Words: PTSD, diagnosis, complex PTSD, culture, DSM, dissociative disorders, complicated bereavement, chronic pain, borderline personality disorder

Introduction

Throughout history, traumatic events such as combat, violent crime, and major natural disasters have been described as causing not only acute negative reactions but, for some, also a more severe and long-lasting psychological syndrome. Posttraumatic stress disorder (PTSD) was formally introduced as a psychiatric diagnosis in the third edition of the *Diagnostic and Statistical Manual* (*DSM-III*; American Psychiatric Association [APA], 1980). Since then, controversies have remained about the validity of the PTSD diagnosis and its boundaries. Detractors have pointed to symptom overlap and high rates of comorbidity with other Axis I (e.g., major depression, generalized anxiety disorder, chronic pain) and Axis II disorders (e.g., borderline personality disorder, anti-social personality disorder; Frueh, Elhai, & Acierno, 2010). Others have criticized PTSD's diagnostic criteria as being too narrow in scope, neglecting the more complex set of symptoms brought on by prolonged interpersonal trauma or complicated grief reactions (Papa, Neria, & Litz, 2008; van der Kolk, Roth, Pelcovitz, Sunday, & Spinazzola, 2005). PTSD has also been criticized as being a socio-political construct that lacks validity and relevance in other contexts and cultures (Frueh et al., 2010; Summerfield, 2001).

In this chapter, we review the current diagnostic criteria of PTSD, pointing out areas of specificity and overlap with other disorders. We then discuss boundaries of the PTSD diagnosis as it currently stands, and its relation to complicated bereavement, dissociative disorders, personality disorders, somatoform disorders, and chronic pain. Next, we describe the proposed syndrome of complex PTSD, designed to capture reactions to prolonged interpersonal trauma. Finally, we discuss cross-cultural features of PTSD.

Diagnostic Criteria

The current formulation of PTSD was introduced to the *Diagnostic and Statistical Manual* (*DSM*) with its third edition (APA, 1980), and the conceptualization and criteria remain mostly the same today (see table 4.1). The first criterion deals with the definition of a traumatic event, in terms of both the objective event itself (A1) and the subjective response of the individual (A2). Issues relating to Criterion A1 are discussed in an earlier chapter within this volume.

Criterion A2, which requires that the response at the time of the event involve fear, helplessness, and/or horror, was added in the fourth edition of the *DSM* (APA, 2000), and is also not without controversy (Bovin & Marx, 2011; Friedman, Resick, Bryant, & Brewin, 2011). One concern is that the current definition of A2 is too narrow. Although many traumas do involve the acute experience of intense fear, helplessness, or horror, events evoking primary emotions of anger or shame can also generate PTSD (Brewin, Andrews, & Rose, 2000). A recent prospective study of individuals with traumatic exposure found that as many as one in four met criteria for PTSD *except* Criterion A2 (O'Donnell, Creamer, McFarlane, Silove, & Bryant, 2010). The majority of A2-negative, PTSD-positive individuals either could not remember their emotional experience during the trauma or reported experiencing emotions other than fear, helplessness, or horror, such as concern for others or frustration. Although individuals who meet Criterion A2 may be at greater risk for psychopathology (Breslau & Kessler, 2001; Creamer, McFarlane, & Burgess, 2005), among individuals for whom traumatic exposure is more routine, such as soldiers and first responders, Criterion A2 may be overly narrow and could therefore limit access to treatment in these populations (Adler, Wright, Bliese, Eckford, & Hoge, 2008).

Another complaint about Criterion A2 focuses on a lack of predictive validity (e.g., Breslau & Kessler, 2001). A number of studies have cited its low positive predictive value, as well as its lack of incremental validity over and above Criterion A1 (reviewed in Bovin & Marx, 2011). Accordingly, some have concluded that Criterion A2 does not

Table 4.1. DSM-IV-TR diagnostic criteria for PTSD

Criterion
A1. Exposure to trauma involving "actual or threatened death or serious injury"
A2. Response to trauma involved "fear, helplessness, or horror"
B. Re-Experiencing. One or more of:
B1. Recurrent intrusive recollections of the event B2. Recurrent distressing dreams of the event B3. Acting or feeling as if the event were recurring B4. Psychological distress to cues symbolizing the event B5. Physiological reactivity to cues symbolizing the event
C. Avoidance and Numbing. Three or more of:
C1. Avoidance of thoughts, feelings, or conversations associated with the event C2. Avoidance of activities, people, or places that arouse recollections of the event C3. Inability to recall significant parts of the event C4. Anhedonia C5. Detachment from others C6. Restricted affect, emotional numbing C7. Sense of a shortened future
D. Hyper-arousal. Two or more of:
D1. Difficulty falling or staying asleep D2. Irritability D3. Difficulty concentrating D4. Hyper-vigilance D5. Exaggerated startle response

sufficiently contribute to diagnostic accuracy and should be excluded from *DSM-5* (Friedman et al., 2011; O'Donnell et al., 2010). However, others have suggested that even in absence of predictive validity, Criterion A2 serves to protect against criterion drift in A1 and should be kept, albeit perhaps with more inclusive wording (Bovin & Marx, 2011). Nevertheless, current proposed changes to PTSD criteria in *DSM-5* exclude Criterion A2, citing its low clinical utility (Frueh et al., 2010; Hinton & Lewis-Fernandez, 2011).

Assuming Criterion A has been met, PTSD currently is characterized by symptoms from three clusters: re-experiencing (Criterion B), avoidance and numbing (Criterion C), and hyper-arousal (Criterion D) (APA, 2000). Symptoms from the three clusters must be present during the past month and must cause "clinically significant distress or impairment in... important areas of functioning" (p. 468). However, emerging evidence from factor analytic studies have not uniformly supported the three cluster structure of PTSD. Initial exploratory (Taylor, Kuch, Koch, Crockett, & Passey, 1998) and confirmatory (Buckley, Blanchard, & Hickling, 1998) factor analyses suggested a two-factor solution, with one factor for re-experiencing and avoidance symptoms and another for hyper-arousal and numbing symptoms. More recent research has supported a four-factor solution, with symptoms of re-experiencing, avoidance, hyper-arousal, and emotional numbing representing separate factors (King, Leskin, King, & Weathers, 1998; Palmieri, Weathers, Difede, & King, 2007), though some have found that a dysphoria factor in place of the emotional numbing factor provides better fit (Simms, Watson, & Doebbelling, 2002; Yufik & Simms, 2010). A confirmatory factor analysis comparing four-, three-, and two-factor models found that all models met standards for reasonable fit, but that the four-factor solution fit the data best (Asmundson et al., 2000). Although no final decisions have been made, it is likely that *DSM-5* will separate the avoidance and emotional numbing symptom sets, consistent with the four-factor models (Forbes et al., 2011; Frueh et al., 2010; Hinton & Lewis-Fernandez, 2011), however, the ideal form of the fourth factor is unclear (Friedman et al., 2011).

Chronic PTSD

PTSD is specified as either chronic or acute, depending on whether symptoms are present for longer than three months. Complete recovery within three months occurs in approximately half of PTSD cases (APA, 2000; Blanchard et al., 1997). Accurate prediction of who is at highest risk for developing chronic PTSD is important because chronic PTSD has been associated with interpersonal functioning problems, such as greater social anxiety and lower social support (Davidson, Hughes, Blazer, & George, 1991). Factors that may predict chronic PTSD include severity of re-experiencing and hyper-arousal symptoms (Brewin, Andrews, Rose, & Kirk, 1999), degree of physical injury and recovery (Blanchard et al., 1997), and cognitive factors such as negative interpretations of intrusions and rumination (Ehlers, Mayou, & Bryant, 1998; Steil & Ehlers, 2000). However, this specification is under consideration to be removed from *DSM-5* due to lack of evidence of its utility (Friedman et al., 2011; Frueh et al., 2010).

Specificity of PTSD Symptoms

The diagnostic criteria for PTSD have been criticized for having relatively high symptom overlap with other psychiatric disorders (Frueh et al., 2010), most prominently major depressive disorder (MDD; see table 4.2). PTSD and MDD frequently co-occur after a trauma, and a MDD is four to seven times more likely in someone with PTSD than in someone without PTSD (Kessler, Sonnega, Bromet, Hughes, & Nelson, 1995). Estimates of rates of MDD in individuals with PTSD have ranged from 26% in the community to 84% in patient samples (Franklin & Zimmerman, 2001). These findings have led some researchers to question whether the co-occurrence of PTSD and MDD represents a general traumatic response, rather than two distinct disorders (Breslau, Davis, Peterson, & Schultz, 2000; O'Donnell, Creamer, & Pattison, 2004). In support of this, factor analytic studies have found that a subset of PTSD criteria, including many of the emotional numbing symptoms within Cluster C, as well as sleep disturbance and irritability criteria from Cluster D, may form a "dysphoria" factor that is equally associated with PTSD and MDD (Grant, Beck, Marques, Palyo, & Clapp, 2008; Simms et al., , 2002; Yufik & Simms, 2010).

However, others have supported the view that co-occurring PTSD and MDD should be classified as two separate comorbid conditions (Franklin & Zimmerman, 2001; Shalev et al., 1998). Anhedonia, sleep disturbance, and concentration difficulties, the most prominently overlapping symptoms in PTSD and MDD, have been shown to be equivalently endorsed

Table 4.2. Symptom overlap among PTSD, MDD, and GAD

PTSD	MDD	GAD
Markedly diminished interest or participation in significant activities	Markedly diminished interest or pleasure in all, or almost all, activities	
Sense of a foreshortened future	Recurrent thoughts of death	
Difficulty falling or staying asleep	Insomnia or hypersomnia	Sleep disturbance
Difficulty concentrating	Diminished ability to think or concentrate	Difficulty concentrating or mind going blank
Hyper-vigilance		Restlessness or feeling keyed up or on edge
Irritability or outbursts of anger		Irritability

in PTSD patients with and without MDD, suggesting that symptom overlap alone cannot account for the high rates of comorbidity between these conditions (Franklin & Zimmerman, 2001). Severity of depressive symptoms has been shown to longitudinally predict worsening of PTSD symptoms, suggesting an important dynamic interplay between the two conditions (King, King, McArdle, Shalev, & Doron-LaMarca, 2009). Factor analytic studies have also generally found that PTSD and MDD are dissociable (Grant et al., 2008).

Generalized anxiety disorder (GAD) is also highly comorbid with PTSD and has symptom overlap with both PTSD and MDD (see table 4.2). Individuals with PTSD are two to six times more likely to have GAD than those without PTSD (Kessler et al., 1995). However, other anxiety disorders may have similar rates of GAD comorbidity as does PTSD (Zayfert, Becker, Unger, & Shearer, 2002), and factor analytic studies have found clear dissociations between PTSD and GAD symptoms (Grant et al., 2008).

Despite the significant overlap in symptom criteria, PTSD also has several unique features. PTSD is the only *DSM* disorder that references the cause of the disorder in its diagnosis (i.e., the traumatic event; North, Suris, Davis, & Smith, 2009; Summerfield, 2001). Not surprisingly then, the symptoms that are specific to PTSD center on the traumatic event itself, such as re-experiencing symptoms, and avoidance of reminders or cues of the traumatic event. Cluster C (avoidance and numbing) has been shown to have the highest specificity of the three *DSM-IV* symptom clusters in identifying individuals with PTSD (North et al., 2009).

In addition, there is evidence supporting the claim that clinicians can reliably distinguish among PTSD, MDD, and GAD (Keane, Taylor, & Penk, 1997). A factor analysis conducted on clinician ratings of psychological symptoms yielded two factors primarily associated with PTSD (ruminations over past events, and difficulty controlling anger and aggression), two factors primarily associated with GAD (physiological reactivity, concern about loss of control), and three factors primarily associated with MDD (pessimistic thinking, disordered thought, and disordered appetitive function; Keane et al., 1997).

In summary, despite a high degree of symptom overlap and comorbidity, particularly with MDD and GAD, PTSD can be differentiated from other Axis I disorders. Symptoms such as dysphoria and disturbances in sleep and concentration are present for many diagnoses, and can be thought of as analogous to a sore throat or fever in general medical practice. Such symptoms are no less distressing, and no less part of each syndrome, when they are present across multiple diagnoses. It is their combination with more specific symptoms (e.g., re-experiencing) that creates the syndrome of PTSD.

Boundaries of PTSD

With the above description of PTSD as a starting point, the remainder of this chapter concerns symptoms and syndromes that push at the boundaries of PTSD as it is currently defined. We discuss complicated bereavement, dissociation, personality disorders, somatoform disorders, and chronic pain, as well as the impact of prolonged interpersonal and/or childhood trauma and cross-cultural features.

Complicated Bereavement

Complicated bereavement, also called complicated grief, traumatic grief, or prolonged grief disorder, has been suggested as a distinct disorder (Papa et al., 2008), with the argument that MDD does not fully capture all complications of bereavement (Prigerson et al., 1999). Although complicated bereavement is not included in *DSM-IV*, proponents of the complicated bereavement diagnosis have argued that grief and loss can act as a traumatic event, with sequelae more similar to PTSD than depression (Prigerson et al., 1999). This conceptualization lies outside the current boundaries of MDD and PTSD and is not fully captured by either diagnosis, or by comorbid diagnoses of both disorders.

Proposed criteria for complicated bereavement (Prigerson et al., 1999) have shown good sensitivity and specificity, and are presented in table 4.3. Proposed symptoms (also see Horowitz et al., 2003 and Papa et al., 2008) include intrusive thoughts about the deceased, emotional numbing, avoidance of reminders of the deceased, and sleep interference, which parallel PTSD symptoms. However, complicated bereavement can be differentiated from PTSD through the nature of the traumatic event itself (i.e., loss in complicated bereavement, threat of death or harm in PTSD). Furthermore, the primary emotion in PTSD is fear, whereas sadness is the primary emotion in complicated bereavement (Shear, Frank, Houck, & Reynolds, 2005).

Table 4.3. Proposed complicated bereavement criteria

A1. Death of a significant other
A2. Three or more of: Intrusive thoughts about the deceased Yearning for the deceased Searching for the deceased Loneliness
B. Four or more of: B1. Purposelessness/futility B2. Numbness/detachment B3. Difficulty acknowledging the death B4. Feeling that life is empty B5. Feeling as though a part of oneself has died B6. Lost sense of security, trust, and/or control B7. Assuming negative behaviors of the deceased person B8. Excessive irritability, bitterness, or anger
C. Duration of at least 2 months
D. Clinically significant impairment in functioning

Source: Prigerson et al. (1999).

Nevertheless, complicated bereavement and PTSD have significant conceptual overlap and clinical co-occurrence. In a study of individuals seeking treatment for complicated grief, 19% also met *DSM-IV* criteria for MDD, 13% met criteria for PTSD, and 36% met criteria for all three conditions (Simon et al., 2007). PTSD Criterion A trauma events can include not only the threat of death or harm to the individual but also the actual death of a friend or loved one, such as a combat veteran who survives a firefight in which members of his or her unit were killed. Such a traumatic event can result in grief and guilt, which complicates PTSD presentation (Neria & Litz, 2004), and increases the risk of additional comorbidity and/or suicidality (Papa et al., 2008). Prior traumatic exposure may also increase the risk of developing complicated bereavement after a loss (Papa et al., 2008). Traumatic grief and trauma-associated guilt are persistent, distressing, and associated with greater PTSD severity and impairment (Simon et al., 2007; Steenkamp et al., 2010).

In summary, complicated bereavement is a proposed mental health syndrome that, although distinct from PTSD, contains significant conceptual overlap and may be an important comorbid condition. Traumatic events that include both loss of a close other *and* threat of death or harm to the individual can be conceptualized as complicated bereavement, PTSD, or MDD, or any combination of these three conditions. Greater clarity regarding the clinical utility (i.e., incremental validity in guiding treatment planning and outcome) of each of these diagnostic options is needed. Further clarity is also needed regarding whether PTSD, MDD, and complicated bereavement represent complications related to a general traumatic stress reaction or whether these are to be considered separate diagnostic entities.

Dissociative Disorders

According to the *DSM-IV* (APA, 2000), dissociative disorders involve "a disruption in the usually integrated functions of consciousness, memory, identity, or perception," (p. 519) and include dissociative amnesia, dissociative identity disorder, and depersonalization disorder. Dissociation also occurs as a symptom within other disorders, including acute stress disorder, PTSD, and somatization disorder. Dissociative disorders are not diagnosed as a separate condition if symptoms occur exclusively as a part of another Axis I disorder (APA, 2000). Dissociation in PTSD can take the form of dissociative flashbacks or severe detachment and numbing and has a considerable negative impact on quality of life (Warshaw et al., 1993).

Prior exposure to trauma and PTSD status are important risk factors for the development of significant dissociative symptoms (Briere, 2006). A history of traumatic events, such as child abuse, has been associated with higher rates of dissociation (Chu & Dill, 1990; Dutra, Bureau, Holmes, Lyubchik, & Lyons-Ruth, 2009). Furthermore, individuals with PTSD have significantly greater dissociative symptoms than do trauma exposed individuals without PTSD (Bremner, Steinberg, Southwick, Johnson, & Charney, 1993). This suggests that PTSD symptom severity, perhaps in combination with poor affect regulation, may mediate the relationship between trauma exposure and dissociation (Briere, 2006).

One line of research has proposed that PTSD be divided into two subtypes based on dissociation (Lanius et al., 2010). Non-dissociative PTSD is thought to be related to underutilization of emotion regulation, leading to dysregulated affect such as hyper-arousal and emotional volatility. In contrast, dissociative PTSD involves overregulation of affect, resulting in emotional numbing and detachment. The presence of these two subtypes is supported by studies indicating differential success of corticolimbic circuitry in modulating affect in the two subtypes (Lanius et al., 2010). Despite this line of research, it is unclear whether the *DSM-5* will incorporate subtype classifiers based on dissociation, as some have asserted that there is insufficient evidence for this distinction (Friedman et al., 2011).

Dissociation can also occur during or immediately after a traumatic event. Dissociation during a severe trauma (i.e., peritraumatic dissociation) may be protective, but persistent dissociation following a traumatic event is a risk factor for the development of PTSD (Briere, Scott, & Weathers, 2005; Spiegel, 1991). The link between persistent dissociation and PTSD is thought to be mediated by a reduced capacity to emotionally process the memory of the traumatic event (Bryant, 2007). Meta-analyses have shown a significant relationship between peritraumatic dissociation and later development of PTSD symptoms, particularly in individuals with a child abuse history, although a causal link between the two has not been established (Lensvelt-Mulders et al., 2008; Ozer, Best, Lipsey, & Weiss, 2003). Severity of the traumatic event and degree of initial PTSD symptoms, particularly physiological arousal, could be confounding factors in the relationship between peritraumatic dissociation and PTSD development (Bryant, 2007; Marshall & Schell, 2002). Because of these potential confounding factors, some have argued that peritraumatic dissociation may not have acceptable sensitivity and specificity to predict PTSD development (Bryant, 2007).

In summary, trauma exposure may be a risk factor for dissociative symptoms, which in turn may be a risk factor for the development of PTSD. Although dissociation is commonly seen in PTSD patients, it is considered an associated feature of PTSD and does not result in a comorbid diagnosis unless a dissociative disorder was preexisting. Dissociation may also be an important consideration in treatment planning. Exposure-based therapy, which has strong empirical support (Bisson et al., 2007; Hofmann & Smits, 2008; Institute of Medicine, 2007; Nemeroff et al., 2006; Ponniah & Hollon, 2009; Solomon, Gerrity, & Muff, 1992), may be less effective in individuals who dissociate or otherwise disengage from trauma memories because of dissociation's ability to block emotional processing of the traumatic memory (Lanius et al., 2010). Therefore, the presence and intensity of dissociative symptoms may need to be assessed and addressed before implementing some evidence-based PTSD interventions.

Personality Disorders

Personality disorders are defined in *DSM-IV* (APA, 2000) as "an enduring pattern of inner experience and behavior that deviates markedly from the expectations of the individual's culture, is pervasive and inflexible, has an onset in adolescence or early adulthood, is stable over time, and leads to distress or impairment" (p. 685). Individuals with PTSD often present with personality disorders or dysfunction in addition to their posttraumatic symptoms.

The high comorbidity of PTSD and personality disorders could be explained by a number of factors. First, traumatic experiences early in life may predispose individuals to the development of both personality dysfunction and PTSD. Alternatively, maladaptive personality traits may increase the risk that individuals will be exposed to a trauma or may increase the risk that they develop PTSD in response to a traumatic event. In addition, there is a relatively high degree of overlap in features of PTSD and many personality disorders, such as anger and irritability, interpersonal difficulties, and cognitive and mood disturbances. This suggests that the development of PTSD symptoms following a traumatic event could exacerbate preexisting personality dysfunction.

One of the personality disorders receiving the most attention as a comorbid condition with PTSD is borderline personality disorder (BDP; up to 76% of PTSD patients; see Southwick, Yehuda, & Giller, 1993). Individuals with BPD frequently report trauma histories, usually involving abuse very early in life or abuse committed by a caregiver (Gunderson & Sabo, 1993). Childhood trauma, particularly sexual abuse or incest, has been shown to be a risk factor for both complex PTSD and BPD (McLean & Gallop, 2003; Pagura et al., 2010). Early childhood trauma, particularly if severe, may therefore predispose individuals to develop both persistent personality dysfunction and PTSD. Individuals with BPD may also be more likely to engage in risky behaviors and therefore experience traumatic events, putting them at greater risk to develop PTSD.

BPD and PTSD share common features of anger and irritability, cognitive disturbances, and dissociative episodes. This overlap suggests that someone with BPD might be more likely to meet full criteria for PTSD following a trauma, given that they may already have a tendency toward PTSD-related symptoms that could be exacerbated by trauma exposure. Indeed, individuals with BPD are as much as twice as likely to develop PTSD in response to a traumatic event (Golier et al., 2003). However, the mechanism of this increased risk remains unclear.

Regardless of the reason for the high co-occurrence, comorbidity between BPD and PTSD is associated with a higher frequency of suicide attempts and poorer life functioning than either condition alone (Harned, Rizvi, & Linehan, 2010; Pagura et al., 2010; Zlotnick et al., 2003). Furthermore, the presence of BPD is associated with poorer PTSD treatment outcome (Feeny, Zoellner, & Foa, 2002; Forbes et al., 2002). There is some suggestion that BPD is best represented as a more severe or complex form of PTSD rather than as a comorbid condition (Herman, Perry, & van der Kolk, 1989), whereas others have maintained that BPD and PTSD should remain distinct diagnoses (Harned et al., 2010). Although BPD and PTSD are most commonly conceptualized as separate conditions, it is clear that they are complexly linked (Gunderson & Sabo, 1993; Zlotnick et al., 2003).

PTSD is also highly comorbid with anti-social personality disorder (ASPD, up to 64% of PTSD patients; e.g., Keane & Kaloupek, 1997). ASPD and PTSD share features of anger and irritability, suspiciousness, and difficulty in relationships (Bailey, 1985). Aggressive tendencies may lead individuals with ASPD to be exposed to an increased number of traumatic events and therefore at increased risk of developing PTSD. Conversely, PTSD features of anger and interpersonal withdrawal may exacerbate subclinical ASPD symptoms. These hypotheses were supported in a study of Vietnam-era veterans, which showed that childhood anti-social traits were associated with increased combat exposure, which in turn was associated with more anti-social traits in adulthood (Resnick, Foy, Donahoe, & Miller, 1989). However, another study of personality dysfunction in PTSD found that anti-social traits were associated with lower PTSD severity than borderline or schizoid characteristics (Hyer, Davis, Albrecht, Boudewyns, & Woods, 1994). Regardless, comorbidity between ASPD and PTSD has been associated with higher rates of substance abuse and suicidality (Goodwin & Hamilton, 2003).

A high incidence of avoidant, paranoid, and obsessive-compulsive personality disorders has also been reported in PTSD (Bollinger, Riggs, Blake, & Ruzek, 2000; Southwick et al., 1993). These may be misinterpretations by clinicians and/or patients of PTSD symptoms such as hypervigilance (mistaken for paranoia) or emotional numbing and interpersonal withdrawal (mistaken for avoidant features; Southwick et al., 1993). Alternatively, traits similar to those found in personality disorders may result from a patient's attempts to adjust to living with PTSD (Southwick et al., 1993).

In summary, traumatic experiences may predispose individuals to personality disorders, and personality disorder traits may be risk factors for the development of PTSD. In general, if left untreated PTSD is unlikely to remit, and so its symptoms, or the patient's attempts to cope with them, may be so persistent as to mimic personality dysfunction. This is especially true if interpersonal characteristics such as social withdrawal and irritability are present. Preexisting personality disorders are a barrier to effective PTSD treatment (Malta, Blanchard, Taylor, Hickling, & Freidenberg, 2002), and are an important comorbidity to research further.

Somatoform Disorders

Somatoform disorders are described in *DSM-IV* (APA, 2000) as "the presence of physical symptoms that suggest a general medical condition... [but] are not fully explained by a general medical condition, by the direct effects of a substance, or by another mental disorder" (p. 485). This can include somatization disorder, hypochondriasis, or body dysmorphic disorder. Somatoform disorders have been linked to PTSD. For instance, in a sample of patients with anxiety symptoms, those with a somatoform disorder were almost three times more likely to have a history of PTSD (Rogers et al., 1996). Furthermore, patients with chronic PTSD were four times more likely to have a somatoform disorder than those whose PTSD remitted (Perkonigg et al., 2005). PTSD has been shown to be related to higher levels of biological markers of immune, cardiovascular, and inflammatory problems (Boscarino, 2004), as well as unexplained somatic symptoms (Hoge, Terhakopian, Castro, Messer, & Engel, 2007).

Taken together, PTSD and somatoform disorders have a high co-occurrence and a complex relationship. The high rates of somatic symptoms in individuals with PTSD may contribute to the greater likelihood of individuals who have experienced traumatic events to seek medical rather than mental health care (Weisberg et al., 2002). Furthermore, the ability to treat both somatic and psychological symptoms of PTSD may be particularly important. In a study of a behavioral medicine treatment for somatization, improvement in somatic symptoms was associated with decreases in anxiety (Nakao et al., 2001). Conversely, treatment of PTSD symptoms may reduce somatization and health care visits (Chemtob, Nakashima, & Carlson, 2002).

Chronic Pain

Chronic pain is frequently present in individuals with PTSD, and PTSD is frequently present in those with chronic pain (Arguelles et al., 2006; Asmundson & Taylor, 2006). Recent reviews have shown that between 30–80% of individuals seeking outpatient treatment for PTSD also report chronic pain (Asmundson & Katz, 2009). Importantly, severity of pain at the time of the trauma has been shown to be a risk factor for the development of PTSD (Norman, Stein, Dimsdale, & Hoyt, 2008). Traumatic events often have physically as well as psychologically damaging sequelae, such as injuries sustained in a motor vehicle accident, natural disaster, assault, first responder duties, or combat, which can result in chronic pain in addition to PTSD. In addition, traumatic brain injury (TBI) is increasingly being recognized as common consequence of many PTSD Criterion A traumas, and has been independently associated with chronic pain (Nampiaparampil, 2008).

Asmundson and Taylor (2006) described three potential explanatory models for the high co-occurrence of PTSD and chronic pain. First, the shared vulnerability model (Asmundson & Taylor, 2006) suggests that anxiety sensitivity is a general predisposing factor to both chronic pain and PTSD. This effect is thought to be mediated by negative interpretations of both pain and hyper-arousal sensations. Anxiety sensitivity has been linked to both PTSD and chronic pain in cross-sectional studies, although longitudinal work is needed to rule out the hypothesis that PTSD and/or chronic pain lead to increases in anxiety sensitivity rather than the reverse (Asmundson & Katz, 2009).

Second, the mutual maintenance model (Sharp & Harvey, 2001) posits that symptoms of PTSD, such as behavioral avoidance and hyper-arousal, can maintain or worsen pain symptoms (e.g., Sherman, Turk, & Okifuji, 2000). At the same time, components of chronic pain, such as catastrophizing cognitions and limited physical activity, can maintain or worsen PTSD. Furthermore, experiencing pain related to injuries that resulted from a traumatic event can be a trigger for the re-experiencing symptoms (Cluster B symptoms) of PTSD. In this way, chronic pain and PTSD maintain each other, leading to a negative spiral of impairment and distress.

Finally, the triple vulnerability model (Asmundson & Taylor, 2006) proposes three risk factors for both PTSD and chronic pain: (1) a biological predisposition to hyper-arousal; (2) a general psychological predisposition to an external locus of control; and (3) a specific predisposition to anxiety reactions. These three factors are hypothesized to create a combined diathesis toward both PTSD and chronic pain that is then activated by a triggering event that causes both psychological trauma and physical pain.

These findings suggest that chronic pain is not only a common complication of PTSD but may also confer risk for and/or maintain PTSD symptoms. Furthermore, the presence or improvement of pain can play an important role in the treatment of PTSD. For example, in a sample of motor vehicle accident survivors, reduction in pain severity was associated with reductions in PTSD symptoms (Fedroff, Taylor, Asmundson, & Koch, 2001). Given that chronic pain frequently co-occurs with PTSD and may negatively affect PTSD treatment response (Taylor et al., 2001), future empirical work examining the models described above will be important.

Complex PTSD

Initial conceptualizations of PTSD were focused on combat experience as the prototypical traumatic event. However, patients with repeated interpersonal trauma such as child abuse, domestic violence, or captivity and torture often have a complex clinical presentation, suggesting that the PTSD diagnosis as it currently stands may be insufficient to capture the full range of posttraumatic symptoms (van der Kolk, Roth, Pelcovitz, Sunday, & Spinazzola, 2005).

To address this issue, complex PTSD has been proposed as a syndrome for survivors of repeated or prolonged traumatic exposure, particularly when the trauma is interpersonal in nature (Briere & Spinazzola, 2005; Herman, 1992). Herman (1992) first described complex PTSD and specified three main areas of disturbance above and beyond "simple" PTSD. First, patients with complex PTSD endorse a greater number of PTSD symptoms, more complex symptoms, and report greater interference from their symptoms. Second, complex PTSD is associated with changes to patients' identity and sense of self, which can include personality changes. Finally, complex PTSD is associated with an increased vulnerability to self-harm behaviors and future traumatic events (i.e., risk of retraumatization). In one study, as many as 70% of individuals meeting criteria for PTSD who also had early childhood abuse met criteria for complex PTSD, as well as 46% of those who met criteria for PTSD due to other types of trauma (van der Kolk et al., 2005).

Symptoms of complex PTSD are currently described in *DSM-IV* (APA, 2000), as an "associated constellation of symptoms [that] may occur and are more commonly seen in association with an interpersonal stressor" including "impaired affect modulation; self-destructive and impulsive behavior; dissociative symptoms; somatic complaints;... impaired relationships with others; or a change from the individual's previous personality characteristics" (p. 465). Therefore complex PTSD symptoms are currently conceptualized in the *DSM* as associated features of the PTSD diagnosis rather than a separate condition.

Some, however, have argued that complex PTSD should be a standalone diagnosis, and have generated provisional diagnostic criteria (Briere & Spinazzola, 2005; Pelcovitz et al., 1997; Taylor, Asmundson, & Carleton, 2006; see table 4.4). Common across conceptualizations are criteria such as (a) difficulty regulating affect; (b) interpersonal problems, often characterized by an inability to trust others; (c) alterations in identity or self-perception; (d) dissociative episodes, often as an avoidance response; (e) somatization; and (f) feelings of hopelessness. Additional proposed features include idealization of the perpetrator, high severity of "simple" PTSD symptoms, mood disturbance, and maladaptive coping strategies such as substance abuse, binge eating, or self-harm behaviors (Briere & Spinazzola, 2005). Complex PTSD has been suggested for inclusion

Table 4.4. Proposed complex PTSD criteria

I.	Poor affect regulation plus one or more of: Poor anger modulation Self-destructive behaviors Suicidal preoccupation Excessive risk taking
II.	Alterations in attention or consciousness (amnesia and/or dissociative episodes)
III.	Alterations in self-perception and identity, including two or more of: Perception of ineffectiveness Sense of being permanently damaged Feelings of guilt Feelings of shame Belief that no one can understand Minimization
IV.	Altered relationships, including at least one of: Inability to trust Revictimization Victimizing others
V.	Somatization, including two or more of: GI problems Chronic pain Cardiopulmonary symptoms Conversion symptoms Sexual symptoms
VI.	Alterations in meaning systems (despair, hopelessness, or loss of sustaining beliefs)

Source: Pelcovitz et al. (1997).

in *DSM-5* under the diagnosis of Disorders of Extreme Stress Not Otherwise Specified (Friedman et al., 2011), however the ultimate fate of complex PTSD in *DSM-5* is unknown at this time.

Prolonged Childhood Trauma

Prolonged childhood trauma is particularly likely to lead to complex PTSD and complicated comorbidity (van der Kolk et al., 2005). Repeated childhood trauma has been associated with a greater risk of comorbid substance abuse (Follette, Polusny, Bechtle, & Naugle, 1996) and BPD (Pagura et al., 2010), which is consistent with the conceptualization of complex PTSD as involving maladaptive coping skills and personality and identity dysfunction.

Repeated traumatic experiences in childhood have also been shown to increase the risk of retraumatization, which is a key proposed consequence of complex PTSD (Follette et al., 1996). Individuals with childhood trauma who experience additional traumas as adults (i.e., retraumatized individuals) show more severe physical and psychological symptoms when compared to those with either childhood or adult trauma alone (McCauley et al., 1997). Therefore, retraumatization can lead to lower functioning, more severe PTSD symptoms, and longer time to remission, which would further complicate the PTSD presentation (Follette et al., 1996).

In summary, complex PTSD often arises from prolonged childhood trauma and is associated with high rates of personality disturbance, particularly BPD, as well as elevated somatization and dissociation. Thus, complex PTSD involves changes at both state (i.e., Axis I) and trait (i.e., Axis II) levels (McLean & Gallop, 2003), and encompasses many of the boundary conditions described previously, such as personality disorders, dissociation, and somatization.

Cross-Cultural Features

Although problematic reactions to traumatic life events, such as fear, helplessness, and horror, occur across cultures (Friedman & Jaranson, 1994), cultures vary widely in the language and "idioms of distress" used to describe the common symptoms and problems after trauma (Hinton & Lewis-Fernandez, 2010). Assessment based on culturally specific idioms may be more sensitive to psychological disturbance than traditional *DSM* diagnoses, and failure to address concerns relating to a patient's broader cultural context can impede treatment success (Hinton & Lewis-Fernandez, 2010). Even within the modern American medical tradition, conceptualization and symptoms associated with the traumatic stress response have shifted over time, highlighting the importance of cultural context in determining what is considered an abnormal response to trauma (Kirmayer, Rousseau, & Measham, 2011).

Variations in cultural dimensions can impact the way in which traumatic events are interpreted, as well as how symptoms are expressed and coped with (Kirmayer et al., 2011). There is extensive variation across cultures in how and whether emotions, particularly negative emotions, are expressed (Matsumoto, 1993), which has clear implications for assessment and treatment of PTSD across cultures. In some cultural contexts, emotional expression is considered inappropriate or otherwise negatively viewed, whereas somatic symptoms are less stigmatized (Nicholl & Thompson, 2004); thus, somatization may be a particularly important variable in cross-cultural assessments of PTSD (Briere & Spinazzola, 2005). For example, somatic complaints seem to be prominent in patients from Southeast Asia, and comorbid panic disorder is common (Hinton & Otto, 2006).

It is important to understand the meaning that an individual patient gives to the traumatic experience, and this meaning is greatly influenced by how the individual's culture interprets that experience in particular and trauma in general (Kirmayer et al., 2011). In cultures where religious practices involve dissociative experiences, dissociation can be an acceptable expression of posttraumatic distress and may therefore occur more commonly (Kirmayer et al., 2011). Help-seeking behavior and disclosure of traumatic experiences are also greatly influenced by the norms of the individual's cultural context (Boehnlein & Kinzie, 1995; see also Hinton & Nickerson, chapter 38, in this volume).

One important cross-cultural context in which to understand PTSD is in refugee populations. The prevalence rate of PTSD is particularly high in refugees (as much as 10 times higher than the general population; Crumlish & O'Rourke, 2010), where an entire culture or society may have communally experienced trauma such as persecution and/or war. Refugees are likely to experience not only specific isolated traumatic events but also high levels of ongoing stress from displacement, isolation, low socioeconomic status, and discrimination associated with their refugee status (Nicholl & Thompson, 2004). Social support and stability are important protective factors against the development of PTSD after a trauma, but migration and relocation can impede the availability of these resources (Kirmayer et al., 2011).

The pervasive traumatic experiences of refugee populations and subsequent high rates of PTSD (e.g., de Jong, Mulhern, Ford, van der Kam, & Kleber, 2000) have led to questions of what is a "normal" compared to a "disordered" response to trauma (Summerfield, 2001). Because of the variations across cultures in how trauma is understood and dealt with, and how distress subsequent to trauma is experienced and expressed, some have argued that the PTSD diagnosis is a uniquely Western phenomenon (Summerfield, 2001). However, many cross-cultural studies of PTSD have shown similar symptoms and symptom clusters across populations varying in socio-political, economic, geographic settings (Mehta, Vankar, & Patel, 2005; Miller et al., 2009; Ruchkin et al., 2005), suggesting cross-cultural validity (Hinton & Lewis-Fernandez, 2011).

Within the United States, rates of PTSD have been shown to vary by ethnic background. For example, in one study of response to a natural disaster, Caucasians had the lowest rates of PTSD, and Spanish-preferring Latinos had the highest (Perilla, Norris, & Lavizzo, 2002). A study of Vietnam-era veterans also found higher rates of PTSD in veterans of Hispanic background (Ruef, Litz, & Schlenger, 2000). Others have found that African Americans have a higher overall prevalence of PTSD in both civilian and military populations (Asnaani, Richey, Dimaite, Hinton, & Hofmann, 2010; Penk et al., 1989). However, in a study of low-income women who experienced domestic violence, no differences in PTSD rates were found across ethnic groups (Vogel & Marshall, 2001). The null finding with regard to ethnicity in this low-income group suggests that socioeconomic factors may play a large role above and beyond ethnicity in conferring PTSD risk. In general, although acculturative stress, overt discrimination, and minority group status may play a role in PTSD vulnerability, these effects have not been disentangled from risks related to socioeconomic variables that also frequently differ by ethnicity.

Conclusion

Despite the longstanding recognition that combat exposure and other major traumatic events can have significant negative effects on mental health, the boundaries of PTSD are still being defined. As with many mood and anxiety disorders in the *DSM*, PTSD symptoms overlap significantly with other psychiatric disorders, such as MDD, GAD, and BPD. This has led to questions of whether the boundaries of PTSD are sufficiently clear, although others have found reasonable differentiation by clinicians. It also remains unclear whether the PTSD diagnosis optimally captures the adverse impact of traumas such as prolonged childhood maltreatment or complicated bereavement, or whether the PTSD diagnosis *should* include room for these conditions. The applicability of the PTSD syndrome across cultural contexts has also been called into question, though others have found it to be reliable, valid, and relatively universal.

Future research should seek to clarify these issues by examining the clinical utility of different boundaries to PTSD, such as changes to Criterion A1 and/or A2, or different factor structures (e.g., Forbes et al., 2011). The syndrome of complex PTSD is listed in *DSM-IV* as a set of possible "associated features" within the PTSD diagnosis. However, more research is needed to determine whether complex PTSD represents a more severe form of PTSD, or whether it should be a specifier or a separate diagnosis unto itself. Cultural variables that can influence the experience and expression of PTSD symptoms following trauma need to be better defined, which could lead to modifications of the criteria in an effort to increase cultural sensitivity of the disorder. Greater understanding of how to best address dissociation, chronic pain, grief, and personality variables in diagnosis is also needed.

Future Directions

1. Should Criterion A2 be defined differently or removed from the *DSM* PTSD diagnosis?
2. Should the PTSD diagnosis encompass complicated bereavement, or should complicated bereavement represent a distinct condition?
3. Is complex PTSD a disorder distinct from PTSD or is complex PTSD simply a more severe form of PTSD?
4. Is PTSD comorbid with BPD conceptually and/or etiologically distinct from complex PTSD?
5. Is PTSD arising from prolonged interpersonal trauma (i.e., complex PTSD) conceptually distinct from PTSD from other traumatic events?
6. Is the PTSD diagnosis valid and relevant across cultures?
7. How do specific cultural features influence the experience and expression of PTSD symptoms?

References

Adler, A. B., Wright, K. M., Bliese, P. D., Eckford, R., & Hoge, C. W. (2008). A2 diagnostic criterion for combat-related posttraumatic stress disorder. *Journal of Traumatic Stress, 21*, 301–308.

American Psychiatric Association. (1980). *Diagnostic and statistical manual of mental disorders* (3rd ed.). Washington, DC: Author.

American Psychiatric Association. (2000). *Diagnostic and statistical manual of mental disorders* (4th ed., text rev.). Washington, DC: Author.

Arguelles, L. M., Afari, N., Buchwald, D. S., Clauw, D. J., Furner, S., & Goldberg, J. (2006). A twin study of posttraumatic stress disorder symptoms and chronic widespread pain. *Pain, 124*, 150–157.

Asmundson, G. J. G., Frombach, I., McQuaid, J., Pedrelli, P., Lenox, R., & Stein, M. B. (2000). Dimensionality of posttraumatic stress symptoms: A confirmatory factor analysis of DSM-IV symptom clusters and other symptom models. *Behaviour Research and Therapy, 38*, 203–214.

Asmundson, G. J. G., & Katz, J. (2009). Understanding the co occurrence of anxiety disorders and chronic pain: State of the art. *Depression and Anxiety, 26*, 888–901.

Asmundson, G. J. G., & Taylor, S. (2006). PTSD and chronic pain: Cognitive-behavioral perspectives and practical implications. In G. Young, A. W. Kane, & K. Nicholson (Eds.), *Psychological knowledge in court: PTSD, pain, and TBI* (pp. 225–241). New York, NY: Springer.

Asnaani, A., Richey, J. A., Dimaite, R., Hinton, D. E., & Hofmann, S. G. (2010). A cross-ethnic comparison of lifetime prevalence rates of anxiety disorders. *The Journal of Nervous and Mental Disease, 198*, 551.

Bailey, J. E. (1985). Differential diagnosis of posttraumatic stress and antisocial personality disorders. *Psychiatric Services, 36*, 881.

Blanchard, E. B., Hickling, E. J., Forneris, C. A., Taylor, A. E., Buckley, T. C., Loos, W. R., et al. (1997). Prediction of remission of acute posttraumatic stress disorder in motor vehicle accident victims. *Journal of Traumatic Stress, 10*, 215–234.

Bisson, J. I., Ehlers, A., Matthews, R., Pilling, S., Richards, D., & Turner, S. (2007). Psychological treatments for chronic post-traumatic stress disorder: Systematic review and meta-analysis. *British Journal of Psychiatry, 190*, 97–104

Boehnlein, J. K., & Kinzie, J. D. (1995). Refugee trauma. *Transcultural Psychiatry, 32*, 223.

Bollinger, A. R., Riggs, D. S., Blake, D. D., & Ruzek, J. I. (2000). Prevalence of personality disorders among combat veterans with posttraumatic stress disorder. *Journal of Traumatic Stress, 13*, 255–270.

Boscarino, J. A. (2004). Posttraumatic stress disorder and physical illness: Results from clinical and epidemiologic studies. *Annals of the New York Academy of Sciences, 1032*, 141–153.

Bovin, M. J., & Marx, B. P. (2011). The importance of peritraumatic experience in defining traumatic stress. *Psychological Bulletin, 137*, 47–67.

Bremner, J. D., Steinberg, M., Southwick, S. M., Johnson, D. R., & Charney, D. S. (1993). Use of the Structured Clinical Interview for DSM-IV Dissociative Disorders for systematic assessment of dissociative symptoms in posttraumatic stress disorder. *American Journal of Psychiatry, 150*, 1011.

Breslau, N., Davis, G. C., Peterson, E. L., & Schultz, L. R. (2000). A second look at comorbidity in victims of trauma: The posttraumatic stress disorder-major depression connection. *Biological Psychiatry, 48*, 902–909.

Breslau, N., & Kessler, R. C. (2001). The stressor criterion in DSM-IV posttraumatic stress disorder: An empirical investigation. *Biological Psychiatry, 50*, 699–704.

Brewin, C. R., Andrews, B., & Rose, S. (2000). Fear, helplessness, and horror in posttraumatic stress disorder: Investigating DSM-IV Criterion A2 in victims of violent crime. *Journal of Traumatic Stress, 13*, 499–509.

Brewin, C. R., Andrews, B., Rose, S., & Kirk, M. (1999). Acute stress disorder and posttraumatic stress disorder in victims of violent crime. *American Journal of Psychiatry, 156*, 360.

Briere, J. (2006). Dissociative symptoms and trauma exposure: Specificity, affect dysregulation, and posttraumatic stress. *Journal of Nervous and Mental Disease, 194*, 78.

Briere, J., Scott, C., & Weathers, F. (2005). Peritraumatic and persistent dissociation in the presumed etiology of PTSD. *American Journal of Psychiatry, 162*, 2295.

Briere, J., & Spinazzola, J. (2005). Phenomenology and psychological assessment of complex posttraumatic states. *Journal of Traumatic Stress, 18*, 401–412.

Bryant, R. A. (2007). Does dissociation further our understanding of PTSD? *Journal of Anxiety Disorders, 21*, 183–191.

Buckley, T. C., Blanchard, E. B., & Hickling, E. J. (1998). A confirmatory factor analysis of posttraumatic stress symptoms. *Behaviour Research and Therapy, 36*, 1091–1099.

Chemtob, C. M., Nakashima, J., & Carlson, J.G. (2002). Brief treatment for elementary school children with disaster-related posttraumatic stress disorder: A field study. *Journal of Clinical Psychology, 58*, 99–112.

Chu, J. A., & Dill, D. L. (1990). Dissociative symptoms in relation to childhood physical and sexual abuse. *American Journal of Psychiatry, 147*, 887.

Creamer, M., McFarlane, A. C., & Burgess, P. (2005). Psychopathology following trauma: The role of subjective experience. *Journal of Affective Disorders, 86*, 175–182.

Crumlish, N., & O'Rourke, K. (2010). A systematic review of treatments for post-traumatic stress disorder among refugees and asylum-seekers. *Journal of Nervous and Mental Disease, 198.*

Davidson, J. R. T., Hughes, D., Blazer, D. G., & George, L. K. (1991). Post-traumatic stress disorder in the community: An epidemiological study. *Psychological Medicine, 21*, 713–721.

de Jong, K., Mulhern, M., Ford, N., van der Kam, S., & Kleber, R. (2000). The trauma of war in Sierra Leone. *Lancet, 355*, 2067–2068.

Dutra, L., Bureau, J. F., Holmes, B., Lyubchik, A., & Lyons-Ruth, K. (2009). Quality of early care and childhood trauma: A prospective study of developmental pathways to dissociation. *Journal of Nervous and Mental Disease, 197*, 383.

Ehlers, A., Mayou, R. A., & Bryant, B. (1998). Psychological predictors of chronic posttraumatic stress disorder after motor vehicle accidents. *Journal of Abnormal Psychology, 107*, 508.

Fedroff, I. C., Taylor, S., Asmundson, G. J. G., & Koch, W. J. (2001). Cognitive factors in traumatic stress reactions: Predicting PTSD symptoms from anxiety sensitivity and beliefs about harmful events. *Behavioural and Cognitive Psychotherapy, 28*, 5–15.

Feeny, N. C., Zoellner, L. A., & Foa, E. B. (2002). Treatment outcome for chronic PTSD among female assault victims with borderline personality characteristics: A preliminary examination. *Journal of Personality Disorders, 16*, 30–40.

Follette, V. M., Polusny, M. A., Bechtle, A. E., & Naugle, A. E. (1996). Cumulative trauma: The impact of child sexual abuse, adult sexual assault, and spouse abuse. *Journal of Traumatic Stress, 9*, 25–35.

Forbes, D., Fletcher, S., Lockwood, E., O'Donnell, M., Creamer, M., Bryant, R. A., et al. (2011). Requiring both avoidance and emotional numbing in DSM-V PTSD: Will it help? *Journal of Affective Disorders, 130*, 483–486.

Forbes, D., Creamer, M., Allen, N., Elliott, P., McHugh, T., Debenham, P. et al. (2002). The MMPI-2 as a predictor of symptom change following treatment for posttraumatic stress disorder. *Journal of Personality Assessment, 79*, 321–336.

Franklin, C. L., & Zimmerman, M. (2001). Posttraumatic stress disorder and major depressive disorder: Investigating the role of overlapping symptoms in diagnostic comorbidity. *The Journal of Nervous and Mental Disease, 189*, 548.

Friedman, M., & Jaranson, J. (1994). The applicability of the posttraumatic stress disorder concept to refugees. In A. J. Marsella, T. Bornemann, S. Ekblad, & J. Orley (Eds.), *Amidst peril and pain: The mental health and wellbeing of the world's refugees* (pp. 207–227). Washington, DC: American Psychological Association.

Friedman, M.J., Resick, P.A., Bryant, R.A. & Brewin, C.R. (2011). Considering PTSD for DSM-5. *Depression and Anxiety, 28*, 750–769.

Frueh, B., Elhai, J., & Acierno, R. (2010). The future of posttraumatic stress disorder in the DSM. *Psychological Injury and Law, 3*, 260–270.

Golier, J. A., Yehuda, R., Bierer, L. M., Mitropoulou, V., New, A. S., Schmeidler, J., et al. (2003). The relationship of borderline personality disorder to posttraumatic stress disorder and traumatic events. *American Journal of Psychiatry, 160*, 2018.

Goodwin, R. D., & Hamilton, S. P. (2003). Lifetime comorbidity of antisocial personality disorder and anxiety disorders among adults in the community. *Psychiatry Research, 117*, 159–166.

Grant, D. M., Beck, J. G., Marques, L., Palyo, S. A., & Clapp, J. D. (2008). The structure of distress following trauma: Posttraumatic stress disorder, major depressive disorder, and generalized anxiety disorder. *Journal of Abnormal Psychology, 117*, 662–672.

Gunderson, J. G., & Sabo, A. N. (1993). The phenomenological and conceptual interface between borderline personality disorder and PTSD. *American Journal of Psychiatry, 150*, 19.

Harned, M. S., Rizvi, S. L., & Linehan, M. M. (2010). Impact of co-occurring posttraumatic stress disorder on suicidal women with borderline personality disorder. *American Journal of Psychiatry, 167*, 1210.

Herman, J. L. (1992). Complex PTSD: A syndrome in survivors of prolonged and repeated trauma. *Journal of Traumatic Stress, 5*, 377–391.

Herman, J. L., Perry, J. C., & van der Kolk, B. A. (1989). Childhood trauma in borderline personality disorder. *American Journal of Psychiatry, 146*, 490–495.

Hinton, D. E., & Lewis-Fernandez, R. (2010). Idioms of distress among trauma survivors: Subtypes and clinical utility. *Culture, Medicine and Psychiatry, 34*, 209–218.

Hinton, D. E. & Lewis-Fernandez, R. (2011). The cross-cultural validity of posttraumatic stress disorder: Implications for DSM-5. *Depression and Anxiety, 28*, 783–801.

Hinton, D. E., & Otto, M. W. (2006). Symptom presentation and symptom meaning among traumatized Cambodian refugees: Relevance to a somatically focused cognitive-behavior therapy. *Cognitive and Behavioral Practice, 13*, 249–260.

Hofmann, S. G., & Smits, J. A. J. (2008). Cognitive-behavioral therapy for adult anxiety disorders: A meta-analysis of randomized placebo-controlled trials. *Journal of Clinical Psychiatry, 69*, 621–632.

Hoge, C. W., Terhakopian, A., Castro, C. A., Messer, S. C., & Engel, C. C. (2007). Association of posttraumatic stress disorder with somatic symptoms, health care visits, and absenteeism among Iraq war veterans. *American Journal of Psychiatry, 164*, 150.

Horowitz, M. J., Siegel, B., Holen, A., Bonanno, G. A., Milbrath, C., & Stinson, C. H. (2003). Diagnostic criteria for complicated grief disorder. *Focus, 1*, 290.

Hyer, L., Davis, H., Albrecht, W., Boudewyns, P., & Woods, G. (1994). Cluster analysis of MCMI and MCMI-II on chronic PTSD victims. *Journal of Clinical Psychology, 50*, 502–515.

Institute of Medicine (2007). *Treatment of posttraumatic stress disorder: An assessment of the evidence.* Washington, DC: National Academies Press.

Keane, T. M., & Kaloupek, D. G. (1997). Comorbid psychiatric disorders in PTSD. *Annals of the New York Academy of Sciences, 821*, 24–34.

Keane, T. M., Taylor, K. L., & Penk, W. E. (1997). Differentiating post-traumatic stress disorder (PTSD) from major depression (MDD) and generalized anxiety disorder (GAD). *Journal of Anxiety Disorders, 11*, 317–328.

Kessler, R. C., Sonnega, A., Bromet, E., Hughes, M., & Nelson, C. B. (1995). Posttraumatic stress disorder in the National Comorbidity Survey. *Archives of General Psychiatry, 52*, 1048.

King, D. W., King, L. A., McArdle, J. J., Shalev, A. Y., & Doron-LaMarca, S. (2009). Sequential temporal dependencies in associations between symptoms of depression and posttraumatic stress disorder: An application of bivariate latent difference score structural equation modeling. *Multivariate Behavioral Research, 44*, 437–464.

King, D. W., Leskin, G. A., King, L. A., & Weathers, F. W. (1998). Confirmatory factor analysis of the clinician-administered PTSD Scale: Evidence for the dimensionality of posttraumatic stress disorder. *Psychological Assessment, 10*, 90–96.

Kirmayer, L. J., Rousseau, C., & Measham, T. (2011). Sociocultural Considerations. In D. M. Benedek & G. H. Wynn (Eds.), *Clinical manual for management of PTSD* (pp. 415–444). Arlington, VA: American Psychiatric Publishing.

Lanius, R. A., Vermetten, E., Loewenstein, R. J., Brand, B., Schmahl, C., Bremner, J. D., et al. (2010). Emotion modulation in PTSD: Clinical and neurobiological evidence for a dissociative subtype. *American Journal of Psychiatry, 167*, 640.

Lensvelt-Mulders, G., van Der Hart, O., van Ochten, J. M., van Son, M. J. M., Steele, K., & Breeman, L. (2008). Relations among peritraumatic dissociation and posttraumatic stress: A meta-analysis. *Clinical Psychology Review, 28*, 1138–1151.

Malta, L. S., Blanchard, E. B., Taylor, A. E., Hickling, E. J., & Freidenberg, B. M. (2002). Personality disorders and posttraumatic stress disorder in motor vehicle accident survivors. *Journal of Nervous and Mental Disease, 190*, 767.

Marshall, G. N., & Schell, T. L. (2002). Reappraising the link between peritraumatic dissociation and PTSD symptom severity: Evidence from a longitudinal study of community violence survivors. *Journal of Abnormal Psychology, 111*, 626.

Matsumoto, D. (1993). Ethnic differences in affect intensity, emotion judgments, display rule attitudes, and self-reported emotional expression in an American sample. *Motivation and Emotion, 17*, 107–123.

McCauley, J., Kern, D. E., Kolodner, K., Dill, L., Schroeder, A. F., DeChant, H. K., et al. (1997). Clinical characteristics of women with a history of childhood abuse: Unhealed wounds. *Journal of the American Medical Association, 277,* 1362.

McLean, L. M., & Gallop, R. (2003). Implications of childhood sexual abuse for adult borderline personality disorder and complex posttraumatic stress disorder. *American Journal of Psychiatry, 160,* 369.

Mehta, K., Vankar, G., & Patel, V. (2005). Validity of the construct of post-traumatic stress disorder in a low-income country: Interview study of women in Gujarat, India. *British Journal of Psychiatry, 187,* 585.

Miller, K. E., Omidian, P., Kulkarni, M., Yaqubi, A., Daudzai, H., & Rasmussen, A. (2009). The validity and clinical utility of post-traumatic stress disorder in Afghanistan. *Transcultural Psychiatry, 46,* 219.

Nakao, M., Myers, P., Fricchione, G., Zuttermeister, P. C., Barsky, A. J., & Benson, H. (2001). Somatization and symptom reduction through a behavioral medicine intervention in a mind/body medicine clinic. *Behavioral Medicine, 26,* 169–176.

Nampiaparampil, D. E. (2008). Prevalence of chronic pain after traumatic brain injury: A systematic review. *Journal of the American Medical Association, 300,* 711.

Nemeroff, C. B., Bremner, J. D., Foa, E. B., Mayberg, H. S., North, C. S., & Stein, M. B. (2006). Posttraumatic stress disorder: A state-of-the-science review. *Journal of Psychiatric Research, 40,* 1–21.

Neria, Y., & Litz, B. T. (2004). Bereavement by traumatic means: The complex synergy of trauma and grief. *Journal of Loss and Trauma, 9,* 73–87.

Nicholl, C., & Thompson, A. (2004). The psychological treatment of post traumatic stress disorder (PTSD) in adult refugees: A review of the current state of psychological therapies. *Journal of Mental Health, 13,* 351–362.

Norman, S. B., Stein, M. B., Dimsdale, J. E., & Hoyt, D. B. (2008). Pain in the aftermath of trauma is a risk factor for post-traumatic stress disorder. *Psychological Medicine, 38,* 533–542.

North, C. S., Suris, A. M., Davis, M., & Smith, R. P. (2009). Toward validation of the diagnosis of posttraumatic stress disorder. *American Journal of Psychiatry, 166,* 34.

O'Donnell, M. L., Creamer, M., McFarlane, A. C., Silove, D., & Bryant, R. A. (2010). Should A2 be a diagnostic requirement for posttraumatic stress disorder in DSM-V? *Psychiatry Research, 176,* 257–260.

O'Donnell, M. L., Creamer, M., & Pattison, P. (2004). Posttraumatic stress disorder and depression following trauma: Understanding comorbidity. *American Journal of Psychiatry, 161,* 1390.

Ozer, E. J., Best, S. R., Lipsey, T. L., & Weiss, D. S. (2003). Predictors of posttraumatic stress disorder and symptoms in adults: A meta-analysis. *Psychological Bulletin, 129,* 52–73.

Pagura, J., Stein, M. B., Bolton, J. M., Cox, B. J., Grant, B., & Sareen, J. (2010). Comorbidity of borderline personality disorder and posttraumatic stress disorder in the US population. *Journal of Psychiatric Research, 44,* 1190–1198.

Palmieri, P. A., Weathers, F. W., Difede, J. A., & King, D. W. (2007). Confirmatory factor analysis of the PTSD Checklist and the Clinician-Administered PTSD Scale in disaster workers exposed to the World Trade Center Ground Zero. *Journal of Abnormal Psychology, 116,* 329.

Papa, A., Neria, Y., & Litz, B. (2008). Traumatic bereavement in war veterans. *Psychiatric Annals, 38,* 686.

Pelcovitz, D., van der Kolk, B., Roth, S., Mandel, F., Kaplan, S., & Resick, P. (1997). Development of a criteria set and a structured interview for disorders of extreme stress (SIDES). *Journal of Traumatic Stress, 10,* 3–16.

Penk, W. E., Robinowitz, R., Black, J., Dolan, M., Bell, W., Dorsett, D., et al. (1989). Ethnicity: Post-traumatic stress disorder (PTSD) differences among black, white, and Hispanic veterans who differ in degrees of exposure to combat in Vietnam. *Journal of Clinical Psychology, 45,* 729–735.

Perilla, J. L., Norris, F. H., & Lavizzo, E. A. (2002). Ethnicity, culture, and disaster response: Identifying and explaining ethnic differences in PTSD six months after Hurricane Andrew. *Journal of Social and Clinical Psychology, 21,* 20–45.

Perkonigg, A., Pfister, H., Stein, M. B., Hofler, M., Lieb, R., Maercker, A., et al. (2005). Longitudinal course of posttraumatic stress disorder and posttraumatic stress disorder symptoms in a community sample of adolescents and young adults. *American Journal of Psychiatry, 162,* 1320.

Ponniah, K., & Hollon, S. D. (2009). Empirically supported psychological treatments for adult acute stress disorder and posttraumatic stress disorder: A review. *Depression and Anxiety, 26,* 1089–1109

Prigerson, H. G., Shear, M. K., Jacobs, S. C., Reynolds, C. F., Maciejewski, P. K., Davidson, J. R., et al. (1999). Consensus criteria for traumatic grief. A preliminary empirical test. *British Journal of Psychiatry, 174,* 67.

Resnick, H. S., Foy, D. W., Donahoe, C. P., & Miller, E. N. (1989). Antisocial behavior and post-traumatic stress disorder in Vietnam veterans. *Journal of Clinical Psychology, 45,* 860–866.

Rogers, M. P., Weinshenker, N. J., Warshaw, M. G., Goisman, R. M., Rodriguez-Villa, F. J., Fierman, E. J., et al. (1996). Prevalence of somatoform disorders in a large sample of patients with anxiety disorders. *Psychosomatics, 37,* 17.

Ruchkin, V., Schwab-Stone, M., Jones, S., Cicchetti, D. V., Koposov, R., & Vermeiren, R. (2005). Is posttraumatic stress in youth a culture-bound phenomenon? A comparison of symptom trends in selected U.S. and Russian communities. *American Journal of Psychiatry, 162,* 538.

Ruef, A. M., Litz, B. T., & Schlenger, W. E. (2000). Hispanic ethnicity and risk for combat-related posttraumatic stress disorder. *Cultural Diversity and Ethnic Minority Psychology, 6,* 235–251.

Shalev, A. Y., Freedman, S., Peri, T., Brandes, D., Sahar, T., Orr, S. P., et al. (1998). Prospective study of posttraumatic stress disorder and depression following trauma. *American Journal of Psychiatry, 155,* 630.

Sharp, T. J., & Harvey, A. G. (2001). Chronic pain and posttraumatic stress disorder: Mutual maintenance? *Clinical Psychology Review, 21,* 857–877.

Shear, K., Frank, E., Houck, P. R., & Reynolds, C. F. (2005). Treatment of complicated grief: A randomized controlled trial. *Journal of the American Medical Association, 293,* 2601.

Sherman, J. J., Turk, D. C., & Okifuji, A. (2000). Prevalence and impact of posttraumatic stress disorder-like symptoms on patients with fibromyalgia syndrome. *Clinical Journal of Pain, 16,* 127.

Simms, L. J., Watson, D., & Doebbelling, B. N. (2002). Confirmatory factor analyses of posttraumatic stress symptoms in deployed and nondeployed veterans of the Gulf War. *Journal of Abnormal Psychology, 111,* 637–647.

Simon, N. M., Shear, K. M., Thompson, E. H., Zalta, A. K., Perlman, C., Reynolds, C. F., et al. (2007). The prevalence and correlates of psychiatric comorbidity in individuals with complicated grief. *Comprehensive psychiatry, 48*, 395–399.

Solomon, S. D., Gerrity, E. T., & Muff, A. M. (1992). Efficacy of treatments for posttraumatic stress disorder. *Journal of the American Medical Association, 268*, 633–638.

Southwick, S. M., Yehuda, R., & Giller Jr, E. L. (1993). Personality disorders in treatment-seeking combat veterans with posttraumatic stress disorder. *American Journal of Psychiatry, 150*, 1020.

Spiegel, D. (1991). Dissociation and trauma. In A.Tasman & S. M. Goldfinger (Eds.), *American Psychiatric Press review of psychiatry* (pp. 261–275). Washington, D. C.: American Psychiatric Press.

Steenkamp, M. M., Litz, B. T., Gray, M. J., Lebowitz, L., Nash, W., Conoscenti, L., et al. (2010). A brief exposure-based intervention for service members with PTSD. *Cognitive and Behavioral Practice, 18*, 98–107.

Steil, R., & Ehlers, A. (2000). Dysfunctional meaning of posttraumatic intrusions in chronic PTSD. *Behaviour Research and Therapy, 38*, 537–558.

Summerfield, D. (2001). The invention of post-traumatic stress disorder and the social usefulness of a psychiatric category. *British Medical Journal, 322*, 95.

Taylor, S., Asmundson, G. J. G., & Carleton, R. N. (2006). Simple versus complex PTSD: A cluster analytic investigation. *Journal of Anxiety Disorders, 20*, 459–472.

Taylor, S., Fedoroff, I. C., Koch, W. J., Thordarson, D. S., Fecteau, G., & Nicki, R. M. (2001). Posttraumatic stress disorder arising after road traffic collisions: Patterns of response to cognitive-behavior therapy. *Journal of Consulting and Clinical Psychology, 69*, 541–551.

Taylor, S., Kuch, K., Koch, W. J., Crockett, D. J., & Passey, G. (1998). The structure of posttraumatic stress symptoms. *Journal of Abnormal Psychology, 107*, 154–160.

van der Kolk, B. A., Roth, S., Pelcovitz, D., Sunday, S., & Spinazzola, J. (2005). Disorders of extreme stress: The empirical foundation of a complex adaptation to trauma. *Journal of Traumatic Stress, 18*, 389–399.

Vogel, L. C. M. & Marshall, L. L. (2001). PTSD symptoms and partner abuse: Low income women at risk. *Journal of Traumatic Stress, 14*, 569–584.

Warshaw, M. G., Fierman, E., Pratt, L., Hunt, M., Yonkers, K. A., Massion, A. O., et al. (1993). Quality of life and dissociation in anxiety disorder patients with histories of trauma or PTSD. *American Journal of Psychiatry, 150*, 1512.

Weisberg, R. B., Bruce, S. E., Machan, J. T., Kessler, R. C., Culpepper, L., & Keller, M. B. (2002). Nonpsychiatric illness among primary care patients with trauma histories and posttraumatic stress disorder. *Psychiatric Services, 53*, 848–854.

Yufik, T., & Simms, L. J. (2010). A meta-analytic investigation of the structure of posttraumatic stress disorder symptoms. *Journal of Abnormal Psychology, 119*, 764–776.

Zayfert, C., Becker, C. B., Unger, D. L., & Shearer, D. K. (2002). Comorbid anxiety disorders in civilians seeking treatment for posttraumatic stress disorder. *Journal of Traumatic Stress, 15*, 31–38.

Zlotnick, C., Johnson, D. M., Yen, S., Battle, C. L., Sanislow, C. A., Skodol, A. E., et al. (2003). Clinical features and impairment in women with borderline personality disorder (BPD) with posttraumatic stress disorder (PTSD), BPD without PTSD, and other personality disorders with PTSD. *Journal of Nervous and Mental Disease, 191*, 706.

CHAPTER

5 Future of Classification in Posttraumatic Stress Disorder

Terence M. Keane *and* Mark W. Miller

Abstract

This chapter reviews the status of modifications to the definition of PTSD and proposed changes for DSM-5. We include a brief history of the diagnosis and trace its evolution in the Diagnostic and Statistical Manual of Mental Disorders (DSM). We discuss some of the current controversies related to the definition of PTSD including its location among the anxiety disorders, the utility of Criterion A and its subcomponents, and the factor structure of the symptoms. We review the rationale for the addition of new symptoms and modifications to existing criteria now and conclude with comments on future directions for research on PTSD.

Key Words: Trauma, PTSD, classification scheme

Introduction

Classification schemes are fundamental methods in science to compare, contrast, and study elements, conditions, and diseases that exist in nature. Diagnostic schemes applied to psychiatric and psychological conditions are now more than one hundred years old. As new information becomes available and as empirical science informs the field of mental health, periodic re-examinations of diagnostic classification systems are needed. The fourth edition of the *Diagnostic and Statistical Manual* (*DSM-IV*) of the American Psychiatric Association is now undergoing such a revision with the intent to improve diagnostic accuracy and enhance assessment, treatment, and future research in the field.

As frequently happens in medicine, the advent of the current wars in the Middle East and Asia (i.e., the Global War on Terrorism, GWOT) and the military actions in Iraq and Afghanistan (i.e., OEF-OIF) promote an interest in the acceleration of methods to evaluate and treat the signature wounds of the contemporary wars. Our involvement in GWOT represents an elevated risk to the mental health of the American and allied forces assigned to these regions. Coupled with impact of the terrorist attacks on the Pentagon and the World Trade Center, the diagnosis of posttraumatic stress disorder (PTSD) is currently receiving increased attention in both the scientific and the popular literature.

Our ultimate understanding of the impact of psychological trauma on the human condition, to include its biological and psychological substrates, is premised on the use of a common definitional framework across scientific and clinical venues. From a historical perspective, great progress in the field was stimulated by the inclusion of the diagnosis of PTSD in the psychiatric nomenclature in 1980 and by several attempts to strengthen the operational criteria employed to define cases and non-cases of people exposed to a traumatic event (*DSM-IV*; American Psychiatric Association [APA], 1994). Our goal in this chapter is to review the status of modifications to the definitional understanding of PTSD and to review some of the proposed changes to the diagnostic criteria to be contained in the *DSM-5*. The objective of this chapter is to contribute to continued instigation of scientific work on trauma that blends the best in behavioral science with the most contemporary models and methods of measuring and understanding the biological and physiological parameters associated with this condition (e.g., Keane, 2008).

Current Definition and Diagnostic Criteria for PTSD.

In its current conception, *DSM* defines PTSD as stemming from an event(s) in which one is exposed to serious threat of injury or death and then experiences extreme fear, helplessness, or horror. Three symptom clusters define the disorder. In addition to recurrent and intrusive recollections and dreams of the event, the re-experiencing cluster includes the experience of flashback episodes wherein an individual experiences a recurrence of at least a portion of the trauma. Hyper-arousal symptoms are characterized by an enhanced startle reaction and difficulty sleeping, concentrating, and controlling anger, as well as hyper-vigilance for danger and a sense of a foreshortened future. Extreme distress and avoidance of cues or reminders of the trauma, as well as an inability to remember aspects of the event, also can accompany this disorder. Additional avoidance symptoms include emotional numbing, described as an inability to feel any positive emotions such as love, contentment, satisfaction, or happiness.

The interpersonal, psychosocial, physical health, and societal consequences of PTSD contribute to the overall costs of developing this condition. People with PTSD are more likely to divorce, report trouble raising their children, engage in intimate partner aggression, experience depression and other psychological problems, report poorer life satisfaction and physical health problems, become involved with the legal system, earn less, and change jobs frequently (Jordan et al., 1992; Koss, Woodruff, & Koss, 1991; Kulka et al., 1990; Schnurr & Green, 2004; Walker et al., 2003). These findings suggest that PTSD constitutes a major public health challenge for this nation and the world, and they highlight the importance of redoubling national and international efforts to enhance our understanding of the biological, psychological, and social factors associated with this condition.

Among the many diagnoses in *DSM-IV*, intentionally, very few invoke etiology in their criteria. Organic mental disorders, substance use disorders, PTSD, acute stress disorder (ASD), and adjustment disorders (AD) are the primary exceptions, and in the former two instances, etiological variables are noted by exception. With regard to the latter three instances, the presumed causal relationship between the stressor and PTSD, ASD, and AD is controversial. Recent empirical work suggests that the relationship of traumatic events to the development of any of these disorders is imperfect, with relatively few people exposed ultimately developing any form of psychopathology, let alone these three conditions specifically. Thus, the predictive validity of exposure to a traumatic event to the development of PTSD, ASD, or AD is quite low. Moreover, the specificity of exposure to the development of one of these three conditions is poor. Conditions such as depression, substance abuse, phobia, generalized anxiety disorder, social anxiety disorder, and the like all commonly follow exposure to traumatic events, albeit most often secondary to the development of PTSD (Kessler et al., 2005; Miller, Resick & Keane, 2009).

Precedents Leading to the Development of Trauma Categories

The earliest cultural works of Western civilization describe the devastating personal impact of exposure to violence, war, and related trauma. The psychological consequences of these experiences are well captured in art, literature, and theatrical plays that describe the human condition through the centuries. Eloquent descriptions of trauma sequelae can be found in reference to the Civil War (e.g., Stephen Crane's description in *The Red Badge of Courage*), the presence of "irritable heart" among soldiers (DaCosta, 1871), Page's (1883) conception of railroad spine (distress following train crashes in the United Kingdom), the psychological consequences of the disastrous 1666 Great Fire of London (Daly, 1983), and even the Trojan War (e.g., the story of Ulysses in Homer's *Iliad*). Anxiety as a specific response to severe or traumatic life stress is described by Oppenheim (1889; cited by Kraepelin, 1896), who labeled this response as "traumatic neurosis," and by Kraepelin (1896), who labeled it *Schreckneurose* (i.e., "fright neurosis"). Other terms commonly used included neurocirculatory asthenia, shell shock, and nostalgia. Each of these early contributors to diagnostic nomenclature recognized something special and perhaps distinct about the psychological disorders that emerge from exposure to traumatic life events.

Despite these common observations throughout history, the scientific study of traumatic responses is a recent enterprise. After World Wars I and II, studies of psychological distress among combatants and concentration camp survivors set the stage for the recognition of the long-term negative effects of trauma exposure. Terms such as "shell shock," "combat fatigue," and "war neurosis" all seemed to capture the essence of war-related PTSD, but the psychological effects of other traumatic life stressors were not recognized in the research literature until Ann Burgess at the famed Boston City Hospital observed the impact of rape on women (Burgess & Holmstrom, 1974). Once advocates for rape survivors and Vietnam veterans teamed with scholars who had studied and treated World War II veterans and concentration camp survivors, the diagnosis of PTSD emerged in the *DSM-III*.

By the late 1970s, clinicians were employing a wide variety of posttraumatic diagnostic options in their clinical practices, although none was recognized in the *DSM-II*. The *DSM-I*, in favor until 1952, contained the ill-defined "gross stress reaction," which provided a useful, but temporary, diagnostic niche for military veterans, ex-prisoners of war, rape victims, and Nazi Holocaust survivors. In *DSM-II*, however, even this diagnostic option was eliminated, so that "situational reaction" was the only diagnosis for people who exhibited clinically significant reactions to catastrophic, life-threatening experiences. Situational reactions were noted to be temporary reactions to extreme life events, and the notion that a contemporary event in adulthood would have life-lasting impact was viewed somewhat skeptically.

The work that led to the development of PTSD in the *DSM-III* recognized that these differently labeled syndromes (e.g., "rape trauma," post-Vietnam, concentration camp syndromes, etc.) were all characterized by a very similar pattern of symptoms that became key components of the PTSD diagnostic criteria. Hence, the emphasis shifted from the specific traumatic stressor to the relatively similar pattern of stress response that could be observed among survivors of an ever expanding list of different, but conceptually similar life-threatening and stressful live events.

Given the consistent historical precedence associated with the notion of a traumatic psychological condition, it is somewhat surprising that controversy regarding its validity emerged during the 1970s and '80s (Figley, 1978; Goodwin & Guze, 1984). Although much of the initial controversy about PTSD's validity has ceased, the nature of the disorder still instigates considerable debate in the field (see Brewin, 2003; Weathers & Keane, 2007a,b). Conceptual issues still exist about the precise definition of PTSD, about which symptoms should define the disorder, how much emphasis should be placed on some of the key features of the disorder, and the proposition that PTSD is simply a social construction, not a psychiatric disorder (McNally, 2004).

Influenced by clinical experience, empirical studies, and evolving conceptual views of PTSD, various subsequent committees altered the original *DSM-III* PTSD criteria. The number of possible symptoms has increased from 12 to 17. Further, the original three symptom clusters (e.g., re-experiencing, numbing, and miscellaneous) were rearranged into re-experiencing, avoidance/numbing, and hyperarousal. Yet through all of this effort at refinement, the fundamental notion that exposure to overwhelming stress can precede the onset of clinically significant and persistent symptoms remains a central feature of this disorder. Epidemiological studies consistently demonstrate that exposure to extreme stress commonly precedes severe and persistent psychopathology (e.g., Breslau, Davis, Andreski, & Peterson, 1991; Kessler, Sonnega, Bromet, Hughes, & Nelson, 1995; Norris & Slone, 2007). Importantly, this research suggests that exposure to traumatic events in Western culture is more normative than exceptional and that the prevalence of psychological disorders that ensue is so high that it represents a major form of disability in contemporary society. The notion that traumatic events are, as stated in the *DSM-III*, "generally outside the range of usual human experience" (p. 236) was simply a gross underestimate of the magnitude of violence, loss, and tragedy in contemporary life.

Location of PTSD in the Anxiety Disorders

PTSD was included within the overarching category of the anxiety disorders when the disorder was initially incorporated in the *DSM-III*. Since the third edition, *DSM* has taken a largely descriptive, as opposed to etiological, approach to defining and classifying disorders. This was consistent with the zeitgeist, given so little was known in 1980 about the etiology of most psychiatric conditions. Although it was clear that there were probable biological diatheses and likely important environmental exposures responsible for many of the conditions, little confirmatory information existed in the late 1970s when the *DSM-III* was constructed. One notable exception to this was the inclusion of an etiological component in the PTSD diagnosis, which specified a causal relationship between trauma exposure and symptom development. Keane (2008), Keane and Miller (2009), Miller et al. (2009), and Resick and Miller, (2009) suggested that the most appropriate location for PTSD in *DSM–5* would be among a class of disorders precipitated by serious adverse life events—that is, a spectrum of traumatic stress disorders. Candidates for inclusion would include PTSD, acute stress disorder, adjustment disorder, a traumatic grief or bereavement-related diagnosis, and possibly complex PTSD. These disorders are the product of an environmental pathogen (i.e., a traumatic stressor) operating on individual diatheses that cross the spectrum of human variation in vulnerability to psychopathology. This diathesis-stress interaction can result in extensive heterogeneity in the phenotypic expression of psychopathology, pathological anxiety being just one manifestation of the process.

At the moment, it is possible and distinctly likely that this categorization of trauma-related conditions within a single overarching traumatic disorders category will appear in the coming edition of the *DSM-5*; there are both conceptual and strategic advantages to such a category. These would include the possibility of further studying how certain subtypes of psychopathology emerge when an individual is exposed to traumatic life events. It also may assist us in understanding the complex array of heterogeneity in symptomatology observed among trauma survivors. At this stage in the *DSM-5* process, it is possible that a trauma subcategory will be incorporated that is separate from the anxiety disorders category, although final decisions will not be reached until the field trials are concluded. Further research on the broad, overarching categories in the *DSM* and the conditions contained within them is clearly needed (Krueger & Markon, 2006).

The present proposal is for PTSD to be included in an overarching category of trauma and stressor related disorders. Included in this category of conditions will be acute stress disorder (for the one-month postexposure disorder), a reactive attachment disorder (for children prior to age five), disinhibited social engagement disorder (for children), and adjustment disorder (for those who are experiencing significant symptoms, but weren't exposed to a traumatic stressor—but, rather, exposed to a significant stressful life event). These collections of disorders are still anxiety and stress disorders by nature, but they are segregated from the other anxiety disorders owing to separate etiological factors and symptom-based experiences. They appear to share more in common with one another than with the other anxiety disorders, yet they retain a strong relationship to anxiety and stress-related conditions more broadly.

Current PTSD Diagnostic Criteria

Exposure to Traumatic Life Event: Criterion A

For recent editions of the *DSM*, Criterion A was divided into objective (A1) and subjective (A2) components in an effort to distinguish aspects of the trauma experience and to determine if one aspect was more influential in determining the extent to which someone develops PTSD. The A1 Criterion resembled the *DSM-III-R* Criterion A, but the number of events that were included as stressor events was expanded. Examples of these included: being diagnosed with a life-threatening illness, child sexual abuse, learning about the sudden unexpected death of a family member or close friend, and learning that one's child has a life-threatening illness. In *DSM-IV*, it was necessary that exposed individuals experience an intense emotional reaction characterized as "fear, helplessness or horror" (Criterion A2).

As we consider the *DSM-IV* Criterion A1, there are several issues that arise, including: (1) Does exposure to a potentially traumatic event cause the development of PTSD? (2) Are stressors readily divided into "traumatic" and "nontraumatic"? and (3) Should the A1 Criterion be eliminated from *DSM-5*? We'll deal with each of these issues in turn.

Does Exposure to a Stressor Cause PTSD?

DSM-III and *DSM-IV* are unclear about the etiological significance of the Criterion A event. They both suggest that traumatic exposure causes PTSD—that is, exposure leads to the symptom picture directly. In addition, they both also suggest that the traumatic event constitutes an experience that temporally precedes the expression of PTSD symptoms.

We know that people differ with regard to resilience and vulnerability so that most people exposed to traumatic events do not develop PTSD (King, Leskin, King, & Weathers, 1998). Epidemiological studies and risk-factor research have identified a number of risk and resiliency variables that differentially affect the susceptibility of individuals to develop PTSD. Resilience is typically defined as a multivariate concept that covers genetic, psychobiological, cognitive, emotional, behavioral, cultural, and social components. It is also clear that traumatic or life-threatening events differ with regard to the conditional probability that PTSD will follow exposure (Kessler, Ormel, Demler, & Stang, 2003). For example, the conditional probability that PTSD will follow rape is much higher than that for exposure to natural disasters. Individual susceptibility and the type of event to which one is exposed determine whether one develops PTSD, depression, or another disorder (or no disorder at all). This diathesis-stress perspective represents a longstanding view on the development of psychopathology broadly, and is readily applicable to the etiology of PTSD (see Keane & Barlow, 2002).

Breslau and Kessler (2001) tested the implications of a broad perspective on the exposure (A1) criterion that included events beyond the most typically considered in psychiatric epidemiological research. Among a representative sample of over 2,000 individuals, lifetime exposure to traumatic events defined by a narrow set of qualifying A1 events was compared to prevalence of exposure to a broad set of events. Narrow events were defined as seven events of "assaultive violence" (e.g., combat, rape, assault, etc.) and seven "other injury events" (e.g., serious accident, natural disaster, witnessing death/serious injury, etc.). Broad events were defined as five events from the category "learning about" traumatic events to close relatives (e.g., rape, assault, accident, etc.). Narrow set exposure was 68.1% compared to broad set exposure of 89.6% in this sample. Importantly, A1 events included within the expanded (broad) A1 criterion contributed 38% of the total PTSD cases. Other investigators found a more trivial impact of examining the broader criterion (Kilpatrick 2008).

Further, Kilpatrick disputed the notion of "bracket/criterion creep" arguments put forth by McNally (2009). He indicated that very few individuals meet PTSD criteria without prior exposure to an A1 event. Non-A1 events most likely to precede the onset of PTSD symptoms were sudden death to close relatives, serious illness, or having a child with a potentially terminal illness. Each of these events seem on the surface of matters to be serious and life threatening and that might well alter the course and trajectory of the lives of people so affected.

SHOULD THE A CRITERION BE ELIMINATED?

Some authors suggest that the total elimination of Criterion A would enhance the reliability of the disorder and mitigate some of the controversy that has followed PTSD since its inception in the *DSM*. Various groups addressed this issue in the past and rejected the elimination of Criterion A owing to concerns that "the loosening of Criterion A may lead to widespread and frivolous use of the concept" (Davidson & Foa, 1991, p. 347). Although some suggest that the full PTSD syndrome may be expressed following nontraumatic events, most of these reports have been dismissed as methodologically flawed because proper clinical interviews were not utilized and because the data merely showed an increase in PTSD symptoms, but not the full diagnosis (Brewin, Lanius, Novac, Schnyder, & Galea, 2009). Indeed, when assessed by a structured clinical interview, there are actually very few examples of individuals who do not meet the A criterion who meet full PTSD diagnostic criteria. Furthermore, it is unclear in most of these reports whether the non-A1 event actually served as a reminder or trigger for a previously experienced traumatic event and, therefore, precipitated a PTSD relapse rather than new-onset PTSD.

Arguments for eliminating the A criterion are: (1) traumatic exposure may sometimes precede onset of other diagnoses (e.g., depression, substance use disorder) rather than PTSD; (2) non-A1 events sometimes do appear to precede onset of PTSD symptoms; (3) it would bring PTSD more in line with other anxiety and affective disorders that do not require that symptom onset be preceded by a specific event; and (4) lack of utility of the A2 criterion (Bovin & Marx, 2010; Weathers & Keane, 2007b).

SPECIAL PROBLEMS WITH TRAUMATIC RESPONSES (A2)

The *DSM-IV* incorporated the need for an individual to experience an intense subjective reaction characterized as "fear, helplessness, or horror" (A2), with the intention of increasing the specificity of Criterion A. The expectation was that few people exposed to low-magnitude (i.e., nontraumatic) events would meet the A2 criterion and therefore limit eligibility for the PTSD diagnosis. Yet, this addition to the A criterion was viewed widely as experimental at the time of its inclusion.

Research suggests that the value of A2 is quite limited. Breslau and Kessler (2001) and Schnurr et al. (2000) in a representative community sample from Detroit, Michigan, and older male military veterans found little value in either sensitivity or specificity in these studies of PTSD prevalence.

Weathers and Keane (2007) summarize this literature and highlight the many reasons A2 adds to the burden of assessment while yielding little in terms of diagnostic accuracy (i.e., accurate prediction of true cases and true noncases of the disorder).

Furthermore, those whose occupation requires frequent traumatic exposure, such as military, police, and emergency medical personnel, may not experience fear, helplessness, or horror during or immediately following a trauma exposure owing to their training and their expectations. In addition, some individuals develop PTSD following mild traumatic brain injury, in which case the person may be unaware of any peritraumatic emotional response because of a loss of consciousness (Bryant, 2001). Clearly, some people can develop PTSD without meeting A2.

Most PTSD cases are evaluated months or years after a traumatic event, and since assessment of A2 requires a retrospective recall of how the person responded during or shortly after the event, many clinicians and researchers share a concern that subsequent recall of acute responses to trauma exposure is unreliable. It is the case that current-day recall is commonly influenced by present-day mood, thus introducing a form of unwanted bias into the assessment process. In conclusion, the accuracy of retrospective A2 reports obtained at varying intervals between trauma exposure and assessment raises multiple thorny assessment issues about the usefulness of A2.

Conceptually, A2's "fear, helplessness and horror" may be too narrow a definition of the traumatic response. Keane and Barlow (2002), in their heuristic model of PTSD, assert that conditioning/learning occurs when a true alarm comprising intense negative emotionality is paired with a traumatic exposure. This alarm can be stress or fear, but may also be anger, shame, guilt, humiliation, and the like. The inclusion of PTSD as an anxiety disorder in the *DSM-III* led to many presumptions about the nature and etiology of the disorder that we now realize are either too limited or even mistaken. The premise that PTSD is a consequence of fear conditioning served many important purposes in the first several decades of research on the topic. Today, fear conditioning is more widely viewed as only one aspect related to the development of PTSD; cognitive models incorporating these intense, aversive emotions are increasingly incorporated into perspectives on the etiology of PTSD (Friedman, Keane, & Resick, 2007; Shiromani, Keane, & LeDoux, 2009).

SUMMARY OF THE STATUS OF THE A CRITERION

Table 5.1 represents the criteria proposed by the *DSM-5* work group for PTSD. There are field trials that are ongoing that will test the changes that are proposed by the work group. The goal is to reduce the ambiguity in the definition of a traumatic event. Current thinking is that A2, the emotional response to exposure to a traumatic event, will be eliminated for all of the reasons elucidated above. Issues like the contribution of Criterion A to the sensitivity and specificity of PTSD are still under discussion by the work group, and it is not likely that these will be resolved by the pending field trials. What is certain at this time is that the response domain that was experimentally included in the *DSM-IV* did not function in the way that the prior group anticipated. Keane, Kaufman, and Kimble (2000) found that the diagnostic function of A2 among combat veterans seemed to be exclusively that its absence predicted the absence of PTSD. Others have replicated this finding in a variety of populations.

Criterion A1 will retain *DSM-IV* language emphasizing that qualifying events must involve direct exposure to actual or threatened death, serious injury, or a threat to the physical integrity of others. Confrontation with the news of a traumatic event that happens to others—the most controversial aspect of the *DSM-IV* PTSD criteria—is limited to learning about the traumatic exposure of a close friend or loved one or learning about aversive details of unnatural deaths, serious injury, or serious assault to others. This includes learning about the homicide of a family member, learning about the gruesome death or grotesque details of rape, genocide, or other abusive violence to others. It also applies to work-related exposure to gruesome and horrific evidence of traumatic events, as with police personnel, firefighters, graves registration workers, and emergency medical technicians. Finally, the revised A criterion excludes witnessing traumatic events through electronic media, television, video games, movies, or pictures.

The B, C, and D Criteria for PTSD

FACTOR STRUCTURE OF PTSD

The precise nature of the factor structure of PTSD has been addressed by many research teams over the past 15 years. The structure of the construct as described in the *DSM-IV* is that PTSD consists of three symptom clusters: B—re-experiencing, C—avoidance/numbing, and D—hyper-arousal. Utilizing confirmatory factor analysis strategies,

Table 5.1. Proposed diagnostic criteria for posttraumatic stress disorder for DSM-5

A. The person was exposed to one or more of the following event(s): death or threatened death, actual or threatened serious injury, or actual or threatened sexual violation, in one or more of the following ways: **

1. Experiencing the event(s) him/herself
2. Witnessing, in person, the event(s) as they occurred to others
3. Learning that the event(s) occurred to a close relative or close friend; in such cases, the actual or threatened death must have been violent or accidental
4. Experiencing repeated or extreme exposure to aversive details of the event(s) (e.g., first responders collecting body parts; police officers repeatedly exposed to details of child abuse); this does not apply to exposure through electronic media, television, movies, or pictures, unless this exposure is work related.

B. Intrusion symptoms that are associated with the traumatic event(s) (that began after the traumatic event(s)), as evidenced by 1 or more of the following:

1. Spontaneous or cued recurrent, involuntary, and intrusive distressing memories of the traumatic event(s). **Note:** In children, repetitive play may occur in which themes or aspects of the traumatic event(s) are expressed.
2. Recurrent distressing dreams in which the content and/or affect of the dream is related to the event(s). **Note:** In children, there may be frightening dreams without recognizable content. ***
3. Dissociative reactions (e.g., flashbacks) in which the individual feels or acts as if the traumatic event(s) were recurring (Such reactions may occur on a continuum, with the most extreme expression being a complete loss of awareness of present surroundings.) **Note:** In children, trauma-specific reenactment may occur in play.
4. Intense or prolonged psychological distress at exposure to internal or external cues that symbolize or resemble an aspect of the traumatic event(s)
5. Marked physiological reactions to reminders of the traumatic event(s)

C. Persistent avoidance of stimuli associated with the traumatic event(s) (that began after the traumatic event(s)), as evidenced by efforts to avoid 1 or more of the following:

1. Avoids internal reminders (thoughts, feelings, or physical sensations) that arouse recollections of the traumatic event(s)
2. Avoids external reminders (people, places, conversations, activities, objects, situations) that arouse recollections of the traumatic event(s).

D. Negative alterations in cognitions and mood that are associated with the traumatic event(s) (that began or worsened after the traumatic event(s)), as evidenced by 3 or more of the following: **Note**: In children, as evidenced by 2 or more of the following:****

1. Inability to remember an important aspect of the traumatic event(s) (typically dissociative amnesia; not due to head injury, alcohol, or drugs).
2. Persistent and exaggerated negative expectations about one's self, others, or the world (e.g., "I am bad," "no one can be trusted," "I've lost my soul forever," "my whole nervous system is permanently ruined," "the world is completely dangerous").
3. Persistent distorted blame of self or others about the cause or consequences of the traumatic event(s)
4. Pervasive negative emotional state—for example: fear, horror, anger, guilt, or shame
5. Markedly diminished interest or participation in significant activities.
6. Feeling of detachment or estrangement from others.
7. Persistent inability to experience positive emotions (e.g., unable to have loving feelings, psychic numbing)

E. Alterations in arousal and reactivity that are associated with the traumatic event(s) (that began or worsened after the traumatic event(s)), as evidenced by 3 or more of the following: **Note**: In children, as evidenced by 2 or more of the following:****

1. Irritable or aggressive behavior
2. Reckless or self-destructive behavior
3. Hypervigilance
4. Exaggerated startle response

(*continued*)

Table 5.1. **Proposed diagnostic criteria for posttraumatic stress disorder for DSM-5** (*continued*)

5. Problems with concentration
6. Sleep disturbance—for example, difficulty falling or staying asleep, or restless sleep.

F. Duration of the disturbance (symptoms in Criteria B, C, D and E) is more than one month.

G. The disturbance causes clinically significant distress or impairment in social, occupational, or other important areas of functioning.

H. The disturbance is not due to the direct physiological effects of a substance (e.g., medication or alcohol) or a general medical condition (e.g., traumatic brain injury, coma).

Specify if:
With Delayed Onset: if diagnostic threshold is not exceeded until 6 months or more after the event(s) (although onset of some symptoms may occur sooner than this).

studies tested whether the three symptom clusters of *DSM-IV* provide the best model for the latent structure of PTSD. In short, the overwhelming majority of studies support a four-factor model. A few studies have supported a two-factor solution. Of the four studies supporting a three-factor model, only one mirrors the three factors found in the *DSM-IV* PTSD diagnostic criteria (Friedman, Resick, Bryant, & Brewin, in press).

Among the four-factor models, re-experiencing, avoidance, and hyper-arousal have emerged as distinct clusters in all of these studies. There has been disagreement, however, about the fourth factor. In many studies, numbing has been identified as the fourth factor, whereas a dysphoria factor has emerged elsewhere. This general dysphoria factor is thought to reflect the common factor underlying disorders of the internalizing spectrum and may account for the high rates of comorbidity observed between PTSD and major depression, dysthymia, and general anxiety disorder (Miller et al., 2009; Slade & Watson, 2006; Watson, 2005).

Principles of diagnostic taxonomy suggest that elements of a specific class, or spectrum, should aggregate more with each other than with elements from another class. Data from hierarchical analyses suggest that PTSD does not fit particularly well into either the anxiety disorders or the mood disorders. This could mean that PTSD would better fit into a trauma disorders category; alternatively, it could mean that neither the anxiety disorders nor the mood disorders categories represents the ideal overarching conceptual model. Results of recent comorbidity studies in the area of PTSD raise questions about where PTSD should be located in future editions of *DSM*. Several factor analyses of diagnostic data from epidemiological and clinical samples (see Miller, Fogler, Wolf, Kaloupek, & Keane, 2008) suggest that PTSD covaries more strongly with disorders defined by anhedonia, worry, and rumination (i.e., the unipolar mood disorders and generalized anxiety disorder) than with ones characterized by pathological fear and avoidance (e.g., the phobias, panic/agoraphobia, and obsessive-compulsive disorder). However, classifying PTSD among these anxious-misery disorders provides a poor fit to the data because PTSD is conditional on trauma exposure and, in new-onset cases, typically develops before its comorbid conditions (Keane & Miller, 2009). For example, when PTSD and major depression co-occur following trauma exposure, PTSD usually precedes or develops concurrently with the depression (Breslau, Davis, Peterson, & Schultz, 2000). Breslau et al. (2000) also learned that new-onset major depression that develops in the wake of trauma rarely precedes or develops in the absence of PTSD. This implies a causal influence of PTSD on comorbid psychopathology and suggests a distinct phenomenology that should be reflected in its diagnostic class membership within *DSM*.

In summary, most confirmatory factor analyses support a four- rather than a three-factor model for PTSD. The majority of studies indicate that serious consideration should be given to including a separate fourth, numbing symptom cluster in *DSM-5*. Finally, there is virtually no evidence in support of *DSM-IV*'s C (avoidance/numbing) criterion, since avoidance and numbing are consistently distinct from one another in both the four- and the two-factor solutions.

Given the factor analytic findings, PTSD criteria in the *DSM-5* may well contain four components in addition to the exposure domain: re-experiencing; arousal and reactivity; negative alterations in cognitions and mood replacing the *DSM-IV* numbing cluster; and avoidance. As table 5.1 suggests, most *DSM-IV* symptoms have been retained, although some are rewritten to enhance clarity and to promote understanding. To accommodate an improved description of each of the four domains, three new symptoms have been introduced, raising the number of symptoms included in the criteria from 17 to 20.

Diagnostic Symptoms Within the Four Domains

Reliving of the Traumatic Experience: Criterion B

Traumatic nightmares (B2) and dissociative flashbacks (B3) are the cardinal symptoms of PTSD. Brewin and his colleagues (2009) argue that intrusive recollections (B1) overlaps conceptually with some forms of rumination observed in major depressive disorder while emotional and physiological arousal following exposure to traumatic reminders (B4 and B5) are too similar to symptoms found in specific and social phobia disorders. Despite these reasonable concerns, the proposed *DSM-5* criteria have retained nightmares, flashbacks, and intrusive recollections as symptom criteria for PTSD.

Physiological reactivity to cues stemming from the traumatic experience are retained in the diagnostic criteria, as it appears that elicitation of emotional and physiological reactivity to trauma-related stimuli is a key characteristic of PTSD. These symptoms were initially included in the diagnostic criteria secondary to extensive research on physiological reactivity (Blanchard, Kolb, Pallmeyer, & Gerardi, 1982; Malloy, Fairbank, & Keane, 1983; Pitman, Orr, Forgue, DeJong & Claiborne, 1987). This is consistent with major fear-conditioning models of the disorder. Most neurobiological studies of PTSD today incorporate the reactivity paradigms developed in the early 1980s and that resulted in key findings about the condition (e.g., Keane et al., 1998). It is the guiding rationale for critical laboratory paradigms in which distinctive alterations in psychological and neurobiological reactivity among PTSD participants can be reliably detected after exposure to trauma-related stimuli. Furthermore, these findings inform our most effective cognitive behavioral therapies where emotions and cognitions elicited by traumatic reminders constitute the premier form of psychological treatment (see Foa, Keane, Friedman, & Cohen, 2009).

Avoidance of the Traumatic Experience: Criterion C

In prior editions of the *DSM*, Criterion C incorporated numbing/avoidance concomitantly. Given the factor analytic data that suggests there are four components to the latent factor structure of PTSD, these two will be divided into two independent criteria. Criterion C will now consist of behavioral and cognitive avoidance strategies. Table 5.1 provides a more complete description of the proposed two items constituting avoidance.

Brewin et al. (2009) summarized data from multiple sources to suggest that these two avoidance components, consistent with the fear model of conditioning previously proposed (Keane & Barlow, 2002; Keane, Zimering, & Caddell, 1985), are the key symptoms associated with PTSD. Efforts to avoid internal reminders associated with the traumatic events (e.g., thoughts, feelings, or physical sensations) and efforts to avoid external reminders of the traumatic event (e.g., people, places, conversations, activities, objects, or situations) constitute the principal avoidance symptoms of PTSD.

Alterations in Cognitions and Mood: Criterion D

Criterion D now contains symptoms associated with catastrophic or maladaptive appraisals that are characteristic of traumatic stress responses associated with disorder or impairment (Ehlers & Clark, 2000). Erroneous cognitions about the causes or consequences of the traumatic event, which leads individuals with PTSD to blame themselves or others, are major therapeutic targets in cognitive behavioral therapy (CBT). Catastrophic thoughts are frequently found among survivors of accident survivors, childhood sexual abuse, rape/assault survivors, torture survivors, and military personnel. Although self-blame is often due to perceived personal failings, inadequacies, or weakness, other cognitive distortions may play a role in the development of PTSD or its maintenance over time. Accordingly, self-blame is now viewed as a symptom that provides incremental discriminative information for making the diagnosis of PTSD.

For many people whose life course is irretrievably altered by exposure to a traumatic event, there develops a sense of foreshortened future. Often interpreted solely as the "belief that one's life will be shorter or changed," the newest version of the *DSM* broadens this definition to more encompassing self-evaluations to include: "I am a bad person; nothing good can happen to me; I can never trust again." They do not expect to have a career, marriage, children, or a normal life span. This symptom suggests that patients with PTSD develop persistent negative expectations across the spectrum of life functions, not just a negative expectation about length of life. There is ample evidence for retaining other symptoms, currently included in the *DSM-IV* numbing cluster. These include dissociative amnesia, diminished interest in significant activities, feeling detached or estranged from others, psychic numbing, and persistent inability to experience positive affect. These are all consistently endorsed by individuals with PTSD as shown in the many confirmatory factor analysis studies reviewed previously.

To summarize, it is proposed that the *DSM-IV* avoidance/numbing cluster be divided into two separate clusters: Criterion C, persistent avoidance of stimuli associated with the trauma; and Criterion D, negative alterations in cognitions and mood associated with the trauma. The dissociative aspects of amnesia are emphasized. The expectation of a foreshortened future has been explicitly expanded to include negative expectations about one's self, others, or one's future. Other *DSM-5* symptoms that are unchanged include diminished interest in significant activities, feeling detached or estranged from others, and psychic numbing. Finally, the empirical literature indicates that two new symptoms should be added: pervasive negative emotional state (e.g., fear, horror, anger, guilt, or shame) and persistent distorted blame of self or others about the cause or consequences of the traumatic event.

Alterations in Arousal and Physiological Reactivity: Criterion E

Four of the five Criterion D symptoms are endorsed frequently by individuals with PTSD and are unchanged in the proposed *DSM-5* criteria. They are insomnia, problems in concentration, hyper-vigilence, and startle reactions. The literature suggests that this symptom cluster is broader than hyper-arousal and should also include psychological and physiological reactivity associated with the traumatic event. Accordingly, two additional symptoms are proposed to be added to this cluster: aggressive behavior and reckless behavior.

Among military veterans especially, PTSD is associated with more than an irritable mood state (cf., *DSM-IV*'s C2). PTSD appears to predict aggressive behavior and violence among military or veteran cohorts following deployment to a war zone (Brewin, Andrews, & Rose, 2000). Brewin et al. also suggest that aggressive behavior is a consequence of surviving floods among women who develop PTSD. This work was the foundation of the aggressive behavior criteria now included.

There is also growing evidence that PTSD is associated with reckless and self-destructive behavior. Reckless driving and risky sexual behavior among individuals with PTSD has been observed by several investigators, most notably by Roemer, Orsillo, Borkovec, and Litz (1998). Finally, risky sexual behavior sometimes associated with HIV risk has been reported among college women, female prisoners, and adult male survivors of childhood sexual abuse (Brief et al., 2004). Accordingly, posttraumatic reckless behavior is proposed to be included as a new symptom in the *DSM-5*.

The Duration (E) Criterion

The *DSM-5* PTSD proposal for the duration of symptoms is a one-month period of time postexposure. This is consistent with versions *III*, *III-R*, and *IV*. Similarly, the committee has proposed retention of a delayed onset type of PTSD in *DSM-5*. Although it is uncommon for people to develop PTSD months or years after the trauma, it is more common for people to develop some symptoms and then with an additional stressor begin to experience the more complete symptom picture that is related to the index traumatic experience. Bryant and Harvey (2002) reported convincing information about the concept of delayed PTSD in their reports a decade ago.

Finally, the present proposal for the *DSM-5* suggests eliminating the acute and chronic distinction for PTSD since the utility of this distinction is not apparent nor has it been empirically examined. Future studies might examine the break point that currently separates acute and chronic disorder (i.e., three months) to see if there is a difference in treatment response, recovery trajectories, or functional impairment.

Functional Impairment: Criterion F

At the present moment, the *DSM* overarching committee is considering the value of the functional impairment criterion across all of the psychiatric conditions. To some, the mere presence of these symptoms (B–E) suggests that people are both distressed and likely impaired in their daily functioning. Others feel that there are people who marshal the strength to cope successfully with their symptomatic response to trauma exposure and should not be labeled with a psychiatric condition. Both points are respectable positions and there may be considerable study of the issue of functional impairment in the near term. The study of functional outcomes associated with psychiatric disorders would present welcome new information to the comparative literature on psychiatric conditions.

Conclusions

The modifications associated with the diagnostic category of PTSD are modest in many respects. The most important change is the creation of a category of trauma and stress-related disorders that will incorporate PTSD and several related conditions for adults and children. This is a great advance and represents decades of work highlighting the importance of traumatic life events on the trajectories of individuals so exposed (cf., Friedman et al., 2007; Shiromani et al., 2009).

Other changes for each of the criteria are delineated above and represent the consensus thinking of the work group assigned the responsibility for synthesizing the literature and proposing alterations in the symptoms associated with each criterion. These individuals worked assiduously to make changes that would reflect the empirical literature, be useful for clinicians in the field, would be concise, and would be helpful. Key to the understanding of diagnosis and classification is an appreciation that diagnostic criteria should provide maximal separation of one condition in the classification scheme (i.e., psychiatric disorders) utilizing the fewest number of symptoms possible in order to accomplish the task. Although most clinicians would prefer the classification scheme to *describe* each disorder, this is an unrealistic objective. Most conditions would lead with anxiety and mood symptoms, as these are common across the preponderance of psychiatric conditions whether they are psychotic, mood, or anxiety based. Anxiety and mood are among the final common pathways for the distress experienced by people who are unable to fulfill their societal roles.

Future Directions

Although there remain many questions to be posed in the young field of psychological trauma, key classification questions include the following:

1. Is the new classification scheme of "Trauma and Stressor Related Disorders" a useful one? Will the empirical data support this category within the classification scheme as distinct and useful?
2. Will the modifications of the diagnostic criteria for PTSD be useful for clinicians? Will the changes provide a more systematic approach for examining patients with this disorder? Does the separation of avoidance and numbing symptoms render the symptoms of PTSD more internally consistent across the criteria?
3. Is the distinction between PTSD and acute stress disorder an important one? Could a preliminary diagnosis of PTSD accomplish the same thing as the inclusion of a separate diagnosis within the classification scheme?

These and other related questions will immediately begin to receive empirical attention in the scientific literature. The future of PTSD and related conditions has never been more firmly established. The remarkably strong scientific literature in this area represents some of the major accomplishments in the psychiatric field over the past 30 years, since its inclusion in the diagnostic nomenclature. The future of the field is, accordingly, a bright one.

References

American Psychiatric Association. (1994). *Diagnostic and statistical manual of mental disorders* (4th ed.). Washington, DC: Author.

Blanchard, E., Kolb, L., Pallmeyer, T., & Gerardi, R. (1982). A psychophysiological study of post traumatic stress disorder in Vietnam veterans. *Psychiatric Quarterly, 54,* 220–229.

Bovin, M. J., & Marx, B. P. (2010). The importance of the peritraumatic experience in defining traumatic stress. *Psychological Bulletin, 137,* 47–67.

Breslau, N., Davis, G., Andreski, P., & Peterson, E. (1991). Traumatic events and posttraumatic stress disorder in an urban population of young adults. *Archives of General Psychiatry, 48,* 216–222.

Breslau, N., Davis, G. C., Peterson, E. L., & Schultz, L. R. (2000). A second look at comorbidity in victims of trauma: The posttraumatic stress disorder-major depression connection. *Biological Psychiatry, 48,* 902–909.

Breslau, N., & Kessler, R. C. (2001). The stressor criterion in DSM-IV posttraumatic stress disorder: An empirical investigation. *Biological Psychiatry, 50,* 699–704.

Brewin, C. R. (2003). *Posttraumatic stress disorder: Malady or myth?* New Haven, CT: Yale University Press.

Brewin, C. R., Lanius, R. A., Novac, A., Schnyder, U., & Galea, S. (2009). Reformulating PTSD for DSM-V: Life after Criterion A. *Journal of Traumatic Stress, 22,* 366–373.

Brewin, C. R., Andrews, B., & Rose S. (2000). Fear, helplessness, and horror in posttraumatic stress disorder: Investigating DSM-IV criterion A2 in victims of violent crime. *Journal of Traumatic Stress, 12,* 499–509.

Brief, D. J., Bollinger, A. R., Vielhauer, M. J., Berger-Greenstein, J. A., Morgan, E. E., Brady, S. M., Buondonno, L. M., & Keane, T. M. (2004). Understanding the interface of HIV, trauma, posttraumatic stress disorder, and substance use and its implications for health outcomes. *AIDS Care, 16*(Suppl.1), 97–120.

Bryant, R. A. (2001) Posttraumatic stress disorder and mild brain injury: Controversies, causes, and consequences. *Journal of Clinical and Experimental Neuropsychology, 23,* 718–728.

Bryant, R.A., Harvey, A.G. (2002). Delayed-onset posttraumatic stress disorder: A prospective evaluation. *Australian and New Zealand Journal of Psychiatry, 36*, 205–209.
Burgess, A., & Holmstrom, L. (1974). Rape trauma syndrome. *The American Journal of Psychiatry, 131*, 981–986.
Crane, S. (1895). *The Red Badge of Courage.* New York: Appleton Press.
Da Costa, J. M. (1871). On irritable heart: A clinical study of a form of functional cardiac disorder and its consequences. *American Journal of the Medical Sciences*, 61, 17–52.
Daly, R. J. (1983). Samuel Pepys and posttraumatic stress disorder. British Journal of Psychiatry, 143, 64–68.
Davidson J. R., & Foa, E. B. (1991). Diagnostic issues in posttraumatic stress disorder: Considerations for the DSM-IV. *Journal of Abnormal Psychology, 100*, 346–355.
Ehlers, A., & Clark, D. (2000). A cognitive model of posttraumatic stress disorder. *Behavior Research and Therapy, 38*, 319–345.
Figley, C. (1978). *Stress disorders among Vietnam veterans: Theory, research, and treatment implications.* New York: Brunner/Mazel.
Foa, E. B., Keane, T. M., Friedman, M. J., & Cohen, J. A. (Eds.). (2009). *Effective treatments for PTSD: Practice guidelines from the International Society for Traumatic Stress Studies* (2nd ed.). New York: Guilford.
Friedman, M. J., Keane, T. M., & Resick, P. A. (Eds.). (2007). *Handbook of PTSD: Science and practice.* New York: Guilford.
Friedman, M. J., Resick, P. A., Bryant, R. A., & Brewin, C. R. (in press). Future of the PTSD diagnostic classification. *Depression and Anxiety.*
Goodwin, D. W., & Guze, S. B. (1984). *Psychiatric diagnosis.* New York: Oxford University Press.
Jordan, B., Marmar, C., Fairbank, J., Schlenger, W., Kulka, R., Hough, R., et al. (1992). Problems in families of male Vietnam veterans with posttraumatic stress disorder. *Journal of Consulting and Clinical Psychology, 60*, 916–926.
Keane, T. M. (2008, March). *Should there be a traumatic stress category in the DSM-V?* Paper presented in plenary symposium on the DSM-V at the Anxiety Disorders Association of America, Savannah, GA.
Keane, T. M., & Barlow, D. H. (2002). Posttraumatic stress disorder. In D. H. Barlow (Ed.), *Anxiety and its disorders* (2nd ed., pp. 418–453). New York: Guilford.
Keane, T. M., Kaufman, M. L., & Kimble, M. O. (2000). Peritraumatic dissociative symptoms, acute stress disorder, and posttraumatic stress disorder: Causation, correlation, or epiphenomenon? In L. Sanchez,-Planell & C. Diez-Quevedo, (Eds.), *Dissociative states* (pp. 21–43). Barcelona: Springer-Verlag Iberica.
Keane, T. M., Kolb, L. C., Kaloupek, D. G., Orr, S. P., Blanchard, E. B., Thomas, R. G., et al. (1998). Utility of psychophysiology measurement in the diagnosis of posttraumatic stress disorder: Results from a department of Veterans Affairs cooperative study. *Journal of Consulting and Clinical Psychology, 66*, 914–923.
Keane, T. M. & Miller, M. W. (2009, August). Perspectives on PTSD for the DSM-V. Paper presented at the meeting of the American Psychological Association. Boston, MA.
Keane, T., Zimering, R., & Caddell, J. (1985). A behavioral formulation of posttraumatic stress disorder in Vietnam veterans. *Behavior Therapist, 8*, 9–12.
Kessler, R., Berglund, P., Demler, O., Jin, R., Merikangas, K., & Walters, E. (2005). Lifetime prevalence and age-of-onset distributions of DSM-IV disorders in the National Comorbidity Survey Replication. *Archives of General Psychiatry, 62*, 593–602.
Kessler, R. C., Sonnega, A., Bromet, E., Hughes, M., & Nelson, C. B. (1995). Posttraumatic stress disorder in the National Comorbidity Survey. *Archives of General Psychiatry, 52*, 1048–1060.
Kessler, R. C., Ormel, H., Demler, H., & Stang, P. E. (2003). Comorbid mental disorders account for the role impairment in commonly occurring chronic physical disorders: Results from the National Comorbidity Survey. *Journal of Occupational and Environmental Medicine, 45*, 1257–1266.
Kilpatrick, D. (2008, March) *Prevalence rates of sexual assault and PTSD in a national sample of women.* Paper presented at the annual meeting of the Anxiety Disorders Association of America, Savannah, GA.
King, D., Leskin, G., King, L., & Weathers, F. (1998). Confirmatory factor analysis of the clinician-administered PTSD Scale: Evidence for the dimensionality of posttraumatic stress disorder. *Psychological Assessment, 10*, 90–96.
Koss, M., Woodruff, W., & Koss, P. (1991). Criminal victimization among primary care medical patients: Prevalence, incidence, and physician usage. *Behavioral Sciences & the Law, 9*, 85–96.
Kraepelin, E. (1896). *Psychiatrie, Vol. 5: Auflage.* Leipzig: Barth.
Krueger, R. F., & Markon, K. E. (2006). Reinterpreting comorbidity: A model-based approach to understanding and classifying psychopathology. *Annual Review of Clinical Psychology, 2*, 111–133.
Kulka, R., Schlenger, W., Fairbank, J., Hough, R., Jordan, B., Marmar, C., et al. (1990). *Trauma and the Vietnam war generation: Report of findings from the National Vietnam Veterans Readjustment Study.* Philadelphia, PA: Brunner/Mazel.
Malloy, P. F., Fairbank, J. A., & Keane, T. M. (1983). Validation of a multimethod assessment of posttraumatic stress disorders in Vietnam veterans. *Journal of Consulting and Clinical Psychology, 51*, 488–494.
McNally, R. J. (2004). Conceptual problems with the DSM-IV criteria for posttraumatic stress disorder. In G. M. Rosen (Ed.), *Posttraumatic stress disorder: Issues and controversies* (pp. 1–14). Chichester, UK: John Wiley.
McNally, R. J. (2009). Can we fix PTSD in the DSM-V? *Depression and Anxiety, 26*, 597–600.
Miller, M. W., Fogler, J., Wolf, E., Kaloupek, D., & Keane, T. (2008). The internalizing and externalizing structure of psychiatric comorbidity in combat veterans. *Journal of Traumatic Stress, 21*, 58–65.
Miller, M. W., Resick, P. A., & Keane, T. M. (2009). DSM-V: Comorbidity studies suggest that PTSD belongs in its own class of traumatic-stress disorders. *British Journal of Psychiatry, 194*, 90.
Norris, F., & Slone, L. B. (2007). The epidemiology of trauma and PTSD. In M. J. Friedman, T. M. Keane, & P. A. Resick, *Handbook of PTSD: Science and practice* (pp 78–99). New York: Guilford.
Oppenheim, B. S. (1889) *Die traumatische Neurosen.* Berlin: Hirschwald.
Page, H.W. (1883). *Injuries of the Spine and Spinal Cord.* Philadelphia: P. Blakinston & Son.
Pitman, R. K., Orr, S. P., Forgue, D. F., DeJong, P. J., & Claiborne, J. (1987) Psychophysiological assessment of posttraumatic stress disorder imagery in Vietnam combat veterans. *Archives of General Psychiatry, 44*, 970–975.

Resick, P. A., & Miller, M. W. (2009). Posttraumatic stress disorder: Anxiety or traumatic-stress disorder? *Journal of Traumatic Stress, 22*, 384–390.

Roemer, L., Orsillo, S. M., Borkovec, T. D., & Litz, B. T. (1998). Emotional response at the time of a potentially traumatizing event and PTSD symptomatology: A preliminary retrospective analysis of the DSM-IV Criterion A-2. *Journal of Behavior Therapy and Experimental Psychiatry, 29*, 123–130.

Schnurr, P. P., Ford, J. D., Friedman, M. J., Green, B., Dain, B. J., & Sengupta, A. (2000). Predictors and outcomes of PTSD in World War II veterans exposed to mustard gas. *Journal of Consulting and Clinical Psychology, 68*, 258–268.

Schnurr, P., & Green, B. (2004). Understanding relationships among trauma, post-traumatic stress disorder, and health outcomes. *Advances in Mind-Body Medicine, 20*, 18–29.

Shiromani, P. J., Keane, T. M., & LeDoux, J. E. (Eds.). (2009). *Post-traumatic stress disorder: Basic science and clinical practice.* Totowa, NJ: Humana Press.

Slade, T., & Watson, D. (2006). The structure of common DSM-IV and ICD-10 mental disorders in the Australian general population. *Psychological Medicine, 36*, 1593–1600.

Walker, E., Katon, W., Russo, J., Ciechanowski, P., Newman, E., & Wagner, A. (2003). Health care costs associated with posttraumatic stress disorder symptoms in women. *Archives of General Psychiatry, 60*, 369–374.

Watson, D. (2005). Rethinking the mood and anxiety disorders: A quantitative hierarchical model for DSM-V. *Journal of Abnormal Psychology, 114*, 522–536.

Weathers, F., & Keane, T. M. (2007a). The crucial role of criterion A: A response to Maier's commentary. *Journal of Traumatic Stress, 20*, 917–919.

Weathers, F. W., & Keane, T. M. (2007b). The Criterion A problem revisited: Controversies and challenges in defining and measuring psychological trauma. *Journal of Traumatic Stress, 20*, 107–121.

PART 3

Epidemiology and Special Populations

CHAPTER

6

The Epidemiology of Acute Stress Disorder and Other Early Responses to Trauma in Adults

Quinn M. Biggs, Jennifer M. Guimond, Carol S. Fullerton, Robert J. Ursano, *and* ASD Workgroup (Christine Gray, Matthew Goldenberg, Dori Reissman, James E. McCarroll, Patcho Santiago, Mary P. Tyler)

Abstract

Acute stress disorder (ASD) is an anxiety disorder characterized by exposure to a traumatic event followed by symptoms of re-experiencing, avoidance, hyper-arousal, peritraumatic dissociation, and impairment in functioning. ASD's time-limited duration (two days to one month) makes it distinct from but related to posttraumatic stress disorder (PTSD), which is diagnosed after one month. ASD's brief duration has contributed to a dearth of large-scale, population-based studies. Smaller studies have sought to determine rates of ASD after specific events in select populations; others have focused on ASD's role in predicting PTSD. Much can be learned from existing epidemiological studies. ASD's prevalence varies from 3% in a population of accident victims to 59% in female sexual assault victims. Female gender is a key risk factor; marital status, ethnicity, and socioeconomic status have also been associated with ASD in some studies. Comorbidities include depressive and anxiety disorders and substance use disorders.

Key Words: Epidemiology, acute stress disorder, posttraumatic stress disorder, acute stress reaction, early responses, anxiety, dissociation, public health

Introduction

"I can't recall all the details of what happened after the explosion. It was unreal; it happened so fast yet everything was in slow motion. I have images of it stuck in my head and horrible dreams about it when I try to sleep. I can still smell the burning Humvee, and I keep thinking about my buddy, Mike—he didn't make it. I really don't want to talk about it anymore," says Sergeant John Patrick to a consulting psychiatrist.

Sergeant Patrick, a 22-year-old soldier, was recently injured by an improvised explosive device (IED) blast while on patrol in Afghanistan. After the blast, he was rushed to emergency surgery in a forward operating base and then quickly evacuated to Landstuhl, Germany, where he had two more surgeries. Two days later, he was transferred to a stateside military hospital for ongoing treatment to try to save his leg. He continues to have insufficient blood perfusion and infection in his leg and remains at risk for above-the-knee amputation. Sergeant Patrick is not sleeping well and reports significant pain despite analgesic therapy.

During the consultation, Sergeant Patrick's mother, who is at his bedside, asks the psychiatrist, "Do you think he has PTSD [posttraumatic stress disorder]?" Sitting up, Sergeant Patrick angrily says to her, "No, Mom. I am not crazy. How would you feel if you got blown up a couple of days ago?"

War and disasters are common throughout the world. Understanding early responses is an important component in developing effective treatments and public health interventions. The soldier quoted above did not have PTSD; however, he did have acute stress disorder (ASD). ASD, an anxiety disorder, was first introduced in the fourth edition of the *Diagnostic and Statistical Manual of Mental Disorders* (*DSM-IV*; American Psychiatric Association [APA], 1994). ASD is a time-limited syndrome characterized by experiencing, witnessing, or being confronted with events that involve actual or threatened death or serious injury, or a threat to the integrity of self or others (Criterion A1) and a response that includes intense fear, helplessness, or horror (Criterion A2). During or after the event, the individual must experience at least three of five dissociative symptoms (Criterion B; subjective sense of numbing, detachment, or absence of emotional responsiveness; a reduction in awareness of surroundings; derealization; depersonalization; or amnesia for an important aspect of the trauma). The individual must have at least one symptom of (1) re-experiencing of the event (Criterion C), often through intrusive thoughts and/or nightmares; (2) avoidance of reminders of the event (Criterion D); and (3) hyper-arousal (Criterion E), which can include exaggerated startle response and poor sleep. Clinically significant distress or impairment in functioning also must be present (Criterion F). These symptoms must occur within a period between two days and four weeks after the traumatic event (Criterion G) and not be due to the effects of a substance or other condition (Criterion H) (APA, 1994).

The diagnostic criteria for PTSD are the same as ASD except: (1) dissociative symptoms are not required; (2) the individual must have three or more avoidance symptoms; (3) two or more hyper-arousal symptoms must be present; and (4) these symptoms must occur one month or more after the traumatic event (APA, 1994). Essentially, a diagnosis of ASD reflects a relatively early onset of significant trauma-related psychological distress symptoms including peritraumatic dissociation within an acute time frame. A diagnosis of PTSD reflects similar trauma-related distress but with a longer course and/or a later onset.

Most people who are exposed to a traumatic event never meet criteria for either ASD or PTSD (Hamaoka, Benedek, Grieger, & Ursano, 2007). However, even those without ASD or PTSD may experience transient psychological reactions that may include fear, sadness, despair, worry, loss of feeling safe, and self-doubt. In general, resilience is the expected outcome following a traumatic event, and some exposed individuals may even experience positive personal growth as a result of the adversity. For those who do develop ASD, treatment has been addressed in several guidelines (for review, see Benedek, Friedman, Zatzick, & Ursano, 2009; Ursano, Bell et al., 2007; Wynn & Benedek, 2010) and in particular the use of psychological first aid is an important part of early intervention planning (Hobfoll et al., 2007; Benedek & Fullerton, 2007).

What populations are most at risk for ASD? Do certain types of trauma seem to affect some individuals more adversely than others? What are the effects of individual factors such as gender or prior history of trauma exposure? What predicts who will bounce back quickly versus who will suffer long-term distress? In this chapter, we will examine these and other questions related to the epidemiology of ASD and other short-term sequelae of traumatic events in adults.

Traumatic Events and Psychological Responses

A traumatic event is an incident that evokes fear, helplessness or horror in the face of a threat to life or serious injury (APA, 1994). Some such events (e.g., tsunami) affect large communities en masse, while other events (e.g., house fire) befall individuals or small groups of people. Traumatic events can be accidental (e.g., motor vehicle crash) or intentional (e.g., rape), naturally occurring (e.g., earthquake) or human-made (e.g., war). Traumatic events are tragically common. The National Comorbidity Survey, a large-scale epidemiological study of psychiatric disorders in the United States, reported a lifetime history of at least one traumatic event for 61% of men and 51% of women; many people (25–50%) experienced two or more such traumas (Kessler, Sonnega, Bromet, Hughes, & Nelson, 1995). Other community-based samples have reported similar exposure rates of at least one traumatic event in 43–92% of men and 37–87% of women (Breslau, Davis, Andreski, & Peterson, 1991; Breslau et al., 1998; Norris et al., 2002; Stein, Walker, Hazen, & Forde, 1997). The most commonly reported traumas are witnessing someone being killed or injured, natural disasters, and life-threatening incidents. In 2005, over 150 million people worldwide were impacted by various disasters, including 105,000 who lost their lives (Saxena, Sharan, Garrido, & Saraceno, 2006).

Some degree of distress following a traumatic event is to be expected. Posttraumatic symptoms may manifest at different times, although symptoms most often appeared within a day (North et al., 1999; North, Smith, & Spitznagel, 1997). Empirically identified responses to traumatic events include numbing, reduced awareness of the environment, derealization, depersonalization, dissociative amnesia, intrusive thoughts, avoidance behaviors, insomnia, concentration deficits, irritability, and autonomic arousal (for review, see Bryant, 2003). An altered sense of time (e.g., feeling that time is either slowed down or sped up) is the most common peritraumatic dissociation symptom (Ursano et al., 1999).

In the aftermath of a trauma, symptoms of depression, and sleep disturbance, as well as diminished functioning in task performance, interpersonal communication, and self-regulation are common (Shalev, 2002). Posttraumatic stress may also manifest as physical symptoms, such as pain (e.g., headaches), gastrointestinal problems, or other somatic complaints (Foa, Stein, & McFarlane, 2006; North, 2007). Some individuals may exhibit increased health risk behaviors, including isolation, alcohol, tobacco, prescription medication or illicit drug use, altered driving patterns, and sleep disturbances. Others may experience irritability, anger, mistrust, or aggression toward others (Benedek, 2007; Foa et al., 2006). When a sudden or violent death occurs, the loss may pose special challenges for surviving loved ones (Fullerton, Ursano, Kao, & Bharitya, 1999; Prigerson et al., 2000; Raphael, Martinek, & Wooding, 2004; Shear, Frank, Houck, & Reynolds, 2005). Even when family members do not directly witness the death, they may develop disturbing intrusive images based on information gleaned from authorities or the media.

Conceptualization of Acute Stress Disorder

For centuries, social scientists, historians, and psychiatrists have recognized that exposure to a traumatic event can profoundly affect an individual's well-being. Over the years, military conflicts increased exposures to traumatic events and spurred formal attempts to conceptualize responses to such events. In 1952, the American Psychiatric Association produced its first version of the *Diagnostic and Statistical Manual of Mental Disorders* (*DSM*; American Psychiatric Association [APA], 1952) using a classification of posttraumatic stress developed by the Armed Forces and Veterans Administration, which assumed that traumatic responses were transient reactions to extreme stress in otherwise nonpathological individuals (Bryant & Harvey, 2000).

It was not until the last few decades, largely as a legacy of the Vietnam War, that more formal conceptualizations and rigorous scientific study of the adverse effects of trauma were undertaken (Shephard, 2001). In 1977, the International Classification of Diseases, Ninth Revision (ICD-9; World Health Organization [WHO], 1977) included diagnostic criteria for an acute stress reaction (ASR). ASR is described as transient disorder that develops, without any other apparent disorder, in response to exceptional physical or mental stress (ICD-10; World Health Organization [WHO], 2007). Symptoms are mixed and evolving with an initial state of "daze," a narrowing of attention, an inability to comprehend stimuli, and disorientation followed by agitation and over-activity. Physical symptoms of panic (tachycardia, sweating, flushing) may also be present and some individuals report partial or complete amnesia for the episode. The symptoms of ASR may appear within minutes of the stressful event and typically disappear within two to three days, although ASR is time-limited to 48 hours in duration (WHO, 2007).

In 1980, PTSD was introduced in the third revision of the *DSM* (*DSM-III*; American Psychiatric Association [APA], 1980). The PTSD diagnosis was developed, in part, as a reflection of the chronic psychological distress and disability that became apparent over time in Vietnam veterans. The *DSM-III* development committee, in an effort to avoid pathologizing individuals who experience transient reactions, defined PTSD as a condition that could be diagnosed only one month or more after a traumatic event. Subsequently, this resulted in a nosologic gap between two days (48 hours) and one month postevent in the diagnostic identification of individuals with severe traumatic reactions.

ASD was added to the *DSM-IV* diagnostic nomenclature for two primary reasons: to identify individuals with severe traumatic reactions who could benefit from early intervention, and to predict who would go on to develop PTSD (Koopman, Classen, Cardena, & Spiegel, 1995). Whether or not ASD appropriately captures the important phenomenology of short-term stress reactions has been a subject of controversy (Bryant, Creamer, O'Donnell, Silove, & McFarlane, 2008). In particular, the diagnostic requirements of fear or horror at the time of the event (A2 criterion) and dissociation (B criterion) are seen by many as problematic. Dissociative phenomena certainly occur in many persons while in the midst of a trauma. Yet reactions to trauma vary, and many do not dissociate. These nondissociating individuals are excluded from the ASD diagnosis despite clinically significant symptoms and dysfunction. Peritraumatic dissociative symptoms have been shown in some studies to predict the later development of PTSD, but are not as strongly predictive as the overall severity of PTSD-related symptoms (re-experiencing, avoidance, hyper-arousal) in the month following trauma (Bryant et al., 2008).

At present, the *DSM-5* is in development. In response to the issues with the A2 and B criteria, the *DSM-5* committee is currently considering revisions to the ASD diagnostic criteria.

Epidemiology of ASD

The epidemiology of ASD differs from PTSD and other psychiatric disorders in that there are no large population-based studies documenting incidence or lifetime prevalence. However, numerous studies have reported the point prevalence of ASD following a variety of traumatic events and in numerous populations (for review of literature on prevalence of ASD, see table 6.1).

Prevalence

As can be seen in table 6.1, rates of ASD following a traumatic exposure vary widely. Victims of violent crime seem to be most at risk for the development of ASD. Studies have found ASD rates as high as 59% in female sexual assault victims seeking service at a rape crisis center (Elklit & Christiansen, 2010) and 16–24% in physical assault victims treated at a hospital emergency department (Elklit & Brink, 2003; Harvey & Bryant, 1999a; Kleim, Ehlers, & Glucksman, 2007). In a community sample that includes victims of physical assault, sexual assault, and bag snatch, 19% met criteria for ASD (Brewin, Andrews, Rose, & Kirk, 1999).

The majority of studies that describe rates of ASD have been conducted with physically injured individuals. In a multisite study of 597 patients admitted to level 1 trauma centers, 6% met criteria for ASD at the time of assessment (Bryant et al., 2008). People

Table 6.1 Prevalence of acute stress disorder: Literature on adult populations from 1990 to 2010

Study	Sample	*N*	Prevalence	Measure	Time since event
Violent Crime					
Brewin et al., 1999	Victims of assault or bag snatch	157	19%	Modified PTSDSS	within 1 month
Classen, Koopman, Hales, & Spiegel, 1998	Employees after workplace Shooting	36	33%	SASRQ	up to 8 days
Elklit & Brink, 2003	Physical assault victims seen in emergency dept	214	24%	HTQ	1–2 weeks
Elklit & Christiansen, 2010	Sexual Assault victims seen at rape crisis center	148	59%	ASDS	up to 6 weeks
Kleim et al., 2007	Physical assault victims seen in emergency dept	222	17%	ASDS	2 weeks
Accidental injury					
Kühn et al., 2006	Trauma center patients	58	7%	SCID-IV	within 6 weeks
Wittmann et al., 2006	Trauma center patients	335	3%	CAPS-IV+PDEQ	M=5 days
Mixed trauma					
Bryant et al., 2008	Trauma center patients	597	6%	ASDI	Within 1 month
Creamer, O'Donnell, & Pattison, 2004	Trauma center patients	307	1%	CAPS-IV	M=8 days
Harvey & Bryant, 1999a	Trauma center patients				
	MVA	32	12%	ASDI	2–29 days
	Assault	25	16%		
	Burns	20	10%		
	Industrial accident	25	12%		
Mellman et al., 2001	Trauma center patients	83	16%	SCID-IV	1–35 days

(*continued*)

Table 6.1 Prevalence of acute stress disorder: Literature on adult populations from 1990 to 2010 (*continued*)

MVA					
Bryant & Harvey, 1999	Trauma center patients				
	mTBI	79	14%	ASDI	2–25 days
	Non-mTBI	92	13%		
Fuglsang et al., 2004	Emergency Dept patients	90	28%	ASDS	2–6 weeks
Hamanaka et al., 2006	Trauma center patients	100	9%	ASDI	within 1 month
Kuhn et al., 2006	Emergency Dept patients	50	10%	ASDI+ASDS	2 weeks
Burns					
Difede et al., 2002	Burn Center patients	83	19%	SASRQ	within 2 weeks
Lambert et al., 2004	Burn Center patients	98	11%	SCID-IV ASD	within 2 weeks
McKibben et al., 2008	Burn Center patients	178	24%	SASRQ	discharge from hospital
Illness					
B. Bryant et al., 2004	Parents of Injured Children	80	16%	PDS	2 weeks
Ginzburg, 2006	Myocardial Infarction patients	116	18%	SASRQ	M = 3.45 days
Kangas et al., 2007	Cancer patients	82	28%	ASDI	7–31 days
Kassam-Adams et al., 2009	Parents of Injured Children	334	12%	SASRQ	within 1 month
Roberge et al., 2008	Myocardial Infarction patients	477	4%	SCID-IV ASD	2–14 days
Shaw et al., 2006	Parents of children in NICU	40	28%	SASRQ	2–4 weeks
Disaster					
Creamer & Manning, 1998	Industrial accident victims	47	6%	SI-PTSD + addl. items	within 2 weeks
Fullerton et al., 2004	Disaster workers after airplane crash				
	exposed	207	26%	IES + additional	1 week
	not exposed	421	2%	items	(retrospective)
Grieger et al., 2000	Disaster workers after airplane crash	45	5%	SASRQ	1 week (retrospective)
Mills et al., 2007	Hurricane Katrina evacuees	132	62%	ASDI+ASDS	within 2 weeks
Staab et al., 1996	Military personnel and their families exposed to typhoons	320	7%	IES + additional items	1 week (retrospective)
Yeh et al., 2002	Military personnel after earthquake				
	Rescue workers	187	9% & 2%	Clinical	assessed twice:
	Other personnel	83	16% & 4%	Interview	within 16 days & 1 month
War/Terrorism					
Biggs et al., 2010	Disaster workers after 9/11 terrorist attacks	90	15%	IES + additional items	2–3 weeks
Blanchard et al., 2004	Undergraduate students after 9/11 terrorist attacks				
	U of Albany, NY	507	28%	ASDS	2 weeks
	Augusta State, GA	336	19%		(retrospective)
	North Dakota, ND	526	10%		

(*continued*)

Table 6.1 Prevalence of acute stress disorder: Literature on adult populations from 1990 to 2010 (*continued*)

Study	Sample	N	Prevalence	Measure	Time since event
Bleich et al., 2003	Representative sample of Israelis	512	<1%	Modified SASRQ	not stated
Cohen & Yahav, 2008	Israelis during the Second Lebanon War				
	Targeted areas	133	7%	ASDI	3 weeks (onset)
	Not Targeted	102	4%		
Grieger et al., 2003	Employees at a DC medical facility after DC Sniper Attacks	382	6%	ASDI	5–19 days after arrest
Musallam et al., 2005	Palestinian Israeli students	148	25%	SASRQ	up to 1 month

ASDI–Acute Stress Disorder Interview (Bryant, Harvey, Dang, & Sackville, 1998).
ASDS–Acute Stress Disorder Scale (Bryant, Moulds, & Guthrie, 2000).
CAPS-IV–Clinician Administered PTSD Scale, Fourth Edition (Blake et al., 1995).
HTQ–Harvard Trauma Questionnaire-Part IV (Mollica et al., 1992).
IES–Impact of Events Scale (Horowitz, Wilner, & Alvarez, 1979).
mTBI–Mild Traumatic Brain Injury.
MVA–Motor Vehicle Accident.
PDEQ–Peritraumatic Dissociative Experiences Questionnaire (Marmar et al., 1994).
PDS–Posttraumatic Stress Diagnostic Scale (Foa, Cashman, Jaycox, & Perry, 1995).
PTSDSS–Posttraumatic Stress Disorder Symptom Scale (Foa, Riggs, Dancu, & Rothbaum, 1993).
SASRQ–Stanford Acute Stress Questionnaire (Cardena, Koopman, Classen, Waelde, & Spiegel, 2000).
SCID–IV–ASD = Structured Clinical Interview for DSM-IV, ASD module (First, Spitzer, Gibbon, & Williams, 1997).

injured in motor vehicle accidents (MVA), as well as household, sports-related, industrial, and work-related accidents, have rates of ASD ranging from 3% to 12% (Harvey & Bryant, 1999a; Kühn et al., 2006; Wittmann, Moergeli, & Schnyder, 2006). Studies specific to MVA survivors have reported higher ASD rates of 9% to 28% (Bryant & Harvey, 1999; Fuglsang, Moergeli, Hepp-Beg, & Schnyder, 2002; Hamanaka et al., 2006; Holeva, Tarrier, & Wells, 2001; Kuhn, Blanchard, Fuse, Hickling, & Broderick, 2006). Patients with severe burns have ASD rates of 11–24% (Difede et al., 2002; Lambert, Difede, & Contrada, 2004; McKibben, Bresnick, Wiechman Askay, & Fauerbach, 2008).

ASD has also been observed in patients who have recently experienced various medical problems including cancer (28%; Kangas, Henry, & Bryant, 2007) and heart attack (4–16%; Ginzburg, Solomon, Dekel, & Bleich, 2006; Roberge, Dupuis, & Marchand, 2008). Parents of hospitalized children are also at risk for the development of ASD (12–28%; B. Bryant, Mayou, Wiggs, Ehlers, & Stores, 2004; Kassam-Adams, Fleisher, & Winston, 2009; Shaw et al., 2006).

In studies of the psychological effects of natural disasters, ASD rates are highly variable; 62% of Hurricane Katrina evacuees met criteria for the diagnosis (Mills, Edmondson, & Park, 2007), as did 22% of tsunami survivors (Tang, 2007), 9% of earthquake victims (Yeh, Leckman, Wan, Shiah, & Lu, 2002), and 7% of typhoon survivors (Staab, Grieger, Fullerton, & Ursano, 1996). Human-made and technological disasters also led to ASD in some exposed individuals. After an airplane crash, 26% of emergency responders (Fullerton, Ursano, & Wang, 2004) and 5% of disaster workers (Grieger et al., 2000) were found to have ASD. Following an industrial accident, 6% of industrial workers had ASD (Creamer & Manning, 1998).

Despite the importance of military populations in the conceptual development of traumatic stress disorders, there are no published studies on rates of ASD following combat exposure. However, a few studies have examined the impact of terrorism and war exposure on affected populations. A national sample of Israelis suggested a point prevalence of ASD of less than 1%, but a large majority of the study sample had not experienced significant exposure to traumatic events (Bleich, Gelkopf, & Solomon, 2003). Another study of Israelis conducted three weeks into the Second Lebanon War (Cohen & Yahav, 2008) reported higher prevalence, possibly because the study participants had more significant trauma exposure. In that study, 7% of respondents in areas targeted by missile attacks and 4% in other areas met criteria for ASD. In the few studies of ASD following the September 11, 2001 (9/11), terrorist attacks on the World Trade Center, ASD rates were 15% among disaster workers (Biggs et al., 2010) and 28% among indirectly exposed upstate New York university students (Blanchard et al., 2004).

If revisions to the ASD diagnostic criteria are implemented in *DSM-5*, future epidemiological studies will need to consider that the prevalence of ASD may change in accordance with the new criteria.

Subclinical Symptoms

In the aftermath of a traumatic event, many individuals experience significant distress and functional impairment without meeting full diagnostic criteria of ASD or PTSD (Stein et al., 1997; Zlotnick, Franklin, & Zimmerman, 2002). Among individuals seen in an emergency ward for injuries due to violence, 21% were classified as subclinical, meaning they lacked one symptom from a full diagnosis (Elklit & Brink, 2003). A similar subclinical syndrome was found among 19% of traffic accident survivors. Most of the cases that did not meet full criteria lacked the dissociation requirement (Harvey & Bryant, 1999a).

The current *DSM-IV* diagnostic system does not have a specific diagnosis with which to categorize distressing symptoms that do not meet full criteria for ASD. For a patient whose symptoms result in dysfunction or distress, but who does not meet full diagnostic criteria for ASD, nonspecific diagnoses such as adjustment disorder or anxiety disorder, not otherwise specified can be considered (APA, 1994). Some clinicians favor designating short-term subsyndromal distress with a V code (e.g., V62.2, Occupational Problem), suggesting a clinically significant problem but no psychiatric diagnosis.

Risk Factors for ASD

Risk factors associated with different traumas and different populations can be useful for identifying individuals who may be more likely to develop ASD and for targeting interventions that may reduce the risk for posttraumatic distress.

Demographics

Female gender and younger age appear to have a strong relationship with risk for ASD. Multiple studies in a variety of settings have demonstrated higher rates of ASD among women: Katrina evacuees (Mills et al., 2007), students in New York affected by the World Trade Center attacks (Blanchard et al., 2004), Israeli residents subject to missile attacks (Cohen, 2008), patients diagnosed with cancer (Kangas et al., 2007), inpatient burn victims (McKibben et al., 2008), hospital personnel following the DC sniper attacks (Grieger, Fullerton, Ursano, & Reeves, 2003), and parents of hospitalized infants (Shaw et al., 2006). Younger age has been identified as a risk factor in a few studies: missile attacks on civilians (Cohen, 2008; Cohen & Yahav, 2008), disaster workers in an airplane crash (Fullerton et al., 2004), and patients diagnosed with cancer (Kangas et al., 2007).

In some studies, marital status, ethnicity, and socioeconomic status have been linked to differential rates of ASD. Unmarried disaster workers who responded to an airplane crash were found to have higher rates of ASD than married disaster workers (Fullerton et al., 2004). Two studies found persons of non-Caucasian ethnicity to have higher rates of ASD than did Caucasians: burn victims (McKibben et al., 2008) and African-American evacuees from Hurricane Katrina (Mills et al., 2007). In addition, after a series of missile attacks, Arab Israelis had higher rates of ASD than Jewish Israelis (20% vs. 5%; Yahav & Cohen, 2007). The rate for Arab Israelis is similar to that of Palestinian Israeli students (25%) during the Palestinian uprising, Intifada Al Aqsa (Musallam, Ginzburg, Lev-Shalem, & Solomon, 2005). More studies are needed to confirm that marital status, ethnicity, and socioeconomic status are consistent risk factors across samples and to determine how these factors may interact with one another in predicting ASD.

Trauma Type, Duration, and Proximity

The risk for developing a trauma-related disorder depends on the qualities of the traumatic exposure itself. Traumatic events that are of longer duration or repeated seem to result in higher rates of posttraumatic distress. Victims of interpersonal violence such as assault or rape tend to have higher rates of distress than those of unintentional accidents, natural disasters, or medical conditions (Kessler et al., 1995; Roberge et al., 2008). For ASD specifically, it can be difficult to study differences in rates based on trauma duration because prolonged traumatic situations, such as intimate partner violence and war exposure, may continue for longer than one month.

Proximity to a traumatic event is likely to increase the potential for exposure to intense experiences and perception of risk for harm. Following the 9/11 World Trade Center attacks, undergraduates at universities in upstate New York, Georgia, and North Dakota experienced different rates of ASD inversely proportional to their distance from New York City (Blanchard et al., 2004). Similarly, another study found that each two-mile increment in distance closer to the World Trade Center site was associated with a 7% increase in anxiety-related diagnoses in Medicaid recipients (DiMaggio, Galea, & Emch, 2010). Anxiety disorders considered in the study included PTSD, adjustment reaction-anxious mood, generalized anxiety disorder, anxiety state, and others. Although ASD was not included, it seems probable that proximity would similarly increase risk for ASD.

Disaster workers are in a unique position to experience high-intensity exposures by the nature of their work. They may or may not be witness to the initial traumatic event, they face danger in rescue efforts, witness severe injuries, and may work with remains of the dead. When disaster workers who responded to an airplane crash were compared to disaster workers from other airports who had not recently been exposed to a crash, the exposed workers had significantly higher rates of ASD (26%) compared to the nonexposed workers (2%; Fullerton et al., 2004). Among disaster workers who responded in the weeks following the 9/11 World Trade Center attacks, "high impact" exposures such as knowing someone who was killed or seriously injured, witnessing someone being killed or seriously injured, and working with the bodies of the dead were associated with the development of ASD (Biggs et al., 2010).

Physical Injury

After a traumatic event, the presence of medical or surgical injuries increases the likelihood that a psychiatric condition will also be present (Rundell, 2007). In current postdisaster algorithms, triage primarily involves detection of medical and not psychiatric conditions. This is unfortunate since there is evidence that early detection of psychiatric casualties through neuropsychiatric triage can decrease medical-surgical treatment burden, decrease inappropriate treatment of patients, and may decrease long-term psychological sequelae (Rundell, 2000).

Although sustaining an injury during a trauma is associated with an ASD diagnosis (Mills et al., 2007), no consistent association has been found between injury severity and an ASD diagnosis (Bryant, Harvey, Guthrie, & Moulds, 2000; Hamanaka et al., 2006; Jones, Harvey, & Brewin, 2005). For example, despite relatively low injury severity, an ASD rate as high as 28% was found in traffic accident survivors (Fuglsang, Moergeli, & Schnyder, 2004). Similarly, source of injury does not appear to make a difference. One study that compared injuries due to MVA (13%), assault (16%), burns (10%), and industrial accidents (12%) found no significant difference in ASD rate (Harvey & Bryant, 1999a). However, another study suggests that injury location may be a factor. Specifically, burns to the hands or head/neck were more likely to be associated with ASD as compared to burns elsewhere on the body (McKibben et al., 2008). Pain has also been identified as a risk factor for ASD and can be a powerful trigger of re-experiencing, thus repeatedly reminding the injured individual of the trauma they have endured (Fuglsang et al., 2002).

Physical injury can complicate the diagnosis of ASD and therefore impact reported rates of ASD (O'Donnell, Creamer, Bryant, Schnyder, & Shalev, 2003). Hyper-arousal symptoms such as sleep disturbance, poor concentration, and irritability may be related to pain, noise in a hospital environment, or the injury itself, rather than traumatic stress. In addition, narcotic pain-control medication may confound accurate recognition of symptoms.

Traumatic brain injury (TBI) can alter the presentation of ASD and make diagnosis more complex (Bryant & Harvey, 1998). Trauma symptoms may resemble those of TBI (e.g., poor concentration, agitation, irritability), and postconcussive symptoms may resemble those of dissociation (e.g., depersonalization, derealization, and dissociative amnesia). In a study of 597 hospitalized traumatic injury patients with and without mild TBI (mTBI), more patients with mTBI (9%) met criteria for ASD that did those without TBI (5%). The authors attributed the difference to a greater number of mTBI patients satisfying the dissociative criterion (28% vs. 12%; Bryant et al., 2008). However, not all studies have found an association between mTBI and ASD (Jones et al., 2005). In theory, insults that cause mTBI may impair consciousness resulting in altered encoding of the trauma memory, which could affect the pattern of intrusive symptoms. Indeed, MVA victims with mTBI were less likely to report fear or helplessness in response to the collision or intrusive memories as compared to those without mTBI (Bryant & Harvey, 1998; Jones et al., 2005).

Prior Trauma, Psychiatric History, and History of Abuse

Several studies have found that a history of previous trauma (e.g., Biggs et al., 2010; Sattler et al., 2006) or a pre-existing mental health problem (e.g., Mills et al., 2007) increases the risk for subsequent ASD. Following the World Trade Center attacks, rates of ASD were higher among students with a history of childhood physical or sexual abuse than among their non-abused peers (Blanchard et al., 2004). A similar study reported that victims of assault who had a history of childhood physical or sexual abuse were at higher risk for ASD than their counterparts not reporting abuse (Elklit & Brink, 2003). MVA survivors were more likely to have ASD if they had a history of prior MVA (Harvey & Bryant, 1999b). History of prior psychiatric treatment was associated with ASD in MVA survivors (Harvey & Bryant, 1999b) and burns victims (McKibben et al., 2008).

The acute trauma phase is more likely to be dominated by preexisting vulnerability factors such as history of previous trauma or psychiatric problems whereas the long-term or chronic posttraumatic phase may be moderated by ongoing posttraumatic problems including adjustment issues, legal, and vocational concerns (Bryant & Harvey, 2000). Prospective epidemiological studies that report ASD prevalence rates for samples with and without prior trauma history or psychiatric history are needed to understand better their impact.

Peritraumatic Factors

The study of peritraumatic factors as predictors of ASD is complicated by the overlap with diagnostic criteria. For example, fear and perception of threat to life has been reported as greater in people with ASD (Fuglsang et al., 2004; Mills et al., 2007). Similarly, it has been suggested that individuals who develop ASD may have a preexisting tendency to dissociate (Bryant & Harvey, 2000). However, these factors are also elements of ASD diagnostic criteria, so such findings may be redundant. Elevated heart rate has been associated with increased ASD symptom severity (Kuhn et al., 2006), although MVA victims with subclinical ASD actually had higher heart rates than those with full ASD or no ASD (Bryant et al., 2000) and one study found no differences at all (Hamanaka et al., 2006). Full ASD, subclinical ASD, and no ASD groups have also been compared on blood pressure, and no differences have been found (Bryant et al., 2000; Hamanaka et al., 2006).

Social Support

The role of social support following trauma has been explored in several studies. Low satisfaction with social support contributed significantly to the prediction of ASD in a study of traffic accident victims (Fuglsang et al., 2004). Similarly, a low score on the Multi-dimensional Scale of Perceived Social Support (MSPSS) predicted ASD in a separate study of MVA victims (Yasan, Guzel, Tamam, & Ozkan, 2009). Future studies might further explore the role of social support as a protective factor against the onset of ASD.

Comorbidity

ASD has been found to be comorbid with depressive and anxiety disorders, general psychological distress, and increased substance use (Grieger et al., 2003; Harvey & Bryant, 1998; Kangas et al., 2007; McKibben et al., 2008; Roberge et al., 2008). These disorders may reflect a reaction to injuries or feelings stimulated by the traumatic event. After a disaster, psychiatric disorders may also be mediated by secondary stressors such as negotiations with insurance companies or unemployment (Epstein, Fullerton, & Ursano, 1998; Vlahov et al., 2002).

Studies of individuals with ASD have found it common to observe depressive disorders at later evaluations. Kühn et al. (2006) assessed comorbidity in a sample of injury survivors with ASD and reported that at six months 25% met full criteria for major depression. Similarly, Staab et al. (1996) reported that eight months after a series of typhoons, 26% of participants with probable ASD met diagnostic criteria for depression.

A few small studies in specific populations have also shown a complex relationship between ASD and substance use. In a study of hospital staff following the Washington, D.C., sniper attacks, respondents with ASD were 5.1 times more likely to endorse increased alcohol use following the attacks (Grieger et al., 2003). Further, for World Trade Center disaster workers, ASD was associated with early (2–3 weeks post 9/11) increased tobacco use (Biggs et al., 2010). Increased substance use (without abuse) can affect morbidity and mortality through such risk behaviors as MVAs, risky sexual behaviors, and family violence (Fullerton et al., 2004; Galea et al., 2002). This comorbid relationship is complicated by the fact that substance intoxication may precipitate an initial traumatic experience or precede further traumatization (McFarlane, 1998).

Limitations of Epidemiological Research

There are several limitations to current epidemiological research on ASD, primarily stemming from its relatively new inclusion in the *DSM* and from the fact that it is typically studied as a precursor to PTSD rather than as a unique disorder in and of itself. Unlike PTSD and other diagnoses, no community-based epidemiological studies using random sampling techniques have been conducted on ASD. Available studies use convenience samples of recently traumatized individuals. Thus, there are no population-based estimates of incidence or lifetime prevalence. The limited duration of ASD makes it difficult to gather such information. In addition to the recall bias inherent in any retrospective study, accurately recalling ASD symptoms is further complicated by the emergence or continuation of any subsequent PTSD symptoms. A cross-sectional study of point prevalence would likely be limited by the willingness and availability of participants who have experienced a trauma during the prior 30 days.

Several factors present challenges to the generalizability of results from studies of ASD. Study outcomes are partially dependent on the studies' inclusion criteria. Studies may include or exclude individuals based on having sustained a mild traumatic brain injury (mTBI), the concurrent use of certain medications (i.e., pain medications), injury severity (emergency room visit versus long-term hospitalization), proficiency with language (written, spoken, or native), and age. Variations such as these may account for the discrepant findings between studies. Existing studies also target individuals who have experienced a specific traumatic event. Sample sizes are often small and depend upon the number of individuals exposed to the event, as well as those willing and available to participate. Circumstances of the traumatic event may make it difficult to contact a significant proportion of those affected. Age may influence participation as, on average, younger individuals tend to decline participation or drop out before completion of the study (Bryant et al., 2008; Kuhn et al., 2006). Finally, most studies are conducted at a single site (e.g., a single hospital or evacuation site). Multisite studies reduce the chance that site-related factors will affect the results.

Several assessment factors affect rates of ASD. Acute stress disorder has been assessed with a variety of measures, some designed specifically for ASD, others for assessing PTSD or other constructs (e.g., PTSD scale with dissociation questions added). The use of unproven measures was a particular problem in the 1990s when the ASD diagnosis was first introduced. Some studies failed to assess ASD Criterion A2 (response of horror, fear, or helplessness). It is unclear whether some individuals meet the B–D criteria without the A2, but it could certainly affect prevalence rates. The timing of assessment is also an important variable. Hospitalized patients are sometimes assessed in a relatively short time after the traumatic event and may not have had time to experience ASD symptoms fully. During their hospitalization, they may be preoccupied with medical procedures, treatments (i.e., surgeries, medications), and other health concerns and perceive the hospitalization as part of the ongoing traumatic event (Roberge et al., 2008). Other studies evaluate individuals months or years after an event. This leads to errors and biases in recall that make it difficult to assess accurately symptoms and trajectory of illness. For all these reasons, caution must be used when comparing results between studies.

The Trajectory of Acute Stress Disorder

ASD and its component symptoms have often been studied as a risk factor for PTSD. One of the controversies of ASD is that those who develop ASD are at greater risk for PTSD, but not all those with ASD go on to develop PTSD. In addition, of those who develop PTSD, not all will have had ASD. Therefore, understanding the trajectory of ASD is important.

Few studies have examined the trajectory of ASD itself. One study that assessed ASD rates at two time points found that of the 31 participants with ASD at 9 to 16 days after an earthquake, 23% continued to meet criteria for ASD at one month (Yeh et al., 2002). Thus, ASD symptoms subsided in the majority of cases. Unfortunately, participants who did not meet ASD criteria during the initial assessment were not reassessed, so it is unknown whether any new cases developed in the interim.

Studies with long-term follow-up have assessed for PTSD in participants with ASD and found variable rates. In injury survivors who had ASD, rates of PTSD were 40% at a six-week follow-up (Mellman, David, Bustamante, Fins, & Esposito, 2001) and 45% at a three-month follow-up (Bryant et al., 2008). Among injured MVA survivors with ASD, rates of PTSD were 78% at six months and 63% at two years (Harvey & Bryant, 1999c). Similarly, 68% of injured assault victims with ASD had PTSD at six months (Kleim et al., 2007), and a reassessment of university students with ASD following the 9/11 World Trade Center terrorist attacks found that 34% met criteria for PTSD 6 to 10 weeks later (Blanchard et al., 2004). These studies suggest that a significant portion of traumatized individuals with ASD meet criteria for PTSD at later assessment. The current literature does not indicate whether symptoms remain continuously elevated or if they wax and wane. Further prospective longitudinal studies are needed to understand better the trajectory of ASD.

Conclusion

Social scientists, historians, and psychiatrists considered the consequences of traumatic experiences on individuals and populations for centuries before the development of the ASD and PTSD diagnoses. Descriptive literature, clinical experience, and case study guided the characterization and treatment of persons suffering from the aftermath of trauma before epidemiologic studies and randomized controlled trials became the standards for disease classification and treatment evaluation. History and scientific investigation have refined our understanding of the mechanisms underlying the range of human response to traumatic events. Such study has led to the characterization and refinement of the diagnosis of ASD and PTSD as distinct but related entities along the continuum of response to traumatic events. Future research should help to identify high-risk individual and group-specific factors or vulnerabilities. Identification of at-risk groups, as well as factors affecting treatment response or adherence, will advance the application of population-based approaches to the recognition and management of ASD and PTSD during and after future traumatic events.

Future Directions

1. ASD and the DSM-5

Though not yet finalized, the *DSM-5* will likely include revisions to the diagnostic criteria for ASD. The current proposal includes the elimination of the A2 criterion of "intense fear, helplessness, or horror" during the traumatic event (APA, 2010). The A2 criterion has generated significant controversy as not all trauma-exposed individuals experience such a response. In a sample of physical assault victims seen in an emergency department, just over half met the A2 criterion (Elklit & Brink, 2003). Rates of the A2 criterion also vary depending upon the type of stressor and the individual's gender (e.g., up to 80% for male sexual assault victims; Weathers & Keane, 2007). In fact, it is not clear that emotional reaction during the event has clinical utility. For example, a soldier may be trained to be "calm and cool under fire," and therefore does not experience intense fear or horror during a firefight. Afterwards, however, he may begin to have clinically significant intrusive thoughts and avoidance symptoms. Perhaps, even those who do not experience an initial emotional response may develop PTSD or suffer significant distress.

Another proposed change is the elimination of the B criterion of dissociation. Like the A2 criterion, many people develop PTSD in the absence of dissociative symptoms during or after the traumatic event (Bryant et al., 2008). In addition, it is proposed that a diagnosis of ASD will require at least eight symptoms in four domains (intrusion, dissociative, avoidance, and arousal). The proposed changes are likely to alter the number of trauma-exposed individuals who meet diagnostic criteria for ASD. Ideally, these changes would result in more readily identifying individuals in posttraumatic distress who may benefit from early intervention.

2. Methodological Issues in the Epidemiology of ASD

ASD has not received much coordinated, large-scale research attention for several reasons; it is a new diagnostic category and much emphasis has been put on its value as a predictor of PTSD rather than its own characteristics. Thus, there is a need for methodological research to help move beyond ad hoc measures and samples of convenience. Future research should consider the following:

- Studies of the validity and reliability of assessment measures
- Comparisons of populations and incident types using established measures
- Community-based random samples to determine base rates of ASD

3. Early Symptoms of Avoidance, Numbing, and Dissociation as Predictors of PTSD

Avoidance and numbing are suspected to be early markers for PTSD (McMillen, North, & Smith, 2000; North et al., 1999). It is not clear whether these symptoms are part of the early response or whether they appear later. Prospective study of the timing of onset of specific symptoms is needed to determine when avoidance and numbing symptoms begin. If they are part of an early symptom response, then they may be useful in early identification of people at high risk for PTSD. Do the dissociative symptoms of ASD predict the avoidance and numbing symptoms of PTSD? If yes, and given the particularly troublesome effects of the avoidance and numbing symptoms, it would strengthen the argument for retaining dissociation in the ASD diagnosis.

4. The Effects of an ASD Diagnosis

The originators of the PTSD diagnosis required that a month elapse before a diagnosis should be made in order to avoid unnecessarily pathologizing normal reactions to severe stress, reducing the resilience of the trauma victim, and preventing unnecessary stigma associated with psychiatric diagnoses. Can reaction to an ASD diagnosis be studied to determine whether an early diagnosis actually has negative or positive effects? Would such a study involve disaster victims or use social psychological methods such as vignettes?

5. New Technological Developments to Better Understand Trauma Symptoms

An altered sense of time, a frequently experienced dissociative symptom, is associated with reductions in cerebellar blood flow (Mathew, Wilson, Turkington, & Coleman, 1998; Ursano, Fullerton, & Benedek, 2007). Recent advances in neuroimaging were critical in identifying the neural link between the cerebellum and basal ganglia involved in the brain timing system (Harrington, Haaland, & Hermanowicz, 1998; Jueptner, Flerich, Weiller, Mueller, & Diener, 1996). Advanced neuroimaging techniques may help us better understand other dissociative symptoms involved in responses to traumatic events. Understanding the neurobiology of early trauma responses and the relationship of events, brain changes and psychology will inform our directions of care (Ursano et al., 2008).

6. Spatial Modeling Analyses

New disease-mapping techniques such as the Bayesian hierarchical spatial model (Richardson, Abellan, & Best, 2006) hold promise for characterization of disease risk where spatial patterning of ecological-level exposures and outcomes may be associated. Analysis of proximity to traumatic events has implications for delivery of interventions to individuals most at risk.

References

American Psychiatric Association. (1952). *Diagnostic and statistical manual: Mental disorders*. Washington, DC: Author.

American Psychiatric Association. (1980). *Diagnostic and statistical manual of mental disorders* (3rd ed.). Washington, DC: Author.

American Psychiatric Association. (1994). *Diagnostic and statistical manual of mental disorders* (4th ed.). Washington, DC: Author.

American Psychiatric Association. (2010). *DSM-5 Development: 308.3 Acute Stress Disorder.* Retrieved May 28, 2010, from http://www.dsm5.org/ProposedRevisions/Pages/proposedrevision.aspx?rid=166#.

Benedek, D. M. (2007). Acute stress disorder and post-traumatic stress disorder in the disaster environment. In R. J. Ursano, C. S. Fullerton, L. Weisaeth, & B. Raphael (Eds.), *Textbook of disaster psychiatry* (pp. 140–163). New York: Cambridge University Press.

Benedek, D. M., Friedman, M. J., Zatzick, D. F., & Ursano, R. J. (2009). Guideline watch: Practice guideline for the treatment of patients with acute stress disorder and posttraumatic stress disorder. *American Psychiatric Association and FOCUS, 7*, 1–9.

Benedek, D. M., & Fullerton, C. S. (2007). Translating five essential elements into programs and practice. *Psychiatry, 70*(4), 345–349.

Biggs, Q. M., Fullerton, C., Reeves, J. J., Grieger, T. A., Reissman, D., & Ursano, R. J. (2010). Acute stress disorder, depression, and tobacco use in disaster workers following 9/11. *American Journal of Orthopsychiatry, 80*(4), 586–592.

Blake, D. D., Weathers, F. W., Nagy, L. M., Kaloupek, D. G., Gusman, F. D., Charney, D. S., et al. (1995). The development of a clinician-administered PTSD scale. *Journal of Traumatic Stress, 8*(1), 75–90.

Blanchard, E. B., Kuhn, E., Rowell, D. L., Hickling, E. J., Wittrock, D., Rogers, R. L., et al. (2004). Studies of the vicarious traumatization of college students by the September 11th attacks: Effects of proximity, exposure and connectedness. *Behaviour Research and Therapy, 42*(2), 191–205.

Bleich, A., Gelkopf, M., & Solomon, Z. (2003). Exposure to terrorism, stress-related mental health symptoms, and coping behaviors among a nationally representative sample in Israel. *Journal of the American Medical Association, 290*(5), 612–620.

Breslau, N., Davis, G. C., Andreski, P., & Peterson, E. (1991). Traumatic events and posttraumatic stress disorder in an urban population of young adults. *Archives of General Psychiatry, 48*(3), 216–222.

Breslau, N., Kessler, R. C., Chilcoat, H. D., Schultz, L. R., Davis, G. C., & Andreski, P. (1998). Trauma and posttraumatic stress disorder in the community: The 1996 Detroit Area Survey of Trauma. *Archives of General Psychiatry, 55*(7), 626–632.

Brewin, C. R., Andrews, B., Rose, S., & Kirk, M. (1999). Acute stress disorder and posttraumatic stress disorder in victims of violent crime. *American Journal of Psychiatry, 156*(3), 360–366.

Bryant, B., Mayou, R., Wiggs, L., Ehlers, A., & Stores, G. (2004). Psychological consequences of road traffic accidents for children and their mothers. *Psychological Medicine, 34*(2), 335–346.

Bryant, R. A. (2003). Early predictors of posttraumatic stress disorder. *Biological Psychiatry, 53*(9), 789–795.

Bryant, R. A., Creamer, M., O'Donnell, M. L., Silove, D., & McFarlane, A. C. (2008). A multisite study of the capacity of acute stress disorder diagnosis to predict posttraumatic stress disorder. *Journal of Clinical Psychiatry, 69*(6), 923–929.

Bryant, R. A., & Harvey, A. G. (1998). Relationship between acute stress disorder and posttraumatic stress disorder following mild traumatic brain injury. *American Journal of Psychiatry, 155*(5), 625–629.

Bryant, R. A., & Harvey, A. G. (1999). The influence of traumatic brain injury on acute stress disorder and posttraumatic stress disorder following motor vehicle accidents. *Brain Injury, 13*(1), 15–22.

Bryant, R. A., & Harvey, A. G. (2000). *Acute stress disorder: A handbook of theory, assessment, and treatment.* Washington, DC: American Psychological Association.

Bryant, R. A., Harvey, A. G., Dang, S. T., & Sackville, T. (1998). Assessing acute stress disorder: Psychometric properties of a structured clinical interview. *Psychological Assessment, 10*(3), 215–220.

Bryant, R. A., Harvey, A. G., Guthrie, R. M., & Moulds, M. L. (2000). A prospective study of psychophysiological arousal, acute stress disorder, and posttraumatic stress disorder. *Journal of Abnormal Psychology, 109*(2), 341–344.

Bryant, R. A., Moulds, M. L., & Guthrie, R. M. (2000). Acute Stress Disorder Scale: A self-report measure of acute stress disorder. *Psychological Assessment, 12*(1), 61–68.

Cardena, E., Koopman, C., Classen, C., Waelde, L. C., & Spiegel, D. (2000). Psychometric properties of the Stanford Acute Stress Reaction Questionnaire (SASRQ): A valid and reliable measure of acute stress. *Journal of Traumatic Stress, 13*(4), 719–734.

Classen, C., Koopman, C., Hales, R., & Spiegel, D. (1998). Acute stress disorder as a predictor of posttraumatic stress symptoms. *American Journal of Psychiatry, 155*(5), 620–624.

Cohen, M. (2008). Acute stress disorder in older, middle-aged and younger adults in reaction to the second Lebanon war. *International Journal of Geriatric Psychiatry, 23*(1), 34–40.

Cohen, M., & Yahav, R. (2008). Acute stress symptoms during the second Lebanon war in a random sample of Israeli citizens. *Journal of Traumatic Stress, 21*(1), 118–121.

Creamer, M., & Manning, C. (1998). Acute stress disorder following an industrial accident. *Australian Psychologist, 33*, 125–129.

Creamer, M., O'Donnell, M. L., & Pattison, P. (2004). The relationship between acute stress disorder and posttraumatic stress disorder in severely injured trauma survivors. *Behaviour Research and Therapy, 42*(3), 315–328.

Difede, J., Ptacek, J. T., Roberts, J., Barocas, D., Rives, W., Apfeldorf, W., et al. (2002). Acute stress disorder after burn injury: A predictor of posttraumatic stress disorder? *Psychosomatic Medicine, 64*(5), 826–834.

DiMaggio, C., Galea, S., & Emch, M. (2010). Spatial proximity and the risk of psychopathology after a terrorist attack. *Psychiatry Research, 176*(1), 55–61.

Elklit, A., & Brink, O. (2003). Acute stress disorder in physical assault victims visiting a Danish emergency ward. *Violence and Victims, 18*(4), 461–472.

Elklit, A., & Christiansen, D. M. (2010). ASD and PTSD in rape victims. *Journal of Interpersonal Violence, 25*(8), 1470–1488.

Epstein, R. S., Fullerton, C. S., & Ursano, R. J. (1998). Posttraumatic stress disorder following an air disaster: A prospective study. *American Journal of Psychiatry, 155*(7), 934–938.

First, M. B., Spitzer, R. L., Gibbon, M., & Williams, J. B. (1997). *Structured Clinical Interview for DSM-IV Axis I Disorders–Patient Edition (SCID-I/P, version 2.0, 4/97 revision).* New York: Biometrics Research Department, New York State Psychiatric Institute.

Foa, E. B., Cashman, L., Jaycox, L., & Perry, K. (1995). The validation of self-report measure of posttraumatic stress disorder: The Posttraumatic Diagnostic Scale. *Psychological Assessment, 9*, 445–451.

Foa, E. B., Riggs, D. S., Dancu, C. V., & Rothbaum, B. O. (1993). Reliability and validity of a brief instrument for assessing post-traumatic stress disorder. *Journal of Traumatic Stress, 6*, 459–473.

Foa, E. B., Stein, D. J., & McFarlane, A. C. (2006). Symptomatology and psychopathology of mental health problems after disaster. *Journal of Clinical Psychiatry, 67*(Suppl. 2), 15–25.

Fuglsang, A. K., Moergeli, H., Hepp-Beg, S., & Schnyder, U. (2002). Who develops acute stress disorder after accidental injuries? *Psychotherapy and Psychosomatics, 71*(4), 214–222.

Fuglsang, A. K., Moergeli, H., & Schnyder, U. (2004). Does acute stress disorder predict post-traumatic stress disorder in traffic accident victims? Analysis of a self-report inventory. *Nordic Journal of Psychiatry, 58*(3), 223–229.

Fullerton, C. S., Ursano, R. J., Kao, T. C., & Bharitya, V. R. (1999). Disaster-related bereavement: Acute symptoms and subsequent depression. *Aviation, Space, and Environmental Medicine, 70*(9), 902–909.

Fullerton, C. S., Ursano, R. J., & Wang, L. (2004). Acute stress disorder, posttraumatic stress disorder, and depression in disaster or rescue workers. *American Journal of Psychiatry, 161*(8), 1370–1376.

Galea, S., Ahern, J., Resnick, H., Kilpatrick, D., Bucuvalas, M., Gold, J., et al. (2002). Psychological sequelae of the September 11 terrorist attacks in New York City. *New England Journal of Medicine, 346*(13), 982–987.

Ginzburg, K. (2006). Life events and adjustment following myocardial infarction: A longitudinal study. *Social Psychiatry and Psychiatric Epidemiology, 41*(10), 825–831.

Ginzburg, K., Solomon, Z., Dekel, R., & Bleich, A. (2006). Longitudinal study of acute stress disorder, posttraumatic stress disorder and dissociation following myocardial infarction. *Journal of Nervous and Mental Disease, 194*(12), 945–950.

Grieger, T. A., Fullerton, C. S., Ursano, R. J., & Reeves, J. J. (2003). Acute stress disorder, alcohol use, and perception of safety among hospital staff after the sniper attacks. *Psychiatric Services, 54*(10), 1383–1387.

Grieger, T. A., Staab, J. P., Cardena, E., McCarroll, J. E., Brandt, G. T., Fullerton, C. S., et al. (2000). Acute stress disorder and subsequent post-traumatic stress disorder in a group of exposed disaster workers. *Depression and Anxiety, 11*(4), 183–184.

Hamanaka, S., Asukai, N., Kamijo, Y., Hatta, K., Kishimoto, J., & Miyaoka, H. (2006). Acute stress disorder and posttraumatic stress disorder symptoms among patients severely injured in motor vehicle accidents in Japan. *General Hospital Psychiatry, 28*(3), 234–241.

Hamaoka, D., Benedek, D., Grieger, T., & Ursano, R. J. (2007). Crisis intervention. In G. Fink (Ed.), *Encyclopedia of stress* (2nd ed., pp. 662–667). London: Elsevier/Academic Press.

Harrington, D. L., Haaland, K. Y., & Hermanowicz, N. (1998). Temporal processing in the basal ganglia. *Neuropsychology, 12*(1), 3–12.

Harvey, A. G., & Bryant, R. A. (1998). Predictors of acute stress following mild traumatic brain injury. *Brain Injury, 12*(2), 147–154.

Harvey, A. G., & Bryant, R. A. (1999a). Acute stress disorder across trauma populations. *Journal of Nervous and Mental Disease, 187*(7), 443–446.

Harvey, A. G., & Bryant, R. A. (1999b). Predictors of acute stress following motor vehicle accidents. *Journal of Traumatic Stress, 12*(3), 519–525.

Harvey, A. G., & Bryant, R. A. (1999c). The relationship between acute stress disorder and posttraumatic stress disorder: A 2-year prospective evaluation. *Journal of Consulting and Clinical Psychology, 67*(6), 985–988.

Hobfoll, S. E., Watson, P., Bell, C. C., Bryant, R. A., Brymer, M. J., Friedman, M. J., et al. (2007). Five essential elements of immediate and mid-term mass trauma intervention: Empirical evidence. *Psychiatry, 70*(4), 283–315.

Holeva, V., Tarrier, N., & Wells, A. (2001). Prevalence and predictors of acute stress disorder and PTSD following road traffic accidents: Thought control strategies and social support. *Behavior Therapy, 32*, 65–83.

Horowitz, M., Wilner, N., & Alvarez, W. (1979). Impact of Event Scale: A measure of subjective stress. *Psychosomatic Medicine, 41*(3), 209–218.

Jones, C., Harvey, A. G., & Brewin, C. R. (2005). Traumatic brain injury, dissociation, and posttraumatic stress disorder in road traffic accident survivors. *Journal of Traumatic Stress, 18*(3), 181–191.

Jueptner, M., Flerich, L., Weiller, C., Mueller, S. P., & Diener, H. C. (1996). The human cerebellum and temporal information processing—results from a PET experiment. *Neuroreport, 7*(15–17), 2761–2765.

Kangas, M., Henry, J. L., & Bryant, R. A. (2007). Correlates of acute stress disorder in cancer patients. *Journal of Traumatic Stress, 20*(3), 325–334.

Kassam-Adams, N., Fleisher, C. L., & Winston, F. K. (2009). Acute stress disorder and posttraumatic stress disorder in parents of injured children. *Journal of Traumatic Stress, 22*(4), 294–302.

Kessler, R. C., Sonnega, A., Bromet, E., Hughes, M., & Nelson, C. B. (1995). Posttraumatic stress disorder in the National Comorbidity Survey. *Archives of General Psychiatry, 52*(12), 1048–1060.

Kleim, B., Ehlers, A., & Glucksman, E. (2007). Early predictors of chronic post-traumatic stress disorder in assault survivors. *Psychological Medicine, 37*(10), 1457–1467.

Koopman, C., Classen, C., Cardena, E., & Spiegel, D. (1995). When disaster strikes, acute stress disorder may follow. *Journal of Traumatic Stress, 8*(1), 29–46.

Kuhn, E., Blanchard, E. B., Fuse, T., Hickling, E. J., & Broderick, J. (2006). Heart rate of motor vehicle accident survivors in the emergency department, peritraumatic psychological reactions, ASD, and PTSD severity: A 6-month prospective study. *Journal of Traumatic Stress, 19*(5), 735–740.

Kühn, M., Ehlert, U., Rumpf, H. J., Backhaus, J., Hohagen, F., & Broocks, A. (2006). Onset and maintenance of psychiatric disorders after serious accidents. *European Archives of Psychiatry and Clinical Neuroscience, 256*(8), 497–503.

Lambert, J. F., Difede, J., & Contrada, R. J. (2004). The relationship of attribution of responsibility to acute stress disorder among hospitalized burn patients. *Journal of Nervous and Mental Disease, 192*(4), 304–312.

Marmar, C. R., Weiss, D. S., Schlenger, W. E., Fairbank, J. A., Jordan, B. K., Kulka, R. A., et al. (1994). Peritraumatic dissociation and posttraumatic stress in male Vietnam theater veterans. *American Journal of Psychiatry, 151*(6), 902–907.

Mathew, R. J., Wilson, W. H., Turkington, T. G., & Coleman, R. E. (1998). Cerebellar activity and disturbed time sense after THC. *Brain Research, 797*(2), 183–189.

McFarlane, A. C. (1998). Epidemiological evidence about the relationship between PTSD and alcohol abuse: The nature of the association. *Addictive Behaviors, 23*(6), 813–825.

McKibben, J. B., Bresnick, M. G., Wiechman Askay, S. A., & Fauerbach, J. A. (2008). Acute stress disorder and posttraumatic stress disorder: A prospective study of prevalence, course, and predictors in a sample with major burn injuries. *Journal of Burn Care and Research, 29*(1), 22–35.

McMillen, J. C., North, C. S., & Smith, E. M. (2000). What parts of PTSD are normal: Intrusion, avoidance, or arousal? Data from the Northridge, California, earthquake. *Journal of Traumatic Stress, 13*(1), 57–75.

Mellman, T. A., David, D., Bustamante, V., Fins, A. I., & Esposito, K. (2001). Predictors of post-traumatic stress disorder following severe injury. *Depression and Anxiety, 14*(4), 226–231.

Mills, M. A., Edmondson, D., & Park, C. L. (2007). Trauma and stress response among Hurricane Katrina evacuees. *American Journal of Public Health, 97*(Suppl. 1), S116–123.

Mollica, R. F., Caspi-Yavin, Y., Bollini, P., Truong, T., Tor, S., & Lavelle, J. (1992). The Harvard Trauma Questionnaire. Validating a cross-cultural instrument for measuring torture, trauma, and posttraumatic stress disorder in Indochinese refugees. *Journal of Nervous and Mental Disease, 180*(2), 111–116.

Musallam, N., Ginzburg, K., Lev-Shalem, L., & Solomon, Z. (2005). The psychological effects of Intifada Al Aqsa: Acute stress disorder and distress in Palestinian-Israeli students. *Israel Journal of Psychiatry and Related Sciences, 42*(2), 96–105.

Norris, F. H., Friedman, M. J., Watson, P. J., Byrne, C. M., Diaz, E., & Kaniasty, K. (2002). 60,000 disaster victims speak: Part I. An empirical review of the empirical literature, 1981–2001. *Psychiatry, 65*(3), 207–239.

North, C. S. (2007). Epidemiology of disaster mental health. In R. J. Ursano, C. S. Fullerton, L. Weisaeth & B. Raphael (Eds.), *Textbook of disaster psychiatry* (pp. 29–47). New York: Cambridge University Press.

North, C. S., Nixon, S. J., Shariat, S., Mallonee, S., McMillen, J. C., Spitznagel, E. L., et al. (1999). Psychiatric disorders among survivors of the Oklahoma City bombing. *Journal of the American Medical Association, 282*(8), 755–762.

North, C. S., Smith, E. M., & Spitznagel, E. L. (1997). One-year follow-up of survivors of a mass shooting. *American Journal of Psychiatry, 154*(12), 1696–1702.

O'Donnell, M. L., Creamer, M., Bryant, R. A., Schnyder, U., & Shalev, A. (2003). Posttraumatic disorders following injury: An empirical and methodological review. *Clinical Psychology Review, 23*(4), 587–603.

Prigerson, H. G., Shear, M. K., Jacobs, S. C., Kasl, S. V., Maciejewski, P. K., Silverman, G. K., et al. (2000). Grief and its relationship to PTSD. In D. Nutt, J. R. T. Davidson, & J. Zohar (Eds.), *Post-traumatic stress disorder: Diagnosis, management and treatment* (pp. 163–177). London, UK: Martin Dunitz.

Raphael, B., Martinek, N., & Wooding, S. (2004). Assessing traumatic bereavement. In J. P. Wilson & T. M. Keane

(Eds.), *Assessing psychological trauma and PTSD* (2nd ed., pp. 492–510). New York: Guilford.

Richardson, S., Abellan, J. J., & Best, N. (2006). Bayesian spatio-temporal analysis of joint patterns of male and female lung cancer risks in Yorkshire (UK). *Statistical Methods in Medical Research, 15*(4), 385–407.

Roberge, M. A., Dupuis, G., & Marchand, A. (2008). Acute stress disorder after myocardial infarction: Prevalence and associated factors. *Psychosomatic Medicine, 70*(9), 1028–1034.

Rundell, J. R. (2000). Psychiatric issues in medical-surgical disaster casualties: A consultation-liaison approach. *Psychiatric Quarterly, 71*(3), 245–258.

Rundell, J. R. (2007). Assessment and management of medical-surgical disaster casualties. In R. J. Ursano, C. S. Fullerton, L. Weisaeth, & B. Raphael (Eds.), *Textbook of disaster psychiatry* (pp. 167–189). New York: Cambridge University Press.

Sattler, D. N., de Alvarado, A. M., de Castro, N. B., Male, R. V., Zetino, A. M., & Vega, R. (2006). El Salvador earthquakes: Relationships among acute stress disorder symptoms, depression, traumatic event exposure, and resource loss. *Journal of Traumatic Stress, 19*(6), 879–893.

Saxena, S., Sharan, P., Garrido, M., & Saraceno, B. (2006). World Health Organization's Mental Health Atlas 2005: Implications for policy development. *World Psychiatry, 5*(3), 179–184.

Shalev, A. Y. (2002). Acute stress reactions in adults. *Biological Psychiatry, 51*(7), 532–543.

Shaw, R. J., Deblois, T., Ikuta, L., Ginzburg, K., Fleisher, B., & Koopman, C. (2006). Acute stress disorder among parents of infants in the neonatal intensive care nursery. *Psychosomatics, 47*(3), 206–212.

Shear, M. K., Frank, E., Houck, P. R., & Reynolds, C. F., 3rd. (2005). Treatment of complicated grief: A randomized controlled trial. *JAMA, 293*(21), 2601–2608.

Shephard, B. (2001). *A war of nerves: Soldiers and psychiatrists in the twentieth century.* Cambridge, MA: Harvard University Press.

Staab, J. P., Grieger, T. A., Fullerton, C. S., & Ursano, R. J. (1996). Acute stress disorder, subsequent posttraumatic stress disorder and depression after a series of typhoons. *Anxiety, 2*(5), 219–225.

Stein, M. B., Walker, J. R., Hazen, A. L., & Forde, D. R. (1997). Full and partial posttraumatic stress disorder: Findings from a community survey. *American Journal of Psychiatry, 154*(8), 1114–1119.

Tang, C. S. (2007). Trajectory of traumatic stress symptoms in the aftermath of extreme natural disaster: a study of adult Thai survivors of the 2004 Southeast Asian earthquake and tsunami. *Journal of Nervous and Mental Disease, 195*(1), 54–59.

Ursano, R. J., Bell, C., Eth, S., Friedman, M., Norwood, A., Pfefferbaum, B., et al. (2007). *Practice guideline for the treatment of patients with acute stress disorder and posttraumatic stress disorder.* Washington, DC: American Psychiatric Association.

Ursano, R. J., Fullerton, C., & Benedek, D. M. (2007). Peritraumatic dissociation: Time perception and cerebellar regulation of psychological, interpersonal, and biological processes. In E. Vermetten, M. J. Dorahy, & D. Spiegel (Eds.), *Traumatic dissociation: Neurobiology and treatment* (pp. 217–230). Arlington, VA: American Psychiatric Publishing.

Ursano, R. J., Fullerton, C. S., Epstein, R. S., Crowley, B., Vance, K., Kao, T. C., et al. (1999). Peritraumatic dissociation and posttraumatic stress disorder following motor vehicle accidents. *American Journal of Psychiatry, 156*(11), 1808–1810.

Ursano, R. J., Li, H., Zhang, L., Hough, C. J., Fullerton, C. S., Benedek, D. M., et al. (2008). Models of PTSD and traumatic stress: The importance of research "from bedside to bench to bedside." *Progress in Brain Research, 167,* 203–215.

Vlahov, D., Galea, S., Resnick, H., Ahern, J., Boscarino, J. A., Bucuvalas, M., et al. (2002). Increased use of cigarettes, alcohol, and marijuana among Manhattan, New York, residents after the September 11th terrorist attacks. *American Journal of Epidemiology, 155*(11), 988–996.

Weathers, F. W., & Keane, T. M. (2007). The Criterion A problem revisited: Controversies and challenges in defining and measuring psychological trauma. *Journal of Traumatic Stress, 20*(2), 107–121.

Wittmann, L., Moergeli, H., & Schnyder, U. (2006). Low predictive power of peritraumatic dissociation for PTSD symptoms in accident survivors. *Journal of Traumatic Stress, 19*(5), 639–651.

World Health Organization (1977). *International statistical classification of diseases, injuries, and causes of death* (9th ed.). Geneva, Switzerland: Author.

World Health Organization (2007). *International statistical classification of diseases and related health problems, F43.0 acute stress reaction.* Retrieved June 16, 2010, from http://apps.who.int/classifications/apps/icd/icd10online/index.htm?gf40.htm+F430.

Wynn, G., & Benedek, D. M. (Eds.). (2010). *Clinical manual for management of PTSD.* Arlington, VA: American Psychiatric Publishing.

Yahav, R., & Cohen, M. (2007). Symptoms of acute stress in Jewish and Arab Israeli citizens during the Second Lebanon War. *Social Psychiatry and Psychiatric Epidemiology, 42*(10), 830–836.

Yasan, A., Guzel, A., Tamam, Y., & Ozkan, M. (2009). Predictive factors for acute stress disorder and posttraumatic stress disorder after motor vehicle accidents. *Psychopathology, 42*(4), 236–241.

Yeh, C. B., Leckman, J. F., Wan, F. J., Shiah, I. S., & Lu, R. B. (2002). Characteristics of acute stress symptoms and nitric oxide concentration in young rescue workers in Taiwan. *Psychiatry Research, 112*(1), 59–68.

Zlotnick, C., Franklin, C. L., & Zimmerman, M. (2002). Does "subthreshold" posttraumatic stress disorder have any clinical relevance? *Comprehensive Psychiatry, 43*(6), 413–419.

Epidemiology of Posttraumatic Stress Disorder in Adults

Naomi Breslau

Abstract

Posttraumatic stress disorder (PTSD) was established in 1980, when it was incorporated in the DSM-III. The PTSD definition brackets a distinct set of stressors—traumatic events—from other stressful experiences and links it causally with a specific response, the PTSD syndrome. Explicit diagnostic criteria in DSM-III made it feasible to conduct large-scale epidemiological surveys on PTSD and other psychiatric disorders, using structured diagnostic interviews administered by nonclinicians. Epidemiologic research has been expanded from Vietnam veterans, who were the center of DSM-III PTSD study, to civilian populations and postwar regions worldwide. This chapter summarizes information on the prevalence estimates of PTSD in U.S. veterans of the Vietnam War, soldiers returning from deployment in Iraq and Afghanistan, and civilian populations. It outlines research findings on the course of PTSD, risk factors, comorbidity with other psychiatric disorders, and the risk for other posttrauma disorders. It concludes with recommendations for future research.

Key Words: Epidemiology, methodology, risk factors, PTSD, civilians, veterans

Introduction

The inclusion of posttraumatic stress disorder (PTSD) in the third edition of the *Diagnostic and Statistical Manual of Mental Disorders* (*DSM-III*), the official classification of psychiatric disorders of the American Psychiatric Association (APA), in 1980, marks the beginning of contemporary epidemiological research on the psychiatric response to trauma. The definition of PTSD in the *DSM-III* and in subsequent *DSM* editions is based on a conceptual model that brackets traumatic (catastrophic) events from other "ordinary" stressful experiences and links them causally with a specific syndrome. The definition of PTSD diverged from the *DSM-III* overarching goal to revolutionize American psychiatry. PTSD was an exception to the rule of creating a classification that is "atheoretical with a regard to etiology" (American Psychiatric Association, 1980). Unlike most diagnoses in the *DSM*, PTSD rests on the assumption of a specific etiology, whereby a distinct category of etiologic events is assumed to be the single most potent contributor to a disorder. Not only did the PTSD definition include an etiologic event, but it incorporates a theory, an underlying process, that connects the syndrome's diagnostic features. Specifically, the trauma creates a pathological memory that, in turn, gives rise to the characteristic symptoms of the disorder. Twenty years ago PTSD was largely confined to psychiatric journals. Now the trauma-PTSD language permeates television, radio talk shows, popular magazines, and fiction. PTSD provides a cultural template of the human response to war, violence, disaster, or very bad personal experiences.

This chapter presents a summary of the epidemiology of PTSD reported in studies of Vietnam veterans, U.S. military personnel of the Iraq and Afghanistan wars, and samples of civilian populations. It outlines methodological issues and summarizes findings on the prevalence of traumatic events and PTSD, risk factors for exposure to traumatic events and PTSD, and the risk for other posttrauma psychiatric disorders.

Methodological Issues

Measurement of Traumatic Events and PTSD

The standard measurement procedure in epidemiologic studies of psychiatric disorders, including PTSD, has been the National Institute of Mental Health-Diagnostic Interview Schedule (NIMH-DIS) and the World Health Organization-Composite International Diagnostic Interview (WHO-CIDI), which is based on the NIMH-DIS (Robins, Cottler, Bucholz, & Compton, 1995; Robins, Helzer, Cottler, & Golding, 1989; World Health Organization [WHO], 1997). These structured interviews are designed to be administered by experienced interviewers with no clinical training so as to enable large-scale studies. The PTSD section inquires about lifetime history of traumatic events. It asks respondents who report multiple events to single out the *worst event* they have ever experienced and elicits information about PTSD symptoms connected with that event. The ascertainment of PTSD is based on that information.

ESTIMATING EXPOSURE TO TRAUMATIC EVENTS AND THE CONDITIONAL PROBABILITY OF PTSD

Published estimates of the prevalence to traumatic events vary according to the inclusiveness of the stressor criterion and the methods used to measure exposure to qualifying stressors. In the *DSM-III* and *DSM-III-R*, qualifying stressors were defined as events that would be "distressing to almost everyone" and as "generally outside the range of usual human experience." Typical PTSD traumas were military combat, rape, physical assault, natural disaster, witnessing violence, and learning about violent injury or a violent death of a loved one. *DSM-IV* has broadened the stressor criterion beyond the earlier definition. According to one study, the impact of the revision on the lifetime prevalence of exposure to traumatic events has been an increase from 68.1% to 89.6% (Breslau & Kessler, 2001). The broadening of the stressor criterion has been controversial (e.g. McNally, 2003).

The conditional probability of PTSD given exposure to traumatic event is derived from information on the prevalence of exposure to one or more qualifying events (the denominator) and the proportion of those exposed who meet criteria for PTSD (the numerator). The majority of exposed persons report more than one event. When multiple qualifying traumas are reported, the standard approach has been to assess PTSD in relation to the traumatic event cited by the respondent as the worst or the most upsetting event ever experienced. This approach is an efficient way to identify persons with PTSD and estimate the prevalence of the disorder. Only a few respondents who fail to meet PTSD diagnostic criteria for their worst trauma meet criteria for other traumatic events they report (Breslau, Davis, Peterson, & Shultz, 1997). However, the approach has been suspected of overstating the conditional risk for PTSD associated with the category of qualifying events as a whole (that is, typical traumatic events not restricted to the worst ones; Kessler et al., 1999; Kessler, Sonnega, Bromet, & Nelson, 1995).

"RANDOM EVENT" VS. THE "WORST EVENT"

Another alternative to inquiring about PTSD symptoms in relation to all reported events, which would impose too great a respondents' burden, involves selecting a random event from the complete list of traumatic events reported by each respondent. Such an approach, together with a weighting procedure to adjust for differences in the selection probabilities of events across respondents, provides a representative sample of qualifying, or typical, traumatic events on which the conditional risk of PTSD is assessed. This method was used in a survey of the general population by Breslau and colleagues, and several reports have been published based on it (for example, Breslau, Chilcoat, Kessler, & Davis, 1999; Breslau et al., 1999; Breslau & Kessler, 2001; Breslau et al., 1998).

A comparison of the estimates based on the two methods—the randomly selected events and the worst events—indicates that the worst-event method moderately overstated the conditional risk of PTSD associated with representative (typical) traumas (Breslau et al., 1998). The modest bias in the estimated overall PTSD risk according to the worst-event method was in large part due to the deviation of the distribution of the worst events from expected values, if all qualifying events had equal prior selection probabilities. With few exceptions, differences between the two methods in the PTSD risk associated with individual event types were minor. Both methods identified the same event types as the most likely to lead to PTSD (rape, held captive/tortured/kidnapped, having been badly beaten, and sexual assault other than rape), and both methods replicated previous findings on the speed of remission of PTSD and the sex difference in the conditional risk of PTSD. It should be noted that, although the random-event method provides an unbiased estimate of the conditional probability of PTSD following typical traumas, it is incapable of identifying all those who met criteria for PTSD following exposure to traumatic events, either in lifetime or during a specified time period. In other words, the randomly selected events cannot replace the worst-event method as a shortcut when an inquiry about all traumatic events is not feasible.

PTSD in U.S. Veterans of the Vietnam War

A congressionally mandated survey of the Vietnam War veterans, the National Vietnam Veterans Readjustment Study (NVVRS), estimated that 30.9% of male veterans developed PTSD (a total 53.4% developed either PTSD or "partial" PTSD) and that 15.2% still suffered from the disorder in the late 1980s, when the survey was conducted (Kulka et al., 1990). These estimates were criticized as implausibly high, for two reasons. First, the Vietnam War was characterized as having had an extremely low rate of proximate psychiatric casualties (then called "combat fatigue" or "combat reaction"; Jones & Wessley, 2005). The high rates of *postcombat* PTSD among veterans were therefore unexpected. Second, only 15% of the men who served in Vietnam were assigned to combat units. Most support personnel were relatively safe from attacks, although some might have been exposed to traumatic events.

A re-evaluation of the NVVRS findings, published 16 years after the initial report (Dohrenwend et al., 2006), addressed several important criticisms of the NVVRS (e.g., the accuracy of self-reports of combat exposure). The researchers used archival data to corroborate self-reports of combat experiences. They also analyzed data from clinical interviews, conducted with a subset of the NVVRS respondents, in order to rule out cases with no functional impairment. The new analysis estimated that 18.7% of male veterans developed war-related PTSD during their lifetime, and 9.1% were still suffering from PTSD in the late 1980s, 11 to 12 years after the war. The level of functional impairment among veterans who continued to suffer from the disorder was mild to moderate. The 40% reduction in the prevalence of PTSD, both lifetime and current at the time of the NVVRS study, confirmed the suspicion that the NVVRS overdiagnosed PTSD among Vietnam veterans. Furthermore, had Dohrenwend et al. (2006) required that PTSD cases show clinically significant functional impairment, rather than mild, the new prevalence estimates would have been even lower (McNally, 2007).

PTSD in Soldiers Returning from Iraq and Afghanistan

The U.S. military operations in Iraq and Afghanistan have involved the first sustained combat warfare since the Vietnam War. In contrast with the research on Vietnam veterans that began years after the end of the war, research on the mental health effects of combat duty in Iraq and Afghanistan began within months of the start of the conflict. Mental health screening pre- and postdeployment conducted by the Department of Defense has become routine. However, estimates of the prevalence of PTSD among U.S. military personnel serving in Iraq and Afghanistan range widely across studies.

An early report on the prevalence of PTSD among U.S. troops returning from operations in Iraq and Afghanistan was based on Army and Marine units assessed three to four months after deployment (Hoge et al., 2004). The study reported similar rates of PTSD in Army and Marine units returning from Iraq—18.0% and 19.9%, respectively. A lower rate of PTSD was reported for an Army unit returning from Afghanistan, 11.5%. Lower estimates were reported when a stricter cut-off on the same screening scale was applied—12.2% and 12.9% for Iraq deployment, Marine and Army, respectively; and 6.2% for the army unit returning from Afghanistan deployment. The study illustrates that variability in case definition is a major source of disparity in the estimates of PTSD across studies. The report found a direct relationship between the number of combat experiences (e.g., being shot at, handling dead bodies, knowing someone who was killed, killing enemy combatants, being responsible for death of noncombatants) and the risk of PTSD. It shows that Marines incurred more combat stressors than Army personnel (especially that of killing enemy combatants, being responsible for the death of noncombatants, and seeing ill or injured women and children) but reported no higher rates of PTSD.

A recent review found that the prevalence estimates of PTSD in nontreatment seeking samples typically range from 5 to 20% (Ramchand et al., 2010). Estimates of less than 5% are chiefly from non-U.S. military (The Netherlands and UK) and deployed personnel who did not report combat. The relationship between level of combat experience and PTSD, reported by Hoge et al. (2004), was found consistently across subsequent studies, as was the difference in the PTSD prevalence between Iraq and Afghanistan deployment.

Mild Traumatic Brain Injury in Soldiers Returning from Iraq

Because of improved protective gear used in the Iraq war, more soldiers survive combat injuries, compared to previous wars. Severe brain injuries have been reported in one quarter of service members evacuated from Iraq and Afghanistan. A major concern has emerged about the effects *of mild* traumatic brain injury (mTBI), claimed to be the "signature" injury of the Iraq and Afghanistan wars (Hoge et al., 2008). TBI is characterized by a self-report of either a brief loss of consciousness or an altered mental status ("dazed," "confused"), resulting mainly from a blast explosion during deployment.

A study of Army soldiers three to four months after returning from one-year deployment in Iraq found that 20.2% reported history of TBI (Hoge et al., 2008). Two-thirds of them reported altered mental status. Elevated rates of PTSD (and major depression) were reported by soldiers who reported TBI, compared with soldiers with other injuries or no injuries. Adjustment for co-occurring PTSD (and major depression) accounted for the physical health problems reported by soldiers with TBI, indicating the importance of co-occurring psychiatric problems, chiefly PTSD, in TBI and its sequelae. The ascertainment of TBI in screening surveys or clinical examinations is problematic because it is based chiefly on self-report of altered mental status, defined by problems that lack specificity and are common in persons who suffered no injury.

Jones, Fear, and Wessely (2007) provide a historical account of "shell shock" during World War I, from the time it was discovered and assumed to be the product of a head injury to subsequent psychological and behavioral explanations of its symptoms. They point out that, although TBI is claimed to be the unique injury of the Iraq and Afghanistan wars, it held a similar position under the label of "shell shock" in World War I. The challenge both then and now is establishing the causal link between the explosion and the symptoms resulting from the shock to the nervous system. As in "shell shock," TBI involves psychological trauma and non specific common physical and psychological symptoms.

The Prevalence of Traumatic Events and PTSD in the Population

In the United States, the vast majority of community residents have experienced one or more PTSD-level events, as defined in the *DSM-IV* (see table 7.1) A similarly high figure has been reported in a Canadian urban community. The lifetime cumulative exposure to any traumatic event in a national sample of the U.S. population, circa 2000, was 82.8%. Much lower estimates of exposure to any traumatic event have been reported in surveys in Germany and Switzerland (20–28%). The estimated prevalence of traumatic events in a Swedish study was similar to the estimates in the United States and Canada.

Table 7.1 also presents estimates of lifetime and/or 12-month prevalence of *DSM-IV* PTSD. The lifetime prevalence in the United States, according to a recent U.S. national study (circa 2000) was 6.8%. The 12-month prevalence in the United States, 3.6%, is higher than in European countries and Australia (table 7.1). The prevalence in Lebanon, a country that suffered war and political violence for decades, was lower than the prevalence in the United States. Even in the United States, where the vast majority of the population has been exposed to one or more traumatic event, only a small minority of the population has ever experienced PTSD.

GENDER DIFFERENCES IN PTSD

A consistent finding across epidemiologic studies is the higher PTSD prevalence in women compared with men. Although men are more likely to experience trauma, the likelihood of developing PTSD following is higher in women. Table 7.2 presents sex-specific data on exposure to traumatic events and PTSD from U.S. community studies published from 1991 to 2005. Variability in exposure across studies reflects differences in the inclusiveness of the stressor criterion that defines "qualifying" events between *DSM-IV* and previous *DSM* editions. They also reflect differences in the methods used to measure exposure to traumatic events, chiefly, whether a list of events was used or a single item that describes (with examples) the type of traumatic events that qualify for

Table 7.1. Cumulative incidence of lifetime and 12 months of DSM-IV PTSD

Study	Sample	Interview	Lifetime	12-Months
			Total	Total
Breslau et al. (1998)	Detroit PMSA, USA Age 18–45 (n = 2181)	WHO-CIDI (telephone interview)	8.3%	-
Breslau et al. (2004)	Mid-Atlantic City, USA Age 19–22 (n = 1698)	WHO-CIDI (personal interview)	7.1%	-
Kessler et al. (2005)	USA National Age ≥ 18 (n = 9282)	WMH-CIDI (personal interview)	6.8%	3.5%
Stein et al. (1997)	Winnipeg, Canada Age > 18 (n = 1002)	PTSD Symptom Scale (telephone interview)	-	2.0%
Hapke et al (2005)	Luebeck, Germany Age 18–64 (n = 4075)	M-CIDI	1.4%	-
Perkonigg et al. (2000)	Munich, Germany Age 14–24 (n = 3021)	WHO-CIDI (personal interview)	1.3%	0.7%
Van Zelst (2003)	The Netherlands Age 55–85 (n = 422)	WHO-CIDI (personal interview)	-	0.9%
Hepp et al (2006)	Zurich, Switzerland Age 34/35 and 40/41	Zurich Cohort Study (personal interview)	-	0.0%
Karam et al (2006)	Lebanon National Age ≥ 18 (n = 308)	WHO-CIDI (personal interview)	-	2.0%
Creamer et al. (2001)	Australia National Age ≥ 18 (n = 10,641)	WHO-CIDI modified (personal interview)	-	1.3%
Frans et al. (2005)	Sweden National Age 18–70 (n = 1824)	DSM-IV based questionnaire (questionnaire)	5.6%	-
Kadri et al. (2007)	Casablanca, Morocco Age 15–80 (n = 800)	MINI (personal interview)	-	3.4%

Abbreviations: CIDI, Composite International Diagnostic Interview; WMH, World Mental Health; *DSM-IV, Diagnostic and Statistical Manual of Mental Disorders*, 4th Edition (1994).
Blanks: not published

diagnosing PTSD. All these studies have reported a higher lifetime prevalence of exposure in men than in women. Although consistent across studies, the sex differences in exposure is modest, with a prevalence ratio in men vs. women of <1.2 to 1. The average number of traumatic events experienced by men exceeds the corresponding average in women. Despite their lower exposure to traumatic events, women consistently have higher risk of PTSD than men.

Some researchers have raised the possibility that females' excess PTSD risk relative to males' (despite overall lower prevalence of exposure to traumatic events) might be explained by sex differences in the *type* of traumatic events—specifically, females' higher risk of experiencing rape and other sexual assault. Epidemiological studies that took into account females' higher risk for sexual trauma found that the sex difference was only slightly attenuated (Breslau et al., 1999; Kessler et al., 1995). The explanation that the sex difference in PTSD was due to females higher risk of sexual trauma was unequivocally rejected in a comprehensive meta-analysis by Tolin and Foa (2006). The results indicate that, although females are more likely to experience sexual assault—a

Table 7.2 Lifetime prevalence of exposure and PTSD (rate/100)

	Exposur		PTSD	
	Males	Females	Males	Females
Breslau (1991)	43.0	36.7	6.0	11.3
Norris (1992)	73.6	64.8	–	–
Resnick (1993)	–	69.0	–	12.3
Kessler (1995)	60.7	51.2	5.0	10.4
Breslau (1997)	–	40.0	–	13.8
Stein (1997)	81.3	74.2	–	–
Breslau (1998)	92.2	87.1	6.2	13.0
Breslau (2004)	87.2	78.4	6.3	7.9
Kessler (2005)	–	–	3.6	9.7

traumatic event associated with a high PTSD risk in both sexes—the sex difference in the exposure to sexual assault did not account for the higher risk of PTSD in females, relative to males. Among victims of specific types of traumatic events other than sexual assault, females exhibited higher PTSD risk. The meta-analysis also confirmed previous findings (Breslau et al., 1998; Breslau, Wilcox, Storr, Lucia, & Anthony, 2004) that the sex difference in the conditional risk of PTSD varies across categories of traumatic events. Specifically, females' excess PTSD risk is due primarily to females' greater susceptibility to PTSD associated with assaultive violence other than sexual.

There is evidence that the gender difference in PTSD among exposed persons is not attributable to gender differences in history of prior traumatic events, preexisting depression (Breslau, Peterson, & Schultz, 2008) or a gender-related bias in reporting PTSD symptoms (Chung & Breslau, 2008).

DIFFERENCES IN PTSD RISK ACROSS EVENT TYPES

The evaluation of the relative severity or magnitude of traumatic events is problematic. However, severity can be inferred from data on the probability of PTSD associated with event types (Tolin & Foa, 2006). A consistent finding across epidemiological studies is that traumatic events involving assaultive violence—rape, sexual assault, physical assault, and military combat (among men)—are associated with a higher risk of PTSD than other event types (e.g., disaster, severe accidents). Table 7.3 illustrates these results, using data from the Detroit Area Study of Trauma (Breslau et al., 1998).

The assaultive violence composite category has the highest probability of PTSD. The composite category of learning about traumatic events experienced by a close friend or relative has the lowest probability of PTSD (table 7.3). The PTSD risk associated with learning of the sudden unexpected death of a close friend/relative is intermediate. Beyond the variability observed across event types, especially between events involving assaultive violence and events that do not, there is no evidence supporting further distinction by severity within event types (Breslau, Peterson, Poisson, Schultz, & Lucia, 2004). An exception to this general observation is military experience.

A relationship between severity and persistent traumatic events and PTSD has been reported consistently in studies of military personnel and veterans, in contrast with civilian studies (Brewin, Andrews, & Valentine, 2000). Studies of veterans of the Vietnam War and the Iraq and Afghanistan wars reported a gradient relationship between the intensity of combat engagement (e.g., number of firefights, ambushes) and the risk of PTSD (Kulka et al., 1990; Hoge et al., 2004). Further, elevated PTSD rates have been reported among deployed soldiers in the Iraq war who participated in combat, but not deployed personnel who did not participate in combat relative to nondeployed personnel (Smith et al., 2008).

Table 7.3 Posttraumatic stress disorder (PTSD) risk associated with specific traumas*

Conditional Risk of PTSD Across Specific Traumas, % PTSD (SE)	
Assaultive violence	20.9 (3.4)
Military combat	0 (0.0)
Rape	49.0 (12.2)
Held captive/tortured/ kidnapped	53.8 (23.4)
Shot/stabbed	15.4 (13.7)
Sexual assault other than rape	23.7 (10.8)
Mugged/threatened with weapon	8.0 (3.7)
Badly beaten up	31.9 (8.6)
Other injury or shock	6.1 (1.4)
Serious car crash	2.3 (1.3)
Other serious accident	16.8 (6.2)
Natural disaster	3.8 (3.0)
Life-threatening illness	1.1 (0.9)
Child's life-threatening illness	10.4 (9.8)
Witnessed killing/ serious injury	7.3 (2.5)
Discovering dead body	0.2 (0.2)
Learning about others	2.2 (0.7)
Close relative raped	3.6 (1.7)
Close relative attacked	4.6 (2.9)
Close relative car crash	0.9 (0.5)
Close relative other accident	0.4 (0.4)
Sudden unexpected death	14.3 (2.6)
Any trauma	9.2 (1.0)

* Labels of traumas are abbreviated

Course of PTSD

The definition of PTSD in *DSM-IV* requires one-month duration of symptoms, a requirement designed to exclude transient (normal) reactions to stressors. *DSM-IV* includes a *subtype of chronic PTSD*, defined as duration of symptoms for six months or more. Epidemiological studies that estimated duration of symptoms based on retrospective data indicate that the majority of cases (>70%) persist for more than six months (Breslau et al., 1998; Kessler et al., 1995). More than one-third of cases persist for five years or longer. Duration of *DSM-IV* PTSD varies by gender and event type. PTSD lasts longer in women and in cases resulting from traumas experienced directly, compared with learning of traumas to a loved one or a sudden unexpected death of a loved one (Breslau et al., 1998).

DSM-IV also includes a *subtype of delayed-onset PTSD*, defined as onset of symptoms six months after exposure. Epidemiological studies in the general population have reported that delayed onset is extremely rare. A recent review confirmed this finding. Although in some cases the full syndrome does not coalesce until a later time, the appearances of some symptoms in cases that develop the disorder typically occur within days or weeks (Andrews, Brewin, Philpott, & Stewart, 2007). Avoidance symptoms and use of alcohol may postpone the emergence of the full syndrome.

Risk Factors for Traumatic Events and PTSD

Risk Factors for Exposure to Traumatic Events

Traumatic events are not random. The prevalence of exposure varies across subgroups of the population. U.S. studies have reported that men, the young, and members of minority groups residing in inner cities have higher lifetime risk for exposure to assaultive violence, compared with women, older persons, and residents of middle-class suburbs (Breslau et al., 1998). Men are also at higher risk than women for exposure to serious accidents and to witnessing violence perpetrated on others. With respect to other event types—events grouped under learning about trauma to others or learning about the unexpected death of a loved one—differences by socio-demographic characteristics are trivial (Breslau, 2002; Breslau et al., 1998). There is evidence that history of exposure to trauma predicts new exposure (Breslau et al., 1995).

Personality traits of neuroticism and extroversion, early conduct problems, family history of psychiatric disorders, and preexisting psychiatric disorders are associated with increased risk for exposure to traumatic events (Breslau et al., 1995; Breslau, Davis, Andreski, & Peterson, 1991; Bromet, Sonnega, & Kessler, 1998).

Risk Factors for PTSD Among Trauma-Exposed Persons

The bracketing of extreme stressors in the definition of PTSD in *DSM-III* implied that, unlike more ordinary stressful life events, the causal effects of extreme stressors are independent of personal vulnerabilities. PTSD was said to be a *normal response to an abnormal event*. The role of stressors in PTSD was compared to the role of force in producing a broken leg (Andreasen, 1980). Therapists and Veterans' advocates rejected any suggestions that predispositions played a part. They saw research on predispositions as leading to blaming the victims for their plight. Breslau and Davis (1987) challenged this assumption and suggested that, in regard to "extreme" stressors, social and individual factors may modify the response in the same way that they modify the response to ordinary stressful life events.

The accumulating epidemiologic evidence has clearly demonstrated the relative rarity of PTSD among trauma victims, and the associations of PTSD with risk factors other than trauma intensity. Far from being a normal response to an abnormal stressor, it is an abnormal response, observed only in some people. Current conceptions of PTSD underscore the role of predispositions in the etiology of PTSD. This emphasis is a radical shift from the formulation of PTSD in *DSM-III* that attributed to the traumatic event the dominant or exclusive role in the development of the disorder (Yehuda & McFarlane, 1995). The shift is not a new development but a return to earlier conceptions that waxed and waned through the history of psychiatry.

Risk factors for PTSD overlap partially with risk factors of exposure to traumatic events. They include the personality trait of neuroticism, family history of psychiatric disorders, preexisting disorders, social support, and intelligence. (Selected risk factors are discussed in more detail below.) Most of the evidence on risk factors of PTSD is based on cross-sectional studies and retrospective self-reports. The few reports on risk factors that are based on longitudinal studies concern cognitive abilities measured before exposure to traumatic events, prior PTSD (vs. prior trauma per se), preexisting psychiatric disorders, and childhood behavior and emotional problems.

A meta-analysis of risk factors of PTSD discovered wide heterogeneity between civilian and veteran studies and across research methods (Brewin et al., 2000). However, three risk factors were uniform across populations and methods: psychiatric history, family psychiatric history, and early adversity (Brewin et al., 2000). Although the effect of each individual risk factor examined in the meta-analysis is relatively small, their sum might outweigh the impact of trauma severity (Brewin et al., 2000).

A subsequent meta-analysis of risk factors for PTSD (or PTSD symptoms) concluded that peritraumatic responses (e.g., dissociation as the immediate response to the stressor) count the most (Ozer, Best, Lipsey, & Weiss, 2003). There is a conceptual problem in this analysis (and similar studies concerning negative appraisal as risk factor) in that peritraumatic responses and appraisal might themselves be aspects of the outcome we wish to explain. Dissociations, negative appraisal, and PTSD are likely to be manifestation of the same psychological process or consequences of a common vulnerability.

Both meta-analysis studies converged on the estimated effect sizes across risk factors. Ozer et al. (2003) classify the results on risk factors for PTSD under two rubrics: (1) characteristics of the individual or life history that were distal to the traumatic event and produced an average small effect size ($r < 0.20$). These include prior trauma, gender, education, SES, IQ, and race; and (2) factors proximal to the traumatic event that yielded effect size $r > 0.20$ (but < 0.40), including perceived life threat, perceived social support, and peritraumatic dissociation. Although effect sizes of factors in the latter category might be large enough to warrant investigations of the mechanisms involved in these relationships (Ozer et al., 2003), there is a conceptual problem concerning the status of these factors as risk factors, rather than aspects of the responses to stressors (including PTSD), as discussed above.

SOCIAL SUPPORT

Several studies have reported higher risk of PTSD in trauma victims with low social support (Brewin et al., 2000; Ozer et al., 2003). The interpretation of the finding is ambiguous in two respects. First, it is unclear whether low social support impedes the resolution of acute PTSD symptoms leading to chronic PTSD or contributes to the development of the symptoms. Second, because social support has been assessed after exposure and the onset of PTSD, it is unclear whether low support plays a causal role in the development or the persistent of PTSD or instead results from poor interpersonal relationship caused by PTSD symptoms.

INTELLIGENCE

Studies conducted on Vietnam veterans reported associations between intelligence test scores and the risk for PTSD (Macklin et al., 1998; McNally & Shin, 1995; Pitman, Orr, Lowenhagen, Macklin, & Altman, 1991). Evidence on the role of intelligence in children's psychiatric response to adversity was reported for a range of disorders including PTSD (Fergusson & Lynskey, 1996; Silva et al., 2000). There is evidence from longitudinal studies that cognitive ability measured in early childhood predicted subsequent exposure to traumatic events and PTSD (following exposure) in general population samples (Breslau, Lucia, & Alvarado, 2006; Koenen, Moffitt, Poulton, Martin, & Caspi, 2007; Storr, Ialongo, Anthony, & Breslau, 2007) Among members of the Vietnam veterans twin registry for whom test scores at enrollment were available, predeployment scores predicted postdeployment PTSD (Kremen et al., 2007). Some of the studies found that a decrease in risk was conferred by high IQ score (e.g., > 1 SD above the mean), and not merely by average IQ (Breslau et al., 2006). These studies suggest the possibility that high IQ plays a protective role. The mechanisms by which high IQ deters the PTSD effects of trauma are unclear. Intelligence involves the ability to reason, plan, solve problems, think abstractly, comprehend complex ideas, learn quickly, and learn from experience. Gilbertson et al. (2006) suggested that high IQ signals a general capacity to effectively and flexibly manipulate verbal information and thus a capacity to place traumatic experiences into meaningful concepts, which may reduce negative emotional impact.

The association of IQ with PTSD is not unique. A recent large-scale Danish study documented lower IQ in pre-morbid psychiatric inpatients relative to hospitalized controls with no psychiatric disorders. IQ at time of military draft, assessed more than one year prior to hospitalization, showed lower IQ in patients with schizophrenia, affective disorders, personality disorders, and neurotic/stress disorders. In each diagnostic category, decreasing IQ was associated with increasing risk of becoming a psychiatric patient (Urfer-Parnas, Mortensen, Saebye, & Parnas, 2010).

PRIOR TRAUMATIC EXPERIENCES

Studies of Vietnam veterans and general population samples have reported higher rates of prior trauma (including childhood maltreatment) among exposed persons who developed PTSD than among exposed persons who did not (Bremner, Southwick, Johnson, Yehuda, & Charney, 1993; Breslau et al., 1999). In these studies, persons with PTSD are asked about traumatic events they had experienced prior to the trauma that triggered their disorder. A major limitation in these studies is the failure to assess how persons had responded to the prior trauma—specifically, whether or not they had developed PTSD in response to the prior trauma. Consequently, it is unclear whether prior trauma per se, or instead prior PTSD, predict an elevated risk for PTSD following a subsequent trauma. A recent prospective study (Breslau et al., 2008) has reported that prior exposure to trauma increased the risk for PTSD *only* if the victim had developed PTSD in response to the prior trauma. Trauma-exposed persons who had not developed PTSD in response to the earlier trauma are not at increased risk for the PTSD effect of a subsequent trauma, compared to persons with no prior trauma (Breslau et al., 2008).

The Role of Risk Factors in High- and Low-magnitude Traumatic Events

The distinction in *DSM-III* between traumatic (extraordinary) stressors and ordinary stressors assumes that the importance of individual predispositions as risk factors is *inversely related to the magnitude of the stressors*. This view reflected standard stress theories as illustrated in a review in *Science*: "the more rigorous and severe the external situation, the less significant are social and individual characteristics in determining the likelihood and nature of response" (Rabkin & Struening, 1976, p. 1018). Along the same line, McNally has recently suggested that the broadening of the stressor criterion in *DSM-IV* to include traumatic events of lower magnitude made it less plausible to assign the causal significance to the stressor itself and more plausible to emphasize personal predispositions (McNally, 2003). However, the available empirical evidence, although limited in volume, does not support this expectation.

Based on data from a follow-up study of Vietnam veterans conducted in the early 1970s, Helzer (1981) examined the effects of antecedent risk factors (failure to graduate from high school, drug use) on depression (PTSD was not examined) across different levels of combat stress. He reported that the influence of these antecedents was marked (and statistically significant) *only* at a high level of combat stress.

A recent meta-analysis of predictors of PTSD found that the relationship between important antecedent risk factors and PTSD following traumatic events varies by type of trauma that constituted the target event (Ozer et al., 2003). There was no evidence supporting the idea that risk factors had a stronger relationship with PTSD when the traumatic event was of a less severe type. To the extent that there were differences in these relationships, the direction was reversed. The results show a stronger relationship between risk factors and PTSD when the target event was assault compared with an event type of less magnitude. Specifically, prior trauma (unspecified as to type) was more strongly correlated with PTSD when the index event involved interpersonal violence (civilian assault, rape, domestic violence) than when it was an accident (effect sizes were r = 0.27 and r = 0.12, respectively). The same pattern was reported for family history of psychopathology (effect sizes were r = 0.31 and r = 0.08, respectively). For prior psychological problems, only a small difference was detected in the same direction as observed for the other factors.

Comorbidity and the Risk of Other Posttrauma Disorders

Epidemiological studies of general population samples have confirmed earlier observations from clinical samples and samples of Vietnam veterans that persons diagnosed with PTSD have high rates of other psychiatric disorders. These include major depression, anxiety disorders other than PTSD, and substance use disorders. Extensive comorbidity is a highly general phenomenon in psychiatry. "Pure" cases that meet criteria for a single disorder are rare. Causal and noncausal explanations have been proposed for the association of PTSD and other disorders. First, preexisting psychiatric disorders may increase the likelihood of PTSD by increasing the risk for exposure to traumatic events of the type that lead to PTSD or increasing susceptibility to the PTSD-inducing effects of trauma. Second, PTSD may be a causal risk factor for other psychiatric disorders. Use of alcohol or drugs to relieve the distressing symptoms of PTSD may increase the likelihood of dependence. Third, the associations may be noncausal, reflecting shared genetic or environmental factors. Genetic factors common to PTSD and substance use disorders as well as depression have been reported.

A suspected shared environmental risk factor for PTSD and other psychiatric disorders is the trauma that gave rise to PTSD. It has been suggested that traumatic events leading to PTSD also induce the onset of other disorders. According to this hypothesis, some trauma victims develop PTSD, whereas others develop major depression or substance use disorder, depending on their preexisting vulnerabilities. Comorbidity of PTSD with other disorders would thus reflect the co-occurrence of distinct diatheses (Breslau, Davis, Peterson, & Schultz, 2000).

The hypothesis that traumatic events increase the risk for other disorders, independent of their PTSD effects, would be supported by evidence of elevated incidence of other disorders in trauma victims who did not develop PTSD, relative to persons who were not exposed to trauma. Conversely, evidence of an increased risk for the subsequent onset of major depression or substance use disorders only in victims with PTSD, relative to persons who did not experience trauma, would suggest that the two disorders share a common underlying vulnerability.

Results from a prospective study showed that the odds ratio for the first onset of *major depression* in persons with preexisting PTSD was 3.0 and in persons who were exposed to trauma but did not develop PTSD, 1.4 (not significant), relative to persons who were not exposed to trauma (Breslau et al., 2000). Neither PTSD nor history of trauma exposure increased the risk of *alcohol use disorder*. However, preexisting PTSD, but not history of trauma exposure, increased the risk for the subsequent onset of *drug use disorder* (Breslau, Davis, & Schultz, 2003). A report from another longitudinal study on the incidence of drug use disorders shows similar results. Increased incidence of drug disorder was found for persons with preexisting PTSD but not for persons with exposure alone (Reed, Anthony, & Breslau, 2007).

These results suggest different explanations across comorbid disorders: (1) the relationship between major depression and PTSD suggests a shared diathesis or shared environmental causes other than the traumatic event (for which there was no evidence); (2) in contrast, drug use disorder, for which there was support for only one direction—from PTSD to drug disorder onset—might be a complication of PTSD.

A general conclusion that can be drawn is that persons who experienced trauma and who did not develop PTSD (i.e., most of those exposed to traumatic events) are not at an elevated risk for major depression and drug use disorders, compared with unexposed persons. The excess incidence of these disorders in persons exposed to trauma is concentrated primarily in the small subset of trauma-exposed persons with PTSD. Reports from other studies on lifetime and current co occurrence of other disorders with trauma and PTSD support this generalization (e.g., Breslau, Chase, & Anthony, 2002; North & Pfefferbaum, 2002). A recent study extends these findings to suicide attempts (Wilcox, Storr, & Breslau, 2009). The study found that PTSD was an independent predictor of a subsequent suicide attempt. However, persons who had been exposed to traumatic events, including high-magnitude events that involve assaultive violence, who did not develop PTSD were not at increased risk of a suicide attempt. A recent study extends these findings to suicide attempts (Wilcox et al., 2009). The study found that PTSD was an independent predictor of a subsequent suicide attempt. However, persons who had been exposed to traumatic events, including high-magnitude events that involve assaultive violence, who did not develop PTSD were not at increased risk of a suicide attempt.

Conclusions

The extensive literature on PTSD, beginning in 1980 with the introduction of PTSD in *DSM-III*, shows that:

1. Estimates of the PTSD effects of the Vietnam War and of the Iraq and Afghanistan wars are controversial. However, there is consistent evidence of a relationship between the intensity of combat exposure and the risk of PTSD.
2. The vast majority of community residents in the United States (>80%) experience one or more traumatic events that qualify for the diagnosis of PTSD (Criterion A) according to *DSM-IV*.
3. Only a small proportion (<10%) of those exposed to traumatic events develop PTSD.
4. Exposure to traumatic events involving assaultive violence (e.g., rape, sexual assault, physical assault) is more likely to result in PTSD than other types of traumatic events.
5. Females are at higher risk of PTSD than males; the gender difference is not due to females higher rates of rape and sexual assault.
6. Risk factors for PTSD following exposure include preexisting psychiatric disorders, family history of psychiatric disorders, cognitive ability, personality traits (neuroticism), and social environment. A subset of risk factors for PTSD following exposure (e.g., cognitive ability, history of psychiatric disorders) also operates indirectly by increasing the risk of exposure to traumatic events.
7. The vast majority of exposed persons, those who do not develop PTSD, are not at an increased risk of other psychiatric disorders; the small proportion of victims who develop PTSD also experience considerably higher risk of major depression and substance use disorders.

The most important impact of the extensive epidemiological literature on PTSD has been a sharp shift away from the original model in *DSM-III* that PTSD was a normal response to an abnormal stressor. The idea that traumatic events would cause PTSD in most victims, regardless of preexisting vulnerabilities, has been refuted. PTSD is seen as a pathological response by a minority of persons. So far, risk factors identified in epidemiological studies have small effects, especially those that are antecedent to exposure to trauma and are not confounded with the PTSD response. With the rise of biological psychiatry, the search for biological markers of PTSD (genetic, brain anatomy, HPA axis, autonomic reactivity) has become a major focus of research designed to distinguish those who develop PTSD from those who do not.

Future Directions

1. PTSD continues to be a challenge for public health. Epidemiological research shows that the majority of community residents in the United States have been exposed to severely traumatic qualifying events. An estimated 10% of trauma-exposed community residents develop PTSD. Previous studies have identified suspected risk factors as causal determinants that might account for PTSD, when it occurs. However, with few exceptions, these studies have been retrospective, limiting greatly causal interpretations. There is a need for longitudinal epidemiological studies to test rival etiological hypotheses, rather than illustrate a plausible idea.
2. One example for future research etiology concerns the potential effects of pre- natal and childhood experiences on PTSD following exposure in late adolescence and adulthood. Despite the continuing reports on the effect of prior trauma and childhood trauma on the PTSD effect of a subsequent trauma, there is little empirical evidence on the mechanisms that might account for these observations. Does prior trauma (e.g., child physical abuse) increase the risk of PTSD from a subsequent trauma directly, even in the absence of prior PTSD or other prior psychopathology?
3. Another etiology to be tested concern intergenerational transmission of PTSD, a hypothesis currently being addressed in biological laboratories on small convenience samples.
4. Epidemiological methods, developed since the 1980s, have been used to estimate

the prevalence of specific psychiatric disorders in populations and their distribution across subgroups. Brief screening scales have been developed to enable the estimation of specific psychiatric disorder in large health surveys that cover a wide range of problems. These methods have been used in recent years to screen members of the U.S. armed forces upon return from Iraq and Afghanistan deployment. The purpose of the screening is to identify soldiers who need help for war-related mental health problems, chiefly PTSD, and ensure that they receive appropriate health care. Screening returning soldiers has not been demonstrated to be effective in reaching the desired outcomes, for two main reasons. The first concerns the inaccuracy of screening instruments used to identify soldiers with PTSD or other mental health problems. The second reason is far more complex and concerns the steps that lead from the identification of soldiers with mental health problems to referral and receipt of effective mental health care. There is a need for accurate screening instruments with minimal false negatives and false positives. The greater challenge, however, is develop a systematic collaborative efforts to translate screening into improved mental health and to test the efficacy of that system. Critics of mass screening programs argue that, in the absence of evidence of efficiency of screening, there is the possibility of inadvertently doing more harm than good. This caveat applies also to post disaster mass screening and early interventions in the United States and across the world.

References

American Psychiatric Association. (1980). *Diagnostic and statistical manual of mental disorders* (3rd ed.). Washington DC: Author.

Andreasen, N. C. (1980). Post-traumatic stress disorder. In A. M. Freedman, H. I. Kaplan, and B. J. Sadock (Eds.), *Comprehensive textbook of psychiatry* (3rd ed.). Baltimore: Williams & Wilkins.

Andrews, B., Brewin, C. R., Philpott, R., & Stewart, L. (2007). Delayed-onset posttraumatic stress disorder: A systematic review of the evidence. *American Journal of Psychiatry, 164*, 1319–1326.

Breslau, N. (2002). Epidemiologic studies of trauma, posttramatic stress disorder, and other psychiatric disorders. *Canadian Journal of Psychiatry, 47*, 923–929.

Breslau, N., Chase, G. A., & Anthony, J. C. (2002). The uniqueness of the DSM definition of post-traumatic stress disorder: Implications for research. *Psychological Medicine, 32*, 573–576.

Breslau, N., & Davis, G. C. (1987). Posttraumatic stress disorder: The stressor criterion. *Journal of Nervous and Mental Disease, 175*: 255–264.

Breslau, N., Davis, G. C., & Andreski, P. (1995). Risk factors for PTSD related traumatic events: A prospective analysis. *American Journal of Psychiatry, 152*, 529–535.

Breslau, N., Davis, G. C., Andreski, P., & Peterson, E. (1991). Traumatic events and posttraumatic stress disorder in an urban population of young adults. *Archives of General Psychiatry, 48*, 216–222.

Breslau, N., Davis, G. C., Peterson, E. L., & Schultz, L. R. (2000). A second look at comorbidity in victims of trauma: The posttraumatic stress disorder major depression connection. *Biological Psychiatry, 48*, 902–909.

Breslau, N., Chilcoat, H. D., Kessler, R. C., & Davis, G. C. (1999). Previous exposure to trauma and PTSD effects of subsequent trauma: Results from the Detroit area survey of trauma. *American Journal of Psychiatry, 156*, 902–907.

Breslau, N., Chilcoat, H. D., Kessler, R. C., Peterson, E. L., & Lucia, V. C. (1999). Vulnerability to assaultive violence: Further specification of the sex difference in post-traumatic stress disorder. *Psychological Medicine, 29*, 813–821.

Breslau, N., Davis, G. C., Peterson, E. L., & Schultz, L. (1997) Psychiatric sequelae of posttraumatic stress disorder in women. *Archives of General Psychiatry, 54*, 81–87.

Breslau, N., Davis, G. C., & Schultz, L. R. (2003). Posttraumatic stress disorder and the incidence of nicotine, alcohol, and other drug disorders in persons who have experienced trauma. *Archives of General Psychiatry, 60*, 289–294.

Breslau, N., & Kessler, R. (2001). The stressor criterion in DSM-IV posttraumatic stress disorder: An empirical investigation. *Biological Psychiatry, 50*, 699–704.

Breslau, N., Kessler, R. C., Chilcoat, H. D., Schultz, L. R., Davis, G. C., & Andreski, P. (1998). Trauma and posttraumatic stress disorder in the community: The 1996 Detroit area survey of trauma. *Archives of General Psychiatry, 55*, 626–632.

Breslau, N., Lucia, V. C., & Alvarado, G. F. (2006). Intelligence and other predisposing factors in exposure to trauma and posttraumatic stress disorder: A follow-up study at age 17 years. *Archives of General Psychiatry, 63*(11), 1238–1245.

Breslau, N., Peterson, E. L., Poisson, L. M., Schultz, L. R., & Lucia, V. C. (2004). Estimating post-traumatic stress disorder in the community: Lifetime perspective and the impact of typical traumatic events. *Psychological Medicine, 34*(5), 889–898.

Breslau, N., Peterson, E. L., & Schultz, L. R. (2008). A second look at prior trauma and the posttraumatic stress disorder effects of subsequent trauma: A prospective epidemiological study. *Archives of General Psychiatry, 65*, 431–437.

Breslau, N., Wilcox, H. C., Storr, C. L., Lucia, V. C., & Anthony, J. C. (2004). Trauma exposure and posttraumatic stress disorder: A study of youths in urban America. *Journal of Urban Health, 81*, 530–544.

Bremner, J. D., Southwick, S. M., Johnson, D. R., Yehuda, R., & Charney, D. S. (1993). Childhood physical abuse and combat-related posttraumatic-stress-disorder in Vietnam veterans. *American Journal of Psychiatry*, 150, 235–239.

Brewin, C. R., Andrews, B., & Valentine, J. D. (2000). Meta-analysis of risk factors for posttraumatic stress disorder in trauma-exposed adults. *Journal of Consulting and Clinical Psychology, 68*(5), 748–766.

Bromet, E., Sonnega, A., & Kessler, R. C. (1998). Risk factors for DSM-III-R posttraumatic stress disorder: Findings from the National Comorbidity Survey. *American Journal of Epidemiology, 147*, 353–361.

Chung, H., & Breslau, N. (2008). The latent structure of posttraumatic stress disorder: Tests of invariance by gender and trauma type. *Psychological Medicine, 38*, 563–573.
Cremer, M., Burgess, P., & McFarlane, A. C. (2001). Posttraumatic stress disorder: Findings from the Australian National Survey of Mental Health and Well-being. *Psychological Medicine, 31*, 1237–1247.
Dohrenwend, B. P., Turner, J. B., Turse, N. A., Adams, B. G., Koenen, K. C., & Marshall, R. (2006). The psychological risks of Vietnam for U.S. veterans: A revisit with new data and methods. *Science, 313*, 979–982.
Fergusson, D. M., & Lynskey, M. T. (1996). Adolescent resiliency to family adversity. *Journal of Child Psychology and Psychiatry, 37*(3), 281–292.
Frans, O., Rimmo, P. A., Aberg, L., & Fredrikson, M. (2005). Trauma exposure and post-traumatic stress disorder in the general population. *Acta Psychiatrica Scandinavica, 111*, 291–299.
Gilbertson, M. W., Paulus, L. A., Williston, S. K., Gurvits, T. V., Lasko, N. B., Pitman, R. K., & Orr, S. P. (2006). Neurocognitive function in monozygotic twins discordant for combat exposure: Relationship to posttraumatic stress disorder. *Journal of Abnormal Psychology, 115*(3), 484–495.
Hapke, U., Schumann, A., Rumpf, H. J., John, U., Konerding, U., & Meyer, C. (2005). Association of smoking and nicotine dependence with trauma and posttraumatic stress disorder in a general population sample. *Journal of Nervous and Mental Disease, 193*, 843–846.
Helzer, J. E. (1981). Methodological Issues in the Interpretations of the Consequences of Extreme Situations (pp 108–129). In B. S. Dohrenwend and B. P. Dohrenwend (Eds.), *Stressful life events and their contexts: Monographs in psychosocial epidemiology*, (vol. 2, pp. xiii, 287). New York: Prodist.
Hepp, U., Gamma, A., Milos, G., Eich, D., Ajdacic-Gross, V., Rossler, W., Angst, J., & Schnyder, U. (2006). Prevalence of exposure to potentially traumatic events and PTSD: The Zurich Cohort Study. *European Archives of Psychiatry and Clinical Neuroscience, 256*, 151–158.
Hoge, C. W., Castro, C. A., Messer, S. C., McGurk, D., Clotting, D. I., & Koffman, R. L. (2004). Combat duty in Iraq and Afghanistan, mental health problems, and barriers to care. *New England Journal of Medicine, 351*, 13–22.
Hoge, C. W., McGurk, D., Thomas, J. L., Cox, A. L., Engel, C. C., & Castro, C. A. (2008). Mild traumatic brain injury in U.S. soldiers returning from Iraq. *New England Journal of Medicine, 358*(5), 453–463.
Jones, E., Fear, N. T., & Wessely, S. (2007). Shell shock and mild traumatic brain injury: A historical review. *American Journal of Psychiatry, 164*(11), 1641–1645.
Jones, E., & Wessely, S. (2005). War syndromes: The impact of culture on medically unexplained symptom. *Medical History, 49*, 55–78.
Kadri, N., Agoub, M., El Gnaoui, S., Berrada, S., & Moussaoui, D. (2007). Prevalence of anxiety disorders: A population-based epidemiological study in metropolitan area of Casablanca, Morroco. *Annals of General Psychiatry, 6*, 6.
Karam, E. G., Mneimneh, Z. N., Karam, A. N., Fayyad, J. A., Nasser, S. C., Chatterji, S., & Kessler, R. C. (2006). Prevalence and treatment of mental disorders in Lebanon: A national epidemiological survey. *Lancet, 367*, 100–1006.
Kessler, R. C., Berglund, P., Demler, O., Jin, R., Merikangas, K. R., & Walters, E. E. (2005). Lifetime prevalence and age-of-onset distributions of DSM-IV disorders in the National Comorbidity Survey Replication. *Archives of General Psychiatry, 62*, 593–602.
Kessler, R. C., Chiu, W. T., Demler, O., Merikangas, K. R., & Walters, E. E. (2005). Prevalence, serverity, and comorbidity of 12-month DSM-IV disorders in the National Comorbidity Survey Replication. *Archives of General Psychiatry, 62*, 617–627.
Kessler, R. C., Sonnega, A., Bromet, E., Hughes, M., Nelson, C. B., & Breslau, N. (1999). Epidemiologic risk factors for trauma and PTSD. In R. Yehuda (Ed.), *Risk factors for posttraumatic stress disorder* (pp. 23–59). Washington, DC: American Psychiatric Press.
Kessler, R. C., Sonnega, A., Bromet, E., & Nelson, C. B. (1995). Posttraumatic stress disorder in the National Comorbidity Survey. *Archives of General Psychiatry, 52*, 1048–1060.
Koenen, K. C., Moffitt, T. E., Poulton, R., Martin, J., & Caspi, A. (2007). Early childhood factors associated with the development of post-traumatic stress disorder: Results from a longitudinal birth cohort. *Psychological Medicine, 37*(2), 181–192.
Kremen, W. S., Koenen, K. C., Boake, C., Purcell, S., Eisen, S. A., Franz, C. E., Tsuang, M. T., & Lyons, M. J. (2007). Pretrauma cognitive ability and risk for posttraumatic stress disorder: A twin study. *Archives of General Psychiatry, 64*(3), 361–368.
Kulka, R. A., Schlenger, W. E., Fairbank, J. A., Hough, R.L., Jordan, B. K., Marmar, C. R., & Weiss, D. S. (1990). *Trauma and the Vietnam War generation: Report of findings from the National Vietnam Veterans Readjustment Study*. New York: Brunner/Mazel.
Macklin, M. L., Metzger, L. J., Litz, B. T., McNally, R. J., Lasko, N. B., Orr, S. P., & Pitman, R. K. (1998). Lower precombat intelligence is a risk factor for posttraumatic stress disorder. *Journal of Consulting and Clinical Psychology*, 66(2), 323–326.
McNally, R. J. (2003). Progress and controversy in the study of posttraumatic stress disorder. *Annual Review of Psychology, 54*, 229–252.
McNally, R. J. (2007). Revisiting Dohrenwend et al.'s revisit of the National Vietnam Veterans Readjustment Study. *Journal of Traumatic Stress, 20*(4), 481–486.
McNally, R. J., & Shin, L. M. (1995). Association of intelligence with severity of posttraumatic stress disorder symptoms in Vietnam Combat veterans. *American Journal of Psychiatry, 152*(6), 936–938.
North, C. S., & Pfefferbaum, B. (2002). Research on the mental health effects of terrorism. *Journal of the American Medical Association, 288*(5), 633–636.
Ozer, E. J., Best, S. R., Lipsey, T. L., & Weiss, D. S. (2003). Predictors of posttraumatic stress disorder and symptoms in adults: A meta-analysis. *Psychological Bulletin, 129*(1), 52–73.
Perkonigg, A., Kessler, R. C., Storz, S., & Wittchen, H. U. (2000). Traumatic events and post- traumatic stress disorder in the community: Prevalence, risk facots and comorbidity. *Acta Psychiatrica Scandinavica, 101*, 46–59.
Pitman, R. K., Orr, S. P., Lowenhagen, M. J., Macklin, M. L., & Altman, B. (1991). Pre-Vietnam contents of posttraumatic stress disorder veterans' service medical and personnel records. *Comprehensive Psychiatry, 32*(5), 416–422.
Rabkin, J. G., & Struening, E. L. (1976). Life events, stress, and illness. *Science, 194* (December 3), 1013–1020.
Ramchand, R., Schell, T. L., Karney, B. R., Osilla, K. C., Burns, R. M., & Caldarone, L. B. (2010). Disparate prevalence estimates of PTSD among service members who served in Iraq

and Afghanistan: Possible explanations. *Journal of Traumatic Stress, 23*, 59–68.
Reed, P. L., Anthony, J. C., & Breslau, N. (2007). Incidence of drug problems in young adults exposed to trauma and posttraumatic stress disorder. *Archives of General Psychiatry, 64*(12), 1435–1442.
Robins, L., Cottler, L., Bucholz, K., & Compton, W. (1995) *Diagnostic interview schedule for DSM-IV.* St. Louis, MO: Washington University.
Robins, L. N., Helzer, J. E., Cottler, L., & Golding, E. (1989). *NIMH Diagnostic interview schedule, version III revised.* St. Louis, MO: Washington University.
Silva, R. R., Alpert, M., Munoz, D. M., Singh, S., Matzner, F., & Dummit, S. (2000). Stress and vulnerability to posttraumatic stress disorder in children and adolescents. *American Journal of Psychiatry, 157*(8), 1229–1235.
Smith, T. C., Ryan, M. A. K., Wingard, D. L., Slymen, D. J., Sallis, J. F., & Kritz-Silverstein, D. (2008). New onset and persistent symptoms of post-traumatic stess disorder self reported after deployment and combat exposures: Prospective population based military cohort study. *British Medical Journal, 336*, 366–371.
Stein, M. B., Walker, J. R., Hazen, A. L., & Forde, D. R. (1997). Full and partial posttraumatic stress disorder: Findings from a community survey. *American Journal of Psychiatry, 154*, 1114–1119.
Storr, C. L., Ialongo, N. S., Anthony, J. C., & Breslau, N. (2007). Childhood antecedents of exposure to traumatic events and posttraumatic stress disorder. *American Journal of Psychiatry, 164*(1), 119–125.
Tolin, D. F., & Foa, E. B. (2006). Sex differences in trauma and posttraumatic stress disorder: A quantitative review of 25 years of research. *Psychological Bulletin, 132*(6), 959–992.
Urfer-Parnas, A., Mortensen, E. L., Saebye, D., & Parnas, J. (2010). Pre-morbid IQ in mental disorders: A Danish draft-board study of 7486 psychiatric patients. *Psychological Medicine, 40*(4), 547–556.
Van Zelst, W. H., De Beurs, E., Beekman, A. T. F., Deeg, D. J. H., & Van Dyck, R. (2003). Prevalence and risk factors of posttramatic stress disorder in older adults. *Psychotherapy and Psychosomatics, 72*, 333–342.
Wilcox, H. C., Storr, C. L., & Breslau, N. (2009). Posttraumatic stress disorder and suicide attempts in a community sample of urban American young adults. *Archives of General Psychiatry, 66*(3), 305–311.
World Health Organization. (1997). *Composite international diagnostic interview (CIDI, Version 2.1.).* Geneva: Author.
Yehuda, R., & McFarlane, A. C. (1995). Conflict between current knowledge about posttraumatic stress disorder & its original conceptual basis. *American Journal of Psychiatry, 152*(12), 1705–1713.
Yehuda, R., McFarlane, A. C., & Shalev, A. Y. (1998). Predicting the development of posttraumatic stress disorder from the acute response to a traumatic event. *Biological Psychiatry, 44*(12), 1305–1313.

CHAPTER

8 Traumatic Stress Disorders in Children and Adolescents

Annette M. La Greca, Cortney J. Taylor, *and* Whitney M. Herge

Abstract

Many children and adolescents who experience potentially traumatic events, such as natural disasters, acts of violence, physical injuries, child abuse, and life-threatening medical illnesses, display significant stress symptoms. In fact, these potentially traumatic events can lead to the development of acute stress disorder (ASD) and/or posttraumatic stress disorder (PTSD) and cause significant psychological impairment. In this chapter, we discuss the types of potentially traumatic events that lead to ASD or PTSD in youth, as well as various aspects of trauma exposure. We next review available evidence on the definition, prevalence, and course of ASD and PTSD in youth, and the risk factors associated with their development. To date, relatively few studies have examined ASD and existing evidence calls into question the validity of dissociative symptoms as part of the existing ASD diagnostic criteria for youth. In contrast, many studies have evaluated PTSD and its symptoms in youth exposed to trauma, although PTSD prevalence rates vary substantially depending on a host of factors, including the type of traumatic event experienced, the degree of exposure to the event, and the informant for PTSD symptoms, among other factors. We also discuss developmental considerations for the ASD and PTSD diagnoses and directions for future research. The chapter closes with a brief summary of proposed changes to the diagnostic criteria for ASD and PTSD in youth that are being considered for the DSM-5.

Key Words: Acute stress disorder, posttraumatic stress disorder, children, adolescents, youth, exposure

Traumatic Stress Disorders in Children and Adolescents

In recent years, considerable attention has been devoted to the impact of traumatic events on children and adolescents. Studies of youths' reactions to devastating natural disasters, acts of violence, motor vehicle and other injuries, and life-threatening medical illnesses reveal that exposure to such events may cause children and adolescents significant distress and psychological impairment (see Bonanno, Brewin, Kaniasty, & La Greca, 2010; Comer & Kendall, 2007; La Greca & Prinstein, 2002; La Greca, Silverman, Vernberg, & Roberts, 2002).

Such findings are troubling in that evidence from large, representative samples suggest that, by age 16, more than two-thirds of youth have experienced at least one traumatic event (Copeland, Keeler, Angold, & Costello, 2007; Costello, Erkanli, Fairbank, & Angold, 2002). Fortunately, potentially traumatic events do not result in psychological disorder in the majority of exposed youth (Bonanno et al., 2010; Copeland et al., 2007), although many traumatized children do experience symptoms of posttraumatic stress disorder (PTSD) or other psychological difficulties (Silverman & La Greca, 2002; Vogel & Vernberg, 1993) that may interfere with their adjustment and functioning.

The present chapter provides a framework for understanding traumatic stress disorders in children and adolescents. In the sections below, we first provide an overview of the most well-studied types of traumatic events and discuss different approaches to understanding youths' exposure to traumatic events. With this background, we go on to describe studies of acute stress disorder (ASD) and of PTSD in youth. Within these later sections, we address the prevalence and course of the disorder, as well as developmental issues and key factors that play a role in the development of ASD and PTSD in youth. We close with a brief summary of the proposed changes to the diagnostic criteria for ASD and PTSD in youth for the *DSM-5*.

What Constitutes Traumatic Stress?

According to the *Diagnostic and Statistical Manual of Mental Disorders*, Fourth Edition–Text Revision (*DSM-IV-TR*; American Psychiatric Association [APA], 2000), traumatic events involve "actual or threatened death or serious injury, or threat to the physical integrity of self or others" (p. 467). Among children and adolescents, the most well studied traumatic events include natural disasters (Goenjian, Karayan, Pynoos, & Minassian, 1997; Goenjian et al., 2001; La Greca & Prinstein, 2002; La Greca, Silverman, Lai, & Jaccard, 2010; Weems et al., 2010), acts of terrorism (Gurwitch, Sitterle, Young, & Pfefferbaum, 2002; Hoven et al., 2005), war (Klingman, 2002; Llabre & Hadi, 2009), life-threatening medical conditions/injuries (Alderfer, Navsaria, & Kazak, 2009; Kassam-Adams, Marsac, & Cirilli, 2010), child physical and sexual abuse (Cohen, Deblinger, Mannarino, & de Arellano, 2001; Deblinger, Mannarino, Cohen, & Steer, 2006), and school shootings and community violence (Kupersmidt, Shahinfar, & Voegler-Lee, 2002; Nader & Mello, 2002; Pynoos et al., 1987). Although less thoroughly studied, many other events also can be potentially traumatic, including residential fires (Jones & Ollendick, 2002) and the sudden death of a parent (Copeland et al., 2007).

Given the breadth of experiences that might be potentially traumatic, there have been efforts to organize or classify potentially traumatic events, although there does not appear to be consensus on how best to do this. Nevertheless, several aspects of traumatic events may be useful to consider when evaluating their impact on youth.

One aspect concerns the scope of the event in terms of the number of individuals who are affected. Some potentially traumatic events affect a large number of individuals, as is the case for community-wide natural disasters (La Greca & Prinstein, 2002), war (Klingman, 2002), and acts of terrorism (Gurwitch et al., 2002; Hoven et al., 2005). Large-scale events often represent significant public health problems, as many individuals are affected yet the enormous scope of the event can interfere with recovery efforts and the delivery of support and psychological services for those in need (Bonanno et al., 2010).

Another important aspect of traumatic events is whether or not they involve violence directed at the individual or at a loved one. In general, events that involve violence, such as the violent death of a loved one, physical or sexual abuse, war, terrorism, or captivity, appear to be associated with higher rates of PTSD in youth than events that do not typically involve violence (Copeland et al., 2007).

Yet another relevant aspect of traumatic events is whether they represent a single incident (e.g., natural disaster, motor vehicle accident, house fire) or a chronic, repeated series of events (e.g., physical abuse, community violence, or ongoing medical treatments). In fact, some investigators have explicitly distinguished between Type I and Type II traumatic events, where Type I refers to single, acute, unpredictable stressors and Type II refers to chronic enduring stressors (Giardino, Harris, & Giardino, 2009). Different risk and resilience factors may come into play for Type I versus Type II traumatic events.

A final consideration is whether or not the event is associated with mass casualties, as may be the case for war, acts of terrorism, and some natural or human-made disasters (e.g., devastating earthquakes in Armenia). Events that involve mass casualties may be associated with significant levels of grief, bereavement, and depression (e.g., Goenjian et al., 1997, 2001), as well as stress reactions. In fact, a recent meta-analysis of children's postdisaster reactions (Furr, Comer, Edmunds, & Kendall, 2010) found that disasters with a high death toll (above 100 individuals) were associated with higher distress levels in children and youth than disasters with little loss of life.

What Constitutes Exposure to a Traumatic Event?

In general, and across many studies, there appears to be a "dose-response" relationship in that the greater a child's exposure to traumatic events, the more severe the stress reaction (Silverman & La Greca, 2002). However, there are several different indices that have been used to capture children's exposure to traumatic events, and some may be more useful and informative than others.

One indicator of exposure is the individual's *proximity* to the traumatic event. The more proximal youth are to a traumatic event, the more intense or severe their stress reactions (e.g., Furr et al., 2010; Nader & Mello, 2002; Pynoos & Nader, 1988; Schuster et al., 2001; Stuber et al., 2002), although this is not consistently the case (e.g., Garner Evans & Oehler-Stinnett, 2006). In fact, even children living very remotely from some traumatic events, such as the 2001 attacks on the World Trade Center, have reported elevated stress reactions (Schuster et al., 2001) and, conversely, children living in the same neighborhood who experience a natural disaster, such as a severe hurricane, have varied considerably in their postdisaster reactions (e.g., La Greca, Silverman, Vernberg, & Prinstein, 1996; La Greca et al., 2010). In essence, proximity is a simplistic proxy for youths' trauma exposure.

Other indicators of exposure that take into account individuals' *subjective reactions* appear to be better indicators of the impact of a potentially traumatic event. This includes youths' *perceptions of life threat* (Silverman & La Greca, 2002), which some have viewed as essential for the emergence of PTSD symptoms (e.g., Green, 1991). Considerable evidence supports the notion that the more children perceive that their lives are threatened, the greater their PTSD symptoms (see Bonanno et al., 2010; Furr et al., 2010; La Greca et al., 2010). This may explain why many children who witness extreme acts of violence, or who experience very catastrophic and destructive disasters, report elevated levels of PTSD symptoms. In fact, such events may elicit the perception of life threat in many children, even though no one may have actually been injured or hurt in that event (Silverman & La Greca, 2002). Moreover, children's threat perceptions are also important with respect to their loved ones. Events that lead to the death of a loved one (e.g., parent, friend, classmate), especially a violent death, have been associated with stress reactions in youth (see Gurwitch et al., 2002; Nader & Mello, 2002).

In addition to perceptions of life threat, youths' *subjective distress* at the time of the potentially traumatic event may be a good indicator of trauma exposure (see Furr et al., 2010; Pfefferbaum, 2005). For example, among youth ages 7 to 16 years who had various traumatic injuries, having panic attacks during the time of the trauma exposure accounted for 28% of the variance in acute stress reactions (Sinclair, Salmon, & Bryant, 2007).

Aside from youths' subjective reactions, the *loss of possessions and disruption of everyday life* in the immediate and ongoing aftermath of a traumatic event may also be a good indicator of trauma exposure, especially following natural disasters. Loss and disruption have been found to contribute to children's PTSD symptoms following disasters, even when controlling for perceptions of life threat (e.g., La Greca et al., 1996, 2010; Vernberg, La Greca, Silverman, & Prinstein, 1996; Yelland et al., 2010). For example, immediately following a destructive hurricane, children may be faced with a cascading series of disaster-related stressors, including loss of home and/or personal property, loss of pets, a change of schools, shifts in parental employment and family finances, friends moving away, altered leisure activities, and so on. Some have referred to such loss/disruption events as "secondary stressors" (e.g., Overstreet, Salloum, & Badour, 2010), as they are secondary to or caused by the traumatic event. Regardless of terminology, these stressors contribute significantly to youths' trauma reactions and may persist for many weeks, months, and even years, depending on the specific traumatic event.

Acute Stress Disorder

Definition

Acute stress disorder (ASD) is an anxiety-based disorder that affects 14–33% of the population (APA, 2000). ASD was introduced into the *DSM-IV* (American Psychiatric Association [APA], 1994) to identify individuals who were at risk for developing later PTSD symptoms (Bryant et al., 2007b).

According to the *DSM-IV Text Revision* (APA, 2000), the essential feature of ASD is "the development of characteristic anxiety, dissociative, and other symptoms that occurs within one month after exposure to an extreme traumatic stressor" (p. 469). ASD can be diagnosed in an individual who is exposed to a traumatic event (i.e., one that involves threat of safety to self or others, or threat to physical integrity) and also displays a reaction involving intense fear, helplessness, or horror. Additional criteria for a diagnosis of ASD include that the individual experiences (1) at least three *dissociative* symptoms, (2) at least one symptom of *re-experiencing* (e.g., recurrent images, thoughts, dreams, or a sense of reliving the experience), (3) marked *avoidance* of trauma-associated stimuli (e.g., avoiding thoughts, people, or places associated with the experience), and (4) marked symptoms of *anxiety or increased arousal* (e.g., problems sleeping, irritability or poor concentration), for a period of at least two days but less than one month following the traumatic event (APA, 2000).

Prevalence of ASD in Children and Adolescents

At the present time, the majority of the research on ASD has been conducted with adults. Evidence for ASD in children and youth is scant, as only a handful of studies have been conducted. Also scant is information regarding general prevalence rates for ASD, which appear to vary depending upon age and type of trauma experienced, among other factors. Specifically, "the prevalence of Acute Stress Disorder in the general population is not known" and in individuals exposed to severe traumas, estimated rates range from 14% to 33% (APA, 2000, p. 470).

Among children and adolescents (ages 5 through 17 years) exposed to various types of traumatic events, studies suggest a similar range of prevalence rates for ASD. To date, available studies of ASD in youth have focused on youth who experienced injuries, such as traffic or motor vehicle accidents (Kassam-Adams & Winston, 2004; Winston et al., 2002) or burns (Saxe et al., 2005).

Symptoms of ASD are very common following such traumatic injuries, with 88% of traffic-injured children aged 5 to 17 years reporting at least one clinically significant symptom of ASD (Winston et al., 2002). Rates of clinical disorder are markedly lower, however. For example, Kassam-Adams and Winston (2004) assessed children aged 8 to 17 years who were hospitalized after a traffic crash, finding that 8% met criteria for ASD and another 14% evidenced subclinical levels of ASD one month after their injury. Somewhat higher rates of ASD (10%) were reported by Bryant and colleagues (2007) in a study of youth aged 7 to 13 years who were treated in a medical emergency setting. A study by Daviss and colleagues (2000) of 54 youth aged 7 to 17 years hospitalized for injuries (e.g., car accidents, auto-pedestrian or auto-bicyclist accidents, falls, accidents related to skiing or snowboarding, accidental gunshots, and burns or explosions) also found that 7% met criteria for ASD and another 22% evidenced subclinical levels of ASD. Among older youth, aged 10 to 16 years, who were seen in an emergency department due to assault or motor vehicle accident, 19% met full criteria for ASD and another 25% met all the symptom criteria for ASD except for dissociation within four weeks of the traumatic event (Meiser-Stedman, Yule, Smith, Glucksman, & Dalgleish, 2005). Together these studies suggest a prevalence rate of 8–19% for ASD among youth seen in emergency medical settings following accidents or assault, but that an additional 14–25% may display clinically elevated levels of ASD that do not meet formal diagnostic criteria. Even higher rates of ASD (31%) have been observed in children aged 7 to 18 years old 10 days after they experienced severe burns (Saxe et al., 2005).

Issues Affecting the Diagnosis and Assessment of ASD in Youth

There are several challenges to evaluating and understanding ASD in youth that will be discussed briefly. These challenges pertain to developmental issues in the expression of ASD symptoms in youth, as well as the difficulty of assessing ASD in youth posttrauma and identifying the best informant for ASD in youth.

DEVELOPMENTAL ISSUES

Although there is evidence that ASD exists in youth, there are questions regarding the applicability of the current diagnostic criteria to children and youth (Meiser-Stedman, Dalgleish, Smith, Yule, Bryant, et al., 2007). Emerging evidence suggests that some features of ASD may be different in youth versus adults.

With respect to the dissociative symptom cluster of ASD, evidence from a large multisite sample suggests that there is less convergence among dissociative symptoms in children than is the case for adult samples (Meiser-Stedman, Dalgleish, Smith, Yule, & Glucksman, 2007). As a result, it appears that the requirement of three dissociative symptoms to "meet criterion" for ASD is excessively strict for youth (Meiser-Stedman et al., 2007). On a related note, studies by Meiser-Stedman et al. (2005) and Dalgleish et al. (2008) found that symptoms of dissociation did not play a significant role in predicting later PTSD among youth involved in physical assaults or motor vehicle accidents.

With respect to the avoidance symptom cluster of ASD, it appears that young children (compared with older children and adults) may not exhibit avoidance symptoms following trauma exposure but instead may show behavioral regression (March, 2003). For example, children may exhibit a loss of recently acquired developmental skills (regression) and display separation anxiety (which may be manifested by anxious clinging; Herbert, 1996; Yule, 1995).

Finally, within the re-experiencing symptom cluster of ASD, children are more likely to endorse frightening dreams *without* recognizable content, whereas adults' frightening dreams are likely to have recognizable content (Stoddard et al., 2006). In addition, a symptom that is unique to children is the presence of trauma-specific reenactment (i.e., behaviorally recreating certain aspects of the trauma such as carrying a weapon after exposure to violence; APA, 1994).

DIFFICULTIES ASSESSING ASD IN YOUTH

A major challenge for assessing and understanding ASD and its symptoms in youth pertains to the timing of assessment. It is extremely difficult to evaluate symptoms of ASD in children within the first few days or weeks after many potentially traumatic events. For example, following community-wide disasters or terrorist events, it may not be possible to assess children's symptoms of ASD during the first month postevent due to extensive rescue and reconstruction efforts (Pfferbaum, 1997) as well as widespread destruction. This challenge explains why existing studies of ASD in youth predominantly have been conducted with children seen in emergency medical settings following accidents or injuries.

Informant issues also complicate the assessment of ASD in youth. It is not clear who the best informant is for children's symptoms of ASD (i.e., is it the parents or the youth?). When child and parent reports of children's ASD symptoms have been compared, parent-child agreement is poor (Meiser-Stedman, Smith, Glucksman, Yule, & Dalgleish, 2008). Moreover, children are significantly more likely to meet criteria for ASD and its symptom clusters based on their own report than when their parent is the informant (Meiser-Stedman et al., 2008), suggesting that parents may underreport ASD symptoms in their children. Daviss and colleagues (2000) similarly found that more children met Criterion A for ASD (i.e., threat of safety to self or others, or threat to physical integrity and a reaction involving intense fear, helplessness, or horror) based on child report (93%) than on parent report (65%).

Based on available evidence, obtaining reports of ASD symptoms from both parents and children seems desirable. Because many symptoms of ASD refer to internal feelings and subjective states that are difficult for adults to detect in children, it may be best to emphasize child report, at least at this early stage of understanding ASD in youth. In this regard, recent work suggests that the Child Stress Disorders Checklist (Saxe et al., 2003) and the 4-item short form of this measure (Bosquet Enlow, Kassam-Adams, & Saxe, 2010) may be useful screening tools in acute trauma settings.

Clinical Course of ASD and Relationship of ASD to PTSD

Acute stress disorder is unique in relation to other anxiety disorders. By definition, ASD has a very clear and distinct clinical course (APA, 2000) with rapid onset and remission. Specifically, an individual can meet criteria for ASD after a minimum of two days following trauma exposure, and symptoms can last a maximum of one month following exposure. After one month, the diagnosis is no longer ASD, although if symptoms persist, a diagnosis of PTSD might be considered (see the next main chapter section, below). At this point in time, however, little data are available on the developmental course of ASD symptoms.

Because ASD is thought to be a precursor to PTSD, studies have examined whether ASD predicts PTSD in youth. The primary differences between ASD and PTSD are (1) the duration of symptoms (i.e., less than one month for ASD and greater than one month for PTSD), and (2) the presence of at least three dissociative symptoms (this is required for a diagnosis of ASD but not for PTSD; APA, 2000).

Among children and adolescents involved in motor vehicle accidents or who were victims of assault, the diagnosis of ASD has moderate success in predicting PTSD; however, a subsyndromal diagnosis of ASD without the dissociative criterion has been found to be as good or even better in predicting PTSD than the full ASD diagnosis (Kassam-Adams & Winston, 2004; Meiser-Stedman et al., 2005). Similarly, among youth aged 6 to17 years who experienced motor vehicle accidents, ASD without dissociation was a significant predictor of PTSD. In fact, subsyndromal ASD was almost three times more sensitive than the full ASD diagnosis in predicting PTSD (Dalgleish et al., 2008). These findings call into question the importance of the dissociative symptoms of ASD in predicting subsequent PTSD in youth who are exposed to traumatic events.

The link between ASD and PTSD has also been examined in youth with serious medical injuries. In a sample of primarily male African-American youth, aged 8 to 17 years, who sustained injuries in a variety of situations (e.g., pedestrian or bicyclist struck by vehicle, motor vehicle passenger in a crash, or bicycle fall), Kassam-Adams and Winston (2004) found that ASD was not a good predictor of PTSD. Specifically, 60% of youth who developed PTSD did not meet criteria for even subsyndromal ASD; however, if the dissociative criteria were removed, the other ASD symptoms displayed sensitivity in predicting PTSD while retaining moderate specificity. Moreover, in another sample of primarily African-American youth (aged 12 to 17 years) who sustained injuries, youths' ratings of depression and acute stress predicted subsequent PTSD symptoms (Pailler, Kassam-Adams, Datner, & Fein, 2007). Taken together, existing findings with youth who are exposed to a traumatic injury suggests that there is "convergent evidence that the ASD diagnosis is overly restrictive" (Salmon, Sinclair, & Bryant, 2007, p. 204). Acute stress symptoms, *other than those that reflect dissociation*, appear to be as good or better predictors of subsequent PTSD than the ASD diagnosis.

Association of ASD with Functional Impairment

There is some limited initial evidence that there are functional impairments in youth with ASD. For example, among adolescents hospitalized for various injuries, the ASD diagnosis was significantly associated with short- and long-term reductions in quality of life (Holbrook et al., 2005).

Although there is scant literature on functional impairment among youth with ASD, adults with ASD have been shown to experience impairment in cognitive functioning, particularly with respect to cognitive biases. For example, Smith and Bryant (2000) found that adults with ASD exhibited negative cognitive biases in three domains: external harm (e.g., "your house will be blacked out"), somatic symptoms (e.g., "your heart will beat faster") and social situations (e.g., "a friend will forget to meet you"). In contrast, adults without an ASD diagnosis did not exhibit cognitive biases in these three areas. Typically, individuals who suffer from anxiety disorders exhibit cognitive biases specific to those disorders (Foa, Franklin, Perry, & Herbert, 1996); for example, individuals with social phobia have anxiety specific to social situations. However, it appears that individuals who experience a traumatic event develop larger fear networks than those suffering from other anxiety disorders, and thus may display event-specific and non-event-specific cognitive biases (Foa, Steketee, & Rothbaum, 1989; Smith & Bryant, 2000).

In general, evidence for functional impairment among youth with ASD is sparse. Further research on functional impairment among youth with ASD will be important and necessary for supporting the validity of the ASD diagnosis in this population.

Risk Factors for ASD

Because ASD may be a pathway to the development of PTSD in traumatized youth, it is important to consider risk and resilience factors that may contribute to ASD. Such information also may inform intervention and prevention programs for youth exposed to trauma. The risk factors studied, thus far, can be organized into those that reflect: (1) the pretrauma characteristics of the child, (2) trauma-specific factors, and (3) other aspects of child and family functioning.

PRETRAUMA CHILD CHARACTERISTICS

Limited data are available regarding the role of pretrauma child characteristics as risk factors for ASD. In one study, female gender was a risk factor for ASD among adolescents hospitalized for traumatic injuries (Holbrook et al., 2005). Further, younger child age was associated with greater ASD symptoms among youth, 7 to 18 years, who experienced injuries due to a variety of sources (e.g., being struck as a pedestrian, motor vehicle accidents, falls, gunshot wounds/stabbings, bicycle accidents, assaults, suffocation; Saxe et al., 2005). At the same time, other studies of youth exposed to assault or motor vehicle accidents have not found associations between pretrauma child characteristics (i.e., previous history of trauma, prior mental health problems, and female sex) and rates of ASD (Meiser-Stedman, Dalgleish, Smith, Yule, Bryant, et al., 2007). Because pretrauma child characteristics are associated with the development of PTSD (Silverman & La Greca, 2002), as discussed later in this chapter, further study of the role of child characteristics in predicting children's ASD reactions appears to be important and desirable.

TRAUMA-RELATED VARIABLES

Variables directly associated with the traumatic event also may contribute to the development of ASD symptoms in youth. For example, Stoddard and colleagues (2006) studied young children (aged 1–4 years) who were burn victims, finding that a larger burn, more pain due to the burn, and a higher mean pulse rate while hospitalized were each associated with acute stress symptoms. Similarly, Saxe et al. (2005) found that children's reports of pain at the time of injury (due to motor vehicle accidents and other events) were associated with symptoms of ASD.

Across several studies, the *subjective severity of the threat* (for assault and motor vehicle accident victims) and *perceived life threat* (due to intentional or violence-related injuries) have been associated with ASD in youth (Holbrook et al., 2005; Meiser-Stedman et al., 2007). Together these findings suggest that life-threatening aspects of the traumatic event are associated with the development of ASD in youth.

OTHER CHILD CHARACTERISTICS: COGNITIVE FACTORS

Several cognitive factors have been associated with the likelihood that children will develop ASD following a traumatic event. For example, in a sample of primarily minority youth, aged 10 to 16 years, who were exposed to assaults or motor vehicle accidents, youths' beliefs about the utility of worry and their tendency to ruminate in response to affective disturbance were associated with early traumatic stress reactions (Meiser-Stedman et al., 2007). Further, in a study of children, aged 7 to 13 years, who were hospitalized after traumatic injury, children's negative appraisals of their vulnerability (i.e., appraisals of being a "feeble person in a scary world") accounted for 44% of the variance in acute stress reactions (Salmon et al., 2007).

Thus, several studies provide some support for the notion that cognitive factors are related to children's symptoms of ASD following traumatic events. Specifically, youths' beliefs about worry, their rumination, and their appraisals of being vulnerable all may influence the development of ASD symptoms.

PARENTAL FUNCTIONING

Finally, parents' psychological functioning and their own stress reactions may influence the development of ASD symptoms in youth. For example, among burn victims, higher parental stress levels were associated with greater ASD symptoms in their children (Stoddard et al., 2006). Also, among youth aged 7 to 18 years who reported various injuries, greater parental psychological distress and higher family strain/life stress were associated with ASD in youth (Saxe et al., 2005).

Conclusions

Overall, there is surprisingly little information on ASD in youth. The existing evidence suggests that: (1) symptoms of ASD do exist in youth although the diagnosis of ASD may be too restrictive for youth; (2) the ASD diagnosis and the ASD symptoms of dissociation are not good predictors of subsequent PTSD in youth exposed to traumatic events; and (3) ASD is associated with poor quality of life for youth, although evidence in this area is very sparse. In light of this comparatively new literature, there are numerous directions for future research on the relevance of the diagnosis and symptoms of ASD in trauma-exposed youth.

First, there is a need for better and more developmentally appropriate criteria for assessing ASD in youth. Second, there is also a need for developmentally appropriate assessment tools for measuring ASD in youth. Third, there are fundamental questions regarding the exact presentation of ASD symptoms in youth, and whether this is a meaningful and relevant diagnosis for youth. Fourth, assuming research continues to support the validity of the ASD diagnosis, there is a need for the development of effective interventions for youth with ASD and other early trauma reactions (e.g., see Cox, Kenardy, & Hendrikz, 2010). Overall, our understanding of ASD in youth is preliminary at this time, and further inquiry is needed to better understand the impact and relevance of ASD in youth.

Posttraumatic Stress Disorder (PTSD)

Definition

When the diagnostic category of PTSD was introduced in the third edition of the American Psychiatric Association's *Diagnostic and Statistical Manual of Mental Disorders*, it was primarily considered to be an adult disorder. However, an increasing awareness that children and adolescents also experience PTSD led to modifications in the diagnosis that are reflected in the *DSM-IV* (published in 1994) and the most recent *DSM-IV-TR* (APA, 2000).

As with ASD, PTSD is an anxiety disorder that may develop after an individual experiences or witnesses an event that involves actual or threatened serious harm or death, either to oneself or to others, and the individual's reaction to the event includes intense fear, helplessness, or horror (APA, 2000). Among children and youth, this latter criterion also may be expressed as disorganized or agitated behavior.

Moreover, for a diagnosis of PTSD, individuals must meet specific criteria for three additional symptom clusters: re-experiencing, avoidance/numbing, and hyper-arousal. *Re-experiencing* symptoms include recurrent or intrusive thoughts or dreams about the event and intense distress at reminders of the event. For young children, re-experiencing may be reflected in repetitive play with traumatic themes or by reenactment of traumatic events in play, drawings, or verbalizations (e.g., Perrin, Smith, & Yule, 2000). *Avoidance or numbing* symptoms include efforts to avoid thoughts, feelings, or conversations about the traumatic event, avoiding reminders of the event, diminished interest in normal activities, and feeling detached or removed from others. *Hyper-arousal* symptoms include difficulty sleeping or concentrating, irritability, angry outbursts, hyper-vigilance, and an exaggerated startle response; these behaviors must represent a change from the individual's prior levels of functioning.

For a diagnosis of PTSD, the above symptoms must be evident for at least one month and be accompanied by significant impairment in functioning (e.g., problems in school, or in social or family relations). If these symptoms persist for less than three months, the diagnosis would be specified as acute, whereas symptoms lasting for more than three months would be specified as chronic (APA, 2000).

Prevalence

Estimating the prevalence of PTSD in youth is extremely difficult because it varies depending on multiple factors, including type of trauma experienced, degree of exposure, child age at exposure, time since the traumatic event occurred, and the measurement method used to evaluate PTSD (La Greca & Silverman, 2006). As with ASD, parents appear to underreport children's symptoms of PTSD (e.g., Meiser-Stedman et al., 2008; Vogel & Vernberg, 1993) so that prevalence rates based on parent report are likely to be substantially lower than those based on child report.

As noted earlier, the experience of trauma in childhood is common, with epidemiological studies reporting that the majority of youth experience one or more traumatic events by 16 or 17 years of age (see Copeland et al., 2007; Costello et al., 2002; Fairbank, 2008; Finkelhor, Ormrod, Turner, & Hamby, 2005; Kilpatrick & Saunders, 1997). At the same time, estimates of PTSD prevalence rates in youth are substantially lower, ranging from 0.5% (see Fairbank, 2008; Heiervang, et al., 2007) to 10.4% (Breslau, Davis, Andreski, & Peterson, 1991). Nevertheless, community prevalence rates may not provide a full picture of the impact of trauma on youth, as such studies do not account for the magnitude of the traumatic event, for the degree to which the child was directly exposed to the event, or for the amount of time that elapsed since the event occurred, among other important variables.

Below, we briefly describe PTSD prevalence rates in youth by the type of traumatic event. The study methodologies have varied substantially, and so gaining a precise estimate of prevalence is exceedingly difficult. In describing the literature we emphasized the well-designed studies, when possible, to provide an approximation of PTSD prevalence rates. In addition, some investigators focus on the diagnosis of PTSD, others on evaluating PTSD symptoms in a continuous or dimensional manner, and still others on combining the two approaches. In summarizing this literature, we attempt to differentiate rates for "clinically significant" PTSD and for the PTSD diagnosis from rates that have been reported for subsyndromal (or subclinical) levels of PTSD symptoms, which also may impair children's functioning. The reader is also referred to two excellent reviews of PTSD in youth (Cohen, Berliner, & Mannarino, 2010; American Academy of Child and Adolescent Psychiatry, 1998).

NATURAL DISASTERS AND ACTS OF TERRORISM

Among youth who are exposed to destructive natural disasters and acts of terrorism, elevated symptoms of PTSD are very common during the first few months postevent (Comer & Kendall, 2007; Silverman & La Greca, 2002). For example, three months after Hurricane Andrew, La Greca and colleagues (La Greca et al., 1996; Vernberg et al., 1996) found that 55% of the children surveyed reported at least moderate levels of PTSD symptom severity and nearly all of the children (90%) reported at least one re-experiencing symptom. After acts of terrorism, such as the 2001 attacks on the World Trade Center, even 10–11-year-olds living outside the

United States (who viewed the events on television) reported symptoms of PTSD (Holmes, Creswell, & O'Connor, 2007).

Much less common, however, are clinically significant levels of PTSD symptoms or PTSD diagnoses. With few exceptions, studies report rates of clinically significant PTSD that are below 30%, and in most studies the rates are 15% or less (see Bonanno et al., 2010) when the time frame is a year or more postdisaster.

In general, rates of clinically significant PTSD are highest in the first few months postdisaster, but then appear to decline over time, especially over the first year postdisaster (see Comer & Kendall, 2007; La Greca & Silverman, 2006; Silverman & La Greca, 2002). For example, three months after a devastating and highly destructive natural disaster (Hurricane Andrew), La Greca and colleagues (1996) found that 39% of the children in their community sample may have "met criteria" for PTSD based on screening measures, but this reduced to 24% at seven months postdisaster, and to 18% by ten months postdisaster. In that study, rates of "clinically significant" PTSD symptom severity (i.e., corresponding to "severe or very severe" levels of posttraumatic stress on the PTSD-Reaction Index, believed to be a good indicator of a PTSD diagnosis) were 29% at three months postdisaster, 18% at seven months postdisaster, and 13% at ten months postdisaster.

Although clinically significant PTSD symptoms decline over the first year postdisaster, it appears that further declines are more gradual. In a recent study of children affected by Hurricane Charley (La Greca et al., 2010), a destructive Category 4 hurricane, 13% of the youth living in affected areas of Charlotte County, Florida, reported clinically significant PTSD at nine months postdisaster, but this was only reduced to 10% a year later (21 months postdisaster). Similarly, Shaw and colleagues (1996) evaluated a small sample of youth who were affected by Hurricane Andrew, finding that most (70%) of the youth who displayed elevated PTSD symptoms at nine months postdisaster continued to display elevated symptoms a year later (21 months postdisaster). Thus, for the most part, children who have not "recovered" almost a year after a disaster event appear to be at high risk for chronic, elevated, and persistent PTSD.

A few studies observed rates of clinically significant PTSD that are substantially higher than the rates reported above (e.g., Goenjian et al., 2000, 2001, 2005; also see Comer & Kendall, 2007); in such cases, the disasters were associated with very severe destruction and substantial loss of life. For example, following an Armenian earthquake that claimed 25,000 casualties, the rate of "likely PTSD" in adolescents living near the area of destruction exceeded 50%; this rate was maintained more than a year following the disaster, and may reflect the magnitude of the event (Goenjian et al., 1995, 1997). Similarly, Goenjian and colleagues (2000) estimated rates of PTSD for 78 Armenian youth exposed to a severe or mild earthquake or to severe violence at 1.5 and 4.5 years postdisaster. Of the youth exposed to the severe disasters/violence, between 73% and 95% reported symptoms consistent with "estimated PTSD" at one of the two time points, in comparison to 13.8% (at 1.5 years) and 6.9% (at 4.5 years) of the youth exposed to a mild earthquake.

Elevated rates of PTSD were also observed among youth who survived the sinking of the cruise ship *Jupiter* off the coast of Greece. With over 400 British students aboard, this ship sank 40 minutes after being struck by a massive tanker. Studies of the survivors revealed that 51.5% developed PTSD at some point following the disaster (Bolton, O'Ryan, Udwin, Boyle, & Yule, 2000; Yule et al., 2000; see Yule, Udwin, & Bolton, 2002 for a review). Such high rates of PTSD likely reflect the severity and magnitude of this event.

Recent work on youth affected by war or terrorism generally supports the notion that rates of PTSD in affected youth are 30% or less, and mostly 15% or less. For example, a study of 2999 Israeli adolescents, who varied with respect to their degree of exposure to terror incidents, found that 4.5% of the boys and 5.6% of the girls reported clinically significant PTSD (i.e., severe to very severe symptoms levels; Laufer & Solomon, 2009). A path analysis revealed that higher levels of fear and exposure both contributed significantly to PTSD symptom levels. Another study of 695 Israeli adolescents exposed to ongoing terrorism (Pat-Horenczyk et al., 2007) found that 7.6% of the youth met criteria for a probable diagnosis of PTSD. Further, a study comparing Israeli and Palestinian youth exposed to ongoing violence found that 6.8% of Israeli youth and 37.2% of Palestinian youth met criteria for PTSD (Pat-Horenczyk et al., 2009). The substantially higher rates of PTSD among Palestinian youth were associated with much higher levels of violence exposure for these youth (Pat-Horenczyk et al., 2009).

PERSONAL INJURY/ACCIDENT

Compared to youth exposed to severe natural disasters and acts of terrorism, studies of youth following personal injuries or accidents reveal a somewhat lower and more restricted range of PTSD prevalence. In general, at six months or more postevent, approximately 6–19% of youth may meet criteria for PTSD following personal injury, such as motor vehicle accidents, accidental injury or physical assault (Bryant, Salmon, Sinclair & Davidson, 2007a, 2007b; Casswell, 1997; Kassam-Adams & Winston, 2004; Meiser-Stedman, Dalgleish, Glucksman, Yule & Smith, 2009; Meiser-Stedman et al., 2008, 2005; Pailler et al., 2007). However, during the first month or two posttrauma, rates of PTSD may be higher (30–35%).

In one of the first large-scale studies of PTSD among youth involved in traffic accidents, Stallard and colleagues (1998) evaluated 119 youth (aged 5 to 18 years) 22 to 79 days after they were seen in an emergency medical setting following a road traffic accident and compared them to 66 children who were treated in the same medical setting for sports injuries. PTSD prevalence rates based on child report were 34.5% for youth involved in road traffic accidents versus 3.0% for those with sports injuries; in this study, youths' perception of life threat was a significant predictor of PTSD.

Kassam-Adams and Winston (2004) assessed children who were hospitalized following motor-vehicle injuries, finding that 6% met criteria for PTSD three or more months postinjury, and another 11% exhibited subsyndromal symptoms. These findings are similar to those of Landolt and colleagues (2005), who examined the prevalence and course of PTSD symptoms in children (N = 68; 6.5–14.5 years of age) after road traffic accidents. They found that the prevalence of moderate to severe PTSD symptoms (which combined clinical and subclinical levels of PTSD) was 16.2% at 4–6 weeks and 17.6% at 12 months posttrauma; children's PTSD symptom scores did not decrease over the course of the study. Finally, a review of 12 studies that evaluated PTSD among children and adolescents injured in accidents (Olofsson, Bunketorp, & Andersson, 2009) found that the prevalence of PTSD was almost 30% at 1 to 2 months posttrauma, but declined to 13% at 3 to 6 months posttrauma.

Taken together, most available evidence is consistent with the child disaster literature, in that rates of clinically significant and subclinical PTSD are often highest during the first few months postinjury, but decline over time. After one year postinjury, it is rare to see rates of PTSD (clinical diagnoses) that exceed 15%.

CHILD ABUSE AND INTERPERSONAL VIOLENCE

Although exact prevalence rates are difficult to estimate, it appears that children and youth exposed to physical abuse, and especially to child sexual abuse, report among the highest levels of PTSD (e.g., Deblinger, McLeer, Atkins, Ralphe, & Foa, 1989; Paolucci, Genuis, & Violato, 2001). For example, the National Center for Posttraumatic Stress Disorder (http://www.ptsd.va.gov/public/pages/ptsd-children-adolescents.asp) indicates that rates of PTSD are as high as 90% among sexually abused children. In a recent study, Carey and colleagues (2008) evaluated 94 South African youth (aged 8–19 years) who were exposed to at least one lifetime trauma. High rates of PTSD were observed (63.8%) and were associated with trauma exposure and especially child sexual abuse. Similarly, Bernard-Bonnin and colleagues (2008) found that girls (aged 6–12 years) who reported sexual abuse in a pediatric setting had a substantially higher prevalence of PTSD clinical scores (46.3%) than girls who did not report such abuse (18.5%).

One methodological problem in research examining the long-term impact of abuse has been that reports of abuse are often assessed retrospectively. However, one recent prospective study (Scott, Smith, & Ellis, 2010) used data from a national child protection agency database to document abuse and examine 12-month and lifetime prevalence of mental health disorders in older adolescents/young adults (aged 16–27 years). Findings revealed that odds of 12-month PTSD were five times higher for abused individuals than for controls, and these odds were even higher when retrospective abuse reports (from control participants) were removed from the study analyses. Such findings clearly document subsequent PTSD in youth who are abused.

Unlike youth who are exposed to natural disasters or other single-incident acute stressors, many abused youth experience multiple forms of trauma, and this additional trauma exposure may also contribute to the high rates of PTSD observed among abused youth. For example, Cohen, Deblinger, Mannarino, and Steer (2004) evaluated the efficacy of trauma-focused cognitive behavioral therapy for sexually abused youth, 8 to 14 years of age. Most (89%) of the 203 youth in the final treatment sample met full criteria for PTSD, and other types of trauma exposure were common among the youth, including the sudden unexpected death or life-threatening illness of a loved one (70%), witnessing domestic violence (58%), being a victim of physical abuse (26%), and being a victim of community violence (17%). In fact, on average, the children experienced 2.66 traumatic events in addition to sexual abuse (Cohen et al., 2004).

Symptoms of PTSD are also common among youth exposed to community violence events (see Kupersmidt et al., 2002), another potentially chronic stressor. Youth exposed to community violence often experience multiple forms of victimization. For example, data from the National Survey of Adolescents (Ford, Elhai, Connor, & Frueh, 2010) revealed that polyvictimization was common among community violence victims (15.5%), as well as victims of physical assault (9%) and abuse (8%). In turn, youth with polyvictimization were more likely to have psychiatric diagnoses, including PTSD, than youth exposed to disaster or accident trauma.

Developmental Issues in the Diagnosis of PTSD

As with ASD, there is an emerging debate about the degree to which current diagnostic criteria apply to children and adolescents. Because the PTSD diagnosis was originally based on symptoms evidenced by adult combat veterans (Grinage, 2003), it is possible, and even likely, that symptoms experienced by youth may differ as a function of development. For example, for the re-experiencing symptom cluster, rather than visual flashbacks, children may re-experience trauma through play or drawing (see Perrin et al., 2000). Additionally, following trauma exposure, children and adolescents may report separation-based anxiety symptoms and become fearful of leaving their parents (see American Academy of Child and Adolescent Psychiatry, 1998; Vogel & Vernberg, 1993). A review of research on the expression of PTSD in youth (Scheeringa, Zeanah, & Cohen, 2010) recommended that developmental manifestations of PTSD be incorporated into the *DSM-5* diagnostic criteria and that the criteria for "avoidance/numbing" be reduced from three to one symptom for preschool children.

Additional evidence suggests that the organization of the PTSD symptom clusters may be different for youth than for adults. Anthony and colleagues (1999) conducted a confirmatory factor analysis of self-reported PTSD symptoms in youth exposed to Hurricane Hugo, finding that the best-fitting model did not match the diagnostic criteria in either *DSM-III-R* or *DSM-IV* (American Psychiatric Association [APA], 1987, 1994). Rather, these researchers identified three symptom clusters—intrusion/active avoidance, numbing/passive avoidance, and arousal—that best accounted for youths' posttrauma symptoms and appeared to be consistent from late childhood to late adolescence. A subsequent investigation (Anthony et al., 2005) cross-validated the model of PTSD in two populations (children exposed to Hurricanes Andrew and Hugo) and demonstrated the model's factorial invariance. In contrast, a study of the factor structure of PTSD symptoms in youth who survived injuries (Kassam-Adams, Marsac, & Cirilli, 2010) revealed a good fit with the traditional three-factor model, but also found a good fit with two alternative four-factor models. Although these exploratory models acknowledge that the structure of PTSD may be different in youth compared to adults, they do not take into account youth-specific symptoms of PTSD.

Other recent studies that included stress symptoms associated with PTSD have identified five- or six-factor models of PTSD in youth. For example, Bulut (2004) analyzed youths' ($N = 152$, aged 6–18 years) stress symptoms following exposure to a tornado, identifying a five-factor model that included: blocking/vigilance (e.g., blocking thoughts and memories of the event), affective/adjustment difficulties (e.g., feeling guilty and/or angry), re-experiencing/intrusion (e.g., intrusive thoughts or dreams), somatic/attachment problems (e.g., separation anxiety), and sense of foreshortened future (e.g., feeling one will not marry or live a long life). Also following tornado exposure, Garner Evans and Oehler-Stinnett (2006) identified a six-factor model of posttraumatic stress among youth (aged 6–12 years) that included avoidance, re-experiencing, interpersonal alienation, interference with daily functioning, physical symptoms/anxiety, and sense of a foreshortened future.

It is possible that these alternate models of PTSD, as described above and elsewhere (e.g., Ford, Elhai, Ruggiero, & Frueh, 2009), may be more relevant for traumatized youth than the current conceptualization of PTSD, although further study is necessary. Existing work has focused almost exclusively on youth affected by natural disasters, and needs to be extended to youth experiencing other types of traumatic events. Further, it should be recognized that even among adults, the symptom structure of

PTSD is somewhat controversial and research has suggested alternate models of PTSD (e.g., Asmundson et al., 2000; Cox, Mota, Clara, & Asmundson, 2008).

Clinical Course of PTSD

Few studies have followed trauma-exposed youth prospectively over an extended period of time, making it difficult to estimate the course of PTSD. However, as noted earlier, at least among high-impact events such as natural disasters and acts of terrorism, it appears that PTSD symptoms may emerge in the days, weeks, or months following the trauma, and can take months or even years, to resolve (Green et al., 1994; Gurwitch et al., 2002; La Greca et al., 1996; La Greca, Silverman, & Wasserstein, 1998; La Greca et al., 2010; Shaw et al., 1996; Vincent, 1997; Yule et al., 2002).

Also as noted earlier, for most youth exposed to disasters, the typical course of PTSD is one of decreasing intensity over time, especially during the first year (Bonanno et al., 2010; La Greca & Silverman, 2006). After that period, PTSD symptoms appear to decline more slowly (e.g., La Greca et al., 2010; Shaw et al., 1996) and may remain persistently elevated in a significant number of youth. For example, of the youth who survived the sinking of the cruise ship *Jupiter*, over 50% met criteria for PTSD following the disaster and most of these youth (70%) reported a PTSD duration of more than a year (Yule et al., 2002). Similarly, among children who reported moderate to severe PTSD symptoms 10 months after Hurricane Andrew, more than 60% continued to show elevated symptoms 42 months after the disaster (Vincent, 1997).

In the longest available follow-up study of children exposed to a disaster, Green and colleagues (1994) evaluated 99 child survivors (initially aged 2–15 years) of the Buffalo Creek dam collapse. At 2 years postdisaster, rates of PTSD were 32% in the youth and declined to 7% at 17 years postdisaster; interestingly, all of the later cases of PTSD were women.

Overall, longitudinal data of youth postdisaster are sparse, yet encouraging (Bonanno et al., 2010). Although further studies are needed, data suggest that the majority of youth recover from disaster-related trauma exposure, although problems persist in a significant minority of youth.

Across studies of youth who experienced abuse or neglect, a somewhat different picture emerges—one of more persistent PTSD. For example, Widom (1999) evaluated a large cohort of victims of child abuse and neglect and a matched group of youth who were not abused or neglected, following the participants (N = 1,196) into adulthood. Widom found that 37.5% of the child sexual abuse victims, 32.7% of the physically abused youth, and 30.6% of the neglected youth met criteria for lifetime PTSD. A subsequent study (Koenen & Widom, 2009) re-examined the 674 individuals in the sample who had documented histories of child abuse or neglect, finding that lifetime prevalence of PTSD differed significantly by gender; rates of PTSD ranged from 15.8% to 25.4% for the male victims of abuse and from 41.8% to 44.7% for female victims, with the highest rates of lifetime PTSD and the greatest gender difference apparent for child sexual abuse victims.

DELAYED ONSET

Studies have not systematically examined whether children display "delayed onset" PTSD. Individuals with delayed onset PTSD do not meet diagnostic criteria for PTSD at six months posttrauma, but do at some later point in time (see Bryant & Harvey, 2002, for a review). Initial research with adults has shown that those with delayed onset PTSD typically show elevated levels of posttraumatic stress (PTS) immediately after the trauma and even six months after the trauma, however their symptoms are subsyndromal and are not sufficient to meet diagnostic criteria (Bryant & Harvey, 2002). Following a deterioration in coping ability over time, or perhaps due to increased stressors, an individual may eventually report enough symptoms, or symptoms of sufficient severity, to warrant a PTSD diagnosis (Bryant & Harvey, 2002).

Some studies suggest a delayed onset of clinically significant PTSD symptoms for a very small percentage of youth who were surveyed following natural disasters or after road traffic accidents (e.g., John, Russell, & Russell, 2007; Landolt et al., 2005), although studies have not systematically evaluated children at multiple time points, using sound diagnostic measures of PTSD (such as clinical interviews). A recent study of child survivors of Hurricane Charley (La Greca et al., 2010) found that only 4% of the youth might be considered "delayed onset" in that they exceeded clinical cutoffs for PTSD symptoms at 21 months but not at 9 months postdisaster; however, several of these youth were close to the clinical cutoffs at 9 months postdisaster. In a review of disaster literature, La Greca and

Silverman (2006) caution that if a child does not report PTSD symptoms within the first few months following trauma exposure, it is unlikely that clinically significant disaster-related PTSD symptoms will develop later on.

Concerning other forms of trauma, research with adult injury survivors assessed at 3 and 12 months posttrauma found that 10% of the sample met criteria for PTSD at 12 months; however, approximately half of those cases were delayed onset (Carty, O'Donnell, & Creamer, 2006). Further, research with adults exposed to the 2001 World Trade Center attacks found that increases in negative life events and decreases in self-esteem over time were related to delayed onset PTSD (Adams & Boscarino, 2009). Similar research needs to be conducted with children and adolescent populations to better understand the parameters of delayed onset PTSD in youth.

COMORBIDITY/OTHER DISORDERS

In addition to PTSD, exposure to traumatic events has been associated with symptoms of grief, depression, anxiety, stress-related health problems, and increased substance use (see Bonanno et al., 2010, for more details). Thus, it is not surprising that PTSD also can be comorbid with these other psychological conditions.

In fact, evidence indicates that PTSD in youth is commonly comorbid with other disorders, especially depression and other anxiety disorders. For example, in a large national sample of adolescents, Kilpatrick and colleagues (2003) found that nearly 75% of the youth who met criteria for PTSD displayed comorbid diagnoses of depression or substance use. High levels of comorbidity between PTSD and depression have been found in youth affected by natural disasters (e.g., Goenjian et al., 1995, 2005), youth residing in refugee camps during war conflict (Thabet, Abed, & Vostanis, 2004), and adolescent survivors of physical abuse (Malmquist, 1986; Pelcovitz et al., 1994). Others have found that PTSD is often comorbid with anxiety disorders (e.g., Kar & Bastia, 2006) and is more likely to develop in youth who are anxious pretrauma (e.g., La Greca et al., 1998; Weems & Carrion, 2007).

Traumatized youth may also display significant behavior problems (Cohen et al., 2010). Moreover, many youth with PTSD experience comorbid complicated bereavement and clinically significant grief reactions, particularly when their trauma exposure involved the death of a loved one (Harris-Hendriks, Black, & Kaplan, 1993; Pynoos, 1992).

Although comorbidity between PTSD and other disorders is high, in many cases the underlying etiological pathways are not well understood. Specifically, it is not clear whether traumatic events lead to both PTSD and other disorders, whether PTSD is more likely to occur in youth with preexisting mental health disorders, or whether the presence of PTSD plays a causal role in the development of other disorders (see Perrin et al., 2000). Some evidence suggests that pretrauma elevations in anxiety and depression can play a role in the development of PTSD in youth exposed to disasters (see Bonanno et al., 2010; La Greca et al., 1998; Weems & Carrion, 2007). Other work suggests that symptoms of depression may develop over time in youth who evidence disaster-related PTSD (see Yule et al., 2002).

Risk Factors for PTSD Symptoms

A number of factors may heighten youths' risk for developing PTSD following trauma exposure. In fact, there is considerable interest in "risk and resilience" factors that play a role in youths' posttrauma reactions, as knowledge of these factors may lead to the development of developmentally appropriate evidence-based interventions for traumatized youth (La Greca, 2008; La Greca & Silverman, 2009). Although a comprehensive review of risk and resilience factors contributing to youths' PTS reactions is beyond the scope of this chapter, below we provide a brief summary of several pretrauma risk factors that contribute to youths' PTSD. The reader is referred to several reviews for further details (Bonanno et al., 2010; Brewin, Andrews, & Valentine, 2000; Fedroff, Taylor, Asmundson, & Koch, 2000; Furr et al., 2010).

Not surprisingly, the most well-studied pretrauma child characteristics include children's age, gender, and ethnicity, as these do not change as a result of trauma exposure, and thus can be assessed accurately even after a traumatic event has occurred. Harder to assess, but also important, are youths' prior trauma exposure and prior mental health functioning.

AGE

The association between child age and the development of PTSD is complex (see Vogel & Vernberg, 1993). For example, the assessment of PTSD in youth is complicated by young children's relative inability to describe their internal states verbally and the consequent reliance on parent reports of symptoms (Vogel & Vernberg, 1993; Stuber, Nader, Yasuda, Pynoos, & Cohen, 1991). This is particularly problematic since parents underestimate children's PTSD symptoms (e.g., Meiser-Stedman et al., 2008; Vogel & Vernberg, 1993).

A comprehensive review of the disaster literature over a 20-year period (Norris et al., 2002) identified children as a vulnerable population for adverse psychological reactions following disasters, compared to adult disaster survivors. Further, although findings are mixed, some evidence indicates that younger children report higher levels of PTSD symptoms following disasters than older youth or adolescents (e.g., Bokszczanin, 2007; McDermott, Lee, Judd, & Gibbon, 2005; Weems et al., 2010; Yelland et al., 2010). For example, a large-scale study (Hoven et al., 2005) of New York City schoolchildren (in grades 4–12), conducted six months after the attacks on the World Trade Center, found that the younger children (those in grades 4 and 5) were the most affected. At the same time, a recent meta-analysis of children's reactions to disasters and terrorist events did not find that child age was significantly associated with youths' PTSD symptoms (Furr et al., 2010).

Given these mixed findings, studies that evaluate youth across a broad age range, use developmentally appropriate measures, and consider multiple types of traumatic events are needed. Such studies will be useful in enhancing our understanding of child age or developmental level as a risk factor for PTSD.

GENDER

Girls typically report more symptoms of PTSD than boys following trauma exposure (Furr et al., 2010; Gurwitch et al., 2002; Hoven et al., 2005; Norris et al., 2002; Weems et al., 2010). However, when gender differences have been found, their magnitude often has been modest (La Greca & Silverman, 2006).

One potential explanation for why girls are at greater risk than boys for developing PTSD or its symptoms is that girls may experience greater subjective life threat during a traumatic event (see Bonanno et al., 2010). For example, in the aftermath of Hurricane Mitch in Nicaragua, Goenjian and colleagues (2001) found that adolescent girls reported more PTS symptoms than boys; however, this association no longer held when adolescents' subjective life threat was controlled in the statistical analyses. Further research that examines the potential mechanisms that contribute to girls' greater vulnerability to PTSD following traumatic events would be important and desirable.

ETHNICITY

Although evidence is mixed (e.g., Garrison, Weinrich, Hardin, Weinrich, & Wang, 1993), community samples of youth exposed to disasters suggests that ethnic minority youth report more PTSD symptoms and have more difficulty recovering from traumatic events than nonminority youth (see La Greca & Silverman, 2006; Rabalais, Ruggiero, & Scotti, 2002). The underlying mechanisms that might account for ethnic differences have not been well studied, but one possibility is that ethnic minority youth and families may have less adequate financial resources to cope with the loss and destruction that is often associated with a major disaster (La Greca & Silverman, 2006). Prior trauma exposure, which might be more common among minority versus nonminority youth, also could play a role in the elevated symptoms of PTSD observed among some minority youth postdisaster (see La Greca & Silverman, 2006). The role of ethnicity and other cultural factors in youth's PTSD is a critical area for further research, and is necessary for developing culturally appropriate clinical interventions.

PRIOR TRAUMA

Prior trauma may play a role in youths' PTSD following a traumatic event. As noted earlier, Ford and colleagues (2010) found that youth in the National Survey of Adolescents who experienced multiple traumas were more likely to have PTSD than youth exposed to single disasters or trauma. Also consistent with this perspective, it appears that a prior history of abuse predicts greater PTSD symptom intensity in adolescents and adults (e.g., Binder et al., 2008; Brewin et al., 2000; Garrison et al., 1993).

BIOLOGICAL/GENETIC MARKERS

Studies have begun to examine biological factors, and especially genetic variables, that may play a role in youths' posttrauma reactions. In general, PTSD is considered a polygenetic disorder, such that multiple genes, and their subsequent interactions, are thought to influence the development of this condition; this perspective is supported by both family studies and twin studies of PTSD (see part IV, chapter 11, of this volume). One gene that may influence the development of PTSD symptoms is 5-HTTLPR (Gotlib, Joorman, Minor, & Hallmayer, 2008). Females who are homozygous for the *s* allele on this gene produce higher and more sustained levels of cortisol when confronted with a stressor, compared to females with at least one *l* allele (Gotlib et al., 2008); such findings suggest that females who are homozygous for the *s* allele might be more likely to develop PTSD following trauma exposure due to their heightened biological reaction. Among adults exposed to a natural disaster, Kilpatrick and colleagues (2007) found that the presence of homozygous *s* alleles on the 5-HTTLPR gene increased risk of PTSD given the conditions of high trauma exposure and low social support. Other work suggests that the FKBP5 polymorphism may interact with the severity of child abuse to produce greater adult PTSD symptom severity (Binder et al., 2008). Studies of gene–environment interactions among youth affected by trauma are underway and are likely to be informative regarding the role of genetic variables in the development of PTSD.

PREEXISTING PSYCHOLOGICAL FACTORS

Despite a number of methodological limitations, such as a reliance on retrospective reporting of pretrauma psychological functioning or use of convenience samples, available evidence indicates that youths' psychological functioning prior to trauma exposure is significantly associated with their stress reactions following a traumatic experience (La Greca et al., 1998; Lonigan et al., 1994; Nolen-Hoeksema & Morrow, 1991; Storr, Ialongo, Anthony, & Breslau, 2007; Weems et al., 2007). Specifically, preexisting anxiety (Asarnow, 1999; La Greca et al., 1998; Lonigan et al., 1994; Weems et al., 2007), as well as pretrauma depression, stress, and ruminative coping styles (Nolen-Hoeksema & Morrow, 1991; Storr et al., 2007; Terranova, Boxer, & Sheffield Morris, 2009) appear to heighten youths' risk for developing PTSD or its symptoms.

OTHER CONTEXTUAL FACTORS: LIFE STRESSORS, SOCIAL SUPPORT, AND FAMILY FUNCTIONING

In addition to pretrauma child characteristics (discussed above), and youths' levels of exposure to the traumatic event (as discussed early in the chapter), several contextual variables will affect the development and persistence of PTSD in youth following trauma. Although a detailed discussion of such factors is beyond the scope of this chapter, a few key points will be noted.

The most well-studied contextual factors influencing youths' PTSD symptoms include major life stressors, the availability of social support, and aspects of family functioning (e.g., see Bonanno et al., 2010). For example, among youth who experience devastating natural disasters, the occurrence of other major life stressors (e.g., death or illness in the family, parental divorce or separation) during the postdisaster period has been associated with greater PTSD symptom severity and slower postdisaster recovery (La Greca et al., 1996, 2010). Moreover, compared to children who do not encounter major life stressors during the first year postdisaster, children who do experience such stressors are significantly more likely to display elevated and persistent PTSD symptoms during the second year postdisaster (La Greca et al., 2010). In essence, life stressors have a "multiplier" effect and markedly interfere with children's posttrauma recovery.

Ample research also has documented the importance of children's social support systems. Youth with greater perceived support from family members and peers fare better in the aftermath of traumatic events, reporting lower levels of PTSD symptoms (e.g., Bernard-Bonnin et al., 2008; Bokszczanin, 2007; La Greca et al., 1996, 2010; Lee, Ha, Kim, & Kwon, 2004; Prinstein, La Greca, Vernberg, & Silverman, 1996). However, children's support systems are complex and dynamic, and thus are potentially disrupted by traumatic events, such as disasters, war, or medical injuries. For example, longitudinal data following Hurricane Charley showed that disaster-related stressors and other major life events (e.g., a family member's illness) adversely affected children's social support levels (La Greca et al., 2010).

Finally, family functioning also plays a key role in youths' posttrauma reactions. Specifically, poor family functioning, family conflicts, or negative family atmosphere have been associated with higher levels of PTSD symptoms in child and adolescent disaster survivors (e.g., Bokszczanin, 2007; Green, 1991; Roussos et al., 2005; Tuicomepee & Romano, 2008; Wasserstein & La Greca, 1998) as well as among adolescent survivors of life-threatening illnesses (e.g., Alderfer et al., 2009).

Conclusions about PTSD

Although there has been tremendous progress in the past 15 to 20 years with respect to our understanding of PTSD in youth, several lines of research appear to be critical for the future. One critical issue relates to the suitability and appropriateness of the current diagnostic criteria for PTSD in youth. Additional research, informed by relevant developmental considerations, will be important and desirable for better understanding the key features of PTSD in youth.

A second issue pertains to causal risk factors that contribute to the development and maintenance of PTSD in youth (see La Greca et al., 2002). In particular, it will be useful to expand work that is investigating the biological and neurological variables that contribute to PTSD, and to examine other potential risk factors (e.g., cultural, economic, etc.) that may help to identify "at risk" youth and inform prevention efforts.

Third, the issue of comorbidity between PTSD and other psychological disorders warrants greater attention (La Greca, 2007). In particular, it would be useful to know how comorbidity affects the course and outcome of PTSD in youth, and how interventions for youth with PTSD might be complicated or affected by the presence of other problems.

Finally, future research might benefit from longitudinal studies of traumatized youth that examine patterns of risk and resilience over time (e.g., Le Brocque, Hendrikz, & Kenardy, 2010; also see Bonanno et al., 2010), as well as variables that mediate and moderate the effects of trauma on youth. Such studies would be useful for identifying youth in need of psychological services posttrauama and developing effective interventions for those who are affected (see La Greca et al., 2002).

Concluding Remarks

This chapter provided an overview of ASD and PTSD in youth. In closing, it is worth noting that, at present, several revisions to the diagnosis of PTSD are under consideration for the *DSM-5* (see American Psychiatric Association [APA], 2010). If accepted, the revisions will result in an additional and separate diagnosis for PTSD in preschool children, and the overall diagnosis of PTSD will contain specific notes with respect to the expression of PTSD-related symptoms in school-aged children and adolescents. Also under consideration is the possibility of including developmental trauma disorder as a new condition.

With respect to ASD, proposed revisions appear to move away from defining symptoms clusters and instead focus on a menu of 14 symptoms, with a threshold number of symptoms (8) that must be present for a diagnosis. The revisions to ASD do not appear to take into account developmental issues at the present time, and dissociative symptoms are still prominent in the proposed revision to ASD. However, the proposed criteria for both ASD and PTSD have greater specificity in terms of what constitutes a traumatic event than is the case for the *DSM-IV*.

References

Adams, R. E., & Boscarino, J. A. (2009). Predictors of PTSD and delayed PTSD after disaster: The impact of exposure and psychosocial resources. *Journal of Nervous and Mental Disease, 194*(7), 485–493.

Alderfer, M. A., Navsaria, N., & Kazak, A. E. (2009). Family functioning and posttraumatic stress disorder in adolescent survivors of childhood cancer. *Journal of Family Psychology, 23*, 717–725.

American Academy of Child and Adolescent Psychiatry. (1998). Practice parameters for the assessment and treatment of children and adolescents with posttraumatic stress disorder. *Journal of the American Academy of Child and Adolescent Psychiatry*, 37(10 Suppl), 4S–26S.

American Psychiatric Association. (1987). *Diagnostic and statistical manual of mental disorders* (3rd. ed., rev.). Washington, DC: Author.

American Psychiatric Association. (1994). *Diagnostic and statistical manual of mental disorders* (4th ed.). Washington, DC: Author.

American Psychiatric Association. (2000). *Diagnostic and statistical manual of mental disorders* (4th ed., text rev.). Washington, DC: Author.

American Psychiatric Association. (2010). *DSM-5 development.* Downloaded from http://www.dsm5.org/ProposedRevisions/Pages/proposedrevision.aspx?rid=165#.

Anthony, J. L., Lonigan, C. J., & Hecht, S. A. (1999). Dimensionality of posttraumatic stress disorder symptoms in children exposed to disaster: Results from confirmatory factor analyses. *Journal of Abnormal Psychology, 108*(2), 326–336.

Anthony, J. L., Lonigan, C. J., Vernberg, E. M., La Greca, A. M., Silverman, W. K., & Prinstein, M. J. (2005). Multisample cross-validation of a model of childhood posttraumatic stress disorder symptomatology. *Journal of Traumatic Stress, 18*, 667–676.

Asarnow, J. (1999). When the earth stops shaking: Earthquake sequelae among children diagnosed for pre-earthquake psychopathology. *Journal of the American Academy of Child and Adolescent Psychiatry, 38*, 1016–1023.

Asmundson, G. J. G., Frombach, I., McQuaid, J., Pedrelli, P., Lenox, R., & Stein, M. B. (2000). Dimensionality of posttraumatic stress symptoms: A confirmatory factor analysis of DSM-IV symptom clusters and other symptom models. *Behaviour Research and Therapy, 38*, 203–214.

Bernard-Bonnin, A-C., Hébert, M., Daignault, I.V.,& Allard-Dansereau, C. (2008). Disclosure of sexual abuse and personal and familial factors as predictors of post-traumatic stress disorder symptoms in school-aged girls. *Journal of Paediatrics and Child Health, 13*(6), 479–486.

Binder, E. B., Bradley, R. G., Liu, W., Epstein, M. P., Deveau, T. C., Mercer, K. B., & Ressler, K. J. (2008). Association of FKBP5 polymorphisms and childhood abuse with risk of posttraumatic stress disorder symptoms in adults. *Journal of the American Medical Association, 299*(11), 1291–1305.

Bokszczanin, A. (2007). PTSD symptoms in children and adolescents 28 months after a flood: Age and gender differences. *Journal of Traumatic Stress, 20*(3), 347–351.

Bolton, D., O'Ryan, D., Udwin, O., Boyle, S., & Yule, W. (2000). The long-term psychological effects of a disaster experienced in adolescence: II. General psychopathology. *Journal of Child Psychology and Psychiatry, 41*, 513–523.

Bonanno, G. A., Brewin, C. R., Kaniasty, K., & La Greca, A. M. (2010). Weighing the costs of disaster: Consequences, risks, and resilience in individuals, families, and communities. *Psychological Science in the Public Interest, 11*(1), 1–49.

Bosquet Enlow, M., Kassam-Adams, N., & Saxe, G. (2010). The Child Stress Disorders Checklist-Short Form: A four-item scale of traumatic stress symptoms in children. *General Hospital Psychiatry, 32*(3), 321–7.

Breslau, N., Davis, G.C., Andreski, P., & Peterson, E.L. (1991). Traumatic events and posttraumatic stress disorder in an urban population of young adults. *Archives of General Psychiatry, 48*, 216–222.

Brewin, C. R., Andrews, B., & Valentine, J. D. (2000). Meta-analysis of risk factors for posttraumatic stress disorder in trauma-exposed adults. *Journal of Consulting and Clinical Psychology, 68*(5), 748–766.

Bryant, R. A. (2004). Assessing acute stress disorder.In J. P. Wilson, & T. M. Keane (Eds.), *Assessing psychological trauma and PTSD* (2nd ed., pp. 45–60). New York: Guilford.

Bryant, R. A., & Harvey, A. G. (2002). Delayed-onset posttraumatic stress disorder: A prospective evaluation. *Australian and New Zealand Journal of Psychiatry, 36*, 205–209.

Bryant, R. A., Salmon, K., Sinclair, E., & Davidson, P. (2007a). A prospective study of appraisals in childhood posttraumatic stress disorder. *Behaviour Research and Therapy, 45*, 2502–2507.

Bryant, R. A., Salmon, K., Sinclair, E., & Davidson, P. (2007b). The relationship between acute stress disorder and posttraumatic stress disorder in injured children. *Journal of Traumatic Stress, 20*(6), 1075–1079.

Bulut, S. (2004). Factor structure of posttraumatic stress disorder in children experienced natural disaster. *Psychologia, 47*, 158–168.

Carey, P.D., Walker, J.L., Rossouw, W., Seedat, S., & Stein, D.J. (2008). Risk indicators in traumatized children and adolescents with a history of sexual abuse. *European Journal of Child and Adolescent Psychiatry, 17*(2), 93–98.

Carty, J., O'Donnell, M. L., & Creamer, M. (2006). Delayed-onset PTSD: A prospective study of injury survivors. *Journal of Affective Disorders, 90*(2–3), 257–261.

Casswell, G. (1997). Learning from the aftermath: The response of mental health workers to a school-bus crash. *Clinical Child Psychology and Psychiatry, 2*, 517–523.

Cohen, J. A., Berliner, L., & Mannarino, A. (2010). Trauma focused CBT for children with co-occurring trauma and behavior problems. *Child Abuse and Neglect, 34*, 215–224.

Cohen, J. A., Deblinger, E., Mannarino, A. P., & deArellano, M. A. (2001). The importance of culture in treating abused and neglected children: An empirical review. *Child Maltreatment, 6*, 148–157.

Cohen, J. A., Deblinger, E., Mannarino, A. P., & Steer, R. A. (2004). A multisite randomized controlled study of sexually abused, multiply traumatized children with PTSD: Initial treatment outcome. *Journal of the American Academy of Child and Adolescent Psychiatry, 43*, 393–402.

Comer, J. S., & Kendall, P. C. (2007). Terrorism: The psychological impact on youth. *Clinical Psychology: Science and Practice, 14*(3), 179–212.

Copeland, W.E., Keeler, G., Angold, A., & Costello, E.J. (2007). Traumatic events and posttraumatic stress in childhood. *Archives of General Psychiatry, 64*, 577–584.

Costello, E.J., Erkanli, A., Fairbank, J.A., & Angold, A. (2002). The prevalence of potentially traumatic events in childhood and adolescence. *Journal of Traumatic Stress, 15*, 99–112.

Cox, C. M., Kenardy, J. A., & Hendrikz, J. K. (2010). A randomized controlled trial of a web- based early intervention for children and their parents following unintentional injury. *Journal of Pediatric Psychology, 35*, 581–592.

Cox, B. J., Mota, N., Clara, I., & Asmudson, G. J. G. (2008). The symptom structure of posttraumatic stress disorder in the National Comorbidity Replication Survey. *Journal of Anxiety Disorders, 22*, 1523–1528.

Dalgleish, T., Meiser-Stedman, R., Kassam-Adams, N., Ehlers, A., Winston, F., Smith, P., & Yule, W. (2008). Predictive validity of acute stress disorder in children and adolescents. *British Journal of Psychiatry, 192*, 392–393.

Daviss, W.B., Racusin, R., Fleischer, A., Mooney, D., Ford, J.D., & McHugo, G.J. (2000). Acute stress disorder symptomatology during hospitalization for pediatric injury. *Journal of the American Academy of Child and Adolescent Psychiatry, 39*(5), 569–575.

Deblinger, E., Mannarino, A. P., Cohen, J. A., & Steer, R. A. (2006). A follow-up study of a multisite, randomized, controlled trial for children with sexual abuse-related PTSD symptoms. *Journal of the American Academy of Child & Adolescent Psychiatry, 45*, 1474–1484.

Deblinger, E., McLeer, S. V., Atkins, M. S., Ralphe, D., & Foa, E. (1989). Post-traumatic stress in sexually abused, physically abused, and nonabused children. *Child Abuse and Neglect, 13*, 403–408.

Fairbank, J. A. (2008). The epidemiology of trauma and trauma related disorders in children and youth. *PTSD Research Quarterly, 19*(1), 1–7.

Fedroff, I. C., Taylor, S., Asmundson, G. J. G., & Koch, W. J. (2000). Cognitive factors in traumatic stress reactions: Predicting PTSD symptoms from anxiety sensitivity and beliefs about harmful events. *Behavioural and Cognitive Psychotherapy, 28*, 5–15.

Finkelhor, D., Ormrod, R., Turner, H., & Hamby, S.L. (2005). The victimization of children and youth: A comprehensive, national survey. *Child Maltreatment, 10*, 5–25.

Foa, E. B., Franklin, M. E., Perry, K. J., & Herbert, J. D. (1996). Cognitive bias in generalized social phobia. *Journal of Abnormal Psychology, 15*, 433–439.

Foa, E. B., Steketee, G., & Rothbaum, B. O. (1989). Behavioural/cognitive conceptualizations of post-traumatic stress disorder. *Behavior Therapy, 20*, 155–176.

Ford, J. D., Elhai, J. D., Connor, D. F., & Frueh, B. C. (2010). Poly-victimization and risk of posttraumatic, depressive, and substance use disorders and involvement in delinquency in a national sample of adolescents. *Journal of Adolescent Health, 46*, 545–552.

Ford, J. D., Elhai, J. D., Ruggiero, K., J., & Frueh, B. C. (2009). Refining posttraumatic stress disorder diagnosis: Evaluation of symptom criteria in the National Survey of Adolescents. *Journal of Clinical Psychiatry, 70*, 748–755.

Furr, J.M., Comer, J. S., Edmunds, J., & Kendall, P.C. (2010). Disasters and youth: A meta-analytic examination of posttraumatic stress. *Journal of Consulting and Clinical Psychology, 78*(6), 765–780.

Garner Evans, L., & Oehler-Stinnett, J. (2006). Structure and prevalence of PTSD symptomology in children who have experienced a severe tornado. *Psychology in the Schools, 43*(3), 283–295.

Garrison, C. Z., Weinrich, M. W., Hardin, S. B., Weinrich, S., & Wang, L. (1993). Post- traumatic stress disorder in adolescents after a hurricane. *American Journal of Epidemiology, 138*, 522–530.

Giardino, A.P., Harris, T. B., & Giardino, E.R. (2009). Child abuse and neglect, posttraumatic stress disorder. Emedicine from WebMD. Downloaded from http://emedicine.medscape.com/article/916007-overview.

Goenjian, A. K., Karayan, I., Pynoos, R. S., & Minassian, D. (1997). Outcome of psychotherapy among early adolescents after trauma. *American Journal of Psychiatry, 154*(4), 536–542.

Goenjian, A. K., Molina, L., Steinberg, A. M., Fairbanks, L. A., Alvarez, M. L., Goenjian, H. A., & Pynoos, R. S. (2001). Posttraumatic stress and depressive reactions among Nicaraguan adolescents after Hurricane Mitch. *American Journal of Psychiatry, 158*, 788–794.

Goenjian, A. K., Pynoos, R. S., Steinberg, A. M., Najarian, L. M., Asarnow, J. R., Asarnow, J. R., Fairbanks, L. A. (1995). Psychiatric comorbidity in children after the 1988 earthquake in Armenia. *Journal of the American Academy of Child and Adolescent Psychiatry, 34*, 1174–1184.

Goenjian, A. K., Steinberg, A. M., Najarian, L. M., Fairbanks, L. A., Tashjian, M., & Pynoos, R. S. (2000). Prospective study of posttraumatic stress, anxiety, and depressive reactions after earthquakes and political violence. *American Journal of Psychiatry, 157*, 911–916.

Goenjian, A. K., Walling, D., Steinberg, A. M., Karayan, I., Najarian, L. M., & Pynoos, R. S. (2005). A prospective study of posttraumatic stress and depressive reactions among treated and untreated adolescents 5 years after a catastrophic disaster. *American Journal of Psychiatry, 162*, 2302–2308.

Gotlib, I. H., Joorman, J., Minor, K. L., & Hallmayer, J. (2008). HPA axis reactivity: A mechanism underlying the associations among 5-HTTLPR, stress, and depression. *Biological Psychiatry, 63*, 847–851.

Green, B. L. (1991). Evaluating the effects of disasters. *Psychological Assessment, 3*, 538–546.

Green, B. L., Korol, M. S., Grace, M. C., Vary, M. G., Kramer, T. L., Gleser, G. C., & Leonard, A. C. (1994). Children of disaster in the second decade: A 17-year follow-up of Buffalo Creek survivors. *Journal of the American Academy of Child and Adolescent Psychiatry, 33*, 71–79.

Grinage, B. D. (2003). Diagnosis and management of Posttraumatic Stress Disorder. *American Family Physician, 68*(12), 2401–2409.

Gurwitch, R. H., Sitterle, K. A., Young, B. H., & Pfefferbaum, B. (2002). The aftermath of terrorism. In A. M. La Greca, W. K. Silverman, E. M. Vernberg, & M. C. Roberts (Eds.), *Helping children cope with disasters and terrorism* (pp. 327–358). Washington, DC: American Psychological Association.

Harris-Hendriks, J., Black, D., & Kaplan, T. (1993). *When father kills mother: Guiding children through trauma and grief.* London, UK: Routledge.

Heiervang, E., Stormark, K.M., Lundervold, A.J., Heimann, M., Goodman, R., Posserud, M., & Gillberg, C. (2007). Psychiatric disorders in Norwegian 8- to 10-year-olds: An epidemiological survey of prevalence, risk factors, and service use. *Journal of the Academy of Child and Adolescent Psychiatry, 46*, 438–447.

Herbert, M. (1996). *Posttraumatic stress disorder in children.* Leicester, UK: British Psychological Society.

Holbrook, T.L., Hoyt, D.B., Coimbra, R., Potenza, B., Sise, M., & Anderson, J. P. (2005). High rates of acute stress disorder impact quality-of-life outcomes in injured adolescents: Mechanism and gender predict acute stress disorder risk. *Journal of Trauma, 59*, 1126–1130.

Holmes, E. A., Creswell, C., & O'Connor, T. G. (2007). Posttraumatic stress symptoms in London school children following September 11, 2001: An exploratory investigation of peri-traumatic reactions and intrusive imagery. *Journal of Behavior Therapy and Experimental Psychiatry, 38*, 474–490.

Hoven, C. W., Duarte, C. S., Lucas, C. P., Wu, P., Mandell, D. J., Goodwin, R. D., & Susser, E. (2005). Psychopathology among New York City public school children 6 months after September 11. *Archives of General Psychiatry, 62*, 545–552.

John, P. B., Russell, S., & Russell, P. S. (2007). The prevalence of posttraumatic stress disorder among children and adolescents affected by tsunami disaster in Tamil Nadu. *Disaster Management and Response, 5*, 3–7.

Jones, R., & Ollendick, T. (2002). Residential fires. In A. M. La Greca, W. K. Silverman, E. M. Vernberg, & M. C. Roberts (Eds.), *Helping children cope with disasters and terrorism* (pp. 175–199). Washington, DC: American Psychological Association.

Kar, N., & Bastia, B. K. (2006). Post-traumatic stress disorder, depression and generalized anxiety disorder in adolescents after a natural disaster: A study of comorbidity. *Clinical Practice and Epidemiology in Mental Health, 2*, 17.

Kassam-Adams, N., Marsac, M. L., & Cirilli, C. (2010). Posttraumatic stress disorder symptom structure in injured children: Functional impairment and depression symptoms in a confirmatory factor analysis. *Journal of the American Academy of Child and Adolescent Psychiatry, 49*, 616–625.

Kassam-Adams, N., & Winston, F.K. (2004). Predicting child PTSD: The relationship between acute stress disorder and PTSD in injured children. *Journal of the American Academy of Child and Adolescent Psychiatry, 43*, 403–411.

Kilpatrick, D. G., Koenen, K. C., Ruggiero, K. J., Acierno, R., Galea, S., Resnick, H. S., & Gelernter, J. (2007). The serotonin transporter genotype and social support and moderation of PTSD and depression in hurricane-exposed adults. *American Journal of Psychiatry, 164*, 1693–1699.

Kilpatrick, D. G., Ruggiero, K. J., Acierno, R., Saunders, B. E., Resnick, H. S., & Best, C. L. (2003). Violence and risk of PTSD, major depression, substance abuse/dependence, and comorbidity: Results from the National Survey of Adolescents. *Journal of Consulting and Clinical Psychology, 71*, 692–700.

Kilpatrick, D.G., & Saunders, B.E. (1997). *Prevalence and consequences of child victimization: Results from the National Survey of Adolescents.* Final Report. (SuDoc No. J 28.24/7:P 92). Washington, DC: U.S. Government Printing Office.

Klingman, A. (2002). Children under stress of war. In A. M. La Greca, W. K. Silverman, E. M. Vernberg, & M. C. Roberts (Eds.), *Helping children cope with disasters and terrorism* (pp. 359–380). Washington DC: American Psychological Association.

Koenen, K. C., & Widom, C. S. (2009). A prospective study of sex differences in the lifetime risk of posttraumatic stress disorder among abused and neglected children grown up. *Journal of Traumatic Stress, 22*, 566–574.

Kupersmidt, J. B., Shahinfar, A., & Voegler-Lee, M. E. (2002). Children's exposure to community violence. In A. M. La Greca, W. K. Silverman, E. M. Vernberg, & M. C. Roberts (Eds.), *Helping children cope with disasters and terrorism* (pp. 381–401). Washington, DC: American Psychological Association.

La Greca, A.M. (2007). Understanding the psychological impact of terrorism on youth: Moving beyond Pottraumatic

Stress Disorder. *Clinical Psychology: Science and Practice, 14*, 219–223.

La Greca, A. M. (2008). Interventions for posttraumatic stress in children and adolescents following natural disasters and acts of terrorism. In R. G. Steele, T. D. Elkin, & M. C. Roberts (Eds.), *Handbook of evidence-based therapies for children and adolescents: Bridging science and practice* (pp. 121–141). New York, NY: Springer.

La Greca, A. M., & Prinstein, M. J. (2002). Hurricanes and earthquakes. In A. M. La Greca, W.K. Silverman, E. M. Vernberg, & M. C. Roberts (Eds.), *Helping children cope with disasters and terrorism* (pp. 107–138). Washington, DC: American Psychological Association.

La Greca, A. M., & Silverman, W. (2006). Treating children and adolescents affected by disasters and terrorism. In P. C. Kendall (Ed.), *Child and adolescent therapy: Cognitive-behavioral procedures* (3rd ed., pp. 356–382). New York: Guilford.

La Greca, A. M., & Silverman, W. (2009). Treatment and prevention of posttraumatic stress reactions in children and adolescents exposed to disasters and terrorism: What is the evidence? *Child Development Perspectives, 3*, 4–10.

La Greca, A.M., Silverman, W., Lai, B., & Jaccard, J. (2010). Hurricane-related exposure experiences and stressors, other life events, and social support: Concurrent and prospective impact on children's persistent posttraumatic stress. *Journal of Consulting and Clinical Psychology, 78*(6), 794–805.

La Greca, A. M., Silverman, W. K., Vernberg, E. M., & Prinstein, M. (1996). Symptoms of posttraumatic stress after Hurricane Andrew: A prospective study. *Journal of Consulting and Clinical Psychology, 64*, 712–723.

La Greca, A. M., Silverman, W. K., Vernberg, E. M., & Roberts, M. C. (Eds.). (2002). *Helping children cope with disasters and terrorism.* Washington, DC: American Psychological Association.

La Greca, A. M., Silverman, W. K., & Wasserstein, S. B. (1998). Children's predisaster functioning as a predictor of posttraumatic stress following Hurricane Andrew. *Journal of Consulting and Clinical Psychology, 66*, 883–892.

Landolt, M. A., Vollrath, M., Timm, K., Gnehm, H. E., & Sennhauser, F. H. (2005). Predicting posttraumatic stress symptoms in children after road traffic accidents. *Journal of the American Academy of Child and Adolescent Psychiatry, 44*, 1276–1283.

Laufer, A., & Solomon, Z. (2009). Gender differences in PTSD in Israeli youth exposed to terror attacks. *Journal of Interpersonal Violence, 24*, 959–976.

Le Brocque R. M., Hendrikz J., & Kenardy J. A. (2010). Parental response to child injury: Examination of parental posttraumatic stress symptom trajectories following child accidental injury. *Journal of Pediatric Psychology, 35*(6), 646–655.

Lee, I., Ha, Y.S., Kim, Y.A., & Kwon, Y.H. (2004). PTSD symptoms in elementary school children after Typhoon Rusa. *Taehan Kanho Hakhoe Chi. 34*(4), 636–645.

Llabre, M. M., & Hadi, F. (2009). War-related exposure and psychological distress as predictors of health and sleep: A longitudinal study of Kuwaiti children. *Psychosomatic Medicine, 71*, 776–783.

Lonigan, C. J., Shannon, M. P., Taylor, C. M., Finch, A. J., & Sallee, F. R. (1994). Children exposed to disaster: II. Risk factors for the development of post-traumatic symptomatology. *Journal of the American Academy of Child Psychiatry, 33*, 94–105.

Malmquist, C. P. (1986). Children who witness parental murder: Post-traumatic aspects. *Journal of the American Academy of Child and Adolescent Psychiatry, 25*, 320–325.

March, J.S. (2003). Acute stress disorder in youth: A multivariate prediction model. *Biological Psychiatry, 53*, 809–816.

McDermott, B. M., Lee, E. M., Judd, M., & Gibbon, P. (2005). Posttraumatic stress disorder and general psychopathology in children and adolescents following a wildfire disaster. *The Canadian Journal of Psychiatry, 50*(3), 137–143.

Meiser-Stedman, R., Dalgleish, T., Glucksman, E., Yule, W., & Smith, P. (2009). Maladaptive cognitive appraisals mediate the evolution of posttraumatic stress reactions: A 6-month follow-up of child and adolescent assault and motor vehicle accident survivors. *Journal of Abnormal Psychology, 118*, 778–787.

Meiser-Stedman, R., Dalgleish, T., Smith, P., Yule, W., Bryant, B., Ehlers, A., Mayou, R.A., Kassam-Adams, N., & Winston, F. (2007). Dissociative symptoms and the acute stress disorder diagnosis in children and adolescents: A replication of the Harvey and Bryant (1999) Study. *Journal of Traumatic Stress, 20*, 359–364.

Meiser-Stedman, R., Dalgleish, T., Smith, P., Yule, W., & Glucksman, E. (2007). Diagnostic, demographic, memory quality, and cognitive variables associated with acute stress disorder in children and adolescents. *Journal of Abnormal Psychology, 116*, 65–79.

Meiser-Stedman, R., Smith, P., Glucksman, E., Yule, W., & Dalgleish, T. (2008). The posttraumatic stress disorder diagnosis in preschool-and elementary school-age children exposed to motor vehicle accidents. *American Journal of Psychiatry, 165*, 1326–1337.

Meiser-Stedman, R., Yule, W., Smith, P., Glucksman, E., & Dalgleish, T. (2005). Acute stress disorder and posttraumatic stress disorder in children and adolescents involved in assaults or motor vehicle accidents. *American Journal of Psychiatry, 162*, 1381–1383.

Nader, K., & Mello, C. (2002). Shootings, hostage takings, and children. In A. M. La Greca, W. K. Silverman, E. M. Vernberg, & M. C. Roberts (Eds.), *Helping children cope with disasters and terrorism* (pp. 301–326). Washington, DC: American Psychological Association.

Nolen-Hoeksema, S., & Morrow, J. (1991). A prospective study of depression and posttraumatic stress symptoms after a natural disaster: The 1989 Loma Prieta earthquake. *Journal of Personality and Social Psychology, 61*, 115–121.

Norris, F. H., Friedman, M. J., Watson, P. J., Byrne, C. M., Diaz, E., & Kaniasty, K. (2002). 60,000 disaster victims speak: Part I. An empirical review of empirical literature, 1981–2001. *Psychiatry: Interpersonal and Biological Processes, 65*, 207–239.

Olofsson, E., Bunkertorp, O., & Andersson, A. L. (2009). Children and adolescents injured in traffic-associated psychological consequences: A literature review. *Acta Paediatrica, 98*, 17–22.

Overstreet, S., Salloum, A., & Badour, C. (2010). A school-based assessment of secondary stressors and adolescent mental health 18 months post-Katrina. *Journal of School Psychology, 48*, 413–431.

Pailler, M.E., Kassam-Adams, N., Datner, E.M., & Fein, J.A. (2007). Depression, acute stress and behavioral risk factors in violently injured adolescents. *General Hospital Psychiatry, 29*, 357–363.

Paolucci, E. O., Genuis, M. L., & Violato, C. (2001). A meta-analysis of the published research on the effects of child sexual abuse. *Journal of Psychology, 135*(1), 17–36.

Pat-Horenczyk, R., Abramovitz, R., Peled, O., Brom, D., Daie, A., & Chemtob, C. M. (2007). Adolescent exposure to recurrent terrorism in Israel: Posttraumatic distress and functional impairment. *American Journal of Orthopsychiatry, 77*, 76–85.

Pat-Horenczyk, R., Qasrawi, R., Lesack, R., Haj-Yahia, H., Peled, O., Shaheen, M., & Abdeen, Z. (2009). Posttraumatic symptoms, functional impairment, and coping among adolescents on both sides of the Israeli-Palestinian conflict: A cross-cultural approach. *Applied Psychology: An International Review, 58*, 688–708.

Pelcovitz, D., Kaplan, S., Goldenberg, G., Mandel, F., Lehane, J., & Guarrero, J. (1994). Post- traumatic stress disorder in physically abused adolescents. *Journal of the American Academy of Child and Adolescent Psychiatry, 33*, 305–312.

Perrin, S., Smith, P., & Yule, W. (2000). Practitioner review: The assessment and treatment of post-traumatic stress disorder in children and adolescents. *Journal of Child Psychology and Psychiatry, 41*(3), 277–289.

Pfefferbaum, B. (1997). Posttraumatic stress disorder in children: A review of the past 10 years. *Journal of the American Academy of Child and Adolescent Psychiatry, 36*, 1503–1511.

Pfefferbaum, B. (2005). Aspects of exposure to childhood trauma: The stressor criterion. *Journal of Traumatic Dissociation, 6*, 17–26.

Prinstein, M. J., La Greca, A. M., Vernberg, E. M., & Silverman, W. K. (1996). Children's coping assistance after a natural disaster. *Journal of Clinical Child Psychology, 25*, 463–475.

Pynoos, R. S. (1992). Grief and trauma in children and adolescents.*Bereavement Care, 2*, 2–10.

Pynoos, R. S., Frederick, C., Nader, K., Arroyo, W., Steinberg, A., Eth, S., & Fairbanks, L. (1987). Life threat and posttraumatic stress disorder in school-age children. *Archives of General Psychiatry, 44*, 1057–1063.

Pynoos, R. S., & Nader, K. (1988). Psychological first aid and treatment approach to children exposed to community violence: Research implications. *Journal of Traumatic Stress, 1*, 445–473.

Rabalais, A. E., Ruggiero, K. J., & Scotti, J. R. (2002). Multicultural issues in the response of children to disasters. In A. M. La Greca, W. K. Silverman, E. M. Vernberg, & M. C. Roberts (Eds.), *Helping children cope with disasters and terrorism* (pp. 73–100). Washington, DC: American Psychological Association.

Roussos, A., Goenjian, A. K., Steinberg, A. M., Sotiropoulou, C., Kakaki, M., Kabakos, C., Karagianni, S., & Manouras, V. (2005). Posttraumatic stress and depressive reactions among children and adolescents after the 1999 earthquake in Ano Liosia, Greece. *American Journal of Psychiatry, 162*, 530–537.

Salmon, K., Sinclair, E., & Bryant, R.A. (2007).The role of maladaptive appraisals in child acute stress reactions. *British Journal of Clinical Psychology, 46*, 203–210.

Saxe, G., Chawla, N., Stoddard, F., Kassam-Adams, N., Courtney, D., Cunningham, K., & King, L. (2003). Child Stress Disorders Checklist: A measure of ASD and PTSD in children. *Journal of the American Academy of Child and Adolescent Psychiatry, 42*, 972–978.

Saxe, G.N., Miller, A., Bartholomew, D., Hall, E., Lopez, C., Kaplow, J., & Moulton, S. (2005). Incidence of and risk factors for acute stress disorder in children with injuries. *Journal of Trauma Injury, Infection, and Critical Care, 59*, 946–953.

Scheeringa, M. S., Zeanah, C. H., & Cohen, J. A. (2010). PTSD in children and adolescents: Toward an empirically based algorithm. *Depression and Anxiety, 28*(9), 770–782.

Schuster, M. A., Stein, B. D., Jaycox, L. H., Collins, R. L., Marshall, G. N., Elliott, M. N., & Berry, S. H. (2001). A national survey of stress reactions after the September 11, 2001, terrorist attacks. *New England Journal of Medicine, 345*, 1507–1512.

Scott, K. M., Smith, D. R., & Ellis, P. M. (2010). Prospectively ascertained child maltreatment and its association with DSM-IV mental disorders in young adults. *Archives of General Psychiatry, 67*, 712–719.

Shaw, J. A., Applegate, B., & Schorr, C. (1996). Twenty-one-month follow-up study of school-age children exposed to Hurricane Andrew. *Journal of the American Academy of Child and Adolescent Psychiatry, 35*, 359–364.

Silverman, W. K., & La Greca, A.M. (2002). Children experiencing disasters: Definitions, reactions, and predictors of outcomes. In A. M. La Greca, W.K. Silverman, E. M. Vernberg, & M.C. Roberts (Eds.), *Helping children cope with disasters*. (pp. 11–34). Washington, DC: American Psychological Association.

Sinclair, E., Salmon, K., & Bryant, R.A. (2007). The role of panic attacks in acute stress disorder in children. *Journal of Traumatic Stress, 20*, 1069–1073.

Smith, K., & Bryant, R.A. (2000).The generality of cognitive bias in acute stress disorder. *Behaviour Research and Therapy, 38*, 709–715.

Stallard, P., Velleman, R., & Baldwin, S. (1998). Prospective study of post-traumatic stress disorder in children involved in road traffic accidents. *British Medical Journal, 7173*, 1619–1623.

Stoddard, F. J., Saxe, G., Ronfeldt, H., Drake, J. E., Burns, J., Edgren, C., & Sheridan, R. (2006). Acute stress symptoms in young children with burns. *Journal of the American Academy of Child and Adolescent Psychiatry, 45*, 87–93.

Storr, C. L., Ialongo, N. S., Anthony, J. C., & Breslau, N. (2007). Childhood antecedents to exposure to traumatic events and posttraumatic stress disorder. *American Journal of Psychiatry, 164*, 119–125.

Stuber, J., Fairbrother, G., Galea, S., Pfefferbaum, B., Wilson-Genderson, M., & Vlahov, D. (2002). Determinants of counseling for children in Manhattan after the September 11 attacks. *Psychiatric Services, 53*, 815–822.

Stuber, M. L., Nader, K., Yasuda, P., Pynoos, R. S., & Cohen, S. (1991). Stress responses after pediatric bone marrow transplantation: Preliminary results of a prospective longitudinal study. *Journal of the American Academy of Child and Adolescent Psychiatry, 30*, 952–957.

Thabet, A. A. M., Abed, Y., & Vostanis, P. (2004). Comorbidity of PTSD and depression among refugee children during war conflict. *Journal of Child Psychology and Psychiatry, 45*, 533–542.

Terranova, A. M., Boxer, P., & Sheffield Morris, A. (2009). Factors influencing the course of posttraumatic stress following a natural disaster: Children's reactions to Hurricane Katrina. *Journal of Applied Developmental Psychology, 30*, 344–355.

Tuicomepee, A. & Romano, J.L. (2008). Thai adolescent survivors 1 year after the 2004 tsunami: A mixed methods study. *Journal of Counseling Psychology, 55*(3), 308–320.

Vernberg, E. M., La Greca, A. M., Silverman, W. K., & Prinstein, M. (1996). Predictors of children's post-disaster functioning

following Hurricane Andrew. *Journal of Abnormal Psychology, 105*, 237–248.
Vincent, N. R. (1997). *A follow-up to Hurricane Andrew: Children's reactions 42 months postdisaster*. Unpublished doctoral dissertation, University of Miami.
Vogel, J. M., & Vernberg, E. M. (1993). Task force report, part 1: Children's psychological responses to disasters. *Journal of Clinical Child Psychology, 22*, 464–484.
Wasserstein, S. B., & La Greca, A. M. (1998). Hurricane Andrew: Parental conflict as a moderator of children's adjustment. *Hispanic Journal of Behavioral Science, 20*, 212–224.
Weems, C.F., & Carrion, V.G. (2007). The association between PTSD symptoms and salivary cortisol in youth: The role of time since the trauma. *Journal of Traumatic Stress, 20*, 903–907.
Weems, C. F., Piña, A. A., Costa, N. M., Watts, S. E., Taylor, L. K., & Cannon, M. F. (2007). Predisaster trait anxiety and negative affect predict posttraumatic stress in youth after hurricane Katrina. *Journal of Consulting and Clinical Psychology, 75*, 154–159.
Weems, C. F., Taylor, L. K., Cannon, M. F., Marino, R. C., Romano, D. M., Scott, B. G., & Triplett, V. (2010). Posttraumatic stress, context, and the lingering effects of the Hurricane Katrina disaster among ethnic minority youth. *Journal of Abnormal Child Psychology, 38*, 49–56.
Widom, C. S. (1999). Posttraumatic stress disorder in abused and neglected children grown up. *American Journal of Psychiatry, 156*, 1223–1229.
Winston, F.K., Kassam-Adams, N., Vivarelli-O'Neill, C., Ford, J., Newman, E., Baxt, C., & Cnaan, A. (2002). Acute stress disorder symptoms in children and their parents after pediatric traffic injury. *Pediatrics, 109*(6), e90.
Yelland, C., Robinson, P., Lock, C., La Greca, A. M., Kokegei, B., Ridgway, V., & Lai, B. (2010). Bushfire impact on youth. *Journal of Traumatic Stress, 23*, 274–277.
Yule, W. (1995). Posttraumatic stress disorders. In M. Rutter, E. Taylor, & L. Hersov (Eds.), *Child and adolescent psychiatry: Modern approaches*. (3rd ed. pp. 392–406). Oxford: Blackwell.
Yule, W., Bolton, D., Udwin, O., Boyle, S., O'Ryan, D., & Nurrish, J. (2000). The long-term psychological effects of a disaster experienced in adolescence. I. The incidence and course of PTSD. *Journal of Child Psychology and Psychiatry, 41*, 503–512.
Yule, W., Udwin, O., & Bolton, D. (2002). Mass transportation disasters. In A. M. La Greca, W. K. Silverman, E. M. Vernberg, & M. C. Roberts (Eds.), *Helping children cope with disasters and terrorism* (pp. 223–240). Washington, DC: American Psychological Association.

CHAPTER

9 Traumatic Stress in Older Adults

Joan M. Cook, Tatyana Biyanova, *and* Diane L. Elmore

Abstract

This chapter focuses on older adult trauma survivors. Information is presented on prevalence of acute stress disorder (ASD) and posttraumatic stress disorder (PTSD); course, functional impairment, suicide risk, and health care utilization in older adults with PTSD; and the impact of demographic factors such as gender, ethnicity, and race on PTSD in older individuals. In general, rates of ASD and PTSD are lower in older adults compared to other age groups. PTSD in older adults has been linked to suicidal ideation and attempts, functional impairment, physical health, and increased healthcare utilization. Although delayed onset of PTSD has been empirically verified in some military samples with World War II veterans and younger adult civilians, it is rare in the absence of any prior symptoms and might more accurately be labeled "delayed recognition." More information on trauma and PTSD in diverse populations of older adults is needed, such as racial and ethnic minorities, those with severe physical or mental impairment, noncommunity-residing groups, and those from nonindustrialized countries.

Key Words: Aged, posttraumatic stress disorder, acute stress disorder, review, epidemiology, delayed-onset posttraumatic stress disorder

Introduction

The number, proportion, and diversity of older adults in the general population are steadily increasing, particularly in industrialized countries, where older adults are expected to constitute 33% of the population by 2050 (United Nations, 2007). Despite this trend, compared to the scientific investigation and clinical attention paid to traumatic exposure and its potential effects in other age groups, much less is known about those aged 65 and over. To date, the majority of the empirical literature on traumatic exposure in older adults comes from one of three groups of survivors: those who experienced trauma earlier in life during military combat/captivity (namely, World War II and the Korean War) or the Holocaust, and those who experienced trauma later in life (i.e., natural and manmade disasters) (for reviews, see Averill & Beck, 2000; Cook & Elmore, 2009; Falk, Hersen, & Van Hasselt, 1994). Relatively less is known about certain aging trauma survivor groups, such as women and minorities, and groups who have experienced other specific traumas—for instance, interpersonal violence or other criminal victimization.

The goals of this chapter are to briefly summarize the epidemiological literature on prevalence and incidence of acute stress disorder (ASD) and posttraumatic stress disorder (PTSD) in older adults; provide information on late-onset PTSD; summarize what is known on the longitudinal course, functional impairment, suicide risk, and healthcare utilization in older adults with PTSD; discuss cross-cultural considerations; and review the impact of demographic characteristics, including gender, ethnicity, and race, on PTSD in this population.

The research literature on older adult trauma survivors reviewed here is likely influenced by cohort variables, specific to certain birth-year–defined groupings, as well as maturation effects attributable to aging. For the current cohort of older adults, trauma that occurred before middle adulthood preceded the 1980 introduction of PTSD into the official psychiatric diagnostic nomenclature (American Psychiatric Association [APA], 1980). This, in conjunction with socialization experiences, likely affected acknowledgment and reporting of traumatic exposure and potential consequences for the current cohort of older adults.

Prevalence, Incidence, and Limitations of Epidemiological Research on ASD in Older Adults

ASD officially entered the psychiatric diagnostic nomenclature in 1994 (American Psychiatric Association [APA], 1994). Since that time, there have only been three empirical investigations that examined the prevalence and correlates of ASD in large samples that contained sufficient numbers of older adults to allow for comparisons (Cardeña, Dennis, Winkel, & Skitka, 2005; Cohen, 2008; Muñoz, Crespo, Pérez-Santos, & Vázquez, 2005). A Web-based survey of a representative sample of adolescents and adults residing in New York City and Washington, D.C., was conducted within the first three weeks following the September 11, 2001, terrorist attacks (Cardeña et al., 2005). A nonlinear relationship was found between age and acute stress symptom severity, with the older adult groups (65–74 and 75+) reporting the lowest ASD symptoms. In contrast, Muñoz and colleagues (2005) found that following the Madrid train bombings in 2004 older adults had 1.7 times greater likelihood of having ASD based on symptom severity. However, there were no significant differences between the age groups when both symptom intensity and functional impairment persisting for longer than a day were taken together. A telephone survey of a randomly selected sample of northern Israeli adults who were subjected to missile attacks during the third week of the second Lebanon war also demonstrated no significant differences in rates of full ASD criteria among three adult age groups (18–40, 41–69, and 70+; Cohen, 2008). Notably, in this small sample, older adults had the lowest rates of subthreshold ASD (Cohen, 2008).

Given only three studies and noting some limitations, it appears that in general older age is associated with lower rates of ASD in the first month after a traumatic event as compared to younger or middle-aged adults. However, there are caveats to this conclusion, and since these limitations apply to PTSD prevalence rates as well, they are covered below.

Prevalence, Incidence, and Limitations of Epidemiological Research on PTSD in Older Adults

Several recent epidemiological studies utilizing representative samples have examined the prevalence of traumatic exposure and rates of PTSD in older adults (Creamer & Parslow, 2008; De Vries & Olff, 2009; Kessler, et al. 2005; Pietrzak, Goldstein, Southwick, & Grant, 2011; Spitzer et al., 2008). These investigations represent an advancement over prevalence rates for older adults in prior research that typically focused on one particular event (i.e., combat, Holocaust, natural disaster), relied on nonrandom or convenience samples, and relegated all older adults to one age category (Cook & Niederehe, 2007).

Results from the National Comorbidity Survey-Replication (NCS-R), one of the largest epidemiological investigations of psychiatric disorders in the United States to date, indicate that lifetime prevalence of PTSD in adults aged 60 and older was 2.5%—significantly lower than in other adult age groups (Kessler et al., 2005). In fact, older adults were five to six times less likely to ever have a PTSD diagnosis.

In another large epidemiological investigation in the United States, Wave 2 of the National Epidemiologic Survey on Alcohol and Related Conditions, those 60 and over were 2.4 to 2.8 times less likely to meet full PTSD criteria than younger age groups and 1.2 to 1.8 times less likely to have subthreshold/partial PTSD (Pietrzak et al., 2011). Overall, the most widely reported worst traumatic events in this age group with either full or partial PTSD were unexpected death, serious illness, or injury of a close person. Those who met criteria for full PTSD diagnoses were significantly more likely to report sexual assault or intimate partner violence as their most distressing event, while those who met criteria for partial PTSD more frequently reported secondary exposure to 9/11 terrorist attacks and injury to a close person as their most stressful events. Large epidemiological studies of community-residing adults outside of the United States show either decreasing rates of PTSD with age (Creamer & Parslow, 2008; De Vries & Olff, 2009) or no differences in rates between young, middle-aged or older adults (Spitzer et al., 2008).

Although, in general, ASD and PTSD prevalence rates are relatively lower in older adults than in other adult age groups, there are specific subsamples within the older adult population that may be particularly vulnerable to the effects of traumatic stress (e.g., older adult survivors of extreme and prolonged stress). In addition, although older adults in the United States and other well-resourced countries may have lower rates of ASD and PTSD after a traumatic event, older adults from less-resourced countries may be more vulnerable. For example, among those older adults who experienced disasters, the least healthy and perhaps the most vulnerable (e.g., physically or emotionally impaired, homebound, or long-term-care residents) had been systematically excluded from investigation (see review by Cook & Elmore, 2009). Thus, any overarching statements that older individuals are the least likely to experience psychiatric distress after a trauma can be potentially misleading and could keep scarce resources from older adults most in need.

Late-Onset PTSD

There have been at least 22 published clinical accounts illustrating what is thought to be late-onset PTSD in older adults, focusing primarily on males who experienced war trauma (for a review, see Hiskey, Luckie, Davies, & Brewin, 2008). Despite this interest, late-onset PTSD in older adulthood has rarely been examined empirically.

Since the introduction of the diagnosis of delayed-onset PTSD, requiring that the onset of symptoms occur six or more months postexposure (APA, 1980), there has been controversy about its existence. Although delayed-onset PTSD has been empirically verified, it is rare in the absence of any prior symptoms. It is likely that delayed-onset is actually a subthreshold PTSD that worsens over time (Andrews, Brewin, Philpott, & Stewart 2008). Indeed, delayed onset PTSD in older adulthood might more accurately be labeled delayed recognition (Pary, Turns, & Tobias, 1986).

A recently reported phenomenon termed late-onset stress symptomatology (LOSS) may be similar to late-onset PTSD (King, King, Vickers, Davison, & Spiro, 2007). In LOSS, older veterans who were exposed to combat in early adulthood and who have had no difficulties in trauma-related functioning throughout most of their lives, experience trauma-related symptoms for the first time in older age. Although qualitative data from a focus group of World War II, Korean War, and Vietnam War combat veterans indicated preliminary evidence for the LOSS phenomena (Davison et al., 2006), empirical investigation is required to verify this construct, differentiate it from delayed onset-PTSD and test its applicability to other older adult trauma populations.

Longitudinal Course, Functional Impairment, Suicide Risk, and Healthcare Utilization in Older Adult Trauma Survivors

Longitudinal Course

Most studies of older adult trauma survivors are cross-sectional, and few investigations of young or middle-aged adult trauma survivors have longitudinally followed individuals into older adulthood. Most of what is known on the course of PTSD symptoms across the life span primarily comes from research on combat veterans (Clipp & Elder, 1996; Dirkzwager, Bramsen, & Van der Ploeg, 2001; Lee, Vaillant, Torrey, & Elder, 1995; Op den Velde et al., 1993) or former prisoners of war (POWs; Port, Engdahl, & Frazier, 2001; Port, Engdahl, Frazier, & Eberly, 2002; Speed, Engdahl, Schwartz, & Eberly, 1989; Zeiss & Dickman, 1989).

The majority of data suggests relative stability of PTSD over time—that is, having PTSD postwar generally predicts PTSD years and even decades later (Clipp & Elder, 1996; Dirkzwager et al., 2001), with one exception. In a study of Harvard University students from 1939–1940, Lee et al. (1995) examined the sequelae of WWII combat and found that there was no temporal relationship between 1946 and 1988 diagnoses of PTSD, possibly due to selective attrition or death of those with PTSD.

Multiple potential trajectories for PTSD symptoms in WWII veterans across their life span were reported: remission, temporal stability of symptoms, subclinical symptoms becoming full and chronic PTSD, delayed-onset possibly after several decades postwar, or waxing and waning of symptoms (Dirkzwager et al., 2001; Op den Velde et al., 1993). Studies involving former POWs yield similar findings, suggesting multiple possible trajectories or fluidity of symptoms (Speed et al., 1989; Zeiss & Dickman, 1989). Despite the findings of variable course of PTSD symptoms, one investigation of community-dwelling WWII and Korean War former POWs found that, in general, symptoms were immediate and intense shortly after captivity, gradually declined for several decades, and increased within the past two decades (Port et al., 2001).

The relative individual variability of the course of PTSD is likely due to influence of contextual factors such as exposure characteristics or life contexts. For example, Speed et al. (1989) reported that younger age at capture and higher percentage of body-weight loss in WWII POWs explained 42% of variance in PTSD severity symptoms decades postwar. Clipp and Elder (1996) reported that the combination of combat and a loss of a friend during combat was associated with a higher rate of stress symptoms. Combat severity and number of physiological symptoms of anxiety experienced during combat predicted PTSD years later (Lee et al., 1995). Social support was also related to improvement in PTSD symptoms (Clipp & Elder, 1996; Port et al., 2002). Contrary to widely held clinical belief, experiencing negative stressful life events does not appear to exacerbate PTSD in old age (Dirkzwager et al., 2001; Port et al., 2002).

Functional Impairment

As adults reach old age, their functional limitations typically increase (e.g., decreased mobility and diminished sensory capacities). However, the relationship between traumatic exposure or PTSD and functional impairments in older adults has also received relatively little attention (Ford et al., 2004; Krause, Shaw, & Cairney, 2004; Shmotkin, Blumstein, & Modan, 2003; Van Zelst, de Beurs, Beekman, van Dyck, & Deeg, 2006). Using data from a national survey of older adults, Krause et al. (2004) examined the relationship between lifetime adverse events characterized as trauma exposure and physical health status in older adults, and found that lifetime trauma events were associated with less favorable health, more acute and chronic health problems, and more difficulties in activities of daily living necessary for fundamental functioning (e.g., ability to bathe, dress, eat, etc.) and instrumental activities of daily living in older adults (e.g., ability to do light housework, prepare meals, etc.). Similarly, older adults with full or partial PTSD reportedly spent more days in bed due to illness and had more days when activities were limited due to health problems than older adults without PTSD (Van Zelst et al., 2006). In contrast, two studies found that despite higher rates of psychiatric problems in Holocaust survivors, functional ability was not impaired (Joffe, Brodaty, Luscombe, & Ehrlich, 2003; Shmotkin et al., 2003). Perhaps these latter findings are due to differential survival of the most physically resilient individuals.

Suicide Risk

A few investigators have examined the relationship of suicidal ideation and trauma in older adulthood, and the findings consistently indicate greater suicidal ideation and/or history of attempts in those who have experienced significant trauma (Barak et al. 2005; Clarke et al., 2004, 2006; Osgood & Manetta, 2001; Rauch, Morales, Zubritsky, Knott, & Oslin, 2006). These findings have been documented in samples ranging from Holocaust survivors, to older veterans, to women who experienced interpersonal victimization. Additionally, in a previously mentioned large epidemiological investigation, after controlling for demographics and psychiatric comorbidities, older adults with PTSD symptoms were twice as likely to attempt suicide than older adults without PTSD (Pietrzak et al., in press).

The findings consistently indicate that history of trauma (e.g., Holocaust, violent victimization) is associated with two to four times higher suicidality in older adult survivors compared to older adults without those traumatic experiences. This relationship is maintained even after adjusting for depression severity and other risk and protective factors (Clarke et al., 2006). Moreover, PTSD in older adults doubles their risk of suicide attempts (Rauch et al., 2006.).

Healthcare Utilization

Both traumatic exposure and PTSD have been linked to poorer self-reported physical health (e.g., Krause et al., 2004; Stein & Barrett-Connor, 2000) and physician-diagnosed medical disorders (Schnurr, Spiro, & Paris, 2000) in older adults. Given these findings, it follows that PTSD in older adults likely also increases service utilization and morbidity. However, the literature on the relationship between age and healthcare utilization in trauma survivors is equivocal (Elhai, North, & Frueh, 2005) and may depend on what type of service is considered (mental and behavioral healthcare versus medical care), the types of healthcare providers, the severity of trauma or PTSD symptoms, comorbid depression, and culture. In some studies, younger age was associated with more frequent mental health service utilization in various traumatized populations (Calhoun, Bosworth, Grambow, Dudley, & Beckham, 2002; Frueh et al., 2007; Koenen, Goodwin, Struening, Hellman, & Guardino, 2003). No relationship was found between age and utilization of mental health services in a sample recruited from general medical practices (Rodriguez et al., 2003).

There are also studies reporting increased mental healthcare utilization in older adults. The psychological effects and help-seeking patterns of survivors of the 2000 Miyake Island volcano eruption in Japan were examined in a random sample of evacuated households (Goto, Wilson, Kahana, & Slane, 2002). Severity of PTSD and depression was associated with an overall higher rate of receiving professional help in the full sample, half of whom were older adults. Compared to younger adults, older individuals reported significantly earlier and more frequent contacts with healthcare professionals and were less likely to seek help from friends and relatives. According to the authors, this may reflect more limited social networks, not realizing their need for help, or not wanting it.

It appears that older adults with PTSD tend to utilize medical services to a greater extent than mental and behavioral health services. For example, in an examination of combat veterans with PTSD, Calhoun and colleagues (2002) found higher rates of general medical services use compared to mental health services use. Frueh and colleagues (2004) reported that the number of primary care visits was three times higher in older than in middle-aged adults. Van Zelst et al. (2006) reported that although older adults with PTSD frequently visited medical specialists, they were rarely treated by psychiatrists or other mental health professionals.

Another predictor of increased healthcare use is severity of trauma. The reviewed data suggest that more severe exposure tends to be associated with higher utilization. Bramsen and van der Ploeg (1999) examined self-reported medical and mental healthcare utilization in WW II survivors in the Netherlands. Although in general there was a relatively low healthcare utilization rate for war-related problems between the 1940s and 1990s (with a peak occurrence in the 1940s), survivors of concentration camps and those with multiple exposures used healthcare services at a higher rate.

In addition to former POWs, Holocaust survivors are another population subjected to severe and prolonged trauma. Levav, Novikov, Grinshpoon, Rosenblum and Ponizovsky (2006) examined medical and mental healthcare utilization in the entire Jewish population of Jerusalem 21 months prior to an intifada through 27 months postterrorist escalation. Utilization of medical services significantly increased for older adults in general, while mental health usage increased for older adults who were already receiving these types of services. Terno, Barak, Hadjez, Elizur, and Szor (1998) also investigated the impact of Holocaust experience on psychiatric inpatients and found that the number and length of hospitalizations varied between groups with Holocaust survivors having more hospitalizations and of longer durations than non-Holocaust survivors.

Finally, traumatic experiences appear to be associated with higher mortality in older adulthood. In a sample of community-dwelling older adults, Lachs, Williams, O'Brien, Pillemer, and Charlson (1998) examined effects of elder abuse and neglect on mortality over a 13-year course. After controlling for demographics, health, cognitive and functional status, social support, depression, and body mass index, that the authors found the chances of dying over the study period tripled in the mistreated group compared to those who did not experience maltreatment or self-neglect. Since mortality was not directly attributable to injuries, the authors hypothesized that negative social support could be one of the factors contributing to mortality. The authors believe that if positive social support is a protective factor, it is possible that the lack of it or negative interactions with the people in the social network could induce a great deal of interpersonal stress and affect mortality.

Although in general the results on the relationships among age, trauma exposure, and mental health utilization are mixed, older adults with severe, prolonged, or multiple traumas may use mental and behavioral health services more frequently than younger or middle-aged adults. In general, older adults use medical care services, especially primary care, more often than mental and behavioral health services. Social support appears to buffer the effect of trauma and PTSD in this population similarly to research with adults of other ages.

Cross-Cultural Considerations in Older Adult Trauma Survivors

There are few empirical investigations examining the influences of trauma on older populations from diverse cultural backgrounds. Contrary to many of the studies involving Caucasian residents of the United States, these investigations have consistently found that older age is related to increased PTSD symptoms in samples from other nations or in immigrant populations. This is observed in northern Croatians from a war zone (Havelka, Lucanin, & Lucanin, 1995), Turkish earthquake survivors (Salcioglu, Basoglu, & Livanou, 2003), Asian and Middle Eastern immigrants of various nationalities who survived the Oklahoma City bombings (Trautman et al., 2002), and Romanian victims of politically motivated violence (Bichescu et al., 2005). Only one study compared older adult survivors from various cultures in regard to their mental health posttrauma (Norris, Kaniasty, Conrad, Inman, & Murphy, 2002). In an examination of PTSD symptoms following disasters in the United States, Mexico, and Poland, there was no one consistent effect of age. There were, however, significant interactions of age with the social, economic, cultural, and historical contexts of the different countries influencing mental health outcomes. Namely, age had a curvilinear association with PTSD among Americans (i.e., middle-aged adults were most distressed); age had a linear and negative relation with PTSD among Mexicans (i.e., young adults were most distressed); and age had a linear and positive relation with PTSD among Poles (i.e., older people were most distressed).

Unlike the results from predominately English-speaking samples or industrialized countries, evidence from other cultures indicates that various traumatic stressors are associated with higher rates of PTSD, depression, somatization, and other problems in older compared to younger adults, be it due to political internment, war-zone exposure, earthquake, or bombing. Thus, there is likely differential impact of various cultural and historical influences on different age groups. Indeed, the only study investigating the expression of trauma simultaneously in several cultures supports this presupposition.

Impact of Demographic Characteristics Including Gender, Ethnicity, and Race in Older Adult Trauma Survivors

Gender

As stated previously, a great deal of the research on older adult trauma survivors comes from male combatants or former POWs. Additionally, although there is a fairly large literature on older adults who experienced the Holocaust or disasters, rarely are gender differences examined or discussed. Over the past decade, there have been a number of research investigations on interpersonal violence—specifically, sexual assault, intimate partner violence and elder abuse, neglect, and exploitation in older females (e.g., Acierno et al., 2007; Bonomi et al., 2007; Fritsch, Tarima, Caldwell, & Beaven, 2005).

As part of a population-based investigation of lifetime physical and sexual assault, Acierno et al. (2007) found that history of physical assault was more likely to be associated with substance abuse, depression, and avoidance and re-experiencing symptoms over the past year, while history of sexual assault was more often associated with autonomic arousal and avoidance symptoms. Although not at diagnostic levels, older women who had been physically or sexually assaulted decades earlier continued to report significant levels of PTSD and other mental health problems.

In smaller convenience samples, the rates of traumatic exposure in older women are even higher and are related to higher levels of depression, anxiety, and worse physical and mental health in both African-American and Caucasian samples (Bechtle-Higgins & Follette, 2002; Paranjape, Sprauve-Holmes, Gaughan, & Kaslow, 2009). Older women who experienced at least one type of abuse (psychological/emotional, physical, sexual, control, threat) since turning 55 were almost four times more likely to report negative health conditions than older women who were not abused (Fisher & Regan, 2006).

Despite lower rates of interpersonal violence in older as compared to younger women, many characteristics of victimization are similar across the age groups (Rennison & Rand, 2003). However, the older women were less likely to report sexual assault to the police than younger women. Fear of retaliation and considering interpersonal violence a private matter were the main reasons for not reporting sexual assault. In addition, certain socialization-related issues for older women, such as perceived loyalty, financial dependency, and fear of stigmatization and loss of social support network, likely also influence reporting and help-seeking behavior.

Ethnicity/Race

Little is known about the differences in rates of traumatic exposure and subsequent mental and physical health effects between older Caucasian adults and older adults from other ethnicities or races. While risk of developing PTSD decreased after young adulthood for non-Hispanic Caucasians, this same risk endured throughout the life course for African Americans and Caribbean blacks (Himle, Baser, Taylor, Campbell, & Jackson, 2009). Utilizing data from two large national surveys, Himle et al. (2009) found that African Americans and Caribbean blacks had a higher risk for PTSD across the life span than did Caucasians. Although the highest risk of PTSD onset was between late teens and early 20s for all three racial groups, risk for PTSD across the rest of the life span was higher among African Americans and Caribbean blacks than among Caucasians. The authors hypothesize that increased vulnerability for PTSD in these two groups is due to higher exposure to trauma and race-related oppression and stressors.

A secondary analysis of two previously examined data sets on victims of recent crime was used to examine rates and differences in PTSD symptoms between community-residing Caucasian and African-American older adults (Mainous, Smith, Acierno, & Geesey, 2005). In general, there were no differences in the prevalence of overall PTSD or its three-symptom clusters (re-experiencing, avoidance, or arousal) between the two groups. However, when data were analyzed separately for those who experienced a physical as opposed to a nonphysical crime, among those reporting a nonphysical trauma, Caucasians were more likely to exceed the PTSD diagnostic threshold for hyper-arousal symptoms. The authors suggest that due to longstanding cultural experiences, African Americans may have had to develop different coping strategies and thus respond to objectively less dangerous situations with less fear-related arousal. These findings were based on self-report, and more research is needed to confirm these results with standardized structured diagnostic interviews.

Conclusion

The limited research indicates lower prevalence rates of ASD and PTSD in older adults as opposed to other age groups. In the majority of studies on longitudinal course of PTSD, which have been primarily conducted on combat veterans and former POWs, there is relative stability across the life span. For some, however, there appears to be a waxing and waning of symptoms and for others, PTSD can reappear or worsen later in life. PTSD in older adults has also been linked to suicidal ideation and attempts, functional impairment, poorer physical health and, in some cases, increased healthcare utilization.

Future Directions

There are significant gaps in the knowledge of trauma and its effects in older adults. Specifically, only three investigations have been conducted on the prevalence and correlates of ASD in older individuals. The overwhelming majority of studies on older adult trauma survivors focus on PTSD, while traumatic exposure has been repeatedly associated with additional mental health consequences, such as depression, in other age groups as well. Longitudinal investigations are important to elucidate the course of PTSD over the life span. For example, such studies would help to illuminate the heterogeneity of mental health trajectories following exposure to a potentially traumatic event in a comprehensive and systematic manner, including the issue of delayed-onset PTSD and the role that cognitive changes play in the onset or exacerbation of PTSD in later life. In addition to basic knowledge needed on the role of race/ethnicity and multicultural issues among older trauma survivors, it would be prudent to understand the relatively higher rates of PTSD among African-American elders. As suggested by Mainous et al. (2005), perhaps historical and cultural factors influence the degree to which older adults experience, interpret, and express trauma-related symptoms specifically related to arousal. Clearly gaining a better understanding of cultural diversity in prevalence, treatment, and recovery is needed.

References

Acierno, R. E., Lawyer, S. R., Rheingold, A. A., Kilpatrick, D. G., Resnick, H. S., & Saunders, B. E. (2007). Current psychopathology in previously assaulted older adults. *Journal of Interpersonal Violence, 22*, 250–258.

American Psychiatric Association. (1980). *Diagnostic and statistical manual of mental disorders* (3rd ed.). Washington, DC: Author.

American Psychiatric Association. (1994). *Diagnostic and statistical manual of mental disorders* (4th ed.). Washington, DC: Author.

Andrews, B., Brewin, C. R., Philpott, R., & Stewart, L. (2008). Delayed onset posttraumatic stress disorder: A systematic review of the evidence. *American Journal of Psychiatry, 164*, 1319–1326.

Averill, P. M., & Beck, J. G. (2000). Posttraumatic stress disorder in older adults: A conceptual review. *Journal of Anxiety Disorders, 14*, 133–156.

Barak, Y., Aizenberg, D., Szor, H., Swartz, M., Maor, R., & Knobler, H. Y. (2005). Increased risk of attempted suicide among aging Holocaust survivors. *American Journal of Geriatric Psychiatry, 13*, 701–704.

Bechtle-Higgins, A., & Follette, V. M. (2002). Frequency and impact of interpersonal trauma in older women. *Journal of Clinical Geropsychology, 8*, 215–226.

Bichescu, D., Schauer, M., Saleptsi, E., Neculau, A., Elbert, T., & Neuner, F. (2005). Long-term consequences of traumatic experiences: An assessment of former political detainees in Romania. *Clinical Practice and Epidemiology in Mental Health, 1*, 1–11.

Bonomi, A. E., Anderson, M. L., Reid, R. J., Carrell, D., Fishman, P. A., Rivara, F. P., et al. (2007). Intimate partner violence in older women. *The Gerontologist, 47*, 34–41.

Bramsen, I., & van der Ploeg, H. M. (1999). Use of medical and mental health care by World War II survivors in the Netherlands. *Journal of Traumatic Stress, 12*, 243–261.

Calhoun, P. S., Bosworth, H. B., Grambow, S. C. Dudley, T. K., & Beckham, J. C. (2002). Medical service utilization by veterans seeking help for posttraumatic stress disorder. *American Journal of Psychiatry, 159*, 2081–2086.

Cardeña, E., Dennis, J. M., Winkel, M., & Skitka, L. J. (2005). A snapshot of terror: Acute posttraumatic responses to the September 11th attack. *Journal of Trauma and Dissociation, 6*, 69–84.

Clarke, D. E., Colantonio, A., Heslegrave, R., Rhodes, A., Links, P., & Conn, D. (2004). Holocaust experience and suicidal ideation in high-risk older adults. *American Journal of Geriatric Psychiatry, 12*, 65–74.

Clarke, D. E., Colantonio, A., Rhodes, A., Conn, D. K., Heslegrave, R., Links, P. S., et al. (2006). Differential experiences during the Holocaust and suicidal ideation in older adults in treatment for depression. *Journal of Traumatic Stress, 19*, 417–423.

Clipp, E. C., & Elder, G., Jr. (1996). The aging veteran of World War II: Psychiatric and life course insights. In P. E. Ruskin & J. A. Talbott (Eds.), *Aging and posttraumatic stress disorder* (pp. 19–51). Washington, DC: American Psychiatric Press.

Cohen, M. (2008). Acute stress disorder in older, middle-aged and younger adults in reaction to the second Lebanon war. *International Journal of Geriatric Psychiatry, 23*, 34–40.

Cook, J. M., & Elmore, D. L. (2009). Disaster mental health in older adults: Symptoms, policy and planning. In Y. Neria, S. Galea, & F. Norris (Eds.), *The mental health consequences of disasters* (pp. 233–263). New York: Cambridge University Press.

Cook, J. M., & Niederehe, G. (2007). Trauma in older adults. In M. J. Friedman, T. M. Keane, & P. A. Resick (Eds.), *PTSD science & practice: A comprehensive handbook* (pp. 252–276). New York: Guilford.

Creamer, M. C., & Parslow, R. A. (2008). Trauma exposure and posttraumatic stress disorder in the elderly: A community prevalence study. *American Journal of Geriatric Psychiatry, 16*, 853–856.

Davison, E. H., Pless, A. P., Gugliucci, M. R., King, L. A., King, D. W., Salgado, D. M., et al. (2006). Late-life emergence of early life trauma: The phenomenon of late-onset stress symptomatology among aging combat veterans. *Research on Aging, 28*, 84–114.

De Vries, G., & Olff, M. (2009). The lifetime prevalence of traumatic events and posttraumatic stress disorder in the Netherlands. *Journal of Traumatic Stress, 22*, 259–267.

Dirkzwager, A. J. E., Bramsen, I., & Van der Ploeg, H. M. (2001). The longitudinal course of posttraumatic stress disorder symptoms among aging military veterans. *Journal of Nervous and Mental Disease, 189*, 846–853.

Elhai, J. D., North, T. C., & Frueh, B. C. (2005). Health service use predictors among trauma survivors: A critical review. *Psychological Services, 2*, 3–19

Falk, B., Hersen, M., & Van Hasselt, V. (1994). Assessment of post-traumatic stress disorder in older adults: A critical review. *Clinical Psychology Review, 14*, 383–415.

Fisher, B. S., & Regan, S. L. (2006). The extent and frequency of abuse in the lives of older women and their relationship with health outcomes. *The Geronotologist, 46*, 200–209.

Ford, J. D., Schnurr, P. P., Friedman, M. J., Green, B. L., Adams, G. A., & Jex, S. (2004). Posttraumatic stress disorder symptoms, physical health, and health care utilization 50 years after repeated exposure to a toxic gas. *Journal of Traumatic Stress, 17*, 185–194.

Fritsch, T. A., Tarima, S. S., Caldwell, G. G., & Beaven, S. (2005). Intimate partner violence against older women in Kentucky. *Journal of the Kentucky Medical Association, 103*, 461–463.

Frueh, B. C., Elhai, J. D., Hamner, M. B., Magruder K. M., Sauvageot, J. A., & Mintzer, J. (2004). Elderly veterans with combat-related posttraumatic stress disorder in specialty care. *Journal of Nervous and Mental Disease, 192*, 75–79.

Frueh, B. C., Grubaugh, A. L., Acierno, R., Elhai, J. D., Cain, G., & Magruder, K. M. (2007). Age differences in posttraumatic stress disorder, psychiatric disorders, and healthcare service use among veterans in Veterans Affairs primary care clinics. *American Journal of Geriatric Psychiatry, 15*, 660–672.

Goto, T., Wilson, J. P., Kahana, B., & Slane, S. (2002). PTSD, depression, and help-seeking patterns following the Miyake Island volcanic eruption. *International Journal of Emergency Mental Health, 4*, 157–172.

Havelka, M., Lucanin, J. D., & Lucanin, D. (1995). Psychological reactions to war stressors among elderly displaced persons in Croatia. *Croatian Medical Journal, 36*, 262–265.

Himle, J. A., Baser, R. E., Taylor, R. J., Campbell, R. D., & Jackson, J. S. (2009). Anxiety disorders among African Americans, blacks of Caribbean descent, and non-Hispanic whites in the United States. *Journal of Anxiety Disorders, 23*, 578–590.

Hiskey, S., Luckie, M., Davies, S., & Brewin, C. R. (2008). The emergence of posttraumatic distress later in life: A review. *Journal of Geriatric Psychiatry, 21*, 232–241.

Joffe, C. F., Brodaty, H., Luscombe,G., & Ehrlich, F. (2003). The Sydney Holocaust study: Posttraumatic stress disorder and other psychosocial morbidity in an aged community sample. *Journal of Traumatic Stress, 16*, 39–47.

Kessler, R. C., Berglund, P., Demler, O., Jin, R., Merikangas, K. R., & Walters, E. E. (2005). Lifetime prevalence and age-of-onset distributions of DSM-IV disorders in the National Comorbidity Survey Replication. *Archives of General Psychiatry, 62*, 593–602.

King, L. A., King, D. W., Vickers, K. S., Davison, E. H., & Spiro, A. (2007). Assessing late-onset stress symptomatology among aging male combat veterans. *Aging and Mental Health, 11*, 175–191.

Koenen, K. C., Goodwin, R., Struening, E., Hellman, F., & Guardino, M. (2003). Posttraumatic stress disorder and treatment seeking in a national screening sample. *Journal of Traumatic Stress, 16*, 5–16.

Krause, N., Shaw, B. A., & Cairney, J. (2004). A descriptive epidemiology of lifetime trauma and the physical health status of older adults. *Psychology and Aging, 19*, 637–648.

Lachs, M. S., Williams, C. S., O'Brien, S., Pillemer, K. A., & Charlson, M. E. (1998). The mortality of elder mistreatment. *Journal of the American Medical Association, 280*, 428–432.

Lee, K. A., Valliant, G. E., Torrey, W. C., & Elder, G. H. (1995). A 50-year prospective study of the psychological sequelae of World War II combat. *American Journal of Psychiatry, 152*, 516–522.

Levav, I., Novikov, I., Grinshpoon, A., Rosenblum, J., & Ponizovsky, A. (2006). Health services utilization in Jerusalem under terrorism. *American Journal of Psychiatry, 163*, 1355–1361.

Mainous, A. G., Smith, D. W., Acierno, R. E., & Geesey, M. E. (2005). Differences in posttraumatic stress disorder symptoms between elderly non-Hispanic whites and African Americans. *Journal of the National Medical Association, 97,* 546–549.

Muñoz, M., Crespo, M., Pérez-Santos, E., & Vázquez, J. J. (2005). Early psychological consequences of the March 11, 2004, terrorist attacks in Madrid, Spain. *Psychological Reports, 97,* 907–920.

Norris, F. H., Kaniasty, K. Z., Conrad, M. L., Inman, G. L., & Murphy, A. D. (2002). Placing age differences in cultural context: A comparison of the effects of age on PTSD after disasters in the United States, Mexico, and Poland. *Journal of Clinical Geropsychology, 8,* 153–173.

Op den Velde, W., Falger, P. R. J., Hovens, J. E., De Groen, J. H. M., Van Duijn, H., Lasschuit, L. J., et al. (1993). PTSD in Dutch resistance veterans from World War II. In J. P. Wilson & B. Rafael (Eds.), *International handbook of traumatic stress syndromes* (pp. 219–230). New York: Plenum.

Osgood, N. J., & Manetta, A. M. (2000–2001). Abuse and suicidal issues in older women. *Omega, 42,* 71–81.

Paranjape, A., Sprauve-Holmes, N. E., Gaughan, J., & Kaslow, N. (2009). Lifetime exposure to family violence: Implications for the health status of older African American women. *Journal of Women's Health, 18,* 171–175.

Pary, R., Turns, D. M., & Tobias, C. R. (1986). A case of delayed recognition of posttraumatic stress disorder. *American Journal of Psychiatry, 143,* 941.

Pietrzak, R. H., Goldstein, R. B., Southwick, S. M., & Grant, B. F. (2011). *Prevalence and Axis I comorbidity of full and partial posttraumatic stress disorder in the United States: Results from Wave 2 of the National Epidemiologic Survey on Alcohol and Related Conditions. Journal of Anxiety Disorders, 25,* 456–465.

Pietrzak, R. H., Goldstein, R. B., Southwick, S. M., & Grant, B. F. (in press). *Psychiatric comorbidity of posttraumatic stress disorder among older adults in the United States: Results from Wave 2 of the National Epidemiologic Survey on Alcohol and Related Conditions. American Journal of Geriatric Psychiatry.*

Port, C. L., Engdahl, B., & Frazier, P. (2001). A longitudinal and retrospective study of PTSD among older POWs. *American Journal of Psychiatry, 158,* 1474–1479.

Port, C. L., Engdahl, B. E., Frazier, P. A., & Eberly, R. E. (2002). Factors related to the long- term course of PTSD in older ex-prisoners of war. *Journal of Clinical Geropsychology, 8,* 203–214.

Rauch, S. A. M., Morales, K. H., Zubritsky, C., Knott, K., & Oslin, D. (2006). Posttraumatic stress, depression, and health among older adults in primary care. *American Journal of Geriatric Psychiatry, 14,* 316–324.

Rennison, C., & Rand, M. (2003). Non-lethal intimate partner violence: Women age 55 or older. *Violence Against Women, 9,* 1417–1428.

Rodriguez, B. F., Weisberg, R. B., Pagano, M. E., Machan, J. T., Culpepper, L., & Keller, M. B. (2003). Mental health treatment received by primary care patients with posttraumatic stress disorder. *Journal of Clinical Psychiatry, 64,* 1230–1236.

Salcioglu, E., Basoglu, M., & Livanou, M. (2003). Long-term psychological outcome for non- treatment-seeking earthquake survivors in Turkey. *Journal of Nervous and Mental Disease, 191,* 154–160.

Schnurr, P. P., Spiro, A., & Paris, A. H. (2000). Physician-diagnosed medical disorders in relation to PTSD symptoms in older male military veterans. *Health Psychology, 19,* 91–97.

Shmotkin, D., Blumstein, T., & Modan, B. (2003). Tracing long-term effects of trauma: A broad-scope view of Holocaust survivors in late life. *Journal of Consulting and Clinical Psychology, 71,* 223–234.

Speed, N., Engdahl, B., Schwartz, J., & Eberly, R. (1989). Posttraumatic stress disorder as a consequence of the POW experience. *Journal of Nervous and Mental Disease, 177,* 147–153.

Spitzer, C., Barnow, S., Völzke, H., John, U., Freyberger, H. J., & Grabe, H. J. (2008). Trauma and posttraumatic stress disorder in the elderly: Findings from a German community study. *Journal of Clinical Psychiatry, 69,* 693–700.

Stein, M. B. & Barrett-Connor, E. (2000). Sexual Assault and Physical health: Findings from a population-based study of older adults. *Psychosomatic Medicine, 62,* 838–843.

Terno, P., Barak, Y., Hadjez, J., Elizur, A., & Szor, H. (1998). Holocaust survivors hospitalized for life: The Israeli experience. *Comprehensive Psychiatry, 39,* 364–367.

Trautman, R. P., Tucker, P. M., Pfefferbaum, B. C., Lensgraf, S. J., Doughty, D. E., Buksh, A., et al. (2002). Effects of prior trauma and age on posttraumatic stress symptoms in Asian and Middle Eastern immigrants after terrorism in the community. *Community Mental Health Journal, 38,* 459–474.

United Nations, Department of Economic and Social Affairs, Population Division (2007). *World population prospects: The 2006 revision, highlights.* Working paper no. ESA/P/WP.202. Retrieved September 28, 2009, from http://www.un.org/esa/population/publications/wpp2006/WPP2006_Highlights_rev.pdf.

Van Zelst, W. H., de Beurs, E., Beekman, A. T. F., van Dyck, R. & Deeg, D. D. H. (2006). Well-being, physical functioning, and use of health services in the elderly with PTSD and subthreshold PTSD. *International Journal of Geriatric Psychiatry, 21,* 180–188.

Zeiss, R. A., & Dickman, H. R. (1989). PTSD 40 years later: Incidence and person-situation correlates in former POWs. *Journal of Clinical Psychology, 45,* 80–87.

CHAPTER

10 Traumatic Stress in Special Populations

Kim T. Mueser *and* Weili Lu

Abstract

Special populations are individuals who by virtue of psychiatric, behavioral, cognitive, or physical disabilities are more likely to be exposed to psychological trauma. Individuals with severe psychiatric disorders, substance use disorders, developmental disabilities, and persons who are incarcerated are more likely to experience trauma throughout their lives, especially interpersonal victimization, and are more likely to develop posttraumatic stress disorder (PTSD). Trauma and PTSD have a negative impact on special populations, often exacerbating psychiatric symptoms and substance abuse, and interfering with community functioning. Despite the high rates of trauma and PTSD in special populations, these problems are often not identified, and when they are, they are rarely treated. Recent progress has been made in adapting treatments developed for PTSD in the general population to special populations, including persons with severe mental illness and individuals with substance use disorders.

Key Words: Severe mental illness, serious mental illness, schizophrenia, bipolar disorder, borderline personality disorder, substance abuse, addiction, prison, incarceration, developmental disabilities, intellectual disabilities

Introduction

Traumatic experiences, such as being physically or sexually assaulted, witnessing violence, the sudden unexpected death of a loved one, or being the victim of a natural disaster or terrorist attack, can happen to anyone. However, this does not mean that everyone is equally vulnerable to trauma or that such events have the same psychological impact on everyone. Some individuals are more likely to be exposed to traumatic events and are more sensitive to the effects of trauma than others. These individuals, or *special populations*, are the focus of this chapter.

For the purposes of this chapter, we define special populations as individuals with developmental, cognitive, behavioral, or emotional disabilities or impairments that are associated with increased exposure to trauma and whose trauma-related disorders are less likely to be recognized and treated. Among the individuals meeting this definition, we focus on those with severe mental illnesses (such as schizophrenia, bipolar disorder, or treatment refractory major depression), addiction, developmental disabilities, or who are incarcerated because of criminal behavior. We recognize that this definition does not include a broader group of special populations who, for reasons related to demographic, situational, or political reasons, may be more susceptible to trauma exposure. For example, racial or ethnic minorities, adolescents or older individuals, refugees, homeless persons, or individuals exposed to mass violence are more likely to experience trauma and less likely to receive treatment, but are not addressed in this chapter for space reasons. We have chosen to focus on this defined subgroup of special populations because their increased vulnerability to trauma is related to who they are as individuals and not to their personal, cultural, or political circumstances, and hence is a relatively immutable aspect of themselves.

Research on the prevalence and treatment of acute stress disorder in special populations is very limited. In contrast, a growing body of research has been conducted examining the prevalence of posttraumatic stress disorder (PTSD) in special populations, and as well as the treatment of PTSD in these individuals (Mueser, Rosenberg, & Rosenberg, 2009; Najavits, 2002). Hence, we focus on PTSD in this chapter. We begin with a review of the epidemiology of PTSD in special populations, followed by a discussion of barriers to obtaining accurate information about trauma and PTSD in these vulnerable persons. Next, to illustrate the challenges caused by trauma and its psychological sequelae, we focus in greater depth on individuals with severe mental illness and the impact of PTSD on the course of illness, as well as the impact of demographic characteristics on PTSD in this population. We briefly highlight recent advances made in the treatment of PTSD in persons with severe mental illness. We conclude with a discussion of future clinical and research directions regarding trauma and PTSD in special populations.

Epidemiology of Trauma and PTSD in Special Populations

Cross-sectional studies of PTSD in the general population conducted in either the United States or Europe tend to report a lifetime prevalence of PTSD in the 6–12% range (Breslau, Peterson, Poisson, Schultz, & Lucia, 2004; Kessler, Chiu, Demler, & Walters, 2005; Kessler, Sonnega, Bromet, Hughes, & Nelson, 1995). Higher rates of PTSD are typically found in developing countries (Zlotnick et al., 2006), where exposure to trauma may be more prevalent. Although a variety of sociodemographic characteristics have been found to be related to PTSD, gender is the most consistent predictor across studies, with women more likely to develop PTSD than men (Tolin & Foa, 2006). By all accounts, studies examining trauma exposure and the prevalence of PTSD in vulnerable populations indicate significantly higher rates than those reported in general population surveys, as briefly reviewed below.

Severe Mental Illness

Severe mental illness, or *serious mental illness*, are widely used terms that refer to the presence of a major psychiatric disorder that is both persistent and disabling to one's ability to work, take care of oneself, or participate actively in social relationships (Schinnar, Rothbard, Kanter, & Jung, 1990), often resulting in the need for financial benefits to compensate for inability to work. Although any psychiatric disorder can be severe enough to lead to disability, the most common ones include schizophrenia, schizoaffective disorder, bipolar disorder, and major depression. Personality disorders can also be severe and disabling, especially borderline and schizotypal personality disorder (Sanislow et al., 2009; Torgersen, Kringlen, & Cramer, 2001).

There is abundant evidence that trauma exposure in childhood increases the chances of a person developing a severe mental illness (Felitti et al., 1998; Read, van Os, Morrison, & Ross, 2005). Furthermore, individuals who develop a severe mental illness are more prone to violent victimization after the onset of their disorder (Goodman, Rosenberg, Mueser, & Drake, 1997; Hiday, Swartz, Swanson, Borum, & Wagner, 1999; Maniglio, 2009). Thus, exposure to multiple traumas is common among people with severe mental illness, to the extent that such exposure can even be considered "normative."

The high rate of trauma in people with severe mental illness has spurred interest in examining PTSD in this population. Most research has examined current PTSD in individuals with a severe mental illness who are receiving inpatient or outpatient mental health services. Most studies of multiepisode persons with severe mental illness have reported rates of current PTSD ranging between 28–53% (i.e., Howgego et al., 2005; McFarlane, Bookless, & Air, 2001; Mueser et al., 1998; Mueser, Salyers, et al., 2004; Switzer et al., 1999).

Two studies have evaluated the prevalence of PTSD in people with a first episode of severe mental illness. One study reported a rate of 16% PTSD in clients admitted to the hospital for treatment of a first episode of psychosis (Neria, Bromet, Sievers, Lavelle, & Fochtmann, 2002). Another study found a rate of 14% PTSD in a sample of adolescents receiving treatment for a first episode of bipolar disorder (Strawn et al., 2010). These two studies are consistent with the previously reviewed research suggesting that higher rates of trauma and PTSD may predispose individuals to the development of a major psychiatric disorder, as well as research indicating increased victimization of persons following the onset of a major psychiatric disorder. The correlates of PTSD in people with severe mental illness, and its impact on the course of the disorder, is considered in more detail later in this chapter.

Substance Use Disorders

A strong association among trauma, PTSD, and substance use disorders has long been noted. Similar to research on trauma and severe mental illness, rates of lifetime trauma exposure are high in persons with an addiction, typically ranging over 80% (Dansky, Saladin, Brady, Kilpatrick, & Resnick, 1995; Mills, Lynskey, Teesson, Ross, & Darke, 2005). As expected from the high rate of trauma exposure, people with an addiction have significantly elevated rates of PTSD compared to the general population. Lifetime estimates of PTSD in people receiving treatment for substance abuse range between 26% and 52% (Jacobson, Southwick, & Kosten, 2001; Mills et al., 2005; Reynolds et al., 2005). Rates of current PTSD among persons in treatment for substance abuse are similarly high, ranging between 15% and 41% (Bonin, Norton, Asmundson, Dicurzio, & Pidlubney, 2000; Clark, Masson, Delucchi, Hall, & Sees, 2001; Dansky et al., 1995; Langeland, Draijer, & van den Brink, 2004; Read, Brown, & Kahler, 2004; Reynolds et al., 2005).

Trauma exposure is an established risk factor for the development of a substance use disorder. To complicate matters further, substance abuse contributes to subsequent traumatization and victimization, for several reasons (Miller, Downs, & Testa, 1993; Najavits, Sonn, Walsh, & Weiss, 2004). First, people are less able to defend themselves when they are under the influence of substances that can alter the accuracy of their perceptions. Second, people are more prone to accidents when using alcohol or drugs. Third, people who abuse substances often spend more time with other people who are more likely to victimize them (e.g., sexual assault or robbery). Fourth, substance use can lead to disinhibition (e.g., sexual relations with a new acquaintance, aggression in response to a minor provocation), resulting in traumatic consequences. Fifth, when people develop a dependence on substances they may engage in behaviors that increase their vulnerability to victimization (e.g., prostitution) or trauma (e.g., robbery) in order to support their habit. Last, people with PTSD are prone to abusing substances in an effort to "self-medicate" their distressing symptoms (Nishith, Resick, & Mueser, 2001; Ouimette, Read, Wade, & Tirone, 2010), often leading to a vicious cycle of increasingly severe PTSD leading to more severe addiction, which results in retraumatization and the further worsening of PTSD symptoms (Chilcoat & Breslau, 1998; Kilpatrick et al., 2003).

The high rate of PTSD in people with an addiction is also associated with a range of other clinical problems. PTSD comorbidity in addiction is associated with an earlier onset of substance abuse (Johnson, Striley, & Cottler, 2006; Read et al., 2004), more severe addiction (Clark et al., 2001; Mills et al., 2005), and abuse of "harder" drugs, such as cocaine, amphetamine, and heroin (Cottler, Compton, Mager, Spitznagel, & Janca, 1992; Mills, Teesson, Ross, & Peters, 2006; Najavits et al., 1998). PTSD in people with substance abuse is also related to higher psychiatric comorbidity (Back et al., 2000; Kessler et al., 1995) and poorer psychosocial functioning and well-being (Mills et al., 2006; Ouimette, Goodwin, & Brown, 2006).

Considering the increased severity of problems related to PTSD for clients with substance use disorders, it is not surprising that these individuals present multiple treatment challenges. Compared to people with substance use disorders only, individuals with substance use disorders and PTSD have greater difficulty engaging and remaining in treatment, and are more likely to relapse back into substance abuse and to require hospitalization (Hien, Nunes, Levin, & Fraser, 2000; Mills et al., 2005; Najavits et al., 2007; Ouimette, Moos, & Finney, 2003). For these reasons, recent efforts have focused on integrating treatment of PTSD and substance abuse (Brady, Dansky, Back, Foa, & Carroll, 2001; McGovern, Lambert-Harris, Acquilano, Weiss, & Xie, 2009; Najavits, 2002).

Incarceration

There is ample evidence that incarcerated individuals are more likely to have been exposed to a wide range of traumatic events in their lifetime. This is in part related to the high rates of mental illness and addiction among incarcerated individuals (Teplin, 1994; Teplin, Abram, & McClelland, 1996). Common traumatic events in this population include childhood physical and sexual abuse, sexual assault and domestic violence (for women), violent loss of a loved one, and witnessing injury or death of another person. Although studies range in their estimates of exposure to specific traumatic events, cumulative trauma exposure rates are typically over 80% (Haugebrook, Zgoba, Maschi, Morgen, & Brown, 2010; Neller, Denny, Pietz, & Tomlinson, 2006; Sarchiapone, Carli, Cuomo,

Marchetti, & Roy, 2009; Saxon et al., 2001; Singer, Bussey, Song, & Lungerhofer, 1995). Childhood sexual abuse among incarcerated women is especially high (Greenfeld & Minor-Harper, 1991; Messina & Grella, 2006; Singer et al., 1995; Zlotnick, 1997).

Research on the prevalence of PTSD in incarcerated populations is limited, but the available evidence indicates higher rates than in the general population (Goff, Rose, Rose, & Purves, 2007). Rates of current PTSD range between 21% and 51% (Butler, Allnutt, Cain, Owens, & Muller, 2005; Gibson et al., 1999; Saxon et al., 2001; Teplin et al., 1996; Warren, Loper, & Komarovskaya, 2009; Zlotnick, 1997). Fewer studies have evaluated lifetime prevalence of PTSD, with research suggesting that about one-third of incarcerated individuals have met criteria for PTSD at some point in their lives (Gibson et al., 1999; Teplin et al., 1996).

PTSD among incarcerated individuals is associated with worse functioning across a range of areas, consistent with the clinical correlates of PTSD in the general population. PTSD among incarcerated individuals is correlated with higher rates of substance abuse, more psychiatric comorbidity, and worse health (Gibson et al., 1999; Saxon et al., 2001; Zlotnick, 1997). Although the treatment of PTSD in jail or prison settings has until recently been a largely neglected need, recent efforts suggest promising results of cognitive-behavioral intervention targeting PTSD and substance abuse in this population (Zlotnick, Johnson, & Najavits, 2009).

Developmental Disabilities

The term *developmental disabilities* refers to a chronic disability that includes a mental or physical impairment, or their combination, that manifests before the age of 22, contributes to significant functional impairment (e.g., language, learning, self-care), and is expected to continue indefinitely (Developmental Disabilities Assistance and Bill of Rights Act, 2000). Examples of developmental disabilities include intellectual disability (mental retardation), cerebral palsy, autism, Down syndrome, and fetal alcohol syndrome. Research on developmental disabilities often focuses on individuals who have an intellectual disability, but not always.

In contrast to the relatively rich database documenting high rates of trauma and PTSD in the aforementioned special populations, less is known about the extent of trauma and rates of PTSD in people with a developmental disability. However, the available research suggests higher rates of physical and sexual abuse than in the general population (Brownridge, 2006; Cloutier, Martin, & Poole, 2002; Hightower & Smith, 2003; Martin et al., 2006; Melcombe, 2003; Sobsey, 1994). Although surveys of trauma history indicate that people with physical disability are more likely to have experienced trauma than people without a disability (McFarlane et al., 2001; Pava, 1994), rates for people with intellectual disability are even higher and suggest increased vulnerability (Furey, 1994; Sobsey & Doe, 1991). For example, some research has reported that among people with an intellectual disability, over 80% of women and over 30% of men have been sexually abused or assaulted (Johnson, 2000; Lumley & Miltenberger, 1997).

A number of factors contribute to the increased rates of exposure to interpersonal violence in people with developmental disabilities. Living in an institutional setting, at distance from traditional supports such as family, can increase vulnerability to abuse by persons who are responsible for their services and supports (McCartney & Campbell, 1998; PAI, 2003; Valenti-Hein & Schwartz, 1995). People with a developmental disability are often raised in an environment in which compliance is expected and demanded, which makes it more difficult to resist physical and sexual intrusions from others (Lumley & Miltenberger, 1997; Tharinger, Horton, & Millea, 1990; Valenti-Hein & Schwartz, 1995). These individuals often lack the resources, physically and cognitively, to defend against abuse. In addition, people with developmental disabilities may give affection that is misunderstood by others and lead to coerced sexual behavior (Kempton & Gochros, 1986).

The consequences of exposure to physical and sexual abuse in people with developmental disabilities are widespread, and include emotional distress, social withdrawal, aggression, sexually inappropriate behavior, and health problems (Mansell, Sobsey, & Moskal, 1998; Sequeira & Hollins, 2003; Sobsey, 1994; PAI, 2003). Less research has evaluated PTSD in this population (King et al., 2004; Newman, 2000; Russell & Shah, 2003). Ryan and colleagues (Ryan, 1994) reported that in a sample of 310 people with intellectual disability who were referred for consultation regarding learning disability, 16% met criteria for PTSD. However, the reliability and validity of PTSD assessments in this population has not been well established (Doyle & Mitchell, 2003; Mevissen & de Jongh, 2010).

Barriers to Acquiring Accurate Data on Trauma and PTSD in Special Populations

Although trauma and PTSD are common in vulnerable populations, they are often not detected, and hence not treated (Hiday et al., 1999; Sobsey & Doe, 1991; Young, Nosek, Howland, Chanpong, & Rintala, 1997). As a result, many individuals who have been multiply traumatized continue to experience high levels of distress, worse symptoms, and impaired psychosocial functioning. Understanding barriers to the accurate detection of trauma and PTSD in special populations is the first step toward improved assessment and treatment.

Three broad types of barriers interfere with accurate detection of trauma and PTSD in special populations, including the failure of professionals to routinely inquire about trauma, the lack of follow-through by professionals on client reports of trauma, and the tendency for clients to not report traumatic events.

Failure of Professionals to Assess Trauma History and PTSD

The most common reason that trauma and PTSD are not detected in special populations is that professionals simply do not routinely screen for these problems when assessing the treatment needs of these individuals. Directly asking clients about their traumatic experiences and PTSD symptoms is the most effective assessment method, yet most professionals working with populations such as persons with severe mental illness, substance abuse, or incarcerated persons fail to do so. Why? There are several reasons.

Professionals often do not understand the importance of trauma and PTSD for their clients' welfare, and thus do not screen for these problems. The nature of special populations is that they have prominent challenges that are the primary focus of treatment efforts (e.g., severe psychiatric disorders, addiction, developmental disability). These conditions can "overshadow" other, less prominent or flagrant conditions, such as PTSD. This problem can be worsened by the fact that all professionals work under significant time constraints and expectations to accomplish more in less time. The assessment of trauma and PTSD is often not viewed as a priority within the clinicians' profession, and thus there is no clear expectation that they should assess it.

Another reason that professionals do not assess trauma exposure and PTSD is a common fear of opening the proverbial "Pandora's box". Many clinicians in the mental health and substance abuse treatment fields have been taught that inquiring into clients' traumatic experiences leads to a significant risk of exacerbating symptoms, substance abuse, and self-injurious behavior (Brown, 1985; Solomon & Davidson, 1997). Although there is now strong evidence from large-scale studies that trauma and PTSD can be safely assessed without worsening psychiatric symptoms or substance abuse (McFarlane et al., 2001; Mueser, Essock, et al., 2004; Mueser, Salyers, et al., 2004; Ouimette et al., 2006), this is only gradually becoming recognized.

Historically, professionals have also not evaluated for trauma history and PTSD symptoms in people with severe mental illnesses because of concerns about the accuracy of clients' self-reports due to the common characteristic symptoms such as delusions and psychotic distortions. However, research on the reliability and validity of trauma history and PTSD in this population indicates that clients can reliably report their traumatic experiences, and that self-reports of PTSD symptoms are strongly related to structured clinical assessments of PTSD (Goodman et al., 1999; Meyer, Muenzenmaier, Cancienne, & Struening, 1996; Mueser et al., 2001). Similarly, professionals often fail to evaluate trauma history in people with developmental disabilities, because they believe that these individuals cannot report reliably about their abuse experiences due to their cognitive impairments (Martorell & Tsakanikos, 2008; Sobsey, 1994). However, reliable and valid measures of trauma exposure have been developed for this population (Valenti-Hein & Schwartz, 1995).

Some professionals may not assess for trauma history and PTSD with their clients because of the lack of adequate training in conducting such assessments, and therefore lack confidence and skills for assessing for these sensitive issues with clients (Cusack, Wells, Grubaugh, Hiers, & Frueh, 2007; Salyers, Evans, Bond, & Meyer, 2004). For professionals who themselves have had significant traumatic experiences in their lives, failure to explore similar experiences in the people they work with may reflect avoidance of dealing with their own experiences. Training in the assessment of trauma history and PTSD is often critical for helping professionals to develop the skills and confidence needed to perform sensitive and effective assessments.

The primary purpose of assessment is to inform treatment planning. For many vulnerable populations, however, the clinical implications of identifying a trauma history and a diagnosis of PTSD are unclear. Much of the literature on treatment research of PTSD has focused on the general population, or on specific traumatic experiences in the general population such as sexual assault or combat exposure, with special populations ruled out by exclusion criteria (Spinazzola, Blaustein, & van der Kolk, 2005). Much less treatment development and research has addressed PTSD and related problems in special populations, with some notable exceptions (Harris & The Community Connections Trauma Work Group, 1998; Mueser et al., 2009; Najavits, 2002; Zlotnick et al., 2009). Thus, trauma may not be evaluated because the treatment implications of identifying a trauma history and/or PTSD may be unclear to the clinician.

Lack of Follow-through by Professionals on Client Reports of Trauma

Even when trauma is correctly identified in special populations, professionals often fail to follow up by evaluating PTSD or making treatment recommendations. For example, police may not believe reports of physical or sexual abuse reported by a person with severe mental illness, and follow up as appropriate (Marley & Buila, 1999). The majority of crimes reported to police by people with developmental disabilities are never prosecuted (Sobsey & Doe, 1991). In addition, clinicians may not know how to act on the information concerning trauma disclosed by clients. In one study, when trauma histories were mandated as part of routine assessment for psychiatric outpatients, although trauma was properly documented in clients' charts, it was rarely incorporated into treatment planning (Eilenberg, Fullilove, Goldman, & Mellman, 1996).

Professionals working in prison settings may have somewhat different reasons for not following through on an incarcerated individual's reports of trauma and PTSD symptoms. In these settings, there is often concern that individuals fabricate traumatic events or exaggerate their experiences in order to escape the legal consequences of their criminal behavior. These professionals may avoid delving into incarcerated individuals' trauma history or following through on reports of traumatic experiences, which they may view as an invitation to avoid blame by presenting themselves as victims who are not responsible for their criminal behavior.

Underreporting of Trauma and PTSD in Special Populations

The problem that professionals often fail to evaluate trauma history and PTSD in special populations, and do not follow through on reports of traumatic events, is compounded by the tendency of people to not report these experiences on their own. One important reason that people avoid talking about trauma and PTSD is that avoidance of trauma-related stimuli is one of the core symptoms of PTSD (American Psychiatric Association [APA], 1994). Thus, many people do not talk about their traumatic experiences unless they are specifically questioned about them.

Another reason that people often do not report traumatic experiences is their fear of not being believed by others. People with severe mental illness in particular are less likely to be believed when they report criminal victimization to law enforcement (Hiday et al., 1999; Maniglio, 2009), and hence crimes against them often go unreported. These individuals often have multiple experiences of being discounted by other people in their lives, and have learned not to report problems to people who question their veracity. Women with substance use disorders may avoid reporting sexual assault for fear that others may blame them for such as event because of their addiction (Dansky et al., 1996).

Individuals with developmental disabilities may not report physical and sexual abuse because their cognitive impairments interfere with their ability to recognize abusive situations (Petersilia, Foote, & Crowell, 2001; Sobsey & Doe, 1991). Abuse from family members or residential staff may be confusing to some individuals with developmental disabilities, who may view it as harmful, but not necessarily wrong or illegal. Further confusion may ensue in those individuals who are affectionate or eager to gain social approval of others, predisposing them to victimization, but reducing their willingness to report when they have been abused by another (Valenti-Hein & Schwartz, 1995).

Unfortunately for many vulnerable populations, trauma is a recurring experience throughout their lives. For some individuals, their family and intimate relationships involve sexual coercion or abuse or physical abuse (Young et al., 1997; Najavits et al., 2004). Although these experiences are unwanted, they also occur in the context of relationships in which the individual may depend upon family members or intimate partners for care. In these circumstances, individuals may be afraid of reporting physical or sexual abuse for fear of reprisal or the loss of valued social and economic supports (Rose et al., 2011).

Illustration of These Issues in Persons with Severe Mental Illness

A history of exposure to trauma is associated with more severe mental illness. Extensive research has shown that physical and sexual abuse in people with severe mental illness in particular is related to greater impairment in psychosocial functioning (e.g., homelessness, social relationships) and more severe psychiatric symptoms, including hallucinations, delusions, depression, anxiety, dissociation, suicidality, and hostility (Briere, Woo, McRae, Foltz, & Sitzman, 1997; Carmen, Rieker, & Mills, 1984; Schenkel, Spaulding, DiLillo, & Silverstein, 2005; Surrey, Swett, Michaels, & Levin, 1990). Furthermore, exposure to interpersonal violence is associated with more frequent hospitalizations, days in the hospital, and emergency room visits (Briere et al., 1997; Carmen et al., 1984; Goodman et al., 1997).

Interestingly, although women are more likely to develop PTSD in the general population (Tolin & Foa, 2006), most studies of PTSD in people with severe mental illness have not found gender differences in prevalence. It is unclear why gender differences have not been found in this research, although the one controlled treatment study of PTSD in this population did report that the majority of participants were women (Mueser et al., 2008), suggesting that women may have more severe PTSD symptoms. Differences in the prevalence of PTSD across racial or ethnic groups have not been found in most studies, although this research has been limited by modest sample sizes. The largest study of PTSD in people with severe mental illness did find higher rates in Whites than minority populations (Mueser, Salyers et al., 2004), which has also been reported in the general population (Brewin, Andrews, & Valentine, 2000). More research is needed to evaluate interactions between gender, race, ethnicity, and PTSD in severe mental illness.

There is also a growing body of research indicating that PTSD contributes to a worse course of severe mental illness. PTSD diagnosis is associated with more severe symptoms, especially anxiety, depression, and psychosis (Howgego et al., 2005; Mueser, Essock, et al., 2004; Resnick, Bond, & Mueser, 2003), as well as greater utilization of psychiatric and emergency services (Calhoun, Bosworth, Stechuchak, Strauss, & Butterfield, 2006; Howgego et al., 2005; Switzer et al., 1999). PTSD is also related to greater psychosocial impairment, such as less adjusted interpersonal relationships and lower levels of employment (Howgego et al., 2005; Mueser, Essock, et al., 2004; Mueser, Salyers, et al., 2004), poorer quality of life (Calhoun et al., 2006; Howgego et al., 2005), and poorer physical health (Mueser, Salyers, et al., 2004).

A Heuristic Model for the Interactions between PTSD and Severe Mental Illness

In order to understand how PTSD may worsen the course of severe mental illness, Mueser and colleagues (2002) developed a model based on the stress-vulnerability model of schizophrenia (Zubin & Spring, 1977) in which they posited both direct and indirect effects of PTSD on the psychiatric disorder. According to this model, PTSD is hypothesized to directly worsen psychotic symptoms and functioning through the core PTSD symptoms of re-experiencing the trauma, avoidance of trauma-related stimuli, and over-arousal. For example, re-experiencing the trauma (e.g., intrusive memories, flashbacks) may serve as a general stressor, precipitating relapses of psychotic symptoms. Avoidance of trauma-related stimuli may lead to social isolation when the traumatic event was interpersonal in nature (e.g., physical or sexual abuse), resulting in receiving less benefit from the buffering effects of social support on stress (Cresswell, Kuipers & Power, 1992) and increased vulnerability to relapses. PTSD over-arousal symptoms may also contribute to relapses in that chronically heightened physiological activity has been linked to a worse prognosis of severe mental illness (Nuechterlein & Dawson, 1984; Zahn, 1986).

There are several hypothesized indirect effects of PTSD on worsening the outcome of severe mental illness. PTSD can contribute to substance abuse (Mueser et al., 2002), which can precipitate relapses (Drake & Brunette, 1998) and lead to further traumatization, which can in turn result in relapses (Bebbington & Kuipers, 1992). In addition, considering the interpersonal distrust common among trauma survivors (Lewis, Kelly, & Allen, 2005), PTSD is hypothesized to impede the development of a good working alliance with treatment providers, leading to receipt of fewer services (e.g., medication checks, case management meetings) and worse overall functioning (Gehrs & Goering, 1994; Neale & Rosenheck, 1995). The implications of this model are that effective treatment of PTSD could improve the course of severe mental illness.

Treatment of PTSD in Severe Mental Illness

Recent efforts have focused on the development of treatments specially designed to address trauma and PTSD in persons with severe psychiatric disorders (Frueh et al., 2004, 2009; Harris & The Community Connections Trauma Work Group, 1998; Mueser et al., 2007, 2009). Common among these interventions is the attempt to address trauma-related problems in an individual or group context that recognizes the high vulnerability of this population to stress, as well as the multitude of other challenges that these individuals experience in their lives (e.g., housing instability, substance abuse, cognitive impairment, ongoing trauma exposure). These programs differ with respect to whether they narrowly focus on PTSD or more broadly seek to address a wider range of trauma-related problems that are not necessarily part of the PTSD syndrome (e.g., poor social skills, body image).

Research on different treatment programs for PTSD in persons with severe mental illness is under way. One randomized controlled trial has been completed, which found positive effects at the six-month follow-up of a 12–16-week individual cognitive-behavioral treatment program compared to usual treatment on PTSD symptoms, depression, other symptoms, trauma-related cognitions, and working alliance with the case manager (Mueser et al., 2008). These findings support the feasibility of treating PTSD in persons with severe mental illness, and suggest that such treatment could improve the course of illness.

Future Directions

The special populations discussed in this chapter are characterized by their increased vulnerability to trauma and PTSD, combined with the relative neglect of these problems by treatment professionals, until recently. Thus, although there are many possible future directions for the field, the most important ones involve assessment and treatment. We briefly consider each of these below.

There is strong evidence that standardized, psychometrically sound instruments developed for the assessment of trauma history and PTSD in the general population are reliable and valid in most special populations, including people with severe mental illness, substance use disorders, and incarcerated individuals. However, despite widespread recognition of the high rate of trauma and PTSD in these vulnerable people, routine screening and assessment are not conducted. Therefore, one important future direction that may increase clinicians' awareness of the importance of assessing trauma and PTSD is to require screening and assessment of trauma and PTSD in routine clinical practice. In addition to informing the need for trauma treatment in vulnerable individuals, routine assessment could also shed light on the impact and interactions among trauma history, PTSD, and the course of severe psychiatric and substance use disorders. At present, few prospective, longitudinal studies have been conducted evaluating interactions between the course of mental illness and PTSD; routine assessment of trauma and PTSD in people entering treatment systems for other disorders would better inform the field about who needs trauma treatment the most and how to integrate different interventions.

There is at present only very limited information about the prevalence of trauma and PTSD in people with intellectual disabilities (Mevissen & de Jongh, 2010). This is at least partly due to the lack of validated instruments for the assessment of these problems in this population. Research is needed to adapt existing instruments or develop new ones that are reliable and valid for assessing trauma and PTSD in persons with intellectual disabilities; before this important work is conducted, it is unlikely that significant treatment advances can be made because of the inability to reliably identify those individuals who need the intervention and to evaluate the impact of treatment on relevant outcomes.

Significant progress is already under way to develop or adapt interventions for the treatment of PTSD or related trauma consequences in persons with severe mental illness, substance use disorders, or in incarcerated individuals, but much work remains to be done. Aside from the need for more research evaluating the effectiveness of interventions that target PTSD in these special populations, there are several other future directions for the field. One unresolved question is determining the staging of trauma-related interventions with respect to the treatment of other psychiatric disorder(s). Substance abuse and more severe psychiatric symptoms tend to worsen PTSD symptoms, and yet clients may be more difficult to engage and retain in trauma treatment when their symptoms are exacerbated. Research is needed to evaluate at what stages of a psychiatric or substance use disorder can clients be most effectively engaged and retained in treatment.

Another question pertains to the integration of trauma treatment and clients' other psychiatric and substance use disorder. Although some degree of integration is presumed to be necessary, it is unclear whether such integration is best accomplished by having the same clinician treat both disorders, or having separate clinicians work with each disorder in a collaborative fashion. Having the same clinician treat both disorders has obvious advantages in terms of addressing the interactions between the disorders, but runs the risk of losing focus on one disorder. This is of particular concern for PTSD, which is partly defined by the avoidance of trauma-related stimuli, suggesting that avoidance of PTSD treatment may be likely to occur when two disorders (rather than one) are being treated. It is possible that some clients will benefit more from integration of both treatments at the level of a single clinician, which requires that only one therapeutic relationship is established, whereas others may benefit more from different clinicians targeting each disorder.

Finally, there is a need for treatment research aimed at examining the relative merits of interventions that focus more narrowly on PTSD symptoms compared to those that seek to address a broader range of trauma consequences, and to explore which groups are most likely to benefit from which type of intervention. For example, the Trauma Recovery and Empowerment model developed by Harris and colleagues (1998) addresses a broad range of trauma consequences (e.g., social skills, sexuality, self-esteem). On the other hand, the cognitive-behavioral program developed by Mueser and colleagues (2009) focuses more narrowly on teaching cognitive restructuring as a self-management skill for dealing with negative feelings and reducing PTSD symptoms. The goals of each program differ, although they are both conceptualized as treatments for trauma-related consequences in people with severe mental illness.

Substantial gains have been made in recent years in recognizing the impact of trauma and PTSD on special populations of individuals who are especially vulnerable to these experiences. Treatments for trauma and PTSD in special populations are in the early stages of evaluation, with preliminary findings showing promise. Much progress has been made in addressing the impact of trauma and PTSD in vulnerable individuals, although there is still much work to be done.

References

American Psychiatric Association. (1994). *Diagnostic and statistical manual of mental disorders* (4th ed.). Washington, DC: Author.

Back, S., Dansky, B. S., Coffey, S. F., Saladin, M. E., Sonne, S., & Brady, K. T. (2000). Cocaine dependence with and without post-traumatic stress disorder: A comparison of substance use, trauma history and psychiatric comorbidity. *American Journal on Addictions, 9*, 51–62.

Bebbington, P. E., & Kuipers, L. (1992). Life events and social factors. In D. J. Kavanagh (Ed.), *Schizophrenia: An overview and practical handbook* (pp. 126–144). London: Chapman & Hall.

Bonin, M. F., Norton, G. R., Asmundson, G. J., Dicurzio, S., & Pidlubney, S. (2000). Drinking away the hurt: The nature and prevalence of PTSD in substance abuse patients attending a community-based treatment program. *Journal of Behavior Therapy and Experimental Psychiatry, 31*, 55–66.

Brady, K. T., Dansky, B. S., Back, S. E., Foa, E. B., & Carroll, K. M. (2001). Exposure therapy in the treatment of PTSD among cocaine-dependent individuals: Preliminary findings. *Journal of Substance Abuse Treatment, 21*, 47–54.

Breslau, N., Peterson, E. L., Poisson, L. M., Schultz, L. R., & Lucia, V. C. (2004). Estimating post-traumatic stress disorder in the community: Lifetime perspective and impact of typical traumatic events. *Psychological Medicine, 34*, 889–898.

Brewin, C. R., Andrews, B., & Valentine, J. D. (2000). Meta-analysis of risk factors for posttraumatic stress disorder in trauma-exposed adults. *Journal of Consulting and Clinical Psychology, 68*, 748–766.

Briere, J., Woo, R., McRae, B., Foltz, J., & Sitzman, R. (1997). Lifetime victimization history, demographics, and clinical status in female psychiatric emergency room patients. *Journal of Nervous and Mental Disease, 185*, 95–101.

Brown, S. (1985). *Treating the alcoholic.* New York: John Wiley.

Brownridge, D. A. (2006). Violence against women with disabilities: Prevalence, risk, and explanations. *Violence Against Women, 12*, 805–822.

Butler, T., Allnutt, S., Cain, D., Owens, D., & Muller, C. (2005). Mental disorder in the New South Wales prisoner population. *Australian and New Zealand Journal of Psychiatry, 39*, 407–413.

Calhoun, P. S., Bosworth, H. B., Stechuchak, K. A., Strauss, J. L., & Butterfield, M. I. (2006). The impact of posttraumatic stress disorder on quality of life and health service utilization among veterans who have schizophrenia. *Journal of Traumatic Stress, 19*, 393–397.

Carmen, E., Rieker, P. P., & Mills, T. (1984). Victims of violence and psychiatric illness. *American Journal of Psychiatry, 141*, 378–383.

Chilcoat, H. D., & Breslau, N. (1998). Posttraumatic stress disorder and drug disorders: Testing causal pathways. *Archives of General Psychiatry, 55*, 913–917.

Clark, H. W., Masson, C. L., Delucchi, K. L., Hall, S. M., & Sees, K. L. (2001). Violent traumatic events and drug abuse severity. *Journal of Substance Abuse Treatment, 20*, 121–127.

Cloutier, S., Martin, S. L., & Poole, C. (2002). Sexual assault among North Carolina women: Prevalence and health risk factors. *Journal of Epidemiology and Community Health, 56*, 265–271.

Cottler, L. B., Compton, W. M., Mager, D., Spitznagel, E. L., & Janca, A. (1992). Posttraumatic stress disorder among

substance users from the general population. *American Journal of Psychiatry, 149*, 664–670.
Cresswell, C. M., Kuipers, L., & Power, M. J. (1992). Social networks and support in long-term psychiatric patients. *Psychological Medicine, 22*, 1019–1026.
Cusack, K. J., Wells, C. B., Grubaugh, A. L., Hiers, T. G., & Frueh, B. C. (2007). An update on the South Carolina trauma initiative. *Psychiatric Services, 58*, 708–710.
Dansky, B. S., Brady, K. T., Saladin, M. E., Killeen, T., Becker, S., & Roitzsch, J. C. (1996). Victimization and PTSD in individuals with substance use disorders: Gender and racial differences. *American Journal of Drug and Alcohol Abuse, 22*, 75–93.
Dansky, B. S., Saladin, M. E., Brady, K. T., Kilpatrick, D. G., & Resnick, H. S. (1995). Prevalence of victimization and posttraumatic stress disorder among women with substance use disorders: Comparison of telephone and in-person assessment samples. *International Journal of the Addictions, 30*, 1079–1099.
Developmental Disabilities Assistance and Bill of Rights Act. (2000). Retrieved from http://www.acf.hhs.gov/programs/add/ddact/DDACT2.html.
Doyle, C., & Mitchell, D. (2003). Post-traumatic stress disorder and people with learning disabilities: A literature based discussion. *Journal of Intellectual Disabilities, 7*, 23–33.
Drake, R. E., & Brunette, M. F. (1998). Complications of severe mental illness related to alcohol and other drug use disorders. In M. Galanter (Ed.), *Recent developments in alcoholism: Consequences of alcoholism* (vol. 14, pp. 285–299). New York: Plenum.
Eilenberg, J., Fullilove, M. T., Goldman, R. G., & Mellman, L. (1996). Quality and use of trauma histories obtained from psychiatric outpatients through mandated inquiry. *Psychiatric Services, 47*, 165–169.
Felitti, V. J., Anda, R. F., Nordenberg, D., Williamson, D. F., Spitz, A. M., Edwards, V., Koss, M. P., & Marks, J. S. (1998). Relationship of childhood abuse and household dysfunction to many of the leading causes of death in adults: The Adverse Childhood Event (ACE) study. *American Journal of Preventive Medicine, 14*, 245–258.
Frueh, B. C., Buckley, T. C., Cusack, K. J., Kimble, M. O., Grubaugh, A. L., Turner, S. M., & Keane, T. M. (2004). Cognitive-behavioral treatment for PTSD among people with severe mental illness: A proposed treatment model. *Journal of Psychiatric Practice, 10*, 26–38.
Frueh, B. C., Grubaugh, A. L., Cusack, K. J., Kimble, M. O., Elhai, J. D., & Knapp, R. G. (2009). Exposure-based cognitive-behavioral treatment of PTSD in adults with schizophrenia or schizoaffective disorder: A pilot study. *Journal of Anxiety Disorders, 23*, 665–675.
Furey, E. M. (1994). Sexual abuse of adults with mental retardation: Who and where. *Mental Retardation, 32*, 173–180.
Gehrs, M., & Goering, P. (1994). The relationship between the working alliance and rehabilitation outcomes of schizophrenia. *Psychosocial Rehabilitation Journal, 18*, 43–54.
Gibson, L. E., Holt, J. C., Fondacaro, K. M., Tang, T. S., Powell, T. A., & Turbitt, E. L. (1999). An examination of antecedent traumas and psychiatric comorbidity among male inmates with PTSD. *Journal of Traumatic Stress, 12*, 473–484.
Goff, A., Rose, E., Rose, S., & Purves, D. (2007). Does PTSD occur in sentenced prison populations? A systematic literature review. *Criminal Behavior and Mental Health, 17*, 152–162.
Goodman, L. A., Rosenberg, S. D., Mueser, K. T., & Drake, R. E. (1997). Physical and sexual assault history in women with serious mental illness: Prevalence, correlates, treatment, and future research directions. *Schizophrenia Bulletin, 23*, 685–696.
Goodman, L. A., Thompson, K. M., Weinfurt, K., Corl, S., Acker, P., Mueser, K. T., & Rosenberg, S. D. (1999). Reliability of reports of violent victimization and PTSD among men and women with SMI. *Journal of Traumatic Stress, 12*, 587–599.
Greenfeld, L. A., & Minor-Harper, S. (1991). *Bureau of Justice Statistics: Special Report: Women in prison*. Washington, DC: U.S. Department of Justice.
Harris, M., & The Community Connections Trauma Work Group. (1998). *Trauma Recovery and Empowerment: A Clinician's Guide for Working with Women in Groups*. New York: Free Press.
Haugebrook, S., Zgoba, K. M., Maschi, T., Morgen, K., & Brown, D. (2010). Trauma, stress, health, and mental health issues among ethnically diverse older adult prisoners. *Journal of Corrections Health Care, 16*, 220–229.
Hiday, V. A., Swartz, M. S., Swanson, J. W., Borum, R., & Wagner, H. R. (1999). Criminal victimization of persons with severe mental illness. *Psychiatric Services, 50*, 62–68.
Hien, D. A., Nunes, E., Levin, F. R., & Fraser, D. (2000). Posttraumatic stress disorder and short-term outcome in early methadone treatment. *Journal of Substance Abuse Treatment, 19*, 31–37.
Hightower, J., & Smith, G. (2003). Aging, disabilities, and abuse. *AWARE: The Newsletter of the BC Institute Against Family Violence, 10*(1), 17–18.
Howgego, I. M., Owen, C., Meldrum, L., Yellowlees, P., Dark, F., & Parslow, R. (2005). Posttraumatic stress disorder: An exploratory study examining rates of trauma and PTSD and its effect on client outcomes in community mental health. *BMC Psychiatry*, 5:21.
Jacobson, L. K., Southwick, S. M., & Kosten, T. R. (2001). Substance use disorders in patients with posttraumatic stress disorder: A review of the literature. *American Journal of Psychiatry, 158*, 1184–1190.
Johnson, C. (2000, August). Violence against women with developmental disabilities: The hidden violence. *TASH Newsletter*, pp. 22–23, 26–27.
Johnson, S. D., Striley, C., & Cottler, L. B. (2006). The association of substance use disorders with trauma exposure and PTSD among African American drug users. *Addictive Behaviors, 31*, 2063–2073.
Kempton, W., & Gochros, J. (1986). The developmentally disabled. In H. L. Gochros, J. S. Gochros, & J. Fisher (Eds.), *Helping the sexually oppressed* (pp. 224–237). Englewood Cliffs, NJ: Prentice-Hall.
Kessler, R. C., Chiu, W. T., Demler, O., & Walters, E. E. (2005). Prevalence, severity, and comorbidity of 12-month DSM-IV disorders in the National Comorbidity Survey Replication. *Archives of General Psychiatry, 62*, 617–627.
Kessler, R. C., Sonnega, A., Bromet, E., Hughes, M., & Nelson, C. B. (1995). Posttraumatic stress disorder in the National Comorbidity Survey. *Archives of General Psychiatry, 52*, 1048–1060.
Kilpatrick, D. G., Ruggiero, K. J., Acierno, R., Saunders, B. E., Resnick, H. S., & Best, C. L. (2003). Violence and risk of PTSD, major depression, substance abuse/dependence, and comorbidity: Results from the National Survey of

Adolescents. *Journal of Consulting and Clinical Psychology, 71*, 692–700.

King, R., Nixon, B., Beatty, K., Szalajko, J., Marwick, L., & Prescott, H. (2004). Posttraumatic stress disorder and phenotype-specific challenging behavior in an individual with Smith-Magenis syndrome: A multimodal approach. *Mental Health Aspects of Developmental Disabilities, 7*, 131–141.

Langeland, W., Draijer, N., & van den Brink, W. (2004). Psychiatric comorbidity in treatment-seeking alcoholics: The role of childhood trauma and perceived parental dysfunction. *Alcoholism: Clinical and Experimental Research, 28*, 441–447.

Lewis, L., Kelly, K., & Allen, J. G. (2005). *Restoring hope and trust: An illustrated guide to mastering trauma*. Baltimore: Sidran Press.

Lumley, V. A., & Miltenberger, R. G. (1997). Sexual abuse prevention for persons with mental retardation. *American Journal on Mental Retardation, 101*, 459–472.

Maniglio, R. (2009). Severe mental illness and criminal victimization: A systematic review. *Acta Psychiatrica Scandinavia, 119*, 180–191.

Mansell, S., Sobsey, D., & Moskal, R. (1998). Clinical findings among sexually abused children with and without developmental disabilities. *Mental Retardation, 36*, 12–22.

Marley, J. A., & Buila, S. (1999). When violence happens to people with mental illness: Disclosing victimization. *American Journal of Orthopsychiatry, 69*, 398–402.

Martin, S. L., Ray, N., Sotres-Alvarez, D., Kupper, L. L., Moracco, K. E., Dickens, P. A., Scandlin, D., & Gizlice, Z. (2006). Physical and sexual assault of women with disabilities. *Violence Against Women, 12*, 823–837.

Martorell, A., & Tsakanikos, E. (2008). Traumatic experiences and life events in people with intellectual disability. *Current Opinion in Psychiatry, 21*, 445–448.

McCartney, J. R., & Campbell, V. A. (1998). Confirmed abuse cases in public residential facilities for persons with mental retardation: A multi-state study. *Mental Retardation, 36*, 465–473.

McFarlane, A. C., Bookless, C., & Air, T. (2001). Posttraumatic stress disorder in a general psychiatric inpatient population. *Journal of Traumatic Stress, 14*, 633–645.

McFarlane, J., Hughes, R. B., Nosek, M. A., Groff, J. Y., Swedlend, N., & Mullen, P. D. (2001). Abuse Assessment Screen–Disability (AAS-D): Measuring frequency, type, and perpetrator of abuse toward women with physical disabilities. *Journal of Women's Health and Gender-Based Medicine, 10*, 861–866.

McGovern, M. P., Lambert-Harris, C., Acquilano, S., Weiss, R. D., & Xie, H. (2009). A cognitive behavioral therapy for co-occurring substance use and posttraumatic stress disorders. *Addictive Behaviors, 34*, 892–897.

Melcombe, L. (2003). Facing up to facts. *AWARE: The Newsletter of the BC Institute Against Family Violence, 10*(1), 8–10.

Messina, N., & Grella, C. (2006). Childhood trauma and women's health outcomes in a California prison population. *American Journal of Public Health 96*, 1842–1848.

Mevissen, L., & de Jongh, A. (2010). PTSD and its treatment in people with intellectual disabilities: A review of the literature. *Clinical Psychology Review, 30*, 308–316.

Meyer, I. H., Muenzenmaier, K., Cancienne, J., & Struening, E. L. (1996). Reliability and validity of a measure of sexual and physical abuse histories among women with serious mental illness. *Child Abuse and Neglect, 20*, 213–219.

Miller, B. A., Downs, W. R., & Testa, M. (1993). Interrelationships between victimization experiences and women's alcohol use. *Journal of Studies on Alcohol, 54*(Suppl. 11), 109–117.

Mills, K. L., Lynskey, M., Teesson, M., Ross, J., & Darke, S. (2005). Post-traumatic stress disorder among people with heroin dependence in the Australian treatment outcome study (ATOS): Prevalence and correlates. *Drug and Alcohol Dependence, 77*, 243–249.

Mills, K. L., Teesson, M., Ross, J., & Peters, L. (2006). Trauma, PTSD, and substance use disorders: Findings from the Australian National Survey of Mental Health and Well-Being. *American Journal of Psychiatry, 163*, 652–658.

Mueser, K. T., Bolton, E. E., Carty, P. C., Bradley, M. J., Ahlgren, K. F., DiStaso, D. R., Gilbride, A., & Liddel, C. (2007). The trauma recovery group: A cognitive-behavioral program for PTSD in persons with severe mental illness. *Community Mental Health Journal, 43*, 281–304.

Mueser, K. T., Essock, S. M., Haines, M., Wolfe, R., & Xie, H. (2004). Posttraumatic stress disorder, supported employment, and outcomes in people with severe mental illness. *CNS Spectrums, 9*, 913–925.

Mueser, K. T., Goodman, L. A., Trumbetta, S. L., Rosenberg, S. D., Osher, F. C., Vidaver, R., Auciello, P., & Foy, D. W. (1998). Trauma and posttraumatic stress disorder in severe mental illness. *Journal of Consulting and Clinical Psychology, 66*, 493–499.

Mueser, K. T., Rosenberg, S. D., Goodman, L. A., & Trumbetta, S. L. (2002). Trauma, PTSD, and the course of schizophrenia: An interactive model. *Schizophrenia Research, 53*, 123–143.

Mueser, K. T., Rosenberg, S. D., & Rosenberg, H. J. (2009). *Treatment of Posttraumatic Stress Disorder in Special Populations: A Cognitive Restructuring Program*. Washington, DC: American Psychological Association.

Mueser, K. T., Rosenberg, S. R., Xie, H., Jankowski, M. K., Bolton, E. E., Lu, W., Hamblen, J. L., et al. (2008). A randomized controlled trial of cognitive-behavioral treatment of posttraumatic stress disorder in severe mental illness. *Journal of Consulting and Clinical Psychology, 76*, 259–271.

Mueser, K. T., Salyers, M. P., Rosenberg, S. D., Ford, J. D., Fox, L., & Carty, P. (2001). A psychometric evaluation of trauma and PTSD assessments in persons with severe mental illness. *Psychological Assessment, 13*, 110–117.

Mueser, K. T., Salyers, M. P., Rosenberg, S. D., Goodman, L. A., Essock, S. M., Osher, F. C., Swartz, M. S., & Butterfield, M. (2004). Interpersonal trauma and posttraumatic stress disorder in patients with severe mental illness: Demographic, clinical, and health correlates. *Schizophrenia Bulletin, 30*, 45–57.

Najavits, L. M. (2002). *Seeking safety: A treatment manual for PTSD and substance abuse*. New York: Guilford.

Najavits, L. M., Gastfriend, D. R., Barber, J. P., Reif, S., Muenz, L., Blaine, J., Frank, A., et al. (1998). Cocaine dependence with and without PTSD among subjects in the National Institute on Drug Abuse Collaborative Cocaine Treatment Study. *American Journal of Psychiatry, 155*, 214–219.

Najavits, L. M., Harned, M. S., Gallop, R. J., Butler, S. F., Barber, J. P., Thase, M. E., & Crits-Christoph, P. (2007). Six-month treatment outcomes of cocaine-dependent patients with and without PTSD in a multisite national trial. *Journal of the Study of Alcohol and Drugs, 68*, 353–361.

Najavits, L. M., Sonn, J., Walsh, M., & Weiss, R. D. (2004). Domestic violence in women with PTSD and substance abuse. *Addictive Behaviors, 29,* 707–715.

Neale, M. S., & Rosenheck, R. A. (1995). Therapeutic alliance and outcome in a VA intensive case management program. *Psychiatric Services, 46,* 719–721.

Neller, D. J., Denney, R. L., Pietz, C. A., & Thomlinson, R. P. (2006). The relationship between trauma and violence in a jail inmate sample. *Journal of Interpersonal Violence, 21,* 1234–1241.

Neria, Y., Bromet, E. J., Sievers, S., Lavelle, J., & Fochtmann, L. J. (2002). Trauma exposure and posttraumatic stress disorder in psychosis: Findings from a first-admission cohort. *Journal of Consulting and Clinical Psychology, 70,* 246–251.

Newman, E. (2000). Developmental disabilities, trauma exposure, and post-traumatic stress disorder. *Trauma, Violence, and Abuse, 1,* 154–170.

Nishith, P., Resick, P. A., & Mueser, K. T. (2001). Sleep disturbances and alcohol use motives in female rape victims with posttraumatic stress disorder. *Journal of Traumatic Stress, 14,* 469–479.

Nuechterlein, K. H., & Dawson, M. E. (1984). Information processing and attentional functioning in the developmental course of schizophrenic disorders. *Schizophrenia Bulletin, 10,* 160–203.

Ouimette, P., Goodwin, E., & Brown, P. J. (2006). Health and well being of substance use disorder clients with and without posttraumatic stress disorder. *Addictive Behaviors, 31,* 1415–1423.

Ouimette, P., Moos, R. H., & Finney, J. W. (2003). PTSD treatment and 5-year remission among patients with substance use and posttraumatic stress disorders. *Journal of Consulting and Clinical Psychology, 71,* 410–414.

Ouimette, P., Read, J. P., Wade, M., & Tirone, V. (2010). Modeling associations between posttraumatic stress symptoms and substance use. *Addictive Behaviors, 35,* 64–67.

PAI. (2003). *Abuse and neglect of adults with developmental disabilities: A public health priority for the State of California.* Los Angeles: Protection and Advocacy, Inc.

Pava, W. S. (1994). Visually impaired persons' vulnerability to sexual and physical assault. *Journal of Visual Impairment and Blindness, 88,* 103–112.

Petersilia, J., Foote, J., & Crowell, N. A. (Eds.). (2001). *Crime victims with developmental disabilities: Report of a workshop.* Washington, DC: National Research Council.

Read, J., van Os, J., Morrison, A. P., & Ross, C. A. (2005). Childhood trauma, psychosis and schizophrenia: A literature review with theoretical and clinical implications. *Acta Psychiatrica Scandinavica, 112,* 330–350.

Read, J. P., Brown, P. J., & Kahler, C. W. (2004). Substance use and posttraumatic stress disorders: Symptom interplay and effects on outcome. *Addictive Behaviors, 29,* 1665–1672.

Resnick, S. G., Bond, G. R., & Mueser, K. T. (2003). Trauma and posttraumatic stress disorder in people with schizophrenia. *Journal of Abnormal Psychology, 112,* 415–423.

Reynolds, M., Mezey, G., Chapman, M., Wheeler, M., Drummond, C., & Baldacchino, A. (2005). Co-morbid posttraumatic stress disorder in a substance misusing clinical population. *Drug and Alcohol Dependence, 77,* 251–258.

Rose, D., Trevillion, K., Woodall, A., Morgan, C., Feder, G., & Howard, L. (2011). Barriers and facilitators of disclosures of domestic violence by mental health service users: A qualitative study. *British Journal of Psychiatry, 198,* 189–194.

Russell, A., & Shah, B. (2003). Posttraumatic stress disorder and abuse. *Developmental Disabilities Digest, 30*(2), 1–8.

Ryan, R. (1994). Posttraumatic stress disorder in persons with developmental disabilities. *Community Mental Health Journal, 30,* 45–54.

Salyers, M. P., Evans, L. J., Bond, G. R., & Meyer, P. S. (2004). Barriers to assessment and treatment of posttraumatic stress disorder and other trauma-related problems in people with severe mental illness: Clinician perspectives. *Community Mental Health Journal, 40,* 17–31.

Sanislow, C. A., Little, T. D., Ansell, E. B., Grilo, C. M., Daversa, M., Markowitz, J. C., Pinto, A., et al. (2009). Ten-year stability and latent structure of the DSM-IV schizotypal, borderline, avoidant, and obsessive-compulsive personality disorders. *Journal of Abnormal Psychology, 118,* 507–519.

Sarchiapone, M., Carli, V., Cuomo, C., Marchetti, M., & Roy, A. (2009). Association between childhood trauma and aggression in male prisoners. *Psychiatry Research, 165,* 187–192.

Saxon, A. J., Davis, T. M., Sloan, K. L., McKnight, K. M., McFall, M. E., & Kiviahan, D. R. (2001). Trauma, symptoms of posttraumatic stress disorder, and associated problems among incarcerated veterans. *Psychiatric Services, 52,* 959–964.

Schenkel, L. S., Spaulding, W. D., DiLillo, D., & Silverstein, S. M. (2005). Histories of childhood maltreatment in schizophrenia: Relationships with premorbid functioning, symptomatology, and cognitive deficits. *Schizophrenia Research, 76,* 273–286.

Schinnar, A. P., Rothbard, A., B., Kanter, R., & Jung, Y. S. (1990). An empirical literature review of definitions of severe and persistent mental illness. *American Journal Psychiatry, 147,* 1602–1608.

Sequeira, H., & Hollins, S. (2003). Clinical effects of sexual abuse on people with learning disability: Critical literature review. *British Journal of Psychiatry, 182,* 13–19.

Singer, M., Bussey, J., Song, L. Y., & Lungerhofer, L. (1995). The psychosocial issues of women serving time in jail. *Social Work, 40,* 103–113.

Sobsey, D. (1994). *Violence and abuse in the lives of people with disabilities.* Baltimore: Paul H. Brookes Publishing.

Sobsey, D., & Doe, T. (1991). Patterns of sexual abuse and assault. *Journal of Sexuality and Disability, 9*(3), 243–259.

Solomon, S. D., & Davidson, J. R. T. (1997). Trauma: Prevalence, impairment, service use, and cost. *Journal of Clinical Psychiatry, 59*(Suppl. 9), 5–11.

Spinazzola, J., Blaustein, M., & van der Kolk, B. A. (2005). Posttraumatic stress disorder treatment outcome research: The study of unrepresentative samples? *Journal of Traumatic Stress, 18,* 425–436.

Strawn, J. R., Adler, C. M., Fleck, D. E., Hanseman, D., Maue, D. K., Bitter, S., Kraft, E. M., et al. (2010). Post-traumatic stress symptoms and trauma exposure in youth with first episode bipolar disorder. *Early Intervention in Psychiatry, 4,* 169–173.

Surrey, J., Swett, C., Jr., Michaels, A., & Levin, S. (1990). Reported history of physical and sexual abuse and severity of symptomatology in women psychiatric outpatients. *American Journal of Orthopsychiatry, 60,* 412–417.

Switzer, G. E., Dew, M. A., Thompson, K., Goycoolea, J. M., Derricott, T., & Mullins, S. D. (1999). Posttraumatic stress disorder and service utilization among urban mental health center clients. *Journal of Traumatic Stress, 12,* 25–39.

Teplin, L. A. (1994). Psychiatric and substance abuse disorders among male urban jail detainees. *American Journal of Public Health, 84*, 290–293.

Teplin, L. A., Abram, K. M., & McClelland, G. M. (1996). Prevalence of psychiatric disorders among incarcerated women. I. Pretrial jail detainees. *Archives of General Psychiatry, 53*, 505–512.

Tharinger, D., Horton, C. B., & Millea, S. (1990). Sexual abuse and exploitation of children and adults with mental retardation and other handicaps. *Child Abuse and Neglect, 14*, 301–312.

Tolin, D. F., & Foa, E. B. (2006). Sex differences in trauma and posttraumatic stress disorder: A quantitative review of 25 years of research. *Psychological Bulletin, 132*, 959–992.

Torgersen, S., Kringlen, E., & Cramer, V. (2001). The prevalence of personality disorders in a community sample. *Archives of General Psychiatry, 58*, 590–596.

Valenti-Hein, D., & Schwartz, L. (1995). *The sexual abuse interview for those with developmental disabilities.* Santa Barbara, CA: James Stanfield.

Warren, J. I., Loper, A. B., & Komarovskaya, I. (2009). Symptom patterns related to traumatic exposure among female inmates with and without a diagnosis of posttraumatic stress disorder. *Journal of the American Academy of Psychiatry and the Law, 37*, 294–305.

Young, M. E., Nosek, M. A., Howland, C., Chanpong, G., & Rintala, D. H. (1997). Prevalence of abuse of women with physical disabilities. *Archives of Physical and Medical Rehabilitation, 78*, S34–S38.

Zahn, T. P. (1986). Psychophysiological approaches to psychopathology. In M. G. H. Coles, E. Donchin, & S. W. Porges (Eds.), *Psychophysiology: Systems, processes and applications* (pp. 508–610). New York: Guilford.

Zlotnick, C. (1997). Posttraumatic stress disorder (PTSD), PTSD comorbidity, and childhood abuse among incarcerated women. *Journal of Nervous and Mental Disease, 185*, 761–763.

Zlotnick, C., Johnson, J., Kohn, R., Vincente, B., Rioseco, P., & Saldivia, S. (2006). Epidemiology of trauma, posttraumatic stress disorder (PTSD) and comorbid disorders in Chile. *Psychological Medicine, 36*, 1523–1533.

Zlotnick, C., Johnson, J., & Najavits, L. M. (2009). Randomized controlled pilot study of cognitive-behavioral therapy in a sample of incarcerated women with substance use disorder and PTSD. *Behavior Therapy, 40*, 325–336.

Zubin, J., & Spring, B. (1977). Vulnerability: A new view of schizophrenia. *Journal of Abnormal Psychology, 86*, 103–126.

4

Contributions from Theory

CHAPTER

11 Genetics and Genomics of Posttraumatic Stress Disorder

Monica Uddin, Ananda B. Amstadter, Nicole R. Nugent, *and* Karestan C. Koenen

Abstract

PTSD is a complex disorder; a range of molecular features likely contribute to individuals' increased risk for, or resilience to, developing PTSD when exposed to trauma. This chapter reviews the existing evidence for genetic and other molecular variation that has been tested for association with PTSD in humans. The authors summarize the 30 candidate gene studies of PTSD published to date, as well as the small but growing literature documenting PTSD-associated gene expression, and the emerging evidence of epigenetic variation that underlies this disorder. This review suggests that genetic and genomic variation contributes to PTSD etiology, with effects at times moderated by the environment; however, robust findings are only arrived at through careful attention to appropriate control selection. Future research in this rapidly evolving area should consider the joint action of molecular and environmental features operating at multiple levels to shape risk for PTSD.

Key Words: Genetic variation, epigenetic variation, gene expression, gene-environment interplay

Introduction

Posttraumatic stress disorder (PTSD) is distinct from other commonly occurring mental disorders in that exposure to a traumatic stressor is a prerequisite for diagnosis. However, although a majority (50–90%) (Kessler, Sonnega, Bromet, Hughes, & Nelson, 1995; Roberts et al., 2011) of adults have been exposed to such events, only a minority go on to develop the disorder: in the United States, lifetime rates of PTSD are estimated at approximately 6.7%, and 12-month prevalence rates at approximately 3.5% (Kessler & Wang, 2008). Among those exposed to a potentially traumatic event (PTE), the conditional risk of PTSD ranges from 8–24% depending on the type of PTE (Kessler et al., 1995; Roberts et al., 2011). These epidemiologic data suggest that preexisting genetic and/or physiologic vulnerabilities may exist among those who develop PTSD in the aftermath of traumatic events. The purpose of this article is to examine the existing evidence for genetic and other molecular variation that has been associated with increased risk for—or resilience to—PTSD in humans. Although we recognize that family and twin studies have made significant contributions to highlighting the role that genetic vulnerability plays to the development of PTSD (reviewed in Koenen, Amstadter & Nugent, 2008; Koenen, Nugent & Amstadter, 2008; Nugent, Amstadter & Koenen, 2008), we focus here on studies that investigate a specific locus or loci that may be associated with this disorder.

Candidate Gene Studies of PTSD

As of this writing, there have been 30 candidate gene studies published that examine genetic variation at loci hypothesized to be involved in the development (or maintenance) of PTSD. Though relatively few in number, studies using the candidate gene design represent the approach most commonly used in the field of PTSD genetics thus far. In this design, allele and/or genotype frequencies at a specific locus are typically compared between a sample of individuals who meet PTSD diagnostic criteria and a sample of individuals who have been trauma exposed but did not go on to develop the disorder. The alleles (i.e., alternative forms of genetic variation—or polymorphisms—at a specific locus) usually take one of two forms: single nucleotide polymorphisms (SNPs), in which the genetic variation occurs at the nucleotide (base pair) level; and variable number of tandem repeats (VNTRs), in which the genetic variation occurs in the number of repetitive sequences (i.e., a length polymorphism). Loci are chosen on the basis of their known or presumed involvement in neurobiological systems that are salient to the development of PTSD and/or posttraumatic stress (PTS) symptoms, and the polymorphisms in question are often associated with known functional differences in the gene.

Table 11.1 summarizes the main characteristics and findings of the 30 candidate gene studies of PTSD to date. Prior to 2009, genes belonging to the dopamine (DA) system were the most heavily represented among these studies. From 2009 onward, however, there has been a steep increase in the number of studies published involving the serotonergic system, as well as other studies involving aspects of alternative neurobiological systems: 10 studies in total have examined variation in serotonergic system genes (only three of these existed prior to 2009), and an additional 12 studies have examined PTSD-associated genetic variation in other systems. This increased interest in investigating genetic correlates of PTSD bodes well for more precisely unpacking the molecular features that contribute to this disorder; however, as described more fully below, the conflicting results produced, at times, by these studies also highlight the challenges inherent to this type of research.

Dopaminergic System Candidate Gene Studies

Both animal and human studies have implicated the dopaminergic (DA) system in the etiology of PTSD. For example, higher levels of plasma (Hamner & Diamond, 1993) and urinary (De Bellis et al., 1999; Lemieux & Coe, 1995) DA have been associated with PTSD in humans. Animal models have demonstrated stress-related responsivity of DA enervation in the amygdala, and have suggested that this response may be modulated by genetically determined adaptation of DA receptors (Puglisi-Allegra & Cabib, 1997). Five of the eight DA-related studies investigated the association between marker alleles at the dopamine receptor DR (*DRD2*) gene region and PTSD (see table 11.1). Three of these five studies found some evidence for an association between PTSD risk and the *TaqIA* SNP, with an excess of "T" allele carriers among those with PTSD (Comings et al., 1991; Comings, Muhleman & Gysin, 1996; Young et al., 2002). Among the remaining two studies that did not find evidence for a PTSD/*TaqIA* association (Gelernter et al., 1999; Voisey et al., 2009), the more recent study did find evidence of a significant association between PTSD and another variant in the *DRD2* gene region (rs6277), and estimated that 14% of susceptibility to PTSD could be attributable to having a "CC" genotype at this locus (Voisey et al., 2009). This recent, positive finding awaits replication. Of note, at the time the earlier (i.e., pre-2008) studies were conducted, the *TaqIA* SNP was thought to occur within the *DRD2* locus; subsequently, however, it was demonstrated that this SNP actually occurs within the coding region of the ankyrin repeat and kinase domain containing 1 (*ANKK1*) gene, located downstream of *DRD2*, and causes a Glu713Lys substitution in the substrate binding domain of the *ANKK1* locus that may change the substrate binding specificity of this gene (Neville, Johnstone & Walton, 2004). Nevertheless, the functional significance of this polymorphism in relation to *DRD2* remains plausible as T allele carriers have been shown to have significantly higher uptake of dopamine precursor L-DOPA in the striatum (Laakso et al., 2005), suggesting increased dopamine synthesis rates in the brains of individuals carrying this allele.

More recently, studies of PTSD-associated genetic variation in DA system genes have expanded beyond investigations focused on the *DRD2* gene region. Two studies have examined a VNTR variation in the 3' untranslated region of the dopamine transporter gene (*DAT1*, also known as *SLC6A3*), with both reporting an excess of the 9-repeat allele among PTSD cases (Drury, Theall, Keats & Scheeringa, 2009; Segman et al., 2002). One additional study examined a VNTR variation in exon 3 of the dopamine receptor D4 (*DRD4*) locus among flood survivors in Poland, finding that the *DRD4* long allele (7 or 8 VNTRs) was associated with significantly more intense PTSD symptoms over-

Table 11.1 **Summary of candidate gene association studies of PTSD**

First author	Year	Trauma-exposed controls?	Trauma type	Gene name (symbol)	Major finding
Dopamine system					
Comings	1991	NSF	Combat	ankyrin repeat and kinase domain containing 1 (*ANKK1*)	Excess *TaqIA* T allele in PTSD cases (p=.007)
Comings	1996	Yes	Combat	ankyrin repeat and kinase domain containing 1 (*ANKK1*)	Excess *TaqIA* T in PTSD cases (p=.0001)
Gelernter	1999	NSF	Combat	ankyrin repeat and kinase domain containing 1 (*ANKK1*)	No significant association between *TaqIA* T allele and PTSD
Young	2002	NSF	Combat	ankyrin repeat and kinase domain containing 1 (*ANKK1*)	Excess *TaqIA* T allele only in PTSD cases with harmful drinking (p < .001)
Voisey	2009	NSF	Combat	Dopamine Receptor D2 (*DRD2*), *ANKK1*	Excess C allele in 957C > T in PTSD (p=.021); no differences in *TaqIA* T allele or −141delC
Dragan	2009	Yes	Flood	Dopamine Receptor D4 (*DRD4*)	Long allele predicted more intense symptoms of PTSD (p=.048)
Segman	2002	Yes	Various	Dopamine Transporter (*DAT1*)	Excess 9-repeat allele in PTSD cases (p=.012)
Drury	2009	Yes	Hurricane	Dopamine Transporter (*DAT1*)	Excess 9-repeat allele in PTSD cases (p < .05)
Serotonin system					
Lee	2005	NSF	Various	Serotonin transporter (*SLC6A4*)	Excess s allele in PTSD cases (p=.04)
Kilpatrick	2007	Yes	Hurricane	Serotonin transporter (*SLC6A4*)	Significant association between s/s genotype and PTSD in adults with high hurricane exposure and low social support (p=.03 for 3-way interaction)
Koenen	2009	Yes	Hurricane	Serotonin transporter (*SLC6A4*)	Significant interaction between genotype and crime rate (p=.03) or unemployment (p=.007) for risk of PTSD. s allele was associated with decreased risk of PTSD in low-risk environments (low crime/unemployment), and increased risk of PTSD in high risk environments
Grabe	2009	Yes	Various	Serotonin transporter (*SLC6A4*)	Individuals with the La/La genotype showed increased risk for PTSD (p < .05). Among individuals with more than 3 traumatic life events an additive interaction was found with the La allele conferring risk (p < .05 for interaction)
Thakur	2009	Yes	MVA	Serotonin transporter (*SLC6A4*)	Excess l/l genotype in chronic PTSD group (p=.052)

(*continued*)

Table 11.1 Summary of candidate gene association studies of PTSD *(continued)*

First author	Year	Trauma-exposed controls?	Trauma type	Gene name (symbol)	Major finding
Xie	2009	Yes	Various	Serotonin transporter (*SLC6A4*)	Significant interaction between genotype and either childhood adversity, adult traumatic events, or both in adults, with the s allele conferring risk (p < .001 in pooled analyses of EAs and AAs in the presence of both events)
Kolassa, Ertl	2010	Yes	Genocide/War	Serotonin transporter (*SLC6A4*)	Main effect of genotype on risk for PTSD, with the s/s genotype showing increased liability (p=.008).
Sayin	2010	Yes	Physical Trauma	Serotonin transporter (*SLC6A4*)	Among those with lifetime PTSD, there was (i) a higher mean (unadjusted) PTSD symptom score among s allele carriers (p=.05) and (ii) significantly milder hyper-arousal symptoms among l allele carriers in unadjusted and adjusted models (p ~ .05). The 12 allele version in intron 2 was associated with more severe avoidance symptoms (p < .05).
Lee	2007	NSF	Not specified	Serotonin receptor 2A (*5-HTR2A*)	Excess GG genotype in females with PTSD (p=.04)
Mellman	2009	Yes	Various	Serotonin receptor 2A (*5-HTR2A*) and *SLC6A4*	No significant association between *SLC6A4* genotype and PTSD. Excess G allele in PTSD cases for the *5HT2A* receptor, (p=.006)
Alternative neurobiological systems					
Freeman	2005	All subjects had PTSD	Combat	Apolipoprotein E (*APOE*)	Presence of *APOE2* allele was associated with worse re-experiencing symptoms (p=.001) and impaired memory function (p < .01)
Lee	2006	NSF	Not specified	Brain derived neurotrophic factor (*BDNF*)	No association between *BDNF* Val66Met and PTSD
Zhang	2006	NSF	Not specified	Brain derived neurotrophic factor (*BDNF*)	No association between three *BDNF* variants and PTSD
Lappalainen	2002	NSF	Combat	Neuropeptide Y (*NPY*)	No association between Leu7Pro and PTSD
Bachmann	2005	Yes	Combat	Glucocorticoid Receptor (*GCCR*)	No association between *GCCR* polymorphisms and PTSD
Mustapic	2007	Yes	Combat	Dopamine beta-hydroxylase (*DBH*)	No association of −1021C/T variant with PTSD. PTSD CC genotype cases had lower DBH activity than non-PTSD CC cases (p < .001)
Lu	2008	NSF	Not Specified	Cannabinoid receptor gene (*CNR1*)	Excess C-A (p=.04) and C-G (p=.01) variants in parents of youth with ADHD who report PTSD.
Binder	2008	NSF	Various	FK506 binding protein 5 (*FKBP5*)	4 SNPs interacted with severity of child abuse to predict adult PTSD symptoms (p < .0004)

(continued)

Table 11.1 Summary of candidate gene association studies of PTSD *(continued)*

First author	Year	Trauma-exposed controls?	Trauma type	Gene name (symbol)	Major finding
Xie	2010	NSF	Various	FK506 binding protein 5 (*FKBP5*)	AA individuals homozygous for T allele at rs9470080 had highest risk for PTSD if they had experienced childhood adversity but lowest risk in the absence of childhood adversity (p=.004)
Amstadter	2009	Yes	Hurricane	Regulator of G-Protein Signaling 2 (*RGS2*)	Significant association between CC genotype and post-hurricane PTS symptoms (p=.029), as well as lifetime PTS symptoms (p < .001) in adults with high hurricane exposure and low social support (p=.029)
Nelson	2009	NSF	Various	γ-aminobutyric acid receptor subunit A2 (*GABRA2*)	Significant interaction between childhood trauma score and individuals homozygous for three of four risk alleles in predicting adult PTSD (p < .05)
Kolassa, Kolassa	2010	Yes	Genocide/ War	Catechol-O-Methyltransferase (*COMT*)	Significant interaction between genotype and number of traumatic events (p=.04). Met/Met genotype carriers were at higher risk for PTSD independent of number of traumatic events, whereas Val/Val and Val/Met showed typical dose-response of traumatic events and risk for PTSD.

*NSF=Not selected for; MVA=Motor vehicle accident
Adapted from: Amstadter et al. (in press).

all (Cohen's $f = 0.2$) and with significantly higher avoidance/numbing symptoms (Cohen's $f = 0.22$; Dragan & Oniszczenko, 2009). Taken together, the weight of evidence suggests that genetic variation in DA system genes may contribute to PTSD etiology.

Serotonin System Candidate Gene Studies

Serotonin system-related genes offer a logical choice for selecting candidate genes involved in the etiology of PTSD, as defects in serotonergic function have been implicated in the hormonal and immune-related changes that accompany anxiety and depression (Leonard, 2006). Among the 10 published studies on genes from this system all but one (Lee, Kwak, Paik, Kang & Lee, 2007) studied the commonly occurring VNTR polymorphism found in the promoter region (*5-HTTLPR*) of the serotonin gene (*SLC6A4*), although some also tested other polymorphisms in this gene region as well (e.g., Sayin et al., 2010). The serotonin transporter protein serves many functions; however, its action has been particularly well studied in the brain where it transports serotonin at synaptic terminals and other neuronal areas (Tao-Cheng & Zhou, 1999) and serves to regulate emotional aspects of behavior (Hariri & Weinberger, 2003). The variants in the promoter region of this gene have traditionally been classified as short (*s*) and long (*l*), with the latter conferring higher expression than the former (Lesch et al., 1996) and the former being associated with greater amygdala activity to fearful stimuli (Hariri et al., 2002). Recently, an A>G SNP within the long *5-HTTLPR* variant has been identified (rs25531), with the l_G variant described as having expression levels similar to the *s* allele (Nakamura, Ueno, Sano, & Tanabe, 2000). This has resulted in some studies using a triallelic classification of this locus, with genotypes classified into functionally similar groups as follows: s/s, s/l_G, l_G/l_G; s/l_A, l_A/l_G; l_A/l_A.. Lack of consideration of the triallelic genotype, however, would be more likely to bias results toward null findings, which do not represent the bulk of published findings for the *5-HTTLPR* locus.

Among the nine studies focusing on *SLC6A4* in relation to PTSD, six in total found evidence for an association between the *s* allele or *s/s* genotype and increased risk for PTSD (Kilpatrick et al., 2007; Koenen et al., 2009; Kolassa, Ertl, et al., 2010; Lee et al., 2005; Xie et al., 2009) or among those with PTSD, higher PTSD symptom scores (Sayin et al., 2010). Importantly, three of these six studies (Kilpatrick et al., 2007; Koenen et al., 2009; Xie et al., 2009) found evidence for this association only in the context of particular environmental exposures—in other words, the *s* allele susceptibility was demonstrated through tests of gene-environment (GxE) interactions. Environmental measures tested in these three studies include hurricane exposure and social support (Kilpatrick et al., 2007), residence in high- vs. low-risk social environments measured at the county level (Koenen et al., 2009), and having a history of either childhood adversity or traumatic events during adulthood (Xie et al., 2009). Stratified analyses in this latter work showed a significant G x childhood adversity interaction for *s* allele carriers among whites but not African Americans, suggesting the possibility of race/ethnic-specific GxE effects. Notably, all three of these GxE studies included trauma-exposed control samples, although in some cases the type of trauma experienced may have differed between those with PTSD relative to those without PTSD.

Despite the preponderance of studies that have found a relation between the *s* allele or *s/s* genotype and PTSD at the serotonin transporter locus, other alleles and/or genotypes have also been implicated in heightening vulnerability to PTSD. Two studies have identified the higher activity *l/l* or L_A/L_A genotypes as conferring increased risk for both chronic (Thakur, Joober, & Brunet, 2009) and lifetime PTSD (Grabe et al., 2009). In addition, one of these two studies provided evidence for a GxE interaction such that individuals with the L_A allele had an excess risk of PTSD if they had experienced three or more PTEs (Grabe et al., 2009). As was the case for the majority of studies identifying the *s* allele as the putative risk variant, these two studies all included trauma-exposed controls but the index trauma may have differed between cases and controls.

Finally, two studies involving the serotonergic system have assessed variation in the serotonin 2A receptor (*5-HTR2A*) gene in relation to PTSD. Both studies focused on a -1438 A/G polymorphism in the promoter region of the gene that had previously been associated with other psychiatric disorders (e.g., Ohara, Nagai, Tsukamoto, Tani, & Suzuki, 1998; Walitza et al., 2002); and both studies found evidence for an excess of the G allele (Mellman et al., 2009) or GG genotype (Lee et al., 2007) among individuals with PTSD.

Alternative Neurobiological System Candidate Gene Studies

The remaining 10 studies published to date on the subject of genetic vulnerability to PTSD have investigated a variety of other neurobiological pathways. Three genes have been investigated that are involved in hypothalamic-pituitary-adrenal (HPA) axis regulation; as with the serotonergic system, genes relating to HPA axis function offer strong candidates for loci involved in PTSD etiology, as the HPA axis is the primary neuroendocrine system that modulates the mammalian stress response. Two studies have focused on the locus encoding the FK506 binding protein 5 (*FKBP5*), which acts as an inhibitor of the glucocorticoid receptor. Both studies provided evidence for PTSD-related GxE interactions at four SNPs in either primary (Binder et al., 2008) or secondary (Xie et al., 2010) analyses: Binder et al. (2008) identified four SNPs that showed significant interaction with experiences of child abuse to predict PTS symptoms, with those who experienced more severe (i.e., greater number) of child abuse events showing increased severity of PTS symptoms; notably, this study was conducted in an almost exclusively low-income, African-American (AA) sample. Consistent with this, Xie et al. (2010) reported a GxE interaction for one of the four SNPS, rs9470080, among AAs exposed to childhood adversity. Interestingly, this interaction was not significant for whites (EAs); however, unlike AAs, EAs showed significant alcohol dependence x G and opioid dependence x G interactions for all four SNPs. Taken together, these and the earlier *5-HTTLPR* results suggest the possibility of race/ethnic-specific GxE effects, the implications of which are discussed in more detail in a subsequent section.

In contrast to the two GxE-based studies involving *FKBP5*, the remaining two studies pertaining to HPA-axis related genes tested only for main effects. Bachman et al. (2005) examined SNP variation of the glucocorticoid receptor (*GCCR*) locus among combat-exposed veterans with and without PTSD, finding only that a subset of PTSD patients ($n = 9$) with the *GG* genotype in intron 2 of *GCCR* showed a significant negative correlation between basal cortisol levels and Clinician-Administered PTSD Scale scores (CAPS). A second study focusing on four SNPs in the cannabinoid receptor gene (*CNR1*) found a significant excess of C-to-A and a deficit of C-to-G variants among those with PTSD among white parents of youth with attention hyperactivity disorder (ADHD; Lu et al., 2008); similar tests in an independent sample of Finnish adolescents, however, did not replicate this finding (Lu et al., 2008).

Genes of the locus coeruleus/noradrenergic systems have been an additional focus of study in the search for candidate genes showing variations associated with PTSD etiology. Noradrenergic hyperactivity in the basolateral amygdala is hypothesized to mediate the overconsoliation of fear memory in PTSD (Deebiec & Ledoux, 2006; Pitman & Delahanty, 2005; Southwick et al., 1999). Furthermore, emotional arousal is associated with enhanced norepinephrine (NE) release in limbic areas, including the amygdala and hippocampus (Cahill & McGaugh, 1996; Cahill, Prins, Weber & McGaugh, 1994; Ferry, Roozendaal & McGaugh, 1999a, 1999b, 1999c;). Preliminary evidence suggests pharmacological agents that block NE receptors prevent the development of PTSD, possibly through attenuation of traumatic memory consolidation (Pitman & Delahanty, 2005). Several genes are involved in synaptic availability of NE including the NE transporter gene (*SLC6A2*, also called *NET1*), the dopamine beta hydroxylase gene (*DBH*), and the catechol O-methytransferase gene (*COMT*).

Studies focused on genes in the locus coeruleus/noradrenergic systems have produced mixed findings. A recent investigation of survivors of the Rwandan genocide detected a significant interaction between *COMT* and number of traumatic events, whereby those with the Met/Met (i.e., higher enzyme activity) genotype were at high risk for PTSD independent of number of traumatic events, whereas Val/Val and Val/Met showed a typical dose-response of traumatic events and risk for PTSD (Kolassa, Kolassa, Ertl, Papassotiropoulos & De Quervain, 2010). In contrast, two additional studies of the neuropeptide Y (*NPY*) and dopamine beta-hydroxylase (*DBH*) loci found no significant association between functional SNP polymorphisms in these loci and PTSD (Lappalainen et al., 2002; Mustapic et al., 2007), although the latter study did detect significantly lower plasma dopamine beta-hydroxylase activity among those with PTSD who carried the *CC* genotype in the promoter region (i.e., *DBH*-1021 C/T) of this locus. Of note, gene-environment interactions were not tested in these latter two studies and, in some cases, control samples were not selected based on trauma exposure (see table 11.1).

Among the four additional studies that have been published to date, two have focused on variation in brain-derived neurotrophic factor (*BDNF*; Lee et al., 2006; Zhang et al., 2006), one has focused on apolioprotein E (*APOE*; Freeman, Roca, Guggenheim, Kimbrell, & Griffin, 2005) and another has focused on gamma-aminobutyric acid receptor subunit 2 (*GABRA2*; Nelson et al., 2009). PTSD has been associated with reduced hippocampal volume and altered function in brain imaging studies (reviewed in Liberzon & Phan, 2003); a polymorphism in the *BDNF* coding region (Val66Met), in turn, has been associated with reduced hippocampal volume and hippocampal deficiencies (Pezawas et al., 2004). However, neither of these two studies has found an association between the Val66Met or other (Zhang et al., 2006) polymorphisms and risk for PTSD. Again, inclusion of control individuals who were not specifically screened for trauma exposure (which occurred in both studies) may have limited their ability to detect a significant association. In contrast, Freeman and colleagues' (2005) study of *APOE* showed a significant association between the *APOE2* allele and increased re-experiencing symptoms and impaired memory function in a sample of male veterans, all of whom had PTSD (Freeman et al., 2005). These results ran counter to expectations that PTSD would show an association with the *APOE4* allele, which had previously been associated with smaller hippocampal volumes (Cohen, Small, Lalonde, Friz, & Sunderland, 2001) and memory impairment (Flory, Manuck, Ferrell, Ryan, & Muldoon, 2000).

Two final studies involving *GABRA2* and *RGS2* identified variants associated with increased susceptibility to PTSD, but only in the context of certain environmental exposures. In *GABRA2*, there was evidence for a significant interaction between childhood trauma and PTSD during adulthood for three of four SNPs tested at the *GABRA2* locus (Nelson et al., 2009). Notably, this effect was only statistically significant among individuals homozygous for the putative risk allele. Similarly, in a study of *RGS2* variation in a sample of hurricane exposed adults, there was evidence for a significant three-way interaction such that individuals with C allele at SNP rs4606, high hurricane exposure, and low social support showed increased risk for higher posthurricane PTS symptoms (Amstadter et al., 2009); a similar interaction was detected when lifetime PTS symptoms was used as the outcome.

Figure 11.1 presents a graph of the polymorphisms, and the loci with which they are associated, that have been tested in at least two studies to date. Among the 21 studies represented in this graph,

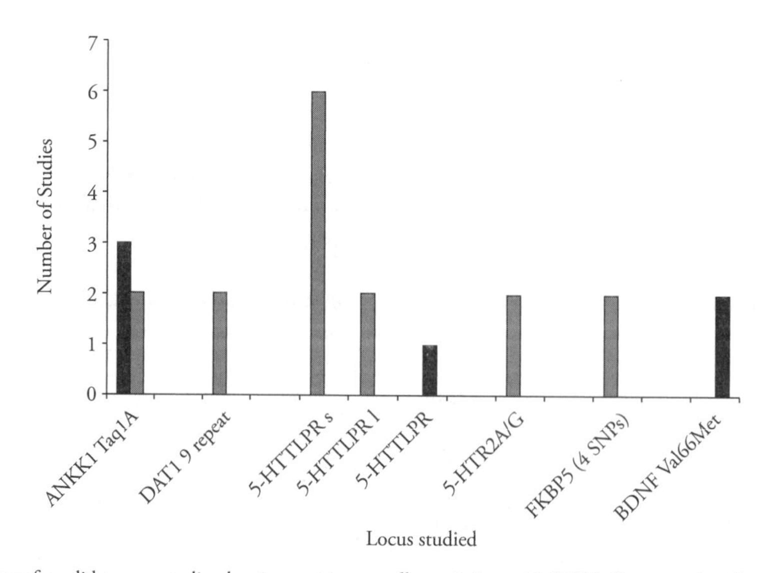

Figure 11.1. Number of candidate gene studies showing positive or null associations with PTSD. Shown are loci for which two or more studies have been published (table 11.1). Positive associations may be derived from secondary analyses not reported in table 11.1.

17 report a positive association with PTSD or PTS symptoms, with some of these presented in secondary analyses, (e.g., Xie et al., 2010) and 5 report no evidence for a significant association with PTSD. The largest proportion (43%) has investigated the *5-HTTLPR* polymorphism. As described in more detail in a following section, this summary must be viewed within the context of the analytic strengths and weaknesses of each study.

Gene-Environment Interplay in PTSD

Among the 30 studies summarized in table 11.1, 11 included one or more tests of GxE interactions, with 10 of these (i.e., all but Dragan & Oniszczenko, 2009) reaching statistical significance. Tests of GxE interactions operate on the premise that individuals with the same underlying genotype will show differing phenotypes (e.g., PTSD) depending on their environmental context. In a seminal article outlining strategies for examining interactions between candidate genes and measured environments, Moffitt and colleagues (2005) provide an overview of the GxE paradigm, recommend steps for conducting GxE research, and highlight the benefits of GxE strategies for understanding the etiology of common mental disorders such as PTSD. Subsequent work by the same group (Rutter, Moffit & Caspi, 2006) broadened the concept of GxE interaction to, instead, GxE interplay in order to draw attention to the variety of ways in which genes and environments act recursively on one another in the etiology of psychopathology. More specifically, the authors suggested that epigenetic effects may, through influences on gene expression, offer one mechanism by which the environment can moderate the effects of genes (Rutter et al., 2006). In the case of PTSD, such epigenetic effects offer a plausible way in which an externally experienced traumatic event may get "under the skin" and translated into adverse psychopathological outcomes. Below we offer a brief review of epigenetics and the nascent literature relating to PTSD in this area.

Epigenetic Studies of PTSD

The term *epigenetics* refers to the regulation of genetic functions mediated through mechanisms that are independent of DNA sequences. Although multiple types of epigenetic modifications have been identified (for a recent review, see Kim, Samaranayake, & Pradhan, 2009), all involve chemical modifications that regulate chromatin structure and/or DNA accessibility, which in turn alters the transcriptional activity of the surrounding loci. Methylation—the covalent modification of DNA in which methyl groups are coupled to cytosine at CpG sites—is perhaps the best studied of these epigenetic mechanisms, due in part to its tractability to study. Recently, work by Uddin et al. (2010) has provided evidence for large-scale differences in methylation profiles among those with relative to those without PTSD. The authors investigated a subsample of 100 individuals from a community-based, representative cohort of adult residents of Detroit. Using DNA derived from whole blood, they assessed the methylation signatures at over 27,000 loci from ~14,500 genes to ascertain whether there were unique methylation profiles that could distinguish between those with vs. without PTSD. Importantly, all 100 individuals tested had been exposed to one or more PTE, with 23 of these individuals meeting PTSD diagnostic criteria. Results showed that the PTSD-affected group was distinguished by relatively lower methylation levels among immune-system related genes, and by increased methylation in genes relating to sensory perception of sound; notably, the immune-system related signal was also observed in genes showing a significant negative correlation with increasing number of PTEs in this group, suggesting that there is a biological effect of cumulative traumatic burden among those with this disorder. In contrast, those without PTSD showed relatively lower methylation levels in genes relating to developmental processes in general, and neurogenesis in particular. These results suggest that those with PTSD are characterized by an activation of immune-system related genes as well as an absence of nervous system related gene activity normally observed in those free of the disorder. The functional implications of this PTSD immune-related profile was also assessed in this work via testing of cytomegalovirus antibody levels in the same 100 individuals tested on the methylation microarray, with results indicating that those with PTSD had a higher antibody response to this normally latent herpesvirus. Taken together, the authors posit that these results suggest a model whereby the external experience of a traumatic event alters the methylation profile of immune-system related genes, which then affects their gene expression and, subsequently, translates into altered immune function.

Although these data provide some evidence of a biologic embedding of posttraumatic stress, it is likely that there are both molecular and environmental features that also render some individuals more susceptible to PTSD. One potential epigenetic example of this phenomenon comes from a recent, finer-grained study of the same 100 individuals described above. Focusing in on the serotonin transporter as a candidate gene, the authors investigated whether *SLC6A4* methylation status interacted with number of PTEs to predict PTSD, controlling for a range of demographic and behavioral characteristics (Koenen et al., 2011). The authors identified a significant interaction whereby *SLC6A4* methylation modified the effect of cumulative trauma on risk for PTSD, such that individuals with higher numbers of PTEs were at increased risk for PTSD at lower methylation levels; however, individuals with more PTEs were protected from this disorder at higher methylation levels. This interaction was also observed when the outcome was PTSD symptom severity or number of PTSD symptoms (Koenen et al., 2011). These results suggest that individuals' preexisting methylation levels at certain loci may moderate their experience of PTEs in a manner salient to PTSD etiology, suggesting potential molecular signatures of increased resilience to this disorder. Future work in this longitudinal cohort will help to shed light on the extent to which such epigenetic marks modify—or are modified by—traumatic stress.

Gene Expression Studies of PTSD

The above-described epigenetic findings provide a snapshot of PTSD-associated differences that are hypothesized to be associated with downstream differences in gene expression. A small but growing literature has provided evidence for actual changes in gene expression patterns among PTSD-affected individuals. The majority of these microarray-based studies have assessed gene expression changes in RNA derived from either peripheral blood mononuclear cells (PBMCs) or whole blood. The earliest work in this area assessed PTSD-associated gene expression signatures among trauma survivors admitted to the emergency room immediately following a traumatic event and again four months after the PTE (Segman et al., 2005). Functional analyses of transcripts that were differentially expressed ($n = 656$) between those with vs. without PTSD showed a reduced expression of transcriptional enhancers, distinct expression signatures of transcripts involved in immune activation, and a significant enrichment of genes that encode neural and endocrine proteins. Notably, although these neural- and endocrine-related genes were detected as differentially expressed in peripheral blood, a larger than expected number of these same genes are known to also be expressed in the amygdala, hippocampus, and HPA axis (Segman et al., 2005), confirming the importance of these brain regions and biologic systems in mediating stress reactivity.

A more recent study used a custom-made "stress/immune" cDNA microarray to assess expression levels of 384 genes among individuals with vs. without PTSD using RNA obtained from whole blood (Zieker et al., 2007). Of note in this study, all of the PTSD-affected individuals had been exposed to the same traumatic event almost 20 years prior to testing (i.e., the Ramstein air show catastrophe of 1989), yet typical PTSD symptoms persisted in this group. Analyses showed a total of 18 differentially expressed transcripts, 4 and 14 of which were up- and down-regulated, respectively (Zieker et al., 2007). The majority of down-regulated transcripts (which were the focus of the study) were associated with immune functions or with reactive oxygen species. Most recently, Yehuda and colleagues (2009) reported whole blood-derived gene expression levels among PTSD-affected and -unaffected individuals who had had exposure to the 9/11 attack on New York City (Yehuda et al., 2009). Differential expression was detected in 16 distinct genes, several of which are involved in signal transduction, brain and immune cell function, and HPA axis activity, including *FKBP5* and signal transducer and activator of transcription 5B (*STAT5B*), both of which were significantly down-regulated in PTSD-affected individuals (Yehuda et al., 2009). *FKBP5* acts as an inhibitor of the glucocorticoid receptor (GR; Wochnik et al., 2005) and *STAT5B* has been shown to delay GR nuclear translocation (Goleva, Kisich & Leung, 2002). The detection of decreased expression in these genes is thus consistent with previous reports of higher GR activity in PTSD (Yehuda, 2006).

The previous studies focused on biological samples obtained from living individuals suffering from PTSD. In a report based on postmortem brain tissues obtained from PTSD-affected and unaffected individuals, gene expression patterns were assessed in the dorsolateral prefrontal cortex (DLPFC) Brodmann area (BA) 46 using a mitochondria-focused cDNA microarray containing ~1,360 genes (Su et al., 2008). A total of 162 genes showed differential expression patterns compared to controls, with fold change values of 1.25 or greater. Among these 162 genes, the mitochondrial dysfunction and oxidative phosphorylation pathways showed the largest number of differentially expressed genes; and 30 differentially expressed genes had known roles in neurological and/or psychiatric disorders (Su et al., 2008). We note, however, that three of the six PTSD-affected individuals assessed in this study were suicide completers, and that suicide completers have been shown to possess epigenetic and gene expression signatures that are distinct from deceased individuals who did not take their own lives (Ernst et al., 2009; McGowan et al., 2008), which may thus affect the generalizability of these results.

Analytic Considerations

The above review confirms that genetic and other molecular features contribute to PTSD etiology. In some cases, specific loci have been implicated in more than one study (figure 11.1). These replications appear to build a case for the relation between specific variants at these loci and risk for PTSD. However, some of these positive findings have been reported in studies that have failed to consider some of the most important aspects of study design in this area (e.g., the inclusion of trauma-exposed controls, see table 11.1). As the literature continues to evolve in this area, careful attention should be paid to the following issues described next.

Control Selection

According to epidemiologic principles (Rothman, 2002), controls should be selected from the same underlying population as the cases, be representative of all controls with respect to exposure, and identical to (or exchangeable with) the exposed cases except for the risk factor in question—in this case, the genetic variant that is under investigation. As noted above and in table 11.1, however, several candidate gene studies, as well as gene expression studies, do not report assessment of trauma exposure in controls. Although it is true that a majority of adults have been exposed to a PTE, the small sample sizes used in many of the above-described studies makes negative associations difficult to interpret; and, further, violation of the exchangeability principle increases the likelihood that confounding factors may underlie any observed positive associations.

Trauma Assessment

Risk for PTSD is influenced by a number of trauma characteristics that should be considered in studies investigating the genetic etiology of this disorder. First, individuals exposed to multiple traumatic events are at greater risk for PTSD than are those exposed to only a single stressor (Hedtke et al., 2008; Neugebauer et al., 2009; Ozer, Best, Lipsey, & Weiss, 2003). Second, type of trauma exposure is associated with differential risk for PTSD. For example, interpersonal violence is associated with higher risk than other types of PTEs, particularly those that do not involve intentionality such as motor vehicle accidents and natural disasters (Kessler et al., 1995; Resnick, Kilpatrick, Dansky, Saunders, & Best, 1993). Third, additional variables and event-related incidents affect risk for PTSD, such as life threat, presence of a weapon, victim-perpetrator relationship and severity (Brewin, Andrews & Valentine, 2000; Galea et al., 2002; Kilpatrick et al., 2003). Therefore, a comprehensive trauma assessment should encompass multiple traumatic experiences across the life course, determine whether traumatic stressors were discrete incidents or chronic in nature, and gather data on incident characteristics.

Developmental Stage and Sex Differences

Accumulating evidence confirms that the effects of stressful experiences will depend on the timing and duration of exposure, as well as on previous exposures to adverse experiences (reviewed in Lupien, McEwen, Gunnar, & Heim, 2009). Indeed, age at trauma exposure may exact distinct psychiatric outcomes (Pollak, 2005). For example, women who experience trauma before age 12 show increased risk for major depression, whereas women who experience trauma between 12–18 years of age develop PTSD more frequently (Maercker, Michael, Fehm, Becker, & Margraf, 2004). Similarly, different patterns of acute and chronic cortisol response have been documented in children relative to adults with PTSD (De Bellis et al., 1999; Delahanty, Nugent, Christopher, & Walsh, 2005). An additional layer of complexity to consider is that genetic factors may contribute to PTSD risk differently between sexes. Epidemiologic investigations have identified a markedly higher prevalence of PTSD in females compared to males in both adult (Breslau, Davis, Andreski, & Peterson, 1991; Davidson, Hughes, Blazer & George, 1991; Kessler et al., 1995) and child/adolescent samples (Cuffe et al., 1998; Singer Anglin, Song, & Lunghofer, 1995). These findings remain when within-trauma type analyses are conducted, suggesting that the greater prevalence of PTSD in females cannot be completely explained by type of trauma. As both age- and sex-dependent GxE effects have been observed for other common mental disorders (e.g., Chipman et al., 2007; Eley et al., 2004; Sjoberg et al., 2006), it is plausible that these may exist for PTSD as well, as suggested by the findings of Lee et al. (2007). Future candidate gene and genomic studies of PTSD should carefully consider these important demographic variables in their study design and, at minimum, avoid continuing the disproportionate reliance on adult, non-Hispanic White males drawn from clinical samples to inform their work.

Conclusion

PTSD is a complex disorder with a range of molecular features that likely underlie individuals' increased risk for, or resilience to, this disorder. No matter what the genetic constitution, epidemiologic evidence confirms that there comes a point at which an individuals' capacity to be resilient in the face of traumatic stressors is completely extinguished (Kolassa, Ertl, et al., 2010; Kolassa, Kolassa, et al., 2010; Neugebauer et al., 2009). Nevertheless, the era of high-throughput genomics offers the chance to more precisely identify the molecular features associated with increased risk for, or resilience to, PTSD—which may, in turn, facilitate the development of pharmacologic interventions targeting those most in need.

Among the above-described studies that specifically included trauma-exposed control samples, the evidence strongly suggests that genetic variation at neurobiologically relevant loci does indeed contribute to PTSD etiology. However, in the case of the gene on which the most studies have been conducted—the transporter region of *SLC6A4*—there is conflicting evidence regarding which allele confers increased susceptibility to PTSD. As this field continues to evolve, it will become increasingly important for studies to adopt comparable, rigorous methodologies in order to replicate, or refute, earlier findings. On the other hand, as has been suggested by GxE studies of depression and other psychological outcomes (Kim et al., 2009; Sjoberg et al., 2006), it is possible that different alleles at the same locus may confer both increased risk for AND resilience to PTSD, depending on the gender and/or environmental context being studied. Careful consideration of the environment is thus clearly warranted in future molecular genetic studies of PTSD.

Furthermore, the explosion of genetic and genomic data will make it increasingly important to consider the joint action of putative risk/resilience alleles at multiple loci that likely interact to shape individuals' risk for PTSD. A limited amount of data on epistatic interactions has been published for other psychopathologies (e.g., Kaufman et al., 2006), and, although twin studies suggest that this mechanism is at work for PTSD, to date no similar work has been published on PTSD. These potentially interacting polymorphisms at multiple loci, in turn, will need to be considered in the context of epigenetic and gene expression variation at these and other, interacting loci, all of which may moderate individuals' response to traumatic stress. Finally, as alluded to previously, early findings by Xie and colleagues (2010) suggest that GxE effects may show population-specific variation at different neurobiologically relevant loci. Given that races can differ on social environmental exposures known to affect psychiatric outcomes, such as assaultive violence (Roberts et al., 2011), an important challenge for future GxE research will be to consider population variation at multiple levels to properly account for putative race-specific effects. Despite these multiple challenges to future investigations, in the context of global and national events involving poverty, war, terrorism and natural disaster, gaining an improved understanding of the molecular factors that may influence vulnerability to PTSD should remain a priority area in public health research.

Future Directions

Our review of the literature and concluding statements suggest the following questions for future research into the genetic etiology of PTSD.

1. What constellation of genetic variation contributes to shape risk for PTSD? Can we uncover epistatic interactions that, given the presence of certain polymorphisms at these loci, will enable us to create an index of genetic risk for PTSD?

2. What are the epigenetic changes induced by exposure to a PTE that are associated with development of PTSD? Do pre-PTE epigenetic signatures at certain loci confer increased risk for, or resilience to, PTSD?

3. Which environmental variables should be included in future GxE investigations of PTSD? How might these GxE effects vary with race, age and sex; and should we be conducting analyses stratified on these variables?

Note

This work was supported by grants DA022720, DA022720-S1 and RC1 MH088283-01 (MU), K01 MH087240 (NRN), HD055885 (ABA), and K08MH070627 and MH078928 (KCK).

References

Amstadter, A. B., Koenen, K. C., Ruggiero, K. J., Acierno, R., Galea, S., Kilpatrick, D. G., & Gelernter, J. (2009). Variant in RGS2 moderates posttraumatic stress symptoms following potentially traumatic event exposure. *Journal of Anxiety Disorders, 23,* 369–373. (doi:10.1016/j.janxdis.2008.12.005)

Amstadter, A. B., Zajax, K., Nugent, N. R. & Koenen, K. C. (2010). Genetic substrates of posttraumatic stress disorder: Review of extant research and neurobiologically informed future directions. In L. Sher & A. Vilens (Eds.), *Neurobiology of post-traumatic stress disorder* (pp. 65–89). Hauppauge, NY: Nova Science Publishers.

Bachmann, A. W., Sedgley, T. L., Jackson, R. V., Gibson, J. N., Young, R. M., & Torpy, D. J. (2005). Glucocorticoid receptor polymorphisms and post-traumatic stress disorder. *Psychoneuroendocrinology, 30,* 297–306. (doi:10.1016/j.psyneuen.2004.08.006)

Binder, E. B., Bradley, R. G., Liu, W., Epstein, M. P., Deveau, T. C., Mercer, K. B., & Ressler, K. J. (2008). Association of FKBP5 polymorphisms and childhood abuse with risk of posttraumatic stress disorder symptoms in adults. *Journal of the American Medical Association, 299,* 1291–1305. (doi:10.1001/jama.299.11.1291)

Breslau, N., Davis, G. C., Andreski, P., & Peterson, E. (1991). Traumatic events and posttraumatic stress disorder in an urban population of young adults. *Archives of General Psychiatry, 48,* 216–222. Retrieved from http://archpsyc.ama-assn.org/.

Brewin, C. R., Andrews, B., & Valentine, J. D. (2000). Meta-analysis of risk factors for posttraumatic stress disorder in trauma-exposed adults. *Journal of Consulting and Clinical Psychology, 68,* 317–336. (doi: 10.1037/0022–006-X.68.5.748)

Cahill, L., & McGaugh, J. L. (1996). The neurobiology of memory for emotional events: Adrenergic activation and the amygdala. *Proceedings of the Western Pharmacology Society, 39,* 81–84. Retrieved from http://www.ncbi.nlm.nih.gov.

Cahill, L., Prins, B., Weber, M., & McGaugh, J. L. (1994). Beta-adrenergic activation and memory for emotional events. *Nature, 371,* 702–704. (doi:10.1038/371702a0)

Chipman, P., Jorm, A. F., Prior, M., Sanson, A., Smart, D., Tan, X., & Easteal, S. (2007). No interaction between the serotonin transporter polymorphism (5-HTTLPR) and childhood adversity or recent stressful life events on symptoms of depression: Results from two community surveys. *American Journal of Medical Genetics Part B: Neuropsychiatric Genetics, 144B,* 561–565. (doi: 10.1002/ajmg.b.30480)

Cohen, R. M., Small, C., Lalonde, F., Friz, J., & Sunderland, T. (2001). Effect of apolipoprotein E genotype on hippocampal volume loss in aging healthy women. *Neurology, 57,* 2223–2228. Retrieved from http://www.neurology.org.

Comings, D. E., Comings, B. G., Muhleman, D., Dietz, G., Shabbahrami, B., & Tast, D. (1991). The dopamine D2 receptor locus as a modifying gene in neuropsychiatric disorder. *Journal of the American Medical Association, 266,* 1793–1800. (doi:10.1001/jama.266.13.1793)

Comings, D. E., Muhleman, D., & Gysin, R. (1996). Dopamine D2 receptor (DRD2) gene and susceptibility to posttraumatic stress disorder: A study and replication. *Biological Psychiatry, 40,* 368–372. (doi:10.1016/0006–3223(95)00519–6)

Cuffe, S. P., Addy, C. L., Garrison, C. Z., Waller, J. L., Jackson, K. L., McKeown, R. E., & Chilappagari, S. (1998). Prevalence of PTSD in a community sample of older adolescents. *Journal of the American Academy of Child and Adolescent Psychiatry, 37,* 147–154. (doi:10.1097/00004583–199802000–00006)

Davidson, J. R., Hughes, D., Blazer, D. G., & George, L. K. (1991). Post-traumatic stress disorder in the community: An epidemiological study. *Psychological Medicine, 21,* 713–721. (doi: 10.1017/S0033291700022352)

De Bellis, M. D., Baum, A. S., Birmaher, B., Keshavan, M. S., Eccard, C. H., Boring, A. M., & Ryan, N. D. (1999). Developmental traumatology part I: Biological stress systems. *Biological Psychiatry, 45,* 1237–1258. (doi:10.1016/S0006–3223(99)00044-X)

Deebiec, J., & Ledoux, J. E. (2006). Noradrenergic signaling in the amygdala contributes to the reconsolidation of fear memory: Treatment implications for PTSD. *Annals of the*

New York Academy of Sciences, *1071*, 521–524. (doi:10.1196/annals.1364.056)

Delahanty, D. L., Nugent, N. R., Christopher, N. C., & Walsh, M. (2005). Initial urinary epinephrine and cortisol levels predict acute PTSD symptoms in child trauma victims. *Journal of Psychoneuroendocrinology*, *30*, 121–128. (doi:10.1016/j.psyneuen.2004.06.004)

Dragan, W. L., & Oniszczenko, W. Ç. (2009). The association between dopamine D4 receptor exon III polymorphism and intensity of PTSD symptoms among flood survivors. *Anxiety, Stress & Coping: An International Journal*, *22*, 483–495. (doi:10.1080/10615800802419407)

Drury, S. S., Theall, K. P., Keats, B. J. B., & Scheeringa, M. (2009). The role of the dopamine transporter (DAT) in the development of PTSD in preschool children. *Journal of Traumatic Stress*, *22*, 534–539. (doi:10.1002/jts.20475)

Eley, T. C., Sugden, K., Corsico, A., Gregory, A. M., Sham, P., McGuffin, P., & Craig, I. W. (2004). Gene-environment interaction analysis of serotonin system markers with adolescent depression. *Molecular Psychiatry*, *9*, 908–915. (doi:10.1038/sj.mp.4001546)

Ernst, C., Deleva, V., Deng, X., Sequeira, A., Pomarenski, A., Klempan, T., & Turecki, G. (2009). Alternative splicing, methylation state, and expression profile of tropomyosin-related kinase B in the frontal cortex of suicide completers. *Archives of General Psychiatry*, *66*, 22–32. (doi:10.1001/archpsyc.66.1.22)

Ferry, B., Roozendaal, B., & McGaugh, J. L. (1999a). Basolateral amygdala noradrenergic influences on memory storage are mediated by an interaction between beta- and alpha1-adrenoceptors. *Journal of Neuroscience*, *19*, 5119–5123. Retrieved from http://www.jneurosci.org.

Ferry, B., Roozendaal, B., & McGaugh, J. L. (1999b). Involvement of alpha1-adrenoceptors in the basolateral amygdala in modulation of memory storage. *European Journal of Pharmacology*, *372*, 9–16. (doi:10.1016/S0014–2999(99)00169–7)

Ferry, B., Roozendaal, B., & McGaugh, J. L. (1999c). Role of norepinephrine in mediating stress hormone regulation of long-term memory storage: A critical involvement of the amygdala. *Biological Psychiatry*, *46*, 1140–1152. (doi:10.1016/S0006–3223(99)00157–2)

Flory, J. D., Manuck, S. B., Ferrell, R. E., Ryan, C. M., & Muldoon, M. F. (2000). Memory performance and the apolipoprotein E polymorphism in a community sample of middle-aged adults. *American Journal of Medical Genetics*, *96*, 707–711. (doi:10.1002/1096–8628(20001204)96:6<707::AID-AJMG1>3.0.CO;2-V)

Freeman, T., Roca, V., Guggenheim, F., Kimbrell, T., & Griffin, W. S. (2005). Neuropsychiatric associations of apolipoprotein E alleles in subjects with combat-related posttraumatic stress disorder. *Journal of Neuropsychiatry and Clinical Neurosciences*, *17*, 541–543. (doi:10.1176/appi.neuropsych.17.4.541)

Galea, S., Ahern, J., Resnick, H., Kilpatrick, D., Bucuvalas, M., Gold, J., & Vlahov, D. (2002). Psychological sequelae of the September 11 terrorist attacks in New York City. *New England Journal of Medicine*, *346*, 982–987. (doi:10.1056/NEJMsa013404)

Gelernter, J., Southwick, S., Goodson, S., Morgan, A., Nagy, L., & Charney, D. S. (1999). No association between D2 dopamine receptor (DRD2) 'A' system alleles, or DRD2 haplotypes, and posttraumatic stress disorder. *Biological Psychiatry*, *45*, 620–625. (doi:10.1016/S0006–3223(98)00087–0)

Goleva, E., Kisich, K. O., & Leung, D. Y. (2002). A role for STAT5 in the pathogenesis of IL-2-induced glucocorticoid resistance. *Journal of Immunology*, *169*, 5934–5940. Retrieved from http://www.jimmunol.org.

Grabe, H. J., Spitzer, C., Schwahn, C., Marcinek, A., Frahnow, A., Barnow, S., Rosskopf, D. (2009). Serotonin transporter gene (SLC6A4) promoter polymorphisms and the susceptibility to posttraumatic stress disorder in the general population. *American Journal of Psychiatry*, *166*, 926–933. (doi:10.1176/appi.ajp.2009.08101542)

Hamner, M. B., & Diamond, B. I. (1993). Elevated plasma dopamine in posttraumatic stress disorder: A preliminary report. *Biological Psychiatry*, *33*, 304–306. (doi:10.1016/0006–3223(93)90302-T)

Hariri, A. R., & Weinberger, D. R. (2003). Functional neuroimaging of genetic variation in serotonergic neurotransmission. *Genes, Brain, and Behavior*, *2*, 341–349. (doi:10.1046/j.1601–1848.2003.00048.x)

Hariri, A. R., Mattay, V. S., Tessitore, A., Kolachana, B., Fera, F., Goldman, D., & Weinberger, D. R. (2002). Serotonin transporter genetic variation and the response of the human amygdala. *Science*, *297*, 400–403. (doi:10.1126/science.1071829)

Hedtke, K. A., Ruggiero, K. J., Fitzgerald, M. M., Zinzow, H. M., Saunders, B. E., Resnick, H. S., & Kilpatrick, D.G. (2008). A longitudinal investigation of interpersonal violence in relation to mental health and substance use. *Journal of Consulting and Clinical Psychology*, *76*, 633–647. (doi:10.1037/0022–006X.76.4.633)

Kaufman, J., Yang, B. Z., Douglas-Palumberi, H., Grasso, D., Lipschitz, D., Houshyar, S., & Gelernter, J. (2006). Brain-derived neurotrophic factor-5-HTTLPR gene interactions and environmental modifiers of depression in children. *Biological Psychiatry*, *59*, 673–680. (doi:10.1016/j.biopsych.2005.10.026)

Kessler, R. C., & Wang, P. S. (2008). The descriptive epidemiology of commonly occurring mental disorders in the United States. *Annual Review of Public Health*, *29*, 115–129. (doi:10.1146/annurev.publhealth.29.020907.090847)

Kessler, R. C., Sonnega, A., Bromet, E., Hughes, M., & Nelson, C. B. (1995). Posttraumatic stress disorder in the National Comorbidity Survey. *Archives of General Psychiatry*, *52*, 1048–1060. Retrieved from http://archpsyc.ama-assn.org/.

Kilpatrick, D. G., Koenen, K. C., Ruggiero, K. J., Acierno, R., Galea, S., Resnick, H. S., & Gelernter, J. (2007). The serotonin transporter genotype and social support and moderation of posttraumatic stress disorder and depression in hurricane-exposed adults. *American Journal of Psychiatry*, *164*, 1693–1699. (doi:10.1176/appi.ajp.2007.06122007)

Kilpatrick, D. G., Ruggiero, K. J., Acierno, R., Saunders, B. E., Resnick, H. S., & Best, C. L. (2003). Violence and risk of PTSD, major depression, substance abuse/dependence, and comorbidity: Results from the National Survey of Adolescents. *Journal of Consulting and Clinincal Psychology*, *71*, 692–700. (doi:10.1037/0022–006X.71.4.692)

Kim, J. K., Samaranayake, M., & Pradhan, S. (2009). Epigenetic mechanisms in mammals. *Cellular and Molecular Life Sciences*, *66*, 596–612. (doi:10.1007/s00018–008–8432–4)

Koenen, K. C., Aiello, A. E., Bakshis, E., Amstadter, A. B., Ruggiero, K. J., Acierno, R., & Galea, S. (2009). Modification of the association between serotonin transporter genotype and risk of posttraumatic stress disorder in adults by county-level social environment. *American Journal of Epidemiology*, *169*, 704–711. (doi:10.1093/aje/kwn397)

Koenen, K. C., Amstadter, A., & Nugent, N. R. (2008). Genetic risk factors for PTSD. In D. L. Delahanty (Ed.), *Psychobiology of trauma and resilience across the lifespan* (pp. 23–46). Lanham, MD: Rowman & Littlefield.

Koenen, K. C., Nugent, N. R., & Amstadter, A. B. (2008). Posttraumatic stress disorder: A review and agenda for gene-environment interaction research in trauma. *European Archives of Psychiatry and Clinical Neuroscience, 258*, 82–96. Retrieved from http://www.springer.com/medicine/psychiatry/journal/406.

Koenen, K. C., Uddin, M., Aiello, A. E., Wildman, D. E., De los Santos, R., Goldmann, E., & Galea, S. (2011). Methylation of SLC6A4 moderates effect of cumulative traumatic burden on risk for PTSD. *Depression and Anxiety, 28*, 639–647. (doi: 10.1002/da.20825)

Kolassa, I.-T., Ertl, V., Eckart, C., Glockner, F., Kolassa, S., Papassotiropoulos, A., & Elbert, T. (2010). Association study of trauma load and SLC6A4 promoter polymorphism in PTSD: Evidence from survivors of the Rwandan genocide. *Journal of Clinical Psychiatry, 71*, 543–547. (doi:10.4088/JCP.08m04787blu)

Kolassa, I. T., Kolassa, S., Ertl, V., Papassotiropoulos, A., & De Quervain, D. J. (2010). The risk of posttraumatic stress disorder after trauma depends on traumatic load and the catechol-o-methyltransferase Val(158)Met polymorphism. *Biological Psychiatry, 67*, 304–308. (doi:10.1016/j.biopsych.2009.10.009)

Laakso, A., Pohjalainen, T., Bergman, J., Kajander, J., Haaparanta, M., Solin, O., & Hietala, J. (2005). The A1 allele of the human D2 dopamine receptor gene is associated with increased activity of striatal L-amino acid decarboxylase in healthy subjects. *Pharmacogenetics and Genomics, 15*, 387–391. (doi:10.1097/01213011–200506000–00003)

Lappalainen, J., Kranzler, H. R., Malison, R., Price, L. H., Van Dyck, C., Rosenheck, R. A., & Gelernter, J. (2002). A functional neuropeptide Y Leu7Pro polymorphism associated with alcohol dependence in a large population sample from the United States. *Archives of General Psychiatry, 59*, 825–831. (doi:10.1001/archpsyc.59.9.825)

Lee, H. J., Kang, R. H., Lim, S. W., Paik, J. W., Choi, M. J., & Lee, M. S. (2006). Short communication: No association between the brain-derived neurotrophic factor gene Val66-Met polymorphism and post-traumatic stress disorder. *Stress and Health, 22*, 115–119. (doi:10.1002/smi.1085)

Lee, H. J., Lee, M. S., Kang, R. H., Kim, H., Kim, S. D., Kee, B. S., & Paik, I. H. (2005). Influence of the serotonin transporter promoter gene polymorphism on susceptibility to posttraumatic stress disorder. *Depression and Anxiety, 21*, 135–139. (doi:10.1002/da.20064)

Lee, H., Kwak, S., Paik, J., Kang, R., & Lee, M. (2007). Association between serotonin 2A receptor gene polymorphism and posttraumatic stress disorder. *Psychiatry Investigations, 4*, 104–108. Retrieved from http://www.psychiatryinvestigation.org.

Lemieux, A. M., & Coe, C. L. (1995). Abuse-related posttraumatic stress disorder: Evidence for chronic neuroendocrine activation in women. *Psychosomatic Medicine, 57*, 105–115. Retrieved from http://www.psychosomaticmedicine.org.

Leonard, B. E. (2006). HPA and immune axes in stress: Involvement of the serotonergic system. *Neuroimmunomodulation, 13*, 268–276. (doi:10.1159/000104854)

Lesch, K. P., Bengel, D., Heils, A., Sabol, S. Z., Greenberg, B. D., Petri, S., & Murphy, D. L. (1996). Association of Anxiety-Related Traits with a Polymorphism in the Serotonin Transporter Gene Regulatory Region. *Science, 274*, 1527–1531. (doi:10.1126/science.274.5292.1527)

Liberzon, I., & Phan, K. L. (2003). Brain-imaging studies of posttraumatic stress disorder. *CNS Spectrums, 8*, 641–650. Retrieved from http://www.cnsspectrums.com.

Lu, A. T., Ogdie, M. N., Jarvelin, M. R., Moilanen, I. K., Loo, S. K., McCracken, J. T., & Smalley, S. L. (2008). Association of the cannabinoid receptor gene (CNR1) with ADHD and post-traumatic stress disorder. *American Journal of Medical Genetics Part B: Neuropsychiatric Genetics, 147B*, 1488–1494. (doi:10.1002/ajmg.b.30693)

Lupien, S. J., McEwen, B. S., Gunnar, M. R., & Heim, C. (2009). Effects of stress throughout the lifespan on the brain, behaviour and cognition. *Nature Reviews Neuroscience, 10*, 434–445. (doi:10.1038/nrn2639)

Maercker, A., Michael, T., Fehm, L., Becker, E. S., & Margraf, J. (2004). Age of traumatisation as a predictor of post-traumatic stress disorder or major depression in young women. *British Journal of Psychiatry, 184*, 482–487. (doi:10.1192/bjp.184.6.482)

McGowan, P. O., Sasaki, A., Huang, T. C., Unterberger, A., Suderman, M., Ernst, C., & Szyf, M. (2008). Promoter-wide hypermethylation of the ribosomal RNA gene promoter in the suicide brain. *PLoS ONE, 3*, e2085. (doi:10.1371/journal.pone.0002085)

Mellman, T. A., Alim, T., Brown, D. D., Gorodetsky, E., Buzas, B., Lawson, W. B., & Charney, D. S. (2009). Serotonin polymorphisms and posttraumatic stress disorder in a trauma exposed African American population. *Depression and Anxiety, 26*, 993–997. (doi:10.1002/da.20627)

Moffitt, T. E., Caspi, A., & Rutter, M. (2005). Strategy for investigating interactions between measured genes and measured environments. *Archives of General Psychiatry, 62*, 473–481. (doi:10.1001/archpsyc.62.5.473)

Mustapic, M., Pivac, N., Kozaric-Kovacic, D., Dezeljin, M., Cubells, J. F., & Mueck-Seler, D. (2007). Dopamine beta-hydroxylase (DBH) activity and-1021C/T polymorphism of DBH gene in combat-related post-traumatic stress disorder. *American Journal of Medical Genetics, 144B*, 1087–1089. (doi:10.1002/ajmg.b.30526)

Nakamura, M., Ueno, S., Sano, A., & Tanabe, H. (2000). The human serotonin transporter gene linked polymorphism (5-HTTLPR) shows ten novel allelic variants. *Molecular Psychiatry, 5*, 32–38. (doi:10.1038/sj.mp.4000698)

Nelson, E. C., Agrawal, A., Pergadia, M. L., Lynskey, M. T., Todorov, A. A., Wang, J. C., & Madden, P. A. F. (2009). Association of childhood trauma exposure and GABRA2 polymorphisms with risk of posttraumatic stress disorder in adults. *Molecular Psychiatry, 14*, 234–235. (doi:10.1038/mp.2008.81)

Neugebauer, R., Fisher, P. W., Turner, J. B., Yamabe, S., Sarsfield, J. A., & Stehling-Ariza, T. (2009). Post-traumatic stress reactions among Rwandan children and adolescents in the early aftermath of genocide. *International Journal of Epidemiology, 38*, 1033–1045. (doi:10.1093/ije/dyn375)

Neville, M. J., Johnstone, E. C., & Walton, R. T. (2004). Identification and characterization of ANKK1: A novel kinase gene closely linked to DRD2 on chromosome band 11q23.1. *Human Mutation, 23*, 540–545. (doi:10.1002/humu.20039)

Nugent, N. R., Amstadter, A. B., & Koenen, K. C. (2008). Genetics of PTSD: Informing clinical conceptualizations and promoting future research. *American Journal of Medical Genetics C Seminars in Medical Genetics, 148*, 127–132. (doi:10.1002/ajmg.c.30169)

Ohara, K., Nagai, M., Tsukamoto, T., Tani, K., & Suzuki, Y. (1998). 5-HT2A receptor gene promoter polymorphism—1438G/A and mood disorders. *Neuroreport, 9*, 1139–1141. (doi:10.1097/00001756-199804200-00033)

Ozer, E. J., Best, S. R., Lipsey, T. L., & Weiss, D. S. (2003). Predictors of posttraumatic stress disorder and symptoms in adults: A meta-analysis. *Psychological Bulletin, 129*, 52–73. (doi:10.1037/0033-2909.129.1.52)

Pezawas, L., Verchinski, B. A., Mattay, V. S., Callicott, J. H., Kolachana, B. S., Straub, R. E., & Weinberger, D. R. (2004). The brain-derived neurotrophic factor val66met polymorphism and variation in human cortical morphology. *Journal of Neuroscience, 24*, 10099–10102. (doi:10.1523/JNEUROSCI.2680-04.2004)

Pitman, R. K., & Delahanty, D. L. (2005). Conceptually driven pharmacologic approaches to acute trauma. *CNS Spectrums, 10*, 99–106. Retrieved from http://www.cnsspectrums.com.

Pollak, S. D. (2005). Early adversity and mechanisms of plasticity: Integrating affective neuroscience with developmental approaches to psychopathology. *Developemental Psychopathology, 17*, 735–752. (doi:10.1017/S0954579405050352)

Puglisi-Allegra, S., & Cabib, S. (1997). Psychopharmacology of dopamine: The contribution of comparative studies in inbred strains of mice. *Progress in Neurobiology, 51*, 637–661. (doi:10.1016/S0301-0082(97)00008-7)

Resnick, H. S., Kilpatrick, D. G., Dansky, B. S., Saunders, B. E., & Best, C. L. (1993). Prevalence of civilian trauma and posttraumatic stress disorder in a representative national sample of women. *Journal of Consulting and Clinical Psychology, 61*, 984–991. (doi:10.1037/0022-006X.61.6.984)

Roberts, A. L., Gilman, S. E., Breslau, J., Breslau, N., & Koenen, K. C. (2011). Race/ethnic differences in exposure to traumatic events, development of post-traumatic stress disorder, and treatment-seeking for post-traumatic stress disorder in the United States. *Psychological Medicine, 41*, 71-83. (doi:10.1017/S0033291710000401)

Rothman, K. J. (2002). *Epidemiology: An introduction.* New York: Oxford University Press.

Rutter, M., Moffit, T. E., & Caspi, A. (2006). Gene-environment interplay and psychopathology: Multiple varieties but real effects. *Journal of Child Psychology and Psychiatry, 47*, 226–261. (doi:10.1111/j.1469-7610.2005.01557.x)

Sayin, A., Kucukyildirim, S., Akar, T., Bakkaloglu, Z., Demircan, A., Kurtoglu, G., & Mergen, H. (2010). A prospective study of serotonin transporter gene promoter (5-HTT gene linked polymorphic region) and intron 2 (variable number of tandem repeats) polymorphisms as predictors of trauma response to mild physical injury. *DNA and Cell Biology, 29*, 71–77. (doi:10.1089/dna.2009.0936)

Segman, R. H., Cooper-Kazaz, R., Macciardi, F., Goltser, T., Halfon, Y., Dobroborski, T., & Shalev, A. Y. (2002). Association between the dopamine transporter gene and posttraumatic stress disorder. *Molecular Psychiatry,7*, 903–907. (doi:10.1038/sj.mp.4001085)

Segman, R. H., Shefi, N., Goltser-Dubner, T., Friedman, N., Kaminski, N., & Shalev, A. Y. (2005). Peripheral blood mononuclear cell gene expression profiles identify emergent post-traumatic stress disorder among trauma survivors. *Molecular Psychiatry, 10*, 500–513, 425. (doi:10.1038/sj.mp.4001636)

Singer, M. I., Anglin, T. M., Song, L. Y., & Lunghofer, L. (1995). Adolescents' exposure to violence and associated symptoms of psychological trauma. *Journal of the American Medical Association, 273*, 477–482. (doi:10.1001/jama.273.6.477)

Sjoberg, R. L., Nilsson, K. W., Nordquist, N., Ohrvik, J., Leppert, J., Lindstrom, L., & Oreland, L. (2006). Development of depression: Sex and the interaction between environment and a promoter polymorphism of the serotonin transporter gene. *International Journal of Neuropsychopharmacology, 9*, 443–449. (doi:10.1017/S1461145705005936)

Southwick, S. M., Paige, S., Morgan, C. A., 3rd, Bremner, J. D., Krystal, J. H., & Charney, D. S. (1999). Neurotransmitter alterations in PTSD: Catecholamines and serotonin. *Seminars in clinical neuropsychiatry, 4*, 242–248.

Su, Y. A., Wu, J., Zhang, L., Zhang, Q., Su, D. M., He, P., & Ursano, R. J. (2008). Dysregulated mitochondrial genes and networks with drug targets in postmortem brain of patients with posttraumatic stress disorder (PTSD) revealed by human mitochondria-focused cDNA microarrays. *International Journal of Biological Science, 4*, 223–235. Retrieved from http://www.biolsci.org/.

Tao-Cheng, J. H., & Zhou, F. C. (1999). Differential polarization of serotonin transporters in axons versus soma-dendrites: An immunogold electron microscopy study. *Neuroscience, 94*, 821–830. (doi:10.1016/S0306-4522(99)00373-5)

Thakur, G. A., Joober, R., & Brunet, A. (2009). Development and persistence of posttraumatic stress disorder and the 5-HTTLPR polymorphism. *Journal of Traumatic Stress, 22*, 240–243. (doi:10.1002/jts.20405)

Uddin, M., Aiello, A.E., Wildman, D.E., Koenen, K.C., Pawelec, G., de los Santos, R., & Galea S. (2010) Epigenetic and immune function profiles associated with posttraumatic stress disorder. *Proceedings of the National Academy of Sciences of the United States of America, 107*, 9470–9475. (doi:10.1073/pnas.0910794107)

Voisey, J., Swagell, C. D., Hughes, I. P., Morris, C. P., van Daal, A., Noble, E. P., & Lawford, B. R. (2009). The DRD2 gene 957C>T polymorphism is associated with posttraumatic stress disorder in war veterans. *Depression and Anxiety, 26*, 28–33. (doi:10.1002/da.20517)

Walitza, S., Wewetzer, C., Warnke, A., Gerlach, M., Geller, F., Gerber, G., & Hinney, A. (2002). 5-HT2A promoter polymorphism -1438G/A in children and adolescents with obsessive-compulsive disorders. *Molecular Psychiatry, 7*, 1054–1057. (doi:10.1038/sj.mp.4001105)

Wochnik, G. M., Ruegg, J., Abel, G. A., Schmidt, U., Holsboer, F., & Rein, T. (2005). FK506-binding proteins 51 and 52 differentially regulate dynein interaction and nuclear translocation of the glucocorticoid receptor in mammalian cells. *Journal of Biological Chemistry, 280*, 4609–4616. (doi:10.1074/jbc.M407498200)

Xie, P., Kranzler, H. R., Poling, J., Stein, M. B., Anton, R. F., Brady, K., & Gelernter, J. (2009). Interactive effect of stressful life events and the serotonin transporter 5-HTTLPR genotype on posttraumatic stress disorder diagnosis in two independent populations. *Archives of General Psychiatry, 66*, 1201–1209. (doi:10.1001/archgenpsychiatry.2009.153)

Xie, P., Kranzler, H. R., Poling, J., Stein, M. B., Anton, R. F., Farrer, L. A., & Gelernter, J. (2010). Interaction of FKBP5 with childhood adversity on risk for post-traumatic stress disorder.

Neuropsychopharmacology. 35, 1684–1692. (doi:10.1038/npp.2010.37)

Yehuda, R. (2006). Advances in understanding neuroendocrine alterations in PTSD and their therapeutic implications. *Annals of the New York Academy of Science, 1071*, 137–166. (doi:10.1196/annals.1364.012)

Yehuda, R., Cai, G., Golier, J. A., Sarapas, C., Galea, S., Ising, M., & Buxbaum, J. D. (2009). Gene expression patterns associated with posttraumatic stress disorder following exposure to the World Trade Center attacks. *Biological Psychiatry, 66*, 708–711. (doi:10.1016/j.biopsych.2009.02.034)

Young, B. R., Lawford, B. R., Noble, E. P., Kanin, B., Wilkie, A., Ritchie, T., & Shadforth, S. (2002). Harmful drinking in military veterans with posttraumatic stress disorder: Association with the D2 dopamine receptor A1 allele. *Alcohol & Alcoholism, 37*, 451–456. (doi:10.1093/alcalc/37.5.451)

Zhang, H., Ozbay, F., Lappalainen, J., Kranzler, H. R., van Dyck, C. H., Charney, D. S., & Gelernter, J. (2006). Brain derived neurotrophic factor (BDNF) gene variants and Alzheimer's disease, affective disorders, posttraumatic stress disorder, schizophrenia, and substance dependence. *American Journal of Medical Genetics B Neuropsychiatric Genetics, 141*, 387–393. (doi:10.1002/ajmg.b.30332)

Zieker, J., Zieker, D., Jatzko, A., Dietzsch, J., Nieselt, K., Schmitt, A., & Gebicke-Haerter, P. J. (2007). Differential gene expression in peripheral blood of patients suffering from post-traumatic stress disorder. *Molecular Psychiatry, 12*, 116–118. (doi:10.1038/sj.mp.4001905)

CHAPTER

12 Biological Contributions to PTSD: Differentiating Normative from Pathological Response

Rachel Yehuda, Laura Pratchett, *and* Michelle Pelcovitz

Abstract

Although the majority of the population will be exposed to trauma, only a small minority will subsequently develop either acute stress disorder (ASD) or posttraumatic stress disorder (PTSD). Efforts to distinguish those at risk for a pathological response have identified certain peritraumatic responses and neuroanatomical and biological variables as candidate indicators. This chapter reviews what is currently known about biological and neuroendocrine features that have been found to correlate with PTSD in efforts to determine whether PTSD is simply a continuation of a normative, acute response to trauma exposure. In particular, the neuroendocrine literature suggests HPA axis alterations in PTSD that are complex and may reflect preexisting risk factors or pathophysiology of the disorder.

Key Words: Catecholamines, cortisol, hypothalamic-pituitary-adrenal axis, glucocorticoid receptors, pathophysiology, negative feedback

Introduction

As the publication of the fifth edition of the *Diagnostic and Statistical Manual of Mental Disorders* (*DSM-5*) approaches, it becomes important to review and consider assumptions about vulnerability to pathology following trauma. The majority of the U.S. population will, at some point in their lives, be exposed to at least one traumatic event, with estimates of prevalence ranging from 58% to 89.6% (Breslau et al., 1998; Kessler, Sonnega, Bromet, Hughes, & Nelson, 1995). However, only a minority will develop and sustain symptoms of posttraumatic stress disorder (PTSD) or other trauma-related psychopathology. There has been much debate about whether long-term psychopathology can be predicted by the profile of either peritraumatic responses or acute responses following trauma exposure. As such, there is limited empirical rationale guiding the field in identifying individuals who would benefit from early intervention.

Although exposure to stress and trauma can result in a range of psychological outcomes and disorders, acute stress disorder (ASD) and PTSD can be differentiated from other disorders in that these diagnoses explicitly require trauma exposure as the major proximal antecedent (American Psychiatric Association [APA], 2000). ASD and PTSD share many symptoms and are generally distinguishable in terms of onset and duration. ASD can be diagnosed if symptoms occur immediately following the trauma and last for no more than four weeks. Although the onset of PTSD may be delayed, the disorder is only diagnosed if symptoms are present for at least one month and the syndrome is typically more chronic. There are some differences in symptoms as well. The critical questions therefore are two: (1) is PTSD a continuation of an acute response to trauma? and (2) should responses to trauma, particularly acute ones, be considered pathological?

This chapter summarizes and reviews these questions in the context of what is known about the pathophysiology of these conditions. We examine the two questions by reviewing acute responses to trauma and the link between ASD and PTSD. To the extent that ASD and PTSD are similar, and PTSD is a continuation of a normative process, ASD might serve to facilitate early identification of risk for chronic posttraumatic pathology. This was the hope in first classifying the disorder. If, however, the conditions are distinct, this informs us about the nature of chronic pathological responses. Then we review some of the current literature on neuroanatomic and neuroendocrine findings associated with PTSD.

Posttrauma Responses and Symptom Trajectories

Longitudinal studies provide the strongest methodology for examining the relationship between acute and chronic responses to trauma. These studies involve examining trauma survivors shortly following trauma exposure and continuing the observations forward for several months or years. This allows us to pose questions regarding similarities and differences in clinical and biological presentations, as well as to examine the extent to which earlier symptoms predict later ones. Longitudinal studies have generally indicated that in trauma-exposed populations, early posttrauma symptoms decline dramatically over time (Galea, Boscarino, Resnik, & Vlahov, 2003; Orcutt, Erickson, & Wolfe, 2002). This phenomenon is well illustrated by results of surveys following the attacks of September 11 in New York City. Five to eight weeks after the attacks, 7.5% of randomly sampled subjects living in the lower half of Manhattan reportedly had developed PTSD (Galea et al., 2002). The results of another randomly sampled group studied six months after the attacks, however, demonstrated that only 0.6% of those in the same locale met full diagnostic criteria for PTSD, while an additional 4.7% met criteria for subsyndromal PTSD (Galea et al., 2003). In specific individuals, who constitute a small minority of the population, PTSD symptoms may not abate and may in fact strengthen. The important question raised by these epidemiological data is the extent to which "PTSD" based on early symptoms therefore reflects a pathological syndrome requiring treatment or is an indication of temporary distress. For those who did not recover, or had persistent features of PTSD even if they partially recovered, these symptoms may have been the earliest manifestations of psychopathology. However, these numbers illustrate the difficulty in determining the extent to which early posttraumatic symptoms are predictive of later ones.

Further highlighting the lack of correspondence between severity of symptoms in the immediate aftermath of a trauma and longer-term adjustment is the observation that, for a small proportion of people, PTSD only develops later in life, sometimes appearing for the first time decades after trauma exposure (Adams & Boscarino 2006; Bryant & Harvey 2002; Carty, O'Donnell, & Creamer, 2006; Gray, Bolton, & Litz, 2004). *DSM-IV* identifies delayed-onset PTSD when the disorder becomes apparent at least six months after the precipitating event. Large-scale studies of civilian trauma have reported delayed onset PTSD in a small minority of cases (around 5%; Bryant & Harvey, 2002; Buckley, Blanchard, & Hickling, 1996; Ehlers, Mayou, & Bryant, 1998; Mayou, Bryant, & Duthrie, 1993). Fear-conditioning models explain this by positing that initial conditioning may persist in a latent form, restrained by new fear extinction learning until sufficient cues, or increased stressors elicit a conditioned response in the form of PTSD (Charney, Deutch, Krystal, Southwick, & Davis, 1993). This suggests that there is some form of fear reaction in the acute phase that, when exacerbated under certain circumstances, reinstates the initial fear-related cues. Indeed, most people who develop delayed-onset PTSD display elevated stress reactions and higher resting heart rates in the acute phase after trauma exposure (Bryant & Harvey, 2002). In addition, most, but not all, experience subsyndromal levels of PTSD symptoms prior to developing the full syndrome (Carty et al., 2006). It is therefore unclear whether delayed-onset PTSD shares a mechanism with the more typical onset of PTSD that begins immediately after trauma exposure. However, the phenomenon seems consistent with the observation that many who recover from PTSD experience a recrudescence or recrudescences at some time(s), generally triggered by an adverse life event or traumatic reminders.

We therefore appear to have multiple trajectories following trauma exposure: those who do not experience significant posttrauma distress either immediately or subsequently; those who initially experience symptoms of "PTSD" but whose symptoms abate within a relatively short period of time; the smaller group who initially experience symptoms of PTSD and whose symptoms become a chronic illness; and the smallest group who develop a delayed-onset PTSD. It would undoubtedly be helpful to understand from an early time which of these groups an individual will fall into.

Can Pathological Responses to Trauma Be Predicted by Responses During the Event?

Although there are no definitive peritraumatic predictors of subsequent psychopathology, our knowledge to date allows an identification of those who are at low risk for subsequent pathology. Since these ultimately constitute the majority of those exposed to trauma, such markers may, in fact, be quite useful. Those with minimal symptoms in the immediate aftermath (hours and days) of a traumatic event are at low risk for the development of subsequent PTSD or other forms of psychopathology (Shalev, 1992). Among those showing a strong emotional response, there appear to be two distinct subgroups: those in whom symptoms will abate within days to weeks, and those in whom symptoms will continue to persist (McFarlane, 1989; Shalev, 1992) but peritraumatic symptoms cannot unfortunately always discern these two groups.

One candidate predictor of long-term psychopathology is peritraumatic dissociation. Peritraumatic dissociation is an experience that occurs at the actual time of the traumatic event and includes features of depersonalization, derealization, and an altered sense of time. For example, persons may have the experience of watching a traumatic event happen to them. Numerous studies have found an association between peritraumatic dissociation and the subsequent development of PTSD (e.g., Ehlers et al., 1998; Koopman, Classen, & Spiegel, 1994; Marmar et al., 1994, 1999; Marmar, Metzler, & Otte, 2004; Marmar et al., 2005; Murray et al., 2002; Shalev et al., 1998). A recent meta-analysis reported that peritraumatic dissociation was the single best predictor of PTSD (r=.35) among trauma-exposed individuals (Ozer, Best, Lipsey, & Weiss, 2003), but this view has not been unanimously supported in prospective studies (e.g., Dancu, Riggs, Hearst-Ikeda, Shoyer, & Foa, 1996; Marshall & Schell, 2002). Rather persistent dissociation, as opposed to peritraumatic dissociation, may be predictive of PTSD, (Briere, Scott, & Weathers, 2005): one explanation of which may be that dissociation is a preexisting trait that leads to peritraumatic and posttraumatic dissociation and to PTSD. Indeed, McNally (2003) notes that many studies do not adequately distinguish between peritraumatic dissociation and subsequent persistent dissociation, and certainly do not generally assess preexisting dissociation. Peritraumatic dissociation may also be mediated by other symptoms such as panic (Fikretoglu et al., 2007). Thus, it may be that peritraumatic dissociation predicts PTSD because it is highly linked with other risk factors, in particular peritraumatic panic (Brunet et al., 2001; Marmar et al., 2005). There is evidence that panic attacks during or immediately after exposure occur in 53–90% of trauma survivors who experience severely traumatic events (Bryant & Panasetis, 2001). More than half of those who meet criteria for ASD report peritraumatic as well as subsequent panic attacks (Nixon & Bryant, 2003). Galea et al. (2002) found peritraumatic panic to be the best predictor of PTSD in the post 9/11 survey of 1008 residents of the lower half of Manhattan. This is consistent with recent observations from a study of police officers, in which panic reactions and related emotional distress during exposure were highly predictive of PTSD symptoms (Brunet et al, 2001); a related prospective study of NYPD officers indicated that peritraumatic panic was also predictive of post 9/11 PTSD symptoms (Marmar et al., 2005).

Peritraumatic panic may indicate a role for neurobiological explanations of the development of subsequent PTSD. Basic science research on memory consolidation and fear conditioning has demonstrated that heightened adrenergic activation can promote the consolidation and retrieval of fear-provoking memories (Bohus & Lissak, 1968). It has been hypothesized that extreme sympathetic arousal at the time of a trauma may result in the release of stress-related neurochemicals (including norepinephrine and epinephrine) in the cortex, mediating an over-consolidation of trauma memories (Pitman, Shalev, & Orr, 2000). Both dissociation (Simeon, Guralnik, Knutelska, Yehuda, & Schmeidler, 2003) and panic reactions (Charney et al., 1993; Southwick et al., 1997) have been associated with increased catecholamine states. It is plausible that persons experiencing panic, dissociation, or other forms of intense emotional distress during and immediately after the trauma have higher levels of catecholamines than those who do not respond in this manner.

An enhanced elevation of catecholamines in the immediate aftermath of a traumatic event may increase the probability of intrusive memories in the first few days and weeks following trauma exposure (Charney et al., 1993; Pitman 1989), as well as promoting the consolidation of the traumatic memory.

Indeed, adrenergic activation in the face of low cortisol has been shown to facilitate "learning" in animals (Cahill, Prins, Weber, & McGaugh, 1994). If this were also occurring in trauma survivors, the memory of the event would not only be strongly encoded, but associated with extreme distress. The distress, in turn, could facilitate the development of altered cognitions in the aftermath of the event, particularly those associated with one's own perception of danger or ability to cope with threat. These altered beliefs could serve to further delay recovery by leading to a failure to modulate fearful responses, thereby strengthening both maladaptive cognitions in response to trauma and fear responses thus perpetuating the intrusive, avoidance, and hyperarousal symptoms of PTSD.

Clarifying the causes of high levels of immediate and long-term symptoms will no doubt lead to ideas about potential preventative treatments. For example, to the extent that panic reactions are associated with increased catecholamine responses at the time of trauma, aggressive intervention with adrenergic blocking agents such as propranolol (Pitman et al., 2002; Vaiva et al., 2004) may be helpful for those who panic at the time of exposure and in the hours immediately following a trauma. Although such clarification is by no means complete, the findings discussed above do seem to begin to point to specific, biological factors that may differentiate the normative from the pathological peritraumatic responses to trauma.

Given the benefits of early identification of pathological responses to trauma, a formal attempt was made to do so by introducing the ASD diagnosis in *DSM-IV* (American Psychiatric Association [APA], 1994). ASD was intended to fill what was considered to be a diagnostic gap because the PTSD diagnosis requires that symptoms be present for at least one month. A second purpose of the diagnosis was to identify acutely traumatized people who were likely to develop chronic PTSD (Koopman, Classen, Cardena, & Spiegel, 1995). The ASD diagnosis therefore attempts to differentiate the majority of trauma survivors who display a transient stress reaction and recover within a few weeks to months from those who are in the initial phase of a chronic disorder.

However, increasingly there are challenges to the validity of ASD as a diagnosis serving this purpose (see part two, chapter 3 of this volume). There are two ways to evaluate the relationship: the proportion of those with ASD who later develop PTSD, or the proportion of those with PTSD who previously had ASD. Although rates differ from study to study, it can generally be noted that among those who meet criteria for ASD, PTSD is a relatively common subsequent trajectory. However, among those who later meet criteria for PTSD, a lower percentage previously had ASD. Therefore, although ASD can be viewed as a relatively good positive predictor of PTSD, it is not a very sensitive predictor.

Biological Predictors of PTSD

Although being able to predict long-term pathology from the acute response would certainly be valuable, even better would be a biological marker, preferably one that is easy to measure from blood, saliva, urine, or a quick radio image. The finding that only a proportion of those exposed to trauma develop short-term symptoms, and only a minority of those with high levels of acute symptoms will develop a chronic severe form of PTSD, justifies a search for such a marker. Alternatively, rather than search for biomarkers of subsequent pathology, it may be useful to identify biological predictors of recovery. A wide variety of risk factors, including developmental, familial, situational, and even genetic risk factors for PTSD, have now been identified, mostly in association with risk (Brewin, Andrews, & Valentine, 2000; McFarlane 1989; Ozer et al., 2003; Yehuda, 1997), but also as correlates for resilience (Morgan et al., 2004; Yehuda, Brand, & Yang, 2006).

Family and genetic studies are pointing toward the role of familial contributions to posttraumatic stress reactions. Adult children of Holocaust survivors with PTSD show a greater prevalence of PTSD to their own traumatic events than adult children of Holocaust survivors without PTSD (Yehuda, Schmeidler, Wainberg, Binder-Brynes, & Duvdevani, 1998). It is difficult to know to what extent that increased vulnerability to PTSD in this population can be attributed to being raised by a parent with this disorder (Yehuda, Halligan, & Bierer, 2001), to exposure of the fetus to the mother's stress hormones during pregnancy implying possibly epigenetic contributions, or to genetic factors such as genotyping. Recent twin studies support the role of genetic contribution, given the increased prevalence of PTSD in monozygotic compared with dizygotic twins (reviewed in Afifi, Asmundson, Taylor, & Yang, 2010), but it has been difficult to differentiate risk for exposure from risk for PTSD in such studies. It is certainly plausible that there is a genetic contribution to variables that increase the risk of exposure to danger including traits like impulsivity, aggression, or substance abuse.

With respect to biology, a recent study compared startle responses in pairs of Vietnam combat veterans and their non-combat-exposed monozygotic twins (Orr et al., 2003). Veterans with PTSD and their non-combat-exposed twins showed evidence of more slowly habituating skin conductance startle responses compared to veterans without PTSD and their non-combat exposed co-twins. This finding suggests that more slowly habituating skin conductance responses to acoustic startle stimuli may represent a pretrauma vulnerability factor for PTSD (Orr et al., 2003). This model is supported by the prospective findings of greater skin conductance and eyeblink EMG startle responses before trauma exposure in firefighter trainees with greater acute stress reactions after duty-related traumatic exposure (Guthrie & Bryant, 2005). These finds are interesting in helping to connect pathophysiological processes associated with PTSD to risk.

It is also possible that there are important individual differences in biologic systems in PTSD. In support of this theory, Southwick and colleagues demonstrated that in certain PTSD patients, panic attacks and flashbacks were elicited by manipulation of the noradrenergic system with yohimbine, whereas in others, they were elicited by manipulation of serotonergic neurotransmission with meta-chlorophenylpiperazine (mCPP) (Southwick et al., 1997). Low gamma-Aminobutyric acid (GABA) plasma levels immediately after trauma are also predictive of subsequent PTSD (Vaiva et al., 2004). GABA agonists reduce fear reactions (Zangrossi, Viana, & Graeff, 1999). Lower GABA levels shortly after trauma may suppress glutamatergic functioning, and thereby lead to PTSD. This interpretation is consistent with the finding that intoxication at the time of trauma can reduce the risk for PTSD (Maes, Delmeire, Mylle, & Altamura, 2001).

It remains to be determined which of these are risk factors and which evolve with exposure to traumatic stressors or with the development of PTSD. It is conceivable that any one of a number of biologic risk factors would have the effect of facilitating a biological sensitization to subsequent traumatic events by allowing for greater physiologic arousal, greater fear during exposure, and as a result stronger fear conditioning and memory consolidation.

Neuroanatomic Predictors of PTSD

Developments in neuroimaging technologies have presented opportunities to examine brain structure and function as markers of PTSD. The hippocampus has been a brain region of focus in such studies owing to both its prominent role in the stress response and to the memory alterations that characterize PTSD (McEwen & Sapolsky 1995; Sapolsky 1994; Landfield & Eldridge 1994). Many, but not all, studies have demonstrated smaller hippocampal volumes in PTSD (for review see Bremner, 2007; Rauch, Shin, & Phelps, 2006). However, the etiology and significance of these findings has yet to be resolved.

Initial explanations for smaller hippocampal volumes in PTSD focused on glucocorticoid toxicity resulting from exposure to trauma (e.g., Bremner et al., 1995, 1997; Gurvits et al., 1996; Stein, Yehuda, Koverola, & Hanna, 1997). This hypothesis was based on demonstrations that repeated stress or glucocorticoid exposure results in decreased hippocampal volume and decreased dendritic branching in animals (McEwen, Gould, & Sakai, 1992; Sapolsky 1994, 2000). However, findings that cortisol levels are not elevated in either the acute or chronic aftermath of trauma in those who develop PTSD has challenged this perspective (reviewed in Yehuda & LeDoux, 2007). In addition, increased glucocorticoid levels or activity have not been shown to relate to hippocampal alterations in PTSD (Neylan et al. 2003; Yehuda, Golier, et al., 2007). A final problem with this explanation is that hippocampal volume has not been shown to change over time in prospective longitudinal studies of individuals following trauma (Bonne et al., 2001).

An alternative explanation—that smaller hippocampal volume is a preexisting risk factor for PTSD—is supported by observations of smaller volumes not only in combat-exposed Vietnam veterans with PTSD but also in their nonexposed identical twins (Gilbertson et al., 2002; Pitman et al., 2006). In addition, smaller hippocampal volume has been observed in veterans who developed PTSD following their first traumatic exposure compared to those who recovered from their first traumatic experiences, but then developed PTSD in response to a subsequent event (Yehuda, Golier, et al., 2007). It is plausible that smaller hippocampal volume may confer risk through an association with other factors that have been observed to increase risk for PTSD (Macklin et al., 1998), such as low IQ (Gilbertson,

Gurvits, Lasko, Orr, & Pitman, 2001; Gurvits et al., 1996). Specifically, this measure may represent a correlate with decreased cognitive capacity necessary for adaptive reinterpretation of traumatic experiences.

Brain regions involved in the neurocircuitry of the fear response, including medial prefrontal cortex (mPFC) (which incorporates the anterior cingulate cortex [ACC]), and amygdala have also been a focus of studies of neuroanatomical risk for PTSD. Such studies have observed reductions in gray matter in the ACC (Rauch et al., 2003; Woodward et al., 2006; Yamasue et al., 2003). One model proposes that this relates to risk for PTSD as it leads to diminished inhibitory regulation of the central nucleus of the amygdala and excessive amygdala activation (Bush, Luu, & Posner, 2000; Shin et al., 2001). Certainly, reduced volume of areas of the mPFC has been found to be associated with reduced fear extinction (Milad et al., 2005). However, one recent study observed that gray-matter density in ACC is reduced in combat-exposed twins with PTSD compared to the non-combat-exposed twin or twin with combat exposure but no PTSD providing some evidence that this reflects pathophysiology rather than risk (Kasai et al., 2008).

Functional neuroimaging techniques (such as fMRI and PET) that measure activity in specific areas of the brain have provided more information on the anomalies in the neurocircuitry of the fear response associated with PTSD. Many of these studies have observed increased amygdala activity in response to threat stimuli in patients with PTSD as compared to those without (Liberzon et al., 1999; Rauch et al., 1996; also for review see Bremner, 2007; Rauch et al., 2006; Yehuda & LeDoux, 2007) and this increased activity is associated with symptom severity (Shin et al., 2004). Decreased activity in response to threatening stimuli has also been found in areas of the mPFC (Bremner et al., 1999; Lanius et al., 2003; Williams et al., 2006; also for review see Bremner, 2007; Rauch et al., 2006; Yehuda & LeDoux, 2007). Reduction in mPFC activity has been observed to be associated with symptom severity (Shin et al., 2004; Williams et al., 2006) and, importantly, is also negatively associated with amygdala activation in response to threat (Shin et al., 2005) supporting the hypothesis that there is a disconnect in the normal modulation of the amygdala by the mPFC. A recent meta-analysis addressed the question of inconsistent findings in these areas (e.g., observations of decreased activation of the amygdala in PTSD [Britton, Phan, Taylor, Fig, & Liberzon, 2005; Phan, Britton, Taylor, Fig, & Liberzon, 2006]) and confirmed that across functional imaging studies increased amygdala and decreased mPFC activation is associated with PTSD (Etkin & Wager, 2007).

Neurobiology of PTSD

The field of neurobiology has also been able to shed some light on the question of whether or not PTSD is merely a prolonged, normative response to trauma. Unfortunately, more is known about the neurobiology of PTSD than of ASD. We have now identified two deficits that suggest a specific neuroendocrine profile of PTSD. Although many studies have replicated these findings of neurobiological correlates of PTSD, investigations have not ruled out the possibility that neurobiological alterations are risk factors rather than pathophysiology of the disorder. However, whether risk factor or pathophysiology, this profile of PTSD seems to be different from that of either healthy controls or of individuals presenting with other psychiatric disorders, and may be helpful in evaluating the question of whether PTSD is simply a continuation of a normative response to trauma. The following sections will discuss two of the major elements of this neuroendocrine profile to assist with answering this question.

Cortisol levels in PTSD

One of the earliest observations was that urinary cortisol excretion is lower in PTSD compared to psychiatric patients in other diagnostic groups and normal controls (Mason, Giller, Kosten, Ostroff, & Podd, 1986).

Table 12.1 presents published studies on 24-hour urinary cortisol levels in PTSD. The majority of these have found evidence of low cortisol in PTSD, but group differences are not always present between subjects with and without PTSD. This is particularly true when samples are from a general civilian population of persons exposed to a wide range of traumatic events, such as in the subjects obtained by Young and Breslau (2004). Because there are numerous sources of potential variability in such studies, samples that are heterogeneous with respect to age, gender, trauma type, PTSD chronicity, and developmental stage at which trauma occurred may obscure overall group differences. But if cortisol levels are related to PTSD risk, and if there are multiple sources of PTSD risk, it would be plausible that not all PTSD patients have low cortisol. The literature

Table 12.1. Summary of data from studies of 24-hour urinary cortisol excretion in adults with PTSD

Author(s), year	Trauma Survivors with PTSD		Trauma w/out PTSD		Normal Comparison		Psychiatric Comparison	
	cortisol µg/day (n)		cortisol µg/day (n)		cortisol µg/day (n)		cortisol µg/day (n)	
Mason et al. 1986[a]	33.3	(n = 9)					48.5	(n=35)
Kosten et al. 1990[a]	50.0	(n=11)			55.0	(n=28)	70.0	(n=18)
Pitman & Orr 1990[b]	107.3	(n=20)	80.5	(n=15)				
Yehuda et al. 1990[a]	40.9	(n=16)			62.8	(n=16)		
Yehuda, Boisoneau et al. 1993[a]	38.6	(n=8)					69.4	(n=32)
Yehuda, Kahana et al. 1995[a]	32.6	(n=22)	62.7	(n=25)	51.9	(n=15)		
Lemieux & Coe 1995[b]	111.8	(n=11)	83.1	(n=8)	87.8	(n=9)		
Maes et al. 1998[b]	840.0	(n=10)			118	(n=17)	591.0	(n=10)
Thaller et al. 1999[a]	130.9	(n=34)			213.9	(n=17)		
Baker et al. 1999	84.4	(n=11)			76.2	(n=12)		
De Bellis et al. 1999[b]	57.3	(n=18)			43.6	(n=24)	56.0	(n=10)
Yehuda et al. 2000[a]	48.3	(n=22)			65.1	(n=15)		
Rasmusson et al. 2001	42.8	(n=12)			34.6	(n=8)		
Glover & Poland, 2002[a, c]	9.8	(n=14)	16.5	(n=7)	12.8	(n=8)		
Otte et al. 2005	52	(n=20)	43	(n=16)				
Bierer et al. 2006[a]	46.3	(n=32)	72.2	(n=10)				
Wheler et al. 2006[a, d]	50.6	(n=10)	73.9	(n=10)				
Yehuda, Golier et al. 2007	30.8	(n=17)	39.1	(n=11)				
Simeon et al. 2007[e]	62	(n=32)			62	(n=56)	83	(n=44)
Lemieux et al. 2008	22.2	(n=11)	48.8	(n=13)	82.2	(n=12)		

[a] findings in which cortisol levels were significantly lower than comparison subjects, or, in the case of Kosten et al., from depression only.
[b] findings in which cortisol levels were significantly higher than comparison subjects.
[c] results are from a 12-hour rather than 24-hour urine collection and are expressed as µg/12 hr.
[d] cortisol levels were significantly lower in PTSD as measured by radioimmunoassay but not by gas chromatography-mass spectroscopy.
[e] no means reported in the text; data estimated from the figures provided.

certainly suggests that at least a significant subgroup show an unusual cortisol profile.

Cortisol as a Pretraumatic Risk Factor

Although cortisol findings in PTSD were initially interpreted as reflecting pathophysiology of the disorder resulting from trauma exposure and/or chronic symptoms, data from prospective longitudinal studies has raised the possibility that low cortisol levels reflect pretraumatic predictors of PTSD. Low cortisol levels in the immediate aftermath of a motor vehicle accident were found to predict the development of PTSD in a group of 35 accident victims presenting to an emergency room (Yehuda, McFarlane, & Shalev, 1998). Delahanty, Raimonde, and Spoonster (2000) also reported that low cortisol levels in the immediate aftermath of a trauma contributed to the prediction of PTSD symptoms at one month. Similarly, in a sample of persons who survived a natural disaster, cortisol levels were found to be lowest in those with highest PTSD scores at one month posttrauma. However, cortisol levels were not predictive of symptoms at one year (Anisman, Griffiths, Matheson, Ravindran, & Merali, 2001). Lower morning but higher evening cortisol levels were observed in 15 subjects with more severe PTSD symptoms five days following a mine accident in Lebanon, compared to 16 subjects with lower levels of PTSD symptoms (Aardal-Eriksson, Eriksson, & Thorell, 2001). In a study examining the cortisol response in the acute aftermath of rape, low cortisol levels were associated with prior rape or assault (Resnick, Yehuda, Pitman, & Foy, 1995), but not with the development of PTSD per se.

These findings suggest that cortisol levels might have been abnormally low even before trauma exposure in survivors who develop PTSD, therefore representing a preexisting risk factor, at least in some persons (e.g., see Pervanidou et al., 2007, who found that elevated evening cortisol within 24 hours of a motor vehicle accident predicted PTSD at six months in children and adolescents). Consistent with this low cortisol level in adult children of Holocaust survivors was associated with the risk factor of parental PTSD, as shown by both 24-hour urine collection (Yehuda, Halligan, & Grossman, 2001) and by plasma samples taken every 30 minutes over 24 hours (Yehuda, Teicher, et al., 2007). The findings suggest that low cortisol may contribute to secondary biological alterations, which ultimately lead to the development of PTSD. In line with these cortisol findings, maternal (but not paternal) PTSD was significantly associated with offspring having PTSD themselves, suggesting that epigenetic mechanisms such as prenatal glucocorticoid programming of HPA axis responsiveness may be involved in transmission of PTSD risk (Yehuda, Bell, Bierer, & Schmeidler, 2008).

Low cortisol levels may impede the process of biological recovery from stress, resulting in a cascade of alterations that lead to intrusive recollections of the event, avoidance of reminders of the event, and symptoms of hyper-arousal. This failure may represent an alternative trajectory to the normal process of adaptation and recovery after a traumatic event. Additionally, it is possible that there is an active process of adaptation and attempt at achieving homeostasis in the period following a trauma before the development of PTSD, and that PTSD symptoms are themselves determined by biological responses, rather than the opposite.

PTSD may arise from any number of circumstances, one of which may be the hormonal milieu at the time of trauma, which itself may reflect an interaction of pre- and peritraumatic influences. These responses may be further modified in the following days and weeks by a variety of other influences. For example, under normal circumstances, corticotropin-releasing factor (CRF) and adrenocorticotropic hormone (ACTH) are activated in response to stress, and ultimately culminate in cortisol release, which negatively feeds back to keep the stress response in check. An attenuated cortisol response to an acute trauma might initially lead to a stronger activation of the pituitary due to increased CRF stimulation resulting in a high-magnitude ACTH response. This in turn could lead to a greater necessity by the pituitary for negative feedback inhibition in order to achieve regulation, for instance via a progressive decline in the ACTH/cortisol ratio, facilitated by accommodations in the sensitivity of glucocorticoid receptors (GRs) and other central neuromodulators, ultimately leading to an exaggerated negative feedback inhibition. Affecting these hormonal responses might also be the demands made by posttraumatic factors. Although such a model is hypothetical, it is consistent with the adaptational process of allostatic load described by McEwen and Seeman (1999): physiologic systems accommodate to achieve homeostasis based on already existing predispositions to stress responses. Thus, the neuroendocrine response to trauma of a person with lower pretrauma cortisol may be fundamentally different from that of someone with a greater adrenal capacity and higher ambient cortisol levels.

One of the most compelling lines of evidence supporting the hypothesis that lower cortisol levels may be an important pathway to the development of PTSD lies in a study by Schelling et al. (2001). Stress doses of hydrocortisone were administered during septic shock and the effects of this treatment on the development of PTSD and traumatic memories were evaluated in a randomized, double-blind study. High doses (determined to be the minimum dose needed to produce a physiological effect in the body) of hydrocortisone were associated with reduced PTSD symptoms compared to the group that received saline. Recent research has further demonstrated the therapeutic implications of the low cortisol–PTSD link—patients with PTSD reported lower intrusive symptoms after treatment with low-dose cortisol for one month (de Quervain & Margraf, 2008).

The Dexamethasone Suppression Test in PTSD

The second area of neuroendocrine alteration associated with PTSD relates to negative feedback inhibition. Results using the dexamethasone suppression test (DST) have presented a relatively consistent view of enhanced cortisol suppression in response to dexamethasone (DEX) administration. The DST provides a direct test of the effects of GR activation in the pituitary on ACTH secretion, and cortisol levels following DEX administration are thus interpreted as an estimate of the strength of negative feedback inhibition, provided that the adrenal response to ACTH is not altered.

When low doses of DEX (0.50 mg and 0.25 mg doses) are administered, a cortisol hypersuppression can clearly be observed, as indicated in table 12.2. Results from these studies, shown in table 12.2, are expressed as the extent of cortisol suppression, evaluated by the quotient of post-DEX cortisol to baseline cortisol. Expressing the data in this manner accounts for individual differences in baseline cortisol levels and allows for a more precise characterization of the strength of negative feedback inhibition as a continuous rather than as a dichotomous variable.

Following the initial studies of cortisol suppression in response to DEX, there has been some debate about whether DST hypersuppression reflects trauma exposure in psychiatric patients, or PTSD per se (Díaz-Marsá et al., 2007; Grossman et al., 2003). One possible explanation for the inconsistent findings was suggested by Yehuda and colleagues (Yehuda, Halligan, Golier, Grossman, & Bierer, 2004), who observed cortisol hypersuppression following DST in subjects with PTSD, both with and without comorbid depression, but noted

Table 12.2 Cortisol suppression to DEX in PTSD and comparison subjects

Author and Year	DEX dose/day	PTSD: % supp	(n)	Comparison:% supp	(n)
Yehuda, Southwick et al. 1993[a]	0.5	87.5	(n=21)	68.3	(n=12)
Stein et al. 1997[a]	0.5	89.1	(n=13)	80.0	(n=21)
Yehuda, Boisoneau et al. 1995[a]	0.5	90.0	(n=14)	73.4	(n=14)
Yehuda, Boisoneau et al. 1995[a]	0.25	54.4	(n=14)	36.7	(n=14)
Kellner et al. 1997[b]	0.50	90.1	(n=7)		
Yehuda et al. 2002[a, c]	0.50	89.9	(n=17)	77.9	(n=23)
Grossman et al. 2003[a, d]	0.50	83.6	(n=16)	63.0	(n=36)
Newport et al. 2004[a, e]	0.50	92.3	(n=16a)	77.78	(n=19)
Yehuda, Halligan et al. 2004[a]	0.50	82.5	(n=19)	68.9	(n=10)
Lange et al. 2005[a, f]	0.50	85.7	(n=12)	65.5	(n=9)
Griffin et al. 2005	0.50	85	(n=42)	75	(n=14)

[a]significantly more suppressed than controls.
[b]no control group was studied.
[c] PTSD group only includes subjects without depression; subjects with both PTSD and MDD (n=17) showed a percent suppression of 78.8, which differs from our previous report (Yehuda, Southwick, et al. 1993) in younger combat veterans.
[d] comparison subjects were those with personality disorders but without PTSD.
[e] it is impossible from this paper to get the correct mean for the actual 15 subjects with PTSD. These 16 subjects had MDD, but 15/16 also had PTSD, so this group also contains 1 subject who had been exposed to early abuse with past, but not current PTSD.
[f] this study compared borderline personality disorder patients with and without comorbid PTSD.

that hypersuppression was particularly prominent in subjects with depression if there had been a prior traumatic experience. Thus, cortisol hypersuppression in response to DEX appears to be associated with PTSD, but in subjects with depression, it may be present as a result of early trauma and, possibly, past PTSD (Yehuda, Halligan, et al., 2004).

Glucocorticoid Receptors in PTSD

Type II GRs are expressed in ACTH- and CRF-producing cells of the pituitary, hypothalamus, and hippocampus, and mediate most systemic glucocorticoid effects, particularly those related to stress responsiveness (deKloet, Joels, Oitzl, & Sutano, 1991). Low circulating levels of a hormone or neurotransmitter can result in increased numbers of available receptors (Sapolsky, Krey, & McEwen, 1984), improving response capacity and facilitating homeostasis. However, alterations in the number and sensitivity of Type II GRs can also significantly influence HPA axis activity, particularly by modulating the strength of negative feedback, thereby regulating hormone levels (Holsboer, Lauer, Schreiber, & Krieg, 1995; Svec, 1985). GRs have therefore been a focus of studies of PTSD, with some studies utilizing lymphocytes which have been found to share similar regulatory and binding characteristics with brain GRs (Lowy, 1989).

Multiple studies have pointed to a role of GRs in the HPA dysregulations observed in PTSD. Greater numbers of mononuclear leukocyte (presumably lymphocyte) Type II GRs have been observed in Vietnam veterans with PTSD compared to a normal comparison group (Yehuda, Lowy, Southwick, Shaffer, & Giller, 1991) and a relationship between low 24- hour urinary cortisol excretion and increased lymphocyte GR numbers in PTSD has been observed (Yehuda, Boisoneau, Mason, & Giller, 1993). Although it is not clear whether alterations in GR number reflect an adaptation to low cortisol levels or some other alteration, the observation of an increased number of lymphocyte GRs provided the basis for the hypothesis of an increased negative feedback inhibition of cortisol secondary to increased receptor sensitivity. Following the administration of DEX, cortisol response has been observed to be accompanied by a concurrent decline in the number of cytosolic lymphocyte receptors (Yehuda, Teicher, Trestman, Levengood, & Siever, 1996).

Observations regarding the cellular immune response in PTSD are also consistent with enhanced GR responsiveness in the periphery. For example, beclomethasone-induced vasoconstriction is increased in female PTSD subjects compared to healthy, non-trauma-exposed comparison subjects (Coupland, Hegadoren, & Myrholm, 2003), and an enhanced delayed-type hypersensitivity of skin-test responses was observed in women who survived childhood sexual abuse versus those who did not (Altemus, Gloitre, & Dhabhar, 2003). Because immune responses, like endocrine ones, can be multiply regulated, these studies provide only indirect evidence of GR responsiveness. However, the observation that PTSD patients show increased expression of the receptors in all lymphocyte subpopulations, despite both a relatively lower quantity of intracellular GR (as determined by flow cytometry) and lower ambient cortisol levels (Gotovac, Sabioncello, Rabatic, Berki, & Dekaris,2003), suggests more convincingly that these findings are due to an enhanced sensitivity of the GR to glucocorticoids.

Finally, one study provided a demonstration of an alteration in target tissue sensitivity in glucocorticoids using an in vitro paradigm. Mononuclear leukocytes isolated from the blood of men with and without PTSD were incubated with a series of concentrations of DEX to determine the rate of inhibition of lysozyme activity. A portion of cells was frozen for the determination of GR. Subjects with PTSD showed evidence of a greater sensitivity to glucocorticoids as reflected by a significantly lower mean lysozyme $IC_{50\text{-}DEX}$. The lysozyme $IC_{50\text{-}DEX}$ was significantly correlated with age at exposure to the first traumatic event in subjects with PTSD. The number of cytosolic GR was correlated with age at exposure to the focal traumatic event (Yehuda, Golier, Yang, & Tischler, 2004).

Although the above studies provide information about cortisol negative feedback inhibition and GR responsiveness in the periphery, the extent to which they reflect changes in central glucocorticoid responsiveness is not clear. To address this question, hydrocortisone was administered and the ACTH response to this was observed. The ACTH response to hydrocortisone is conceptually similar to the cortisol response to DEX, but DEX does not cross the blood brain barrier, and acts mostly at the level of the pituitary. A greater ACTH decline was observed in combat veterans with, compared to those without, PTSD, implying that both peripheral and central GR are more responsive (Yehuda, Yang, Buchsbaum & Golier, 2006). Importantly, this single dose was found to affect memory performance (Yehuda, Harvey, Buchsbaum, Tischler, & Schmeidler, 2007) suggesting that enhanced glucocorticoid responsiveness may contribute to PTSD pathophysiology.

Putative Models of HPA Axis Alterations in PTSD

The neuroendocrine profile of PTSD is, therefore, certainly not always clear but some general findings allow us to begin to formulate a model of HPA axis alterations. Cortisol levels are most often found to be abnormally low in PTSD, but can also be similar to or greater than those in comparison subjects. This suggests that although cortisol levels may be generally lower, the adrenal gland is certainly capable of producing adequate amounts of cortisol in response to challenge.

The model of enhanced negative feedback inhibition discussed in this chapter is compatible with the idea that there may be transient elevations in cortisol, but it suggests that when present, these increases will be shorter lived owing to a more efficient containment of ACTH release as a result of enhanced GR activation. Thus, there may be chronic or transient elevations in CRF in PTSD that stimulate pituitary release of ACTH, which in turn stimulates the adrenal release of cortisol. However, increased GR number and sensitivity can result in reduced cortisol levels under ambient conditions (Yehuda et al., 1996). This model of enhanced negative feedback inhibition in PTSD is in large part descriptive and currently offers little explanation for why some individuals show such alterations of the HPA axis following exposure to traumatic experiences while others do not. It nonetheless represents an important development in the field of neuroendocrinology of PTSD by accounting for a substantial proportion of the findings observed, and can be put to further hypothesis testing.

Conclusions

The literature reviewed in this chapter now allows us to return to answer the two questions originally posed: (1) is PTSD a continuation of an acute response to trauma? and (2) should responses to trauma, particularly acute ones, be considered pathological? In the absence of definitive markers of risk, resilience, and recovery from PTSD, recent studies evaluating peritraumatic indicators of risk, and neuroanatomical and biological variables associated with increased risk suggest that PTSD is not simply a continuation of a normative acute response to trauma exposure. In addition, the poor sensitivity of ASD in predicting PTSD suggests that while the disorders may be related, PTSD is unlikely to be a mere continuation of ASD. In response to the second question, the literature to date would appear to indicate that while certain acute (and peritraumatic) responses to trauma are pathological, the majority of the population will recover from such symptoms suggesting that, for most, these acute responses are normative rather than pathological.

The neuroendocrine literature does allow us to begin to examine some of the factors that differentiate PTSD from other psychiatric disorders and from those with trauma exposure and no psychopathology. In particular, HPA axis alterations in PTSD are complex and may be associated with different aspects of the disorder, including pre-existing risk factors. The wide range of findings on the neuroendocrinology of PTSD underscore that in psychiatric disorders, neuroendocrine alterations may be subtle; consequently, it is not always likely that standard tools for assessing endocrine alterations will reveal all the alterations consistent with a neuroendocrine explanation of the pathology in tandem. Additionally, disparate results may be observed within the same patient group owing to a stronger compensation or re-regulation of the HPA axis following challenge.

The next generation of studies should aim to apply more rigorous neuroendocrine tests to the investigation of PTSD, in consideration of appropriate developmental issues, the longitudinal course of the disorder, and individual differences that affect relevant processes. No doubt such studies will require a closer examination of a wide range of biologic responses, including the cellular and molecular mechanisms involved in adaptation to stress, and an understanding of the relationship between the endocrine findings and other identified biologic alterations in PTSD.

References

Aardal-Eriksson, E., Eriksson, T. E., & Thorell, L. (2001). Salivary cortisol, posttraumatic stress symptoms and general health in the acute phase and during 9-month follow-up. *Biological Psychiatry 50*, 986–993.

Adams, R. E., & Boscarino, J. A. (2006). Predictors of PTSD and delayed PTSD after disaster: The impact of exposure and psychosocial resources. *Journal of Nervous and Mental Disease, 194*(7), 485–493.

Afifi, T., O., Asmundson, G., J., Taylor, S., & Jang, K., L. (2010). The role of genes and environment on trauma exposure and posttraumatic stress disorder symptoms: A review of twin studies. *Clinical Psychology Review, 30*(1), 101–112.

Altemus, M., Cloitre, M., & Dhabhar, F. R. (2003). Enhanced cellular immune responses in women with PTSD related to childhood abuse. *American Journal of Psychiatry, 160(9)*, 1705–1707.

American Psychiatric Association. (2000). *Diagnostic and statistical manual of mental disorders* (4th ed., text rev.). Washington, DC: Author.

American Psychiatric Association. (1994). *Diagnostic and statistical manual of mental disorders* (4th ed.). Washington, DC: Author.

Anisman, H., Griffiths, J., Matheson, K., Ravindran, A. V., & Merali, Z. (2001). Posttraumatic stress symptoms and salivary cortisol levels. *American Journal of Psychiatry, 158*(9), 1509–1511.

Baker, D. G., West, S. A., Nicholson, W. E., Ekhator, N. N., Kasckow, J. W., Hill, K. K., et al. (1999). Serial CSF corticotropin-releasing hormone levels and adrenocortical activity in combat veterans with posttraumatic stress disorder *American Journal of Psychiatry, 156*, 585–588.

Bierer, L., M., Tischler, L., Labinsky, E., Cahill, S., Foa, E., & Yehuda, R. (2006) Clinical correlates of 24-hr. cortisol and norepinephrine excretion among subjects seeking treatment following the world trade center attacks on 9/11. *Annals of the New York Academy of Sciences, 1071*, 514–520.

Bohus, B., & Lissak, K. (1968). Adrenocortical hormones and avoidance behaviour of rats. *International Journal of Neuropharmacology, 7*(4), 301–306.

Bonne, O., Brandes, D., Gilboa, A., Gomori, J. M., Shenton, M. E., Pitman, R. K., et al. (2001). *American Journal of Psychiatry, 158*(8), 1248–1251.

Bremner, J. D. (2007) Functional neuroimaging in posttraumatic stress disorder. *Expert Review of Neurotherapeutics, 7*, 393–405.

Bremner, J. D., Randall, P., Scott, T. M., Bronen, R. A., Seibyl, J. P., Southwick, S. M., et al. (1995). MRI-based measurement of hippocampal volume in patients with combat-related posttraumatic stress disorder. *American Journal of Psychiatry, 152*(7), 973–981.

Bremner, J. D., Randall, P., Vermetten, E., Staib, L., Bronen, R. A., Mazure, C., et al. (1997). Magnetic resonance imaging-based measurement of hipoocampal colume in posttraumatic stress disorder related to childhood physical and sexual abuse—a preliminary report. *Biological Psychiatry, 41*(1), 23–32.

Bremner, J. D., Staib, L. H., Kaloupek, D., Southwick, S. M., Soufer, R., & Charney, D. S. (1999). Neural correlates of exposure to traumatic pictures and sound in Vietnam combat veterans with and without posttraumatic stress disorder: A positron emission tomography study. *Biological Psychiatry, 45*(7), 806–816.

Breslau, N., Kessler, R. C., Chilcoat, H. D., Schultz L. R., Davis, G. C., & Andreski, P. (1998). Trauma and posttraumatic stress disorder in the community: The 1996 Detroit Area Survey of Trauma. *Archives of General Psychiatry, 55*(7), 626–632.

Brewin, C. R., Andrews, B., & Valentine, J. D. (2000). Meta-analysis of risk factors for posttraumatic stress disorder in trauma-exposed adults. *Journal of Consulting and Clinical Psychology, 68*(5), 748–766.

Briere, J., Scott, C., & Weathers, F. (2005). Peritraumatic and persistent dissociation in the presumed etiology of PTSD. *American Journal of Psychiatry, 162*(12), 2295–2301.

Britton, J. C., Phan, K. L., Taylor, S. F., Fig, L. M., & Liberzon, I. (2005). Corticolimbic blood flow in posttraumatic stress disorder during script-driven imagery. *Biological Psychiatry, 57*(8), 832–840.

Brunet, A., Weiss, D. S., Metzler, T. S., Best, S. R., Neylan, T. C., Rogers, C., et al. (2001). The Peritraumatic Distress Inventory: A proposed measure of PTSD Criterion A2. *American Journal of Psychiatry, 158*(9), 1480–1485.

Bryant, R. A. (2003). Early predictors of posttraumatic stress disorder. *Biological Psychiatry, 53*, 789–795.

Bryant, R. A., & Harvey A. G. (2002). Delayed-onset posttraumatic stress disorder: A prospective evaluation. *Australian and New Zealand Journal of Psychiatry, 36*(2), 205–209.

Bryant, R. A., & Panasetis, P. (2001). Panic symptoms during trauma and acute stress disorder. *Behaviour Research Therapy, 39*, 961–966.

Buckley, T. C., Blanchard, E. B., & Hickling, E. J. (1996). A prospective examination of delayed onset PTSD secondary to motor vehicle accidents. *Journal of Abnormal Psychology, 105*, 617–625.

Bush, G., Luu, P., & Posner, M. I. (2000). Cognitive and emotional influences in anterior cingulate cortex. *Trends in Cognitive Sciences, 4*(6), 215–222.

Cahill, L., Prins, B., Weber, M., & McGaugh, J. L. (1994). Beta-adrenergic activation and memory for emotional events. *Nature, 371*(6499), 702–704.

Carty, J., O.'Donnell, M. L., & Creamer, M. (2006). Delayed-onset PTSD: A prospective study of injury survivors. *Journal of Affective Disorders, 90*, 257–261.

Charney, D. S., Deutch, A. Y., Krystal, J. H., Southwick, S. M., & Davis, M. (1993). Psychobiologic mechanisms of posttraumatic stress disorder. *Archives of General Psychiatry, 50*(4), 295–305.

Coupland, N. J., Hegadoren, K. M., & Myrholm, J. (2003). Increased beclomethasone-induced vasoconstriction in women with posttraumatic stress disorder. *Journal of Psychiatric Research, 37*(3), 221–228.

Dancu, C., V., Riggs, D. S., Hearst-Ikeda, D., Shoyer, B. G., & Foa, E. B. (1996). Dissociative experiences and posttraumatic stress disorder among female victims of criminal assault and rape. *Journal of Traumatic Stress, 9*(2), 253–267.

De Bellis, M. D., Baum, A. S., Birmaher, B., Keshavan, M. S., Eccard, C. H., Boring, A. M., et al. (1999). A. E. Bennett Research Award. Developmental traumatology. Part I: Biological stress systems. *Biological Psychiatry, 45*(10), 1259–1270.

de Kloet, E. R., Joels, M., Oitzl, M., & Sutanto, W. (1991). Implication of brain corticosteroid receptor diversity for the adaptation syndrome concept. *Methods and Achievements in Experimental Pathology, 14*, 104–132.

Delahanty, D. L., Raimonde, A. J., & Spoonster, E. (2000). Initial posttraumatic urinary cortisol levels predict subsequent PTSD symptoms in motor vehicle accident victims. *Biological Psychiatry, 48*, 940–947.

de Quervain, D. J., & Margraf, J. (2008). Glucocorticoids for the treatment of post-traumatic stress disorder and phobias: A novel therapeutic approach. *European Journal of Pharmacology, 583*, 365–371.

Díaz-Marsá, M., Carrasco, J. L., Basurte, E., Pastrana, J. I., Sáiz-Ruiz, J., & López-Ibor, J. J. (2007). Findings with 0.25 mg dexamethasone suppression test in eating disorders: Association with childhood trauma. *CNS Spectrums, 12*(9), 675–680.

Ehlers, A., Mayou, R. A., & Bryant, B. (1998). Psychological predictors of chronic PTSD after motor vehicle accidents. *Journal of Abnormal Psychology, 107*(3), 508–519.

Etkin, A., & Wager, T., D. (2007). Functional neuroimaging of anxiety: A meta-analysis of emotional processing in PTSD, social anxiety disorder, and specific phobia. *American Journal of Psychiatry, 164*, 1476–1488.

Fikretoglu, D., Brunet, A., Best, S. R., Metzler, T. J., Delucchi, K., Weiss, D. S., et al. (2007). Peritraumatic fear, helplessness and horror and peritraumatic dissociation: Do physical and cognitive symptoms of panic mediate the relationship between the two? *Behaviour Research and Therapy, 45*(1), 39–47.

Galea, S., Ahern, J., Resnick, H., Kilpratric, D., Bucuvalas, M., Gold, J., et al.(2002). Psychological sequelae of the September 11 terrorist attacks. *New England Journal of Medicine, 346*(13), 982–987.

Galea, S., Boscarino, J., Resnik, H., & Vlahov, D. (2003). Trends of probable post-traumatic stress disorder in New York City after the September 11 terrorist attacks. *American Journal of Epidemiology, 158*(6), 514–524.

Gilbertson, M. W., Gurvits, T. V., Lasko, N. B., Orr, S. P., & Pitman, R. K. (2001). Multivariate assessment of explicit memory function in combat veterans with posttraumatic stress disorder. *Journal of Traumatic Stress, 14*(2), 413–432.

Gilbertson, M. W., Shenton, M. E., Ciszewski, A., Kasai, K., Lasko, N. B., Orr, S. P., et al. (2002). Smaller hippocampal volume predicts pathologic vulnerability to psychological trauma. *Nature Neuroscience, 5*(11), 1242–1247.

Glover, D., & Poland, R. (2002) Urinary cortisol and catecholamines in mothers of child cancer survivors with and without PTSD. *Psychoneuroendocrinology, 27*(7), 805–819.

Gotovac, K., Sabioncello, A., Rabatic, S., Berki, T., & Dekaris, D. (2003). Flow cytometric determination of glucocorticoid receptor (GCR) expression in lymphocyte subpopulations: Lower quantity of GCR in patients with post-traumatic stress disorder (PTSD). *Clinical and Experimental Immunology, 131*(2), 335–339.

Gray, M., J., Bolton, E. E., & Litz, B. T. (2004). A. longitudinal analysis of PTSD symptom course: Delayed-onset PTSD in Somalia peacekeepers. *Journal of Consulting and Clinical Psychology, 72*(5), 909–913.

Griffin, M. G., Resick, P. A., & Yehuda, R. (2005) Enhanced cortisol suppression following dexamethasone administration in domestic violence survivors. *American Journal of Psychiatry, 162*(6), 1192–1199.

Grossman, R., Yehuda, R., New, A., Schmeidler, J., Silverman, J., Mitropoulous, V., et al. (2003). Dexamethasone suppression test findings in subjects with personality disorders: Associations with posttraumatic stress disorder and major depression. *American Journal of Psychiatry, 160*(7), 1291–1298.

Gurvits, T. V., Shenton, M. E., Hokama, H., Ohta, H., Lasko, N. B., Gilbertson, M. W., et al. (1996). Magnetic resonance imaging study of hippocampal volume in chronic, combat-related posttraumatic stress disorder. *Biological Psychiatry, 40*(11), 1091–1099.

Guthrie, R. M., & Bryant, R. A. (2005). Auditory startle response in firefighters before and after trauma exposure. *American Journal of Psychiatry, 162*(2), 283–290.

Harvey, A. G., & Bryant, R. A. (2002). Acute stress disorder: A synthesis and critique. *Psychological Bulletin, 128*(6), 886–902.

Holsboer, F., Lauer, C. J., Schreiber, W., & Krieg, J. C. (1995). Altered hypothalamic-pituitary-adrenocortical regulation in healthy subjects at high familial risk for affective disorders. *Neuroendocrinology, 62*(4), 340–347.

Kasai, K., Yamasue, H., Gilbertson, M. W., Shenton, M. E., Rauch, S. L., & Pitman, R. K. (2008). Evidence for acquired pregenual anterior cingulated gray matter loss from a twin study of combat-related posttraumatic stress disorder. *Biological Psychiatry, 63*(6), 550–556.

Kellner, M., Baker, D. G., & Yehuda, R. (1997). Salivary cortisol in Operation Desert Storm returnees. *Biological Psychiatry, 42*(9), 849–850.

Kessler, R. C., Sonnega, A., Bromet, E., Hughes, M., & Nelson, C. B. (1995). Posttraumatic stress disorder in the National Comorbidity Survey. *Archives of General Psychiatry, 52*(12), 1048–1060.

Koopman, C., Classen, C., Cardena, E., & Spiegel, D. (1995). When disaster strikes, acute stress disorder may follow. *Journal of Traumatic Stress, 8*(1), 29–46.

Koopman, C., Classen, C., & Spiegel, D. (1994). Predictors of posttraumatic stress symptoms among survivors of the Oakland/Berkeley, Calif., firestorm. *American Journal of Psychiatry, 151*(6), 888–894.

Kosten,T. R., Wahby, V., Giller, E., & Mason, J. (1990). The dexamethasone suppression test and thyrotropin-releasing hormone stimulation test in posttraumatic stress disorder. *Biological Psychiatry, 28*, 657–664.

Landfield, P. W., & Eldridge, J. C. (1994). The glucocorticoid hypothesis of age-related hippocampal neurodegeneration: Role of dysregulated intraneuronal calcium. *Annals of the New York Academy of Sciences, 746*, 308–312.

Lange, W., Wulff, H., Berea, C., Beblo, T., Saavedra, A. S., Mensebach, C., et al. (2005). Dexamethasone suppression test in borderline personality disorder—Effects of posttraumatic stress disorder. *Psychoneuroendocrinology, 30*(9), 919–923.

Lanius, R. A., Williamson, P. C., Hopper, J., Densmore, M., Boksman, K., Gupta, M. A., et al. (2003). Recall of emotional states in posttraumatic stress disorder: An fMRI investigation. *Biological Psychiatry, 53*(3), 204–210.

Lemieux, A. M., & Coe, C. L. (1995) Abuse-related posttraumatic stress disorder: Evidence for chronic neuroendocrine activation in women. *Psychosomatic Medicine*, 57(2), 105–115.

Lemieux, A., Coe, C. L., & Carnes, M. (2008). Symptom severity predicts degree of T cell activation in adult women following childhood maltreatment. *Brain, Behavior, and Immunity, 22*(6), 994–1003.

Liberzon, I., Taylor, S. F., Amdur, R., Jung, T. D., Chamberlain, K. R., Minoshima, S., et al. (1999). Brain activation in PTSD in response to trauma-related stimuli. *Biological Psychiatry, 45*(7), 817–826.

Lowy, M. T. (1989). Quantification of type I. and II adrenal steroid receptors in neuronal, lymphoid and pituitary tissues. *Brain Research, 503*(2), 191–197.

Macklin, M. L., Metzger, L. J., Litz, B. T., McNally, R. J., Lasko, N. B., Orr, S. P., et al. (1998). Lower precombat intelligence is a risk factor for posttraumatic stress disorder. *Journal of Consulting and Clinical Psychology, 66*(2), 323–326.

Maes, M., Delmeire, L., Mylle, J., & Altamura, C. (2001). Risk and preventive factors of post-traumatic stress disorder (PTSD): Alcohol consumption and intoxication prior to a traumatic event diminishes the relative risk to develop PTSD in response to that trauma. *Journal of Affective Disorders, 63*, 113–121.

Maes, M., Lin, A., Bonaccorso, S., van Hunsel, F., Van Gastel, A., Delmeire, L., et al. (1998) Increased 24-hour urinary cortisol excretion in patients with post-traumatic stress disorder and patients with major depression, but not in patients with fibromyalgia. *Acta Psychiatrica Scandinavica, 98*(4), 328–335.

Marmar, C., Metzler, T., Chemtob, C., Delucchi, K., Liberman, A., Fagan, J., et al. (2005, July). *Impact of the World Trade Center attacks on New York City police officers; A prospective study*. Annual Conference on Criminal Justice Research and Evaluation, Washington, DC.

Marmar, C. R., Metzler, T. J., & Otte, C. (2004). The Peritraumatic Dissociative Experiences Questionnaire. In J. P. Wilson and T. M. Keane (Eds), *Assessing psychological trauma and PTSD* (pp.). New York: Guilford.

Marmar, C. R., Weiss, D. S., Metzler, T. J., Delucchi, K. L., Best, S. R., & Wentworth, K. A. (1999). Longitudinal course and predictors of continuing distress in emergency services Personnel. *Journal of Nervous and Mental Disease, 187*, 15–22.

Marmar, C., Weiss, D., Schlenger, W., Fairbank, J., Jordan, B., Kulka, R., et al. (1994). Peritraumatic dissociation and posttraumatic stress in male Vietnam theater veterans. *American Journal of Psychiatry, 151*(6), 902–907.

Marshall, G. N., & Schell, T. L. (2002). Reappraising the link between peritraumatic dissociation and PTSD symptom severity: Evidence from a longitudinal study of community violence survivors. *Journal of Abnormal Psychology, 111*(4), 626–636.

Mason, J. W., Giller, E. L., Kosten, T. R., Ostroff, R. B., & Podd, L. (1986). Urinary free-cortisol levels in posttraumatic stress disorder patients. *Journal of Nervous and Mental. Disease, 174*(3), 145–159.

Mayou, R., Bryant, B., & Duthrie, R. (1993). Psychiatric consequences of road traffic accidents. *British Medical Journal, 307*, 647–651.

McEwen, B. S., Gould, E. A., & Sakai, R. R. (1992). The vulnerability of the hippocampus to protective and destructive effects of glucocorticoids in relation to stress. *British Journal of Psychiatry, 15*(Suppl.), 18–23.

McEwen, B. S., & Sapolsky, R. M. (1995). Stress and cognitive function. *Current Opinion in Neurobiology, 5*(2), 205–216.

McEwen, B. S., & Seeman, T. (1999). Protective and damaging effects of mediators of stress: Elaborating and testing the concepts of allostasis and allostatic load. *Annals of the New York Academy of Sciences, 896*, 30–47.

McFarlane A. C. (1989). The aetiology of post-traumatic morbidity: Predisposing, precipitating and perpetuating factors. *British Journal of Psychiatry, 154*, 221–228.

McNally R. J. (2003). Psychological mechanisms in acute response to trauma. *Biological Psychiatry, 53*(9), 779–788.

Milad, M. R., Quinn, B. T., Pitman, R. K., Orr, S. P., Fischl, B., & Rauch, S. L. (2005). Thickness of ventromedial prefrontal cortex in humans in correlated with extinction memory. *Proceedings of the National Academy of Sciences of the United States of America, 102*(30), 10706–10711.

Morgan, C. A. 3rd, Southwick, S., Hazlett, G., Rasmusson, A., Hoyt, G., Zimolo, Z., et al. (2004). Relationships among plasma dehydroepiandrosterone sulfate and cortisol levels, symptoms of dissociation, and objective performance in humans exposed to acute stress. *Archives of General Psychiatry, 61*(8), 819–825.

Murray, J., Ehlers, A., & Mayou, R. A. (2002). Dissociation and post-traumatic stress disorder: Two prospective studies of road traffic accident survivors. *British Journal of Psychiatry, 180*, 363–368.

Newport, D. J., Heim, C., Bonsall, R., Miller, A. H., & Nemeroff, C. B. (2004). Pituitary-adrenal responses to standard and low-dose dexamethasone suppression tests in adult survivors of child abuse. *Biological Psychiatry, 55*(1), 10–20.

Neylan, T. C., Schuff, N., Lenoci, M., Yehuda, R., Weiner, M. W., & Marmar, C. R. (2003). Cortisol levels are positively correlated with hippocampal N-acetylaspartate. *Biological Psychiatry, 54*(10), 1118–1121.

Nixon, R. D., & Bryant, R. A. (2003). Peritraumatic and persistent panic attacks in acute stress disorder. *Behaviour Research and Therapy, 41*(10), 1237–1242.

Orr, S. P., Metzger, L. J., Lasko, N. B., Macklin, M. L., Hu, F. B., Shalev, A. Y. et al. (2003). Physiologic responses to sudden, loud tones in monozygotic twins discordant for combat exposure: Association with posttraumatic stress disorder. *Archives of General Psychiatry, 60*(3), 283–288.

Orcutt, H. K., Erickson, D. J., & Wolfe, J. (2002). A prospective analysis of trauma exposure: The mediating role of PTSD symptomatology. *Journal of Traumatic Stress, 15*(3), 259–266.

Otte, C., Lenoci, M., Metzler, T., Yehuda, R., Marmar, C. R., & Neylan, T. C. (2005). Hypothalamic-pituitary-adrenal axis activity and sleep in posttraumatic stress disorder. *Neuropsychopharmacology, 30*(6), 1173–1180.

Ozer, E. J., Best, S. R., Lipsey, T. L., & Weiss, D. S. (2003). Predictors of posttraumatic stress disorder and symptoms in adults: A meta-analysis. *Psychological Bulletin, 129*, 52–73.

Pervanidou, P., Kolaitis, G., Charitaki, S., Margeli, A., Ferentinos, S., Bakoula, C., et al. (2007). Elevated morning serum interleukin (IL)-6 or evening salivary cortisol concentrations predict posttraumatic stress disorder in children and adolescents six months after a motor vehicle accident. *Psychoneuroendocrinology, 32*, 991–999.

Phan, K. L., Britton, J. C., Taylor, S. F., Fig, L. M., & Liberzon, I. (2006). Corticolimbic blood flow during nontraumatic emotional processing in posttraumatic stress disorder. *Archives of General Psychiatry, 63*(2), 184–192.

Pitman, R. K. (1989). Post-traumatic stress disorder, hormones, and memory. *Biological Psychiatry, 26*, 221–223.

Pitman, R. K., Gilbertson, M. W., Gurvits, T. V., May, F. S., Lasko, N. B., Metzger, L. J., et al. (2006). Clarifying the origin of biological abnormalities in PTSD through the study of identical twins discordant for combat exposure. *Annals of the New York Academy of Sciences, 1071*, 242–254.

Pitman, R. K., & Orr, S. P. (1990) Twenty-four hour urinary cortisol and catecholamine excretion in combat-related posttraumatic stress disorder. *Biological Psychiatry, 27*(2), 245–247.

Pitman, R. K., Sanders, K. M., Zusman, R. M., Healy, A. R., Cheema, F., Lasko, N. B., et al. (2002). Pilot study of secondary prevention of posttraumatic stress disorder with propranolol. *Biological Psychiatry, 51*(2), 189–192.

Pitman, R. K., Shalev, A. Y., & Orr, S. P. (2000). Posttraumatic stress disorder: Emotion, conditioning, and memory. In M. D. Corbetta & M. S. Gazzaniga (Eds.), *The new cognitive neurosciences* (pp. 687–700). New York: Plenum Press.

Rasmusson, A. M., Lipschitz, D. S., Wang, S., Hu, S., Vojvoda, D., Bremner, J. D., et al. (2001). Increased pituitary and adrenal reactivity in premenopausal women with posttraumatic stress disorder. *Biological Psychiatry, 50*(12), 965–977.

Rauch, S. L., Shin, L. M., & Phelps, E. A. (2006). Neurocircuitry models of posttraumatic stress disorder and extinction: Human neuroimaging research—Past, present, and future. *Biological Psychiatry, 60*(4), 376–382.

Rauch, S. L., Shin, L. M., Segal, E., Pitman, R. K., Carson, M. A., McMullin, K., et al. (2003). Selectively reduced regional cortical volumes in post-traumatic stress disorder. *Neuroreport, 14*(7), 913–916.

Rauch, S. L., van der Kolk, B. A., Fisler, R. E., Alpert, N. M., Orr, S. P., Savage, C. R., et al. (1996). A symptom provocation study of posttraumatic stress disorder using positron emission topography and script-driven imagery, *Archives of General Psychiatry, 53*(5), 380–387.

Resnick, H. S., Yehuda, R., Pitman, R. K., & Foy D. W. (1995). Effect of previous trauma on acute plasma cortisol level following rape. *American Journal of Psychiatry, 152*(11), 1675–1677.

Sapolsky, R. M. (1994). The physiological relevance of glucocorticoid endangerment of the hippocampus. *Annals of the New York Academy of Sciences, 746*, 294–304.

Sapolsky, R. M., (2000). Glucocorticoids and hippocampal atrophy in neuropsychiatric disorders. *Archives of General Psychiatry, 57*(10), 925–935.

Sapolsky, R. M., Krey, L. C., & McEwen, B. S. (1984). Stress down-regulates corticosterone receptors in a site-specific manner in the brain. *Endocrinology, 114*, 287–292.

Schelling, G., Briegel, J., Roozendaal, B., Stoll, C., Rothenhausler, H. B., & Kapfhammer, H. P. (2001). The effect of stress doses of hydrocortisone during septic shock on posttraumatic stress disorder in survivors. *Biological Psychiatry, 50*(12), 978–985.

Shalev, A. Y. (1992). Posttraumatic stress disorder among injured survivors of a terrorist attack: Predictive value of early intrusions and avoidane symptoms. *Journal of Nervous and Mental Disease, 180*, 505–509.

Shalev, A. Y., Sahar, T., Freedman, S., Peri, T., Glick, N., Brandes, D., et al. (1998). A prospective study of heart rate response following trauma and the subsequent development of posttraumatic stress disorder. *Archives of General Psychiatry, 55*, 553–559.

Shin, L. M., Orr, S. P., Carson, M. A., Rauch, S. L., Macklin, M. L., Lasko, N. B., et al. (2004). Regional cerebral blood flow in the amygdala and medial prefrontal cortex during traumatic imagery in male and female veterans with PTSD. *Archives of General Psychiatry, 61*(2), 168–176.

Shin, L. M., Whalen, P. J., Pitman, R. K., Bush, G., Macklin, M. L., Lasko, N. B., et al. (2001). An fMRI study of anterior cingulate function in posttraumatic stress disorder. *Biological Psychiatry, 50*(12), 932–942.

Shin, L. M., Wright, C. I., Cannistraro, P. A., Wedig, M. M., McMullin, K., Martis, B., et al. (2005). A functional magnetic resonance imaging study of amygdala and medial prefrontal cortex responses to overtly presented fearful faces in posttraumatic stress disorder. *Archives of General Psychiatry, 62*(3), 273–281.

Simeon, D., Guralnik, O., Knutelska, M., Yehuda, R., & Schmeidler, J. (2003). Basal norepinephrine in depersonalization disorder. *Psychiatry Research, 121*, 93–97.

Simeon, D., Knutelska, M., Yehuda, R., Putnam, F., Schmeidler, J., & Smith, L. M. (2007). Hypothalamic-pituitary-adrenal axis function in dissociative disorders, post-traumatic stress disorder, and healthy volunteers. *Biological Psychiatry, 61*(8), 966–973.

Southwick, S. M., Krystal, J. H., Bremner, J. D., Morgan, C. A., 3rd, Nicolaou, A. L., Nagy, L. M., et al. (1997). Noradrenergic and serotonergic function in posttraumatic stress disorder. *Archives of General Psychiatry, 54*(8), 749–758.

Spiegel, D., Classen, C., & Cardena, E. (2000). New DSM-IV diagnosis of acute stress disorder. *American Journal of Psychiatry, 157*(11), 1890–1891.

Stein, M. B., Koverola, C., Torchia, M. G., & McClarty, B. (1997). Hippocampal volume in women victimized by childhood sexual abuse. *Psychological Medicine, 27*(4), 951–959.

Stein, M. B., Yehuda, R., Koverola, C., & Hanna, C. (1997). Enhanced dexamethasone suppression of plasma cortisol in adult women traumatized by childhood sexual abuse. *Biological Psychiatry, 42*(8), 680–686.

Svec, F. (1985). Glucocorticoid receptor regulation. *Life Sciences, 36*(25), 2359–2366.

Thaller, V., Vrkljan, M., Hotujac, L., & Thakore, J. (1999). The potential role of hypocortisolism in the pathophysiology of PTSD and psoriasis. *Collegium Antropologicum, 23*(2), 611–619.

Vaiva, G., Thomas, P., Ducrocq, F., Fontaine, M., Boss, V., Devos, P., et al. (2004). Low posttrauma GABA plasma levels as a predictive factor in the development of acute posttraumatic stress disorder. *Biological Psychiatry, 55*(3), 250–254.

Wheler, G. H., Brandon, D., Clemons, A., Riley, C., Kendall, J., Loriaux, D. L., et al. (2006). Cortisol production rate in posttraumatic stress disorder. *Journal of Clinical Endocrinology and Metabolism, 91*(9), 3486–3489.

Williams, L. M., Kemp, A. H., Felmingham, K., Barton, M., Olivieri, G., Peduto, A., et al. (2006). Trauma modulates amygdale and medial prefrontal responses to consciously attended fear. *Neuroimage, 29*(2), 347–257.

Woodward, S. H., Kaloupek, D. G., Streeter, C. C., Martinez, C., Schaer, M., & Eliez, S. (2006). Decreased anterior cingulate volume in combat-related PTSD. *Biological Psychiatry, 59*(7), 582–587.

Yamasue, H., Kasai, K., Iwanami, A., Ohtani, T., Yamada, H., Abe, O., et al. (2003). Voxel-based analysis of MRI reveals anterior cingulated gray-matter volume reduction in posstraumatic stress disorder due to terrorism. *Proceedings of the National Academy of Sciences in the United States, 100*(15), 9039–9043.

Yehuda, R. (1997) Sensitization of the hypothalamic-pituitary-adrenal axis in posttraumatic stress disorder. *Annals of the New York Academy of Sciences 821*, 57–75.

Yehuda, R., Bell, A., Bierer, L. M., & Schmeidler, J. (2008). Maternal, not paternal, PTSD is related to increased risk for PTSD in offspring of Holocaust survivors. *Journal of Psychiatric Research, 42*(13), 1104–1111.

Yehuda, R., Bierer, L. M., Schmeidler, J., Aferiat, D. H., Breslau, I., & Dolan, S. (2000). Low cortisol and risk for PTSD in adult offspring of holocaust survivors. *American Journal of Psychiatry, 157*(8), 1252–1259.

Yehuda, R., Boisoneau, D., Lowy, M. T., & Giller, E. L. (1995). Dose-response changes in plasma cortisol and lymphocyte glucocorticoid receptors following dexamethasone administration in combat veterans with and without posttraumatic stress disorder. *Archives of General Psychiatry, 52*(7), 583–593.

Yehuda, R., Boisoneau, D., Mason, J. W., & Giller, E. L. (1993). Glucocorticoid receptor number and cortisol excretion in mood, anxiety, and psychotic disorders. *Biological Psychiatry, 34*, 18–25.

Yehuda, R., Brand, S., & Yang, R. K. (2006). Plasma neuropeptide Y concentrations in combat exposed veterans: Relationship to trauma exposure, recovery from PTSD, and coping. *Biological Psychiatry, 59*(7), 660–663.

Yehuda, R., Golier, J. A., Tischler, L., Harvey, P. D., Newmark, R., Yang, R. K., et al. (2007). Hippocampal volume in aging combat veterans with and without post-traumatic stress disorder: Relation to risk and resilience factors. *Journal of Psychiatric Research, 41*(5), 435–445.

Yehuda, R., Golier, J. A., Yang, R. K., & Tischler, L. (2004). Enhanced sensitivity to glucocorticoids in peripheral mononuclear leukocytes in posttraumatic stress disorder. *Biological Psychiatry, 55*(11), 1110–1116.

Yehuda, R., Halligan, S. L., & Bierer, L. M. (2001). Relationship of parental trauma exposure and PTSD to PTSD, depressive and anxiety disorders in offspring. *Journal of Psychiatric Research, 35*(5), 261–269.

Yehuda, R., Halligan, S. L., & Grossman, R. (2001). Childhood trauma and risk for PTSD: Relationship to intergenerational effects of trauma, parental PTSD and cortisol excretion. *Development and Psychopathology, 13*(3), 733–753.

Yehuda, R., Halligan, S. L., Grossman, R., Golier, J. A., & Wong, C. (2002). The cortisol and glucocorticoid receptor response to low dose dexamethasone administration in aging combat veterans and Holocaust survivors with and without posttraumatic stress disorder. *Biological Psychiatry, 52*(5), 393–403.

Yehuda, R., Halligan, S. L., Golier, J. A., Grossman, R., & Bierer, L. M. (2004). Effects of trauma exposure on the cortisol response to dexamethasone administration in PTSD and major depressive disorder. *Psychoneuroendocrinology, 29*(3), 389–404.

Yehuda, R., Harvey, P. D., Buchsbaum, M., Tischler, L., & Schmeidler, J. (2007). Enhanced effects of cortisol administration on working memory in PTSD. *Neuropsychopharmacology, 32*(12), 2581–2591.

Yehuda, R., Kahana, B., Binder-Brynes, K., Southwick, S. M., Mason, J. W., & Giller, E. L. (1995). Low urinary cortisol excretion in Holocaust survivors with posttraumatic stress disorder. *American Journal of Psychiatry, 152*(7), 982–986.

Yehuda, R., & LeDoux, J. (2007). Response variation following trauma: A translational neuroscience approach to understanding PTSD. *Neuron Review, 56*, 19–32.

Yehuda, R., Lowy, M. T., Southwick, S., Shaffer, D., & Giller, E. L. (1991). Lymphocyte glucocorticoid receptor number in posttraumatic stress disorder. *American Journal of Psychiatry, 148*(4), 499–504.

Yehuda, R., McFarlane, A. C., & Shalev A. Y. (1998b). Predicting the development of posttraumatic stress disorder from the acute response to a traumatic event. *Biological Psychiatry, 44*(12), 1305–1313.

Yehuda, R., Morris, A., Labinsky, E., Zemelman, S., & Schmeidler, J. (2007). Ten-year follow-up study of cortisol levels in aging Holocaust survivors with and without PTSD. *Journal of Traumatic Stress, 20*(5), 757–761.

Yehuda, R., Southwick, S. M., Krystal, J. H., Bremner, D., Charney, D. S., & Mason, J. W. (1993). Enhanced suppression of cortisol following dexamethasone administration in posttraumatic stress disorder. *American Journal of Psychiatry, 150*, 83–86.

Yehuda, R., Southwick, S. M., Nussbaum, G., Wahby, V., Giller, E. L., & Mason J. W. (1990). Low urinary cortisol excretion in patients with posttraumatic stress disorder. *Journal of Nervous and Mental Disease, 178*(6), 366–369.

Yehuda, R., Schmeidler, J., Wainberg, M., Binder-Brynes, K., & Duvdevani, T. (1998). Vulnerability to posttraumatic stress disorder in adult offspring of Holocaust survivors. *American Journal of Psychiatry, 155*(9), 1163–1171.

Yehuda, R., Teicher, M. H., Seckl, J. R., Grossman, R. A., Morris, A., & Bierer L. M. (2007). Parental posttraumatic stress disorder as a vulnerability factor for low cortisol trait in offspring of holocaust survivors. *Archives of General Psychiatry, 64*(9), 1040–1048.

Yehuda, R., Teicher, M. H., Trestman, R. L., Levengood, R. A., & Siever L. J. (1996). Cortisol regulation in posttraumatic stress disorder and major depression: A chronobiological analysis. *Biological Psychiatry, 40*(2), 79–88.

Yehuda, R., Yang, R. K., Buchsbaum, M. S., & Golier J. A. (2006). Alterations in cortisol negative feedback inhibition as examined using the ACTH response to cortisol administration in PTSD. *Psychoneuroendocrinology, 31*(4), 447–451.

Young, E. A., & Breslau, N. (2004). Cortisol and catecholamines in posttraumatic stress disorder: An epidemiologic community study. *Archives of General Psychiatry, 61*(4), 394–401.

Zangrossi, H., Jr., Viana, M. B., & Graeff, F. G. (1999). Anxiolytic effect of intra-amygdala injection of midazolam an 8-hydroxy-2-(di-n-propylamino) tetralin in the elevated T-maze. *European Journal of Pharmacology, 369*(3), 267–270.

CHAPTER

13 Learning Models of PTSD

Shmuel Lissek *and* Christian Grillon

Abstract

Of all anxiety disorders, PTSD may be most clearly attributable to discrete, aversive learning events capable of evoking both conditioned fear responding to stimuli associated with the event and more general overreactivity—or failure to adapt—to intense, novel, or fear-related stimuli. The relatively straightforward link between PTSD and these basic, evolutionarily old, learning processes of conditioning, sensitization, and habituation affords models of PTSD comprising fundamental, experimentally tractable mechanisms of learning that have been well characterized across a variety of mammalian species including humans. Though such learning mechanisms have featured prominently in explanatory models of psychological maladjustment to trauma for at least 90 years, much of the empirical testing of these models has occurred only in the past two decades. The current chapter delineates the variety of theories forming this longstanding tradition of learning-based models of PTSD, details empirical evidence for such models, attempts an integrative account of results from this literature, and delineates limitations of, and future directions for, studies testing learning correlates of PTSD.

Key Words: PTSD, fear conditioning, extinction, contextual anxiety, overgeneralization, sensitization, habituation

Introduction

Learning, defined as the alteration of behavioral tendencies through experience, is of central importance to any account of posttraumatic stress disorder (PTSD). From a conditioning perspective, symptoms of PTSD are promoted by maladaptive learning acquired as a direct consequence of traumatic experiences. Such learning manifests in both *associative* and *nonassociative* forms. Through associative fear conditioning (Pavlov, 1927), neutral stimuli (people, places, and things) associated with the aversive trauma acquire the capacity to trigger and maintain anxiety well after the occurrence of the traumatic episode. This conditioning process is thought to contribute centrally to the re-experiencing (e.g., distressing recollections) and avoidance symptom-clusters that are often triggered by exposure to benign stimuli that resemble aspects of the trauma. Maladaptive forms of nonassociative learning in PTSD are evidenced by broad anxious reactivity—to novel, intense, or fear-relevant stimuli in the environment—that is both resistant to degradation via *habituation* and susceptible to intensification through *sensitization.* These nonassociative learning correlates of PTSD promote sustained sympathetic activation thought to result in such hyper-arousal symptoms of PTSD as hypervigilance, exaggerated startle, difficulty concentrating, and irritability.

During the course of this chapter, we will explore, in depth, the variety of learning mechanisms implicated in the onset and maintenance of PTSD through outlining associative and nonassociative learning models of PTSD; detailing extant empirical support for such models; and delineating the research limitations and future directions for the field.

Description of Learning Models

Associative Fear Conditioning

Fear conditioning, the learning process whereby a naturally benign conditioned stimulus (CS) acquires anxiogenic properties by virtue of its repeated pairing with a naturally aversive unconditioned stimulus (US), has long figured prominently in accounts of maladaptive psychological reactions to trauma (Pavlov, 1927; Watson & Rayner, 1920). During this period, a variety of mechanisms through which fear conditioning exerts pathological influence have been theorized, including: (1) resistance to extinguish conditioned fear, (2) Mowrer's two-stage learning, (3) stimulus generalization, (4) hyper-conditionability, and (5) associative-learning deficits leading to contextual anxiety. The first section of the review is dedicated to the description of this rich assortment of associative learning theories of PTSD.

RESISTANCE TO EXTINCTION

Many conditioning models of PTSD posit a resistance to extinguish conditioned fear as the central pathogen. In the context of fear conditioning, extinction refers to a decline in fear responding to a conditioned danger-cue (i.e., CS) presented one or more times in the absence of the aversive US. Failure to extinguish entails the persistence of fear to stimuli that are no longer indicative of environmental danger, and thus constitutes a maladaptive expression of anxiety. Importantly, extinction is a new learning that inhibits, rather than erases, the acquired CS/US association (for a review, see Bouton, 2004). Specifically, extinction involves the encoding of a second learning experience with the CS (i.e., the CS as benign) that competes for activation with the original acquisition learning experience (i.e., the CS as a signal of danger: Bouton & Swartzentruber, 1991). Extinction of conditioned responding occurs only when the extinction learning is strong enough to inhibit activation of the fear memory encoded at acquisition (see figure 13.1).

From this competition-theory perspective, extinction accounts of PTSD derive from two mechanisms through which the inhibitory influences of extinction are outstripped by excitatory influences of fear acquisition. The first results from elevated levels of acquisition that overpower the inhibitory effects of extinction. The second involves a deficit in extinction (inhibitory) learning that confers a competitive edge to the fear acquisition memory. Drawing from the first of these two mechanisms, the *conditionability* theory by Pitman and colleagues (e.g., Orr et al., 2000) imputes PTSD to hyper-conditionability: a disposition toward forming aversive associations instantiated by abnormally strong acquisition and a resulting resistance to extinguish. The second mechanism is reflected in theories by Davis and colleagues (Davis, Falls, & Gewirtz, 2000) and Jovanovic and Ressler (2010) linking PTSD to deficits in extinction, and other forms of inhibitory fear learning, resulting in the failure to suppress what are otherwise normative levels of fear acquisition.

An additional formulation of the extinction model comes from Eysenck (1979), who argues that

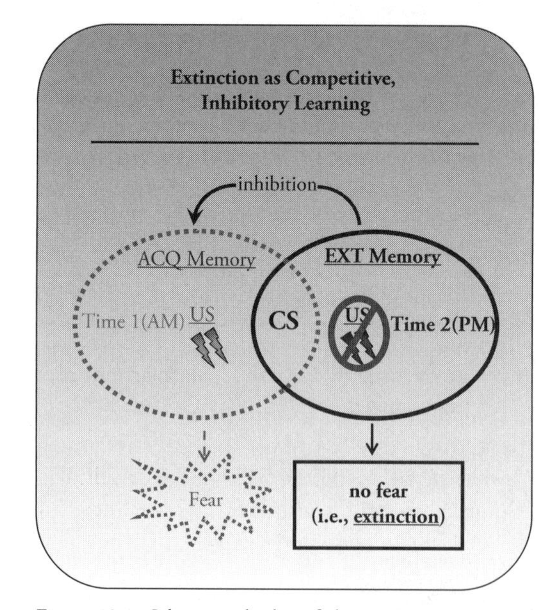

Figure 13.1. Schematic display of the competing nature of acquisition (ACQ) and extinction (EXT) memories of the conditioned stimulus (CS). In this example, ACQ of conditioned fear follows from presentations of the CS together with an electric-shock US during a morning (AM) testing session. The EXT memory is encoded later that afternoon (PM) during a testing session in which the CS is repeatedly presented in the absence of the US. These ACQ and EXT learning experiences generate two competing memories of the CS, with the former representing the CS as an anxiogenic predictor of aversive shock and the latter characterizing the CS as a benign stimulus associated with no aversive outcome. Activation of the ACQ memory of the CS elicits fear, while activation of the EXT memory of the CS elicits no fear. Successful EXT learning depends on an EXT memory of the benign CS that is strong enough to outcompete the ACQ memory for excitation, thereby inhibiting both activation of the ACQ memory and the associated fear reactivity to the CS.

the conditioned response (i.e., an internal state of fear) is sufficiently "nocive," or uncomfortable, in those disposed toward clinical anxiety to serve as an aversive US substitute in the absence of the genuine US. That is, extinction of fear to a CS previously paired with an aversive outcome may be slowed or prevented in those for whom anxiety reactions to the CS are sufficiently strong to function as aversive reinforcement of the CS during extinction learning. Eysenck not only predicts slowed extinction but goes further by expecting a kind of "incubation," or enhancement of the conditioned fear response, in the absence of the genuine US in those disposed to anxiety. Such incubation is proposed to operate through a positive feedback loop whereby repeated reinforcement of the CS by the fear response strengthens the aversive valence of the CS, which subsequently increases levels of fearful CS-reactivity and provides further aversive reinforcement of the CS. To illustrate extinction failure in the context of PTSD, consider the example of a combat soldier who acquires conditioned fear to a roadside, box-shaped object (CS) used to encase an improvised explosive device (US) by which he is injured while on street patrol in Iraq. Though, upon return to civilian life, the initial display of conditioned fear to roadside objects is normative, failure to extinguish fear through repeated exposure to benign roadside objects (i.e., the CS in the absence of the US) is thought to be the maladaptive consequence of either: (1) an overly strong acquisition memory (i.e., *conditionability hypothesis*); (2) an insufficiently strong extinction memory (i.e., *failure-to-inhibit hypothesis*); or (3) an especially nocive conditioned response that continues to aversively reinforce roadside objects (i.e., *incubation hypothesis*).

ASSOCIATIVE-LEARNING DEFICITS AND SUSTAINED CONTEXTUAL ANXIETY

In dramatic contrast to the *conditionability* theory of Pitman and colleagues (Orr et al., 2000), this model attributes PTSD to an *impaired* ability to form aversive associations through classical conditioning (Grillon, 2002). During a traumatic experience, this deficit is said to prevent the individual from learning environmental cues predicting danger. To not know cues for danger is to be unaware of safety in their absence, leaving the individual in a chronic state of anxiety (Seligman & Binik, 1977). Furthermore, the absence of threat cues leads the individual to more generally associate the unpleasant US with the environment in which the US is experienced, resulting in heightened contextual anxiety—a form of learning further contributing to chronic anxiety by maintaining diffuse anxiety for the duration of exposure to the traumatic milieu. Thus on this view, chronic anxiety—fueled by both the absence of safety periods and contextual conditioning—is the pathologic consequence of associative learning deficits in those with, or disposed toward, PTSD (Grillon, 2002).

TWO-STAGE LEARNING

A variant of extinction theory, the two-stage learning model, views avoidance of the CS as the primary force behind extinction failure. Specifically, classically conditioned fear is proposed to act as a drive that motivates and reinforces avoidance of the CS, thereby denying an individual the opportunity to extinguish via exposure to the CS in the absence of the US (Eysenck, 1976, 1979; Eysenck & Rachman, 1965; Miller, 1948; Mowrer, 1947, 1960). The explanatory power of this model derives largely from its clinical and intuitive appeal. Specifically, avoidance of learned trauma cues is central to the clinical presentation of PTSD, which by definition denies patients the exposure necessary to extinguish conditioned fear.

In terms of the competitive learning model of extinction detailed in figure 13.1, such avoidance results in an acquisition memory of the CS that receives no competition from an inhibitory extinction memory, leaving only the memory of the CS as a danger cue available for activation. In our example, the returning veteran may avoid driving or walking on streets to avert conditioned fear elicited by roadside objects resembling improvised explosive device (IED) encasements encountered during combat. By so doing, the veteran is denied the opportunity to extinguish this conditioned response in their now safe postdeployment environment through exposure to roadside objects in the absence of dangerous outcomes.

OVERGENERALIZATION

Conditioned responses have long been known to transfer, or generalize, to stimuli resembling the original CS (Pavlov, 1927). Evidence linking the conditioned generalization process to pathologic anxiety dates back to Watson and Rayner (1920), who famously demonstrated generalization of conditioned fear to all things furry in a toddler ("Little Albert") following acquisition of fear conditioning to a white rat. This kind of conditioned generalization has since been adopted as a core feature of PTSD, through which fear during a traumatic event extends to safe conditions "resembling" the distressing event (American Psychiatric Association [APA], 2000). The pathogenic contribution of conditioned generalization follows from the undue proliferation of trauma cues in the individual's environment. That is, generalization results in the spreading of traumatic reactions to stimuli that resemble the CS, but are themselves benign. Precipitating this proliferation of trauma cues may be an underlying disposition toward reduced thresholds for threat reactivity, resulting in less danger information (i.e., less resemblance to the CS) required for activation of the fear circuit among those with, or prone toward, clinical anxiety (Lissek et al., 2010).

The maladaptive effects of this generalization process can be illustrated by an IED-exposed combat veteran with PTSD. Though conditioned fear was acquired to a box-shaped encasement of the IED, the veteran's fears may generalize to such other roadside objects in his postdeployment environment as trash cans, fire hydrants, or other roadside debris. This may promote frequent trauma-related anxiety in his benign posttraumatic environment because of the ubiquity of these roadside objects in his neighborhood and town.

FAILURE TO INHIBIT FEAR

This final associative learning theory links PTSD to impaired mechanisms of fear inhibition, resulting in the expression of fear in the presence of safety cues (Davis et al., 2000; Jovanovic & Ressler, 2010). This model comes as a logical corollary of the above described theory of extinction from Davis and colleagues (2000) and Jovanovic and Ressler (2010), according to which impaired mechanisms of inhibitory fear conditioning in PTSD are responsible for extinction failure. From this perspective, all processes dependent on fear inhibition—including but not limited to extinction—should be compromised in PTSD. Safety learning in the traumatic context is one such process because cues signaling periods of safety are effective only if inhibition of ongoing anxiety to the ambient threat of the environment is achieved. This model thus links PTSD to an inability to suppress fear in the presence of safety cues.

On this view, our IED-exposed veteran, who continues to display conditioned fear to roadside objects upon return to his benign predeployment environment, is suffering the effects of failed inhibition of fear in the presence of safety signals. Specifically, such roadside objects are experienced coincident with many potential environmental cues of safety, including neighborhood people, shops, parks, and houses associated with what may have been the relative safety of his childhood years. Such safety cues are, however, unable to exert inhibitory control over the conditioned response to roadside objects, leading to a continuation of the traumatic response in the benign, civilian context.

Nonassociative Fear Learning

In contrast to fear conditioning, nonassociative fear learning involves changes in reactivity to environmental stimuli with no acquired link to the presence or absence of aversive outcomes. In the context of PTSD, nonassociative mechanisms are thought to generate increases, or resistance to decreases, in fear reactivity to novel, intense, or fear-relevant stimuli. Contrasting the multiplicity of associative models of PTSD, nonassociative accounts largely center on two mechanisms of learning: habituation and sensitization.

HABITUATION

One of the most fundamental and ubiquitous forms of learning is *habituation*, whereby responding progressively declines with repeated stimulation (Groves & Thompson, 1970). In the context of traumatic responding, habituation refers to decreases in autonomic, behavioral, or neural responses to repeatedly presented novel, intense, or fear-relevant (unconditioned) stimuli. The failure of this type of habituation is proposed as a central contributor to the hyper-arousal cluster of PTSD symptoms (e.g., hyper-vigilance, exaggerated startle, and difficulty concentrating). For example, hyper-vigilance and exaggerated startle may be maintained in the benign posttraumatic context through persistent autonomic responding to reoccurring, and more or less irrelevant, stimuli. Additionally, the inability to filter out these reoccurring sensory stimuli likely compromises concentration by exhausting attentional resources otherwise available for processing more consequential stimulus events.

SENSITIZATION

The direct inverse of habituation is *sensitization*: a nonassociative learning mechanism whereby responses are *amplified* through repeated stimulation (Groves & Thompson, 1970). In the context of fear and anxiety, sensitization generally refers to the increase in fear-related responses to novel, intense, or fear-relevant stimuli following activation of the fear system (Marks & Tobena, 1990). Essentially, fear sensitization is thought to arise from a fear system rendered hyper-excitable by previous activation (Rosen & Schulkin, 1998).

A large body of work in animals has documented stress-related sensitization with some elucidation of its underlying mechanisms. The most common approach involves assessing changes in fear-relevant behaviors in rats following exposure to highly stressful conditions. In one such line of work, defensive responding, which is operationalized by startle reactivity to intense bursts of white noise, is reliably enhanced in rats after administration of strong electric foot shocks (e.g., Davis, 1989). This startle potentiation, referred to as *shock sensitization*, may model the nonassociative hyper-reactivity to intense, novel stimuli seen in PTSD, though it is worth noting that the nonassociative nature of this effect has been brought into question by evidence imputing shock sensitization to associative fear of the context in which shock was delivered (for a review, see Richardson & Elsayed, 1998).

A second line of work exposing rats to aversive electric shocks in the service of assessing sensitization demonstrates the imperative of stressor *uncontrollability* for displays of stress-related sensitization (for a review, see Maier & Watkins, 2005). Specifically, rats exposed to inescapable (uncontrollable) versus escapable (controllable) shocks exhibit time-limited enhancement (sensitization) of such stress-related processes as avoidance of cat odors (Williams & Groux, 1993), avoidance of novel situations and flavors (Job & Barnes, 1995; Minor, 1990), fear-conditioning (Desiderato & Newman, 1971), suppression of appetitive behaviors (Maier & Watkins, 1998), and avoidance of social interactions (Short & Maier, 1993). Importantly, these effects of uncontrollable stress are likely due to nonassociative sensitization, as they occur in contexts with no apparent resemblance to the shock-delivery environment and, as such, are unlikely the result of contextual conditioning. The possibility thus exists that oversensitivity to novel, intense, or fear-relevant stimuli of the kind seen in PTSD stems from trauma-induced stress sensitization that is dependent on the uncontrollable nature of the trauma. The plausibility of this theory is supported by the view that the uncontrollable nature of trauma is central to the etiology of PTSD (e.g., Foa, Zinbarg, & Rothbaum, 1992; Volpicelli, Balaraman, Hahn, Wallace, & Bux, 1999).

One final related animal model induces sensitization through electrically stimulating, or partially kindling, the amygdala-based fear circuit with the aim of increasing the excitability of this circuit (for a review, see Rosen & Schulkin, 1998)[1]. Indeed, a number of studies document increases in fear-related behaviors following amygdala kindling in animals (e.g., Adamec & Morgan, 1994). For example, Rosen and colleagues (1996) found partial kindling (only two stimulations) of the amygdala to enhance fear potentiated startle (Rosen, Hamerman, Sitcoske, Glowa, & Schulkin, 1996): the amygdala-dependent enhancement of the startle reflex when an organism is in a state of fear (Davis & Astrachan, 1978; Grillon, Ameli, Woods, Merikangas, & Davis, 1991; Pissiota et al., 2003).

Additionally, affective consequences of epileptic discharges in the human temporal lobe (the cerebral structure encasing the amygdala) are marked by increases in reported fear and anxiety (e.g., Gloor, 1978). These findings support the theory that trauma-evoked anxiety sensitizes the fear system through a partial kindling of the amygdala, leaving it hyper-reactive to future traumatic encounters and conferring risk for PTSD from subsequent trauma. Consistent with this idea are findings demonstrating a heightened incidence of PTSD among those with previous histories of trauma-exposure (e.g., Bremner, Southwick, Johnson, Yehuda, & Charney, 1993; Breslau, Chilcoat, Kessler, & Davis, 1999; Davidson, Hughes, & Blazer, 1991).

Empirical Evidence

The wealth of learning accounts of PTSD described above have, historically, not been matched by an equally rich empirical literature on the subject. Indeed, early 20th-century conditioning accounts of psychological maladaptation to trauma (e.g., Watson & Raynor, 1920) received sparse experimental attention for the ensuing 70 years. The late 1990s brought a rejuvenated interest in testing conditioning models of clinical anxiety. This development was in part attributable to emerging discoveries in animals elucidating the neurobiology of conditioned fear and the potential for neural characterizations of conditioning abnormalities in the anxiety disorders such animal findings presented. Fortunately, this recent experimental attention has resulted in a fairly sizable literature offering some means by which to validate learning contributions to PTSD. The following section reviews this literature as well as other clinical and correlational data with implications for associative and nonassociative learning accounts of PTSD.

Associative Fear Conditioning

FAILURE TO EXTINGUISH

Much support for the role of extinction in PTSD derives from the clinical effectiveness of "extinction-like" exposure therapy for the treatment of PTSD (e.g., Rothbaum & Davis, 2003; Rothbaum & Foa, 2002). Specifically, the use of this treatment is predicated on the notion that patients manifest a resistance to extinguish trauma-related fear that is surmountable through clinical facilitation of the extinction process. Unfortunately, the lab-based evidence is less convincing, with some but not other experiments demonstrating weaker extinction learning in PTSD (e.g., Blechert, Michael, Vriends, Margraf, & Wilhelm, 2007; Orr et al., 2000; Wessa & Flor, 2007, vs. Grillon & Morgan, 1999; Peri, Ben Shakhar, Orr, & Shalev; 2000). This heterogeneity in extinction results is difficult to disentangle given the absence of methodological or sample characteristics that clearly differentiate studies producing positive versus null findings. For example, findings are inconsistent for: (1) studies assessing extinction psychophysiologically (compare Orr et al., 2000, and. Peri et al., 2000) or through subjective ratings (compare Wessa & Flor, 2007, and Blechert et al., 2007); (2) studies employing electric shock (Orr et al., 2000, vs. Grillon & Morgan, 1999) or more mild aversive events (Wessa & Flor, 2007, vs. Peri et al., 2000) as unconditioned stimuli; and (3) studies testing patients with combat-related PTSD (Milad et al., 2008, vs. Grillon & Morgan, 1999) or noncombat-related PTSD (Wessa & Flor, 2007, vs. Bremner et al., 2005).

More recently, interest has accrued in studying PTSD-control differences in retention of extinction learning (Milad et al., 2008, 2009; Orr et al., 2006). Two of three such studies document impaired recall of extinction learning in PTSD patients during a second day of testing, in the absence of abnormalities in the original extinction learning (Milad et al., 2008, 2009). Twin data from one such study (Milad et al., 2008) characterizes deficient extinction recall in PTSD as a consequence of traumatic exposure rather than a preexisting risk factor. Such findings link PTSD to an intact ability to extinguish conditioned fear during the course of extinction (exposure) training, but a trauma-induced impairment in maintaining benefits of this training over time. Whether impaired extinction recall emerges as a more replicable marker of PTSD awaits further testing. For now these results seem to highlight the importance of repeated follow-up assessments of PTSD, and repeated treatment sessions if needed, for patients undergoing exposure-based treatments.

As portrayed in figure 13.1, the competition theory of extinction implies two mechanisms by which extinction failure might occur: (1) an overly strong acquisition memory of the CS as threatening that is refractory to the inhibitory effects of the extinction memory, as implied by the hyper-conditionability theory (e.g., Orr et al., 2000); or (2) an insufficiently strong, inhibitory extinction memory of the CS as benign that is unable to outcompete the acquisition memory for activation, as posited by the failure-to inhibit theory (e.g., Davis et al., 2000). A degree of doubt is cast on the former mechanism by a strong majority of lab-based conditioning studies evidencing normative levels of fear acquisition to the CS in PTSD (Blechert et al., 2007; Grillon & Morgan, 1999; Milad et al., 2008, 2009; Peri et al., 2000). Such findings suggest that extinction failure in PTSD—via dominance of the acquisition memory over the extinction memory—is unlikely attributable to unduly strong, initial levels of acquisition in patients. That retention of extinction may constitute a more robust marker of PTSD leaves open the possibility for abnormally strong retention of acquisition in patients that, over time, results in acquisition memories too strong for inhibition by extinction memories. Importantly, the absence of abnormally strong conditioned responding immediately following acquisition among those with PTSD, in the presence of heightened retention of conditioned fear over time, seems consistent with the observation that retention of PTSD symptoms, rather than the initial acquisition of such symptoms, distinguishes trauma survivors with PTSD from those without PTSD (e.g., Rothbaum & Foa, 1993). Indeed, the majority of trauma survivors (65–94%) display posttraumatic symptoms in the early aftermath of the trauma and only a minority of survivors meet diagnostic criteria for PTSD (11–42%) by retaining such symptoms beyond the first few months posttrauma (estimated percentages from Rothbaum & Foa, 1993). Though the weight of available data suggest no abnormalities in acquisition of conditioned fear to the conditioned danger cue in PTSD, such data, by and large, reflect levels of conditioning during and immediately following acquisition. Future studies assessing retention of fear to conditioned danger cues in PTSD are needed before ruling out heightened responding to learned danger cue as a conditioning marker of PTSD.

The second mechanism, imputing extinction failure in PTSD to inadequate inhibition of the acquisition memory, has begun to receive support from results suggesting impaired processes of fear inhibition in PTSD (for a review, see Jovanovic & Ressler, 2010). Because these data are directly relevant to both *failure-to-extinguish* and *failure-to-inhibit* theories of PTSD, such data will be discussed in the context of both models in the following section. Of note, though Eysenck's *incubation* version of extinction theory is appealing on its face, no empirical support for this model in PTSD has been garnered to date.

IMPAIRED INHIBITION

Support for the role of deficient fear inhibition in PTSD-related conditioning abnormalities draws from neuroimaging data linking poor retention of extinction in PTSD to an underfunctioning medial-prefrontal cortex (mPFC; Milad et al., 2009): a brain region thought to subserve fear reduction through its demonstrated inhibition of amygdaloid neurons (e.g., Quirk, Likhtik, Pelletier, & Pare, 2003; Rosenkrantz, Moore, & Grace, 2003). Further support for impaired mPFC engagement by fear-inducing stimuli in PTSD, that may instantiate compromised fear inhibition, is found by neuroimaging studies documenting reduced mPFC activation in those with versus those without PTSD during exposure to traumatic pictures and sounds (Bremner, et al., 1999), script-driven traumatic imagery (Shin et al., 1999), and fearful faces (Shin et al., 2005; Williams et al., 2006). Additionally, two such studies found inverse relations between the severity of PTSD symptomatology and mPFC responses in PTSD patients (Shin et al., 2005; Williams et al., 2006), supporting the clinical relevance of decreased mPFC engagement during fear evocations.

A final line of work supporting impaired inhibition of fear in PTSD comes from studies applying a *conditioned inhibition* paradigm designed to assess the degree to which conditioned fear to a conditioned danger cue is reduced when presented in tandum with a conditioned safety cue. Results provide evidence for both decreased inhibition of fear-potentiated startle in the presence of a conditioned safety cue and less transfer of that inhibition during the combined (configural) presentation of the conditioned danger and safety cue (Jovanovic et al., 2010).

ASSOCIATIVE LEARNING DEFICITS LEADING TO SUSTAINED CONTEXTUAL ANXIETY

Whereas evidence for associative learning deficits in PTSD is mixed, with support coming from some studies (Burriss, Ayers, Ginsberg, & Powell, 2008) but not others (Burriss, Ayers & Powell, 2007; Geuze, Vermetten, Ruf, de Kloet, Westenberg, 2008; Werner et al., 2009),the psychopathological endpoint of this model (sustained contextual anxiety) is substantiated by startle studies evidencing heightened contextual anxiety in PTSD. For example, the previously discussed pattern of results across multiple studies in which heightened startle magnitudes in PTSD are found in aversive, but not benign, experimental contexts (for a review, see Grillon & Baas, 2003) links PTSD with an enhanced sensitivity to contextual anxiety. Moreover, a study by our group further studied this link (Grillon et al., 2009) using an instructed threat paradigm designed for within-subject manipulations of contextual danger (Grillon, Baas, Lissek, Smith, & Milstein, 2004). Specifically, startle magnitudes were assessed during three sustained contexts (duration = 2 minutes) of increasing aversiveness: (1) a neutral (N) context where no unpleasant events were possible; (2) a mildly aversive context where unpleasant stimuli were presented predictably (P); (3) and a more highly aversive context in which unpleasant stimuli were presented unpredictably (U). As can be seen in figure 13.2, fear-potentiated startle to the most aversive context (U) relative to the least (N), is significantly stronger in PTSD patients. Because this enhanced *contextual potentiation* in patients was derived from startle responses collected across the 2-minute duration of N, P, and U conditions; such data link PTSD with *sustained* contextual anxiety. Importantly, this result was accompanied by normative levels of startle potentiation to discrete (noncontextual) cues reliably predicting imminent delivery of unpleasant stimulation, specifically linking PTSD to abnormal processes of sustained contextual anxiety rather than more phasic, discretely cued fear responses. Consistently, a prospective study of police cadets exposed to police-related trauma found pretrauma levels of subjective anxiety to contextual threat, but not discretely cued threat, to be predictive of posttrauma symptoms of PTSD (Pole et al., 2009). Such results also implicate increased contextual anxiety as a premorbid risk factor for PTSD.

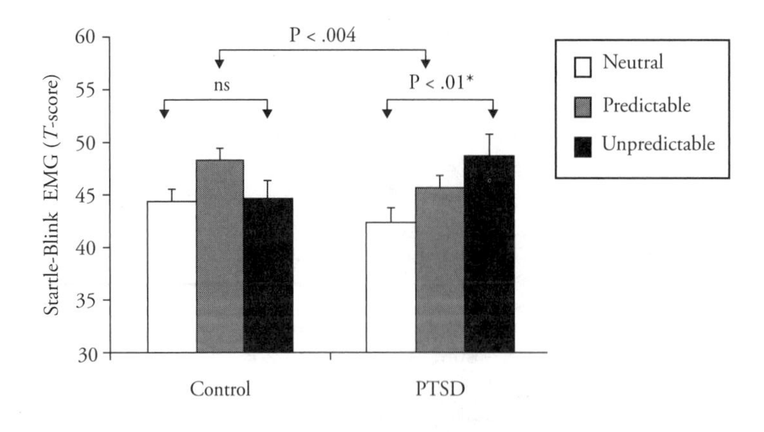

Figure 13.2 Average startle magnitudes in PTSD patients and healthy controls across three levels of contextual aversiveness: (1) neutral context (low threat), during which no unpleasant stimulation was delivered; (2) predictable context (moderate threat) during which unpleasant stimulation was given predictably; and (3) unpredictable context during which unpleasant stimulation could be given at any time.

TWO-STAGE LEARNING

Although the first *classical fear-conditioning stage* of this model has received substantial experimentation in PTSD (see above), the extent to which this initial conditioning motivates the second *instrumental avoidance stage* has been the target of little lab-based testing. Indeed, most assessments of avoidance in PTSD have explored correlations between PTSD symptom severity and *experiential avoidance*: the intrapsychic attempt to evade thoughts, emotions, and sensations related to the trauma (e.g., Marx & Sloan, 2005; Simpson, Jakupcak, & Luterek, 2006). Though this work has helped elucidate the contribution of mental avoidance to the onset and course of PTSD, it has not allowed for systematic assays of learning mechanisms subserving the more objectively measurable, behavioral constituents of avoidance in PTSD. Future studies are needed to assess the way acquisition of lab-based classic fear conditioning antecedes instrumental, behavioral avoidance of conditioned stimuli.

OVERGENERALIZATION

Though generalization of conditioned fear has featured prominently in etiologic accounts of maladaptive anxiety at least since Watson and Raynor's "Little Albert" experiment (1920), lab-based testing of this idea has been sparse (for a review, see Lissek et al., 2008). More recently, this idea has been the target of increased empirical attention, prompted—in part—by meta-analytic results implicating overgeneralization of conditioned fear as one of the more robust conditioning correlates of clinical anxiety generally, and PTSD in particular (Lissek et al., 2005). Specifically, those with PTSD were found overreactive to safety cues sharing stimulus features (e.g., shape, size, duration, spatial location) with the conditioned danger cue, an effect implying heightened transfer, or generalization, of conditioned fear from the learned danger cue to resembling stimuli in PTSD patients. In further pursuit of this finding, our group developed a conditioned fear-generalization paradigm incorporating systematic methods developed and tested in animals (e.g., Armony, Servan-Schreiber, Romanski, Cohen, & LeDoux, 1997) in which fear responses are assessed to both the conditioned danger cue and generalization stimuli (GS) parametrically varying in similarity to the danger cue. As in work with animals, such methods applied to humans yielded *generalization gradients*, or slopes, with the highest level of fear responding to the conditioned danger cue and gradually decreasing levels of fear generalization to GSs of decreasing similarity to the danger cue (Lissek et al., 2008). The steepness of this gradient indexes generalization, with less steep downward gradients indicating more generalization. A more detailed description of this method as well as preliminary results, suggesting less steep gradients of generalization in PTSD versus healthy comparisons, can be found in figure 13.3.

As illustrated in figure 13.3, findings of less steep gradients of responding in PTSD patients are unlikely due purely to overgeneralization of conditioned fear but, rather, seem to reflect the combined influence of (associative) generalization and (nonassociative) sensitization processes. Specifically, generalization is evidenced by the downward slope in PTSD responses as the presented, ring-shaped stimulus increasingly differentiates in size from the conditioned danger cue, and sensitization is evidenced by the degree to which PTSD responding to most classes of ringed stimuli (i.e., GS_3, GS_2, GS_1, & CS-) is elevated relative to healthy comparisons. The possibility, however, exists that elevated responding to most ring sizes in PTSD, seemingly reflecting a

(A) Conditioned and Generalization Stimuli

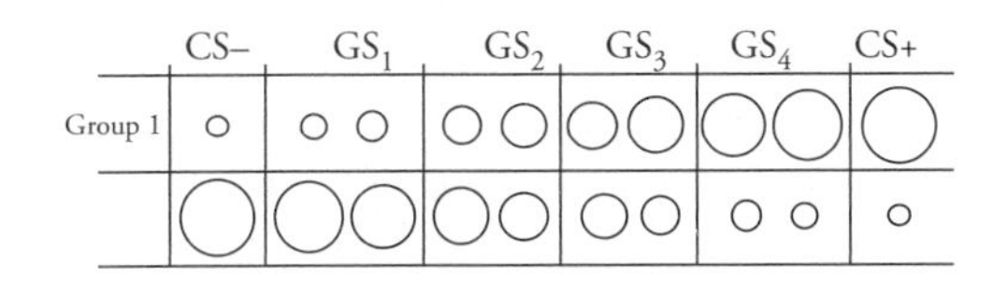

(B) Generalization Results

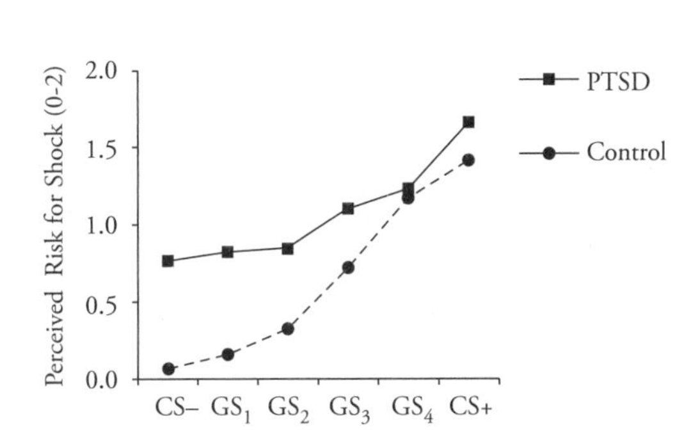

Figure 13.3. **(A)** Conditioned and generalization stimuli included 10 rings of gradually increasing size with extremes serving as the conditioned danger-cue paired with electric shock (CS+) and the conditioned safety-cue unpaired with shock (CS-). For half of participants (Group 1), the largest ring was the CS+ and the smallest was the CS-, and for the other half (Group 2) this was reversed. The eight rings of intermediary size served as generalization stimuli (GSs) and created a continuum-of-similarity from CS+ to CS-. Before analysis, responses to every two intermediaries were collapsed into a single class of stimulus, leaving four classes of generalization stimuli (GS^1, GS^2, GS^3, GS^4). Collapsing was implemented to avoid an unduly large number of trials while maintaining a gradual continuum-of-size across rings. Immediately following presentation of each ring, participants were asked to rate their perceived risk for receiving a shock on a scale of 0–2 (where 0 = *no risk*, 1 = *some risk*, and 2 = *a lot of risk*) to assess the degree to which the conditioned threat value of the CS+ generalized to resembling GSs. **(B)** Generalization results for 13 adult PTSD patients with mixed traumatic histories (sexual abuse [$n = 2$], physical assault [$n = 4$], car accident [$n = 3$], other [$n = 4$]) and 13 age- and sex-matched healthy comparisons indicate less steep gradients of perceived risk in the PTSD group (Group x Stimulus-type interaction, $p = .003$). Though this suggests over-generalization in patients, higher overall risk ratings in PTSD patients ($p = .02$) imply the additional influence of nonassociative sensitization on the shape of response gradients in patients.

sensitization process, actually stems from conditioned responding that has generalized from the ring-shaped danger cue to all ringed stimuli. This possibility is currently being tested with a modified version of this paradigm including assessment of responses to a nonringed, control stimulus. Results reflecting general elevations in responding to all ring sizes in PTSD, in the absence of overresponding to the nonringed control, impute general elevations in PTSD to an overgeneralization process. Clinically, the link between PTSD and overgeneralization prescribes a therapeutic focus on stimulus events resembling features of the traumatic encounter in addition to the actual features of the encounter. Specifically, exposure treatments might focus on reducing fear reactivity to both stimuli associated with the trauma and stimuli approximating those associated with the trauma.

Nonassociative Learning

HABITUATION

The failure-to-habituate theory of PTSD receives support from the well-replicated finding of less steep habituation slopes to repeatedly presented intense acoustic tones in trauma survivors with versus without PTSD when assessing habituation with the skin conductance response (SCR; e.g., Orr, Lasko, & Metzger, 1995; Orr et al., 1997; Shalev, Orr, Peri, Schreiber, & Pitman, 1992): an index of sympathetic arousal. Indeed, a recent meta-analysis identified this SCR habituation effect as the most robust psychophysiological correlate of PTSD (Pole, 2007). These findings link PTSD to an impaired ability to autonomically adapt, or habituate, to intense environmental stimuli, and serve as experimental analogues of the sustained hyper-arousal and hyper-vigilance seen clinically. Although such data do not provide clarification on whether decreased SCR habituation in PTSD precedes or follows the traumatic exposure, a recent prospective study provides support for reduced SCR habituation as a pretraumatic risk factor for PTSD (Pole et al., 2009). These data are further supported by findings in monozygotic twins documenting strong genetic contributions to rates of SCR habituation, thus supporting SCR habituation as a premorbid, dispositional trait (Lykken, Iacono, Haroian, McGue, & Bouchard, 1988). Unlike SCR measures of habituation, the weight of habituation effects assessed by heart-rate (HR) and eyeblink-startle responses to intense tones do not evidence attenuated habituation in PTSD (Pole, 2007). The reason for these differences across measures is unclear, though the presence of habituation effects in PTSD when measured with SCR (an index of sympathetic activation, but not HR, a measure that is sensitive to both sympathetic and parasympathetic influences) suggests that reduced habituation in PTSD is attributable to sympathetic abnormalities.

SENSITIZATION

Perhaps the strongest evidence for greater sensitization of fear-related autonomic responses in PTSD is psychophysiology studies assessing HR responses to repeatedly presented, high-intensity acoustic stimuli, the majority of which document larger average HR responses in PTSD patients (e.g., Carson et al., 2007; Jovanovic, Norrholm, Sakoman, Esterajher, & Kozarić-Kovacić, 2009; Metzger et al., 1999; Orr et al., 1995, 1997, 2003; Shalev et al., 1992, 2000). Several studies have also found stronger SCR to these same acoustic stimuli in PTSD (e.g., Shalev et al., 1992, 1997), though somewhat less robustly than HR elevations (for a review, see Pole, 2007). Because these psychophysiological results were largely found in trauma exposed individuals with versus without PTSD, such findings represent viable support for stronger, trauma-related sensitization of the autonomic nervous system as a nonassociative learning correlate of PTSD. Although it could be argued that this type of increased HR responding is due to risk factors predating the trauma (e.g., genetic predisposition) rather than de novo learning, both behavioral-genetic data (Orr et al., 2003) and prospective assessments (Shalev et al., 2000) characterize this effect as an acquired (e.g., learned) marker of PTSD rather than a preexisting risk factor conferred by heredity or the pretraumatic environment.

In contrast to HR findings, enhanced psychophysiological activation to high-intensity acoustic stimuli is not consistently found in PTSD when operationalized by baseline measures of the startle-blink reflex (Grillon & Baas, 2003). The mixed nature of these results is surprising given that exaggerated startle is a diagnostic feature of PTSD (APA, 2000). Indeed, findings in rodents and humans reliably demonstrate the potentiation of startle magnitudes when an organism is in a state of anxious arousal (Davis & Astrachan, 1978; Grillon et al., 1991), an emotional state clearly axiomatic to the PTSD diagnosis. Importantly, a review of this literature reveals an interesting pattern of results whereby elevated baseline startle magnitudes in PTSD are found in experimental contexts in which stressful procedures ensue (e.g., threat of electric shock), but are not found in contexts relatively free of experimental stress (Grillon & Baas, 2003). This dissociation may best be understood from a kindling perspective on PTSD (e.g., Pitman, Orr, & Shalev, 1993; Post & Weiss, 1998; Rosen & Schulkin, 1998), according to which psychological trauma sensitizes the fear system among those prone to PTSD, and renders the amygdala-based fear circuit hyper-excitable to such future fear-evoking situations as stressful experimental contexts. On its face, this conceptualization seems at odds with findings of null differences in startle potentiation between survivors with and without PTSD to instructed, discrete cues signaling imminent delivery of aversive stimulation (e.g., Grillon, Morgan, Davis, & Southwick, 1998; Grillon et al., 2009). That is, the kindling model would predict greater trauma-related sensitization of the fear circuit in PTSD leaving the circuit hyper-excitable to threat, and culminating in stronger fear-potentiated startle to both contextual and discretely cued signals of danger. This apparent inconsistency may be reconciled within the *strong situation* framework (Lissek, Pine, & Grillon, 2006), whereby *strong* threats constitute cues of potent, imminent, and certain danger that evoke the adaptive fear response among anxiety patients and healthy controls alike; and *weaker* threats constitute cues of less potent, imminent, and certain danger to which those with an anxiety disorder are hyper-reactive.

In our instance, the *situational strength* of discrete threat cues is stronger than that of contextual threat by virtue of the increased imminence and certainty of the discretely cued danger. Thus, discrete threat cues should elicit a fear response regardless of whether or not the individual's fear system has been made excitable through stress sensitization, and regardless of whether or not the individual has PTSD. By contrast, such weak situations as contextual threat may elicit fear only in individuals for whom hyper-excitability of the fear system was achieved through sensitization (e.g., PTSD patients), with all others experiencing only subthreshold levels of fear activation. Increased baseline startle in stressful contexts found in PTSD, therefore, supports a role for sensitization via kindling in the disorder, despite null patient-control differences in startle potentiation to discrete threat cues.

Further findings consistent with the kindling model of PTSD derive from neuroimaging studies tracking the neural correlates of fearful-face processing across those with and without PTSD. Presentations of fearful-facial expressions reliably activate the human amygdala (e.g., Hariri, Mattay, Tessitore, Fera, & Weinberger, 2003; Morris et al., 1996; Phillips et al., 1997), and have become a noninvasive means of probing amygdala function in the intact human brain. If, as held by the kindling model, trauma-evoked fear renders the amygdala-based fear circuit hyper-excitable in survivors who develop PTSD, posttraumatic presentations of fearful faces should produce stronger amygdala reactions in those with PTSD. Several studies confirm this prediction, with fearful faces (vs. happy faces) evoking stronger amygdala reactions in trauma survivors with PTSD compared to those without PTSD (e.g., Rauch et al., 2000; Shin et al., 2005; Felmingham et al., 2010). It should be noted that the increased amygdala reactivity in PTSD may reflect a premorbid risk factor rather than abnormal stress sensitization of this circuit; prospective research on amygdala responses to fearful faces in PTSD is needed to clarify this issue.

The above described experimental support for the sensitization-by-kindling hypothesis of PTSD is well complemented by phenomenological data revealing greater risk for PTSD among survivors with a history of previous traumatic exposures (e.g., Breslau et al., 1999; Brewin, Andrews, & Valentine, 2000; Ozer, Best, Lipsey, & Weiss, 2003). These findings suggest that psychological trauma kindles the fear system and renders it maladaptively hyper-reactive to future trauma.

The final sensitization theory reviewed herein imputes nonassociative learning correlates of PTSD to the uncontrollable nature of the stressor (trauma). This theory of PTSD has received little experimental testing, which is unfortunate given the general view that uncontrollability and unpredictability are critical features of PTSD-inducing events (e.g., Foa et al., 1992; Mineka & Zinbarg, 2006; Volpicelli et al., 1999). This general view stems largely from animal data documenting behavioral consequences of uncontrollable and unpredictable threat that are analogous to many symptoms of PTSD (for a review, see Foa et al., 1992). Nonexperimental evidence for this perspective derives from studies documenting inverse relations between perceptions of control and PTSD symptoms among survivors of sexual victimization (Bolstad & Zinbarg, 1997; Regehr, Cadell, & Jansen, 1999) and criminal assault (Kushner, Riggs, Foa, & Miller, 1993). Extant experimental support comes from initiatives testing the relation between clinical anxiety and threat predictability (e.g., Grillon et al., 2008), which is a characteristic of threat distinct from, but highly related to, controllability. In a recent study conducted by Grillon et al. (2009), PTSD patients displayed normative levels of fear-potentiated startle to threat cues signaling imminent aversive noises (e.g., predictable threat), but elevated fear-potentiated startle during a sustained period in which aversive noises were delivered at random (i.e., unpredictable threat). These findings demonstrate a heightened reactivity to threat unpredictability in PTSD, and provide a degree of support for the hypothesis that uncontrollable/unpredictable threat differentially sensitizes the fear system of those with versus without PTSD.

Toward an Integrated Account of Learning Findings in PTSD

Studies reviewed herein report a variety of results across a multiplicity of stress-related learning mechanisms with proposed relevance to PTSD. Although no unified conceptualization of these results is readily obvious, the social psychological concept of the *strong situation* may provide an interpretive framework with which to deduce the beginnings of a unified account. As described previously, the strong threat situation represents an experimental condition that unambiguously signals aversive events of high certainty and imminence, and evokes the adaptive fear response among anxiety patients and healthy controls alike. *Weakening* the experimental situation by reducing the temporal proximity of the stressor, decreasing the predictive value of the danger cue, and/or increasing the ambiguity of the threat information are predicted to facilitate the emergence of patient-control differences in anxious reactivity.

In our context, the discrete conditioned danger cue is something of a strong situation by virtue of its relatively unambiguous signaling of certain and imminent danger. Contextual threat, unpredictable threat, and cues resembling threat cues (to which fear generalizes) may be thought to constitute weaker threats. That is, compared to discrete conditioned danger cues, contextual threat communicates danger of less imminence; unpredictable threat signals danger of less certainty; and cues approximating the likeness of the danger cue constitute threats of greater ambiguity. Consistent with predictions of the strong situation framework, PTSD-control differences in anxious reactivity have not been reliably found to the *stronger* discrete conditioned danger cue and seem to emerge under *weaker* situations of contextual threat (e.g., Grillon & Baas, 2003), unpredictable threat (Grillon et al., 2009), and perceptually degraded danger cues (Lissek et al., 2010). Although this perspective does not thoroughly account for the rich variety of findings in the literature, it may help set the stage for future, more comprehensive, integrative explanations.

Research Limitations and Future Directions

The past two decades have seen substantial increases in lab-based testing of associative and nonassociative learning abnormalities in PTSD. Although tests of extinction failure in PTSD are well represented in this recent literature, the variety of other promising learning theories of PTSD detailed herein have, to date, have received relatively little empirical attention. Specifically, tests of learning models predicting PTSD abnormalities in contextual anxiety, conditioned generalization, failure to inhibit fear to safety cues, and instrumental avoidance are in need of further testing.

In addition to this problem of investigative scope, existing studies often identify PTSD–related learning abnormalities that are not unambiguously attributable to a single learning mechanism. For example, overresponding to the conditioned safety cue (CS-) repeatedly found in PTSD patients could reflect overresponding to all novel cues (i.e., sensitization), heightened transfer of responding to cues resembling the CS+ (overgeneralization), an impaired ability to accurately learn the link between the CS+ and US (associative learning deficits), or failure to inhibit fear to safety cues. Additionally, resistance to extinguish fear could reflect overly strong excitation learning to the CS+ at acquisition or too little learned fear inhibition to the CS+ at extinction. Some of these interpretive problems can be addressed by way of improved experimental design. For example, further tests of overreactivity to the CS- in PTSD would benefit from use of generalization methods in which fear responding is assessed to CS- that are perceptually similar and dissimilar to the CS+. That is, overresponding in PTSD patients to perceptually similar but not dissimilar CS- reflects an overgeneralization process rather than a general overresponding to either all CS- (as predicted by the failure-to-inhibit hypothesis) or all novel stimuli (as predicted by the sensitization hypothesis).

Other efforts to link specific learning abnormalities to PTSD may benefit from brain imaging techniques. For example, the contributions of fear excitation versus fear inhibition processes toward extinction abnormalities in PTSD may be dissociated by the specific brain correlates of these abnormalities, with perturbed activation in areas attributed to fear excitation (e.g., amygdala, anterior insula) implicating excitatory abnormalities and perturbations in brain areas associated with fear inhibition (e.g., ventromedial prefrontal cortex) suggestive of inhibitory abnormalities. This approach has begun to yield fruit, with brain imaging results attributing deficiencies in extinction recall to perturbations in circuitry associated with fear inhibition (Milad et al., 2009).

An additional limitation of this literature that besets much of experimental psychopathology is whether abnormalities in patients generated by lab-based testing reflect premorbid risk factors or ongoing disease processes. The dissociation of the former from the latter is facilitated by prospective data relating premorbid to postmorbid findings, as well as behavioral genetic methods designed to disentangle the influence of genetic risk from that of environment, on onset and maintenance of the disorder. The available data of this type in the PTSD literature on learning abnormalities characterizes effects of poor recall of extinction and oversensitization as acquired markers of PTSD (Milad et al., 2008; Orr et al., 2003; Shalev et al., 2000), and enhanced contextual anxiety and deficient habituation as pretrauma risk factors for PTSD (Pole et al., 2009). Nevertheless, more data are needed before conclusions can be drawn, with confidence, regarding the value of a given learning abnormality as a vulnerability factor for, versus a diagnostic marker of, PTSD.

FUTURE DIRECTIONS

One fortuitous consequence of the cross-species relevance of associative and nonassociative learning processes implicated in the etiology of PTSD is the availability of rich neuroscience findings in animals from which to generate and test psychobiological accounts of PTSD. For example, data in animals suggest that sensitization-like PTSD symptoms in the hyper-arousal cluster are, in part, instantiated by the activation of a subset of serotonergic neurons in the dorsal raphe nucleus (DRN) projecting to the basolateral amygdala during uncontrollable stress (for a review, see Maier & Watkins, 2005). Additionally, fear-conditioning research in animals employing lesion and single-cell recording methods have linked extinction and its retention to the vmPFC (e.g., Milad & Quirk, 2002; Quirk, Russo, Barron, & Lebron, 2000), which is a brain region strongly implicated in fear reduction through inhibitory influences on the amygdala (Quirk et al., 2003; Rosenkranz et al., 2003). These animal findings have inspired a fruitful line of human work testing the medial prefrontal cortex as a neural locus of extinction abnormalities in PTSD (Milad et al., 2009). Future studies testing learning models of

PTSD should continue to test neural hypotheses informed by the animal literature. For example, animal findings suggest the importance of testing the role of the bed-nucleus-of-the-stria-terminalis, hippocampus, and vmPFC in putative, PTSD abnormalities in contextual anxiety, overgeneralization of conditioned fear, and failure to inhibit fear, respectively. Additionally, animal data have important implications for up and down regulation of these learning processes and should be brought to bear by efforts to develop novel treatments for PTSD.

In addition to the importance of future efforts to neurally characterize learning correlates of PTSD, genetic work in this area is needed. Although historically, learning theories posit stimulus-response accounts of behavior that draw exclusively on environmental causes of behavior (e.g., Skinner, 1953), the emergence of PTSD among some survivors of comparable traumas is evidence of gene by environment interactions. As such, modern learning theories of PTSD must account for the genetic liabilities that dispose some trauma survivors to maladaptive learning following traumatic encounters. Though this effort is under way (for a review see Amstadter, Nugent, & Koenen, 2009), more work of this kind is needed.

Concluding Thoughts

A rich array of learning-based theories of PTSD has emerged during the century following Watson and Rayner's seminal experiment on "Little Albert" (1920). Such learning models have offered mechanized accounts of PTSD based on basic learning processes that are readily probed and objectively quantified in the laboratory environment. It is thus surprising that empirical testing of these models has occurred primarily in the most recent two decades. During this time, evidence for a variety of PTSD-related abnormalities in basic learning processes have been found, the most promising of which include slowed habituation, heightened sensitization, failure to retain extinction learning, overgeneralization of conditioned fear, heightened contextual anxiety, and deficits inhibiting fear to safety cues. Importantly, the cross-species relevance of such learning processes brings to bear a wealth of animal data from which to infer the neural basis of these PTSD-related abnormalities. This translational bridge between animal and PTSD findings promises to contribute essentially to the field's dedicated efforts toward future brain-based diagnostics and neurally targeted interventions for PTSD.

Note

This work was supported by the Intramural Research Program of the National Institute of Mental Health.

1. Full kindling produces seizures in the activated tissue while partial kindling is usually limited to only two stimulations and produces no behavioral signs of seizure.

References

Adamec, R. E., & Morgan, H. D. (1994). The effect of kindling of different nuclei in the left and right amygdala on anxiety in the rat. *Physiology and Behavior, 55*, 1–12.

American Psychiatric Association. (2000). *Diagnostic and statistical manual of mental disorders* (4th ed., text rev.). Washington, DC: Author.

Amstadter, A. B., Nugent, N. R., & Koenen, K. C. (2009). Genetics of PTSD: Fear Conditioning as a Model for Future Research. *Psychiatric Annals, 39*, 358–367.

Armony, J. L., Servan-Schreiber, D., Romanski, L. M., Cohen, J. D., & LeDoux, J. E. (1997). Stimulus generalization of fear responses: Effects of auditory cortex lesions in a computational model and in rats. *Cerebral Cortex, 7*, 157–165.

Blechert, J., Michael, T., Vriends, N., Margraf, J., & Wilhelm, F. H. (2007). Fear conditioning in posttraumatic stress disorder: Evidence for delayed extinction of autonomic, experiential, and behavioural responses. *Behaviour Research and Therapy, 45*, 2019–2033.

Bolstad, B., & Zinbarg, R. (1997). Sexual victimization, generalized perception of control, and posttraumatic stress disorder symptom severity. *Journal of Anxiety Disorders, 11*, 523–540.

Bouton, M. E. (2004). Context and behavioral processes in extinction. *Learning and Memory, 11*, 485–494.

Bouton, M. E., & Swartzentruber, D. (1991). Sources of relapse after extinction in Pavlovian and instrumental learning. *Clinical Psychology Review, 11*(2), 123–140.

Bremner, J. D., Southwick, S. M., Johnson, D. R., Yehuda, R., & Charney, D. S. (1993). Childhood physical abuse and combat-related posttraumatic stress disorder in Vietnam veterans. *American Journal of Psychiatry, 150*, 235–239.

Bremner, J. D., Staib, L. H., Kaloupek, D., Southwick, S. M., Soufer, R., & Charney, D. S. (1999). Neural correlates of exposure to traumatic pictures and sound in Vietnam combat veterans with and without posttraumatic stress disorder: A positron emission tomography study. *Biological Psychiatry, 45*, 806–816.

Bremner, J. D., Vermetten, E., Schmahl, C., Vaccarino, V., Vythilingam, M., Afzal, N., et al. (2005). Positron emission tomographic imaging of neural correlates of a fear acquisition and extinction paradigm in women with childhood sexual-abuse-related post-traumatic stress disorder. *Psychological Medicine, 35*, 791–806.

Breslau, N., Chilcoat, H. D., Kessler, R. C., & Davis, G. C. (1999). Previous exposure to trauma and PTSD effects of subsequent trauma: Results from the Detroit Area Survey of Trauma. *American Journal of Psychiatry, 156*, 902–907.

Brewin, C. R., Andrews, B., & Valentine, J. D. (2000). Meta-analysis of risk factors for posttraumatic stress disorder in trauma-exposed adults. *Journal of Consulting and Clinical Psychology, 68*, 748–766.

Burriss, L., Ayers, E., Ginsberg, J., & Powell, D. A. (2008). Learning and memory impairment in PTSD: Relationship to depression. *Depression and Anxiety, 25*, 149–157.

Burriss, L., Ayers, E., & Powell, D. A. (2007). Combat veterans show normal discrimination during differential trace eyeblink conditioning, but increased responsivity to the conditioned and unconditioned stimulus. *Journal of Psychiatric Research, 41*, 785–794.

Carson, M. A., Metzger, L. J., Lasko, N. B., Paulus, L. A., Morse, A. E., Pitman, R. K., & Orr, S. P. (2007). Physiologic reactivity to startling tones in female Vietnam nurse veterans with PTSD. *Journal of Traumatic Stress, 20*, 657–666.

Davidson, J. R. T., Hughes, D., & Blazer, D. G. (1991). Posttraumatic stress disorder in the community: An epidemiological study. *Psychological Medicine, 21*, 713–721.

Davis, M. (1989). Sensitization of the acoustic startle reflex by footshock. *Behavorial. Neuroscience, 103*, 495–503.

Davis, M., & Astrachan, D. I. (1978). Conditioned fear and startle magnitude: Effects of different footshock or backshock intensities used in training. *Journal of Experimental Psychology: Animal Behavior Processes, 4*, 95–103

Davis, M., Falls, W. A., & Gewirtz, J. (2000). Neural systems involved in fear inhibition: Extinction and conditioned inhibition. In M. Myslobodsky & I. Weiner (Eds.), *Contemporary issues in modeling psychopathology* (pp. 113–142). Boston: Kluwer Academic.

Desiderato, O., & Newman, A. (1971). Conditioned suppression produced in rats by tones paired with escapable or inescapable shock. *Journal of Comparative Physiology and Psychology, 77*, 427–443.

Eysenck, H. J. (1976). The learning theory model of neurosis: A new approach. *Behaviour Research and Therapy, 14*, 251–267.

Eysenck, H. J. (1979). The conditioning model of neurosis. *Behavioral and Brain Sciences, 2*, 155–199.

Eysenck, H. J., & Rachman, S. J. (1965). *Causes and cures of neurosis*. London: Routledge & Kegan Paul.

Felmingham, K., Williams, L. M., Kemp, A. H., Liddell, B., Falconer, E., Peduto, A., et al. (2010). Neural responses to masked fear faces: Sex differences and trauma exposure in posttraumatic stress disorder. *Journal of Abnormal Psychology, 119*, 241–247.

Foa, E. B., Zinbarg, R., and Rothbaum, B. O. (1992). Uncontrollability and unpredictability in post-traumatic stress disorder: An animal model, *Psychological Bulletin, 112*, 218–238.

Geuze, E., Vermetten, E., Ruf, M., de Kloet, C. S., & Westenberg, H. G. (2008). Neural correlates of associative learning and memory in veterans with posttraumatic stress disorder. *Journal of Psychiatriac Research, 42*, 659–669.

Gloor, P. (1978). *Inputs and outputs of the amygdala: What the amygdala is trying to tell the rest of the brain*. New York: Plenum Press.

Grillon, C. (2002). Associative learning deficits increase symptoms of anxiety in humans. *Biological Psychiatry, 51*, 851–858.

Grillon, C., Ameli, R., Woods, S. W., Merikangas, K., & Davis, M. (1991). Fear-potentiated startle in humans: Effects of anticipatory anxiety on the acoustic blink reflex. *Psychophysiology, 28*, 588–595.

Grillon, C., & Baas, J. (2003). A review of the modulation of the startle reflex by affective states and its application in psychiatry. *Clinical Neurophysiology, 114*, 1557–1579.

Grillon, C., Baas, J. P., Lissek, S., Smith, K., & Milstein, J. (2004). Anxious responses to predictable and unpredictable aversive events. *Behavioral Neuroscience, 118*, 916–924.

Grillon, C., Lissek, S., Rabin, S., McDowell, D., Dvir, S., & Pine, D. S. (2008). Increased anxiety during anticipation of unpredictable but not predictable aversive stimuli as a psychophysiologic marker of panic disorder. *American Journal of Psychiatry, 165*, 898–904.

Grillon, C., & Morgan, C. A., III (1999). Fear-potentiated startle conditioning to explicit and contextual cues in Gulf War veterans with posttraumatic stress disorder. *Journal of Abnormal Psychology, 108*, 134–142.

Grillon, C., Morgan, C. A., Davis, M., and Southwick, S. M. (1998). Effects of experimental context and explicit threat cues on acoustic startle in Vietnam veterans with post-traumatic stress disorder, *Biological Psychiatry, 44*, 1027–1036.

Grillon, C., Pine, D. S., Lissek, S., Rabin, S., Bonne, O., & Vythilingam, M. (2009). Increased anxiety during anticipation of unpredictable aversive stimuli in posttraumatic stress disorder but not in generalized anxiety disorder. *Biological Psychiatry, 66*, 47–53.

Groves, P. M., & Thompson, R. F. (1970). Habituation: A dual process theory. *Psychological Review, 77*, 419–450.

Hariri, A. R., Mattay, V. S., Tessitore, A., Fera, F., & Weinberger, D. R. (2003). Neocortical modulation of the amygdala response to fearful stimuli, *Biological. Psychiatry, 53*, 494–501.

Job, R. F., & Barnes, B. W. (1995). Stress and consumption: Inescapable shock, neophobia, and quinine finickiness in rats. *Behavioral Neuroscience, 109*, 106–116.

Jovanovic, T., & Ressler, K. J. (2010). How the neurocircuitry and genetics of fear inhibition may inform our understanding of PTSD. *American Journal of Psychiatry, 167*, 648–662.

Jovanovic. T., Norrholm, S.D., Blanding, N.Q., Davis, M., Duncan, E., Bradley, B., et al. (2010). Impaired fear inhibition is a biomarker of PTSD but not depression. *Depression and Anxiety, 27*, 244–251.

Jovanovic, T., Norrholm, S. D., Sakoman, A. J., Esterajher, S., & Kozarić-Kovačić, D. (2009). Altered resting psychophysiology and startle response in Croatian combat veterans with PTSD. *International Journal of Psychophysiology, 71*, 264–268.

Kushner, M. G., Riggs, D. S., Foa, E. B., & Miller, S. M. (1993). Perceived controllability and the development of posttraumatic stress disorder (PTSD) in crime victims. *Behaviour Research and Therapy, 31*, 1105–110.

Lissek, S., Biggs, A. L., Rabin, S., Cornwell, B. R., Alvarez, R. P., Pine, D. S., & Grillon, C. (2008). Generalization of conditioned fear-potentiated startle in humans: Experimental validation and clinical relevance. *Behaviour Research and Therapy, 46*, 678–687.

Lissek, S., Pine, D. S., & Grillon, C. (2006). The *strong situation*: A potential impediment to studying the psychobiology and pharmacology of anxiety disorders. *Biological Psychology, 72*, 265–270.

Lissek, S., Powers, A. S., McClure, E. B., Phelps, E. A., Woldehawariat, G., Grillon, C., & Pine, D. S. (2005). Classical fear-conditioning in the anxiety disorders: A meta-analysis. *Behaviour Research and Therapy, 43*, 1391–1424.

Lissek, S., Rabin, S. J., Heller, R. E., Luckenbaugh, D., Geraci, M., Pine, D. S., & Grillon, C. (2010). Overgeneralization of conditioned fear as a pathogenic marker of panic disorder. *American Journal of Psychiatry, 167*, 47–55.

Lykken, D. T., Iacono, W. G., Haroian, K., McGue, M., & Bouchard, T. J. (1988). Habituation of the skin conductance responses to strong stimuli: A twin study. *Psychophysiology, 25*, 4–15.

Maier, S. F., & Watkins, L. R. (1998). Stressor controllability, anxiety, and serotonin. *Cognitive Therapy an Research, 22,* 595–613.
Maier, S. F., & Watkins, L. R. (2005). Stressor controllability and learned helplessness: The roles of the dorsal raphe nucleus, serotonin, and corticotropin-releasing factor. *Neuroscience and Biobehavoral Reviews, 29,* 829–841.
Marks, I., & Tobena, A. (1990). Learning and unlearning fear: A clinical and evolutionary perspective. *Neuroscience and Biobehavioral Reviews, 14,* 365–384.
Marx, B. P., and Sloan, D. M. (2005). Peritraumatic dissociation and experiential avoidance as predictors of posttraumatic stress symptomatology. *Behaviour Research and Therapy, 43,* 569–583.
Metzger, L. J., Orr, S. P., Berry, N. J., Ahern, C. E., Lasko, N. B., & Pitman, R. K. (1999). Physiologic reactivity to startling tones in women with PTSD. *Journal of Abnormal Psychology, 108,* 347–352.
Milad, M. R., Orr, S. P., Lasko, N. B., Chang, Y., Rauch, S. L., & Pitman, R. K. (2008). Presence and acquired origin of reduced recall for fear extinction in PTSD: Results of a twin study. *Journal of Psychiatric Research, 42,* 515–520.
Milad, M. R., Pitman, R. K., Ellis, C. B., Gold, A. L., Shin, L. M., Lasko, N. B., et al. (2009). Neurobiological basis of failure to recall extinction memory in posttraumatic stress disorder. *Biological Psychiatry, 66,* 1075–1082.
Milad, M. R., & Quirk, G. J. (2002). Neurons in medial prefrontal cortex signal memory for fear extinction. *Nature, 420,* 70–74.
Miller, N. E. (1948). Studies of fear as a learnable drive: I. Fear as motivation and fear reduction as reinforcement in the learning of new responses. *Journal of Experimental Psychology, 38,* 89–101.
Mineka, S., & Zinbarg, R. (2006). A contemporary learning theory perspective on the etiology of anxiety disorders: It's not what you thought it was. *American Psychologist, 61,* 10–26.
Minor, T. R. (1990). Conditioned fear and neophobia following inescapable shock. *Animal Learning and Behavior, 18,* 222–226.
Morris, J. S., Frith, C. D., Perrett, D. I., Rowland, D., Young, A. W., Calder, A. J., et al. (1996). A differential neural response in the human amygdala to fearful and happy facial expressions. *Nature, 383,* 812–815.
Mowrer, O. H. (1947). On the dual nature of learning: A reinterpretation of "conditioning" and "problem solving." *Harvard Educational Review, 17,* 102–148.
Mowrer, O. H. (1960). *Learning theory and behavior.* New York: John Wiley.
Orr, S. P., Lasko, N. B., Shalev, A. Y., Pitman, R. K. (1995). Physiologic responses to loud tones in Vietnam veterans with posttraumatic stress disorder. *Journal of Abnormal Psychology, 104,* 75–82.
Orr, S. P., Metzger, L. J., Lasko, N. B., Macklin, M. L., Hu, F. B., Shalev, A.Y., et al. (2003). Physiologic responses to sudden loud tones in monozygotic twins discordant for combat exposure: Association with posttraumatic stress disorder. *Archives of General Psychiatry, 60,* 283–288.
Orr, S. P., Metzger, L. J., Lasko, N. B., Macklin, M. L., Peri, T., & Pitman, R. K. (2000). De novo conditioning in trauma-exposed individuals with and without posttraumatic stress disorder. *Journal of Abnormal Psychology, 109,* 290–298.
Orr, S. P., Milad, M. R., Metzger, L. J., Lasko, N. B., Gilbertson, M. W., Pitman, R. K. (2006). Effects of beta blockade, PTSD diagnosis, and explicit threat on the extinction and retention of an aversively conditioned response. *Biological Psychology, 73,* 262–271.
Orr, S. P., Solomon, Z., Peri, T., Pitman, R. K., Shalev, A. Y. (1997). Physiologic responses to loud tones in Israeli veterans of the 1973 Yom Kippur War. *Biological Psychiatry, 41,* 319–326.
Ozer, E., Best, S., Lipsey, T., & Weiss, D. (2003). Predictors of posttraumatic stress disorder and symptoms in adults: A meta-analysis. *Psychological Bulletin, 129,* 52–73.
Pavlov, I. (1927). *Conditioned reflexes.* London: Oxford University Press.
Peri, T., Ben Shakhar, G., Orr, S. P., & Shalev, A. Y. (2000) Psychophysiologic assessment of aversive conditioning in postraumatic stress disorder. *Biological Psychiatry, 47,* 512–519.
Phillips, M. L., Young, A. W., Senior, C., Brammer, M., Andrew, C., Calder, A. J., et al. (1997). A specific neural substrate for perceiving facial expressions of disgust. *Nature, 389,* 495–498.
Pissiota, A., Frans, O., Michelgard, A., Appel, L., Langstrom, B., Flaten, M. A., et al. (2003). Amygdala and anterior cingulate cortex activation during affective startle modulation: A PET study of fear. *European Journal of Neuroscience, 18,* 1325–1331.
Pittman, R. K., Orr, S. P., & Shalev, A. Y. (1993). Once bitten, twice shy: Beyond the conditioning model of PTSD. *Biological Psychiatry, 44,* 193–206.
Pole, N. (2007). The psychophysiology of posttraumatic stress disorder: A meta-analysis. *Psychological Bulletin, 133,* 725–746.
Pole, N., Neylan, T. C., Otte, C., Henn-Hasse, C., Metzler, T. J., & Marmar, C. R. (2009). Prospective prediction of posttraumatic stress disorder symptoms using fear potentiated auditory startle responses. *Biological Psychiatry, 65,* 235–240.
Post, R. M., & Weiss, S. R. B. (1998). Sensitization and kindling phenomena in mood, anxiety, and obsessive–compulsive disorders: The role of serotonergic mechanisms in illness progression. *Biological Psychiatry, 44,* 193–206.
Quirk, G. J., Likhtik, E., Pelletier, J. G., & Pare, D. (2003). Stimulation of medial prefrontal cortex decreases the responsiveness of central amygdala output neurons. *Journal of Neuroscience, 23,* 8800–8807.
Quirk, G. J., Russo, G. K., Barron, J. L., & Lebron, K. (2000). The role of ventromedial prefrontal cortex in the recovery of extinguished fear. *Journal of Neuroscience, 20,* 6225–6231.
Rauch, S. L., Whalen, P. J., Shin, L. M., McInerney, S. C., Macklin, M. L., Lasko, N. B., et al. (2000). Exaggerated amygdala response to masked facial stimuli in posttraumatic stress disorder: A functional MRI study, *Biological Psychiatry, 47,* 769–776.
Regehr, C., Cadell, S., & Jansen, K. (1999). Perceptions of control and long-term recovery from rape. *American Journal of Orthopsychiatry, 69,* 110–115.
Richardson, R., & Elsayed, H. (1998). Shock sensitization of startle in rats: The role of contextual conditioning. *Behavioral Neuroscience, 112,* 1136–1141.
Rosen, J. B., Hamerman, E., Sitcoske, M., Glowa, J. R., & Schulkin, J. (1996). Hyperexcitability: Exaggerated

fear-potentiated startle produced by partial amygdala kindling. *Behavioral Neuroscience, 110*, 43–50.

Rosen, J. B., & Schulkin, J. (1998). From normal fear to pathological anxiety. *Psychological Review, 105*, 325–350.

Rosenkranz, J. A., Moore, H., & Grace, A. A. (2003). The prefrontal cortex regulates lateral amygdala neuronal plasticity and responses to previously conditioned stimuli. *Journal of Neuroscience, 23*, 11054–11064.

Rothbaum, B. A., & Foa, E. B. (1993). Subtypes of posttraumatic stress disorder and duration of symptoms. In J. R. Davidson & E. B. Foa (Eds.), *Posttraumatic stress disorder: DSM-IV and beyond.* (pp. 23–35). Washington, DC: American Psychiatric Press.

Seligman M. E. P., & Binik Y. M. (1977). The safety signal hypothesis. In H. Davis & H. M. B. Hurwitz (Eds.) *Operant-Pavlovian interactions* (pp. 165–187). New York: Hillsdale.

Shalev, A. Y., Orr, S. P., Peri, T., Schreiber, S., & Pitman, R. K. (1992). Physiologic responses to loud tones in Israeli patients with posttraumatic stress disorder. *Archives of General Psychiatry, 49*, 870–875.

Shalev, A. Y., Peri, T., Brandes, D., Freedman, S., Orr, S. P., Pitman, R. K. (2000). Auditory startle response in trauma survivors with posttraumatic stress disorder: A prospective study. *American Journal of Psychiatry, 157*, 255–261.

Shalev, A. Y., Peri, T., Orr, S. P., Bonne, O., Pitman, R. K. (1997). Auditory startle responses in help-seeking trauma survivors. *Psychiatry Research, 69*, 1–7.

Shin, L. M., , Wright, C. I., Cannistraro, P. A., Wedig, M. M., McMullin, K., Martis, B., et al. (2005). A functional magnetic resonance imaging study of amygdala and medial prefrontal cortex responses to overtly presented fearful faces in posttraumatic stress disorder, *Archives of General Psychiatry, 62*, 273–281.

Shin, L. M., McNally, R. J., Kosslyn, S. M., Thompson, W. L., Rauch, S. L., Alpert, N. M., et al. (1999). Regional cerebral blood flow during script-driven imagery in childhood sexual abuse-related PTSD: A PET investigation. *American Journal of Psychiatry, 156*, 575–584.

Short, K. R., & Maier, S. F. (1993). Stressor controllability, social interaction, and benzodiazepine systems. *Pharmacology, Biochemistry and Behavior, 45*, 1–9.

Simpson, T., Jakupcak, M., & Luterek, J. A (2006). Fear and avoidance of internal experiences among patients with substance use disorders and PTSD: The centrality of anxiety sensitivity. *Journal of Traumatic Stress, 19*, 481–491.

Skinner, B. F. (1953). *Science and human behavior*. New York: Macmillan.

Volpicelli, J., Balaraman, G., Hahn, J., Wallace, H., & Bux, D. (1999). The role of uncontrollable trauma in the development of PTSD and alcohol addiction. *Alcohol Research & Health, 23*, 256–262.

Watson, J. B., & Rayner, R. (1920). Conditioned emotional reactions. *Journal of Experimental Psychology, 3*, 1–14.

Werner, N. S., Meindl, T., Engel, R. R., Rosner, R., Riedel, M., Reiser, M., et al. (2009). Hippocampal function during associative learning in patients with posttraumatic stress disorder. *Journal of Psychiatric Research, 43*, 309–318.

Wessa, M., & Flor, H. (2007). Failure of extinction of fear responses in posttraumatic stress disorder: Evidence from second-order conditioning. *American Journal of Psychiatry, 164*, 1684–1692.

Williams, J. L., & Groux, M. L. (1993). Exposure to various stressors alters preferences for natural odors in rats *(Rattus norvegicus). Journal of Comparative Psychology, 107*, 39–47.

Williams, L. M., Kemp, A. H., Felmingham, K., Barton, M., Olivieri, G., Peduto, A., et al. (2006). Trauma modulates amygdala and medial prefrontal responses to consciously attended fear. *NeuroImage, 29*, 347–357.

CHAPTER

14 Information Processing in Posttraumatic Stress Disorder

Anke Ehlers, Thomas Ehring, *and* Birgit Kleim

Abstract

The chapter reviews the contribution of information processing models to understanding the development and maintenance of posttraumatic stress disorder. Individual differences in cognitive processing during the trauma and basic memory mechanism, such as priming and associative learning, may help explain why people with PTSD involuntarily re-experience parts of the trauma in a wide range of situations. Individual differences in how people remember traumatic events may influence the likelihood of developing PTSD. Attentional bias to trauma-related cues and threatening interpretations of the trauma or its aftermath help explain why people with PTSD have many symptoms of anxiety even though the trauma is over. Cognitive strategies people use to deal with memories of the trauma, such as effortful suppression of trauma memories and rumination, help explain why some develop chronic PTSD whereas many recover from trauma. Finally, there may be cognitive vulnerability factors that increase the probability of developing PTSD in response to trauma. Directions for future research are outlined.

Key Words: Posttraumatic stress disorder, cognition, selective attention, memory, priming, appraisal, conditioning, rumination, thought suppression

Several of the symptoms of posttraumatic stress disorder (PTSD) defined in the *Diagnostic and Statistical Manual of Mental Disorders* (*DSM-IV*; American Psychiatric Association [APA], 1994) point to problems in information processing. These include amnesia for an important part of the traumatic event, involuntary re-experiencing of aspects of the trauma, concentration problems, chronic hyper-vigilance, and cognitive avoidance of trauma reminders.

The interest in information processing during and after trauma and its relation to psychopathology has a long tradition in clinical psychology and psychiatry. For example, Sigmund Freud saw memories of trauma at the core of neurosis, and Pierre Janet highlighted a lack of an integrated narrative of the traumatic experience in posttrauma psychopathology (see Gersons & Carlier, 1992; van der Kolk, Weisaeth, & van der Hart, 1996). Horowitz (1986) presented an early information processing account of posttrauma adaptation. He proposed that trauma leads to information overload and the need to subsequently process trauma-related information. This information is thought to remain in active memory and result in re-experiencing symptoms, until it is fully processed and reconciled with the individual's existing cognitive schemas.

Contemporary clinical researchers have built on advances in learning theory and experimental cognitive science to explain the symptoms of PTSD. In the following, we will review how information processing may help explain how PTSD develops and how its symptoms are maintained. In particular, we are going to address contributions of information processing theories and empirical findings to answering the following questions:

1. Why do people with PTSD involuntarily re-experience parts of the trauma in a wide range of situations?
2. How do people remember traumatic events, and how does this influence the likelihood of developing PTSD?
3. Why do people with PTSD have many symptoms of anxiety even though the trauma is over?
4. Why do some people recover from trauma while others develop chronic PTSD?
5. What makes people vulnerable to developing PTSD?

1. Information Processing and Re-experiencing

One of the core questions that information processing theories aim to answer is why people with PTSD keep re-experiencing parts of their traumatic experience long after the trauma is over. Re-experiencing includes intrusive memories, flashbacks, nightmares, and strong emotional and physiological responses to trauma reminders. Intrusive memories commonly take the form of vivid and distressing sensory impressions from the trauma that suddenly pop into one's mind and appear to come 'out of the blue' (Hackmann, Ehlers, Speckens & Clark, 2004; Michael, Ehlers, Halligan, & Clark, 2005). For example, a motor vehicle accident (MVA) survivor may re-experience the sight of headlights coming toward him, just like before the crash, or an assault survivor may re-experience a glimpse of the assailant standing before him with a knife, just like during the assault. The content of the intrusive memories appears to happen in the 'here and now' (e.g., Michael, Ehlers, Halligan, et al., 2005) and is accompanied by the same emotions as the individual experienced during the trauma (Foa & Rothbaum, 1998). Most dramatically, in a posttraumatic flashback people may lose all contact with current reality and respond as if the trauma were happening at that moment (see Ehlers, Hackmann & Michael, 2004, for examples).

Clinical observations suggest that a wide range of stimuli trigger re-experiencing (e.g., Brewin, Dalgleish, & Joseph, 1996; Foa, Steketee, & Rothbaum, 1989). Interview and questionnaire studies found that triggers of re-experiencing often are perceptually similar to the intrusive content or have *sensory* similarities with stimuli that signaled the onset of these moments (e.g., similar color, shape, smell, or body sensation; Ehlers et al., 2002; Michael, Ehlers, Halligan, et al., 2005). A key question is how and why re-experiencing is so easily triggered in PTSD.

Theoretical Explanations of Re-experiencing

Theories drawing on learning theory and experimental cognitive science offer possible explanations of re-experiencing and its triggers. We will give a few examples of these theories in this section. In the following sections, we discuss several hypotheses that can be derived from these and related information processing models and review the empirical evidence available so far.

Note that most information processing theories of PTSD do not see re-experiencing as a sign of psychopathology per se. Several authors have noted that re-experiencing is common in the immediate aftermath of the trauma and may initially indicate adaptive cognitive processing (e.g., Creamer, Burgess, & Pattison, 1992; Ehlers & Steil, 1995; Horowitz, 1986). Thus, the emphasis of most information theories is on explaining why re-experiencing *persists* in PTSD.

Building on Lang's (1977) associative network model of emotion, Foa et al. (1989) proposed that the trauma is represented as a fear structure in memory (a program to escape danger) that contains stimulus (e.g., stimuli associated with the traumatic event such as features of the perpetrator), response (e.g., fear, physiological reactions, and avoidance), and meaning elements (e.g., dangerous). The authors suggested that the fear memory structure in PTSD is characterized by (1) particularly strong response elements, (2) unrealistic associations including benign stimuli and danger- or fear-related stimulus, response and meaning elements, and (3) an especially large number of stimulus elements. Re-experiencing occurs through spreading activation in this large associative network if one of its components is activated. This leads to information about the trauma entering consciousness (intrusive memories) and the strong response elements of the structure being activated (fear, hyper-arousal, avoidance). The triggers can include stimuli that are objectively safe. Other associative fear network models of PTSD have been proposed by Chemtob, Roitblat, Hamada, Carlson, and Twentyman (1988) and Creamer et al. (1992). Common to these approaches is the idea that re-experiencing and fear result from easy or chronic activation of an associative network laid down during the trauma.

Brewin et al. (1996) proposed that traumatic events are represented in two parallel memory systems named the *situationally accessible memory system* (containing detailed sensory information that can only be accessed involuntarily) and the *verbally accessible memory system* (containing abstract records of the experience that can be deliberately retrieved). Re-experiencing is thought to result if some aspects of the trauma are only encoded into the situationally accessible memory system, so that they cannot be accessed voluntarily but are being triggered by situational cues. Brewin, Gregory, Lipton, and Burgess (2010) presented an updated version of this model that links its central concepts to cognitive neuroscience. The term *verbally accessible memories* has been replaced by *contextual memory representations* (abstract, contextually bound representations) that are supported by the medial temporal lobe system for declarative memory. The concept of situationally accessible memories has been replaced by sensation-based memory representations that are supported by early sensory cortical and subcortical areas and the insula. A central hypothesis is that flashbacks in PTSD are due to the creation of a strong sensation-based memory representation, a weak contextually bound representation, and an impaired association between the two representations. Re-experiencing is thought to result from bottom-up activation of the sensation-based representation by situational cues that is relatively uninfluenced by corresponding contextual representations.

Ehlers and Clark (2000) focus on memory processes rather than representations. These authors suggested that re-experiencing and the ease with which it is triggered in PTSD can be explained by (1) what is encoded in memory, and (2) a combination of memory processes that facilitate (or fail to inhibit) cue-driven retrieval. Data-driven processing (i.e., primarily processing sensory impressions) and a lack of self-referent processing (i.e., impression that one is no longer the same person or cut off from one's past) during trauma are thought to put people at risk for subsequent intrusive memories. Cue-driven retrieval of moments from the trauma is facilitated by strong perceptual priming and strong associative learning, and poorly inhibited due to poor memory elaboration (binding with other information in autobiographical memory). This model further emphasizes that problematic appraisals and dysfunctional strategies contribute to the maintenance of re-experiencing symptoms.

One important difference between information processing models described in this section and other approaches that aim to explain involuntary memories of trauma by general mechanisms of autobiographical memory retrieval (Berntsen, 2009; Rubin, Boals, & Berntsen, 2008) is the range of memory phenomena under consideration. Whereas information processing models of PTSD were developed with the aim to explain the full range of intrusive re-experiencing symptoms, including those that lack autonoetic awareness (i.e., the awareness of the self in the past), Rubin, Boals, et al. (2008) and Berntsen (2009) only include the involuntary retrieval of memory content that is recognized by the individual as a trauma memory. Berntsen (2009) explicitly excludes involuntary auditory and visual imagery that is not deemed autobiographical and "phenomena in which the involuntary mental contents overrule reality more or less completely" (p. 15). Thus, many of the phenomena that information processing models of PTSD aim to explain (such as flashbacks where patients lose all contact with current reality, other intrusions that are not recognized by the individual as a memory, re-experiencing strong emotions, physiological reactions or behavior from the trauma without recollection of the trauma) are excluded from consideration in these models. However, these phenomena are important for understanding PTSD and for developing effective treatments.

Note that several information processing theories of PTSD do not exclusively rely on memory processes or representations to explain re-experiencing, but also include problematic meanings of the trauma as a causal factor (Ehlers & Clark, 2000; Foa et al., 1989; Foa & Riggs, 1993). Dalgleish (2004) suggested that schemas are one of a minimum of three levels of representations needed to explain PTSD, with associative networks and verbal/propositional representations constituting the other two levels. It is thought that the trauma memory is initially characterized by high internal cohesion of these representations and not assimilated into existing memory representations, with the consequence that external triggers can trigger the whole network, resulting in re-experiencing. We come back to the role of problematic meanings of the trauma in a later section and focus on re-experiencing and its triggers here. The wide range of re-experiencing symptoms under consideration explains why information processing models emphasize memory processes that facilitate cue-driven re-experiencing—namely, priming and associative learning.

Associative Learning and Re-experiencing

Predictions from Information Processing Theories

Several information processing models of PTSD emphasize the role of associative learning in re-experiencing, especially in explaining the physiological arousal and negative emotions that people with PTSD show when confronted with reminders (e.g. Ehlers & Clark, 2000; Foa et al., 1989; Keane, Zimering & Caddell, 1985). It is hypothesized that during trauma (unconditioned stimulus), Pavlovian conditioning leads to an association between the unconditioned emotional responses to the trauma and stimuli (conditioned stimuli) that are present at the time. Subsequently, the conditioned stimuli evoke conditioned fear responses. Associative learning models of PTSD further suggest that the conditioned fear responses generalize more broadly to stimuli and situations that resemble the original trauma, thus explaining the wide range of stimuli that can trigger emotional and physiological responses. Finally, a failure to extinguish the learned fear response, whether due to avoidance or deficits in extinction learning, may play a role in maintaining PTSD.

Does the Content of Re-experiencing Fit with Associative Learning Models?

In systematic interviews, patients with PTSD reported that they re-experienced brief moments from the trauma, such as "hearing footsteps behind me" or "seeing the perpetrator stand before me with a knife" (Ehlers et al., 2002). Further analysis of these intrusions indicated that they represented sensory impressions that signaled the onset of the trauma or the onset of its worst moments. In line with modern associative learning models that highlight the information value of conditioned stimuli in predicting the unconditioned stimuli (Rescorla, 1988), Ehlers et al. (2002) therefore suggested that the intrusions had functional significance in that they represented stimuli that *predicted* the worst moments of trauma and had thus acquired the status of warning signals. Evidence for this hypothesis comes from interview studies of PTSD patients and violent offenders who had intrusive memories of their crime, showing that the majority of intrusive memories were about moments predicting either the onset of the trauma or a moment when the meaning of the event changed for worse (Hackmann et al., 2004; Evans, Ehlers, Mezey, & Clark, 2007b; Speckens, Ehlers, Hackmann, Ruths, & Clark, 2007). Ehlers et al.'s (2002) emphasis that the sensory impressions that are later re-experienced *preceded* the trauma or its worst moments has been interpreted by some authors (e.g., Berntsen, 2009; Berntsen & Rubin, 2008) as meaning that they needed to *finish* before trauma onset. However, consistent with what is known about conditioned stimuli in Pavlovian conditioning (Rescorla, 1988), the hypothesis concerns sensory impressions that *started* just before the trauma or worst moment and thus had *predictive* information value. They may well have still been present during the worst moment. Furthermore, it is important to note that the worst moments of the trauma are defined from the perspective of the traumatized person with PTSD, not from the perspective of an outside observer who—in the absence of information about the person's subjective experience—may define the onset and end of trauma or its worst moments differently. Furthermore, in prolonged trauma, there are usually several moments when the meaning of the event changed for the worse, and each of them may be represented in re-experiencing. The latter two points explain why a study of tsunami survivors (Berntsen & Rubin, 2008) showed that only a minority of survivors had intrusive memories of the tsunami wave itself. Intrusions were mainly from the period when they were trying to escape the wave or searching for lost ones, presumably because the most traumatic moments—for example, thinking that they may drown or that their loved ones had died—occurred during these periods. The subjectively most traumatic moments were unfortunately not assessed in this study.

Physiological Responses to Trauma Reminders

Associative learning accounts of re-experiencing would suggest that people with PTSD show greater physiological responses to trauma reminders than those without PTSD. A recent meta-analysis by Pole (2007) supported this prediction. Physiological responses (including heart rate (HR), skin conductance, EMG, or blood pressure) to standardized trauma-related cues identified PTSD with a mean sensitivity of 77% and a mean specificity of 91%; and responses to idiographic trauma cues identified PTSD with a mean sensitivity of 65% and mean specificity of 83%. Although most of the studies included in the meta-analysis were cross-sectional so that it remains unclear whether the physiological responses were a cause or consequence of having chronic PTSD, several recent studies suggest that physiological responses to trauma reminders measured soon after trauma distinguish between trauma survivors with and without PTSD. Elsesser, Sartory, and Tackenberg (2004) found that chronic PTSD patients and recent trauma survivors who met criteria for acute stress disorder at six weeks after the trauma showed HR acceleration to individualized trauma-related pictures, whereas nontraumatized controls and survivors without acute stress disorder showed HR deceleration. The groups did not differ in HR responses to generally threatening or neutral pictures. Elsesser, Sartory, and Tackenberg (2005) followed up 35 recent trauma survivors and found that greater HR responses to the individualized trauma-related pictures predicted PTSD symptoms three months later. Blanchard et al. (1996) studied MVA survivors at about 2.5 months after the trauma and found that HR responses to audiotaped individualized scripts describing the participants' accidents, but not responses to other stressors, distinguished survivors with PTSD from those without PTSD and nontraumatized controls. These results are in line with the notion that in the initial months after trauma, PTSD is characterized by strong learned fear responses to reminders of the trauma. HR acceleration to individualized MVA scripts predicted chronicity of PTSD at one year in 48 participants who had PTSD at the initial assessment.

Acquisition, Extinction, and Generalization of Fear Responses

Several studies investigated whether individual differences in the ease with which conditioned responses are acquired or extinguished are related to PTSD. Although some studies found that participants with PTSD were more likely to acquire conditioned responses to new stimuli (e.g., Orr et al., 2000), others failed to replicate this result (e.g. Orr et al., 2006). There is more consistent evidence for impaired extinction learning in PTSD (e.g., Blechert, Michael, Vriends, Margraf, & Wilhelm, 2007; Peri, Ben-Shakar, Orr, & Shalev, 2000). In a prospective study of firefighters, Guthrie and Bryant (2006) found that reduced extinction learning predicted later PTSD symptoms. A recent study also points to a possible impairment in discrimination learning in PTSD (Mauchnik, Ebner-Priemer, Bohus, & Schmahl, 2010).

There is some evidence that individual differences in stimulus generalization may be related to PTSD. Two studies found that at one month after the trauma, assault and accident survivors with PTSD showed greater HR responses to standardized trauma-related pictures than those without PTSD, even though they rated these pictures as dissimilar to their own trauma; but not to general threat or neutral pictures. HR response to trauma-related pictures also predicted PTSD severity six months later (Ehlers et al., 2010; Sündermann, Ehlers, Böllinghaus, Gamer, & Glucksman, 2010). These results are in line with the hypothesis that generalized fear responses to stimuli loosely associated with the trauma contribute to the maintenance of PTSD. Wessa and Flor (2007) paired neutral stimuli with trauma reminders to investigate second-order conditioning as a potential mechanism of stimulus generalization. Participants with PTSD acquired greater conditioned responses to the neutral stimuli and showed slower extinction than trauma survivors without PTSD. Nontraumatized controls, on the other hand, did not acquire a conditioned response to the neutral stimuli. Michael et al. (2010) found that such second-order conditioning may occur in PTSD even if the individual is unaware of the contingency between the neutral stimulus and trauma reminder.

Priming and Triggers of Re-experiencing

Predictions from Information Processing Theories

Priming is a form of implicit memory that comprises facilitated processing of a stimulus because the same stimulus, or a related one, has been processed before (Bowers & Turner, 2003; Schacter, Dobbins, & Schnyer, 2004). Perceptual priming is very stable, can last as long as 17 years (Mitchell, 2006), and transfers to different contexts (McKone & French, 2001). Ehlers and Clark (2000) suggested that trauma survivors with PTSD show heightened perceptual priming for trauma-related stimuli. Priming may influence the development of PTSD in two ways. First, people may vary in the degree to which stimuli that are present *during* trauma are primed. Heightened perceptual priming for stimuli encountered during trauma may increase the risk of PTSD, as priming results in a lowered perceptual threshold and a processing advantage for similar stimuli, with the consequence that such stimuli are more likely noticed than other stimuli in the environment and trigger trauma memories through unintentional, cue-driven memory retrieval (Ehlers & Clark, 2000). Second, some trauma survivors may also show greater priming for trauma-related cues they encounter in the aftermath of traumas than other survivors. Such enhanced *posttrauma* priming of trauma-related cues may be involved in the development of chronic PTSD as it would extend the range of trauma-related cues that are preferentially processed and may serve as generalized potential triggers for PTSD-related symptoms.

Priming during Trauma

Experimental analogue studies provided initial support for the role of perceptual priming *during* trauma in the development of analogue intrusive trauma memories in healthy volunteers. In these studies, visual stimuli were embedded in traumatic and neutral picture stories, and perceptual priming was assessed later with a picture-identification task. Several studies found that stimuli that occurred in a traumatic context were more strongly primed than those occurring in a neutral context (Arntz, de Groot & Kindt, 2005; Ehlers, Mauchnik & Handley, 2010; Ehlers, Michael, Chen, Payne & Shan, 2006; Michael & Ehlers, 2007). Furthermore, the degree of priming for objects from the trauma stories indeed predicted subsequent intrusive re-experiencing (Ehlers et al., 2006; Michael & Ehlers, 2007).

Kleim, Ehring, and Ehlers (2011) gave a blurred picture identification task to trauma survivors. Participants with PTSD, but not those without PTSD, identified trauma-related pictures, but not general threat pictures, with greater likelihood than neutral pictures. There were no group differences in response bias. In a second prospective study, they replicated these results for assault survivors who had acute stress disorder at two weeks after the trauma. Furthermore, the relative processing advantage for trauma-related pictures predicted PTSD at follow-up.

Priming after Trauma

There is some evidence for enhanced posttrauma priming of trauma-related stimuli in PTSD. In several cross-sectional studies using a range of different paradigms (e.g., word-stem completion test; perceptual word identification paradigm; white noise paradigm; visual clarity rating task), trauma survivors with PTSD showed greater posttrauma priming for trauma-related stimuli than for neutral stimuli, whereas trauma survivors without PTSD did not show differential priming (Amir, Leiner, & Bomyea, 2010; Amir, McNally, & Wiegartz, 1996; Michael, Ehlers, & Halligan, 2005). However, other studies did not find such enhanced priming effects in PTSD (Golier, Yehuda, Lupien, & Harvey, 2003; McNally & Amir, 1996).

The inconsistent results may in part be due to differences in the sensitivity of the paradigms used to assess priming. For example, an early study used a perceptual identification paradigm to investigate whether Vietnam veterans with PTSD exhibit an enhanced implicit memory bias for trauma-related sentences (Amir et al., 1996). Combat veterans were asked to listen to a number of trauma-related and neutral sentences. Some of these sentences were later repeated, embedded within different levels of white noise, and participants rated the volume of the noise. Priming in this paradigm shows in lower noise ratings. A differential effect was only found for the highest volume of white noise. The PTSD group rated the volume of noise that accompanied the "old" trauma-related sentences as less loud than that accompanying the neutral sentences, indicating greater priming.

Michael, Ehlers, and Halligan (2005) used a word-stem completion task designed to increase task sensitivity. In the standard version of the word-stem completion test, target words are presented in an encoding phase. Word stems of these words and new words that have not been shown in the encoding phase are presented in the test phase. Priming shows in a greater completion rate of the previously presented words. In the new version of the task, Michael, Ehlers, and Halligan (2005) presented target words as well as matched neutral words with the same word stem and frequency in the encoding phase. Target and matched neutral words are thought to compete for processing resources in the subsequent test phase, thus increasing sensitivity in detecting processing biases. Assault survivors who had PTSD at eight weeks posttrauma showed greater priming for assault-related words in this task, but not for general threat or neutral words than those without PTSD. Priming for assault-related words also predicted PTSD symptom severity six months later. Ehring and Ehlers (2011) tested MVA survivors at two weeks after the trauma with an adapted version of the modified word-stem completion test. Participants who later developed chronic PTSD (at six months) showed enhanced completion of trauma-related words at two weeks. Interestingly, the enhanced priming for trauma-related words was not associated with acute stress disorder. This pattern of results rules out that the enhanced priming was an epiphenomenon of having early PTSD symptoms and suggests that it is one of the processes involved in the development of chronic PTSD symptoms.

As intrusive trauma memories and their triggers appear to be primarily visual (Ehlers et al., 2002), studies of the priming hypothesis using visual stimuli are particularly interesting. Amir et al. (2010) used picture clarity ratings as a measure of implicit memory for previously encoded trauma-related, negative and neutral pictures. Trauma survivors with PTSD showed a greater implicit memory bias for trauma and negative pictures relative to neutral pictures than those without PTSD.

Encoding during Trauma

Several information processing models suggest that strong encoding of perceptual information and relatively weak encoding of contextual information during trauma predicts the development of re-experiencing symptoms (e.g., Brewin et al., 1996, 2010; Ehlers & Clark, 2000). Other authors have emphasized the role of dissociation (a complex concept involving a lack of integration of subjective experiences including depersonalization, derealization, altered time perception, and emotional numbing) in the development of re-experiencing (e.g., van der Kolk & Fisler, 1995). Dissociation and perceptual processing may overlap to a certain extent (Ehlers & Clark, 2000).

In line with a role of cognitive processing during trauma in the development of re-experiencing symptoms, several studies have shown that self-reports of peritraumatic data-driven processing (preferential processing of perceptual information as opposed to conceptual information) assessed shortly after the trauma predicted subsequent PTSD (e.g., Halligan, Michael, Clark, & Ehlers, 2003; Ehring, Ehlers, & Glucksman, 2006, 2008). Similarly, self-reported dissociation during trauma has repeatedly been found to predict PTSD (see Ozer, Best, Lipsey, & Weiss, 2003, for a review).

A limitation of assessing cognitive processing during trauma through self-reports is that they are retrospective, even if taken soon after the trauma, and recall may be biased—for instance, by current PTSD symptoms. Researchers have therefore attempted to experimentally manipulate cognitive processing during analogue traumatic stressors or have studied the effect of individual differences in cognitive processing styles on the response to such analogue stressors. Halligan, Clark and Ehlers (2002) found that participants who reported more data-driven processing while watching a videotape of traffic accidents and those who scored high on habitual data-driven processing subsequently developed more frequent re-experiencing of the video and other analogue PTSD symptoms than those with low data-driven processing scores. Similar results were obtained by Kindt, van den Hout, Arntz, and Drost (2008). Further experimental studies found a similar pattern of results for dissociation during exposure to an aversive film (Kindt & van den Hout, 2003; Kindt, van den Hout, & Buck, 2005). Holmes and colleagues (e.g., Bourne, Frasquilho, Roth, & Holmes, 2010; Holmes, Brewin & Hennessy, 2004) presented a series of studies showing that performing a visuospatial task during exposure to a trauma film reduced the frequency of subsequent intrusive memories. The authors also found that performing a distracting verbal task during the film increased subsequent intrusions, and impaired recognition memory (Bourne et al., 2010). Thus, a task that interfered with verbal/conceptual processing predicted poor intentional recall, but more frequent unintentional retrieval, as predicted by Brewin et al.'s (1996) and Ehlers and Clark's (2000) models.

Conclusions: Information Processing and Re-experiencing

Overall, there is empirical support that perceptual processing during trauma, associative learning, and perceptual priming plays a role in the development of re-experiencing symptoms, and in the generalization of triggers of re-experiencing after trauma. However, the observed effect sizes in the studies are small so that their clinical significance remains to be investigated further.

The content of intrusive memories and the enhanced physiological responses to trauma reminders observed in people with PTSD compared to those without PTSD are consistent with associative learning accounts of re-experiencing. Experimental investigations point to a possible role of delayed extinction of fear responses to conditioned stimuli and second-order conditioning in PTSD. A limitation is that standard Pavlovian conditioning experiments involve repeated pairings of the unconditioned stimulus with the conditioned stimulus, whereas single traumatic events can be sufficient to induce PTSD. Studies of conditioned emotional and physiological responses after single presentations of aversive stimuli would be of interest.

There is evidence from analogue studies and studies with trauma survivors that stimuli that are perceived in the context of trauma are more strongly primed than other stimuli, leading to a lower perceptual threshold for trauma-related perceptual cues similar to those encountered during trauma. This may contribute to the involuntary triggering of intrusive trauma memories in PTSD. Despite some negative findings, there is also some evidence for enhanced posttrauma priming for trauma-related cues in PTSD. Enhanced posttrauma priming of trauma-related cues may contribute to stimulus generalization of triggers of trauma memories as it results in a processing advantage for a wide range of trauma-related stimuli that may serve as triggers of trauma memories, negative affect, or rumination.

Finally, there is consistent evidence showing that high levels of perceptual processing during trauma are associated with later re-experiencing. However, the causal nature of this association remains still to be investigated.

In addition to peritraumatic perceptual processing, perceptual priming, and associative learning, it has been suggested that re-experiencing in PTSD is caused by a lack of elaboration and contextualization of the trauma memory (see Brewin et al., 1996, 2010; Ehlers & Clark, 2010). In order to test this hypothesis, researchers have investigated characteristics of intentional trauma recall in PTSD that we discuss in the next section.

2. Recalling the Trauma in PTSD

PTSD is a disorder that is about a past event. It is therefore not surprising that many experts see the memory for the traumatic event at the core of PTSD. "Among the anxiety syndromes, PTSD is most dramatically a disorder of memory" (McNally, 1998, p. 971). Nevertheless, the nature of trauma memories is perhaps the most controversial area in PTSD research.

Predictions from Information Processing Theories

Clinical observations suggest that trauma survivors with PTSD are often confused about details of what happened during the trauma and have problems with giving a coherent narrative account of the traumatic event (e.g., Zoellner & Bittinger, 2004). The *Diagnostic and Statistical Manual of Mental Disorders* (APA, 1994) includes amnesia for parts of the traumatic event among the diagnostic criteria. Building on such observations of problems in recalling the trauma, several information processing models suggested that disturbances in the memory for the traumatic event contribute to PTSD. The nature of the proposed memory disturbance has been a matter of debate. In one of the strongest formulations, van der Kolk and Fisler (1995) postulated that trauma memories are fragmented and initially recollected in a sensory form "without any semantic representation" and "experienced primarily as fragments of the sensory components of the event" (p. 513). Other authors refer to milder forms of memory disturbances (often termed *memory disorganization*) that show as gaps in memory, lack of coherence, and/or problems remembering the temporal order of events (e.g., Foa & Riggs, 1993; Halligan et al., 2003).

The fragmentation and memory disorganization concepts have been questioned on theoretical grounds. It has been suggested that fragmentation might simply be an artifact of the method used, as every autobiographical memory encoding is incomplete and the recalled memory therefore fragmented in some way (e.g., Berntsen, 2009; McNally, 2003; Rubin, Berntsen, & Bohni, 2008). McNally (2003) argued that instead of postulating special processes for trauma memories, the memory characteristics observed in PTSD could instead be accounted for by well-known processes identified in cognitive psychology, such as attentional narrowing as a consequence of stress (Christianson, 1992; Easterbrook, 1959).

Ehlers and Clark (2000) and Brewin et al. (1996, 2010) proposed that both perspectives may be correct—namely, that (1) trauma memories in PTSD can be understood by general memory processes identified in cognitive psychology and neuroscience, and (2) there are systematic differences in how the trauma is laid down in memory between people with and without PTSD that explain re-experiencing and other symptoms. For example, Ehlers and Clark (2000) built on Roediger's (1990) transfer appropriate processing account when they suggested that a lack of conceptual and self-referent processing during trauma would explain the relative disorganization and confusion in recalling the trauma observed in PTSD. In particular, it should lead to relatively poor links between the traumatic experience and other relevant information in autobiographical memory (see also the suggested lack of association with contextual memory, Brewin et al., 2010). Poor elaboration is thought to contribute to PTSD in two ways. First, poor elaboration leads to poor inhibition of cue-driven retrieval and thus makes re-experiencing more likely. Second, poor elaboration contributes to problematic appraisals such as "I am to blame for the event." Ehlers et al. (2004) further specified that poor elaboration would mainly be expected for the (subjectively) worst moments of the trauma that are later re-experienced. These moments are thought to be disjointed in memory from other information (e.g., "I did not die/still live with my children/my body has healed") that updated impressions and predictions at the time (e.g., "I am going to die/never see my children again/be paralyzed"). The overall disorganization of the trauma memory may influence appraisals about responsibility for the event, but is thought to be less relevant in predicting re-experiencing symptoms than the disorganization of the worst moments.

It is noteworthy that the term *memory elaboration* as used by Ehlers and Clark (2000) differs from the way it is interpreted by Rubin, Berntsen, and Bohni (2008). Rubin, Berntsen, et al. (2008) suggested an *enhanced* elaboration in that the trauma becomes a central component of identity and reference point for other autobiographical experiences. The hypotheses are not mutually exclusive. Several studies showed that both memory disorganization and appraisals of being permanently changed by the trauma predict PTSD (e.g., Dunmore, Clark & Ehlers, 2001; Ehlers, Maercker, & Boos, 2000; Halligan et al., 2003). The permanent change concept is very similar to Rubin, Berntsen, et al.'s (2008) centrality of event concept.

In the following, we discuss the evidence for trauma-induced amnesia, other problems in intentional recall of the trauma memory, their relationship with encoding during trauma, and other problems in autobiographical and general memory in PTSD.

Trauma-induced Amnesia?

Several case reports suggest that after trauma some people may develop retrograde psychogenic amnesia (an inability to remember a period of their lives including the trauma; e.g., Christianson 1992; Markowitsch et al., 1998). This involves an inability to remember who they are, and may include inability to remember semantic knowledge acquired during that part of their lives such as a language. Markowitsch and colleagues termed this extremely rare condition *mnestic block syndrome* (see Brand & Markowitsch, 2010, for a review). For example, Markowitsch et al. (1998) described the case of a young man who discovered a fire at home and suddenly was unable to remember the preceding six years of his life. It later emerged that the patient had observed a man dying in a burning car when he was four years old. Apparently, the house fire induced a massive stress reaction as it represented a sensory reminder of the earlier traumatic experience. Markowitsch and colleagues further found that patients with retrograde psychogenic amnesia show abnormalities in metabolic and functional brain activity (see Brand & Markowitsch, 2010, for a review). For example, when patients listened to descriptions of events from their personal past they showed a pattern of activation typical of listening to unfamiliar events and they lacked the activation of the right hippocampus and amygdala usually observed when people listen to descriptions of events from their lives.

A more specific form of amnesia, the inability to remember the traumatic event, has been implicated in PTSD and has attracted much interest (e.g., Brown, Scheflin, & Whitfield, 1999). A review by McNally (2003) concluded that it is often difficult to disentangle psychogenic causes of amnesia from organic causes such as head injury, hypoxia, starvation, alcohol blackout, or other substance-induced amnesia. McNally (2003) found that many of the studies and case reports cited in support of traumatic amnesia do not provide convincing evidence, as there are a range of alternative explanations for why people may not recall certain aspects of their traumas. These include failure to encode the information, forgetting, avoidance, or simulation. A recent study of individuals who claimed to have experienced amnesia for a past traumatic event during a period of their lives but were now able to remember it, investigated whether there was independent corroboration for the fact that the trauma had taken place (Geraerts et al., 2007). Corroboration rates for individuals who had spontaneously retrieved a discontinuous trauma memory outside of therapy were the same as for those who had continuous trauma memories. However, low levels of corroboration were found for discontinuous memories retrieved in therapy. Although this suggests that accurate trauma memories can be discontinuous, mechanisms other than amnesia may account for these findings, such as forgetting of previous recollections, failure to think about the trauma, or absence of triggers for recollection (see McNally & Geraerts, 2009).

Another interesting example is that amnesia has been reported in people who committed violent crimes such as murder (e.g., Kopelman, 1987). A problem is that the interviews usually took place before the offenders were convicted so that their report of being unable to remember their violent act may be motivated by the expectation of lenience in their upcoming trial. A recent study by Evans, Mezey, and Ehlers (2009) assessed 105 young offenders *after* they had been convicted of seriously harming or killing other people. The authors found that only one participant reported complete amnesia, and 20 reported gaps in their memory of the offense. Memory gaps were related to high alcohol intake, emotional ties to the victim, and more dissociation and less self-referent processing during the assault. Thus, in line with McNally's (2003) conclusion, this study showed that complete amnesia is very rare and may be related to organic causes such as high alcohol use rather than psychogenic causes. The more subtle gaps in memory reported by participants may also be due to a range of reasons other than irreversible memory loss or a problem in accessing information by intentional recall, such as avoidance of thinking or talking about the worst moments of the assault. It is possible that some of the material may be accessible using other modes of retrieval, such as picture cues or a visit to the scene of the assault.

Intentional Recall of Trauma Memories

The hypothesis that trauma memories in PTSD are fragmented or disorganized has been investigated with a range of methods. Whereas some researchers focused on self-report measures asking participants to rate the degree to which they perceive their trauma memory to be fragmented or disorganized, others used objective indices.

Self-reported Memory Disorganization

Most studies using self-report questionnaires and interviews to assess memory fragmentation or disorganization compared characteristics of the trauma memory in trauma survivors with versus without PTSD. In the majority of these studies, a diagnosis of PTSD and/or PTSD symptom severity was indeed related to reports that the recollection of the traumatic experience was more fragmented and less clear, to have more gaps and to follow less of a meaningful order (e.g., Engelhard, van den Hout, Kindt, Arntz, & Schouten, 2003; Halligan et al., 2003; Koss, Figueredo, Bell, Tharan, & Tromp, 1996; Murray, Ehlers, & Mayou, 2002), although discrepant results have also been reported (Berntsen, Willert, & Rubin, 2003).

A second group of studies investigated whether trauma survivors or nonclinical participants describe their trauma memories as more fragmented or disorganized than control memories of nontraumatic events. Results from this line of research are mixed. Some studies indeed found that trauma memories were described as significantly more disorganized than memories for nontraumatic events (Byrne, Hyman, & Scott, 2001; Tromp, Koss, Figueredo, & Tharan, 1995; van der Kolk & Fisler, 1995), whereas other studies reported no significant differences (Peace, Porter, & ten Brinke, 2008; Porter & Birt, 2001; Rubin, Feldman, & Beckham, 2004).

In order to test whether disorganization is specific to trauma memories in PTSD, it appears necessary to combine both of these approaches and use a 2 (type of memory) x 2 (PTSD vs. no PTSD group) design. The results are inconsistent. Halligan et al. (2003) found a main effect of memory type and an interaction with PTSD. Trauma memories were described as more disorganized than other unpleasant memories, and this difference was more pronounced in the PTSD group. Another study showed main effects of memory type, but no significant interaction (Jelinek, Randjbar, Seifert, Kellner, & Moritz, 2009); trauma survivors with PTSD reported more memory disorganization than the control group; and trauma memories were generally rated as more disorganized than non-traumatic control memories (independent of group). Two studies found no significant main effects or interactions (Megías, Ryan, Vaquero, & Frese, 2007; Rubin; Boals, & Berntsen, 2008).

In sum, the evidence from studies using self-report measures of memory disorganization is mixed. The wording of the questions used to assess disorganization and the extent to which the studies used clinical or student populations may have contributed to this variability. The psychometric properties of the measures used in the studies are in most cases unknown. It is noteworthy that several of the negative studies used single items to assess memory disorganization (e.g., Berntsen et al., 2003; Rubin et al., 2004). In addition, the majority of studies using student populations showed negative results whereas most studies on clinical or community samples of trauma survivors supported of the trauma memory disorganization hypothesis.

Objective Measures of Memory Disorganization

Efforts to assess memory disorganization objectively have mainly concentrated on the analysis of transcripts of trauma narratives. Foa, Molnar, and

Cashman (1995) obtained narratives of rape survivors with PTSD in their first and last imaginal exposure to the trauma memory during therapy. Narrative segments (defined as one thought, action, or speech utterance) were coded by blind raters for indicators of fragmentation versus organization. In line with the fragmentation/disorganization hypothesis, narratives from the last imaginal exposure contained significantly more segments that were rated as 'organized thoughts' than those from the first imaginal exposure. Although a total fragmentation score was not reduced over the course of the treatment, a significant correlation between the fragmentation score and the reduction of PTSD symptoms over treatment was found. In a study aiming to replicate these results, van Minnen, Wessel, Dijkstra, and Roelofs (2002) did not find an effect of treatment on the number of organized thoughts or the overall fragmentation index. However, the posttreatment narrative contained significantly fewer 'disorganized thoughts' than the pretreatment narratives. In addition, this reduction was significantly related to treatment response.

In five further cross-sectional studies, the Foa et al. (1995) coding scheme (or variants of it) were used to compare trauma survivors with versus without acute stress disorder (Harvey & Bryant, 1999; Jones, Harvey, & Brewin, 2007), PTSD (Hagenaars, van Minnen, Hoogduin, & Verbraak, 2009; Halligan et al., 2003, study 1; Jones et al., 2007), or intrusive memories (Evans, Ehlers, Mezey & Clark, 2007a). As expected, symptomatic participants had more disorganized trauma narratives than nonsymptomatic participants. Furthermore, results of five prospective longitudinal studies showed that objective measures of trauma memory disorganization taken in the initial weeks after the trauma predicted the severity of PTSD symptoms at follow-up, either using variants of Foa et al.'s narrative coding method (Ehring, 2004; Halligan et al., 2003, study 2; Jones et al., 2007) and/or using a global observer rating of narrative disorganization (Buck, Kindt, van den Hout, Steens, & Linders, 2007; Ehring, 2004; Halligan et al., 2003, study 2; Murray et al., 2002).

Three studies tested whether disorganization is specific to trauma memories in PTSD and analyzed narratives of the trauma and other events. Jelinek et al. (2009) found a significant interaction between PTSD group and type of event; participants with PTSD showed significantly greater trauma memory disorganization than those without PTSD, whereas no group difference emerged for a nontrauma control narrative. In a study by Ehring (2004), trauma narratives were more disorganized than narratives of another very unpleasant life event, and participants with PTSD showed greater disorganization than those without PTSD, but there was no interaction between PTSD group and event type. Rubin (in press) did not find any significant main effects for PTSD group status, type of event, or a significant interaction. However, it should be noted that the sample size was rather small in this study (n = 15 per cell) and comprised undergraduate students, both of these design features may have led to reduced power.

A few studies used reading levels to measure trauma memory fragmentation. Amir, Stafford, Freshman, and Foa (1998) asked assault survivors to give a narrative of their traumatic experience two weeks following the trauma. The authors found that low reading levels of trauma narratives predicted PTSD symptom severity at 12 weeks following the assault. Gray and Lombardo (2001) replicated the relationship between PTSD and low reading level of trauma narratives. However, when the authors statistically controlled for scores obtained from tests of verbal intelligence and writing skills, the effect of diagnostic group was no longer significant. This raises the possibility that general cognitive abilities influence the degree of organization with which trauma memories are laid down in memory. For the analysis of narrative disorganization, corresponding data are largely lacking, although in Halligan et al.'s (2003) studies, the correlation between memory disorganization and concurrent and subsequent PTSD severity remained significant when level of education (a correlate of intelligence) was partialed out.

Encoding and Memory Disorganization

The objective measures of problems in trauma memory recall discussed above share an important problem: as many details of the event are usually not known to the raters, it is difficult for them to spot possible indicators of problems in recall such as gaps in memory or missing details. Thus, narratives may appear complete, coherent, and following the order of events even if there are subtle gaps in memory. Experimental studies have therefore tested memory for aversive films in healthy volunteers to test for possible relationships with encoding during trauma, recall of the aversive material, and PTSD symptoms. Halligan et al. (2002) showed participants a film of road traffic accidents and asked them later to describe everything they could recall about the film in the correct order. They found that data-driven processing during an aversive film was related to self-reported memory disorganization, and to less coherent and less complete recall of the film one week later (but not immediately after the film). Memory incoherence was also related to hyper-arousal symptoms. Kindt and van den Hout (2003) and Kindt et al. (2005) found that dissociation during film exposure correlated with self-reported memory fragmentation, but not with a sequential memory task performed four hours after the film. The task required participants to put a range of clips seen previously into the correct order. Thus, the evidence for objective deficits in recall from experimental studies is mixed and may depend on the time interval and the measures used.

Disjointedness of Worst Moments from Other Autobiographical Information

In support of Ehlers et al.'s (2004) suggestion that the disjointedness of trauma memory from other autobiographical information may be most pronounced for the worst moments of the trauma, Evans et al. (2007a) found that narratives of the moments that were re-experienced were more disorganized than other segments of the trauma narrative that were not; furthermore, in 23% of the cases these moments were not included in the narrative at all. This finding was replicated by Ehring (2004) and partly replicated by Jelinek et al. (2010). In a study by Kleim, Wallott, and Ehlers (2008), assault survivors with and without PTSD completed an autobiographical memory retrieval task during script-driven imagery of (a) the assault and (b) an unrelated negative event. When listening to a taped imagery script of the worst moment of their assault, survivors with PTSD took longer to retrieve unrelated nontraumatic autobiographical information than those without PTSD, but not when listening to a taped script of the worst moment of another negative life event. The effects were not due to differences in arousal or general retrieval latencies.

Overgeneral Autobiographical Memory in PTSD

People with major depression show difficulty in retrieving specific autobiographical memories (for a review, see J. M. G. Williams et al., 2007). When asked to remember a specific event from their lives in response to a cue word (e.g., "happy"), individuals with depression show an *overgeneral memory bias* (OGM)—that is, they tend to reply with descriptions that summarize several different events (e.g., "I am always happy when I visit friends") rather than a specific instance ("I was happy when my school friend rang me last week").

Some, but nor all studies, found a relationship between OGM and trauma (see Moore & Zoellner, 2007, for a review). Several studies reported that trauma survivors with PTSD or acute stress disorder (ASD) show less specific autobiographical memory retrieval than those without PTSD or ASD (Bryant, Sutherland, & Guthrie, 2007; Harvey & Bryant, 1999; Kangas, Henry, & Bryant, 2005; McNally, Lasko, Macklin, & Pitman, 1995; Schönfeld & Ehlers, 2006; Schönfeld, Ehlers, Böllinghaus, & Rief, 2007). In line with these cross-sectional studies, Kleim and Ehlers (2008) found that assault survivors with ASD or major depression at two weeks, but not those with phobia, retrieved fewer specific autobiographical memories than those without the respective disorder. Reduced memory specificity at two weeks also predicted subsequent PTSD and major depression at six months over and above what could be predicted from initial diagnoses and symptom severity. Sutherland and Bryant (2007) reported that with successful treatment of PTSD, memory specificity increased. These studies suggest that PTSD is characterized by OGM, which may contribute to changes in self-perception commonly observed in this condition, such as being 'frozen' at the time of the traumatic event (e.g., Herman, 1992) and perceptions that one is permanently changed (e.g., Ehlers, Maercker, & Boos, 2000; Schönfeld & Ehlers, 2006; Schönfeld et al., 2007; Kleim & Ehlers, 2008).

Poor Memory for Neutral Information?

Patients with PTSD have problems concentrating and often also report that they have difficulty remembering things. These clinical observations and findings of a small hippocampus in people with PTSD (see McNally, 2006, for a review) further contributed to the hypothesis that people with PTSD may show general impairment in their neuropsychological performance including memory tasks. Brewin, Kleiner, Vasterling, and Field (2007) conducted a meta-analysis of studies of memory for emotionally neutral information in PTSD. Overall, they found that people with PTSD show a decrement in memory performance, with a small to moderate effect size. The impairment was stronger for verbal material than for visual material. The pattern of results suggested that the impairment could not be accounted for by head injury.

Conclusions: Memory Recall and PTSD

Research on memory recall in PTSD has shown inconsistent results. Complete amnesia for the traumatic event appears to be extremely rare. Much of the inconsistency in the empirical work on memory fragmentation and disorganization appears to be due to methodological differences. Studies using more reliable measures and samples with strict definitions of trauma and clinically significant levels of PTSD symptoms tend to find more positive results than other studies. Studies of student or unselected volunteer samples found little support of the fragmentation or disorganization hypotheses, possibly because of a less strict definition of trauma and a restriction in the variance of PTSD symptoms. In contrast, the majority of studies with clinical samples supported trauma memory disorganization as one of the contributing factors to PTSD symptom development. However, several studies suggested that the observed disorganization of memory recall in PTSD may not be specific to trauma narratives and may therefore be due to a more general impairment. Possibilities include that people with PTSD show a general disturbance in autobiographical memory (see also the findings on low specificity of autobiographical memories in PTSD), a general deficit in memory (see also the findings on impaired memory for neutral material), or generally lower verbal intelligence (see McNally & Shin, 1995).

Overall, deficits in trauma memory recall observed in PTSD appear to be subtle and effect sizes are small. It appears that most trauma survivors are able to verbalize the gist of what happened to them. This is in contrast to the extreme formulation of the fragmentation hypothesis by van der Kolk and Fisler (1995). Several recent studies showed that memory disorganization may mainly apply to those parts of the trauma memory that are re-experienced, which is in line with Ehlers et al.'s (2004) suggestions. Not all aspects of fragmentation or disorganization relate equally well to PTSD and recovery. General measures of narrative complexity such as number of details do not seem to bear a close relationship to PTSD symptoms (e.g., Porter & Birt, 2001). Aspects of the narrative such as speech fillers or unfinished sentences may also be less useful in assessing memory disorganization, possibly because they mainly reflect general verbal abilities (Halligan et al., 2003; Ehring, 2004). Van Minnen et al.'s (2002) finding that the change in the number of disorganized segments in the trauma narrative was most closely related to treatment outcome parallels findings from prospective studies of accident and assault survivors in that the number of disorganized segments had the greatest predictive power (Ehring, 2004; Halligan et al., 2003).

The controversy about amnesia for traumatic events and trauma memory disorganization highlights some conceptual problems. Different researchers have used terms such as fragmentation, disorganization, or memory elaboration in different ways and have chosen different measures. Clearer hypotheses about what aspects of disorganization are relevant to PTSD, what part of the trauma memory they apply to, and by what mechanism they lead to PTSD symptoms are needed to advance the field. A clearer distinction between features of memory and appraisals of memories is also needed. Finally, it may remain difficult to distinguish whether observed behavior such as errors in remembering the order of events during trauma is a feature of deficient memory access, a result of what was encoded, or a reflection of cognitive avoidance.

3. Information Processing and Persisting Anxiety in PTSD

Many of the symptoms of PTSD (e.g., avoidance, hyper-vigilance) overlap with those of other anxiety disorders. This raises an interesting question: anxiety is an emotional response to future threat; however, the trauma is a past event, so why does the anxiety response persist long after trauma in people with PTSD? We have discussed above that conditioned fear responses, generalization of conditioned triggers of anxiety, failure to extinguish learned fear responses and posttrauma priming may play a role in maintaining anxiety responses to a wide range of stimuli in PTSD. In this section, we address two further relevant processes: attentional bias and threatening interpretations.

Attentional Bias to Threat

Predictions from Information Processing Theories

An attentional bias to threatening information has been identified in a range of anxiety disorders (e.g., Bar-Haim, Lamy, Pergamin, Bakermans-Kranenburg, & van Ijzendoorn, 2007; J. M. G. Williams, Mathews & McLeod, 1997). Several information processing theories of PTSD highlight the potential role of selective attention to threat. These theories posit a PTSD-specific selective processing bias that automatically favors trauma-relevant information. Such a bias may contribute to the generalized fear responses that people with PTSD show in a wide range of situations (e.g., Chemtob et al., 1988; Dalgleish, 2004; Litz & Keane, 1989) and make it more likely for the individual to detect potential triggers of intrusive memories (Ehlers & Steil, 1995).

Information processing theories of anxiety disorders further suggest a biphasic vigilance-avoidance response to threat. The initial phase is characterized by enhanced vigilance to threat so that possible danger cues are easily detected. This is followed by early avoidance, which prevents full processing of the threat cue and prevents correction of the impression that there is danger in cases of false alarm (e.g., Mogg, Bradley, Miles, & Dixon, 2004; J. M. G. Williams, Watts, MacLeod, & Mathews, 1997).

Attentional Bias—Experimental Findings

The emotional Stroop task is the most commonly used paradigm to study attentional bias in PTSD. Participants are asked to name the colors of trauma-related and control words. Attentional bias to the emotional content of the words interferes with color-naming and shows in delayed responses. Several reviews suggested that across studies, trauma survivors with PTSD showed greater interference when color-naming trauma-related words than those without PTSD, but not for other words (see Buckley, Blanchard, & Neill, 2000, or Constans, 2005, for reviews). For example, Foa, Feske, Murdock, Kozak, and McCarthy (1991) asked rape victims to name the colors of rape-related, general threat, neutral words, and nonwords. Rape victims with PTSD, but not those without PTSD, took longer to color-name the rape-related words than the other word types. Stroop interference tends to increase as congruence between the stimuli used in the task and the dominant concern of participants increases (Riemann & McNally, 1995). Vietnam veterans with PTSD, for instance, were slower to react to words that were strongly related to the trauma compared to words that were only moderately related to the trauma, such as "firefight" versus "death" (Vrana, Roodman, & Beckham, 1995). A recent review, however, has called for caution regarding the emotional Stroop effect in PTSD (Kimble, Frueh, & Marks, 2009), and concluded that only 44% of the peer-reviewed literature actually found the emotional Stroop effect in PTSD. Furthermore, a study of changes in Stroop performance with cognitive-behavioral treatment did not find an association between symptom change and changes in interference (Devineni, Blanchard, Hickling, & Buckley, 2004). Nevertheless, the emotional Stroop effect remains among the most widely cited findings in the attentional bias literature in the PTSD field.

Other paradigms such as the dot-probe task have shown mixed results. Unlike the Stroop task, this task involves allocation of visual attention to discrete areas of the visual field. Participants are required to respond to probes that occur in the same or a different spatial location as the experimental cues of interest. Attentional bias to threat shows in a faster response to probes that occur in the same spatial location as trauma-related cues. In Bryant and Harvey's (1997) study, an attentional bias to mild threat words was observed in MVA survivors with PTSD, whereas Elsesser et al. (2004) reported negative findings. One possible problem with this inconclusive pattern of results is that these studies used words as threat cues, which are different from the threat cues that trigger anxiety in everyday life.

Recent research has concentrated on the question of whether the attentional bias in PTSD represents an enhanced detection of threatening stimuli or a difficulty in disengaging from the threatening stimuli, which then interferes with the primary task. Data from visual search tasks for verbal cues supported an enhanced difficulty in disengaging from trauma-related cues in trauma survivors with PTSD compared to those without PTSD, but not an enhanced detection of threat (e.g., Pineles, Shipherd, Welch, & Yovel, 2007; Pineles, Shipherd, Mostoufi, Abramovitz, & Yovel, 2009). Eye-tracking methodology may provide additional clues in answering this question. A recent eye-tracking study on visual attention to threatening stimuli in veterans of the Iraq War found that those endorsing more PTSD symptoms showed a trend for preferential attention to Iraq images compared to negative and neutral pictures (Kimble, Fleming, Brady, Kim, & Zambetti, 2010). There was also a trend for those higher in PTSD scores to look at trauma-related and negative pictures first, but no support for avoidance of trauma-related stimuli in this population. There is some evidence for the specifity of the Stroop effect. For example, Beck, Freeman, Shipherd, Hamblen, and Lacker (2001) found that MVA survivors with PTSD and pain showed delayed responses when color-naming both accident and pain-related words, whereas those with pain and no PTSD showed delays to pain-related stimuli only. Sveen, Dyster-Aas, and Willebrand (2009) reported that almost 80% of a sample of burns survivors displayed a burn-specific interference at one year following the trauma. This bias was related to earlier and concurrent PTSD symptoms, but not to symptoms of general anxiety or depression.

There is evidence that the results of studies of attentional bias are moderated by real-life threat (e.g., Constans, McCloskey, Vasterling, Brailey, & Mathews, 2004). Bar-Haim et al. (2010) indexed imminence of war-related threat in Israel as the time available for seeking shelter from rocket attacks in different areas bordering the Gaza strip. Participants who lived in most imminent threat displayed an attentional bias away from threat in the dot-probe task. Participants living outside this zone, on the other hand, displayed a bias toward threat. Greater attentional bias away from threat was associated with PTSD symptom severity in the imminent threat group. In one of the few studies of attentional bias in PTSD using threatening images, Pine et al. (2005) showed maltreated children and controls photographs of neutral, angry/threatening, and happy faces in a dot-probe task. Attention away from threatening faces was associated with PTSD.

Information processing theories suggest that the attentional bias in anxiety disorders is automatic (e.g., J. M. G. Williams, Watts, et al., 1997). Paradigms designed to measure automatic processing of verbal threat cues (e.g., the masked Stroop task), however, failed to produce consistent evidence for a pre-stimulus identification attentional bias to threat in PTSD on the behavioral level (for a review, see Buckley, Blanchard, & Neill, 2000). However, there is some evidence from EEG and fMRI studies that threatening faces are preferentially processed at a preattentive level by individuals with PTSD.

Attentional Bias—Neuroscience Findings

From a cognitive neuroscience perspective, attentional bias to threat in PTSD has been conceptualized as hyper-responsiveness of emotional and memory systems, and as a dysfunction in top-down regulatory systems (Etkin & Wager, 2007; Liberzon & Martis, 2006; Shin, Rauch & Pitman, 2006). Functional neuroimaging studies have aimed to establish the neural circuits underlying the increased interference in the emotional Stroop task in PTSD. Based on the conceptualization of the rostral anterior cingulate cortex (ACC) as a regulatory area that is activated during normal processing of emotional stimuli, Shin et al. (2001) hypothesized that patients with PTSD may fail to show significant activation in this area while attending to disorder-relevant words. In line with this prediction, the PTSD group in this study did not show significant activation in rostral ACC areas while presented with trauma-related words in an emotional Stroop task. They did show an activation of the dorsal region of the ACC, which has consistently been shown to be activated in interference paradigms. Those without PTSD, on the other hand, showed increased activation in the rostral ACC when trauma versus general negative word conditions were compared. Bremner et al. (2004) replicated these findings in a sample of women with PTSD who had been abused, who also showed lower blood flow response in the ACC compared to those without PTSD. In Bremner et al.'s (2004) study, emotional Stroop performance was also associated with decreased activity in visual areas, such as the visual association cortex, cuneus, and the inferior parietal lobe, which are involved in the processing in visual imagery and memory. In both studies, deficits in ACC areas were specific to the presentation of emotional material and were not shown in a nonemotional color Stroop task. Taken together, these findings point to a dysfunction in the ACC in PTSD. The ACC inhibits the amydala and may play a crucial role in the extinction of conditioned fear responses and the solution of emotional conflict (for a review see McNally, 2006). Conflict adaptation paradigms revealed an ACC-prefrontal sensory cortex cognitive control loop that ensures the protection of task-relevant processing from interference by task-irrelevant stimuli (e.g., Kerns et al., 2004), which may be dysfunctional in PTSD.

In line with an increased vigilance to threat cues, several studies have found a hyper-reactivity of the amygdala to subliminally presented and supraliminally presented negative pictures in participants with PTSD compared to healthy controls (Bryant et al., 2008; L. Williams et al., 2006). Recent studies point to a biphasic cortical response to threat with PTSD. In contrast to the hypo-responsivity of the medial prefrontal cortex in PTSD observed with supraliminal stimulus presentations (Shin et al., 2001), Bryant et al. (2008) and L. Williams et al. (2006) found increased medial prefrontal activity in PTSD with subliminal presentations of fearful faces. The pattern of results across studies may reflect a vigilance-avoidance response suggested by information processing theories of anxiety (e.g., J. M. G. Williams et al., 1997). Adenauer et al. (2010) presented a magnetoencephalography study that is consistent with this interpretation. Compared to traumatized and nontraumatized controls, participants with PTSD showed elevated cortical activity in right prefrontal areas in response to aversive pictures as early as 130–160 ms after stimulus onset, followed by decreased activity in the parieto-occipital cortex at 206–256 ms.

Threatening Personal Meanings (Interpretations, Appraisals, Beliefs, Schemas)

Predictions from Information Processing Theories of PTSD

Several information processing theories of PTSD highlighted the fact that a traumatic experience is often incompatible with preexisting schemas of the world and the self, thus requiring effortful processing to assimilate information from the trauma into these schemas and/or accommodate the schemas (Horowitz, 1986; Joseph, Williams, & Yule, 1995; McCann & Pearlman, 1990). Janoff-Bulman's (1992) concept of shattered assumptions is a prominent example of schema accommodation theories. Foa and Riggs (1993) and Resick and Schicke (1993) proposed that these trauma-related cognitions may reflect either a confirmation or shattering of previously held beliefs.

Several theorists have suggested that individual differences in the meanings people ascribe to the trauma contribute to the development and maintenance of PTSD. For people with PTSD, the trauma has threatening meanings that go beyond what everyone would find horrific about the experience. For example, Foa and Riggs (1993) specified two schemas involved in chronic PTSD "I am entirely incompetent" and "The world is entirely dangerous." Ehlers and Clark (2000) assigned a central role to the personal meaning of the traumatic event and its sequelae for the maintenance of PTSD. They suggested that persistent PTSD occurs only if individuals process the traumatic experience in a way that produces a sense of a serious current threat. Two key processes are thought to lead to a sense of current threat: (1) excessively negative appraisals of the event and/or its sequelae, and (2) the memory processes discussed above.

Empirical Evidence—Questionnaires Measuring View of the Self and the World

The role of problematic beliefs/appraisals about the meaning of traumatic event and its aftermath has mainly been assessed with questionnaire and interview studies assessing the individual's view of the self and the world. A series of cross-sectional studies (e.g., Clohessy & Ehlers, 1999; Dunmore, Clark, & Ehlers, 1997, 1999; Ehring, Ehlers, & Glucksman, 2006; Foa, Ehlers, Clark, Tolin, & Orsillo, 1999; Halligan et al., 2003; Mechanic & Resick, 1993; Resick, Schnicke, & Markway, 1991; Steil & Ehlers, 2000) showed that such beliefs/appraisals consistently distinguished between traumatized people with and without PTSD. Questionnaires such as the Personal Beliefs and Reactions Scale (PBRS; Resick et al., 1991) and the Posttraumatic Cognitions Inventory (PTCI; Foa et al., 1999), showed high specificity and sensitivity in identifying traumatized people with PTSD (Foa et al., 1999). Note that the World Assumption Scale (Janoff-Bulman, 1989), another widely used questionnaire measuring the concept of shattered assumptions, did not distinguish well between trauma survivors with PTSD and those without PTSD but, rather, distinguished trauma survivors from nontraumatized controls (Foa et al., 1999). Thus, although traumatic experiences universally require accommodation of existing cognitive schemas, only excessive or dysfunctional interpretations of the traumatic experience are related to psychopathology.

In line with the hypothesis that excessively negative appraisals of the trauma and its aftermath maintain PTSD, prospective longitudinal studies (Andrews, Brewin, Rose, & Kirk, 2000; Dunmore, Clark, & Ehlers, 2001; Ehlers, Mayou, & Bryant, 1998; Ehring, Ehlers, & Glucksman, 2008; Halligan et al., 2003; Kleim, Ehlers, & Gluckman, 2007, in press) found that dysfunctional appraisals measured soon after the trauma predicted chronic PTSD. Problematic appraisals of the initial PTSD symptoms predict over and above initial symptom severity (Dunmore et al., 2001; Ehlers et al., 1998) and over and above what can be predicted from trauma severity and other known risk factors (e.g., Ehring, Ehlers, et al., 2008; Halligan et al., 2003; Kleim et al., in press). The cross-sectional studies by Dunmore et al. (1997, 1999) and Halligan et al. (2003, study 1) further found that these appraisals distinguished between people with persistent PTSD and those that had recovered from PTSD.

Some authors emphasized that it is important to distinguish between explicit and implicit trauma-related appraisals (e.g., Dalgleish, 2004). Despite the widespread application of implicit measures in other areas of clinical psychology (see Wiers, Teachman, & de Houwer, 2007), there is a lack of research to date assessing implicit trauma-related appraisals in PTSD. In one of the few studies on this topic,

Engelhard, Huijding, van den Hout, and de Jong (2007) used an implicit association test (IAT) assessing implicit assumptions of the self as vulnerable in soldiers before and after their deployment to Iraq. In line with cognitive appraisal models, a cross-sectional association between implicit representations of the self as vulnerable and PTSD was found postdeployment. However, IAT scores assessed pretrauma did not predict posttrauma psychopathology.

Empirical Evidence—Biases in Interpretations and Probability Judgments

A minority of studies assessed probability estimates as an indicator of interpretation biases in PTSD. Dalgleish et al. (1997) found that children with PTSD gave higher probability judgments for general negative events than those without PTSD. Warda and Bryant (1998) reported that MVA survivors with ASD overestimated the cost and probability of future negative events compared to those without ASD. Similarly, White, McManus, and Ehlers (2008) found that adults with PTSD overestimated the probability and cost of future stressful life events. This judgment bias was reduced after successful therapy, and ratings were similar to those of controls.

Few studies to date have measured interpretation bias with objective tasks. One example is Kimble et al.'s study (2002) using a sentence-completion task. Veterans with and without PTSD were first exposed to trauma reminders and then had to complete sentences that could have either military or neutral endings. Veterans with PTSD produced more trauma-related endings than those without PTSD. Amir, Coles, and Foa (2002) used a homograph task and found that trauma survivors showed less inhibition of threatening meanings of homographs than traumatized participants without PTSD.

Conclusions: Attentional Bias and Threatening Interpretations

Both threatening interpretations of the trauma and its consequences and attentional bias are thought to contribute to the subjective impression of being under threat and thus maintain anxiety. The evidence supports both hypotheses. Evidence for the role of threatening interpretations of the trauma and of initial PTSD symptoms in PTSD is strong. Research using questionnaire measures of such appraisals has shown large effect sizes in predicting chronic PTSD. It is noteworthy that the problematic interpretations can concern both internal (e.g., "I am inadequate," "I am a bad person") and external threat (e.g., "I will be attacked again"), and that those relating to threat to one's view of the self appear to be especially powerful in predicting PTSD. There is relatively little work on objective measures of interpretation biases or implicit trauma-related appraisals in PTSD.

The relatively large literature on attentional bias to threat in PTSD has given somewhat inconsistent findings. Studies of Stroop interference for color naming of trauma-related words largely accord with the predicted increased attention to trauma-related and threatening material in PTSD, whereas results for other paradigms such as the dot-probe paradigm are less clear. Further research on the temporal pattern of attentional bias in PTSD is needed. Some studies using the dot-probe paradigm show attention to threat cues whereas others point to avoidance, and it remains unclear whether the avoidance is preceded by initial attention to the threat cues as information processing theories would predict (J. M. G. Williams, Watts, et al., 1997). Recent neuroscience findings appear to support such a biphasic response to threat in PTSD (e.g., Adenauer et al., 2010). Further research is needed to disentangle the contribution of enhanced detection of threatening stimuli versus difficulty disengaging from threatening stimuli and problematic avoidance in maintaining PTSD. Prospective studies that predict chronic PTSD from early attentional bias are largely lacking (Elsesser, Sartory, & Tackenberg, 2005). Finally, studies of moderators of attentional bias are of interest. PTSD is often comorbid with depression, and depression has been shown to moderate the effects of anxiety on attentional bias in some, but not all studies (Musa, Lepine, Clark, Mansell, & Ehlers, 2003, see Bar-Haim et al., 2007, for a review). Furthermore, attentional bias paradigms have largely relied on verbal material that represents external threat. Work on threatening meanings of the trauma, however, indicates that the perceived threat is often a threat to the self (e.g., "I am inadequate," "I am a bad person"). This may require a refinement of the stimulus materials used in attentional bias studies of PTSD.

4. Cognitive Responses to Trauma Memories that Maintain PTSD

Parallel to other anxiety disorders, avoidance of situational trauma reminders is a core symptom of PTSD and is considered to be one of the mechanisms that maintain PTSD. Cognitive avoidance is also common (Horowitz, 1986; Litz & Keane, 1989). Although early theories highlighted the role of avoidance in maintaining anxiety, more recent information processing models emphasize that avoidance prevents disconfirmation of maladaptive appraisals and processing of the trauma memory (e.g., Ehlers & Clark, 2000; Foa & Riggs, 1993). If people avoid thinking and talking about the trauma, then they will not correct misperceptions about what happened and what it means about themselves and the world. Ehlers and Steil (1995) suggested that PTSD maintaining behaviors go beyond avoidance and involve a range of responses, including substance misuse; excessive precautions (safety behaviors), scanning for signs of danger, thought suppression, or rumination about the event. We focus on the latter two in this section.

Thought Suppression

Predictions from Information Processing Theories of PTSD

Building on Wegner's seminal work on the paradoxical effects of thought suppression (e.g., Wegner, Schneider, Carter, & White, 1987), several authors suggested that effortful suppression of intrusive trauma memories leads to paradoxical increases of intrusions or rebound effects that maintain PTSD. For example, Ehlers and Steil (1995) suggested that that negative interpretations of initial PTSD symptoms motivate some trauma survivors to engage in cognitive strategies that are meant to control their symptoms, but maintain the disorder, such as thought suppression. Interpretations of initial symptoms and cognitive control strategies should therefore predict subsequent PTSD severity over and above what can be explained from initial severity. Wells (2000) suggested that cognitive strategies to control unwanted thoughts interfere with processing the trauma and thus lead to PTSD symptoms.

Empirical Evidence

A first group of studies used self-report measures to assess the frequency with which trauma survivors engage in suppression of trauma-related memories and thoughts. PTSD correlated with self-report levels of suppressing trauma-related thoughts and memories (Bennett, Beck, & Clapp, 2009; Clohessy & Ehlers, 1999; Ehring et al., 2006; Vázquez, Hervás, & Pérez-Sales, 2008), as well as a trait tendency to suppress unwanted thoughts in general (Amstadter & Vernon, 2008; Cameron, Palm, & Follette, 2010; Rosenthal & Follette, 2007; Vázquez et al., 2008; Yoshizumi & Murase, 2007). In addition, levels of thought suppression predicted PTSD in prospective longitudinal studies (Ehlers et al., 1998; Ehring, Ehlers et al., 2008; Kleim, Ehlers & Glucksman, in press; Morgan, Matthews, & Winton, 1995).

A second group of studies used experimental designs to test the effects of suppressing trauma memories and/or trauma-related thoughts in trauma survivors with acute stress disorder or PTSD. Results showed that the intentional suppression of intrusive trauma memories or thoughts leads to a rebound in intrusions (Amstadter & Vernon, 2006; Beck, Gudmundsdottir, Palyo, Miller, & Grant, 2006; Harvey & Bryant, 1998; Shipherd & Beck, 1999, 2005). Whereas in most of these studies the rebound effect emerged only in PTSD sufferers and not trauma survivors without the disorder, Beck et al. (2006) found a rebound effect following trauma-related thought suppression in trauma survivors irrespective of PTSD status. A recent thought-suppression study with combat veterans showed that PTSD was also related to an increased rebound effect following the suppression of a neutral thought (Aikins et al., 2009). Importantly, suppressing neutral thoughts also led to an enhancement of trauma-related intrusions in veterans with PTSD. This suggests that the suppression of trauma-related as well as non-trauma-related thoughts may maintain intrusions in PTSD.

A further group of studies used the trauma-film paradigm to test the effect of thought suppression on trauma-related intrusions. In these studies, healthy nontraumatized participants were exposed to a film depicting traumatic experiences (e.g., accidents, rape) and assessed the number of film-related intrusive memories participants developed afterwards. Results showed that the degree to which individuals reported suppressing film-related thoughts and memories was positively correlated to the number of film-related intrusions experienced in the days after the session (Nixon, Nehmy & Seymour, 2007; Regambal & Alden, 2009). Davies and Clark (1998) found experimental evidence for a causal role of thought suppression in the maintenance of intrusive memories. Participants who were instructed to suppress film-related thoughts subsequently reported significantly more intrusive memories regarding the film than those not suppressing the memories. However, Buck, Kindt, and Van Den Hout (2009) failed to replicate this finding. These inconsistent findings may be due to different control conditions used in these two studies (recording thoughts versus conceptual processing). Alternatively, they may suggest that thought suppression is not always equally dysfunctional. There is evidence showing that the ability to successfully suppress negative thoughts is a stable individual difference factor (Nixon, Flood, & Jackson, 2007), which may be related to weak inhibitory control (Verwoerd & Wessel, 2007; Verwoerd, Wessel & de Jong, 2009; Wessel, Overwijk, Verwoerd, & de Vrieze, 2008). Low thought-suppression ability and/or weak cognitive control may therefore be a risk factor for the development of PTSD, especially when individuals frequently use this strategy for coping with trauma-related memories. In order to test this hypothesis, Wessel, Huntjens, and Verwoerd (2010) manipulated cognitive control capacity by testing participants either at an optimal or a non-optimal time of the day. Participants were shown a stressful film and then asked to suppress film-related memories. Results partially supported the hypotheses, showing that trait inhibitory control was negatively correlated with intrusive memories following suppression on the non-optimal, but not on the optimal time of the day.

The effects of thought suppression may also depend on the context in which participants are engaging in this strategy. Importantly, research has shown the ability to successfully suppress negative thoughts is reduced when cognitive load demands are placed on the individual—for example, by a concurrent task (see Wenzlaff & Wegner, 2000). Nixon, Cain, Nehmy, and Seymour (2009b) used an experimental 2 (cognitive load: concurrent task versus none) x 2 (thought suppression versus none) design to test the effect of cognitive load on the effects of suppressing thoughts related to a trauma film. In line with the hypotheses, the highest number of intrusions emerged in the condition in which participants were instructed to suppress film-related thoughts while engaging in a concurrent task (but see also Nixon, Cain, Nehmy, & Seymour, 2009a, who did not replicate this finding using a slightly different design).

Rumination

Predictions from Information Processing Theories of PTSD

Although *DSM-IV* (APA, 1994) classifies ruminative thoughts about the trauma such as "Why did it happen to me" or "If only I had..." as a part of re-experiencing, some theorists distinguish between intrusive memories and rumination about the trauma (Ehlers & Clark, 2000; Ehlers & Steil, 1995; Joseph et al., 1995). Rumination is seen as a maladaptive way of coping with the trauma. Ehlers and Clark (2000) suggested that rumination maintains PTSD in several ways: (1) by strengthening problematic appraisals of the trauma (e.g., "The trauma has ruined my life"); (2) by interfering with the formation of an updated trauma memory because it focuses on "what if..." questions rather than what actually happened and what the outcome was; (3) by increasing feelings of nervous tension, dysphoria, or hopelessness; and (4) by providing internal retrieval cues for intrusive memories of the traumatic event.

An important issue in the rumination literature concerns the question of how maladaptive rumination can be distinguished from adaptive forms of repeated thinking. It has been suggested that dysfunctional rumination is characterized by abstract thinking, defined as decontextualized, aggregated and ambiguous, whereas functional forms of processing are more concrete, defined as experiential, specific and unambiguous (see Ehring & Watkins, 2008).

Empirical Evidence

Evidence is accumulating that intrusive memories and rumination about the trauma are phenomenologically and functionally distinct. In interview studies, intrusive memories were described as predominantly sensory experiences of short duration, whereas rumination was described as predominantly a train of thoughts of longer duration (e.g. Evans et al. 2007b; Hagenaars, Brewin, van Minnen, Holmes, & Hoogduin, 2010; Speckens et al., 2007). Michael, Halligan, Clark, and Ehlers (2007) identified a number of characteristics of trauma-related rumination that predicted PTSD in a prospective study, including the compulsion to continue rumination, "why" and "what if" type questions and the degree of negative emotions before and after rumination.

Results from cross-sectional studies using self-report questionnaires of trauma-related rumination show that rumination is associated with PTSD (e.g., Clohessy & Ehlers, 1999; Ehring et al., 2006; Michael et al., 2007; Moore, Zoellner, & Mollenholt, 2008). In line with the hypothesis that rumination maintains PTSD, rumination predicted future PTSD in a series of prospective longitudinal studies (e.g., Ehlers et al., 1998; Ehring, Ehlers, et al., 2008; Kleim et al., 2007; Michael et al., 2007; Murray et al., 2002). Importantly, rumination still predicted future PTSD when initial symptom levels were statistically controlled (Ehring, Ehlers, et al., 2008; Kleim et al., 2007; Michael et al., 2007).

The cross-sectional and prospective relationship between rumination and PTSD was also replicated when using an adapted version of the Catastrophizing Interview (CI) as an objective indicator of repetitive thinking (Ehring, Frank, & Ehlers, 2008). The CI asks participants to elaborate a worrisome topic in an iterative procedure, whereby the degree of repetitive thinking is operationalized as the number of steps completed in the interview.

The hypothesis that rumination is causally involved in the maintenance of PTSD symptoms was tested in a number of experimental studies where participants are randomly assigned to either a condition in which rumination was induced or to a number of different control conditions (e.g., distraction, imagery, memory integration). Ehring, Fuchs, and Kläsener (2009) asked participants to provide a detailed narrative of a recent distressing life event, followed by either rumination or distraction. In the rumination condition, intrusive memories and negative mood produced by the narrative task lasted longer than distraction. Several studies used distressing films with healthy nontraumatized participants to study the effects of rumination. Rumination led to significantly more analogue PTSD symptoms and/or a significantly slower recovery from the film than the control conditions (Butler, Wells, & Dewick, 1995; Wells & Papageorgiou, 1995; Zetsche, Ehring, & Ehlers, 2009).

Ehring, Szeimies, and Schaffrick (2009) tested whether the abstractness of rumination is a critical component in its maladaptive effects. After seeing a distressing film, participants were randomly assigned to either an abstract rumination condition, a condition that induced concrete thinking about the same content, or a distraction condition. Abstract rumination led to significantly longer maintenance of negative mood and arousal triggered by a trauma film than concrete thinking and distraction. In two studies of MVA survivors, Ehring, Frank, et al. (2008) found that a combination of abstractness of ruminative thinking and self-reported rumination frequency predicted symptom severities better than rumination frequency alone.

Conclusions: Maintaining Cognitive Reactions

There is strong evidence from self-report data and moderate support from experimental data that rumination is an important factor in the maintenance of intrusive memories and negative mood after trauma. Correlational and experimental studies in trauma survivors further support the hypothesis that suppressing trauma-related thoughts and memories maintains intrusions in PTSD. Results from experimental analogue studies suggest that the effects of thought suppression may be moderated by individual's cognitive control capacity and situational demands.

5. Cognitive Vulnerabilities that Predict the Development of PTSD

Not everyone develops PTSD symptoms after trauma. This raises the question of whether there are cognitive vulnerability factors that predict whether or not people develop PTSD. Two groups of cognitive factors have been studied: (1) measures of cognitive capacity, and (2) measures of personality and coping styles.

There is evidence that a high intelligence level is a protective factor and low hippocampal volume a vulnerability factor for the development of PTSD (see McNally, 2006, for a review). The mechanisms by which cognitive capacity affects vulnerability to PTSD remain to be studied. One hypothesis is that people with greater cognitive ability are better able to cope with the high cognitive processing demands of the trauma so that they are better able to continue conceptual as opposed to data-driven processing of the trauma (Ehlers & Clark, 2000). They may also be less likely to overestimate the threat that the trauma poses (Buckley et al., 2000). Furthermore, they may use better coping strategies in the aftermath of trauma (McNally, 2006). Of the personality factors that may influence the development of PTSD, neuroticism has gained the most consistent support (e.g., Engelhard & van den Hout, 2007). In a recent review, Elswood, Hahn, Olatunji, and Williams (2009) suggested that a negative attributional style, anxiety sensitivity, a tendency to ruminate, and a looming cognitive style are vulnerability factors for the development of PTSD. Prospective studies that assess these traits before trauma exposure are needed to support their status as vulnerability factors. In one of the very few studies of this kind, Bryant and Guthrie (2007) found that maladaptive appraisals as measured with the PTCI (Foa et al., 1999) predicted the development of PTSD symptoms in newly recruited firefighters.

Future Directions

The above review showed that there is evidence that information processing models can help explain the characteristic re-experiencing symptoms in PTSD, why people with PTSD continue to be anxious although the trauma is over, and what maintains PTSD.

Nevertheless, there are important gaps in current knowledge. As discussed above, there are some contradictive findings in the literature—for example, in the discussion about the nature of trauma memories or in the direction of attentional bias—that need to be addressed in future research before any firm conclusions can be drawn. In addition, overall effect sizes for differences between people with and without PTSD in experimental studies of information processing are typically small. This raises the question of whether they are clinically significant. A number of directions appear promising to further improve our understanding of information processing in PTSD, resolve current controversies, and illuminate the relevance of the findings.

First, it appears that some of the existing problems regarding contradictive findings can be resolved by greater conceptual clarity about the constructs under investigation. For example, research has shown that although they were originally considered the same symptom, intrusive memories and rumination about the trauma are phenomenologically and functionally different. Similarly, better distinctions between helpful and unhelpful ways of thinking about the trauma and between different aspects of memory disorganization in PTSD may prove fruitful in the future. There is already some evidence that it may be necessary to distinguish between the memory for those parts of the traumatic event that are re-experienced and those parts that are not.

Second, methodological refinements may be necessary to solve some of the inconsistencies in the literature. For example, in interpreting the findings, one has to consider the stimulus material used in the tasks. Most experiments used standardized stimuli such as word lists. As traumatic experiences differ widely, individualized stimuli may yield larger effect sizes (e.g., Elsesser et al., 2004). Furthermore, the predominance of verbal information processing tasks in the field is a concern as intrusive memories of trauma are predominantly visual. Visual stimuli that have been used in experimental studies typically represent external threat rather than threat to self. Tasks with greater ecological validity, such as pictures of threatening interpersonal cues in victims of interpersonal violence (e.g., Pine et al., 2005; Kleim et al., 2011) or stimulus material that represents the perceived threat to the self reported by individuals with PTSD may yield larger effect sizes. Furthermore, there is scope for developing more sensitive experimental tasks (see, for example, the modified word stem task, Michael, Ehlers, et al., 2005).

Third, inconsistent results should be interpreted taking the population under investigation into account. For example, descriptions of memories of upsetting events given by college students may systematically differ from those of patients seeking treatment for PTSD following traumatic events that meet *DSM* criteria. In addition, the majority of studies to date have focused on survivors of single traumatic events in adulthood. Future research will need to test whether the results can be replicated in PTSD following repeated or chronic traumas early in life, such as childhood physical or sexual abuse, when information processing of trauma can be expected to be influenced by developmental processes.

Fourth, methodological improvements are needed to draw firmer conclusions about causal effects of information processing in PTSD. The majority of studies remain cross-sectional and are thus limited in their conclusiveness. More prospective studies and experimental studies that manipulate the information processes under investigation are needed. However, not all cognitive variables described in this chapter can be manipulated in trauma survivors (e.g., cognitive processing during the trauma). Therefore, it appears promising to systematically combine studies with trauma survivors, in which an association between information processing variables and PTSD is established, with experimental analogue studies in healthy individuals to establish causality (see Ehring et al., 2011, for a discussion). Advances in neuroscience are likely to help in clarifying the neurophysiological basis of re-experiencing and memory problems in PTSD. In addition, studies that assess participants before exposure to trauma are sparse and much needed to investigate hypotheses about cognitive risk factors for PTSD.

Fifth, it may be also be productive to study moderators of the effects of information processing on PTSD symptoms. There is a renewed interest in sex differences in PTSD, and differences in information processing may play a role (Olff, Langeland, Draijer & Gersons, 2007). There is also some initial evidence that neurophysiological responses differ between people who dissociate when reminded of the trauma and those who show a strong fear response (Lanius et al., 2010). Furthermore, the effects of comorbidity on patterns of information processing need to be systematically studied.

Finally, investigations of the mediators of effective treatments of PTSD may help support the role of information processing further. Conversely, theories and empirical findings on information processing in PTSD may inspire novel treatment procedures. For example, Cognitive Therapy for PTSD, a version of trauma-focused cognitive behavior therapy that builds on Ehlers and Clark's (2000) model of PTSD, includes several procedures that build directly on the work described in this chapter. Building on the work on perceptual priming and stimulus generalization after trauma, *stimulus discrimination training* helps patients identify sensory triggers of intrusive memories and discriminate them from those occurring during the trauma. Building on the work on disjointedness of the worst moments of the trauma in memory, the *updating memories procedure* involves identifying updating information that puts the meaning of the worst moments into a less threatening perspective and explicitly linking these moments in memory with the updating information. Building on the work on problematic appraisals in PTSD, cognitive restructuring of the appraisals of the trauma and its sequelae that induce a sense of current threat is a major emphasis of the treatment. Building on the work on the role of maintaining behaviors, the effects of thought suppression, rumination, and safety behaviors (excessive precautions) are demonstrated in experiential exercises and the patient is encouraged to experiment with dropping these behaviors. The treatment program has been shown to be effective in several randomized controlled trials (Duffy, Gillespie, & Clark, 2007; Ehlers, Clark, Hackmann, McManus, & Fennell, 2005; Ehlers et al., 2003, 2010; Smith et al., 2007). Investigations on mechanisms of treatment are under way.

References

Adenauer. H., Pinösch, S., Catani, C., Gola, H., Keil, J., Kißler, J., & Neuner, F. (2010). Early processing of threat cues in posttraumatic stress disorder: Evidence for a cortical vigilance-avoidance reaction. *Biological Psychiatry, 68*, 451–458.

Aikins, D. E., Johnson, D. C., Borelli, J. L., Klemanski, D. H., Morrissey, P. M., Benham, T. L., et al. (2009). Thought suppression failures in combat PTSD: A cognitive load hypothesis. *Behaviour Research and Therapy, 47*, 744–751.

American Psychiatric Association. (1994). *Diagnostic and statistical manual of mental disorders* (4th ed.). Washington, DC: Author.

Amir, N., Coles, M. E., & Foa, E. B. (2002). Automatic and strategic activation and inhibition of threat-relevant information in posttraumatic stress disorder. *Cognitive Therapy and Research, 26*, 645–655.

Amir, N., Leiner, A. S., & Bomyea, J. (2010), Implicit memory and posttraumatic stress symptoms. *Cognitive Therapy and Research, 34*, 49–58.

Amir, N., McNally, R. J., & Wiegartz, P. S. (1996). Implicit memory bias for threat in posttraumatic stress disorder. *Cognitive Therapy and Research, 20*, 625–635.

Amir, N., Stafford, J., Freshman, M. S., & Foa, E. B. (1998). Relationship between trauma narratives and trauma pathology. *Journal of Traumatic Stress, 11*, 385–392.

Amstadter, A. B., & Vernon, L. L. (2006). Suppression of neutral and trauma targets: Implications for posttraumatic stress disorder. *Journal of Traumatic Stress, 19*, 517–526.

Amstadter, A. B., & Vernon, L. L. (2008). A preliminary examination of thought suppression, emotion regulation, and coping in a trauma-exposed sample. *Journal of Aggression, Maltreatment and Trauma, 17*, 279–295.

Andrews, B., Brewin, C. R., Rose, S., & Kirk, M. (2000). Predicting PTSD symptoms in victims of violent crime: The role of shame, anger, and childhood abuse. *Journal of Abnormal Psychology, 109*, 69–73.

Arntz, A., de Groot, C., & Kindt, M. (2005). Emotional memory is perceptual. *Journal of Behavior Therapy and Experimental Psychiatry, 36*, 19–34.

Bar-Haim, Y., Holoshitz, Y., Eldar, S., Frenkel. T. I., Muller, D., Charney, D. S., et al. (2010). Life-threatening danger and suppression of attention bias to threat. *American Journal of Psychiatry, 167*, 694–698.

Bar-Haim, Y., Lamy, D., Pergamin, L., Bakermans-Kranenburg, M. J., & van IJzendoorn, M. H. (2007). Threat-related attentional bias in anxious and nonanxious individuals. *Psychological Bulletin, 133*, 1–24.

Beck, J. G., Freeman, J, B., Shipherd, J.C., Hamblen, J.L., & Lacker, J.M. (2001). Specificity of Stroop interference in patients with pain and PTSD. *Journal of Abnormal Psychology, 110*, 536–543.

Beck, J. G., Gudmundsdottir, B., Palyo, S. A., Miller, L. M., & Grant, D. M. (2006). Rebound effects following deliberate thought suppression: Does PTSD make a difference? *Behavior Therapy, 37*, 170–180.

Bennett, S. A., Beck, J. G., & Clapp, J. D. (2009). Understanding the relationship between posttraumatic stress disorder and trauma cognitions: The impact of thought control strategies. *Behaviour Research and Therapy, 47*, 1018–1023.

Berntsen, D. (2009). *Involuntary autobiographical memories.* Cambridge, UK: Cambridge University Press.

Berntsen, D., & Rubin, D. C. (2008). The reappearance hypothesis revisited: Recurrent involuntary memories after traumatic events and in everyday life. *Memory and Cognition, 36*, 449–460.

Berntsen, D., Willert, M., & Rubin, D. C. (2003). Splintered memories or vivid landmarks? Qualities and organization of traumatic memories with and without PTSD. *Applied Cognitive Psychology, 17*, 675–693.

Blanchard, E. B., Hickling, E. J., Buckley, T. C., Taylor, A. E., Vollmer, A., & Loos, W. R. (1996). Psychophysiology of posttraumatic stress disorder related to motor vehicle accidents: Replication and extension. *Journal of Consulting and Clinical Psychology, 64*, 742–751.

Blechert, J., Michael, T., Vriends, N., Margraf, J., & Wilhelm, F. (2007). Fear conditioning in posttramatic stress disorder: Evidence for delayed extinction of autonomic, experiential, and behavioural responses. *Behaviour Research and Therapy, 45*, 2019–2033.

Bourne, C., Frasqilho, F., Roth, A. D., & Holmes, E. A. (2010). Is it mere distraction? Peri-traumatic verbal tasks can increase analogue flashbacks, but reduce voluntary memory performance. *Journal of Behavior Therapy and Experimental Psychiatry, 41*, 316–324.

Bowers, J. S., & Turner, E. L. (2003). In search of perceptual priming in a semantic classification task. *Journal of Experimental Psychology: Learning, Memory, Cognition, 29*, 1248–1255.

Brand, M., & Markowitsch, H. J. (2010). Environmental influences on autobiographical memory. The mnestic block syndrome. In L. Bäckman & L. Nyberg (Eds.), *Memory, aging and the brain* (pp. 229–263). Hove, UK: Psychology Press.

Bremner, J. D., Vermetten, E., Vythilingam, M., Afzal, N., Schmahl, C., Elzinga, B., & Charney, D. S. (2004). Neural correlates of the classic color and emotional Stroop in women with abuse-related posttraumatic stress disorder. *Biological Psychiatry, 55*, 612–620.

Brewin, C. R., Dalgleish, T., & Joseph, S. 1996. A dual representation theory of posttraumatic stress disorder. *Psychological Review, 103*, 670–686.

Brewin, C. R., Gregory, J. D., Lipton, M., & Burgess, N. (2010). Intrusive images in psychological disorders: Characteristics, neural mechanisms, and treatment implications. *Psychological Review, 117*, 210–232.

Brewin, C. R., Kleiner, J. S., Vasterling, J. J., & Field, A. P. (2007). Memory for emotionally neutral information in posttraumatic stress disorder. *Journal of Abnormal Psychology, 116*, 448–463.

Brown, D., Scheflin, A. W., & Whitfield, C. L. (1999). Recovered memories: The current weight of the evidence in science and in the courts. *Journal of Psychiatry and Law, 27*, 5–156.

Bryant, R. A., & Guthrie, R. M. (2007). Maladaptive self-appraisals before trauma exposure predict posttraumatic stress disorder. *Journal of Consulting and Clinical Psychology, 75*, 812–815.

Bryant, R. A., & Harvey, A. G. (1997). Attentional bias in posttraumatic stress disorder. *Journal of Traumatic Stress, 10*, 635–644.

Bryant, R. A., Kemp, A. H., Felmingham, K. L., Liddell, B., Olivieri, G., Peduto, A., et al. (2008). Enhanced amygdala and medial prefrontal activation during nonconscious processing of fear in posttraumatic stress disorder: An fMRI study. *Human Brain Mapping, 29*, 517–523.

Bryant, R. A., Sutherland, K., & Guthrie, R. M. (2007). Impaired specific autobiographical memory as a risk factor for posttraumatic stress after trauma. *Journal of Abnormal Psychology, 116*, 837–841.

Buck, N., Kindt, M., & Van Den Hout, M. (2009). The effects of conceptual processing versus suppression on analogue PTSD symptoms after a distressing film. *Behavioural and Cognitive Psychotherapy, 37*, 195–206.

Buck, N., Kindt, M., van den Hout, M., Steens, L., & Linders, C. (2007). Perceptual memory representations and memory fragmentation as predictors of post-trauma symptoms. *Behavioural and Cognitive Psychotherapy, 35*, 259–272.

Buckley, T. C., Blanchard, E. B., & Neill, W. T. (2000). Information processing and PTSD: A review of the empirical literature. *Clinical Psychology Review, 28*, 1041–1065.

Butler, G., Wells, A., & Dewick, H. (1995). Differential effects of worry and imagery after exposure to a stressful stimulus: A pilot study. *Behavioural and Cognitive Psychotherapy, 23*, 45–56.

Byrne, C. A., Hyman, I. E., Jr., & Scott, K. L. (2001). Comparisons of memories for traumatic events and other experiences. *Applied Cognitive Psychology, 15*, S119-S133.

Cameron, A., Palm, K., & Follette, V. (2010). Reaction to stressful life events: What predicts symptom severity? *Journal of Anxiety Disorders, 24*, 645–649.

Christianson, S. A. (1992). Remembering emotional events: Potential mechanisms. In S.A. Christianson (Ed.), *The handbook of emotion and memory: Research and theory* (pp. 307–340). Hillsdale, NJ: Lawrence Erlbaum.

Chemtob, C., Roitblat, H. L., Hamada, R. S., Carlson, J. G., & Twentyman, C. T. (1988). A cognitive action theory of posttraumatic stress disorder. *Journal of Anxiety Disorders, 2*, 253–275.

Clohessy, S., & Ehlers, A. (1999). PTSD symptoms, response to intrusive memories and coping in ambulance service workers. *British Journal of Clinical Psychology, 38*, 251–265.

Constans, J. I., McCloskey, M. S., Vasterling, J. J., Brailey, K., & Matthews, A. (2004). Suppression of attentional bias in PTSD. *Journal of Abnormal Psychology, 113*, 315–323,

Creamer, M., Burgess, P., & Pattison, P. (1992). Reaction to trauma: A cognitive processing model. *Journal of Abnormal Psychology, 101*, 165–174.

Dalgleish, T. (2004). Cognitive approaches to posttraumatic stress disorder: The evolution of multirepresentational theorizing. *Psychological Bulletin, 130*, 228–260.

Dalgleish, T., Neshat-Doost, H., Taghavi, R., Moradi, A., Yule, W., & Canterbury, R. (1997). Information processing in clinically depressed and anxious children and adolescents. *Journal of Child Psychology and Psychiatry, 38*, 535–541.

Davis, M. I., & Clark, D.M. (1998). Thought suppression produces a rebound effect with analogue post-traumatic intrusions. *Behaviour Research and Therapy, 36*, 571–582.

Devineni, T., Blanchard, E. B., Hickling, E. J., & Buckley, T. C. (2004). Effect of psychological treatment on cognitive bias in motor vehicle accident-related Posttraumatic Stress Disorder. *Journal of Anxiety Disorders. 18*, 211–231.

Duffy, M., Gillespie, K., & Clark D. M. (2007). Post-traumatic stress disorder in the context of terrorism and other civil conflict in Northern Ireland: Randomised controlled trial. *British Medical Journal, 334*, 1147–1150.

Dunmore, E., Clark, D. M., & Ehlers, A. (1997). Cognitive factors in persistent versus recovered post-traumatic stress disorder after physical or sexual assault: A pilot study. *Behavioural and Cognitive Psychotherapy, 25*, 147–159.

Dunmore, E., Clark, D. M., & Ehlers, A. (1999). Cognitive factors involved in the onset and maintenance of posttraumatic stress disorder after physical or sexual assault. *Behaviour Research and Therapy, 37*, 809–829.

Dunmore, E., Clark, D. M., & Ehlers, A. (2001). A prospective study of the role of cognitive factors in persistent posttraumatic stress disorder after physical or sexual assault. *Behaviour Research and Therapy, 39*, 1063–1084.

Easterbrook, J. A. (1959). The effect of emotion on cue utilization and the organization of behavior. *Psychological Review, 66*, 183–201.

Ehlers, A., & Clark, D. M. (2000). A cognitive model of posttraumatic stress disorder. *Behaviour Research and Therapy, 38*, 319–345.

Ehlers, A., Clark, D. M., Hackmann, A., McManus, F., & Fennell, M. (2005). Cognitive therapy for PTSD: Development and evaluation. *Behaviour Research and Therapy, 43*, 413–431.

Ehlers, A., Clark, D. M., Hackmann, A., McManus F., Fennell, M., Herbert, C., & Mayou, R. (2003). A randomized controlled trial of cognitive therapy, self-help booklet, and repeated assessment as early interventions for PTSD. *Archives of General Psychiatry, 60*, 1024–1032.

Ehlers, A., Hackmann, A., & Michael, T. (2004). Intrusive re-experiencing in post-traumatic stress disorder: Phenomenology, theory, and therapy. *Memory, 12*, 403–415.

Ehlers, A., Hackmann, A., Steil, R., Clohessy, S., Wenninger, K., & Winter, H. (2002). The nature of intrusive memories after trauma: The warning signal hypothesis. *Behaviour Research and Therapy, 40*, 995–1002.

Ehlers, A., Maercker, A., & Boos, A. (2000). Posttraumatic stress disorder following political imprisonment: The role of mental defeat, alienation, and perceived permanent change. *Journal of Abnormal Psychology, 109*, 45–55.

Ehlers, A., Mauchnik, J., & Handley, R. (2010). Reducing unwanted trauma memories by imaginal exposure or autobiographical memory elaboration: An analogue study of memory processes. *Journal of Behavior Therapy and Experimental Psychiatry.* advance online publication, doi:10.1016/j.jbtep.2010.12.009

Ehlers, A., Mayou, R. A., & Bryant, B. (1998). Psychological predictors of chronic posttraumatic stress disorder after motor vehicle accidents. *Journal of Abnormal Psychology, 107*, 508–519.

Ehlers, A., Michael, T., Chen, Y. P., Payne, E., & Shan, S. (2006). Enhanced perceptual priming for neutral stimuli in a traumatic context: A pathway to intrusive memories? *Memory, 14*, 316–328.

Ehlers, A., & Steil, R. (1995). Maintenance of intrusive memories in Posttraumatic Stress Disorder: A cognitive approach. *Behavioural and Cognitive Psychotherapy, 23*, 217–249.

Ehlers, A., Sündermann, O., Böllinghaus, I., Vossbeck-Elsebusch, A., Gamer, M., Briddon, E., et al. (2010). Heart rate responses to standardized trauma-related pictures in acute posttraumatic stress disorder. *International Journal of Psychophysiology, 78*, 27–34.

Ehring, T. (2004). Psychological consequences of road traffic accidents: The prediction of PTSD, phobias and depression. Ph.D. thesis, King's College London.

Ehring, T., & Ehlers, A. (2011). Enhanced primin.g for trauma-related words predicts posttraumatic stress disorder. *Journal of Abnormal Psychology, 120*, 234–239. doi: 10.1037/a0021080

Ehring, T., Ehlers, A., & Glucksman, E. (2006). Contribution of cognitive factors to the prediction of posttraumatic stress disorder, phobia and depression after road traffic accidents. *Behaviour Research and Therapy, 44*, 1699–1716.

Ehring, T., Ehlers, A., & Glucksman, E. (2008). Do cognitive models help in predicting the severity of posttraumatic stress disorder, phobia and depression after motor vehicle accidents? A prospective longitudinal study. *Journal of Consulting and Clinical Psychology, 76*, 219–230.

Ehring, T., Frank, S., & Ehlers, A. (2008). The role of rumination and reduced concreteness in the maintenance of posttraumatic stress disorder and depression following trauma. *Cognitive Therapy and Research, 33*, 488–506.

Ehring, T., Fuchs, N., & Kläsener, I. (2009). The effects of experimentally induced rumination versus distraction on analogue posttraumatic stress symptoms. *Behavior Therapy, 40*, 403–413.

Ehring, T., Kleim, B, & Ehlers, A. (2011). Combining clinical studies and analogue experiments to investigate cognitive mechanisms in posttraumatic stress disorder. *International Journal of Cognitive Therapy, 4*, 165–177

Ehring, T., Szeimies, A. K., & Schaffrick, C. (2009). An experimental analogue study into the role of abstract thinking in trauma-related rumination. *Behaviour Research and Therapy, 47*, 285–293.

Ehring, T., & Watkins, E. R. (2008). Repetitive negative thinking as a transdiagnostic process. *International Journal of Cognitive Therapy, 1*, 192–205.

Elswood, L. S., Hahn, K. S., Olatunji, B. O., & Williams, N. L. (2009). Cognitive vulnerabilities to the development of PTSD: A review of four vulnerabilities and the proposal of an integrative vulnerability model. *Clinical Psychology Review, 29*, 87–100.

Elsesser, K., Sartory, G., & Tackenberg, A. (2004). Attention, heart rate, and startle response during exposure to trauma-relevant pictures: A comparison of recent trauma victims and patients with posttraumatic stress disorder. *Journal of Abnormal Psychology, 113*, 289–301.

Elsesser, K., Sartory, G., & Tackenberg, A. (2005). Initial symptoms and reactions to trauma-related stimuli and the development of posttraumatic stress disorder. *Depression and Anxiety, 21*, 61–70.

Engelhard, I. M., Huijding, J., van den Hout, M. A., & de Jong, P. J. (2007). Vulnerability associations and symptoms of post-traumatic stress disorder in soldiers deployed to Iraq. *Behaviour Research and Therapy, 45*, 2317–2325.

Engelhard, I. M., & Van den Hout, M. A. (2007) Preexisting neuroticism, subjective stressor severity, and posttraumatic stress in soldiers deployed to Iraq. *The Canadian Journal of Psychiatry, 52*, 505–509.

Engelhard, I. M., Van den Hout, M. A., Kindt, M., Arntz, A., & Schouten, E. (2003). Peritraumatic dissociation and posttraumatic stress after pregnancy loss: A prospective study. *Behaviour Research and Therapy, 41*, 67–78.

Etkin, A., & Wager, T. D. (2007). Functional neuroimaging of anxiety. A meta-analysis of emotional processing in PTSD, social phobia, and specific phobia. *American Journal of Psychiatry, 164*, 1476–1488.

Evans, C., Ehlers, A., Mezey, G., & Clark, D. M. (2007a). Intrusive memories in perpetrators of violent crime: Emotions and cognitions. *Journal of Consulting and Clinical Psychology, 75*, 134–144.

Evans, C., Ehlers, A., Mezey, G., & Clark, D. M. (2007b). Intrusive memories and ruminations related to violent crime among young offenders: Phenomenological characteristics. *Journal of Traumatic Stress, 20*, 183–196.

Evans, C., Mezey, G., & Ehlers, A. (2009). Amnesia for violent crime. *Journal of Forensic Psychiatry and Psychology, 20*, 85–106.

Foa, E. B., Ehlers, A., Clark, D. M., Tolin, D., & Orsillo, S. (1999). The Post-traumatic Cognitions Inventory (PTCI). Development and validation. *Psychological Assessment, 11*, 303–314.

Foa, E. B., Feske, U., Murdock, T. B, Kozak, M. J., & McCarthy, P. R. (1991). Processing of threat-related information in rape victims. *Journal of Abnormal Psychology, 100*, 156–162.

Foa, E. B., Molnar, C., & Cashman, L. (1995). Change in rape narratives during exposure therapy for posttraumatic stress disorder. *Journal of Traumatic Stress, 8*, 675–690.

Foa, E. B., & Riggs, D. S. (1993). Posttraumatic stress disorder and rape. In J. M. Oldham, M. B. Riba & A. Tasman (Eds.),

American Psychiatric Press Review of Psychiatry (pp. 273–303). Washington, DC: American Psychiatric Press.

Foa, E. B., & Rothbaum, B. O. (1998). *Treating the trauma of rape. Cognitive-behavior therapy for PTSD.* New York: Guilford.

Foa, E. B., Steketee, G., & Rothbaum, B. O. (1989). Behavioral/cognitive conceptualizations of post-traumatic stress disorder. *Behavior Therapy, 20,* 155–176.

Geraerts, E., Schooler, J., Merckelbach, H., Jelicic, M., Hauer, B. J. A., & Ambadar, Z. (2007). The reality of recovered memories: Corroborating continuous and discontinuous memories of childhood sexual abuse. *Psychological Science, 18,* 564–568.

Gersons, B. P. R., & Carlier, I. V. E. (1992). Post-traumatic stress disorder: The history of a recent concept. *British Journal of Psychiatry, 161,* 742–748.

Golier, J., Yehuda, R., Lupien, S. J., & Harvey, P. D. (2003). Memory for trauma-related information in Holocaust survivors with PTSD. *Psychiatry Research, 121,* 133–143.

Gray, M. J., & Lombardo, T. W. (2001). Complexity of trauma narratives as an index of fragmented memory in PTSD: A critical analysis. *Applied Cognitive Psychology, 15,* S171-S186.

Guthrie, R. M., & Bryant, R. A. (2006). Extinction learning before trauma and subsequent posttraumatic stress. *Psychosomatic Medicine, 68,* 307–311.

Hackmann, A., Ehlers, A., Speckens, A., & Clark, D. M. (2004). Characteristics and content of intrusive memories in PTSD and their changes with treatment. *Journal of Traumatic Stress, 17,* 231–240.

Hagenaars, M. A., Brewin, C. R., van Minnen, A., Holmes, E., & Hoogduin, K. A. L. (2010). Intrusive images and intrusive thoughts as different phenomena: Two experimental studies. *Memory, 18,* 76–84.

Hagenaars, M. A., van Minnen, A., Hoogduin, C. A. L., & Verbraak, M. (2009). A transdiagnostic comparison of trauma and panic memories in PTSD, panic disorder, and healthy controls. *Journal of Behavior Therapy and Experimental Psychiatry, 40,* 412–422.

Halligan, S. L., Clark, D. M., & Ehlers, A. (2002). Cognitive processing, memory, and the development of PTSD symptoms: Two experimental analogue studies. *Journal of Behavior Therapy and Experimental Psychiatry, 33,* 73–89.

Halligan, S. L., Michael, T., Clark, D. M., & Ehlers, A. (2003). Posttraumatic stress disorder following assault: The role of cognitive processing, trauma memory, and appraisals. *Journal of Consulting and Clinical Psychology, 71,* 419–431.

Harvey, A. G. & Bryant, R. A. (1998). The effect of attempted thought suppression in acute stress disorder. *Behaviour Research and Therapy, 36,* 583–590.

Harvey, A. G. & Bryant, R. A. (1999). A qualitative investigation of the organization of traumatic memories. *British Journal of Clinical Psychology, 38,* 401–405.

Harvey, A. G., Bryant, R. A., & Dang, S. T. (1998). Autobiographical memory in acute stress disorder. *Journal of Consulting and Clinical Psychology, 66,* 500–506.

Herman, J. L. (1992). Complex PTSD: A syndrome in survivors of prolonged and repeated trauma. *Journal of Traumatic Stress, 5,* 377–391.

Holmes, E. A., Brewin, C. R., & Hennessy, R. G. (2004). Trauma films, information processing, and intrusive memory development. *Journal of Experimental Psychology: General, 133,* 3–22.

Horowitz, M. J. (1986). *Stress response syndromes* (2nd ed.). Northvale, NJ: Jason Aronson.

Janoff-Bulman, R. (1989). Assumptive worlds and the stress of traumatic events: Applications of the schema construct. *Social Cognition, 7,* 113–136.

Janoff-Bulman, R. (1992). *Shattered assumptions: Towards a new psychology of trauma.* New York: Free Press.

Jelinek, L., Randjbar, S., Seifert, D., Kellner, M., & Moritz, S. (2009). The organization of autobiographical and non-autobiographical memory in posttraumatic stress disorder (PTSD). *Journal of Abnormal Psychology, 118,* 288–298.

Jelinek, L., Stockbauer, C., Randjbar, S., Kellner, M., Ehring, T., & Moritz, S. (2010). Characteristics and organization of the worst moment of trauma memories in posttraumatic stress disorder. *Behaviour Research and Therapy, 48,* 680–685.

Jones, C., Harvey, A. G., & Brewin, C. R. (2007). The organisation and content of trauma memories in survivors of road traffic accidents. *Behaviour Research and Therapy, 45,* 151–162.

Joseph, S., Williams, R., & Yule, W. (1995). Psychosocial perspectives on post-traumatic stress. *Clinical Psychology Review, 15,* 515–544.

Kangas, M., Henry, J. L., & Bryant, R. A. (2005). A prospective study of autobiographical memory in posttraumatic stress disorder following cancer. *Journal of Consulting and Clinical Psychology, 73,* 292–299.

Keane, T. M., Zimering, R. T., & Caddell, J. M. (1985). A behavioral formulation of posttraumatic stress disorder in Vietnam veterans. *Behavior Therapist, 8,* 9–12.

Kerns, J. G., Cohen, J. D., MacDonald, A. W., Cho, R.Y., Stenger, V.A., & Carter, C.S. (2004). Anterior cingulate conflict monitoring and adjustments of control. *Science, 303,* 1023–1026.

Kimble, M. O., Fleming, K., Bandy, C., Kim, J., & Zambetti, A. (2010). Eye tracking and visual attention to threatening stimuli in veterans of the Iraq war. *Journal of Anxiety Disorders, 24,* 293–299.

Kimble, M. O., Frueh, C. B., & Marks, L. (2009). Does the modified Stroop effect exist in PTSD? Evidence from dissertation abstract and the peer reviewed literature. *Journal of Anxiety Disorders, 23,* 650–655.

Kimble, M. O., Kaufman, M. L., Leonard, L. L., Nestor, P. G., Riggs, D. S., Kaloupek, D. G., & Bahcrach, P. (2002). Sentence completion test in combat veterans with and without PTSD: Preliminary findings. *Psychiatry Research, 113,* 303–307.

Kindt, M., & van den Hout, M. (2003) Dissociation and memory fragmentation: Experimental effects on meta-memory but not on actual memory performance. *Behaviour Research and Therapy, 41,* 167–178.

Kindt, M., Van den Hout, M., Arntz, A., & Drost, J. (2008). The influence of data-driven versus conceptually-driven processing on the development of PTSD-like symptoms. *Journal of Behavior Therapy and Experimental Psychiatry, 39,* 546–557.

Kindt, M., Van den Hout, M., & Buck (2005). Dissociation related to subjective memory fragmentation and intrusions but not to objective memory disturbances. *Journal of Behavior Therapy and Experimental Psychiatry, 36,* 43–59.

Kleim, B., & Ehlers, A. (2008). Reduced autobiographical memory specificity predicts depression and posttraumatic stress disorder after recent trauma. *Journal of Consulting and Clinical Psychology, 76,* 231–242.

Kleim, B., Ehlers, A., & Glucksman, E. (2007). Early predictors of posttraumatic stress disorder in assault survivors. *Psychological Medicine, 37,* 1457–1467.

Kleim, B., Ehlers, A., & Glucksman, E. (in press). Investigating cognitive pathways to psychopathology: Predicting depression and posttraumatic stress disorder from early responses after assault. *Psychological Trauma: Theory, Research, Practice, and Policy.*

Kleim, B., Ehring, T, & Ehlers, A. (2011). Perceptual processing advantages for trauma-related visual cues in post-traumatic stress disorder. *Psychological Medicine.* advance online publication, doi:10.1017/S0033291711001048

Kleim, B., Wallott, F., & Ehlers, A. (2008). Are trauma memories disjointed from other autobiographical memories in PTSD? An experimental investigation. *Behavioural and Cognitive Psychotherapy, 36,* 221–234.

Kopelman, M. (1987). Crime and amnesia: A review. *Behavioural Sciences and the Law, 5,* 323–342.

Koss, M. P., Figueredo, A. J., Bell, I., Tharan, M., & Tromp, S. (1996). Traumatic memory characteristics: A cross-validated mediational model of response to rape among employed women. *Journal of Abnormal Psychology, 105,* 421–432.

Lang, P. M. (1977). Imagery in therapy: An information processing analysis of fear. *Behavior Therapy, 8,* 862–886.

Lanius, R. A., Vermetten, E., Loewenstein, R. J., Brand, B., Schmahl, C., Bremner, J. D., & Spiegel, D. (2010). Emotion modulation in PTSD: Clinical and neurobiological evidence for a dissociative subtype. *American Journal of Psychiatry, 167,* 640–647.

Liberzon, I., & Martis, B. (2006). Neuroimaging studies of emotional responses in PTSD. *Annual Review New York Academy of Sciences, 1071,* 87–109.

Litz, B. T., & Keane, T. M. (1989). Information processing in anxiety disorders: Application to the understanding of post-traumatic stress disorder. *Clinical Psychology Review, 9,* 243–257.

Markowitsch, H. J., Kessler, J., Van der Ven, C., Weber-Luxemburger, G., Albers, M., & Heiss, W. D. (1998). Psychic trauma causing grossly reduced brain metabolism and cognitive deterioration. *Neuropsychologia, 36,* 77–82.

Mauchnik, J., Ebner-Priemer, U. W., Bohus, M., & Schmahl, C. (2010). Classical conditioning in borderline personality disorder with and without posttraumatic stress disorder. *Zeitschrift für Psychologie, 218,* 80–88.

McCann, I. L., & Pearlman, L. A. (1990). Vicarious traumatization: A framework for understanding the psycholgical effects of working with victims. *Journal of Traumatic Stress, 3,* 131–149.

McKone, E., & French, B. (2001). In what sense is implicit memory episodic? The effect of reinstating environmental context. *Psychonomic Bulletin and Review, 8,* 4, 806–811.

McNally, R. J. (1998). Experimental approaches to cognitive abnormality in posttraumatic stress disorder. *Clinical Psychology Review, 18,* 971–982.

McNally, R. J. (2003). *Remembering trauma.* Cambridge, MA: Belknap Press/Harvard University Press.

McNally, R. J. (2006). Cognitive abnormalities in post-traumatic stress disorder. *Trends in Cognitive Sciences, 10,* 271–277.

McNally, R. J., & Amir, N. (1996). Perceptual implicit memory for trauma-related information in post-traumatic stress disorder. *Cognition and Emotion, 10,* 551–556.

McNally, R. J., & Geraerts, E. (2009). A new solution to the recovered memory debate. *Perspectives in Psychological Science, 4,* 126–134.

McNally, R. J., Lasko, N. B., Macklin, M. L., & Pitman, R. K. (1995). Autobiographical memory disturbance in combat-related posttraumatic stress disorder. *Behaviour Research & Therapy, 33,* 619–630.

McNally, R. J., Litz, B. T., Prassas, A., Shin, L. M., & Weathers, F. W. (1994). Emotional priming of autobiographical memory in post-traumatic stress disorder. *Cognition and Emotion, 8,* 351–367.

McNally, R. J., & Shin, L. M. (1995). Association of intelligence with severity of posttraumatic stress disorder symptoms in Vietnam combat veterans. *American Journal of Psychiatry, 152,* 936–938.

Mechanic, M. B., & Resick, P. A. (1993, November). *The personal beliefs and reactions scale: Assessing rape-related cognitive schemata.* Paper presented at the 9th annual meeting of the International Society for Traumatic Stress Studies, San Antonio, TX.

Megías, J. L., Ryan, E., Vaquero, J. M. M., & Frese, B. (2007). Comparisons of traumatic and positive memories in people with and without PTSD profile. *Applied Cognitive Psychology, 21,* 117–130.

Michael, T., & Ehlers, A. (2007). Enhanced perceptual priming for neutral stimuli occurring in a traumatic context: Two experimental investigations. *Behaviour Research and Therapy, 45,* 341–358.

Michael, T., Ehlers, A., & Halligan, S.L. (2005). Perceptual priming for trauma-related material in posttraumatic stress disorder. *Emotion, 5,* 103–112.

Michael, T., Ehlers, A., Halligan, S., & Clark, D. M. (2005). Unwanted memories of assault: What intrusion characteristics predict PTSD? *Behaviour Research and Therapy, 43,* 613–628

Michael, T., Halligan, S., Clark, D. M., & Ehlers, A. (2007). Rumination in posttraumatic stress disorder. *Depression and Anxiety, 24,* 307–317.

Michael, T., Vriends, N., Blechert, J., Meyer, A. H., Zetsche, U., Margraf, J., & Wilhelm, F. (2010). *Strong associative learning between neutral and trauma-related stimuli in posttraumatic stress disorder in the absence of contingency awareness.* Manuscript submitted for publication.

Mitchell, D. B. (2006). Nonconscious priming after 17 years. Invulnerable implicit memory? *Psychological Science, 17,* 925–929.

Mogg, K., Bradley, B. P., Miles, F., & Dixon, R. (2004). Time course of attentional bias or threat scenes: Testing the vigilance-avoidance hypothesis. *Cognition and Emotion, 18,* 689–700.

Moore, S.A., & Zoellner, L. A. (2007). Overgeneral autobiographical memory and traumatic events: An evaluative review. *Psychological Bulletin, 133,* 419–437.

Moore, S.A., Zoellner, L. A., & Mollenholt, N. (2008). Are expressive suppression and cognitive reappraisal associated with stress-related symptoms? *Behaviour Research and Therapy, 46,* 993–1000.

Morgan, I. A., Matthews, G., & Winton, M. (1995). Coping and personality as predictors of post-traumatic intrusions, numbing, avoidance and general distress: A study of victims of the Perth Flood. *Behavioural and Cognitive Psychotherapy, 23,* 251–264.

Murray, J., Ehlers, A., & Mayou, R. A. (2002). Dissociation and posttraumatic stress disorder: Two prospective studies of road traffic accident victims. *British Journal of Psychiatry, 180,* 363–368.

Musa, C., Lepine, J. P., Clark, D. M., Mansell, W., & Ehlers, A. (2003). Selective attention in social phobia and the moderating effect of a concurrent depressive disorder. *Behaviour Research and Therapy, 41,* 1043–1054.

Nixon, R. D. V., Cain, N., Nehmy, T., & Seymour, M. (2009a). Does post-event cognitive load undermine thought suppression and increase intrusive memories after exposure to an analogue stressor? *Memory, 17,* 245–255.

Nixon, R. D. V., Cain, N., Nehmy, T., & Seymour, M. (2009b). The influence of thought suppression and cognitive load on intrusions and ,memory processes following an analogue stressor. *Behavior Therapy, 40,* 368–379.

Nixon, R. D. V., Flood, J., & Jackson, K. (2007). The generalizability of thought suppression ability to novel stimuli. *Personality and Individual Differences, 42,* 677–687.

Nixon, R. D. V., Nehmy, T., & Seymour, M. (2007). The effect of cognitive load and hyperarousal on negative intrusive memories. *Behaviour Research and Therapy, 45,* 2652–2663.

Olff, M., Langeland, W., Drijer N., & Gersons, B. P. R. (2007). Gender differences in posttraumatic stress disorder. *Psychological Bulletin, 133,* 183–204.

Orr, S. P., Metzger L. J., Lasko, N. B., Macklin, M. L., Peri, T., & Pitman, R. K. (2000). De novo conditioning in trauma-exposed individuals with and without posttraumatic stress disorder. *Journal of Abnormal Psychology, 109,* 290–298.

Orr, S. P., Milad, M. R., Metzger L. J., Lasko, N. B., Gilbertson, M. W., & Pitman, R. K. (2006). Effects of beta blockade, PTSD diagnosis, and explicit threat on the extinction and retention of an aversively conditioned response. *Biological Psychology. 73,* 262–271.

Ozer, E. J., Best, S. R., Lipsey, T. L., & Weiss, D. S. (2003). Predictors of posttraumatic stress disorder and symptoms in adults: A meta-analysis. *Psychological Bulletin, 129,* 52–73.

Peace, K. A., Porter, S., & ten Brinke, L. (2008). Are memories for sexually traumatic events "special"? A within-subjects investigation of trauma and memory in a clinical sample. *Memory, 16,* 10–21.

Peri, T., Ben-Shakar, G., Orr, S. P., & Shalev, A. (2000). Psychophysiologic assessment of aversive conditioning in posttraumatic stress disorder. *Biological Psychiatry, 47,* 512–519.

Pine, D. S., Mogg, K., Bradley, B. P. Montgomery, L., Monk, C. S., McClure, E., et al. (2005). Attentional bias to threat in maltreated children: Implications for vulnerability to stress-related psychopathology. *American Journal of Psychiatry, 162,* 291–296.

Pineles, S. L., Shipherd, J. C., Mostoufi, S. M., Abramovitz, S. M., & Yovel, I. (2009). Attentional biases in PTSD: More evidence for interference. *Behaviour Research and Therapy, 47,* 1050–1057.

Pineles, S. L., Shipherd, J. C., Welch, L., & Yovel, I. (2007). The role of attentional biases in PTSD: Is it interference or facilitation ? *Behaviour Research and Therapy, 45,* 1903–1913.

Pole, N. (2007). The psychophysiology of posttraumatic stress disorder: A meta-analysis. *Psychological Bulletin, 133,* 725–746.

Porter, S., & Birt, A. R. (2001). Is traumatic memory special? A comparison of traumatic memory characteristics with memory for other emotional life experiences. *Applied Cognitive Psychology, 15,* S101-S117.

Regambal, M. J., & Alden, L. E. (2009). Pathways to intrusive memories in a trauma analogue paradigm: A structural equation model. *Depression and Anxiety, 26,* 155–166.

Rescorla, R.A. (1988). Pavlovian conditioning. It's not what you think it is. *American Psychologist, 43,* 151–160.

Resick, P. A, & Schnicke, M. K. (1993). *Cognitive processing therapy for rape victims.* Newbury Park, CA: Sage.

Resick, P. A., Schnicke, M. K., & Markway, B. G. (1991, November). *The relationship between cognitive content and posttraumatic stress disorder.* Paper presented at the Annual Meeting of the Association for Advancement of Behavior Therapy, New York.

Riemann, B., & McNally, R. J. (1995). Cognitive processing of personally relevant information. *Cognition and Emotion, 9,* 325–340.

Roediger, H. L. (1990). Implicit memory: Retention without remembering. *American Psychologist, 45,* 1043–1056.

Rosenthal, M. Z., & Follette, V. M. (2007). The effects of sexual assault-related intrusion suppression in the laboratory and natural environment. *Behaviour Research and Therapy, 45,* 73–87.

Rubin, D. C. (in press). The coherence of memories for trauma: Evidence from posttraumatic stress disorder. *Consciousness and Cognition.*

Rubin, D. C., Berntsen, D., & Bohni, M. K. (2008). A memory-based model of posttraumatic stress disorder: Evaluating basic assumptions underlying the PTSD diagnosis. *Psychological Review, 115,* 985–1011.

Rubin, D. C., Boals, A., & Berntsen, D. (2008). Memory on posttraumatic stress disorder: Properties of voluntary and involuntary, traumatic and nontraumatic autobiographical memories in people with and without posttraumatic stress disorder symptoms. *Journal of Experimental Psychology: General, 137,* 591–614.

Rubin, D. C., Feldman, M. E., & Beckham, J. C. (2004). Reliving, emotions, and fragmentation in the autobiographical memories of veterans diagnosed with PTSD. *Applied Cognitive Psychology, 18,* 17–35.

Schacter, D. L., Dobbins, I. G. & Schnyer, D. M. (2004). Specificity of priming: A cognitive neuroscience perspective. *Nature Neuroscience, 5,* 853–862.

Schönfeld, S., & Ehlers, A. (2006). Overgeneral memory extends to pictorial retrieval cues and correlates with cognitive features in posttraumatic stress disorder. *Emotion, 6,* 611–622.

Schönfeld, S., Ehlers, A., Böllinghaus, I., & Rief, W. (2007). Overgeneral memory and suppression of trauma memories in posttraumatic stress disorder. *Memory, 15,* 339–352.

Shin, L. M., Rauch, S. L., & Pitman, R. K. (2006). Amygdala, medial prefrontal cortex, and hippocampal function in PTSD. *Annals of the New York Academy of Sciences, 1071,* 67–69.

Shin, L. M., Whalen, P. J., Pitman, R. K., Bush, G., Macklin, M. L., Lasko, N. B., et al. (2001). An fMRI study of anterior cingulate function in posttraumatic stress disorder. *Biological Psychiatry, 50,* 932–942.

Shipherd, J. C., & Beck. J. G. (1999). The effects of suppressing trauma-related thoughts on women with rape-related posttraumatic stress disorder. *Behaviour Research and Therapy, 37,* 99–112.

Shipherd, J. C., & Beck. J. G. (2005). The role of thought suppression in posttraumatic stress disorder. *Behavior Therapy, 36,* 277–287.

Smith, P., Yule, W., Perrin, S., Tranah, T., Dalgleish, T., & Clark, D. M. (2007). Cognitive-behavioral therapy for PTSD in children and adolescents: A preliminary randomized controlled trial. *Journal of the American Academy of Child and Adolescent Psychiatry, 46,* 1051–1061.

Speckens, A, Ehlers, A., Hackmann, A., Ruths, F. & Clark, D. M. (2007). Intrusions and rumination in patients with posttraumatic stress disorder: A phenomenological study. *Memory, 15*, 249–257.

Steil, R., & Ehlers, A. (2000). Dysfunctional meaning of posttraumatic intrusions in chronic PTSD. *Behaviour Research and Therapy, 38*, 537–558.

Sunderland, K., & Bryant, R. B. (2007). Autobiographical memoriy in posttraumatic stress disorder before and after treatment. *Behaviour Research and Therapy, 45*, 2915–2923.

Sündermann, O., Ehlers, A., Böllinghaus, I., Gamer, M., & Glucksman, E. (2010). Early heart rate responses to standardized trauma-related pictures predict posttraumatic stress disorder – a prospective study. *Psychosomatic Medicine, 72*, 302–310.

Sveen, J., Dyster-Aas, J., & Willebrand, M. (2009). Attentional bias and symptoms of posttraumatic stress disorder one year after burn injury. *Journal of Nervous and Mental Disease, 197*, 11, 850–855.

Tromp, S., Koss, M. P., Figueredo, A. J., & Tharan, M. (1995). Are rape memories different? A comparison of rape, other unpleasant, and pleasant memories among employed women. *Journal of Traumatic Stress, 8*, 607–627.

van der Kolk, B. A., & Fisler, R. (1995). Dissociation and the fragmentary nature of traumatic memories: Overview and exploratory study. *Journal of Traumatic Stress, 8*, 505–525.

van der Kolk, B.A., Weisaeth, L., & van der Hart, O. (1996). History of trauma in psychiatry. In B. A. van der Kolk, A. C. McFarlane, & L. Weisaeth (Eds.), *Traumatic stress* (pp. 47–74). New York: Guilford.

van Minnen, A., Wessel, I., Dijkstra, T., & Roelofs, K. (2002). Changes in PTSD patients' narratives during prolonged exposure therapy: A replication and extension. *Journal of Traumatic Stress, 15*, 255–258.

Vázquez, C., Hervás, G., & Pérez-Sales, P. (2008). Chronic thought suppression and posttraumatic symptoms: Data from the Madrid March 11, 2004 terrorist attack. *Journal of Anxiety Disorders, 22*, 1326–1336.

Verwoerd, J., & Wessel, I. (2007). Distractibility and individual differences in the experience of involuntary memories. *Personality and Individual Differences, 42*, 325–334.

Verwoerd, J., Wessel, I., & de Jong, P. J. (2009). Individual differences in experiencing intrusive memories: The role of the ability to resist proactive interference. *Journal of Behavior Therapy and Experimental Psychiatry, 40*, 189–201.

Vrana, S. R, Roodman, A., & Beckham, J. C. (1995). Selective processing of trauma-relevant words in posttraumatic stress disorder. *Journal of Anxiety Disorders, 9*, 515–530.

Warda, G., & Bryant, R. A. (1998). Cognitive bias in acute stress disorder. *Behaviour Research and Therapy, 36*, 1177–1183.

Wegner, D. M., Schneider, D. J., Carter, S. R., & White, T. L. (1987). Paradoxical effects of throught suppression. *Journal of Personality and Social Psychology, 53*, 5–13.

Wells, A. (2000). Emotional disorders and metacognition: Innovative cognitive therapy. Chichester, UK: John Wiley.

Wells, A., & Papageorgiou, C. (1995). Worry and the incubation of intrusive images following stress. *Behaviour Research and Therapy, 33*, 579–583.

Wenzlaff, R. M., & Wegner, D. M. (2000). Thought suppression. *Annual Review of Psychology, 51*, 59–91.

Wessel, I., Huntjens, R. J. C., & Verwoerd, J. R. L. (2010). Cognitive control and suppression of memories of an emotional film. *Journal of Behavior Therapy and Experimental Psychiatry, 41*, 83–89.

Wessa, M., & Flor, H. (2007). Failure of extinction of fear responses in posttraumatic stress disorder: Evidence from second-order conditioning. *American Journal of Psychiatry, 164*, 1684–1692.

Wessel, I., Overwijk, S., Verwoerd, J., & de Vrieze, N. (2008). Pre-stressor cognitive control is related to intrusive cognition of a stressful film. *Behaviour Research and Therapy, 46*, 496–513.

Wiers, R. W., Teachman, B. A., & De Houwer, J. (2007). Implicit cognitive processes in psychopathology: An introduction. *Journal of Behavior Therapy and Experimental Psychiatry, 38*, 95–104.

Williams, J. M. G., Barnhofer, T., Crane, C., Hermans, D., Raes, F., Watkins, E. & Dalgleish, T. (2007). Autobiographical memory specificity and emotional disorder. *Psychological Bulletin, 133*, 122–148.

Williams, J. M. G., Mathews, A., & MacLeod, C. (1997). The emotional Stroop task and psychopathology. *Psychological Bulletin, 120*, 3–24.

Williams, J. M. G., Watts, F. N., MacLeod, C., & Mathews, A. (1997). *Cognitive psychology and the emotional disorders.* (2nd ed.). Chichester, UK: John Wiley.

Williams, L. M., Liddell, B. J., Kemp, A. H., Bryant, R.A., Meares, R. A., Peduto, A. S., & Gordon, E. (2006). Amygdala-prefrontal dissociation of subliminal and supraliminal fear. *Human Brain Mapping, 27*, 652–661.

White, M., McManus, F., & Ehlers, A. (2008). An investigation of whether patients with PTSD overestimate the probability and cost of future negative events. *Journal of Anxiety Disorders, 22*, 1244–1254.

Yoshizumi, T., & Murase, S. (2007). The effect of avoidant tendencies on the intensity of intrusive memories in a community sample of college students. *Personality and Individual Differences, 43*, 1819–1828.

Zetsche, U., Ehring, T., & Ehlers, A. (2009). The effects of rumination on mood and intrusive memories after exposure to traumatic material: An experimental study. *Journal of Behavior Therapy and Experimental Psychiatry, 40*, 499–514.

Zoellner, L. A., & Bittenger, J. N. (2004). On the uniqueness of trauma memories in PTSD. In G. M. Rosen (Ed.), *Posttraumatic stress disorder: Issues and controversies* (pp. 147–162). Chicester: John Wiley.

CHAPTER

15 Family Models of Posttraumatic Stress Disorder

Candice M. Monson, Steffany J. Fredman, Rachel Dekel, *and* Alexandra Macdonald

Abstract

This chapter reviews the extant literature on the interpersonal aspects of posttraumatic stress disorder (PTSD), with a focus on couple and family models of PTSD. Topics include the association of PTSD with a variety of family relationship problems in a range of traumatized populations. The role of relevant interpersonal constructs in the development and maintenance of PTSD (e.g., social support, attachment) and the psychological effects of PTSD symptoms on family members and their relations are discussed. In addition, models that take into account a range of relationship variables and the likely bi-directional association between individual and family functioning in PTSD are presented. Future directions for theory and research, as well as the clinical implications of this work are outlined.

Key Words: Posttraumatic stress disorder, PTSD, family, couples Family Models of Posttraumatic Stress Disorder

There is compelling evidence establishing an association between PTSD and myriad couple and family problems, but only limited efforts to develop theoretical models that account for the association between PTSD and family relationship dysfunction. The available research suggests that there is a bi-directional association between PTSD and close relationships such that PTSD affects the relationships of those with the disorder and is itself affected by those relationships. Under ideal conditions, couple and family relationships facilitate recovery and perhaps even prevent PTSD after exposure to trauma. In contrast, a negative interpersonal environment characterized by conflict and hostility may impede recovery by increasing the traumatized individual's stress and undermining motivation to do the difficult work of treatment. As discussed, the ways that family members respond to someone with PTSD and the way the traumatized individual reacts to loved ones can have important implications for each individual's well-being and quality of the relationships that they share. In this chapter, we provide a brief description of the associations among PTSD symptoms and problems in family relationships, discuss theoretical constructs and models explaining these associations, and consider future directions for research in this area.

Empirical Research on PTSD and Couple/Family Relationships

Much of the research on PTSD and family functioning has been descriptive in nature. Epidemiological research indicates that individuals with PTSD are as likely to marry as those without the disorder but are three to six times more likely to divorce than are those without PTSD (Davidson, Hughes, Blazer, & George, 1991; Kessler, Sonnega, Bromet, Hughes, & Nelson, 1995). A diagnosis of PTSD is also associated with relationship distress. For instance, a large community study of nearly 5,000 couples in Canada investigated the association between nine mental health diagnoses and the presence/absence of marital distress (Whisman, Sheldon, & Goering, 2000). A diagnosis of PTSD was associated with a 3.8 times greater likelihood of having relationship discord compared with couples in which neither partner had a mental health diagnosis; these odds of relationship discord with PTSD were comparable to the strong associations between relationship distress and major depression, panic disorder, and generalized anxiety disorder.

Natural Disaster Samples

Research with natural disaster victims suggests that being married generally functions as a protective factor for men's individual postdisaster mental health, but as a risk factor for women's mental health (e.g., Brooks & McKinlay, 1992; Fullerton, Ursano, Kao, & Bharitya, 1999; Gleser, Green, & Winget, 1981; Solomon, 2002; Ursano, Fullerton, Kao, & Bhartiya, 1995). In fact, Solomon (2002) found that women who perceived themselves to have excellent spouse support were actually more likely to experience mental health problems than were women with weaker spouse support. She interpreted these findings as an indication that the social ties and obligations that accompany spouse support can also serve as a source of stress for married women.

Several cross-sectional studies of postdisaster mental health have found that husbands' and wives' postdisaster symptoms were associated. For instance, Vila and colleagues (2001) studied families affected by an industrial accident in France and observed that husbands' and wives' individual postdisaster symptoms were correlated with each other. Studying the Buffalo Creek dam collapse, Gleser and colleagues (1981) found that husbands' and wives' mental health symptoms predicted each other after controlling for the severity of trauma exposure and demographic variables. However, they also found that husbands' symptoms were more predictive of the wives' symptoms than vice versa, which is consistent with the literature on the differential influence of intimate relationships on women's versus men's mental health problems more generally (e.g., Dawson, Grant, Chou, & Stinson, 2007; Steelman, 2007).

In a sample of heterosexual couples who experienced a severe flood in the Midwestern United States, Monson and colleagues (2009) found that husbands' assumptions about the benevolence of the world moderated the association between wives' assumptions about the benevolence of the world and the wives' PTSD symptoms. Specifically, wives of husbands with less benevolent world assumptions showed an expected inverse relation between their own benevolent world assumptions and PTSD symptoms (that is, lower levels of benevolent world assumptions were associated with higher levels of PTSD symptoms). However, wives of husbands who held more benevolent world assumptions did not exhibit an association between their assumptions and PTSD symptoms. These findings suggest that cognitions held by one member of a couple may affect the strength of the association between trauma-related beliefs and PTSD symptoms in the other member.

Drawing from a larger set of women who experienced the same flood, Fredman and colleagues (in press) used structural equation modeling to investigate associations among characteristics of the disaster (threat/harm versus loss), relationship adjustment, and PTSD symptoms. Although the threat/harm and loss dimensions of the flood were significantly associated with each other, they were differentially related to relationship adjustment and PTSD symptoms. As expected, threat/harm and PTSD symptoms were positively and significantly related. However, loss was not significantly associated with PTSD symptoms and was instead *positively* and significantly associated with relationship adjustment. Relationship adjustment was negatively and significantly related to PTSD symptoms. These data suggest that some aspects of disaster exposure can actually have a mobilizing and positive effect on intimate relationships and that positive intimate relationships may mitigate the severity of PTSD symptoms.

Veteran Samples

Research on veterans and their significant others consistently indicates that veterans diagnosed with PTSD and their partners report more numerous and severe relationship problems, more parenting problems, and overall worse family adjustment than trauma-exposed veterans without PTSD and their significant others (Jordan et al., 1992). Compared with trauma-exposed veterans without PTSD, male veterans with PTSD have been found to be less self-disclosing and less emotionally expressive with their partners (Carroll, Rueger, Foy, & Donahoe, 1985) and to have greater anxiety related to intimacy (Riggs, Byrne, Weathers, & Litz, 1998). Male veterans diagnosed with PTSD, compared with those without PTSD, are also more likely to perpetrate verbal and physical aggression against their partners and children (Carroll et al., 1985; Glenn, Beckham, Feldman, et al., 2002; Jordan et al., 1992; Verbosky & Ryan, 1988). According to Byrne and Riggs (1996), rates of aggression are as high as 63% for performing at least one act of physical violence in the past year, and the severity of violent behavior has been shown to be positively correlated with PTSD symptom severity (Byrne & Riggs, 1996; Glenn, Beckham, Feldman et al., 2002).

Research on veterans from the current conflicts in Iraq and Afghanistan indicates that this most recent cohort is also experiencing postdeployment interpersonal impairment. For example, in a longitudinal study of over 88,000 soldiers who served in Iraq, Milliken and colleagues (Milliken, Auchterlonie, & Hoge, 2007) found a fourfold increase in reported interpersonal problems from the first to second waves of assessment (median time between assessments was six months). Sayers and colleagues (Sayers, Farrow, Ross, & Oslin, 2009) found high rates of family difficulties among recently returned veterans who screened positive for mental health problems in an outpatient Veterans' Administration (VA) treatment clinic. Specifically, they found that more than three-quarters of married/partnered service members reported difficulties with partners or children and that PTSD and major depression were particularly associated with difficulties in family adjustment.

Findings from other samples of recently returned veterans also support an association between service members' PTSD symptoms and intimate relationship functioning. In a sample of male National Guard veterans, Nelson Goff and colleagues (Nelson Goff, Crow, Reisbig, & Hamilton, 2007) found a negative association between service members' self-reported PTSD symptom severity and their marital satisfaction. Other posttraumatic sequelae were also associated with each partners' dyadic adjustment, such as the veterans' sleep problems, dissociation, and sexual problems. In another sample of National Guard members, Renshaw, Rodrigues, and Jones (2009) observed significant inverse associations between soldiers' self-reported PTSD symptoms and relationship satisfaction, as well as between PTSD symptoms and perceived social support. A similar pattern of findings was observed for soldiers' self-reported depressive symptoms. Of note, although combat exposure severity was significantly related to both PTSD and depressive symptoms, it was not significantly related to either marital satisfaction or perceived social support, suggesting that it is the mental health problems secondary to combat exposure rather than combat exposure per se that drives this association.

Potential Mechanisms

Several investigations have been undertaken to explicate mechanisms accounting for the associations between PTSD symptoms and intimate relationship difficulties. In the National Vietnam Veterans Readjustment Study (NVVRS), Jordan and colleagues (1992) found that the veterans' PTSD symptoms accounted for variance in their intimate relationship distress above and beyond other factors known to be associated with intimate relationship dysfunction (e.g., childhood behavioral problems, low parental affection, parental violence/abuse). Riggs and colleagues (1998) found that the avoidance/numbing PTSD symptom cluster was most strongly associated with the ability of veterans diagnosed with PTSD to express emotions in their relationships. Other investigators have also noted an association between the avoidance/numbing cluster and problems with intimacy and intimate relationship dissatisfaction (e.g., Evans, McHugh, Hopwood, & Watt, 2003; Solomon, Dekel, & Mikulincer, 2008), and findings suggest that diminished self-disclosure may help to account for this association (Koenen, Stellman, Sommer, & Steelman, 2008; Solomon et al., 2008). Among Vietnam veterans, avoidance/numbing symptom severity is also negatively related to parenting satisfaction (Berz, Taft, Watkins, & Monson, 2008; Glenn, Beckham, Sampson et al., 2002; Ruscio, Weathers, King, & King, 2002; Samper, Taft, King, & King, 2004).

Each partner's perception of relationship processes also appear to be related to the association between PTSD symptoms and relationship adjustment. For example, studying a sample of couples in which the husbands were active duty Army soldiers, Allen, Rhoades, Stanely, and Markman (2010) attempted to parse the unique association between PTSD symptoms and relationship satisfaction for the husband soldiers and their civilian wives. They found that each partner's self-report of negative communication, positive bonding, and parenting alliance at least partially mediated the association between husbands' self-reported PTSD symptoms and each partner's relationship satisfaction.

Several studies have evaluated the role of cognitive and emotional processes in the association between veterans' PTSD and romantic relationship functioning. Miterany (2004), using a modified Stroop methodology, found that being primed with positive interpersonally oriented words (e.g., *love*) decreased the reaction time to trauma-relevant words among participants with PTSD symptoms, suggesting that evoking positive interpersonally oriented cognitions or emotions might potentiate an individuals' ability to moderate threat-relevant cues. In a study with National Guard members who had served in Iraq and their wives, Renshaw, Rodrigues, and Jones (2008) explored the moderating impact of wives' assessments of their husbands' combat experiences. They found that, when wives believed that their husbands had experienced lower levels of combat exposure but their husbands reported high levels of PTSD symptoms, the wives reported higher levels of relationship distress. The authors interpreted these findings as a suggestion that one partner's attributions about the other partner's trauma-related symptoms can influence how they feel about the relationship. Given that relationship distress can interfere with recovery from PTSD, psychoeducation about trauma and its effects, as well as communication skills to promote a shared understanding of traumatic experiences by patients and their loved ones, offers the potential to facilitate recovery from PTSD. Cognitive-behavioral conjoint therapy for PTSD (CBCT for PTSD; Monson & Fredman, in press) is one such treatment and has shown promise in ameliorating PTSD and relationship distress in both veteran and community samples (Monson, Schnurr, Stevens, & Guthrie, 2004; Monson, Stevens, & Schnurr, 2005; Monson et al., 2010).

Several studies have sought to identify factors accounting for the association between PTSD and intimate aggression perpetration. Using structural equation modeling with NVVRS data, Orcutt, King, and King (2003) found that PTSD was directly related to the male veterans' perpetration of physical violence against their female partners. Early family stressors and childhood antisocial behavior, factors previously found to be associated with intimate aggression perpetration, were indirectly related to violence perpetration through their contribution to the likelihood of having PTSD. Interestingly, after taking into account the association between combat trauma exposure and PTSD, higher trauma exposure was associated with less intimate violence perpetration. Similar to the above mentioned study by Renshaw and colleagues (2009), it appears that PTSD versus trauma exposure is unique in potentiating intimate aggression. Moreover, this research suggests that trauma exposure without consequent PTSD may decrease the likelihood of perpetrating intimate partner aggression. Though the exact mechanism by which PTSD increases risk of intimate partner aggression has yet to be specified, there is some evidence to suggest that heightened arousal may account for this relationship. Savarese, Suvak, King, and King (2001) found that partners' reports of psychological and physical violence victimization was particularly associated with veterans' self-reported hyper-arousal symptom severity.

PTSD with at least one comorbid condition is the rule rather than the exception (Kessler, Sonnega, Bromet, Hughes, & Nelson, 1995). The most commonly occurring comorbidities are depression, substance use disorders, and personality disorders (e.g., Kessler, McGonagle, & Shanyang, 1994). Well-established literatures document the interpersonal aspects of the onset, course, and treatment of each of these common comorbidities (e.g., O'Farrell & Fals-Stewart, 2006; O'Leary & Beach, 1990). A few studies have examined the shared and unique associations among PTSD, these conditions, and interpersonal variables. For example, Savarese and colleagues' (2001) study on the association between PTSD and perpetration of intimate aggression, as noted above, found that hyper-arousal symptoms were specifically associated with intimate aggression perpetration. This relationship, however, was moderated by alcohol use patterns such that more frequent but smaller quantities of alcohol use diminished the association between hyper-arousal symptoms and PTSD. Larger quantities of alcohol paired with more frequent use strengthened the association between hyper-arousal symptoms and PTSD.

When examining the role of depression in the association between PTSD and relationship problems, Taft and colleagues (2007) found that, in a sample of male combat veterans seeking diagnostic assessment of PTSD, dysphoria directly, and through PTSD, was associated with the veterans' perpetration of aggression. Beck, DeMond, Grant, Clapp, and Palyo (2009) found different results in a sample of predominantly female motor vehicle accident survivors. They used hierarchical regression analyses to investigate the relative contribution of depression and PTSD symptoms in predicting interview-rated interpersonal functioning and self-reported social support. They found that overall interpersonal functioning was predicted by depression, but not PTSD. Social support was predicted by both the emotional numbing symptoms of PTSD and depression. The difference in these findings across these two studies may be at least partly attributable to sample (e.g., gender, type of trauma), as well as differences in assessment methodology. Additional research designed to address the role of comorbid conditions in the association between PTSD and interpersonal relationship problems is needed.

Theoretical Constructs and Models Accounting for PTSD and Close Relationship Problems

Several constructs and theories have been proposed to account for the associations among trauma exposure, PTSD, and close relationship functioning. We have organized them by the presumed direction of causality among the significant other(s), the individual who has been traumatized or has PTSD, and their close relationship functioning. We first review those addressing the effect of close others on persons who have been traumatized or have PTSD. We then discuss processes presumed to exert a negative effect of PTSD on others in close relation to an individual with PTSD. Lastly, we describe theories that posit reciprocal effects among significant others, the individual with PTSD, and the shared impact of their relationship functioning.

Effect of Close Others on Trauma Recovery and PTSD

SOCIAL SUPPORT

According to meta-analyses, social support is one of the most consistently and strongly associated variables with PTSD symptomatology (Brewin, Andrews, & Valentine, 2000; Ozer, Best, Lipsey, & Weiss, 2003). In particular, perceived support appears to be more important than objective support, and negative "support" seem to be a more powerful risk factor than positive support is a protective factor (see Charuvastra & Cloitre, 2008, for review).

Although the research establishing an association between social support and PTSD is well developed, there are still gaps in the literature regarding the specific aspects of social support that account for its association with PTSD symptoms. Some have argued that significant others' trauma appraisals have important implications for survivors' coping abilities and emotional states by influencing survivors' own appraisals of traumatic events (Joseph, Williams, & Yule, 1997; Williams & Joseph, 1999). However, additional work is needed to more fully elaborate the precise mechanisms through which this process may operate.

In addition, although originally conceptualized as an interpersonal variable impacting the traumatized individual, evidence suggests that chronic stress and chronic PTSD can actually diminish the availability and quality of social support. Several researchers have found that certain types of chronic traumatic stressors can erode social support, independent of PTSD symptoms (Kaniasty & Norris, 1993; Lepore, Evans, & Schneider, 1991), as can the symptoms of PTSD themselves. For example, a large study of Gulf War I veterans revealed that PTSD symptoms 18 to 24 months after return from service were negatively associated with social support five years later. However, social support at the first assessment was not associated with PTSD symptoms five years later (King, Taft, King, Hammond, & Stone, 2006). These findings suggest that chronic, untreated PTSD has the potential to "burn out" close others and negatively impact the receipt of social support. Results from nonveteran samples are also consistent with this interpretation. For instance, Kaniasty and Norris (2008) completed a study with survivors of severe mudslides and flooding in Mexico and found that 6 to12 months after the disaster, higher levels of familial social support predicted lower levels of individual PTSD symptoms. Between 12 and 18 months postexposure, social support and PTSD symptoms were reciprocally associated. By 18 to 24 months postdisaster, higher levels of PTSD symptoms predicted lower levels of social support, but social support did not predict PTSD.

Recent gene-by-environment (G X E) studies (Moffitt, Caspi, & Rutter, 2005) have expanded upon the research on social support by investigating the interaction of social support and genetic risk factors for PTSD (for a thorough review of genetics and PTSD, see chapter 11 of this volume). Two genes that have been implicated in the etiology of PTSD are the regulator of the G-protein signaling gene (*RGS2*) and the serotonin transporter gene (*SLC6A4*; Amstadter, Nugent, & Koenen, 2009). In their study of the predictors of PTSD in hurricane victims, Kilpatrick and colleagues (2007) found no main effects for high hurricane exposure, low social support, or the polymorphism 5-HTTLPR, nor did they find two-way interactions between any of the combination of risk factors (e.g., 5-HTTLPR by severity of hurricane exposure). When they examined the three-way interaction, however, they found that participants who had high hurricane exposure, the 5-HTTLPR polymorphism, and low social support were over four times more likely to meet criteria for a diagnosis of PTSD than those who did not have these risk factors. Using this same sample of hurricane victims, Amstadter and colleagues (2009) also found this three-way interaction of risk with the *RGS2* polymorphism. Although questions still remain regarding the exact mechanisms by with *RGS2* and 5-HTTLPR may exert their influences on the development of PTSD, these studies suggest that it is the *interplay* among exposure, social support and biological vulnerability that may afford the most thorough understanding of risk factors for the etiology of PTSD.

ADULT ATTACHMENT

As originated by Bowlby (e.g., 1983), attachment theory primarily dealt with understanding the effect of caregivers' responsiveness and attentiveness on the socio-emotional health of infants and children. Bowlby's theory was subsequently extended to adult intimate relationships by Hazan and Shaver (1994). They argue that, similar to healthy caregiver-child relationships, security in adult intimate relationships facilitates emotion regulation, effective cognitive processing of information, and clear communication.

Adult attachment theory may help to explain the effects of PTSD on relationships with others in at least two ways. First, adult attachment may contribute to one's ability to cope with traumatic events. Specifically, insecure attachment that develops in childhood and extends into adulthood is a risk factor that can reduce resilience in times of stress, foster negative affectivity, and contribute to emotional problems, maladjustment, and psychopathology when presented with stress (Mikulincer, Shaver, & Horesh, 2006). Second, the effects of trauma on attachment and interpersonal relations may increase the need for protective attachments and simultaneously undermine the ability to trust and, therefore, to build such attachments (Johnson & Makinen, 2003). The negative impact of these interpersonal difficulties can produce a relational cycle of distance and disconnection between partners, reducing the secure attachment necessary for healthy functioning and recovery from stressful events (Johnson, 2002).

Several cross-sectional studies of adults have found positive associations among self-reported adult attachment insecurity, difficulties coping with traumatic events, and PTSD (e.g., (Dieperink, Leskela, Thuras, & Engdahl, 2001; Solomon, Ginzburg, Mikulincer, Neria, & Ohry, 1998). A more recent longitudinal study has raised questions about whether adult attachment problems are a risk factor or consequence of PTSD symptoms. In a sample of Israeli prisoners of war, Solomon and colleagues (Solomon et al., 2008) assessed PTSD and attachment dimensions at two occasions. PTSD symptoms at the initial assessment predicted attachment patterns at the second assessment better than vice versa. These findings support prior studies questioning the stability of attachment patterns over time (Fraley, 2002), They also suggest that, over time, PTSD symptoms may be equally or more likely to negatively affect attachment within intimate relationships than the converse. Additional empirical research is needed to clarify the directionality of the associations among adult attachment, trauma exposure, PTSD, and interpersonal relationships.

Effect of Trauma and PTSD on Close Others

SECONDARY/VICARIOUS TRAUMATIZATION

The effects of trauma-related symptoms, including PTSD, often extend beyond just the trauma-exposed individual. Several authors have theorized that close others, including intimate partners, children, close friends, and therapists, may themselves experience trauma-related symptoms (e.g., McCann & Pearlman, 1990b; Solomon et al., 1992). According to Figley (1989), these symptoms may develop through a process of secondary traumatization. This starts with the efforts of close others to emotionally support their traumatized loved ones, which then leads to attempts to understand their feelings and experiences and, from there, to empathize with them. Through the process of information gathering, significant others can take on the traumatized person's feelings, experiences, and even memories as their own, leading to symptom development. In this conceptualization, it is the loved ones' overidentification with the traumatized individual (Catherall, 1992; Figley, 1995) that leads to development of symptoms similar to those experienced by the trauma survivor (Maloney, 1988; Solomon et al., 1992).

Prior to reviewing this literature, which has been mostly done with male combat veterans and their female partners, it is important to consider some limitations in study methodology. Some studies ask the female partners of those with PTSD to report their own symptoms related to the PTSD identified partner's trauma. Other studies have not anchored the female partner's report of symptoms to her partner's trauma(s), making it difficult to determine if the woman responded based on her own history of trauma exposure, nontraumatic stressors, or without a particular index event that she or her partner experienced. Although there has been some evidence that secondary traumatization can result in trauma-related symptoms manifested by the loved ones that "mimic" those of trauma survivors, others believe that secondary traumatization can include a wide range of symptoms of distress (Dekel & Solomon, 2006), resulting in a relative lack of construct clarity.

Cross-sectional research has documented an association between PTSD in one partner and general mental health problems and compromised life satisfaction in the other partner. Using this broad definition of secondary/vicarious traumatization, researchers have found that female partners of veterans with PTSD, compared with female partners of veterans without PTSD, have reported more mental health symptoms (e.g., depression, anxiety), lower quality of life, greater feelings of demoralization, and more impaired and unsatisfying social relations (Jordan et al., 1992; Waysman, Mikulincer, Solomon, & Weisenberg, 1993; Westerink & Giarratano, 1999).

CAREGIVER BURDEN

Caregiver burden refers to the extent to which caregivers perceive their emotional or physical health, social life, or financial status to be affected by their caring for an impaired relative (Zarit, Todd, & Zarit, 1986). Although this construct initially emerged in the literature on caregivers of chronically physically ill and mentally ill individuals (Chakrabarti & Kulhara, 1999; Cuijpers & Stam, 2000; Loukissa, 1995; Piccinato & Rosenbaum, 1997), it has also been applied to female romantic partners of combat veterans with PTSD. Several studies have shown an association between wives' perceived caregiving burden and their husbands' combat-related PTSD, as well a relationship between caregiving burden and the wives' level of individual distress (Beckham, Lytle, & Feldman, 1996; Ben Arzi, Solomon, & Dekel, 2000; Calhoun, Beckham, & Bosworth, 2002; Dekel, Solomon, & Bleich, 2005; Manguno-Mire et al., 2007).

AMBIGUOUS LOSS

Ambiguous loss refers the perception or "feeling" of loss of a loved one, despite the continued physical presence within the relationship. This model suggests that there are two different experiences of perceived loss associated with ambiguity: (1) there is a physical absence with psychological presence, and (2) there is a psychological absence with physical presence (Boss, 1999, 2007). In both cases, the uncertainty or lack of information about the whereabouts or status of a loved one as absent or present is difficult for most individuals, couples, and families. The ambiguity is hypothesized to freeze the grief process and prevent cognitive processing, thus blocking coping and decision-making processes (Boss, 1999). PTSD in a relationship has been considered to fit the second type of ambiguous loss (Dekel, Goldblatt, Keidar, Solomon, & Polliack, 2005). The ambiguity regarding the psychological absence of a loved one, and subsequent feeling of loss, may lead significant others to experience symptoms of depression, anxiety, guilt, and distressing dreams.

Beyond the potential impact of ambiguous loss on an individual significant other, there also can be disruptions to the overall dynamics of a family. Family members may be uncertain as to who is in or out of the family and who is performing which roles and tasks within the family system. This could result in immobilization of the family, such that decisions are put on hold, more tasks are taken on by the "healthier" partner, or children assume roles that are beyond their capacities (Boss, 1999). A qualitative study of wives of Israeli veterans with PTSD provides some support for ambiguous loss associated with PTSD. Wives' concerns included questions about whether the spouse was a husband or another child; other concerns included questions of whether he was an independent adult or a dependent. The authors found that this ambiguity was associated with psychological distress in the wives (Dekel, Solomon, et al., 2005).

INTERGENERATIONAL TRANSMISSION OF PTSD

The idea that PTSD in one generation or proband can translate into risk for PTSD in subsequent generations was originally raised with regard to Holocaust survivors and their offspring. Many of the studies with this population examined risk based on exposure to Holocaust experiences, as opposed to the PTSD status of the Holocaust survivor. In a meta-analysis of studies involving over 4,000 participants, there was minimal evidence that parents' traumatic Holocaust experiences alone were associated with PTSD symptomatology in their offspring

(Van IJzendoorn, Bakermans-Kranenburg, & Sagi-Schwartz, 2003). A few studies of parental PTSD related to Holocaust experiences have revealed that parental PTSD (Kellerman, 2007), and especially maternal PTSD (Yehuda, Bell, Bierer, & Schmeidler, 2008), is associated with general mental health problems in their offspring. Researchers have also attempted to identify cross-generational biological markers associated with PTSD in this population. For example, several studies have found lower cortisol levels among the offspring of Holocaust survivors who have PTSD (Yehuda et al., 2000; Yehuda, Blair, Labinsky, & Bierer, 2007; Yehuda, Halligan, & Bierer, 2002).

The studies of intergenerational transmission of combat veterans' PTSD to their offspring reveal inconsistent findings. For example, Davidson, Smith, and Kudler (1989) found that children of male veterans with PTSD had received more mental health treatment, had more eating and communication disorders, and had more academic and behavior problems than children in a control group of fathers without PTSD. In another study, Ahmadzadeh and Malekian (2004) found higher rates of aggression and anxiety among Iranian children whose fathers were veterans with PTSD compared with children of nonveteran fathers. In a sample of help-seeking veterans with PTSD, Beckham and colleagues (1997) found that these veterans' children reported high levels of illegal drug use, behavioral problems, PTSD symptoms, and hostility. A more recent study of the effects of combat deployment on the spouses and children of U.S. active-duty and recently returned veterans from Iraq and Afghanistan (Lester et al., 2010) found that the children of these service members experienced high levels of anxiety compared with community norms. In addition, the authors observed that mental health symptoms in the service member, but also in the at-home caregiving parent, predicted child adjustment problems and that the risk of adverse child outcomes (e.g., depression, externalizing problems) increased with the length of parental combat deployment. Other studies of the children of veterans with PTSD have not found differences in emotional distress (Davidson & Mellor, 2001; Souzzia & Motta, 2004; Westerink & Giarratano, 1999), social development, (Ahmadzadeh & Malekian, 2004), or self-esteem (Davidson & Mellor, 2001; Westerink & Giarratano, 1999) when compared with children from various control groups.

Research on the intergenerational transmission of PTSD would benefit from using more sophisticated behavioral genetic methods designed to parse the environmental and genetic factors that operate to place someone at risk for PTSD. Moreover, because the investigations have tended to identify nonspecific mental health problems in offspring rather than the specific risk of PTSD intergenerationally, it has been difficult to determine whether the possible intergenerational risk for PTSD is due to an increased likelihood of traumatic exposure in these families, psychological factors, shared genetic risk, or an interaction of these factors.

Reciprocal Influences of PTSD and Close Relationship Functioning

COUPLE ADAPTATION TO TRAUMATIC STRESS MODEL

The CATS model (Nelson Goff & Smith, 2005) provides a description of how individuals and couples are jointly affected when trauma occurs. The model proposes that adaptation to traumatic stress in the couple is dependent on the dynamic interaction of three factors: individual level of functioning of each partners, predisposing factors and resources, and couple functioning. The model posits that a trauma survivor's level of functioning or trauma symptoms sets in motion a systemic response that can potentially yield secondary traumatic stress symptoms in the partner. Given the bi-directionality of couples' interactions, partners' symptoms may potentiate trauma-related symptoms in the survivor. Individual and couple functioning are each influenced by predisposing factors and resources (McClubbin & Patterson, 1982), such as individual characteristics or unresolved stress experienced by either partner prior to the trauma. The "couple functioning" component of the model, which refers to the level and quality of variables such as relationship satisfaction, support/nurturance, intimacy, communication, and conflict, also influences the individual components of the dyad system.

Recent findings described by Hamilton, Nelson Goff, Crow, and Reisberg (2009) are consistent with this model. Studying a sample of male Army soldiers and their female partners, the authors found that the partners' PTSD symptoms related to their own prior history of trauma predicted their own and soldiers' relationship satisfaction. Specifically, partners' re-experiencing symptoms were inversely related to their own relationship satisfaction, and partners' hyperarousal symptoms were negatively related to the soldiers' relationship satisfaction. The authors interpreted the former finding as a suggestion that the context of being in a relationship with someone recently returned from war and grappling with the effects of combat could serve to remind the women of their own traumatic experiences and contribute to feeling unsafe in the relationship, which in turn leads to diminished relationship satisfaction. Regarding the latter finding, they suggested that, for the soldiers, being in a relationship with someone who is chronically hyperaroused and emotionally reactive could feel threatening and, thereby, contribute to decreased satisfaction.

COGNITIVE-BEHAVIORAL INTERPERSONAL THEORY OF PTSD

Monson and colleagues (Monson, Fredman, & Dekel, 2010; Monson et al., 2005) have previously outlined a cognitive-behavioral theory accounting for the association between intimate relationship problems and PTSD. As illustrated in the model depicted in figure 15.1, we assert the existence of behavioral, cognitive, and emotional variables that interact within each individual and between members of a dyad to contribute to a shared relationship milieu that, in turn, feeds back on the individuals existing in that milieu.

In behavioral conceptualizations of PTSD, classical conditioning processes help to explain why certain stimuli associated with trauma later provoke distress; operant conditioning, and in particular, the negative reinforcing value of avoidance, accounts for the maintenance of the distress response (Mowrer, 1960). From an interpersonal perspective, well-intended caretaking behaviors by partners, children, and other family members (e.g., being careful not to make loud noises in order to avoid startling the patient or making excuses for patients' behaviors to others) can "accommodate" and, thereby, maintain avoidant behavior and PTSD more generally. Behavioral accommodation can take many forms, ranging from avoiding topics that might upset the patient to buying alcohol for the patient and encouraging drinking as a way to feel less distressed in the moment. We also worked with a couple in which the partner agreed to be available by cell phone at all times so that the patient would not worry that something bad had happened to him.

Behavioral accommodation can also negatively impact intimate relationship satisfaction through decreased engagement in shared pleasurable activities (e.g., going to movies), less affective expression, and limited self-disclosure, including trauma-related disclosure. Poor communication and conflict management, coupled with avoidance, lessen the probability of effective trauma disclosure. This has important implications for recovery, given that trauma disclosure in an encouraging and supportive

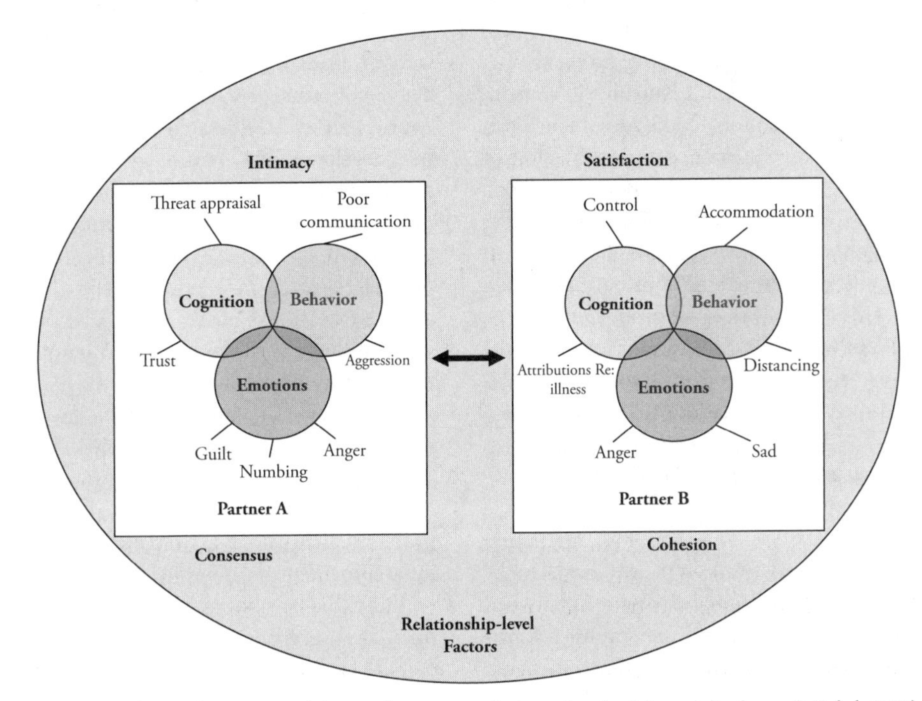

Figure 15.1. Cognitive-behavioral interpersonal theory of posttraumatic stress disorder (Monson, Fredman, & Dekel, 2010).

environment can lead to the development of a more cogent trauma narrative and emotional processing of traumatic memories. Impaired conflict management and problem-solving skills are also hypothesized to mediate the association between the hyperarousal symptoms of PTSD and aggressive relationship behavior.

We theorize that there are interrelated cognitive processes and thematic content that account for the association between PTSD and intimate relationship problems. Individual and dyadic impairment are theorized to arise from reliance on enduring, rigid, and maladaptive schemas in making meaning of experiences and the environment (Young, 1994). Borrowing from earlier work by McCann and Pearlman (1990a), which is also found in cognitive processing therapy (Resick, Monson, & Chard, 2007), themes such as safety, trust, power, esteem, and intimacy are disrupted as a result of the trauma and are pertinent to close relationship functioning. An example of an interpersonally oriented cognition with close relationship implications comes from a sexual abuse survivor whose traumatic event involved incest by a close family member. As a result, she avoided both emotional and physical intimacy with her partner, believing "if I trust anyone and let my guard down, they will hurt me."

Research shows that the emotional disturbances associated with traumatization extend beyond anxiety. There is strong evidence that individuals with PTSD experience disruption in a range of emotions in addition to fear, including guilt, shame, anger, grief, sadness, etc. (e.g., Kubany & Watson, 2002; Novaco & Chemtob, 2002). Avoidance can also generalize to the experience and expression of emotions more generally in PTSD (Boeschen, Koss, Figueredo, & Coan, 2001). Emotional process disturbances such as alexithymia and difficulties with identifying and expressing emotions have also been associated with PTSD (Price, Monson, Callahan, & Rodriguez, 2006) and have important interpersonal implications, such as emotional communication deficits and their related relationship impairments.

Conclusions and Future Directions

There is a solid evidence base documenting the association between PTSD symptoms and family relationship problems. Although we have highlighted the likely bi-directional associations between PTSD and family dysfunction, the empirical foundation of this assumption is not yet well established. With a few exceptions, most studies have been cross-sectional in nature and, therefore, cannot address the directionality of the various associations that have been found. Further prospective studies are sorely needed to understand the longitudinal association between these individual and interpersonal problems.

As reviewed in this chapter, much of what is known about PTSD and family relationships, with exception of the role of social support in trauma recovery, mostly relates to romantic relationships. Less is known about the association between PTSD and problems in other family relationships and in other significant close relationships. Moreover, much of the research has been conducted on male veterans with PTSD. The associations among family problems and PTSD in other trauma populations, and the potential for gender differences in these associations, have not been fully examined.

We presented several constructs and theories seeking to explain the familial risk and resilience factors and consequences of PTSD. Yet, minimal research has tested these theories, and as described, there are construct validity issues with some. With family problems associated with PTSD well documented, our research agenda needs to move toward theory-driven research that can begin to elucidate the mechanisms accounting for the associations. As an example, further longitudinal research on the association between behavioral accommodation and PTSD would help to clarify the processes through which significant others' accommodative behavior is both affected by and moderates the association between trauma exposure and the development and course of PTSD. Research that takes into account the developmental nature of intimate relationships and PTSD would also advance understanding in the field. There may be different associations between these variables depending on when the trauma occurred in relation to the couple initiating their relationship, the presence of other familial stressors such as the transition to parenthood, and the presence of mental health problems in spouses and children. In addition, there may be family problems that are associated with variables associated with trauma exposure. For example, deployment in and of itself, apart from the mental health problems that can arise from trauma exposure during deployment, is a familial stressor that may lead to individual problems in service members' loved ones. In a recent large study of wives of Army soldiers, Mansfield and colleagues (2010) found that deployment itself was associated with increased mental health diagnoses (e.g., depressive disorders, sleep problems, anxiety, acute stress reaction, and adjustment disorders) among the wives, compared with wives whose husbands were not deployed. The results were even more pronounced when deployment lasted for more than 11 months.

Greater understanding of the interpersonal nature of PTSD, the longitudinal course of the links between PTSD and family problems, and the mechanisms that account for those links will ultimately be of valuable to developing and refining interpersonally oriented PTSD prevention and treatment strategies. Although social support appears to be one of the most important resilience factors in warding off PTSD, few efforts have been made to capitalize on this factor in prevention efforts. We argue that it would be beneficial to help traumatized persons and their loved ones to martial social support, use it effectively, and prevent burn-out of their support network in order to prevent PTSD and associated relationship problems. In addition, application of existing conjoint treatments for PTSD (e.g., Monson & Fredman, in press; Sautter, Glynn, Thompson, Franklin, & Han, 2009) to nonromantic significant others is another important avenue to pursue in order to reach the widest number of patients and their loved ones with PTSD. Finally, it is important to consider how technology (e.g., Web sites, teletherapy) might be used to incorporate significant others who are otherwise unwilling or unable to participate in existing treatments but who could greatly facilitate their significant other's PTSD treatment. These interventions have the added benefit of addressing a range of barriers to care (e.g., stigma, transportation, proximity to healthcare settings with expertise in these interventions).

It is marvelous to witness greater appreciation of the familial context of PTSD and efforts to address family relationships to improve the strength of families and the health and well-being of the individuals that comprise them. A fuller appreciation of the interpersonal factors that affect and are affected by PTSD should only enhance the study and treatment of PTSD and ultimately benefit traumatized individuals and their loved ones who are affected by the disorder.

References

Ahmadzadeh, G., & Malekian, A. (2004). Aggression, anxiety, and social development in adolescent children of war veterans with PTSD versus those of non-veterans. *Journal of Research in Medical Sciences, 9*, 33–36.

Allen, E. S., Rhoades, G. K., Stanley, S. M., & Markman, H. J. (2010). Hitting home: Relationships between recent deployment, posttraumatic stress symptoms, and marital functioning for army couples. *Journal of Family Psychology, 24*, 280–288.

Amstadter, A. B., Koenen, K. C., Ruggiero, K. J., Acierno, R., Galea, S., Kilpatrick, D. G., et al. (2009). Variant in RGS2 moderates posttraumatic stress symptoms following potentially traumatic event exposure. *Journal of Anxiety Disorders, 23*, 369–373.

Amstadter, A. B., Nugent, N. R., & Koenen, K. C. (2009). Genetics and PTSD: Fear conditioning as a model for future research. *Psychiatric Annals, 39*, 358–367.

Beck, G. J., DeMond, M. G., Clapp, J. D., & Palyo, S. A. (2009). Understanding the interpersonal impact of trauma: Contributions of PTSD and depression. *Journal of Anxiety Disorders, 23*, 443–450.

Beckham, J. C., Braxton, L. E., Kudler, H. S., Feldman, M. E., Lytle, B. L., & Palmer, S. (1997). Minnesota Multiphasic Personality Inventory profiles of Vietnam combat veterans with posttraumatic stress disorder and their children. *Journal of Clinical Psychology, 53*, 847–852.

Beckham, J. C., Lytle, B. L., & Feldman, M. E. (1996). Caregiver burden in partners of Vietnam War veterans with posttraumatic stress disorder. *Journal of Consulting and Clinical Psychology, 64*, 1068–1072.

Ben Arzi, N., Solomon, Z., & Dekel, R. (2000). Secondary traumatization among wives of PTSD and post-concussion casualties: Distress, caregiver burden and psychological separation. *Brain Injury, 14*, 725–736.

Berz, J. B., Taft, C. T., Watkins, L., & Monson, C. M. (2008). Associations between PTSD symptoms and parenting satisfaction in a female veteran sample. *Journal of Psychological Trauma, 7*, 37–45.

Boeschen, L. E., Koss, M. P., Figueredo, A. J., & Coan, J. A. (2001). Experiential avoidance and post-traumatic stress disorder: A cognitive mediational model of rape recovery. *Journal of Aggression, Maltreatment and Trauma, 4*, 211–245.

Boss, P. (1999). *Ambiguous loss: Learning to live with unresolved grief.* Cambridge, MA: Harvard University Press.

Boss, P. (2007). Ambiguous loss theory: Challenges for scholars and practitioners. *Family Relations, 56*, 105–111.

Bowlby, J. (1983). Attachment and loss: Retrospect and prospect. *Annual Progress in Child Psychiatry & Child Development*, 29–47.

Brewin, C. R., Andrews, B., & Valentine, J. D. (2000). Meta-analysis of risk factors for posttraumatic stress disorder in trauma-exposed adults. *Journal of Consulting and Clinical Psychology, 68*, 748–766.

Brooks, N., & McKinlay, W. (1992). Mental health consequences of the Lockerbie Disaster. *Journal of Traumatic Stress, 5*, 527–543.

Byrne, C. A., & Riggs, D. S. (1996). The cycle of trauma: Relationship aggression in male Vietnam veterans with symptoms of posttraumatic stress disorder. *Violence and Victims, 11*, 213–225.

Calhoun, P. S., Beckham, J. C., & Bosworth, H. B. (2002). Caregiver burden and psychological distress in partners of veterans with chronic posttraumatic stress disorder. *Journal of Traumatic Stress, 15*, 205–212.

Carroll, E. M., Rueger, D. B., Foy, D. W., & Donahoe, C. P. (1985). Vietnam combat veterans with posttraumatic stress disorder: Analysis of marital and cohabitating adjustment. *Journal of Abnormal Psychology, 94*, 329–337.

Catherall, D. R. (1992). *Back from the brink: A family guide to overcoming traumatic stress*. New York: Bantam.

Chakrabarti, S., & Kulhara, P. (1999). Family burden of caring for people with mental illness. *British Journal of Psychiatry, 174*, 463.

Charuvastra, A., & Cloitre, M. (2008). Social bonds and posttraumatic stress disorder. *Annual Review of Psychology, 59*, 301–328.

Cuijpers, P., & Stam, H. (2000). Burnout among relatives of psychiatric patients attending psychoeducational support groups. *Psychiatric Services, 51*, 375–379.

Davidson, A. C., & Mellor, D. J. (2001). The adjustment of children of Australian Vietnam veterans: Is there evidence for the transgenerational transmission of war-related trauma? *Australian and New Zealand Journal of Psychiatry, 35*, 345–351.

Davidson, J. R., Hughes, D., Blazer, D. G., & George, L. K. (1991). Post-traumatic stress disorder in the community: An epidemiological study. *Psychological Medicine, 21*, 713–721.

Davidson, J. R., Smith, R., & Kudler, H. (1989). Familial psychiatric illness in chronic posttraumatic stress disorder. *Comprehensive Psychiatry, 30*, 339–345.

Dawson, D. A., Grant, B. F., Chou, S. P., & Stinson, F. S. (2007). The impact of partner alcohol problems on women's physical and mental health. *Journal of Studies on Alcohol and Drugs, 68*, 66–75.

Dekel, R., Goldblatt, H., Keidar, M., Solomon, Z., & Polliack, M. (2005). Being a wife of a veteran with posttraumatic stress disorder. *Family Relations, 54*, 24–36.

Dekel, R., & Solomon, Z. (2006). Secondary traumatization among wives of Israeli POWs: The role of POWs' distress. *Social Psychiatry and Psychiatric Epidemiology, 41*, 27–33.

Dekel, R., Solomon, Z., & Bleich, A. (2005). Emotional distress and marital adjustment of caregivers: Contribution of level of impairment and appraised burden. *Anxiety, Stress, and Coping, 18*, 71–82.

Dieperink, M., Leskela, J., Thuras, P., & Engdahl, B. (2001). Attachment style classification and posttraumatic stress disorder in former prisoners of war. *American Journal of Orthopsychiatry, 71*, 374–378.

Evans, L., McHugh, T., Hopwood, M., & Watt, C. (2003). Chronic posttraumatic stress disorder and family functioning of Vietnam veterans and their partners. *Australian and New Zealand Journal of Psychiatry, 37*, 765–772.

Figley, C. (1995). Compassion fatigue as secondary traumatic stress disorder: An overview. In C. Figley (Ed.), *Compassion fatigue: Coping with secondary traumatic stress disorder in those who treat the traumatized* (pp. 1–20). New York: Brunner/Mazel.

Figley, C. R. (1989). *Helping traumatized families*. San Francisco: Jossey-Bass.

Fraley, C. R. (2002). Attachment stability from infancy to adulthood: Meta-analysis and dynamic modeling of developmental mechanisms. *Personality and Social Psychology Review, 6*, 123–151.

Fredman, S. J., Monson, C. M., Schumm, J. A., Adair, K. C., Taft, C. T., & Resick, P. A. (2010). Associations among disaster exposure, intimate relationship adjustment, and PTSD symptoms: Can disaster exposure enhance a relationship? *Journal of Traumatic Stress, 23*, 446–451.

Fullerton, C. S., Ursano, R. J., Kao, T. C., & Bharitya, V. R. (1999). Disaster-related bereavement: Acute symptoms and subsequent depression. *Aviation, Space, and Environmental Medicine, 70*, 902–909.

Glenn, D. M., Beckham, J. C., Feldman, M. E., Kirby, A. C., Hertzberg, M. A., & Moore, S. D. (2002). Violence and hostility among families of Vietnam veterans with combat-related posttraumatic stress disorder. *Violence and Victims, 17*, 473–489.

Glenn, D. M., Beckham, J. C., Sampson, W. S., Feldman, M. E., Hertzberg, M. A., & Moore, S. D. (2002). MMPI-2 profiles of Gulf and Vietnam combat veterans with chronic posttraumatic stress disorder. *Journal of Clinical Psychology, 58*, 371–381.

Gleser, G. C., Green, B. L., & Winget, C. N. (1981). *Prolonged psychological effects of disaster: A study of Buffalo Creek*. New York: Academic Press.

Hamilton, S., Nelson Goff, B. S., Crow, J. R., & Reisbig, A. M. J. (2009). Primary trauma of female partners in a military sample: Individual symptoms and relationship satisfaction. *The American Journal of Family Therapy, 37*, 336–346.

Hazan, C., & Shaver, P. R. (1994). Attachment as an organizational framework for research on close relationships. *Psychological Inquiry, 5*, 1–22.

Johnson, S. M. (2002). *Emotionally focused couple therapy with trauma survivors: Strengthening attachment bonds*. NY: Guilford.

Johnson, S. M., & Makinen, J. (2003). Posttraumatic Stress. In D. K. Snyder & M. A. Whisman (Eds.), *Treating Difficult Couples* (pp. 308–329). New York: Guilford.

Jordan, B. K., Marmar, C. R., Fairbank, J. A., Schlenger, W. E., Kulka, R. A., Hough, R. L., et al. (1992). Problems in families of male Vietnam veterans with posttraumatic stress disorder. *Journal of Consulting and Clinical Psychology, 60*, 916–926.

Joseph, S., Williams, R., & Yule, W. (1997). *Understanding posttraumatic stress*. New York: John Wiley.

Kaniasty, K., & Norris, F. H. (1993). A test of the social support deterioration model in the context of natural disaster. *Journal of Personality and Social Psychology, 64*, 395–408.

Kaniasty, K., & Norris, F. H. (2008). Longitudinal linkages between perceived social support and posttraumatic stress symptoms: Sequential roles of social causation and social selection. *Journal of Traumatic Stress, 21*, 274–281.

Kessler, R.C., McGonagle, K.A., & Shanyang, Z. (1994). Lifetime and 12-month prevalence of DSM-III-R psychiatric disorders in the United States: Results from the National Comorbidity Survey. *Archives of General Psychiatry, 51*, 8–19.

Kessler, R. C., Sonnega, A., Bromet, E., Hughes, M., & Nelson, C. B. (1995). Posttraumatic stress disorder in the National Comorbidity Survey. *Archives of General Psychiatry, 52*, 1048–1060.

Kilpatrick, D. G., Koenen, K. C., Ruggiero, K. J., Acierno, R., Galea, S., Rensick, H. S., et al. (2007). The serotonin transporter genotype and social support and moderation of posttraumatic stress disorder and depression in hurricane-exposed adults. *American Journal of Psychiatry, 164*, 1693–1699.

King, D. W., Taft, C. T., King, L. A., Hammond, C., & Stone, E. R. (2006). Directionality of the association between social support and posttraumatic stress disorder: A longitudinal investigation. *Journal of Applied Social Psychology, 36*, 2980–2992.

Koenen, K. C., Stellman, S., Sommer, J., & Steelman, J. (2008). Persisting posttraumatic stress disorder symptoms and their relationship to functioning in Vietnam veterans: A 14-year follow-up. *Journal of Traumatic Stress, 21*, 49–57.

Kubany, E. S., & Watson, S. B. (2002). Cognitive trauma therapy for formerly battered women with PTSD: Conceptual bases and treatment outlines. *Cognitive and Behavioral Practice, 9*, 111–127.

Lepore, S. J., Evans, G. W., & Schneider, M. L. (1991). Dynamic role of social support in the link between chronic stress and psychological distress. *Journal of Personality and Social Psychology, 61*, 899–909.

Lester, P., Peterson, K., Reeves, J., Knauss, L., Glover, D., Mogil, C., et al. (2010). The long war and parental combat deployment: Effects on military children and at-home spouses. *Journal of the American Academy of Child and Adolescent Psychiatry, 49*, 310–320.

Loukissa, D. A. (1995). Family burden in chronic mental illness: A review of research studies. *Journal of Advanced Nursing, 21*, 248–255.

Maloney, L. J. (1988). Post traumatic stresses on women partners of Vietnam veterans. *Smith College Studies in Social Work, 58*, 122–143.

Manguno-Mire, G., Sautter, F., Lyons, J. A., Myers, L., Perry, D., Sherman, M., et al. (2007). Psychological distress and burden among female partners of combat veterans with PTSD. *Journal of Nervous & Mental Disease, 195*, 144–151.

Mansfield, A. J., Kaufman, J. S., Marshall, S. W., Gaynes, B. N., Morrissey, J. P., & Engel, C. C. (2010). Deployment and the use of mental health services among U.S. army wives. *The New England Journal of Medicine, 362*, 101–109.

McCann, L., & Pearlman, L. A. (1990a). *Psychological trauma and the adult survivor: Theory, therapy, and transformation.* New York: Brunner/Mazel.

McCann, L., & Pearlman, L. A. (1990b). Vicarious traumatization: A framework for understanding the psychological effects of working with victims. *Journal of Traumatic Stress, 3*, 131–149.

McClubbin, H. I., & Patterson, J. M. (1982). Family adaptation to crisis. In H. I. McClubbin, A. E. Cauble & J. M. Patterson (Eds.), *Family stress, coping and social support* (pp. 26–47). Springfield, IL: Charles C. Thomas.

Mikulincer, M., Shaver, P. R., & Horesh, N. (2006). Attachment bases of emotion regulation and posttraumatic adjustment. In D. K. Snyder, J. A. Simpson & J. N. Hughes (Eds.), *Emotion regulation in families: Pathways to dysfunction and health* (pp. 77–99). Washington, DC: American Psychological Association.

Milliken, C. S., Auchterlonie, J. L., & Hoge, C. W. (2007). Longitudinal assessment of mental health problems among active and reserve component soldiers returning from the Iraq war. *Journal of the American Medical Association, 298*, 2141–2148.

Miterany, D. (2004). *The healing effects of the contextual activation of the sense of attachment security: The case of posttraumatic stress disorder.* Unpublished master's thesis, Bar-Ilan University, Ramat-Gan, Israel.

Moffitt, T. E., Caspi, A., & Rutter, M. (2005). Strategy for investigating interactions between measured genes and measured environments. *Archives of General Psychiatry, 62*, 473–481.

Monson, C. M., & Fredman, S. J. (in press). *Cognitive-behavioral conjoint therapy for posttraumatic stress disorder: Therapist's manual.* New York: Guilford Press.

Monson, C. M., Fredman, S. J., Adair, K. C., Stevens, S. P., Resick, P. A., Schnurr, P. P., MacDonald, H. Z., & Macdonald, A. (2011). Cognitive-behavioral conjoint therapy for PTSD: Initial results from a community sample. *Journal of Traumatic Stress, 24*, 97–101..

Monson, C. M., Fredman, S. J., & Dekel, R. (2010). Posttraumatic stress disorder in an interpersonal context. In J. G. Beck (Ed.), *Interpersonal processes in the anxiety disorders: Implications for understanding psychopathology and treatment* (pp. 179–208). Washington, DC: American Psychological Association.

Monson, C. M., Gradus, J. L., La Bash, H., & Resick, P. A. (2009). The role of couples' interacting trauma-related cognitions in post-disaster PTSD. *Journal of Traumatic Stress, 22*, 276–281.

Monson, C. M., Schnurr, P. P., Stevens, S. P., & Guthrie, K. A. (2004). Cognitive-behavioral couple's treatment for posttraumatic stress disorder: Initial findings. *Journal of Traumatic Stress, 17*, 341–344.

Monson, C. M., Stevens, S. P., & Schnurr, P. P. (2005). Cognitive-behavioral couple's treatment for posttraumatic stress disorder. In T. A. Corales (Ed.), *Focus on posttraumatic stress disorder research* (pp. 251–280). Hauppague, NY: Nova Science.

Mowrer, O. A. (1960). *Learning theory and behavior.* New York: John Wiley.

Nelson Goff, B. S., Crow, J. R., Reisbig, A. M. J., & Hamilton, S. (2007). The impact of individual trauma symptoms of deployed soldiers on relationship satisfaction. *Journal of Family Psychology, 21*, 334–353.

Nelson Goff, B. S., & Smith, D. B. (2005). Systemic traumatic stress: The couple adaptation to traumatic stress model. *Journal of Marital and Family Therapy, 31*, 145–157.

Novaco, R. W., & Chemtob, C. M. (2002). Anger and combat-related posttraumatic stress disorder. *Journal of Traumatic Stress, 15*, 123–132.

O'Farrell, T. J., & Fals-Stewart, W. (2006). *Behavioral couples therapy for alcoholism and drug abuse.* New York: Guilford.

O'Leary, K. D., & Beach, S. R. H. (1990). Marital therapy: A viable treatment for depression and marital discord. *American Journal of Psychiatry, 147*, 183–186.

Ozer, E. J., Best, S. R., Lipsey, T. L., & Weiss, D. S. (2003). Predictors of posttraumatic stress disorder and symptoms in adults: A meta-analysis. *Psychological Bulletin, 129*, 52–73.

Piccinato, J. M., & Rosenbaum, J. N. (1997). Caregiver hardiness explored within Watson's theory of human caring in nursing. *Journal of Gerontological Nursing, 23*, 32–39.

Price, J. L., Monson, C. M., Callahan, K., & Rodriguez, B. F. (2006). The role of emotional functioning in military-related PTSD and its treatment. *Journal of Anxiety Disorders, 20*, 661–674.

Renshaw, K. D., Rodrigues, C. S., & Jones, D. H. (2008). Psychological symptoms and marital distress in spouses of Operation Iraqi Freedom veterans: Relationships with spouses' perceptions of veterans' experiences and symptoms. *Journal of Family Psychology, 22*, 586–594.

Renshaw, K. D., Rodrigues, C. S., & Jones, D. H. (2009). Combat exposure, psychological symptoms, and marital satisfaction in National Guard soldiers who served in Operation Iraqi Freedom from 2005 to 2006. *Anxiety, Stress & Coping, 22*, 101–115.

Resick, P. A., Monson, C. M., & Chard, K. M. (2007). *Cognitive processing therapy: Veteran/military version.* Washington, DC: Department of Veterans Affairs.

Riggs, D. S., Byrne, C. A., Weathers, F. W., & Litz, B. T. (1998). The quality of the intimate relationships of male Vietnam veterans: Problems associated with posttraumatic stress disorder. *Journal of Traumatic Stress, 11*, 87–101.

Ruscio, A., Weathers, F., King, L., & King, D. (2002). Male warzone veteran's perceived relationships with their children: The importance of emotional numbing. *Journal of Traumatic Stress, 15*, 351–357.

Samper, R., Taft, C. T., King, D. W., & King, L. A. (2004). Posttraumatic stress disorder and parenting satisfaction among a national sample of male Vietnam veterans. *Journal of Traumatic Stress, 17*, 311–315.

Sautter, F., Glynn, S., Thompson, K. E., Franklin, C. L., & Han, X. (2009). A couple-based approach to the reduction of PTSD avoidance symptoms: Preliminary findings. *Journal of Marital and Family Therapy, 35*, 343–349.

Savarese, V. W., Suvak, M. K., King, L. A., & King, D. W. (2001). Relationships among alcohol use, hyperarousal, and marital abuse and violence in Vietnam veterans. *Journal of Traumatic Stress, 14*, 717–732.

Sayers, S. L., Farrow, V., Ross, J., & Oslin, D. W. (2009). Family problems among recently returned military veterans. *Journal of Clinical Psychiatry, 70*, 163–170.

Solomon, S. D. (2002). Gender differences in response to disaster. In G. Weidner, M. S. Kopp, & M. Kristenson (Eds.), *Heart disease: Environment, stress and gender* (pp. 267–274). Amsterdam: IOS Press.

Solomon, Z., Dekel, R., & Mikulincer, M. (2008). Complex trauma of war captivity: A prospective study of attachment and post-traumatic stress disorder. *Psychological Medicine, 7*, 1–8.

Solomon, Z., Ginzburg, K., Mikulincer, M., Neria, Y., & Ohry, A. (1998). Coping with war captivity: The role of attachment style. *European Journal of Personality, 12*, 271–285.

Solomon, Z., Waysman, M., Levy, G., Fried, B., Mikulincer, M., Benbenishty, R., et al. (1992). From front line to home front: A study of secondary traumatization. *Family Process, 31*, 289–302.

Souzzia, J. M., & Motta, R. (2004). The relationship between combat exposure and the transfer of trauma-like symptoms to offspring of veterans. *Traumatology, 10*, 17–37.

Steelman, J. R. (2007). Relationship dynamics: Understanding married women's mental health. *Advances in Nursing Science, 30*, 151–158.

Taft, C. T., Vogt, D. S., Marshall, A. D., Panuzio, J., & Niles, B. L. (2007). Aggression among combat veterans: Relationships with combat exposure and symptoms of posttraumatic stress disorder, dysphoria, and anxiety. *Journal of Traumatic Stress, 20*, 135–145.

Ursano, R. J., Fullerton, C. S., Kao, T. C., & Bhartiya, V. R. (1995). Longitudinal assessment of posttraumatic stress disorder and depression after exposure to traumatic death. *Journal of Nervous and Mental Disease, 183*, 36–42.

Van IJzendoorn, M. H., Bakermans-Kranenburg, M. J., & Sagi-Schwartz, A. (2003). Are children of Holocost survivors less well-adapted? No meta-analytic evidence for secondary traumatization. *Journal of Traumatic Stress, 16*, 459–469.

Verbosky, S. J., & Ryan, D. A. (1988). Female partners of Vietnam veterans: Stress by proximity. *Issues in Mental Health Nursing, 9*, 95–104.

Vila, G., Witkowski, P., Tondini, M. C., Perez-Diaz, F., Mouren-Simeoni, M. C., & Jouvent, R. (2001). A study of posttraumatic disorders in children who experienced an industrial disaster in the Briey region. *European Child and Adolescent Psychiatry, 10*, 10–18.

Waysman, M., Mikulincer, M., Solomon, Z., & Weisenberg, M. (1993). Secondary traumatization among wives of posttraumatic combat veterans: A family typology. *Journal of Family Psychology, 7*, 104–118.

Westerink, J., & Giarratano, L. (1999). The impact of posttraumatic stress disorder on partners and children of Australian Vietnam veterans. *Australian & New Zealand Journal of Psychiatry, 33*, 841–847.

Whisman, M. A., Sheldon, C. T., & Goering, P. (2000). Psychiatric disorders and dissatisfaction with social relationships: Does type of relationship matter? *Journal of Abnormal Psychology, 109*, 803–808.

Williams, R., & Joseph, S. (1999). Conclusions: An integrative psychosocial model of PTSD. In W. Yule (Ed.), *PTSD: Concepts and theory* (pp. 297–314). Chichester, England: Wiley.

Yehuda, R., Bell, A., Bierer, L., & Schmeidler, J. (2008). Maternal, not paternal, PSTD is related to increased risk for PTSD in offspring of Holocaust surviors. *Journal of Psychiatric Research, 42*, 1104–1111.

Yehuda, R., Bierer, L. M., Schmeidler, J., Aferiat, D. H., Breslau, I., & Dolan, S. (2000). Low cortisol and risk for PTSD in adult offspring of holocaust survivors. *American Journal of Psychiatry, 157*, 1252–1259.

Yehuda, R., Blair, W., Labinsky, E., & Bierer, L. M. (2007). Effects of parental PTSD on the cortisol response to dexamethansone administration in their adult offspring. *American Journal of Psychiatry, 164*, 163–166.

Yehuda, R., Halligan, S. L., & Bierer, L. (2002). Cortisol levels in adult offspring of Holocaust survivors: Relation to PTSD symptom severity in the parent and child. *Psychoneuroendocrinology, 27*, 171–180.

Young, J. E. (1994). *Cognitive therapy for personality disorders: A schema focused approach.* Sarasota, FL: Professional Resource Press.

Zarit, S. H., Todd, P. A., & Zarit, J. M. (1986). Subjective burden of husbands and wives as caregivers: A longitudinal study. *The Gerontologist, 26*, 260–266.

PART 5

Assessment

CHAPTER

16 Assessing PTSD Symptoms

Michelle J. Bovin *and* Frank W. Weathers

Abstract

Posttraumatic stress disorder (PTSD) is a serious and prevalent mental disorder that poses a number of significant challenges for accurate assessment and diagnosis. In this chapter we describe some of the most widely used PTSD assessment tools for adult trauma survivors, including structured interviews, self-report measures, and psychophysiological methods. We also discuss several key issues in PTSD assessment, including identifying an index traumatic event for symptom inquiry, linking symptoms to the index event, and detecting exaggerated symptom reporting. We conclude with a brief discussion of future directions for research on PTSD assessment.

Key Words: PTSD, assessment, interview, self-report, psychophysiology, malingering

Assessing PTSD Symptoms

Posttraumatic stress disorder (PTSD) is a serious and prevalent mental disorder that may develop following exposure to catastrophic life events such as combat, sexual assault, natural disasters, and life-threatening accidents. As currently conceptualized in *DSM-IV-TR* (American Psychiatric Association [APA], 2000), PTSD is a multifaceted syndrome, with 17 characteristic symptoms grouped into three clusters, including reexperiencing the traumatic event (e.g., intrusive thoughts, nightmares, and dissociative flashbacks), avoidance and numbing (e.g., avoidance of trauma-related thoughts and feelings; restricted range of affect), and hyper-arousal (hypervigilance, exaggerated startle). PTSD, particularly in its chronic form, is associated with extensive comorbidity with other mental disorders (Kessler, Sonnega, Bromet, Hughes, & Nelson, 1995; Koenen et al., 2008; Kulka et al., 1991) and physical health problems (Schnurr & Green, 2004) as well as marked impairment in social and occupational functioning (Kuhn, Blanchard, & Hickling, 2003; Ruscio, Weathers, King, & King, 2002; Schnurr, Hayes, Lunney, McFall, & Uddo, 2006; Smith, Schnurr, & Rosenheck, 2005; Stein, McQuaid, Pedrelli, Lenox, & McCahill, 2000; Stein, Walker, Hazen, & Forde, 1997). PTSD has been estimated to affect between 8–12% of the general population (Kessler et al., 1995; Norris & Slone, 2007), with higher rates for at risk populations (e.g., combat veterans; Kulka et al., 1990). Thus, PTSD is a significant public health problem, and its complex clinical presentation poses a number of significant challenges for accurate assessment and diagnosis in clinical and research settings.

In this chapter we first provide an overview of some of the most widely used measures for assessing PTSD in adult trauma survivors, including structured diagnostic interviews, self-report measures, and psychophysiological methods. Next, we outline several key issues in PTSD assessment, including assessment of Criterion A (i.e., the precipitating traumatic stressor); and assessment of response bias, especially malingering or symptom exaggeration.

Finally, we discuss several unresolved questions and future directions for PTSD assessment.

PTSD Assessment Instruments

In this section we briefly review a number of the most widely used PTSD assessment instruments (see Elhai, Gray, Kashdan, & Franklin, 2005, for a more comprehensive list and estimates of frequency of use). These measures vary in terms of method of administration (e.g., interview, self-report); wording of items; number and type of response options; and time frame assessed. In addition, these measures vary in explicit coverage of *DSM* diagnostic criteria. Whereas all interviews are based directly on *DSM* criteria, self-report measures can be divided into those that: (a) correspond exactly to *DSM* criteria; (b) assess core and associated features of PTSD but do not correspond exactly to *DSM* criteria; and (c) were derived empirically from existing instruments and correspond substantially less to *DSM* criteria (Weathers & Keane, 1999). We review PTSD assessment instruments by category, beginning with interviews and following up with each of the three types of self-report measures.

Interviews

STRUCTURED CLINICAL INTERVIEW FOR *DSM-IV* AXIS I DISORDERS (SCID-I), CLINICIAN VERSION

The SCID-I (First, Spitzer, Williams, & Gibbon, 2000) is a comprehensive structured interview that assesses all major Axis I disorders. The SCID PTSD module, which can be administered as a part of a full SCID or as a stand-alone measure, follows *DSM-IV* criteria exactly, providing a standard prompt question for each of the 17 PTSD symptoms based on the respondent's worst trauma. Interviewers rate symptom presence as: *? = inadequate information*, *1 = absent*, *2 = subthreshold*, or *3 = threshold*.

The SCID PTSD module has good reliability and convergent validity. Kulka et al. (1991) found a kappa for interrater reliability of .93, although Keane et al. (1998) found a lower interrater kappa of .68. More recently, Zanarini et al. (2000) found a kappa of .88 for interrater reliability and .78 for test-retest reliability; and Zanarini and Frankenburg (2001) found kappas of 1.0 for both interrater and test-retest reliability, indicating perfect diagnostic agreement across raters and occasions. Schlenger et al. (1992) provided evidence of convergent validity, reporting moderate positive correlations between the SCID PTSD module and the Mississippi Scale for Combat-Related PTSD (kappa = .53) and the PK Scale of the MMPI (kappa = .48). They also provided evidence of excellent diagnostic utility, reporting a sensitivity of .81, specificity of .98, and kappa of .82 when the SCID PTSD module was used to predict a criterion based on a composite PTSD diagnosis. One limitation of the SCID PTSD module is that it yields essentially dichotomous present/absent ratings for symptoms and diagnostic status, and thus does not provide a continuous measure of PTSD symptom severity.

CLINICIAN ADMINISTERED PTSD SCALE (CAPS)

Since its development in 1990 at the National Center for PTSD, the CAPS (Blake et al., 1990, 1995) has become the most widely used structured interview for PTSD. The CAPS consists of 30 items, including 17 items assessing the *DSM-IV* PTSD symptoms; 5 items assessing onset and duration of symptoms, subjective distress, and functional impairment; 3 items assessing response validity, overall severity, and improvement since a previous assessment; and 5 optional items assessing trauma-related guilt and dissociation. The CAPS also includes the Life Events Checklist, which screens for exposure to a wide range of traumatic stressors, and a trauma inquiry section to assess Criterion A, the stressor criterion for PTSD.

Unlike the SCID, the CAPS provides dichotomous and continuous scores for individual symptoms, symptom clusters, and for the full PTSD syndrome. The frequency and intensity of each symptom are rated on separate five-point (0–4) rating scales. These can be summed to create a nine-point (0–8) symptom severity score, which in turn can be summed across symptoms to create a total severity score. A number of scoring rules for the CAPS have been developed for converting symptom ratings into a PTSD diagnosis (Weathers, Ruscio, & Keane, 1999). These rules vary from relatively lenient to relatively stringent, permitting greater flexibility for different assessment tasks across different settings.

The CAPS has been investigated extensively and has excellent psychometric properties (see Weathers, Keane, & Davidson, 2001, for a review). Because it yields both a PTSD diagnosis and a continuous measure of PTSD symptom severity, it is well suited for a variety of assessment tasks. The main limitations of the CAPS are that it typically takes longer to administer than other PTSD interviews and it requires more extensive training and experience to master its administration and scoring.

PTSD SYMPTOM SCALE INTERVIEW (PSS-I)

The PSS-I (Foa, Riggs, Dancu, & Rothbaum, 1993) is a structured interview consisting of 17 items corresponding to the 17 PTSD symptoms. Symptom severity is rated on a four-point scale. In the original *DSM-III-R* version, the anchors were: *0 = not at all, 1 = a little bit, 2 = somewhat,* and *3 = very much*. These were revised for *DSM-IV* to incorporate both frequency and intensity (e.g., *1 = once per week or less/a little; 3 = five or more times per week/very much*), which allows interviewers to consider the more relevant severity dimension for a given symptom (e.g., frequency for nightmares, intensity for hyper-vigilance). The PSS-I yields both diagnostic and symptom severity information. Diagnostic status is determined by considering items rated 1 or higher as exceeding the symptom threshold and following the *DSM* diagnostic rule (i.e., one reexperiencing symptom, three avoidance symptoms, and two arousal symptoms). Total severity is determined by summing the 17 items. Severity for each symptom cluster also may be calculated by summing the appropriate items.

The PSS-I has strong psychometric properties. Foa et al. (1993) found high internal consistency for both the whole measure (alpha = .85) and for the three symptom clusters (alphas = .65–.71). These investigators also found good test-retest reliability (.80), high interrater reliability for PTSD diagnostic status (kappa = .91), and an intraclass correlation of .97 for total severity. In addition, the PSS-I showed good convergent validity—for example, correlating .69 with the Impact of Event Scale (IES; Horowitz, Wilner, & Alvarez, 1979) intrusion score, and .67 with the Rape Aftermath Symptom Test (RAST; Kilpatrick, 1988). The PSS-I also demonstrated strong diagnostic utility against the SCID PTSD module, with a sensitivity of .88, specificity of .96, and efficiency of .94. Foa and Tolin (2000) confirmed these initial positive results, reporting a full-scale alpha of .86, full-scale interrater reliability of .93, and kappas of .65 against the CAPS and .56 against the SCID PTSD module. They also found that the PSS-I was significantly briefer than the CAPS (22 vs. 33 minutes).

The PSS-I has several advantages and is a very useful measure for assessing PTSD. It is relatively brief; it provides information about PTSD diagnostic status as well as symptom severity; it has strong psychometric properties; and it can be administered by clinicians or other trained interviewers. However, the PSS-I also has a few disadvantages. The instrument itself provides only a single question per symptom (although additional questions are suggested in the manual; see Hembree, Foa, & Feeny, 2002), it assesses symptoms over a two-week interval, rather than the one-month interval required by *DSM*, and its original scoring rule appears to be too lenient, yielding substantially higher prevalence rates than even the most lenient CAPS scoring rule (Foa & Tolin, 2000).

STRUCTURED INTERVIEW FOR PTSD (SI-PTSD)

The SI-PTSD was developed in 1989 by Davidson, Smith, and Kudler to assess the presence of both current and lifetime PTSD diagnostic status, as well as the severity of the syndrome, as described by *DSM-III* and *DSM-III-R* criteria. In 1997, the interview was updated to reflect *DSM-IV* criteria, and the acronym was changed to SIP (Davidson, Malik, & Travers, 1997). The SIP can be administered by either a clinician or a trained lay interviewer, and takes 10–30 minutes to complete. It includes 17 individual items that correspond to *DSM-IV* PTSD criteria, as well as two additional items that assess survival and behavioral guilt. Each item is rated on a five-point scale (0–4). For diagnostic purposes, items that are rated as greater than or equal to 2 meet criteria for the symptom. Items can also be summed to create a continuous measure of symptom severity.

The SI-PTSD possesses excellent psychometric properties. In the initial analysis of its reliability and validity, Davidson et al. (1989) reported an overall full-scale alpha of .94, test-retest reliability of .71, and interrater reliability ranging from .97–.99, with perfect diagnostic agreement. Investigations of the SIP have been equally promising. Davidson, Malik, et al. (1997) reported an alpha of .80, test-retest reliability of .89, and interrater reliability of .90. They also found that a cutoff score of 20 on the SIP had perfect diagnostic agreement with the SCID PTSD module. The advantages of the SIP are that it provides follow-up prompts and explicit rating scale descriptors to help clarify administration and scoring, it yields a PTSD diagnosis as well a measure of symptom severity, and it appears to be psychometrically sound. The disadvantages are that only one rationally derived scoring rule has been evaluated and, overall, investigation of the psychometric properties has been somewhat limited.

SUMMARY

The four interview measures we have reviewed vary in several ways, including administration time, type of rating scale, and information provided. Because of this, each measure can be appropriate depending upon the goals of the assessment. The SCID PTSD module is relatively brief and is useful for establishing PTSD diagnostic status, but does not yield information about symptom severity. The PSS-I and SIP are also relatively brief and provide information regarding PTSD diagnostic status as well symptom severity, although the two-week time frame for the PSS-I (rather than the one-month time frame indicated in *DSM*) makes it less useful for establishing an initial PTSD diagnosis. The PSS-I and SIP are well suited for repeated administrations—for example, for tracking symptom severity in treatment outcome studies. The CAPS also provides information regarding PTSD diagnostic status and symptom severity, but is more complex and takes longer to administer than the other interviews. It is useful for eliciting detailed information about PTSD symptoms, and thus is well suited for initial diagnosis, functional analysis of symptoms, and treatment planning. Because they yield a continuous measure of PTSD symptom severity, the PSS-I, SIP, and CAPS provide a flexible metric for research applications involving, for example, comparisons of mean PTSD severity or correlations between PTSD and other constructs.

Self-Report Measures: DSM-correspondent

DAVIDSON TRAUMA SCALE (DTS)

The DTS was developed in 1997 as a self-rating scale for PTSD (Davidson, Book et al., 1997). It includes 17 items that correspond to the *DSM-IV* criteria for PTSD. Each item is rated for both frequency and severity on five-point scales, using a past-week time frame. The DTS was designed to yield a continuous score of PTSD severity, with scores ranging from 0–136. The DTS has excellent psychometric properties. In their initial examination of the measure, Davidson, Book, et al. (1997) found strong internal consistency (.97–.99) and test-retest reliability (.86). In addition, the DTS correlated highly with other measures of PTSD, including the CAPS (.78) and the IES (.64). When a cutoff score of 40 was used, the authors reported a sensitivity of .69, a specificity of .95, and an overall efficiency of .83. Subsequent examinations of the psychometric properties of the DTS have yielded equally strong results (e.g., McDonald, Beckham, Morey, & Calhoun, 2009), although lower cutoff scores have been found to be more effective. Based on its excellent psychometric properties and ease of use, the DTS is well suited for the assessment of PTSD symptom severity.

PTSD CHECKLIST (PCL)

The PCL (Weathers, Litz, Herman, Huska, & Keane, 1993; Weathers, 2008) was developed at the National Center for PTSD for use in establishing construct validity for the CAPS. Originally designed to reflect *DSM-III-R* criteria, it was revised in 1994 to assess PTSD as described by the *DSM-IV*. The PCL consists of 17 items rated on a five-point scale. Respondents indicate how bothered they were by each of the items over the past month. There are currently three versions of the PCL, which differ only in the phrase describing the index trauma for the first eight items: the civilian version (PCL-C) refers to "a stressful experience from the past," the military version (PCL-M) refers to "a stressful military experience," and the specific version (PCL-S) refers to "the stressful experience," which is identified by the respondent before completing the scale. For all three versions of the PCL, severity scores for symptom clusters and the full syndrome may be calculated by summing across corresponding items. A dichotomous PTSD diagnosis is calculated by counting items rated *3 = moderately* or above as symptoms endorsed, then following the *DSM* diagnostic rule.

The PCL is one of the most widely used self-report measures of PTSD and has consistently displayed excellent psychometric properties across a wide range of research and clinical settings. In the earliest report, Weathers et al. (1993) found high internal consistency (full-scale alpha = .97), and excellent test-retest reliability (.96) in male combat veterans. They also found strong correlations between the PCL and other PTSD measures, including the Mississippi Scale (.93), PK Scale (.77) and IES (.90), and good diagnostic utility against the SCID PTSD module, with a sensitivity of .82, specificity of .83 and kappa of.64. The strong psychometric properties of the PCL have been replicated in a number of subsequent investigations with other populations, including survivors of motor vehicle accidents, sexual assault (Blanchard, Jones-Alexander, Buckley, & Forneris, 1996) and college students with mixed civilian traumas (Adkins, Weathers, McDevitt-Murphy, & Daniels, 2008; Ruggiero, Del Ben, Scotti, & Rabalais, 2003). The

PCL is also the most commonly used measure in the growing factor-analytic literature on PTSD (e.g., Palmieri, Weathers, Difede, & King, 2007), so its factor structure has been extensively cross-validated and helped challenge the three-factor model of PTSD implicit in *DSM-IV* criteria.

One limitation of the PCL is that there are three versions, and although they differ only slightly, the question of the comparability across versions has not been resolved. Another limitation is that it only assesses the 17 PTSD symptoms, and does not assess trauma exposure, course, or functional impairment. Finally, the optimal cutoff score for predicting a PTSD diagnosis has varied widely across studies, so the choice of a cutoff score for a given assessment task in a specific population still needs further investigation.

POSTTRAUMATIC STRESS DIAGNOSTIC SCALE (PDS)

The PDS, a revised version of the PTSD Symptom Scale-Self-Report Version (PSS-SR; Foa et al., 1993), is a comprehensive self-report measure that assesses all six *DSM-IV* PTSD criteria (i.e., Criteria A-F; Foa, Cashman, Jaycox, & Perry, 1997). The PDS consists of 49 items divided into four parts. Part 1 consists of a 12-item checklist of traumatic events as well as a single item that asks the respondent to identify the single event that has disturbed him/her the most in the last month. Part 2 consists of four dichotomous items that assess whether the event identified in Part 1 meets Criterion A. Part 3 assesses the frequency over the last month of the 17 PTSD symptoms on a four-point scale. Part 4 includes nine items that assess the impact of symptoms on various aspects of functioning. The PDS provides both a dichotomous diagnostic score and a continuous symptom severity score. Individual PTSD symptoms are counted as present if the corresponding PDS item is endorsed as 1 or higher.

The PDS, like the PCL, boasts excellent psychometric properties. In their original examination of the reliability and validity of the PDS, Foa and her colleagues (1997) used the PDS with a normative sample of adults in a variety of clinical and research settings. The authors reported high test-retest reliability for symptom severity for both the total scale (.83) and the individual symptom clusters (.77–.85). Further, diagnostic agreement between the two administrations produced a kappa of .74. Internal consistency was also high for both the total scale (.92) and the symptom clusters (.78–.84). Diagnostic utility (against the SCID) produced a sensitivity of .89, a specificity of .75, an efficiency of .79, and a kappa of .65 (i.e., 82% agreement). The PDS also demonstrated excellent convergent validity with both the IES-R intrusion (.78) and avoidance subscales (.66), as well as the RAST (.81). The discriminant validity of the PDS was more questionable; the measure produced a correlation of .79 with the Beck Depression Inventory (BDI). However, recent studies have reported that the PDS does have good discriminant validity. For instance, Adkins et al. (2008) reported that correlations ranged from only .32–.60 with measures of depression, anxiety, and social phobia. The overall strength of the psychometric properties of the PDS has been supported by other studies as well (e.g., Griffin, Uhlmansiek, Resick, & Mechanic, 2004). The PDS has a number of advantages as a self-report measure of PTSD. It has been translated into a number of languages and widely used in a variety of different trauma populations.

DETAILED ASSESSMENT OF POSTTRAUMATIC STRESS (DAPS)

The DAPS (Briere, 2001) is another comprehensive self-report measure that assesses all *DSM-IV* diagnostic criteria for PTSD. In addition, the DAPS assesses other important trauma-related responses and outcomes, including peritraumatic distress and dissociation, trauma-specific dissociation, substance abuse, and suicidality. Further, the DAPS is the only self-report PTSD measure that assesses positive and negative response bias. The DAPS consists of 104 items that yield two response validity scales and 11 clinical scales. Scores are reported as T-scores based on a normative sample of trauma survivors, with T-scores above 65 considered clinically significant.

The DAPS appears to have excellent psychometric properties. The professional manual reports conceptually consistent levels of internal consistency and good convergent and discriminant validity across all scales. The manual also reports strong diagnostic utility against the CAPS, with a sensitivity of .88, specificity of .86, and kappa of .73. The DAPS is a promising measure. It provides full coverage of core and associated features of PTSD, assesses response bias, and provides a dimensional profile of PTSD severity based on a normative sample. It is longer than most self-report PTSD measures and may not be appropriate in assessment contexts requiring a brief screening tool, but it has much to offer and has become increasingly popular in both clinical and research settings (Elhai et al., 2005).

Self-Report Measures: PTSD-focused, Non-DSM-correspondent

MISSISSIPPI SCALE FOR COMBAT-RELATED PTSD (MISSISSIPPI SCALE)

The Mississippi Scale (Keane, Caddell, & Taylor, 1988), a 35-item self-report measure of PTSD and associated problems, is one of the first and most widely used measures of combat-related PTSD. Respondents rate items on a five-point scale using verbal anchors that vary according to item content (e.g., indicating frequency or the extent to which an item is true for the respondent). Items are summed to yield a continuous measure of PTSD symptom severity.

The Mississippi Scale has been thoroughly evaluated and empirical evidence indicates that its psychometric properties are strong. In their initial examination of the measure, Keane et al. (1988) reported high internal consistency (.94) and test-retest reliability (.97). The strong reliability of the Mississippi Scale was confirmed by other investigations (e.g., Kulka et al., 1991; McFall, Smith, Mackay, & Tarver, 1990). Keane et al. (1988) also reported that, with a cutoff score of 107, the Mississippi Scale yielded a sensitivity of .93, a specificity of .89, and an efficiency of .90 against a consensus clinical diagnosis of PTSD. The validity of the measure has been further supported by other studies. For example, McFall et al. (1990) reported strong correlations between the Mississippi Scale and the PK Scale, the SCID, and the IES. In addition, Kulka et al. (1991) reported that the Mississippi Scale was able to correctly classify more combat veterans in the NVVRS than either the PK Scale or the IES.

A civilian version of the Mississippi Scale (Civilian Mississippi Scale, or CMS) has also been developed. Unlike the Mississippi Scale, the psychometric properties of the CMS have been somewhat inconsistent. Studies have generally supported the reliability of the CMS. For example, studies have reported internal consistency ranging from .86 to .90 (Rosenberger, 2007) and test-retest reliability ranging from .84–.86 (Adkins et al., 2008). However, the findings for the validity of the CMS are not as strong. For example, Lauterbach, Vrana, King, and King (1997) found that the CMS had poor construct validity in that it correlated more strongly with measures of general distress than with measures of PTSD. Similarly, Adkins et al. (2008) found that the CMS tended to have lower discriminant validity and somewhat lower convergent validity relative to other PTSD measures. In contrast, however, Rosenberger (2007) found that the CMS correlated more strongly with measures of PTSD (.75 with the PCL) than with non-PTSD measures of general anxiety (.47–.55), depression (.51) and global distress (.62). Rosenberger suggested that her findings may differ from Lauterbach et al.'s (1997) owing to the use of the PCL and higher rates of PTSD in her sample. Nonetheless, Rosenberger acknowledged that her findings indicated strong correlations between the CMS non-PTSD measures, suggesting that this is likely due to the inclusion of associated features of PTSD in the CMS, making it a less "pure" measure of PTSD than *DSM*-correspondent measures such as the PCL.

IMPACT OF EVENT SCALE (IES)

The IES (Horowitz et al., 1979) is the first standardized self-report measure of reactions to extreme stressors, and continues to be one of the most widely used instruments for assessing posttraumatic symptomatology. It was developed based on Horowitz's (1976) conceptual model of responses to stressful life events. The IES includes 15 items, 7 of which assess intrusive symptoms and 8 which assess avoidance symptoms. Respondents first specify a stressful event, and then rate the frequency of each IES item over the last week on a four-point scale. The IES does not correspond directly to *DSM-IV* criteria, and most notably, does not include items assessing Criterion D (the hyper-arousal cluster). In 1997, Weiss and Marmar revised the IES to more directly assess PTSD symptoms. Their revision, the 22-item Impact of Event Scale–Revised (IES-R), incorporates a number of significant alterations, including the addition of items corresponding to Criterion D and dissociative reexperiencing, and the adoption of a five-point scale, with ratings based on subjective distress rather than frequency. Despite these changes, the IES-R still does not assess some PTSD criteria at all (e.g., diminished interest, foreshortened future), and only indirectly assesses other symptoms (restricted range of affect, inability to recall important aspects of the traumatic event).

In their initial examination of the IES, Horowitz et al. (1979) reported high test-retest reliability within a one-week interval (.87 for the intrusion scale, .79 for the avoidance scale) and internal consistency (.79 for the intrusion scale, .82 for the avoidance scale). Other researchers have supported these findings. For example, Sundin and Horowitz (2002) conducted a comprehensive review of 23 studies that have utilized the IES over the last

20 years. These authors found the reliability of the measure to be consistent with that reported by Horowitz et al. (1979). Specifically, the authors found the internal consistency of the intrusion scale to be .86 (range of .72–.92) and the avoidance scale to be .82 (range of .65–.90). However, Sundin and Horowitz found that test-retest reliability of the IES was affected by the interval between testings; shorter time intervals (i.e., < 6 months) were associated with higher estimates of stability than longer intervals (i.e., > 1 year).

Sundin and Horowitz (2002) also examined the validity of the IES. Of the 12 studies that assessed content validity, the authors reported an average correlation of .63 between the intrusion and avoidance subscales. Although this is somewhat higher than the correlation reported by Horowitz et al. (1979; .41); Sundin and Horowitz argued that this still provides evidence that the two subscales are relatively independent of one another. In their examination of convergent validity, the authors found that the two subscales of the IES varied widely in their correlations with both similar and dissimilar measures. The authors concluded that the moderate correlations between measures of PTSD and both the IES intrusion subscale (range of .49–.79) and the avoidance subscale (range of .29–.80) provide evidence that the IES subscales tap aspects of posttraumatic reactions that are not captured by *DSM*-correspondent measures.

Several researchers have also examined the psychometric properties of the IES-R. For example, in their original investigation of the scale, Weiss and Marmar (1997) found that the three subscales of the IES-R yielded good internal consistency (.87–.92 for intrusion symptoms; .84–.86 for avoidance symptoms; .79–.90 for hyper-arousal symptoms), and acceptable test-retest reliability (.57–.94 for intrusion symptoms; .51–.89 for avoidance symptoms; .59–.92 for hyper-arousal symptoms). The strong reliability of the IES-R has been confirmed by several other studies (e.g., Adkins et al., 2008; Beck et al., 2008; Shapinsky, Rapport, Henderson, & Axelrod, 2005). In addition, the IES-R appears to have high levels of validity. For example, among a sample of motor vehicle accident survivors, Beck et al. (2008) found that the three subscales of the IES-R were correlated with other measures of PTSD (range of .39–.86). The IES-R also appears to have strong discriminant validity. Shapinsky et al. (2005) reported that the correlations of the IES-R with measures of affect were weaker than those with measures of PTSD. These findings were also supported by other investigators (e.g., Adkins et al., 2008; Beck et al., 2008).

Self-Report Measures: Empirically Derived

PK SCALE OF THE MMPI AND MMPI-2

The PK Scale of the Minnesota Multiphasic Personality Inventory (MMPI) was originally developed by Keane, Malloy, and Fairbank (1984). It consists of 49 MMPI items that were found to statistically differentiate Vietnam combat veterans with and without PTSD. When the MMPI was revised in 1989 (MMPI-2), two minor modifications were made to the PK Scale (Lyons & Keane, 1992). The revised measure consists of 46 MMPI items. Both versions of the PK Scale use a true-false format and provide continuous measures of symptomatology.

Empirical investigations have provided evidence that the original PK Scale has strong psychometric properties. For example, Keane et al. (1984) found that a cutoff score of 30 correctly classified 82% of veterans in both the validation and cross-validation samples. The utility of the PK Scale in discriminating between both veterans and civilians with and without PTSD has been supported by other empirical studies (e.g., Koretzky & Peck, 1990).

The revised version of the PK Scale has also demonstrated excellent psychometric properties. For example, in the normative testing of the MMPI-2, the revised PK Scale demonstrated good internal consistency (.85–.87) and test-retest reliability (.86–.89). The revised PK Scale has also been examined as both an embedded measure (within the MMPI-2) and as a stand-alone measure. Researchers found that both versions showed strong reliability (e.g., Herman, Weathers, Litz, & Keane, 1996; Lyons & Scotti, 1994). However, the validity of the stand-alone measure has been equivocal. Although several researchers have demonstrated that the PK Scale shows strong convergent validity (e.g., Neal et al., 1994), Adkins et al. (2008) found that the convergent validity of the PK Scale with the CAPS was weaker than that of six other self-report measures. In addition, the PK Scale has demonstrated weak discriminant validity, correlating highly with measures of depression, anxiety, social phobia and general distress (e.g., Adkins et al., 2008; Neal et al., 1994). Despite this, the PK Scale does appear to discriminate both veterans and civilians with and without PTSD (e.g., Herman et al., 1996).

SYMPTOM CHECKLIST-90-R (SCL-90-R) PTSD SCALES

The SCL-90-R (Derogatis, 1977) is a commonly used 90-item self-report symptom inventory. Items are scored on a five-point scale. The SCL-90-R includes nine subscales and can be administered in 15—20 minutes. Several PTSD scales have been empirically derived from the SCL-90-R, including the Crime-Related PTSD scale (CR-PTSD; Saunders, Arata, & Kilpatrick, 1990) and the War-Zone-Related PTSD scale (WZ-PTSD; Weathers et al., 1996).

The CR-PTSD scale is a 28-item measure that was originally shown to discriminate between female crime victims with and without PTSD (Saunders et al., 1990). In the same study, it showed strong internal consistency (.93) and was able to correctly classify 89% of the sample. Subsequent empirical investigations have supported the strong psychometric properties of the measure (e.g., Arata, Saunders, & Kilpatrick, 1991). However, the CR-PTSD does not appear to perform better than the SCL-90-R Global Severity Index (GSI). For example, Dutton, Hohnecker, Halle, and Burghardt (1994) found that forensic and clinical samples of battered women differed significantly on the CR-PTSD. However, the difference found by the CR-PTSD was no greater than that obtained by the GSI. This calls the precision of the CR-PTSD into question.

The WZ-PTSD scale is a 25-item measure that shares fewer than half of its items with the CR-PTSD scale. Weathers et al. (1996) found that the WZ-PTSD scale discriminated combat veterans with and without PTSD above and beyond the other SCL-90-R items. The authors reported that the psychometric properties were generally strong; the WZ-PTSD yielded high internal consistency and efficiency. However, similar to the CR-PTSD, the WZ-PTSD did not discriminate participants in the study with more efficiency than the GSI. The authors argued that this may have been a product of the high distress of the sample. Similar to the PK Scale, both the CR-PTSD scale and the WZ-PTSD scale have utility in that they are derived from a measure that is commonly administered; as such, PTSD can be assessed at no additional cost. In addition, both scales are useful in that they are derived from a measure that requires a relatively short amount of time for administration.

SUMMARY

As with the PTSD interviews, the various self-report PTSD measures have different features that make them appropriate for different assessment purposes. All of the *DSM*-correspondent measures are appropriate for directly assessing *DSM* PTSD symptom severity. The PDS and DAPS, however, are the only self-report measures that assess all PTSD diagnostic criteria, not just the symptoms, and thus provide a more comprehensive evaluation. Further, the DAPS also includes an assessment of response bias, which helps identify potentially invalid responses. The PTSD-focused measures, while not corresponding directly to *DSM* criteria, have been shown to be valid indicators of severity of trauma-related symptoms and impairment and thus are appropriate as adjunct or convergent measures in a PTSD assessment battery. The empirically derived measures are the least strongly associated with *DSM* PTSD criteria. They should not be considered for use as a primary measure in a PTSD assessment, and are probably best limited to situations in which they are an adjunct measure or the only available PTSD measure—for example, when the parent instrument is administered routinely in a given setting, or in an archival data set.

Psychophysiological Procedures

Thus far, we have discussed exclusively self-report and interview measures that can be used for the purposes of diagnosing PTSD. One method that deviates from this format is the assessment of psychophysiological reactivity. Psychophysiological procedures are not psychometric measures per se, but non-self-report, behavioral measures that can provide evidence of trauma-related conditioned emotional reactions. PTSD is uniquely suited to psychophysiological measurement because many of the individual symptoms required by *DSM-IV* involve physiological arousal. In fact, researchers have found that individuals with PTSD show heightened psychophysiologic reactivity to trauma cues in comparison to individuals without PTSD (Orr, McNally, Rosen, & Shalev, 2004). Researchers initially explained this increased reactivity by using a classical conditioning framework. Within this framework, the initial traumatic event serves as the unconditioned stimulus, and the accompanying emotional reaction is the unconditioned response (e.g., Keane, Fairbank, Caddell, Zimering, & Bender, 1985; Kolb & Multalipassi, 1982; Orr, McNally, et al., 2004; Pitman, 1988). Exposures to reminders of the trauma then serve to elicit the conditioned emotional response (i.e., heightened reactivity).

However, this conceptualization was criticized due to its inability to explain why the emotional responses are resistant to extinction. Lang's (1985) bioinformational theory of emotion more fully explains the longevity of the reactivity associated with the disorder. According to Lang, PTSD consists of one or more pathological emotion networks that produce reactivity when activated and that can maintain their integrity over long periods of time (Orr, McNally, et al., 2004).

Although the paradigms for assessing physiological arousal vary, two methods are most commonly utilized: a paradigm involving the presentation of standardized audiovisual trauma-relevant stimuli and individually constructed script-driven imagery of the trauma event using a paradigm originally advanced by Lang (1979). In a standardized audiovisual trauma-relevant stimuli paradigm, a fixed set of stimuli (e.g., light flashes, combat sounds, pictures of combat pictures) are presented to a participant while physiological responses are recorded. In contrast, individually constructed script-driven imagery is specifically designed to reflect the trauma experienced by the individual participant. In this paradigm, various scripts are prepared that portray actual or hypothetical experiences of the person being assessed, including the two most stressful trauma-related experiences they can recall. Scripts are then recorded in a neutral voice by the experimenter; the participant listens to these scripts while physiological responses are recorded. With either approach, responses during resting baseline and/or neutral intervals are compared to those obtained during processing of trauma-related stimuli. Psychophysiological measurements that are recorded vary, but typically include at least one of the following: cardiovascular measures (e.g., heart rate), electrodermal measures (e.g., skin conductance), electromyographic measures (e.g., corrugator facial electromyography), and electocortical measures (e.g., electroencephalographic; Orr, McNally, et al., 2004).

Several researchers have attempted to use psychophysiological measures to assess for PTSD. Although certain measures (e.g., heart rate) do tend to consistently distinguish between individuals with and without PTSD (e.g., Bryant, Creamer, O'Donnell, Silove, & McFarlane, 2008), researchers have been less successful using these measures to assign a PTSD diagnosis. The largest study to date that examined the utility of psychophysiological measures in determining PTSD diagnostic status was conducted by Keane et al. (1998) in a Cooperative Studies Program of the Department of Veteran Affairs. The authors derived an equation to predict PTSD status on the basis of four physiological variables. However, this equation was only able to correctly classify approximately two-thirds of the veterans with PTSD. Smaller studies have demonstrated somewhat more impressive rates of classification (e.g., Orr, 1997), possibly because unlike Keane et al. (1998), these studies did not exclude individuals who were taking psychoactive medications (and may have been those with the most severe levels of PTSD). However, even the most inclusive studies cannot correct for the fact that roughly 40% of individuals who meet criteria for PTSD show little or no physiologic reactivity (Orr, McNally, et al., 2004). This finding makes the use of physiological reactivity for diagnostic purposes particularly challenging.

Overall, assessment of physiological reactivity offers a number of strengths. In addition to providing a more "objective" measure than some of the other methods we have discussed, it also provides an avenue for individuals who have difficulty reporting on their subjective state to provide evidence of PTSD symptomatology (Keane, Brief, Pratt, & Miller, 2007). However, measuring psychophysiological reactivity is not without its drawbacks. First, although the methodology has become much simpler than it once was, physiological assessment still requires both technical skills and expensive equipment. In addition, physiological assessment can be affected by a number of factors, including the appropriateness of trauma cue presentation, participant compliance with protocol demands, participant dissociation, individual biological influences, and pharmacological agents (Orr, Metzger, Miller, & Kaloupek, 2004). Finally, and perhaps most importantly, a substantial minority of individuals who meet criteria for PTSD do not show increased physiological reactivity. Despite these limitations, physiological responding may offer a useful avenue for PTSD assessment, potentially in combination with other methods. However, in order for psychophysiological assessment methods to have utility, specific individual cutoff scores must be defined. Currently, there is no accepted rubric for defining "heightened" reactivity or "exaggerated" startle for the individual patient. Defining pathological levels of reactivity would increase the utility of psychophysiological measurement in identifying individuals with PTSD symptoms.

Additional Issues in the Assessment of PTSD

Criterion A

The measures we have presented thus far assess PTSD symptoms, and thus are relevant to the three symptom clusters (Criteria B, C, D) for PTSD. However, a diagnosis of PTSD cannot be assigned unless Criterion A—that is, exposure to a traumatic stressor—is met. Further, in addition to documenting trauma exposure for Criterion A, PTSD symptoms also must be linked to the traumatic event. Eight PTSD symptoms (the five reexperiencing symptoms, two effortful avoidance symptoms, and amnesia) are inherently linked to the event, so for these symptoms the task is straightforward. However, the remaining nine symptoms (numbing and hyper-arousal symptoms) are not inherently linked to the event, and thus an effort must be made to establish that they are functionally related to the event in some way. In some cases this can be challenging, and can be further complicated by the fact that individuals often experience multiple traumatic events, making it difficult to determine with certainty which PTSD symptoms are attributable to which traumatic events. Currently, only the CAPS provides a means for assessing the symptom-event link explicitly. For the nine symptoms not inherently linked to a traumatic event, the CAPS provides a trauma-related query to allow the interviewer to evaluate whether the symptom is definitely, probably, or unlikely the result of the trauma.

Several of the measures reviewed in this chapter (i.e., SCID, CAPS, PDS) include an assessment of Criterion A. For measures that do not include this feature, a number of other measures have been developed to assess for exposure to traumatic events. These measures differ on a number of qualities, including format (i.e., interview, self-report), number of events assessed, and conformity to Criterion A. Several of them have shown strong test-retest reliability and high kappa coefficients. For example, the Traumatic Events Questionnaire (TEQ; Vrana & Lauterbach, 1994) assesses 11 Criterion A1 events; however, this measure does not assess Criterion A2 (i.e., the experience of fear, helplessness, or horror during the traumatic event). In contrast, the Life Stressor Checklist-Revised (LSC-R; Wolfe, Kimerling, Brown, Chrestman, & Levin, 1996) assesses 30 events and both Criterion A1 and A2 (see Norris & Hamblen, 2004, for a review of self-report measures of trauma exposure).

Malingering

The measures discussed in this chapter were designed to assess the presence of PTSD. However, examining the elevations of these scales can only tell us whether respondents endorse PTSD symptoms; they do not tell us whether the respondents are being truthful about their experiences. Unfortunately, false reporting of psychological symptoms is not an uncommon occurrence (APA, 2000). This phenomenon, known as malingering, is defined by the *DSM-IV* as "the intentional production of false or grossly exaggerated physical or psychological symptoms, motivated by external incentives such as avoiding military duty, avoiding work, obtaining financial compensation, evading criminal prosecution, or obtaining drugs," (American Psychiatric Association [APA], 1994, p. 683). Rates of malingering are difficult to determine because malingerers must either be caught or have confessed for researchers to be sure of their status. Despite this, rates have been estimated as ranging from 7–50%, depending on the setting (e.g., Rogers, Harrell, & Liff, 1993; Rogers, Sewell, & Goldstein, 1994).

PTSD is particularly vulnerable to malingering for several reasons (Butcher, 2007; Guriel & Fremouw, 2003). First, PTSD symptoms are easily simulated because the symptoms are subjective. In addition, information on PTSD is widely available, providing a rich literature to which a potential malingerer can refer. Finally, there are significant external incentives in several situations that can make malingered PTSD a tempting possibility.

The cost to society by malingerers in terms of misused healthcare or legal resources, loss of taxpayer dollars, and other expenses is high (APA, 2000; Butcher, 2007). In an effort to reduce these costs, several researchers have developed measures for detecting malingered PTSD. Several of these measures are embedded in PTSD assessment measures (i.e., validity scales), whereas others are stand-alone instruments. Although the assessment of malingered PTSD is in its infancy, several measures have shown promise in discriminating honest responders from malingerers. In terms of embedded scales, two of the MMPI validity scales (Fp and Ds) have consistently outperformed the others in detecting malingerers of PTSD (e.g., Greene, 2008; Rogers, Sewell, Martin, & Vitacco, 2003). Several stand-alone instruments also appear to have utility. For example, both the Structured Interview of Reported Symptoms (SIRS; Rogers, 1992) and the Morel Emotional Numbing Test for PTSD-Revised

(MENT-R; Morel, 1998) have demonstrated success at identifying malingered PTSD in a range of settings (e.g., Morel & Shepherd, 2008; Rogers, Payne, Berry, & Granacher, 2009).

Several researchers have proposed that measuring physiological reactivity may be particularly useful in identifying malingerers. The ability of this method to discriminate between individuals with and without PTSD has been equivocal. Orr and Pitman (1993) found that they could correctly classify 75% of individuals with and without PTSD using measures of skin conductance and corrugator facial electromyography. In addition, Laor et al. (1998) found that whereas veterans with PTSD were able to alter their physiological reactions to appear less reactive, veterans without PTSD were not able to appear more reactive. In contrast, Gerardi, Blanchard, and Kolb (1989) found that veterans without PTSD were able to increase their reactivity so as not to differ from those with PTSD on several measures, whereas veterans with PTSD were not able to alter their responses. More research is needed to determine the utility of psychophysiological measurement in detecting malingerers.

Conclusion

In this chapter, we have reviewed a selection of the most frequently used measures for assessing PTSD symptoms, including interviews, self-report measures, and psychophysiological methods. Each type of measure has both benefits and drawbacks, and thus is well suited for some assessment tasks but not others. For example, structured interviews administered by an experienced clinician are essential for establishing a PTSD diagnosis, but may be too time-consuming and costly for initial screening or repeated assessments. Self-report measures are time- and cost-efficient and are particularly useful for quantifying PTSD symptom severity, but are more subject to various forms of response bias. Psychophysiological methods provide more objective evidence of PTSD severity in a behavioral assessment context, but primarily assess only one aspect of the PTSD syndrome—that is, conditioned fear responses.

Thus, a multimodal assessment, involving one or more of each type of measure, is likely the best approach, in that the limitations of a given type of measure are offset by the strengths of the other types. Such an approach has been central to evidence-based assessment of PTSD since the disorder was first officially recognized in *DSM-III* (Keane et al., 1985; Keane, Wolfe, & Taylor, 1987; Kulka et al, 1991), and is also advocated in the assessment of psychopathology more broadly (Anthony & Barlow, 2002). Empirical support for this approach to assessing PTSD has been established. For example, Monson et al. (2008) examined the longitudinal association between clinician and patient ratings of PTSD using the CAPS and the PCL. Although they found significant overlap between the two measures, they were not perfectly concordant. Rather, changes on the CAPS were typically two-thirds to three-quarters of the changes on the PCL. This suggests that measures that differ in format (e.g., interview versus self-report) may provide different estimates of PTSD symptom severity.

Despite the advantages of the multimodal approach, it may not always be feasible to implement fully. Thus, in selecting PTSD assessment measures for a given clinical or research application, it is essential to clarify the assessment question and goals, the population to be evaluated, and the resources available. If at all possible, however, the assessment of PTSD should include a structured diagnostic interview. Structured interviews are considered the gold standard for assessing psychopathology, especially with respect to establishing diagnostic status, and are useful for obtaining detailed information relevant to treatment planning. Further, several available PTSD interviews yield both a PTSD diagnosis and a continuous measure of symptom severity and thus can be used to measure changes in symptom level over time, as in treatment outcome studies.

Although much progress has been made in the evidence-based assessment of PTSD, more remains to be done. First, additional validation studies are needed, particularly for promising newer measures, focusing on evidence regarding convergent and discriminant validity, factor structure, optimal scoring rules and diagnostic utility, sensitivity to clinical change, and generalizability. Even well-established measures require additional empirical support, particularly with respect to their generalizability across different trauma populations and assessment contexts. Second, several areas of research show promise for the development of new assessment techniques. For example, a number of researchers have suggested that behavioral observation of individuals with PTSD (e.g., agitation or tearfulness when discussing the traumatic event) may be useful as a measure of treatment outcome (e.g., Fairbank, Gross, and Keane, 1983; Saigh, 1978, 1987). Despite these findings, recent studies have not employed these measures. This may be because no standardized tool exists to assess these behaviors. However, based on the findings reported by Fairbank et al. (1983) and Saigh (1978, 1987), the development of such a measure might have utility for the assessment of PTSD. In addition, researchers have provided evidence that brain substrates and brain function (e.g., Hedges & Woon, 2010; Werner et al., 2009) as well as cortisol levels (e.g., Marshall & Garakani, 2002) may discriminate between individuals with and without PTSD; these may be useful avenues to pursue in assessing PTSD as well. Finally, the upcoming publication of *DSM-5* will likely have a significant impact on PTSD assessment. The new diagnostic criteria for PTSD will contain some substantial revisions to the *DSM-IV* criteria, reflecting the evolving conceptual and empirical understanding of the disorder. Existing measures will need to be updated to incorporate these revisions, and a new wave of psychometric evaluation will need to be undertaken. As the field of traumatic stress continues to develop, researchers and clinicians will need to remain informed consumers of the literature regarding the evidence-based assessment of PTSD so they can utilize the most scientifically sound methods for identifying and treating individuals suffering the toxic effect of trauma exposure.

References

Adkins, J. W., Weathers, F. W., McDevitt-Murphy, M., & Daniels, J. B. (2008). Psychometric properties of seven self-report measures of posttraumatic stress disorder in college students with mixed civilian trauma exposure. *Journal of Anxiety Disorders, 22,* 1393–1402.

American Psychiatric Association. (1994). *Diagnostic and statistical manual of mental disorders* (4th ed.). Washington, DC: Author.

American Psychiatric Association. (2000). *Diagnostic and statistical manual of mental disorders* (4th ed., text revision.). Washington, DC: Author.

Anthony, M. A., & Barlow, D. H. (2002). *Handbook of assessment and treatment planning for psychological disorders.* New York: Guilford.

Arata, C., Saunders, B., & Kilpatrick, D. (1991). Concurrent validity of a crime-related post-traumatic stress disorder scale for women within the Symptom Checklist-90—Revised. *Violence and Victims, 6,* 191–199.

Beck, J. G., Grant, D. M., Read, J. P., Clapp, J. D., Coffey, S. F., Miller, L. M., & Palyo, S. A. (2008). The Impact of Event Scale-Revised: Psychometric properties in a sample of motor vehicle accident survivors. *Anxiety Disorders, 22,* 187–198.

Blake, D. D., Weathers, F. W., Nagy, L. M., Kaloupek, D. G., Klauminizer, G., Charney, D. S., & Keane, T. M. (1990). A clinical rating scale for assessing current and lifetime PTSD: The CAPS-1. *Behavior Therapist, 18,* 187–188.

Blake, D. D., Weathers, F. W., Nagy, L. M., Kaloupek, D. G., Gusman, F. D., Charney, D. S., & Keane, T. M. (1995). The development of a Clinician-Administered PTSD Scale. *Journal of Traumatic Stress, 8,* 75–90.

Blanchard, E. B., Jones-Alexander, J., Buckley, T. C., & Forneris, C. A. (1996). Psychometric properties of the PTSD Checklist (PCL). *Behaviour Research and Therapy, 34,* 669–673.

Briere, J. (2001). *Detailed Assessment of Posttraumatic Stress (DAPS).* Odessa, FL: Psychological Assessment Resources.

Bryant, R. A., Creamer, M., O'Donnell, M., Silove, D., & McFarlane, A. C. (2008). A multisite study of initial respiration rate and heart rate as predictors of posttraumatic stress disorder. *Journal of Clinical Psychiatry, 69,* 1694–1701.

Butcher, J. J. (2007). *Malingering strategies used to feign posttraumatic stress disorder on the Trauma Symptom Inventory.* Doctoral dissertation. Retrieved from PsycINFO database.

Davidson, J. R. T., Book, S. W., Colket, J. T., Tupler, L. A., Roth, S., David, D., & Feldman, M. E. (1997). Assessment of a new self-rating scale for post-traumatic stress disorder. *Psychological Medicine, 27,* 153–160.

Davidson, J. R. T., Malik, M. A., & Travers, J. (1997). Structured Interview for PTSD (SIP): Psychometric validation for DSM-IV criteria. *Depression and Anxiety, 5,* 127–129.

Davidson, J., Smith, R., & Kudler, H. (1989). Validity and reliability of the DSM-III criteria for posttraumatic stress disorder: Experience with a structured interview. *Journal of Nervous and Mental Disease, 177,* 336–341.

Derogatis, L. (1977). *SCL-90: Administration, scoring, and procedure manual for the revised version.* Baltimore, MD: John Hopkins University School of Medicine.

Dutton, M., Hohnecker, L., Halle, P., & Burghardt, K. (1994). Traumatic responses among battered women who kill. *Journal of Traumatic Stress, 7,* 549–564.

Elhai, J., Gray, M., Kashdan, T., & Franklin, C. (2005). Which instruments are most commonly used to assess traumatic event exposure and posttraumatic effects?: A survey of traumatic stress professionals. *Journal of Traumatic Stress, 18,* 541–545.

Fairbank, J. A., Gross, R. T., and Keane, T. M. (1983). Treatment of posttraumatic stress disorder: Evaluating outcome with a behavioral code. *Behavioral Modification,* 7, 557–568.

First, M., Spitzer, R., Williams, J., & Gibbon, M. (2000). Structured Clinical Interview for DSM-IV Axis I Disorders (SCID-I). In American Psychiatric Association (Ed.), *Handbook of psychiatric measures* (pp. 49–53). Washington DC: American Psychiatric Association.

Foa, E. B., Cashman, L., Jaycox, L., & Perry, K. (1997). The validation of a self-report measure of posttraumatic stress disorder: The Posttraumatic Diagnostic Scale. *Psychological Assessment, 9,* 445–451.

Foa, E. B., Riggs, D. S., Dancu, C. V., & Rothbaum, B. O. (1993). Reliability and validity of a brief instrument for assessing post-traumatic stress disorder. *Journal of Traumatic Stress, 6,* 459–473.

Foa, E., & Tolin, D. (2000). Comparison of the PTSD Symptom Scale-Interview Version and the Clinician-Administered PTSD Scale. *Journal of Traumatic Stress, 13,* 181–191.

Gerardi, R. J., Blanchard, E. B., & Kolb, L. C. (1989). Ability of Vietnam veterans to dissimulate a psychophysiological assessment for post-traumatic stress disorder. *Behavior Therapy, 20,* 229–243.

Greene, R. L. (2008). Malingering and defensiveness on the MMPI-2. In R. Rogers (Ed.), *Clinical assessment of malingering and deception* (pp. 159–181). New York: Guilford Press.

Griffin, M. G., Uhlmansiek, M. H., Resick, P. A., & Mechanic, M. B. (2004). Comparison of the posttraumatic stress disorder scale versus the clinician-administered posttraumatic stress disorder scale in domestic violence survivors. *Journal of Traumatic Stress, 17,* 497–503.

Guriel, J., & Fremouw, W. (2003). Assessing malingered posttraumatic stress disorder: A critical review. *Clinical Psychology Review, 23,* 881–904.

Hedges, D., & Woon, F. (2010). Premorbid brain volume estimates and reduced total brain volume in adults exposed to trauma with or without posttraumatic stress disorder: A meta-analysis. *Cognitive and Behavioral Neurology, 23,* 124–129.

Hembree, E. A., Foa, E. B., & Feeny, N. C. (2002). Manual for the administration and scoring of the PTSD Symptom Scale – Interview (PSS-I). Unpublished manuscript, available online at www.istss.org/resources/browse.cfm.

Herman, D. S., Weathers, F. W., Litz, B. T., & Keane, T. M. (1996). Psychometric properties of the embedded and stand-alone versions of the MMPI-2 Keane PTSD Scale. *Assessment, 3,* 437–442.

Horowitz, M. J. (1976). *Stress response syndromes.* Oxford, England: Jason Aronson.

Horowitz, M. J., Wilner, N., & Alvarez, W. (1979). Impact of Event Scale: A measure of subjective stress. *Psychosomatic Medicine, 41,* 209–218.

Keane, T. M., Brief, D. J., Pratt, E. M., & Miller, M. W. (2007). Assessment of PTSD and its comorbidities in adults. In M. J. Friedman, T. M. Keane, & P.A. Resick (Eds.), *Handbook of PTSD: Science and practice* (pp. 279–305). New York: Guilford.

Keane, T. M., Caddell, J. M., & Taylor, K. L. (1988). Mississippi Scale for Combat-Related Posttraumatic Stress Disorder: Three studies in reliability and validity. *Journal of Consulting and Clinical Psychology, 56,* 85–90.

Keane, T. M., Fairbank, J. A., Caddell, J. M., Zimering, R. T., & Bender, M. E. (1985). A behavioral approach to assessing and treating post-traumatic stress disorder. In C. R. Figley (Ed.), *Trauma and its wake: The study and treatment of post-traumatic stress disorder* (pp. 257–294). New York: Brunner/Mazel.

Keane, T. M., Kolb, L. C., Kaloupek, D. G., Orr, S. P., Blanchard, E. B., Thomas, R. G., & Lavori, P. W. (1998). Utility of psychophysiology measurement in the diagnosis of posttraumatic stress disorder: Results from a department of Veteran's Affairs cooperative study. *Journal of Consulting and Clinical Psychology, 66,* 914–923.

Keane, T. M., Malloy, P. F., & Fairbank, J. A. (1984). Empirical development of an MMPI subscale for the assessment of combat-related posttraumatic stress disorder. *Journal of Consulting and Clinical Psychology, 52,* 888–891.

Keane, T., Wolfe, J., & Taylor, K. (1987). Post-traumatic stress disorder: Evidence for diagnostic validity and methods of psychological assessment. *Journal of Clinical Psychology, 43,* 32–43.

Kessler, R., Sonnega, A., Bromet, E., Hughes, M., & Nelson, C. (1995). Posttraumatic stress disorder in the National Comorbidity Survey. *Archives of General Psychiatry, 52,* 1048–1060.

Kilpatrick, D. G. (1988). Rape Aftermath Symptom Test. In M. Hersen & A. S. Bellack (Eds.), *Dictionary of behavioral assessment techniques* (pp. 366–367). Oxford: Pergamon Press.

Koenen, K. C., Moffitt, T. E., Capsi, A., Gregory, A., Harrington, H., & Poulton, R. (2008). The developmental mental-disorder histories of adults with posttraumatic stress disorder: A prospective longitudinal birth cohort study. *Journal of Abnormal Psychology, 117,* 460–466.

Kolb, L. C., & Multalipassi, L. R. (1982). The conditioned emotional response: A sub-class of the chronic and delayed post-traumatic stress disorder. *Psychiatric Annals, 12,* 979–987.

Koretzky, M. B., & Peck, A. H. (1990). Validation and cross-validation of the PTSD Subscale of the MMPI with civilian trauma victims. *Journal of Clinical Psychology, 46,* 296–300.

Kuhn, E., Blanchard, E. B., & Hickling, E. J. (2003). Posttraumatic stress disorder and psychosocial functioning within two samples of MVA survivors. *Behaviour Research and Therapy, 41,* 1105–1112.

Kulka, R. A., Schlenger, W. E., Fairbank, J. A., Hough, R. L., Jordan, B. K., Marmar, C. R., & Weiss, D. S. (1990). *Trauma and the Vietnam war generation: Report of findings from the National Vietnam Veterans Readjustment Study.* New York: Brunner/Mazel.

Kulka, R. A., Schlenger, W. E., Fairbank, J. A., Jordan, B. K., Hough, R. L., Marmar, C. R., & Weiss, D. S. (1991). Assessment of posttraumatic stress disorder in the community: Prospects and pitfalls from recent studies of Vietnam veterans. *Psychological assessment, 3,* 547–560.

Lang, P. (1979). A bio-informational theory of emotional imagery. *Psychophysiology, 16,* 495–512.

Lang, P. (1985). The cognitive psychophysiology of emotion: Fear and anxiety. In A. Tuma & J. Maser (Eds.), *Anxiety and anxiety disorders* (pp. 131–170). Hillsdale, NJ: Lawrence Erlbaum.

Laor, N., Wolmer, L., Wiener, Z., Reiss, A., Muller, U., Weizman, R., & Ron, S. (1998). The function of image control in the psychophysiology of posttraumatic stress disorder. *Journal of Traumatic Stress, 11,* 679–696.

Lauterbach, D., Vrana, S., King, D. W., & King, L. A. (1997). Psychometric properties of the Civilian Version of the Mississippi PTSD scale. *Journal of Traumatic Stress, 10,* 499–513.

Lyons, J. A., & Keane, T. M. (1992). Keane PTSD Scale: MMPI and MMPI—2 update. *Journal of Traumatic Stress, 5,* 111–117.

Lyons, J. A., & Scotti, J. R. (1994). Comparability of two administration formats of the Keane Posttraumatic Stress Disorder Scale. *Psychological Assessment, 6,* 209–211.

Marshall, R., & Garakani, A. (2002). Psychobiology of the acute stress response and its relationship to the psychobiology of post-traumatic stress disorder. *Psychiatric Clinics of North America, 25,* 385–395.

McDonald, S. D., Beckham, J. C., Morey, R. A., & Calhoun, P. S. (2009). The validity and diagnostic efficiency of the Davidson Trauma Scale in military veterans who have served since September 11th, 2001. *Journal of Anxiety Disorders, 23,* 247–255.

McFall, M. E., Smith, D. E., Mackay, P. W., & Tarver, D. J. (1990). Reliability and validity of Mississippi Scale for Combat-Related Posttraumatic Stress Disorder. *Psychological Assessment: A Journal of Consulting and Clinical Psychology, 2,* 114–121.

Monson, C. M., Gradus, J. L., Young-Xu, Y., Schnurr, P. P., Price, J. L., & Schumm, J. A. (2008). Change in posttraumatic stress disorder symptoms: Do clinicians and patients agree? *Psychological Assessment, 20,* 131–138.

Morel, K. R. (1998). Development and preliminary validation of a forced-choice test of response bias for posttraumatic stress disorder. *Journal of Personality Assessment, 70,* 299–314.

Morel, K. R., & Shepherd, B. E. (2008). Meta-analysis of the Morel Emotional numbing Test for PTSD: Comment on Singh, Avasthi, and Grover. *German Journal of Psychiatry, 11,* 128–131.

Neal, L. A., Busuttil, W., Rollins, J., Herepath, R., Strike, P., & Turnbull, G. (1994). Convergent validity of measures of post-traumatic stress disorder in a mixed military and civilian population. *Journal of Traumatic Stress, 7,* 447–455.

Norris, F. H., & Hamblen, J. L. (2004). Standardized self-report measures of civilian trauma and PTSD. In J. P. Wilson & T. M. Keane (Eds.), *Assessing psychological trauma and PTSD* (2nd ed., pp. 63–102). New York: Guilford.

Norris, F., & Slone, L. (2007). The epidemiology of trauma and PTSD. *Handbook of PTSD: Science and practice* (pp. 78–98). New York: Guilford.

Orr, S. (1997). Psychophysiologic reactivity to trauma-related imagery in PTSD. Diagnostic and theoretical implications of recent findings. *Psychobiology of posttraumatic stress disorder* (pp. 114–124). New York: New York Academy of Sciences.

Orr, S. P., McNally, R. J., Rosen, G. M., & Shalev, A. Y. (2004). Psychophysiologic reactivity: Implications for conceptualizing PTSD. In G. M. Rosen (Ed.), *Posttraumatic stress disorder: Issues and controversies* (pp. 101–126). West Sussex, England: John Wiley.

Orr, S. P., Metzger, L. J., Miller, M. W., & Kaloupek, D. G. (2004). Psychophysiological assessment of PTSD. In J. P. Wilson & T. M. Keane (Eds.), *Assessing psychological trauma and PTSD* (2 ed., pp. 289–343). New York: Guilford.

Orr, S. P., & Pitman, R. K. (1993). Psychophysiologic assessment of attempts to simulate posttraumatic stress disorder. *Biological Psychiatry, 33,* 127–129.

Palmieri, P., Weathers, F., Difede, J., & King, D. (2007). Confirmatory factor analysis of the PTSD Checklist and the Clinician-Administered PTSD Scale in disaster workers exposed to the World Trade Center Ground Zero. *Journal of Abnormal Psychology, 116,* 329–341.

Pitman, R. K. (1988). Post-traumatic stress disorder: Conditioning and network theory. *Psychiatric Annals, 18,* 182–189.

Rogers, R. (1992). *Structured Interview of Reported Symptoms.* Odessa, FL: Psychological Assessment Resources.

Rogers, R., Harrell, E. H., & Liff, C. D. (1993). Feigning neuropsychological impairment: A critical review of methodological and clinical considerations. *Clinical Psychology Review, 13,* 255–274.

Rogers, R., Payne, J. W., Berry, D. T. R., & Granacher, R. P. (2009). Use of the SIRS in compensation cases: An examination of its validity and generalizability. *Law and Human Behavior, 33,* 213–224.

Rogers, R., Sewell, K. W., & Goldstein, A. M. (1994). Explanatory models of malingering: A prototypical analysis. *Law and Human Behavior, 18,* 543–552.

Rogers, R., Sewell, K. W., Martin, M. A., & Vitacco, M. J. (2003). Detection of feigned mental disorders: A meta-analysis of the MMPI-2 and malingering. *Assessment, 10,* 160–177.

Rosenberger, S. R. (2007). An evaluation of the psychometric properties and diagnostic utility of the Mississippi scale for PTSD-Civilian Version. Doctoral dissertation. Retrieved from PsycINFO database.

Ruggiero, K., Del Ben, K., Scotti, J., & Rabalais, A. (2003). Psychometric Properties of the PTSD Checklist—Civilian Version. *Journal of Traumatic Stress, 16,* 495–502.

Ruscio, A. M., Weathers, F. W., King, L. A., & King, D. W. (2002). Male war-zone veterans' perceived relationships with their children: The importance of emotional numbing. *Journal of Traumatic Stress, 15,* 351–357.

Saigh, P. A. (1978). In vitro flooding of childhood posttraumatic stress disorders: A systematic replication. *Professional School Psychology, 2,* 135–146.

Saigh, P. A. (1987). In vitro flooding of an adolescent posttraumatic stress disorder. *Journal of Clinical and Child Psychology, 16,* 147–150.

Saunders, B. E., Arata, C. M., & Kilpatrick, D. G. (1990). Development of a Crime-Related Post-Traumatic Stress Disorder scale for women within the Symptom Checklist-90-Revised. *Journal of Traumatic Stress, 3,* 439–448.

Schlenger, W. E., Kulka, R. A., Fairbank, J. A., Hough, R. L., Jordan, B. K., Marmar, C.R., & Weiss, D. S. (1992). The prevalence of post-traumatic stress disorder in the Vietnam generation: A mulitmethod, multisource assessment of psychiatric disorder. *Journal of Traumatic Stress, 5,* 333–363.

Schnurr, P. P., & Green, B. L. (Eds.). (2004). *Trauma and health: Physical consequences of exposure to extreme stress.* Washington, DC: American Psychological Association.

Schnurr, P. P., Hayes, A. F., Lunney, C. A., McFall, M., & Uddo, M. (2006). Longitudinal analysis of the relationship between symptoms and quality of life in veterans treated for posttraumatic stress disorder. *Journal of Consulting and Clinical Psychology, 74,* 707–713.

Shapinsky, A. C., Rapport, L. J., Henderson, M. J., & Axelrod, B. N. (2005). Civilian PTSD scales: Relationships with trait characteristics and everyday distress. *Assessment, 12,* 220–230.

Smith, M. W., Schnurr, P. P., & Rosenheck, R. M. (2005). Employment outcomes and PTSD symptom severity. *Mental Health Services Research, 7,* 89–101.

Stein, M. B., McQuaid, J. R., Pedrelli, P., Lenox, R., & McCahill, M. E. (2000). Posttraumatic stress disorder in the primary care medical setting. *General Hospital Psychiatry, 22,* 261–269.

Stein, M. B., Walker, J. R., Hazen, A. L., & Forde, D. R. (1997). Full and partial posttraumatic disorder: findings from a community survey. *American Journal of Psychiatry, 154,* 1114–1119.

Sundin, E. C., & Horowitz, M. J. (2002). Impact of Event Scale: Psychometric properties. *British Journal of Psychiatry, 180,* 205–209.

Vrana, S., & Lauterbach, D. (1994). Prevalence of traumatic events and posttraumatic psychological symptoms in a nonclinical sample of college students. *Journal of Traumatic Stress, 7,* 289–302.

Weathers, F. W. (2008). Posttraumatic Stress Disorder Checklist. In G. Reyes, J. D. Elhai, & J. D. Ford (Eds.), *Encyclopedia of psychological trauma* (pp. 491–494). Hoboken, NJ: John Wiley.

Weathers, F. W., & Keane, T. M. (1999). Psychological assessment of traumatized adults. *Posttraumatic stress disorder: A comprehensive text* (pp. 219–247). Needham Heights, MA: Allyn & Bacon.

Weathers, F. W., Keane, T. M., & Davidson, J. R. T. (2001). Clinician-Administered PTSD Scale: A review of the first ten years of research. *Depression and Anxiety, 13,* 132–156.

Weathers, F. W., Litz, B. T., Herman, D. S., Huska, J. A., & Keane, T. M. (1993, October). *The PTSD Checklist (PCL): Reliability, validity, and diagnostic utility.* Paper presented at the annual meeting of the International Society for Traumatic Stress Studies, San Antonio, CA.

Weathers, F. W., Litz, B. T., Keane, T. M., Herman, D. S., Steinberg, H. R., Huska, J. A., & Kraemer, H. C. (1996). The utility of the SCL-90 for the diagnosis of war-zone-related posttraumatic stress disorder. *Journal of Traumatic Stress, 9,* 111–128.

Weathers, F. W., Ruscio, A. M., & Keane, T. M. (1999). Psychometric properties of nine scoring rules for the Clinician-Administered Posttraumatic Stress Disorder Scale. *Psychological Assessment, 11,* 124–133.

Weiss, D. S., & Marmar, C. R. (1997). The Impact of Event Scale—Revised. *Assessing psychological trauma and PTSD* (pp. 399–411). New York: Guilford.

Werner, N., Meindl, T., Engel, R., Rosner, R., Riedel, M., Reiser, M., & Fast, K. (2009). Hippocampal function during associative learning in patients with posttraumatic stress disorder. *Journal of Psychiatric Research, 43,* 309–318.

Wolfe, J., Kimerling, R., Brown, P. J., Chrestman, K. R., & Levin, K. (1996). Psychometric review of the Life Stressor Checklist – Revised. In B. H. Stamm (Ed.), *Measurement of stress, trauma, and adaptation* (pp. 198–201). Lutherville, MD: Sidran Press.

Zanarini, M. C., & Frankenburg, F. R. (2001). Attainment and maintenance of reliability of Axis I and II disorders over the course of a longitudinal study. *Comprehensive Psychiatry, 42,* 369–374.

Zanarini, M. C., Skodol, A. E., Bender, D., Dolan, R., Sanislow, C., Schaefer, E. Gunderson, J. G. (2000). The Collaborative Longitudinal Personality Disorders Study: Reliability of Axis I and II diagnoses. *Journal of Personality Disorders, 14,* 291–299.

Assessing Acute Traumatic Stress Symptoms

Richard A. Bryant

Abstract

There is significant change in acute stress reactions in the weeks after exposure to a traumatic event, which raises challenges for assessing the responses in the acute posttraumatic period. This chapter reviews the assessment tools and strategies that are appropriate in the acute period. It focuses initially on acute stress disorder (ASD) as a description of acute posttraumatic stress and as a predictor of subsequent PTSD. Psychometrically-validated scales are reviewed for both diagnostic and symptom responses in the acute period, with a critique of the limited ability of these measures to identify most people who are at high risk for subsequent PTSD. Finally, this chapter identifies mechanisms that may enhance our ability to identify maladaptive responses in the acute phase, and specific populations that need particular attention in the immediate period following trauma exposure.

The weeks following exposure to a traumatic event are often characterized by considerable distress, fluctuating emotions, and changing environmental factors. This lack of emotional and contextual stability raises significant challenges for assessment of psychological states shortly after trauma. This chapter aims to provide an overview of assessment of psychological responses in the weeks after trauma. It commences with a review of the current evidence about the nature of acute posttraumatic stress reactions and discusses the different goals of assessment at this stage. Established psychometric instruments are then reviewed, including structured clinical interviews, self-report measures, and other tools relevant to acute reactions. The review then turns to other factors that can be assessed, including cognitive and biological factors, occurring in the acute posttraumatic period. Finally, the chapter outlines other procedural issues that need to be considered when assessing trauma survivors in the acute phase.

Key Words: Acute stress disorder, posttraumatic stress disorder, assessment, diagnosis, screening

The Nature of Acute Posttraumatic Stress Reactions

There is very strong evidence that most people who are recently exposed to a traumatic experience commonly report a diverse range of posttraumatic stress reactions in the initial weeks after trauma. There are reports of high rates of emotional numbing (Feinstein, 1989; Noyes & Kletti, 1977), reduced awareness of one's environment (Berah, Jones, & Valent, 1984; Hillman, 1981), derealization (Cardeña & Spiegel, 1993; Noyes & Kletti, 1977; Sloan, 1988), depersonalization (Cardeña & Spiegel, 1993; Noyes & Kletti, 1977), dissociative amnesia (Cardeña & Spiegel, 1993; Feinstein, 1989; Madakasira & O'Brien, 1987), intrusive thoughts (Cardeña & Spiegel, 1993; Feinstein, 1989; Sloan, 1988), avoidance behaviors (Cardeña & Spiegel, 1993; North, Smith, McCool, & Lightcap, 1989), insomnia (Cardeña & Spiegel, 1993; Feinstein, 1989; Sloan, 1988), concentration deficits (Cardeña & Spiegel, 1993; North et al.,

1989), irritability (Sloan, 1988), and autonomic arousal (Feinstein, 1989; Sloan, 1988). These rates highlight the common occurrence of different forms of distress in the weeks after a traumatic experience.

Although posttraumatic stress responses are common immediately after trauma exposure, there is much evidence that these reactions subside in the following weeks and months in most individuals. For example, whereas 94% of rape victims displayed posttraumatic stress disorder (PTSD) symptoms two weeks posttrauma, this rate dropped to 47% eleven weeks later (Rothbaum, Foa, Riggs, Murdock, & Walsh, 1992). In another study, 70% of women and 50% of men were diagnosed with PTSD at an average of 19 days after an assault; the rate of PTSD at four-month follow-up dropped to 21% for women and zero for men (Riggs, Rothbaum, & Foa, 1995). Similarly, half of a sample meeting criteria for PTSD shortly after a motor vehicle accident had remitted by six months and two-thirds had remitted by one year posttrauma (Blanchard, Hickling, Barton, & Taylor, 1996). A similar pattern was observed in community studies of residents of New York following the terrorist attacks on the World Trade Center. Whereas 8.8% of residents reported PTSD within one month after the attacks (Galea, Resnick, et al., 2002), the rate dropped to 3.8% four months later (Galea, Ahern, et al., 2002). These patterns suggest that the normative response to trauma is to gradually adapt after displaying initial PTSD symptoms.

It is important to understand that there is not a uniform trajectory following trauma, and especially disaster. The most salient example of this point is the phenomenon of delayed-onset PTSD. Delayed-onset PTSD refers to PTSD reactions that develop at least six months after the trauma. Delayed-onset is a rare occurrence in civilian populations, although there is increasing evidence that it is more common in military contexts (Andrews, Brewin, Philpott, & Stewart, 2007). Despite the finding that delayed-onset PTSD is a minority response following trauma, it reminds us that a proportion of people will develop PTSD at some point after trauma exposure that do not initially display acute stress reactions. This trajectory is not well understood and there is a paucity of evidence concerning acute markers of delayed-onset psychological problems.

The Goals of Early Assessment

It is important to note that one can assess a recently traumatized individual for different reasons. One goal is to identify people who are suffering severe acute stress reactions with the intention of singling out individuals who require assistance in the immediate aftermath of trauma exposure. In this sense, the assessment attempts to simply describe the severity and nature of the acute psychological response. A second goal of early assessment is to attempt identification of people who will subsequently develop more persistent PTSD. This has been a very difficult task because, as noted above, the majority of trauma survivors experience some degree of traumatic stress in the weeks following exposure but most of these symptoms subside in the following months (Bryant, 2003). Accordingly, the challenge for assessment tools has been to discriminate between transient stress reactions and stress responses that represent the precursor of chronic PTSD. A major motivation to achieve accurate early identification is the evidence that early intervention can prevent the majority of high-risk individuals from developing PTSD. Brief forms of cognitive behavior therapy provided within the initial weeks after trauma have been shown to reduce subsequent PTSD relative to other forms of counseling (Bisson, Shepherd, Joy, Probert, & Newcombe, 2004; Bryant, Harvey, Dang, Sackville, & Basten, 1998; Bryant, Mastrodomenico et al., 2008; Bryant, Sackville, Dang, Moulds, & Guthrie, 1999).

Acute Stress Disorder

Acute stress disorder (ASD) was introduced in *DSM-IV* as a new diagnosis to describe acute stress reactions that may precede posttraumatic stress disorder (PTSD). This diagnosis was introduced for two primary reasons: to describe acute stress reactions that occur in the initial month after trauma exposure, and to identify trauma survivors who are at high risk for developing subsequent PTSD (Harvey & Bryant, 2002). One motivation for the introduction of the ASD diagnosis was that PTSD can only be diagnosed at least one month following trauma, resulting in a diagnostic gap within the initial month of trauma. There has been concern that some trauma survivors may not readily have access to mental health services because they lacked a formal diagnosis, and therefore the ASD diagnosis would address this potential problem.

DSM-IV defines ASD after a fearful response to experiencing or witnessing a threatening event that elicits fear, helplessness, or horror (Cluster A). The requisite symptoms to meet criteria for ASD include three dissociative symptoms (Cluster B), one reexperiencing symptom (Cluster C), marked avoidance (Cluster D), marked arousal (Cluster E), and evidence of significant distress or impairment

(Cluster F). The disturbance must last for a minimum of two days and a maximum of four weeks (Cluster G), after which time a diagnosis of PTSD can be considered. Major differences between the criteria for ASD and PTSD are the time frame and the former's emphasis on dissociative reactions to the trauma. A diagnosis of ASD requires that the individual have at least three of the following: (a) a subjective sense of numbing or detachment, (b) reduced awareness of one's surroundings, (c) derealization, (d) depersonalization, or (e) dissociative amnesia either during the traumatic event or in the following month.

The Descriptive Role of Acute Stress Disorder

In terms of describing acute trauma reactions, the ASD diagnosis has been criticized by some people by being too focused on fear responses and neglecting other psychological reactions. The ASD focus can be distinguished from the construct of acute stress reactions (ASR), described in the tenth edition of the *International Classification of Diseases* (World Health Organization, 1995). The *ICD-10* conceptualizes acute stress reaction as a transient reaction that can be evident immediately after the traumatic event and usually resolves within 2–3 days after trauma exposure. The *ICD* description of acute stress reaction includes dissociative (daze, stupor, amnesia), anxiety (tachycardia, sweating, flushing), anger, or depressive reactions. Some commentators propose that this broader description of responses may have more utility for clinicians than the more focused *DSM-IV* criteria (Isserlin, Zerach, & Solomon, 2008). This approach presumes that the initial period after trauma exposure may result in a rather amorphous state of distress that can include many emotional responses that cannot be readily classified into different responses (Yitzhaki, Solomon, & Kotler, 1991).

The Predictive Role of Acute Stress Disorder

A secondary goal of the ASD diagnosis is to discriminate between recent trauma survivors who are experiencing transient stress reactions and those who are suffering reactions that will persist into long-term PTSD (Koopman, Classen, Cardeña, & Spiegel, 1995). There are currently 22 prospective studies of trauma survivors who were assessed for ASD in the initial month after trauma, and were subsequently assessed for PTSD months or years later (for a review, see (Bryant, 2011) A recent review of these studies indicates at least half of trauma survivors with ASD subsequently meet criteria for PTSD (Bryant, 2011). In contrast, the majority of survivors who eventually developed PTSD did not initially meet ASD criteria. This pattern suggests that if a major goal of ASD is to predict people who will subsequently develop PTSD, it is failing to identify half of those who will meet criteria for PTSD at some later time.

One ramification of this finding is that if the goal of assessing trauma survivors in the acute phase after trauma is to identify people who are at high risk for developing subsequent PTSD, one needs to be cognizant that the ASD diagnosis, and assessment tools based on this diagnosis, has modest capacity of accurately identify the majority of people who will eventually develop PTSD.

In this context it is worth noting that the proposed revision of ASD in *DSM-5* has strategically abandoned the goal of identifying people who are at high risk for PTSD. The convergent evidence that most people who develop PTSD do not initially display ASD has led to the conclusion that early prediction of high-risk individuals may be more accurately achieved by employing a broader array of biological and cognitive factors (Bryant, Friedman, Spiegel, Ursano, & Strain, 2011). In the proposed revision of ASD, the goal is to describe severe acute stress reactions that may benefit from mental health intervention. It is explicitly noted that this reaction may represent a precursor of PTSD or may be a transient stress reaction (Bryant et al., 2011).

The Predictive Role of Peritraumatic Dissociation

As noted earlier, a prevailing model of acute trauma response posits that dissociative responses occurring during or immediately following the traumatic event are predictive of subsequent PTSD because these responses purportedly impede emotional processing of the experience (Spiegel, Koopmen, Cardeña, & Classen, 1996). Supporting this view are many studies that have reported an association between peritraumatic dissociation and chronic PTSD (Ehlers, Mayou, & Bryant, 1998; Koopman, Classen, & Spiegel, 1994; Murray, Ehlers, & Mayou, 2002; Ozer, Best, Lipsey, & Weiss, 2003; Shalev, Freedman, Peri, Brandes, & Sahar, 1997). This issue has relevance to assessment in the acute phase because it suggests that one should be particularly sensitive to dissociative responses as a marker of longer term PTSD. More recent analyses have suggested that this relationship may not be linear. Two meta-analyses have suggested that whereas peritraumatic dissociation does predict PTSD, the majority of longitudinal studies indicate that peritraumatic dissociation has not emerged as an independent predictor but, rather, is mediated by other variables (Breh & Seidler, 2007; Velden et al., 2006). An alternate model has been proposed that suggests that peritraumatic dissociation is a function of elevated arousal in the immediate aftermath of trauma exposure, and in this sense dissociation is an epiphenomenon of heightened peritraumatic arousal (Friedman, 2000; Gershuny & Thayer, 1999). Indirect support for this view comes from evidence that the relationship between peritraumatic dissociation and acute stress depends on the levels of peritraumatic panic (Fikretoglu et al., 2006, 2007). It should also be noted that there is considerable evidence that people typically have dissociative experiences during experiences involving high arousal that are not associated with any current or subsequent psychopathology (Bryant, 2007; Sterlini & Bryant, 2002). In summary, these data suggest that the relationship between peritraumatic dissociation and subsequent PTSD is not linear, and that emphasis on the predictive role of acute dissociation in acute assessment may result in inaccurate prediction of PTSD because it may neglect other important mediating variables.

It is worth noting that dissociative amnesia is apparently distinctive in trauma response. In a factor analysis of ASD symptoms, dissociative amnesia did not load strongly onto the dissociative cluster (Brooks et al., 2008). This finding is consistent with evidence from confirmatory factor analyses of chronic PTSD (King, Leskin, King, & Weathers, 1998). Dissociative amnesia tends to load weakly across different instruments (Palmieri et al., 2007), which suggests that it is not a clearly articulated construct. In the context of acute trauma response, dissociative amnesia may reflect impaired encoding of the experience, normal forgetting, cognitive avoidance, or inability to access memories that were encoded (McNally, 2003). Assessing amnesia in the acute phase requires caution because one needs to recognize that a person's inability to report some aspect of the event may be attributed to many reasons, and need not necessarily reflect a dissociative response.

Structured Clinical Interviews

Clinical Interview of Acute Stress Disorder

The Acute Stress Disorder Interview (ASDI; Bryant, Harvey, Dang, & Sackville, 1998) is a structured clinical interview that is based on *DSM-IV* criteria. The ASDI contains 19 dichotomously scored items that relate to the dissociative (Cluster B, 5 items), reexperiencing (Cluster C, 4 items), avoidance (Cluster D, 4 items), and arousal (Cluster E, 6 items) symptoms of ASD. Summing the affirmative responses to each symptom provides a total score indicative of acute stress severity (range 1–19). The ASDI possesses good internal consistency (r = .90), test-retest reliability (r = .88), sensitivity (91%) and specificity (93%) relative to independent clinician diagnosis of ASD, based on *DSM-IV* criteria. A confirmatory factor analysis of the ASDI completed by 587 trauma survivors indicated that the interview structure was best described by the four clusters described by *DSM-IV* (Brooks et al., 2008). The ASDI has been used in numerous prospective studies that have attempted to identify recently trauma-exposed people who are at high risk for developing PTSD (Bryant, Creamer, O'Donnell, Silove, & McFarlane, 2008b; Bryant & Harvey, 1998; Harvey & Bryant, 2000).

Structured Clinical Interview for DSM-IV Dissociative Disorders

Although not intentionally developed as a measure of ASD, the Structured Clinical Interview for *DSM-IV* Dissociative Disorders (SCID-D; Steinberg, Cicchetti, Buchanan, Hall, & Rounsaville, 1993) has been offered as a structured interview for ASD (Steinberg, 1995). This structured interview was developed to diagnose dissociative disorders, and it has been evaluated comprehensively in this context (Steinberg et al., 1993). It asks about five core dissociative symptoms: amnesia, depersonalization, derealization, identity confusion, and identity alteration. Although the SCID-D has been shown to index dissociative symptoms, the emphasis it places on dissociation results in relatively little attention given to reexperiencing, avoidance, and arousal symptoms. There have been no studies validating the SCID-D as a measure of ASD, and accordingly it is not recommended as an index of either acute trauma reactions or as a predictive tool of subsequent PTSD.

Self-Report Measures of Acute Stress Disorder

Stanford Acute Stress Reaction Questionnaire

The first measure to be developed was the Stanford Acute Stress Reaction Questionnaire (SASRQ). The original version of the SASRQ (Cardeña, Classen, & Spiegel, 1991) was a self-report inventory that indexed dissociative (33 items), intrusive (11 items), somatic anxiety (17 items), hyper-arousal

(2 items), attention disturbance (3 items), and sleep disturbance (1 item) symptoms; and different versions of this measure have been employed by the authors across a range of studies (Cardeña & Spiegel, 1993; Classen, Koopman, Hales, & Spiegel, 1998; Koopman et al., 1994). Each item asks respondents to indicate the frequency of each symptom on a six-point Likert scale (0 = "not experienced," 5 = "very often experienced") that can occur during and immediately following a trauma. The SASRQ possesses high internal consistency (Cronbach alpha = .90 and .91 for dissociative and anxiety symptoms, respectively) and concurrent validity with scores on the Impact of Event Scale (r = .52–.69; Cardeña, Koopman, Classen, Waelde, & Spiegel, 2000; Koopman et al., 1994). Different versions of the SASRQ have been employed in a number of studies conducted by the authors (Classen et al., 1998; Koopman et al., 1994). The current version of the SASRQ (Cardeña et al., 2000) is a 30-item self-report inventory that encompasses each of the ASD symptoms.

Acute Stress Disorder Scale

The Acute Stress Disorder Scale (ASDS; Bryant, Moulds, & Guthrie, 2000) is another self-report inventory that is based on the same items described in the ASDI. Each item on the ASDS is scored on a five-point scale that reflects degrees of severity. It was validated against the Acute Stress Disorder Interview on 99 civilian trauma survivors assessed between 2 and 10 days posttrauma. Using a formula to identify ASD caseness that incorporates satisfying the dissociative, reexperiencing, avoidance, and arousal clusters of the ASD diagnosis, the ASDS possessed good sensitivity (95%) and specificity (83%). Test-retest reliability was evaluated on 107 bushfire survivors 3 weeks posttrauma, with a readministration interval of 2 to 7 days. Test-retest reliability of the ASDS scores was strong (r = .94). Predictive ability of the ASDS was investigated in 82 trauma survivors who completed the ASDS and were subsequently assessed for PTSD 6 months posttrauma. A cut-off score of 56 on the ASDS predicted 91% of those who developed PTSD and 93% of those who did not. The major limitation of the ASDS in predicting PTSD, however, was that one-third of people who scored above the cut-off did not develop PTSD.

Posttraumatic Adjustment Scale

In recognition of the finding that, in addition to PTSD, depression frequently occurs after trauma (Shalev et al., 1998), the Posttraumatic Adjustment Scale (PAS; O'Donnell et al., 2008) was developed to screen recently trauma-exposed people who were at risk of developing PTSD or depression. The PAS comprises 10 items that are each scored on a five-point scale. This scale was developed such that a summation of scores of all 10 items was predictive of PTSD (PAS-P), and the summation of 5 of these items was predictive of subsequent depression (PAS-D). In terms of predicting subsequent PTSD 12 months after trauma, the PAS-P had a sensitivity of .82 and a specificity of .84, positive predictive power of .28, and negative predictive power of .96. These authors compared the PAS to the ASDI, and found that the two instruments had comparable predictive utility. In terms of predicting subsequent depression, the PAS-D had a sensitivity of .72 and a specificity of .74, positive predictive power of .30, and negative predictive power of .91.

Trauma Screening Questionnaire

The Trauma Screening Questionnaire (TSQ; Brewin et al., 2002) was developed as a screening measure to identify people with probable PTSD, and was intended to serve as a brief screen that would facilitate identification of those who warranted fuller assessment. Derived from the PTSD Symptom Scale–Self-Report Version (Foa, Riggs, Dancu, & Rothbaum, 1993), the TSQ is a 10-item measure that is answered on a dichotomous basis and indexes re-experiencing and arousal symptoms of PTSD. The TSQ has been evaluated as a predictive tool to determine the extent to which it can identify acutely traumatized people who will subsequently develop PTSD. In a study of 562 people admitted to an emergency unit after assault (Walters, Bisson, & Shepherd, 2007), the TSQ was administered between 1–3 weeks after admission and PTSD was assessed six months later with the Davidson Trauma Scale (Davidson et al., 1997). Adopting the prescribed cut-off of reporting at least 6 reexperiencing or arousal symptoms, the TSQ had sensitivity of .88, specificity, .78, positive predictive power of .33, and negative predictive power of .98 in predicting PTSD at six months.

Peritraumatic Dissociative Experiences Questionnaire (PDEQ)

The PDEQ (Marmar, Weiss, & Metzler, 1997) was developed to index dissociative responses during and immediately following a trauma. It consists of nine items that index depersonalization, derealization, and amnesia. Reviews of studies that have employed the PDEQ have shown that it possesses acceptable internal consistency, reliability, and validity (Marmar, Metzler, & Otte, 2004). The scale has been found to be positively associated with posttraumatic stress responses and dissociative coping style, but not correlated with general psychopathology (Marmar et al., 2004). Numerous studies have also found that the PDEQ administered within the initial weeks of trauma exposure is associated with subsequent PTSD (Shalev, Peri, Canetti, & Schreiber, 1996). A factor analysis of the PDEQ found two distinct factors: lack of awareness and derealization (Brooks et al., 2009). Whereas lack of awareness was not associated with acute stress reactions, the derealization factor was. This pattern is consistent with the proposal that alterations in awareness that occur at the time are common and not necessarily indicative of elevated posttraumatic stress; in contrast, altered perceptions of oneself or one's environment may reflect more severe stress reactions.

Peritraumatic Distress Scale

The Peritraumatic Distress Scale (PDS; Brunet et al., 2001) was developed as a companion to the PDEQ and is intended to assess the emotional responses experienced during a traumatic experience, such as fear, horror, helplessness, grief, anger, and panic. It comprises 13 items that are scored on a five-point scale. The PDS has been shown to have sound psychometric properties, including internal consistency (standardized alpha = .74), test-retest reliability (r = .74), and convergent validity with the PDEQ (r = .59) and the Impact of Event Scale–Revised (IES-R; Weiss & Marmar, 1997) subsales of intrusions (r = .47), avoidance (r = .47), and arousal (r = .42; Brunet et al., 2001). The PDS does appear to be a very relevant index of the level of distress that recent trauma survivors experience. There is limited evidence concerning the extent to which the PDS immediately after trauma predicts subsequent PTSD. One study of French assault survivors found that elevated scores on the PDS provided additive predictive power beyond baseline IES-R scores in predicting PTSD severity six months later (Jehel, Paterniti, Brunet, Louville, & Guelfi, 2006).

Other Indices of Risk for PTSD

Assessment of Cognitive Factors

In the wake of concerns about the predictive value of the ASD diagnosis, increasing attention has focused on other factors that may be predictive of subsequent PTSD. Much attention has focused on cognitive responses in the acute phase after trauma. Although these factors do not necessarily enhance assessment of ASD, they can provide the clinician with useful insights into cognitive processes in the acutely traumatized person that may impede optimal adaptation. Identifying these factors in the acute phase can directly lead to cognitive interventions that can alleviate distress.

A central tenet of cognitive models of trauma response proposes that the transition from acute stress reaction to chronic PTSD is strongly influenced by people's cognitive styles. Ehlers and Clark (2000) suggest that PTSD is strongly influenced by excessively negative appraisals of the trauma and its aftermath. It is proposed that catastrophic interpretations about the likelihood of future harm, one's role in the trauma, or about one's reactions in the immediate weeks after trauma will determine the severity of subsequent PTSD. Consistent with this proposition, people with ASD exaggerate both the probability of future negative events occurring and the adverse effects of these events compared to non-ASD participants (Smith & Bryant, 2000; Warda & Bryant, 1998). There is also evidence that negative appraisals in the period after trauma exposure predicts subsequent PTSD (Ehlers et al., 1998; Engelhard, van den Hout, Arntz, & McNally, 2002). There is also evidence that the attributions of responsibility for a trauma that trauma survivors make in the acute posttrauma phase (e.g., blaming others or feeling shame) influences subsequent PTSD (Andrews, Brewin, Rose, & Kirk, 2000; Delahanty et al., 1997). Identifying these cognitive distortions shortly after the event has the potential advantage of (a) identifying people who are more likely to develop PTSD, and (b) provide the opportunity for brief cognitive interventions that can correct maladaptive appraisals and possibly limit PTSD or depression development.

Assessment of Biological Factors

Arguably the most influential theory of posttraumatic stress reactions involves fear conditioning models. These models posit that the fear elicited during a traumatic event results in conditioning in which subsequent reminders of the trauma elicit anxiety in response to trauma reminders (conditioned stimuli; Milad, Rauch, Pitman, & Quirk, 2006). This model proposes that extreme sympathetic arousal at the time of a traumatic event may result in the release of stress neurochemicals (including norepinephrine and epinephrine), mediating an overconsolidation of trauma memories (Pitman, 1989). Fear-conditioning models are supported by considerable evidence that people with chronic PTSD are hyper-responsive to trauma reminders (Pitman et al., 1990).

Fear-conditioning models have led to several attempts to identify acute markers of people who are at high risk for PTSD by indexing markers that would reflect stronger unconditioned or conditioned responses. Probably the most studied acute marker of subsequent PTSD is resting heart rate. Increased sympathetic nervous system (or reduced parasympathetic activation) occurring after trauma exposure may contribute to fear conditioning, and this increase may be reflected in faster resting heart rate. A series of studies have assessed resting heart rate in the initial days after trauma exposure and determined the relationship between heart rate and subsequent PTSD. These studies have generally found that adults and children who subsequently develop PTSD display higher resting HR initially than those who do not develop PTSD (for a review, see Bryant, 2006). There is also evidence that elevated respiration rate in the immediate period after trauma can predict subsequent PTSD, which again is consistent with the predictions of fear conditioning models (Bryant, Creamer, O'Donnell, Silove, & McFarlane, 2008).

One model proposes that PTSD develops, and is maintained, by excessive sympathetic nervous system response to the traumatic event as a result of impaired modulation by the hypothalamic-pituitary-adrenal (HPA) axis (Yehuda, 1997). This model posits that hypocorticolism represents a risk factor for PTSD development because it is associated with reduced negative feedback function of the HPA axis (Yehuda, 2003). Consistent with this proposal, numerous studies have found an association between lower levels of cortisol in the immediate period following trauma exposure and subsequent PTSD (Aardal-Eriksson, Eriksson, & Thorell, 2001; Delahanty, Raimonde, & Spoonster, 2000; Ehring, Ehlers, Cleare, & Glucksman, 2008; McFarlane, Atchison, & Yehuda, 1997), although this appears to be influenced by degree of prior trauma exposure (Delahanty, Royer, Spoonster, & Raimonde, 2001; Resnick, Yehuda, Pitman, & Foy, 1995). It should be noted, however, that not all studies have found this relationship (Bonne et al., 2003); one study found elevated cortisol in children who subsequently developed PTSD (Delahanty, Nugent, Christopher, & Walsh, 2005).

In summary, although there is considerable evidence of statistical relationships between acute psychophysiological responses after trauma, such as heart rate, respiration rate, and lower cortisol level, and subsequent PTSD, there is inadequate evidence to indicate that any of these measures have proven specificity, sensitivity, and predictive power to reliably identify people in the acute phase who may be at high risk for PTSD development. There have been reports of other potential indices of subsequent PTSD that can be measured immediately after trauma, such as lower GABA levels (Vaiva et al., 2006, 2004) and impaired sleep patterns immediately prior to trauma exposure (Bryant, Creamer, O'Donnell, Silove, & McFarlane, 2010). It appears that many of these variables are mediated by other factors, including individual differences, and at this point in time they cannot be relied on to accurately predict recently trauma-exposed people who are at high risk for PTSD.

Factors Impacting Acute Assessment

Timing of Assessment

Psychological reactions to trauma are very fluid in the initial period after exposure, and so the timing of a psychological assessment is critical. One current problem with the ASD time frame is that the definition of dissociation states that dissociation in ASD can occur "either during or after experiencing the distressing event" (American Psychiatric Association [APA], 1994, p. 431) The ambiguity concerning the time frame for dissociation is highly problematic because transient dissociation (peritraumatic dissociation) and persistent dissociation may reflect distinct psychological reactions. This is an important distinction because evidence suggests that the majority of trauma survivors experience transient dissociative reactions that do not persist beyond the trauma (Noyes & Kletti, 1977).

Cognitive models of trauma would predict that persistent dissociation would be maladaptive and would be associated with subsequent PTSD because it impedes retrieval of emotional memories that are required for adaption (Foa & Kozak, 1986). In contrast, transient dissociation at the time of the trauma may be a normal response under stress, and could even serve a protective function because it may limit the encoding of traumatic experiences. In this context, it is worth noting that persistent dissociation is more predictive of ASD (Panasetis & Bryant, 2003) and subsequent PTSD (Briere, Scott, & Weathers,

2005) than dissociation that only occurs at the time of the traumatic experience.

DSM-IV stipulates that the ASD diagnosis can be made two days after trauma exposure. There is no empirical basis for this time frame. The prevalence of transient stress reactions following trauma underscores that the sooner one identifies a trauma survivor as being at high risk for subsequent PTSD, the more likely that false a positive diagnosis will be made. There is some evidence from a study of civilians involved in the Gulf War that many people experience immediate posttraumatic stress reactions in the initial days after trauma exposure, but that these reactions subsequently remit (Solomon, Laor, & McFarlane, 1996). Confirming that more accurate identification of high-risk individuals can be achieved by delaying assessment of recently trauma-exposed people, one prospective study found that delaying assessment of ASD to four weeks after exposure led to increased predictive power relative to assessments conducted in the initial period after exposure (Murray et al., 2002).

Another critical issue in the timing of the acute assessment is consideration of the ongoing traumatic context. *DSM-IV* defined ASD as occurring at least two days after the traumatic event. Implied in this definition is the notion that traumatic events are discrete incidents that terminate in a definitive manner; after the "offset" of the trauma, the clinician can calculate the period of time since the traumatic event to determine when ASD can be assessed. This temporal framework can be problematic in situations where the traumatic event is ongoing because of ongoing threats, social upheaval, or community destruction. For example, following Hurricane Katrina, many people's lives were massively disrupted for lengthy periods because of relocation, lack of housing, and loss of basic infrastructures. The impact of this persistent stress following a trauma is highlighted by evidence that rates of PTSD actually *increased* over time in New Orleans, arguably because the unresolved, or increasing, stress involved in the aftermath created further psychological strain (Kessler et al., 2008). Assessing acute psychological reactions needs to recognize that responses will be heavily influenced by the presence of current stressors. Although it is reasonable to assess current stress reactions in these circumstances, it is problematic to attempt identification of people who are at high risk for subsequent disorder because many survivors will be experiencing transient stress reactions that will abate after the stressors reduce.

The Range of Psychological Reactions

One limitation of the focus on ASD is that it potentially directs assessment toward fear-based reactions, and PTSD reactions in particular. There is increasing recognition that trauma can precipitate a range of psychological disorders, including depression, generalized anxiety disorder, panic disorder, agoraphobia, social phobia, and substance abuse (Bryant, Creamer, O'Donnell, Silove, Clark, & McFarlane, 2010). There is also increasing evidence that in the acute phase trauma survivors can experience a range of emotional responses, such as anger, guilt, grief, and shame (Brewin, Andrews, & Rose, 2000). There are no structured assessments of the different emotional responses following trauma, and they are probably unnecessary. In the process of indexing acute stress response, it is important for the assessor to be aware that a range of emotional responses can be present beyond fear and anxiety.

Traumatic Brain Injury

Special care needs to be taken when assessing ASD in the wake of traumatic brain injury (TBI), analgesic medications administered to injured patients, medical conditions that involve coma or impaired awareness, and substance abuse because these conditions may all create alterations in awareness that can appear similar to dissociative experiences. For example, morphine is commonly prescribed to injured patients to manage acute pain; however, this medication can result in reduced awareness, derealization, depersonalization, or amnesia as a direct result of the analgesic. *DSM-IV* explicitly states that a diagnosis of ASD should not be made if the symptoms can be explained by medical or chemically induced conditions.

Probably the most common differential diagnosis for ASD is mild traumatic brain injury (MTBI) because the effects of MTBI can closely mimic a range of ASD symptoms. Depersonalization, derealization, reduced awareness, and dissociative amnesia can present similarly to the impaired consciousness observed following TBI (Grigsby & Kaye, 1993; Gronwall & Wrightson, 1980). Further, a number of the arousal symptoms described in the ASD criteria can be observed among the postconcussive symptoms following brain injury (Bohnen & Jolles, 1992). Considering the traumatic circumstances that surround the occurrence of many TBI injuries, it is likely that many of these individuals may be vulnerable to ASD development. Interestingly, prospective studies of MTBI patients have found that meeting ASD criteria is predictive of subsequent PTSD (Bryant & Harvey, 1998; Harvey & Bryant, 2000). Despite differential diagnosis challenges, it appears that meeting the criteria that include the reexperiencing and avoidance (as well as dissociative and arousal) clusters is nonetheless indicative of subsequent PTSD. One symptom that is particularly difficult to interpret is amnesia in the wake of MTBI because it is typically present following MTBI. There are no reliable means to differentiate between dissociative amnesia and amnesia secondary to MTBI (Bryant, 2001). In recognition of this problem, several commentators have recommended that calculating presence of ASD and PTSD following MTBI should not include dissociative amnesia as a eligible symptom (O'Donnell, Creamer, Bryant, Schnyder, & Shalev, 2003). Diagnosing ASD in patients with moderate or severe TBI is not recommended because these patients, by definition, have more pervasive disturbances in consciousness that will overlap markedly with stress reactions, and are typically unable or have difficulty to monitor and report their psychological states.

Summary

This review highlights that our field has much to learn about key issues of assessing trauma survivors in the acute phase after exposure. The clinician must initially decide if the goal is to describe current levels of posttraumatic stress or to attempt prediction of persistent disorder. If the goal is the former, there are numerous scales of acute dissociative and stress reactions available. If the goal is the latter, then several interview and self-report scales exist with adequate psychometric strengths, but they are all limited by modest predictive capacity. As we learn that the relationship between initial response and subsequent adjustment is not linear, there is increasing awareness that attempts at acute identification of high-risk individuals will inevitably be flawed. Nonetheless, the availability of proven secondary prevention strategies that can limit subsequent PTSD underscores the merits of refining these early identification assessment techniques.

References

Aardal-Eriksson, E., Eriksson, T. E., & Thorell, L. H. (2001). Salivary cortisol, posttraumatic stress symptoms, and general health in the acute phase and during 9-month follow-up. *Biological Psychiatry, 5*, 986–993.

American Psychiatric Association. (1994). *Diagnostic and statistical manual of mental disorders* (4th ed.). Washington, DC: Author.

Andrews, B., Brewin, C. R., Philpott, R., & Stewart, L. (2007). Delayed-onset posttraumatic stress disorder: A systematic review of the evidence. *American Journal of Psychiatry, 164*, 1319–1326.

Andrews, B., Brewin, C. R., Rose, S., & Kirk, M. (2000). Predicting PTSD symptoms in victims of violent crime: The role of shame, anger, and childhood abuse. *Journal of Abnormal Psychology, 109*, 69–73.

Berah, E. F., Jones, H. J., & Valent, P. (1984). The experience of a mental health team involved in the early phase of a disaster. *Australian and New Zealand Journal of Psychiatry, 18*, 354–358.

Bisson, J. I., Shepherd, J. P., Joy, D., Probert, R., & Newcombe, R. G. (2004). Early cognitive-behavioural therapy for post-traumatic stress symptoms after physical injury. Randomised controlled trial.[see comment]. *British Journal of Psychiatry, 184*(Suppl.), 63–69.

Blanchard, E. B., Hickling, E. J., Barton, K. A., & Taylor, A. E. (1996). One-year prospective follow-up of motor vehicle accident victims. *Behaviour Research and Therapy, 34*, 775–786.

Bohnen, N., & Jolles, J. (1992). Neurobehavioral aspects of postconcussive symptoms after mild head injury. *Journal of Nervous & Mental Disease, 180*, 183–192.

Bonne, O., Brandes, D., Segman, R., Pitman, R. K., Yehuda, R., & Shalev, A. Y. (2003). Prospective evaluation of plasma cortisol in recent trauma survivors with posttraumatic stress disorder. *Psychiatry Research, 119*, 171–175.

Breh, D. C., & Seidler, G. H. (2007). Is peritraumatic dissociation a risk factor for PTSD? *Journal of Trauma Dissociation, 8*, 53–69.

Brewin, C. R., Andrews, B., & Rose, S. (2000). Fear, helplessness, and horror in posttraumatic stress disorder: Investigating DSM-IV criterion A2 in victims of violent crime. *Journal of Traumatic Stress, 13*, 499–509.

Brewin, C. R., Rose, S., Andrews, B., Green, J., Tata, P., McEvedy, C., et al. (2002). Brief screening instrument for post-traumatic stress disorder. *British Journal of Psychiatry, 181*, 158–162.

Briere, J., Scott, C., & Weathers, F. (2005). Peritraumatic and persistent dissociation in the presumed etiology of PTSD. *American Journal of Psychiatry, 162*, 2295–2301.

Brooks, R., Bryant, R. A., Silove, D., Creamer, M., O'Donnell, M., McFarlane, A. C., et al. (2009). The latent structure of the Peritraumatic Dissociative Experiences Questionnaire. *Journal of Traumatic Stress, 22*, 153–157.

Brooks, R., Silove, D., Bryant, R., O'Donnell, M., Creamer, M., & McFarlane, A. (2008). A confirmatory factor analysis of the acute stress disorder interview. *Journal of Traumatic Stress, 21*, 352–355.

Brunet, A., Weiss, D. S., Metzler, T. J., Best, S. R., Neylan, T. C., Rogers, C., et al. (2001). The Peritraumatic Distress Inventory: A proposed measure of PTSD criterion A2. *American Journal of Psychiatry, 158*, 1480–1485.

Bryant, R. A. (2001). Posttraumatic stress disorder and traumatic brain injury: Can they co-exist? *Clinical Psychology Review, 21*, 931–948.

Bryant, R. A. (2003). Early predictors of posttraumatic stress disorder. *Biological Psychiatry, 53*, 789–795.

Bryant, R. A. (2006). Longitudinal psychophysiological studies of heart rate: Mediating effects and implications for treatment. In R. Yehuda (Ed.), *Psychobiology of posttraumatic stress disorder: A decade of progress* (Vol. 1071, pp. 19–26). New York: New York Academy of Science.

Bryant, R. A. (2007). Does dissociation further our understanding of PTSD? *Journal of Anxiety Disorders, 21,* 183–191.
Bryant, R.A. (2011). Acute stress disorder as a predictor of posttraumatic stress disorder: A systematic review. Journal of Clinical Psychiatry,72, 233-239.

Bryant, R. A., Creamer, M., O'Donnell, M., Silove, D., & McFarlane, A. C. (2008a). A multisite study of initial respiration rate and heart rate as predictors of posttraumatic stress disorder. *Journal of Clinical Psychiatry, 69,* 1694–1701.

Bryant, R. A., Creamer, M., O'Donnell, M. L., Silove, D., & McFarlane, A. C. (2008b). A multisite study of the capacity of acute stress disorder diagnosis to predict posttraumatic stress disorder. *Journal of Clinical Psychiatry, 69,* 923–929.

Bryant, R. A., Creamer, M., O'Donnell, M., Silove, D., & McFarlane, A. C. (2010). Sleep disturbance immediately prior to trauma predicts subsequent psychiatric disorder. *Sleep, 33,* 69–74.

Bryant, R. A., Creamer, M., O'Donnell, M., Silove, D., Clark, C. R., & McFarlane, A. C. (2010). The psychiatric sequelae of traumatic injury. *American Journal of Psychiatry, 167,* 312–320.

Bryant, R.A., Friedman, M.J., Spiegel, D., Robert, R., & Strain, J. (2011). A review of acute stress disorder in DSM-V. Depression and Anxiety, 28, 802-817.

Bryant, R. A., & Harvey, A. G. (1998). Relationship between acute stress disorder and posttraumatic stress disorder following mild traumatic brain injury. *American Journal of Psychiatry, 155,* 625–629.

Bryant, R. A., Harvey, A. G., Dang, S. T., & Sackville, T. (1998). Assessing acute stress disorder: Psychometric properties of a structured clinical interview. *Psychological Assessment, 10,* 215–220.

Bryant, R. A., Harvey, A. G., Dang, S. T., Sackville, T., & Basten, C. (1998). Treatment of acute stress disorder: A comparison of cognitive-behavioral therapy and supportive counseling. *Journal of Consulting and Clinical Psychology, 66,* 862–866.

Bryant, R. A., Mastrodomenico, J., Felmingham, K. L., Hopwood, S., Kenny, L., Kandris, E., et al. (2008). Treatment of acute stress disorder: A randomized controlled trial. *Archives of General Psychiatry, 65,* 659–667.

Bryant, R. A., Moulds, M., Guthrie, R. (2000). Acute stress disorder scale: A self-report measure of acute stress disorder. *Psychological Assessment, 12,* 61–68.

Bryant, R. A., Sackville, T., Dang, S. T., Moulds, M., & Guthrie, R. (1999). Treating acute stress disorder: An evaluation of cognitive behavior therapy and supportive counseling techniques. *Amercian Journal of Psychiatry, 156,* 1780–1786.

Cardeña, E., Classen, C., & Spiegel, D. (1991). *Stanford acute stress reaction questionnaire.* Stanford, CA: Stanford University Medical School.

Cardeña, E., Koopman, C., Classen, C., Waelde, L. C., & Spiegel, D. (2000). Psychometric properties of the Stanford Acute Stress Reaction Questionnaire (SASRQ): A valid and reliable measure of acute stress. *Journal of Traumatic Stress, 13,* 719–734.

Cardeña, E., & Spiegel, D. (1993). Dissociative reactions to the San Francisco Bay Area earthquake of 1989. *American Journal of Psychiatry, 150,* 474–478.

Classen, C., Koopman, C., Hales, R., & Spiegel, D. (1998). Acute stress disorder as a predictor of posttraumatic stress symptoms. *American Journal of Psychiatry, 155,* 620–624.

Davidson, J., Book, S., Colket, J., Tupler, L., et al. (1997). Assessment of a new self-rating scale for post-traumatic stress disorder. *Psychological Medicine, 27,* 153–160.

Delahanty, D. L., Herberman, H. B., Craig, K. J., Hayward, M. C., Fullerton, C. S., Ursano, R. J., et al. (1997). Acute and chronic distress and posstraumatic stress disorder as a function of responsibility for serious motor vehicle accidents. *Journal of Consulting and Clinical Psychology, 65,* 560–567.

Delahanty, D. L., Nugent, N. R., Christopher, N. C., & Walsh, M. (2005). Initial urinary epinephrine and cortisol levels predict acute PTSD symptoms in child trauma victims. *Psychoneuroendocrinology, 30,* 121–128.

Delahanty, D. L., Raimonde, A. J., & Spoonster, E. (2000). Initial posttraumatic urinary cortisol levels predict subsequent PTSD symptoms in motor vehicle accident victims. *Biological Psychiatry, 48,* 940–947.

Delahanty, D. L., Royer, D. K., Spoonster, E., & Raimonde, J. (2001). Initial cortisol levels after a motor vehicle accident mediate the relationship between prior trauma history and subsequent symptoms of PTSD. *Psychosomatic Medicine, 63,* 1106.

Ehlers, A., & Clark, D. M. (2000). A cognitive model of posttraumatic stress disorder. *Behaviour Research & Therapy, 38,* 319–345.

Ehlers, A., Mayou, R. A., & Bryant, B. (1998). Psychological predictors of chronic posttraumatic stress disorder after motor vehicle accidents. *Journal of Abnormal Psychology, 107,* 508–519.

Ehring, T., Ehlers, A., Cleare, A. J., & Glucksman, E. (2008). Do acute psychological and psychobiological responses to trauma predict subsequent symptom severities of PTSD and depression? *Psychiatry Research, 161,* 67–75.

Engelhard, I. M., van den Hout, M. A., Arntz, A., & McNally, R. J. (2002). A longitudinal study of "intrusion-based reasoning" and posttraumatic stress disorder after exposure to a train disaster. *Behaviour Research & Therapy, 40*(, 1415–1424.

Feinstein, A. (1989). Posttraumatic stress disorder: A descriptive study supporting DSM-III—R criteria. *American Journal of Psychiatry, 146,* 665–666.

Fikretoglu, D., Brunet, A., Best, S., Metzler, T., Delucchi, K., Weiss, D. S., et al. (2006). The relationship between peritraumatic distress and peritraumatic dissociation. *Journal of Nervous and Mental Disease, 194,* 853–858.

Fikretoglu, D., Brunet, A., Best, S. R., Metzler, T. J., Delucchi, K., Weiss, D. S., et al. (2007). Peritraumatic fear, helplessness and horror and peritraumatic dissociation: Do physical and cognitive symptoms of panic mediate the relationship between the two? *Behaviour Research and Therapy, 45,* 39–47.

Foa, E. B., & Kozak, M. J. (1986). Emotional processing of fear: Exposure to corrective information. *Psychological Bulletin, 99,* 20–35.

Foa, E. B., Riggs, D. S., Dancu, C. V., & Rothbaum, B. O. (1993). Reliability and validity of a brief instrument for assessing post-traumatic stress disorder. *Journal of Traumatic Stress, 6,* 459–473.

Friedman, M. J. (2000). What might the psychobiology of posttraumatic stress disorder teach us about future approaches to pharmacotherapy? *Journal of Clinical Psychiatry, 61* (Suppl. 7), 44–51.

Galea, S., Ahern, J., Resnick, H., Kilpatrick, D., Bucuvalas, M., Gold, J., et al. (2002). Psychological sequelae of the September 11 terrorist attacks in New York City. *New England Journal of Medicine, 346,* 982–987.

Galea, S., Resnick, H., Ahern, J., Gold, J., Bucuvalas, M., Kilpatrick, D., et al. (2002). Posttraumatic stress disorder in Manhattan, New York City, after the September 11th terrorist attacks. *Journal of Urban Health, 79*, 340–353.

Gershuny, B. S., & Thayer, J. F. (1999). Relations among psychological trauma, dissociative phenomena, and trauma-related distress: A review and integration. *Clinical Psychology Review, 19*, 631–657.

Grigsby, J., & Kaye, K. (1993). Incidence and correlates of depersonalization following head trauma. *Brain Injury, 7*, 507–513.

Gronwall, D., & Wrightson, P. (1980). Duration of post-trauma amnesia after mild head injury. *Journal of Clinical Neuropsychology, 2*, 51–60.

Harvey, A. G., & Bryant, R. A. (2000). Two-year prospective evaluation of the relationship between acute stress disorder and posttraumatic stress disorder following mild traumatic brain injury. *American Journal of Psychiatry, 157*, 626–628.

Harvey, A. G., & Bryant, R. A. (2002). Acute stress disorder: A synthesis and critique. *Psychological Bulletin, 128*, 886–902.

Hillman, R. G. (1981). The psychopathology of being held hostage. *American Journal of Psychiatry, 138*, 1193–1197.

Isserlin, L., Zerach, G., & Solomon, Z. (2008). Acute stress responses: A review and synthesis of ASD, ASR, and CSR. *American Journal of Orthopsychiatry, 78*, 423–429.

Jehel, L., Paterniti, S., Brunet, A., Louville, P., & Guelfi, J. D. (2006). Peritraumatic distress prospectively predicts PTDS symptoms in assault victims. *Encephale, 32*(6 Pt 1), 953–956.

Kessler, R. C., Galea, S., Gruber, M. J., Sampson, N. A., Ursano, R. J., & Wessely, S. (2008). Trends in mental illness and suicidality after Hurricane Katrina. *Molecular Psychiatry, 13*, 374–384.

King, D. W., Leskin, G. A., King, L. A., & Weathers, F. W. (1998). Confirmatory factor analysis of the clinician-administered PTSD Scale: Evidence for the dimensionality of posttraumatic stress disorder. *Psychological Assessment, 10*, 90–96.

Koopman, C., Classen, C., Cardeña, E., & Spiegel, D. (1995). When disaster strikes, acute stress disorder may follow. *Journal of Traumatic Stress, 8*, 29–46.

Koopman, C., Classen, C., & Spiegel, D. A. (1994). Predictors of posttraumatic stress symptoms among survivors of the Oakland/Berkeley firestorm. *American Journal of Psychiatry, 151*, 888–894.

Madakasira, S., & O'Brien, K. F. (1987). Acute posttraumatic stress disorder in victims of a natural disaster. *Journal of Nervous and Mental Disease, 175*, 286–290.

Marmar, C. R., Metzler, T.J., & Otte, C. (2004). The Peritraumatic Dissociative Experiences Questionnaire. In J. P. Wilson & T. M. Keane (Eds.), *Assessing psychological trauma and PTSD* (2nd ed., pp. 144–167). New York: Guilford.

Marmar, C. R., Weiss, D. S., & Metzler, T. J. (1997). The Peritraumatic Dissociative Experiences Questionnaire. In J. P. Wilson & T. M. Keane (Eds.), *Assessing psychological trauma and PTSD* (pp. 412–428). New York: Guilford.

McFarlane, A. C., Atchison, M., & Yehuda, R. (1997). The acute stress response following motor vehicle accidents and its relation to PTSD. *Annals of the New York Academy of Sciences, 821*, 437–441.

McNally, R. (2003). *Remembering trauma.* Cambridge, MA: Harvard University Press.

Milad, M. R., Rauch, S. L., Pitman, R. K., & Quirk, G. J. (2006). Fear extinction in rats: Implications for human brain imaging and anxiety disorders. *Biological Psychology, 73*, 61–71.

Murray, J., Ehlers, A., & Mayou, R. A. (2002). Dissociation and post-traumatic stress disorder: Two prospective studies of road traffic accident survivors. *British Journal of Psychiatry, 180*, 363–368.

North, C. S., Smith, E. M., McCool, R. E., & Lightcap, P. E. (1989). Acute postdisaster coping and adjustment. *Journal of Traumatic Stress, 2*, 353–360.

Noyes, R., Jr., & Kletti, R. (1977). Depersonilization in response to life-threatening danger. *Comprehensive Psychiatry, 18*, 375–384.

O'Donnell, M. L., Creamer, M., Bryant, R. A., Schnyder, U., & Shalev, A. (2003). Posttraumatic disorders following injury: An empirical and methodological review. *Clinical Psychology Review, 23*, 587–603.

O'Donnell, M. L., Creamer, M. C., Parslow, R., Elliott, P., Holmes, A. C., Ellen, S., et al. (2008). A predictive screening index for posttraumatic stress disorder and depression following traumatic injury. *Journal of Consulting and Clinical Psychology, 76*, 923–932.

Ozer, E. J., Best, S. R., Lipsey, T. L., & Weiss, D. S. (2003). Predictors of posttraumatic stress disorder and symptoms in adults: A meta-analysis. *Psychological Bulletin, 129*, 52–73.

Palmieri, P. A., Weathers, F. W., Difede, J., & King, D. W. (2007). Confirmatory factor analysis of the PTSD Checklist and the Clinician-Administered PTSD Scale in disaster workers exposed to the World Trade Center Ground Zero. *Journal of Abnormal Psychology, 116*, 329–341.

Panasetis, P., & Bryant, R. A. (2003). Peritraumatic versus persistent dissociation in acute stress disorder. *Journal of Traumatic Stress, 16*, 563–566.

Pitman, R. K. (1989). Post-traumatic stress disorder, hormones, and memory. *Biological Psychiatry, 26*, 221–223.

Pitman, R. K., Orr, S. P., Forgue, D. F., Altman, B., de Jong, J. B., & Herz, L. R. (1990). Psychophysiologic responses to combat imagery of Vietnam veterans with posttraumatic stress disorder versus other anxiety disorders. *Journal of Abnormal Psychology, 99*, 49–54.

Resnick, H. S., Yehuda, R., Pitman, R. K., & Foy, D. W. (1995). Effect of previous trauma on acute plasma cortisol level following rape. *American Journal of Psychiatry, 152*, 1675–1677.

Riggs, D. S., Rothbaum, B. O., & Foa, E. B. (1995). A prospective examination of symptoms of posttraumatic stress disorder in victims of nonsexual assault. *Journal of Interpersonal Violence, 10*, 201–214.

Rothbaum, B. O., Foa, E. B., Riggs, D. S., Murdock, T., & Walsh, W. (1992). A prospective examination of post-traumatic stress disorder in rape victims. *Journal of Traumatic Stress, 5*, 455–475.

Shalev, A. Y., Freedman, A., Peri, T., Brandes, D., Sahara, T., Orr, S., et al. (1998). Prospective study of posttraumatic stress disorder and depression following trauma. *American Journal of Psychiatry, 155*, 630–637.

Shalev, A. Y., Freedman, S., Peri, T., Brandes, D., & Sahar, T. (1997). Predicting PTSD in trauma survivors: Prospective evaluation of self-report and clinician-administered instruments. *British Journal of Psychiatry, 170*, 558–564.

Shalev, A. Y., Peri, T., Canetti, L., & Schreiber, S. (1996). Predictors of PTSD in injured trauma survivors: A prospective study. *American Journal of Psychiatry, 153*, 219–225.

Sloan, P. (1988). Post-traumatic stress in survivors of an airplane crash-landing: A clinical and exploratory research intervention. *Journal of Traumatic Stress, 1*(2), 211–229.

Smith, K., & Bryant, R. A. (2000). The generality of cognitive bias in acute stress disorder. *Behaviour Research and Therapy, 38*, 709–715.

Solomon, S., Laor, N., & McFarlane, A. (1996). Acute posttraumatic reactions in soldiers and civilians. In B. A. Van der Kolk, A. C. McFarlane, & L. Weisaeth (Eds.), *Traumatic stress: The effects of overwhelming experience on mind, body and society* (pp. 102–114). New York: Guilford.

Spiegel, D., Koopmen, C., Cardeña, C., & Classen, C. (1996). Dissociative symptoms in the diagnosis of acute stress disorder. In L. K. Michelson & W. J. Ray (Eds.), *Handbook of dissociation* (pp. 367–380). New York: Plenum Press.

Steinberg, M. (1995). *Handbook for the assessment of dissociation: A clinical guide.*

Steinberg, M., Cicchetti, D., Buchanan, J., Hall, P., & Rounsaville, B. (1993). Clinical assessment of dissociative symptoms and disorders: The structured clinical interview for DSM-IV dissociative disorders (SCID-D). *Dissociation, 6*, 3–15.

Sterlini, G. L., & Bryant, R. A. (2002). Hyperarousal and dissociation: A study of novice skydivers. *Behaviour Research and Therapy, 40*, 431–437.

Vaiva, G., Boss, V., Ducrocq, F., Fontaine, M., Devos, P., Brunet, A., et al. (2006). Relationship Between posttrauma GABA plasma levels and PTSD at 1-year follow-up. *American Journal of Psychiatry, 163*(8), 1446–1448.

Vaiva, G., Thomas, P., Ducrocq, F., Fontaine, M., Boss, V., Devos, P., et al. (2004). Low posttrauma GABA plasma levels as a predictive factor in the development of acute posttraumatic stress disorder. *Biological Psychiatry, 55*, 250–254.

Velden, P. G. v. d., Kleber, R. J., Christiaanse, B., Gersons, B. P. R., Marcelissen, F. G. H., Drogendijk, A. N., et al. (2006). The independent predictive value of peritraumatic dissociation for postdisaster intrusions, avoidance reactions, and PTSD symptom severity: A 4-year prospective study. *Journal of Traumatic Stress, 19*, 493–506.

Walters, J. T. R., Bisson, J. I., & Shepherd, J. P. (2007). Predicting post-traumatic stress disorder: Validation of the Trauma Screening Questionnaire in victims of assault. *Psychological Medicine, 37*, 143–150.

Warda, G., & Bryant, R. A. (1998). Cognitive bias in acute stress disorder. *Behaviour Research and Therapy, 36*, 1177–1183.

Weiss, D. S., & Marmar, C. R. (1997). The Impact of Event Scale—Revised. In J. P. Wilson & T. M. Keane (Eds.), *Assessing psychological trauma and PTSD* (pp. 399–411). New York: Guilford.

World Health Organization. (1995). *The ICD-10 classification of mental and behavioural disorders: Clinical descriptions and diagnostic guidelines.* Geneva: Author.

Yehuda, R. (1997). Sensitization of the hypothalamic-pituitary-adrenal axis is posttraumatic stress disorder. In R. Yehuda & A. C. McFarlane (Eds.), *Psychobiology of posttraumatic stress disorder* (pp. 57–75). New York: New York Academy of Sciences.

Yehuda, R. (2003). Adult neuroendocrine aspects of PTSD. *Psychiatric Annals, 33*, 30–36.

Yitzhaki, T., Solomon, Z., & Kotler, M. (1991). The clinical picture of acute combat stress reaction among Israeli soldiers in the 1982 Lebanon war. *Military Medicine, 156*, 193–197.

CHAPTER

18 Assessing Trauma-related Symptoms in Children and Adolescents

Sonja March, Alexandra De Young, Belinda Dow, *and* Justin Kenardy

Abstract

The literature concerning the assessment of posttrauma reactions is well developed for adults, but this is not so for children and adolescents, especially young children. This chapter covers some key trauma-assessment issues in the child and adolescent population, which includes derivation and validation problems, the influence of developmental factors, applicability of current diagnostic classification, and the use of multiple informants. The range of available assessment measures is then reviewed, including semi-structured and self-report measures of posttraumatic stress disorder, acute stress disorder, and dissociation. Available screening measures and physiological measures are also reviewed. Directions for future work in this area are made.

Key Words: Assessment, posttraumatic stress disorder, child, adolescent, preschool, school-aged, dissociation, acute stress disorder, heart rate

Assessing Trauma-related Symptoms in Children and Adolescents

It is now well established that children and adolescents can experience posttraumatic stress symptoms (PSS) and posttraumatic stress disorder (PTSD) following a variety of traumatic events (Brown, Madan-Swain, & Lambert, 2003; Goenjian et al., 1995). Accurate assessment of trauma-related symptoms in youth is extremely important, as untreated trauma reactions are associated with poor long-term psychological and developmental outcomes (Scheeringa, Zeanah, Myers, & Putnam, 2005; Yates, Dodds, Sroufe, & Egeland, 2003). Therefore, we need to identify assessment tools that aid in the accurate identification of traumatic stress reactions so that early intervention can prevent the deleterious consequences associated with untreated PTSD.

Guidelines for the assessment of PSS in children and adolescents have been previously described (American Academy of Child and Adolescent Psychiatry [AACAP], 1998), and several researchers have now published detailed reviews of PTSD measures for children and adolescents (Hawkins & Radcliffe, 2006; McNally, 1996; Nader, 2004; Newman, 2002; Ohan, Myers, & Collett, 2002; Stover & Berkowitz, 2005; Strand, Sarmiento, & Pasquale, 2005). Overall, assessment procedures and measures are far less developed and validated for the assessment and diagnosis of PTSD or PSS in youth than in adults, although significant progress has been made in recent years. This chapter provides an overview of the issues to consider when assessing trauma-related symptoms in youth and describes available measures, with consideration of psychometric properties, clinical utility, and usefulness of the measures. In particular, some of the more widely used measures, as well as some newly developed scales, are reviewed.

Issues Relating to Assessment of Trauma-related Symptoms in Youth

Diagnostic Classification Issues

The *Diagnostic and Statistical Manual* (*DSM-IV-TR*; American Psychiatric Association [APA], 2000) remains the most widely used diagnostic classification system for mental health disorders, including PTSD. However, concerns have been raised regarding the suitability and validity of the PTSD criteria for youth, as the criteria have been mostly defined, researched, and validated in adult populations (Postert, Averbeck-Holocher, Beyer, Muller, & Furniss, 2009). Only minimal modifications to the *DSM-IV* (American Psychiatric Association [APA], 1994) criteria were made to accommodate the unique developmental differences in symptom manifestation in youth, and no children under the age of 15 were included in *DSM-IV* field trials (Kilpatrick et al., 1998).

Recent research has indicated that the *DSM-IV-TR* PTSD criteria do not adequately capture the symptom manifestation experienced by children, particularly infants and preschoolers, and underestimate the number of children experiencing considerable posttraumatic distress and impairment (Carrion, Weems, Ray, & Reiss, 2002; Meiser-Stedman, Smith, Glucksman, Yule, & Dalgleish, 2008; Scheeringa, Zeanah, Myers, & Putnam, 2003). A number of alternative diagnostic algorithms and modifications to existing criteria have therefore been proposed to take into account the distinct differences in how trauma is experienced, how affect is expressed, and how symptoms may present in youth of different ages (Aaron, Zaglul, & Emery, 1999; Pynoos et al., 2009; Scheeringa et al., 2003; Steinberg, Brymer, Decker, & Pynoos, 2004; Winston, Kassam-Adams, Garcia-España, Ittenbach, & Cnaan, 2003).

In particular, Scheeringa and colleagues (e.g., Scheeringa et al., 2003; Scheeringa, Wright, Hunt, & Zeanah, 2006; Scheeringa & Zeanah, 2008) have demonstrated that their alternative PTSD algorithm (PTSD-AA) for young children provides a more reliable, valid, and developmentally sensitive measure of PTSD than the *DSM-IV* criteria. The PTSD-AA includes modification to *DSM-IV* PTSD symptom wording to make it more developmentally sensitive to young children, the removal of Criterion A2 and two avoidance symptoms that were deemed developmentally inappropriate, and adjustment to the avoidance cluster such that only one symptom is required instead of three (Scheeringa et al., 2003). While further work is warranted to reach a consensus on a developmentally sensitive classification system for infants, children, and adolescents, consideration should be given to these alternative approaches when assessing PTSD and PSS in youth.

Psychometric Issues

There are several issues that must be noted with respect to the psychometric integrity of measures for the assessment of trauma-related symptoms in youth. First, in many cases, measures were adapted from adult scales rather than developed to reflect the specific manifestation of trauma symptoms in children and adolescents. Such tools have typically been adapted through simplifications of text, item concepts, and language (Hawkins & Radcliffe, 2006). Although such modifications aid comprehension, it is unlikely that they adequately capture the PTSD construct in youth. Therefore, assessment tools that account for youth-specific symptom manifestations are necessary.

Second, few of the available measures have undergone rigorous systematic psychometric evaluation in child and adolescent samples. Measures validated in adults are often assumed to be valid and reliable for use with youth, although these measures have most often not been examined in such contexts. Further, psychometric properties of many of the youth-specific measures have only been formally examined on one occasion or with one specific population and require replication to demonstrate validity and reliability in other populations. Finally, many of the available assessment tools do not have normative data to support their use.

Measurement of Trauma-related Symptoms across Different Ages

In addition to issues with psychometric validation for youth, many of the available instruments fail to take into consideration subtle developmental differences between children of different ages. Scales are often designed for broad age groups (e.g., 8–16), which may fail to account for the many developmental and cognitive changes that occur over this developmental period. Failure to consider these differences could affect the administration, interpretation, meaning, and use of such instruments. The differences among preschoolers, school-aged children, and adolescents necessitate the development of measures that not only assess different symptom manifestations but also match their administration methods to the developmental and cognitive capabilities of the young person.

Many of the existing measures have not adequately considered the ways in which trauma reactions may differ depending on the young person's level of cognitive, social, and emotional maturity and developmental milestones. An assessment of trauma-related symptoms in younger children and school-aged children should therefore also consider assessment of externalizing behaviors (e.g., attention, oppositional behavior, aggression, hyperactivity, learning problems), internalizing difficulties (e.g., anxiety, depression, somatization, withdrawal, self-regulation), and social competence. Preadolescents and adolescents may require measures that assess for risky behavior, self-harm, substance use, impulse control, consideration for others, responsibility, self-efficacy, and optimism.

Some of the more commonly used adult-assessment procedures (e.g., pen and paper) may not be suitable for all youth. Rather, child-friendly and age-appropriate approaches are preferable. As noted by Scheeringa, Zeanah, Drell, and Larrieu (1995), many of the *DSM-IV* criteria for PTSD necessitate the young person to provide verbal descriptions of experiences and emotions in order for criteria to be met (e.g., numbing and withdrawal), which may not be possible in very young children. Thus, practitioners need to consider alternative assessment measures that are suitable for younger children (e.g., measures that are less reliant on verbal or written skills, shorter in duration, and less complex, or measures that are conducted with parents). Unfortunately, very few measures have been developed and tested specifically for children under the age of 10.

The Use of Multiple Informants

Assessment of trauma-related symptoms in youth may require information to be obtained from multiple informants (e.g., caregiver, child) in order to provide a comprehensive understanding of the young person's history and an indication of symptoms that cannot be expressed accurately by children. Although there is typically low agreement between parent and child reports on diagnostic interviews (Choudhury, Pimentel, & Kendall, 2003; Jensen, Rubio-Stipec, Canino, & Bird, 1999; Rapee, Barrett, Dadds, & Evans, 1994), a combined parent-child report may provide the most accurate description of child trauma symptoms (Meiser-Stedman et al., 2008; Scheeringa et al., 2006). The importance of child and parent reports may differ according to the child's age and developmental level, the type of assessment tool administered, and the type of traumatic event experienced by the child. However, it is clear that both parent and child may offer valuable information important to the conceptualization of the disorder and that a combination of sources may be best (De Bellis & Van Dillen, 2005; Grills & Ollendick, 2002; Jensen et al., 1999). Unfortunately, very few of the current measures include reports for multiple informants (e.g., youth, parent, and teacher) and this may influence the selection of appropriate assessment tools.

Measures for the Assessment of Trauma-related Symptoms in Young People

The following provides an overview of measures for the assessment of trauma-related symptoms in young people, including those administered by clinicians and those completed by youth and their caregivers. A review of every measure assessing PTSD or PSS in youth is beyond the scope of this chapter. Rather, we aim to provide evaluations of the most widely used, recognizable, and/or psychometrically sound instruments and provide discussion of the advantages, disadvantages, and utility associated with these measures. Instruments are reviewed according to categories (e.g., diagnostic instruments, self-report questionnaires, screening measures, physiological measures) and in order from those suited for very young infants and children, through to adolescents.

Diagnostically oriented Instruments

A thorough assessment of PSS in young people should ideally include a clinical interview either with the young person, parent, or both. While there are many structured diagnostic interviews available that provide assessment of PTSD as part of their overall packages, there are also some diagnostic tools that focus solely on the assessment and diagnosis of PTSD. For some youth, a broad diagnostic tool may be necessary to examine symptoms in addition to PTSD symptoms. Further, the choice of interview may depend on whether the clinician chooses to interview the parent and/or child. Some of the more widely used tools for diagnostic assessment are reviewed in table 18.1, which provides specific information relating to administration requirements and psychometric properties of diagnostic-oriented measures for youth.

DIAGNOSTIC INSTRUMENTS FOR VERY YOUNG CHILDREN

The following provides a discussion of diagnostic instruments for very young children, from one to six years of age.

Table 18.1 Summary of diagnostically oriented instruments

Measure	Age range	General information/Purpose	Administration/Length/Scoring	Psychometric Properties
PTSD Semi-structured Interview and Observational Record for Infants and Young Children (PTSD-SSI-ORIYC; Scheeringa & Zeanah, 1994)	1–6 years	• Screens for presence of traumatic event & PTSD symptoms • Provides DSM-IV PTSD diagnosis? Yes, *DSM-IV* & PTSD-AA criteria • Other information: Dutch, German, Spanish & Hebrew translations	• Format: Semi-structured interview • Administered by: Clinician • Conducted with: primary caregiver, child present. Optional child observation • Length of administration: 45 mins • Requirements: Training & supervision	• Reliability: IRR: PTSD-AA diagnosis κ=.74–.79; PTSD-AA items range κ=.29-1.0; median κ=.71–.75. • Other: Observation component only detected 12% of PTSD symptoms • (Scheeringa, et al., 2001; Scheeringa, et al., 2003, 2005)
Preschool Age Psychiatric Assessment (PAPA; Egger, et al., 2006)	2–5 years	• Assesses for broad range of psychological disorders including PTSD • Provides PTSD diagnosis? Yes, *DSM-IV* & RDC-PA criteria • Other information: Spanish, Romanian & Norwegian translations	• Format: Structured interview • Administered by: Clinician • Conducted with: primary caregiver • Length of administration: Avg 100 mins • Requirements: Graduate, training & supervision	• Reliability: TR: PTSD ICC α=.56; PTSD κ=.73 • (Egger, et al., 2006)
Diagnostic Infant and Preschool Assessment (DIPA; Scheeringa & Haslett, 2010)	1–6 years	• Assesses psychopathology in childhood (13 *DSM-IV* Axis-I disorders) • Provides PTSD diagnosis? Yes, *DSM-IV* & PTSD-AA criteria • Other information: Used in clinical & research settings	• Format: Semi-structured interview • Administered by: Clinician • Conducted with: primary caregiver • Length of administration: 517 questions • Requirements: Training & supervision	• Reliability: TR: PTSD-AA ICC α=.87; PTSD-AA κ=.56 • Validity: CONV w/CBCL PTSD Scale: • Continuous: r=.15-.24 for PTSD-AA • Categorical: r=.48 for PTSD-AA-RA, .12 for PTSD-AA-Clinician • (Scheeringa & Haslett, 2010)
Clinician Administered PTSD Scale for Children and Adolescents (CAPS-CA; Newman et al. 2004)	8–15 years	• Assesses PTSD symptoms relating to traumatic events • Provides PTSD diagnosis? Yes • Other information: • Current & lifetime diagnoses • Assesses functioning & associated symptoms	• Format: Semi-structured interview • Administered by: Clinician • Conducted with: Child • Length of administration: 30min-2hrs • Requirements: Training & supervision	Psychometrics from CAPS-C or CAPS-CA: • Reliability: ICC: α=.97, IC: Total symptom score α=.89 • Validity: CONC: w/PTSD-RI, r=.51; w/Child PTSD Checklist, r=.64. • (Carrion, et al., 2002; Daviss et al., 2000)

(*continued*)

Table 18.1 Summary of diagnostically oriented instruments (*continued*)

Measure	Age range	General information/Purpose	Administration/Length/Scoring	Psychometric Properties
Children's PTSD Inventory (CPTSDI; Saigh et al. 2000)	7–18 years	• Assesses presence of PTSD symptoms in relation to specific events • Provides PTSD diagnosis? Yes • Other information: • Can diagnose acute PTSD, chronic PTSD & Delayed onset PTSD • Items incorporate youth feedback	• Format: Semi-structured interview • Administered by: Clinician • Conducted with: Child • Length of administration: 5- 15mins • Requirements: Training & supervision	• Reliability: IRR: total (α=.95); subscales (α=.53-.89); subtest ICC's α=.88-.96; TR: κ=.91, ICC α=.88 • Validity: SENS (.87–1.00), SPEC (.92–.99), PPV (.65–.96), NPV (.95–1.00), diagnostic efficiency (.93–.95); CONV: w/RCMAS (r=0.70), w/CBCL Internalising (r=0.55) • (Saigh et al., 2000; Yasik et al., 2001)
Kiddie Schedule for Affective Disorders and Schizophrenia for School-Age Children – Present and Lifetime Version (K-SADS-PL; Kaufman et al. 1997)	7–17 years	• Assesses broad psychopathology in childhood (32 *DSM-IV* Axis I disorders) • Provides PTSD diagnosis? Yes, *DSM-III* & *DSM-IV* criteria • Other information: • Assesses present, lifetime, full & partial PTSD • Integrates child & parent report	• Format: Semi-structured interview • Administered by: Clinician • Conducted with: Child & parent • Length of administration: 35mins-1.25hrs each for child & parent • Requirements: Intensive training in diagnostic classification & differential diagnosis	• Reliability: IRR=present & lifetime dx range 93%-100%; TR: present dx κ=.63–1.00, lifetime dx κ=.55–1.00; Present PTSD=.67, lifetime PTSD=.60 • (Kaufman, Birmaher, Brent, Rao, & et al., 1997)
Anxiety Disorders Interview Schedule, Child and Parent versions (ADIS – C/P; Silverman & Albano, 1996)	7–17 years	• Assesses for a variety of anxiety, mood & behavioral disorders • Provides PTSD diagnosis? Yes • Other information: Child & parent versions	• Format: Semi-structured interview • Administered by: Clinician • Conducted with: Child &/or parent • Length of administration: 1.5 hrs each for child & parent (entire schedule) • Requirements: Training & supervision	• Reliability: IRR κ=.84 ADIS-C; κ=.78 ADIS-P, κ=.78 composite dx; TR: 7–14 days child κ=.61–.80, parent κ=.65–1.00, & combined κ=.62–1.00; Parent-child agreement PTSD scale, κ=.21 • (Meiser-Stedman, Smith, Glucksman, Yule, & Dalgleish, 2007; Silverman, Saavedra, & Pina, 2001; Wood, Piacentini, Bergman, McCracken, & Barrios, 2002)

Note: CBCL=Child Behavior Checklist; CONC=Concurrent validity; CONV=Convergent validity; Dx=diagnosis; IC=Internal consistency; ICC=Intraclass correlation statistic; IRR: interrater reliability; NPV=Negative Predictive Value; PPV=Positive Predictive Value; *rs*=Pearson *rs*; PTSD-AA = Alternative PTSD algorithm; PTSD-RI=PTSD-Reaction Index; RA=Research Assistant; Research Diagnostic Classification System – Preschool Age; RCMAS = Revised Children's Manifest Anxiety Scale; SENS=Sensitivity; SPEC=Specificity; TR=test-retest reliability; w/=with.

The Posttraumatic Stress Disorder Semi-structured Interview and Observational Record for Infants and Young Children (PTSD-SSIORIYC; Scheeringa & Zeanah, 1994). The PTSD-SSIORIYC is a clinician-administered interview, conducted with a caregiver, which assesses for PTSD symptoms following exposure to trauma in children under the age of six. The interview allows for additional inquiry regarding symptoms commonly seen in very young, traumatized children and provides a rating of functional impairment and distress associated with the overall symptoms. Further, the PTSD-SSIORIYC allows for a diagnosis of PTSD to be made using both the *DSM-IV* and PTSD-AA criteria. The PTSD-SSI demonstrates good to excellent interrater reliability for the PTSD-AA diagnosis and acceptable reliability for the individual PTSD items (Scheeringa, Peebles, Cook, & Zeanah, 2001; Scheeringa et al., 2003). Observations of the child during the interview can be used to supplement this measure; however, they do not add to the interview's ability to assess diagnostic symptoms (Scheeringa et al., 2001). The psychometric properties of this measure have only been examined by the group who developed the measure, and administration requires training, strong clinical skills, and an understanding of child development, which may limit its usefulness in some settings.

Preschool Age Psychiatric Assessment (PAPA; Egger & Angold, 2004). The PAPA is a structured diagnostic interview conducted with the primary caregiver and provides diagnostic algorithms for various childhood psychiatric disorders, including PTSD. The PAPA is widely used and includes specific developmental modifications (e.g., questions worded to reflect how symptoms typically manifest in young children) to aid the assessment of symptoms in two- to five-year-olds. It also provides a measure of the degree of disability or impairment the child's symptoms have on their functioning in activities or relationships. The psychometric properties of the PAPA have been reported in one study to date and demonstrate good test-retest reliability and fair intraclass coefficients (ICCs) for the PTSD diagnostic category (Egger et al., 2006). However, further evaluation of its psychometric properties is needed to ensure generalizability to various trauma situations. The PAPA is time-consuming to administer and requires extensive training, which may limit its usefulness in some settings. It is possible to only administer the PTSD module; however, two of the symptoms (sense of foreshortened future and diminished interests) need to be extracted from the MDD module (Scheeringa & Haslett, 2010).

Diagnostic Infant Preschool Assessment (DIPA; Scheeringa & Haslett, 2010). The DIPA is a diagnostic interview conducted with the primary caregiver of children aged between one and six years old. As with the PAPA, the DIPA includes empirically validated developmental modifications and provides a categorical diagnosis or continuous measure of various *DSM-IV* disorders, including PTSD. The DIPA is the first measure to be evaluated with children under the age of two, is concise in its questioning, and allows for an assessment of child distress and functional impairment related to the identified symptoms. The psychometric properties of the DIPA have been reported in one study, with acceptable reliability and validity (as a diagnostic measure), as well as fair to excellent test-retest reliability (Scheeringa & Haslett, 2010). However, the DIPA demonstrated questionable concurrent criterion validity between the PTSD-AA and CBCL PTSD Scale, although this may be because the CBCL PTSD Scale was not designed to specifically measure PTSD (Scheeringa & Haslett, 2010). These findings are comparable to the PAPA, which is the only other broad diagnostic measure for young children. Although it requires further psychometric evaluation, the DIPA offers promise as a developmentally sensitive, broad, diagnostic tool for very young children.

DIAGNOSTIC INSTRUMENTS FOR SCHOOL-AGED CHILDREN

The following provides an overview of diagnostic instruments for children aged 7 to 18 years.

The Clinician-Administered PTSD Scale for Children and Adolescents (CAPS-CA; Newman et al., 2004). The CAPS-CA is a clinician-administered scale for the assessment of PTSD symptoms in youth (8–15 years) that was developmentally modified from the Clinician-Administered PTSD Scale (CAPS; Blake et al., 1990). The CAPS-CA is a specific measure that assesses current and lifetime instances of traumatic events as well as the frequency and intensity of PTSD symptoms relating to these events. It has the distinct advantage of also assessing associated symptoms in children and adolescents. It is easy to use, allows for an assessment of both partial and full PTSD, and provides descriptions of impairment in functioning. Further, the CAPS is the preferred diagnostic tool for adults, and previous versions of the child interview have demonstrated sound psychometric properties (e.g., Carrion et al., 2002; Daviss et al., 2000). Subsequently, it is favored by many researchers. However, there is very little psychometric evidence currently published for the revised CAPS-CA, nor is there information regarding a normative base. Given its ability to evaluate exposure to trauma, assess for subclinical PTSD and provide detailed information about the child's trauma reactions, the CAPS-CA offers particular promise in the assessment of youth PTSD. Users should be cautious of the limited psychometric data available for the current interview version and the training and time required administering the interview.

The Children's PTSD Inventory (CPTSDI: Saigh et al., 2000). The CPTSDI is a brief clinician-administered instrument to assess the presence of PTSD symptoms (in relation to specific events) in youth aged 7–18 years and provides scores on five subscales. Of note, the items of this measure were trialed with youth and modified following feedback to ensure developmental appropriateness and relevance. This inventory is one of the most thoroughly evaluated scales for the assessment of PTSD in youth and is supported by strong psychometric properties. The measure allows for an examination of problem severity as well as information on the presence or absence of PTSD. Significant advantages of this measure are that it is brief in nature, developmentally suitable for youth, requires only two hours of training to administer, has scoring built into the measure, and allows for diagnosis based on *DSM-IV* criteria. Although the psychometric properties of the scale have now been established, its applicability to various trauma situations requires further confirmation in the literature. Nonetheless, the CPTSDI appears to be one of most widely researched assessment measures that offer significant utility to researchers and clinicians.

The Kiddie Schedule for Affective Disorders and Schizophrenia for School-Aged Children – Parent and Lifetime Version (K-SADS-PL; Kaufman et al., 1997). The K-SADS-PL is a clinician-administered interview designed to assess for broad psychopathology in childhood (7–17 years). As part of this interview, clinicians are able to assess for present and lifetime PTSD according to *DSM-IV* criteria. Strengths of this measure are that it allows for the identification of various traumatic events, assesses for both full and partial PTSD, and also provides information about comorbid disorders. Further, it allows for the clinician to use information from both child self-report and parental reports of observable behavior. However, drawbacks include extensive administration time and significant training needed for administration. The K-SADS generally demonstrates sound psychometric properties. The PTSD Scale, however, has demonstrated poor test-retest reliability (i.e., $\kappa = .67$ present diagnosis; $\kappa = .60$ lifetime diagnosis), which is also lower than that of other K-SADS scales (Kaufman et al., 1997).

The Anxiety Disorders Interview Schedule, Child and Parent Versions (ADIS-C/P: Silverman & Albano, 1996). The ADIS is a widely used clinician-administered interview for the assessment of anxiety disorders in childhood and adolescence (7–17 years). It comprises a child and parent interview schedule that can be combined to provide an overall diagnosis. Although the ADIS has the advantage of providing information about common comorbid anxiety, mood, and behavioral disorders, it lacks specific assessment of PTSD symptom clusters, frequency or duration of symptoms, and no differentiation between full and partial PTSD. The ADIS allows for identification of lifetime or present exposure to specific traumatic events, and then assesses for *DSM-IV* symptoms of PTSD related to the specific traumatic event. It is easy to administer and score, provides a rating of overall PTSD impairment, and has demonstrated good psychometric properties for the anxiety scales. Specific psychometric data for the PTSD Scale are less well described, although available data suggest excellent interrater reliability, but only fair parent-child agreement (Meiser-Stedman, Smith, Glucksman, Yule, & Dalgleish, 2007). Administration of both child and parent interview schedules is extremely time-intensive and may limit the usefulness of this interview.

Self-Report Questionnaires

In times when diagnostic instruments are too time-intensive or additional information is required, it may also be valuable to consider various self-report measures of trauma-related symptoms. There are now several useful self-report measures that can be completed by the caregiver, teacher, or young person, depending on their age. Detailed information regarding these measures and their psychometric properties is described next and an overview is provided in table 18.2.

SELF-REPORT QUESTIONNAIRES FOR THE ASSESSMENT OF VERY YOUNG CHILDREN

Although the use of self-report questionnaires with very young children is generally limited to a

Table 18.2 Summary of self-report measures

Measure	Age range	General Information/Purpose	Administration/length/scoring	Psychometric Properties
The Trauma Symptom Checklist for Young Children (TSCYC; Briere, 2005)	3–12 years	• Assesses posttraumatic symptoms & comorbid difficulties. • Provides PTSD diagnosis? No • Other information: • 9 subscales: 4 PTSD-related, Sexual Concerns, Anxiety, Depression, Dissociation & Anger/Aggression. • Contains two rater validity scales • Spanish & Swedish translations	• Format: Observer-report questionnaire • Items: 90 items rated on a 4-point scale. • Completed by: Primary caregiver • Length: 15 mins (+8 mins to score) • Scoring: • Norms based on sex & age (3–4, 5–9, 10–12) • Manual available? Yes • Requirements: Graduate training	• Reliability: IC: α=.55-.93, • Validity: CONV: w/TSCC scales for PTS-I, ANX, DEP, ANG, & SC (.18-.30) but not for PTS-AV or PTS-AR; DISC: TSCC PTS scale best predictor of PTSD status on the TSCYC. • (Becker-Blease, Freyd, & Pears, 2004; Briere, 2005; Briere et al., 2001; Finkelhor, Ormrod, & Turner, 2009; Lanktree et al., 2008)
Child Behavior Checklist (CBCL; Achenbach & Rescorla, 2000, 2001)	1 1/2–5 6–18	• Broad measure of child functioning • Provides PTSD diagnosis? No • Other information: • Generates Externalising, Internalising & Total Problems Scales, Syndrome Scales including post-hoc PTSD syndrome scale • Multiple translations • Can be used in diverse populations.	• Format: Observer-report questionnaire • Items: 100 (younger) - 120 (older), rated on a 3-point scale • Completed by: Primary caregiver (Teacher- & youth-report also available (11–18yrs) • Length: 10–15 mins • Scoring: Norms based on sex & age • Manual available? Yes • Requirements: Interpretation requires knowledge of standardised assessment.	PTSD Scale: • Reliability: IC: α=.67–.89 for 4–18yrs & .80–.83 for 2-3yrs. • Validity: CONV: *r*=.66 with PTSD-SSIORIYC & *r*=.57 with K-SADS-E; Cut-off=9 (CBCL/1.5-5): SENS=75%; SPEC=84%; Cut-off=8 (CBCL/4-18): SENS=87%; SPEC=61.5% • (Ayer et al., 2009; Dehon & Scheeringa, 2006; Levendosky, Huth-Bocks, Semel, & Shapiro, 2002; Ruggiero & McLeer, 2000)
Trauma Symptom Checklist for Children (TSCC; Briere, 1996)	8–16	• Assesses PTSD symptoms & other psychological difficulties following trauma. • Provides PTSD diagnosis? No • Other information: • Typically used to assess children's responses to sexual abuse, but can exclude sexual concern items (TSCC-A) • Contains two rater validity scales • Multiple translations	• Format: Self-report questionnaire • Items: 54 rated on a 4-point scale; 44 items for TSCC-A • Completed by: Young person • Length: 10–15 mins • Scoring: • Normed on over 3000 children • Norms based on sex & age (8-12; 13–16) • Manual available? Yes • Requirements: Graduate training	• Reliability: IC: main subscales α=.82-.89, total α=.89 • Validity: CONV w/MMPI *r*=.69; w/ TSCYC PTS-I *r*=.11 & ANX *r*=.24 • (e.g. Lanktree, et al., 2008; Sadowski & Friedrich, 2000)

(*continued*)

Table 18.2 Summary of self-report measures (*continued*)

Measure	Age range	General Information/Purpose	Administration/length/scoring	Psychometric Properties
Child PTSD Reaction Index (CPTSD-RI; Pynoos et al., 1987) UCLA PTSD Index for *DSM-IV* (UPID: Pynoos et al., 1998)	6–17 7–18	CPTSD-RI: • Assesses frequency of posttraumatic symptoms following exposure. • Provides PTSD diagnosis? No • Other information: Multiple translations UPID: • Revision of the CPTSD-RI. • Assesses exposure to traumatic events, frequency of PTSD, & associated symptoms • Provides PTSD diagnosis? Not intended • Other information: • Multiple translations • Child, adolescent, & parent versions. • Can be read aloud as interview (if>8yrs)	• Format: Self-report questionnaire • Items: 20 items rated on 5-point scale • Completed by: Young person • Length: 5–10 mins • Format: Self-report questionnaire, parent report also available • Items: 48 items • Completed by: Young person or parent • Length: 15–20mins	• Reliability: IC: α=0.70–0.80; IRR: κ=.89 • Validity: CONV w/clinician r=.91 • (Pynoos et al., 1987; Nader et al., 1990) • Reliability: IC: α=.69-.90; IRR: α=.88 total; TR: α=.93 (1 week), agreement between total score & PTSD dx=.91 • Validity: CONV w/K-SADS PTSD module r=.70; w/CAPS-CA r=.82; SENS=.93, SPEC .87 at cut-off 38 • (e.g. Steinberg, et al., 2004)
Child PTSD Symptom Scale (CPSS: Foa et al. 2001)	8–18	• Assesses frequency & severity of PTSD symptoms & functional impairment • Provides PTSD diagnosis? Yes, *DSM-IV* criteria • Other information: Child version of the Posttraumatic Diagnostic Scale (1993)	• Format: Self-report questionnaire • Items: 24 items rated on a 4-point scale. • Completed by: Young person • Length: 20–30 mins • Scoring: can calculate a symptom severity score	• Reliability: Symptom severity score: IC: α=.89, TR α=.84; Dx TR: κ=.55; agreement 84% • Validity: CONV w/CPTSD-RI: r=.80 • (Foa, Johnson, Feeny, & Treadwell, 2001)

Note: ANG = Anger; ANX = Anxiety; CAPS-CA = Clinician Administered PTSD Scale for Children and Adolescents; CONV = Convergent validity; CPTSD-RI = Children's PTSD Inventory; DEP = Depression; DISC = Discriminant validity; Dx = diagnosis; ECBI = Eyberg Child Behavior Inventory; IC = Internal consistency; ICC = Intraclass correlation statistic; IRR = Interrater reliability; KSADS = Kiddie Schedule for Affective Disorders and Schizophrenia for School-Age Children - Epidemiological Version; MMPI = Minnesota Multiphasic Personality Inventory; PTS-AR = Posttraumatic stress arousal; PTS-AV = Posttraumatic stress avoidance; PTS-I = Posttraumatic stress-intrusion; PTSD-SSIORIYC = PTSD Semi-structured Interview and Observational Record for Infants and Young Children; *rs* = Pearson *rs*; SC = Sexual concerns; SENS = Sensitivity; SPEC = Specificity; TR = Test-retest reliability; w/ = With.

caregiver report, there are several questionnaires worth considering for use.

Trauma Symptom Checklist for Young Children (TSCYC; Briere, 2005). The TSCYC assesses posttrauma reactions in 3- to 12-year-olds through caregiver report. It produces nine clinical scales and provides a tentative PTSD diagnosis with the summary Posttraumatic Stress-Total (PTS-TOT) Scale. There are several advantages to the TSCYC; it was designed specifically for young traumatized children, it provides a comprehensive measure of trauma symptoms as well as comorbid conditions, and has established norms that enable interpretations to be made based on clinical cut-offs. Further, the TSCYC incorporates scales to check the validity of caregiver report, is quick to administer and score, and can be used in combination with the Trauma Symptom Checklist (TSCC; Briere, 1996) to provide a multi-informant assessment. Psychometric properties of the TSCYC have been reported in several studies, with acceptable scale internal consistency, moderate convergent and discriminant validity with child report (8–12 years) on the TSCC, and good construct validity for the posttraumatic stress scales. However, the TSCYC is still a relatively new measure requiring further psychometric evaluation. Other limitations are that the standardization sample only contained a small number of 3- to 4-year-olds, it does not include trauma symptoms that typically manifest in young children (Stover & Berkowitz, 2005) and the TSCYC cannot be used with children under the age of 3.

Child Behavior Checklist for 1.5-5 & 6-18 (CBCL/1.5-5, CBCL/6-18; Achenbach & Rescorla, 2000, 2001). The CBCL is one of the most widely used measures of emotional and behavioral functioning, with versions for parents of youth aged 6 to 18 years and also for young children aged 1.5 to 5 years. An advantage of the CBCL is its ability to provide an overall measure of general distress, internalizing and externalizing difficulties, and more specific *DSM*-oriented scales. Although the CBCL was not specifically designed to measure PTSD, it has been proposed that a subset of items can be combined to provide a PTSD subscale (Wolfe, Gentile, & Wolfe, 1989). In some studies, the CBCL PTSD Scale has shown acceptable internal consistency, some evidence of convergent validity with PTSD diagnostic interviews, and the ability to screen for the presence of PTSD symptoms. However, other studies have reported questionable convergent validity as well as poor discriminant validity (Ayer et al., 2009; Levendosky, Huth-Bocks, Semel, & Shapiro, 2002; Ruggiero & McLeer, 2000), suggesting that the CBCL PTSD Scale may not offer the best measure of trauma-related symptoms. The CBCL-PTSD items are administrated within the context of assessing behavioral change rather than traumatic stress responses specifically, and may therefore provide an assessment of generic rather than trauma-related distress (Briere et al., 2001; Levendosky et al., 2002; Sim et al., 2005). Therefore, the CBCL-PTSD Scale is not recommended as a specific measure of PTSD symptoms; however, it may be useful as a measure of general distress or when specific comorbid problems are evident.

Pediatric Emotional Distress Scale (PEDS; Saylor, Swenson, Reynolds, & Taylor, 1999). Alternatively, if an assessment of comorbid difficulties is required, the PEDS may be worth considering. This very brief caregiver report allows for the assessment of general behavior items following trauma and has some psychometric support (Page & Nooe, 1999; Saylor et al., 1999; Spilsbury et al., 2005; Spilsbury, Fletcher, Creeden, & Friedman, 2008).

SELF-REPORT QUESTIONNAIRES FOR SCHOOL-AGED CHILDREN AND ADOLESCENTS

The following describes some of the more commonly used self-report measures for children over the age of 6.

The Trauma Symptom Checklist for Children (TSCC; Briere, 1996). The TSCC assesses PTSD symptoms, as well as other psychological difficulties, following acute or chronic trauma, in children aged 8–16 years old. Although it has typically been used to assess responses to sexual-related trauma, the checklist can be delivered without the sexual concern items and incorporates six clinical scales (anxiety, depression, anger, posttraumatic stress, sexual concerns, and dissociation). The TSCC can be administered relatively quickly and has been normed in over 3,000 children. It has undergone extensive psychometric evaluation and, overall, has demonstrated strong psychometric properties, including good validity in a number of settings and high internal consistency (Lanktree et al., 2008; Sadowski & Friedrich, 2000; Wolpaw, Ford, Newman, Davis, & Briere, 2005). The TSCC is one of the most validated self-report trauma measures for children and may be particularly useful for assessing responses to trauma across a variety of domains. However, the TSCC does not provide a measure of all PTSD symptoms and may be more useful for screening current trauma reactions, or when other trauma responses are evident (e.g., anxiety, depression, anger).

The Child PTSD Reaction Index (CPTSD-RI; Pynoos, et al., 1987) and UCLA PTSD Index for *DSM-IV* (UPID; Pynoos, Rodriguez, Steinberg, Stuber, & Frederick, 1998). The UPID is a revised version of the CPTSD-RI; both will be discussed here. The UPID and CPTSD-RI assess for the presence and frequency of posttraumatic symptoms following trauma exposure in youth aged between 6 and 18 years old. The original CPTSD-RI was a shorter measure that was widely used and demonstrated strong psychometric properties; however, the CPTSD-RI did not assess all PTSD symptoms. The UPID is a revised version that incorporates child, adolescent, and parent versions of the inventory. The UPID assesses exposure to 26 types of traumatic events and assesses all *DSM-IV* diagnostic criteria (including associated symptoms). Although psychometric evaluation of the UPID is not as extensive as some other measures, it has particular promise given the strong evidence base for the original CPTSD-RI. A particular strength of this measure is its developmentally appropriate nature and its potential to incorporate reports from an accompanying caregiver. Further, it is able to describe the young person's history of exposure to traumatic events and has been translated into several other languages. It is recommended as a specific measure of PTSD symptoms following trauma. However, this measure is not as brief as other available measures.

The Child PTSD Symptom Scale (CPSS; Foa, Johnson, Feeny, & Treadwell, 2001). The CPSS is based on the widely used Posttraumatic Diagnostic Scale for adults (Foa, 1995) and assesses for the presence, frequency, and severity of *DSM-IV* PTSD symptoms in the past month for youth (aged 8–18 years old) exposed to traumatic events. The CPSS is developmentally appropriate, is quick to administer, and is able to yield a diagnosis. Further, it provides an indication of functional impairment related to PTSD symptoms. Strong psychometric properties are reported for the CPSS, with good internal and test-retest reliability for total symptom severity, as well as good convergent validity with other measures of PTSD (e.g., CPTSD-RI; Foa et al., 2001). Overall, the CPSS is a developmentally appropriate and efficient instrument that may be particularly useful when assessing specific symptoms of PTSD. It has the added advantage that it is able to provide an indication of severity along with diagnosis of PTSD.

Dissociation Measures

In addition to instruments assessing PTSD symptoms, it is may be useful to consider measures of associated features of PTSD, such as dissociation.

The Child Dissociative Checklist (CDC; Putnam, Helmers, & Trickett, 1993). The CDC is a 20-item, observer- or parent-report screen of dissociative behaviors displayed in children aged 5–12 years. Items were derived from the author's experience and from predictor lists of symptoms circulated among child maltreatment professionals. The items were designed to assess six domains of dissociation: dissociative amnesia, rapid shifts in demeanor and abilities, spontaneous trance states, hallucinations, identity alterations, and aggression or sexualized behaviors. However, recent factor analysis analysis suggests the CDC can be reduced into three components: pathological dissociation, variability, and externalizing (Wherry, Neil, & Taylor, 2009). The measure is brief; has shown good to excellent internal reliability in mixed clinical and nonclinical samples (internal consistency: $\alpha = .95$; split half reliability $r = .88$); has been shown to distinguish among children with dissociative disorders, healthy children, and children with a history of maltreatment; and has shown moderate test-retest reliability (1-year, $\rho = .69$; Putnam et al., 1993). However, low to moderate validity has been reported with other child dissociation scales. Thus, scores must be considered within a broader clinical context. The CDC is best utilized as a screening measure indicating the presence or absence of dissociative symptoms in children.

The Adolescent Dissociative Experience Scale (A-DES: Armstrong, Putnam, Carlson, Libero, & Smith, 1997). The A-DES is a relatively brief, 30-item self-report scale developed specifically for youth between 12 and 18 years. It assesses for normal and pathological dissociative symptoms and contains subscales of dissociative amnesia, absorption/imaginal involvement, passive influence, and depersonalization/derealization. However, a factor analysis has reported only a single factor solution (Farrington, Waller, Smerden, & Faupel, 2001). A total dissociative score can also be calculated for the A-DES. The A-DES demonstrates very good internal reliability ($\alpha = .92$; split-half reliability $r = .92$; Armstrong et al., 1997), and good test-retest reliability (2-week, $\rho = .77$; Smith & Carlson, 1997) and is able to distinguish between normal adolescents and those with clinical diagnoses, as well as those with and without a history of sexual abuse (Armstrong et al., 1997; Seeley, Perosa, & Perosa, 2004). The A-DES is recommended if the researcher/clinician wishes to gain more information about the young person's dissociative symptoms.

Acute Stress Disorder Measures

A brief discussion of acute stress disorder (ASD) assessment measures is also warranted, as recent developments have led to some practical, brief, and psychometrically strong measures that may be very useful to the clinician or researcher involved in assessing early post-trauma reactions in youth.

Acute Stress Disorder Module of the Diagnostic Interview for Children and Adolescents (DICA-ASD; Miller, Enlow, Reich, & Saxe, 2009). The DICA-ASD is a 58-item semi-structured clinical interview that assesses acute traumatic stress symptoms and provides a diagnosis of ASD in children and adolescents aged 7 to 18 years. The DICA-ASD was adapted from the PTSD module of the DICA, which has strong psychometric properties (Reich, 2000). The DICA-ASD consists of the PTSD module in addition to five *DSM-IV* symptom clusters related to dissociation and requires approximately 15 minutes to administer. The DICA-ASD shows high internal consistency ($\alpha = .97$) and perfect interrater agreement at the diagnostic level ($\kappa = 1.00$; Miller et al., 2009). Advantages of the measure include the use of child report of symptoms, ability to assess diagnostic criteria, and the convenience of assessing other disorders within the DICA. Disadvantages to the measure are the level of clinical training required (minimum of master's level) and the limited studies and psychometric data available with different child groups, but at this early stage the measure appears promising.

Acute Stress Checklist for Children (ASC-Kids; Kassam-Adams, 2006). The ASC-Kids is a 29-item self-report measure of acute traumatic stress symptoms in youths aged 8–17. A total symptom severity score and *DSM-IV* diagnostic criteria can be derived. The measure has demonstrated good psychometric properties, with strong internal consistency (Cronbach $\alpha = .86$) and test-retest reliability ($r = .83$), strong correlation with a concurrent PTSD measure (Child and Adolescent Trauma Survey [CATS] acute, $r = .77$) and moderate correlation with a parent-report ASD measure (Child Stress Disorder Checklist, $r = .37$; Kassam-Adams, 2006). The ASC-Kids also shows good predictive validity, correlating with PTSD symptom severity three months later (CATS follow-up, $r = .61$; Kassam-Adams, 2006). The ASC-Kids has a brief, 5–10-minute administration time and is a very promising measure of ASD for use in clinical and research settings.

Screening Instruments

There are several screening instruments that have been utilized in young populations that are described next and presented in table 18.3. Although these instruments are used for screening those at risk of developing PTSD, they may also be useful in identifying current PTSD symptoms. However, given that they are very brief instruments and their psychometric properties have typically been examined within a screening context, they should be considered primarily as screening instruments rather than self-report measures of trauma symptoms.

The Impact of Event Scale (IES: Horowitz, Wilner, & Alvarez, 1979). The IES is a 15-item self-report questionnaire that was originally designed to assess the psychological impact of trauma in adults. It is one of the most widely used measures and has demonstrated adequate psychometric properties in adult populations (Joseph, 2000). The original 15-item IES (IES-15) has also been used with children and adolescents exposed to a variety of traumas; however, only a limited number of studies have investigated whether it is psychometrically sound when used with youth (Dyregrov, Kuterovac, & Barath, 1996; Sack, Seeley, Him, & Clarke, 1998; Yule, Ten Bruggencate, & Joseph, 1994).

Children's Revised Impact of Event Scale (CRIES-8; Yule, 1997). Problems with the application of the IES to child and adolescent populations led to the development of a revised eight-item child-friendly version now referred to as the Children's Revised Impact of Event Scale (CRIES-8). The CRIES-8 consists of four intrusion and four avoidance items. Analyses by Smith, Perrin, Dyregrov, and Yule (2003) have confirmed that the intrusion and avoidance factors are robust and have satisfactory internal consistency. A cut-off of 17 has demonstrated moderate to excellent sensitivity and specificity for identifying concurrent PTSD in accident and clinical samples (Perrin, Meiser-Stedman, & Smith, 2005; Stallard, Velleman, & Baldwin, 1999). However, the predictive performance of the CRIES-8 was inadequate for identifying full and subsyndromal PTSD at one and six months following accidental injury (Kenardy, Spence, & Macleod, 2006).

Children's Revised Impact of Event Scale (CRIES-13; Smith, Perrin, Dyregov, & Yule, 2003).

Table 18.3 Summary of screening instruments

Measure	Age	General Information/Purpose	Administration/length/scoring	Psychometric Properties
Impact of Event Scale (IES-15; Horowitz et al., 1979)	Developed for adults	• Measures intrusive & avoidance symptoms relating to specific traumatic event. • Not child specific	• Format: Self-report questionnaire • Items: 15 rated on a 4 point scale • Completed by: Young person • Length: 10–15 mins • Scoring: Scores ≥30 indicate a positive screen for trauma symptoms	• Reliability: IC: Intrusion α=.72–.90; Avoidance α=.61–.82; Numbing α=.60; Total α=.92 • Validity: CONV r=.41–.78 subscales w/measures of anxiety & depression; SENS=.66-.74 SPEC=.63-.87; PPV=.30–.63; NPV=.90–.89; OE=.85 • (Dyregrov, et al., 1996; Sack, et al., 1998; Yule, et al., 1994)
Children's Revised Impact of Event Scale 8-item (CRIES-8; Yule, 1997)	8–18 years	• Screens for intrusive & avoidance symptoms but not hyper-arousal symptoms	• Format: Self-report questionnaire • Items: 8 rated on a 4 point scale • Completed by: Young person • Length: 5 mins • Scoring: Scores ≥ 17 indicate a positive screen for trauma symptoms	• Reliability: IC: Intrusion α=.70; Avoidance α=.73; Total α=.75 • Validity: CONV w/CTSQ=.56; CONC predictive utility: SENS=.69–1.0; SPEC=.59-.83; PPV=.30–.55; NPV=.83–1.0; OE=.75–.83; Predictive utility: SENS=.55-.69; SPE=.58; PPV=.11-.15; NPV=.93–.95; OE=.58–.59. • (Kenardy, Spence, & Macleod, 2006; Perrin, Meiser-Stedman, & Smith, 2005; Smith, et al., 2003; Stallard, Velleman, & Baldwin, 1999)
Children's Revised Impact of Event Scale 13-item (CRIES-13; Smith et al., 2003)	8–18 years	• Screens for PTSD symptoms: intrusion, avoidance & hyper-arousal symptoms • Available for free in 19 different languages.	• Format: Self-report questionnaire • Items: 13 rated on a 4 point scale • Completed by: Young person • Length: 5-10 mins • Scoring: Scores ≥ 17 indicate a positive screen for trauma symptoms	• Reliability: IC: Intrusion α=.70-.82; Avoidance α=.73-.82; Hyper-arousal α=.60–.70; Total α=.80-.87 • Validity: CONV w/CPTS-RI=.79; SENS=.86-.91; SPEC=.65-.73; PPV=.29-.84; NPV=.79-.98; OE=.75-.83 • (Giannopoulou et al., 2006; Perrin, et al., 2005; Smith, et al., 2003)

Child Trauma Screening Questionnaire (CTSQ; Kenardy et al., 2006)	6–16 years	• Screens for intrusive & hyper-arousal symptoms following trauma	• Format: Self-report questionnaire • Items: 10 rated on a dichotomous Yes/No scale • Completed by: Young person • Length: 5–10 mins • Scoring: Scores ≥ 5 indicate a positive screen for trauma symptoms.	• Reliability: IC: α=.69 • Validity: CONV w/CRIES-8=.56; SENS=.82-.85; SPEC=.74–.75; PPV=.23-.26; NPV=.98; OE=.75-.76. • Other: The CTSQ was more accurate than the CRIES-8 • (Kenardy, et al., 2006)
Screening Tool for Early Predictors of PTSD (STEPP; Winston et al., 2003)	8–17 years	• Screens for parent & child posttraumatic stress after child injury. • Can only be administered in acute care, injury context.	• Format: Clinician administered questionnaire • Items: 12 • Conducted with: 4 items: Parent, 4 items: child & 4 items: medical record • Length: <2mins	• Reliability: TR: child κ=.86; parent κ=.67 • Validity: Child: SENS=.88; Spec=.48; PPV=.25; NPV=.95; OE=.54; Parent: SENS=.96; Spec=.53; PPV=.27; NPV=.99; OE=.59. • (Winston, et al., 2003)

Note: CONC = Concurrent validity, CONV = Convergent validity; CPTS-RI = Child Posttraumatic Stress Reaction Index; IC = Internal consistency; NPV = Negative Predictive Value; OE: Overall E8 ciency; PPV = Positive Predictive Value; *rs* = Pearson *rs*; SENS = Sensitivity; SPEC = Specificity; TR = test-retest; w/ = with.

The CRIES-8 was subsequently expanded to include an additional five items to assess the additional hyper-arousal symptom cluster (Children and War Foundation, 2005). Factor analyses have generally found support for a three-factor structure (i.e., intrusion, avoidance and hyper-arousal) and general PTSD factor (Giannopoulou et al., 2006; Smith et al., 2003). However, Smith et al. (2003) found the arousal factor had poor internal consistency and was highly correlated with intrusion. The CRIES-13 has demonstrated adequate internal consistency for the intrusion, avoidance, and total scales (Giannopoulou et al., 2006; Smith et al., 2003) and convergent validity with the CPTSD-RI (Giannopoulou et al., 2006). Using a cut-off of 30 or more, the CRIES-13 has demonstrated adequate sensitivity and specificity, correctly classifying 75–83% of cases (Perrin et al., 2005). However, the overall efficiency of the CRIES-8 and CRIES-13 were comparable in this study, with no apparent advantage of including the additional five arousal symptoms when screening large samples of children (Perrin et al., 2005). It seems that the CRIES-8 will provide sufficient screening of PTSD symptoms and has the advantage of shorter administration and scoring time.

The CRIES-8 and CRIES-13 have several advantages, including that they are brief measures that are quick, easy to administer and score, can be administered by both professionals and nonprofessionals, and have been translated into multiple languages. The CRIES-8 would be particularly beneficial when screening large numbers of children for the presence of concurrent PTSD symptoms, whereas the CRIES-13 would be most appropriate to specifically screen for the presence of the three PTSD clusters.

Child Trauma Screening Questionnaire (CTSQ: Kenardy et al., 2006). The CTSQ is a 10-item self-report screen adapted for children from the adult Trauma Screening Questionnaire (TSQ; Brewin et al., 2002). The CTSQ assesses for the presence of re-experiencing (5 items) and hyper-arousal symptoms (5 items) following a traumatic event. A cut-off score of 5 or more indicates a positive screen for trauma symptoms. To date, the psychometric properties of the CTSQ have only been examined on one occasion (Kenardy et al., 2006), although further evaluation is under way. The CTSQ showed acceptable internal consistency and convergent validity with the CRIES-8. The predictive performance of the CTSQ was promising, with preliminary analyses indicating that the CTSQ demonstrated acceptable sensitivity and specificity for predicting the development of full and subsyndromal PTSD diagnosis at one and six months postaccidental injury (correctly classifying 74–82% of cases). The authors found the CTSQ was more accurate than the widely used CRIES-8.

Screening Tool for Early Predictors of PTSD (STEPP; Winston et al., 2003). The STEPP is another brief, stand-alone screening tool for use by clinicians in acute trauma care settings to identify children and parents at risk of persistent posttraumatic stress symptoms. The STEPP was derived from empirically validated risk factors for child and parent posttraumatic stress and consists of a total of 12 questions. The child answers four questions, the parent answers four, and four questions are obtained from medical records. A child score of 4 or more and a parent score of 3 or higher is considered a positive screen. The test-retest reliability for the presence of a positive screen for children was excellent and good for parents (Winston et al., 2003). The authors found the STEPP demonstrated good to excellent sensitivity for predicting children and parents suffering from traumatic stress a mean of six months postaccident. However, the specificity and overall efficiency of the STEPP was fair, with only 54–59% of cases correctly identified.

Physiological Assessment Measures

Research investigating heart rate as a predictor of PTSD in children has found that elevated heart rate during emergency medical services transportation, emergency department triage, or 24 hours following admission significantly predicts PTSD symptoms at six weeks (Nugent, Christopher, & Delahanty, 2006a), emotional numbing at six weeks and six months (Nugent, Christopher, & Delahanty, 2006b), and PTSD diagnosis (full or subsyndromal) at approximately six months following hospitalization for accidental injury, even after controlling for age, gender, and injury severity (Bryant, Salmon, Sinclair, Psychol, & Davidson, 2007; De Young, Kenardy, & Spence, 2007; Kassam-Adams, Garcia-España, Fein, & Winston, 2005; Nugent et al., 2006a). Elevated heart rate (defined as 1 SD above the age and sex mean) during emergency department triage or the first 24 hours of hospital admission has demonstrated modest predictive utility as a screen (sensitivity = .47–.88; specificity = .63–.84; positive predictive value = .17–.53; negative predictive value = .81–.98, and overall efficiency = .65–.78; Bryant et al., 2007; De Young et al., 2007; Kassam-Adams et al., 2005). Olsson, Kenardy, De Young, and Spence (2008) demonstrated that when heart rate is combined with the CTSQ, it is more efficient than the use of the CTSQ or heart rate alone at identifying children at risk of developing PTSD six months following an accident. When heart rate was combined with the CTSQ, it correctly classified PTSD diagnostic status for 89–90% of children at six months postaccident.

The advantage of using heart rate as a screening tool is that, in comparison to psychological measures, it is an objective, noninvasive, cost-effective measure that is routinely obtained during vital-sign assessments. The use of heart rate as an indicator of risk may also be particularly useful for preverbal or nonverbal children. Additionally, heart rate appears to improve the predictive utility of psychological self-report screening tools. A limitation of relying solely on heart rate is that it may be influenced by a number of factors, including pain, medication, injury severity, treatment procedures, and premorbid factors (e.g., preexisting anxiety disorder, trauma history). Further research is still needed to determine the utility of heart rate; however, the preliminary findings to date suggest that elevated heart rate, particularly when combined with a psychological instrument, could be used as a screening tool in an acute-care setting to efficiently identify children in need of further assessment and intervention following accidental injury. Furthermore, heart rate is routinely assessed in medical situations and is accessible in most emergency settings.

Summary of Assessment Measures and Recommendations

There are several recommendations that can be made to guide the selection of instruments when conducting an assessment of trauma-related symptoms in young people.

Preschool-aged Children

For a structured interview that assesses only PTSD symptoms with consideration of age-related symptom manifestations, the PTSD-SSI appears to be a valid and reliable instrument for clinicians and researchers. Alternatively, based on preliminary research, the PAPA and DIPA are promising clinician-administered interviews that provide a developmentally sensitive measure of PTSD, as well as a range of other preschool emotional and behavioral disorders commonly seen following trauma. For parent-report measures, the TSCYC provides a reliable and valid measure of trauma symptoms and comorbid conditions and allows for comparison to normative data.

School-aged Children

The clinician-administered CPTSDI is a very quick and psychometrically sound measure that allows diagnosis of PTSD and ratings of clinical impairment. The CAPS-CA is developmentally appropriate and allows the interviewer to obtain more detailed information regarding frequency, duration, and intensity of PTSD symptoms; however, it is quite long and may only be suitable in certain contexts. Should an assessment of comorbid conditions be required, the K-SADS or ADIS may offer viable alternatives, although it may be advisable to pair with the CPTSDI. For self-report measures, the CPSS would be ideal for initial assessment given its relatively brief nature and ability to provide specific details regarding the frequency and intensity of PTSD symptoms. The CPTSD-RI or UPID may offer value in those instances where cultural sensitivity is of concern and the TSCC is recommended when an assessment of various other trauma responses (e.g., anxiety and depression) is required.

When assessing dissociative symptoms, the very brief CDC may be useful for children 5–12 years of age; however, it may best be utilized as a screening tool. The A-DES is more suitable for adolescents and is able to distinguish between normal adolescents and those with clinical diagnoses. For the assessment of early posttrauma reactions, the ASD module of the DICA is able to provide a diagnosis of ASD; however, it requires substantial training. The ASC-Kids allows for self-report of acute traumatic stress symptoms in children, and may be useful in a number of research and clinical contexts given its brief nature.

Screening Instruments and Physiological Assessments

The CRIES-8, CRIES-13, and the CTSQ appear to be the most suitable screening instruments for use with youth, each demonstrating comparable overall efficiency rates. The CRIES has the advantage of being more widely used and validated in several cultures, ages, and trauma populations. However, the CTSQ demonstrates greater accuracy predicting PTSD, which is one of the most important characteristics of a screening tool. Finally, the inclusion of heart rate, assessed immediately following trauma exposure, in combination with screening instruments may improve PTSD predictive ability.

Conclusion

It is clear that no one measure will be suitable for every researcher or clinician in every circumstance. Instrument selection should be guided by evaluation of psychometric properties, the age and developmental level of the child, purpose of the assessment, and context within which the assessment is to take place. Although further empirical evaluation is needed, there are now a number of assessment tools available for the assessment of PTSD and PSS in youth that demonstrate acceptable and in some cases, excellent psychometric properties and offer great utility in clinical and research settings.

Future Directions

Recommendations regarding the best practice in assessment for trauma-related symptoms may change over time as more scales are introduced and are further empirically evaluated. Given the current uncertainty regarding methods of diagnostic classification in children, it will be necessary to reexamine the structure and properties of scales over time. This is particularly important for those instances in which different versions of scales are created, but not subjected to empirical investigation. This will ensure that the scales reflect current understanding of the disorder and that goals of the assessment tool are in line with such understanding (Myers & Winters, 2002). Further, although many of the current scales may provide some indications of PTSD or PSS symptoms and severity, their ability to accurately inform assessment and treatment planning is far from established. Development of instruments that take into account the differences in symptom manifestation and diverse administration methods required for children at different developmental stages is also necessary. As consensus regarding diagnostic classifications is reached and new diagnostic criteria are introduced (e.g., *DSM-5*), it will also be necessary for existing measures to be updated accordingly and psychometrically reevaluated, as well as expanding normative databases for assessment tools to enable comparisons and aid clinical interpretation.

References

Aaron, J., Zaglul, H., & Emery, R. E. (1999). Posttraumatic stress in children following acute physical injury. *Journal of Pediatric Psychology, 24*(4), 335–343. (doi: 10.1093/jpepsy/24.4.335)

Achenbach, T. M., & Rescorla, L. A. (2000). *Manual for the ASEBA Preschool Forms & Profiles.* Burlington, VT: University of Vermont, Research Center for Children, Youth, & Families.

Achenbach, T. M., & Rescorla, L. A. (2001). *Manual for the ASEBA School-Age Forms & Profiles.* Burlington, VT: University of Vermont, Research Center for Children, Youth, Families.

American Academy of Child & Adolescent Psychiatry. (1998). Practice parameters for the assessment and treatment of children and adolescents with posttraumatic stress disorder. *Journal of the American Academy of Child & Adolescent Psychiatry, 37*, 4S-26S.

American Psychiatric Association. (1994). *Diagnostic and statistical manual of mental disorders* (4th ed.). Washington, DC: Author.

American Psychiatric Association. (2000). *Diagnostic and statistical manual of mental disorders* (4th ed., text rev.). Washington, DC: Author.

Armstrong, J. G., Putnam, F. W., Carlson, E. B., Libero, D. Z., & Smith, S. R. (1997). Development and validation of a measure of adolescent dissociation: The Adolescent Dissociative Experiences Scale. *Journal of Nervous and Mental Disease, 185*(8), 491–497.

Ayer, L., Althoff, R., Ivanova, M., Rettew, D., Waxler, E., Sulman, J., et al. (2009). Child Behavior Checklist Juvenile Bipolar Disorder (CBCL-JBD) and CBCL Posttraumatic Stress Problems (CBCL-PTSP) scales are measures of a single dysregulatory syndrome. *Journal of Child Psychology and Psychiatry, 50*(10), 1291–1300.

Becker-Blease, K. A., Freyd, J. J., & Pears, K. C. (2004). Preschoolers' memory for threatening information depends on trauma history and attentional context: Implications for the development of dissociation. *Journal of Trauma & Dissociation, 5*(1), 113–131.

Blake, D. D., Weathers, F. W., Nagy, L. M., Kaloupek, D. G., Klauminzer, G., Charney, D. S., et al. (1990). A clinician rating scale for assessing current and lifetime PTSD: The CAPS-1. *Behavior Therapist, 13*, 187–188.

Brewin, C. R., Rose, S., Andrews, B., Green, J., Tata, P., McEvedy, C., et al. (2002). Brief screening instrument for post-traumatic stress disorder. *British Journal of Psychiatry, 181*(2), 158–162.

Briere, J. (1996). *Trauma symptom checklist for children.* Odessa, FL: Psychological Assessment Resources.

Briere, J. (2005). *Trauma Symptom Checklist for Young Children (TSCYC): Professional manual.* Odessa, FL: Psychological Assessment Resources.

Briere, J., Johnson, K., Bissada, A., Damon, L., Crouch, J., Gil, E., et al. (2001). The trauma symptom checklist for young children (TSCYC): Reliability and association with abuse exposure in a multi-site study. *Child Abuse & Neglect, 25*(8), 1001–1014.

Brown, R. T., Madan-Swain, A., & Lambert, R. (2003). Posttraumatic stress symptoms in adolescent survivors of childhood cancer and their mothers. *Journal of Traumatic Stress, 16*, 309–318.

Bryant, R. A., Salmon, K., Sinclair, E., Psychol, M., & Davidson, P. (2007). Heart rate as a predictor of posttraumatic stress disorder in children. *General Hospital Psychiatry, 29*(1), 66–68.

Carrion, V. G., Weems, C. F., Ray, R., & Reiss, A. L. (2002). Toward an empirical definition of pediatric PTSD: The phenomenology of PTSD symptoms in youth. *Journal of the American Academy of Child & Adolescent Psychiatry, 41*(2), 166–173. (doi: 10.1097/00004583–200202000–00010)

Choudhury, M. S., Pimentel, S. S., & Kendall, P. C. (2003). Childhood anxiety disorders: Parent-child (dis)agreement using a structured interview for the DSM-IV. *Journal of the American Academy of Child and Adolescent Psychiatry, 42*, 957–964.

Daviss, W. B., Mooney, D., Racusin, R., Ford, J. D., Fleischer, A., & McHugo, G. J. (2000). Predicting posttraumatic stress after hospitalization for pediatric injury. *Journal of the American Academy of Child & Adolescent Psychiatry, 39*(5), 576–583.

De Bellis, M. D., & Van Dillen, T. (2005). Childhood posttraumatic stress disorder: An overview. *Child and Adolescent Psychiatric Clinics of North America, 14*(4), 745–772.

De Young, A. C., Kenardy, J. A., & Spence, S. H. (2007). Elevated heart rate as a predictor of PTSD six months following accidental pediatric injury. *Journal of Traumatic Stress, 20*(5), 751–756.

Dehon, C., & Scheeringa, M. S. (2006). Screening for preschool posttraumatic stress disorder with the Child Behavior Checklist. *Journal of Pediatric Psychology, 31*(4), 431–435.

Dyregrov, A., Kuterovac, G., & Barath, A. (1996). Factor analysis of the Impact of Event Scale with children in war. *Scandinavian Journal of Psychology, 37*(4), 339–350.

Egger, H. L., & Angold, A. (2004). The Preschool Age Psychiatric Assessment (PAPA): A structured parent interview for diagnosing psychiatric disorders in preschool children. In R. DelCarmen-Wiggins & A. Carter (Eds.), *Handbook of infant, toddler, and preschool mental health assessment* (pp. 223–243). New York: Oxford University Press.

Egger, H. L., Erkanli, A., Keeler, G., Potts, E., Walter, B. K., & Angold, A. (2006). Test-retest reliability of the Preschool Age Psychiatric Assessment (PAPA). *Journal of the American Academy of Child & Adolescent Psychiatry, 45*(5), 538–549.

Farrington, A., Waller, G., Smerden, J., & Faupel, A. W. (2001). The Adolescent Dissociative Experiences Scale: Psychometric properties and difference in scores across age groups. *Journal of Nervous and Mental Disease, 189*(10), 722–727.

Finkelhor, D., Ormrod, R. K., & Turner, H. A. (2009). Lifetime assessment of poly-victimization in a national sample of children and youth. *Child Abuse & Neglect, 33*(7), 403–411.

Foa, E. B., Johnson, K. M., Feeny, N. C., & Treadwell, K. R. H. (2001). The Child PTSD Symptom Scale: A preliminary examination of its psychometric properties. *Journal of Clinical Child Psychology, 30*(3), 376–384.

Foa, E.B. (1995). *Posttraumatic Stress Diagnostic Scale Manual.* Minneapolis, MN: National Computer Systems.

Giannopoulou, I., Smith, P., Ecker, C., Strouthos, M., Dikaiakou, A., & Yule, W. (2006). Factor structure of the Children's Revised Impact of Event Scale (CRIES) with children exposed to earthquake. *Personality and Individual Differences, 40*(5), 1027–1037.

Goenjian, A. K., Pynos, R. S., Steinberg, A. M., Najarian, L. M., Asarnow, J. R., & Karayan, I. (1995). Psychiatric comorbidity in children after the 1988 earthquake in Armenia. *Journal of the American Academy of Child & Adolescent Psychiatry, 34*, 1174–1184.

Grills, A. E., & Ollendick, T. H. (2002). Issues in parent-child agreement: The case of structured diagnostic interviews. *Clinical Child and Family Psychology Review, 5*(1), 57–83. (doi: 10.1023/a:1014573708569)

Hawkins, S. S., & Radcliffe, J. (2006). Current measures of PTSD for children and adolescents. *Journal of Pediatric Psychology, 31*(4), 420–430.

Horowitz, M. J., Wilner, N., & Alvarez, W. (1979). Impact of Event Scale: A measure of subjective stress. *Psychosomatic Medicine, 41*(3), 209–218.

Jensen, P. S., Rubio-Stipec, M., Canino, G., & Bird, H. R. (1999). Parent and child contributions to diagnosis of mental disorder: Are both informants always necessary? *Journal of the American Academy of Child & Adolescent Psychiatry, 38*, 1569–1579.

Joseph, S. (2000). Psychometric evaluation of Horowitz's Impact of Event Scale: A review. *Journal of Traumatic Stress, 13*(1), 101–113.

Kassam-Adams, N. (2006). The Acute Stress Checklist for Children (ASC-Kids): Development of a child self-report measure. *Journal of Traumatic Stress, 19*(1), 129–139.

Kassam-Adams, N., Garcia-España, J. F., Fein, J. A., & Winston, F. K. (2005). Heart rate and posttraumatic stress in injured children. *Archives of General Psychiatry, 62*(3), 335–340.

Kaufman, J., Birmaher, B., Brent, D., Rao, U., et al. (1997). Schedule for Affective Disorders and Schizophrenia for School-Age Children-Present and Lifetime version (K-SADS-PL): Initial reliability and validity data. *Journal of the American Academy of Child & Adolescent Psychiatry, 36*(7), 980–988.

Kenardy, J. A., Spence, S. H., & Macleod, A. C. (2006). Screening for posttraumatic stress disorder in children after accidental injury. *Pediatrics, 118*(3), 1002–1009.

Kilpatrick, D., Resnick, H., Freedy, J., Pelcovitz, D., Resick, P., Roth, S., et al. (1998). Posttraumatic stress disorder field trial: Evaluation of the PTSD construct - Criteria A through E. In T. Widiger, A. Frances, H. Pincus, R. Ross, M. First, W. Davis & M. Kline (Eds.), *DSM-IV sourcebook* (pp. 803–844). Washington, DC: American Psychiatric Association.

Lanktree, C. B., Gilbert, A. M., Briere, J., Taylor, N., Chen, K., Maida, C. A., et al. (2008). Multi-informant assessment of maltreated children: Convergent and discriminant validity of the TSCC and TSCYC. *Child Abuse & Neglect, 32*(6), 621–625.

Levendosky, A. A., Huth-Bocks, A. C., Semel, M. A., & Shapiro, D. L. (2002). Trauma symptoms in preschool-age children exposed to domestic violence. *Journal of Interpersonal Violence, 17*(2), 150–164.

McNally, R. (1996). Assessment of posttraumatic stress disorder in children and adolescents. *Journal of School Psychology, 34*(2), 147–161.

Meiser-Stedman, R., Smith, P., Glucksman, E., Yule, W., & Dalgleish, T. (2007). Parent and child agreement for acute stress disorder, post-traumatic stress disorder and other psychopathology in a prospective study of children and adolescents exposed to single-event trauma. *Journal of Abnormal Child Psychology, 35*, 191–201.

Meiser-Stedman, R., Smith, P., Glucksman, E., Yule, W., & Dalgleish, T. (2008). The posttraumatic stress disorder diagnosis in preschool- and elementary school-age children exposed to motor vehicle accidents. *The American Journal of Psychiatry, 165*(10), 1326–1337.

Miller, A., Enlow, M. B., Reich, W., & Saxe, G. (2009). A diagnostic interview for acute stress disorder for children and adolescents. *Journal of Traumatic Stress. Special Issue: Innovations in trauma research methods, 22*(6), 549–556.

Myers, K., & Winters, N. (2002). Ten-year review of rating scales. I: Overview of scale functioning, psychometric properties, and selection. *Journal of Amer Academy of Child & Adolescent Psychiatry, 41*(2), 114–122.

Nader, K. O. (2004). Assessing traumatic experiences in children and adolescents: Self-reports of DSM PTSD Criteria B-D symptoms. In J. P. Wilson & T. M. Keane (Eds.), *Assessing psychological trauma and PTSD* (2nd ed., pp. 513–537). New York: Guilford.

Nader, K., O. Pynoos, R., Fairbanks, L., & Frederick, C. (1990). Children's PTSD reactions one year after a sniper attack at their school. *American Journal of Psychiatry, 147*, 1526–1530.

Newman, E. (2002). Assessment of PTSD and trauma exposure in adolescents. *Journal of Aggression, Maltreatment & Trauma, 6*(1), 59–77.

Newman, E., Weathers, F. W., Nader, K., Kaloupek, D. G., Pynoos, R., & Blake, D. D. (2004). *Clinician-Administered PTSD Scale for Children and Adolescents (CAPS-CA)*. Los Angeles: Western Psychological Services.

Nugent, N. R., Christopher, N. C., & Delahanty, D. L. (2006a). Emergency medical service and in-hospital vital signs as predictors of subsequent PTSD symptom severity in pediatric injury patients. *Journal of Child Psychology and Psychiatry, 47*(9), 919–926.

Nugent, N. R., Christopher, N. C., & Delahanty, D. L. (2006b). Initial physiological responses and perceived hyperarousal predict subsequent emotional numbing in pediatric injury patients. *Journal of Traumatic Stress, 19*(3), 349–359.

Ohan, J. L., Myers, K., & Collett, B. R. (2002). Ten-year review of rating scales. IV: Scales assessing trauma and its effects. *Journal of the American Academy of Child & Adolescent Psychiatry, 41*(12), 1401–1422.

Olsson, K. A., Kenardy, J. A., De Young, A. C., & Spence, S. H. (2008). Predicting children's post-traumatic stress symptoms following hospitalization for accidental injury: Combining the Child Trauma Screening Questionnaire and heart rate. *Journal of Anxiety Disorders, 22*(8), 1447–1453.

Page, T. F., & Nooe, R. M. (1999). Relationships between psychosocial risks and stress in homeless children. *Journal of Social Distress & the Homeless, 8*(4), 255–267.

Perrin, S., Meiser-Stedman, R., & Smith, P. (2005). The children's revised impact of event scale (CRIES): Validity as a screening instrument for PTSD. *Behavioural and Cognitive Psychotherapy. Special Issue: A Festschrift for William Yule, 33*(4), 487–498.

Postert, C., Averbeck-Holocher, M., Beyer, T., Muller, J., & Furniss, T. (2009). Five systems of psychiatric classification for preschool children: Do differences in validity, usefulness and reliability make for competitive or complimentary constellations? *Child Psychiatry and Human Development, 40*(1), 25–41.

Putnam, F., Helmers, K., & Trickett, P. (1993). Development, reliability, and validity of a child dissociation scale. *Child Abuse & Neglect, 17*, 731–741.

Pynoos, R., Frederick, C., Nader, K., Arroyo, W., Steinberg, A., Eth, S., Nunez, F., & Fairbanks, L. (1987), Life threat and posttraumatic stress in school-age children. *Archives of General Psychiatry, 44*, 1057–1063.

Pynoos, R., Rodriguez, N., Steinberg, A., Stuber, M., & Frederick, C. (1998). *The UCLA PTSD reaction index for DSM-IV (Revision 1)*. Los Angeles: UCLA Trauma Psychiatry Program.

Pynoos, R., Steinberg, A. M., Layne, C. M., Briggs, E. C., Ostrowski, S. A., & Fairbank, J. A. (2009). DSM-V PTSD diagnostic criteria for children and adolescents: A developmental perspective and recommendations. *Journal of Traumatic Stress, 22*(5), 391–398.

Rapee, R. M., Barrett, P. M., Dadds, M. R., & Evans, L. (1994). Reliability of the DSM-III—R childhood anxiety disorders using structured interview: Interrater and parent-child agreement. *Journal of the American Academy of Child & Adolescent Psychiatry, 33*(7), 984–992.

Reich, W. (2000). Diagnostic Interview for Children and Adolescents (DICA). *Journal of the American Academy of Child & Adolescent Psychiatry, 39*(1), 59–66.

Ruggiero, K. J., & McLeer, S. V. (2000). PTSD Scale of the Child Behavior Checklist: Concurrent and discriminant validity with non-clinic-referred sexually abused children. *Journal of Traumatic Stress, 13*(2), 287–299.

Sack, W. H., Seeley, J. R., Him, C., & Clarke, G. N. (1998). Psychometric properties of the Impact of Events Scale in traumatized Cambodian refugee youth. *Personality and Individual Differences, 25*(1), 57–67.

Sadowski, C., & Friedrich, W. (2000). Psychometric properties of the Trauma Symptom Checklist for children (TSCC) with psychiatrically hospitalized adolescents. *Child Maltreatment, 5*(4), 364–372.

Saigh, P. A., Yasik, A. E., Oberfield, R. A., Green, B. L., Halamandaris, P. V., Rubenstein, H., et al. (2000). The children's PTSD Inventory: Development and reliability. *Journal of Traumatic Stress, 13*(3), 369–380.

Saylor, C. F., Swenson, C. C., Reynolds, S. S., & Taylor, M. (1999). The Pediatric Emotional Distress Scale: A brief screening measure for young children exposed to traumatic events. *Journal of Clinical Child Psychology, 28*(1), 70–81.

Scheeringa, M. S., & Haslett, N. (2010). The reliability and criterion validity of the Diagnostic Infant and Preschool Assessment: A new diagnostic instrument for young children. *Child Psychiatry and Human Development, 41*(3), 299–312.

Scheeringa, M. S., Peebles, C. D., Cook, C. A., & Zeanah, C. H. (2001). Toward establishing procedural, criterion, and discriminant validity for PTSD in early childhood. *Journal of the American Academy of Child & Adolescent Psychiatry, 40*(1), 52–60.

Scheeringa, M. S., Wright, M. J., Hunt, J. P., & Zeanah, C. H. (2006). Factors affecting the diagnosis and prediction of PTSD symptomatology in children and adolescents. *American Journal of Psychiatry, 163*(4), 644–651.

Scheeringa, M. S., & Zeanah, C. H. (1994). *PTSD semi-structured interview and observational record for Infants and Young Children*. New Orleans, LA: Department of Psychiatry and Neurology, Tulane University Health Sciences Center.

Scheeringa, M. S., & Zeanah, C. H. (2008). Reconsideration of harm's way: Onsets and comorbidity patterns of disorders in preschool children and their caregivers following Hurricane Katrina. *Journal of Clinical Child and Adolescent Psychology, 37*(3), 508–518.

Scheeringa, M. S., Zeanah, C. H., Drell, M. J., & Larrieu, J. A. (1995). Two approaches to the diagnosis of posttraumatic stress disorder in infancy and early childhood. *Journal of the American Academy of Child & Adolescent Psychiatry, 34*(2), 191–200.

Scheeringa, M. S., Zeanah, C. H., Myers, L., & Putnam, F. W. (2003). New findings on alternative criteria for PTSD in preschool children. *Journal of the American Academy of Child & Adolescent Psychiatry, 42*(5), 561–570.

Scheeringa, M. S., Zeanah, C. H., Myers, L., & Putnam, F. W. (2005). Predictive validity in a prospective follow-up of PTSD in preschool children. *Journal of the American Academy of Child & Adolescent Psychiatry, 44*(9), 899–906.

Seeley, S. M. K., Perosa, S. L., & Perosa, L. M. (2004). A validation study of the Adolescent Dissociative Experiences Scale. *Child Abuse & Neglect, 28*(7), 755–769.

Silverman, W. K., & Albano, A. M. (1996). *Anxiety Disorders Interview Schedule for Children for DSM-IV: Child and parent versions.* San Antonio, TX: The Psychological Corporation, Harcourt, Brace.

Silverman, W. K., Saavedra, L. M., & Pina, A. A. (2001). Test-retest reliability of anxiety symptoms and diagnoses with the anxiety disorders interview schedule for DSM-IV: Child and parent versions. *Journal of the American Academy of Child & Adolescent Psychiatry, 40,* 937–944.

Sim, L., Friedrich, W. N., Davies, W. H., Trentham, B., Lengua, L., & Pithers, W. (2005). The Child Behavior Checklist as an indicator of posttraumatic stress disorder and dissociation in normative, psychiatric, and sexually abused children. *Journal of Traumatic Stress, 18*(6), 697–705.

Smith, P., Perrin, S., Dyregrov, A., & Yule, W. (2003). Principal components analysis of the Impact of Event Scale with children in war. *Personality and Individual Differences, 34*(2), 315–322.

Smith,S., & Carlson, E. (1997). Reliability and validity of the Adolescent Dissociative Experiences Scale. *Dissociation, 9,* 125–129.

Spilsbury, J. C., Drotar, D., Burant, C., Flannery, D., Creeden, R., & Friedman, S. (2005). Psychometric properties of the Pediatric Emotional Distress Scale in a diverse sample of children exposed to interpersonal violence. *Journal of Clinical Child and Adolescent Psychology, 34*(4), 758–764.

Spilsbury, J. C., Fletcher, K. E., Creeden, R., & Friedman, S. (2008). Psychometric properties of the Dimensions of Stressful Events Rating Scale. *Traumatology, 14*(4), 116–130.

Stallard, P., Velleman, R., & Baldwin, S. (1999). Psychological screening of children for post-traumatic stress disorder. *Journal of Child Psychology and Psychiatry, 40*(7), 1075–1082.

Steinberg, A., Brymer, M., Decker, K., & Pynoos, R. (2004). The University of California at Los Angeles post-traumatic stress disorder reaction index. *Current Psychiatry Reports, 6*(2), 96–100.

Stover, C. S., & Berkowitz, S. (2005). Assessing violence exposure and trauma symptoms in young children: A critical review of measures. *Journal of Traumatic Stress, 18*(6), 707–717.

Strand, V. C., Sarmiento, T. L., & Pasquale, L. E. (2005). Assessment and screening tools for trauma in children and adolescents: A review. *Trauma, Violence, & Abuse, 6*(1), 55–78.

Wherry, J. N., Neil, D., & Taylor, T. (2009). Pathological dissocation as measured by the Child Dissociative Checklist. *Journal of Child Sexual Abuse, 18,* 93–102.

Winston, F. K., Kassam-Adams, N., Garcia-España, F., Ittenbach, R., & Cnaan, A. (2003). Screening for risk of persistent posttraumatic stress in injured children and their parents. *Journal of the American Medical Association, 290*(5), 643–649.

Wolfe, V. V., Gentile, C., & Wolfe, D. A. (1989). The impact of sexual abuse on children: A PTSD formulation. *Behavior Therapy, 20*(2), 215–228.

Wolpaw, J. M., Ford, J. D., Newman, E., Davis, J. L., & Briere, J. (2005). Trauma Symptom Checklist for Children. In T. Grisso, G. Vincent, & D. Seagrave (Eds.), *Handbook of mental health screening and assessment for juvenile justice* (pp. 152–165). New York: Guilford.

Wood, J. J., Piacentini, J. C., Bergman, R. L., McCracken, J., & Barrios, V. (2002). Concurrent validity of the anxiety disorders section of the Anxiety Disorders Interview Schedule for DSM-IV: Child and parent versions. *Journal of Clinical Child and Adolescent Psychology, 31*(3), 335–342.

Yasik, A. E., Saigh, P. A., Oberfield, R. A., Green, B., Halamandaris, P., & McHugh, M. (2001). The validity of the children's PTSD Inventory. *Journal of Traumatic Stress, 14*(1), 81–94.

Yates, T. M., Dodds, M. F., Sroufe, L. A., & Egeland, B. (2003). Exposure to partner violence and child behavior problems: A prospective study controlling for child-directed abuse and neglect, child cognitive ability, socioeconomic status, and life stress. *Development and Psychopathology, 15,* 199–218.

Yule, W. (1997). Anxiety, depression, and posttraumatic stress disorder in children. In I. Sclare (Ed.), *The NFER Child Portfolio.* Windsor: NFER-Nelson.

Yule, W., Ten Bruggencate, S., & Joseph, S. A. (1994). Principal components analysis of the Impact of Events Scale in adolescents who survived a shipping disaster. *Personality and Individual Differences, 16*(5), 685–691.

CHAPTER

19 Psychometric Concerns in the Assessment of Trauma-related Symptoms in Older Adults

Willeke H. van Zelst *and* Aartjan T. F. Beekman

Abstract

Assessment of PTSD in older adults is still in its infancy despite reflections on this subject in past literature. Factors that influence assessment are: traumas that occurred long in the past, lower prevalence, the fact that older people complain less, more misinterpretation of avoiding and intrusion, more somatic comorbidity and higher risk of cognitive impairment. The Clinician Administered PTSD Scale (CAPS) is mostly used to diagnose PTSD, but less researched in older age. Only two screening instruments have been validated, the PTSD Checklist (PCL) and the Self Rating Inventory for PTSD (SRIP), but cross-validation has still to be done. The PCL scale has been used more often and is also suitable for clinician rating, which is considered more appropriate for older adults. Biological measures have not yet been adapted for assessment in the complex biological systems of older age. Multimethod assessment is becoming more important and can address many of the difficulties in this field. Finally, much can be learned from knowledge already acquired from younger adults.

Key Words: PTSD, assessment, elderly, validation, efficiency, prevalence, cognitive

Psychometric Concerns in the Assessment of Trauma-related Symptoms in Older Adults

General Considerations

Assessing posttraumatic stress disorder (PTSD) in older adults is still in its infancy, although various investigators illuminated the issue in the past and called for more research (Cook & O'Donell, 2005; Falk, Hersen, & Van Hasselt, 1994; Hyer et al., 1992; Neal, Hill, Hughes, Middleton, & Busuttil, 1995). Well-considered concepts of how to measure PTSD in the elderly, as well as psychometric instruments designed specifically for the old (e.g., 70+) or very old (e.g., 80+), are conspicuously missing (Cook, Elhai, & Arean, 2005). However, there are five factors that deserve consideration when PTSD is investigated in older persons (Averill & Beck, 2000; Falk et al., 1994; Owens, Baker, Kasckow, Ciesla, & Mohamed, 2005).

First, older persons are less accurate in reporting their events as traumatic (Acierno et al., 2002); have fewer complaints (Acierno, Ruggiero, Kilpatrick, Resnick, & Galea, 2006); and they tend to have subthreshold symptoms instead of full PTSD more often than younger adults (van Zelst, de Beurs, Beekman, Deeg, & van Dyck, 2003). Prevalence rates are lower (Creamer & Parslow, 2008; de Vries & Olff, 2009; Frueh et al., 2007; Gum & Cheavens, 2008; Kohn, Vicente, Saldivia, Rioseco, & Torres, 2008; Norris, 1992), even in special groups (Flint et al., 2010), although there are ethnic differences (Jimenez, Alegria, Chen, Chan, & Laderman, 2010). This may be the result of selection bias or the fact that older adults report other forms of psychopathology, such as more isolated anxiety symptoms or depression or personality changes (Cook, 2002). The consequences of low prevalence rates imply that measurement instruments need to be very sensitive to detect PTSD in older adults.

Second, older adults report their symptoms of anxiety and depression less accurately (Wetherell et al., 2009). They tend to classify symptoms as neither anxiety nor depression. This suggests that older adults might be less able to identify, and therefore seek appropriate treatment for, their complaints. Consequently, measurements should facilitate recognition and choices between clear-cut affective items.

Third, cognitive problems can interfere with posttraumatic symptoms (Carlson, Lauderdale S, Hawkins, & Sheikh, 2008; Colenda et al., 2010; Cook, Ruzek, & Cassidy, 2003; Yaffe et al., 2010), not only because memory impairment is more general in old age as was conceptualized by earlier research (Barrett, Green, Morris, Giles, & Croft, 1996; Zeiss & Dickman, 1989), but also because of increased memory impairment accompanying PTSD itself (Yaffe et al., 2010). Therefore, instruments should help to shape features in items that are easily recognized by older individuals. Additionally, PTSD with memory impairment is often accompanied by aggressive behavior (Carlson et al., 2008; Verma et al., 2001). Although research is limited and only executed in long-term care facilities, aggression appeared to be a component of PTSD and was not due to cognitive impairment itself (Carlson et al., 2008). Older trauma survivors entering a long-term care setting are already upset by retirement, loss of independence, and health, and they may be faced with trauma reminders that reactivate PTSD (e.g., seeing bedridden patients, hearing delirant moaning and shouting, hearing loud-speaking care providers). Questionnaires should include measurements of aggression either internally manifested or overtly expressed (Carlson et al., 2008).

Fourth, older persons have more somatic complaints, which they express more readily and which may mask existing PTSD symptoms (Hyer, Summers, Braswell, & Boyd, 1995; Sperr, Sperr, Craft, & Boudewyns, 1990; van Zelst, de Beurs, Beekman, van Dyck, & Deeg, 2006). To overcome this problem in assessment, somatic complaints should be phrased in terms of the physical consequences of tension and burdensome thoughts concerning traumatic events.

Finally, there is a failure to assess a broad range of stressor events (Breslau & Kessler, 2001; Elklit & O'Connor, 2005; Resnick, Falsetti, & Kilpatrick, 1996; Weathers & Keane, 2007). It is recognized that there is no one-to-one relationship between exposure to a stressor and the development of PTSD and that we can only identify the proximal event that activates the disorder (Averill & Beck, 2000). However, there are events that have happened in the distant past (Acierno et al., 2007) and events that happen in old age itself. In the case of past events, there may be an episodic course to PTSD and recent triggers that cause symptoms to resurface (van Zelst, deBeurs, Beekman, Deeg, Bramsen, et al., 2003). In particular, factors associated with aging may be retraumatizing (Sadavoy, 1997). Recent distress reinforces memories of past traumatic experiences and can trigger new feelings of loss, stress, and grief (Busuttil, 2004; Lantz & Buchalter, 2001). Unresolved conflicts may resurface in the face of new stressors (Salerno & Nagy, 2002). Even the death of a pet can instigate PTSD (Adrian, Deliramich, & Frueh, 2009). These factors broaden the range of stressor events in old age.

Another aspect of current approaches to defining traumatic events is the fact that somatic illnesses are typically excluded in the lists of possible traumatic events; increasingly, life-threatening illness is recognized as traumatic, especially over the life course (Alonzo, 2000). Additionally, somatic events are more frequent in old age (van Zelst et al., 2006). Because distressing public events influence the mean scores on a PTSD rating scale (van Zelst, de Beurs, & Smit, 2003), cumulative life-event distress suggests that the present impact of past trauma should be considered in a life span perspective (Elder & Clipp, 1989; Kahana & Kahana, 1998). Even with the same background of being a war veteran, major differences in outcome exist between experiences in Korea or other combat theaters (Brooks & Fulton, 2010). Instruments should enable a broad range of possible events to be kept in mind when checking the features of potentially traumas. As already mentioned, the problem is that older people may not label events as traumatic (Acierno et al., 2002; Cook, 2002). However, research has supported better reporting of trauma exposure when queries are more specific (Cook, Elhai, Cassidy, et al., 2005) or when respondents are prompted by a trauma questionnaire (Witteveen, Bramsen, Hovens, & van der Ploeg, 2005).

Factors that may be important in the use of any assessment instrument in older age are: use of plain language, questions that are not confusing in relation to somatic complaints, and questions that do not give reason for shame or guilt (Falk et al., 1994). Older adults are not acquainted with the specific terminology of younger generations and phrasing should be prudent. The length of the self-report or interview needs to be limited in order to reduce fatigue in older subjects who also are disabled, dysphasic, or cognitively impaired. In the practical implementation of tests for older adults, self-rating may be unrealistic.

Measuring PTSD

Approaches to measuring PTSD can be divided into a clinical interview approach and a psychometric approach that can be either rational (e.g., assessing whether symptoms necessary for a *DSM* diagnosis are present or absent) or empirical (e.g., symptom descriptions, statements, and other stimuli are used that can identify cases empirically and that are found by comparing individuals with and without PTSD). This empirical approach is elaborated in the statistical approach, which will be discussed at the end of this chapter.

Diagnostically Oriented Instruments (Clinician-administered, Self-report)

Structured Clinical Interview for the DSM

Although PTSD was introduced to the *DSM-III* in 1980, the module targeted to that disorder in the Structured Clinical Interview for the *DSM* (SCID; Spitzer & Williams, 1984) was only published after the arrival of the *DSM-III-R* in 1992, although it was already used for veterans in the National Vietnam Veterans Readjustment (NVVR) study (Kulka et al., 1990). At this point, the SCID had not been used often with older adults. Furthermore, to date there are very little data on its psychometric properties, or regarding its successor, the SCID-I (First, Spitzer, Gibbon, & Williams, 1996), either in general or on the PTSD section, let alone in older adults. However, this instrument often is used to standardize other instruments (Wilson & Keane, 2004). It may be that the scale is beyond psychometric testing because it was the first scale ever and is simply asking whether a symptom of the *DSM* is present or absent. That is exactly the idea behind the *DSM*: one should make an inventory of symptoms that are evident and there is no other way than posing the question to determine if it is present. As noted by Meehl (1995), this approach is the consequence of the evidentiary approach instead of the definatory approach of the *DSM-IV*). Kulka et al. (1991) assessed the reliability of SCID diagnosis for PTSD by reviewing 437 audiotaped sessions with Vietnam veterans with known clinical diagnosis who were interviewed by very experienced assessors. It resulted in changing the SCID diagnosis in only 10 (2.3%) because a clerical or clinical error was found. Subsequent blinded rescoring indicated high reliability (κ = .933). Hovens and colleagues (1992) compared SCID ratings with clinician ratings based on *DSM-III* criteria in 147 Dutch World War II Resistance veterans aged 60 to 65 years and found no statistical difference. Psychometric properties were calculated from the published results and are shown in table 19.1a and 1b. The SCID was used by Lenze et al. (2000) to investigate PTSD prevalence in a clinical and primary-care population of older adults.

Table 19.1a. Diagnostic instruments: psychometric properties in older age

Instrument/Study/Population	GS	Sens.	Spec.	PPV	NPV	Effic.	Remark
SI-PTSD/(Amaya-Jackson et al., 1999; Davidson et al., 1989) middle aged to old	SCID	.96	.80	.89	.92	.90	
SI-PTSD (Hovens, Bramsen, et al., 1994) mean age 50 years	CAPS	.85	.70			.76	α .96 49 items
SCID (Hovens et al., 1992) 147 male WWII Resistance mean age 64 years	Clinical Diagnosis	.92	.77	.79	.91	.94	
CAPS (Hovens,Klaarenbeek, et al., 1994) 76 Dutch traumatized Aged 60-65 years mean 60 years	Clinical Diagnosis	.74	.84				
CAPS (Blake et al., 1995)		.84	.95			.89	cut off: 65
CAPS-1 (Hyer & Boyd, 1996) 125 older KC and combat veterans mean age 70 years	SCID-DTREE	.90	.95	.92	.93	.93	prev. 40% at least 1 resp.2 on freq/ intensity

GS = Gold Standard; Sens. = Sensitivity; Spec. = Specificity; PPV = Positive Predictive Value; NPV = Negative Predictive Value; Effic. = Efficiency.

Table 19.1b. Diagnostic instruments: psychometric properties concerning validity in older age correlations

Instrument/population	Convergent Validity	Criterion Validity	Inter-rater	Crohn-bach's α	Test-retest
SI-PTSD (Hovens, Bramsen, et al., 1994)	M-PTSD .70 MMPI –PTSD .72 IES .61	.73			
SCID PTSD (Kulka et al., 1991) 437 NVVR veterans		Clinician review	.933		
CAPS (Blake et al., 1990) cut off:65 Pilot 25 (younger) veterans	M-PTSD .70 MMPI-PTSD .84		.77–.96	.85–.87	.90–.98
CAPS (Blake, 1994) 125 (younger) veterans	M-PTSD 0.91 MMPI-PTSD .77 BDI 0.74 MMPI-DEP .69	SCID .89		.94	
CAPS (Hovens, Klaaren-beek, et al., 1994) 76 traumatized subjects Mean age 60	IES 0.62 M-PTSD .73 MMPI-PTSD .74			Intr. .63 Av. .78 Hyp..79 Tot. .89	
CAPS (Hyer et al., 1996) 125 veterans Mean age 70 years	IES .81 M-PTSD .61	SCID-DTREE	excellent	.95 T .88 I .87A .88 H	

The SCID-I was recently used to measure the prevalence of anxiety disorders in older people in Turkey (Kirmizioglu, Dogan, Kugu, & Akyuz, 2009). See table 19.2.

Clinician Administered PTSD Scale

The Clinician Administered PTSD Scale (CAPS; Blake et al., 1990) has been the most widely used structured interview for diagnosis in adults (Weathers, Keane, & Davidson, 2001). However, publications related to older age are limited. The advantages of this scale include the possibility to assess a range of rating options instead of merely the presence or absence of symptoms. These options allow rating on a continuous scale. Frequency and intensity are assessed separately, which makes it possible to follow presence and intensity of PTSD symptoms in time and tracking the lifetime course of PTSD. With a five-point Likert scale for 17 *DSM*-based questions and 8 additional behavior-anchored questions, the total score on the CAPS can range from 0 to 136. Originally, this instrument covered *DSM-III-R* criteria and now the CAPS 1 is based on the *DSM-IV*, determining current (previous month) and lifetime PTSD. From the beginning, the CAPS covered Criterion F, concerning distress or impaired functioning in important areas of life. In the first pilot study, interrater reliability was .92 to .99, which may have been inflated because ratings were made during the same interview (Weathers & Litz, 1994). The CAPS 2 was designed to assess symptoms in the previous week and was meant for frequent application (Blake, 1994; Blake et al., 1995). Currently, the CAPS consists of 30 carefully worded interview questions that target *DSM-IV* criteria for PTSD without leading the respondent. These items assess core PTSD symptoms and related issues. The scale also offers an optional Life Events Checklist, with 17 items, that can be completed by the patient to help identify precipitating traumatic events. Content, criterion, and construct validity are considered to be quite good in general, but not especially in relation to older adults. A possible disadvantage of the CAPS is the need for an additional trauma questionnaire. However, the Life Events Checklist, which accompanies the CAPS, does measure the presence or absence of traumatic life events.

Table 19.2. **Diagnostic interviews for PTSD used in research of older persons**

Diagnostic interview	Authors	Population	PTSD prevalence/ Remark
SI-PTSD	Davidson et al., 1990	25 younger Vietnam veterans and 19 older WWII veterans mean age 63	
DIS	Davidson et al., 1991	444 elderly Piedmont USA	0.4
CAPS (Blake, 1994)	Schnurr et al. 2002	436 Veteran Affair/Normative Aging Study	0.5 current 1.5 lifetime
CAPS	Magruder et al., 2005	Veterans in 4 centers primary care. 210 65–74 yr 109 75–79 yr	3.3 1-month 10.1 1-month
SCID	Lenze et al., 2000	182 depressed primary care aged 60-93	Current 0.6 Lifetime 1.7
SCID-I	Kirmizioglu et al., 2009	462 Turkey elderly 65–69 70–74 75–79 >80	2.4 1.4 1.4 0.0 Total 1.9
SCID DSMIV-TR (First et al., 1996)	Flint et al., 2010	60 + participants of a RCT in MD + psychotic features	Strong selected group: 2.1
DSM-III questions by telephone	Acierno et al., 2002	55+ women National Women Study	Lifetime Avoidance 16.6 Arousal 21.1 Re-experience 11.5
CIDI	Kohn et al, 2005	103 60+ after Hurricane Mitch	13.6
CIDI	Ford et al., 2007	African Americans 364 55–64 283 64–74 139 ≥75	12- month PTSD 2.85
WMH-CIDI (Kessler & Ustun, 2004)	Alegria et al., 2007	231 older American Latinos	Lifetime/12-month anxiety diagnosis including PTSD
CIDI	Trollor et al., 2007	1792 Australian NMHWS 65+	12- month PTSD: 0.2 1-month PTSD: 0.2
CIDI	Creamer et al., 2008	1792 Australian NMHWS 65+	12- month PTSD: 0.2
CIDI	de Vries et al., 2009	180 representative elderly Netherlands 65–80 yr	Lifetime 2.7
CIDI	Gum et al., 2009	5692 NCS-R (USA) 65–74 75+	12-month PTSD 0.4 (0.6) (0.2)
CIDI	Sharon et al., 2009	145 Holocaust survivors Israel WMHS	Lifetime 3.8
WMH-CIDI (Kessler et al., 2004)	Jimenez et al., 2010	2375 community and noninstitutional different older ethnic minorities	12-month PTSD: 0.4–2.2 Lifetime 2.3–4.8

(continued)

Table 19.2. Diagnostic interviews for PTSD used in research of older persons (*continued*)

Diagnostic interview	Authors	Population	PTSD prevalence/ Remark
WMH-CIDI(Kessler et al., 2004)	Byers et al., 2010	NCS–R 55-64 NCS–R 65-74 NCS–R 75-85 NCS–R 85+	1114: 12-month 4.7 813: 12-month 0.6 526: 12-month 0.1 122: 12-month 0.7
WMH-CIDI(Kessler et al., 2004)	Sharon et al., 2009	145 community-dwelling Holocaust survivors mean age 75	Lifetime and 12-month anxiety rate including PTSD 7 rep 23 x higher
DSM-IV hierarchy-free	Kim & Choi, 2010	223 older Asian 60+	12-month
DSM-IV PTSD	Simpson et al., 1996	350 consecutive patients Old Age Psychiatry Manchester	Crime-related prevalence 1.4
ICD-9-CM (World Health Organisation, 1992)	Yaffe et al., 2010	181093 veterans 55+ (53155 PTSD+)	Study not suitable for measurement of prevalence
ICD-10	Trollor et al., 2007	1792 Australian 65+	12 month 1.0 1-month 0.5
DSM-IV checklist for PTSD (own design) Score/IES	Joffe et al., 2003	Sydney Holocaust Study Holocaust survivors N = 100 age: 74.1 Refugees N=50 age: 75.5 Australian/English N=50 age: 76.6	 39% (IES:32.5) 12% (IES:10.3) 4% (IES:2.1)
ICD-10 PTSD checklist (own design)	Bowing et al., 2008	German clinic for gerontopsychiatry 12 psychotic 22 nonpsychotic	Late PTSD mean age 80 mean age 74

WMH = World Mental Health.

Concerning older persons, the CAPS was first used by Hyer and colleagues (1992; Hyer, Summers, Boyd, Litaker, & Boudewyns, 1996) in older combat veterans. See table 19.1a and 19.1b. These investigators concluded that older veterans might have a different symptom presentation and intensity level of PTSD. Besides, prevalence rates may differ as function of various settings, type of sample, and intensity of trauma. Moreover, Hyer et al. (1992) cautioned that norming the CAPS solely on Vietnam veterans may be inadequate for other older persons. Another weakness mentioned was the fact that comorbidity was not addressed. However, the subjects in the sample were not seeking compensation and were generally healthy (Hyer et al., 1996). Soon after its introduction, the CAPS was used as the gold standard to measure convergent validity of other PTSD scales (e.g., the Impact of Event Scale, the Minnesota Multiphasic Personality Inventory, and the Mississippi Scale) in older persons (Neal et al., 1995). In a small study with 30 former prisoners of war, one-third had PTSD as measured with the CAPS. In 179 Cambodian refugees (mean age 55 years), 65% had PTSD according to *DSM-IV*. Importantly, the CAPS performed well in this study. Coefficient α was .92 and scores of cases and noncases were wide apart: mean score 65.3 (SD 18.1) versus 13.9 (SD 16.7) (Hinton et al., 2006).

Composite International Diagnostic Interview, Diagnostic Interview Sschedule, and Structured Interview for PTSD

Another structured interview based on the *DSM* proposed by the WHO is the Composite

International Diagnostic Interview (CIDI; Andrews & Peters, 1998) for trained lay interviewers. The CIDI is often used in epidemiological studies. It was the gold standard in the Longitudinal Aging Study Amsterdam (LASA), the first epidemiologic study to investigate the prevalence of PTSD in community-dwelling older adults (van Zelst, de Beurs, Beekman, Deeg, & van Dyck, 2003) and was used in several prevalence studies in older adults (Creamer & Parslow, 2008; de Vries & Olff, 2009; Ford et al., 2007; Gum, King-Kallimanis, & Kohn, 2009; Trollor, Anderson, Sachdev, Brodaty, & Andrews, 2007). See table 19.2.

Its predecessor, the Diagnostic Interview Schedule (DIS; Robins, Helzer, Croughan, & Ratcliff, 1981) was never used widely and was questioned for its sensitivity when administered by a nonclinician (Kulka et al., 1988). It was used in one of the first prevalence studies by Davidson (Davidson, Hughes, Blazer, & George, 1991), which contained 447 elderly persons, comprising 15% of the total sample of a larger study (see table 19.2). Psychometric properties for the PTSD section of the DIS in elderly are not published.

The Structured Interview for PTSD (later SIP) has not been used in the oldest old, but was developed with 116 middle-aged and older veterans by Davidson and colleagues (Davidson, Smith, & Kudler, 1989). It contains 13 items, each ranging from 0 to 4 and each symptom can be rated for present state and for worst ever. Validated against the SCID, it performed well (for worst ever state) in 51 veterans (Davidson et al., 1989). Davidson and colleagues also used the SIP in 19 WWII veterans (mean age 63) who had a mean score of 22.9 (Davidson, Kudler, Saunders, & Smith, 1990). The SIP was used by Hovens and colleagues (Hovens, van der Ploeg, Bramsen, et al., 1994) for the development of a screening instrument, the (Dutch) Self-rating Inventory for PTSD, which followed the *DSM-III* and was used in 135 inhabitants of the Netherlands with trauma, including 76 older military war survivors (Hovens, van der Ploeg, Bramsen, et al., 1994).The SIP consists of 47 items. It should be noted that the 22-item *DSM-III-R* subscale was developed into a screening instrument: the Self-Rating Inventory for PTSD (SRIP), which was validated for older adults (see below). Several studies used other diagnostic interviews for older adults (see table 19.2), but these studies provided no information concerning validity of the instruments that were used.

Self-report Instruments

The Impact of Event Scale

The Impact of Event Scale (IES), and later IES-Revised (IES-R; Weiss, 2004), comprises 22 items rated on a five-point Likert-type scale (0–4). The IES was originally designed to assess the degree of symptomatic response to a specific traumatic exposure in the previous week (Horowitz, Wilner, & Alvarez, 1979). However, the IES was not designed as a diagnostic instrument because hyper-arousal items were not included in the original questionnaire, although threshold scores are often provided (Joseph, 2000). Moreover, in older adults (mean age 60 years), the IES-R was not found to be a good screening instrument (Witteveen et al., 2005). It was recommended in pharmacological trials to identify and monitor individuals who need treatment (Sundin & Horowitz, 2002). The IES was first researched in older individuals by Neal and colleagues (Neal et al., 1995). The CAPS intrusion subscales and the IES intrusion subscales are highly correlated ($r = .71$). However, contrary to what might be expected, the IES avoidance subscale was moderately correlated with the CAPS intrusion subscales ($r =.61$), but poorly ($r = .42$) with the avoidance/numbing subscale of the CAPS. In contrast, both IES subscales correlated even better with each other in older individuals ($r = .71$) than in younger subjects ($r = .42$; Horowitz et al., 1979). The authors speculated that this elderly population had misinterpreted the meaning of avoidance subscale questions and tended to respond as if the questions were about intrusive symptoms.

Furthermore, it was found that with the recommended cut-off score, sensitivity was low in the IES (and the Mississippi-PTSD scale). However, with cut-off scores at maximum sensitivity of 100%, the specificity and positive predicted values became unacceptably low: .38 and .41, respectively. In populations with lower prevalence rates, these figures would be even worse. These findings were replicated by Witteveen et al. (2005). See table 19.3 and table 19.4. In the later revised form (Weiss, 2004) the internal consistency of the total score of the IES, as well as the subscales, was high for a late middle-aged population of Vietnam veterans aged 51.1 on average (SD 4.4; Creamer, Bell, & Failla, 2003). However, in a confirmatory factor analysis, the three-factor model did not obtain good fit indices, whereas a one- or two-factor model seemed to show a better level of fit. This was

Table 19.3. **Other self-report instruments: psychometric properties in older age**

Instrument/study	GS	Sensitivity	Specificity	PPV	NPV	Effic.	Remark
MMPI-PK (Query et al., 1986) 69 POWs Mean age 63		.67	.88	.67	.88		Cut-off:17 Prev.: 26%
MMPI- PK (Kulka et al., 1991) 130 veterans preliminary NVVRS	SCID and chart diagnosis	.901	.688			.815	κ: .605 Cut-off:14
MMPI- PK (Kulka et al., 1991) 343 Vietnam Theater Veterans (NVVRS)	SCID	.72	.82				κ: .478 cut-off:14
MMPI-PK (Hyer et al., 1992) 15 PTSD inpatients 20 POW > 60 years	DSM-III-R	.83	.79	.92	.69	.80	Cut-off:34
MMPI-PK (Neal et al., 1994) 30 POW mean age 75 (70–85)	CAPS	.89 1.00	.62 .42				Cut-off:17 30% PTSD Cut-off:13
IES (Lillywhite & Neal, 1993; Neal et al., 1994) 30 POW mean age 75 (70–85)	CAPS	.67 1.00	.57 .38				Cut-off:35 Cut-off:16
IES (Witteveen et al., 2005) 74 older adults with war trauma mean age 60 years. Same as (Hovens et al., 1994b)	CAPS	.91.77 .63 .31 .29 .03	.33 .51 .61 .92 97 1.00	.55 .59 .58 .79 .90 1.00	.81 .71 .63 .60 .60 .53		Cut-off:15 Cut-off:36 Cut-off:40 Cut-off:52 Cut-off:60 Cut-off:70
M-PTSD (Kulka et al., 1991) 225 veterans preliminary NVVRS	SCID and chart diagnosis	.940	.787			.889	κ: .753 Cut-off:89
M-PTSD (Kulka et al., 1991) 343 Vietnam Theater Veterans (NVVRS)	SCID	.77	.83				K: .528 Cut-off:89
M-PTSD (Hyer et al., 1992) 15 PTSD inpatients 20 POW > 60 years;	DSM-III-R	1.00	.93	.88	.74	.97	Cut-off:100
M-PTSD (Neal et al., 1995)	CAPS	.33 100	1.00 .42				Cut-off:107 Cut-off:79

GS = Gold Standard, PPV = Positive Predictive Value, NPV = Negative Predictive Value; Effic. = Efficiency.

thought to be due to the sample, who had suffered traumas in the distant past. Subsequent research by Beck et al. (2008) with 182 victims of a serious motor vehicle accident aged 18 to 79 years (mean 49. 9) demonstrated that the IES-R is still not an optimal screening instrument, but a sound measure for both clinical and research purposes. The measure showed good psychometric properties. It had a five-factor model in a large cross-validated war sample (Morina et al., 2010). The scale was recommended to measure posttrauma phenomena that can augment related assessments, but no further research in elderly adults has been conducted to date.

Table 19.4. Other self-report instruments used in research with older people

Instrument	Authors	Population	PTSD prevalence/remark
MMPI-2-PK	Kubzansky et al., 2007	Normative Aging Study 944 elderly Mean age 60 years	Cut-off:28. Low prevalence. Correlation with risk CHD
M-PTSD	Kubzansky et al., 2007	Normative Aging Study 944 elderly Mean age 60 years	Cut off:9. Low prevalence Correlation with risk CHD
M-PTSD	Cook, Cassidy, et al., 2005	Long-term care 65+ veterans	Cut-off:89
M-PTSD	James et al., 2007	291 older nurses	Association impact with age
M-PTSD	Rintamaki et al., 2009	157 older POWs of WWII	
IES	Witteveen et al., 2005	Same as Hovens, Klaarenbeek, et al., 1994. 74 veterans	Int. subscale Avoid. subcale Intercorrelated $r=.79$
IES	Strug et al. 2009	24 older Hispanic citizens of New York	
TSI	Higgins & Follette, 2002	102 60+ women mean age 74	40 item 4-point scale

Int. = Intrusion; Avoid. = Avoidance. CHD = Coronary Heart Disease.

The Mississippi Scale

The Mississippi Scale for Combat-Related PTSD (M-PTSD; Keane, Caddell, & Taylor, 1988), later named Civilian Mississippi Scale (CMS; Lauterbach, Vrana, King, & King, 1997) is a 35-item measure of PTSD symptoms and associated features. Items are rated on a five-point Likert scale and scores range from 35 to 175. A diagnostic cut-off score of 89 has been supported (Kulka et al., 1990). It was validated in older subjects (Hyer et al., 1992; Neal et al., 1995). See table 19.3.The mean score in long-term care older veterans was 71.12 (SD 16.79), as noted by Cook and colleagues (Cook, Elhai, Cassidy, et al., 2005) and the M-PTSD correlated well with the PTSD checklist (0.70). Unfortunately, the complicated response format was not easily understood by this population, who struggled with response options shifting direction and wording. However, it was used in convergent validation of other studies. See table 19.1b.

The Minnesota Multiphasic Personality Inventory–PTSD Subscale

The Minnesota Multiphasic Personality Inventory–PTSD (MMPI-PTSD) will be discussed here because it is often researched together with the self-report scales such as the IES and the M-PTSD, but in the strictest sense of the word it is not a self-report scale. The MMPI-PTSD was one of the first scales tested to identify PTSD in older adults with a single index instead of a multimethod approach (Query, Megran, & McDonald, 1986). This 49-item subscale was developed by Keane and colleagues in Vietnam veterans and had a sensitivity of .82 with a cut-off point of 30 (Keane, Malloy, & Fairbank, 1984). In 69 older POWs (mean age around 63 years), this cut-off had to be lowered to 17 where it correctly identified 67% of the PTSD+ subjects. However, 12% of the PTSD-subjects also scored above this cut-off (Query et al., 1986). The scale was used for convergent validation in older subjects in several studies. See table 19.1b. Its successor, the MMPI-2, was based on larger samples, more representative for the general U.S. population, and it showed a high degree of comparability in relation to the PTSD subscale (Litz et al., 1991). The MMPI-2-PK contains 46 items and also is named Keane PTSD Scale. However, it should not be used as the sole basis for a diagnosis. To date, cut-off scores of 28 (Lyons & Wheeler-Cox, 1999) and 30 points (Scotti, Sturges, & Lyons, 1996) have been recommended. It was used in elderly in the Normative Aging Study (Kubzansky, Koenen, Spiro III, Vokonas, & Sparrow, 2007) to research whether PTSD is associated with increased risk of coronary heart disease. See table 19.4. The other subscale for PTSD in the MMPI-2, the PS from Schlenger and Kulka (1987), which has 14 additional items, needs more research (Lyons & Wheeler-Cox, 1999).

Screening Instruments

The advantages of screening instruments in older adults are their brevity, which make them suitable even in the elderly who may fatigue easily, and their broad applicability to assess trauma-related symptoms following all kinds of stressors. Screening instruments are accepted well in this age group and can be a first probe for the presence of PTSD, which may be diagnosed subsequently using a more extensive assessment instrument. In addition, if severity measures are used, they can serve to track the longitudinal course of PTSD. Although many screeners have been developed, only two have been validated in older adults. Psychometric properties of screening instruments used in older adults are listed in table 19.5.

PTSD Checklist

The PTSD Checklist (PCL) was originally developed by Weathers (Weathers, Litz, Huska, & Keane, 1994). It follows the 17 items of the *DSM-IV* and is rated on a five-point Likert scale measuring severity in the previous month (e.g., 1 = not at all; 5 = extremely). Three adult versions exist: a military (PCL-M) version, a specified civilian version (PCL-S), and an unspecified civilian version (PCL-C). Test-retest reliability was .88 and internal consistency was .94 in younger populations of motor vehicle accidents and sexual assault (Blanchard, Jones-Alexander, Buckley, & Forneris, 1996). In 2005, Cook reported on the psychometric properties of the PCL in community-dwelling older adults attending primary care services (Cook, Elhai, & Arean, 2005). The researchers selected 142 older adults

Table 19.5a. Screening instruments: psychometric properties in older age

Instrument/study	GS	Sensitivity	Specificity	PPV	NPV	Effic.	Remark
PCL (Cook, Cassidy, et al., 2005) 142 primary care 65+	PCL-algorithm	.96	.92	.71	.99	.93	Post-hoc cut-off:37
PCL (Hudson et al., 2008) 100 65+ patients	CAPS	.4 .9	.97 .87	.45			Cut-off:50 Cut-off:36
PCL (Yeager et al., 2007) 840 mixed age (stratified)	CAPS	81.05 52.63	81.22 94.90	35.49 56.82	97.11 94.02	81.19 90.12	Cut-off:31 Cut-off:50
SPAN (Yeager et al., 2007) 840 mixed age mean >54 years (stratified)	CAPS	73.68	81.99	34.28	95.07	81.05	Cut-off:5
SRIP (van Zelst, Bramsen, et al., 2003) 1721 community-dwelling older adults	CIDI (in 422 older adults	22.6 74.2	97.8 81.4	17.1 7.4	98.4 99.4	.90	Cut-off:52 Cut-off:39 two phase sample design

Table 19.5b. Screening instruments: psychometric properties concerning validity

Instrument/study	Convergent*	Criterion*	Inter-rater	Crohnbachs'α	Test-retest
PCL (Cook,Cassidy, et al., 2005) 35 long-term care veterans	M-PTSD .70			.87	
PCL (Schinka et al., 2007) 153 post-hurricane CCHAS participants 66–90				.87	
SRIP (Hovens, Bramsen, et al., 1994) Mixed-age population, cut-off:52	M-PTSD 0.83 MMPI-PK .78 IES .63	CAPS .75		(.92)	(.92)

CCHAS: Charlotte County Healthy Aging Study four-factor model intercorrelated χ^2 334.81.

from 1197 participants of a large western U.S. city who had traumatic events in the past, but no mental or substance use therapy. Potential participants were screened and selected if they were older than 65, had no current use of mental health or substance use, reported good cognitive functioning (Short Blessed Test < 17), and obtained any of the following: general health questionnaire ≥ 3, recent (binge) drinking, and suicidal ideation. The PCL algorithm diagnosis served as the gold standard instead of an interview-based diagnosis, which was acknowledged as a weakness of the study. With a Receiver Operating Characteristics analysis, the optimal cut-off was 37 points. PCL total scores for area under the curve was .98 (SE = .1). The same was found by Hudson, Beckford, Jackson, & Philpot (2008). They validated the PCL in 100 65+ elderly medical/psychiatric hospital cases and corrected the cut-off from 50 to 36 points with a ROC analysis against the CAPS. In this analysis, the sensitivity was good, but positive predictive value was poor. Yeager, Magruder, Knapp, Nicholas, & Frueh (2007) confirmed that the threshold of the PCL should be lowered to 31 in a large mixed-age sample (529 Caucasian veterans mean age 62.7 and 311 African-American veterans mean age 54.3). Surprisingly, ROC curves differed for race across age groups, but in the 65–80 age group no racial differences were noted. There were no differences for gender. As can be expected from the discussion above, in this non-PTSD- treatment-seeking population, cut-off scores were lower than in the treatment-seeking survivors of accidents in previous studies. Optimal threshold scores vary with the prevalence of PTSD in the researched populations. Remarkably, Hudson and colleagues (2008) found no effect on psychometric results of the PCL when analyses were repeated excluding those with organic impairment. Also, separating results for older adults with psychiatric versus medical disorders did not have appreciable differences.

In another study of Cook, Elhai, Cassidy, et al. (2005) among 35 long-term care veterans, the PCL and Mississippi-PTSD (M-PTSD) correlated well (r = .70), but both scales had nonsignificant correlations with the number of trauma types endorsed. However, the study was underpowered and would have had medium effect size correlations for PCL and number of trauma types if additional participants had been included.

In 2007, the confirmatory factor analysis of the PCL-C was researched in a sample of older hurricane survivors by Schinka, Brown, Borenstein, and Mortimer (2007). They examined nine models and found slightly stronger support for a four-factor intercorrelated model. This implies that there is a greater heterogeneity in symptom profiles among older adults when using this measure. However, in a four-factor intercorrelated model the following dimensions can be distinguished: re-experiencing, avoiding, numbing, and arousal.

Self Rating Inventory for PTSD

In an overview of published and diagnostically compared screening instruments (Brewin, 2005), only the Self Rating Inventory for PTSD (SRIP) was researched for application in older adults. This instrument was developed by Hovens and colleagues (Hovens, van der Ploeg, Bramsen, et al., 1994) and assesses *DSM* symptoms on a four-point scale (1 = not at all; 4 = extremely). In a well-documented sample of mixed-age adults with a trauma history and psychiatric outpatients, the cut-off scores were 52, but in 1721 community-dwelling elderly of the Longitudinal Aging Study Amsterdam, the optimal cut-off determined by Receiver Operating Characteristics analysis was 39 (van Zelst, de Beurs, Beekman, Deeg, Bramsen, et al., 2003). Decline of sensitivity has typically been observed in moving from clinical to community-based samples (Kulka et al., 1990). Several reviewers of PTSD instruments discussed the problem of diversity in validity samples in which screening instruments are developed (Kubany, Leisen, Kaplan, & Kelly, 2000; Norris & Riad, 1997). However, the SRIP had been validated in several categories of patients and high-risk populations (e.g., psychiatric patients and treatment-seeking as well as non-treatment-seeking traumatized veterans). Normative tables were published in more than 7000 older and younger adults (Hovens, Bramsen, & van der Ploeg, 2000). Test retest reliability was .92 and internal consistency was high (Crohnbach's α: .92). See table 19.5.

Other Screening Instruments Closely Following the DSM

The PTSD-Scale based on the *DSM-III-R* criteria adapted from Horowitz, Wilner, Kaltreider, and Alvarez (1980) was used in a small study comparing older adults who were child Holocaust survivors and who, respectively, did not know their biological ancestry (Amir & Lev-Wiesel, 2001). In this scale, 17 *DSM* items are rated on a four-point Likert scale and concern the last month. Crohnbach's α was .74, .83, and 0.83, respectively, for intrusion, avoidance, and arousal. No further validation was examined.

The Posttraumatic Symptom Scale (PSS), developed by Foa and colleagues (Foa, Riggs, Dancu, & Rothbaum, 1993) begins with a 12-item checklist of events and administers four questions on Criterion A2 before following with17 *DSM-III-R* items on a four-point Likert scale. It provides the opportunity to score severity. It has not yet been validated for older subjects.

Later, the Posttraumatic Diagnostic Scale (PDS) (Foa, 1995) appeared, which was based on *DSM-IV*. The PDS, also referred to as PTDS, was validated in a wide range of trauma victims aged 18–65 years (Foa, Cashman, Jaycox, & Perry, 1997).

No validated instrument was used in the study of Potts (1994) who examined civilian internees of Japan in WWII, including 72% of the sample aged 60 or older. Potts used a 22-item *DSMIII-R*-based questionnaire with a four-point scale ranging from 0 (never) to 3 (very often). The internal consistency was high: Crohnbach's α was .97 and .96, respectively, for scales concerning the past (six months immediate after release) and the present (most recent six months).

Likewise Brodaty, Joffe, Luscombe, and Thompson (2004), Joffe, Brodaty, Luscombe, and Ehrlich (2003) devised their own *DSM-IV*–based checklist of symptoms in their study of Holocaust survivors in Australia.

The Screen for Posttraumatic Stress Symptoms (SPTSS; Carlson, 2001) follows the 17 items of the *DSM* without a key to a particular trauma. The items are worded very simply, which provides a very low reading level. The average of 17 item scores is calculated, with each item rated on a 0–10 scale. The SPTSS was validated against the SI-PTSD in a mixed population of 136 inpatients and performed moderately with a sensitivity of .94 and specificity of .60 at cut-off score of 4,5. Its readability may be an advantage for older adults, but the scale has not been validated specifically for this population. See table 19.6.

Other Screening Instruments

The M-3 Checklist (Gaynes et al., 2010) combined a 27-item one-page screening tool for all anxiety disorders including PTSD and affective disorders, and was validated in 647 consecutive primary-care patients aged 18–92. It shows good properties, but no separate information on elderly was provided.

The SPAN, the four-item test (for Startle, Physiologic arousal, Anger, and Numbness) derived

Table 19.6. Screening instruments used in research with older people

Screening instrument	Authors	Population	PTSD prevalence remark
PCL	Magruder et al., 2004	203 65+ (40% of sample)/	
PCL-C	Hankin et al. 1999	2160 Veteran Health Study mean 62 yrs	20% PTSD with screener; true prevalence?
PCL Mississippi	Schnurr et al., 2002	436 Veteran Affair/Normative Aging Study/0.5%	Low PCL scores (20.6–25.1)
HTQ (Mollica et al., 1992)	Elklit et al., 2005	55 bereaved in Denmark/27% PTSD	Internal consistency .91
TSC (Briere et al., 1989)	Elklit et al., 2005	55 bereaved in Denmark/27% PTSD	Internal consistency .92
Potts PTS scale	Potts, 1994	184 Internees of Japanese in WWII	Internal consistency Present .96 Past .97
PTSS-10/IES R	Maercker, 2002	3 cases	
PTSS screen for cognitively Impaired	Carlson et al., 2008	32 long-term care	Observer reported vs. self-report only 2 current cases. No validation
BAI-PC	Mori et al., 2003	313 outpatients mean age 64 year	Cut-off:5 Good screener for PCL+ participants

from the Davidson Trauma Scale (Meltzer-Brody, Churchill, & Davidson, 1999), was researched in a large mixed-age group (529 Caucasian veterans mean age 62.7 and 311 African-American veterans mean age 54.3) and performed well at a cut-off score of 5 (Yeager et al., 2007). Sensitivity was 73.68 and specificity was 81.99 against the CAPS. There were no differences in ROC curves across age groups (<50; 50–64; 65–80) for race or gender. However, it was concluded from ROC curves that PCL performed better in identifying PTSD in this sample.

The Beck Anxiety Inventory—Primary Care version (BAI-PC)—was used as a PTSD screener in a mixed-age population of 313 Veteran Affairs outpatients in Boston with a mean age of 63.3 (SD 13.2) years (Mori et al., 2003). The seven items of BAI-PC correlated well ($r = .74$) with the full BAI. With a cut-off score of 5, the sensitivity of the BAI-PC was 97.2, specificity 72.6, and efficiency 0.75 against a PCL score of > 50 as the gold standard.

The Trauma Symptom Checklist (TSC) was used in a Danish study of bereaved elderly with an average age of 75 years (Elklit & O'Connor, 2005). It was developed to measure the impact of childhood abuse on later adult functioning. It consists of 33 items, but the TSC was slightly adapted; 3 questions were added and 3 questions on sexual activity were removed from the scale. Internal consistency was very good for the total score and acceptable for subscores except for interpersonal sensitivity and hostility. Other screening instruments were used in older adults in several studies (see table 19.5), but none published psychometrics separately.

Psychophysiological and Biological (e.g., Cortisol) Assessment

Studies that use psychophysiological or biological assessment in older adults are lacking. This is not surprising, as the research in this area is a minefield of confounding risk factors, contradictory findings, and overlapping outcomes. For example, Tucker and colleagues (2007) found higher blood pressure readings compared to controls during and after an interview in middle-aged survivors of the Oklahoma City bombing. However, the effect is only visible for the whole group and cannot be a diagnostic help in the individual, let alone in the older adult with more complex physiology and confounding medication use.

Facial EMG was once favored to determine PTSD (Carlson, Singelis, & Chemtob, 1997), but no subsequent publications were found. Orr and Pitman (1993) measured several physiological responses (heart rate, skin conductance, lateral frontalis electromyogram, corrugators electromyogram) during script-induced traumatic imagery in 25 middle-aged war veterans and found that skin-conductance response was the most reliable in discriminating PTSD+ patients from non-PTSD participants. However, the use of medication may have created a confound in this study. The medication problem exactly reflects the drawback in the application of these tests in older adults. Besides, the issue of arousal of sympatic nerve system is more complex than previously thought, because studies in younger PTSD subjects suggested that parasympatic influences on basal heart rate have to be taken into account also (Hopper, Spinazzola, Simpson, & van der Kolk, 2006).

With regard to physiology, researchers underscore the possibility of accelerated aging in PTSD with features of hippocampal damage (Bremner et al., 1995). This is probably the result of stress (LeDoux, 1996), but may be also a vulnerability factor (Gilbertson et al., 2002) and is related to subsequent dementia (Yaffe et al., 2010). High cortisol levels were found in cerebrospinal fluid of (presenile) demented individuals (Swaab et al., 1994). By contrast, in PTSD, down regulation of the hypothalamic-pituitary-adrenal axis was postulated (Yehuda, Halligan, Grossman, Golier, & Wong, 2002). However, down regulation was not found in female nurse Vietnam veterans (Metzger et al., 2008).

In PTSD, learning processes are compromised. Associative learning, using simple Pavlovian delay eyeblink conditioning as a startle response, was not found to discriminate for combat experience (Ayers, White, & Powell, 2003), but delay eyeblink conditioning by air puffs discriminates PTSD in older veterans (mean age > 53 years; Ginsberg, Ayers, Burriss, & Powell, 2008). See Table 19.7. Although interest has been expressed regarding the physiology of older individuals, no further studies have been conducted. Olfactory Identification (O.I.; Dileo, Brewer, Hopwood, Anderson, & Creamer, 2008) becomes another field of interest for research in older individuals. War veterans with PTSD who had a mean age of 58 years exhibited significant OI deficits (OIDs) despite good cognitive functioning. These deficits were significant predictors of aggression and impulsivity. It was concluded that the orbito-prefrontal dysfunction in the pathophysiology depicts underlying PTSD. How this test

Table 19.7. Other psychophysiological and biological assessments used in older age

Instrument	Author	Population	Outcome	Remark
Blood pressure	Tucker et al., 2007	60 survivors Oklahoma City bombing	Higher HR and blood pressures	Psychiatric reliance Middle aged
Olfactory identification	Dileo et al., 2008	31 war veterans	Correlation with PTSD and aggression	mean age 58 years
HR, SC, facial EMG	Orr et al., 1990; Orr et al., 1993	25 Vietnam veterans;18 healthy participants	Correlation with psychometric scales	Middle aged
Delay eyeblink conditioning (air puff)	Ginsberg et al., 2008	20 combat PTSD+ 16 combat PTSD- 30 noncombat	PTSD had deficits in EB conditioning	Correlation with HRV Mean age > 53 years

HR = Heart Rate; SC = Skin conductance; EMG = Electromyogram, EB = Eyeblink. HRV Heart rate variability.

performs in older populations is still unknown, but crucial for its potential use in the aged.

Behavioral Assessment and Assessment of Associated Features

Among older adults, behavioral assessment focusing on PTSD has targeted aggression in cognitively impaired elderly. Although aggression is fairly common in elderly patients with dementia (Brodaty & Low, 2003), aggression in PTSD is not found to be associated with the problem of cognitive impairment itself (Carlson et al., 2008). Moreover, prospective research does not support an increased risk of aggression in patients with a coexisting diagnosis of newly diagnosed dementia and PTSD (Ball et al., 2009). Therefore, aggression in cognitively impaired older adults with PTSD seems to be a problem depending on the setting in which they are located (e.g., long-term care facilities). For these settings, the scale for PTSD with aggression and cognitive impairment is useful, but still premature, because no validation has been published (Carlson et al., 2008).

Another phenomenon researched in older adults with PTSD is the intense and vivid relived intrusive memories that reappear after a very long silent interval with intense clarity and feeling of "nowness" across all sensory elements (Hiskey, Luckie, Davies, & Brewin, 2008). Components of this type of intrusion were always visual memories (e.g., seeing flames; seeing other people with injuries) and in more than half of the participants, physical memories (the shock of a gunshot wound, knotting of the stomach) and auditory memories (gunfire, the whiz of bombs). In one-third of the participants, olfactory intrusions (scorching flesh) were reported. These components of the memories can be scored on an analogical scale for vividness and nowness.

Shame and fear are features that are often cited in the literature related to PTSD in older individuals (Falk et al., 1994). The shame and fear may present true dissimilarities, but may also reflect cohort effects. Older participants are not used to self-disclosure (Fontana & Rosenheck, 1994) and have learned to "keep up appearances." Even more, self-disclosure was not socially accepted in their formative years and mental illness has had a stigma of weakness as long as they know (Nichols & Czirr, 1986). Men were expected to show self-reliance and women had to be subservient, and both ways of behavior prevent reporting traumas (Wolkenstein & Sterman, 1998). However, measuring shame as an associated feature did not differentiate between PTSD and non-PTSD according to the CAPS in the research of Hovens and colleagues (Hovens, van der Ploeg, Bramsen, et al., 1994). Some investigators suggested that in spite of that shame should be part of Criterion A2, which was extensively reviewed by Weathers and Keane (2007).

Future Directions

In the field of psychometrics of PTSD, more research is sorely needed. There is a dearth of information on the use of diagnostic and self-report instruments in old age. Commonly used screening instruments ought to be validated for older persons in independent populations. To date, scales have been adapted with post-hoc analyses (e.g., PCL, SRIP), but no further research has been conducted with these adapted scales. Other promising screening instruments have to be entirely adapted for older persons. Among these are the Penn Inventory (Hammarberg, 1992), the Davidson Trauma Scale (DTS; Davidson, Tharwani, & Connor, 2002; Sijbrandij, Olff, Opmeer, Carlier, & Gersons, 2008), the Short Posttraumatic Stress Disorder Rating Interview (SPRINT; Connor & Davidson, 2001), the Distressing Event Questionnaire (DEQ; Kubany et al., 2000), and BPTSD-12 and BPTSD-6 (Fullerton et al., 2000). Scales can be used depending on the research questions. Clustering of symptoms can help to identify suitable cases for treatment (Ehring, Kleim, Clark, Foa, & Ehlers, 2007). Multimodal assessments, using the strong features of each method (e.g., self-report, clinician interviews, and psychophysiological tests), and overcoming the psychometric limitations of a single instrument, can be developed to maximize correct diagnoses and add information particularly when measuring change (Cook, 2002; Monson et al., 2008). Moreover, a single-item PTSD screener performed very poorly in spite of the success of single-item screeners in depression (Gore, Engel, Freed, Liu, & Armstrong, 2008). A new development in the field concerns statistical prediction instruments. This approach uses the history of cases with known outcome to determine which risk factor is relevant given a diagnostic decision and to what extent (Marx et al., 2008). These approaches are especially promising in the elderly because of their long history colored by numerous, potential risk factors. The field of biological and psychophysiological assessments is still in its infancy and should be further developed before being used in older persons who already have a complex physiology and multi-morbidity, which may be partly due to a lifetime of stress factors. In short, the future of psychometrics of PTSD in older adults is useful and promising, but considerable work has to be done. Finally, future research of PTSD in older adults should go beyond a simple inventory of PTSD symptoms to examine in detail the life course of older subjects with PTSD, including early childhood trauma, distressing events, and psychiatric and somatic illnesses.

References

Acierno, R., Brady, K., Gray, M., Kilpatrick D., Resnick, H., & Best, C. (2002). Psychopathology following interpersonal violence: A comparison of risk factors in older and younger adults. *Journal of Clinical Geropsychology, 8*, 13–23.

Acierno, R., Lawyer, S. R., Rheingold, A., Kilpatrick, D. G., Resnick, H. S., & Saunders, B. E. (2007). Current psychopathology in previously assaulted older adults. *Journal of Interpersonal Violence, 22*, 250–258.

Acierno, R., Ruggiero, K. J., Kilpatrick, D. G., Resnick, H. S., & Galea, S. (2006). Risk and protective factors for psychopathology among older versus younger adults after the 2004 Florida hurricanes. *American Journal of Geriatric Psychiatry, 14*, 1051–1059.

Adrian, J. A., Deliramich, A. N., & Frueh, B. C. (2009). Complicated grief and posttraumatic stress disorder in humans' response to the death of pets/animals. *Bulletin of the Menninger Clinic, 73*, 176–187.

Alegria, M., Mulvaney-Day, N., Torres, M., Polo, A., Cao, Z., & Canino, G. (2007). Prevalence of psychiatric disorders across Latino subgroups in the United States. *American Journal of Public Health, 97*, 68–75.

Alonzo, A. A. (2000). The experience of chronic illness and post-traumatic stress disorder: The consequences of cumulative adversity. *Social Science & Meicine, 50*, 1475–1484.

Amaya-Jackson, L., Davidson, J. R., Hughes, D. C., Swartz, M., Reynolds, V., George, L. K., et al. (1999). Functional impairment and utilization of services associated with post-traumatic stress in the community. *Journal of Traumatic Stress, 12*, 709–724.

Amir, M., & Lev-Wiesel, R. (2001). Does everyone have a name? Psychological distress and quality of life among child Holocaust survivors with lost identity. *Journal of Traumatic Stress, 14*, 859–869.

Andrews, G., & Peters, L. (1998). The psychometric properties of the Composite International Diagnostic Interview. *Social Psychiatry and Psychiatric Epidemiology, 33*, 80–88.

Averill, P. M., & Beck, J. G. (2000). Posttraumatic stress disorder in older adults: A conceptual review. *Journal of Anxiety Disorders, 14*, 133–156.

Ayers, E. D., White, J., & Powell, D. A. (2003). Pavlovian eye-blink conditioning in combat veterans with and without post-traumatic stress disorder. *Integrative Physiological and Behavioral Science, 38*, 230–247.

Ball, V. L., Hudson, S., Davila, J., Morgen, R., Walder, A., Greham, D. P., Snow, A. L. & Kunik, M. E. (2009). Post-traumatic stress disorder and prediction of aggression in persons with dementia. *International Journal of Geriatric Psychiatry, 24*, 1285–1290.

Barrett, D. H., Green, M. L., Morris, R., Giles, W. H., & Croft, J. B. (1996). Cognitive functioning and posttraumatic stress disorder. *American Journal of Psychiatry, 153*, 1492–1494.

Beck, J. G., Grant, D. M., Read, J. P., Clapp, J. D., Coffey, S. F., Miller, L. M., et al. (2008). The Impact of Event Scale-Revised: Psychometric properties in a sample of motor vehicle accident survivors. *Journal of Anxiety Disorders, 22*, 187–198.

Blake, D. D. (1994). Rationale and development of the Clinician-Administered PTSD-scales. *PTSD-Research Quarterly, 5*, 1–8.

Blake, D. D., Weathers, F. W., Nagy, L. M., Kaloupek, D. G., Gusman, F. D., Charney, D. S., et al. (1995). The development of a Clinician-Administered PTSD Scale. *Journal of Traumatic Stress, 8*, 75–90.

Blake, D. D., Weathers, F. W., Nagy, L. M., Kaloupek, D. G., klauminzer, G., Charney, D. S., et al. (1990). A clinician rating scale for assessing current and lifetime PTSD: The CAPS-I. *Behavior Therapy, 18*, 187–188.

Blanchard, E. B., Jones-Alexander, J., Buckley, T. C., & Forneris, C. A. (1996). Psychometric properties of the PTSD Checklist (PCL). *Behaviour Research and Therapy, 34,* 669–673.

Bowing, G., Schmidt, K. U., Juckel, G., & Schroder, S. G. (2008). Psychosis in elderly post-traumatic stress disorder patients. *Nervenarzt, 79,* 73–79.

Bremner, J. D., Randall, P., Scott, T. M., Bronen, R. A., Seibyl, J. P., Southwick, S. M., et al. (1995). MRI-based measurement of hippocampal volume in patients with combat-related posttraumatic stress disorder. *American Journal of Psychiatry, 152,* 973–981.

Breslau, N., & Kessler, R. C. (2001). The stressor criterion in DSM-IV posttraumatic stress disorder: An empirical investigation. *Biological Psychiatry, 50,* 699–704.

Brewin, C. R. (2005). Systematic review of screening instruments for adults at risk of PTSD. *Journal of Traumatic Stress, 18,* 53–62.

Briere, J., & Runtz, M. (1989). The Trauma Symptom Checklist (TSC-33): Early data on a new scale. *Journal of Interpersonal Violence, 4,* 151–163.

Brodaty, H., Joffe, C., Luscombe, G., & Thompson, C. (2004). Vulnerability to post-traumatic stress disorder and psychological morbidity in aged Holocaust survivors. *International Journal of Geriatric Psychiatry, 19,* 968–979.

Brodaty, H., & Low, L. F. (2003). Aggression in the elderly. *Journal of Clinical Psychiatry, 64* (Suppl, 4), 36–43.

Brooks, M. S., & Fulton, L. (2010). Evidence of poorer life-course mental health outcomes among veterans of the Korean War cohort. *Aging and Mental Health, 14,* 177–183.

Busuttil, W. (2004). Presentations and management of post traumatic stress disorder and the elderly: A need for investigation. *International Journal of Geriatric Psychiatry, 19,* 429–439.

Byers, A. L., Yaffe, K., Covinsky, K. E., Friedman, M. B., & Bruce, M. L. (2010). High occurrence of mood and anxiety disorders among older adults: The National Comorbidity Survey Replication. *Archives of General Psychiatry, 67,* 489–496.

Carlson, E. B. (2001). Psychometric study of a brief screen for PTSD: Assessing the impact of multiple traumatic events. *Assessment, 8,* 431–441.

Carlson, E. B., Lauderdale S, Hawkins, J., & Sheikh, J. I. (2008). Posttraumatic stress and aggression among veterans in long-term care. *Journal of Geriatric Psychiatry and Neurology, 21,* 61–71.

Carlson, J. G., Singelis, T. M., & Chemtob, C. M. (1997). Facial EMG responses to combat-related visual stimuli in veterans with and without posttraumatic stress disorder. *Applied Psychophysiological Biofeedback, 22,* 247–259.

Colenda, C. C., Legault, C., Rapp, S. R., DeBon, M. W., Hogan, P., Wallace, R., et al. (2010). Psychiatric disorders and cognitive dysfunction among older, postmenopausal women: Results from the Women's Health Initiative Memory Study. *American Journal of Geriatric Psychiatry, 18,* 177–186.

Connor, K. M. & Davidson, J. R. (2001). SPRINT: A brief global assessment of post-traumatic stress disorder. *International Journal of Clinical Psychopharmacology, 16,* 279–284.

Cook, J. M. (2002). Traumatic exposure and PTSD in older adults: Introduction the special issue. *Journal of Clinical Geropsychology, 18,* 149–152.

Cook, J. M., Elhai, J. D., & Arean, P. A. (2005). Psychometric properties of the PTSD Checklist with older primary care patients. *Journal of Traumatic Stress, 18,* 371–376.

Cook, J. M., Elhai, J. D., Cassidy, E. L., Ruzek, J. I., Ram, G. D., & Sheikh, J. I. (2005). Assessment of trauma exposure and post-traumatic stress in long-term care veterans: Preliminary data on psychometrics and post-traumatic stress disorder prevalence. *Military Medicine, 170,* 862–866.

Cook, J. M., & O'Donnell, C. (2005). Assessment and psychological treatment of posttraumatic stress disorder in older adults. *Journal of Geriatric Psychiatry Neurology, 18,* 61–71.

Cook, J. M., Ruzek, J. I., & Cassidy, E. (2003). Practical geriatrics: Possible association of posttraumatic stress disorder with cognitive impairment among older adults. *Psychiatric Services, 54,* 1223–1225.

Creamer, M., & Parslow, R. (2008). Trauma exposure and posttraumatic stress disorder in the elderly: A community prevalence study. *American Journal of Geriatric Psychiatry, 16,* 853–856.

Creamer, M., Bell, R., & Failla, S. (2003). Psychometric properties of the Impact of Event Scale—Revised. *Behaviour Research and Therapy, 41,* 1489–1496.

Davidson, J., Smith, R., & Kudler, H. (1989). Validity and reliability of the DSM-III criteria for posttraumatic stress disorder. Experience with a structured interview. *Journal of Nervous and Mental Disease, 177,* 336–341.

Davidson, J. R., Hughes, D., Blazer, D. G., & George, L. K. (1991). Post-traumatic stress disorder in the community: An epidemiological study. *Psychological Medicine, 21,* 713–721.

Davidson, J. R., Kudler, H. S., Saunders, W. B., & Smith, R. D. (1990). Symptom and comorbidity patterns in World War II and Vietnam veterans with posttraumatic stress disorder. *Comprehensive Psychiatry, 31,* 162–170.

Davidson, J. R., Tharwani, H. M., & Connor, K. M. (2002). Davidson Trauma Scale (DTS): Normative scores in the general population and effect sizes in placebo-controlled SSRI trials. *Depression and Anxiety, 15,* 75–78.

de Vries, G. J., & Olff, M. (2009). The lifetime prevalence of traumatic events and posttraumatic stress disorder in the Netherlands. *Journal of Traumatic Stress, 22,* 259–267.

Dileo, J. F., Brewer, W. J., Hopwood, M., Anderson, V., & Creamer, M. (2008). Olfactory identification dysfunction, aggression and impulsivity in war veterans with post-traumatic stress disorder. *Psychoogical Medicine, 38,* 523–531.

Ehring, T., Kleim, B., Clark, D. M., Foa, E. B., & Ehlers, A. (2007). Screening for posttraumatic stress disorder: What combination of symptoms predicts best? *Journal of Nervous and Mental Disease, 195,* 1004–1012.

Elder, G. H., & Clipp, E. C. (1989). Combat experience and emotional health: Impairment and resilience in later life. *Journal of Psychiatric Research, 57,* 311–341.

Elklit, A., & O'Connor, M. (2005). Post-traumatic stress disorder in a Danish population of elderly bereaved. *Scandinavian Journal of Psychology, 46,* 439–445.

Falk, B., Hersen, M., & Van Hasselt, V. (1994). Assessment of posttraumatic stress disorder in older adults: A critical review. *Clinical Psychology Review, 14,* 383–415.

First, M. B., Spitzer, R. L., Gibbon, M., & Williams, J. B. (1996). *Structured Clinical Interview for the DSM-IV Axis I Disorders (SCID-I), Clinician Version.* Washington, DC: American Psychiatric Association.

Flint, A. J., Peasley-Miklus, C., Papademetriou, E., Meyers, B. S., Mulsant, B. H., Rothschild, A. J., et al. (2010). Effect of age on the frequency of anxiety disorders in major depression with psychotic features. *American Journal of Geriatric Psychiatry, 18,* 404–412.

Foa, E. B. (1995). *Posttraumatic Stress Diagnostic Scale manual.* Minneapolis, MN: National Computer Systems Inc.

Foa, E. B., Cashman, L., Jaycox, L., & Perry, K. (1997). The validation of a self-report measure of posttraumatic stress disorder: The Posttraumatic Diagnostic Scale. *Psychological Assessment: A Journal of Consulting and Clinical Psychology, 9*, 445–451.

Foa, E. B., Riggs, D. S., Dancu, C. V., & Rothbaum, B. O. (1993). Reliability and validity of a brief instrument for assessing post-traumatic stress disorder. *Journal of Traumatic Stress, 6*, 459–473.

Fontana, A., & Rosenheck, R. (1994). Traumatic war stressors and psychiatric symptoms among World War II, Korean, and Vietnam War veterans. *Psychological Aging, 9*, 27–33.

Ford, B. C., Bullard, K. M., Taylor, R. J., Toler, A. K., Neighbors, H. W., & Jackson, J. S. (2007). Lifetime and 12-month prevalence of Diagnostic and Statistical Manual of Mental Disorders, Fourth Edition, disorders among older African Americans: Findings from the National Survey of American Life. *American Journal of Geriatric Psychiatry, 15*, 652–659.

Frueh, B. C., Grubaugh, A. L., Acierno, R., Elhai, J. D., Cain, G., & Magruder, K. M. (2007). Age differences in posttraumatic stress disorder, psychiatric disorders, and healthcare service use among veterans in Veterans Affairs primary care clinics. *American Journal of Geriatric Psychiatry, 15*, 660–672.

Fullerton, C. S., Ursano, R. J., Epstein, R. S., Crowley, B., Vance, K., Craig, K. J., et al. (2000). Measurement of posttraumatic stress disorder in community samples. *Nordic Journal of Psychiatry, 54*, 5–12.

Gaynes, B. N., Veaugh-Geiss, J., Weir, S., Gu, H., MacPherson, C., Schulberg, H. C., et al. (2010). Feasibility and diagnostic validity of the M-3 checklist: A brief, self-rated screen for depressive, bipolar, anxiety, and post-traumatic stress disorders in primary care. *Annals of Family Medicine, 8*, 160–169.

Gilbertson, M. W., Shenton, M. E., Ciszewski, A., Kasai, K., Lasko, N. B., Orr, S. P., et al. (2002). Smaller hippocampal volume predicts pathologic vulnerability to psychological trauma. *Nature Neuroscience, 5*, 1242–1247.

Ginsberg, J. P., Ayers, E., Burriss, L., & Powell, D. A. (2008). Discriminative delay Pavlovian eyeblink conditioning in veterans with and without posttraumatic stress disorder. *Journal of Anxiety Disorders, 22*, 809–823.

Gore, K. L., Engel, C. C., Freed, M. C., Liu, X., & Armstrong, D. W., III. (2008). Test of a single-item posttraumatic stress disorder screener in a military primary care setting. *General Hospital Psychiatry, 30*, 391–397.

Gum, A. M., & Cheavens, J. S. (2008). Psychiatric comorbidity and depression in older adults. *Current Psychiatry Reports, 10*, 23–29.

Gum, A. M., King-Kallimanis, B., & Kohn, R. (2009). Prevalence of mood, anxiety, and substance-abuse disorders for older Americans in the national comorbidity survey-replication. *Americal Journal of Geriatric Psychiatry, 17*, 769–781.

Hammarberg, M. (1992). Penn Inventory for Posttraumatic Stress Disorder: Psychometric properties. *Psychological Assessment: A Journal of Consulting and Clinical Psychology, 4*, 67–76.

Hankin, C. S., Spiro, A., III, Miller, D. R., & Kazis, L. (1999). Mental disorders and mental health treatment among U.S. Department of Veterans Affairs outpatients: The Veterans Health Study. *American Journal of Psychiatry, 156*, 1924–1930.

Higgins, A. B., & Follette, V. M. (2002). Frequency and Impact of Interpersonal Trauma in Older Women. *Journal of Clinical Geropsychology, 8*, 215–226.

Hinton, D. E., Chhean, D., Pich, V., Pollack, M. H., Orr, S. P., & Pitman, R. K. (2006). Assessment of posttraumatic stress disorder in Cambodian refugees using the Clinician-Administered PTSD Scale: Psychometric properties and symptom severity. *Journal of Traumatic Stress, 19*, 405–409.

Hiskey, S., Luckie, M., Davies, S., & Brewin, C. R. (2008). The phenomenology of reactivated trauma memories in older adults: A preliminary study. *Aging and Mental Health, 12*, 494–498.

Hopper, J. W., Spinazzola, J., Simpson, W. B., & van der Kolk, B. A. (2006). Preliminary evidence of parasympathetic influence on basal heart rate in posttraumatic stress disorder. *Journal of Psychosomatic Research, 60*, 83–90.

Horowitz, M. J., Wilner, N., & Alvarez, W. (1979). The Impact of Event Scale. *Psychosomatic Medicine, 41*, 209–218.

Horowitz, M. J., Wilner, N., Kaltreider, N., & Alvarez, W. (1980). Signs and symptoms of posttraumatic stress disorder. *Archives of General Psychiatry, 37*, 85–92.

Hovens, J. E., Bramsen, I., & van der Ploeg, H. M. (2000). *Zelfinventarisatielijst Posttraumatische Stress Stoornis ZIL Handleiding.* Lisse: Swets Test Publishers.

Hovens, J. E., van der Ploeg, H. M., Bramsen, I., Klaarenbeek, M. T., Schreuder, J. N., & Rivero, V. V. (1994). The development of the Self-Rating Inventory for Posttraumatic Stress Disorder. *Acta Psychiatrica Scandavica, 90*, 172–183.

Hovens, J. E., van der Ploeg, H. M., Klaarenbeek, M. T., Bramsen, I., Schreuder, J. N., & Rivero, V. V. (1994). The assessment of posttraumatic stress disorder: With the Clinician Administered PTSD Scale: Dutch results. *Journal of Clinical Psychology, 50*, 325–340.

Hovens, J. E., Falger, P. R. J., Op Den Velde, W., Schouten, E. G. W., De Groen, J. H. M., & van Duijn, H. (1992). Occurrence of current post traumatic stress disorder among Dutch World War II resistance veterans according to the SCID. *Journal of Anxiety Disorders, 6*, 147–157.

Hudson, S. A., Beckford, L. A., Jackson, S. D., & Philpot, M. P. (2008). Validation of a screening instrument for posttraumatic stress disorder in a clinical sample of older adults. *Aging and Mental Health, 12*, 670–673.

Hyer, L., & Boyd, S. (1996). Personality scales as predictors of older combat veterans with posttraumatic stress disorder. *Psychological Reports, 79*, 1040–1042.

Hyer, L., Summers, M. N., Boyd, S., Litaker, M., & Boudewyns, P. (1996). Assessment of older combat veterans with the clinician-administered PTSD scale. *Journal of Traumatic Stress, 9*, 587–593.

Hyer, L., Summers, M. N., Braswell, L., & Boyd, S. (1995). Posttraumatic stress disorder: Silent problem among older combat veterans. *Psychotherapy, 32*(2), 1–17.

Hyer, L., Walker, C., Swanson, G., Sperr, S., Sperr, E., & Blount, J. (1992). Validation of PTSD measures for older combat veterans. *Journal of Clinical Psychology, 48*, 579–588.

James, N. T., Miller, C. W., Nugent, K., Welch, C., Cabanna, M., & Vincent, S. (2007). The impact of Hurricane Katrina upon older adult nurses: An assessment of quality of life and psychological distress in the aftermath. *Journal of the Mississippi State Medical Association, 48*, 299–307.

Jimenez, D. E., Alegria, M., Chen, C. N., Chan, D., & Laderman, M. (2010). Prevalence of psychiatric illnesses in older ethnic minority adults. *Journal of American Geriatric Society, 58*, 256–264.

Joffe, C., Brodaty, H., Luscombe, G., & Ehrlich, F. (2003). The Sydney Holocaust study: Posttraumatic stress disorder and other psychosocial morbidity in an aged community sample. *Journal of Traumatic Stress, 16*, 39–47.

Joseph, S. (2000). Psychometric evaluation of Horowitz's Impact of Event Scale: A review. *Journal of Traumatic Stress, 13*, 101–113.

Kahana, B., & Kahana, E. (1998). Toward a temporal-spatial model of cumalative life stress: Placing late-life stress effect in a life course perspective. In J. Lomranz (Ed.), *Handbook of aging and mental health; An integrative approach* (pp. 153–178). New York: Plenum.

Keane, T. M., Caddell, J. M., & Taylor, K. L. (1988). Mississippi Scale for Combat-Related Posttraumatic Stress Disorder: Three studies in reliability and validity. *Journal of Consulting and Clinical Psychology, 56*, 85–90.

Keane, T. M., Malloy, P. F., & Fairbank, J. A. (1984). Empirical development of an MMPI subscale for the assessment of combat-related posttraumatic stress disorder. *Journal of Consulting and Clinical Psychology, 52*, 888–891.

Kessler, R. C., & Ustun, T. B. (2004). The World Mental Health (WMH) Survey Initiative Version of the World Health Organization (WHO) Composite International Diagnostic Interview (CIDI). *International Journal of Methods Psychiatry Research, 13*, 93–121.

Kim, J., & Choi, N. G. (2010). Twelve-month prevalence of DSM-IV mental disorders among older Asian Americans: Comparison with younger groups. *Aging Mental Health, 14*, 90–99.

Kirmizioglu, Y., Dogan, O., Kugu, N., & Akyuz, G. (2009). Prevalence of anxiety disorders among elderly people. *International Journal of Geriatric Psychiatry, 24*, 1026–1033.

Kohn, R., Levav, I., Garcia, I. D., Machuca, M. E., & Tamashiro, R. (2005). Prevalence, risk factors and aging vulnerability for psychopathology following a natural disaster in a developing country. *International Journal of Geriatric Psychiatry, 20*, 835–841.

Kohn, R., Vicente, B., Saldivia, S., Rioseco, P., & Torres, S. (2008). Psychiatric epidemiology of the elderly population in Chile. *American Journal of Geriatric Psychiatry, 16*, 1020–1028.

Kubany, E. S., Leisen, M. B., Kaplan, A. S., & Kelly, M. P. (2000). Validation of a brief measure of posttraumatic stress disorder: The Distressing Event Questionnaire (DEQ). *Psychological Assessment, 12*, 197–209.

Kubzansky, L. D., Koenen, K. C., Spiro, A., III, Vokonas, P. S., & Sparrow, D. (2007). Prospective study of posttraumatic stress disorder symptoms and coronary heart disease in the Normative Aging Study. *Archives of General Psychiatry, 64*, 109–116.

Kulka, R. A., Schlenger, W. E., Fairbank, J. A., Hough, R. L., Jordan, B. K., Marmar, C. R., et al. (1990). *Trauma and the Vietnam war generation; Report of findings from the National Vietnam Veterans Readjustment Study.* New York: Brunner/Mazel.

Kulka, R. A., Schlenger, W. E., Fairbank, J. A., Howard, R., Jordan, B. K., Marshall, R. D., et al. (1988). *National Vietnam Veterans Readjustment Study (NVVRS): Discription, current status and initial PTSD prevalence estimate.* Research Triangle Park, NC: Research Triangle Institute.

Kulka, R. A., Schlenger, W. E., Fairbank, J. A., Jordan, B. K., Hough, R. L., Marmar, C. R., et al. (1991). Assessment of postraumatic stress disorder in the community: Prospects and pitfalls from recent studies of Vietnam veterans. *Psychological Assessment: A Journal of Consulting and Clinical Psychology, 3*, 547–560.

Lantz, M. S., & Buchalter, E. N. (2001). Posttraumatic stress. Helping older adults cope with tragedy. *Geriatrics, 56*, 35–36.

Lauterbach, D., Vrana, S., King, D. W., & King, L. A. (1997). Psychometric properties of the civilian version of the Mississippi PTSD Scale. *Journal of Traumatic Stress, 10*, 499–513.

LeDoux, J. E. (1996). *The emotional brain; the mysterious underpinnings of emotional life.* New York: Simon and Schuster.

Lenze, E. J., Mulsant, B. H., Shear, M. K., Schulberg, H. C., Dew, M. A., Begley, A. E., et al. (2000). Comorbid anxiety disorders in depressed elderly patients. *American Journal of Psychiatry, 157*, 722–728.

Lillywhite, A. R., & Neal, L. A. (1993). The importance of severity as a factor in post-traumatic stress disorder. *British Journal of Psychiatry, 163*, 837.

Litz, B. T., Penk, W. E., Walsh, S., Hyer, L., Blake, D. D., Marx, B., et al. (1991). Similarities and differences between MMPI and MMPI-2 applications to the assessment of posttraumatic stress disorder. *Journal of Personality Assessment, 57*, 238–253.

Lyons, J. A., & Wheeler-Cox, T. (1999). MMPI, MMPI-2 and PTSD: Overview of scores, scales, and profiles. *Journal of Traumatic Stress, 12*, 175–183.

Maercker, A. (2002). Life review technique in the treatment of PTSD in elderly patients: Rationale and three single case studies. *Journal of Clinical Geropsychology* 8(3), 239–249.

Magruder, K. M., Frueh, B. C., Knapp, R. G., Davis, L., Hamner, M. B., Martin, R. H., et al. (2005). Prevalence of posttraumatic stress disorder in Veterans Affairs primary care clinics. *General Hospital Psychiatry, 27*, 169–179.

Magruder, K. M., Frueh, B. C., Knapp, R. G., Johnson, M. R., Vaughan, J. A., III, Carson, T. C., et al. (2004). PTSD symptoms, demographic characteristics, and functional status among veterans treated in VA primary care clinics. *Journal of Traumatic Stress, 17*, 293–301.

Marx, B. P., Humphreys, K. L., Weathers, F. W., Martin, E. K., Sloan, D. M., Grove, W. M., et al. (2008). Development and initial validation of a statistical prediction instrument for assessing combat-related posttraumatic stress disorder. *Journal of Nervous and Mental Disease, 196*, 605–611.

Meehl, P. E. (1995). Bootstraps taxometrics. Solving the classification problem in psychopathology. *American Psychologist, 50*, 266–275.

Meltzer-Brody, S., Churchill, E., & Davidson, J. R. (1999). Derivation of the SPAN, a brief diagnostic screening test for posttraumatic stress disorder. *Psychiatry Research, 88*, 63–70.

Metzger, L. J., Carson, M. A., Lasko, N. B., Paulus, L. A., Orr, S. P., Pitman, R. K., et al. (2008). Basal and suppressed salivary cortisol in female Vietnam nurse veterans with and without PTSD. *Psychiatry Research, 161*, 330–335.

Mollica, R. F., Caspi-Yavin, Y., Bollini, P., Truong, T., Tor, S., & Lavelle, J. (1992). The Harvard Trauma Questionnaire. Validating a cross-cultural instrument for measuring torture, trauma, and posttraumatic stress disorder in Indochinese refugees. *Journal of Nervous andMental Disease, 180*, 111–116.

Monson, C. M., Gradus, J. L., Young-Xu, Y., Schnurr, P. P., Price, J. L., & Schumm, J. A. (2008). Change in posttraumatic stress disorder symptoms: Do clinicians and patients agree? *Psychological Assessment, 20*, 131–138.

Mori, D. L., Lambert, J. F., Niles, B. L., Orlander, D. J., Grace, M. C., & LoCastro, J. S. (2003). The BAI-PC as a screen for anxiety, depression and PTSD in primary care. *Journal of Clinical Psychology in Medical Settings, 10*(3), 187–192.

Morina, N., Böhme, H. F., Ajdukovic, D., Bogic, M., Franciskovic, T., Galeazzi, G. M., et al. (2010). The structure of posttraumatic stress symptoms in survivors of war: Confirmatory factor analyses of the Impact of Event Scale—Revised. *Journal of Anxiety Disorders, 24*, 606–611.

Neal, L. A., Busuttil, W., Rollins, J., Herepath, R., Strike, P., & Turnbull, G. (1994). Convergent validity of measures of post-traumatic stress disorder in a mixed military and civilian population. *Journal of Traumatic Stress, 7*, 447–455.

Neal, L. A., Hill, N., Hughes, J., Middleton, A., & Busuttil, W. (1995). Convergent validity of measures of PTSD in an elderly population of former prisoners of war. *International Journal of Geriatric Psychiatry, 10*, 617–622.

Nichols, B. L., & Czirr, R. (1986). Posttraumatic stress disorder: Hidden syndrome in elders. *Clinical Gerontologist, 5*, 417–433.

Norris, F. H. (1992). Epidemiology of trauma: Frequency and impact of different potentially traumatic events on different demographic groups. *Journal of Consulting and Clinical Psychology, 60*, 409–418.

Norris, F. H., & Riad, J. K. (1997). Standardized self-report measures of civilian trauma and posttraumatic stress disorder. In J. Wilson & T. Keane (Eds.), *Assessing psychological trauma and posttraumatic stress disorder: A practitioner's handbook* (pp. 7–42). New York: Guilford.

Orr, S. P., Claiborn, J. M., Altman, B., Forgue, D. F., de Jong, J. B., Pitman, R. K., et al. (1990). Psychometric profile of posttraumatic stress disorder, anxious, and healthy Vietnam veterans: Correlations with psychophysiologic responses. *Journal of Consulting and Clinical Psychology, 58*, 329–335.

Orr, S. P., & Pitman, R. K. (1993). Psychophysiologic assessment of attempts to simulate posttraumatic stress disorder. *Biological Psychiatry, 33*, 127–129.

Owens, G. P., Baker, D. G., Kasckow, J., Ciesla, J. A., & Mohamed, S. (2005). Review of assessment and treatment of PTSD among elderly American armed forces veterans. *International Journal of Geriatric Psychiatry, 20*, 1118–1130.

Potts, M. K. (1994). Long-term effects of trauma: Post-traumatic stress among civilian internees of the Japanese during World War II. *Journal of Clinical Psychology, 50*, 681–698.

Query, W. T., Megran, J., & McDonald, G. (1986). Applying posttraumatic stress disorder MMPI subscale to World War II POW veterans. *Journal of Clinical Psychology, 42*, 315–317.

Resnick, H. S., Falsetti, S. A., & Kilpatrick, D. G. (1996). Assessment of rape and other civilian trauma-related posttraumatic stress disorder: Emphasis on assessment of potentially traumatic events. In T. W. Miller (Ed.), *Theory and assessment of stressful life events* (pp. 235–271). Madison, CT: International Universities Press.

Rintamaki, L. S., Weaver, F. M., Elbaum, P. L., Klama, E. N., & Miskevics, S. A. (2009). Persistence of traumatic memories in World War II prisoners of war. *Journal of the American Geriatric Society, 57*, 2257–2262.

Robins, L. N., Helzer, J. E., Croughan, J., & Ratcliff, K. S. (1981). National Institute of Mental Health Diagnostic Interview Schedule. Its history, characteristics, and validity. *Archives of General Psychiatry, 38*, 381–389.

Sadavoy, J. (1997). Survivors. A review of the late-life effects of prior psychological trauma. *American Journal of Geriatric Psychiatry, 5*, 287–301.

Salerno, J. A., & Nagy, C. (2002). Terrorism and aging. *The Journals of Gerontology Series A Biological Sciences and Medical Sciences, 57*, M552–M554.

Schinka, J. A., Brown, L. M., Borenstein, A. R., & Mortimer, J. A. (2007). Confirmatory factor analysis of the PTSD checklist in the elderly. *Journal of Traumatic Stress, 20*, 281–289.

Schlenger, W. E., & Kulka, R. A. (1987). Performance of the Keane-Fairbank MMPI scale and other self-report measures in identifying postttraumatic stress disorder. Conference Proceeding APA, New York.

Schnurr, P. P., Spiro, A., III, Vielhauer, M. J., & Findler, M. N., Hamblen, J. L. (2002). Trauma in the lives of older men: Findings from the Normative Aging Study. *Journal of Clinical Geropsychology, 8*(3), 175–187.

Scotti, J. R., Sturges, L. V., & Lyons, J. A. (1996). The Keane PTSD Scale extracted from the MMPI: Sensitivity and specificity with Vietnam veterans. *Journal of Traumatic Stress, 9*, 643–650.

Sharon, A., Levav, I., Brodsky, J., Shemesh, A. A., & Kohn, R. (2009). Psychiatric disorders and other health dimensions among Holocaust survivors 6 decades later. *British Journal of Psychiatry, 195*, 331–335.

Sijbrandij, M., Olff, M., Opmeer, B. C., Carlier, I. V., & Gersons, B. P. (2008). Early prognostic screening for posttraumatic stress disorder with the Davidson Trauma Scale and the SPAN. *Depression and Anxiety., 25*, 1038–1045.

Simpson, S., Morley, M., & Baldwin, B. (1996). Crime-related posttraumatic stress disorder in elderly psychiatric patients: A case series. *International Journal of Psychophysiology, 11*, 879–882.

Sperr, E., Sperr, S., Craft, R. B., & Boudewyns, P. (1990). MMPI profiles and post-traumatic symptomatology in former prisoners of war. *Journal of Traumatic Stress, 3*, 369–378.

Spitzer, R. L., & Williams, R. B. W. (1984). *Structured Clinical Interview for DSM-III disorders (SCID-P 5/1/84)*, 3 ed. New York, NY: Biometrics Research Department, New York State Psychiatric Institute.

Strug, D. L., Mason, S. E., & Auerbach, C. (2009). How older Hispanic immigrants in New York City cope with current traumatic stressors: Practice implications. *Journal of Gerontologic Social Work, 52*, 503–516.

Sundin, E. C. & Horowitz, M. J. (2002). Impact of Event Scale: Psychometric properties. *British Journal of Psychiatry, 180*, 205–209.

Swaab, D. F., Raadsheer, F. C., Endert, E., Hofman, M. A., Kamphorst, W., & Ravid, R. (1994). Increased cortisol levels in aging and Alzheimer's disease in postmortem cerebrospinal fluid. *Journal of Neuroendocrinology, 6*, 681–687.

Trollor, J. N., Anderson, T. M., Sachdev, P. S., Brodaty, H., & Andrews, G. (2007). Prevalence of mental disorders in the elderly: The Australian National Mental Health and Well-Being Survey. *American Journal of Geriatric Psychiatry, 15*, 455–466.

Tucker, P. M., Pfefferbaum, B., North, C. S., Kent, A., Burgin, C. E., Parker, D. E., et al. (2007). Physiologic reactivity despite emotional resilience several years after direct exposure to terrorism. *American Journal of Psychiatry, 164*, 230–235.

van Zelst, W., de Beurs, E., & Smit, J. H. (2003). Effects of the September 11th attacks on symptoms of PTSD on

community-dwelling older persons in the Netherlands. *International Journal of Geriatric Psychiatry, 18*, 190.
van Zelst, W. H., de Beurs, E., Beekman, A. T., Deeg, D. J., Bramsen, I., & van Dyck, R. (2003). Criterion validity of the self-rating inventory for posttraumatic stress disorder (SRIP) in the community of older adults. *Journal of Affective Disorders, 76*, 229–235.
van Zelst, W. H., de Beurs, E., Beekman, A. T., Deeg, D. J., & van Dyck, R. (2003). Prevalence and risk factors of posttraumatic stress disorder in older adults. *Psychotherapy and Psychosomatics, 72*, 333–342.
van Zelst, W. H., de Beurs, E., Beekman, A. T., van Dyck, R., & Deeg, D. D. (2006). Well-being, physical functioning, and use of health services in the elderly with PTSD and subthreshold PTSD. *International Journal of Geriatric Psychiatry, 21*, 180–188.
Verma, S., Orengo, C. A., Maxwell, R., Kunik, M. E., Molinari, V. A., Vasterling, J. J., et al. (2001). Contribution of PTSD/POW history to behavioral disturbances in dementia. *International Journal of Geriatric Psychiatry, 16*, 356–360.
Weathers, F. W., & Keane, T. M. (2007). The Criterion A problem revisited: Controversies and challenges in defining and measuring psychological trauma. *Journal of Traumatic Stress, 20*, 107–121.
Weathers, F. W., Keane, T. M., & Davidson, J. R. (2001). Clinician-administered PTSD scale: A review of the first ten years of research. *Depression and Anxiety, 13*, 132–156.
Weathers, F. W., & Litz, B. T. (1994). Psychometric properties of the clinician-administered PTSD Scale, CAPS I. *PTSD Research Quarterly, 5*, 2–6.
Weathers, F. W., Litz, B. T., Huska, J. A., & Keane, T. M. (1994). *PTSD Checklist-Civilian version*. Boston: National Center for PTSD, Behavioral Science Division.
Weiss, D. S. (2004). The Impact of Event Scale-Revised. In J. P. Wilson & T. M. Keane (Eds.), *Assessing psychological trauma and PTSD* (pp. 168–189). New York: Guilford.
Wetherell, J. L., Petkus, A. J., McChesney, K., Stein, M. B., Judd, P. H., Rockwell, E., et al. (2009). Older adults are less accurate than younger adults at identifying symptoms of anxiety and depression. *Journal of Nervous and Mental Disease, 197*, 623–626.
Wilson, J., & Keane, T. M. (2004). *Assessing psychological trauma and PTSD* (2nd ed.). New York: Guilford.
Witteveen, A. B., Bramsen, I., Hovens, J. E., & van der Ploeg, H. M. (2005). Utility of the Impact of Event Scale in screening for posttraumatic stress disorder. *Psychological Reports, 97*, 297–308.
Wolkenstein, B. H., & Sterman, L. (1998). Unmet needs of older women in a clinical population: The discovery of possible long-term sequelae of domestic violence. *Professional Psychology, Research and Practice, 29*, 341–348.
World Health Organization (1992). *International classification of diseases (9th ed.): Clinical Modification (ICD-CM)*. Geneva, Switzerland: Author.
Yaffe, K., Vittinghoff, E., Lindquist, K., Barnes, D., Covinsky, K. E., Neylan, T., et al. (2010). Posttraumatic stress disorder and risk of dementia among US veterans. *Archives of General Psychiatry, 67*, 608–613.
Yeager, D. E., Magruder, K. M., Knapp, R. G., Nicholas, J. S., & Frueh, B. C. (2007). Performance characteristics of the posttraumatic stress disorder checklist and SPAN in Veterans Affairs primary care settings. *General Hospital Psychiatry, 29*, 294–301.
Yehuda, R., Halligan, S. L., Grossman, R., Golier, J. A., & Wong, C. (2002). The cortisol and glucocorticoid receptor response to low dose dexamethasone administration in aging combat veterans and Holocaust survivors with and without posttraumatic stress disorder. *Biological Psychiatry, 52*, 393–403.
Zeiss, R. A., & Dickman, H. R. (1989). PTSD 40 years later: Incidence and person-situation correlates in former POWs. *Journal of Clinical Psychology, 45*, 80–87.

CHAPTER

20 Assessment of PTSD in Non-Western Cultures: The Need for New Contextual and Complex Perspectives

Boris Droždek,, John P. Wilson, *and* Silvana Turkovic

Abstract

Posttraumatic psychological impacts to non-Western populations cannot be assessed and understood solely within a biomedical paradigm and described primarily by the diagnosis of posttraumatic stress disorder. Instead, a more holistic assessment framework is critical. This chapter presents such a holistic assessment framework that incorporates clinical, psychological, and psychometric perspectives. In assessment of trauma populations, a contextual framework has to be applied. Psychological consequences should be approached as a spectrum of changes to individual psychosocial processes and patterns of adjustment. Assessment procedures should be culture sensitive and the instruments applied should address survivors' cultural realities and historical experiences within the disaster or trauma experience itself. The context of the traumatic event within a cultural matrix is essential to an accurate diagnostic picture, and this endeavor requires special knowledge of cultural differences in everyday life, traditions of daily living, and cultural community-based approaches for healing and recovery.

Key Words: Trauma, asylum seekers, refugees, complex PTSD, assessment, cultural sensitivity

Introduction

The issue of the assessment of psychological trauma is a complex and multifaceted one that requires knowledge of both scientifically validated measures and critiques of objective and subjective assessment techniques, processes, and standardized protocols. How does the clinician or researcher determine that his or her approach to assessment is applicable to non-Western cultures? Do Western standardized techniques for trauma assessment and posttraumatic stress disorder (PTSD) equate across cultures and have transcultural validity? These considerations raise fundamental concerns about the cross-cultural applications of Western, mostly American, procedures of assessment in non-Western populations. The purpose of this chapter is to identify and outline the central focal points in the assessment of critical psychological aspects of trauma and PTSD. As such, this chapter creates a conceptual framework, one that we believe is applicable to therapists, clinicians, researchers, educators, and others concerned with the processes of psychobiological evaluations of traumatic impacts to personality and PTSD.

Why Create New Frameworks for Cross-cultural Assessment of Trauma and PTSD?

What is the complex and conceptual framework of assessing cross-cultural trauma and PTSD? First, it should be recognized that this issue, while relatively new, has emerged out of several demands on nations, cultures, and legal authorities. To wit, refugees, war victims, asylum seekers, and others have struggled, on a worldwide basis, to find and secure new homes and niches in host countries given the political turmoil, violence, and political dismemberment or radical transformation of their previous existences.

The stressful uprooting of refugees and displaced persons, and their adaptation to a host country, poses enormous psychosocial and existential challenges to everyday life and efforts to learn the "rules" and acceptable, "normative ways" of living. In the broadest context, these adaptational challenges are easily subsumed under the rubric of "secondary stressors" after trans-mobilization—that is, geographical movement from one culture or one country to another. While the primary, secondary, and tertiary stressors may be profoundly stressful and result in disruptive impacts, the sum total of these reality-based requirements with which to cope may be psychologically overwhelming and significantly influence the survivors' ability to discuss the trauma and relocation stressors. Moreover, these stressors may limit these persons' capacity to articulate the entire nature of their personal journey (Wilson & Thomas, 2004). The refugees or asylum seekers may, consequently, experience helplessness in many forms, both personally and culturally (Wilson & Tang, 2007). The specific relevance of these issues to psychological assessments of trauma impacts, PTSD, and comorbid conditions, is that the clinician (i.e., assessor, psychiatrist, clinical psychologist, social worker, clergy, etc.) needs to have an informed complex and contextual framework in which to correctly and specifically conduct an evaluation process in order to render an ethically respectful and empirically valid set of conclusions about the specific ways that a traumatic event impacted a human life.

In the way of an overarching overview, the complex-critical cross-cultural context of psychological evaluation, assessment, and diagnosis has some fundamental premises based on our empirical review of the literature (Drožđek, 2007; Wilson & Tang, 2007). To establish a framework for the chapter, the following guidepoints are suggested:

- Cultures differ in complexity, diversity, and idiosyncratic dimensions.
- Cultural ideologies and predominant religious beliefs shape systems of meaning and normative expectations for behavior.
- Cultures have different views of gender roles, insights, and expectations regarding freedom, rights, and entitlements (e.g., see Afghanistan in reference to women's roles and rights for a current example).
- Cultures have different levels of norms about what is acceptable and unacceptable in choices and behaviors (e.g., political systems of governance, sexual behavior, drug use, etc.).
- Cultures differ in their definitions of medical illness and mental illnesses (Wilson & Tang, 2007). There are overlaps and radical differences in definitions of psychiatric disorders and their etiology. The conceptual premises of illness (e.g., traditional Chinese medicine, or TCM) result in different views of how illness is manifested (Wilson & Tang, 2007).

The recognition and cultural awareness of distinct and diversified cultural variables necessitates an understanding of how these critically essential elements exert a profound influence on the nature, context (i.e., the assessment situation or clinical setting) or the clinical and personal definitional reality for the person being evaluated. For example, many non-Western cultures do not have specialized psychiatric clinics, mental health facilities, specialized hospital facilities, community mental health centers, or designated and approved governmental agencies to assist in determining the level of disaster and trauma impacts (Wilson & Tang, 2007). Next, we will present some specific considerations from our collective clinical and research experiences.

Case Illustration and Generative Assessment Questions

In a brief, focused form:

- Do Bosnian Muslim females who were tortured and raped in raping camps by Serbian perpetrators manifest the symptoms of PTSD, depression, anxiety, or dissociation in a similar way as war victims who survived the four-year siege of Sarajevo but without torture and rape experiences? How do mental health professionals determine differences in complex comparative analyses such as this case illustrates?
- By what criteria do researchers determine what, if any, psychometric procedures and assessment tools are scientifically, and globally, valid for the assessment of trauma's impact and resultant consequences, that are either normal or pathological responses?

• Are Western psychometric questionnaires developed to evaluate the "big" and "specific" measures of personality, psychopathology, and PTSD cross-culturally validated, standardized, or applicable to the non-Western cultures that vastly outnumber the Western ones? In an era of worldwide globalization, we (Drožđek, 2007; Wilson & Tang, 2007) have suggested that the emergent growth curve of efforts to address this most relevant cross-cultural effort is both theoretically and scientifically essential, as the issues of whether or not PTSD and prolonged stress response syndromes are universal in psychobiological manifestations or driven primarily by culture, genetics, or social cultural factors. The critical question remains: What are the interactive cultural dimensions that shape human response to significant psychological trauma events, disasters, and other extreme stress experiences? And, how best to assess their capacity to influence personality, the self-structure, and personal identity (Wilson, 2006)?

• Is there a necessary reconceptualization of the assumptions of psychological test development for non-Western cultures? In the simplest formulation, Is what works here applicable there? How do we know? What culturally based reconceptualizations are necessary?

• Do Western statistical tests have universality in non-Western cultures? If so, how to prove the generality of measures and, more importantly, the underlying assumptions of the procedures and their mathematical bases of analysis and construction?

Empirically Based Studies and Factual Groundworks

In recent years there has been an emphasis to rely on the language of "empirically based evidence" for some focal points of scientific inquiry in the psychological literature, especially that reported in the American Psychological Association (APA) professional publications. The idea of evidence-based scientific outcomes in research studies has an appeal transparent of controlled scientific inquiry and proper methodology to validate the outcome measures. Although this culturally popular trend has gained an unchallenged success, it has marginally investigated of cross-cultural differences in psychometric assessment procedures or the suggestion that only Western cultural psychometric studies are applicable to research designs, protocol driven outcomes standards, and future endeavors of new developments (Drožđek, 2007; Wilson & Tang, 2007).

As Summerfield (1997) and others (Drožđek, 2007; Wilson & Tang, 2007) have indicated, the most complete approach to assessing psychic trauma needs to be embedded within a hierarchically nested set of boxes of cultural parameters that shape and influence how the trauma survivor perceives and processes an extremely stressful life—event such as the atomic bombing of Hiroshima, or the 2003 tsunami devastation in Asia and the South Pacific region. In other words, the context in which traumatic events occur cannot be separated from the culture in which they happen.

Moreover, traumatic experiences are a part of a survivor's life cycle and cannot be understood as a disembodied construct (Wilson, 2006). To focus more precisely, it is important to consider when the traumatic event occurred in the life-cycle and what are its consequences to psychosocial development, adjustment and patterns of adaptation in the culture (Wilson, 2006).

Although this approach to assessing trauma impact is obvious in many ways, the interwoven nature of the cultural context of an extreme life event is a conceptual foundation for accurate psychological/medical diagnosis. How can the professional prediction establish a reliable and scientifically defensible diagnosis without a culturally sensitive and intelligently informed basis of the minimum considerations of cultural influences that shape stress responses?

To fully understand the impact of different forms of traumatic events to the individual survivor requires a culture-specific phenomenological perspective, and a life-span epigenetic framework of personality factors, self-structure, and identity (Aronoff & Wilson, 1985; Wilson, 1989, 2006). Contextual analysis assumes that professionals who are responsible for psychological assessment have knowledge of the population and persons they evaluate. The failure to know details of what the survivor endured or experienced may lead to counterproductive responses, and result in inaccurate clinical analyses and psychiatric/psychological reports, court testimonies, and other recommendations based on inadequate, and perhaps inappropriate, psychological evaluations (Wilson & Lindy, 1994; Wilson & Thomas, 2004).

The abovementioned issues should represent the future of empirical studies for understanding of the complex nature of posttraumatic stress syndromes (Wilson, 2006). At present, this type of research has just begun. We encourage greater empirical activity on cultural influences to assessment.

Is PTSD a Psychiatric Category or a Spectrum of Prolonged Stress Response Syndromes?

Given the capacity of traumatic events to impact adaptive behavior, including the inner and outer worlds of psychic activity (Wilson, 2006), it is critically important to look beyond diagnostic criteria of PTSD to identify both *pathogenic* and *salutogenic* outcomes as individuals cope with the effects of trauma in their lives (Wilson, 1989, 2006).

Some investigators suggest that the PTSD concept is an individualized, medicalized, and reified perspective of posttraumatic damage (van Dijk 2006). Individualization focuses exclusively on the impact of trauma on the survivor's individual psychology, to the exclusion of the impact of trauma on society. Medicalization of social suffering has been extensively and critically discussed by Summerfield (1997). He states that all refugees need social justice and some may need psychological treatment for experienced difficulties in relocation and adaptation (i.e., the bigger psychosocial and sociological picture of trauma's psychological impact).

Researchers in the field of cross-cultural psychology have emphasized the diversity of human emotions that are expressed among ethnic groups (Shweder, 2001; Shweder & Haidt, 2000). In the broadest sense, they distinguish an *emic* from an *etic* procedure in cross-cultural analyses (Pike, 1954). Although the *emic* approach examines a culture's phenomena from an "inward" perspective—that is, in terms of the culture itself—the *etic* approach aims at developing universal or generic categories that meet the requirements of most cultures in terms of universal phenomena observed. Triandis (1972) pointed out the dangers of the *pseudoetic* approach in cross-cultural research. Nevertheless, researchers are continuing to construct appropriate *etic* measures of PTSD and related constructs (e.g., depression), and to globalize Western assessment procedures.

The PTSD concept does not necessarily include the sociopolitical and cultural context in which trauma occurs, although the cultural embedding is central to how people recover from trauma (Wilson, 1989). The context of trauma is shaped, and in turn shapes, worldviews, cultural norms, constructions of society, and victims' perceptions of trauma and future outlooks. After trauma, there are individually constructed changes in value priorities and assumptive behaviors (Wilson, 2006). Trauma is not a disembodied construct. It is inseparable from cultural influences and cultural healing alternatives. Trauma and its effects on the psyche are inevitably wedded to cultural forces and should be perceived as a spectrum of prolonged stress response syndromes (Drožđek, 2007).

The Role of Culture in Assessment of PTSD: The Multifaceted Considerations

The relationship between trauma and culture is critical because traumatic experiences demand a response from culture in terms of medical care, healing, culturally based treatments, interventions, counseling, and other forms of professional care. To understand this relationship requires a broad overview, what some have termed an orbital space satellite overview (Marsella & White, 1989; Wilson & Tang, 2007). It is important to understand how cultures utilize different mechanisms to assist those injured by extreme stress experiences (Wilson & Tang, 2007). The critical question is, How, specifically, do they do it within the parameters and traditions of non-Western cultures?

Throughout the years, in a superordinate perspective, research has demonstrated that the causes, expectable courses, and outcomes of major psychiatric disorders, including PTSD, are influenced by cultural factors (Kirmayer, 2001; Kleinman, 1988; Leff, 2001; Lopez & Guarnaccia, 2000). Attitudes and assumptions based on cultural background govern the perspectives that the patient and clinician bring to the clinical encounter (Kirmayer, Rousseau, Jarvis & Guzder, 2008). For example, Smith, Lin, and Mendoza (1993) state:

> Humans in general have an inherent need to make sense out of and explain their experiences. This is especially true when they are experiencing suffering and illness. In the process of this quest for meaning, culturally shaped beliefs play a vital role in determining whether a particular explanation and associated treatment plan will make sense to the patient.... Numerous studies in medical anthropology have documented that indigenous systems of health beliefs and practices persist and may even flourish in all societies after exposure to modern Western medicine.... These beliefs and practices exert profound influences in patients' attitudes and behavior. (p. 38)

Kirmayer (1996) noted that non-Western societies do not share the dualism of body versus mind that is characteristic of the Western medical perspective, emphasizing somatic as opposed to psychological complaints as manifestations of distress. Marsella,

Kaplan, and Suarez (2002) noted that somatic components are known worldwide as essential elements of the symptomatology pertaining to anxiety and affective disorders, including PTSD. This noted, patients from collectivistic societies place value on interpersonal balance with an emphasis on avoiding interpersonal conflict (Renner, Salem, & Ottomeyer, 2007). Therefore, to non-Western survivors, somatic symptoms may seem more acceptable and easier to communicate than psychological symptoms.

Culture determines the understanding and the conceptualizing of suffering in all of its varied forms (Wilson & Raphael, 1993). Although symptoms of PTSD are found in most populations exposed to traumatic stress, other symptoms of distress may be of greater concern to affected individuals and govern their help-seeking behavior (Miller et al., 2009). For the most part, culture defines what is seen as acceptable in private and public pain (Helman, 1994). Using culturally inappropriate or insensitive instruments traps clinicians into what Kleinman (1977) refers to as a category fallacy. This common "fallacy" is that the investigator defines the Western psychiatric category and then starts looking for it in a non-Western culture leading to that which has to be validated. This is a process of reification—that is, finding self-validating processes and hypotheses. However, if one carefully listens to narratives, the reported emotional and distressing complaints in non-Western survivors may not match those of Western categories of psychiatric diagnoses.

Toward a New Paradigm for Understanding Trauma Damage: Implications for Proper Psycho-cultural Assessments

In the field of psychosocial and traumatic/medical stress studies, there is a polarization between the universalists and the cultural relativists. In many cases, the first claim is that PTSD is a universal reaction to traumatic experiences. From the other perspective, many agree that culture shapes the ways in which survivors experience, express, and suffer from posttraumatic impact and that cultural, political, and social factors are critical to understanding (Wilson, 1989; Wilson & Tang, 2007). These researchers suggest that although some reaction patterns may be universal, their significance and importance vary considerably among different cultures (Bracken & Petty, 1998; Wilson & Tang, 2007). Marsella and Yamada (2000) discussed the oversimplified medical model in psychiatry and clinical psychology, and advocated for a more comprehensive culturally sensitive view. To quote, "our realities, including our scientific realities, are all constructed." (p. 7). In a similar view, Summerfield (1999) observed that in non-Western societies, trauma related distress is commonly understood as a consequence of a disrupted "social and moral order" (p. 1455).

Scholars and practitioners can easily be confused by the polarization of universalist and relativist standpoints regarding the psychological assessment of trauma, PTSD and other considerations of research and treatment. In this context, trauma and PTSD assessments include identification of psychopathological symptoms and disorders mediated by psychiatric diagnosis and leading primarily to medicalized interventions. In our collective experience, insufficient attention is paid, for example, to translation of the refugee experiences into personal, idiosyncratic, culture-specific idioms of distress (Dana, 2007; Drožđek, 2007). Therefore, survivors may be stigmatized by the host culture and secondarily victimized by the treating professionals and labeled as persons who somatize their problems, the ones who cannot follow the strict pathways of treatment protocols and who are present as different and difficult to treat (Drožđek, 2007; Wilson & Tang, 2007).

Thus far, we have discussed the PTSD concept and diagnosis from the perspective of cultural psychology/psychiatry and proposed a new, complex, contextual paradigm for understanding the trauma and phenomenological damage to the self, personality, and adaptive behavior. The advantages of the contextual assessment procedures and processes, as well as its special considerations and complications, are presented next.

Contextual Assessment: Its Critical Contextual Cross-cultural Importance

To fully understand the complexity of traumatic life events, it is essential to frame them in what Bronfenbrenner (1981, pp. 22–26) called "the ecological environment" of critical analysis. As a pioneer, Bronfenbrenner (1981) described the social-cultural environment as a nested arrangement of concentric structures, each contained within the next. In this metaphor, there is a hierarchical set of "cultural boxes, nests or events, encompassing the phenomena." In building on Bronfenbrenner's work and others (e.g., Antonovsky, 1972), it is important to understand that "the ecological environment" is a dynamic system that can change over time. In the case of asylum seekers and refugees or other non-Western people, the time line can include the premigratory and the postmigratory periods, as well as the period of forced migration and resettlement. Included in these intervals are many secondary stressors and intersecting variables that effect patterns of posttraumatic adaptations and disposition to the development of PTSD (Drožđek, 2007; Drožđek, Wilson, & Turkovic, 2012).

Another important step toward understanding the impact of trauma and other life events on survivors is awareness of the traumatic impact to self and resources of resilience. When assessing trauma, the clinician should be cognizant that traumatic experiences are complex in nature (Wilson, Friedman & Lindy, 2001). In essence, the current *DSM-IV-TR* (American Psychiatric Association [APA], 2004) definition of PTSD is an algorithm built around a minimum of 17 diagnostic symptoms divided into three categories of pre- and post-trauma related symptoms (Wilson & Keane, 2004).

In the assessment of trauma in asylum seekers and refugees, the clinician should also give attention to the causality principle and what the pre- and post-trauma stress experiences are that relate to a diagnosis of PTSD. Asylum seekers and refugees present with a broad array of problems (e.g., social, economic, spiritual, existential), and the process of adaptation to forced migration itself can lead to significant psychological problems in the posttraumatic environment. Therefore, it is critical to differentiate primary (i.e., traumatic experiences) from secondary or tertiary stressor events of many types and dimensional impacts when conducting a proper psychological or psychiatric assessment.

Cross-cultural/Contextual Heuristic Advantages in Assessments, Treatments, and Measurement Outcomes

Applying a cross-cultural contextual analysis in the assessment of posttraumatic damage in asylum seekers and refugees has several advantages. Key considerations include:

1. Avoidance of the "either/or" dichotomy (PTSD or another diagnostic category), and application of the "and/and" paradigm (PTSD as a continuum with many different facets), serves to create a broader view of survivors' problems and helps understand the person in the wholeness of human existence.
2. This paradigm automatically invites a clinician to inquire into relational aspects of individual survivor (e.g., partner, family, society), thereby anchoring consequences of trauma in a context that goes beyond intrapsychic conflicts per se.
3. Using the contextual paradigm, a clinician establishes better contact with the survivor because his or her conceptualization may be more congruent with the survivor's perception of what he or she has endured within a culture-specific event.
4. Inclusion of cultural, political, and social issues in the assessment process is important as poverty, marginalization, unemployment, and powerlessness may cause psychological and psychiatric problems regardless of existence of traumatic experiences and influence identity and dispositions toward help-seeking behavior.

Considerations of Psychological and Psychiatric Assessment Procedures and Determinations of Diagnoses, Syndromes, and Normal Prolonged Stress-Response Patterns

For clients coming from cultures where disclosing personal problems to a professional stranger (e.g., a Western psychiatrist or clinical psychologist) is not a common way of healing, the first contact with an agency representative or a therapist can be a fearful and anxiety-provoking experience and can lead to avoidance behaviors, with the client deciding not to return again out of fear and uncertainty (Drožđek & Wilson, 2004; Wilson & Tang, 2007). It is important that the assessor provide the client with essential educational information about the agency and the expectations for assessment. The assessor should explain transparently the possibilities and risks of the assessment process and try to alleviate the stigma of being a "psychiatric" or traumatized patient. Indeed, to the non-Western patient, this entire process may be experienced as foreign, difficult, and uncomfortable to comprehend, or just "strange or weird." For many, especially victims of torture, oppression, and politically driven interrogations, the assessment process may feel like a torture interrogation or a reactivation of a past experience of a coercive interrogation.

Drožđek and Wilson (2004) defined five important factors for establishing a therapeutic alliance. First, a mutually respectful relationship between assessor/clinician and client is needed. Second, the creation of trust and safety is essential and promoted by transparency, calmness, and predictability of action. Reasons for the assessment and the procedure for the assessment should be presented to the client at the very beginning of involvement. Third, assessment guidelines have to be respected and "secret agendas" among responsibilities in authority are not permitted. Fourth, where possible, assessors should exhibit tolerance and have the capacity to "decode messages" from their clients about their trauma experiences. These messages are sometimes "hidden" owing to different cultural backgrounds. Fifth, a culturally sensitive attitude must be adopted by assessors in its complex forms.

Cultural sensitivity, per se, is not about specific clinical assessment procedures or treatment techniques but instead is about the attitude and disposition of the clinician. Cultural competence involves the clinician's keen sense of the restrictions of his or her limited knowledge, a respect for cultural differences, and a tolerance for uncertainty about deficiencies in knowledge. To state the issue differently, How many Western clinicians and researchers have the education and training to know how to approach cross-cultural critical issues to understand PTSD and associated conditions? (Wilson & Tang, 2007). The answer at this time is transparent, but it is also promising for future professional development programs. The term *cultural competence* is not a buzz word but a reality.

Key elements of transcultural clinical encounters have been suggested by Drožđek and Wilson (2004) and Kirmayer et al. (2008). Clinicians are cautioned not to diagnose pathology where there is simply a cultural difference between client and clinician. Openness, empathy, curiosity, interest in cultural differences, respect, awareness of ones' own mental processes, a capacity for containment and maintaining proper boundaries, and ability to deal with basic emotional exhortations such as anger, love, rage, and doubt (van der Veer & van Waning 2004) are important. Capacity for self-criticism is also useful because each society has blind spots regarding the forms of social suffering that it produces (Kleinman, Das & Lock, 1997). Cultures encompass practices that may help or hinder trauma survivors aggravate or ameliorate psychopathology at different historical moments, depending on the complex interplay of history, culture, and the context of what happened to the person at a given moment in space, time, and existential reality.

Assessment often includes and necessitates an interpreter. The use of interpreters influences the length of the assessment process and, more important, its quality. There are several models of working with interpreters (Westermeyer, 1989). An interpreter can provide translations only or serve as a go-between, an active intermediary with autonomy or possibly a "culture broker" who provides both the patient and the clinician with the cultural context needed to understand each other's meanings. Interpreters must be trained in the refinement of the assessment process as this can sensitize them to the nuances of language necessary for understanding the world of emotional suffering and fear, and view the spectrum of PTSD symptoms and other disorders. When the issue of psychological assessment via standardized protocols emerges, the translator must be trained in the knowledge of understanding the clinical assessment instrument and be able to correctly use it in clinical interventions.

Cultural Issues in Social Greetings and Nonverbal Behavior

Some clinically based data may help therapists in understanding the behavior, functioning, and posttraumatic symptoms of non-Western persons. This literature (Drožđek, 2007; Drožđek & Wilson, 2004; Kirmayer et al., 2008; Wilson & Tang, 2007) can inform non-Western clinicians as to the damaging potential of cross-cultural malfeasance and insensitivity.

For example, ultra-orthodox Jewish and Muslim men and women do not shake hands with a person of the opposite gender. Females from patriarchal cultures may avoid eye contact with male clinicians, thereby showing their culturally embedded respect. A Western professional should avoid wearing sexually appealing clothes while meeting clients from other cultures, because of the differences in attributions of dressing styles. A Western professional may view dynamics in patriarchal families as oppressive to women and the styles of child rearing in other cultures as aggressive, domineering, and abusive. Familiarity with culturally appropriate greetings and styles of interaction is essential for cultural sensitivity. For example, signs of respect that a client shows toward a clinician can vary from culture to culture, from putting a hand on the chest after shaking hands in the Middle East or North Africa to kissing hands or a shoulder in Afghanistan and Iran. Reticence upon entering a clinical/medical counseling or examination room before the clinician is also a sign of respect. It is important that knowing these customs conveys understanding between client and assessor/clinician that extends beyond words, and it underscores the need for a cross-cultural framework of trauma and PTSD and a fundamental respect for the "other."

Potential Complications in the Assessment Procedure

There are many factors that complicate the assessment process of trauma experiences in asylum seekers, refugees, and others seeking psychosocial assistance, benefits, and medical or psychological help:

1. Assessment itself may lead to re-experiencing of trauma and an ensuing decompensation and therefore be avoided by a survivor (Crumlish & O'Rourke, 2010). Assessment might also lead to avoidance behavior by the survivor out of fear, uncertainty, lack of trust, or anxiety about culture-specific expectations for compliance with regulated procedures.
2. Lack of existential safety and ongoing fear of deportation in asylum seekers.
3. Uncertainty about the accuracy of memories recalled, problems with concentration, shame, the stigma of being a psychiatric patient, psychic and emotional numbing, altered spatial and time perception in relation to a trauma story, therapist bias, and cultural differences in explanatory models (Droždek, 2007).
4. Secondary gain in asylum seekers (Jaranson et al., 2001), based on their desire to be diagnosed with PTSD or a trauma-related psychiatric disorder so as to improve their chances of achieving refugee status on humanitarian grounds. In these cases, differential diagnoses must be subjected to careful psychometric and clinical scrutiny.
5. In individuals from cultures where acknowledging or expressing distressing emotions reflecting psychological suffering is discouraged, assessment may result in decreasing rates of psychological and psychiatric distress (Miller, Omidian, Rasmussen, Yaqubi, & Daudzai, 2008).
6. Health professionals burdened with issues of prejudice, suspicion, stereotypes, and cynicism toward the client may avoid trauma stories out of fear for vicarious traumatization or for breaking the rules of politeness and conduct (Rousseau, Crépeau, Foxen, & Houle, 2002; Wilson & Lindy, 1994; Wilson & Thomas, 2004). These dispositional tendencies inevitably result in deficits and errors in the assessment process (Wilson & Thomas, 2004).
7. Lack of transculturally validated diagnostic instruments for assessment (Hollifield et al., 2002; Miller et al., 2009) is a paramount issue for research scientists in the field of trauma and PTSD. At present, there does not exist a single volume to document scientific cross-cultural, psychometric, and other reference measures and their relevant cross-cultural applicability. However, an initial effort was indicated and described by Wilson and Tang (2007).
8. The necessity to use interpreters, which may interfere with the quality of communication (Farooq & Fear, 2003) and disable the communication of empathy (Pugh & Vetere, 2009), requires empirical research and critical evaluation.

Use of Assessment Instruments and Their Validity

The *DSM-IV-TR* (APA, 2004) diagnostic criteria cannot be reasonably applied to indigenous populations simply by translating them into foreign languages. Berry, Poortinga, Segall, and Dasen (1992) have stated three prerequisites for a diagnostic instrument to be transferred to another culture and to be translated into another language: (1) behavior addressed by the assessment instrument must have equivalent meanings in both cultures; (2) the statistical factorial structure and item intercorrelations have to be similar in both versions of the instrument and among both samples; and (3) the quantitative results obtained by the instrument must be equivalent—that is, in the case of a psychometric instrument, its norms must be comparable in both populations along with descriptions of variance, mean scores, t-scores, and other normative data. At present, the field of cross-cultural validation of psychometric measures is in its infancy, but with globalization, the door is now open for such necessary research which will take decades to complete, as described by Wilson and Tang (2007).

In a more global and comprehensive view, Marsella, Dubanoski, Hamada, and Morse (2000) warned of possible ethnocentric bias with respect to Western diagnostic instruments being "transferred" to other cultures. These authors called for important aspects of *cross-cultural equivalence of psychometric measures*, as we mentioned above. They pointed out the importance of the cultural, linguistic, conceptual, scale properties, and normative equivalence, the factorial validity of instruments across cultures, and the problems arising from self-reports (e.g., Asian cultures not speaking openly about oneself and feelings regarded as egotistic, inappropriate, or shameful).

In respect to established methods of clinical diagnoses, these limitations suggest that qualitative and quantitative approaches should be employed side by side in order to assess symptoms of trauma in a culture sensitive way (Renner, Salem, & Ottomeyer, 2007). Qualitative methods are less biased by the preconceptions of Western culture than traditional psychometric instruments (Wilson & Tang, 2007). In our view, these assessments, based on open questions, should be conducted without theoretical assumptions. Most ideally, diagnostic interviews should be carried out by clinicians knowledgeable about the culture-specific peculiarities of the population involved and normative reactions to extreme stress experience (Wilson, 1989; Wilson & Tang, 2007).

Self-report instruments currently used in the trauma field are concerned with the intrapsychic aspects of trauma experience and subsequent symptoms, while placing less emphasis on the role of contextual cultural variables (e.g., Briere & Spinnazzola, 2005; Courtois, 2004). Moreover, there are only few psychometric measures of trauma and PTSD that are cross-culturally validated (see Wilson & Tang, 2007, for a review). Stamm (1996) provided a summary and evaluation of instruments for assessing stress, trauma, and adaptation, and found only a few measures available in languages other than English. Until recently, we did not have any cross-culturally validated instruments designed to assess associated features of PTSD, such as guilt, anger or shame, and resilience. As discussed by Wilson and Tang (2007), questions of posttraumatic abuse, anxiety, and guilt showed complicated results on various forms of posttraumatic adaptational styles and psychopathology across cultures.

Crumlish and O'Rourke (2010) provided an overview of the PTSD assessment tools that have been used in studies inquiring into PTSD treatment among asylum seekers and refugees. Most commonly, types of trauma were assessed with the Communal Traumatic Experiences Inventory (Weine et al., 1995) and the 31-item checklist (Karunakara et al., 2004). PTSD diagnosis and its severity were assessed with the PTSD Symptoms Scale (PSS; Foa, Riggs, Dancu, & Rothbaum, 1993), the Clinician-Administered PTSD Scale (CAPS; Blake et al., 1995), the Impact of Event Scale-Revised (IES-R; Weiss, 2007), the Structured Clinical Interview for *DSM-IV* (SCID; First, Spitzer, & Gibbon, 1995), the CIDI (World Health Organization, 1997), the Post-Traumatic Stress Diagnostic Scale (PDS; Foa, Cashman, Jaycox, & Perry, 1997), and the Harvard Trauma Questionnaire (HTQ; Mollica et al., 1992). Also, the Peritraumatic Dissociative Experiences Questionnaire (PDEQ; Marmar et al., 2007) has been utilized in many different cultural settings with disaster and refugee populations (see Wilson & Keane, 2004; Wilson & Tang, 2007, for a review).

The WHO Disability Assessment Scale-II (WHODAS-II; World Health Organization, 2000) has been used in assessment of functional impairment, whereas the WHO-Quality of Life (WHO-QOL; World Health Organization, 1998) has been suggested as an instrument that provides information about daily functioning in life, social stress and risk factors, quality of life, and perceived control of one's existence. This instrument, although widely used, is not translated and validated in many non-Western languages. Similarly, the Sense of Coherence (SOC) scale provides a psychosocial measure serving to index the quality of overt behaviors under different stressful conditions. Among other studies, the SOC has been used with Chinese Americans (Ying, Lee, & Tsai, 2000) and Southeast Asian refugees (Ying, Akutsu, Zhang, & Huang, 1997).

Briere and Spinazzola (2005) recommended the combined use of two psychometric measures, including one with a cultural-ecological focus and one with a clinical interview in the psychometric assessment of trauma. Examples of psychometric instruments that reflect an ecological emphasis are the measures of community cohesion (Buckner, 1988) and collective efficacy (Sampson, Raudenbush, & Earls, 1997; for discussion, see Hoshmand, 2007).

In order to examine cultural dimensions of clinical assessment, *DSM-IV* (American Psychiatric Association [APA], 1994) introduced an outline for a cultural formulation of psychiatric diagnoses. This complex, thoughtful, and integrated formulation helps to account for symptomatology, diagnosis, prognosis, and appropriate treatment options (Lewis-Fernandez, 1996). The manual explains criteria and explores a broad range of social and cultural issues relevant for assessing post traumatic well-being. These criteria are divided into five areas: (1) ethnocultural identity (including language, religious, and spiritual practices); (2) explanatory models of illness and help-seeking; (3) psychosocial environment (family, age, gender roles, social and power structures, activities and routines, etc.); (4) meaning for levels of adaptive functioning; and (5) the relationship between the individual and the clinician, and an overall integrative assessment of cultural and social aspects that can guide diagnosis and treatment. These criteria and narrative suggestions clearly point to the obvious need to make empirical studies of all assessment instruments and psychometric procedures, until scientific standardization can be determined and achieved. These future tasks are critical for advancement of empirical data, test development and theory revision.

The Explanatory Model Interview (Kleinman, Eisenberg, & Good, 1978) is another useful tool for eliciting explanatory models of problems with which patients present. Within culturally sensitive frameworks, this is an open-ended, nonjudgmental interview aiming at reconstructing the events surrounding symptoms and the illness experience.

At present, research clinicians, policymakers, grant agencies, foundations, and federal agencies need to recognize the gap of knowledge in the relevance of Western validated tools for non-Western populations. The evidence is scant and partial as is the approachability to non-Western cultures.

The Development of Culturally Grounded Assessment Measures

Research on the consequences of exposure to significant or massive trauma in non-Western populations has used assessment tools developed in the West (i.e., mostly the United States), and has been insufficient in questioning the cross-cultural validity and reliability of the PTSD concept, possible cross-cultural validity, and much more (Wilson & Tang, 2007). The measures used were, in general, capable of assessing core human psychological responses and some levels of psychological distress. However, they were not meant to capture *culturally specific indicators* and *idioms of distress* or culture-specific meanings of traumatic impacts, which are often more salient for local communities. Nevertheless, there is no doubt that assessing culturally specific idioms of distress is important (de Jong, 2002; Miller et al., 2006; van der Put & Eisenbruch, 2004; Wessels & Monteiro, 2004) because it assists understanding the *emic* perspectives on distress in non-Western communities and shapes adequate mental health policies and practices.

Until recently, the cross-cultural literature provided little guidance as to the development of culturally based and grounded assessment measures. In the methodological review of the mental health literature, Hollifield et al. (2002) found that half of the studies reviewed did not question construct, concurrent with other forms of validity of PTSD, and provided no information regarding psychometric properties of the measures used in specific non-Western populations.

The use of a contextual theoretical and pragmatic cultural paradigm implies the necessity for the development and cross-cultural validation of culturally grounded assessment measures (Wilson & Tang, 2007). These measurement and assessment procedures should be and can be developed from the ecological and social constructivist perspective in order to grasp the complexity of trauma impact on non-Western trauma and disaster survivors. What this requires is cross-cultural nomothetic and idiosyncratic specialized techniques of assessment in all of their permutations and metric styles to be utilized in the cross-cultural assessment of trauma impacts, PTSD, and more, as necessary to hypothesis testing and research hypotheses.

Miller et al. (2006, 2009) described a methodology for developing *culturally grounded* assessment measures in conflict and postconflict situations of all types. Similar methodology has been utilized by Bolton and Tang (2002) and Hubbard and Pearson (2004). In this multimethod approach, qualitative and quantitative methods were combined and eight steps of the developmental process were distinguished:

1. Identification of *emic* indicators of well-being and distress by qualitative methods (e.g., how people talk about distress), and a content analysis of material obtained, revealing indicators of poor mental health in three domains of human functioning, (e.g., within the community, within the family, and on an individual psychological level).
2. Selection of the most commonly mentioned indicators of distress in the narratives, and the creation of an instrument that assesses frequency of experiencing distress.
3. Translation and back-translation of the assessment instrument, critical to the empirical validation of measurement protocols and empirically derived procedures.
4. Peer and cross-cultural group review of appropriateness and ease of comprehension of the instrument's items.
5. Pilot-testing of the instrument (i.e., self-report tool, etc.) in relevant epidemiology of cross-cultural populations.
6. Use of the instrument developed in large surveys across different cultural populations.
7. Scientific assessment of the construct validity and reliability of the instrument tools.
8. Examination of the factor structure of various instruments (with an exploratory principal components factor analysis with varimax rotation) in order to establish ways in which commonly experienced symptoms tend to cluster among variables and measures. The caveat here is whether

or not such factor analytic solutions are conceptually applicable within a specific cultural context.

Conclusion

It is generally understood that the assessment of trauma in non-Western populations needs to be culturally sensitive. The survivors' experiential world and cultural context must be reconstructed simultaneously from the inside out and from the outside in. Posttraumatic psychological injuries cannot simply be reduced to a diagnosis of PTSD and be exclusive to other Axis I and Axis II diagnoses and cultural idioms of distress. Adequate assessment tools can be developed and standardized across cultures, although the process is in its infancy. The contextual model of assessment is recommended as one that includes the complexity of the refugee experience and is among the most adequate, comprehensive, and inclusive ways beyond a simple, expectable PTSD paradigm, per se.

The limitations of traditional psychometric assessment procedures include a broad array of considerations that extend beyond the traditional assumptions of largely American standards of scientific validation and acceptability. We should ask ourselves how non-Western persons can even understand test items for measure of PTSD, and the like, when such concepts do not exist within their culturally based belief systems of meaning.

Future Directions

1. Fundamental conceptual revision of approaches to understanding and studying trauma need to occur. They should include multiple realities determined by contextual factors and insightful theoretical perspectives that embrace anthropology and archaeology.

2. The prevailing pathogenic-disease paradigm requires supplementation by a positive psychology advocating holistic health within culturally derived techniques of treatment and healing (Wilson, 2006).

3. Further research should be done considering applicability and transfer of psychological treatments developed in one culture to another (Wilson & Tang, 2007). What works here may not work there, and vice versa.

4. Assessment instruments that address cultural realities should be created (Wilson & Tang, 2007) and be idiosyncratic in terms of the specificity of items.

5. Qualitative research and ethnographic approaches should be promoted and re-enter the realm of the Western science in order to enlarge our understanding of non-Western traumatized individuals and communities. The qualitative nature of research opens new doors to the future and the evolution of ethnography, psychology, anthropology, sociology, and so much more. In the end, these important considerations ask the question of how humans from different cultures will come to know each other with respect, humility, and love for differences, including the most basic archetypal appreciation of psychic trauma and its potential impact to humanness.

References

American Psychiatric Association (APA). (1994). *Diagnostic and statistical manual of mental disorders* (4th ed.). Washington, DC: Author.

American Psychiatric Association (APA). (2004). *Diagnostic and statistical manual of mental disorders* (4th ed., text rev.). Washington, DC: Author.

Antonovsky, A. (1972). Breakdown: A needed fourth step in the conceptual armamentarium of modern medicine. *Social Science and Medicine*, 6, 537–544.

Aronoff, J., & Wilson, J. P. (Eds.). (1985). *Personality in the social process.* Hillsdale: Lawrence Erlbaum.

Berry, J. W., Poortinga, Y. H., Segall, M. H., & Dasen, P. R. (1992). *Cross-cultural psychology. Research and applications.* Cambridge: Cambridge University Press.

Blake, D. D., Weathers, F. W., Nagy, L. M., Kaloupek, D. G., Gusman, F. D., Charney, D. S., & Keane, T. M. (1995). The development of a clinician-administered PTSD scale. *Journal of Traumatic Stress, 8*, 75–90.

Bolton, P., & Tang, A. (2002). An alternative approach to cross-cultural function assessment. *Social Psychiatry and Psychiatric Epidemiology, 37*, 537–543.

Briere, J., & Spinazzola, J. (2005). Phenomenology and psychological assessment of complex posttraumatic states. *Journal of Traumatic Stress, 18*, 401–412.

Bracken, P. J., & Petty, C. (Eds.). (1998). *Rethinking the trauma of war.* London: Free Association Books.

Bronfenbrenner, U. (1981). *The ecology of human development: Experiments by nature and design* (4th ed.). Cambridge, MA: Harvard University Press.

Buckner, J. C. (1988). The development of an instrument to measure neighborhood cohesion. *American Journal of Community Psychology, 16*, 771–791.

Courtois, C. A. (2004). Complex trauma, complex reactions: Assessment and treatment. *Psychotherapy: Theory, Research, Practice, Training, 41*, 412–425.

Crumlish, N., & O'Rourke, K. (2010). A systematic review of treatments for post-traumatic stress disorder among refugees and asylum seekers. *Journal of Nervous and Mental Disease, 198*, 237–251.

Dana, R. H. (2007). Refugee assessment practices and cultural competency training. In J. P. Wilson, & C. Tang (Eds.), *Cross-cultural assessment of psychological trauma and PTSD* (pp. 91–112). New York: Springer.

de Jong, J. (Ed.). (2002). *Trauma, war and violence: Public mental health in socio-cultural context.* New York: Plenum Press

Drožđek, B. (2007). The rebirth of contextual thinking in psychotraumatology. In B. Drožđek, & J. P. Wilson (Eds.), *Voices of trauma: Treating survivors across cultures* (pp. 1–26). New York: Springer.

Droždek, B., & Wilson, J. P. (2004). Uncovering: Trauma-focused treatment techniques with asylum seekers. In J. P. Wilson & B. Droždek (Eds.), *Broken spirits: The treatment of traumatized asylum seekers, refugees, war and torture victims* (pp. 243–276). New York: Brunner-Routledge.

Droždek, B., Wilson, J. P., & Turkovic, S. (2012). PTSD and psychopathology in refugees: A reflective cross-cultural contextual view of mental health interventions. In U. A. Segal, & D. Elliott (Eds.), *Refugees worldwide.* Westport, CT/London: Praeger (in press).

Farooq, S., & Fear, F. (2003). Working through interpreters. *Advances in Psychological Treatment, 9,* 104–109.

First, M. B., Spitzer, R. L., & Gibbon, M. G. (1995). *Structured clinical interview for DSM-IV Axis I disorders.* New York: New York State Psychiatric Institute.

Foa, E. B., Riggs, D. S., Dancu, C. V., & Rothbaum, B. O. (1993). Reliability and validity of a brief instrument for assessing post-traumatic stress disorder. *Journal of Traumatic Stress, 6,* 459–473.

Foa, E., Cashman, L., Jaycox, L., & Perry, K. (1997). The validation of a self-report measure of PTSD: The Posttraumatic Diagnostic Scale. *Psychological Assessments, 9,* 445–451.

Helman, C. G. (1994). *Culture, health and illness.* Oxford: Butterworth Heinemann.

Hollifield, M., et al. (2002). Measuring trauma and health status in refugees: A critical review. *Journal of the American Medical Association, 288,* 611–621.

Hoshmand, L.T. (2007). Cultural-ecological perspectives on the understanding and assessment of trauma. In J. P. Wilson, & C. Tang (Eds.), *Cross-cultural assessment of psychological trauma and PTSD* (pp. 31–50). New York: Springer.

Hubbard, J., & Pearson, N. (2004). Sierra Leonean refugees in Guinea: Addressing the mental health effects of massive community violence. In K. E. Miller, & L. M. Rasco (Eds.), *The mental health of refugees: Ecological approaches to healing and adaptation* (pp. 95–132). Mahwah, NJ: Lawrence Erlbaum.

Jaranson, J. M., Kinzie, J. D., Friedman, M., Ortiz, D., Friedman, M. J., Southwick, S., & Mollica, R. (2001). Assessment, diagnosis and intervention. In E. Gerrity, T. M. Keane, & F. Tuma (Eds.), *The mental health consequences of torture* (pp. 249–275). New York: Kluwer Academic.

Karunakara, U. K., Neuner, F., Schauer, M., Singh, K., Hill, K., Elbert, T., & Burnham, G. (2004). Traumatic events and symptoms of post-traumatic stress disorder amongst Sudanese nationals, refugees and Ugandans in the West Nile. *African Health Science, 4,* 83–93.

Kirmayer, L. J. (1996). Confusion of the senses: Implications of ethnocultural variations in somatoform and dissociative disorders for PTSD. In A. J. Marsella, M. J. Friedman, E. T. Gerrity, & R. M. Scurfield (Eds.), *Ethnocultural aspects of posttraumatic stress disorder. Issues, research, and clinical applications* (pp. 131–163). Washington, DC: American Psychiatric Association.

Kirmayer, L. J. (2001). Cultural variations in the clinical presentation of depression and anxiety: Implications for diagnosis and treatment. *Journal of Clinical Psychiatry, 62*(Suppl 13), 22–28.

Kirmayer, L. J., Rousseau, C., Jarvis, G. E., & Guzder, J. (2008). The cultural context of clinical assessment. In A. Tasman, M. Maj, M. B. First, J. Kay, & J. Lieberman (Eds.), *Psychiatry* (3rd ed., pp. 54–66). New York: John Wiley.

Kleinman, A. (1977). Depression, somatization and the new cross cultural psychiatry. *Social Science and medicine, 11,* 3–10.

Kleinman, A. (1988). *Rethinking psychiatry.* New York: Free Press.

Kleinman, A., Das, V., & Lock, M. (Eds.). (1997). *Social suffering.* Berkeley, CA: University of California Press.

Kleinman, A., Eisenberg, L., & Good, B. (1978). Culture, illness and care: Clinical lessons from anthropologic and cross-cultural research. *Annals of Internal Medicine, 88,* 251–258.

Leff, J. (2001). *The unbalanced mind.* New York: Columbia University Press.

Lewis-Fernandez, R. (1996). Cultural formulation of psychiatric diagnosis. *Culture, Medicine and Psychiatry, 20,* 133–144.

Lopez, S., & Guarnaccia, P. J. (2000). Cultural psychopathology: Uncovering the social world of mental illness. *Annual Review of Psychology, 51,* 571–598.

Marmar, C. R., Metzler, T. J., Otte, C., McCaslin, S., Inslicht, S., & Haase, C. H. (2007). The Peritraumatic Dissociative Experiences Questionnaire: An international perspective. In J. P. Wilson, & C. Tang (Eds.), *Cross-cultural assessment of psychological trauma and PTSD* (pp. 197–218). New York: Springer.

Marsella, A. J., Dubanoski, J., Hamada, W. C., & Morse, H. (2000). The measurement of personality across cultures. Historical, conceptual, and methodological issues and considerations. *American Behavioral Scientist, 44,* 41–62.

Marsella, A. J., Kaplan, A., & Suarez, E. (2002). Cultural considerations for understanding, assessing, and treating depressive experience and disorder. In M. A. Reinecke & M. R. Davison (Eds.), *Comparative treatments of depression* (pp. 47–78). New York: Springer.

Marsella, A. J., & White, G. M. (1989). *Cultural conceptions of mental health and therapy.* Boston, MA: G. Reidel.

Marsella, A. J., & Yamada, A. M. (2000). Culture and mental health: An introduction and overview of foundations, concepts, and issues. In I. Cuéllar & F. A. Paniagua (Eds.), *Handbook of multicultural mental health* (pp. 3–24). San Diego: Academic Press.

Miller, K. E., Omidian, P., Kulkarni, M., Yaqubi, A., Daudzai, H., & Rasmussen, A. (2009). The validity and clinical utility of post-traumatic stress disorder in Afghanistan. *Transcultural Psychiatry, 46,* 219–237.

Miller, K.E., Omidian, P., Quraishy, A.S., Quraishy, N., Nasiry, M. N., Nasiry, S., & Yaqubi, A. A. (2006). The Afghan Symptom Checklist: A culturally grounded approach to mental health assessment in a conflict zone. *American Journal of Orthopsychiatry, 76,* 423–433.

Miller, K. E., Omidian, P., Rasmussen, A., Yaqubi, A., & Daudzai, H. (2008). Daily stressors, war experiences, and mental health in Afghanistan. *Transcultural Psychiatry, 45,* 611–638.

Mollica, R. F., Caspi-Yavin, Y., Bollini, P., Truong, T., Tor, S., & Lavelle, J. (1992). The Harvard Trauma Questionnaire. Validating a cross-cultural instrument for measuring torture, trauma and posttraumatic stress disorder in Indochinese refugees. *Journal of Nervous and Mental Disease, 180,* 111–116.

Pike, K. L. (1954). Emic and etic standpoints for the description of behavior. In K. L. Pike (Ed.), *Language in relation to a unified theory of the structure of human behavior* (pp. 8–28). Glendale, CA: Summer Institute of Linguistics.

Pugh, M. A., & Vetere, A. (2009). Lost in translation: An interpretative phenomenological analysis of mental health professionals' experiences of empathy in clinical work with an interpreter. *Psychological Psychotherapy, 82*, 305–321.

Put van de, W. A. C. M., & Eisenbruch, M. (2004). Internally displaced Cambodians: Healing trauma in communities. In K. E. Miller & L. M. Rasco (Eds.), *The mental health of refugees: Ecological approaches to healing and adaptation* (pp. 133–160). Mahwah, NJ: Lawrence Erlbaum.

Renner, W., Salem, I., & Ottomeyer, K. (2007). Posttraumatic stress in asylum seekers from Chechnya, Afghanistan, and West Africa: Differential findings obtained by quantitative and qualitative methods in three Austrian samples. In J. P. Wilson & C. Tang (Eds.), *Cross-cultural assessment of psychological trauma and PTSD* (pp. 239–275). New York: Springer.

Rousseau, C., Crépeau, F., Foxen, P., & Houle, F. (2002). The complexity of determining refugeehood: A multidisciplinary analysis of the decision-making process of the Canadian Immigration and Refugee Board. *Journal of Refugee Studies, 15*, 43–70.

Sampson, R. J., Raudenbush, S. W., & Earls, F. (1997). Neighborhoods and violence crime: A multi-level study of collective efficacy. *Science, 277*, 918–923.

Shweder, R. A. (2001). *Thinking through cultures. Expeditions in cultural psychology*. Cambridge, MA: Harvard University Press.

Shweder, R. A., & Haidt, J. (2000). The cultural psychology of the emotions: Ancient and new. In M. Lewis & J. M. Haviland-Jones (Eds.), *Handbook of emotions* (2nd ed., pp. 397–414). New York: Guilford.

Smith, M., Lin, M. K., & Mendoza, R. (1993). Non biological issues affecting psychopharmacology: Cultural considerations. In K. M. Lin, R. E. Poland, & G. Nalcasali (Eds.), *Psychopharmacology and psychobiology of ethnicity* (pp. 37–58). Washington, DC: American Psychiatric Press.

Stamm, B. H. (Ed.). (1996). *Measurement of stress, trauma and adaptation*. Lutherville, MD: Sidran Press.

Summerfield, D. (1997). The impact of war and atrocity on civilian populations. In D. Black, M. Newman, J. Harris-Hendricks, & G. Mezey (Eds.), *Psychological trauma: A developmental approach* (pp. 148–155). London: Gaskell.

Summerfield, D. (1999). A critique of seven assumptions behind psychological trauma programs in war-affected areas. *Social Science and Medicine, 48*, 1449–1462.

Triandis, H. C. (1972). *The analysis of subjective culture*. New York: John Wiley.

van der Veer, G., & van Waning, A. (2004). Creating a safe therapeutic sanctuary. In J. P. Wilson & B. Drožđek (Eds.), *Broken spirits: The treatment of traumatized asylum seekers, refugees, war and torture victims* (pp. 187–220). New York: Brunner-Routledge.

Van Dijk, R. (2006). Cultuur, trauma en PTSS: Kanttekeningenbij de cultuurgebondenheid van de posttraumatische stresstoornis. Cultuur Migratie en Gezondheid, 4/5, 20–31.

Weine, S. M., Becker, D. F., McGlashan, T. H., Laub, D., Lazrove, S., Vojvoda, D., & Hyman, L. (1995). Psychiatric consequences of "ethnic cleansing": Clinical assessments and trauma testimonies of newly resettled Bosnian refugees. *American Journal of Psychiatry, 152*, 536–542.

Weiss, D S. (2007). The Impact of Event Scale-Revised. In J. P. Wilson & C. Tang (Eds.), *Cross-cultural assessment of psychological trauma and PTSD* (pp. 219–238). New York: Springer.

Wessells, M., & Monteiro, C. (2004). Internally displaced Angolans: A child-focused, community-based intervention. In K. E. Miller & L. M. Rasco (Eds.), *The mental health of refugees: Ecological approaches to healing and adaptation* (pp. 67–94). Mahwah, NJ: Lawrence Erlbaum.

Westermeyer, J. (1989). *Psychiatric care of migrants: A clinical guide*. Washington, DC: American Psychiatric Press.

Wilson, J. P. (Ed.). (1989). *Trauma, transformation and healing*. New York: Brunner/Mazel.

Wilson, J. P. (2006). *The posttraumatic self: Restoring meaning and wholeness to personality*. New York: Brunner Routledge.

Wilson, J. P., Friedman, M. J., & Lindy, J. D. (Eds.). (2001). *Treating psychological trauma and PTSD*. New York: Guilford.

Wilson, J. P., & Keane, T. M. (Eds.). (2004). *Assessing psychological trauma and PTSD*. New York: Guilford.

Wilson, J. P., & Lindy, J. D. (Eds.). (1994). *Countertransference in the treatment of PTSD*. New York: Guilford.

Wilson, J. P., & Raphael, B. (Eds.). (1993). *International handbook of traumatic stress syndrome*. New York: Plenum.

Wilson, J. P., & Thomas, R. B. (2004). *Empathy in the treatment of trauma and PTSD*. New York: Brunner Routledge.

Wilson, J. P., & Tang, C. (Eds.). (2007). *Cross-cultural assessment of psychological trauma and PTSD*. New York: Springer.

World Health Organization. (1997). *Composite international diagnostic interview (CIDI)*. Geneva: Author.

World Health Organization. (1998). The World Health Organization Quality of Life Assessment (WHOQOL): Development and general psychometric properties. *Social Science and Medicine, 46*, 1569–1585.

World Health Organization. (2000). World Health Organization Disability Scale-II (WHODAS-II) 12 Item Version. Geneva: Author.

Ying, Y-W, Akutsu, P. D., Zhang, X., & Huang, L. N. (1997). Psychological dysfunction in Southeast Asian refugees as mediated by sense of coherence. *American Journal of Community Psychology, 25*, 839–859.

Ying, Y-W, Lee, P. A., & Tsai, J. L. (2000). Cultural orientation and racial discrimination: Predictors of coherence in Chinese American young adults. *Journal of Community Psychology, 28*, 427–442.

CHAPTER

21 Assessing PTSD-related Functional Impairment and Quality of Life

Darren W. Holowka *and* Brian P. Marx

Abstract

Previous research has shown that PTSD is associated with impairments in functioning across a variety of domains and decrements in quality of life. In this chapter, we review the literature on the assessment of PTSD-related impairments in functioning and quality of life. We first discuss the importance of assessing PTSD-related impairments in quality of life and functioning. We then review some important methodological concerns related to the assessment of these constructs. Finally, we review some of the most commonly used assessment tools and discuss recent efforts to develop and validate a new assessment tool to assess PTSD-related functional impairment.

Key Words: Trauma, posttraumatic stress disorder, functional impairment, quality of life, assessment

Assessing PTSD-related Functional Impairment and Quality of Life

According to the *Diagnostic and Statistical Manual for Mental Disorders* (*DSM*-IV; American Psychiatric Association [APA], 2000), in order for a posttraumatic stress disorder (PTSD) diagnosis to be rendered, the individual must not only endorse the requisite number of PTSD symptoms (i.e., at least one re-experiencing symptom, three avoidance and numbing symptoms, and two hyper-arousal symptoms) but also report that these symptoms have resulted in additional psychological distress and/or social or occupational impairment. Previous research has shown that PTSD is associated with impairments across a range of functional outcomes, including occupational functioning (e.g., Hoge et al., 2008; Resnick & Rosenheck, 2008; Rona et al., 2009), marital, family and interpersonal functioning (e.g., Kuhn, Blanchard, & Hickling, 2003; Rona et al., 2009; Sayers, Farrow, Ross, & Oslin, 2009) and subjective (e.g., Gudmundsdottir, Beck, Coffey, Miller, & Palyo, 2004; Paunović & Öst, 2004; Rapaport, Clary, Fayyad, & Endicott, 2005) and objective indicators (e.g., homelessness, unemployment) of quality of life (O'Connell, Kasprow & Rosenheck, 2008; Schnurr, Hayes, Lunney, McFall, & Uddo, 2006).

Although the majority of the research in this area is cross-sectional, there is some available research showing that PTSD and impairments in functioning and quality of life are prospectively related to one another (e.g., Golden-Kreutz et al., 2005; Koenen, Stellman, Sommer, & Stellman, 2008; Solomon & Mikulincer, 2007; Taylor, Wald, & Asmundson, 2006). Schnurr et al. (2006) found that increases in PTSD symptom severity were associated with increases in both psychosocial and physical health-related functional impairments. Lunney and Schnurr (2007) reported that clinically significant improvements in PTSD symptoms were associated with improvements in multiple domains of quality of life. Ramchand, Marshall, Schell, and

Jaycox (2008) found that, among survivors of community violence, greater PTSD symptoms within one week of the event predicted lower quality of life at 3 months posttrauma. In addition, quality of life at 3 months posttrauma predicted greater PTSD symptoms at 12 months posttrauma. These findings suggest a reciprocal relationship between PTSD and impairments in functioning and quality of life.

Further complicating our understanding of these associations is the fact that various PTSD symptoms appear to be differentially associated with functional impairments. Intrusive recollections, psychological distress caused by trauma reminders, sleep and concentration difficulties, and hyper-vigilence are the most frequently reported PTSD symptoms among those with functional impairments (Norman, Stein, & Davidson, 2007). Other research has found that PTSD reexpeeriencing symptoms have been associated specifically with impairments in occupational functioning (Taylor et al., 2006) as well as in play, learning, and creativity (Lunney & Schnurr, 2007). Avoidance and numbing symptoms have been associated specifically with impairments in parenting (Samper, Taft, King, & King, 2004), relationship distress and difficulties (e.g., Litz, 1992; Litz & Gray, 2002; Riggs, Byrne, Weathers, & Litz, 1998), role functioning impairments (Kuhn et al., 2003; Lunney & Schnurr, 2007), reduced self-esteem (Lunney & Schnurr, 2007), and physical health problems (Lunney & Schnurr, 2007; Woods & Wineman, 2004). Hyper-arousal symptoms have been associated with impairments in occupational and major role functioning (Kuhn et al., 2003; Taylor et al., 2006), as well as physical health problems (Kimerling, Clum, & Wolfe, 2000; Woods & Wineman, 2004).

A number of recent studies have compared the impact of PTSD and other anxiety disorders on functional outcomes. For example, Rapaport et al. (2005) found that individuals with PTSD reported functional impairments that were both more likely to be severe and more pervasive compared to those with other anxiety disorders. A recent meta-analysis of quality of life in anxiety disorders (Olatunji, Cisler, & Tolin, 2007) found large effect sizes for PTSD across multiple domains of quality of life. Although they found no differences in overall quality of life, they did find that impairments in some domains might be different across anxiety disorders. In particular, there was some evidence to suggest that not all anxiety disorders were associated with the same type and severity of impairments and that, in relation to other anxiety disorders, PTSD was always associated with lesser quality of life.

One of the striking features of the studies on functional outcomes associated with PTSD is the variety of instruments used to measure and describe these outcomes. For example, two recent reviews of quality of life in the anxiety disorders (Mendlowicz & Stein, 2000; Mogotsi, Kaminer, & Stein, 2000) included findings on subjective quality of life, psychosocial impairment, and physical health functioning. These authors noted that, although there is no agreed-upon definition of quality of life, there is broad agreement that a good measure should include subjective and objective assessments across a variety of domains. Given the possibility that particular symptoms or characteristics of different disorders may have distinctive effects on quality of life and functioning, these authors also suggested that researchers consider developing disorder-specific scales.

In the remainder of this chapter, we review the literature on the assessment of PTSD-related impairments in functioning and quality of life. We first discuss the importance of assessing PTSD-related impairments in quality of life and functioning. We then review some important methodological concerns related to the assessment of these constructs. Finally, we provide an overview of some of the most commonly used assessment tools, as well as discuss recent efforts to develop and validate a new assessment tool to assess PTSD-related functional impairment.

The Importance of Accurately Measuring PTSD-related Functional Impairment and Quality of Life

Our ability to adequately and competently assess PTSD-related functional impairment and quality of life has great importance for the field of PTSD research. First, the means and methods by which we assess PTSD-related functional impairment affect our understanding of how frequently the disorder occurs among those exposed to trauma (e.g., prevalence of the disorder). This point is highlighted by a recent discussion in the literature regarding the Dohrenwend et al. (2006) reanalysis of the National Vietnam Veterans Readjustment Study (NVVRS). In the original analysis of the (NVVRS) data, the prevalence of current PTSD was estimated at 15.2% and 8.5%, whereas the lifetime prevalence was 30.9% and 26.9%, respectively. However, in the reanalysis, after adjusting for documentation of trauma exposure and level of reported impairment, Dohrenwend and colleagues reported prevalence estimates of 9.1% for current PTSD and 18.7% for lifetime PTSD among male Vietnam Veterans. Although the reanalysis lowered the prevalence estimates of PTSD among Vietnam Veterans, critics complained that the estimated rate of PTSD was still too high because the measure of functioning that was used (the Global Assessment of Functioning; GAF) was heavily skewed toward identifying impairment (Frueh, 2007; McNally, 2007). McNally (2007) stated that if the NVVRS reanalysis had used just a slightly more stringent cutoff score on the GAF for determining functional impairment, the prevalence of current PTSD would have dropped by 65% relative to the original NVVRS prevalence estimate. Importantly, the purpose of the Dohrenwend et al. study was not to recalculate the prevalence of PTSD in the NVVRS but to arrive at confirmation of war-zone stress exposure variables.

Second, the means and methods by which we assess PTSD-related impairment in functioning and quality of life also are important for determining the extent to which various therapies may be considered beneficial for PTSD. For example, two recent large-scale VA Cooperative Studies examining the effects of group therapy (Schnurr et al., 2003) and individual cognitive-behavior therapy (CBT; Schnurr et al., 2007) showed that, although PTSD symptoms improved significantly, neither study found improvements on either the Medical Outcomes Study Short Form (SF-36; Ware & Sherbourne, 1992) or the Quality of Life Inventory (QOLI; Frisch, Cornell, Villanueva, & Retzlaff, 1992). These results suggest that either (1) the treatment did not improve functioning or quality of life, or (2) the measures that are currently being used to assess functioning and quality of life are not sufficiently sensitive to assess improvements in these constructs.

Finally, the means and methods by which we assess PTSD-related impairment also have implications for compensation and pension procedures and decisions for those contending that they are suffering impairments related to their PTSD. Related to this point are the recent findings of a committee convened by the Institute of Medicine (Institute of Medicine [IOM], 2007) to address ongoing concerns about the current procedures used to assess PTSD among Veterans in compensation and pension examinations. Among other things, the committee was asked to review the utility of the GAF in evaluating impairment associated with PTSD. The committee found that the GAF score has limited utility in the assessment of disability for PTSD compensation for Veterans. The score is only marginally relevant to PTSD because of its emphasis on the symptoms of mood disorders and schizophrenia and its limited range of symptom content. Given that the means and methods by which we measure psychiatric-related functional impairment have enormous value from a healthcare perspective in terms of identifying individuals with the disorder, and for promoting more efficient allocation of resources and efforts toward those who are in most need, the IOM committee recommended that the Department of Veterans Affairs ultimately identify and implement an appropriate replacement for the GAF, although they did not specifically identify any such replacement.

General Issues in the Assessment of Functional Impairment and Quality of Life

One of the first question that arises with respect to measurement of functional impairment and quality of life is whether the self-report methodology is adequate or appropriate. Katschnig (2006) noted that, especially among individuals with mental illness, the reliability of self-report may be questionable. Furthermore, transitory affective states associated with mental disorders may diminish the capacity to reliably report on one's own functioning and quality of life. Nonetheless, quality of life by definition must incorporate some level of subjective self-report into its assessment.

Although the functional impairment construct is central to the notion of what constitutes a mental disorder within the *DSM* classification system, the term is never explicitly defined anywhere in the *DSM*. An important consequence of this fact is that it introduces additional error into an already somewhat unreliable diagnostic process. Although diagnostic reliability is relatively good when using structured interviews or assessments, such formal assessments are not commonly conducted in most clinical settings. Under less rigorous conditions, reliability of diagnosis is less well understood. Of course, many factors are likely contributors to such variance, but it is reasonable to expect that a criterion lacking an operational definition is at least partly responsible. Anecdotally, many clinicians will ignore the functional impairment requirement and rather opt to endorse its proxy, "clinically significant distress," which some clinicians assume through the mere presence at a clinical evaluation, thereby effectively ignoring the criterion altogether. Other clinicians may use any number of unstandardized metrics whereby they assign significance to impairment.

Interestingly, the functional impairment criterion is handled differently by the *DSM* and the World Health Organization (WHO) International Family of Classifications (Madden, Sykes, & Ustün, 2007). Within the WHO classification system, a distinction is drawn between diseases for which diagnoses are assigned and disability, which is considered a separate outcome from the diagnosis itself. In the WHO system, disorders are defined by the *International Classification System of Disorders* (*ICD*), whereas disability is defined by the *International Classification Functioning, Disability and Health* (*ICF*) system (World Health Organization [WHO], 2001). Thus, in contrast to the *DSM* classification system, the *ICD* does not include a functional impairment criterion for PTSD (Ustün & Kennedy, 2009). Although the Impairment and Disability Study Group for *DSM-5* has recommended harmonizing the *DSM-5* classification with the WHO classification system (recommended changes as of May 2010), at present, it appears that *DSM-5* is poised to continue with the inclusion of distress or disability as a criterion for diagnosis of disorders in general and of PTSD in particular.

The fact that the WHO system classifies disability separately from disorders and/or diseases gives credence to the possibility that these outcomes may be separate, albeit related, but equally important sequelae to trauma exposure. Some, however, have argued that functioning may even be more important than symptomatology (e.g., McKnight & Kashdan, 2009). Although this may or may not be the case, if indeed symptoms are the cause of the impairments in functioning and quality of life, it is at least worth noting that improvements in symptomatology without concomitant gains in functioning may indicate that further intervention is needed. More specifically, it may not be possible to affect functioning and quality of life without treating symptoms, but treating symptoms may not be sufficient to ameliorate functional impairments or improve quality of life. At a minimum, functioning and quality of life are important outcome measures that are both relevant to the lived experiences of those suffering the aftermath of trauma exposure.

As noted earlier with respect to the controversy surrounding the NVVRS and compensation and pension benefits among Veterans, one of the most contentious issues with regard to the assessment of functional impairment involves the use of the standard measure of functioning in *DSM*, the GAF (Endicott, Spitzer, Fleiss, & Cohen, 1976). The GAF is a clinician-rated index of functioning that ranges from 0 to 100, with higher scores indicating better functioning. Originally developed to assess the severity of mood and psychotic disorder, this index has been incorporated into Axis V of the *DSM-IV* for the purpose of establishing an individual's level of overall functioning.

Given its origins, a primary concern about the GAF is that it may be only marginally relevant to PTSD because of its emphasis on the symptoms of mood disorders and schizophrenia and its limited range of symptom content. Another concern related to using the GAF is that, although it combines symptomatology and social-occupational functioning into one score (Goldman, 2005), these constructs may be orthogonal. Some research has suggested that GAF scores correlate more strongly with symptom severity than with functional impairment per se (Moos, Nichol, & Moos, 2002) and that they may not be very reliable at the individual level (Söderberg, Tungström, & Armelius, 2005). Additionally, because the GAF is a single-item measure, its psychometric properties are of concern (Nunnally, 1978). These limitations have led to revisions of the GAF, such as the Social and Occupational Functioning Assessment Scale (Goldman, Skodol, & Lave, 1992) and Mental Illness Research Education and Clinical Center Global Assessment of Functioning (Niv, Cohen, Sullivan, & Young, 2007).

Measures of Functional Impairment and Quality of Life

A large number of extant measures of functional impairment and quality of life are available for clinical and research purposes. Table 21.1 provides information regarding many of the most widely used measures. Among the more commonly used measures to assess functional impairment and quality of life are the World Health Organization Disability Assessment Scale-II (WHODAS-II; Epping-Jordan, Chatterji, & Ustün, 2000; World Health Organization [WHO], 1988), the Medical Outcomes Study Short Form 36-item (SF-36; McHorney, Ware, & Raczek, 1993; Ware, 1999) and the Quality of Life Inventory (Frisch et al., 1992).

Table 21.1. **Measures of functional impairment and quality of life**

Measure	Domains Assessed	Description	Items
World Health Organization Disability Assessment Schedule-II (WHODAS-II; WHO, 2000)	1. Understanding and communicating 2. Mobility 3. Self-Care 4. Getting along with others 5. Life activities 6. Participation in society	A revised version of the WHODAS (World Health Organization, 1988), the WHODAS-II is a measure of impairment due to military or health- related problems experienced in the past 30 days. It provides a profile of functioning across six activity domains, as well as a general disability score. It can be administered as a self-report questionnaire or in interview form.	36
Medical Outcomes Study Short Form (SF-36; Ware et al., 1993)	1. Physical functioning 2. Role functioning 3. Energy 4. Emotional well-being 5. Social functioning 6. Pain 7. General health 8. Health change 9. Mental Health	A generic widely used measure of health status. The 8 domains included in the SF-36 were selected from the 40 used in the Medical Outcomes Study (Stewart & Ware, 1992). A short form is also available (SF-12).	36
International Classification of Functioning, Disability and Health Checklist (ICF; WHO, 2003)	1. Functioning & Disability a. Body functions b. Mental functions 2. Contextual Factors a. Environmental Factors b. Personal Factors	The ICF is a comprehensive rating system for assessing health disability and functioning. The ICF checklist is a guideline for clinician-administered assessment of health status and health related functioning. It includes a brief questionnaire that may be administered by an interviewer of used as a self-report instrument. Its comprehensive nature requires sufficient training to administer effectively.	Extensive
Global Assessment of Functioning (GAF; APA, 2000)		The GAF is a clinician-rated barometer of overall functioning, taking into account symptom severity and social and occupational functioning. It is rated on a 100-point scale, divided into 10-point ranges. Examples of levels of symptomatology and impairment are provided as anchors.	1
Social and Occupational Functioning Assessment Scale (SOFAS; APA, 2000; Morosini et al., 2000)	1. Social 2. Occupational functioning	Similar in to the GAF, however it focuses exclusively on social and occupational functioning.	1
MIRECC GAF Department of Veterans Affairs (Niv et al., 2007)	1. Occupational 2. Social 3. Symptom	Another modification of the GAF, it was expanded to include 3 separate 100-point scales for each of constructs measured.	3
Sheehan Disability Scale (Sheehan, 1983)	1. Work/School 2. Social 3. Family	Respondent rates difficulties due to symptoms in each of 3 domains on a 10-point scale with verbal anchors.	3

(*continued*)

Table 21.1. Measures of functional impairment and quality of life (*continued*)

Measure	Domains Assessed	Description	Items
Sheehan Work Disability Scale (SWDS; Sheehan, 1983)	1. Physical work 2. Mental work (thinking, planning, using your brain) 3. Work closely and effectively with others	Respondent rates difficulties in occupational functioning due to his or her symptoms on a 10-point scale with anchors.	3
Sheehan Disability Scale for Women (SDS-W; Sheehan, 2003)	1. Work/school 2. Social life 3. Family life/home responsibilities 4. Balance between personal life and career	Respondent rates the extent to which he or she experiences problems in each of these four domains due to his or her symptoms on a 10-point visual analog scale.	4
The Longitudinal Interval Follow-up Evaluation (LIFE; Keller et al., 1987)	1. Work 2. Relationships 3. Sexual 4. Household 5. Recreation 6. Overall life satisfaction. 7. Family 8. Marital Status 9. Global Social Adjustment 10. GAF	An integrated system for assessing the long-term course of psychiatric disorders. The interviewer grades impairment for each domain on a monthly basis within a set time period (typically 6 to 12 months). Higher ratings denote more severe impairment.	13; additional items for different familial relationships
Range of Impaired Functioning Tool (LIFE-RIFT; Leon et al., 1999)	1. Work 2. Interpersonal relations 3. Satisfaction 4. Recreation	A brief version of the LIFE that can be administered by a clinician or trained layperson in 5 minutes. The interviewer must be able to distinguish impairment resulting from psychopathology versus other life issues (e.g., caring for a sick relative).	5
Health and Work Performance Questionnaire (HPQ; WHO, 2002)	1. Absenteeism 2. Presenteeism	A self-report measure that assesses the work- related consequences of illness including absenteeism, presenteeism, and workplace accidents.	4
Work Limitation Questionnaire (WLQ; Lerner et al., 2001)	1. Work-related time management 2. Physical demands 3. Interpersonal/mental Demands 4. Productivity demands	The WLQ evaluates the level of limitation the patient is experiencing in the workplace due to health problems. The patient reports his/her ability or inability to execute work tasks and related loss of productivity.	25 (there is also an 8-item version)
Work productivity and Activity Impairment (WPAI; Reilly et al., 1993)	1. Hours absent from work due to health issues 2. Hours absent for other reasons 3. Hours worked 4. Impact of health on productivity 5. Impact of health on productivity outside of work	Assesses the impact of health problems on work productivity	6

(*continued*)

Table 21.1. Measures of functional impairment and quality of life (*continued*)

Measure	Domains Assessed	Description	Items
Social Adjustment Scale (SAS-SR; Weissman & Bothwell, 1976)	1. Work 2. Social/leisure activities 3. Relationships with extended family 4. Roles as spouse, parent, and member of a family unit	Self-report which allows the routine assessment of the patient's social adjustment, especially in the case of depression. It is also a useful method as part of the detection of even mild depressions, regular aftercare evaluation of out-patients or as an outcome measure in longitudinal studies. Does not ask for specific time period (e.g., in the past 30 days...)	54
Health and Daily Living form (HDL; Moos, Cronkite, & Finney, 1983)	1. Health-related functioning 2. Social functioning and resources family functioning 3. Indices of life change	Structured assessment that gauges drinking problems and depressions. The measure also assesses availability of social supports, social functioning, and life stressors (chronic and acute).	
Life Stressors and Social Resources Inventory (LISRES; Moos & Moos, 1994)	1. Physical health 2. Spouse/partner 3. Finances 4. Work 5. Home/Neighborhood 6. Children 7. Friends & social activities 8. Extended family	A self-report measure that gauges ongoing life stressors and social resources as well as changes over time.	200
Disability Profile (DP; Schneier et al., 1994)	1. School 2. Work 3. Family 4. Marriage/dating 5. Friendships 6. Other interests 7. Activities of daily living 8. Suicidal Behavior	The DP is a clinician-rated instrument with items assessing current and most severe lifetime impairment due to social phobia in 8 domains.	8
Liebowitz Self-Rated Disability Scale (Schneier et al., 1994)	1. School 2. Work 3. Family 4. Marriage/dating 5. Friendships 6. Other interests 7. Activities of daily living 8. Suicidal behavior	Similar to DP, but self-report.	11
Social Functioning Questionnaire (Tyrer et al., 2005)	1. Work and home tasks 2. Financial concerns 3. Relationships/family 4. Sexual activities 5. Social contacts 6. Spare time activities	A short self-report measure adapted from the Social Functioning Schedule (SFS) to gauge the respondent's perception of his/her social functioning.	8
UCLA Social Attainment Scale (SAS; Goldstein, 1978)	Social Functioning	Assess level of social functioning. Used mostly in assessing functional impairment in psychotic populations.	7

(continued)

Table 21.1 Measures of functional impairment and quality of life (*continued*)

Measure	Domains Assessed	Description	Items
Quality of Life Inventory (QOLI; (Frisch et al., 1992)	1. Health 2. Self-esteem 3. Goals & values 4. Money 5. Work 6. Play 7. Learning 8. Creativity 9. Helping 10. Love 11. Friends 12. Children 13. Relatives 14. Home 15. Neighborhood 16. Community	A measure of general life satisfaction, it requires respondents to indicate the level of importance of each area on a 3-point scale, and their level of satisfaction with that area of their life. Brief descriptions/definitions are provided of each domain prior to each pair of items.	32
Inventory of Psychosocial Functioning (IPF; Marx et al., 2009)	1. Romantic relationships 2. Family relationships 3. Work 4. Friendships and socializing 5. Parenting 6. Education 7. Self-care	New self-report instrument designed to assess functional impairment across the spectrum of domains.	80 items on full scale; 7 items on brief scale
Quality of Well Being Scale (QWB; Kaplan et al., 1989)	1. Physical symptoms (36 items) 2. Psychological symptoms (14 items) 3. Self-care (2 items) 4. Mobility (3 items) 5. Physical activity (8 items) 6. Usual activity (3 items) 7. Overall self-rating of health (3 items) 8. Demographics (4 items)	An interviewer administered measure assessing problems in the past 3 days. Psychological symptoms assessed include symptoms of anxiety and depression. Also available in self-report form.	73
Quality of Life Enjoyment and Satisfaction Questionnaire (Q-LES-Q; Endicott et al., 1993)	1. Physical health (13 items) 2. Subjective feelings (14 items) 3. Leisure time activities (6 items) 4. Social relationships (11 items) 5. General activities (14 items) 6. Work (13 items) 7. Household duties (10 items) 8. School/course work (10 items) 9. Medication (1 item) 10. Overall life satisfaction and contentment (1 item)	A self-report questionnaire intended to measure the level of enjoyment/satisfaction across several elements of daily functioning over the past week (5 days).	93
Life Functioning Questionnaire (LFQ; Altshuler, et al., 2002)	1. Duties at work/school 2. Duties at home 3. Leisure time with family 4. Leisure time with friends	A two-part assessment that examines "role function" over the past month. Part 1 focuses on all 4 domains, part 2 focuses on work only.	14 core items (part 1) 5 items (part 2)

The WHODAS-II is based on the *ICF* and assesses a wide range of impairment and disability dimensions using multi-item scales, including understanding and communicating, mobility, self care, family burden, getting along with others, household and work activities and work loss, and participation in society. It is used across countries and population groups, has high test-retest reliability and correlates with other measures of functioning, such as the SF-36. The WHODAS-II is becoming widely used in investigations of functional disability across wide-ranging populations, including the physically ill (i.e., rheumatology, pulmonary, primary care cohorts) and severely mentally ill (schizophrenic cohorts).

The SF-36 is a relatively brief measure of health-related quality of life. It is a short form that assesses 8 areas selected from the 40 used in the Medical Outcomes Study (Stewart & Ware, 1992). Most items are measured on three-point scales (from "not limited at all" to "limited a lot"), five- or six-point scales (from "none of the time" to "all of the time"), and five-point scales (from "definitely true" to "definitely false"). The SF-36 provides eight domain scores indexing physical functioning, physical role, bodily pain, general health, vitality, social functioning, emotional role, and mental health; in addition, summary physical and mental health scores may be computed. Also, the SF-36 offers norm-based scoring that may aid in interpretation of scores. It consistently has shown good reliability with internal consistency and test-retest reliabilities greater than .80 (McHorney et al., 1993). The validity of its subscales has been known to vary, with some subscales being more strongly associated with related variables than others, but overall it has displayed good content, concurrent, and predictive validity.

The Quality of Life Index (QOLI) is a measure of life satisfaction that was designed for use in treatment planning and outcome assessment. Items target 16 areas of life, (e.g., health, self-regard, work, friendships, romantic and family relationships) and are rated for both importance (three-point Likert scale from "not important" to "extremely important") and satisfaction (seven-point Likert scale from -3 "very dissatisfied" to +3 "very satisfied"). For each domain indicated to be important, responses on both questions are multiplied and domains indicated as not important are excluded. The QOLI has shown good convergent validity with other measures of subjective well-being. Furthermore, it has displayed excellent test-retest reliability (ranging from .80 to .91) and good internal consistency (alphas ranging from .77 to .91).

Specific Limitations of Current Measures Used to Assess PTSD-related Functioning and Quality of Life

Although there are many measures of functioning and quality of life from which to choose, each measure has its strengths and weaknesses that must be considered before selecting which to use. It is also important to keep in mind that, despite the fact that research has found repeated and strong associations between PTSD and functional impairment and quality of life difficulties, there are no universally accepted measures of functional impairment and quality of life for use with individuals with PTSD. It was noted earlier that one of the difficulties with assessment of functional impairment and reduced quality of life due to mental illness is the lack of reliability of self-report. Interview-based measures promote the use of clinical judgment in determining the degree to which specific symptoms may be related to difficulties in functioning and quality of life, as well as for determining whether an individual may be over or underreporting symptoms for secondary gain purposes. On the other hand, interview measures can be time and resource-intensive (e.g., Range of Impaired Functioning Tool, LIFE-RIFT; Leon et al., 1999). Minimally, they require the presence of an interviewer or observer, which may not be feasible under all circumstances and certainly limits the number of patients or research participants who can be assessed using this methodology. Even the briefest of measures, such as the GAF, requires some degree of clinical contact and thus may not be appropriate in all settings.

Another concern for researchers and clinicians is the burden associated with having patients and participants completing lengthy assessments. Lengthy measures (e.g., ICF checklist, LISRES; Moos, Fenn, & Billings, 1988) may not be practical or desirable in many healthcare settings or in large-scale survey studies when many measures are frequently administered. In these instances, researchers usually prefer brief measures of constructs, as longer measures may lead to inaccurate measurement resulting from lapses in attention or motivation.

On the other hand, questionnaires that are too brief pose their own problems. Problems with the single-item GAF have already been noted, but similarly, other questionnaires, while requiring little time to administer and score, may be too simple or narrow in scope to capture the full range of impairments associated with PTSD and other disorders or to adequately assess all domains of impairment. For instance, the Sheehan Disability Scale (SDS; Sheehan, 1983) contains only three items that evaluate separate domains of functioning (Work/School, Social, and Family). Similarly, the Social and Occupational Functioning Assessment Scale (SOFAS; Goldman et al., 1992) is a single-item measure similar to the GAF, but is focused on social and occupational functioning and rates these together on a 0–100 scale, with anchor points.

Available short- to medium-length self-report questionnaires evaluate only a narrow range of functioning domains and thus provide an incomplete assessment of the entire spectrum of functioning. For instance, the Work Limitation Questionnaire (WLQ; Lerner et al., 2001) the Work Productivity and Activity Impairment (WPAI; Reilly, Zbrozek, & Dukes, 1993) and the Health and Work Performance Questionnaire (HPQ; Kessler et al., 2003) are specific to difficulties in occupational functioning. Measures such as the Social Attainment Scale (SAS; Goldstein, 1978) and the Social Functioning Questionnaire (SFQ; Tyrer et al., 2005) similarly only address impairments in social functioning. Trauma survivors are known to exhibit deficits in many areas, and unless research or clinical questions are fairly narrow, many of these measures would not be appropriate to assess the broad spectrum of functioning deficits and quality of life difficulties that arise in the wake of trauma exposure.

Another difficulty with several of the measures of functioning pertains to the fact that many of the available scales focus on physical health-related impairment and health-related quality of life (HRQOL) and physical symptoms, (e.g., SF-36, WHODAS-II, Quality of Well-Being Scale (QWB); Anderson, Kaplan, Berry, & Bush, 1989). Although there is certainly a need for measures that evaluate deficits in functioning in relation to physical illness, the consequences of mental illness may be different from those arising from physical illness. For instance, items on the WHODAS-II assess difficulty in mobility or getting dressed. Such impairments are less likely the result of psychiatric symptoms and precious assessment time could perhaps be better spent.

Although there is certainly some overlap between symptoms and impairment, researchers have not paid sufficient attention to disentangling the two constructs for the purpose of measurement. As a result, some measures unfortunately confound impairment with symptomatology (e.g., QWB, SF-36, Health and Daily Living form). For instance, there are items on the SF-36 that inquire whether respondents "felt so down in the dumps that nothing could cheer you up" or whether they have "been very nervous" in the past four weeks.

Another issue that arises with respect to the assessment of functioning is the causal link between the PTSD symptoms and the experienced functional impairments and reduced quality of life. Much like the causal link that must be inferred between exposure to the stressor and PTSD symptoms, a similar link is presumed to exist between symptoms and impairment. Researchers have chosen to address this problem in various ways. For instance, rather than asking the respondent to make the causal inference, some researchers may prefer to focus solely on impairment and assume that these limitations are due to the symptoms (e.g., LIFE-RIFT, QOLI, Social Adjustment Scale–Self Report; Weissman & Bothwell, 1976). Other researchers may require an explicit attribution of causality be made by the respondent. There are several measures of functioning that take this approach and instruct the individual completing the form to only endorse items if he or she attributes the impairment to the condition in question. For instance, on the Liebowitz Self-Rated Disability Scale (LSRDS; Schneier, Heckelman, Garfinkel, & Campeas, 1994), instructions to the questionnaire cue respondents with the following question: "How much does your emotional problem limit your ability to do each of the following?" In contrast, measures such as the SF-36 do not distinguish between different sources or causes of impairment. Some items contain phrasing such as "to what extent has your physical health or emotional problems interfered with...."

Unfortunately, research has shown that asking respondents to make attributions regarding sources of impairment is not advised, since people frequently make errors in attribution and engage in self-serving biases (e.g., Anderson, Krull, & Weiner, 1996; McNally, 2007). For instance, in the case of trauma exposure, attributions of the source of symptoms and functional impairment may be attempts at financial or other secondary gain (Resnick, West, & Payne, 2008). The difficulty lies in whether respondents themselves can accurately differentiate the source of their impairments, which not only has not been established empirically but also it is unclear whether such information is even objectively knowable. In reality, there could be any number of causes for the functional impairments associated with trauma exposure, as trauma exposure can be associated with numerous physical and psychological sequelae. In fact, if it *is* possible to gauge, it is likely that some trauma survivors are more able than others to accurately identify such differences, which would introduce even more measurement error.

Although much of the psychopathology research literature focuses on individual syndromes, clinically speaking, comorbidity is the norm. Although PTSD is emblematic of the psychological aftermath of trauma exposure, PTSD is only one of the disorders known to develop in the aftermath of an extreme stressor. Adjustment disorders, mood disorders, substance use disorders, and other anxiety disorders are some of the symptom profiles that are known to arise in response to trauma. According to the National Comorbidity Survey (Kessler, Sonnega, Bromet, & Hughes, 1995), the most commonly associated comorbidities are depression (48%) and substance abuse (40%), both of which are also known to be associated with impairments in functioning (McKnight & Kashdan, 2009) and quality of life (Hansson, 2002; Rapaport et al., 2005; Rudolf & Watts, 2002). In fact, some studies have shown that psychological comorbidity may be associated with lower quality of life (Forman-Hoffman et al., 2005; Norberg, Diefenbach, & Tolin, 2008; Rudolf & Watts, 2002; Zayfert, Dums, Ferguson, & Hegel, 2002) and specifically, some researchers have observed more functional impairment in the presence of comorbid PTSD and depression (Momartin, Silove, Manicavasagar, & Steel, 2004) as well as comorbid PTSD and substance abuse disorders (Mills, Teesson, Ross, & Peters, 2006; Najavits, Weiss, & Shaw, 1999; Ouimette, Goodwin, & Brown, 2006). Given that these disorders co-occur at such high rates, this poses an additional problem for the assessment of functional impairment in the context of PTSD—namely, that it is impossible to tell whether the impairments are due to one disorder or another, or to the combination of disorders. Of course, it is possible that the other disorders are also sequelae to trauma and thus all of the impairment may be distally attributable to the trauma exposure, if not the PTSD per se. Nonetheless, at least in some cases the comorbid disorders may have a separate etiology, and questions remain about how best to understand or partition the causes of functional impairment.

This state of affairs suggests that the development of a new measure of psychiatric-related functional impairment for use with trauma-exposed individuals is warranted. Importantly, any new measure should assess all the pertinent domains of functioning with sufficient breadth and depth without requiring respondents to make attributions regarding the cause of the impairments.

The Inventory of Psychosocial Functioning (IPF; Marx et al., 2009) is a newly developed 80-item self-report measure designed to assess functional impairment across multiple domains. Unlike the other instruments described here, the IPF is easy to use and score, is not disorder specific but has relevant content for impairment associated with PTSD and other psychiatric disorders, distinguishes between symptoms and impairment, does not require attributions regarding the cause of the impairments, and is usable in both research and clinical contexts.

The IPF asks respondents to rate their functioning over the past 30 days. Items are rated on a seven-point scale ranging from 1 ("never") to 7 ("always"). The IPF yields a mean score for each of seven scales: romantic relationships with a spouse or partner, family relationships, work, friendships and socializing, parenting, education, and self-care. A mean functional impairment score is computed by calculating the mean of the scores for each completed scale (IPF grand mean). Because functioning over the past 30 days is assessed, respondents skip sections of the instrument that do not apply to them.

Currently, the psychometric properties of the IPF are being tested with male and female Veterans. Thus far, based on data collected from 285 participants, the IPF is demonstrating excellent psychometric properties. The IPF scales demonstrate strong internal consistency, with Cronbach alphas ranging from .79 to .90. The IPF scales and IPF grand mean score all correlate significantly with a number of other self-report measures of impairment and quality of life, such as the SDS, WHODAS-II, SF-36V (Kazis et al., 1999), QOLI, and the GAF.

The IPF grand mean score and scale scores all correlate significantly with PTSD symptom severity, as assessed using the Clinician Administered PTSD Scale for *DSM-IV* (CAPS; Blake et al., 1990), such that greater functional impairment is associated with more severe PTSD symptoms. The IPF grand mean also correlates significantly with major depression symptom severity, assessed using the module for Major Depressive Episode (current) from the M.I.N.I. International Neuropsychiatric Interview (Sheehan et al., 1998), such that greater functional impairment is associated with more depression symptoms. In terms of discriminant validity, the IPF grand mean score correlates less strongly with the total score from the Psychopathic Personality Inventory-Short Form and its subscales (PPI-SF; Lilienfeld & Andrews, 1996; Marx et al., 2009).

These preliminary findings suggest that the IPF is already a viable option for clinicians and researchers who need to assess psychiatric-related functional impairment. However, continued research is needed to refine the instrument and determine the extent to which it will be helpful to both clinicians and researchers in the future.

Conclusions

In sum, it is clear that trauma can lead to PTSD, which may be associated with impairments in functioning and quality of life. Evidence from numerous sources indicates that the impact of trauma exposure and subsequent PTSD frequently includes difficulties in various areas. The present *DSM* diagnostic system includes functional impairment as one criterion for the assignment of a diagnosis. Particular forms of impairments may not be specific to PTSD, but are perhaps attributable to mental health difficulties more generally. In addition, these impairments may be transitory or longstanding, and as yet, it is unclear which factors may influence their severity or course.

Functional impairment and decreases in quality of life are important outcomes of interest following exposure to potentially traumatic events and are in need of further study. The level of impairment, severity, and course of impairment over time is not understood and may reveal interesting aspects of trauma and recovery that have yet to be observed or elucidated. To date this has not been adequately assessed among traumatized populations due, in part, to an absence of appropriate measurement instruments.

No measure to date has proven adequate to the assessment of functional impairments. Problems with existing measures include length (either too long or too brief), requiring an independent clinical interviewer or rater, focus on too few aspects of impairment, or requiring respondents to make causal attributions. Efforts are under way in the creation of a new measure of functional impairment that avoids some of the pitfalls that have made the assessment of mental health related functional impairment so difficult to date.

Future Directions

In order for research to proceed in this area, it will first be important to arrive at a consensus regarding the definitions of terms. Especially given the fact that functional impairment will likely continue to be a key element of psychological diagnosis, it behooves the field to provide an adequate definition as a starting point. Once key terms are defined, it will be important to validate measures of functional impairment that assess mental-health specific constructs in trauma-exposed populations. Of particular utility to the field would be a general consensus on a small number of measures that are more or less widely accepted so that comparisons can be made across studies. Of course, specific research questions may necessitate the use of focused measures, but as can be seen in other areas of research, there is utility in standardizing measures to a point.

Regardless of whether the field agrees on standardized measurement, an important next step in research in this area will be to continue to establish whether there are domain-specific challenges among those with PTSD by comparing the disability profiles of those with PTSD to those with other disorders. The relationship between symptoms of PTSD and functional impairment is arguably the most important endeavor in this area.

It will also be important to identify potential mediators and moderators of the impairments in particular domains, as these may then reasonably become targets for psychotherapeutic interventions. Indeed, we must also evaluate whether current interventions adequately improve functioning; and if so, whether they affect global functioning, or whether they differentially ameliorate functioning in specific domains. Similiarly, it will also be important to determine whether specific components of those therapies influence global functioning and specific areas of impairment. The program of research proposed here is certainly ambitious and will require the contributions of many individuals. Nonetheless, it is only through the elucidation of the complex relationships among trauma, psychopathology, and quality of life that we will be in a position to help survivors of trauma on the path to recovery and reclaiming their lives.

References

Altshuler, L., Mintz, J., & Leight, K. (2002). The life functioning questionnaire (LFQ): A brief, gender-neutral scale assessing functional outcome. *Psychiatry Research, 112,* 161–182. (doi: 10.1016/S0165–1781(02)00180–4)

American Psychiatric Association. (2000). *Diagnostic and statistical manual of mental disorders* (4th ed.). Washington, DC: Author.

Anderson, C. A., Krull, D. S., & Weiner, B. (1996). Explanations: Processes and consequences. In E. T. Higgins & A. W. Kruglanski (Eds.), *Social psychology: Handbook of basic principles.* (pp. 271–296). New York: Guilford.

Anderson, J. P., Kaplan, R. M., Berry, C. C., & Bush, J. W. (1989). Interday reliability of function assessment for a health status measure: The Quality of Well-Being scale. *Medical Care, 27,* 1076–1084. (doi: 10.1097/00005650–198911000–00008)

Blake, D. D., Weathers, F. W., Nagy, L. M., Kaloupek, D. G., Klauminzer, G., & Charney, D. S. (1990). A clinician rating scale for assessing current and lifetime PTSD: The CAPS-1. *Behavior Therapist, 13,* 187–188.

Dohrenwend, B. P., Turner, J. B., Turse, N. A., Adams, B. G., Koenen, K. C., & Marshall, R. (2006). The psychological risks of Vietnam for U.S. veterans: A revisit with new data and methods. *Science, 313,* 979–982. (doi: 10.1126/science.1128944)

Endicott, J., Nee, J., Harrison, W., & Blumenthal, R. (1993). Quality of life enjoyment and satisfaction questionnaire: A new measure. *Psychopharmacology Bulletin, 29,* 321–326.

Endicott, J., Spitzer, R. L., Fleiss, J. L., & Cohen, J. (1976). The Global Assessment Scale: A procedure for measuring overall severity of psychiatric disturbance. *Archives of General Psychiatry, 33,* 766–771.

Epping-Jordan, J. E., Chatterji, S., & Ustun, T. B. (2000, July). *The World Health Organization Disability Assessment Schedule II. (WHO DAS II): A tool for measuring clinical outcomes.* Oral presentation at NIMH Mental Health Services Research Meeting, Washington, DC.

Forman-Hoffman, V. L., Carney, C. P., Sampson, T. R., Peloso, P. M., Woolson, R. F., Black, D. W., et al. (2005). Mental health comorbidity patterns and impact on quality of life among veterans serving during the first Gulf War. *Quality of Life Research: An International Journal of Quality of Life Aspects of Treatment, Care & Rehabilitation, 14,* 2303–2314. (doi: 10.1007/s11136–005–6540–2)

Frisch, M. B., Cornell, J., Villanueva, M., & Retzlaff, P. J. (1992). Clinical validation of the Quality of Life Inventory. A measure of life satisfaction for use in treatment planning and outcome assessment. *Psychological Assessment, 4,* 92–101.

Frueh, B. C. (2007). PTSD and Vietnam veterans. *Science, 315,* 184–187.

Golden-Kreutz, D. M., Thornton, L. M., Wells-Di Gregorio, S., Frierson, G. M., Jim, H. S., Carpenter, K. M., et al. (2005). Traumatic stress, perceived global stress, and life events: Prospectively predicting quality of life in breast cancer patients. *Health Psychology, 24,* 288–296. (doi: 10.1037/0278–6133.24.3.288)

Goldman, H. H. (2005). 'Do you walk to school, or do you carry your lunch?' *Psychiatric Services, 56.* (doi: 10.1176/appi.ps.56.4.419)

Goldman, H. H., Skodol, A. E., & Lave, T. R. (1992). Revising Axis V for DSM-IV: A review of measures of social functioning. *American Journal of Psychiatry, 149,* 1148–1156.

Goldstein, M. J. (1978). Further data concerning the relation between premorbid adjustment and paranoid symptomatology. *Schizophrenia Bulletin, 4,* 236–243.

Gudmundsdottir, B., Beck, J. G., Coffey, S. F., Miller, L., & Palyo, S. A. (2004). Quality of life and post trauma symptomatology in motor vehicle accident survivors: The mediating effects of depression and anxiety. *Depression and Anxiety, 20,* 187–189. (doi: 10.1002/da.20037)

Hansson, L. (2002). Quality of life in depression and anxiety. *International Review of Psychiatry, 14,* 185–189. (doi: 10.1080/09540260220144966)

Hoge, C. W., McGurk, D., Thomas, J., Cox, A. L., Engel, C. C., & Castro, C. A. (2008). Mild traumatic brain injury in U.S. soldiers returning from Iraq. *New England Journal of Medicine, 358,* 453–463. (doi: 10.1056/NEJMoa072972)

Institute of Medicine. (2007). *PTSD compensation and military service.* Washington, DC: National Academies Press.

Kaplan, R. M., Anderson, J. P., Wu, A., Mathews, W., Kozin, F., & Orenstein, D. (1989). The Quality of Well-being Scale: Applications in AIDS, cystic fibrosis, and arthritis. *Medical Care, 27,* S27–43.

Katschnig, H. (2006). How useful is the concept of quality of life in psychiatry? In H. Katschnig, H. Freeman, & N. Sartorius (Eds.), *Quality of life in mental disorders* (2nd ed., pp. 3–17). New York: John Wiley.

Kazis, L. E., Ren, X. S., Lee, A., Skinner, K., Rogers, W., Clark, J., et al. (1999). Health status in VA patients: Results from the Veterans Health Study. *American Journal of Medical Quality, 14,* 28–38.

Keller, M. B., Lavori, P. W., Friedman, B., Nielsen, E., Endicott, J., McDonald-Scott, P., et al. (1987). The Longitudinal Interval Follow-up Evaluation: A comprehensive method for assessing outcome in prospective longitudinal studies. *Archives of General Psychiatry, 44,* 540–548.

Kessler, R. C., Barber, C., Beck, A., Berglund, P., Cleary, P. D., McKenas, D., et al. (2003). The World Health Organization Health and Work Performance Questionnaire (HPQ). *Journal of Occupational and Environmental Medicine, 45,* 156–174.

Kessler, R. C., Sonnega, A., Bromet, E., & Hughes, M. (1995). Posttraumatic stress disorder in the National Comorbidity Survey. *Archives of General Psychiatry, 52,* 1048–1060.

Kimerling, R., Clum, G. A., & Wolfe, J. (2000). Relationships among trauma exposure, chronic posttraumatic stress disorder symptoms, and self-reported health in women: Replication and extension. *Journal of Traumatic Stress, 13,* 115–128. (doi: 10.1023/A:1007729116133)

Koenen, K. C., Stellman, S. D., Sommer, J. F., Jr., & Stellman, J. M. (2008). Persisting posttraumatic stress disorder symptoms and their relationship to functioning in Vietnam Veterans: A 14-year follow-up. *Journal of Traumatic Stress, 21,* 49–57. (doi: 10.1002/jts.20304)

Kuhn, E., Blanchard, E. B., & Hickling, E. J. (2003). Posttraumatic stress disorder and psychosocial functioning within two samples of MVA survivors. *Behaviour Research and Therapy, 41,* 1105–1112. (doi: 10.1016/S0005-7967(03)00071-8)

Leon, A. C., Solomon, D. A., Mueller, T. I., Turvey, C. L., Endicott, J., & Keller, M. B. (1999). The Range of Impaired Functioning Tool (LIFE-RIFT): A brief measure of functional impairment. *Psychological Medicine: A Journal of Research in Psychiatry and the Allied Sciences, 29,* 869–878. (doi: 10.1017/S0033291799008570)

Lerner, D., Amick, B. C., III, Rogers, W. H., Malspeis, S., Bungay, K., & Cynn, D. (2001). The Work Limitations Questionnaire. *Medical Care, 39,* 72–85. (doi: 10.1097/00005650-200101000-00009)

Lilienfeld, S. O., & Andrews, B. P. (1996). Development and preliminary validation of a self-report measure of psychopathic personality traits in noncriminal populations. *Journal of Personality Assessment, 66,* 488–524.

Litz, B. T. (1992). Emotional numbing in combat-related post-traumatic stress disorder: A critical review and reformulation. *Clinical Psychology Review, 12,* 417–432. (doi: 10.1016/0272-7358(92)90125-R)

Litz, B. T., & Gray, M. J. (2002). Emotional numbing in posttraumatic stress disorder: Current and future research directions. *Australian and New Zealand Journal of Psychiatry, 36,* 198–204. (doi: 10.1046/j.1440-1614.2002.01002.x)

Lunney, C. A., & Schnurr, P. P. (2007). Domains of quality of life and symptoms in male veterans treated for posttraumatic stress disorder. *Journal of Traumatic Stress, 20,* 955–964. (doi: 10.1002/jts.20269)

Madden, R., Sykes, C., & Ustun, T. B. (2007). *World Health Organization Family of International Classifications: Definition, scope and purpose.* Geneva: World Health Organization.

Marx, B. P., Schnurr, P. P., Rodriguez, P., Holowka, D. W., Lunney, C. A., Weathers, F. W., et al. (2009, November). Development of a functional impairment scale for active duty service members and veterans. In K. M. Lester (Chair), *Beyond PTSD symptom reduction: Social and health-related benefits of trauma focused treatment.* Symposium conducted at the meeting for the International Society for Traumatic Stress Studies, Atlanta, GA.

McHorney, C. A., Ware, J. E., & Raczek, A. E. (1993). The MOS 36-Item Short-Form Health Survey (SF-36): II. Psychometric and clinical tests of validity in measuring physical and mental health constructs. *Medical Care, 31,* 247–263. (doi: 10.1097/00005650-199303000-00006)

McKnight, P. E., & Kashdan, T. B. (2009). The importance of functional impairment to mental health outcomes: A case for reassessing our goals in depression treatment research. *Clinical Psychology Review, 29,* 243–259. (doi: 10.1016/j.cpr.2009.01.005)

McNally, R. J. (2007). Can we solve the mysteries of the National Vietnam Veterans Readjustment Study? *Journal of Anxiety Disorders, 21,* 192–200. (doi: 10.1016/j.janxdis.2006.09.005)

Mendlowicz, M. V., & Stein, M. B. (2000). Quality of life in individuals with anxiety disorders. *American Journal of Psychiatry, 157,* 669–682. (doi: 10.1176/appi.ajp.157.5.669)

Mills, K. L., Teesson, M., Ross, J., & Peters, L. (2006). Trauma, PTSD, and substance use disorders: Findings from the Australian National Survey of Mental Health and Well-Being. *American Journal of Psychiatry, 163,* 651–658. (doi: 10.1176/appi.ajp.163.4.652)

Mogotsi, M., Kaminer, D., & Stein, D. J. (2000). Quality of life in the anxiety disorders. *Harvard Review of Psychiatry, 8,* 273–282. (doi: 10.1093/hrp/8.6.273)

Momartin, S., Silove, D., Manicavasagar, V., & Steel, Z. (2004). Comorbidity of PTSD and depression: Associations with trauma exposure, symptom severity and functional impairment in Bosnian refugees resettled in Australia. *Journal of Affective Disorders, 80,* 231–238. (doi: 10.1016/S0165-0327(03)00131-9)

Moos, R. H., Cronkite, R. C., & Finney, J. W. (1983). *Health and Daily Living Form manual.* Palo Alto, CA: Department of Veterans Affairs.

Moos, R. H., Fenn, C. B., & Billings, A. G. (1988). Life stressors and social resources: An integrated assessment approach. *Social Science & Medicine, 27,* 999–1002. (doi: 10.1016/0277-9536(88)90291-2)

Moos, R. H., & Moos, B. S. (1994). *The Life Stressors and Social Resources Inventory: Adult form manual.* Odessa, FL: Psychological Assessment Resources.

Moos, R. H., Nichol, A. C., & Moos, B. S. (2002). Global Assessment of Functioning ratings and the allocation and outcomes of mental health services. *Psychiatric Services, 53,* 730–737. (doi: 10.1176/appi.ps.53.6.730)

Morosini, P.-L., Magliano, L., Brambilla, L., Ugolini, S., & Pioli, R. (2000). Development, reliability and acceptability of a new version of the DSM-IV Social and Occupational Functioning Assessment Scale (SOFAS) to assess routine social functioning. *Acta Psychiatrica Scandinavica, 101,* 323–329.

Najavits, L. M., Weiss, R. D., & Shaw, S. R. (1999). A clinical profile of women with posttraumatic stress disorder and substance dependence. *Psychology of Addictive Behaviors, 13,* 98–104. (doi: 10.1037/0893-164X.13.2.98)

Niv, N., Cohen, A. N., Sullivan, G., & Young, A. S. (2007). The MIRECC version of the global assessment of functioning scale: Reliability and validity. *Psychiatric Services, 58,* 529–535. (doi: 10.1176/appi.ps.58.4.529)

Norberg, M. M., Diefenbach, G. J., & Tolin, D. F. (2008). Quality of life and anxiety and depressive disorder comorbidity. *Journal of Anxiety Disorders, 22,* 1516–1522. (doi: 10.1016/j.janxdis.2008.03.005)

Norman, S. B., Stein, M. B., & Davidson, J. R. T. (2007). Profiling posttraumatic functional impairment. *Journal of Nervous and Mental Disease, 195,* 48–53. (doi: 10.1097/01.nmd.0000252135.25114.02)

Nunnally, J. C. (1978). *Psychometric theory* (2nd ed.). New York: McGraw-Hill.

O'Connell, M. J., Kasprow, W., & Rosenheck, R. A. (2008). Rates and risk factors for homelessness after successful housing in a sample of formerly homeless veterans. *Psychiatric Services, 59,* 268–275. (doi: 10.1176/appi.ps.59.3.268)

Olatunji, B. O., Cisler, J. M., & Tolin, D. F. (2007). Quality of life in the anxiety disorders: A meta-analytic review. *Clinical Psychology Review, 27,* 572–581. (doi: 10.1016/j.cpr.2007.01.015)

Ouimette, P., Goodwin, E., & Brown, P. J. (2006). Health and well being of substance use disorder patients with and without posttraumatic stress disorder. *Addictive Behaviors, 31*, 1415–1423. (doi: 10.1016/j.addbeh.2005.11.010)

Paunović, N., & Öst, L.-G. (2004). Clinical Validation of the Swedish version of the quality of life inventory in crime victims with posttraumatic stress disorder and a nonclinical sample. *Journal of Psychopathology and Behavioral Assessment, 26*, 15–21. (doi: 10.1023/B:JOBA.0000007452.65270.13)

Ramchand, R., Marshall, G. N., Schell, T. L., & Jaycox, L. H. (2008). Posttraumatic distress and physical functioning: A longitudinal study of injured survivors of community violence. *Journal of Consulting and Clinical Psychology, 76*, 668–676. (doi: 10.1037/0022–006X.76.4.668)

Rapaport, M. H., Clary, C., Fayyad, R., & Endicott, J. (2005). Quality-of-life impairment in depressive and anxiety disorders. *American Journal of Psychiatry, 162*, 1171–1178. (doi: 10.1176/appi.ajp.162.6.1171)

Reilly, M. C., Zbrozek, A. S., & Dukes, E. M. (1993). The validity and reproducibility of a work productivity and activity impairment instrument. *Pharmacoeconomics, 4*, 353–365.

Resnick, P. J., West, S., & Payne, J. W. (2008). Malingering of posttraumatic disorders. In R. Rogers (Ed.), *Clinical assessment of malingering and deception* (3rd ed., pp. 109–127). New York: Guilford.

Resnick, S. G., & Rosenheck, R. A. (2008). Integrating peer-provided services: A quasi-experimental study of recovery orientation, confidence, and empowerment. *Psychiatric Services, 59*, 1307–1314. (doi: 10.1176/appi.ps.59.11.1307)

Riggs, D. S., Byrne, C. A., Weathers, F. W., & Litz, B. T. (1998). The quality of the intimate relationships of male Vietnam veterans: Problems associated with posttraumatic stress disorder. *Journal of Traumatic Stress, 11*, 87–101. (doi: 10.1023/A:1024409200155)

Rona, R. J., Jones, M., Iversen, A., Hull, L., Greenberg, N., Fear, N. T., et al. (2009). The impact of posttraumatic stress disorder on impairment in the UK military at the time of the Iraq War. *Journal of Psychiatric Research, 43*, 64–55. (doi: 10.1016/j.jpsychires.2008.09.006)

Rudolf, H., & Watts, J. (2002). Quality of life in substance abuse and dependency. *International Review of Psychiatry, 14*, 19–97. (doi: 10.1080/09540260220144975)

Samper, R. E., Taft, C. T., King, D. W., & King, L. A. (2004). Posttraumatic stress disorder symptoms and parenting satisfaction among a national sample of male Vietnam veterans. *Journal of Traumatic Stress, 17*, 31–15. (doi: 10.1023/B:JOTS.0000038479.30903.ed)

Sayers, S. L., Farrow, V. A., Ross, J., & Oslin, D. W. (2009). Family problems among recently returned military veterans referred for a mental health evaluation. *Journal of Clinical Psychiatry, 70*, 16–70. (doi: 10.4088/JCP.07m03863)

Schneier, F. R., Heckelman, L. R., Garfinkel, R., & Campeas, R. (1994). Functional impairment in social phobia. *Journal of Clinical Psychiatry, 55*, 32–31.

Schnurr, P. P., Friedman, M. J., Engel, C. C., Foa, E. B., Shea, M. T., Chow, B. K., et al. (2007). Cognitive behavioral therapy for posttraumatic stress disorder in women: A randomized controlled trial. *Journal of the American Medical Association, 297*, 82–30. (doi: 10.1001/jama.297.8.820)

Schnurr, P. P., Friedman, M. J., Foy, D. W., Shea, M. T., Hsieh, F. Y., Lavori, P. W., et al. (2003). Randomized trial of trauma-focused group therapy for posttraumatic stress disorder: Results from a Department of Veterans Affairs cooperative study. *Archives of General Psychiatry, 60*, 48–89. (doi: 10.1001/archpsyc.60.5.481)

Schnurr, P. P., Hayes, A. F., Lunney, C. A., McFall, M., & Uddo, M. (2006). Longitudinal analysis of the relationship between symptoms and quality of life in veterans treated for posttraumatic stress disorder. *Journal of Consulting and Clinical Psychology, 74*, 70–13. (doi: 10.1037/002–06-X.74.4.707)

Sheehan, D. V. (1983). *The anxiety disease.* New York: Scribner.

Sheehan, D. V. (2003). *Sheehan Disability Scale-W (SDS-W).* Unpublished instrument.

Sheehan, D. V., Lecrubier, Y., Sheehan, K. H., Amorim, P., Janavs, J., Weiller, E., et al. (1998). The Mini-International Neuropsychiatric Interview (M.I.N.I): The development and validation of a structured diagnostic psychiatric interview for DSM-IV and ICD-10. *Journal of Clinical Psychiatry, 59*, 2–3.

Söderberg, P., Tungström, S., & Armelius, B. (2005). Reliability of global assessment of functioning ratings made by clinical psychiatric staff. *Psychiatric Services, 56*, 43–38. (doi: 10.1176/appi.ps.56.4.434)

Solomon, Z., & Mikulincer, M. (2007). Posttraumatic intrusion, avoidance, and social functioning: A 20-year longitudinal study. *Journal of Consulting and Clinical Psychology, 75*, 31–24. (doi: 10.1037/002–06X.75.2.316)

Stewart, A. L., & Ware, J. E. (1992). *Measuring functioning and well-being: The medical outcomes study approach.* Durham, NC: Duke University Press.

Taylor, S., Wald, J., & Asmundson, G. J. G. (2006). Factors associated with occupational impairment in people seeking treatment for posttraumatic stress disorder. *Canadian Journal of Community Mental Health, 25*, 28–01.

Tyrer, P., Nur, U., Crawford, M., Karlsen, S., McLean, C., Rao, B., et al. (2005). The Social Functioning Questionnaire: A Rapid and Robust Measure of Perceived Functioning. *International Journal of Social Psychiatry, 51*, 26–75. (doi: 10.1177/0020764005057391)

Ustün, B., & Kennedy, C. (2009). What is "functional impairment"? Disentangling disability from clinical significance. *World Psychiatry, 8*, 82–85.

Ware, J. E. (1999). SF-36 Health Survey. In M. E. Maruish (Ed.), *The use of psychological testing for treatment planning and outcomes assessment* (2nd ed., pp. 122–246). Mahwah, NJ: Lawrence Erlbaum.

Ware, J. E., & Sherbourne, C. D. (1992). The MOS 36-item short-form health survey (SF-36): I. Conceptual framework and item selection. *Medical Care, 30*, 47–83. (doi: 10.1097/0000565–9920600–0002)

Ware, J. E., Snow, K. K., Kosinski, M., & Gandek, B. (1993). *SF-36 Health Survey manual and interpretation guide.* Boston: New England Medical Center, The Health Institute.

Weissman, M. M., & Bothwell, S. (1976). Assessment of social adjustment by patient self-report. *Archives of General Psychiatry, 33*, 111–115.

Woods, S. J., & Wineman, N. M. (2004). Trauma, posttraumatic stress disorder symptom clusters, and physical health symptoms in post-abused women. *Archives of Psychiatric Nursing, 18*, 2–4. (doi: 10.1053/j.apnu.2003.11.005)

World Health Organization. (1988). *WHO Psychiatric Disability Assessment Schedule (WHO/DAS).* Albany, NY: Author.

World Health Organization. (2000). *World Health Organization Disability Assessment (WHODASII).* Geneva: Author.

World Health Organization. (2001). *International classification of functioning, disability and health: ICF.* Geneva: Author.

World Health Organization. (2002). *World Health Organization Health and Performance Questionnaire (HPQ): Clinical trials baseline version.* Geneva: Author.

World Health Organization. (2003). *ICF Checklist.* Geneva: Author..

Zayfert, C., Dums, A. R., Ferguson, R. J., & Hegel, M. T. (2002). Health functioning impairments associated with posttraumatic stress disorder, anxiety disorders, and depression. *Journal of Nervous and Mental Disease, 190*, 23–40. (doi: 10.1097/0000505–0020400–0004)

PART 6

Prevention/Early Intervention

CHAPTER

22 Risk and Protective Factors for Traumatic Stress Disorders

Lynda A. King, Anica P. Pless, Jennifer L. Schuster, Carrie M. Potter,
Crystal L. Park, Avron Spiro, III, *and* Daniel W. King

Abstract

This chapter provides an overview of risk and protective factors that may account for posttraumatic responses. In addition to risk and protective factors specifically for posttraumatic stress disorder (PTSD), the outcomes of resilience and posttraumatic growth are considered. Emphasis is placed on the importance of a longitudinal and especially a lifespan developmental framework to understand both the short- and long-term implications of trauma exposure and the factors that influence its consequences. A brief introduction to methodological approaches for documenting longitudinal change is presented, followed by suggestions for future research.

Key Words: Risk factor, protective factor, PTSD, resilience, posttraumatic growth, longitudinal methods, lifespan perspective

Risk and Protective Factors for Traumatic Stress Disorders

Current thinking and empirical evidence argue for multivariate explanations for the consequences of exposure to traumatic life events, including acute stress disorder (e.g., Saxe et al., 2005), posttraumatic stress disorder (PTSD; e.g., King, King, Foy, Keane, & Fairbank, 1999), the absence of stress reactions (lack of PTSD, or resilience; e.g., Bonanno, Galea, Bucciarelli, & Vlahov, 2007), associated physical health symptoms (e.g., Schnurr & Spiro, 1999), or positive psychological change (posttraumatic growth; e.g., Wilson & Boden, 2008). The etiology of PTSD in particular and trauma-related outcomes in general is complex, and the "causes" of posttraumatic sequelae encompass a broad array of variables that may amplify or mitigate outcomes. A common event, like a community-wide disaster, elicits varying responses and degrees of disturbance across persons: Most trauma-exposed people do not suffer symptoms; many have fleeting discomfort or experience distress that diminishes over time; and a noteworthy minority have enduring negative reactions (Kessler, Sonnega, Bromet, Hughes, & Nelson, 1995; Kulka et al., 1990). The purpose of this chapter is to identify risk and protective factors for traumatic stress disorders and other outcomes, place these factors in a longitudinal and especially a lifespan developmental framework, and suggest methodological approaches to better understand their effects over time.

We define a *risk factor* as a characteristic of the person, environment, or traumatic event that initiates, exacerbates, or maintains a negative response. A *protective factor* is a characteristic of the person, environment, or traumatic event that prevents, decreases, or contains a negative response. The two terms may (but not necessarily) be simply the inverse of one another (Bonnano, 2004; King, Vogt, & King, 2004). For example, if female gender is a risk factor for PTSD following a natural disaster, then male gender can be viewed as a protective factor. Likewise, if training and preparedness is a protective factor for a stress reaction in the face of combat, then lack of such training and preparedness could be considered a risk factor.

In past summaries of the literature (e.g., King et al., 2004), protective factors were called *resilience factors*. With recent emphasis on positive psychology (Seligman, 1991) and increased popularity of resilience research, however, there has been a clarification and specification imposed on the term *resilience* in the study of trauma (see later discussion), reflecting a shift in definition from predictor to outcome. Consistent with a long tradition in the developmental sciences, primarily the study of children who successfully thrived despite disadvantage and adversity, resilience is currently conceptualized as a process, a longitudinal trend or trajectory of a variable that signifies continued favorable functioning (Bonanno, 2004, 2005; Masten & Wright, 2010). Thus, posttraumatic resilience may be operationalized as the absence of psychopathology *over time* or the presence of a healthy state *over time*.

In similar manner, the present chapter emphasizes any response to a traumatic event as a longitudinal dynamic process, a continuous action or series of changes taking place in a systematic manner toward some end. This process emerges from an identifiable starting point, trauma exposure, and extends forward in time. Outcomes of interest are those that document this developmental progression or unfolding process. The study of this progression or process of responding to the event may be restricted to dense or intensive measurement observations over a brief interval (Walls & Schafer, 2006). It may encompass a more extended time frame—months or perhaps a few years—to capture trends toward recovery or chronicity (King, King, Salgado, & Shalev, 2003). Or, it may incorporate a larger lifespan developmental perspective wherein the consequences of exposure to trauma in earlier life potentially influence and are influenced by events and circumstances occurring in later years (Chatterjee, Spiro, King, King, & Davison, 2009). Importantly, risk and protective factors influencing the unfolding process of health or disease may differ or play different roles depending on the segment of the life course under study. In this chapter, we give particular attention to this longitudinal dynamic process following a traumatic event and encourage trauma researchers to consider a lifespan developmental perspective.

In the sections to follow, we first overview the literature on risk and protective factors for PTSD and provide additional commentary on posttraumatic resilience and growth. We next underscore the importance of a lifespan developmental perspective. We then present methodological approaches to document longitudinal change following trauma and how risk and protective factors may influence this change process. We close with a number of suggestions for future research.

Overview of the Literature

Risk and Protective Factors for PTSD

Many people who are exposed to traumatic events do not experience prolonged stress reactions or develop traumatic stress disorders. Although 50–60% of the general population is exposed to trauma at some point over the life course, only 5–15% develop PTSD, depending on the trauma type (Ozer, Best, Lipsey, & Weiss, 2003). In the field of traumatic stress, research with various populations has examined differences among characteristics of individuals, environments, and traumatic events to determine factors that initiate or, conversely, prevent negative responses. As a result, a variety of risk and protective factors for the development of traumatic stress disorders have been identified in the literature.

Research has conceptualized risk and protective factors as belonging to one of three categories: pretrauma variables, features of the traumatic experience, and posttrauma variables (Brewin, Andrews, & Valentine, 2000; Ozer et al., 2003). Regarding the pretrauma category, various demographic characteristics have been studied, and evidence suggests that female gender, younger age, and racial/ethnic minority status serve as risk factors for PTSD (Brewin et al., 2000). Several studies have also examined the role of cognitive ability, with findings indicating that lower intelligence is associated with higher rates of PTSD (e.g., Baily & Elmore, 1999).

Another pretrauma factor found to relate to PTSD is prior trauma exposure. For instance, number of previously experienced traumatic events was positively related to PTSD symptom severity in a large sample of male Vietnam combat veterans (King, King, Foy, & Gudanowski, 1996). This direct dose-response contribution of prior trauma history to the development of PTSD has also been found among other populations, such as sexual assault survivors (e.g., Nishith, Mechanic, & Resick, 2000) and motor vehicle accident victims (e.g., Delahanty, Raimonde, Spoonster, & Cullado, 2003). This relationship may not be straightforward, however; Regehr, Hill, and Glancy (2000) found that firefighters exposed to more traumatic events reported higher levels of self-efficacy. This finding suggests that some types of cumulative trauma might be protective, especially if the experiences help individuals to build a sense of mastery or control for confronting subsequent traumatic events (Hoge, Austin, & Pollack, 2007).

Other pretrauma characteristics of the individual and the environment influence posttrauma psychological functioning. Individuals with a family history of psychiatric problems are more likely to experience PTSD symptoms following trauma exposure (e.g., Breslau, Davis, Andreski, & Peterson, 1991). In the meta-analysis conducted by Ozer et al. (2003), the effect size for this relationship, indexed as an average sample size-weighted correlation (r^*) was .17. Psychological functioning of individuals prior to a traumatic event also influences their response; those who have more severe mental health problems prior to trauma (e.g., anxiety, affective disorders) are at higher risk for developing stress reactions (Blanchard, Hickling, Taylor, & Loos, 1995; Bromet, Sonnega, & Kessler, 1998); Ozer et al. (2003) reported $r^* = .17$. Dysfunction in the family of origin—for example, child abuse/neglect or family instability—also creates increased risk for later traumatic stress disorders (Andrews, Brewin, Rose, & Kirk, 2000; King et al., 1996). Since such risk factors are likely to co-occur in the lives of individuals (Masten & Wright, 2010), it may be helpful to view the amalgamation of pretrauma characteristics of the person and the environment as constituting a more general vulnerability factor, portending higher levels of susceptibility following a stressful life experience (Ozer et al., 2003).

Evidence suggests that individuals who experienced more severe trauma report more severe posttraumatic stress symptomatology (e.g., Fairbank, Keane, & Molloy, 1983), but the strength of this finding differs depending on the population assessed. In fact, Brewin et al.'s (2000) meta-analysis suggested that the impact of trauma severity may be stronger in military samples ($r^* = .26$) than in civilian samples ($r^* = .18$). In addition, the effect was less consistent across types of civilian traumas—stronger for crime, disaster, and motor vehicle accidents ($r^* = .20–.26$), but weaker for burn victims and other specific traumas ($r^* = .10–.14$). These differences based on population or trauma types may serve to explain some of the discrepancies in the overall literature regarding the role of trauma severity (and other) risk and protective factors in the emergence and understanding of posttrauma sequelae.

Other features of the traumatic event, such as perceived threat and emotional response during the event, are related to the likelihood of developing stress symptoms (King et al., 2003; Ozer et al., 2003). A study of Vietnam War combat veterans showed that perceived threat of injury or death was a more potent predictor of PTSD symptom severity than was a more objective tally of actual combat events (King, King, Gudanowski, & Vreven, 1995). A small to moderate effect ($r^* = .26$) for perceived life threat was reported in Ozer et al.'s (2003) meta-analysis, such that those individuals who thought their lives were in danger during the event reported more PTSD symptoms afterward. Additionally, those individuals who reported more severe negative emotionality (e.g., shame, guilt, generalized fear) occurring during or soon after the event experienced higher levels of later PTSD symptomatology ($r^* = .26$; Ozer et al., 2003). Dissociation during an index trauma also influences subsequent psychopathology (Bremner, Southwick, Brett, & Fontana, 1992; Fontana & Rosenheck, 1993). Dissociation is a defense that separates anxiety-provoking reactions from an individual's awareness during a traumatic event; it is associated with amnesia for event details, derealization, or depersonalization and it keeps one from feeling overwhelmed in the moment. Although it may serve a protective function during a traumatic event, dissociation is linked to the later development of PTSD ($r^* = .35$; Ozer et al., 2003).

Coping in the face of trauma (emotion-focused or avoidance coping versus problem-focused or approach coping) also has been shown to affect psychological adjustment. Avoidance coping involves strategies to release tension or distract or calm oneself. Approach coping is more active in nature and involves attempts to seek information and manage a threatening situation. Sharkansky et al. (2000) found that Gulf War veterans who used higher percentages of approach coping (relative to avoidance coping) in combat reported fewer postdeployment stress symptoms. In contrast, other studies have found avoidance coping to be helpful, especially where controllability is low (e.g., in extremely high-level combat; Suvak et al., 2002). Generally, controllability of the environment moderates the influence of stressful situations on a variety of psychological outcomes across populations (e.g., Forsythe & Compas, 1987; Park, Armeli, & Tennen, 2004).

Recent evidence from King et al. (2010) suggested that coping strategies applied during conditions of extreme stress may interact with severity of the stressor to predict later physical and mental health. They used data from a sample of repatriated U.S. prisoners of the Vietnam War who were assessed in 1973 and reexamined almost 30 years later. Avoidance coping led to better long-term physical health for men exposed to higher levels of physical torture during captivity and poorer physical health for men exposed to lower levels of physical torture during captivity. Approach coping led to better mental health for men who sustained lower levels of injuries at time of capture and to poorer mental health for men who sustained higher levels of injuries at capture. These findings substantiate significant patterns of relationships over a remarkably long time interval and reveal that trauma exposure and the methods used to cope with it earlier in life can have effects that reverberate through the lifespan.

Factors that are present posttrauma can also influence risk for developing stress symptomatology. Social support is one important posttrauma variable. Ozer et al. (2003) reported findings from 11 studies suggesting that individuals who experienced higher levels of social support following trauma reported fewer PTSD symptoms ($r^* = .28$). Again, this finding appears to be stronger within military ($r^* = .43$) than within civilian ($r^* = .30$) samples (Brewin et al., 2000) and perhaps, according to King, King, Fairbank, Keane, and Adams (1998), stronger for women than for men. The experience of additional life stressors following an index trauma also is related to poorer psychological outcomes (e.g., Green & Berlin, 1987; King et al., 1998). The average effect for this relationship in the Brewin et al. (2000) meta-analysis was $r^* = .32$. From a lifespan developmental perspective, King, King, Vickers, Davison, and Spiro (2007) demonstrated that older veterans' concerns about retirement, a normative late-life stressor, was associated with combat-related stress symptomatology.

The ways that individuals appraise and reappraise their trauma and its consequences may influence symptomatology. More negative appraisals of stress symptoms (e.g., Mayou, Bryant, & Ehlers, 2001) or of the impact of the event on one's life (e.g., Fairbrother & Rachman, 2006) are related to PTSD. In a recent study of college students, Park, Mills, and Edmondson (in press) found that appraisals of the extent to which the trauma violated beliefs and goals predicted levels of stress symptoms. Furthermore, Aldwin, Levenson, and Spiro (1994) found that the relationship between combat exposure in early life and PTSD symptoms in later life was partially mediated by positive and negative appraisals of military service. Specifically, perceiving more undesirable effects of military service was related to more symptoms, while acknowledging more positive aspects of the military experience was related to fewer symptoms, after controlling for level of combat. These findings reinforce a lifespan developmental orientation: Later-life perspectives can influence the outcomes of trauma exposure as individuals mature and possibly reinterpret their traumatic experience.

Increasing Emphasis on Posttraumatic Resilience and Growth

Although research on responses to traumatic events mostly has focused on negative outcomes, there is a growing interest in the study of *posttraumatic resilience. Resilience* can be defined as the maintenance of a relatively stable trajectory of healthy functioning following exposure to a trauma (Bonanno, 2004, 2005). Bonanno (2004, 2005) emphasizes that resilience is more than the simple absence of psychopathology; rather, it represents a particular pattern of responding. He argues that individuals who experience significant or even subthreshold symptoms following trauma and then display improvement would not be resilient. Instead, resilient individuals experience only mild and short-lived posttraumatic symptoms following the traumatic event and generally maintain healthy functioning over time. Bonanno asserts that resilience is the most common outcome following exposure to a traumatic event, and that most individuals show sustained functioning typical of the resilience trajectory. This notion is supported by the fact that few individuals exposed to traumatic events develop posttraumatic stress disorder. Bonanno's model emphasizes that resilience is distinct from *recovery*, which is defined by initial moderate to severe psychological symptoms that significantly impair normal functioning and take many months to decline to pretrauma levels. On the other hand, Masten and Wright (2010) would tend to characterize a recovery pattern as a form of resilience.

Early efforts in studying resilience were focused on understanding qualities of resilient children. In the developmental literature, resilience has been described as a dynamic process of adaptive functioning that emerges in response to aversive life circumstances, such as poverty or enduring abuse (Luthar, Cicchetti, & Becker, 2000). In contrast, adult resilience typically has been characterized as an outcome reflecting adaptive functioning in the face of an isolated and relatively brief traumatic event (Bonanno, 2004). However, recent theorizing suggests that, even in adulthood, resilience should not be conceptualized as a static individual trait. Since adversity can occur at any point in life, a lifespan developmental perspective is necessary to understand resilience fully, and as such resilience should be characterized as a process of positive adaptation in the context of significant life threat (Masten & Wright, 2010). Some current research on resilience attempts to capture this distinction by examining resilience as a process that changes over time (e.g., Ong, Bergeman, & Boker, 2009).

Multiple factors have been shown to promote resilience. Early research in children identified broad categories of characteristics that serve as buffers against adversity. These include personal attributes, such as temperament, and socio-contextual factors, such as family relationships and support from the wider social environment (Masten & Garmezy, 1985). Research on adults also indicates that multiple risk and protective factors may influence the likelihood of resilience following adversity (Mancini & Bonanno, 2010). For instance, male gender, older age, and more education were associated with resilience following exposure to the September 11, 2001, World Trade Center disaster (Bonanno et al., 2007). Ethnic minority status is another demographic factor that might be related to resilience, although research in this area is equivocal. One study found significantly higher rates of resilience among Asians than among whites following disaster (Bonanno et al., 2007), yet racial-ethnic differences in PTSD often are diminished when socioeconomic status is controlled (e.g., Adams & Boscarino, 2005).

Social and personal resources also have been shown to be related to resilience. Social support has been correlated with resilience, in that individuals with lower levels of perceived support were less likely to be resilient (Bonanno et al., 2007). Several coping styles have been associated with resilience. Pragmatic, goal-directed coping and flexible adaptation both predicted superior adjustment following traumatic events (Bonanno, 2005). Surprisingly, resilience also has been found among individuals who habitually use repressive coping, or cognitive and emotional strategies to ignore or avoid negative stimuli despite increased psychological arousal in response to those stimuli (Bonanno & Singer, 1990). One explanation for this finding is that repressive coping is largely an automatic process distinct from more conscious and effortful strategies to manage thoughts and feelings, such as deliberate cognitive avoidance (Bonanno, Keltner, Holen, & Horowitz, 1995). This effortless orientation away from threatening stimuli appears to mitigate the potentially overwhelming and threatening nature of a traumatic event without expending cognitive resources, so that the individual may use these resources to employ more active, problem-focused coping strategies in response to the stressor (Mancini & Bonanno, 2010). Another factor shown to contribute to resilience is self-enhancement bias, a dispositional tendency to view the self in highly favorable terms (Taylor & Armor, 1996).

Posttraumatic growth has recently been discussed in the context of resilience following trauma (e.g., Lepore & Revenson, 2006; Meichenbaum, 2006). *Posttraumatic growth* refers to positive life changes that people often report following highly stressful events (Park, 2009): developing closer relationships with significant others, becoming more confident and capable of coping with stress, appreciating life more and developing a deeper spiritual perspective, and becoming more compassionate following traumatic events such as motor vehicle accidents, terrorist attacks, combat, and sexual assault (see the meta-analysis by Helgeson, Reynolds, & Tomich, 2006).

Although posttraumatic resilience and posttraumatic growth are similar in that both reference a favorable outcome following trauma, they are distinguished in several ways: First, resilience refers to an individual's change trajectory with regard to psychological and physical adjustment (e.g., levels of depression or PTSD symptoms; Bonanno, 2004) while posttraumatic growth refers to an individual's change trajectory with regard to personal and social characteristics (e.g., philosophy of life, social support; Tedeschi & Calhoun, 2004). Second, resilience is defined as a *lack of change* in functioning, while posttraumatic growth denotes *improvement.* That is, although resilience implies essentially no (or minimal) change on adjustment measures (e.g., no depressive or PTSD symptoms following a traumatic bereavement; Mancini & Bonanno, 2010), posttraumatic growth implies notable change (in a positive direction) on some personal characteristic (e.g., more appreciation for life, deeper social connections).

How are these two constructs—posttraumatic resilience and posttraumatic growth—empirically associated with one another? It appears that many individuals who encounter traumatic events may be resilient regardless of whether they report experiencing posttraumatic growth (Westphal & Bonanno, 2007). For example, in one study, prostate cancer survivors reported very low levels of distress (suggesting resilience) and also reported very little posttraumatic growth (Blank & Bellizzi, 2008). Other studies have found that significant numbers of people report both PTSD symptoms and posttraumatic growth following significant stressful experiences, such as the 9/11 terrorist attacks (Park, Aldwin, Fenster, & Snyder, 2008), the Holocaust (Lev-Wiesel & Amir, 2003), motor vehicle accidents (Salter & Stallard, 2004), and natural disasters (Cryder, Kilmer, Tedeschi, & Calhoun, 2006). Still other studies find inverse relationships between PTSD and posttraumatic growth (e.g., Ickovics et al., 2006).

Thus, it appears that experiences of posttraumatic distress are inconsistently related to posttraumatic growth. They have been found to be positively related (e.g., Park et al., 2008), but sometimes found to be inversely related (e.g., Frazier, Conlon, & Glaser, 2001). Other studies have found no relationship between PTSD symptoms and reports of growth (see Zoellner & Maercker, 2006, for a review). Although one would desire that self-reports of posttraumatic growth be accurate reflections of change, some evidence indicates that reports of growth may be attempts to cope with continued distress; these latter findings, not surprisingly, are linked to poorer adjustment (Zoellner & Maercker, 2006). There is also evidence for a possible interaction between PTSD symptom severity and posttraumatic growth: In the context of high PTSD symptom severity, posttraumatic growth appears to be related to higher levels of distress and lower quality of life, while for low PTSD symptom severity, posttraumatic growth is favorably related to indices of adjustment (e.g., Morrill et al., 2007; Park et al., in press).

Research into posttraumatic growth has proliferated in recent years, and a fairly consistent set of its predictors has emerged across studies. Among trauma characteristics, time since the event tends to be unrelated to growth, although event severity is related to growth (Helgeson et al., 2006). Demographic characteristics such as female gender, younger age, and minority racial status are related to more perceived growth (Helgeson et al., 2006), as are personality characteristics such as optimism, religiousness, and internal locus of control (Zoellner & Marcker, 2006). Further, several coping strategies have been linked to higher levels of reported growth, especially religious coping and positive reappraisal coping (Helgeson et al., 2006).

Lifespan Developmental Perspective

The consequences of trauma exposure can reverberate throughout a lifetime, potentially altering development across multiple domains over the short and long term (Masten & Wright, 2010). Accordingly, its impact might best be approached from a lifespan developmental perspective (Chatterjee et al., 2009). First and foremost, traumatic events may interfere with the successful resolution of developmental tasks. A good deal of research (e.g., Chapman, Dube, & Anda, 2007) has focused on the relation between trauma experienced during childhood (e.g., sexual abuse, neglect) and long-term psychopathology (e.g., anxiety disorders, personality disorders, and substance use disorders). A traumatic event can occur at any point in the lifespan, however, and its impact on and interaction with developmental processes depend largely on the *age-salient developmental tasks* facing the individual at that stage of life (Masten & Wright, 2010). For example, experiencing a traumatic event may interfere with an adolescent's developmental task of performing well in school. The failure to complete earlier developmental tasks (e.g., dropping out of school) can lead to problems with later competence (e.g., multiple instances of unemployment in adulthood). Furthermore, how one views and appraises a prior traumatic event varies with developmental perspective. As individuals mature, they may gain new understanding and insights and reinterpret their earlier experiences, altering the influence of those events and circumstances on longer term outcomes. For example, an adult who successfully manages the mid-life developmental task of family relationship formation may gain the maturity to reassess his or her own childhood and reinterpret and forgive a dysfunctional parent's behavior.

One class of potentially traumatic experiences, military service, often is a "hidden variable" in aging research, influencing the trajectory of positive and negative outcomes that develop over the life course (Spiro, Schnurr, & Aldwin, 1997). Elder and Clipp (1988) pioneered a lifespan developmental framework in their longitudinal studies of aging World

War II and Korean War veterans and documented risk and protective factors for traumatic stress disorders. Their findings suggested that military experience makes an impact across the life course and that stress reactions in response to earlier combat trauma may intensify as individuals confront risk factors (e.g., personal or material loss, retirement) or decline as they cultivate protective factors (e.g., social support, positive environment). Aging is not just a late-life process but, rather, is ongoing throughout a lifetime. Taking a lifespan developmental approach to the study of trauma exposure, therefore, requires tracing both positive and negative influences and positive and negative outcomes forward in time to fully understand the implications of trauma exposure (Chatterjee et al., 2009).

It is also important to consider how the historical-social context can influence trauma and its long-term consequences (Settersten, 2006). The context surrounding a traumatic event can affect how that event is interpreted by different cohorts. For example, the experience of returning home from war differed for Vietnam veterans and World War II veterans. Many returning Vietnam veterans experienced the hostility and opposition surrounding the Vietnam War, while most World War II veterans were greeted as heroes. Thus, it is likely that levels of family, community, and societal support were more available to World War II veterans than to Vietnam veterans, thus enabling this protective factor to aid in resolving war-related distress. Furthermore, World War II veterans had access to a generous "structural intervention" (Settersten, 2006, p. 19) in terms of a G.I. Bill, affording educational, occupational, housing, and other opportunities after their service, that was unavailable to earlier cohorts of returning veterans (and, to that extent, not since). For many World War II veterans, therefore, the infusion of these social resources clearly benefited them over their life course.

Davison and colleagues (2006) and King and colleagues (2007) have approached the examination of traumatic stress from a lifespan developmental perspective in their research on *late-onset stress symptomatology* (LOSS). Based on qualitative evidence collected from focus groups with aging veterans, Davison et al. conceptualized LOSS as occurring among older combat veterans who (a) have functioned successfully since their military experience, but (b) as they confront normative late-life developmental tasks and concomitant stressors (e.g., retirement, bereavement, physical decline), and attempt to make meaning of their lives, they (c) begin to exhibit increased reminiscences about their wartime experience, possibly accompanied by some distress. LOSS once again highlights the interaction between trauma history and lifespan development; here, combat exposure influences a veteran's progression through late-life developmental tasks, and the aging process elicits increased emotionality about earlier traumatic experiences. Just as the interaction of trauma exposure and developmental processes in later life can lead to LOSS, sequelae of trauma exposure may surface at other critical points in the lifespan.

Methodological Tools

A lifespan developmental perspective on trauma and its consequences mandates attention to documenting change or operationalizing process via longitudinal design and analysis. Indeed, many contemporary tools for the study of change have been offered by quantitatively oriented developmentalists (see Collins & Sayer, 2001). Our purpose in this section is to introduce several longitudinal approaches to operationalize change over time in PTSD or other trauma-related outcomes and to document how risk and protective factors may be shown to affect such change. Rather than predicting an individual's score on a variable of interest at a particular moment in one's posttrauma life, these methods emphasize the description and prediction of individual dynamic change functions or mathematical statements about how an individual's score on an outcome changes over time. To borrow from Browne and Nesselroade (2004), *dynamic change* refers to forces (such as risk and protective factors) that drive or impact within-person or intraindividual change in some outcome, the process variable (PTSD or another trauma-related effect). Such models are largely adapted from developmental psychology and fit well with our emphasis on a longitudinal and especially a lifespan perspective on the consequences of trauma exposure.

The most intuitively appealing and straightforward means of documenting change in an individual over time is to calculate a *simple difference score*, subtracting the person's score on a variable at an earlier time point from that person's score on the same variable at a subsequent time point. Historically, some methodologists (e.g., Cronbach & Furby, 1970) cautioned against the use of simple difference scores, claiming that difference scores lack reliability (and using unreliable measures results in bias in parameter estimates—in particular, in regression coefficients). The assertion of the unreliability of difference scores arises from the assumption that the dispersion (variance or standard deviation) of scores at each of the two time points remains constant, based on classical test theory's formulation of parallel tests.

Other methodologists (e.g., Nesselroade & Cable, 1974), however, noted that the expectation of equal dispersion over repeated assessments often is not tenable. Typically, there is either a fan spread or increase in score variability or a constriction or decrease in score variability from occasion to occasion. As demonstrated by Williams and Zimmerman (1996), the greater the difference in variability for the two assessments (other factors held constant), the more reliable will be the difference score. Hence, simple difference scores should not be dismissed and may be considered reasonable representations of within-person or intraindividual change.

One recent example of a trauma study using simple difference scores as the outcome is Vasterling et al.'s (2010) examination of war-zone and postwar stressors predicting Iraq War veterans' pre- to postdeployment change in PTSD symptom severity. These researchers found that increases in PTSD symptom severity (simple difference scores from pre- to postdeployment) were significantly associated with five key risk factors: exposure to combat events, exposure to highly stressful aftermath-of-battle experiences, perceived threat in the war zone, concerns about family and life disruption during deployment, and additional stressful events occurring after return from the war zone, all controlling for baseline PTSD symptom severity. Moreover, difference scores (or increases in symptoms) for deployed military personnel were significantly higher than those for a comparison nondeployed group. Also, Taft, Murphy, King, Dedeyn, and Musser (2005) computed simple difference scores for PTSD symptom severity and for a variety of indices for physical and psychological abuse using a sample of female partners of men undergoing treatment for perpetrating domestic violence. Change in the female partners' PTSD symptom severity was positively related to change in their reports of the frequency of their psychological abuse; those women reporting decreases in psychological abuse from their male partners likewise reported decreases in PTSD symptom severity. These significant associations between simple difference scores were observed both from pre- to posttreatment (over 16 weeks) and from posttreatment to follow-up (over six months).

Another approach to indexing process or intraindividual change in PTSD or other trauma-related outcomes is a *residualized change score*, also called a *partialed change score*: the difference between a person's observed score on a measure at a particular time and the score predicted for that person from a prior score on the same measure. In turn, this residualized change score (say, for PTSD) is typically regressed on scores on another variable of interest (a risk factor, such as trauma severity, or a protective factor, such as available social support). A significant relationship between the risk or protective factor (trauma severity or social support) and the residualized change score (for PTSD) suggests the efficacy of that factor as a predictor of change. Computationally, this partialing or baseline-adjusted process is accomplished in a multiple regression context, wherein scores at the later time point are multiply regressed on scores for that variable at the earlier time point and simultaneously on the putative risk or protective factor. Salience of the risk or protective factor is found in the significance of its partial regression weight. For example, King et al. (2000) found intensity of combat exposure was positively associated with residualized change in PTSD symptom severity 1.5 to 2 years later for a sample of Gulf War veterans. An important assumption of this approach is that the difference between PTSD status predicted from Time 1 scores and actual PTSD status on Time 2 scores is solely attributable to the influence of the putative risk or protective factor and that there is no natural trend or other unmeasured variables (e.g., meaning-making, coping style, additional life stressors) responsible for change over time. This assumption, labeled *stationarity*, is easily challenged in tracking longitudinal trends for postttrauma sequelae and complicates interpretation of a residualized change approach. Prediction of residualized change usually is conducted over a sample of reasonable size assessed on but a handful of occasions; the objective is to derive a group-based common set of parameter estimates.

There is another class of analytic procedures, *time series analysis*, that uses data generated by a single individual assessed over many occasions (Browne & Nesselroade, 2004). One can predict an individual's residualized change occasion to occasion in a time series analysis from previous or lagged scores on the same variable and previous or lagged scores on a potential predictor variable. Resulting parameter estimates calculated over occasions can be considered attributes of the individual. An example might be the partial regression coefficient representing social support's prediction of later residualized change in PTSD for a person. Thus, it is possible to begin to think of the *association between two variables* as a dynamic individual difference characteristic that distinguishes one person from another, just as a score on a measure is intended to differentiate one person from another. Returning to group data, such a partial regression coefficient describing a dynamic prediction process between two variables (e.g., social support and PTSD) for each individual, in turn, could be predicted by yet another individual difference characteristic that varies across persons, a between-persons or interindividual risk or protective factor (e.g., gender). A significant relationship between the within-person dynamic process and the between-persons variable would signify a more complex interaction between two risk or protective factors—the within-person factor and the between-persons factor—in predicting change. To continue the hypothetical example, the dynamic association between social support and PTSD symptom severity over time for individuals may depend upon the gender of the trauma victim, such that, for women, social support appears to be a stronger protective factor than for men. Analyses of this general type, using repeated assessments within individuals nested within multiple persons, can be accomplished using multilevel regression, also referred to as mixed-effects regression, random coefficients regression, or hierarchical linear modeling (see Raudenbush & Bryk, 2002; Singer & Willett, 2003).

To document and predict dynamic change, one may also use the class of procedures known as *growth curve modeling*, which also relies on a multilevel data structure. The goal of growth curve modeling is to describe a trajectory of scores on an outcome variable of interest over a particular time interval, such that the score on the outcome is a function of time since some starting point. The procedure uses within-person repeated assessments and the times of assessment to generate a series of parameter estimates that describe a regression line that best fits the data for each study participant. In the simplest case of straight-linear regression, at least two parameters are estimated for each person: intercept (most frequently the score at initial assessment) and slope (amount of change in the outcome per unit change in time). In turn, associations between other individual difference characteristics and these intercept and slope variables may be examined. Of course, a best-fitting function describing the relationship between scores on an outcome and time is not necessarily straight-linear, and more complex trajectories of change can be considered.

The textbooks by Duncan, Duncan, Strycker, Li, and Alpert (1999) and Raudenbush and Bryk (2002) provide detailed guidance on the growth curve methodology. The former adopts a structural equation modeling orientation while the latter relies on random coefficients regression. Each of these alternative strategies has its own advantages. Structural equation modeling allows for more complex multivariate models, potentially including the consideration of simultaneous trajectories for multiple outcomes. This flexibility comes at the cost of assuming that each study participant is systematically assessed on the same occasions over time. Although there may be missing data, and this can be accommodated, the time structure that underlies the analyses must be consistent over individuals. Random coefficients regression is much more flexible with regard to the time structure. The timing of assessment occasions for each individual can be unique and varied, but the technique is typically univariate with regard to the outcome. That is, change or growth is usually restricted to one outcome at a time (but see MacCallum, Kim, Malarkey, & Kiecolt-Gleser, 1997, for a possible exception).

There has been increasing though still quite limited application of growth curve techniques in the trauma literature over the past decade. A nice example that emphasizes the role of risk and protective factors in the prediction of change in PTSD symptom severity was offered by Murphy, Johnson, Chung, and Beaton (2003). These researchers followed parents of children who had succumbed to violent death prospectively over five years. Parents' individual PTSD intercepts (at initial status) and slopes (change over time) were regressed on nine risk and protective factors (e.g., concurrent mental distress, coping, gender, social support). Though six of the nine factors predicted the intercept, only parent gender and social support predicted reduction in PTSD symptoms, illustrating the contrast between a static single-occasion prediction of intercept and a process or change-based orientation in the prediction of slope to the potential impact of risk and protective factors. In their study, Murphy et al. (2003) chose a straight-linear function for change in PTSD over time, whereas others have proposed a curvilinear function, where symptoms are expected to diminish but at a more rapid rate initially, followed by a decreasing rate of change as time progresses. For example, deRoon-Cassini, Rusch, Mancini, and Bonanno (2010) used a power-polynomial specification for curvilinear change to document trajectories in depression and PTSD symptom severity following serious injury. They also incorporated an exploratory technique called growth mixture modeling, a structural equation modeling procedure to reveal different classes of individuals based on patterns of responding. They reported four distinct patterns or trends: resilience, recovery, chronicity, and delayed response. Their findings regarding risk and protective factors in predicting these trajectories were mixed. Koss and Figueredo (2004) and Resnick et al. (2007), both studying rape victims, used an alternative growth curve approach to documenting curvilinearity. In place of power polynomials, they regressed each participant's PTSD symptom severity scores on the natural log of the time since trauma exposure. Koss and Figueredo (2004) were able to document the efficacy of attributions and beliefs as mediators or protective factors associated with reduction in symptoms over time, and Resnick et al. (2007) pointed to the importance of prior rape as a risk factor for PTSD over time.

An interesting variation on curvilinear growth curve patterns is *spline regression*, sometimes called *piecewise regression*. Conceptually, spline regression disaggregates a curvilinear trend into a series of two or more slopes such that there is one or more distinct "turning points" marking the separation of different rates of change over adjacent time intervals. In other words, there is a regression discontinuity at a particular point along the time dimension where an abrupt shift in slope occurs: an alteration of the change in the outcome per unit change in time. Again, of course, each slope is an individual difference characteristic available to be predicted or regressed on other variables, and even the turning point or point of inflection, though normally fixed, could likewise be a personal attribute to be predicted. King et al. (2003) demonstrated spline regression on data from emergency room patients and showed that the average rate of decrease in PTSD symptom severity from time of the traumatic event to 30 days was five times greater than the average rate of decrease after 30 days. Just as spline regression has proved useful to index critical shifts in cognitive functioning over the life course (McArdle, Ferrer-Caja, Hamagami, & Woodcock, 2002), trauma researchers might find it beneficial in exploring turning points in mid- to later-life that may be influenced by trauma exposure in childhood, adolescence, or early adulthood (see the methodological volume on turning points [Cohen, 2008] for various applications).

Latent difference score analysis (McArdle, 2001) likewise is used to disaggregate a trend or trajectory of change over time into a series of segments, each of which defines a change in the value of an outcome over that particular time interval. Latent difference score models use a structural equation modeling framework. They have three advantages. First, the difference scores are represented as differences between two perfectly reliable latent variables, thereby optimizing the reliability of the difference scores themselves. Second, the model allows for the control of the effects of prior status on the outcome variable. And, third, the model controls for the influence of extraneous unmeasured variables, eliminating the need to assume stationarity. In the trauma literature, this methodology has been used in two studies. King et al. (2006) investigated longitudinal trends in PTSD among severely injured children and adolescents and documented different rates of decline in PTSD symptom severity as a function of age at time of trauma and the influence of ongoing family disruptions and conflict following the event. For the most distal time segment (beyond roughly 200 days posttrauma), adolescents tended to exhibit less negative change or diminution in symptom severity than younger children, a finding that the authors interpreted as possibly influenced by differential stages in biological development. Moreover, family strains were most influential on symptom severity in the 100–200 day interval, which corresponded to the potential stress of hospital discharge and family and community reintegration. King, King, McArdle, Shalev, and Doron-LaMarca (2009) applied latent difference score analysis to longitudinal data from emergency room patients and found level of depression symptom severity to be positively associated with subsequent changes in PTSD symptom severity. Higher scores on depression anticipated a worsening or increase in PTSD scores, but the reverse pattern did not obtain.

The goal of these and related methods is to better understand the short- and long-term reverberations of traumatic events through the life course. From understanding comes knowledge that can be used to ameliorate symptoms whether at or soon after the event, or even later in life when symptoms become exacerbated owing to various circumstances.

Directions for Future Research

In this chapter, we attempt to promote a lifespan developmental perspective to understand the consequences of traumatic events and the risk and protective factors that influence them. Relatedly, we emphasize the value of contemporary methods for longitudinal inquiry incorporating repeated assessments, whether they be over days, weeks, months, or years. Indeed, our overriding recommendation for future research is to operationalize outcomes as process variables reflecting longitudinal intraindividual change over time. We also urge researchers to consider the developmental stages, tasks, and challenges that define their study participants; how those stages, tasks, and challenges interact with the traumatic experience; and if stage transitions might influence trauma victims' retrospective appraisals of the experience. Age-related psychosocial, cognitive, and physiological changes all deserve consideration. Moreover, we encourage researchers to recognize the historical-social context that defines and differentiates distinct age cohorts and that suggests potential cohort-specific vulnerabilities and strengths that filter responses to trauma. And, importantly, we ask researchers to think broadly and distally about how early trauma may have repercussions to multiple life domains into the middle and later years.

One avenue for future research relates to the various patterns of response to trauma proposed in the literature (e.g., Bonanno, 2004): a generally persistent healthy state of functioning after exposure, with mild or initial short-lived symptoms (resilience), symptoms that appear just after exposure and remit after a specified time (recovery), symptoms that appear early but do not remit (chronicity), and symptoms that emerge after a recognizable symptom-free period (delayed response). We need to track outcomes repeatedly across time to verify the efficacy of these proposed response trajectories heretofore uncovered via exploratory means (deRoon-Casini et al., 2010). Modern diary methods for data collection may prove useful (Bolger, Davis, & Rafaeli, 2003). It also seems fitting to bring more empirical evidence to bear on the difference between resilience and recovery. As currently conceptualized, there is some degree of vagueness as to the distinction between the two. How mild can symptoms be or how brief an interval must one manifest posttraumatic symptoms and still be declared resilient as opposed to recovered? From the panoply of risk and protective factors, which differentiate between these two patterns?

In addition, clarification is needed as to whether the risk and protective factors that predict resilience (e.g., low trauma severity, high social support, lack of additional life stressors; see Bonanno et al., 2007) are merely the inverse of the predictors of chronicity (e.g., high trauma severity, low social support, additional life stressors; see King et al., 1999). It would be interesting to simultaneously examine multiple types of outcome variables (e.g., indices of psychopathology, physical stamina, perceived quality of life, satisfaction with life). Is it possible to manifest psychopathology in one domain but appear to manifest resilience in another domain—for example, to tolerate and manage generally persistent PTSD symptoms and still report acceptable levels of life satisfaction? Do risk and protective factors operate differentially, depending upon the dimension of functioning under scrutiny? Finally, with regard to longitudinal patterns of response to traumatic events, posttraumatic growth deserves continued attention, and a crucial need is to document a change score-based representation of this construct rather than a single-occasion self-report assessment that relies on retrospective and possibly biased judgments of change.

In closing, we recommend more attention to the mechanisms by which risk and protective factors make their independent and joint contributions to change following trauma. We also caution that a longitudinal and lifespan developmental perspective must accommodate two ongoing time-based processes, one being time since the trauma and the other being the stage of development through which the individual passes, each of which operates with other factors to influence health and well-being. The search for mechanisms, therefore, can be quite complex. Vogt, King, and King (2007), adopting a risk factors framework proposed by Kraemer and colleagues (Kraemer, Stice, Kazdin, Offord, & Kupfer, 2001), outlined strategies to understand etiological process in traumatic stress studies—specifically, how risk and protective factors may work together to impact outcomes. In the context of resilience research, Ong et al. (2009) also encouraged studies to elucidate the mechanisms underlying response to trauma and adversity, with special attention to determining which risk and protective factors are modifiable and hence available to intervention.

Note

This work was supported by the National Center for Posttraumatic Stress Disorder—Behavioral Science Division, and the Massachusetts Veterans Epidemiology Research and Information Center, VA Boston Healthcare System, via their assistance to the Stress, Health, and Aging Research Program (SHARP).

References

Adams, R., & Boscarino, J. (2005). Differences in mental health outcomes among whites, African Americans, and Hispanics following a community disaster. *Psychiatry: Interpersonal and Biological Processes, 68*, 25–65.

Aldwin, C. M., Levenson, M. R., & Spiro, A., III. (1994). Vulnerability and resilience to combat exposure: Can stress have lifelong effects? *Psychology and Aging, 9*, 3–4.

Andrews, B., Brewin, C., Rose, S., & Kirk, M. (2000). Predicting PTSD symptoms in victims of violent crime: The role of shame, anger, and childhood abuse. *Journal of Abnormal Psychology, 109*, 6–3.

Baily, D., & Elmore, R. (1999, August). *PTSD symptom severity: Differences in demographic characteristics among combat veterans.* Paper presented at the 107th American Psychological Association Annual Convention, Boston, MA.

Blanchard, E., Hickling, E., Taylor, A., & Loos, W. (1995). Psychiatric morbidity associated with motor vehicle accidents. *Journal of Nervous and Mental Disease, 183*, 49–04.

Blank, T. O., & Bellizzi, K. M. (2008). A gerontologic perspective on cancer and aging. *Cancer, 112*, 2569–2576.

Bolger, N., Davis, A., & Rafaeli, E. (2003). Diary methods: Capturing life as it is lived. *Annual Review of Psychology, 54*, 57–16.

Bonanno, G. A. (2004). Loss, trauma, and human resilience: Have we underestimated the human capacity to thrive after extremely aversive events? *American Psychologist, 59*, 2–8.

Bonanno, G. A. (2005). Clarifying and extending the construct of adult resilience. *American Psychologist, 60*, 26–67.

Bonanno, G. A., Galea, S., Bucciarelli, A., & Vlahov, D. (2007). What predicts psychological resilience after disaster? The role of demographics, resources, and life stress. *Journal of Consulting and Clinical Psychology, 75*, 67–82.

Bonanno, G. A., Keltner, D., Holen, A., & Horowitz, M. J. (1995). When avoiding unpleasant emotions might not be such a bad thing: Verbal-automatic response dissociation and midlife conjugal bereavement. *Journal of Personality and Social Psychology, 69*, 97–89.

Bonanno, G. A., & Singer, J. L. (1990). Repressive personality style: Theoretical and methodological implication for health and pathology. In J. L. Singer (Ed.), *Repression and dissociation: Implication for personality theory, psychopathology, and health* (pp. 43–70). Chicago, IL: University of Chicago Press.

Bremner, J., Southwick, S., Brett, E., & Fontana, A. (1992). Dissociation and posttraumatic stress disorder in Vietnam combat veterans. *American Journal of Psychiatry, 149*, 32–32.

Breslau, N., Davis, G. C., Andreski, P., & Peterson, E. (1991). Traumatic events and posttraumatic stress disorder in an urban population of young adults. *Archives of General Psychiatry, 48*, 216–222.

Brewin, C. R., Andrews, B., & Valentine, J. D. (2000). Meta-analysis of risk factors for posttraumatic stress disorder in trauma-exposed adults. *Journal of Consulting and Clinical Psychology, 68*, 748–766.

Bromet, E., Sonnega, A., & Kessler, R. C. (1998). Risk factors for DSM-III-R posttraumatic stress disorder: Findings from the national comorbidity survey. *American Journal of Epidemiology, 147*, 353–361.

Browne, M. W., & Nesselroade, J. R. (2004). Representing psychological processes with dynamic factor models: Some promising uses and extensions of autoregressive moving average time series models. In A. Maydeu-Olivares, & J. J. McArdle (Eds.), *Contemporary psychometrics: A festschrift for Roderick P. Mcdonald* (pp. 40–47). Mahwah, NJ: Lawrence Erlbaum.

Chapman, D., Dube, S., & Anda, R. (2007). Adverse childhood events as risk factors for negative mental health outcomes. *Psychiatric Annals, 37*, 35–64.

Chatterjee, S., Spiro, A., III, King, L. A., King, D. W., & Davison, E. H. (2009). Research on aging military veterans. Lifespan implications of military service. *PTSD Research Quarterly, 20*, 1–7.

Cohen, P. (2008). *Applied data analytic techniques for turning points research.* London: Taylor & Frances.

Collins, L. M., & Sayer, A. G. (2001). *New methods for the analysis of change.* Washington, DC: American Psychological Association.

Cronbach, L., & Furby, L. (1970). How we should measure 'change': Or should we? *Psychological Bulletin, 74*, 6–0.

Cryder, C., Kilmer, R., Tedeschi, R., & Calhoun, L. (2006). An exploratory study of posttraumatic growth in children following a natural disaster. *American Journal of Orthopsychiatry, 76*, 6–9.

Davison, E. H., Pless, A. P., Gugliucci, M. R., King, L. A., King, D. W., Salgado, D. M., Bachrach, P. (2006). Late-life emergence of early-life trauma. The phenomenon of late-onset stress symptomatology among aging combat veterans. *Research on Aging, 28*, 8–15.

Delahanty, D. L., Raimonde, A., Spoonster, E., & Cullado, M. (2003). Injury severity, prior trauma history, urinary cortisol levels and acute PTSD in motor vehicle accident victims. *Journal of Anxiety Disorders, 17*, 14–64.

deRoon-Cassini, T. A., Mancini, A. D., Rusch, M. D., & Bonanno, G. A. (2010). Psychopathology and resilience following traumatic injury: A latent growth mixture model analysis. *Rehabilitation Psychology, 55*, 1.

Duncan, T. E., Duncan, S. C., Strycker, L. A., Li, F., & Alpert, A. (1999). *An introduction to latent variable growth curve modeling: Concepts, issues, and applications.* Mahwah, NJ: Lawrence Erlbaum.

Elder, G., & Clipp, E. (1988). Combat experience, comradeship, and psychological health. In J. P. Wilson, Z. Harel, & B. Kahana (Eds.), *Human adaptation to extreme stress: From the Holocaust to Vietnam* (pp. 13–56). New York: Plenum Press.

Fairbank, J. A., Keane, T. M., & Malloy, P. F. (1983). Some preliminary data on the psychological characteristics of Vietnam veterans with posttraumatic stress disorder. *Journal of Consulting and Clinical Psychology, 51*, 91–19.

Fairbrother, N., & Rachman, S. (2006). PTSD in victims of sexual assault: A test of a major component of the Ehlers-Clark theory. *Journal of Behavior Therapy and Experimental Psychiatry, 37*, 7–3.

Fontana, A., & Rosenheck, R. (1993). A causal model of the etiology of war-related PTSD. *Journal of Traumatic Stress, 6*, 47–00.

Forsythe, C. J., & Compas, B. E. (1987). Interaction of cognitive appraisals of stressful events and coping: Testing the

goodness of fit hypothesis. *Cognitive Therapy and Research, 11*, 47–85.
Frazier, P., Conlon, A., & Glaser, T. (2001). Positive and negative life changes following sexual assault. *Journal of Consulting and Clinical Psychology, 69*, 104–055.
Green, M. A., & Berlin, M. A. (1987). Five psychosocial variables related to the existence of post-traumatic stress disorder symptoms. *Journal of Clinical Psychology, 43*, 64–49.
Helgeson, V. S., Reynolds, K. A., & Tomich, P. L. (2006). A meta-analytic review of benefit finding and growth. *Journal of Consulting and Clinical Psychology, 74*, 79–16.
Hoge, E. A., Austin, E. D., & Pollack, M. H. (2007). Resilience: Research evidence and conceptual considerations for posttraumatic stress disorder. *Depression and Anxiety, 24*, 139–152.
Ickovics, J. R., Meade, C. S., Kershaw, T. S., Milan, S., Lewis, J. B., & Ethier, K. A. (2006). Urban teens: Trauma, posttraumatic growth, and emotional distress among female adolescents. *Journal of Consulting and Clinical Psychology, 74*, 841–850.
Kessler, R. C., Sonnega, A., Bromet, E., Hughes, M., & Nelson, C. B. (1995). Posttraumatic stress disorder in the national comorbidity survey. *Archives of General Psychiatry, 52*, 1048–1060.
King, D. W., King, L. A., Erickson, D. J., Huang, M. T., Sharkansky, E. J., & Wolfe, J. (2000). Posttraumatic stress disorder and retrospectively reported stressor exposure: A longitudinal prediction model. *Journal of Abnormal Psychology, 109*, 624–633.
King, L. A., King, D. W., Fairbank, J. A., Keane, T. M., & Adams, G. A. (1998). Resilience-recovery factors in post-traumatic stress disorder among female and male Vietnam veterans: Hardiness, postwar social support, and additional stressful life events. *Journal of Personality and Social Psychology, 74*, 420–434.
King, D. W., King, L. A., Foy, D. W., & Gudanowski, D. M. (1996). Prewar factors in combat-related posttraumatic stress disorder: Structural equation modeling with a national sample of female and male Vietnam veterans. *Journal of Consulting and Clinical Psychology, 64*, 520–531.
King, D., King, L., Foy, D., Keane, T., & Fairbank, J. (1999). Posttraumatic stress disorder in a national sample of female and male Vietnam veterans: Risk factors, war-zone stressors, and resilience-recovery variables. *Journal of Abnormal Psychology, 108*, 164–170.
King, D., King, L., Gudanowski, D., & Vreven, D. (1995). Alternative representations of war zone stressors: Relationships to posttraumatic stress disorder in male and female Vietnam veterans. *Journal of Abnormal Psychology, 104*, 184–196.
King, D. W., King, L. A., McArdle, J. J., Shalev, A. Y., & Doron-LaMarca, S. (2009). Sequential temporal dependencies in associations between symptoms of depression and posttraumatic stress disorder: An application of bivariate latent difference score structural equation modeling. *Multivariate Behavioral Research, 44*, 437–464.
King, L. A., King, D. W., McArdle, J. J., Saxe, G. N., Doron-LaMarca, S., & Orazem, R. J. (2006). Latent difference score approach to longitudinal trauma research. *Journal of Traumatic Stress, 19*, 771–785.
King, L. A., King, D. W., Salgado, D., & Shalev, A. (2003). Contemporary longitudinal methods for the study of trauma and posttraumatic stress disorder. *CNS Spectrums, 8*, 686–692.
King, L. A., King, D. W., Vickers, K., Davison, E. H., & Spiro, A., III. (2007). Assessing late-onset stress symptomatology among aging male combat veterans. *Aging & Mental Health, 11*, 175–191.
King, D. W., Potter, C. M., Pless, A. P., Schuster, J. L., Park, C. L., King, L. A., Moore, J. L. (2010, May). Coping during capitivity and long-term physical and mental health: Vietnam repatriated prisoners of war (RPWs). Poster presented at the Association for Psychological Science 22nd annual convention, Boston, MA.
King, D. W., Vogt, D. S., & King, L. A. (2004). Risk and resilience factors in the etiology of chronic PTSD. In B. T. Litz (Ed.), *Early interventions for trauma and traumatic loss in children and adults: Evidence-based directions* (pp. 34–64). New York: Guilford.
Koss, M. P., & Figueredo, A. J. (2004). Change in cognitive mediators of rape's impact on psychosocial health across 2 years of recovery. *Journal of Consulting and Clinical Psychology, 72*, 1063–1072.
Kraemer, H. C., Stice, E., Kazdin, A., Offord, D., & Kupfer, D. (2001). How do risk factors work together? Mediators, moderators, and independent, overlapping, and proxy risk factors. *American Journal of Psychiatry, 158*, 848–856.
Kulka, R., Schlenger, W., Fairbank, J., Hough, R., Jordan, B., Marmar, C. R., & Weiss, D. S. (1990). *Trauma and the Vietnam War generation: Report of findings from the National Vietnam Veterans Readjustment Study*. Philadelphia, PA: Brunner/Mazel.
Lepore, S., & Revenson, T. (2006). Resilience and posttraumatic growth: Recovery, resistance, and reconfiguration. In L. G. Calhoun & R. G. Tedeschi (Eds.), *Handbook of posttraumatic growth: Research & practice* (pp. 24–46). Mahwah, NJ: Lawrence Erlbaum.
Lev-Wiesel, R., & Amir, M. (2003). Posttraumatic growth among Holocaust child survivors. *Journal of Loss & Trauma, 8*, 229–237.
Luthar, S., Cicchetti, D., & Becker, B. (2000). The construct of resilience: A critical evaluation and guidelines for future work. *Child Development, 71*, 543–562.
MacCallum, R. C., Kim, C. Malarky, W. B., & Kiecolt-Gleser, J. K. (1997). Studying multivariate change using multilevel models and latent curve models. *Multivariate Behavioral Research, 32*, 215–253.
Mancini, A. D., & Bonanno, G. A. (2010). Resilience to potential trauma: Toward a lifespan approach. In J. W. Reich, A. J. Zautra, & J. S. Hall (Eds.), *Handbook of adult resilience* (pp. 258–282). New York: Guilford.
Masten, A. S., & Garmezy, N. (1985). Risk, vulnerability, and protective factors in the developmental psychopathology. In B. B. Lahey & A. E. Kazdin (Eds.), *Advances in clinical child psychology*, Vol. 8 (pp. 1–51). New York: Plenum.
Masten, A. S., & Wright, M. O. (2010). Resilience over the lifespan: Developmental perspectives on resistance, recovery, and transformation. In J. W. Reich, A. J. Zautra, & J. S. Hall (Eds.), *Handbook of adult resilience* (pp. 213–237). New York: Guilford.
Mayou, R., Bryant, B., & Ehlers, A. (2001). Prediction of psychological outcomes one year after a motor vehicle accident. *American Journal of Psychiatry, 158*, 1231–1238.
McArdle, J. J. (2001). A latent difference score approach to longitudinal dynamic structural analyses. In R. Cudeck, S. DuToit, & D. Sorbom (Eds.), *Structural equation modeling: Present and future* (pp. 342–380). Lincolnwood, IL: Scientific Software International.

McArdle, J. J., Ferrer-Caja, E., Hamagami, F., & Woodcock, R. W. (2002). Comparative longitudinal structural analyses of the growth and decline of multiple intellectual abilities over the life span. *Developmental Psychology, 38,* 115–142.

Meichenbaum, D. (2006). Resilience and posttraumatic growth: A constructive narrative perspective. *Handbook of posttraumatic growth: Research & practice* (pp. 355–367). Mahwah, NJ: Lawrence Erlbaum.

Morrill, F., Brewer, N. T., O'Neill, S. C., Lillie, S. E., Dees, E. C., Carey, L. A., & Rimer, B. K. (2007). The interaction of post-traumatic growth and post-traumatic stress symptoms in predicting depressive symptoms and quality of life. *Psycho-Oncology, 17,* 948–953.

Murphy, S. A., Johnson, L., Chung, I., & Beaton, R. (2003). The prevalence of PTSD following the violent death of a child and predictors of change 5 years later. *Journal of Traumatic Stress, 16,* 17–25.

Nesselroade, J. R., & Cable, D. G. (1974). 'Sometimes, it's okay to factor differences scores'-The separation of state and trait anxiety. *Multivariate Behavioral Research, 9,* 273–281.

Nishith, P., Mechanic, M. B., & Resick, P. A. (2000). Prior interpersonal trauma: The contribution to current PTSD symptoms in female rape victims. *Journal of Abnormal Psychology, 109,* 20–25.

Ong, A., Bergeman, C., & Boker, S. (2009). Resilience comes of age: Defining features in later adulthood. *Journal of Personality, 77,* 1777–1804.

Ozer, E., Best, S., Lipsey T., & Weiss, D. (2003). Predictors of posttraumatic stress disorder and symptoms in adults: A meta analysis. *Psychological Bulletin, 129,* 52–73.

Park, C. L. (2009). Overview of theoretical perspectives. In C. L. Parl, S. C. Lechner, M. H. Antoni, & A. L. Stanton (Eds.), *Medical illness and positive life change: Can crisis lead to personal transformation?* (pp. 11–30). Washington, DC: American Psychological Association.

Park, C. L., Aldwin, C. M., Fenster, J. R., & Snyder, L. B. (2008). Pathways to posttraumatic growth versus posttraumatic stress: Coping and emotional reactions following the September 11, 2001, terrorist attacks. *American Journal of Orthopsychiatry, 78,* 300–312.

Park, C. L., Armeli, S., & Tennen, H. (2004). Appraisal-coping goodness of fit: A daily Internet study. *Personality and Social Psychology Bulletin, 30,* 558–569.

Park, C. L., Mills, M., & Edmondson, D. (in press). PTSD as meaning violation: A test of a cognitive worldview perspective. *Psychological Trauma: Theory, Research, Practice, and Policy.*

Raudenbush, S. W., & Bryk, A. S. (2002). *Hierarchical linear models: Applications and data analysis methods* (2nd ed.). Thousand Oaks, CA: Sage.

Regehr, C., Hill, J., & Glancy, G. (2000). Individual predictors of traumatic reactions in firefighters. *Journal of Nervous and Mental Disease, 188,* 333–339.

Resnick, H. S., Acierno, R., Waldrop, A. E., King, L., King, D., Danielson, & C. Kilpatrick, D. (2007). Randomized controlled evaluation of an early intervention to prevent post-rape psychopathology. *Behaviour Research and Therapy, 45,* 2432–3447.

Salter, E., & Stallard, P. (2004). Posttraumatic growth in child survivors of a road traffic accident. *Journal of Traumatic Stress, 17,* 335–340.

Saxe, G. N., Miller, A., Bartholomew, D., Hall, E., Lopez, C., Kaplow, J., Moulton, S., et al. (2005). Incidence and risk factors for acute stress disorder in children with injuries. *Journal of Trauma: Injury, Infection, and Critical Care, 59,* 946–953.

Schnurr, P., & Spiro, A. (1999). Combat disorder, posttraumatic stress disorder symptoms, and health behaviors as predictors of self-reported physical health in older veterans. *Journal of Nervous and Mental Disease, 187,* 353–359.

Seligman, M. E. P. (1991). *Learned optimism: How to change your mind and your life.* New York: Knopf.

Settersten, R. (2006). When nations call: How wartime military service matters for the life course and aging. *Research on Aging, 28,* 12–36.

Sharkansky, E., King, D. W., King, L. A., Wolfe, J., Erickson, D., & Stokes, L. (2000). Coping with Gulf War combat stress: Mediating and moderating effects. *Journal of Abnormal Psychology, 109,* 188–197.

Singer, J. D., & Willett, J. B. (2003). *Applied longitudinal data analysis: Modeling change and event occurrence.* New York: Oxford University Press.

Spiro, A., III, Schnurr, P., & Aldwin, C. (1997). A life-span perspective on the effects of military service. *Journal of Geriatric Psychiatry, 30,* 91–128.

Suvak, M. K., Vogt, D. S., Savarese, V. W., King, L. A., & King, D. W. (2002). Relationship of war-zone coping strategies to long-term general life adjustment among Vietnam veterans: Combat exposure as a moderator variable. *Personality and Social Psychology Bulletin, 28,* 974–985.

Taft, C. T., Murphy, C. M., King, L. A., DeDeyn, J. M., & Musser, P. H. (2005). Posttraumatic stress disorder symptomatology among partners of men in treatment for relationship abuse. *Journal of Abnormal Psychology, 114,* 259–268.

Taylor, S., & Armor, D. (1996). Positive illusions and coping with adversity. *Journal of Personality, 64,* 873–898.

Tedeschi, R. G., & Calhoun, L. G. (2004). Posttraumatic growth: Conceptual foundations and empirical evidence. *Psychological Inquiry, 15,* 1–18.

Vasterling, J. J., Proctor, S. P., Friedman, M. J., Hoge, C. W., Heeren, T., King, L. A., & King, D. W. (2010). PTSD symptom increases in Iraq-deployed soldiers: Comparison with nondeployed soldiers and associations with baseline symptoms, deployment experiences, and postdeployment stress. *Journal of Traumatic Stress, 23,* 41–51.

Vogt, D., King, D., & King, L. (2007). Risk pathways for PTSD: Making sense of the literature. In M. J. Friedman, T. M. Keane, & P. A. Resick (Eds.), *Handbook of PTSD: Science and practice* (pp. 99–115). New York: Guilford.

Walls, T., & Schafer, J. (2006). *Models for intensive longitudinal data.* New York: Oxford University Press.

Westphal, M., & Bonanno, G. A. (2007). Posttraumatic growth and resilience to trauma: Different sides of the same coin or different coins? *Applied Psychology: An International Review, 56,* 417–427.

Williams, R. H., & Zimmerman, D. W. (1996). Are simple gain scores obsolete? *Applied Psychological Measurement, 20,* 59–69.

Wilson, J., & Boden, J. (2008). The effects of personality, social support and religiosity on posttraumatic growth. *Australasian Journal of Disaster and Trauma Studies, 2008*(1).

Zoellner, T., & Maercker, A. (2006). Posttraumatic growth in clinical psychology—A critical review and introduction of a two component model. *Clinical Psychology Review, 26,* 626–653.

CHAPTER

23 Community-based Early Intervention with Trauma Survivors

Josef I. Ruzek

Abstract

The numbers of individuals affected by frequently occurring traumatic events such as accidents and assaults, as well as large-scale traumas such as war and disaster, call for systematic, comprehensive community-based responses to manage mental health consequences of such exposure. Comprehensive early response by the community to its trauma-exposed members requires integration of several key response components. Communities should develop immediate response services, educate the affected community, reach out to survivors, engage in efficient early identification of those at risk, implement community-wide early intervention counseling services, monitor those at risk, train and support providers, monitor the well-being and needs of the affected population, and provide additional large-community interventions and programs. These services should encompass both trauma survivors and their family members and should target a range of potential negative outcomes, including posttraumatic stress disorder, depression, substance abuse, and impairments in functioning. Increased attention should be given to training and supporting providers, integration of online interventions into community-based service delivery, and program monitoring and evaluation. Those who serve sexual assault survivors, crime victims, deployed military personnel, physically injured assault and motor vehicle accident survivors, and disaster-affected groups can potentially learn much from one another, and efforts should be under taken to ensure that "cross-fertilization" of perspectives can occur in the service of creating integrated and comprehensive community-based responses to trauma.

Key Words: Trauma, PTSD, community, early intervention, prevention, disaster

Although most traumas affect a small number of individuals and their loved ones, some events such as disasters and wars affect large numbers of individuals over a short span of time. Other kinds of traumas, such as sexual assaults, violence, and motor vehicle accidents, affect large numbers of individuals over the course of time in most communities. The number of individuals affected by these large-scale events and continuously occurring traumas along with the magnitude of cumulative mental health impact on survivor populations call for systematic, comprehensive community-based responses. In communities, the capability for many kinds of helpful responses exists, to include delivery of individual and small-group interventions, promotion of self-help activities, media applications, and development of larger community programs and public ceremonies. In this chapter, best practices in early intervention and community-based services aimed at preventing development of posttrauma psychological problems are reviewed. Large numbers of community members may perceive the impact of traumatic events on their perceived quality of life, confidence in the future, and beliefs and emotions, but the focus here is on prevention of mental/behavioral health problems (e.g., posttraumatic stress disorder, depression, problem drinking) and problems of functioning in those exposed to traumas, rather than overall population wellness. Selected illustrative applications in the contexts of disaster, war-related deployment stresses, and sexual and nonsexual assault are explored, and challenges in response to community-wide traumas that cut across types of trauma are discussed. Finally, some suggestions for future directions in the development of services are highlighted.

Comprehensive early response by the community to its trauma-exposed members requires integration of several key response components. Adequate attention to these components means that communities should undertake, when possible, to develop capacity/capability to provide immediate response services, educate and inform the affected community, reach out to survivors, engage in efficient early identification of those who are likely to require assistance, implement community-wide early intervention counseling services (including Web services), monitor those at risk, train and support providers, monitor the well-being and needs of the affected population, and provide additional large-community interventions and programs.

Identification of Survivors at Risk for Problems

A major challenge in the delivery of early post-trauma community services is identifying those with problems and engaging them in helping services. However, in many settings where recent trauma survivors may be found, routine procedures for proactively identifying those at risk for trauma-related mental health problems are absent. For example, in hospitals, many injured trauma survivors have high levels of symptomatic distress that are inconsistently evaluated and treated (Zatzick et al., 2005).

Unfortunately, it is not at present possible to reliably identify individuals within the first few days of trauma exposure who will go on to develop posttraumatic stress disorder (PTSD) or other problems. Therefore, rather than initiating intervention, a useful approach is to offer periodic brief follow-ups for those considered at risk (Brewin, 2003). Periodic phone contacts or visits can enable contacts at a later time when problems can be more reliably identified and when initiation of care may be more clearly warranted. Screening tools are becoming available that can be used after the first few weeks following a range of traumas (Brewin et al., 2002), including disaster (Norris, Hamblen, Brown, & Schinka, 2008), or injury requiring a hospital visit (Richmond et al., in press; O'Donnell et al., 2009). Brewin and colleagues (2002) developed the Trauma Screening Questionnaire (TSQ), a 10-item measure designed to predict development of PTSD. In separate studies of rail crash survivors and crime victims, endorsement of at least six re-experiencing or arousal symptoms on the TSQ was found to predict PTSD as diagnosed using a structured clinical interview with high levels of specificity and sensitivity. The feasibility of using the TSQ to screen disaster survivors has been demonstrated by Brewin et al., (2008). Following the July 7, 2005, bombings in the London transport system, a dedicated screening team was established to identify persons with bombing-related mental disorders. A telephone hotline provided consultation and referral of appropriate callers to the screening team. Those receiving professional or hotline referrals or who were self-referring were sent materials including the TSQ. Individuals screening positive were invited for a more detailed assessment that included diagnostic interviews, and those with identified disorder or significant distress or impairment were referred for treatment. For those deemed not to require immediate initiation of mental health care, repeated screenings at 3-, 6-, and 9-month intervals were instituted to guard against development of delayed-onset PTSD or gradual symptom worsening. Thus, 906 individuals were sent the screening instrument, and 596 completed the questionnaire. Of these, 370 were invited for and 346 received the more detailed assessment; 26% were judged to require only monitoring, and 74% were referred for treatment.

Many individuals who are reluctant to seek formal mental health support, owing to logistical barriers, perceptions of social stigma, and/or a desire to self-manage their responses, may be more receptive to support from other sources, include chaplains or physicians. The latter groups are especially important in helping to identify those who may require additional services. A key, but often underused, resource is the primary-care medical service sector. PTSD screening tools such as the Primary Care PTSD screen are available and have been validated in some primary-care settings (Ouimette, Wade, Prins, & Schon, 2008; Prins et al., 2003). Such tools could be used to better identify those in need of more careful assessment. Such primary-care-based screening programs have been implemented within the Department of Defense and the Veterans Healthcare Administration to identify individuals experiencing symptoms of deployment-related PTSD.

Because many survivors in distress will not seek mental health counseling, it is important to reach out to them actively. In disasters, outreach efforts are routinely mounted, with workers knocking on doors and the "marketing" of services in the media. Proactive outreach is also seen in Sexual Assault Nurse Examiner (SANE) programs, in which forensic nurses offer 24-hour, first-response medical care and crisis-intervention services to rape survivors in either hospitals or clinic settings. Outreach contacts provide opportunities for making potential users aware of available services, as well as providing education about postdisaster coping. To reach trauma survivors, it is important that trauma-related education and services be offered in the places where recently traumatized individuals can be found. Attention should be given to identifying key environments where survivors may congregate and matching the interventions to these environments. For many survivors of industrial and motor vehicle accidents, sexual and physical assault, and sudden, unexpected bereavement, this may mean, in part, providing services in hospitals.

Design of Services and Phased Intervention

Some general considerations related to delivery of community-based early intervention programs should be noted. First, these programs should target a range of potentially negative outcomes. In addition to PTSD, survivors of disaster and terrorist attack or other traumas can develop problems with depression, other anxiety disorders, and substance abuse (Ruzek, Maguen, & Litz, 2006). In addition, they may experience significant impairment of ability to work or benefit from schooling, and diminished functioning as a family member, partner, or parent. Second, problems extend beyond the individual trauma survivor to include those close to him or her. As community-based early intervention systems are developed, they should encompass family members, both to harness familial resources in the recovery of the traumatized individual and to prevent or reduce emotional and behavioral problems in affected spouses/partners, children, and other family members.

Third, the community-wide provision of information and coping advice should be a routine part of community response to trauma. Receipt of accurate, planned communications about the traumatic event, adaptive coping, and available support services can reduce uncertainty and calm survivors. Care must be taken in design of survivor education because, although there is little evidence on this subject, it is possible that some kinds of educational approaches (e.g., presentation of "shopping lists" of psychological symptoms) may in fact worsen reactions by labeling common reactions negatively and encouraging selective attention to sensations and symptoms following trauma (Wessely et al., 2008). Methods of proactive risk communication will be especially important during events that continue to unfold, such as natural disasters or influenza pandemics. Accurate information that includes useful, relevant advice should be provided by trusted sources; the challenge is to avoid creating unnecessary anxiety while presenting facts about any risks and guidance about what these risks mean for day-to-day living (Rogers, Amlot, Rubin, Wessely, & Krieger, 2007). To be useful, communications should demonstrate openness and transparency, focus on the concerns and priorities of specific populations, and actively promote self-efficacy about coping behaviors (Vaughan & Tinker, 2009). Systematic community-wide risk communication and constructive media coverage and media campaigns may influence psychological outcomes by promoting adaptive coping, accurate understanding of events, and appropriate self- and other referral to helping services. Accurate information may help prevent or correct negative trauma-related appraisals and reduce worry and anxiety. Media coverage holds promise for modeling adaptive response to trauma, destigmatizing help seeking, and increasing expectations of recovery in those impacted.

Response to the needs of trauma survivors varies according to the time posttrauma. In the first hours and days, immediate help is needed to calm survivors and their families, mobilize social support, and provide pragmatic assistance. In the next weeks and months, brief preventive counseling services can be made available that focus on the psychological impact of the event and the reduction of continuing symptoms and problems. With the passage of time, access to treatment for enduring problems caused by the traumatic events must be part of the fabric of care.

Immediate Support

There is little empirical research to guide the selection of services in the first hours and days after trauma exposure. Simple provision of self-help information appears not to reduce risk for developing PTSD. Recently traumatized patients attending an accident and emergency department who received a self-help booklet did not show reduced PTSD or anxiety symptoms compared with those who did not receive such materials (Turpin, Downs, & Mason, 2005), and this same lack of efficacy was observed with individuals at higher risk due to symptoms of acute stress disorder (ASD; Scholes, Turpin, & Mason, 2007). Studies of the most used immediate intervention, psychological debriefing, and meta-analyses of those studies have failed to demonstrate its efficacy in reduction of posttraumatic stress reactions or prevention of development of PTSD (Bisson, McFarlane, Rose, Ruzek, & Watson, 2009; Rose, Bisson, & Wessely, 2003). In some studies (e.g., Bisson, Jenkins, Alexander, & Bannister, 1997; Mayou, Ehlers, & Hobbs, 2000), those receiving debriefing have actually fared worse than those receiving no intervention. Although negative outcomes have not been consistently found, it has been hypothesized that recitation of traumatic experiences during the debriefing process may increase distress and arousal. Accordingly, the recommendation in several clinical practice guidelines (e.g., Department of Veterans Affairs & Department of Defense, 2004) is that psychological debriefing not be used following exposure to traumatic events.

In the absence of empirically validated approaches to immediate care, psychological first aid (PFA; Brymer et al., 2006; Ruzek et al., 2007) has increasingly been endorsed via expert consensus processes (Hobfoll et al., 2007; National Institute of Mental Health, 2002). PFA comprises eight core helping actions: contact and engagement, safety and comfort, stabilization, information gathering, practical assistance, connection with social supports, information on coping support, and linkage with collaborative services. Increasingly, disaster response organizations (e.g., Medical Reserve Corps, American Red Cross) are training their providers in PFA to enable widespread delivery and online training that can be accessed "just in time" by entire communities is now available (National Child Traumatic Stress Network, National Center for PTSD, and National Association of County and City Health Officials, 2008). While PFA requires systematic evaluation, it represents an approach designed to minimize potential for negative effects of intervention while mobilizing helping processes thought to be effective in prevention.

Brief Counseling after the Immediate Period

The interpersonal support, stress-related education, and normalization of acute stress responses that take place under the label of PFA are unlikely to address the full range of survivor needs, especially following events characterized by high-intensity individual exposure to potentially traumatic events. Many individuals will require more than PFA. Recent research has begun to demonstrate the effectiveness of specific, brief early interventions in reducing posttraumatic stress reactions and preventing development of PTSD when they are delivered starting at two weeks posttrauma (Litz & Bryant, 2009). These four- to five-session cognitive-behavioral interventions have included several helping components, including education, breathing training/relaxation, imaginal and in vivo (real-world) exposure, and cognitive restructuring. Randomized controlled trials have demonstrated their potential effectiveness with survivors of sexual and nonsexual assault (Foa, Hearst-Ikeda, & Perry, 1995) and motor vehicle and industrial accidents (Bryant, Harvey, Dang, Sackville, & Basten, 1998; Bryant, Sackville, Dang, Moulds, and Guthrie, 1999; Bryant et al., 2008). When interventions have been targeted at all trauma survivors, regardless of levels of stress reaction, they have not been found to be effective in reducing and preventing posttraumatic stress symptoms. It is when trauma-focused CBT has been targeted at those with significant symptom levels, especially those meeting criteria for ASD, that intervention has been effective (Roberts, Kitchiner, Kenardy, & Bisson, 2009). These findings highlight the importance of identifying those at risk following trauma exposure.

Unfortunately, at present the posttrauma counseling services that may be available across communities do not incorporate these emerging early intervention approaches. Instead, they offer education, support, and brief coping advice. Education and support, while important and useful, are likely if used alone to be ineffective in preventing PTSD in those at risk for developing problems. Social support has been studied as a control condition in the intervention trials conducted by Bryant and colleagues, and has not effectively prevented development of PTSD (e.g., Bryant et al., 1998). The challenge, then, is to bring methods found effective in research into community-based secondary prevention initiatives (Ruzek, 2006).

Treatment for Trauma-related Problems

Although not typically conceptualized as an element of early intervention, treatment for those who develop mental health problems following trauma exposure is part of a comprehensive community response and will be indicated within two to three months of trauma exposure for some survivors. Effective treatments for PTSD (see Foa, Keane, Friedman, & Cohen, 2009) and other mental health disorders exist, but at present, the mental health treatment provided in most communities is not consistent with best practices as recommended in practice guidelines (Hughes & Barlow, 2010), so communities affected by traumatic events may need to plan for training and support of mental health professionals as they learn evidence-based treatments.

Participation in Trauma-related Community Activities

Although evidence is lacking, there is reason to believe that participation in community activities intended to support those affected by a particular trauma may be helpful to trauma survivors. Such activities, often initiated by community agencies and self-help organizations for survivors and their families, include ceremonies (e.g., memorial events, parades), fund-raising projects, and establishment of legal and financial support services. Participation in services and activities that help address social disruption (e.g., family tracing and reunification services, re-initiation of schooling, establishment of safe play spaces) may be especially important in the context of extreme stressors and settings in which health-care infrastructures are largely absent (van Ommeren, Morris, & Shekhar, 2008). Involvement in mutual support and social activities may help reduce the negative psychological impact of traumas via several hypothetical mechanisms. First, they may conserve or increase resources available to survivors. The Conservation of Resources theory of stress (e.g., Hobfoll, 2006) holds that stress occurs when resources—important possessions, conditions of living, personal characteristics, and tools to acquire other resources—are threatened, and research has indicated that resource loss is correlated with symptom severity in disaster survivors (Freedy, Shaw, Jarrell, & Masters, 1992). Activities that reduce resource loss or bring significant new resources to survivors may reduce perceived stress and accompanying psychological symptoms. Second, community activities may serve to increase perceptions of social support. Following disasters, individuals often experience deterioration in social support owing to disruptions of support availability (Kaniasty & Norris, 1993). Support may be disrupted, for example, by displacement of communities, death of loved ones, or loss of access to routine daily activities. Lower perceived social support is associated with PTSD symptoms in trauma survivors (Brewin, Andrews, & Valentine, 2000). Community activities can provide opportunities for the exchange of social support and may increase perceptions that support is available. A third way in which participation in community activities may reduce problems is by influencing key trauma-related appraisals. For example, traumatic stressors are by definition associated with perceptions of helplessness; joining a self-help group, participating in legal proceedings, or working toward legislative reform may sometimes increase perceptions of control among individuals and groups.

Some Domains of Community-based Early Posttrauma Intervention

Disaster Mental Health Response

Disaster crisis counseling services are generally targeted at the short-term needs of affected individuals by providing active outreach to community survivors, educating them about stress reactions, normalizing reactions, providing social support, promoting positive coping, and providing referral for more intensive help if needed. Such services have been available in the United States for many years (Flynn, 1994), but until recently (Donahue, Jackson, Shear, Felton, & Essock, 2006; Norris & Bellamy, 2009), there has been little formal evaluation of disaster-related crisis counseling services. Since the September 11, 2001, World Trade Center terrorist attacks, observers have suggested that there is a need to provide mental health services more intensive than crisis counseling after severe disasters or for those most at risk (Gibson, Hamblen, Zvolensky, & Vujanovic, 2006; Pfefferbaum, North, Flynn, Norris, & DeMartino, 2002). Some enhanced programs have been described and evaluated. Jones, Allen, Norris, and Miller (2009) surveyed Mississippi-based Hurricane Katrina survivors who used Regular (RCCS; $N = 237$) and Specialized Crisis Counseling Services (SCCS; $N = 41$) between January and March of 2007. SCCS programming included added cognitive-behavioral interventions and procedures for linking survivors with community resources and, compared with RCCS counseling, resulted in increased survivor ratings of benefits of counseling (quality of information received, help with social functioning, growth in confidence in their abilities to help themselves, and reassurance that their feelings were okay). A group of 129 SCCS participants who were interviewed on two occasions showed large reductions in disaster-related distress. Within the SCCS, participation in larger numbers of counseling encounters was associated with greater perceived benefits and larger reductions in survivor distress. A cross-site evaluation of 2,850 disaster survivors receiving crisis counseling services after Hurricanes Katrina, Rita, and Wilma indicated that programs that provide more referrals for psychological counseling are perceived more positively by survivors (Norris, Hamblen, & Rosen, 2009), but psychological treatment referrals are relatively uncommon in crisis counseling programs, suggesting a significant gap between rates of psychological referral and need for counseling (Rosen, Matthieu, & Norris, 2009).

The 2005 terrorist bombing attack on the London transportation system led to implementation of a centralized public health program to screen and refer survivors for evidence-based treatments and to monitor outcomes using standardized instruments (Brewin et al., 2008). Treatments were trauma-focused cognitive-behavioral therapy and Eye Movement Desensitization and Reprocessing. Preliminary outcome data on 82 individuals meeting criteria for PTSD diagnosis indicated significant reductions in PTSD symptoms, with a large effect size of $d = 2.5$. The study demonstrated that a public health response to disaster could include use of validated screening measures, empirically supported treatments, and outcomes monitoring using standardized measures. A similar demonstration of the ability to train community-based crisis counselors in an effective cognitive-behavioral intervention was seen following Hurricane Katrina in the United States. A disaster-specific 10-session intervention (Cognitive Behavioral Therapy for Postdisaster Distress or CBT-PD; Hamblen, Gibson, Mueser, & Norris, 2006), specifically targeting not PTSD, but postdisaster distress, CBT-PD includes psychoeducation, breathing retraining, behavioral activation, and cognitive restructuring, and clients receive a workbook and complete assignments to reinforce the skills they have learned in session. For 88 adult survivors of Hurricane Katrina who received the intervention 18–30 months after the hurricane, CBT-PD was associated with significant reductions in distress with a large effect size ($d = 1.4$); prevalence of severe distress was reduced from 61% at pretreatment to 14% at posttreatment (Hamblen et al., 2009).

Other development efforts are under way. The National Center for PTSD, National Child Traumatic Stress Network, and Dr. Richard Bryant have developed a brief cognitive-behavioral secondary prevention intervention termed Skills for Psychological Recovery (SPR). SPR comprises briefer, simplified applications of interventions found effective in other service contexts that should be relatively simple to rapidly teach to community-based professional and paraprofessional service providers of all disciplines: problem-solving training, positive activity scheduling, skills training in management of trauma reminders and emotional distress, cognitive reframing, and social support. The brief intervention is intended to enable disaster mental health counselors to help survivors identify their most pressing current needs and concerns and teach and support them as they master skills to address those needs. Although formal evaluation will be necessary to establish the effectiveness of SPR, training in SPR has been extremely well received by counselors working in the Louisiana Spirit (Hurricane Katrina) Specialized Crisis Counseling Services; they reported that the skills were highly practical and improved their ability to serve their clients. In a study by Forbes et al. (in press), 342 Australian providers representing a range of health-care disciplines were trained in SPR following the 2009 Victoria bushfires. Those trained were satisfied with the training, considered SPR as relevant to their work, were confident in their ability to use SPR with survivors, and believed that their clients found the interventions to be useful.

School- and workplace-based programs are important following disasters in part because of their ability to reach affected individuals. Gelkopf and Berger (2009) demonstrated the effectiveness of a program designed to help Israeli middle-school children deal with the threat of terrorism, as well as reduce stress-related symptoms. Twelve classroom sessions, delivered as part of the school curriculum, were used to educate children about terrorism and its impact and to train them in skills for managing stress and resiliency strategies. Compared to a wait-list group, children assigned to the intervention condition reported significantly less posttraumatic symptomatology, depression, somatic symptoms, and functional problems three months after the class. There has also been some indication that one to three brief worksite sessions can be effective in reducing a range of negative outcomes, including alcohol dependence, binge drinking, depression, PTSD, and anxiety symptoms (Boscarino, Adams, Foa, & Landrigan, 2006).

In some large-scale disasters, the support needs of affected individuals will exceed the capacity of available counseling resources. In such circumstances, to reach large numbers of survivors, technologies are increasingly being harnessed to reduce reliance on human providers or enable them to effectively serve more persons. More than 53 million people accessed the Internet following the terrorist attacks of 9/11 to seek information about the attacks (Rainie & Kalsnes, 2001). Moreover, Internet-based interventions have been found to be effective as treatments for a range of mental health problems (Marks, Cavanagh, & Gega, 2007), including anxiety (Reger & Gahm, 2009), and are increasingly being developed and evaluated for treatment (e.g., Lange et al., 2003; Litz, Engel, Bryant, & Papa, 2007; Knaevelsrud & Maercker, 2007, 2010) and prevention (Benight, Ruzek, & Waldrep, 2008) of PTSD and other trauma-related problems (e.g., complicated grief; Wagner & Maercker, 2007). Ruggiero and colleagues (2006) demonstrated the feasibility of delivering an Internet mental health intervention for disaster-affected populations. After the terrorist attacks of September 11, 2001, 285 participants were recruited from the New York City area and, depending on their performance on online screening instruments, invited to use self-help educational modules addressing problems relevant to them. Modules addressed posttraumatic stress/panic, depression, generalized anxiety, alcohol use, marijuana use, drug use, and cigarette use. Users were educated about common emotional and behavioral reactions to traumatic stressors, as well as effective coping strategies. Once participants screened into and entered a particular module, they were administered extended screeners that were used to tailor content to their needs and motivational level. Results indicated significant positive knowledge change and high participant satisfaction. Another Web application, Journey to Trauma Recovery (Benight et al., 2008), incorporates principles of social learning theory to focus on strengthening perceived self-efficacy for coping with traumas. The site has been translated into several languages and has been versioned for general trauma and firefighter populations, as well as disaster survivors.

Although Web-based technology is likely to be increasingly important in reaching large numbers of community survivors, more traditional technologies, such as video and telephone, should also be used more proactively. Telephone hotlines, for example, have been established following some major disasters and are widely used to serve sexual assault survivors. The potential for measurable impact of such technologies has been suggested in some pilot demonstration studies. A single session of telephone-delivered anxiety management training decreased anxiety among Israeli citizens who were worried about the possibility of a missile attack (Somer, Tamir, Maguen, & Litz, 2005) more than standard hotline counseling (unconditional positive regard, empathic listening, validation, social support).

Military Deployment

With the large number of active-duty personnel and veterans experiencing postdeployment stress symptoms, many programs have been put in place to support resilience and prevent development of more chronic problems. What is perhaps most salient about these evolving efforts is their comprehensiveness, in that they include pre- and postdeployment education that is military culture–specific, screening for mental health difficulties, and postdeployment interventions. Interventions and services can target those deployed, their families, and their leaders. Individuals returning from deployments are screened for PTSD and other problems via questionnaire, and they participate in a face-to-face health assessment with a trained health-care provider on two occasions: within 30 days of returning home (Post-Deployment Health Assessment) and again three to six months later (Post-Deployment Health Reassessment). In these interviews, service members' current health and mental health issues and concerns are discussed; if indicated, standard PTSD assessment instruments are used and/or referrals for medical consultation are made (Deployment Health Clinical Center, 2010).

A variety of programs implemented soon after return from deployment are intended to educate personnel and reduce likelihood of problem development and/or continuation. The Army Battlemind program (Adler, Castro, & McGurk, 2009) includes training components for soldiers, leaders, family members, and caregivers that are delivered at several points in time (before deployment, within two weeks of returning home, and at 90–120 days postdeployment). Battlemind reframes challenges associated with the transition to civilian life (including PTSD symptoms) as combat skills that, while effective in the war zone, are problematic in the home civilian environment. Adler, Bliese, McGurk, Hoge, and Castro (2009) studied the Battlemind approach, randomly assigning 2297 returnees in platoons to one of four intervention conditions. Compared to those exposed to brief stress education (a 40–50 minute PowerPoint presentation delivered to groups of 51–257 persons), active-duty soldiers returning from a 12-month combat deployment to Iraq who received Battlemind debriefing (one 50-minute session conducted in groups of 20–32), small group Battlemind training (one 40-minute PowerPoint presentation to groups of 18–45), or large group Battlemind training (presentation to groups of 126–225) reported fewer posttraumatic stress symptoms at four-month follow-up. However, these effects were only seen in that third of the sample exposed to high levels of trauma exposure. Also, only 1060 subjects completed the follow-up assessment. The Army is also implementing a Comprehensive Soldier Fitness program whose goal is to enhance the physical, cognitive, social, and spiritual fitness of every soldier and family member in the Army (U.S. Army, 2010).

Another major initiative is the Navy–Marine Corps Stress Continuum Model, designed to help line leaders and their medical, mental health, and religious ministry personnel to assess the stress level of an individual or unit at any point in time (Nash, Krantz, Stein, Westphal, & Litz, 2011). The Stress Continuum divides the spectrum of possible stress states into four color-coded stress zones, each of which corresponds to a level of stress and functioning. Prevention programs built on the Stress Continuum Model include educational modules provided for all Marines, sailors, leaders, caregivers, and family members throughout the deployment cycle. Leaders, support personnel, and Marines and sailors themselves use the Stress Continuum to identify individuals who have become symptomatic because of a stress injury. The Navy and Marine Corps also apply principles of Combat and Operational Stress First Aid (COSFA; Nash, Westphal, Watson, & Litz, 2008). Based on the Psychological First Aid approach developed by the National Center for PTSD and the National Child Traumatic Stress Network (Brymer et al., 2006), COSFA includes seven key actions: Check: assess and reassess; Coordinate: inform others and refer for additional care, as needed; Cover: get to safety and keep safe; Calm: reduce physiological and emotional arousal; Connect: ensure or restore social support from peers and family; Competence: restore self-efficacy and occupational and social competence; and Confidence: restore self-esteem and hope.

As with disasters, Web-delivered materials are being developed to serve active-duty military personnel, veterans, and their families. Afterdeployment.org (www.afterdeployment.org) is a congressionally mandated Internet site designed to assist those returning from Iraq and Afghanistan (and their families) to self-manage postdeployment stress and recognize the need for self-referral for counseling. Although Web-based interventions can be used entirely as self-management tools for survivors, practitioner support significantly increases likelihood that individuals will complete such materials (Marks et al., 2007).

Sexual and Physical Assault

Although they are not mass events in the sense of a discrete trauma affecting large numbers of persons during the same time frame, rape and sexual assaults are very common in most communities and affect very large numbers of individuals over the course of a year. To support the many community members who experience assault each year, it is important that community programs be implemented to provide effective early intervention. Unfortunately, existing postassault contact with community systems sometimes exacerbates rather than reduces rape victims' psychological and physical health distress. Campbell, Wasco, Ahrens, Sefl, and Barnes (2001) found that the majority of rape survivors who reported their assault to the legal or medical system did not receive needed services, and these difficulties with service delivery were associated with both perceived and objective measures of negative health outcomes.

Rape crisis centers are widely available as a community-based resource for sexual assault survivors, providing a range of potential services including telephone hotlines, counseling, community education, and public advocacy. These important community resources for sexual assault survivors can also provide a needed infrastructure to disseminate information about and conduct trainings in the most effective early interventions (Vickerman & Margolin, 2009). To date, however, they have received little formal evaluation in treatment outcome studies. Foa et al. (2005) demonstrated that master's degree social work or counseling clinicians working in a community clinic for rape survivors can be trained to deliver Prolonged Exposure (PE) treatment for PTSD and achieve patient outcomes that match or exceed those obtained by experts in the treatment.

Also widely available as early intervention community services are the sexual assault nurse examiner (SANE) programs. Campbell, Patterson, and Lichty (2005) reviewed the literature on these programs, concluding that preliminary evidence suggests that SANE programs are effective in promoting improved outcomes in several domains: psychological recovery of survivors, postrape medical care (e.g., emergency contraception, sexually transmitted disease prophylaxis), documentation of forensic evidence, prosecution of sexual assault cases, and creation of community change by bringing multiple service providers together to provide comprehensive care. The authors noted that conclusions are tentative at present because most published studies have not included adequate methodological controls. Brief psycho-education and skills interventions have also been designed to reduce risk for sexual assault revictimization, with positive findings in one study (Marx, Calhoun, Wilson, & Meyerson, 2001), and no impact on revictimization rates in the other (Hanson & Gidycz, 1993).

Resnick and colleagues (2007) showed 68 female victims of sexual assault a video within 72 hours of their assault, prior to their forensic medical examination. Video content included education about posttrauma stress reactions, as well as orientation to forensic gynecological examination processes. Among women with a prior rape history, those viewing the video reported lower scores on measures of PTSD and depression six weeks later than those in a standard care condition. At six-month follow-up, depression scores were also lower among those with a prior rape history who were shown the video. However, the intervention showed no significant benefit for women who had not experienced a prior rape.

The frequency of nonsexual physical assault also demands a systematic community response, and some approaches have been developed that show how such a response can be implemented for specific populations of assault survivors. For example, Stein et al. (2003) demonstrated the effectiveness of a school-based 10-session cognitive-behavioral group intervention (5–8 children per group) to reduce symptoms of PTSD and depression, and to improve psychosocial functioning and classroom behavior, in middle-school students who have been exposed to violence and show clinical levels of PTSD symptoms. Students in the study had experienced a mean of 2.8 violent events in the last year: they had witnessed 5.9 violent events. They were randomly assigned to the intervention or to a delayed intervention group for comparison. The intervention included education about common reactions to stress/trauma and instruction in skills (e.g., combating negative thoughts, exposure to traumatic memories, problem-solving). At a three-month follow-up assessment, those participating in the group had lower PTSD, depression, and psychosocial dysfunction symptom scores. At six months, after the delayed intervention group had received the treatment, there were no significant differences between the groups.

Like schools, the workplace provides an important setting for delivery of early intervention services. The Assaulted Staff Action Program (ASAP) developed by Flannery (2001; 2008) illustrates the potential for systematic organizational response to violence against staff members who have been assaulted in the course of their work. A voluntary, peer-administered crisis intervention service was established that includes a range of different kinds of intervention, including individual, group, family outreach, and referral to specialist care if needed. More generally, employee assistance programs provide important platforms for reaching employees subjected to traumatic experiences, especially when they serve those employed in high-risk occupations (e.g., bank workers). These programs provide a comprehensive range of services that can be implemented before, during, and after traumatic events (Paul & Blum, 2005). Key challenges, as with many other kinds of community-based early intervention approaches, are to ensure delivery of evidence-based best practices within these programs and to establish formal program evaluation. Collaborations between researchers and program leadership are needed to strengthen the empirical basis of these programs.

Core Challenges in Community-based Early Intervention

Training and Supporting Providers

A relatively overlooked element of effective community response to traumas is the training of mental health providers (Young & Ruzek, in press).

Many of the component skills of effective response, including PFA and the brief cognitive-behavioral interventions described above, are largely new to the professional community. Moreover, the processes of training that exist in most communities (e.g., workshops) are unlikely to enable mental health personnel to master the needed skills (e.g., Jensen-Doss, Cusack, & de Arellano, 2008), and training is unlikely to change provider behavior in a sustained way.

To ensure effective training in PFA, SPR, and other skills-based interventions, processes of training should include formal instruction in the intervention via "hands-on" workshops in which all participants practice key elements of the intervention via role-play and receive individual feedback and coaching related to their performance (Fixsen, Naoom, Blasé, Friedman, & Wallace, 2005; Grol & Grimshaw, 2003). Following this, all participants should receive regular supervision from instructors as they deliver the interventions in real-world settings. Supervision can be provided in weekly or bi-weekly face-to-face meetings, or via scheduled telephone supervision sessions. When organizations conduct disaster exercises, care should be taken to include opportunity to observe providers as they deliver PFA, and to provide individualized feedback following the exercise.

Several research demonstrations suggest that community providers can be effectively trained if such procedures are established (e.g., Foa et al., 2005; Gillespie, Duffy, Hackmann, & Clark, 2002). For example, CBT-PD was rapidly disseminated to community-based clinicians (Hamblen, Norris, Gibson, & Lee, 2010). Trainees attended a two-day training in CBT-PD that included lectures, practice exercises, expert demonstrations (including live and video demonstrations), and role-plays, and also participated in ongoing telephone case consultation. Therapists showed significant improvements in their ratings of the importance of various elements of cognitive-behavioral therapy, knowledge, and confidence that they could use skills effectively. Immediately following the training, 90% of therapists demonstrated excellent retention of CBT-PD.

Issues of training may be especially important when services use both professional and paraprofessional counselors. In their study of crisis counseling programs serving survivors of Hurricane Katrina, Norris et al. (2009) found that providers with advanced degrees received higher participant ratings because they offered greater service intensity and made referrals more frequently, both of which were related to perceived benefits. The authors acknowledge that their finding does not allow a conclusion that professional counselors are better counselors than paraprofessionals, but they recommended that programs employ professional counselors to provide supervision and support to counselors and assist survivors whose needs may be greater than the paraprofessionals are trained to meet.

Although training presents a challenge in any community response to trauma, it is especially important in the context of large disasters. Such events call for a significant "scaling-up" of services, training must be offered in a limited window of time, and in most situations, there will not be enough skilled human resources. A potentially cost-effective training method that may prove useful in such circumstances is Web-based training, wherever possible supplemented by ongoing telephone or face-to-face consultation/supervision.

In addition to training in skills, it is important that organizations develop systems to monitor and support the mental health functioning of their providers. Outreach, PFA, counseling, and other response activities are potentially stressful experiences, due both to the nature of the working environments and to vicarious exposure to emotional suffering, loss, and death. Mental health professionals, paraprofessionals, volunteers, and disaster responders (including leaders) are at risk for stress-related problems (Creamer & Liddle, 2005; Lesaca, 1996) and it is incumbent on organizations to monitor the well-being of their staff members and offer services intended to prevent problems and address them should they occur. One study found a relationship between provider levels of job stress and disaster survivor perceptions of service benefit; areas where providers were more stressed received poorer ratings of services (Norris et al., 2009). Periodic anonymous staff member surveys can help examine potential difficulties. Staff training and supervision should include formal focus on self-management of stresses, peer mutual support methods, and management responsibilities for establishing systems of care.

Program Monitoring and Evaluation

A much needed but often neglected aspect of community-based early response to traumas is program evaluation. This is because skills required for evaluation are often not found within helper agencies, and because resources are needed to conduct ongoing evaluation activities. Planners, therefore, should anticipate evaluation needs and establish required collaborations and resourcing prior to implementation of services, when possible.

One kind of evaluation that is important in ongoing design of intervention is the needs assessment of affected individuals and groups. It is important that organizations listen to their user audiences (and to the mental health providers who interact with them) via focus groups, survey administration, and other measures. Understanding the concerns of the end users of services is crucial to effectively addressing their needs and to designing services in ways that will attract use. Careful assessment of concerns has the potential to strengthen the relationship between provider and survivor (Zatzick et al., 2007).

It is also crucial that early intervention services be evaluated in terms of their effectiveness in helping trauma survivors. Generally, lack of formal evaluation is a weakness of community-based early intervention programs for trauma populations. Established programs serving military personnel and civilian survivors of assault and injury have rarely been evaluated in methodologically adequate ways that can reassure the provider organization and those being helped, and inform ongoing redesign of programs to improve services. Disaster crisis counseling programs have been evaluated, but it is only recently that evaluation has been more formally undertaken and reported. Media campaigns, public risk communication, public ceremonies, self-help organizations, and other large-scale interventions require careful evaluation and research attention if they are to be improved and justify resource expenditure. Broadly, in the field of early post-trauma intervention, there is a real need to establish an "evaluation culture" with stable evaluation infrastructures and institutionalized program evaluation (Norris & Rosen, 2009).

Some Conclusions and Future Directions

To maximize effectiveness, it is important that the various components of community-based early intervention be integrated to form comprehensive, organized systems of care. Such systems are now being conceptualized, for example, in relation to events involving hospital visits for treatment of physical injury and for management of disaster trauma. A more comprehensive U.S. system for management of war-related trauma is rapidly arising, following the advent of the Iraq and Afghanistan conflicts. More broadly, there is an increasing awareness of the need to create trauma-informed systems of care (e.g., Ko et al., 2008).

Physical injuries, like disasters, affect great numbers of individuals each year and represent an important public health priority. O'Donnell, Bryant, Creamer, and Carty (2008) outlined a health system model of early intervention following traumatic injury. Their model includes screening for vulnerability in the hospital itself, monitoring those at risk and screening again at one month post-trauma (when identification of those who will continue to experience problems is more accurate), and initiating early psychological interventions for those experiencing significant impairment. Shalev, Freedman, Israeli, Shalev, Frenkiel-Fishman, and Adessky (2005) demonstrated the feasibility of implementing such a model in a hospital emergency department in Israel.

With regard to disaster, the European Network for Traumatic Stress (TENTS) developed guidelines for comprehensive provision of psychosocial aftercare for victims (Bisson et al., 2010; European Network for Traumatic Stress, 2008). Intended as a nonmandatory model for the delivery of care in all European countries, the guidelines target provision of psychosocial care for areas with a population of 250,000 to 500,000 people, but can be adapted for larger or smaller areas. The comprehensive approach covers several broad areas of operation, including planning, preparation and management, general components, and specific components to be included at particular phases of the response. The guidelines also stress the importance of establishing services that provide evidence-based care. In recognition that non-evidence-based interventions are still widely offered, they developed an evidence-based model of psychosocial care that is currently being disseminated and implemented across all involved European countries. The TENTS proposal is innovative in terms of its aims to build a community-wide network of expertise on posttraumatic stress management for victims of natural and other disasters, and in its establishment of a multicountry collaboration to produce and disseminate a sustainable evidence-based model of care.

As noted above, the U.S. military now addresses postdeployment stress (including the stresses of trauma exposure) in ways that incorporate (but are not limited to) many of the components listed above, including preparation for exposure/deployment, psychological support in the potentially traumatic environment, routine screening postdeployment, widely available support services for families, military community-wide educational programming, Web-based self-management resources, integration of mental health programming in primary care, leadership training, and training in evidence-based treatments interventions for mental health professionals. The evolving challenge will be to demonstrate the effectiveness of these elements, incorporate emerging evidence-based best practices into the system, and ensure effective integration of the response elements. In fact, a comprehensive response to those returning from military deployments must involve the Department of Defense, Veterans Healthcare Administration, and community-based services in an interactive system of care (Ruzek & Batten, in press). The potential for creative community integration initiatives is illustrated by recent efforts to establish statewide community coalitions of stakeholders (e.g., Kudler & Straits-Tröster, 2009; Slone, Pomerantz, & Friedman, 2009) serving returnees and their families to increase collaboration and integration of efforts.

Development of procedures to accomplish the adoption and sustained implementation of best practices in posttrauma care is an important public health priority (Ruzek & Rosen, 2009), and this is especially true of early preventive interventions. It is only recently that early interventions have been researched. Efficacy trials have suggested that some cognitive-behavioral interventions may prevent development of PTSD in those with high levels of acute stress reactions (e.g., meeting criteria for acute stress disorder), but these methods have not been extended to all survivor groups nor have they been evaluated in the real-world of service delivery. An exception is seen in work by Shalev and colleagues (Shalev et al., 2005), who implemented an early intervention program in the context of hospital emergency medical care, offering screening and counseling services to the population of patients seen in that environment. Many emerging best practices (e.g., PFA) have not yet been evaluated, so that research in this area is much needed. Despite a lack of good evidence, services are being widely provided and it is important that providers be trained in ways consistent with best current thinking. As noted above, evidence-based training methods should be incorporated into the preparation of providers. For this to happen, organizations will need to develop more systematic training programs and explore the complementary systems changes necessary to support providers in delivering state-of-the-art interventions.

A key area of innovation in posttrauma early intervention will be the integration of online interventions into community-based service delivery. Efforts to develop and test online services that provide information and, perhaps more importantly, access to self-management interventions for trauma survivors are under way. An emerging challenge will be to combine these services with existing models of outreach, PFA, and especially brief cognitive-behavioral interventions for ASD, SPR, and other methods of brief counseling. In the future, it seems likely that counseling activities will bring together provider, survivor, and Internet program (or other technology) in ways that simultaneously increase the convenience of services for survivors and engage their interest, increase access to best practices, and enable providers to serve more affected individuals and families.

To foster innovation, it will be helpful if program developers and administrators look beyond the confines of their familiar operations and populations served and consider features of early intervention services emerging from other delivery contexts. Those who serve sexual assault survivors, crime victims, deployed military personnel, physically injured assault and motor vehicle accident survivors, and disaster-affected groups can potentially learn much from one another, and efforts should be undertaken to ensure that such "cross-fertilization" of perspectives can occur.

References

Adler, A. B., Bliese, P. D., McGurk, D., Hoge, C. W., & Castro, C. A. (2009). Battlemind debriefing and Battlemind training as early interventions with soldiers returning from Iraq: Randomization by platoon. *Journal of Consulting and Clinical Psychology, 77*, 928–940.

Adler, A. B., Castro, C. A., & McGurk, D. (2009). Time-driven Battlemind psychological debriefing: A group-level early intervention in combat. *Military Medicine, 174*, 21–28.

Benight, C. C., Ruzek, J. I., & Waldrep, E. (2008). Internet interventions for traumatic stress: A review and theoretically-based example. *Journal of Traumatic Stress, 21*, 513–520.

Bisson, J. I., Jenkins, P. L., Alexander, J., & Bannister, C. (1997). Randomized controlled trial of psychological debriefing for victims of acute burn trauma. *British Journal of Psychiatry, 171*, 78–81.

Bisson, J. C., McFarlane, A. I., Rose, S., Ruzek, J. I., & Watson, P. J. (2009). Psychological debriefing for adults. In E. B. Foa, T. M. Keane, M. J. Friedman, & J. Cohen (Eds.), *Effective treatments for PTSD: Practice guidelines from the International Society for Traumatic Stress Studies* (pp. 83–105). New York: Guilford.

Bisson, J. I., Tavakoly, B., Witteveen, A. B., Ajdukovic, D., Jehel, L., Johansen, V. J., & Olff, M. (2010). TENTS guidelines: Development of post-disaster psychosocial care guidelines

through a Delphi process. *British Journal of Psychiatry, 196*, 69–74.
Boscarino, J. A., Adams, R. E., Foa, E. B., & Landrigan, P. J. (2006). A propensity score analysis of brief worksite crisis interventions after the World Trade Center disaster: Implications for intervention and research. *Medical Care, 44*, 454–462.
Brewin, C. R. (2003). *Post-traumatic stress disorder: Malady or myth?* London: Yale University Press.
Brewin, C. R., Andrews, B., & Valentine, J. D. (2000). Meta-analysis of risk factors for posttraumatic stress disorder in trauma-exposed adults. *Journal of Consulting and Clinical Psychology, 68*, 748–766.
Brewin, C. R., Rose, S., Andrews, B., Green, J., Tata, P., McEvedy, C., & Foa, E. B. (2002). Brief screening instrument for post-traumatic stress disorder. *British Journal of Psychiatry, 181*, 158–162.
Brewin, C. R., Scragg, P., Robertson, M., Thompson, M., d'Ardenne, P., & Ehlers, A. (2008). Promoting mental health following the London Bombings: A screen and treat approach. *Journal of Traumatic Stress, 21*, 3–8.
Bryant, R. A., Harvey, A. G., Dang, S. T., Sackville, T., & Basten, C. (1998). Treatment of acute stress disorder: A comparison of cognitive-behavioral therapy and supportive counseling. *Journal of Consulting and Clinical Psychology, 66*, 862–866.
Bryant, R. A., Mastrodomenico, J., Felmingham, K. L., Kenny, L., Cahill, C., Creamer, M., & Hopwood, S. (2008). Treatment of acute stress disorder: A randomized controlled trial. *Archives of General Psychiatry, 65*, 659–667.
Bryant, R. A., Sackville, T., Dang, S. T., Moulds, M., & Guthrie, R. (1999). Treating acute stress disorder: An evaluation of cognitive behavior therapy and supportive counseling techniques. *American Journal of Psychiatry, 156*, 1780–1786.
Brymer, M., Jacobs, A., Layne, C., Pynoos, R., Ruzek, J., Steinberg, A., Watson, P. 2006. National Child Traumatic Stress Network and National Center for PTSD. *Psychological first aid: Field operations guide* (2nd ed.). Available from www.nctsn.org and www.ncptsd.va.gov.
Campbell, R., Patterson, D., & Lichty, L. F. (2005). The effectiveness of Sexual Assault Nurse Examiner (SANE) programs: A review of psychological, medical, legal, and community outcomes. *Trauma, Violence, and Abuse, 6*, 313–329.
Campbell, R., Wasco, S. M., Ahrens, C. E., Sefl, T., & Barnes, H. E. (2001). Preventing the "second rape": Rape survivors' experiences with community service providers. *Journal of Interpersonal Violence, 16*, 1239–1259.
Creamer, T. L., & Liddle, B. J. (2005). Secondary traumatic stress among disaster mental health workers responding to the September 11 attacks. *Journal of Traumatic Stress, 18*, 89–96.
Department of Veterans Affairs/Department of Defense (2004). *Clinical practice guidelines for the management of post-traumatic stress* (Version 1.0.). Washington, DC: Authors.
Deployment Health Clinical Center (2010). Enhanced post-deployment health assessment (PDHA) process. Available from http://www.pdhealth.mil/dcs/DD_form_2796.asp.
Donahue, S., Jackson, C., Shear, M. K., Felton, C., & Essock, S. (2006). Outcomes of enhances counseling services provided to adults through Project Liberty. *Psychiatric Services, 57*, 1298–1303.
European Network for Traumatic Stress. (2008). The TENTS guidelines for psychosocial care following disasters and major incidents. Retrieved from http://www.tentsproject.eu/_site1264/dbfiles/document/_-64-TENTS_Full_guidelines_booklet_A5_FINAL_24–04.pdf.
Fixsen, D. L., Naoom, S. F., Blase, K. A., Friedman, R. M., & Wallace, F. (2005). *Implementation research: A synthesis of the literature*. Tampa, FL: University of South Florida, Louis de la Parte Florida Mental Health Institute, The National Implementation Research Network (FMHI Publication #231).
Flannery, R. B. (2001). The Assaulted Staff Action Program (ASAP): Ten year empirical support for critical incident stress management (CISM). *International Journal of Emergency Mental Health, 3*, 5–10.
Flannery, R. B. (2008). Crisis intervention services and empirical data: Lessons learned from the Assaulted Staff Action Program (ASAP). *International Journal of Emergency Mental Health, 10*, 271–274.
Flynn, B. W. (1994). Mental health services in large scale disasters: An overview of the Crisis Counseling Program. *NCP Clinical Quarterly, 4*, 1–4.
Foa, E. B., Hearst-Ikeda, D., & Perry, K. J. (1995). Evaluation of a brief cognitive-behavioral program for the prevention of chronic PTSD in recent assault victims. *Journal of Consulting and Clinical Psychology, 63*, 948–955.
Foa, E. B., Hembree, E. A., Cahill, S. P., Rauch, S. A., Riggs, D. S., Feeny, N. C., & Yadin, E. (2005). Randomized trial of prolonged exposure for PTSD with and without cognitive restructuring: Outcome at academic and community clinics. *Journal of Consulting and Clinical Psychology, 73*, 955–964.
Foa, E. B., Keane, T. M., Friedman, M. J., & Cohen, J. (2009). *Effective treatments for PTSD: Practice guidelines from the International Society for Traumatic Stress Studies*. New York: Guilford.
Forbes, D., Fletcher, S., Wolfgang, B., Varker, T, Creamer, M., Brymer, M., Ruzek, J., Watson, P. & Bryant, R. A. (in press). Practitioner perceptions of Skills for Psychological Recovery: A training program for health practitioners in the aftermath of the Victorian bushfires. *Australian and New Zealand Journal of Psychiatry*.
Freedy, J. R., Shaw, D., Jarrell, M., & Masters, C. (1992). Towards an understanding of the psychological impact of natural disasters: An application of the conservation resources stress model. *Journal of Traumatic Stress, 5*, 441–454.
Gelkopf, M., & Berger, R. (2009). A school-based, teacher-mediated prevention program (ERASE-Stress) for reducing terror-related traumatic reactions in Israeli youth: A quasi-randomized controlled trial. *Journal of Child Psychology and Psychiatry, 50*, 962–971.
Gibson, L., Hamblen, J., Zvolensky, M., &Vujanovic, A. (2006). Evidence-based treatments for traumatic stress: An overview of the research literature with an emphasis on disaster settings. In F. Norris, S. Galea, M. Friedman, & P. Watson (Eds.), *Methods for disaster mental health research* (pp. 208–225). New York: Guilford.
Gillespie, K., Duffy, M., Hackmann, A., & Clark, D. M. (2002). Community based cognitive therapy in the treatment of post-traumatic stress disorder following the Omagh bomb. *Behaviour Research and Therapy, 40*, 345–357.
Grol, R., & Grimshaw, J. (2003). From best evidence to best practice: Effective implementation of change in patients' care. *Lancet, 362*, 1225–1230.
Hamblen, J., Gibson, L., Mueser, K., & Norris, F. (2006). Cognitive behavioral therapy for prolonged disaster distress. *Journal of Clinical Psychology: In Session, 62*, 1043–1052.

Hamblen, J., Norris, F., Gibson, L., & Lee, L. (2010). Training community therapists to deliver cognitive behavioral therapy in the aftermath of disaster. *International Journal of Emergency Mental Health*, *12*, 33–40.

Hamblen, J. L., Norris, F. H., Pietruszkiewicz, S., Gibson, L. E., Naturale, A., & Louis, C. (2009). Cognitive behavioral therapy for postdisaster distress: A community based treatment program for survivors of Hurricane Katrina. *Administration and Policy in Mental Health and Mental Health Services Research*, *36*, 206–214.

Hanson, K. A., & Gidycz, C. A. (1993). Evaluation of a sexual assault prevention program. *Journal of Consulting and Clinical Psychology*, *61*, 1046–1052.

Hobfoll, S. E. (2006). Guiding community intervention following terrorist attack. In Y. Neria, R. Gross, R. Marshall, & E. Susser (Eds.), *9/11: Mental health in the wake of terrorist attacks* (pp. 215–228). New York: Cambridge University Press.

Hobfoll, S. E., Watson, P., Bell, C. C., Bryant, R. A., Brymer, M. J., Friedman, M. J., & Ursano, R. J. (2007). Five essential elements of immediate and mid-term mass trauma intervention: Empirical evidence. *Psychiatry*, *70*, 283–315.

Hughes, R. K., & Barlow, D. H. (2010). The dissemination and implementation of evidence-based psychological treatments: A review of current efforts. *American Psychologist*, *65*, 73–84.

Jensen-Doss, A., Cusack, K. J., & de Arellano, M. A. (2008). Workshop-based training in trauma-focused CBT: An in-depth analysis of impact on provider practices. *Community Mental Health Journal*, *44*, 227–244.

Jones, K., Allen, M., Norris, F., & Miller, C. (2009). Piloting a new model of crisis counseling: Specialized Crisis Counseling Services in Mississippi after Hurricane Katrina. *Administration and Policy in Mental Health and Mental Health Services Research*, *36*, 195–205.

Kaniasty, K., & Norris, F. (1993). A test of the social support deterioration model in the context of natural disaster. *Journal of Personality and Social Psychology*, *64*, 395–408.

Knaevelsrud, C., & Maercker, A. (2007). Internet-based treatment for PTSD reduces distress and facilitates the development of a strong therapeutic alliance: A randomized controlled clinical trial. *BMC Psychiatry*, *7*, 13

Knaevelsrud, C., & Maercker, A. (2010). Long-term effects of an Internet-based treatment for posttraumatic stress. *Cognitive Behaviour Therapy*, *39*, 72–77.

Ko, S. J., Ford, J. D., Kassam-Adams, N., Berkowitz, S. J., Wilson, C., Wong, M., & Layne, C. M. (2008). Creating trauma-informed systems: Child welfare, education, first responders, health care, juvenile justice. *Professional Psychology: Research and Practice*, *39*, 396–404.

Kudler, H., & Straits-Tröster, K. (2009). Partnering in support of war zone veterans and their families. *Psychiatric Annals*, *39*, 64–70.

Lange, A., Rietdijk, D., Hudcovicova, M., Van de Ven, J-P., Schrieken, B., & Emmelkamp, P. M. G. (2003). Interapy: A controlled randomized trial of the standardized treatment of posttraumatic stress through the internet. *Journal of Consulting and Clinical Psychology*, *71*, 901–909.

Lesaca, T. (1996). Symptoms of stress disorder and depression among trauma counselors after an airline disaster. *Psychiatric Services*, *47*, 424–426.

Litz, B. T., & Bryant, R. (2009). Early cognitive-behavioral interventions for adults. In E. Foa, M. Friedman, T. Keane & J. Cohen (Eds.), *Effective treatments for PTSD: Practice guidelines from the International Society for Traumatic Stress Studies* (2nd ed., pp. 117–135). New York: Guilford.

Litz, B. T., Engel, C. C., Bryant, R. A., & Papa, A. (2007). A randomized, controlled proof-of-concept trial of an Internet-based, therapist-assisted self-management treatment for posttraumatic stress disorder. *American Journal of Psychiatry*, *164*, 1676–1683.

Marks, I. M., Cavanagh, K., & Gega, L. (2007). *Hands-on help: Computer-aided psychotherapy*. Hove, East Sussex: Psychology Press.

Marx, B. P., Calhoun, K. S., Wilson, A. E., & Meyerson, L. A. (2001). Sexual revictimization prevention: An outcome evaluation. *Journal of Consulting and Clinical Psychology*, *69*, 25–32.

Mayou, R., Ehlers, A., & Hobbs, M. (2000). Psychological debriefing for road traffic accident victims: Three-year follow-up of a randomized controlled trial. *British Journal of Psychiatry*, *176*, 589–593.

Nash, W. P., Krantz, L., Stein, N., Westphal, R. J., & Litz, B. (2011). The evolving challenges of mental health prevention in the military, and two approaches to meet them: Army Battlemind and the Navy–Marine Corps Stress Continuum. In J. Ruzek, J. Vasterling, P. Schnurr, & M. Friedman (Eds.), *Caring for Veterans with deployment-related stress disorders: Iraq, Afghanistan, and beyond* (pp. 193–214). Washington, DC: American Psychological Association Press.

Nash, W. P., Westphal, R. J., Watson, P., & Litz, B. T. (2008, November). Combat and operational stress first aid (COSFA): A toolset for military leaders. Presented at the Defense Centers of Excellence For Psychological Health and Traumatic Brain Injury Warrior Resilience Conference, Fairfax, VA.

National Child Traumatic Stress Network, National Center for PTSD, and National Association of County and City Health Officials (2008). *Psychological First Aid Online*. Available from http://learn.nctsn.org/course/category.php?id=11.

National Institute of Mental Health. (2002). Mental health and mass violence: Evidenced-based early psychological intervention for victims/survivors of mass violence. A workshop to reach consensus on best practices. NIM publication no. 02-5138. Washington, DC: U.S. Government Printing Office.

Norris, F. H, & Bellamy, N. (2009). Evaluation of a national effort to reach Hurricane Katrina survivors and evacuees: The Crisis Counseling Assistance and Training Program. *Administration and Policy in Mental Health and Mental Health Services Research*, *36*, 165–175.

Norris, F., Hamblen, J., Brown, L., & Schinka, J. (2008). Validation of the Short Post-traumatic Stress Disorder Rating Interview (Expanded Version, Sprint-E) as a measure of postdisaster distress and treatment need. *American Journal of Disaster Medicine*, *3*, 201–212.

Norris, F. H., Hamblen, J. L., & Rosen, C. S. (2009). Service characteristics and counseling outcomes: Lessons from a cross-site evaluation of crisis counseling after Hurricanes Katrina, Rita, and Wilma. *Administration and Policy in Mental Health and Mental Health Services Research*, *36*, 176–185.

Norris, F. H. & Rosen, C. S. (2009). Innovations in disaster mental health services and evaluation: National, state, and local responses to Hurricane Katrina (Introduction to the special issue). *Administration and Policy in Mental Health and Mental Health Services Research*, *36*, 159–164.

O'Donnell, M. L., Bryant, R. A., Creamer, M., & Carty, J. (2008). Mental health following traumatic injury: Toward a health system model of early psychological intervention. *Clinical Psychology Review, 28*, 387–406.

O'Donnell, M. L., Creamer, M. C., Parslow, R., Elliott, P., Holmes, A. C. N., Ellen, S., & Bryant, R. A. (2009). A predictive screening index for posttraumatic stress disorder and depression following traumatic injury. *Journal of Consulting and Clinical Psychology, 76*, 923–932.

Ouimette, P., Wade, M., Prins, A., & Schon, M. (2008). Identifying PTSD in primary care: Comparison of the Primary Care-PTSD screen (PC-PTSD) and the General Health Questionnaire-12 (GHQ). *Journal of Anxiety Disorders, 22*, 337–343.

Paul, J., & Blum, D. (2005). Workplace disaster preparedness and response: The Employee Assistance Program continuum of services. *International Journal of Emergency Mental Health, 7*, 169–178.

Pfefferbaum, B., North, C. S., Flynn, B. W., Norris, F. H., & DeMartino, R. (2002). Disaster mental health services following the 1995 Oklahoma City bombing: Modifying approaches to address terrorism. *CNS Spectrums, 7*, 575–579.

Prins, A., Ouimette, P., Kimerling, R., Cameron, R. P., Hugelshofer, D. S., Shaw-Hegwer, J., & Sheikh, J. I. (2003). The primary care PTSD screen (PC-PTSD): Development and operating characteristics. *Primary Care Psychiatry, 9*, 9–14.

Rainie, L., & Kalsnes, B. (2001). The commons of the tragedy: How the Internet was used by millions after the terror attacks: To grieve, console, share news, and debate the country's response. Pew Internet and American Life Project, Washington, D.C. Retrieved from http://www.eric.ed.gov/ERICWebPortal/custom/portlets/recordDetails/detailmini.jsp?_nfpb=true&_&ERICExtSearch_SearchValue_0=ED462072&ERICExtSearch_SearchType_0=no&accno=ED462072, April 23, 2010.

Reger, M. A., & Gahm, G. A. (2009). A meta-analysis of the effects of internet- and computer-based cognitive-behavioral treatments for anxiety. *Journal of Clinical Psychology, 65*, 53–75.

Resnick, H., Acierno, R., Waldrop, A. E., King, L., King, D., Danielson, C., & Kilpatrick, D. (2007). Randomized controlled evaluation of an early intervention to prevent post-rape psychopathology. *Behaviour Research and Therapy, 45*, 2432–2447.

Richmond, T. S., Ruzek, J., Wiebe. D., Winston, F., & Kassam-Adams, N. (in press). Predicting the future development of depression or PTSD after injury. *General Hospital Psychiatry.*

Roberts, N. P., Kitchiner, N. J., Kenardy, J., & Bisson, J. I. (2009). Systematic review and meta-analysis of multiple-session early interventions following traumatic events. *American Journal of Psychiatry, 166*, 293–301.

Rogers, M. B., Amlot, R., Rubin, G. J., Wessely, S., & Krieger, K. (2007). Mediating the social and psychological impacts of terrorist attacks: The role of risk perception and risk communication. *International Review of Psychiatry, 19*, 279–288.

Rose, S., Bisson, J., & Wessely, S. (2003). A systematic review of single psychological interventions ('debriefing') following trauma. Updating the Cochrane review and implications for good practice. In R. Orner & U. Schnyder (Eds.), *Reconstructing early intervention after trauma: Innovations in the care of survivors* (pp. 24–39). Oxford: Oxford University Press.

Rosen, C., Matthieu, M., & Norris, F. (2009). Factors predicting crisis counselor referrals to other crisis counseling, disaster relief, and psychological services: A cross-site analysis of post-Katrina programs. *Administration and Policy in Mental Health and Mental Health Services Research.* doi: 10.1007/s10488-009-0216-0.

Ruggiero, K. J., Resnick, H. S., Acierno, R., Carpenter, M. J., Kilpatrick, D. G., Coffey, S. F., Galea, S. (2006). Internet-based intervention for mental health and substance use problems in disaster-affected populations: A pilot feasibility study. *Behavior Therapy, 37*, 190–205.

Ruzek, J. I. (2006). Bringing cognitive-behavioral psychology to bear on early intervention with trauma survivors: Accident, assault, war, disaster, mass violence, and terrorism. In V. F. Follette & J. I. Ruzek (Eds.), *Cognitive-behavioral therapies for trauma* (2nd ed., pp. 433–462). New York: Guilford.

Ruzek, J. I. & Batten, S. J. (in press). Enhancing systems of care: From private practice to large healthcare systems. In J. I. Ruzek, J. J. Vasterling, P. P. Schnurr, & M. J. Friedman (Eds.), *Caring for Veterans with deployment-related stress disorders: Iraq, Afghanistan, and beyond.* Washington, D.C.: Americbryan Psychological Association Press.

Ruzek, J. I., Brymer, M. J., Jacobs, A. K., Layne, C. M., Vernberg, E. M., & Watson, P. J. (2007). Psychological First Aid. *Journal of Mental Health Counseling, 29*, 17–49.

Ruzek, J. I., Maguen, S., & Litz, B. T. (2006). Evidence-based interventions for survivors of terrorism. In B. Bongar, L. Beutler, P. Zimbardo, L. Brown, & J. Breckenridge (Eds.), *Psychology of terrorism* (pp. 247–272). Oxford: Oxford University Press.

Ruzek, J. I. & Rosen, R. C. (2009). Disseminating evidence-based treatments for PTSD in organizational settings: A high priority focus area. *Behaviour Research and Therapy, 47*, 980–989.

Scholes, C., Turpin, G., & Mason, S. (2007). A randomised controlled trial to assess the effectiveness of providing self-help information to people with symptoms of acute stress disorder following a traumatic injury. *Behaviour Research and Therapy, 45*, 2527–2536.

Shalev, A. Y., Freedman, S., Israeli-Shalev, Y., Frenkiel-Fishman, S., & Adessky, R. (2005). Treatment of trauma survivors with acute stress disorder: Achievements of systematic outreach. In S. Wessely & V. Krasnov (Eds.), *Psychological responses to the new terrorism: A NATO-Russia dialogue* (pp. 171–183). Amsterdam: IOS Press.

Silverman, W. K., Ortiz, C. D., Viswesvaran, C., Burns, B. J., Kolko, D. J., Putnam, F. W., & Amaya-Jackson, L. (2008). Evidence-based psychosocial treatments for children and adolescents exposed to traumatic events. *Journal of Clinical Child and Adolescent Psychology, 37*, 156–183.

Somer, E., Tamir, E., Maguen, S., & Litz, B. T. (2005). Brief cognitive-behavioral phone-based intervention targeting anxiety about the threat of attack: A pilot study. *Behaviour Research and Therapy, 43*, 669–679.

Stein, B. D., Jaycox, L. H., Kataoka, S. H., Wong, M., Tu, W., Elliott, M. N., & Fink, A. (2003). A mental health intervention for schoolchildren exposed to violence: A randomized controlled trial. *Journal of the American Medical Association, 290*, 603–611.

Turpin, G., Downs, M., & Mason, S. (2005). Effectiveness of providing self-help information following acute traumatic injury: Randomised controlled trial. *British Journal of Psychiatry, 187*, 76–82.

U.S. Army (2010, July 1). *Comprehensive soldier fitness*. Retrieved from http://www.army.mil/csf/.

van Ommeren, M., Morris, J., & Shekhar, S. (2008). Social and clinical interventions after conflict or other large disaster. *American Journal of Preventive Medicine, 35*, 284–286.

Vaughan, E., & Tinker, T. (2009). Effective health risk communication about pandemic influenza for vulnerable populations. *American Journal of Public Health*, , *99*(Suppl. 2), S324–S332.

Vickerman, K. A., & Margolin, G. (2009). Rape treatment outcome research: Empirical findings and state of the literature. *Clinical Psychology Review, 29*, 431–448.

Wagner, B., & Maercker, A. (2007). A 1.5-year follow-up of an internet-based intervention for complicated grief. *Journal of Traumatic Stress, 20*, 625–629.

Wessely, S., Bryant, R. A., Greenberg, N., Earnshaw, M., Sharpley, J., & Hughes, J. H. (2008). Does psychoeducation help prevent post traumatic psychological distress? *Psychiatry, 71*, 287–302.

Young, B. H. & Ruzek, J. I. (in press). Disaster mental health services: Implementation, training, and sustainability. In J. Framingham & M. Teasley (Eds.), *Behavioral health response to disasters*. Philadelphia: Taylor & Francis.

Zatzick, D. F., Russo, J., Rajotte, E., Uehara, E., Roy-Byrne, P., Ghesquire, A., & Rivara, F. (2007). Strengthening the patient—provider relationship in the aftermath of physical trauma through an understanding of the nature and severity of posttraumatic concerns. *Psychiatry: Interpersonal and Biological Processes, 70*, 260–273.

Zatzick, D., Russo, J., Rivara, F., Roy-Byrne, P., Jurkovich, G., & Katon, W. (2005). The detection and treatment of posttraumatic distress and substance intoxication in the acute care inpatient setting. *General Hospital Psychiatry, 27*, 57–62.

CHAPTER

24 Individual Approaches to Prevention and Early Intervention

Teresa M. Au, Caroline Silva, Eileen M. Delaney, *and* Brett T. Litz

Abstract

This chapter provides an overview of individual and small group-based approaches for prevention and early intervention of posttraumatic stress disorder (PTSD). Using the Institute of Medicine's (IOM) classification system for preventive interventions of mental disorders (universal, selective, and indicated), we describe individual and small group early interventions and review the effectiveness of these strategies. Specifically, psychological debriefing, psychological first aid, and psychoeducation have been used as selective interventions targeting individuals exposed to trauma with varying degrees of success. However, there is strong empirical support for using cognitive behavioral therapy as an indicated preventive intervention to help symptomatic individuals in the weeks or months following traumatic exposure. A review of the literature also suggests that future research should explore different modes of delivery and devote more attention to determining the best time to intervene after traumatic exposure.

Key Words: Individual, small group, prevention, early intervention, posttraumatic stress, PTSD

Individual Approaches to Prevention and Early Intervention

Traumatic life events can have a devastating impact on individuals, families, and communities. Intervening soon after exposure to trauma has the potential to prevent long-term suffering and disability. The need for early/preventive interventions is underscored by the ubiquity of trauma exposure, as indicated by epidemiological studies estimating that 51–90% of the U.S. population experience at least one traumatic event in their lifetime (Breslau et al., 1998; Kessler, Sonnega, Bromet, Hughes, & Nelson, 1995). Although most trauma-exposed individuals exhibit resilience or recover from transient distress using their own resources, many others suffer greatly and develop chronic mental and behavioral health problems (e.g., Bonanno, 2004).

One of the most enduring and destructive long-term consequences of trauma is posttraumatic stress disorder (PTSD). Approximately 9% of trauma-exposed individuals develop PTSD, although the rate of PTSD can exceed 50% for particularly egregious types of trauma, such as rape (Breslau et al., 1998; Kessler et al., 1995). Considering the tragically high prevalence of traumatic life events, this statistic translates into a significant amount of individual distress and a substantial public health burden. In addition, PTSD can persist for years, exerting a crippling toll on individuals across the life span (Kessler, 2000). Many individuals with PTSD do not seek treatment owing to stigma, financial barriers, uncertainty about where to go for treatment, and other personal and logistical concerns (Kessler, 2000). Without appropriate treatment, they endure considerable emotional, interpersonal, and economic consequences (Kessler, 2000). Even with treatment, over 30% of PTSD cases persist for more than five years (Breslau et al., 1998; Kessler et al., 1995). Given the intractable and damaging nature of PTSD, preventing this disorder before it emerges and becomes ingrained is of great importance.

There are many considerations when implementing early interventions, including who to treat (i.e., who is vulnerable), when to intervene, and what interventions to use. Although researchers have begun to examine these issues, conclusive best practice recommendations await more empirical research, especially randomized clinical trials (RCTs). Thankfully, recent research has made substantial progress in elucidating which interventions are most effective for alleviating immediate distress and promoting lasting recovery. Because not all trauma-exposed individuals need early intervention (Bonanno, 2004; Litz & Bryant, 2009), research has focused on developing evidence-based early interventions for those who are most vulnerable to chronic posttraumatic difficulties and therefore most likely to benefit from prevention efforts. When evaluating these early interventions, it is important to bear in mind that trauma occurs in the context of interwoven personal, social, cultural, and environmental factors. Determining the best course of action in the midst of such complexity is formidable. Nevertheless, understanding the theory, evidence, and limitations behind current preventive strategies will help guide best practices in diverse settings.

In this chapter, we review models of preventive intervention, describe individual and small group early intervention strategies that are currently in use, and review the empirical evidence for those methods. We conclude with comments on future directions and a call for further research on early interventions.

Models of Intervention

In developing and evaluating early interventions, it is essential to weigh the likelihood of long-term posttraumatic impairment against the potential costs of intervening. For example, a given intervention may be highly effective at preventing a disorder, but it may not be worth implementing if the risk of developing the disorder is very low while the costs associated with intervening are high (e.g., financial burden, investment of time, energy, and resources, or unintended, negative iatrogenic effects). The Institute of Medicine (IOM) Committee on Prevention of Mental Disorders provides a useful organizing framework for conceptualizing the complex interactions between risk factors and outcomes. It defines prevention or early interventions as those that target individuals with no impairment or subclinical symptoms at most (Muñoz, Mrazek, & Haggerty, 1996). In the context of trauma, these interventions seek to prevent the onset of chronic PTSD and other enduring, negative psychological sequelae.

According to the IOM classification system, prevention can be categorized as universal, selective, or indicated, depending on who the intervention targets. All three types of preventive interventions can be implemented before or after a traumatic event. Universal preventive interventions target the general public or an entire subgroup (e.g., children, the elderly), regardless of individual risk (Mrazek & Haggerty, 1994). Examples of universal prevention include mass-media public health campaigns and school programs. Since universal prevention is the most inclusive strategy and may be applied even to those with little individual risk, the benefits should greatly outweigh the potential costs. The goal of universal prevention for PTSD is to prevent exposure to various preventable traumatic life experiences (e.g., car accidents) and to limit the impact of traumatic events that could affect anyone in the general population. Currently, there are no universal preventive interventions for PTSD that target the general public. However, within certain high-risk occupations there are universal prevention programs aimed at promoting resilience among all members, irrespective of individual risk (e.g., the Army's Comprehensive Total Fitness program; Geren & Casey, 2009).

Selective preventive interventions target high-risk groups, regardless of individual risk within the group. Biological, psychological, social, or environmental risk factors associated with the onset of a diagnosable mental health disorder can be used to identify these high-risk groups. Selective intervention does not entail individual assessment but, rather, infers risk simply from an individual's membership in a high-risk group. Considering the group's increased risk, interventions that incur moderate costs and minimal negative effects may be justified. In terms of preventing PTSD, some selective interventions target anyone exposed to trauma, irrespective of the event's individual impact. Targeting individuals with an elevated risk of PTSD, such as those with a history of childhood abuse, is another example of selective intervention.

Indicated preventive interventions specifically target individuals with detectable pre-clinical signs or symptoms of a mental disorder, but who do not meet diagnostic criteria at the time of examination. Indicated interventions to prevent PTSD would target individuals displaying pre-clinical signs of psychological distress and impairment as a result of their exposure to trauma. Indicated interventions attempt not only to prevent the onset of PTSD and other trauma-related disorders but also to reduce the duration and severity of early traumatic stress symptoms. The disadvantage of some indicated interventions is that they may be high in cost or risk, without producing discernable benefits until months or years later.

The IOM taxonomy encourages an empirical, risk-benefit approach that weighs the costs and risks of an intervention against an individual's risk of acquiring a disorder (Mrazek & Haggerty, 1994). In contrast, other prevention models may not adequately differentiate between prevention categories, collapsing selective and indicated interventions into one category. The IOM framework therefore allows for more precise identification of individuals who may benefit from early intervention.

Description of Preventive/Early Interventions

For the remainder of this chapter, we discuss individual and small group selective and indicated early interventions for preventing chronic PTSD. Given that the onset of PTSD may be delayed (e.g., Andrews, Brewin, Philpott, & Stewart, 2007) and that trauma-related problems can last for years or even decades (Kessler et al., 1995), preventive/early interventions for PTSD can be employed in the time frame of hours, weeks, or several months following traumatic exposure (Litz & Gray, 2004). In the next section, we describe four main categories of interventions that have been applied to individuals and small groups to prevent long-term psychopathology shortly after traumatic exposure: (1) psychological debriefing, (2) psychological first aid, (3) psychoeducation, and (4) cognitive behavioral therapy. Later in the chapter, we review the empirical research findings for each of these early intervention categories.

Psychological Debriefing

Psychological Debriefing (PD) is a semi-structured, selective intervention that targets all individuals who have been exposed to a potentially traumatic event, regardless of their symptoms (Bisson, McFarlane, Rose, Ruzek, & Watson, 2009). PD normalizes posttraumatic stress symptoms, guides individuals to describe their thoughts, feelings, and symptoms resulting from the event, suggests coping strategies, and provides information on additional treatment options.

Although the PD category includes a diverse array of interventions, the most common form is Critical Incident Stress Debriefing (CISD), a single-session individual or small group-based discussion of the traumatic event. For nearly three decades, CISD has been widely disseminated and used throughout the world, with the goals of reducing acute distress and preventing long-term psychiatric morbidity in individuals exposed to traumatic events. CISD developers recommend using CISD only within the context of Critical Incident Stress Management (CISM), a comprehensive program that includes a diverse array of services, from feeding work crews to conducting family crisis interventions (Mitchell, 2004). However, in practice, CISD is most commonly administered as a stand-alone preventive intervention (McNally, Bryant, & Ehlers, 2003).

CISD is delivered shortly after traumatic exposure and provides a venue for survivors to engage in "emotional ventilation" by discussing their emotional reactions to the traumatic event (Everly, Flannery, & Mitchell, 2000). This discussion is led by a CISD facilitator who does not use formal psychotherapy techniques (Mitchell, 2003). Rather, the facilitator asks survivors to discuss what happened during the traumatic event and then to share what they thought and felt as it was occurring (Mitchell & Everly, 1996). Group members then identify and discuss any posttraumatic symptoms they may have experienced since the event (Mitchell & Everly, 1996). CISD also provides psychoeducation on common reactions to trauma and adaptive coping strategies (Mitchell & Everly, 1996). Proponents of CISD posit that the intervention reduces distress and helps survivors reestablish a sense of mastery and meaning by creating a social support system, promoting emotional ventilation, and teaching coping strategies (Everly et al., 2000).

Psychological debriefing has also been utilized in a military setting, in the form of a selective intervention called Battlemind Debriefing. Emphasizing a strength-based approach, the intervention uses the word *battlemind* to refer to service members' capacity for mental resilience. Battlemind Debriefing seeks to help military service members with the transition back to duty after they experience a potentially traumatic event during deployment. Similar to other types of PD, Battlemind Debriefing does not screen for symptoms and includes the entire group (e.g., everyone in a platoon) that was directly or indirectly exposed to the event, regardless of symptom presentation. Battlemind Debriefings are administered in a group format and ideally use two facilitators, including one who is a trusted, well-respected fellow service member (Adler, Castro, & McGurk, 2009). By involving all ranks of the platoon, including leadership, Battlemind Debriefing seeks to promote a strong peer support system. Facilitators guide service members in acknowledging significant combat or deployment events, reviewing common reactions, and discussing actions that can be taken to facilitate their transition back to duty. In contrast to CISD, Battlemind Debriefing avoids recounting traumatic events in a detailed manner, increases expectations of resilience and functioning, and emphasizes use of natural social supports including peers, leaders, and family (Adler et al., 2009).

Psychological First Aid

Psychological First Aid (PFA) is a selective intervention that utilizes evidence-informed helping actions to reduce immediate distress and promote short- and long-term functioning in trauma-exposed individuals (Brymer et al., 2006; Ruzek et al., 2007). Due to the lack of evidence supporting CISD (discussed later in this chapter), PFA has become the prescriptive approach to early intervention for direct victims, first responders, and care providers in the aftermath of disasters. PFA is designed to address individuals' acute needs in the hours or days after a traumatic event, although the time frame may vary depending on whether or not there is continued exposure to an ongoing traumatic event, as in the case of a natural disaster. Mental health and disaster response workers can deliver PFA in a variety of settings, including shelters, emergency rooms, family assistance centers, and triage centers.

As described in the PFA Field Operations Guide (Brymer et al., 2006), PFA adopts a nonintrusive, flexible, and pragmatic approach. Using practical, hands-on strategies, PFA helps survivors navigate through the chaos, confusion, and disorganization that often accompany potentially traumatic events. Rather than focusing on emotional disclosure and details of the event as in CISD, PFA attends to basic needs in the present and provides practical assistance (Ruzek et al., 2007). It acknowledges that experiencing a wide variety of physical, psychological, and behavioral reactions is common and does not always lead to psychopathology or lasting impairment (Brymer et al., 2006). To avoid pathologizing normative, acute distress, PFA providers do not use jargon and terms such as "symptom" or "disorder." PFA also respects developmental and cultural differences, detailing specific ways that providers can practice cultural sensitivity and adapt their strategies for child, adolescent, and elderly populations (Brymer et al., 2006).

PFA intervention strategies fall into eight main categories, or core actions. These eight core actions are derived from research and theory on risk and resiliency after potentially traumatic events. A large body of research indicates that feeling safe, calm, efficacious, connected, and hopeful promotes adaptive functioning in trauma survivors (reviewed in Hobfoll et al., 2007; Ozer, Best, Lipsey, & Weiss, 2003). PFA techniques therefore center on reducing perceived threat, attenuating heightened emotionality and physiological reactivity, fostering belief in one's ability to manage the traumatic event, promoting social support, and instilling positive expectations (Hobfoll et al., 2007; Ruzek, 2008).

The first core action, contact and engagement, involves initiating contact with survivors in a compassionate, nonintrusive manner to establish the PFA provider as a potential source of help. The second core action, safety and comfort, assists survivors with practical concerns and basic needs (e.g., locating medical care) and offers emotional support. Stabilization, the third helping action, targets individuals whose stress reactions significantly interfere with basic functioning or important responsibilities (e.g., sleeping, eating, parenting). To stabilize these individuals, PFA providers may use "grounding" techniques that orient individuals to nondistressing sights, sounds, and sensations. The fourth essential component of PFA, information gathering, involves asking survivors for information in a culturally and contextually appropriate manner to identify acute needs and concerns, assess risk, and assist future planning. Nonintrusive information-gathering techniques (e.g., inquiring about social support and substance use in a normalizing, respectful manner) can be used to systematically assess factors known to increase likelihood of posttraumatic difficulties (Brymer et al., 2006). The fifth core action, practical assistance, employs strategies to help survivors prioritize their needs and develop a concrete action plan. PFA's sixth core action, connecting with social supports, focuses on identifying family members, friends, or members of the community who can provide the individual with ongoing emotional support, guidance, a sense of connectedness, or assistance with practical tasks. The seventh core component of PFA, information on coping, provides trauma survivors with information on psychological and physiological stress reactions, healthy ways of coping, and maladaptive coping responses to avoid or monitor. The final core action, linkage with collaborative services, connects survivors with further services (as appropriate) and facilitates a smooth transition to these services.

Psychoeducation

Psychoeducation generally entails providing information about stress and trauma; behavioral, psychological, and physiological reactions to trauma; and coping techniques (Kilpatrick, Cougle, & Resnick, 2008; Ruzek, 2008). It is employed as part of an overall "package" in most forms of early intervention, including PFA (Brymer et al., 2006), CISD (Mitchell & Everly, 1996), and cognitive behavioral therapy (e.g., Bryant, Harvey, Dang, Sackville, & Basten, 1998). However, psychoeducation has also been used as a stand-alone preventive strategy, often in the form of self-help booklets, handouts in hospitals and clinics, or brief videos (Creamer & O'Donnell, 2008; Resnick, Acierno, Kilpatrick, & Holmes, 2005; Wessely et al., 2008). More recently, informational material on trauma and PTSD has proliferated on the Internet, appearing on web sites for health organizations such as the Centers for Disease Control and Prevention (CDC), National Institute of Mental Health (NIMH), World Health Organization (WHO), and The National Center for PTSD, exponentially increasing the number of people who have access to this information (e.g., National Institute of Mental Health [NIMH], 2008). Considering its ubiquity as a stand-alone preventive strategy, psychoeducation can be conceptualized as an intervention in itself.

At the broadest level, psychoeducation seeks to help trauma survivors understand and manage their reactions to trauma (Ruzek, 2008). By normalizing transient stress reactions, psychoeducation aims to reassure individuals who have those symptoms and reduce their distress (Wessely et al., 2008). Providing accurate information about posttraumatic reactions has the potential to correct maladaptive appraisals regarding the traumatic event and its sequelae (Ehlers et al., 2003; Wessely et al., 2008). Psychoeducation also helps individuals identify and assess trauma-related problems and directs them to appropriate resources, presumably making it more likely that they will seek help if needed (Hobfoll et al., 2007; Pratt et al., 2005).

Psychoeducation materials lend themselves well to a self-help format, which may be more palatable for individuals who would not normally seek help for personal, social, financial, or logistical reasons (Kessler, 2000). Incorporating some contact with healthcare professionals could enhance the benefits of psychoeducation, since they can tailor the information to the needs of the individual and ensure that the individual understands the material (Ruzek, 2008). Sophisticated web sites can also assess comprehension, provide feedback, and offer individualized, interactive educational experiences (Hobfoll, Walter, & Horsey, 2008).

Cognitive Behavioral Therapy

In recent years, cognitive behavioral therapy (CBT) techniques have been increasingly used in indicated preventive interventions. Exposure-based CBT is a well-validated treatment for chronic PTSD (Ponniah & Hollon, 2009) and has been adapted to prevent chronic PTSD in trauma-exposed individuals exhibiting posttraumatic symptoms. Preventive and treatment strategies differ in the timing of the intervention (i.e., when it is initiated), whether individuals currently meet criteria for PTSD, and the overall aim of the intervention (i.e., preventing vs. alleviating the disorder).

Used as an early intervention, CBT typically includes the following techniques: psychoeducation, anxiety management, exposure, and cognitive restructuring (e.g., Bryant et al., 1998; Sijbrandij et al., 2007). Although these CBT strategies are most often used together, they have also been employed separately (e.g., Bryant, Sackville, Dang, Moulds, & Guthrie, 1999; Bryant et al., 2008). Another related technique that has been used as an early intervention is Behavioral Activation (BA), which is derived from behavioral therapy (Wagner, Zatzick, Ghesquiere, & Jurkovich, 2007). Whichever form it takes, CBT uses a collaborative, action-oriented approach that emphasizes homework completion outside of therapy sessions to enhance patients' self-efficacy and encourage them to utilize CBT skills in their daily lives. CBT interventions are highly structured yet are usually tailored to meet individual needs.

CBT preventive interventions usually begin with psychoeducation. As described earlier, psychoeducation is not unique to CBT but is nearly always included in CBT interventions. In addition to providing general information about the stress response and common reactions to trauma, CBT-based psychoeducation teaches patients about the relationships among thoughts, feelings, and behaviors, and how they work together to maintain posttraumatic symptoms. This understanding provides a rationale and framework for subsequent CBT techniques, such as cognitive restructuring and exposure.

Most CBT interventions also include an anxiety management component. Patients learn techniques such as deep, slow diaphragmatic breathing and progressive muscle relaxation, which they are instructed to practice daily. Patients are also shown how to use these strategies to manage negative affect and arousal when they encounter trauma-related triggers (Litz & Bryant, 2009).

A pivotal component of most CBT interventions is cognitive restructuring or exposure, or a combination of the two. Cognitive restructuring rests on the premise that the interpretation of an event, not the event itself, determines emotional states (Beck, Rush, Shaw, & Emery, 1979). From this perspective, PTSD symptoms are considered to be caused by distorted and unhelpful thoughts regarding the traumatic experience and its aftermath. Therapists teach a variety of cognitive restructuring techniques to help patients alter maladaptive thoughts and beliefs, such as examining evidence for and against their belief. It is believed that once patients begin using these techniques to challenge and ultimately replace their unhelpful cognitions, they will also experience emotional and behavioral changes. Beliefs that are targeted often include appraisals of safety, trust, power, control, esteem, and intimacy (e.g., McCann & Pearlman, 1990).

Exposure therapy is a key component of most CBT preventive interventions. During exposure exercises, patients are guided by the therapist to recount the traumatic event in the present tense (i.e., imaginal exposure) and gradually confront situations that are typically avoided because they trigger disturbing memories, thoughts, or emotions about the trauma (i.e., graded in vivo exposure; e.g., Foa et al., 1999). During exposure exercises, patients are prevented from engaging in avoidance behaviors. Once avoidance is no longer reinforced, conditioned responses, such as intrusive memories and anxiety, are extinguished through habituation. By approaching situations that were once avoided, patients gradually learn to tolerate trauma-related cognitions and situations, increasing the opportunities for corrective life experiences and subsequently modifying maladaptive trauma-related appraisals (e.g., engaging in positive social interactions will challenge the belief "I will never be able to trust anyone again").

Behavioral Activation (BA), a type of behavioral therapy, has also shown promise as a preventive intervention (Wagner et al., 2007). Originally employed as a component of cognitive therapy to treat depression, BA has proved to be an effective stand-alone intervention (Jacobson et al., 1996) and has recently been adapted for preventing and treating PTSD (Jakupcak et al., 2006; Mulick & Naugle, 2004; Wagner et al., 2007). BA prompts individuals to identify and complete reinforcing activities that move them toward their long-term goals (Kanter et al., 2010). As they progress through treatment, patients are encouraged to be proactive rather than reactive to their moods and thoughts and to monitor their moods as they engage in different types of activities. Similar to exposure therapy, BA targets avoidance behaviors, which produce reinforcing, short-term reductions in anxiety but maintain elevated levels of anxiety in the long term by blocking habituation (Keane, Fairbank, Caddell, Zimering, & Bender, 1985). Unlike exposure, BA does not focus exclusively on activities that are avoided due to their potential to provoke fear and anguish (Mulick & Naugle, 2004; Wagner et al., 2007). Rather, BA seeks to identify and increase activities based on what is important to the individual and in line with his or her goals, which may or may not include trauma-related activities or situations that are avoided out of fear. Like other CBT preventive strategies, BA is brief and cost-effective (Wagner et al., 2007). Compared to cognitive restructuring and exposure, BA is relatively straightforward, does not require as much specialty training by the therapist, and may be easier for the patient to tolerate (Mulick & Naugle, 2004; Wagner et al., 2007).

Empirical Research Findings

In the following section, we discuss the empirical evidence for PD, PFA, psychoeducation, and CBT as preventive/early interventions. In evaluating the efficacy of these preventive interventions, a number of methodological issues frequently arise. Ethical, practical, and economic considerations often limit researchers' ability to conduct controlled trials immediately after a traumatic event. For instance, randomizing trauma survivors to different intervention conditions (e.g., no-treatment control conditions) may not be feasible or ethical. Despite these constraints, there is a push for greater methodological rigor. As argued by Foa and Meadows (1997), even where randomized controlled trials (RCTs) are not possible, studies should strive to clearly specify the targeted symptoms, use psychometrically sound measures, demonstrate reliable and valid assessment procedures, employ manualized and replicable interventions, and evaluate treatment adherence.

Psychological Debriefing

Single-session psychological debriefing (PD) delivered in the immediate aftermath of trauma has great intuitive appeal but has not been supported by well-controlled studies. Initially, uncontrolled studies suggested that CISD was effective in reducing distress and promoting recovery in the aftermath of trauma (reviewed in Everly, Flannery, & Eyler, 2002; Everly et al., 2000). Proponents of CISD hailed its success across thousands of debriefings and claimed that empirical studies had definitively proved CISD's effectiveness (Mitchell & Everly, 2001). However, since the majority of these studies were not scientifically rigorous, the observed benefits could not be attributed to CISD versus natural recovery processes. In addition, many of these studies were cross-sectional and only assessed participants at a single time point after the intervention (reviewed in Everly et al., 2000; Gray & Litz, 2005).

In recent years, RCTs have challenged the efficacy of CISD. These studies have used rigorous methodology, including random assignment to treatment, psychometrically validated outcome measures, and structured clinical interviews for assessments (reviewed in Litz, Gray, Bryant, & Adler, 2002). In these RCTs, trauma survivors randomly assigned to receive CISD exhibited reductions on several measures of psychological distress (Conlon, Fahy, & Conroy, 1999; Deahl et al., 2000; Rose, Brewin, Andrews, & Kirk, 1999), as previously observed in uncontrolled studies supporting CISD. However, these RCTs found that no-treatment control conditions resulted in equivalent improvements, indicating that CISD was no more effective than receiving no treatment at all. Furthermore, several RCTs found that CISD was associated with worse outcomes compared to no-treatment (Bisson, Jenkins, Alexander, & Bannister, 1997; Hobbs, Mayou, Harrison, & Worlock, 1996; Mayou, Ehlers, & Hobbs, 2000). Meta-analytic studies have confirmed that single-session PD is no better, and in some cases slightly worse, than no-treatment or educational control groups at reducing distress, general psychological morbidity, PTSD, depression, and anxiety (Rose, Bisson, Churchill, & Wessely, 2002; van Emmerik, Kamphuis, Hulsbosch, & Emmelkamp, 2002). Collectively, these findings argue against applying CISD as a blanket preventive intervention for individuals exposed to trauma.

Various theories have been proposed to explain why CISD has had a small detrimental effect on trauma survivors in some cases. One explanation is that CISD may unintentionally interfere with natural recovery processes by substituting preexisting support networks with an artificial source of support (van Emmerik et al., 2002). Deleterious outcomes associated with CISD may also be due to its medicalization of normal distress. Although CISD aims to reduce distress by normalizing posttraumatic stress symptoms, it may paradoxically heighten distress by increasing participants' expectations that they will develop these symptoms (Devilly, Gist, & Cotton, 2006). Another possibility is that CISD prompts individuals to relive their traumatic experience and engage in emotional ventilation but does not incorporate sufficient repetition to habituate them to trauma-related cues (McNally et al., 2003). Without adequate follow-up care, this process may only exacerbate distress. Indeed, a dismantling study found that emotional ventilation increased PTSD symptoms among trauma survivors with high initial hyper-arousal symptoms, compared to those who received psychoeducation debriefing or no treatment (Sijbrandij, Olff, Reitsma, Carlier, & Gersons, 2006). These findings suggest that emotional ventilation can prolong or even escalate psychological and physiological arousal in individuals who have increased reactivity immediately after a traumatic event (Sijbrandij et al., 2006).

Proponents of CISD have rebutted that the RCTs showing null or adverse effects did not adequately evaluate CISD because they neglected clinically important outcomes, did not adhere to prescribed CISD procedures, and misapplied the intervention to primary (direct) victims of trauma instead of high-risk occupational groups, for which CISD was originally devised. A RCT addressing these issues, however, was still unable to find clear evidence that CISD produced better outcomes than no treatment or a psychoeducational stress management class (Adler et al., 2008). Supporters of CISD further counter that CISD was never intended as a single-session treatment but as part of the larger Critical Incident Stress Management (CISM) package (Mitchell, 2004). However, as noted by McNally et al. (2003), CISM does not readily lend itself to empirical investigation since it is not an intervention but an administrative framework with disparate components determined by the specific context. Furthermore, despite the developers' recommendation, CISD is almost always administered as a stand-alone treatment without implementing other parts of CISM (McNally et al., 2003). Owing to the lack of evidence for CISD's efficacy, current policy guidelines in the United Kingdom and United States now advise against its use (e.g., National Institute for Health and Clinical Excellence, 2005).

On the other hand, non-CISD forms of single-session PD have shown some promise. In particular, a recent study showed that Battlemind Debriefing reduces negative psychological sequelae in soldiers following combat exposure (Adler et al., 2009). In this study, platoons were randomized to receive either standard postdeployment stress education or Battlemind Debriefing. Follow-up assessment four months after the intervention revealed that soldiers who received Battlemind Debriefing had fewer PTSD symptoms, depressive symptoms, and sleep problems compared to the stress education group, but only for those exposed to high levels of combat. In contrast to studies showing adverse effects of CISD, Battlemind Debriefing did not increase symptoms immediately after the intervention or at the four-month follow-up assessment. However, since effect sizes in this study were small and a no-intervention control group was not included, firm conclusions about the efficacy of Battlemind Debriefing cannot be made at this time. Although this study suggests that non-CISD PD may be helpful—or at least not harmful—for at-risk occupational groups, further studies are needed to replicate these results and evaluate the efficacy of specific Battlemind Debriefing components.

Psychological First Aid

Psychological First Aid (PFA) is based on a solid conceptual framework (Litz, 2008) and a broad evidence base from the risk and resilience literature (Hobfoll et al., 2007). Because its core components are informed by empirical evidence, there is a growing consensus among disaster mental health experts that PFA is the "acute intervention of choice" (Brymer et al., 2006, p. 5). Although PFA as a whole has not been systematically investigated, research on stress, coping, and positive adaptation following traumatic events support the utility of the core components (Hobfoll et al., 2007, Ozer et al., 2003; Ruzek et al., 2007; Vernberg et al., 2008). One of the challenges in empirically evaluating PFA is that it seeks to produce short- and long-term outcomes that are not conventionally assessed. For example, PFA aims to increase survivors' sense of safety and connectedness with others, reduce immediate distress, enhance self-efficacy for addressing immediate practical needs and making important decisions, and increase help-seeking behavior (Ruzek et al., 2007). Researchers are currently developing appropriate tools to measure these outcomes and evaluate provider adherence to PFA guidelines (Vernberg et al., 2008).

Psychoeducation

It is commonly assumed that providing psychoeducation as a stand-alone preventive intervention is beneficial or at least does no harm. Unfortunately, only a handful of studies have directly evaluated the efficacy of psychoeducation and have found equivocal results (reviewed in Wessely et al., 2008). In one RCT, civilian trauma victims were randomized to receive a psychoeducational self-help booklet that provided information on typical posttraumatic symptoms and the benefits of social support and nonavoidance (Turpin, Downs, & Mason, 2005). Despite participant reports that the psychoeducation material was helpful, the psychoeducation group did not report greater reductions in PTSD symptoms, depression, or anxiety compared to those who received no psychoeducation. Furthermore, at six-month follow-up, participants in the psychoeducation condition had experienced smaller reductions in depression than those in the no-treatment control condition. In addition, among participants who initially met criteria for PTSD, fewer participants in the psychoeducation group improved relative to those in the control group, although this difference did not reach statistical significance. This study suggests that the use of self-help psychoeducational material alone is ineffective for reducing psychological distress after traumatic exposure, and like CISD, it may actually impede natural recovery processes. Similarly, another RCT that randomized participants with acute stress disorder to receive either a self-help psychoeducational booklet or no information found no differences between the two conditions in terms of PTSD, anxiety, or depression, yet participants rated the self-help information favorably (Scholes, Turpin, & Mason, 2007).

Other evidence suggests that psychoeducation may be helpful in certain situations. For instance, Resnick et al. (2007) found that a short psychoeducation video produced reductions in PTSD and depression symptoms for sexual assault survivors with a prior history of assault, compared to survivors in a no-intervention control group. Since having a history of prior rape is a risk factor for PTSD, this finding indicates that a brief psychoeducation intervention could benefit at-risk populations. However, this positive result is tempered by the concerning finding that women without a history of sexual assault experienced slight elevations in PTSD and anxiety symptoms after watching the psychoeducation video, compared to no-intervention controls, although this difference was no longer apparent at six-month follow-up.

As a whole, these findings indicate that even a seemingly innocuous intervention such as psychoeducation must be applied with caution, as it may lead to adverse consequences if applied indiscriminately to all individuals exposed to a traumatic event. Preliminary evidence suggests that psychoeducation may benefit only those who are more at risk for developing PTSD (Resnick et al., 2007). These findings speak to the need for more studies to investigate the effect of psychoeducation on different populations. Additionally, the content of psychoeducation varies considerably, with some emphasizing expectations of resilience (Resnick et al., 2007) and others providing detailed instructions on imaginal exposure (Scholes et al., 2007). Given this heterogeneity among psychoeducation interventions, future studies are needed to systematically refine and evaluate the content, format, and delivery of psychoeducation (Kilpatrick et al., 2008; Ruzek, 2008). There is also a need to measure outcomes that psychoeducation supposedly targets, such as help-seeking behavior (Wessely et al., 2008).

Cognitive Behavioral Therapy

Most cognitive behavioral therapy (CBT) preventive interventions have used an indicated approach, targeting those who have early signs or symptoms of PTSD but do not yet meet criteria for chronic PTSD. Symptomatic individuals have been targeted due to economic and logistical constraints, as well as evidence that selective preventive interventions applied to all trauma-exposed individuals irrespective of symptoms are ineffective (Roberts, Kitchiner, Kenardy, & Bisson, 2009). Inclusion criteria for CBT preventive interventions vary across studies, from acute symptoms of psychological distress (e.g., Bisson, Shepherd, Joy, Probert, & Newcombe, 2004; Zatzick et al., 2004), to acute stress disorder (ASD; e.g., Bryant et al., 1998), or acute PTSD (e.g., van Emmerik, Kamphuis, & Emmelkamp, 2008). Treatments for ASD can be conceptualized as indicated prevention for PTSD since prospective studies have shown that approximately 80% of people with ASD meet criteria for chronic PTSD six months after the trauma (Harvey & Bryant, 1998). A diagnosis of ASD can therefore be used to identify trauma victims who are less likely to recover without intervention.

Several well-designed trials have demonstrated that trauma survivors with ASD benefit more from preventive CBT than from supportive counseling (SC). In one of the earliest trials, when civilian trauma survivors with ASD received either five sessions of CBT or SC, only 8% of individuals in the CBT condition were diagnosed with PTSD at posttreatment, compared to 83% in the SC condition (Bryant et al., 1998). At six-month follow-up, 17% of participants in the CBT condition met criteria for PTSD compared to 67% in SC. At both posttreatment and follow-up, CBT was more effective in reducing depressive, avoidance, and intrusive symptoms compared to SC.

The same research group has replicated these findings across several trials, in each case showing the superiority of CBT over SC (Bryant, Moulds, Guthrie, & Nixon, 2005; Bryant et al., 1999). Long-term benefits from these interventions have also been observed. For example, one follow-up study found that 8% of trauma survivors who participated in a brief CBT preventive intervention were diagnosed with PTSD four years after traumatic exposure, compared to 25% of SC patients (Bryant, Moulds, & Nixon, 2003). In addition, severity of PTSD symptoms, particularly avoidance behaviors, remained lower for the CBT group relative to the SC group at four-year follow-up assessment (Bryant et al., 2003).

Since the above studies compared CBT to SC and not to an untreated control group, it is possible that CBT only appears effective because SC disrupts natural recovery processes (Ehlers & Clark, 2003; Litz & Bryant, 2009). However, other trials comparing CBT to no-treatment or other control groups have also observed greater beneficial outcomes associated with CBT. For instance, one RCT found that rape victims with acute PTSD who completed a five-session CBT intervention reported fewer PTSD symptoms at 12-month follow-up than those who received only relaxation training (Echeburua, de Corral, Sarasua, & Zubizarreta, 1996). In another study, individuals in acute psychological distress 5–10 weeks after a traumatic physical injury were randomized to a four-session CBT intervention or to a standard-care condition (Bisson et al., 2004). At 13-month follow-up, CBT patients reported greater reductions in PTSD symptoms compared to standard-care patients. However, the effect size was modest and there were no between-group differences in anxiety or depressive symptoms.

Clearer differences between CBT and no treatment were found in a RCT that tested a cognitive restructuring-focused CBT intervention on motor vehicle accident (MVA) survivors suffering from acute PTSD (Ehlers et al., 2003). In this trial, at three-month follow-up, participants in the CBT intervention group reported the greatest reductions in functional impairment and PTSD, depression, and anxiety symptoms, compared to those who received a CBT-based self-help booklet and those who were repeatedly assessed but received no treatment. These gains remained at nine-month follow-up, with fewer participants in the CBT group meeting criteria for PTSD compared to the other two groups.

Nearly all of the RCTs evaluating CBT as a preventive intervention have employed a variety of techniques, commonly using both cognitive restructuring and exposure techniques, thereby precluding any clear conclusions about possible agents of change. To evaluate the individual efficacy of different techniques for preventing chronic PTSD in patients with ASD, Bryant et al. (2008) compared exposure therapy, trauma-focused cognitive restructuring, and a wait-list control condition. Both cognitive restructuring and exposure were effective at reducing PTSD compared to wait-list controls, but exposure resulted in better outcomes than cognitive restructuring. At posttreatment, 33% of exposure participants met criteria for PTSD, compared to 63% of individuals treated with cognitive restructuring and 77% of the wait-list control group. Compared to cognitive restructuring, exposure also produced significantly larger reductions in PTSD, anxiety, and depressive symptoms. Nevertheless, since cognitive restructuring was more effective than no treatment, it may still be useful on its own, as an alternative for those who are unwilling or unable to tolerate exposure therapy.

In another dismantling study, an exposure-only condition was compared against exposure with anxiety management (Bryant et al., 1999). Six months later, the incidence of PTSD was lower in both the exposure-only and exposure with anxiety management conditions (15% and 23%, respectively), compared to SC. The two exposure groups did not differ significantly on any outcome measures, suggesting that anxiety management does not enhance the benefits of exposure. This result is consistent with the chronic PTSD treatment literature, which has found that anxiety management alleviates distress in the short term but that exposure yields more lasting reductions in PTSD symptoms (Foa, Rothbaum, Riggs, & Murdock, 1991).

There is emerging evidence that other CBT tools such as BA may also be useful as an indicated preventive intervention. A small-scale randomized effectiveness trial found that BA, consisting of up to six sessions, was more effective at reducing PTSD symptoms than treatment as usual for ASD patients (Wagner et al., 2007). However, BA was not associated with greater reductions in depressive symptoms compared to the control group. Considering that many clinicians may avoid using exposure because of the distress it can cause in the short-term (Rosen et al., 2004), it is important to continue evaluating non-exposure-based forms of CBT such as BA. Future studies are needed to replicate Wagner et al.'s findings and compare BA against other CBT strategies, such as exposure.

Although the evidence in favor of using CBT strategies to prevent chronic PTSD is compelling, some findings have been mixed. Sijbrandij et al. (2007) found that one week after treatment, people with acute PTSD who had received four sessions of CBT (consisting of psychoeducation, anxiety management, imaginal and in vivo exposure, and cognitive restructuring) experienced reductions in PTSD symptoms compared to wait-list controls. However, the two groups did not differ significantly on PTSD, anxiety, or depression at four-month follow-up. These data suggest that CBT hastened recovery from acute PTSD, but these benefits were not maintained at long-term follow-up. The authors speculated that the lack of efficacy at follow-up could be due to the fewer number of sessions compared to other early interventions (e.g., Bryant et al., 1999; Ehlers et al., 2003).

Similarly, Foa, Hearst-Ikeda, and Perry (1995) found that a four-session CBT intervention initially reduced PTSD symptoms, so that at posttreatment, only 10% of CBT participants met PTSD criteria compared to 70% of those in the no-treatment control group. At 5.5-month follow-up, CBT participants reported significantly fewer depressive symptoms relative to those in the control group. However, by this point, the control group had improved in terms of PTSD symptoms and no longer differed from the CBT group on PTSD diagnosis. This study supports the notion that CBT accelerates recovery even if it does not produce lasting prevention against chronic PTSD. In a larger trial, Foa, Zoellner, and Feeny (2006) found that a four-session CBT intervention, administered to individuals with acute PTSD several weeks after traumatic exposure, did not lead to long-term differences in PTSD, depression, or anxiety symptoms compared to SC or a no-treatment, assessment-only condition. However, there was some evidence that the CBT intervention accelerated recovery for sexual-assault survivors with severe PTSD symptoms. The authors proposed several factors that may account for the lack of long-term benefit associated with CBT, including demographics, type of trauma, and reduced homework compliance.

These null findings notwithstanding, a recent meta-analysis of 15 early interventions found that CBT produced better outcomes at posttreatment than wait-list or SC for individuals with traumatic stress symptoms (Roberts et al., 2009). All of the studies included in the meta-analysis had evaluated indicated interventions administered within three months of trauma exposure. The largest reductions in traumatic stress symptoms were seen in individuals who met criteria for ASD or acute PTSD before receiving CBT. In a separate analysis, Roberts et al. (2009) also investigated the efficacy of multiple-session interventions applied globally to all trauma-exposed individuals, regardless of their symptoms. In contrast to the positive outcomes produced by the indicated interventions targeting symptomatic individuals, no evidence was found for the efficacy of selective interventions targeting trauma-exposed individuals irrespective of their symptoms.

Although the evidence that CBT effectively prevents chronic PTSD and other negative psychological sequelae is compelling, there are many remaining questions. Although the empirical data strongly indicate that CBT is effective while psychological debriefing is not, it remains unclear precisely which components account for this difference. Factors that may explain this differential efficacy include CBT's prolonged, systematic method of disclosure and processing, targeted nature, increase in structure, longer duration of treatment, and homework exercises assigned between sessions, which likely promote self-efficacy and generalization of acquired skills. Determining the critical components of CBT is complicated by the heterogeneity among CBT interventions, in terms of specific techniques used, amount of exposure, duration, timing, and population targeted. Although most CBT preventive interventions incorporate exposure strategies, others focus more on cognitive techniques (Ehlers et al., 2003), and still others do not include an exposure element at all (Bryant et al., 1999; Wagner et al., 2007). Additional dismantling studies would help to identify possible change agents in preventive CBT interventions.

Limitations and Promising Future Directions

Much progress has been made in identifying and evaluating interventions for preventing chronic psychopathology after traumatic events. Although early intervention research has focused primarily on determining which particular intervention strategies are most effective, several related areas need to be explored. Possible areas that require further examination include intervention content and form (e.g., different modes of delivery, other potentially effective treatments), assessment issues (e.g., measuring other outcomes of interest, how to best screen individuals for distress), and logistical concerns (e.g., when is the best time to intervene).

There is strong empirical support for using CBT as a brief, indicated preventive intervention to help symptomatic individuals in the weeks or months following traumatic exposure. However, additional research is needed to better understand how CBT works (i.e., what are the change agents) and whether it is more effective for certain types of events or for particular subgroups of individuals. It remains unclear what factors mediate symptom reduction and improvements in functioning. Potential mediators that could be examined in future studies include process variables, such as instilling hope, self-efficacy, and acceptance, as well as learning specific strategies/behaviors, such as nonavoidance and cognitive restructuring (Litz, 2008).

Further attention should also be paid to the particular contexts for which early CBT interventions may be most efficacious. CBT has been tested and has proved effective for symptomatic civilians who have survived industrial accidents, nonsexual assault, and motor vehicle accidents (e.g., Bryant et al., 1998, 1999; Ehlers et al., 2003). However, early interventions for female sexual assault survivors have been effective in some studies (Echeburua et al., 1996) but ineffective in others (Foa et al., 2006), emphasizing the need for more research on adapting preventive interventions to treat other types of trauma, such as sexual assault and combat trauma. Additionally, as a preventive intervention, CBT has only been tested in an individual therapy format. Adapting CBT to a group format would conserve resources and potentially expand the reach of CBT early interventions.

Although RCTs have provided solid evidence in support of using CBT, there is still a need to develop and evaluate additional early intervention strategies. Compared to other early interventions, CBT is resource-intensive, requiring greater logistical coordination, therapist expertise, and investment of time. For these reasons, CBT is not appropriate as an immediate intervention in the initial hours or days after trauma, when survivors may be preoccupied with more urgent, practical concerns. Furthermore, existing RCTs have mostly compared CBT to supportive counseling or wait-list control conditions. It would be informative to broaden the types of comparison groups to include interventions that focus on sleep, diet, or exercise to determine if CBT's benefits exceed those of simply improving self-care (Litz & Bryant, 2009).

As CBT does not seem well suited as an immediate intervention, it is less clear which interventions may be effective in the immediate aftermath of a potentially traumatic event. As discussed in this chapter, psychological debriefing, psychological first aid, and psychoeducation have been used as selective interventions targeting individuals exposed to trauma, with varying degrees of success. Since RCTs have failed to support the efficacy of CISD, it is no longer recommended by the International Society for Traumatic Stress Studies (ISTSS) and National Institute of Mental Health (NIMH; Bisson et al., 2009; NIMH, 2008). While there is some evidence that other types of PD such as Battlemind Debriefing may be more effective, further evaluation is needed. Institutions such as the ISTSS now recommend PFA as a nonintrusive, flexible approach to alleviating distress and promoting long-term adaptive functioning. PFA is particularly suited to disasters and mass trauma, when a large number of survivors may be grief-stricken and too beleaguered with addressing basic needs to benefit from other interventions. Importantly, early interventions such as CBT and PFA are not mutually exclusive and may complement one another. It is essential that future studies evaluate PFA empirically to further inform the trauma field of its merits as a preventive intervention. Psychoeducation as a stand-alone intervention constitutes another form of selective prevention that is widely used and assumed to be beneficial, or at worst innocuous, but requires empirical validation. Although preliminary research on psychoeducation has been discouraging (Scholes et al., 2007; Turpin et al., 2005), further investigations are needed to make firm conclusions about its efficacy.

Currently, most early interventions such as PFA and CBT depend on direct contact with mental health providers. Since trauma survivors may encounter financial, personal, or logistical barriers that prevent them from accessing these services (Kessler, 2000), there is great interest in using innovative methods for delivering early interventions, including the Internet (Benight, Ruzek, & Waldrep, 2008), telephone (Phipps, Byrne, & Deane, 2007), and self-help (Bugg, Turpin, Mason, & Scholes, 2009). These different forms of delivery have been highlighted as simple, inexpensive, and easily accessible. These tools have the potential to reach more people in need of services because they place less demand on professional resources and provide instant communication, unlimited by geographic barriers (Benight et al., 2008; Phipps et al., 2007). Internet-based interventions have been used to treat PTSD (Lange et al., 2003; Litz, Engel, Bryant, & Papa, 2007), but further research is needed to determine how Internet-based interventions could be employed within the prevention framework. Interventions delivered via telephone are also promising, as a phone-based CBT intervention has been shown to reduce anxiety in Israeli citizens following the threat of a terrorist attack (Somer, Tamir, Maguen, & Litz, 2005). Additionally, in a study directly aimed at preventing PTSD in MVA survivors, participants who received a phone-based intervention were less likely to meet criteria for PTSD and reported fewer PTSD symptoms than controls at three- to four-month follow-up (Gidron et al., 2001). Preventive interventions can also be delivered through self-help methods, from detailed booklets with CBT techniques to writing paradigms, although early findings have not supported the efficacy of these techniques (Bugg et al., 2009; Ehlers et al., 2003). Well-controlled studies are needed to compare the efficacy of preventive interventions delivered via conventional, direct contact with clinicians versus those delivered through Internet, telephone, or self-help methods. In addition, concerns over unique ethical considerations and guidelines when using these different forms of delivery (e.g., patient confidentiality, consent, liability issues, appropriateness for psychiatric emergencies) must be seriously considered (Hsiung, 2002).

Early intervention research may also benefit from adapting other treatments that have proven effective for treating chronic PTSD. For example, Eye Movement Desensitization and Reprocessing (EMDR) is efficacious for treating PTSD (reviewed in Ponniah & Hollon, 2009), although it may be less practical to implement than CBT. Cognitive Processing Therapy (CPT) could be a helpful preventive intervention for sexual assault survivors, since research has found it to be effective for treating chronic PTSD in this population (Chard, 2005; Resick, Nishith, Weaver, Astin, & Feuer, 2002;). Other treatments, such as hypnotherapy, may serve as useful adjuncts to CBT (Ponniah & Hollon, 2009). Thus far, early intervention research has not found that hypnotic induction preceding exposure confers additional long-term benefits over CBT alone (Bryant et al., 2005, 2006), but interest remains in exploring different ways that hypnosis could enhance outcomes.

Although the field of PTSD prevention has focused mainly on psychological interventions, there is also growing interest in pharmacological strategies. It is well established that stressful and traumatic events trigger a cascade of acute physiological changes that constitute the "flight-or-fight" response. Dysregulation of the acute stress response may contribute to the onset and maintenance of enduring difficulties including PTSD (Yehuda & Golier, 2009). Hydrocortisone, propranolol, benzodiazepines, and morphine have all been used in attempts to regulate the stress response and prevent overconsolidation of trauma-related memories (Bryant, Creamer, O'Donnell, Silove, & McFarlane, 2009; Feldner, Monson, & Friedman, 2007). There is some evidence that administering propranolol to patients with elevated physiological arousal decreases PTSD symptoms (Pitman et al., 2002; Vaiva et al., 2003). However, other studies have found no significant differences in PTSD for either propranolol or benzodiazepines compared to placebo (Gelpin, Bonne, Peri, Brandes, & Shalev, 1996; Mellman, Bustamante, David, & Fins, 2002; Stein, Kerridge, Dimsdale, & Hoyt, 2007). Acute administration of morphine shortly after traumatic injury has been associated with lower rates of PTSD (Holbrook, Galarneau, Dye, Quinn, & Dougherty, 2010) and decreases in PTSD severity (Bryant et al., 2009), but these studies did not use a randomized placebo-controlled design, limiting the ability to draw firm conclusions about morphine's use as an early intervention.

Although some studies have found preliminary evidence for using pharmacotherapy to reduce PTSD symptoms (Bryant et al., 2009; Pitman et al., 2002; Vaiva et al., 2003), rigorous RCTs are needed before conclusions can be made about the efficacy of pharmacotherapy for preventing PTSD. Medications offer potential as a preventive intervention since they are easily administered (i.e., they do not require a professional trained in trauma treatment) and consist of a simple regimen for the patient. However, several issues should be considered in assessing medications' utility as an early intervention. For example, potential benefits would need to be weighed against possible side effects of the medication. Other important considerations include determining dosage, establishing screening criteria and procedures, and training medical personnel or mental healthcare workers. Additionally, administering medications as prophylaxis may only be possible in medical facilities, which would limit this early intervention to those who present to a hospital setting shortly after traumatic exposure.

In addition to further evaluating the form and content of preventive interventions, future research should also explore other areas such as how to measure and target additional outcomes of interest (rather than traditional PTSD variables), how to identify those most in need, and how soon to initiate these interventions. In determining the efficacy of preventive interventions, there is growing interest in assessing not only maladaptive functioning but also other outcomes that reflect how well individuals are actually functioning in their daily lives, relationships, and occupational roles. Measuring outcomes that reflect long-term adaptive adjustment, such as increased help-seeking or social support, could also provide valuable information on the efficacy of these interventions. To this end, it is essential to create brief, reliable, and well-validated instruments that can be used in the aftermath of trauma for assessing these outcomes.

Comorbidity is another important issue related to early intervention of PTSD. Epidemiological findings indicate that 88% of men and 79% of women with PTSD meet criteria for at least one other disorder in their lifetime (Kessler et al., 1995). PTSD is especially likely to co-occur with other anxiety disorders, depression, and substance use disorders. Despite these high rates of comorbidity, early intervention research has yet to address how patients presenting with specific patterns of comorbidity differ from patients who are only experiencing symptoms of PTSD. There is some evidence that early interventions incorporating collaborative case management, pharmacological treatment, and separate psychological interventions targeting PTSD and substance abuse are feasible and effective, but more research is needed in this area (Zatzick et al., 2001, 2004).

Another remaining challenge lies in identifying individuals who are most vulnerable to lasting posttraumatic impairment and are therefore most in need of early intervention. Since resources are often limited, it is essential to allocate these resources wisely by accurately identifying those who are most likely to develop serious posttraumatic difficulties. Administering early interventions to all trauma-exposed individuals would not only be impractical and wasteful of scarce resources but could also interfere with natural resiliency and recovery processes (McNally et al., 2003). However, identifying those who would benefit from early intervention is complicated by the difficulty of predicting later dysfunction from initial symptoms. That is, individuals who exhibit immediate, acute distress or impaired functioning often recover fully, while others who initially give little indication of dysfunction may experience delayed-onset PTSD (Andrews et al., 2007; Bonanno, 2004).

To aid in identifying those in need of clinical care, effective screening tools are needed for distinguishing normal, transient dysfunction from symptoms that indicate severe distress that is likely to persist. A variety of potential risk factors that may be germane to chronic posttraumatic difficulties have been studied (reviewed in Brewin, Andrews, & Valentine, 2000; McNally et al., 2003). Cross-sectional studies have found significant associations between PTSD and factors that existed prior to trauma exposure (e.g., personality traits, family psychiatric history, childhood abuse, cognitive ability), characteristics of the trauma itself (e.g., type of trauma, duration of traumatic exposure, trauma severity), and peri- and posttrauma variables (e.g., ASD, dissociation, hyper-arousal, lack of social support) (Brewin et al., 2000). To date, only a few posttrauma variables, such as number of posttraumatic stress symptoms and ASD diagnosis, have been used as screening criteria for indicated early interventions (e.g., Bryant et al., 1998). Prospective and longitudinal risk and resiliency research could play an important role in further examining these factors as well as identifying other potential screening variables (Litz, 2008).

It also remains unclear how soon interventions should be implemented after a traumatic event (Litz, 2008). Because victims of trauma often increase their contact with health services in the hours, days, and weeks following a traumatic event, there is more opportunity to intervene during this time, rather than waiting months after traumatic exposure when problems have become entrenched. However, although it is often assumed that sooner is better, survivors may have more pressing, practical concerns immediately after a traumatic event that would be unethical to neglect. They may also be too acutely distressed to process and benefit from new information (Litz & Bryant, 2009). Existing early interventions range from days (Bryant et al., 1999) to months (Ehlers et al., 2003) after trauma exposure. There is some evidence that participants receiving CBT within the first month after traumatic exposure experience better outcomes, compared to those who receive CBT one to three months after the traumatic event (Sijbrandij et al., 2007). Future RCTs should devote more attention to determining the best time to intervene after traumatic exposure. Such research would undoubtedly increase our ability to effectively and efficiently facilitate recovery and prevent long-term suffering in trauma survivors.

References

Adler, A. B., Castro, C. A., & McGurk, D. (2009). Time-driven Battlemind psychological debriefing: A group-level early intervention in combat. *Military Medicine, 174*, 21–28.

Adler, A. B., Litz, B. T., Castro, C. A., Suvak, M., Thomas, J. L., Burrell, L., et al. (2008). A group randomized trial of critical incident stress debriefing provided to U.S. peacekeepers. *Journal of Traumatic Stress, 21*, 253–263.

Andrews, B., Brewin, C. R., Philpott, R., & Stewart, L. (2007). Delayed-onset posttraumatic stress disorder: A systematic review of the evidence. *American Journal of Psychiatry, 164*, 1319–1326.

Beck, A.T., Rush, A.J., Shaw, B.F., & Emery, G. (1979). *Cognitive therapy of depression*. New York: Guilford.

Benight, C. C., Ruzek, J. I., & Waldrep, E. (2008). Internet interventions for traumatic stress: A review and theoretically based example. *Journal of Traumatic Stress, 21*, 513–520.

Bisson, J. I., McFarlane, A. C., Rose, S., Ruzek, J. I., & Watson, P. J. (2009). Psychological debriefing for adults. In E. B. Foa, T. M. Keane, M. J. Friedman, & J. A. Cohen (Eds.), *Effective treatments for PTSD: Practice guidelines from the International Society for Traumatic Stress Studies* (2nd ed., pp. 83–105). New York: Guilford.

Bisson, J. I., Shepherd, J. P., Joy, D., Probert, R., & Newcombe, R. G. (2004). Early cognitive-behavioural therapy for post-traumatic stress symptoms after physical injury: Randomised controlled trial. *British Journal of Psychiatry, 184,* 63–69.

Bisson, J., Jenkins, P., Alexander, J., & Bannister, C. (1997). A randomized controlled trial of psychological debriefing for victims of acute burn trauma. *British Journal of Psychiatry, 171,* 78–81.

Bonanno, G. A. (2004). Loss, trauma, and human resilience: Have we underestimated the human capacity to thrive after extremely aversive events? *American Psychologist, 59,* 20–28.

Breslau, N., Kessler, R. C., Chilcoat, H. D., Schultz, L. R., Davis, G. C., & Andreski, P. (1998). Trauma and posttraumatic stress disorder in the community: The 1996 Detroit Area Survey of Trauma. *Archives of General Psychiatry, 55,* 626–632.

Brewin, C. R., Andrews, B., & Valentine, J. D. (2000). Meta-analysis of risk factors for posttraumatic stress disorder in trauma-exposed adults. *Journal of Consulting and Clinical Psychology, 68,* 748–766.

Bryant, R. A., Creamer, M., O'Donnell, M., Silove, D., & McFarlane, A. C. (2009). A study of the protective function of acute morphine administration on subsequent posttraumatic stress disorder. *Biological Psychiatry, 65,* 438–440.

Bryant, R. A., Harvey, A. G., Dang, S. T., Sackville, T., & Basten, C. (1998). Treatment of acute stress disorder: A comparison of cognitive-behavioral therapy and supportive counseling. *Journal of Consulting and Clinical Psychology, 66,* 862–866.

Bryant, R. A., Mastrodomenico, J., Felmingham, K. L., Hopwood, S., Kenny, L., Kandris, E., et al. (2008). Treatment of acute stress disorder: A randomized controlled trial. *Archives of General Psychiatry, 65,* 659–667.

Bryant, R., Moulds, M., & Nixon, R. (2003). Cognitive behavior therapy of acute stress disorder: A four-year follow-up. *Behaviour Research and Therapy, 41,* 489–494.

Bryant, R. A., Moulds, M. L., Guthrie, R. M., & Nixon, R. D. (2005). The additive benefit of hypnosis and cognitive-behavioral therapy in treating acute stress disorder. *Journal of Consulting and Clinical Psychology, 73,* 334–40.

Bryant, R. A., Moulds, M. L., Nixon, R. D., Mastrodomenico, J., Felmingham, K., & Hopwood, S. (2006). Hypnotherapy and cognitive behavior therapy of acute stress disorder: A 3-year follow-up. *Behavioral and Research Therapy, 44,* 1331–1335.

Bryant, R. A., Sackville, T., Dang, S. T., Moulds, M., & Guthrie, R. (1999). Treating acute stress disorder: An evaluation of cognitive behavior therapy and supportive counseling techniques. *American Journal of Psychiatry, 156,* 1780–1786.

Brymer, M., Jacobs, A., Layne, C., Pynoos, R., Ruzek, J., Steinberg, A., et al. (2006). *Psychological first aid field operations guide.* Washington, DC: National Child Traumatic Stress Network and National Center for PTSD.

Bugg, A., Turpin, G., Mason, S., & Scholes, C. (2009). A randomised controlled trial of the effectiveness of writing as a self-help intervention for traumatic injury patients at risk of developing post-traumatic stress disorder. *Behaviour Research and Therapy, 47,* 6–12.

Chard, K. M. (2005). An evaluation of cognitive processing therapy for the treatment of posttraumatic stress disorder related to childhood sexual abuse. *Journal of Consulting and Clinical Psychology, 73,* 965–971.

Conlon, L., Fahy, T. J., & Conroy, R. (1999). PTSD in ambulant RTA victims: A randomized controlled trial of debriefing. *Journal of Psychosomatic Research, 46,* 37–44.

Creamer, M., & O'Donnell, M. (2008). The pros and cons of psychoeducation following-trauma: Too early to judge? *Psychiatry: Interpersonal and Biological Processes, 71,* 319–321.

Deahl, M., Srinivasan, M., Jones, N., Thomas, J., Neblett, C., & Jolly, A. (2000). Preventing psychological trauma in soldiers: The role of operational stress training and psychological debriefing. *British Journal of Medical Psychology, 73,* 77–85.

Devilly, G. J., Gist, R., & Cotton, P. (2006). Ready! Fire! Aim! The status of psychological debriefing and therapeutic interventions: In the work place and after disasters. *Review of General Psychology, 10,* 318–345.

Echeburua, E., de Corral, P., Sarasua, B., & Zubizarreta, I. (1996). Treatment of acute posttraumatic stress disorder in rape victims An experimental study. *Journal of Anxiety Disorders, 10,* 185–199.

Ehlers, A., & Clark, D. M. (2003). Early psychological interventions for adult survivors of trauma: A review. *Biological Psychiatry, 53,* 817–826.

Ehlers, A., Clark, D. M., Hackmann, A., McManus, F., Fennell, M., Herbert, C., et al. (2003). A randomized controlled trial of cognitive therapy, a self-help booklet, and repeated assessments as early interventions for posttraumatic stress disorder. *Archives of General Psychiatry, 60,* 1024–1032.

Everly, G. S., Flannery, R. B., & Eyler, V. A. (2002). Critical incident stress managment (CISM): A statistical review of the literature. *Psychiatric Quarterly, 73,* 171–182.

Everly, G. S., Flannery, R. B., & Mitchell, J. T. (2000). Critical incident stress management (CISM): A review of the literature. *Aggression and Violent Behavior, 5,* 23–40.

Feldner, M. T., Monson, C. M., & Friedman, M. J. (2007). A critical analysis of approaches to targeted PTSD prevention: Current status and theoretically derived future directions. *Behavior Modification, 31,* 80–116.

Foa, E. B., Dancu, C. V., Hembree, E. A., Jaycox, L. H., Meadows, E. A., & Street, G. P. (1999). A comparison of exposure therapy, stress inoculation training, and their combination for reducing posttraumatic stress disorder in female assault victims. *Journal of Consulting and Clinical Psychology, 67,* 194–200.

Foa, E. B., Hearst-Ikeda, D., & Perry, K. J. (1995). Evaluation of a brief cognitive-behavior program for the prevention of chronic PTSD in recent assault victims. *Journal of Consulting and Clinical Psychology, 63,* 948–955.

Foa, E. B., & Meadows, E. A. (1997). Psychosocial treatments for post-traumatic stress disorder: A critical review. In J. Spence, J. M. Darley, & D. J. Foss (Eds.), *Annual review of psychology* (pp. 449–480). Palo Alto, CA: Annual Reviews.

Foa, E. B., Rothbaum, B. O., Riggs, D., & Murdock, T. (1991). Treatment of post-traumatic stress disorder in rape victims: A comparison between cognitive-behavioral procedures and counseling. *Journal of Consulting and Clinical Psychology, 59,* 715–723.

Foa, E. B., Zoellner, L. A., & Feeny, N. C. (2006). An evaluation of three brief programs for facilitating recovery after assault. *Journal of Traumatic Stress, 19,* 29–43.

Gelpin, E., Bonne, O., Peri, T., Brandes, D., & Shalev, A. Y. (1996). Treatment of recent trauma survivors with benzodiazepines: A prospective study. *Journal of Clinical Psychiatry, 57*, 390–394.

Geren, P., & Casey, G. W., Jr. (2009, May 7). Army posture statement: Comprehensive soldier fitness program. In *Online information papers* (Addenda A). Retrieved June 28, 2010, from http://www.army.mil/aps/09/information_papers/comprehensive_soldier_fitness_program.html.

Gidron, Y., Gal, R., Freedman, S., Twiser, I., Lauden, A., Snir, Y., et al. (2001). Translating research findings to PTSD prevention: Results of a randomized-controlled pilot study. *Journal of Traumatic Stress, 14*, 773–780.

Gray, M. J., & Litz, B. T. (2005). Behavioral interventions for recent trauma: Empirically informed practice guidelines. *Behavior Modification, 29*, 189–215.

Harvey, A. G., & Bryant, R. A. (1998). The relationship between acute stress disorder and posttraumatic stress disorder: A prospective evaluation of motor vehicle accident survivors. *Journal of Consulting and Clinical Psychology, 66*, 507–512.

Hobbs, M., Mayou, R., Harrison, B., & Worlock, P. (1996). A randomized controlled trial of psychological debriefing for victims of road traffic accidents. *British Medical Journal, 313*, 1438–1439.

Hobfoll, S. E., Walter, K. H., & Horsey, K. J. (2008). Dose and fit are vital to intervention success. *Psychiatry: Interpersonal and Biological Processes, 71*, 308–318.

Hobfoll, S. E., Watson, P., Bell, C. C., Bryant, R. A., Brymer, M. J., Friedman, M. J., et al. (2007). Five essential elements of immediate and mid-term mass trauma intervention: Empirical evidence. *Psychiatry, 70*, 283–315.

Holbrook, T. L., Galarneau, M. R., Dye, J. L., Quinn, K., & Dougherty, A. L. (2010). Morphine use after combat injury in Iraq and post-traumatic stress disorder. *New England Journal of Medicine, 362*, 110–117.

Hsiung, R. C. (2002). Suggested principles of professional ethics for e-therapy. In R. C. Hsiung (Ed.), *E-therapy: Case studies, guiding principles, and the clinical potential of the Internet* (pp. 150–165). New York: W. W. Norton.

Jacobson, N. S., Dobson, K. S., Truax, P. A., Addis, M. E., Koerner, K., Gollan, J. K., et al. (1996). A component analysis of cognitive-behavioral treatment for depression. *Journal of Consulting and Clinical Psychology, 64*, 295–304.

Jakupcak, M., Roberts, L. J., Martell, C., Mulick, P., Michael, S., Reed, R., et al. (2006). A pilot study of behavioral activation for veterans with posttraumatic stress disorder. *Journal of Traumatic Stress, 19*, 387–391.

Kanter, J. W., Manos, R. C., Bowe, W. M., Baruch, D. E., Busch, A. M., & Rusch, L. C. (2010). What is behavioral activation? A review of the empirical literature. *Clinical Psychology Review, 30*, 608–620.

Keane, T. M., Fairbank, J. A., Caddell, J., Zimering, R. T., & Bender, M. (1985). A behavioral approach to assessing and treating post-traumatic stress disorder in Vietnam veterans. In C. R. Figley (Ed.), *Trauma and its wake: The study and treatment of post-traumatic stress disorder* (pp. 257–294). New York: Brunner/Mazel.

Kessler, R. C. (2000). Posttraumatic stress disorder: The burden to the individual and to society. *Journal of Clinical Psychiatry, 61*(Suppl. 5), 4–14.

Kessler, R. C., Sonnega, A., Bromet, E., Hughes, M., & Nelson, C. B. (1995). Posttraumatic Stress Disorder in the National Comorbidity Survey. *Archives of General Psychiatry, 52*, 1048–1060.

Kilpatrick, D. G., Cougle, J. R., & Resnick, H. S. (2008). Reports of the death of psychoeducation as a preventative treatment for posttraumatic psychological distress are exaggerated. *Psychiatry: Interpersonal and Biological Processes, 71*, 322–328.

Lange, A., Rietdijk, D., Hudcovicova, M., van de Ven, J.-P., Schrieken, B., & Emmelkamp, P. M. G. (2003). Interapy: A controlled randomized trial of the standardized treatment of posttraumatic stress through the Internet. *Journal of Consulting and Clinical Psychology, 71*, 901–909.

Litz, B. T. (2008). Early intervention for trauma: Where are we and where do we need to go? A commentary. *Journal of Traumatic Stress, 21*, 503–506.

Litz, B. T., & Bryant, R. A. (2009). Early cognitive-behavioral interventions for adults. In E. B. Foa, T. M. Keane, M. J. Friedman, & J. A. Cohen (Eds.), *Effective treatments for PTSD: Practice guidelines from the International Society for Traumatic Stress Studies* (2nd ed., pp. 117–135). New York: Guilford.

Litz, B. T., Engel, C. C., Bryant, R. A., & Papa, A. (2007). A randomized, controlled proof-of-concept trial of an Internet-based, therapist-assisted self-management treatment for posttraumatic stress disorder. *American Journal of Psychiatry, 164*, 1676–1684.

Litz, B. T., & Gray, M. J. (2004). Early intervention for trauma in adults: A framework for first aid and secondary prevention. In B. T. Litz (Ed.), *Early intervention for trauma and traumatic loss* (pp. 87–111). New York: Guilford.

Litz, B. T., Gray, M. J., Bryant, R. A., & Adler, A. B. (2002). Early intervention for trauma: Current status and future directions. *Clinical Psychology: Science and Practice, 9*, 112–134.

Mayou, R. A., Ehlers, A., & Hobbs, M. (2000). Psychological debriefing for road traffic accident victims: Three-year follow-up of a randomised controlled trial. *British Journal of Psychiatry, 176*, 589–593.

McCann, L., & Pearlman, L. A. (1990). Constructivist self-development theory as a framework for assessing and treating victims of family violence. In S. M. Stith, M. B. Williams, & K. H. Rosen (Eds.), *Violence hits home: Comprehensive treatment approaches to domestic violence* (pp. 305–329). New York: Springer.

McNally, R. J., Bryant, R. A., & Ehlers, A. (2003). Does early psychological intervention promote recovery from posttraumatic stress? *Psychological Science in the Public Interest, 4*, 45–79.

Mellman, T. A., Bustamante, V., David, D., & Fins, A. I. (2002). Hypnotic medication in the aftermath of trauma. *Journal of Clinical Psychiatry, 63*, 1183–1184.

Mitchell, J.T. (2003, February 1). *Crisis intervention and CISM: A research summary*. Retrieved July 7, 2010, from http://www.icisf.org/articles/cism_research_summary.pdf

Mitchell, J. T. (2004). A response to the Devilly and Cotton article, "Psychological Debriefing and the Workplace…" *Australian Psychologist, 39*, 24–28.

Mitchell, J. T., & Everly, G. S., Jr. (1996). *Critical incident stress debriefing: An operations manual for the prevention of traumatic stress among emergency services and disaster workers* (2nd ed.). Ellicott City, MD: Chevron.

Mitchell, J.T., & Everly, G. S., Jr. (2001). *Critical incident stress debriefing: An operations manual for CISD, defusing and other group crisis intervention services* (3rd ed.). Ellicott City, MD: Chevron.

Mrazek, P. B., & Haggerty, R. J. (Eds.). (1994). *Reducing risks for mental disorders: Frontiers for preventive intervention research.* Washington, DC: National Academy Press.

Mulick, P. S., & Naugle, A. E. (2004). Behavioral activation for comorbid PTSD and major depression: A case study. *Cognitive and Behavioral Practice, 11*, 378–387.

Muñoz, R. F., Mrazek, P. J., & Haggerty, R. J. (1996). Institute of Medicine report on prevention of mental disorders: Summary and commentary. *American Psychologist, 51*, 1116–1122.

National Institute for Health and Clinical Excellence. (2005, June). *Brief debriefing – doesn't help, might harm. In Gems from Cochrane: Mental Health.* Retrieved July 7, 2010, from http://www.cks.nhs.uk/knowledgeplus/gems_from_cochrane/previous_gems_by_clinical_category/mental_health/brief_debriefing_doesnt_help_might_harm#

National Institute of Mental Health. (2008). *Post-traumatic stress disorder (PTSD)* (No. 08 6388). Retrieved July 7, 2010, from http://www.nimh.nih.gov/health/publications/post-traumatic-stress-disorder-ptsd/nimh_ptsd_booklet.pdf.

Ozer, E. J., Best, S. R., Lipsey, T. L., & Weiss, D. S. (2003). Predictors of posttraumatic stress disorder and symptoms in adults: A meta-analysis. *Psychological Bulletin, 129*, 52–73.

Phipps, A. B., Byrne, M. K., & Deane, F. P. (2007). Can volunteer counsellors help prevent psychological trauma? A preliminary communication on volunteers skill using the 'orienting approach' to trauma counselling. *Stress and Health, 23*, 15–21.

Pitman, R. K., Sanders, K. M., Zusman, R. M., Healy, A. R., Cheema, F., Lasko, N. B., et al. (2002). Pilot study of secondary prevention of posttraumatic stress disorder with propranolol. *Biological Psychiatry, 51*, 189–192.

Ponniah, K., & Hollon, S. D. (2009). Empirically supported psychological treatments for adult acute stress disorder and posttraumatic stress disorder: A review. *Depression and Anxiety, 26*, 1086–1109.

Pratt, S. I., Rosenberg, S., Mueser, K. T., Brancato, J., Salyers, M., Jankowski, M. K., et al. (2005). Evaluation of a PTSD psychoeducational program for psychiatric inpatients. *Journal of Mental Health, 14*, 121–127.

Resick, P. A., Nishith, P., Weaver, T. L., Astin, M. C., & Feuer, C. A. (2002). A comparison of cognitive-processing therapy with prolonged exposure and a waiting condition for the treatment of chronic posttraumatic stress disorder in female rape victims. *Journal of Consulting and Clinical Psychology, 70*, 867–879.

Resnick, H., Acierno, R., Kilpatrick, D. G., & Holmes, M. (2005). Description of an early intervention to prevent substance abuse and psychopathology in recent rape victims. *Behavior Modification, 29*, 156–188.

Resnick, H., Acierno, R., Waldrop, A. E., King, L., King, D., Danielson, C., et al. (2007). Randomized controlled evaluation of an early intervention to prevent post-rape psychopathology. *Behaviour Research and Therapy, 45*, 2432–2447.

Roberts, N. P., Kitchiner, N. J., Kenardy, J., & Bisson, J. I. (2009). Systematic review and meta-analysis of multiple-session early interventions following traumatic events. American *Journal of Psychiatry, 166*, 293–301.

Rose, S., Bisson, J., Churchill, R., & Wessely, S. (2002). Psychological debriefing for preventing post traumatic stress disorder (PTSD). *Cochrane Database of Systematic Reviews* (2), CD000560.

Rose, S., Brewin, C. R., Andrews, B., & Kirk, M. (1999). A randomized controlled trial of individual psychological debriefing for victims of violent crime. *Psychological Medicine, 29*, 793–799.

Rosen, C. S., Chow, H. C., Finney, J. F., Greenbaum, M. A., Moos, R. H., Sheikh, J. I., et al. (2004). VA practice patterns and practice guidelines for treating posttraumatic stress disorder. *Journal of Traumatic Stress, 17*, 213–222.

Ruzek, J. I. (2008). Commentary on "Does Psychoeducation Help Prevent Posttraumatic Psychological Distress?" *Psychiatry: Interpersonal and Biological Processes, 71*, 332–338.

Ruzek, J. I., Brymer, M. J., Jacobs, A. K., Layne, C. M., Vernberg, E. M., & Watson, P. J. (2007). Psychological first aid. *Journal of Mental Health Counseling, 29*, 17–49.

Scholes, C., Turpin, G., & Mason, S. (2007). A randomised controlled trial to assess the effectiveness of providing self-help information to people with symptoms of acute stress disorder following a traumatic injury. *Behaviour Research and Therapy, 45*, 2527–2536.

Sijbrandij, M., Olff, M., Reitsma, J. B., Carlier, I. V. E., de Vries, M. H., & Gersons, B. P. R. (2007). Treatment of acute posttraumatic stress disorder with brief cognitive behavioral therapy: A randomized controlled trial. *American Journal of Psychiatry, 164*, 82–90.

Sijbrandij, M., Olff, M., Reitsma, J. B., Carlier, I. V., & Gersons, B. P. (2006). Emotional or educational debriefing after psychological trauma. Randomised controlled trial. British *Journal of Psychiatry, 189*, 150–155.

Somer, E., Tamir, E., Maguen, S., & Litz, B. T. (2005). Brief cognitive-behavioral phone-based intervention targeting anxiety about the threat of attack: A pilot study. *Behaviour Research and Therapy, 43*, 669–679.

Stein, M. B., Kerridge, C., Dimsdale, J. E., & Hoyt, D. B. (2007). Pharmacotherapy to prevent PTSD: Results from a randomized controlled proof-of-concept trial in physically injured patients. *Journal of Traumatic Stress, 20*, 923–932.

Turpin, G., Downs, M., & Mason, S. (2005). Effectiveness of providing self-help information following acute traumatic injury: Randomised controlled trial. *British Journal of Psychiatry, 187*, 76–82.

Vaiva, G., Ducrocq, F., Jezequel, K., Averland, B., Lestavel, P., Brunet, A., et al. (2003). Immediate treatment with propranolol decreases posttraumatic stress disorder two months after trauma. *Biological Psychiatry, 54*, 947–949.

van Emmerik, A. A. P., Kamphuis, J. H., Hulsbosch, A. M., & Emmelkamp, P. M. G. (2002). Single session debriefing after psychological trauma: A meta-analysis. *Lancet, 360*, 766–771.

van Emmerik, A. A. P., Kamphuis, J. H., & Emmelkamp, P. M. G. (2008). Treating acute stress disorder and posttraumatic stress disorder with cognitive behavioral therapy or structured writing therapy: A randomized controlled trial. *Psychotherapy and Psychosomatics, 77*, 93–100.

Vernberg, E. M., Steinberg, A. M., Jacobs, A. K., Brymer, M. J., Watson, P. J., Osofsky, J. D., et al. (2008). Innovations in disaster mental health: Psychological first aid. *Professional Psychology: Research and Practice, 39*, 381–388.

Wagner, A. W., Zatzick, D. F., Ghesquiere, A., & Jurkovich, G. J. (2007). Behavioral activation as an early intervention for posttraumatic stress disorder and depression among physically injured trauma survivors. *Cognitive and Behavioral Practice, 14*, 341–349.

Wessely, S., Bryant, R. A., Greenberg, N., Earnshaw, M., Sharpley, J., & Hughes, J. H. (2008). Does psychoeducation help prevent post traumatic psychological distress? *Psychiatry: Interpersonal and Biological Processes, 71,* 287–302.

Yehuda, R., & Golier, J. (2009). Is there a rationale for cortisol-based treatments for PTSD? *Expert Review of Neurotherapeutics, 9,* 1113–1115.

Zatzick, D. F., Roy-Byrne, P., Russo, J. E., Rivara, F. P., Koike, A., Jurkovich, G. J., et al. (2001). Collaborative interventions for physically injured trauma survivors: A pilot randomized effectiveness trial. *General Hospital Psychiatry, 23,* 114–123.

Zatzick, D., Roy-Byrne, P., Russo, J., Rivara, F., Droesch, R., Wagner, A., et al. (2004). A randomized effectiveness trial of stepped collaborative care for acutely injured trauma survivors. *Archives of General Psychiatry, 61,* 498–506.

CHAPTER

25 Prevention and Early Intervention Programs for Children and Adolescents

Melissa J. Brymer, Alan M. Steinberg, Patricia J. Watson, *and* Robert S. Pynoos

Abstract

This chapter provides a review of basic concepts essential to understanding the nature and role of factors that may mediate or moderate the relationship between traumatic stress and a broad range of outcomes. Such intervening factors, including risk, vulnerability, protective, and resilience factors, can be conveniently accommodated within the categories of child intrinsic factors, family factors, and community ecology factors. Community-level and individual/family early interventions for children and adolescents after trauma are critically reviewed. Although many of these early interventions hold promise, a good deal more methodologically sound research using standardized measures is needed. Increased knowledge of risk, vulnerability, and resilience factors can facilitate the development of enhanced evidence-based early and intermediate interventions, clinical treatments, public policy, and trauma-informed services for traumatized children and their families across stages of recovery.

Key Words: Traumatic stress, children and adolescents, prevention, early intervention, resilience

Prevention and Early Intervention Programs for Children and Adolescents

Terms such as "risk," "vulnerability," "protective factor," "resistance," "resilience," "adjustment," and "maladjustment" have not been uniformly employed across discussions of the impact of traumatic stress on children and adolescents or in the literature on prevention and early intervention strategies. This chapter will offer definitions of these key concepts. It will also provide a classification system and overview of factors that have been posited to mediate or moderate the relationship between trauma, post-trauma consequences, and intervention approaches, including child intrinsic, family, and community ecology factors. In addition, it will provide a review of the empirical literature on community, individual, and family-based early interventions that have been used to remediate the impact of traumatic stress. Based on the available literature, recommendations are made for improvements in early intervention research, especially regarding components of promising early interventions that warrant further testing.

Risk, Vulnerability, and Resilience

In regard to factors that potentially moderate and/or mediate the impact of traumatic stress on children and adolescents, the following key concepts and their definitions in Table 25.1 deserve special attention (see Cicchetti, 1996; Pynoos & Steinberg, 2006; Steinberg & Ritzmann, 1990).

Over the years, a variety of factors have been posited that may moderate and/or mediate the relationship between trauma exposure and

Table 25.1. Key concepts and definitions for understanding the impact of traumatic stress on children and adolescents

ADJUSTMENT: The use of appropriate and effective efforts by children and adolescents to recover from traumatic experiences and their impact over time.
MALADJUSTMENT: The use of ineffective efforts by children and adolescents to recover from traumatic experiences and their impact.
PROTECTIVE FACTOR: Those factors that mitigate or buffer the adverse effects of trauma and its aftermath and promote both resistance and resilience.
RESILIENCE The capacity of children and adolescents for early and effective adjustment after exposure to trauma.
RESISTANCE: The capacity of children and adolescents to buffer the detrimental effects typically associated with exposure to trauma, thereby maintaining biological, psychological, behavioral, functional, and developmental progression.
RISK: Either the increased potential of children and adolescents for exposure to trauma, or the increased susceptibility among children and adolescents to adverse biological, psychological, behavioral, functional, and developmental outcomes after exposure to trauma.
VULNERABILITY: An increased susceptibility among children and adolescents to adverse biological, psychological, behavioral, functional, and developmental outcomes after exposure to trauma.

posttrauma outcomes among children and adolescents. These factors can be conveniently accommodated within the following three categories: child intrinsic factors, family factors, and community ecology factors. Table 25.2 presents as comprehensive a list of potential moderating and mediating factors as can be gleaned from the child/adolescent trauma literature.

Of course, these intervening factors need to be considered against a broad range of outcomes, many of which are beginning to be intensively investigated, as each factor may operate differently depending on the specific outcome under consideration. In addition, many of these factors may themselves be affected by traumatic stress, and as such, may be conceived as potential outcome variables. To date, in addition to factors that relate specifically to the onset and severity of PTSD, outcomes of trauma in children and adolescents that have been studied have been quite varied and cover a range of psychological reactions and psychiatric disorders, as well as biological alterations, behavioral disturbances, functional impairments, alterations in a sense of safety and protection, alteration in expectations and aspirations for the future, cognitive and emotional development, physical health and well-being, and disturbances in moral development and conscience functioning (see Fairbank, Putnam & Harris, 2007; Goenjian et al., 2005).

Epidemiological research has indicated that many youth experience exposure to one or more traumatic events in their lifetimes, and that children exposed to multiple traumas are particularly vulnerable to a range of psychological, behavioral, and emotional problems (Paolucci, Genuis, & Violato, 2001), social maladjustment (Schwartz & Proctor, 2000), and academic failure (Delaney-Black et al., 2002). Risk factors for exposure to violence have indicated that adolescents, as compared with other age groups, are at increased risk of being victimized, involved in incidents outside of the home, experiencing threat to life, and suffering physical injuries, with girls more likely to be victimized than boys (Harpaz-Rotem, Murphy, Berkowitz, Marans, & Rosenheck, 2007). The cumulative epidemiological evidence indicates that the adverse effects of traumatic stress experienced from infancy through adolescence may extend well into adulthood, increasing the risk for lifelong problems such as depression, posttraumatic stress disorder (PTSD), substance abuse, marital discord, low occupational attainment, and poor physical and mental health (Felitti et al., 1998).

Some of the factors that have been most consistently linked with increased risk for PTSD following exposure to a trauma are the nature and severity of the traumatic experience, the nature and severity of posttrauma stresses and adversities (including exposure to trauma and loss reminders), and parental reaction to the traumatic event (Layne et al., 2006). In general, most studies find that children and adolescents who report experiencing the most severe traumas also report the highest levels of PTSD symptoms, known as a "dose of exposure" effect (Pynoos et al., 1987). Studies also show that recovery from a traumatic experience is likely to be negatively influenced by having a family member who was also exposed to the event, experiencing the death of a parent or another significant person, having mental health or learning problems before the event, and lacking a strong social support network (Scheering & Zeanah, 2001). Sex is another factor that has consistently been found to affect the severity of PTSD, with girls showing more severe

Table 25.2. **Posited factors that moderate and/or mediate the relationship between traumatic stress and outcome**

Category	Moderating and/or Mediating Factor	
Child-Intrinsic	Gender	Ethnicity
	Age	Intelligence
	Temperament	Genetics
	Self-Esteem	Self-Efficacy
	Self-Confidence	Coping Repertoire/Skills
	Support Seeking Attitudes/Skills Religiosity	School Functioning/Performance
	Physical Health	Social/Communication Skills
	Subsequent Trauma/Loss	History of Trauma and Loss
	Locus of Control	Attachment Style
	Developmental Level	Cultural Identity
		Motivation
Family	Family History of Psychopathology	Parent Communication Style
	Parent Educational Level	Family Attachment Relationships
	Parenting Style	Parental Alcohol/Drug Use
	Family Support	Family Structure
	Family Values	Caregiver Functioning
	Caregiver Physical Health	Family Financial Status
	Family Living Conditions	Family Functioning
Community Ecology	Peer/Mentor Relationships	Community/Cultural Ecology
	Community Support Systems	Community Involvement
	School/Classroom Milieu	Ongoing Threats
	Ongoing Legal Proceedings	Media Exposure
	Exposure to Trauma Reminders	Exposure to Loss Reminders

PTSD symptoms as compared with boys (American Academy of Child and Adolescent Psychiatry [AACAP], 2010; Fairbank et al., 2007), although more research is needed to determine if this finding is related to a greater willingness on the part of girls to endorse symptoms. It remains unclear how a child's age at the time of exposure to a traumatic event affects the onset or severity of PTSD, as there have been mixed findings (AACAP, 2010; Fairbank et al., 2007). These discrepant findings may be related to differences in the way that PTSD is measured and manifested in children and adolescents of different ages and developmental levels.

Recent literature reviews have identified intervening protective and vulnerability variables as some of the best predictors of long-term posttraumatic adaptation (Brewin, Andrews, & Valentine, 2000; Cicchetti & Schneider-Rosen, 1984; Masten, Best, & Garmezy, 1990; Silverman & La Greca, 2002). Of particular note is Brewin and colleagues' (2000) meta-analysis of risk factors for the development of PTSD in adulthood, showing that the absence of social support and higher levels of contextual life stress are two of the top risk factors, with larger effect sizes than traditionally emphasized variables such as child abuse history, intelligence, socioeconomic status, lack of education, and sex.

In summary, risk factors for the development of PTSD include multiple trauma exposure (actually a causal factor rather than a moderator or mediator), exposure to posttrauma stress and adversity, female sex, preexisting psychiatric disorder, parental psychopathology, and lack of social support (Pine & Cohen, 2002). Adaptive or resilience factors include social support, self-efficacy, and positive family environment (Graham-Berman, Gruber, Howell & Girz, 2009). In regard to research among children and adolescents in the area of disasters, studies have indicated that, in addition to trauma exposure variables, severity of postdisaster stresses and adversities, frequency of exposure to trauma and loss reminders, parental mental health and reactions, and poor social relationships and support are associated with increased severity of PTSD and depression (Goenjian et al., 2005; Layne et al., 2001; McFarlane, Policansky & Irwin, 1987). Studies have also indicated that increased television viewing of disaster-related material is associated with the development and severity of PTSD symptoms in children (Hoven et al., 2005; Pfefferbaum et al., 1999). Many of the findings from studies of risk, vulnerability, and resilience factors have been used to inform prevention and early intervention efforts. These efforts can be divided into community-based programs and individual/family intervention approaches.

Community-based Programs

Community-based programs fall on a continuum from providing services to meet the basic needs of an entire population affected by a traumatic event to offering specialized services for those needing psychological or psychiatric treatment. Implementation of these approaches depends largely on the type and magnitude of the traumatic event and the specific needs of the affected population or community. Services can range from providing training to parents and teachers about common reactions of children after traumatic events to providing more structured acute, intermediate, or tertiary-level interventions.

In terms of basic psycho-education, many organizations have developed talking points or websites for parents about the effects of trauma on children and recommended parental support (Kassam-Adams, 2008; La Greca & Silverman, 2009); however, there is limited research on the use and effectiveness of these materials. For example, one group (Marsac, Kassam-Adams, Hildenbrand, Kohser, & Winston, 2011), studied 50 parents of children who had suffered injuries within the past two months and placed parents in a Web-based or video intervention (www.aftertheinjury.org). Demonstrating the potential helpfulness of these types of materials, parents at postintervention showed high levels of knowledge about psychological injury-related reactions, were able to generate new, positive strategies to help their child recover, and identified specific traumatic stress reactions to monitor in their child.

Kazak and colleagues (2006) reported on a promising hospital system-based program for hospitalized injured children. It is a stepped-care intervention program designed to provide continuity of care, beginning with screening during hospitalization for risk factors or current distress, subsequent follow-up contacts to monitor recovery, psycho-education to promote effective coping assistance from parents, specific support for adherence to follow-up medical care, and evidence-based psychological treatment if distress is severe or persistent (Kazak et al., 2006). Results from a randomized control trial have been presented (Kassam-Adams, Marsac, & Garcia-Espana, 2009) indicating that screening provided information to predict later PTSD status, and that the stepped intervention was highly welcomed by families during the inpatient stay. The impact on posttraumatic stress and depression remain under investigation.

In addition to efforts on behalf of injured and medically ill children, community-based programs have also included secondary-prevention strategies for children exposed to violence. One, the Child Development Community Policing (CD-CP) program, involves integrated training and consultation between mental health professionals and police officers, and acute intervention and follow-up services to children exposed to violence (Marans, Murphy, & Berkowitz, 2002). CD-CP includes the Child and Family Traumatic Stress Intervention (CFTSI; Berkowitz & Marans 2005), a four-session model designed to decrease distress symptoms and prevent chronic PTSD by increasing family communication and facilitating parents' support to potentially traumatized children who have experienced a wide array of adverse events. A randomized pilot study of CFTSI was conducted with 112 youth aged 7–16 assigned to either CFTSI or a psycho-educational and supportive comparison group within 30 days of an event. The CFTSI group was significantly less likely to develop partial or full PTSD at follow-up, with a reduced odds ratio of 73%. Also, the CFTSI group showed significantly reduced severity of PTSD and anxiety symptoms compared to controls at follow-up (Berkowitz, Stover, & Marans, 2011).

Using a community empowerment model, the Community Crisis Response Team (CCRT; Harvey, Mondesir, & Aldrich, 2007) provides a different example of a community-level intervention in response to community-wide trauma. This model is time limited and stresses the importance of enlisting team members from the community targeted for response. The model promotes empowerment by designing intervention strategies with community members, making positive contributions to the community's crisis response resources, and enhancing relationships between affected individuals and community members and resources. In addition to providing direct assistance, the CCRT provides consultation to school administrators, workplace managers, and neighborhood representatives on how to deal with the media; how to handle rumor control; and if, when, and how to structure community meetings and group interventions. Interventions include informative community meetings, traumatic stress debriefing, stress workshops, peer support, and follow-up.

Little controlled research has been conducted on community-level intervention following disasters and war, but a number of models have emerged in the past six years. For example, Laor, Wiener, Spirman, and Wolmer (2005) report on the Tel Aviv Model, a promising practice of implementing community-level interventions under the continual threat of terrorism in Israel. Within this model, behavioral health teams were deployed to regional trauma centers specializing in screening and evaluation, treatment, and community interventions. These authors specifically note that effective intervention requires collaboration with teachers, nurses, social workers, educational counselors, and other providers. They recommend that the appropriate role for behavioral health specialists is to lead these interdisciplinary teams, and provide training and support, thus allowing for screening and initial assistance in a variety of accessible settings.

The Post-Traumatic Stress Management (PTSM) program has been employed immediately after disasters, political violence, and other critical incidents that have had a high impact on communities. PTSM offers a continuum of services and encourages community members to play a key role in its implementation (Macy et al., 2004). One intervention strategy used in PTSM is a Classroom/Community/Camp-based Intervention (CBI), a psychosocial intervention that includes a series of highly structured expressive-behavioral activities for children who are facing difficult life circumstances (e.g., living with political conflict, living in refugee camps) or who have been involved in a critical incident. The overall aim of CBI is to identify existing coping and social support resources among these children and to sustain utilization of resources over time. Two recent randomized controlled studies using CBI with children exposed to armed conflict and political violence showed improved PTSD symptoms compared with controls (Tol et al., 2008) and prosocial behavior among girls, reduction of aggression among boys, and increased hope for older children (Jordans et al., 2010). However, neither study found a reduction in stress-related physical symptoms, depression, anxiety, or functional impairment. Across studies of CBI, most children and service providers overwhelmingly viewed the intervention positively with high levels of perceived problem-reduction, improved emotional well-being, and positive behavioral and social changes (Jordans, Tol, Komproe, & de Jong, 2009).

The FEMA Funded Crisis Counseling and Training Program (CCP) is a model designed to support, rather than supplant, natural community support systems after presidentially declared disasters in the United States. It is a broad-based community program that serves a full spectrum of children, adolescents, parents or caregivers, families, and adults in communities affected by disasters, as well as businesses and other organizations, neighborhoods, and communities as a whole. The CCP mostly utilizes lay professionals along with some licensed counselors to provide a number of services, including brief educational or supportive contacts, linking survivors to resources, individual, group, and family counseling, and public education, with the goal of enhancing individual, family, and community resilience. Despite its 30-year history, there is little systematic evidence of the benefits of crisis counseling or the justification of program assumptions. Recently an extensive cross-site evaluation has been conducted of the services provided under CCP after Hurricanes Katrina, Rita, and Wilma. Norris and Bellamy (2009) reported findings from 19 CCP programs and noted that survivors were generally positive about their experiences with the program. These responses were strongly positively correlated with intensity and duration of services. Frequency of psychological referrals was also associated with higher ratings of benefit (Norris, Hamblen, & Rosen, 2009). In addition, across CCP programs there was wide variability in type and intensity of services provided and the extent of reach and penetration. The next stage of cross-site CCP evaluation should separate children from adult data to determine the unique service needs, perceptions of benefits, and outcome of services in broad domains appropriate for children.

Individual/Family Interventions

Many of the child, adolescent, and family-based centered components of community-based programs have been derived from those employed in individual and family-based approaches. The goal of most early interventions is to stabilize the child and family, teach and enhance the use of positive coping strategies, and prevent chronic distress, functional impairment, and psychopathology. In intervening early, children and families can be assisted with managing and reducing their current reactions; those most at risk for more serious disorder or developmental disruption can be identified; and referrals for more intensive or specialized services can be made. Specific early intervention strategies targeted for children and adolescents have included: psycho-education; bereavement support; various forms of psychological debriefing; Eye Movement Desensitization and Reprocessing (EMDR); various cognitive behavioral approaches; discussion of thoughts and feelings; reinforcing adaptive coping; teaching problem-solving and stress management skills; promotion of safety behaviors and use of support systems; structured and unstructured art and play activities; massage; and pharmacological treatments (see Brymer et al., 2009; La Greca & Silverman, 2009). Early interventions have been delivered using a variety of modalities, including individual, family, group, and classroom sessions, provision of psycho-educational materials, establishment of crisis hotlines, and Internet-based interventions.

To date, there is scant evidence for the effectiveness of early interventions for children exposed to trauma, and there have been no controlled outcome studies conducted in the short-term recovery phase after disasters (La Greca & Silverman, 2009). No doubt this is because of the many challenges and obstacles to conducting research in chaotic crisis situations. In addition, those studies that have been conducted suffer from significant methodological flaws (Brymer et al., 2009; Steinberg, Brymer, Steinberg, & Pfefferbaum 2006). Nevertheless, there are several promising early intervention approaches that have been developed and these will be briefly reviewed.

Trauma- and grief-focused cognitive behavioral approaches have been widely utilized among children and adolescents and are among those with the most empirical support in long-term recovery (Silverman et al., 2008). Cognitive behavioral approaches utilize components summarized by the acronym PRACTICE, including psycho-education and parenting skills, relaxation, affective modulation, cognitive coping and processing, trauma narrative, in vivo mastery of trauma reminders, conjoint child-parent sessions, and enhancement of future safety and development (Cohen, Mannarino, & Deblinger, 2006; Stein et al., 2003). Further research is needed on the effectiveness of these approaches in the early aftermath of traumatic events, across settings, and with children of different ages, ethnic, and cultural groups.

Psychological First Aid (PFA) approaches include many of the intervention strategies that comprise other early intervention protocols for children and families, including trauma-informed cognitive behavioral strategies. PFA allows tailoring of these interventions to meet the specific needs of children and families. Many of the strategies of PFA are supported by research and clinical literature that demonstrates the utility of enhancing coping, social support, self and community efficacy, and problem solving in the wake of crises and stressful events (Hobfoll et al., 2007). Although PFA has not yet been systematically studied, the PFA Field Operations Guide by National Child Traumatic Stress Network and the National Center for PTSD (NCPTSD) was found to be acceptable to, and well received by, children and caregivers who were provided PFA services (Allen et al., 2010; Brymer et al., 2006).

In addition to the PFA Field Operations Guide, NCTSN/NCPTSD have developed a second field operations guide for the intermediate stage of disaster response, Skills for Psychological Recovery (SPR; Berkowitz et al., 2010). This guide was developed to meet specific criteria for the FEMA/SAMHSA Crisis Counseling Program. SPR providers assist survivors with learning and using a set of empirically based skills, including problem solving, positive activity scheduling, managing reactions, promoting helpful thinking, and rebuilding healthy social connections. Research suggests that a skills-building approach is more effective than supportive counseling (Beutler, 2009; Bryant, Harvey, Dang, Sackville, & Basten, 1998; Bryant, Sackville, Dang, Moulds., & Guthrie, 1999), and consequently SPR embodies a problem- and solution-focused approach. Each module begins with a rationale for the importance of the skill, followed by a step-by-step procedure to implement the skill. There are clear guidelines on how to gather information, to prioritize problems and concerns, to enhance motivation for change, and to address obstacles to using the SPR skills. In addition, SPR includes handouts and worksheets to support children, adults, and families in implementing the skills. This intervention has been used in several postdisaster programs, including in Louisiana after Hurricanes Katrina, Rita, and Gustav and after the 2010 Deepwater Horizon oil spill; in Australia after the 2009 Victorian bushfires, and in American Samoa after the 2009 earthquake/tsunami. Evaluation reports from Louisiana and Australia indicate that the intervention was favorably perceived by providers as an acceptable and useful intervention for disaster survivors and that the intervention was implemented without difficulty, with most reporting that they would use the intervention in the event of a future disaster (Fletcher et al., 2010; Hansel, 2011).

Although there has been a plethora of studies of EMDR among traumatized individuals, very few methodologically sound studies have been conducted among children in the acute aftermath of a traumatic event. Jarero, Artigas, and Hartung (2006) reported on several pilot projects using EMDR group treatment and found a significant reduction in trauma symptoms, although no standard PTSD measure was used. Three months after an initial EMDR group intervention, Aduriz, Bluthgen, and Knopfler (2009) used a one-session EMDR group protocol with 124 children who had been impacted by a massive flood in Argentina in 2003. Again, results of the one-session treatment showed significant reduction of symptoms postintervention and at three-month follow-up. However, no standardized PTSD outcome measure was used nor was there a comparison or control group. These studies lay the groundwork for future randomized controlled studies using standardized PTSD outcome measures.

The current evidence indicates that debriefing cannot be advocated as effective in preventing the subsequent development of PTSD or other anxiety disorders in traumatized children and adolescents (Stallard et al. 2006; Vila, Porche, & Mouren-Simeoni, 1999; Yule 1992). In the most rigorous study, Stallard and colleagues (2006) compared the effectiveness of debriefing using a randomized control design including 70 experimental subjects and 62 controls. Children assigned to the experimental condition were provided with a manualized debriefing intervention four weeks after road traffic accidents, while the children assigned to the control group were engaged in a non-accident focused discussion. Children in both groups showed significant pre/post improvements in PTSD, depression, and anxiety, with the only between group difference being that children in the experimental group reported fewer behavioral and emotional problems. There were no significant between-group differences in PTSD diagnosis, depression, and anxiety at posttreatment. The authors concluded that debriefing as an early intervention for children is not effective.

Various forms of art and massage therapies have been employed separately or in combination with other types of interventions with acutely traumatized children. Field, Seligman, Scafidi, and Schanberg (1996) compared eight sessions of massage therapy to a video-attention control condition provided to 60 grade-school-age children within the first month after being exposed to a hurricane. Children in the massage condition experienced greater reduction in anxiety, depression, and cortisol levels, and an increase in positive feelings relative to children in the video-attention control condition. The authors did not measure PTSD at postintervention. Chapman, Morabito, Ladakakos, Schreier, and Knudson (2001) conducted a randomized controlled study of the effectiveness of manualized art therapy compared with hospital care as usual. Participants had experienced traumatic injuries that required hospitalization for a minimum of 24 hours. There were no between-group differences in PTSD scores as measured at one week and one month posttreatment. Studies of art and massage interventions would clearly benefit from greater attention to methodological and measurement issues, including stratification of study participants by exposure levels, employment of intervention protocols with fidelity checks, expanded use of valid and reliable instrumentation, application of statistics proper for sample size, and extended follow-up.

Family-centered approaches have been developed and used to assist children in the aftermath of trauma (Landau, Mittal, & Wieling, 2008). For instance, Walsh's family resilience approach attempts to strengthen family capacities (Walsh, 1996, 2006). Providers help families to deal more effectively with stressful situations, search for positive examples of success in overcoming past adversities, and encourage family members to use mentors in their kin network to support their recovery. The framework calls for providers to facilitate adaptive functioning within three domains: family belief systems, organization patterns, and communication processes (Walsh, 2006). While this approach is based on family theory and extrapolation from general research on effective coping strategies, at this time there are no controlled studies.

Additionally, new interventions are being developed to assist military families where there have been multiple deployments, combat-related injury and stress, and adversities for the family (Cohen, Mannarino, Gibson et al., 2006; Cozza et al., 2010). In general, family-centered approaches have been shown to have a positive impact on parent and child adjustment and in strengthening the use of effective coping skills (Compas, Phares, & Ladoux, 1989). Based on evidence for interventions for families at risk, the FOCUS (Families Over Coming Under Stress) program provides preventive intervention for military families. The intervention has been manualized and piloted at Camp Pendleton in California (Saltzman & Lester et al., 2009). FOCUS is a strength-based resilience training approach that provides psycho-education, training on trauma-informed coping skills, and strategies to strengthen parent and child social, behavioral, and emotional adjustment (Lester et al., 2011). This program is now being implemented as a large-scale demonstration project for the U.S. Marine Corps and Navy, and at selected Army and Air Force installations. The project includes comprehensive program evaluation encompassing the effectiveness of an outreach process that addresses the multiple barriers to behavioral health services in military settings and the effectiveness of the intervention on multiple outcome domains.

Suggestions for Improvement in Early Intervention Research

As noted above, much of the research on early interventions for traumatized children and adolescents to date has suffered from a number of methodological problems in subject selection and stratification, research design, statistical approaches, and metrics. In addition to the need for more randomized controlled studies with adequate sample sizes that include the use of standardized measures, suggestions for critically needed advances include: (a) increased research on special populations, including diverse age, ethnic, racial, cultural, and social groups, and those with physical disability, illness, or injury; (b) expansion of the range of intervention outcomes beyond distress measures to include behavioral, functional, developmental, and physical health outcomes; (c) addressing the question of which intervention components are effective in regard to which outcomes and under what conditions; (d) consideration of the contribution of traumatic bereavement to intervention outcome, with inclusion of measures and interventions to address grief and associated depressive reactions and separation anxiety; and (e) increased studies of the acceptability and effectiveness of early pharmacological interventions for children and adolescents.

Summary and Conclusion

Increased knowledge of risk, vulnerability, protective, and adjustment factors, whether in the child, family, or community, holds enormous promise for the development of enhanced evidence-based acute and intermediate interventions, clinical treatments, and trauma-informed practices and services to assist traumatized children, adolescents, and their families across stages of recovery. In addition, with greater knowledge of these factors, public policy can be developed to support those characteristics that promote early identification, intervention, and recovery (Fairbank et al., 2007). For many of the potential mediators and moderators listed in table 25.2, valid and reliable measures will need to be developed to permit research investigating these factors (Cicchetti & Hinshaw, 2003; Kazdin & Nock, 2003). For example, improved measures relating to ongoing exposure to trauma and loss reminders, psychological and physiological reactivity to them, and strategies used to cope with reminders will allow for better determination of the extent to which such exposures and reactivity exacerbate and prolong posttraumatic stress reactions (Layne, Warren, Watson, & Shalev, 2007). Another important area relates to the interaction of trauma and loss, and improved measures will need to be developed to better understand ways in which grief reactions may interfere with the resolution of posttraumatic stress reactions. In addition, more powerful research designs and statistical methods—for example, the use of structural equation modeling—will be needed in order to draw valid causal inferences in investigations of the mechanisms by which these factors affect outcome.

Based on the available literature, a number of components can be recommended for inclusion in community-based public mental health approaches to providing early interventions for traumatized children and their families. First, public mental health approaches should include the use of systematic needs assessment, triage, and surveillance measures that can facilitate the provision of appropriate levels of early and ongoing intervention to meet the needs of differentially affected child populations. Triage protocols should not only take into account the child's exposure and current distress and functioning but also include parental functioning, available social support, and secondary adversities. Second, communities need to build response and recovery resources to ensure the availability of trained personnel who can deliver early and intermediate interventions that can assist children and families in the aftermath of traumatic events, including identifying and supporting available child and family service systems. Third, after a community-wide event, community planners need to map the ecology of an event in order to have a comprehensive understanding of the impact on the community and the nature and extent of resources that are needed. Fourth, community response needs to include a continuum of services to ensure that an appropriate level of service is available for children who are differentially impacted. Fifth, early intervention programs should incorporate developmental and cultural perspectives in their response strategies. Addressing developmental issues means not only taking into account a child's age and cognitive level but also intervening to support the role of parents in the family's recovery and ensuring that developmental disruptions are addressed (Berkowitz, 2003; Brymer & Kassam-Adams, 2008).

There are currently a number of different early intervention models for traumatized children and adolescents. The NCTSN/NCPTSD Psychological First Aid is considered a sound initial early intervention, as it does not assume pathology, assesses current needs and concerns, identifies future service requirements, links with collaborative services, has a cultural and developmental perspective, and identifies the role of parents as a primary source for supporting a child's recovery. For children needing a more in-depth intervention, skill-based and cognitive-behavioral approaches are indicated. The employment of systemic community-based approaches can ensure that early interventions are embedded in community infrastructure and resources and utilize state-of-the-art intervention strategies. Currently, the evidence suggests that debriefing cannot be recommended with children, and more research is needed to further refine and establish the evidence base for other early intervention models.

Establishing the evidence base for acute and intermediate interventions (such as PFA and SPR) will need to be done in progressive stages that correspond to a number of basic research questions. Among the overarching research questions include those relating to: (a) the types of training methods and resources that are needed (including the use of learning communities and on-line courses) to effectively disseminate these interventions; (b) how best to ensure that providers can be trained to implement these interventions with fidelity; (c) whether these interventions can be effectively delivered and received by survivors in community settings; (d) whether implementing the intervention leads to improved outcomes as compared to other intervention practices; and (e) whether implementing the intervention in a community setting improves the overall effectiveness and efficiency of the community response. Addressing these research questions will require the use of a variety of research strategies and metrics, including the use of drills, focus groups, and prospective longitudinal and randomized controlled studies. Attention should also be directed toward identifying and assessing intervention components that may benefit traumatized children and their families after the intervention has ended, including: (a) linkage with collaborative services, (b) use of handouts by survivors over time, and (c) ongoing use by children and families of knowledge and skills acquired during the intervention.

Future Directions

There are a number of critical questions that need to be addressed in regard to the advancement of early prevention programs and interventions for traumatized children and their families. First, we need to develop an array of assessment tools, including those for needs assessment, triage, surveillance, clinical assessment, clinical outcome, and program evaluation that can provide the data needed for developing more effective public mental health response and recovery programs (see Balaban et al., 2005). Such data will allow for the accurate identification of those whose exposure to trauma, loss, and posttrauma adversities greatly increases risk for severe, persisting distress, behavioral problems, functional impairment, and developmental disturbance. In addition, data collection should include items that relate to potential mediating or moderating factors so as to better identify those at risk and specific targets of intervention.

Second, the field of child and adolescent trauma needs to not only identify those factors that moderate or mediate the impact of traumatic stress but gain a better understanding of their mechanisms of action, how they operate to facilitate resilience and adjustment. This understanding will allow for the development of much improved intervention strategies and techniques that rely on a more in-depth appreciation of adaptive coping mechanisms and skills that should be a focus of both primary and secondary prevention.

Third, there has been extremely limited research on the impact of biological, chemical, and radiological terrorism on children, adolescents, and families, and inadequate preparation for the unique national challenges presented to schools, communities, and the public mental health system (Pynoos, Steinberg, Schreiber, & Brymer, 2006). In addition, there has not been adequate behavioral research to identify potential mental health consequences for children and their families, along with risk, protective, and resilience factors, especially those related to aspects of health care seeking behavior in the event of pandemic flu. Such a research base for these types of catastrophic events is needed to inform community-based resilience and recovery programs, mental health providers, and public decision makers in regard to strategies of response, including how factors like the dissemination of public health information and family compliance with public health directives may represent important behavioral health areas for mitigation of impact.

References

Aduriz, M. E., Bluthgen, C., & Knopfler, C. (2009). Helping child flood victims using group EMDR intervention in Argentina: Treatment outcome and gender differences. *International Journal of Stress Management, 16*, 138–153.

American Academy of Child and Adolescent Psychiatry (2010). Practice parameter for the assessment and treatment of children and adolescents with posttraumatic stress disorder, *Journal of the American Academy of Child and Adolescent Psychiatry, 49*, 414–430.

Allen, B., Brymer, M. J., Steinberg, A. M., Vernberg, E. M., Jacobs, A., Speier, A., & Pynoos, R. S. (2010). Perceptions of use of Psychological First Aid among providers responding to Hurricanes Gustav and Ike. *Journal of Traumatic Stress, 23*, 509–513.

Balaban, V. F., Steinberg, A. M., Brymer, M. J., Layne, C. M., Jones, R. T., & Fairbank, J.A. (2005). Screening and assessment for children's psychosocial needs following war and terrorism. In M. J. Friedman & A. Mikus-Kos (Eds.), *Promoting the psychosocial well-being of children following war and terrorism* (pp. 121–161). Netherlands: IOS Press.

Berkowitz, S. J. (2003). Children exposed to community violence: The rationale for early intervention. *Clinical Child and Family Psychological Review, 6*, 293–302.

Berkowitz, S., Bryant, R., Brymer, M., Hamblen, J., Jacobs, A., Layne, C., et al., National Center for PTSD and National Child Traumatic Stress Network. (2010). *Skills for Psychological Recovery: Field Operations Guide*. Available at: www.nctsn.org and www.ncptsd.va.gov.

Berkowitz, S. J., Stover, C., & Marans, S. (2011). The Child and Family Traumatic Stress Intervention: Secondary prevention for youth at risk of developing PTSD. *The Journal of Child Psychology and Psychiatry, 52*, 676–685.

Berkowitz, S. J., & Marans, S. (2005). *Child and Family Traumatic Stress Intervention Manual.* Unpublished manuscript.

Beutler, L. E. (2009). Making science matter in clinical practice: Redefining psychotherapy. *Clinical Psychology: Science and Practice, 16*, 301–317.

Brewin, C. R., Andrews, B., & Valentine, J. D. (2000). Meta-analysis of risk factors for posttraumatic stress disorder in trauma-exposed adults. *Journal of Consulting and Clinical Psychology, 68*, 748–766.

Bryant, R. A., Harvey, A. G., Dang, S. T., Sackville, T., & Basten, C. (1998). Treatment of acute stress disorder: A comparison of cognitive-behavioral therapy and supportive counseling. *Journal of Consulting and Clinical Psychology, 66*, 862–866.

Bryant, R. A. Sackville, T., Dang, S. T., Moulds, M., & Guthrie, R. (1999). Treating acute stress disorder: An evaluation of cognitive behavior therapy and supportive counseling. *American Journal of Psychiatry, 156*, 1780–1786.

Brymer, M. J., & Kassam-Adams, N. (2008). Crisis Interventions for Children. In G. Reyes, J. Elhai, & J. Ford (Eds.), *Encyclopedia of psychological trauma* (pp. 179–182). Hoboken, NJ: John Wiley.

Brymer, M., Layne, C., Jacobs, A., Pynoos, R., Ruzek, J., Steinberg, A., et al. (2006). *Psychological first aid field operations guide* (2nd ed.). Available at: www.nctsn.org and www.ncptsd.va.gov.

Brymer, M. J., Steinberg, A. M., Vernberg, E. M., Layne, C. M., Watson, P. J., Jacobs, A., et al. (2009). Acute Interventions for children and adolescents exposed to trauma. In E. Foa, T. Kean, M. Friedman, & J. Cohen (Eds.), *Effective treatments for PTSD* (2nd ed., pp. 106–116). New York: Guilford.

Chapman, L, Morabito, D., Ladakakos, C., Schreier, H., & Knudson, M. (2001). The effectiveness of art therapy interventions in reducing posttraumatic stress disorder (PTSD) symptoms in pediatric trauma patients. *Art-Therapy, 18*, 100–104.

Cicchetti, D. (1996). Developmental theory: Lessons from the study of risk and psychopathology. In S. Matthysse, D.L. Levy, J. Kagan, & F. M. Benes (Eds.), *Psychopathology: The evolving science of mental disorder* (pp. 253–284). New York: Cambridge University Press.

Cicchetti, D., & Hinshaw, S. (Eds.). (2003). Conceptual, methodological, and statistical issues in developmental psychopathology: A special issue in honor of Paul E. Meehl. *Development and Psychopathology, 15*, 497–832.

Cicchetti, D., & Schneider-Rosen, K. (1984). Toward a transactional model of childhood depression. In D. Cicchetti & K. Schneider-Rosen (Eds.), *Childhood depression* (pp. 5–27). San Francisco: Jossey Bass.

Cohen, J. A., Mannarino, A. P., & Deblinger, E. (2006). *Treating trauma and traumatic grief in children and adolescents.* New York: Guilford.

Cohen, J. A., Mannarino, A. P., Gibson L. E., Cozza, S., Brymer, M. J., & Murray, L. (2006). Interventions for children and adolescents following disasters. In E. C. Ritchie, P. J. Watson, & M. J. Friedman (Eds.), *Interventions following mass violence and disasters: Strategies for mental health practice* (pp. 227–256). New York: Guilford.

Compas, B. E., Phares, V., & Ledoux, N. (1989). Stress and coping prevention intervention with children and adolescents. In L. A. Bond & B. E. Compass (Eds.), *Primary prevention and promotion in the schools* (pp. 60–89). Beverly Hills, CA: Sage.

Cozza, S. J., Guimond, J. M., McKibben, J. B. A., Chun R. S., Arata-Maiers, T. L., Schneider, B., Maiers, A., Fullerton, C. S., & Ursano, R. J. (2010). Combat-injured service members and their families: The relationship of child distress and spouse-perceived family distress and disruption. *Journal of Traumatic Stress, 23*, 112–115.

Delaney-Black, V., Covington, C., Ondersma, S. J., Nordstrom-Kee, B., Templin, T., Ager, J. et al. (2002). Violence exposure, trauma, and IQ and/or reading deficits among urban children. *Archives of Pediatric Adolescent Medicine, 156,* 280–285.

Fairbank, J. A., Putnam, F. W., & Harris, W. W. (2007). The prevalence and impact of traumatic stress. In M. J. Friedman, T. M. Keane, & P. A. Resick (Eds.), *Handbook of PTSD: Science and practice* (pp. 229–251). New York: Guilford.

Felitti, V. J., Anda, R. F., Nordenberg, D., Williamson, D. F., Spitz, A M., Edwards, V., et al. (1998). Relationship of childhood abuse and household dysfunction to many of the leading causes of death in adults: The adverse childhood experiences (ACE) study. *American Journal of Preventive Medicine, 14,* 245–258

Field, T., Seligman, S., Scafidi, F., & Schanberg, S. (1996). Alleviating posttraumatic stress in children following Hurricane Andrew. *Journal of Applied Developmental Psychology, 17,* 37–50.

Fletcher, S., Forbes, D., Wolfgang, B., Varker, T., Creamer, M., Brymer, M., et al. (2010). Practitioner perceptions of Skills for Psychological Recovery: A training program for health practitioners in the aftermath of the Victorian bushfires. *Australian and New Zealand Journal of Psychiatry, 44,* 1105–1111.

Goenjian, A. K., Walling, D. Steinberg, A. M., Karavan, I., Najarian, L. M., & Pynoos, R. (2005). A prospective study of posttraumatic stress and depressive reactions among treated and untreated adolescents 5 years after a catastrophic disaster. *American Journal of Psychiatry, 162,* 2302–2308.

Graham-Bermann, S. A., Gruber, G., Howell, K. H., & Girz, L. (2009). Factors discriminating among profiles of resilience and psychopathology in children exposed to intimate partner violence. *Child Abuse and Neglect, 33*(9), 648–660.

Hansel, T. C., Osofsky H., Steinberg, A. M, Brymer, M. J, Landis R., Riise, K. S., Gilkey, S., Osofsky, J., & Speier, A. (2011). Louisiana Spirit Specialized Crisis Counseling: Counselor perceptions of training and services. *Psychological Trauma: Theory, Research, Practice, and Policy, 3,* 276–282.

Harpaz-Rotem, I., Murphy, R. A., Berkowitz, S., Marans, S., & Rosenheck, R. A. (2007). Clinical epidemiology of urban violence: Responding to children exposed to violence in ten communities. *Journal of Interpersonal Violence, 22,* 1479–1490.

Harvey, M. R., Mondesir, A.V., & Aldrich, H. (2007). Fostering resilience in traumatized communities: A community empowerment model of intervention. *Journal of Aggression, Maltreatment and Trauma, 14,* 265–285.

Hobfoll, S. E., Watson, P. E., Bell, C. C., Bryant, R. A., Brymer, M. J., Friedman, M. J., et al. (2007). Five essential elements of immediate and mid-term mass trauma intervention: Empirical evidence. *Psychiatry: Interpersonal and Biological Processes, 70,* 283–315.

Hoven, C. W., Duarte, C. S., Lucas, C. P., Wu, P., Mandell, D. J., Goodwin R. D., et al. (2005). Psychopathology among New York City public school children 6 months after September 11. *Archives of General Psychiatry, 62,* 545–552.

Jarero, I., Artigas, L., & Hartung, J. (2006). EMDR integrative group treatment protocol: A postdisaster trauma intervention for children and adults. *Traumatology, 12,* 121–129.

Jordans, M. J. D., Komproe, I. H., Tol, W. A., Kohrt, B., Luitel, N., Macy R. D., & de Jong, V. T. M. (2010). Evaluation of a classroom–based psychosocial intervention in conflict-affected Nepal: A cluster randomized controlled trial. *Journal of Child Psychology and Psychiatry, 51,* 818–826.

Jordans, M. J. D., Tol, W. A., Komproe, I. H., & de Jong V. T. M. (2009). Systematic review of evidence and treatment approaches: Psychosocial and mental health care of children in war. *Child and Adolescent Mental Health, 14,* 2–14.

Kassam-Adams, N. (2008). Prevention, child. In G. Reyes, J. Elhai, & J. Ford (Eds.), *Encyclopedia of psychological trauma* (pp. 511–516). Hoboken, NJ: John Wiley.

Kassam-Adams, N., Marsac, M., & Garcia-Espana (2009, November). *Evaluating screening and secondary prevention in the pediatric medical setting.* Poster presented at the 25th International Society for Traumatic Stress Studies Annual Meeting, Atlanta, GA.

Kazdin, A. E., & Nock, M. K. (2003). Delineating mechanisms of change in child and adolescent therapy: Methodological issues and research recommendations. *Journal of Child Psychology and Psychiatry, 44,* 1116–1129.

Kazak, A. E., Kassam-Adams, N., Schneider, S., Zelikovsky, N., Alderfer, M. A., & Rourke, M. (2006). An integrative model of pediatric medical traumatic stress. *Journal of Pediatric Psychology, 31,* 343–355.

Laor, N., Wiener, Z., Spiriman, S., & Wolmer, L. (2005). Community mental health in emergencies and mass disasters: The Tel-Aviv model. *Journal of Aggression, Maltreatment and Trauma, 10,* 681–694.

La Greca, A. M., & Silverman, W. K. (2009). Treatment and prevention of posttraumatic stress reactions in children and adolescents exposed to disasters and terrorism: What is the evidence? *Child Development Perspectives, 3,* 4–10.

Landau, J., Mittal, M., & Wieling, E. (2008). Linking human systems: Strengthening individuals, families, and communities in the wake of mass trauma. *Journal of Marital and Family Therapy, 34*(2), 193–209.

Layne, C. M., Pynoos, R. S., Saltzman, W. R., Arslanagic, B., Black, M., Savjak, N., et al. (2001). Trauma/grief-focused group psychotherapy: School-based postwar intervention with traumatized Bosnian adolescents. *Group Dynamics-Theory Research and Practice, 5,* 277–290.

Layne, C. M., Warren, J. S., Saltzman, W. R., Fulton, J. B., Steinberg, A. M., & Pynoos, R. S. (2006). Contextual influences on posttraumatic adjustment: Retraumatization and the roles of victimization, posttraumatic adversities, and distressing reminders. In L. A. Schein, H. I. Spitz, G. M. Burlingame, & P. R. Mushkin (Eds.), *Psychological effects of catastrophic disasters: Group approaches to treatment* (pp. 235–286). New York: Haworth.

Layne, C. M., Warren, J. S., Watson, P. J., & Shalev. A. (2007). Risk, vulnerability, resistance, and resilience: Toward an integrative conceptualization of posttraumatic adaptation. In M. J. Friedman T. M. Keane, & P. A. Resick (Eds.), *Handbook of PTSD: Science and practice* (pp. 497–520). New York: Guilford.

Lester, P., Leskin, G., Woodward, K., Saltzman, W., Nash, W., Mogil, C., Paley B., & Beardslee, W. (2011). Wartime deployment and military children: Applying prevention to science to enhance family resilience. In S. Mac Dermid Wadsworth & D. Riggs (Eds.), *Risk and Resilience in U.S. Military Families* (pp. 149–173). New York, NY: Springer Science & Business Media.

Macy, R. D., Behar, L., Paulson, R., Delman, J., Schmid, L., & Smith, S. F. (2004). Community-based, acute posttraumatic stress management: A description and evaluation of a psychosocial-intervention continuum. *Harvard Review of Psychiatry, 12,* 217–228.

Marans, S., Murphy, R., & Berkowitz, S. (2002). Police-mental health responses to children exposed to violence: The child development-community policing program. In M. Lewis

(Ed.), *Child and adolescent psychiatry: A comprehensive textbook* (3rd ed., pp. 1406–1416). Baltimore, MD: Lippincott, Williams and Wilkins.

Marsac, M., Kassam-Adams, N., Hildenbrand, A., Kohser, K., & Winston F. (2011). After the Injury: Initial evaluation of a web-based intervention for parents of injured children. *Health Education Research, 26*, 1–12.

Masten, A. S., Best, K. M., & Garmezy, N. (1990). Resilience and development: Contributions from the study of children who overcome adversity. *Development & Psychopathology, 2*, 425–444.

McFarlane, A., Policansky, S. K., & Irwin C. (1987). A longitudinal study of the psychological morbidity in children due to a natural disaster. *Psychological Medicine, 17*, 727–738.

Norris, F. H., & Bellamy, N. D. (2009). Evaluation of a national effort to reach Hurricane Katrina survivors and evacuees: The Crisis Counseling Assistance and Training Program. *Administration and Policy in Mental Health and Mental Health Services Research, 36*, 165–175.

Norris, F. H., Hamblen, J. L., & Rosen, C. S. (2009). Service characteristics and counseling outcomes: Lessons from a cross-site evaluation of crisis counseling after Hurricanes, Katrina, Rita, and Wilma. *Administration and Policy in Mental Health and Mental Health Services Research, 36*, 176–185.

Paolucci, E. O., Genuis, M. L., & Violato C. (2001). A meta-analysis of the published research on the effects of child sexual abuse. *Journal of Psychology, 135*(1), 17–36.

Pfefferbaum B., Nixon S. J., Krug R. S., Tivis, R., Moore, V. L., Brown, J. M., et al. (1999). Clinical needs assessment of middle and high school students following the 1995 Oklahoma City bombing. *American Journal of Psychiatry, 156*, 1069–1074.

Pine D. S., & Cohen J. A. (2002). Trauma in children and adolescents: Risk and treatment of psychiatric sequelae. *Biological Psychiatry, 51*, 519–531.

Pynoos, R. S., Frederick, C., Nader, K., Arroyo, W., Steinberg, A., Eth, S., et al. (1987). Life threat and posttraumatic stress in school-age children. *Archives of General Psychiatry, 44*(12), 1057–1063.

Pynoos, R. S., & Steinberg, A.M. (2006). Recovery of children and adolescents after exposure to violence: A developmental ecological framework. In A. F. Liberman & A. F. DeMartino (Eds.), *Interventions for children exposed to violence* (pp.17–43). New Brunswick, NJ: Johnson & Johnson Pediatric Roundtable, Series 6.

Pynoos, R. S., Steinberg, A. M., Schreiber M. D. & Brymer M. (2006). Children and families: A new framework for preparedness and response to danger, terrorism and trauma. In L. A. Schein, H. I. Spitz, G. M. Burlingame, & P. R. Mushkin (Eds.), *Psychological effects of catastrophic disasters: Group approaches to treatment* (pp. 85–112). New York: Haworth.

Saltzman, W. R. & Lester, P., Pynoos, R., Mogil, C., Green, S., Layne, C. M., & Beardslee, W. (2009). *FOCUS for Military Families: Individual Family Resiliency Training Manual* (2nd ed.). Unpublished manuscript.

Scheering, M. S., & Zeanah. C. H. (2001). A relational perspective on PTSD in early childhood. *Journal of Traumatic Stress, 14*(4), 799–815.

Schwartz, D., & Proctor, L. (2000). Community violence exposure and children's social adjustment in the school peer group: The mediating roles of emotion regulation and social cognition. *Journal of Consulting and Clinical Psychology, 68*, 670–683.

Silverman, W. K., & La Greca, A. M. (2002). Children experiencing disasters: Definitions, reactions, and predictors of outcomes. In A. M. La Greca, W. K. Silverman, E. M. Vernberg, & M. C. Roberts (Eds.), *Helping children cope with disasters and terrorism* (pp. 11–33). Washington, DC: American Psychological Association.

Silverman, W. K., Ortiz, C. D., Viswesvaran, C., Burns, B. J., Kolko, Putnam, F. W., & Amaya-Jackson, L. (2008). Evidence-based psychosocial treatment for children and adolescents exposed to traumatic events. *Journal of Clinical Child & Adolescent Psychology, 37*, 156–183.

Stallard, P., Velleman, R., Salter, E., Howse, I., Yule, W., & Taylor, G. (2006). A randomised controlled trial to determine the effectiveness of an early psychological intervention with children involved in road traffic accidents. *Journal of Child Psychology and Psychiatry and Applied Disciplines, 47*, 127–134.

Stein, B. D., Jaycox, L. H., Kataoka, S., Wong, M., Tu, W., Elliott, M. N., & Fink, A. (2003). A mental health intervention for school children exposed to violence: A randomized controlled trial. *Journal of the American Medical Association, 290*, 603–611.

Steinberg, A. M., Brymer, M. J., Steinberg J. R., & Pfefferbaum, B. (2006). Conducting research on children and adolescents after mass trauma. In F. Norris, M. Friedman, S. Galea, & P. Watson (Eds.), *Methods for disaster mental health research* (pp. 243–253). New York: Guilford.

Steinberg, A. M., & Ritzmann, R. F. (1990). A living systems approach to understanding the concept of stress. *Behavioral Science, 35*,138–146.

Tol, W. A., Komproe, I. H., Susanty, D., Jordans, M. J. D., Macy, R. D., & De Jong, J. T. V. M. (2008). School-based mental health intervention for political violence-affected children in Indonesia: A cluster randomized trial. *Journal of the American Medical Association, 300*, 655–662.

Vila, G., Porche L., & Mouren-Simeoni M. (1999). An 18-month longitudinal study of posttraumatic disorders in children who were taken hostage in their school. *Psychosomatic Medicine, 61*, 746–754.

Walsh, F. (1996). The concept of family resilience: Crisis and challenge. *Family Process, 35*, 261–281.

Walsh, F. (2006). *Strengthening Family Resilience* (2nd ed.). New York: Guilford.

Yule, W. (1992). Post traumatic stress disorders in child survivors of shipping disasters: The sinking of the 'Jupitor.' *Psychotherapy and Psychosomatics, 57*, 200–205.

CHAPTER

26 Prevention and Early Intervention Programs for Older Adults

Martha Strachan, Lisa S. Elwood, Ananda B. Amstadter, *and* Ron Acierno

Abstract

Although older age appears to be a protective factor against developing psychopathology subsequent to trauma exposure, factors associated with the aging process may complicate identification and treatment of PTSD in older persons. This chapter reviews the risk and protective factors associated with posttraumatic stress disorders in older adults, describes research on secondary prevention and early intervention programs for older adults exposed to potentially traumatic events, and provides recommendations for adaptation of extant early traumatic stress treatment programs to meet the needs of older adults.

Key Words: Older adults, trauma exposure, PTSD, risk and resiliency factors, early intervention

Introduction

Although approximately 65% of adults age 60 and older report they have experienced at least one potentially traumatic event (PTE) during their lifetime (Acierno et al., 2010; Norris, 1992), little is known about the correlates and outcomes associated with proximal PTE exposure in this population. Furthermore, experiences that typify aging (e.g., loss of social support, declining health) may complicate the development, course, presentation, and treatment of traumatic stress disorders. As such, it is unclear whether secondary prevention/early intervention programs developed for and evaluated on younger adult populations will be effective for elderly persons. This chapter reviews the extant literature on the factors associated with course and treatment of trauma-related psychopathology in older adults following PTE exposure. First, we review research examining the risk and resiliency factors associated with developing traumatic stress disorders in aging populations. Second, we summarize the available literature on existing community- and individual-level secondary prevention and early intervention programs that target older adults. Finally, we consider how evidence-based strategies for prevention of trauma-related psychiatric disorders in younger adult populations can be applied to design effective early programming for older adult populations.

Risk and Resiliency Factors in Older Adults Following PTE Exposure

Investigations examining correlates of PTSD in the general adult population suggest that female gender, poor social support, prior trauma exposure, and low socioeconomic status (SES) increase the risk of developing the disorder, while perceived social support, higher education, and higher income are associated with more positive health outcomes (e.g., Acierno et al., 2007; Brewin, Andrews & Valentine, 2000; Kilpatrick, et al., 2003). Studies that make explicit, age-based comparisons between older and younger adults suggest that older age is predictive of better mental health outcomes following PTEs, and that correlates associated with psychiatric health vary according to event type. The following sections consider the risk and protective factors associated with developing traumatic stress disorders in older adults following exposure to catastrophic events, physical and sexual assault, and elder mistreatment.

Following Exposure to Natural Disasters and Catastrophic Events

Older age appears to be a protective factor against trauma-related psychopathology following disaster exposure. In their review of the risk and protective factors associated with traumatic stress symptoms, Norris and colleagues (2002) found that older adults were less likely to experience significant emotional problems in the aftermath of a disaster (i.e., hurricane, terroristic attack, etc.) than younger adults. Similarly, among New York City residents exposed to the September 11th terrorist attacks, older adults were less likely to endorse PTSD symptoms than all other age groups (Galea et al., 2002). Furthermore, in a specific examination of age-related differences associated with mental health problems secondary to multiple hurricane exposure in one year, older Florida residents were less likely to endorse PTSD, generalized anxiety disorder, and major depressive disorder (MDD) symptoms than younger adults (Acierno, Ruggiero, Kilpatrick, Resnick, & Galea, 2006). Although low social support, poor health status, and prior exposure to traumatic events predicted psychiatric symptoms across age groups, socioeconomic risk factors (i.e., low income, postinsurance monetary losses, duration of displacement from one's home, etc.) increased the risk of psychopathology in older adults but not in younger adults. The researchers hypothesized that older adults are more likely to experience economic challenges (i.e., living on a fixed income) that prevent recovery from the unexpected financial expenditures commonly associated with natural disasters. The investigators reasoned that the inability to regain financial security contributed to hopelessness, depressive symptoms, and posttraumatic stress symptoms.

Following Exposure to Sexual and Physical Assault

Incident characteristics associated with physical and sexual assault appear to differ across age groups. Specifically, among sexual assault victims, older adults are more likely to be victimized by strangers at home and to require medical attention than are younger adults. Among physical assault victims, older adults are more likely to be victimized by armed or multiple assailants than are younger adults (e.g., Acierno et al., 2001).

To the extent that these factors increase the life-threatening nature of the traumatic event, one might assume that older adults experience higher rates of psychiatric problems following criminal victimization as compared to younger adults. However, large-scale epidemiological investigations that assess the prevalence of PTSD and related disorders, as well as studies that compare risk and protective factors associated with post-assault-related psychopathology, suggest that older age is once again a protective factor against the development of psychiatric problems following exposure to interpersonal violence. For example, results from the National Women's Study (Acierno et al., 2001) found that of women who had experienced physical or sexual assault, older women (i.e., those 55 and older) were less likely to develop PTSD or MDD than younger women (i.e., those ages 18 through 34). Furthermore, among older women, sexual assault and physical assault predicted only PTSD symptom clusters C (avoidance) and B (re-experiencing), respectively, whereas these assault types predicted full PTSD and MDD diagnostic criteria among younger women. Finally, unlike investigations examining risk factors associated with mental health sequelae postdisaster exposure, low income was correlated with increased avoidance and depressive symptoms in the younger but not older age groups and self-reported health status was not associated with increased risk of psychopathology in either age group.

Following Exposure to Elder Mistreatment

Research examining the risk and protective factors associated with the onset of trauma-related psychopathology following elder mistreatment (defined as the physical, sexual, emotional, or financial mistreatment or neglect of an older adult by a trusted other) is less well developed. It may be that certain subtypes of elder mistreatment (i.e., emotional and financial mistreatment, neglect), although known to be related to emotional distress, are not currently characterized by researchers or health professionals as sufficient PTSD Criterion A stressors (i.e., in that these events involved real or imagined life threat, and the victim responded with fear, horror, and/or helplessness); thus, these events are less likely to be reported to or identified by legal authorities and healthcare professionals. Investigations that demonstrate a relationship between elder mistreatment and traumatic stress disorders will provide a solid foundation for the adaptation and evaluation of treatment programs for abused older adults. Until such data are available, health providers, social service workers, and community educators should utilize current knowledge about victim and perpetrator characteristics to improve the identification of at-risk older adults.

VICTIM CHARACTERISTICS

Risk factors for elder mistreatment vary across gender, race, SES, prior victimization history, psychiatric history, and substance use (Bachman, 1994; Biggs, Manthorpe, Tinker, Doyle, & Erens, 2009; Breslau, Davis, Andreski, & Peterson, 1991; Hanson, Kilpatrick, Falsetti, & Resnick, 1995; Laumann, Leitsch, & Waite, 2008; Norris, 1992). In general, female gender, poor health status, low social support, physical and/or cognitive impairment, living with a spouse or family member, prior PTE exposure, and low SES increase the risk for elder mistreatment while strong social support, good health status, and higher SES were protective factors (Acierno et al., 2010; Biggs et al., 2009; Pillemer & Finkelhor, 1988; Racic, Kusmuk, Kozomara, Develnogic, & Tepic., 2006; Yaffe, Weiss, Wolfson, & Lithwick, 2007).

PERPETRATOR CHARACTERISTICS

Older adults are more likely to be abused by spouses or family members than by nursing aids and/or other health professionals (Biggs et al., 2009; Moon, Lawson, Carpiac, & Spaziano, 2006; Tatara, 1997; Zink & Fisher, 2007). Perpetrators of mistreatment are more likely to be male, older, and may have histories of substance use and social isolation (Biggs et al., 2009; Reay & Brown, 2001). Thus, psychological problems of individuals in an older adult's immediate environment may represent risk for mistreatment.

Community-level Prevention: Improving Access to Care, Detection, and Provider Education

To our knowledge, no studies have validated the use of community-level prevention programming to address the emotional health needs of older adults during the initial weeks following PTE exposure; thus, our discussion here is limited to summarizing those strategies that may reduce risk of PTSD in older adults by proxy of (a) increasing access to care, (b) improving screening efforts, and (c) training health professionals to recognize risk factors for traumatic stress disorders in older populations.

Access to Care

Older adults may be more likely than younger adults to experience barriers to mental healthcare (e.g., Bartels et al., 2004). Indeed, less than 3% of older adults report seeing a mental health professional, a rate lower than any other age group (Olfson & Pincus, 1996). First, older adults appear to perceive more stigma associated with receipt of psychiatric services than do younger adults (e.g., Zeitlin, Katona, D'Ath, & Katona, 1997). Second, older adults may experience limitations of physical mobility (e.g., chronic health conditions, ambulatory problems, and lack of transportation) that impede their ability to attend psychiatric services in person. Third, relative to younger adults, a higher percentage of older adults live in rural areas where psychiatric services may be unavailable (e.g., Smalley et al., 2010). Fourth, older adults may be unlikely to disclose victimization to health, social service, and legal professionals because the perpetrators of interpersonal violence are often the very individuals (i.e., spouses, children, and other cohabitants) on whom they rely for care. Indeed, relative to older adult self-report of mistreatment, agency reports appear to underestimate the prevalence of elder mistreatment. Fourth, physicians may be unlikely to diagnose older adults with PTSD or MDD or refer them to psychiatric services because they perceive common symptoms of these disorders (e.g., sleep and appetite disturbance, reduced participation in social activities) to be part of the normal aging process (e.g., German, Shapiro, & Skinner, 1985). Fifth, cohort effects associated with this generation (e.g., a "grin and bear it" attitude in the face of adversity, disdain for self-disclosure, etc.) may predispose older adults to a reluctance to endorse emotional symptoms.

INTEGRATED-CARE MODELS

Collaborative-care models of service delivery, sometimes referred to as patient-centered care, or "medical home"–styled care, may increase the likelihood that older adults will engage in mental health treatment (e.g., Bartels et al., 2004; Katon et al., 1997). Bartels and colleagues (2004) found that older adults with depression or substance use problems who received integrated health services (i.e., patients received psychiatric services administered by mental health professionals within the primary-care setting) were more likely to attend mental health appointments than older adults who received enhanced referral services (i.e., patients were referred by their primary care physician to receive psychiatric services at a mental health clinic, were given assistance with transportation and cost, and were afforded a short wait time between primary-care referral and the first appointment).

TARGETED OUTREACH MODELS

Targeted outreach and gatekeeper programs (e.g., Psycho-geriatric Assessment and Treatment in City Housing; the "PATCH" program) can facilitate older adult engagement in psychiatric services (e.g., McCarthy et al., 2009; Rabins et al., 2000). These programs train health professionals, peers, and "case finders" (i.e., individuals in the community such as bank tellers, supermarket cashiers, maintenance workers) to identify and refer older persons in need of psychiatric services. Successful models generally include the following components: (a) training of "lay" individuals to identify older adults at risk for developing psychiatric disorders, (b) referral to psychiatric nurses or other mental health professionals, and (c) in-home psychiatric evaluation. As mentioned, these are "proxy" interventions in that they are not focused on victims of PTEs per se but, rather, on the larger community of older adults.

Targeted outreach and collaborative care models of service delivery have typically focused on older adults with serious mental illness and depression, respectively. However, when informed by the research-identified, event-specific correlates of PTSD presented earlier in this chapter, such programs may effectively increase access to care for PTE-exposed older adults. Specifically, trauma-focused targeted outreach programs should emphasize training community case finders to (a) identify older adults most at risk for developing traumatic stress disorders (i.e., those who have been exposed to trauma, are poor, have low social support, have chronic health conditions, require assistance with activities of daily living; (b) notify the appropriate agency in the aftermath of criminal victimization (e.g., police), interpersonal violence (e.g., adult protective services), catastrophic event, or natural disaster (e.g., Red Cross); and (c) refer at-risk older adults for psychiatric evaluation via community outreach. Trauma-focused collaborative-care models should focus on training mental health professionals to provide evidence-based assessment and treatment for PTSD within the primary care or "medical home" setting.

ACCESS TO TRANSPORTATION

Older adults, particularly those with disabilities, have limited transportation options and thus are often unable to access social support, practical assistance, and/or medical care during the aftermath of a PTE. Specifically, physical and cognitive disability, declining vision, and worsening coordination or ambulation may prevent older adults from driving or from using public transportation without assistance. Furthermore, a high percentage of older adults live in rural areas that are often poorly served by public transportation. Thus, the provision of transportation to older adults (i.e., to medical appointments, the grocery store, social gatherings) following a PTE may serve as an informal, yet effective "prevention initiative" to reduce PTSD risk in older persons. National organizations such as Project ACTION and the National Center on Senior Transportation can provide disaster recovery teams with a valuable prevention resource: the coordination of transportation for at-risk seniors.

Detection

Efforts to facilitate the identification of traumatized older adults via reducing barriers to care will be effective only insofar as health and social service professionals are armed with sensitive screening measures to detect trauma exposure and related mental health symptoms. The following sections describe efforts to enhance identification of traumatized older adults who may be in need of psychiatric services.

SCREENING

Several investigations suggest that common PTSD screening instruments are valid for use with aging populations (Cook, Elhai, & Arean, 2005; van Zelst et al., 2003); thus, perhaps the most significant "screening" challenge that health providers face is not the detection of PTSD symptoms once an older adult patient discloses a PTE but the disclosure of the PTE itself, as event disclosure generally prompts medical professionals to administer behavioral health screens. Indeed, specific screening approaches may be required to facilitate PTE disclosure in older populations. With regard to the detection of elder mistreatment, research suggests that screening measures that use behaviorally specific, closed-ended questions increase the likelihood that older adults will disclose acts of interpersonal violence, emotional neglect, and financial exploitation (Acierno et al., 2010).

SPECIAL CONSIDERATIONS FOR COGNITIVELY IMPAIRED OLDER ADULTS

Cognitively impaired older adults may be unable to provide valid self-report about past trauma history. As such, health and social service providers should adopt a flexible, multi-informant assessment approach when cognitive impairment is present. Importantly, although early research indicated some usefulness of proxy reports (e.g., Pillemer & Finkelhor, 1988), more recent research suggests that the individuals who live with and/or provide care to older adults may in fact underestimate the incidence of mistreatment events (Strachan, Amstadter, & Acierno, 2010). Moreover, a recent study found that older adults with dementia can provide accurate and reliable information about past emotional events; thus, the presence of cognitive impairment should not deter professionals from interviewing vulnerable elders about traumatic events (Wiglesworth et al., 2010). Sentinels (i.e., individuals trained to identify elder mistreatment) may provide corroborative information with which to verify elder and proxy-informant reports.

PROFESSIONAL EDUCATION INITIATIVES

Training programs designed to enhance provider awareness of the prevalence, correlates, presentation, and course of traumatic stress symptoms in older patient populations may increase the identification and referral of older adults in need of psychiatric treatment. These curricula should include event-specific information about risk and resiliency factors associated with the development of psychopathology in trauma-exposed older adults.

Related to elder mistreatment, physicians report fewer than 2% of all elder mistreatment cases, despite the fact that older adults are frequently in contact with medical doctors, suggesting they may be unaware of warning signs for elder abuse and/or unsure how to execute mandatory reporting statutes (Rosenblatt, Cho, & Durance, 1996). Internal and emergency medicine residency programs are less likely to include elder-abuse education than family-medicine programs, suggesting that initiatives to increase physician awareness should target these programs first (Wagenaar, Rosenbaum, Herman, & Page, 2009). Furthermore, although 75% of hospital emergency departments in the United States have protocols for handling suspected child abuse and domestic violence, less than 30% have protocols for handling suspected elder mistreatment (McNamara, Rousseau, & Sanders, 1992). Thus, elder-abuse education programs should include information about mandatory reporting statutes and referral mechanisms for suspected cases. Indeed, research suggests that educational programs that focus on reporting procedures increase the likelihood that social service and health professionals will identify and refer positive cases (Anetzberger et al., 2000; Richardson, Kitchen, & Livingston, 2002).

Early Intervention Approaches: Adaptations for Older Adult Populations

In summary, if community-level initiatives improve the identification of older adults who would benefit from psychiatric services subsequent to PTE exposure (i.e., those who present with specific risk factors and who endorse traumatic stress symptoms), then health, social service, and legal professionals can refer these individuals to early interventions designed to mitigate the course of trauma-related psychopathology.

Research suggests that brief, cognitive-behavioral protocols delivered to individuals during the early aftermath of trauma exposure can alleviate the development of PTSD and related psychiatric disorders in at-risk populations (e.g., Bryant, Harvey, Dang, Sackville, & Basten, 1998; Litz, 2008). Although early findings are promising, few studies have tested these strategies on trauma-exposed older adults. Thus, here, we describe promising early interventions strategies for PTE-exposed older adults and consider how researchers may adapt extant protocols to address the needs of older populations.

Factors Associated with Aging: Content, Process, and Delivery of Treatment

Older adults may differ from younger adults across variables relevant to the content, process, and delivery of treatment (e.g., Gallagher-Thompson & Thompson, 1996). Related to treatment content, older adults tend to emphasize the somatic symptoms of PTSD or MDD over emotional and cognitive symptoms (e.g., Gray & Acierno, 2002). Thus, early interventions should include strategies that improve sense of physical well-being such as education about sleep hygiene, relaxation training, and deep breathing. Additionally, older adults may be less likely than younger adults to characterize certain events (e.g., physical or sexual mistreatment by a spouse or family member) as "traumatic" (e.g., Lindesay, 1996) reducing the likelihood they will disclose these events to health professionals or legal authorities. Thus, primary-care physicians and other "gatekeepers" to psychiatric services should provide older adult patients with psycho-education about health consequences associated with PTE exposure. Related to treatment process, the ability to retain and learn new information sometimes declines with advancing age, particularly for those at higher risk of assault (i.e., cognitively impaired adults). Thus, therapists may consider adopting the following strategies when delivering early PTSD treatment to older adults: (a) frequent repetition of therapeutic rationales and important concepts, (b) presentation of material through both visual and auditory modalities, and (c) selection of concrete treatment goals.

Finally, related to service delivery, older adults may experience limitations to physical mobility (e.g., chronic health conditions, ambulatory problems, lack of transportation) that prevent them from attending weekly, office-based therapy. Thus, evidence-based protocols delivered via community outreach, telehealth, the Internet, and/or other multimedia (e.g., video, DVD) formats, may provide effective contexts for service delivery to the subgroup of older adults (e.g., those who are physically impaired) who might otherwise be unable to receive psychiatric treatment.

Early Intervention for Catastrophic Event Exposure: Psychological First Aid

Researchers have criticized large-scale intervention initiatives to prevent postdisaster PTSD such as Critical Incident Stress Debriefing, citing the fact that such initiatives pathologize normal reactions to catastrophic events and characterize "traumatic stress" symptoms (e.g., emotional numbing, avoidance) as "maladaptive." Indeed, research presented earlier in this chapter suggests that these approaches may not best serve older victims of catastrophic events to the extent that they prioritize mental health needs over basic financial, medical, and housing needs. If older adults are the least likely age group to endorse PTSD symptoms in the months following disaster exposure, and if socioeconomic and health-related variables increase the likelihood that older adults will develop diagnostic symptom levels, then psychological first aid (e.g., Brymer et al., 2005) rather than formal debriefing approaches, may provide a viable "first response" approach to reduce negative mental health outcomes in this population. Psychological first aid approaches emphasize adaptive coping strategies and practical assistance, rather than formal individual or group counseling interventions; thus, these approaches are consistent with identified correlates of PTSD in postdisaster exposed older adults (e.g., low SES, poor health). First responders may employ a multiwave assessment/referral strategy to identify those older adults most at risk for developing traumatic stress disorders following a catastrophic event. At Wave 1 (several days to several weeks postdisaster), first responders should assess the health, financial, and housing status of older adults and route them to appropriate services. At Wave 2 (several weeks to several months postdisaster), first responders should assess the mental health status of older adults; those who endorse traumatic stress symptoms should be referred to psychiatric professionals for follow-up and possible therapeutic services.

Early Intervention for Criminal Victimization: Psycho-education and Coping Skills Training

To our knowledge, only one study has specifically examined an early intervention strategy in an older adult sample exposed to criminal victimization. Acierno and colleagues (2004) (examined a brief, video-based intervention for older adult (age 55 and older) victims of crime. Individuals who reported criminal victimization to local authorities within the previous four weeks viewed a 15-minute video and were provided with a corresponding brochure. The video included psycho-education about normal responses to trauma, safety planning, and coping skills training (e.g., increased participation in pleasant events, in vivo exposure to trauma cues) to prevent development of traumatic stress symptoms. Participants who received the intervention displayed better understanding of (a) negative consequences of behavioral avoidance, (b) positive consequences of behavioral activation, (c) typical emotional responses to exposure-based treatment for anxiety, (d) substance abuse prevention strategies, and (e) safety planning skills. However, despite knowledge gains, participants in both the active and control conditions reported comparable levels of PTSD and MDD symptoms six weeks postintervention. Importantly, despite presumptions that older adults may find technology-based interventions aversive, 96% of the participants who received the active condition described the video as helpful.

Early Intervention for Complicated Bereavement: Behavioral Activation and Therapeutic Exposure

Complicated bereavement (CB) refers to a heightened emotional response following the death of a loved one that includes traumatic stress symptoms (e.g., numbing, sense of foreshortened future, etc.) along with grief specific responses (Prigerson et al., 1999). Some hypothesize that CB is a variant of PTSD (Windholz, Marmar & Horowitz, 1985). Indeed, bereavement and PTSD share a common symptom presentation, course, and response to treatment (Acierno et al., 2006; Parkes & Weiss, 1983; Reed, 1998; Windholz et al., 1985). In their review of grief counseling programs, Allumbaugh and Hoyt (1999) noted that effective programs generally emphasize behavioral strategies and are brief in duration.

Acierno and colleagues (2011) investigated the effectiveness of a brief, behavioral-activation and exposure-based protocol for adults experiencing complicated bereavement. Behavioral Activation and Therapeutic Exposure (BA-TE), a five-session, multimedia-based intervention was delivered to 26 older adults who recently experienced the death of a loved one. At posttreatment, participants displayed fewer symptoms of depression and traumatic stress. Furthermore, participants reported increased quality of life. Although no control condition was included, this pilot study provides preliminary evidence that (a) interventions targeting behavioral avoidance and withdrawal can reduce negative mental health and functional outcomes when delivered during the initial weeks following the death of a loved one, and (b) older adults tolerate technology-based models of service delivery.

Early Intervention for Elder Mistreatment: Social Support and ADL Management

As little research has investigated development of psychiatric disorders subsequent to elder mistreatment, early interventions for elder mistreatment should focus on strengthening factors that will promote resiliency: improving social support and managing activities of daily living (ADLs).

SOCIAL SUPPORT

Programs that increase social engagement have been linked to improved cognitive acuity, increased longevity, and better quality of life in older adults (e.g., Dupuis-Blanchard, Neufeld, & Strang, 2009; Zunzunegui, Alvarado, Teldoro, & Otero, 2003). By definition social support initiatives have characteristically "low threshold" inclusion criteria for involvement and referral; indeed, older adults do not require a mental health diagnosis or professional referral in order to volunteer for local non-profit organizations, attend religious services, or have weekly coffee dates with friends or neighbors. Such initiatives may circumvent the barriers to care often experienced by older adults (e.g., low disclosure rates) because health and social service professionals do not have to identify high-risk cases to recommend increased social participation.

ADL MANAGEMENT

Older adults who require assistance with ADLs may benefit from interventions that improve independent living skills. Programs to increase self-efficacy and reduce reliance on others for daily care (e.g., Phelan, Williams, Penninx, LoGerfo, & Leveille, 2004) have been effective when delivered in primary care (e.g., Leveille et al., 1998); thus, provider trainings and dissemination efforts to bring these interventions to primary-care clinics may provide an additional "low threshold" prevention effort to reduce risk of elder mistreatment.

Furthermore, physicians who treat impaired older adults are in a unique position to refer caregivers, often the perpetrators of mistreatment, to social support services as these individuals typically accompany their loved ones to healthcare appointments. Some research suggests that even Internet-based social support networks relieve stress associated with caregiver burden (Colvin, Chenowith, Bold, & Harding, 2004). To the extent that caregiver burden is associated with either the frequency or intensity of elder mistreatment, these programs may offer primary prevention for elder mistreatment.

Summary and Conclusions

Current understanding of effective secondary prevention and early intervention strategies to reduce the development of traumatic stress disorders in at-risk older adults is limited by lack of research on the effects of trauma exposure on aging populations. Thus, researchers should prioritize investigations that compare the correlates, symptom presentation, and course of PTSD across age groups and traumatic event types. These data will inform the adaptation of evidence-based prevention and early intervention protocols for PTE-exposed older adults.

Research reviewed in the current chapter suggests the following:

1. Older adults present with unique risk and resiliency factors. Older adults present with unique risk and resiliency factors related to the

development and course of traumatic stress disorders following PTE exposure; these factors vary across event type.

2. Identification and referral of at-risk older adults requires increasing access to care. Community-level prevention and early intervention initiatives should focus on increasing access to care, improved screening for PTE exposure and traumatic stress symptoms in medical settings, and provider trainings to enhance the identification of PTSD in aging populations. Collaborative care and targeted outreach models of service delivery may increase detection of mentally ill seniors and improve engagement in psychiatric services. Informal community initiatives such as provision of transportation to vulnerable seniors may promote resiliency during the aftermath of a PTE.

3. Older adults respond well to interventions that promote engagement in social activities. Researchers should adapt evidence-based early intervention programs to meet the needs of seniors. Informed by factors associated with aging and the current knowledge base on risk and resiliency in PTE-exposed older adults, these programs may reduce risk of PTSD and related disorders. Current findings indicate that video-based early intervention programs that include behavioral activation components that emphasize social interaction are feasible and likely to be well received by older crime victims and older adults who have recently lost a loved one (Acierno et al., 2011).

4. Informal prevention and intervention strategies may provide the best "treatment" alternative for older adults. Given that older age is a protective factor against PTSD, informal strategies may provide necessary and sufficient prevention of traumatic stress symptoms in PTE-exposed seniors. Specifically, offering one's older neighbor a ride to the grocery store, medical appointment, or church may promote resiliency in the aftermath of a traumatic event. Furthermore, efforts to promote social engagement (e.g., taking one's older neighbor to the movies) may provide a simple low threshold "intervention" solution for a patient population who may be unlikely to disclose PTEs or emotional distress to health, legal, or social service professionals. Indeed, research on older adults following disasters, interpersonal violence, and mistreatment indicates that social support may be the most consistent predictor of resiliency and recovery. Fortunately, it is also among the least expensive and simplest community-based interventions to initiate.

References

Acierno, R., Rheingold, A., Amstadter, A., Kurent, J., Amella, E., Resnick, H.,...Lejuez, C.. Behavioral activation and therapeutic exposure for bereavement in older adults. *American Journal of Hospice and Palliative Medicine*, Published online before print June 17, 2011, doi: 10.1177/1049909111411471.

Acierno, R., Gray, M., Best, C., Resnick, H., Kilpatrick, D., Saunders, B., et al. (2001). Rape and physical violence: Comparison of assault characteristics in older and younger adults in the National Women's Study. *Journal of Traumatic Stress, 14*, 685–695.

Acierno, R., Hernandez, M., Amstadter, A., Resnick, H., Steve, K., Muzzy, W., et al. (2010). Prevalence and correlates of emotional, physical, sexual, neglectful, and financial abuse in the United States: The National Elder Mistreatment Study. *American Journal of Public Health, 100*, 292–297.

Acierno, R., Rheingold, A., Resnick, H., & Stark-Riemer, W. (2004). Preliminary evaluation of a video-based intervention for older adult victims of violence. *Journal of Traumatic Stress, 17*, 535–541.

Acierno, R., Ruggiero, K., Galea, S., Resnick, H. S., Koenen, K., Roitzsch, J., et al. (2007). Psychological sequelae resulting from the 2004 Florida Hurricanes: Implications for postdisaster intervention. *Research and Practice, 97*, S103-S108.

Acierno, R., Ruggiero, K., Kilpatrick, D., Resnick, H., & Galea, S. (2006). Risk and protective factors for psychopathology among older versus younger adults after the 2004 Florida hurricanes. *American Journal of Geriatric Psychiatry, 14*, 1051–1059.

Allumbaugh, D., & Hoyt, W. (1999). Effectiveness of grief therapy: A meta-analysis. *Journal of Counseling Psychology, 46*, 370–380.

Anetzberger, G., Palmisano, B., Sanders, M., Bass, D., Dayton, C., Eckert, S., et al. (2000). A model intervention for elder abuse and dementia. *The Gerontologist, 40*, 492–497.

Bachman, R. (1994). *Violence against women. A national crime victimization survey report.* NCJ Publication No. 145325. Rockville, MD: Justice Statistics Clearinghouse/NCJRS.

Bartels, S., Coakley, E., Zubritsky, C., Ware, J., Miles, K., Arean, P., et al. (2004). Improving access to geriatric mental health services: A randomized trail comparing treatment engagement with integrated versus enhanced referral care for depression, anxiety and at-risk alcohol use. *American Journal of Psychiatry, 161*, 1455–1462.

Biggs, S., Manthorpe, J., Tinker, A., Doyle, M., & Erens, B. (2009). Mistreatment of older people in the United Kingdom: Findings from the first national prevalence study. *Journal of Elder Abuse and Neglect, 21*, 1–14.

Breslau N., Davis C., Andreski P., & Peterson, E. (1991). Traumatic events and posttraumatic stress disorder in an urban population of young adults. *Archives General Psychiatry, 48*, 216–222.

Brewin, C., Andrews, B., & Valentine, J. (2000). Meta-analysis of risk factors for posttraumatic stress disorder in trauma-exposed adults. *Journal of Consulting and Clinical Psychology, 68*, 748–766.

Bryant, R., Harvey, A., Dang, S., Sackville, T., & Basten, C. (1998). Treatment of acute stress disorder: A comparison of cognitive-behavioral therapy and supportive counseling. *Journal of Consulting and Clinical Psychology, 66*, 862–866.

Brymer, M., Jacobs, A., Layne, C., Pynoos, R., Ruzek, J., Steinberg, A.,...Watson, P. (National Child Traumatic Stress

Network/National Center for PTSD) (2005). *Psychological first aid: Field operations guide, 2nd Edition.* July 2006. Available at: www.nctsn.org and www.ncptsd@va.gov

Colvin, J., Chenowith, L., Bold, M., & Harding C. (2004). Caregivers of older adults: Advantages and disadvantages of Internet-based social support. *Family Relations, 53,* 49–57.

Cook, J., Elhai, J., & Arean, P. (2005). Psychometric properties of the PTSD Checklist with older primary care patients. *Journal of Traumatic Stress, 4,* 371–376.

Dupuis-Blanchard, S., Neufeld, A., & Strang, V. (2009). The significance of social engagement in relocated older adults. *Quality Health Research, 19,* 1186–1195.

Galea, S., Ahern, J., Resnick, H., Kilpatrick, D., Bucuvalas, M., Gold, J., et al. (2002). Psychological sequelae of the September 11 terrorist attacks in New York City. *New England Journal of Medicine, 346,* 982–987.

Gallagher-Thompson, D. & Thompson, L. (1996). Applying cognitive-behavioral therapy to the psychological problems of later life. In S. Zarit & B. Knight (Eds.), *A guide to psychotherapy and aging: Effective clinical interventions in a life-stage context* (pp. 61–82). Washington, DC: American Psychological Association.

German, P., Shapiro, S., & Skinner, E. (1985). Mental health of the elderly: Use of health and mental health services. *Journal of American Geriatric Society, 33,* 247–252.

Gray, M., & Acierno, R. (2002). Symptom presentations of older adult crime victims: Description of a clinical sample. *Journal of Anxiety Disorders, 16,* 299–309.

Hanson, R., Kilpatrick, D., Falsetti, S., & Resnick, H. (1995). Violent crime and mental health. In J. R. Freedy & S. E. Hobfoll (Eds.), *Traumatic stress: From theory to practice* (pp. 129–161). New York: Plenum Press.

Katon, W., Von Korff, M., Lin, E., Simon, G., Walker, E., Bush, T., et al., (1997). Collaborative management to achieve depression treatment guidelines. *Journal of Clinical Psychiatry, 58,* 20–23.

Kilpatrick, D., Ruggiero, K., Acierno, R., Saunders, B., Resnick, H., & Best C. (2003). Violence and risk of PTSD, major depression, substance use/dependence, and comorbidity: Results from the national survey of adolescents. *Journal of Clinical and Consulting Psychology, 71,* 692–700.

Laumann, E., Leitsch, S., & Waite, L. (2008). Elder mistreatment in the United States: Prevalence estimates from a nationally representative study. *Journal of Gerontology, 63,* S248-S254.

Leveille, S., Wagner, E., Davis, C., Davios, C., Grothaus, L., Wallace, J., LoGerfo, M., & Kent, D. (1998). Preventing disability and managing chronic illness in frail older adults: A randomized trial of a community-based partnership with primary care. *Journal of the American Geriatrics Society, 46,* 1191–1198.

Lindesay, J. (1996). Elderly people and crime. *Reviews in Clinical Gerontology, 6,* 199–204.

Litz, B. (2008). Early intervention for trauma: Where are we and where do we need to go? A commentary. *Journal of Traumatic Stress, 21,* 503–506.

McCarthy, J., Valenstein, M., Dixon, L., Visnic, S., Blow, F., & Slade, E. (2009). Initiation of assertive community treatment among veterans with serious mental illness: Client and program factors. *Psychiatric Services, 60,* 196–201.

McNamara R., Rousseau E., & Sanders A. (1992). Geriatric emergency medicine: A survey of practicing emergency physicians. *Annals of Emergency Medicine, 21,* 796–801.

Moon, A., Lawson, K., Carpiac, M., & Spaziano, E. (2006). Elder abuse and neglect among veterans in greater Los Angeles: Prevalence, types, and intervention outcomes. *Journal of Gerontological Social Work, 46,* 187–204.

Norris, F. (1992). Epidemiology of trauma: Frequency and impact of different potentially traumatic events on different demographic groups. *Journal of Clinical and Consulting Psychology, 60,* 409–418.

Norris, F., Friedman, M., Watson, P., Byrne, C., Diaz, E., & Kaniasty, K. (2002). 60,000 Disaster Victims Speak: Part 1 An Empirical Review of the Empirical Literature 1981–2001. *Psychiatry, 65,* 207–239.

Olfson, M., & Pincus, H. (1996). Outpatient mental health care in nonhospital settings: Distribution of patients across provider groups. *American Journal of Psychiatry, 153,* 1353–1356.

Parkes, C., & Weiss, R. (1983). *Recovery from bereavement.* New York: Basic Books

Phelan, E., Williams, B., Penninx, B., LoGerfo, J., & Leveille, S. (2004). Activities of daily living function and disability in older adults in a randomized trial of the Health Enhancement Program. *Journals of Gerontology Series A: Biological Sciences and Medical Sciences, 59,* 838–843.

Pillemer, K. & Finkelhor, D. (1988). The prevalence of elder abuse: A random sample survey. *The Gerontologist, 28,* 51–57.

Prigerson, H., Shear, M., Jacobs, S., Reynolds, C., Maciejewski, P., Davidson, J., et al. (1999). Consensus criteria for traumatic grief. A preliminary empirical test. *British Journal of Psychiatry, 174,* 67–73.

Rabins,V., Black, B., Roca, R., German, P., McGuire, M., Robbins, B., et al. (2000). Effectiveness of a nurse-based outreach program for identifying and treating psychiatric illness in the elderly. *Journal of the American Medical Association, 283,* 2802–2809.

Racic, M., Kusmuk, S., Kozomara, L., Develnogic, B., & Tepic, R. (2006). The prevalence of mistreatment among the elderly with mental disorders in primary healthcare settings. *Journal of Adult Protection, 8,* 20–24.

Reay, A., & Brown, K. (2001). Risk factor characteristics in careers who physically abuse or neglect their elderly dependents. *Aging and Mental Health, 5,* 56–62.

Reed, M. (1998). Predicting grief symptomatology among the suddenly bereaved. *Suicide and Life-Threatening Behavior, 28,* 285–301.

Richardson, B., Kitchen, G., & Livingston, G. (2002). The effect of education on knowledge and management of elder abuse: A randomized controlled trial. *Age and Ageing, 31,* 335–341.

Rosenblatt D., Cho K., & Durance, P. (1996). Reporting mistreatment of older adults: The role of physicians. *Journal of the American Geriatric Society, 4,* 65–70.

Smalley, K., Yancey, C., Warren, J., Naufel, K., Ryan, R., & Pugh, J. (2010). Rural mental health and psychological treatment: A review for practitioners. *Journal of Clinical Psychology, 66,* 479–489.

Strachan, M., Amstadter, A., & Acierno, R. (2010). Proxy versus older adult report of elder mistreatment: The National Elder Mistreatment Study. Paper presented at the annual convention of the *American Psychology-Law Society,* Vancouver, BC.

Tatara, T. (1997). *The National Elder Abuse Incidence Study: Executive Summary.* New York: Human Services Press.

van Zelst, W., de Beurs, E., Beekman, D., Beekman, A., Deeg, D., Bramsen, I., et al. (2003). Criterion validity of the self-rating inventory for posttraumatic stress disorder in the community of older adults. *Journal of Affective Disorders, 76*, 229–235.

Wagenaar, D, Rosenbaum, R., Page, C., & Herman, S. (2009). Elder abuse education in residency programs: How well are we doing? *Academic Medicine, 84*, 611–618.

Wiglesworth, A., Mosqueda, L.,Mulnard, R., Liao, S., Gibbs, L., & Fitzgerald, W. Screening for abuse and neglect of people with dementia. *Journal of the American Geriatrics Society, 58*(3), 493–500.

Windholz, M., Marmar, C., & Horowitz, M. (1985). A review of the research on conjugal bereavement: Impact on health and efficacy of intervention. *Comprehensive Psychiatry, 26*, 433–447.

Yaffe, M., Weiss, D., Wolfson, C., & Lithwick, M. (2007). Detection and prevalence of abuse of older males: Perspectives from family practice. *Journal of Elder Abuse and Neglect, 19*, 47–60.

Zeitlin, D., Katona, C., D'Ath, P., & Katona, P. (1997). Attitudes to depression in primary care attenders: Effects of age and depressive symptoms. *Primary Care Psychiatry, 3*, 17–20.

Zink, T., & Fisher, B. (2007). Older women living with intimate partner violence. *Aging Health, 3*, 257–265.

Zunzunegui, M., Alvarado, A, Teldoro, D., & Otero, A. (2003). Social networks, social integration, and social engagement determine cognitive decline in community-dwelling Spanish older adults. *Journals of Gerontology, 58*, S93–S100.

CHAPTER

27 Prevention and Early Intervention Programs for Special Populations

Heather E. Baldwin *and* B. Heidi Ellis

Abstract

Special populations have unique issues that need to be considered in the development and delivery of prevention and early intervention models. For these individuals, social context or stressors and support within their social environments may be particularly critical to consider in the wake of a traumatic exposure. In this chapter, we will discuss some of the environmental factors that are important to consider when planning and implementing prevention and early intervention programs for special populations and explore these factors in the case of refugee children.

Key Words: Special populations, trauma, prevention, early intervention, refugee, social environment

Introduction

Although some approaches to prevention and early intervention may be broadly applicable with trauma survivors, special populations have unique issues that need to be considered in the development and delivery of prevention and early intervention models. Special populations may include racial and ethnic minorities, refugees or immigrants, homosexual individuals, victims of domestic violence, young children, prisoners, cognitively impaired individuals, homeless individuals, and individuals with developmental disabilities (Flaskerund & Winslow, 1998; McGarry, Clarke, Landau, & Cyr, 2008; Redman, 2007). Although these populations are heterogeneous and likely to present with very different needs in the aftermath of a traumatic exposure, they share an increased vulnerability to health disparities due to their marginalized social status. For these individuals, social context or stressors and support within their social environments may be particularly critical to consider in providing prevention and early intervention in the wake of a traumatic exposure.

This chapter uses the socio-ecological model to describe the ways in which prevention and early intervention programs may benefit from taking into account the social context as experienced by special populations. The socio-ecological model (see figure 27.1) is based on Bronfennbrenner's (1977) ecology of human development. Bronfennbrenner (1977) divides an individual's environment into progressively broader levels including the microsystem, mesosystem, exosystem, and macrosystem. In this chapter, we will focus primarily on the microsystem. The microsystem encompasses the immediate settings within which an individual resides (Bronfennbrenner, 1977), including home, school, work, neighborhood, and any other settings with which the individual has direct interactions with others. In this model, the individual is embedded within the family, his or her institutions (i.e., work, school), and the person's community. The health and functioning of the individual is in part determined by his or her interactions with the different levels of the social ecology; disruptions within these layers of

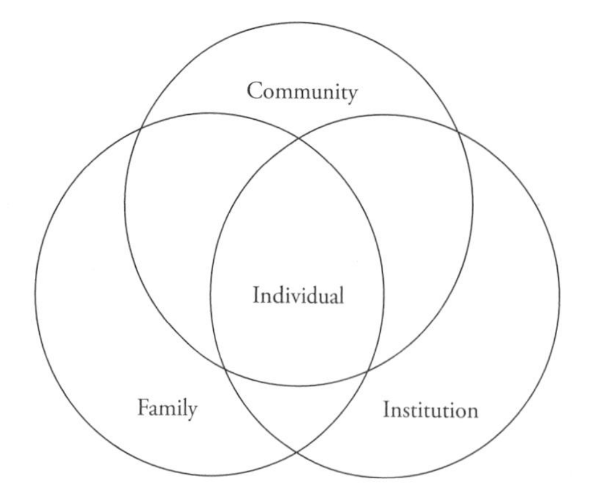

Figure 27.1. Overlapping microsystems in an individual's social ecology.

the social ecology can have profound implications for the individual.

Hobfoll and colleagues (1995) have suggested that trauma leads to a loss of resources across multiple levels of the social ecology, and that these losses must be attended to as fundamental aspects of prevention and early intervention. Such loss of resources may be layered on top of an already disadvantaged status of certain populations. Individuals who have been marginalized within society often face increased stress within the various levels of the social ecology, and may have less access to resources (Link & Phelan, 2001). Layering traumatic events and associated loss of resources on top of an already disadvantaged status may place individuals at particularly high risk for the development of mental health problems.

Prevention and early intervention efforts with these populations must, therefore, include a focus not only on the individuals but also on their environments. Prevention programs with a focus on the environment may even reduce the likelihood that the individuals will be exposed to further potentially traumatic events (PTEs). Early intervention programs can help individuals to cope with exposure through enhancing and leveraging the existing capabilities of these individuals' environment to support healthy recovery and processing of their experiences.

In this chapter, we will first discuss some of the environmental factors that are important to consider when planning and implementing prevention and early intervention programs for special populations. We will then explore these factors in the case of refugee children and present some current prevention and intervention programs that address these environmental factors.

The Social Ecology of Trauma

Posttraumatic Stress Disorder (PTSD) is intrinsically linked to the social environment; embedded in the definition is both exposure to a traumatic event within the social environment and the presence of symptoms in response to reminders of the event. PTSD also appears to be more likely to develop in the context of exposure to ongoing nontraumatic stressors, as is illustrated through the developmental psychopathology trauma model described by Pynoos, Steinberg, and Piacentini (1999). In this model, the development of PTSD is determined jointly by exposure to a traumatic event and exposure to stressors in the proximal and distal aftermath of the event. There is evidence within special populations that stressors in the social environment contribute to the likelihood of experiencing mental health problems. For example, in a sample of Somali adolescent refugees, the number of traumatic events experienced was significantly related to PTSD and depression symptoms, but once social environmental stressors such as discrimination were taken into account, the strength of the association between trauma exposure and mental health symptoms diminished for PTSD and became nonsignificant for depression (Ellis, MacDonald, Lincoln, & Cabral, 2008). Katz and Nevid (2005) found, through bivariate correlations, that for women diagnosed with HIV, more physical symptoms, more past traumatic events, lower satisfaction with social support, higher negative current life change, and higher perceived stigma were all associated with PTSD symptomatology. Hierarchical multiple regression revealed that past traumatic events were not predictive of PTSD symptomotolgy. In fact, the significant predictors were all environmental factors: current negative life change, number of HIV physical symptoms, and stigma.

Immediate Needs

In the wake of certain types of trauma, the ability to meet an individual's basic needs may be profoundly disrupted. Natural disasters such as Hurricane Katrina may leave individuals without access to basic food and shelter. Gaining access to resources to meet these basic needs may be particularly challenging for individuals who are already disadvantaged. For example, someone with a physical disability may have trouble moving around in a rubble-strewn street and may be unable to leave the home in order to reach temporary shelters (Brodie, Weltzien, Altman, Blendon, & Benson, 2006).

Individuals with cognitive disabilities may have difficulty understanding what services and resources they are entitled to receive. Immigrants who do not speak English may similarly have difficulty identifying where and how to access resources that have been put in place. Attention to how early intervention is made accessible to special populations needs to be considered. In these cases, interventions such as the Specialized Crisis Counseling Services (SCCS) provided by the Mississippi Department of Mental Health in the wake of Hurricane Katrina may be particularly effective. The SSCS program linked individuals with resources to meet their postdisaster immediate needs in addition to mental health counseling services (Jones, Allen, Norris, & Miller, 2009). In this intervention, each client was served by a team that included a resource coordinator who helped clients to access local community resources associated with housing, employment, financial assistance, physical health, transportation, social support, and recreation. In an evaluation of the program, Jones and colleagues (2009) found that clients were significantly more satisfied with the SSCS intervention than with a comparable intervention that focused only on mental health counseling. This indicates that the provision of access to resources for immediate needs may have been an important aspect of client satisfaction with the intervention.

Other types of trauma may affect the individual but not change the basic availability of resources. For individuals who are already struggling to have their basic needs met, however, the urgency of these basic needs may remain a primary target of early intervention. For instance, for homeless individuals, basic housing is their first and most important need (Goodman, Saxe, & Harvey, 1991) and may need to be addressed before focusing on trauma and traumatic responses.

Although mental health professionals do not always provide basic services (e.g., housing, transportation, help seeking employment, provisions for food) for their clients, this can often be an important barrier that individuals face in overcoming traumatic stress. In fact, some of these needs may cause further traumatization in the form of homelessness, malnutrition, or isolation. Clients may even be forced to live in neighborhoods where they are daily witnesses to and occasionally victims of violence and aggression. These circumstances may also serve as triggers that remind the individual of a traumatic event, such as past abuse or hardship (Saxe, Ellis, & Kaplow, 2007). As such, meeting these basic needs or helping the individual to succeed in having these needs met may be an important first step in providing care for vulnerable individuals.

The Family

Social support has been identified as a critical factor in facilitating recovery from trauma exposure (Charuvastra & Cloitre, 2008). Although family is often a central source of social support, within some populations family support may be compromised. For some individuals such as victims or witnesses of domestic violence, the family may be the location of the traumatic exposure. For these families, interventions such as Parent-Child Interaction Therapy (PCIT) may be an important first step in trauma prevention. The PCIT model, originally developed for children with disruptive behaviors, has been adapted for physically abusive families by Chaffin and colleagues (2004). The intervention was found to be significantly more effective at reducing rates of future child abuse than standard community-based groups (Chafin et al., 2004). By focusing on reducing rates of abuse and thus exposure to PTEs, this intervention may also prove effective in preventing trauma-related symptoms.

A family's ability to provide support may also be compromised by its own exposure to traumatic events (Barenbaum, Ruchkin, & Schwab-Stone, 2004). This is particularly true for families exposed to violent neighborhoods, such as the urban poor (Kiser & Black, 2005); families exposed to natural disasters, such as Hurricane Katrina (Rowe & Liddle, 2008); and families exposed to war, such as refugees (Weine, 2008). In these cases, addressing the needs of the individual may also entail addressing the needs of his or her immediate family members in order to reduce the individual's exposure either directly or vicariously to trauma.

For others, the family can provide invaluable support and help individuals to exhibit remarkable resilience in the face of PTEs (Gerwitz, Forgatch, & Weiling, 2008). For these families, prevention and early intervention programs can leverage the family strengths in order to help individuals who have been exposed to PTEs. Programs with these families may focus on educating them about PTSD and the ways in which they can recognize symptoms and provide support for their family members. Leveraging social support has been recommended as an area to explore in early intervention for trauma generally (Litz, Gray, Bryant, & Adler, 2006), and may hold particular applicability in working with special populations where the family system may be under stress. The community-based intervention provided for adolescent survivors of the *Ehime Maru* sea accident is an example of a program that helped build family capacity to support traumatized adolescents. The accident involved a Japanese training vessel and resulted in the deaths of several high school students. Nurses and psychiatrists working with the Uwajima Health Center and the Uwijima Psychiatric Hospital were tasked by the Ehime prefectural government with the provision of services to the nine adolescent survivors of the accident. This early intervention included home visits every two to three weeks, weekly group meetings for the families, and intensive psychiatric treatment for the adolescents. The adolescents who received this intervention showed a significant decrease in their PTSD symptoms as measured by the Impact of Event Scale-Revised after eight months. Three years after the accident, the prevalence of PTSD had decreased. The authors attribute the success of the intervention to the combination of the treatments and attest to the importance of including a component to enhance families' self-help function.

Institutions

Institutions are often where individuals spend the majority of their time on a day-to-day basis. For children, this may be the school; for prisoners, it is the prison; and for immigrants, it may be their workplace. Although the family is clearly important to individuals' well-being, they may actually spend more of their time in this immediate institutional environment. The institution, like the family, can be both the source of PTEs such as bullying or sexual abuse (Carney, 2008; Struckman-Johnson, Struckman-Johnson, Rucker, Bumby, & Donaldson, 1996) and an important opportunity for strength and resilience building. If the institutional environment is the source of the trauma (e.g., the client is being abused by someone in the institution), prevention and early intervention programs must work with these institutions, when possible, to prevent the occurrence of these PTEs. For example, children with disabilities are particularly susceptible to bullying in the school environment because they are often different from their peers in some noticeable way (Hoover & Stenhjem, 2003). For these students, school-wide interventions such as the Olweus Bullying Prevention Program (OBPP) may be an effective method to reduce the extent to which all students, including those with disabilities, experience bullying.

The OBPP prevention targets the individual, the school, the classroom, and the community. Activities at the school level include school-wide teacher meetings and trainings for the entire staff, parent/teacher discussions, enhanced supervision during recreational activities/periods, improvement of children's play spaces, a formal survey, and the creation of an OBPP group to coordinate intervention activities (Ttofi, Farrington, & Baldry, 2008). In a meta-analysis of 59 bullying intervention programs, researchers found that several iterations and adaptations of the OBPP effectively reduced both bullying and victimization in schools across North America and Europe (Ttofi, Farrington, & Baldry, 2008). In some cases where workers in the organization are overworked or seldom present, an important aspect of these programs may be alerting the institution to the presence of these harmful instances.

The immediate environment may be particularly important for individuals who do not experience a supportive family life. In these cases, prevention and early intervention programs can educate staff at the institution on how to recognize the symptoms and consequences of exposure to PTEs. Staff can also be trained to help reduce potential trauma triggers in the environment of the institution. Ideally these programs can work with institution staff and administrators to create an environment that fosters the individual's own strengths and resilience.

The Community

The community refers to the broader socio-cultural context in which an individual resides. This may include a neighborhood, a religious community, a cultural community, or other groups with which an individual and his or her family are affiliated. In the case of individuals living in an unhealthy environment such as a violent neighborhood, the community may be the source of PTEs. Ethnic minorities and immigrants may be particularly likely to live in impoverished communities where community violence is present (Capps, Fix, Ost, Reardon-Anderson, & Passel, 2004). In these cases, prevention and early intervention programs should, when possible, address the systemic and overarching issues that lead to neighborhood violence. These programs may also include helping individuals to advocate for themselves and their community at higher levels of administration.

The community can also be a source of great strength and comfort for individuals who experience PTEs. Individuals may find that the support of their community and their beliefs provide them with the fortitude they need to deal with many different PTEs. Prevention and early intervention programs that focus on the community should work to connect individuals with their community and build on rather than refute cultural beliefs and practices. In this way, individuals can be supported in facing the PTEs in ways that are in line with their beliefs and their understanding of the way the world works.

The ADAPT (Adaptation and Development After Persecution and Trauma) early intervention model, used primarily with East Timorese refugees, is particularly relevant for early interventions in communities that are affected by trauma such as warfare or natural disasters (Silove, 2006). This model proposes that early interventions should focus on helping individuals feel safe, enhancing existing bonds between family and community members, highlighting issues of social injustices, offering valuable activities in the form of training for employment, and linking the families and community members to institutions that are meaningful, like mosques or community-run organizations (Silove, 2006). This model of early intervention has been used in Australia.

Case Example: Refugee Children as a Special Population

For the remainder of the chapter, we will focus on issues of prevention and early intervention for a particularly vulnerable population refugee children. According to the United Nations High General Assembly (1951) a refugee is someone who "owing to a well-founded fear of being persecuted for reasons of race, religion, nationality, membership of a particular social group or political opinion, is outside the country of nationality, and is unable to, or owing to such fear, is unwilling to avail himself of the protection of that country" (p. 137). In the year 2008 alone (United Nations High Commissioner for Refugees [UNHCR], 2009), there were 15.2 million refugees worldwide and 348,776 refugees and asylum seekers were residing in the United States (UNHCR, 2009). Worldwide children under 18 represent about 44% of all refugees and asylum seekers (UNHCR, 2009). Thus, in 2008, there were approximately 153,000 refugee and asylum-seeking children currently living in the United States.

By definition, refugee children and their families have been exposed to persecution and/or violence. This may include witnessing, perpetrating, or being victims of violence and warfare; internal displacement within their countries of origin; loss of family members and loved ones through death or separation; life in overcrowded refugee camps; abject poverty; life-threatening journeys out of their countries of origin; and many other potentially traumatic events (Amnesty International, 1999; Hodes, Jagdev, Chandra, & Cunniff, 2008). Thus, refugee youth can be considered a group that could benefit from selective prevention and early intervention programs.

In addition to their past exposure to potentially traumatic events, refugee children and their families who have relocated to the United States are faced with stress associated with acculturation. Some of the stresses associated with acculturation include having to learn a new culture and language, loss of social support, difficulties finding employment and achieving financial independence, and changes in traditional family roles (Lustig et al., 2004). In fact, some researchers argue that these ongoing stressors are as important, if not more important, to refugee children's current mental health and well-being as their past exposures to potentially traumatic events (Ellis et al., 2008; Miller et al., 2002).

Not all refugee children suffer negative psychological consequences as a result of their experiences. Factors such as being accompanied by their parents, lower exposures to potentially traumatic events, parent mental health, family cohesion, access to schools, social support, and active participation in the design and implementation of programs designed to help refugee children have been shown to increase their resilience (Barenbaum et al., 2004; de Berry & Boyden, 2000; Hodes et al., 2008). Despite some children's resilience, children and adolescents who are exposed to war, chronic violence, and forced migration are at risk for myriad psychological, physical, and behavioral consequences, such as traumatic stress disorders, depression, anxiety, psychic numbing, paranoia, insomnia, somatization, academic difficulties, and violent/problem behaviors (Birman et al.,; 2005; Lustig et al., 2004). In a meta-analysis of refugee mental disorders, Fazel, Wheeler, and Danesh (2005) found that 11% of refugee children were diagnosed with PTSD.

Despite the high prevalence rates of trauma-associated disorders in refugee youth, there is an alarming lack of evidence-based prevention and intervention programs. It is not within the scope of this chapter to review all of the existing mental health programs for refugees; this has been done elsewhere (Birman et al., 2005). In this chapter, we will highlight several prevention and early intervention programs that specifically address different aspects of the refugee child's social ecology.

Early Intervention and Prevention Programs for Refugee Youth

Addressing Immediate Needs: Case Management as an Early Intervention

International Family, Adult, and Child Environment Services (FACES) is a community-based refugee mental health program established in 1999 (Birman et al., 2008). The program was built from a longstanding history of providing services for multiple refugee and immigrant communities in the Chicago area. This initial exposure to the refugee communities and their establishment as an agency that meets many refugee needs (not just mental health needs) make this program unique. In addition to individual and family counseling, this program offers case-management services that help the families to meet their basic needs and communicate their experiences to other service providers.

In an assessment of the effectiveness of the International FACES program (Birman et al., 2008), the researchers reported that the largest percentage of the staff's time (22%) was spent not on mental health interventions but on case-management activities. Furthermore, the authors found that participants improved over the course of treatment on the Child and Adolescent Functional Assessment Scale (CAFAS). This suggests that an important part of a successful intervention with refugee children is helping families meet their immediate needs, as well as providing mental health specific interventions.

Bolstering Family Support as a Form of Selective Prevention

Weine (2008) argues that interventions that target only refugee children without taking into account the entire family will be limited in their ability to help the child. Weine and colleagues (2008) have developed a prevention model that focuses on the refugee family rather than on the child alone. The aim of this prevention is to target individuals who are at risk for developing a mental disorder, or individuals who have begun to show minimal symptoms of mental disorders, and provide services that focus on the strengths of the individual's family in order to prevent the development of mental disorders.

Youth CAFES was created to address the needs of Bosnian refugee 11–15-year-old adolescents living in Chicago, as expressed by the youth, their parents, and the Bosnian community in Chicago. Although the stated goal of the program is not to address symptoms of traumatic stress, the target behaviors of the program—high-risk behaviors—have been linked to trauma exposure in other refugee populations (Agaibi & Wilson 2005). The program consists of seven meetings with a group of refugee families; each meeting focuses on a predetermined topic, including (1) introductions and priority concerns, (2) urban adolescents and their families, (3) school life, (4) city life, (5) family talk, (6) family values and beliefs, and (7) planning and celebrating the future.

Weine and colleagues (2008) do not report on the effectiveness of these groups for reducing youth high-risk behaviors. However, in other research, Weine (2008) found that similar CAFES with adults with PTSD increased participants' access to mental health services. Further studies are indicated to determine if this family-based prevention/early intervention is effective in reducing youths' symptoms associated with exposure to trauma.

Integrating Early Intervention and Selective Prevention into the School Setting

Rousseau and Guzder (2008) contend that the school is the primary gateway through which refugee and immigrant youth access mental health treatment. As such, the school is an ideal setting for primary prevention and early intervention programs (Baan, 2007; Fazel & Stein, 2008; Gong-Guy, Cravens, & Patterson, 1991). One such program has been implemented in Bosnia and Herzegovina with adolescents exposed to war trauma (Layne et al., 2008). Although these adolescents are not refugees, they have been exposed to many of the same PTEs and thus have similar trauma histories as many refugee adolescents in the United States.

Layne and colleagues' (2008) school-based group psychotherapy program for war-exposed adolescents (TCGT) consists of approximately 20 sessions that fall into four modules: (1) psycho-education, (2) processing of PTEs; (3) beneficial grieving of losses, and (4) adaptive development. The goal of the program is to treat adolescents who have been exposed to potentially traumatic events and are at risk for the development of traumatic stress disorders.

In a randomized controlled trial with 127 students (66 in the full treatment condition) students attending secondary schools in Bosnia and Herzegovina, Layne and colleagues (2008) compared students who received the entire TCGT with students who participated only in the first two modules. They found that both the full and the abbreviated version of the program predicted reductions in PTSD and depression symptoms, and the full version predicted significant reductions in symptoms of maladaptive grief. In addition, participants in both conditions had significant improvement in PTSD symptoms four months after the treatment was finished. These results are very promising and represent one of the few rigorously evaluated school-based programs for children who have experienced war trauma.

It should be noted that the students in the above research were not refugees and were living in an environment where the majority of their peers had been exposed to similar PTEs (Layne et al., 2001). Implementing this program in a school setting where the majority of the students may not have been exposed to PTEs should involve careful consideration for refugee-specific issues that may arise. For example, Rousseau and Guzder (2008) suggests that trauma-focused groups for refugees in a school setting may place the children at risk for being stigmatized by other students and by their community. As such, some school-based programs, such as Pharos (Baan, 2007), intentionally avoid a focus on trauma and instead address general challenges and commonalities that refugee children share (Watters & Ingleby, 2004). Pharos is a school-based mental health program designed to reduce socio-emotional problems and enhance youths' resilience. The program was adapted and implemented in Sweden, Italy, the United Kingdom, Germany, Austria, and the Netherlands to address the needs of refugee school-age youth in each country. Unfortunately, there is no published evaluation data on the effectiveness of Pharos and other more general school-based programs in reducing traumatic stress and associated symptoms in refugee children.

Integrating Care Across Levels of the Social Ecology

Project SHIFA is a program serving Somali adolescents and provides services along a continuum of care and across different levels of the social ecology (Ellis, Miller, Baldwin, & Abdi, in press). Although delivery of a specific intervention model, termed Trauma Systems Therapy (Saxe et al., 2007) for youth who have developed trauma-related mental health problems is part of the model, access to this higher level of care is facilitated by the coordinated provision of prevention and early intervention broadly within the community. For the purpose of this chapter, we focus on early intervention aspects of the program.

One of the barriers that refugee youth face in accessing mental health care is the fact that in many refugee communities, mental health is rarely talked about and is highly stigmatized (Ellis et al., in press; Mann & Fazil, 2006). Refugees may thus be reluctant to seek out mental health services for their children. One way that services providers have found to address this challenge is to use a community-based participatory method and develop community partnerships (Ellis, Kia-Keating, Yusuf, Lincoln, & Nur, 2007). The implementation of this program thus begins with the community and the family's basic needs, and then addresses the proximal environment and the family and child's specific mental health needs. The community outreach component of Project SHIFA includes psycho-education in social group settings. These gatherings include members of the community at all levels and are not restricted to family members of Project SHIFA's patients. In this way, the program strives to build the understanding of mental health and children's needs at a broad community level, and to build on a community strength of supporting and advocating for the community's youth.

The intervention also engages refugee families by seeking active family involvement from the Somali community. This includes a parent advisory board that provides input on all aspects of the intervention, including the needs of their children and feedback on the previous activities of the intervention. Project SHIFA also works across the child's social ecology to connect the parents and families to the child's school. In a description of the program, Ellis and colleagues (in press) explain that parent involvement in school affairs is eschewed in Somali culture. Thus, encouraging this type of interaction with the school is an important aspect of helping to work across all levels of the child's social ecology in an effort to meet the best interests of the youth.

Project SHIFA is also located within a school setting where the clinicians lead skill-based group therapy. These groups focus on addressing specific stressors known to affect refugee youth and on building skills in emotion regulation. In addition to helping students develop necessary skills for succeeding in the school environment, the groups also allow staff members to get to know the students and their families. In addition to providing direct intervention in the school setting, project SHIFA works with school staff to provide an environment that supports the mental health of the Somali youth.

Future Directions

Given their marginalized status in society, special populations may experience and be affected by trauma in unique ways; early intervention and prevention efforts must take this into account. Any program developed for these populations must, therefore, work with community members to better understand the specific needs of that community. For refugee children, this means learning about cultural beliefs and values, and striving to help the community meet the needs that they prioritize. This cultural knowledge can help providers to contextualize trauma experiences and better understand the ways in which individuals' environments may hinder or support prevention and early intervention efforts.

Currently, there is insufficient research to understand the treatment needs of many special populations. Research with these populations is fraught with challenges that researchers working with mainstream populations do not have to face. In fact, the very fact of their "vulnerability" makes it more challenging to conduct the necessary research trials. For example, in research with patients with "mental disorders" that may affect their decision-making capabilities, there are questions about their ability to even consent to be part of a research study given their potentially limited ability to understand consent processes (Oldham, Haimowitz, & Delano, 1999). Despite the challenges associated with this research, high-quality prevention and early intervention programs require that we better understand how established models of early intervention and prevention work with these groups and if other models successfully meet the needs of these groups in the wake of a trauma.

In agreement with Hobfoll's (1991) suggestion that early intervention efforts specifically address resource losses, we have provided one lens for understanding commonalities across special populations and the importance of intervening in the social environment as a means of prevention/early intervention. This is particularly relevant as individual, psychologically based early interventions have not proved effective for all individuals exposed to PTEs (Litz et al., 2002). In order to fully understand the effectiveness of these resource-based prevention and early intervention programs, further research is needed to investigate how specific early intervention and prevention in the social ecology helps mitigate the effect of trauma in these disparate groups.

Finally, we need to consider how these special populations may have unique strengths and resiliencies that can be leveraged. For example, a child's parents can help to buffer the effects of PTEs (Thabet, Ibraheem, Shivram, Winter, & Vostanis, 2009). Family unity has been identified as an important family strength among Somali refugees (Detzner, Senyurekli, Yang, & Sheikh, 2009). This sense of family unity may help parents to buffer the effects that forced displacement, refugee camp conditions, and the challenges of resettlement and acculturation may have on Somali refugee children. Schwartzberg (1994) writes about the vitality and growth associated with gay men's HIV diagnosis. He reports that, as a result of HIV, the respondents were able to "discover internal resources that had never previously been put to the test." (Schwartzberg, 1994, p. 597). The respondents all demonstrated a renewed sense of belonging to a broader community, an enhanced appreciation of time and taking advantage of the time they had, and increased involvement in altruistic behaviors (Schwartzberg, 1994). Thus, as a result of their diagnosis, these men were able to experience growth and renewal that were directly related to their exposure to a PTE (Schwartzberg, 1994). This suggests the importance of leveraging and encouraging these strengths when designing prevention and early intervention programs for special populations.

References

Agaibi, C., & Wilson, J. P. (2005). Trauma, PTSD, and resilience. *Trauma, Violence, & Abuse, 6,* 195–216. (doi: 10.1177/1524838005277438)

Amnesty International (1999). *In the firing line.* London: Ennisfield Print and Design.

Baan, J. (2007). *Listen to them: Supporting refugee and asylum-seeking children at school* (final report of the project). Retrieved from Pharos Web site: http://www.pharos.nl/uploads/_site_1/English/Final%20report%20Supporting%20refugee%20and%20asylum%20seeking%20children%20at%20school.pdf.

Barenbaum, J., Ruchkin, V., & Schwab-Stone, M. (2004). The psychosocial aspects of children exposed to war: Practices and policy initiatives. *Journal of Child Psychology and Psychiatry, 45,* 41–62. (doi: 10.1046/j.0021–9630.2003.00304.x)

Birman, D., Beehler, S., Harris, E. M., Everson, M. L., Batia, K., Liautaud, J., & Cappella, E. (2008). International family, adult, and child enhancement services (FACES): A community-based comprehensive services model for refugee children in resettlement. *American Journal of Orthopsychiatry, 78,* 121–132. (doi:10.1037/0002–9432.78.1.121)

Birman, D., Ho, J., Pulley, E., Batia, K., Everson, M. L., Ellis, H., & Gonzalez, A. (2005). *Mental health interventions for refugee children in resettlement* (white paper ii). Retrieved from National Child Traumatic Stress Network (NCSTN) Web site: http://www.nctsn.org/nctsn_assets/pdfs/promising_practices/MH_Interventions_for_Refugee_Children.pdf.

Brady, S. S., Gorman-Smith, D., Henry, D. B., & Tolan, P. H. (2008). Adaptive coping reduces impact of community violence exposure on violent behavior among African American and Latino male adolescents. *Journal of Abnormal Child Psychology, 36,* 105–115. (doi: 10.1007/s10802–007–9164-x)

Brodie, M., Weltzien, E., Altman, D., Blendon, R. J., & Benson, J. M. (2006). Experiences of Hurricane Katrina evacuees in Houston shelters: Implications for future planning. *American Journal of Public Health, 96,* 1402–1408. (doi: 10.2105/AJPH.2005.084475)

Bronfenbrenner, U. (1977). Toward an experimental ecology of human development. *American Psychologist, 32,* 513–531. (doi:10.1037/0003-066X.32.7.513)

Capps, R., Fix, M., Ost, J., Reardon-Anderson, J., & Passel, J. S. (2004). *The health and well-being of young children of immigrants.* Retrieved from Urban Institute Web site: http://www.urban.org/UploadedPDF/311139_ChildrenImmigrants.pdf.

Carney, J. V. (2008). Perceptions of Bullying and associated trauma during adolescence. *Professional School Counseling, 11,* 179–188.

Chaffin, M., Silovsky, J. F., Funderbunk, B., Valle, L. A., Brestan, E. V., Balachova, T., & Bonner, B. L. (2004). Parent-child interaction therapy with physically abusive parents: Efficacy for reducing future abuse reports. *Journal of Consulting and Clinical Psychology, 72,* 500–510. (doi: 10.1037/0022-006-X.72.3.500)

Charuvastra, A., & Cloitre, M. (2008). Social bonds and post-traumatic stress disorder. *Annual Review of Psychology, 59,* 301–328. (doi:10.1146/annurev.psych.58.110405.085650)

de Berry, J., & Boyden, J. (2000). Children in adversity. *Forced Migration, 9,* 1–4.

Detzner, D. F., Senyurekli, A. R., Yang, P. N. D., & Sheikh, K. S. (2009). Family strengths of Hmong and Somali refugees in the United States. In R. L. Dalla, J. DeFrain, J. Johnson, & D. A. Abbott (Eds.), *Strengths and challenges of new immigrant families: Implications for research, education, policy, and service* (pp. 135–155). Retrieved from http://books.google.com/books?id=DwWs-fSyEFAC&pg=PA135&dq=Family+strengths+of+Hmong+and+Somali+refugees+in+the+United+States.&hl=en&ei=RcQsTNLfA4OB8gaBh7CCDg&sa=X&oi=book_result&ct=result&resnum=1&ved=0CCsQ6AEwAA#v=onepage&q=Family%20strengths%20of%20Hmong%20and%20Somali%20refugees%20in%20the%20United%20States.&f=false.

Ellis, B. H., Kia-Keating, M., Yusuf, S. A., Lincoln, A., & Nur, A. (2007). Ethical research in refugee communities and the use of community participatory methods. *Transcultural Psychiatry, 44,* 459–481. (doi: 10.1177/1363461507081642)

Ellis, B. H., MacDonald, H. Z., Lincoln, A., Cabral, H. (2008). Mental health of Somali adolescent refugees: The role of trauma, stress, and perceived discrimination. *Journal of Consulting and Clinical Psychology, 76,* 184–193. (doi: 10.1037/0022-006X.76.2.184)

Ellis, B.H., Miller, A, Baldwin, H., Abdi, S. (2011). New directions in refugee youth mental health services: Overcoming barriers to engagement. *Journal of Child and Adolescent Trauma,* 4(1), 69-85.

Fazel, M., & Stein, A. (2008). The mental health of refugee children. *Archives of Disease in Childhood, 87,* 366–370. (doi:10.1136/adc.87.5.366)

Fazel, M., Wheeler, J., & Danesh, J. (2005). Prevalence of serious mental disorder in 7000 refugees resettled in western countries: a systemic review. *Lancet, 365,* 1309–1314. (doi:10.1016/S0140-6736(05)61027-6)

Flaskerud, J. H., & Winslow, B. J. (1998). Conceptualizing vulnerable populations' health-related research. *Nursing Research, 47,* 69–78.

Gerwitz, A., Forgatch, M., & Wieling, E. (2008). Parenting practices as potential mechanisms for child adjustment following mass trauma. *Journal of Marital and Family Therapy, 34,* 177–192. (doi: 10.1111/j.1752-0606-.2008.00063.x)

Gong-Guy, E., Cravens, R. B., & Patterson, T. E. (1991). Clinical issues in mental health service delivery to refugees. *American Psychologist, 46,* 642–648.

Goodman, L., Saxe, L., & Harvey, M. (1991). Homelessness as psychological trauma: Broadening perspectives. *American Psychologist, 46,* 1219–1225.

Hobfoll, S. E., Dunahoo, C. A., & Monnier, J. (1995). Conservation of resources and traumatic stress. In J. R. Freedy & S. E. Hobfoll (Eds.), *Traumatic stress: From theory to practice* (pp. 29–42). New York: Plenum Press.

Hobfoll, S. E., Spielberger, C. D., Breznitz, S., Figley, C., Folkman, S., Lepper-Green, B., & van der Kolk, B. (1991). War-related stress: Addressing the stress of war and other traumatic events. *American Psychologist, 46(8),* 848-855. doi:10.1037/0003-066X.46.8.848

Hodes, M., Jagdev, D., Chandra, N., & Cunniff, A. (2008). Risk and resilience for psychological distress amongst unaccompanied asylum seeking adolescents. *Journal of Child Psychology and Psychiatry, 49,* 723–732. (doi: 10.1111/j.1469-7610-.2008.01912.x)

Hoover, J., & Stenhjem, P. (2003, December). *Bullying and teasing of youth with disabilities: Creating positive school environments for effective inclusion* (Issue Brief 2 [3]). Minneapolis, MN: National Center on Secondary Education and Transition.

Jones, K., Allen, M., Norris, F. H., & Miller, C. (2009). Piloting a new model of crisis counseling: Specialized crisis counseling services in Mississippi after hurricane Katrina. *Administration and Policy in Mental Health, 36,* 195–205. (doi: 10.1007/s10488-009-0214-2)

Katz, S., & Nevid, J. S. (2005). Risk factors associated with posttraumatic stress disorder symptomatology in HIV-infected women. *AIDS Patient Care and STDs, 19,* 110–120. (doi:10.1089/apc.2005.19.110)

Kiser, L., & Black, M. (2005). Family processes in the midst of urban poverty: What does the trauma literature tell us? *Aggression and Violent Behavior, 10,* 715–750. (doi:10.1016/j.avb.2005.02.003)

Layne, C. M., Pynoos, R. S., Saltzman, W. R., Arslanagic, B., Black, M., Savjak, N., & Houston, R. (2001). Trauma/grief focused group psychotherapy: School-based postwar intervention with traumatized Bosnian adolescents. *Group Dynamics: Theory, research, and Practice, 5,* 277–290. (doi: 10.1037///1089-2699.5.4.277)

Layne, C. M., Saltzman, W. R., Poppleton, L., Burlingame, G. M., Pasalic, A., Durakovic, E., & Pynoos, R. S. (2008). Effectiveness of a school-based group psychotherapy program for war-exposed adolescents: A randomized controlled trial. *Journal of the American Academy of Child and Adolescent Psychiatry, 47,* 1048–1062. (doi:10.1097/CHI.0b013e31817eecae)

Link, B. G., & Phelan, J. C. (2001). Conceptualizing stigma. *Review of Sociology, 27,* 363–385. (doi:10.1146/annurev.soc.27.1.363)

Litz, B. T., Gray, M. J., Bryant, R. A., & Adler, A. B. (2002). Early intervention for trauma: Current status and future directions. *Clinical Psychology: Science and Practice, 9,* 112–134. (doi: 10.1093/clipsy.9.2.112)

Lustig, S. L., Kia-Keating, M., Knight, W. G., Geltman, P., Ellis, H., Kinzie, D., & Saxe, G. (2004). Review of child and adolescent refugee mental health. *Journal of the Academy of Child and Adolescent Psychiatry, 43,* 24–36. (doi:10.1097/00004583-200401000-00012)

Mann, C. M., & Fazil, Q. (2006). Mental illness in asylum seekers and refugees. *Primary Care Mental Health, 4(1),* 57-66.

McGarry, K. A., Clarke, J. G., Landau, C., & Cyr, M. G. (2008). Caring for vulnerable populations: Cirricula in U.S. Internal Medicine Residencies. *Journal of Homosexuality, 54,* 225–232. (doi: 10.1080/08873260801982064)

Miller, K. E., Weine, S. M., Ramic, A., Brkic, N., Bjedic, Z. D., Smajkic Worthington, G. (2002). The relative contribution of war experiences and exile-related stressors to levels of psychological distress among Bosnian refugees. *Journal of Traumatic Stress, 15(5),* 377-387.

Oldham, J. M., Haimowitz, S., & Delano, S. J. (1999). Protection of persons with mental disorders from research risk. *Archives of General Psychiatry, 56,* 688–693.

Pynoos, R. S., Steinberg, A. M., & Piacentini, J. C. (1999). A developmental psychopathology model of childhood traumatic stress and intersection with anxiety disorders. *Biological Psychiatry, 46,* 1542–1554. (doi:10.1016/S0006-3223(99)00262-0)

Redman, R. W. (2007). Vulnerable populations and health care disparities. *Research and Theory for Nursing Practice: An International Journal, 21,* 153–155.

Rousseau, C., & Guzder, J. (2008). School-based prevention programs for refugee children. *Child and Adolescent Psychiatric Clinics of North America, 17,* 533–549. (doi:10.1016/j.chc.2008.02.002)

Rowe, C. L. & Liddle, H. A. (2008). When the levee breaks: Treating adolescents and families in the aftermath of Hurricane Katrina. *Journal of Marital and Family Therapy, 34,* 132–148. (doi: 10.1111/j.1752-0606.2008.00060.x)

Saxe, G. N., Ellis, B. H., & Kaplow, J. B. (2007). Collaborative treatment of traumatized children and teens. New York: Guilford.

Silove, D. (2006). The impact of mass psychological trauma on psychosocial adaptation among refugees. In G. Reyes & G. A. Jacobs (Eds.), *Handbook of International disaster psychology* (vol. 3, pp. 1–18). Retrieved from http://books.google.com/books?id=3vpE2UyBrFIC&pg=PR21&dq=Handbook+of+International+disaster+psychology&ei=Qs8sTIfFL4GqM7_7oOoD&cd=2#v=onepage&q&f=false.

Schwartzberg, S. (1994). Vitality and growth in HIV-infected gay men. *Social Science Medicine, 38,* 593–602. (doi:10.1016/0277-9536(94)90256-9)

Struckman-Johnson, C., Struckman-Johnson, D., Rucker, L., Bumby, L., & Donaldson, S. (1996). Sexual coercion reported by men and women in prison. *Journal of Sex Research, 33,* 67–76. (doi: 10.1080/00224499609551816)

Thabet, A. A, Ibraheem, A.N., Shivram, R., Winter, E. A. & Vostanis, P. (2009). Parenting support and PTSD in children of a war zone. *International Journal of Social Psychiatry, 55,* 226–237. (doi: 10.1177/0020764008096100)

Ttofi, M. M., Farrington, D. P., & Baldry, A. C. (2008). *Effectiveness of programmes to reduce school bullying.* Retrieved from Swedish National Council for Crime Prevention Web site: http://www.bra.se/extra/measurepoint/?module_instance=4&name=Effectiveness_of_programmes_to_reduce_school_bullying_webb.pdf&url=/dynamaster/file_archive/081023/04395cbc57201c39fa6c7f78319ea2ab/Effectiveness%255fof%255fprogrammes%255fto%255freduce%255fschool%255fbullying%255fwebb.pdf.

United Nations High General Assembly (1951). *Convention Relating to the Status of Refugees.* (Treaty Series, vol. 189, p. 137). Retrieved from the United Nations High Commissioner for Refugees (UNHCR), Refworld Web site: http://www.unhcr.org/refworld/docid/3be01b964.html.

United Nations High Commissioner for Refugees (UNHCR). (2010). Asylum levels and trends in industrialized countries 2009: Statistical overview of asylum applications lodged in Europe and selected non-European countries. Division of Programme Support and Management. Retrieved from http://www.unhcr.org/4d8c5b109.html

Watters, C., & Ingleby, D. (2004). Locations of care: Meeting the mental health needs of refugees in Europe. International *Journal of Law and Psychiatry, 27,* 549–570. (doi: 10.1016/j.ijlp.2004.08.004)

Weine, S. (2008) Family roles in refugee youth resettlement from a prevention perspective. *Child and Adolescent Psychiatric Clinics of North America, 17,* 515–532. (doi:10.1016/j.chc.2008.02.006)

Weine, S., Kulauzovic, Y., Klebic, A., Besic, S., Mujagic, A., Muzurovic, J., & Rolland, J. (2008). Evaluating a multiple-family group access intervention for refugees with PTSD. *Journal of Marital and Family Therapy, 34,* 149–164. (doi: 10.1111/j.1752-0606.2008.00061.x)

Treatment

CHAPTER 28

PTSD Treatment Research: An Overview and Evaluation

Jessica L. Hamblen, Erin R. Barnett, Barbara A. Hermann, *and* Paula P. Schnurr

Abstract

This chapter provides an overview of key concepts in designing and evaluating clinical trials. Our focus is on randomized controlled trials for PTSD. In the first section we discuss design elements and how they influence the conclusions that can be drawn from a study. Examples from the trauma literature are provided when available to illustrate concepts. In the second section we explore newer developments in PTSD treatment trials. Specifically, we discuss treatment and design considerations related to common comorbid conditions of PTSD, cultural issues in PTSD, and optimizing the delivery of treatments. Our goal is to improve both clinicians and researchers ability to critically review PTSD clinical trials.

Key Words: PTSD, treatment, randomized controlled trials, research methodology

In 2008, the Institute of Medicine (IOM) convened a panel to review the PTSD treatment literature. The committee found support for the efficacy of cognitive behavioral therapy (CBT) that included exposure as a component, such as Prolonged Exposure (PE) and Cognitive Processing Therapy (CPT). However, they identified significant methodological weaknesses in studies of other treatments that prevented conclusions regarding the efficacy of these treatments. Overall, they concluded that "the scientific evidence on treatment modalities for PTSD [did] not reach the level of certainty that would be desired for such a common and serious condition" and concluded that "additional high-quality research is essential for every treatment modality" (Institute of Medicine [IOM], 2008, p. 14).

In this chapter, we discuss essential issues in evaluating clinical trials and emerging issues in trauma treatment research. Our goal is to provide clinicians with a guide for how to critically review treatment trials and help them to be more aware of issues that can limit findings. For researchers, we highlight elements we believe are essential to consider when designing a trial. Although we touch on many of the key issues discussed in Schnurr (2007), we refer readers to the original article for a more detailed review of these issues.

Essential Issues in Evaluating Clinical Trials

The design of a clinical trial determines the conclusions that can be drawn from its findings. For example, it is difficult to determine a cause-and-effect relationship between treatment and outcome without randomization. Several groups have outlined what they see as critical design issues (e.g., Borkovec, 1993; Foa, Keane, Friedman, & Cohen, 2009; Foa & Meadows, 1997; IOM, 2008; Schnurr, 2007). Here we review the elements we believe are most important.

Efficacy, Effectiveness, and Practical Trials

There are several types of clinical trials, each designed to answer a different question. The majority are efficacy studies that aim to determine whether a treatment works. These trials strive to maximize internal validity and utilize tight controls such as random assignment, rigorous control for the nonspecific benefits of treatment, manualized treatment and monitoring of therapists' fidelity to the manual, well-defined outcomes, the exclusion of patients with multiple comorbidities, and fixed assessment intervals. However, as pointed out by Seligman (1995), these trials do not necessarily tell us whether the treatment will work in a clinical setting, only that the treatment works under carefully controlled circumstances.

Effectiveness trials are aimed at evaluating how a treatment works under the conditions in which it will typically be used. These trials strive to maximize external validity. The strict controls required for efficacy trials are loosened to reflect what takes place in clinical practice. Treatments may be flexible in length and assessments may be conducted when the therapist notices changes or is considering switching treatments. Patients even may not be randomized to treatment but may instead choose which treatment they receive.

Rounsaville, Carroll, and Onken (2001) suggested a stage model for treatment development in which the question being addressed moves from questions of feasibility and piloting (stage 1), to treatment efficacy (stage 2), and ultimately to treatment effectiveness (stage 3). Thus, the stage of a treatment's development and the question being asked directly affect the design of the study. Therefore, one type of study is not inherently better or worse than another; they simply answer different questions and permit different conclusions. For example, a randomized controlled trial (RCT) utilizing nonexpert therapists may be a premature strategy for a stage 2 efficacy trial evaluating the benefits of virtual reality therapy for PTSD. In this case, expert therapists are necessary to ensure that the treatment in question is being accurately delivered as competently as possible. However, using nonexpert clinicians is a good strategy for a stage 3 effectiveness study evaluating their ability to deliver virtual reality therapy with the same success as trained study therapists.

Ideally, research would progress through this stage model. In reality, treatment evaluation studies are often conducted in a more random fashion. For example, because it can take so long for studies to be conducted and published, a major trial could be under way that investigators are unaware of during the planning of their new trials. This can sometimes make it difficult to evaluate the "state of affairs" for a given treatment.

Practical trials combine elements of efficacy and effectiveness studies (Schnurr, 2007). They are specifically designed to help patients, clinicians, payers, administrators, and policymakers make decisions about healthcare (Tunis, Stryer, & Clancy, 2003). They optimize real-world conditions by introducing heterogeneity while maintaining enough control from randomization to permit meaningful conclusions about treatment outcome. Most utilize standardized treatments and careful measurement (efficacy elements) that are implemented with clinically relevant comparison groups, diverse populations, and heterogeneous practice settings (effectiveness elements). As reviewed in Schnurr, 2007, Cooperative Study #494 (Schnurr et al., 2005, 2007) is an example of a practical trial. In this study, 284 female veterans and active-duty personnel were randomized to either PE (Foa & Rothbaum, 1998) or Present-Centered Therapy, a credible therapeutic alternative treatment that controlled for nonspecific therapeutic benefits. To increase the generalizability of the findings, the study took place at 12 different sites, including VA hospitals, vet centers, and a military hospital, and used local therapists who were not experts in cognitive behavioral therapy. It also utilized more lenient inclusion and exclusion criteria, designed to maximize patient heterogeneity. For example, significant comorbidity was allowed and exclusion criteria were limited to factors that would affect patient safety. This design allowed investigators to control what therapy was being delivered but did so under conditions as close as possible to real-world practice.

Comparison Groups

Schnurr (2007) discussed how the choice of a comparison group affects the inferences that may be drawn from a study (see also Borkovec, 1993, for a similar analysis). The first design examined uses an untreated comparison group. Here, the treatment under study is compared with no treatment. These comparisons are also called waitlist comparisons when participants are offered treatment at the end of the observation period. These designs control for most threats to internal validity such as history, maturation, selection, etc. (Cook & Campbell, 1979). They answer the question of whether the treatment being tested is better than what would have happened if there were no intervention at all. This is an appropriate question when a new treatment is being developed or an established treatment is being used in a new population. For example, Monson et al. (2006) randomized veterans with combat-related PTSD to CPT or waitlist. At this time, although there was strong evidence for the effects of CPT in sexual assault survivors, there were no trials with veterans. Results indicated that CPT was superior to waitlist.

The next control group reviewed by Schnurr (2007) is a nonspecific comparison group that does not involve any of the active mechanisms of the target intervention. Treatment as usual comparisons are also considered nonspecific controls. Both types of treatment groups control for attention, as well as for the nonspecific benefits of treatment, and allow investigators to draw conclusions about the added benefit of the target treatment over and above the benefits of seeing a general therapist. The Schnurr et al. (2007) practical trial reviewed above compared female veterans and active-duty personnel who received PE to those who received Present-Centered Therapy, a nonspecific comparison treatment, and found PE to be superior.

Dismantling and additive studies are the next class of studies discussed by Schnurr (2007) and are specifically designed to determine the active components of a treatment. There have been a few dismantling studies of Eye Movement Desensitization and Reprocessing (EMDR). In these studies, EMDR conducted with fixed eyes was compared to EMDR with the bilateral eye movements. Results from these studies indicated that the eye movements may not be necessary (Davidson & Parker, 2001; Spates, Koch, Cusack, Pagoto, & Waller, 2009), suggesting that some other component of EMDR may be the mechanism of action. Additive designs also help isolate key therapeutic elements. In additive trials, two effective techniques are combined and then compared to each alone. Later in this chapter, we discuss design issues to be aware of in additive studies and provide an example.

Active treatment controls provide the next level of control and help answer questions such as whether one treatment is better than another. For example, Resick and colleagues (2002) compared CPT with PE and a minimal attention control. No differences were found between the two active treatments and both were more effective than the control condition (Resick, Nishith, Weaver, Astin, & Feuer, 2002).

Schnurr (2007) also discussed how choice of the comparison group affects effect sizes, using the findings from EMDR as an example. The largest effects (between 1.0 and 2.7) were observed in studies that used a waitlist comparison group, whereas smaller effects (roughly 0.70 to 1.0) were observed when nonspecific treatments or treatment as usual were compared with EMDR. Two of the three smallest effect sizes were observed in dismantling studies (0.03 and 0.31), that attempted to determine whether the eye movements were necessary. This makes sense because the effect size is dependent on the amount of variation that is being controlled for; the smaller the difference between the comparison groups, the smaller the expected effect size.

Lack of attention to the type of comparison group can result in conclusions being drawn from a study that goes beyond what is actually being tested by the design. For example, if an active treatment is shown to be more effective than a nonspecific comparison treatment or treatment as usual, all that can be determined is that the treatment has effects greater than the effects of therapy in general. However, the mechanism through which the treatment works cannot be established. If both treatments work equally well (i.e., there is no difference between the active and comparison conditions), you have to accept the null hypothesis that the treatments are the same.

Attrition and Missing Data

The handling of missing data due to attrition and lack of participation in assessment in both pharmacologic and psychotherapy trials received significant attention in the IOM (2008) report. Participant attrition is certainly not unique to PTSD treatment research and in fact is comparable to attrition in studies of treatment for other mental disorders. The IOM found median attrition was 26% from PTSD medication trials (IOM, 2008) as compared with 35% in a review of trials of antidepressants in general (Khan, Schwartz, Redding, Kolts, & Brown, 2007) or 32% in an earlier meta-analysis of medication trials for PTSD (van Etten & Taylor, 1998). For PTSD psychotherapy trials, median attrition was 20% (IOM, 2008), as compared to 19% in a nationally representative sample of outpatients seen by mental health professionals (Olfson et al., 2009). Attrition does not appear to differ among various forms of CBT for PTSD, either (Hembree et al., 2003).

The IOM (2008) found that the most common strategy for handling missing data due to attrition or lack of participation in assessment in PTSD treatment trials was to use the last observation carried forward (LOCF) method. In LOCF, in the event of missing data, a participant's last assessment score on a given measure is used to replace all subsequently missing values on that measure. LOCF is based on a number of unlikely assumptions that make it a poor data analytic strategy (IOM, 2008). First, it assumes that a participant's outcome would not change between observation points. Second, it assumes that a participant who drops out will have the same outcome as one who completes all assessments. And finally, it assumes that the dropout itself is not connected to the participant's outcome. This approach can bias results in either direction, particularly in cases where there is significant dropout. In the IOM report, studies with more than 10% missing outcome data that utilized LOCF were considered poorer quality than those that used other missing data analytic methods such as multiple imputation or mixed-model repeated measurement (IOM, 2008).

The IOM report provides a good example of how attrition can influence outcomes (see IOM, 2008). It describes a trial in which the active intervention and the control condition both yield a true rate of improvement of 50%. So in a trial in which 100 participants start and finish each condition, 50 in each condition would improve. Assume that 50% in the active treatment group who fail to improve do not complete the post assessment (n = 25) while only 10% of those who fail to improve in the control group do not complete the postassessment (n = 5). If analyses only include those who complete the postassessment, the active condition improvement rate will appear to be 67% (50/75) and the control condition will appear to be 53% (50/90) when in fact there is no actual difference in efficacy between the conditions. The influence of missing data on conclusion regarding outcome is evident.

Not only should every effort be made to collect follow-up data from all participants, but investigators also need to consider how to handle data from participants who do not complete a full course of treatment. We know that many patients will not attend all of the scheduled therapy sessions, but it is important that all participants who are randomized be included in the analyses regardless of whether they received any treatment. These analyses, called intention-to-treat (ITT) analyses, are critical when estimating the effect of the treatment in the population of interest. Completer analyses can also be conducted to examine the effect of the treatment on people in the population who receive a full course of treatment.

Sample Size and Design Choice

With the increasing number of evidence-based treatments available for PTSD, investigators frequently compare one treatment to another. However, in many cases these studies have been considerably underpowered. Schnurr (2007) provides guidelines for estimating sample sizes as a function of comparison group. While small samples (approximately 26 per group; p = .05, two-tailed) often have enough power to detect large effects such as what would be observed when comparing an active treatment to a waitlist, the sample size needed to maintain adequate power grows considerably when comparing two treatments. Moderate samples (approximately 64 per group; p = .05, two-tailed) are needed to detect a difference between an active treatment and a nonspecific control, and very large samples (approximately 393 per group) are required to detect a small effect such as what would be observed when comparing two active comparisons (Schnurr, 2007).

As an example, we review two additive PTSD trials that failed to find differences between treatment groups. Glynn et al. (1999) compared exposure therapy alone (n = 12) with exposure therapy followed by behavioral family therapy (n = 17), and Arntz, Tiesema, and Kindt (2007) compared imaginal exposure alone (n = 42) with imaginal exposure plus imagery rescripting (n = 29). In both cases, the sample size was not large enough to detect a small effect, as would be expected when comparing two active treatments. When sample sizes are too small to detect significant effects, investigators can present effect sizes as a method of demonstrating the actual difference between two treatments (even if the p-value is nonsignificant). However, effect sizes for these two studies were between 0.06 and 0.20 (depending on the measure), suggesting that if there was an effect, it was likely to be clinically insignificant.

Sometimes the question being asked is how a new treatment compares with the standard of practice. For example, is a brief version of PE as effective as the standard dose? It is tempting to conclude that the new treatment is comparable to the standard if the difference between them is not statistically significant—in short, to accept the null hypothesis. It may be possible to tentatively interpret the lack of difference, even though this is technically not correct, if the study is powered to find a meaningful effect and the observed effect is much smaller. However, the correct analytic approach is to use a noninferiority design, which uses a one-sided test of the null hypothesis that the new treatment is inferior by a prespecified amount (i.e., that the treatments are not equal). A related approach using a two-tailed test can be used to compare the equivalence of two active treatments, which may be more appropriate than testing whether one treatment is better than the other. There are good sources of information about the specifics of these designs (e.g., Piaggio et al., 2006), including a review by Greene, Morland, Durkalski, and Frueh (2008) that focuses specifically on trauma research.

As in superiority designs that compare active treatments, noninferiority and equivalence trials also require large samples but permit greater assurance in interpreting a lack of difference between two treatments. Greene et al. (2008) found few examples of well-designed and adequately powered noninferiority or equivalence trials in mental health research in general. The authors discussed one study in the PTSD literature, their own ongoing noninferiority trial examining the clinical effectiveness of using a telemental health service delivery mode to provide a cognitive behavioral therapy for treating combat related PTSD (Morland, Greene, Rosen, Mauldin, & Frueh, 2009). They are testing the hypothesis that CPT delivered by video teleconferencing is "not inferior" to CPT delivered in person.

Controlling for Clustering Effects

Group treatment for PTSD offers benefits over individual treatment in terms of optimum use of clinical resources, patient access, facilitation of social support, and increased treatment compliance (Beck, Coffey, Foy, Keane, & Blanchard, 2009; Ruzek, Young, & Walser, 2003; Schnurr et al., 2003). However, the very fact that the group can influence individual members in these positive ways means that participants' outcomes are not statistically independent, as required in conventional analytic approaches such as ANOVA and MANOVA. When observations are clustered within treatment groups, the dependency among observations can be measured as the intraclass correlation, or ICC. Schnurr et al. (2003) reported an ICC of 0.04 in one study of group therapy for PTSD, but Creamer, Morris, Biddle, and Elliot (2004) reported ICCs ranging from 0.10 to 0.13, depending on outcomes.

The correct analysis of clustered data statistically takes this dependency into account. Failing to do so can exaggerate the effects of a treatment (Baldwin, Murray, & Shadish, 2005; Schnurr, 2007). Baldwin et al. illustrated the problem dramatically, using data from 33 studies of group psychotherapy on the American Psychological Association's list of empirically supported group treatments (Task Force, 1998). All treatments had been chosen for the list based on evidence from published studies demonstrating their efficacy. After Baldwin et al. corrected for degrees of freedom (which should be based on the number of groups, not subjects), only 51–68% of the previously significant findings were still significant, depending on other assumptions. And after correcting for even a small ICC (0.05), the investigators found that just 35–43% of the tests remained significant.

Only two studies of group therapy for PTSD have used such adjustments. One is Schnurr and colleagues' (2003) study comparing cognitive behavioral group therapy to a present-centered process group treatment in 360 Vietnam veterans. The other study is Beck et al.'s (2009) trial of cognitive behavioral group therapy for PTSD, which was compared to a waitlist control condition in a sample of 33 motor vehicle accident survivors. As a consequence, little can be said about the effectiveness of group therapy for PTSD; there simply are not enough studies on which to base definitive conclusions.

The same statistical problem occurs when participants are clustered within individual therapists. Just as groups can influence the outcomes of individual members, so can therapists; good therapists have better outcomes than average or poor therapists. Failing to account for such therapist effects can optimistically bias the estimate of the treatment effect. Crits-Christoph et al. (1991) conducted a meta-analysis of data from 141 therapists in 15 studies that included 27 treatment conditions. Therapist effects accounted for an average of 8.6% variance in outcomes (range = 0–49%). According to multivariate analysis, the use of a manual and greater therapist experience were associated with small differences between therapists, whereas more inexperienced therapists and lack of a treatment manual were associated with larger therapist effects (Crits-Christoph et al., 1991).

The correct approach to analysis should account for therapists in the statistical model to provide an unbiased estimate of treatment outcome. Schnurr (2007) also discusses design strategies that can help to standardize treatment and minimize the extent of individual therapist variation in treatment delivery: randomly assigning therapists to treatment, training them in the use of a manualized protocol, and providing ongoing supervision of therapists. These strategies also serve to ensure consistent delivery between treatments and enhance validity and replicability. Unfortunately, trials with a limited number of therapists may not be able to randomly assign therapists to treatment and need to control bias through especially careful training and supervision (Schnurr, Friedman, Lavori, & Hsieh, 2001; Schnurr et al., 2005).

Measuring PTSD Outcomes

The IOM reported a lack of agreement across treatment studies on how to measure PTSD outcomes or what constitutes "recovery" (IOM, 2008). They note that improvement in PTSD is measured in a variety of ways including a change in PTSD status and loss of diagnosis (e.g., Beck et al., 2009; Ehlers et al., 2003), clinically meaningful improvement in PTSD symptoms (e.g., Foa & Meadows, 1997), and multiple domain measures used to determine positive end-state functioning (Ehlers, Clark, Hackmann, McManus, & Fennell, 2005; Foa et al., 1999; IOM, 2008). There is little consistency in how each of these domains is measured. Therefore, the committee recommended that outcome studies utilize a set of core, valid outcomes measures that can be used to assess patients over time.

Zayfert and colleagues (2005) suggest that different definitions of recovery may be appropriate for different situations. For example, in clinical settings the decision to end treatment may be when the patient and therapist determine that they have met their PTSD treatment goals. Using this definition, significantly fewer PTSD patients are "recovered" compared to those who completed a specified length of treatment. For example, in their clinical sample of 115 patients with primary PTSD, only 28% recovered according to their definition (Zayfert et al., 2005).

Emerging Issues in PTSD Treatment Research

The first section of the chapter drew attention to issues relevant to evaluating clinical trials. In this section, we highlight some of the newer developments in PTSD treatment trials. Specifically, we discuss treatment and design considerations related to common comorbid conditions of PTSD, cultural issues in PTSD, and optimizing the delivery of treatments.

Comorbidities and Associated Features

Nearly 80% of individuals with PTSD have at least one additional psychiatric disorder (Kessler, Sonnega, Bromet, Hughes, Nelson, 1995). Given the high rates of comorbidity, it is important to know whether these co-occurring conditions interfere with the effects of PTSD treatments and, relatedly, if these treatments can be modified to address the additional clinical issues. There is increased recognition that many people being treated for another condition may also have PTSD.

Approximately 30–40% of patients with substance use disorders meet criteria for current PTSD (Brady, Back, & Coffey, 2004; Ouimette, Moos, & Brown, 2003). Historically, addiction treatment programs have not addressed PTSD out of concern that targeting the PTSD would exacerbate re-experiencing symptoms and jeopardize early and unstable periods of abstinence (Killeen et al., 2008; McGovern, Lambert-Harris, Acquilano, Alterman, & Weiss, 2009). The opposite argument has also been proposed. Evidence in support of the self-medication theory indicates that people use substances as a means to control their re-experiencing symptoms (Chilcoat & Breslau, 1998a, 1998b). Therefore, ignoring the PTSD may lead to increased relapse and poorer outcome.

A number of PTSD clinical trials have allowed participants with substance abuse to participate (e.g., Foa & Cahill, 2002; Monson et al., 2006; Schnurr et al., 2003). Recently, though, pilot trials have included patients with substance dependence. Preliminary results suggest that both PE and CPT can be effective in treating PTSD in such cases (E. Foa, personal communication, October 14, 2009; K. Chard, personal communication, October 6, 2009).

Several treatments specifically target both PTSD and substance use disorders (e.g., Brady, Dansky, Back, Foa, & Carroll, 2001; Donovan, Padin-Rivera, & Kowlaiw, 2001; McGovern et al., 2009; Triffleman, Carroll, & Kellogg, 1999). Seeking Safety, which has generated the most interest, is a present centered therapy that focuses on teaching coping skills that are relevant to both PTSD and substance use disorders. RCTs of Seeking Safety have been inconclusive. Findings indicated significant reductions in PTSD symptoms, but not more so than the active control conditions. Moreover, outcomes related to substance use have been inconsistent (Hien, Cohen, Miele, Litt, & Capstick, 2004; Najavits, Gallop, & Weiss, 2006; Zlotnick, Johnson, & Najavits, 2009).

PTSD is also highly comorbid with severe mental illness (Mueser, Rosenbeg, Goodman, & Trumbetta, 2002). An estimated 42% of individuals with SMI also have PTSD (Mueser et al., 1998). As in the case of substance use disorders, authors have expressed concern that treating the PTSD would risk stability in patients with SMI (e.g., Frueh, Cusack, Grubaugh, Sauvageot, & Wells, 2006). However, Mueser et al. (2007) found that cognitive behavioral treatment for PTSD safely improved PTSD symptoms in people with serious mental illness.

TBI has been coined the "signature injury" of the wars in Afghanistan and Iraq (Okie, 2006). Over a third of individuals with TBI meet criteria for either PTSD or depression (Tanielian & Jaycox, 2008). Anecdotally, we have heard clinicians discuss whether veterans with mild TBI can engage in PE or CPT. They question if these veterans have the cognitive capacity to challenge their cognitions and the emotional capacity to tolerate exposure. Preliminary findings suggest both PE and CPT may be as effective for veterans with PTSD and mild TBI as they are for veterans with PTSD alone (Rauch et al., 2011; McIlvain Chard, & Bailey, 2011).

Another condition that has received considerable attention is complex PTSD, a group of symptoms commonly seen in response to chronic interpersonal trauma that include affect dysregulation, dissociation, and markedly impaired interpersonal relationships (Herman, 1992). It has been argued that complex trauma is a unique condition requiring its own treatment (Courtois, Ford, & Cloitre, 2009) and many patients with suicidal and nonsuicidal self-injury behaviors are excluded from PTSD trials (Bradley, Green, Russ, Dutra, & Westen, 2005; Stirman, DeRubeis, Crits-Christoph, & Rothman, 2005).

However, some preliminary research findings indicate that current evidence-based treatments for PTSD work well for individuals with borderline personality disorder, a condition with significant overlap with complex PTSD. For example, in the Mueser, Rosenberg, and Xie (2008) RCT of cognitive behavioral therapy for PTSD in people with severe mental illness, the 27 participants with borderline personality disorder did not differ in treatment response to the 81 participants without the disorder.

There is concern though that even if people with complex presentations can be treated with evidence-based PTSD treatments, they may be more likely to drop out (Zayfert et al., 2005). Several investigators have focused efforts on increasing stability and tolerability of PTSD among patients with more complex presentations. Many of these treatments utilize Dialectical Behavior Therapy techniques (DBT; Linehan, 1993a, 1993b) as strategies to prepare clients for evidence-based trauma-focused treatments (e.g., Becker & Zayfert, 2001; Cloitre, Koenen, Cohen, & Han, 2002; Wagner, Rizvi, & Harned, 2007). Cloitre and colleagues developed a sequential treatment for women with PTSD related to childhood abuse that involves an initial phase of skills training in affect and interpersonal regulation followed by a second phase of exposure (Cloitre et al., 2002). They conducted an RCT in women with PTSD related to childhood abuse to determine whether the use of skills training proceeding exposure would produce outcomes better than exposure alone (Cloitre et al., 2010). Not only were outcomes improved in the combined condition, but women were less likely to drop out of treatment if they received the skills training (Cloitre et al, 2010).

In sum, the evidence suggests that PTSD can be treated in a wide range of trauma survivors, including those with significant comorbidities or chronic presentations. In some cases these standard treatments have been modified to address the comorbid concerns. In other cases, new components have been added to treatments to enhance tolerability of treatments for at-risk populations.

Cultural Considerations

An important question is whether our current treatments for PTSD are equally effective for patients from varying cultural backgrounds. Alternatively, does each cultural group need its own version of the treatment or its unique intervention? The vast majority of studies utilizing evidence-based treatments for PTSD have been conducted with members of majority and minority groups alike and have shown successful outcomes (e.g., Rauch et al., 2009; Resick et al., 2002; Schnurr et al., 2007; Zoellner, Feeny, Fitzgibbons, & Foa, 1999). For example, in Cooperative Study #494 (Schnurr et al., 2007), 45% of participants were non-white. Another trial examined whether African-American and Caucasian women fared similarly following PE, and indeed both groups did (Zoellner et al., 1999). There is also considerable diversity in participants enrolled in two successful PE trials. In both cases, more than 60% of participants had incomes below $30,000 (a third of whom were below $10,000) and more than a third were African American (Foa et al., 1999; Foa & Cahill, 2002).

In other studies, existing PTSD treatments with some modifications have been evaluated in participants from other cultures. For example, PE was piloted in 10 Japanese patients with PTSD. Patients were comfortable expressing overwhelming emotion and showed significant improvements (Asukai, Saito, Tsuruta, & Kishimoto, 2008). In the United States, CPT, again with some adaptations and assessment translations, has been successfully adapted for Bosnian and other foreign-born refugee trauma survivors (Schulz, Resick, Huber, & Griffin, 2006; Schulz, Huber, & Resick, 2006).

Together these trials demonstrate the evidence-based treatments for PTSD have been tested in a diverse sample of participants. Preliminary studies of participants from other cultures suggest that many of these treatments are effective in reducing symptoms of PTSD. The next step is to conduct a randomized control trial with an adequate control group.

Optimizing Treatment Delivery

There is considerable interest in how to improve the effectiveness of evidence-based treatments for PTSD. One approach is to use an additive design to determine if therapeutic elements can be combined to enhance their separate effects. Another approach is to use a dismantling design in order to better understand the effect of separate elements. A third approach is to use a parametric design to determine the optimal amount of treatment. Other topics of interest focus on treatment matching, how to sustain the benefits of treatments, and how to enhance delivery by making it easier or more efficient.

COMBINING PTSD INTERVENTIONS

Several trials have examined whether current PTSD treatments could be enhanced by adding a component. Stress inoculation training (Foa et al., 1999), cognitive restructuring (Foa et al., 2005), behavioral family therapy (Glynn et al., 1999), and imagery rescripting (Arntz et al., 2007) have been added to PE to see if the combination was more effective than exposure alone. In each case, the combined or added components did not enhance PTSD outcomes more than the stand-alone PTSD treatment. However, there are several important design considerations for any study of this type. First, is the study underpowered to detect small differences between groups (this was in fact not the case in the studies above)? Second, if the two treatments were combined, were the overall amounts of those treatments reduced so that the combined treatment would last the same amount of time as the individual treatments? If so consider whether the combined treatment contained adequate amounts of the original treatments.

A better design would be to deliver a full dose of each treatment while still controlling for amount of therapy. A more recent study by Bryant et al. (2008) utilized this procedure. Participants were randomized to one of four treatments: imaginal exposure, in vivo exposure, imaginal plus in vivo exposure, and imaginal and in vivo exposure plus cognitive restructuring. In each case, participants received the full dose of the active treatment plus supportive counseling to equate the total amount of therapy. The combined treatment resulted in the largest effects suggesting that the optimal treatment outcome may be achieved by adding cognitive restructuring to exposure therapy.

DETERMINING EFFECTIVE TREATMENT ELEMENTS

Another approach to improving outcomes is to better understand the effectiveness of a treatment's individual components. Dismantling studies allow researchers to identify the most critical components of a treatment and those that may have little utility. For example, Resick and colleagues compared the full CPT protocol to its components: cognitive therapy and written exposure (Resick et al., 2008). All treatment groups improved over the course of treatment and the combined treatment fared no better than either component alone. However, the fastest improvement was observed in cognitive treatment alone.

DETERMINING THE OPTIMAL DOSE OF TREATMENT

Despite the practical implications of failing to understand what the appropriate dose of treatment is, no trials have been designed specifically to answer this question. There are various approaches one could take to examine length of treatment. For example, a study could be designed to determine if a brief treatment is as good as the standard length. Or, one could look at the incremental benefits or decrements of more versus fewer sessions.

A few studies have allowed length of treatment to vary. For example, in one study (Foa et al., 2005) participants in the active treatment group who reached at least 70% improvement in self-reported PTSD symptoms completed treatment after nine sessions. The rest were offered up to 12 sessions. Of the participants who completed treatment, 42% terminated at session 8 or 9 (short treatment), and 58% received between 10 and 12 sessions (long treatment). Of those who received the short treatment, about two-thirds had met the criterion for early termination and one-third declined additional sessions. Results suggest that the majority of participants required additional sessions than commonly prescribed for PE and that the additional sessions resulted in continued improvement in symptoms (Foa et al., 2005).

LONG-TERM OUTCOME

Few trials provide sufficient follow-up to examine long-term outcomes. At the time of the IOM report, six studies were identified with one year follow-up and only five with 15 months or more (IOM, 2008). Few trials provide sufficient follow-up to examine long-term outcomes. PE and CPT have two trials each with follow-up of one year or longer, and EMDR has one trial. In general, gains were maintained through follow-up in these trials. However, in one design with exceptionally long follow-up comparing PE to cognitive therapy, there was a clear superiority for cognitive therapy over PE after five years, despite no differences at posttreatment or six-month follow-up (Tarrier & Sommerfield, 2004). These findings demonstrate the importance of extended follow-up to reveal the sustainability of gains following different treatments so that interventions can be enhanced to promote maintained improvement.

PREDICTORS OF RESPONSE AND TREATMENT MATCHING

A final strategy to enhance outcomes is to identify predictors of treatment response and match clients to the treatments that will be most effective for them. It would be useful to know in advance who will respond well to which evidence-based treatments for PTSD. However, to date, the field of PTSD treatment has been limited by studies with inadequate power to detect significant differences, as mentioned above, and investigations examining predictors based on theoretical considerations have been rare (Rizvi, Vogt, & Resick, 2009). The majority of these studies have examined predictors of response to exposure therapy and found few consistent and stable predictors of outcome beyond pretreatment symptom severity (e.g., Ehlers et al., 2005; Foa, Riggs, Massie, & Yarczower, 1995; Forbes, Creamer, Hawthorne, Allen, & McHugh, 2003; Hagenaars, van Minnen, & Hoogduin, 2010; van Minnen, Arntz, & Keijsers, 2002). The exceptions include investigations of therapy attendance (Tarrier, Sommerfield, Pilgrim, & Faragher, 2000), hostile expressed emotion in relatives (Barrowclogh, Greg, & Tarrier, 2008), homework compliance (Mueser et al., 2008), and therapeutic alliance (Cloitre, Stovall-McClough, Miranda, & Chemtob, 2004). The latter study is noteworthy due to its use of a two-phase longitudinal design showing that changes in alliance early in treatment predicted improvement in PTSD symptoms at posttreatment.

Resick and colleagues (2002) conducted secondary analyses to examine the effect of different treatments on guilt. They compared three groups: PE, CPT, and a minimal attention control. Both PE and CPT showed more reductions in global guilt than the minimal attention group. However, CPT was slightly better at reducing certain aspects of guilt (hindsight bias and lack of justification) than PE (Resick et al., 2002). These findings may suggest matching patients with higher guilt to CPT over PE; however, these effect sizes were relatively small and should be interpreted as such.

Conclusion

Publications on trauma have increased substantially since 1980, when PTSD was first recognized in the *Diagnostic and Statistical Manual of Mental Disorders* (American Psychiatric Association, 1980) until today (Schnurr, 2010). Despite these efforts, there are a number of critical design issues that impact the conclusions that may be drawn from these studies. We end with a list of recommendations for future PTSD treatment trials. First, and most important, trial design should match the state of the knowledge. There is no one best design for a treatment trial. As suggested by Rounsaville et al. (2001), treatment trials should progress from pilot to efficacy to effectiveness. Similarly, the comparison groups selected for the study and the study design (i.e., superiority, inferiority, equivalence) should be influenced by what studies have already taken place. Investigators must understand how their study extends previous research to determine an appropriate design and be precise in the question they are attempting to answer. For example, a small pilot study comparing a novel treatment (such as meditation) to a waitlist is appropriate early on to see if there is any effect of meditation. But ultimately, the question to answer is probably whether meditation is as effective as evidence-based trauma-focused treatments.

Next, we encourage investigators to appropriately size and power their studies. Although it can be tempting to conduct small trials and hope the effect is large enough to reach significance, this is a poor strategy that often leads to null findings. Multisite studies are one solution to the problem of small sample size and should be considered whenever investigators are comparing two or more active treatments.

Finally, we suggest that when possible, investigators work with a biostatistician to design their studies and plan their analyses. Today there are sophisticated data analytic techniques that are expected for even the most basic clinical trial. Sample size and missing data are two places where a biostatistician can be invaluable, but they are also helpful when investigators attempt to answer more complex questions such as what predicts outcome and what is the rate of change in a study.

We challenge researchers to continue to push the field of PTSD treatment research forward. At the same time, we encourage the use of more practical trials to ensure that these treatments will ultimately be effective in the real-world conditions confronting clinicians. As treatments are developed, major dissemination and implementation efforts are required to help translate this new knowledge into practice.

References

American Psychiatric Association. (1980). *Diagnostic and statistical manual of mental disorders* (3rd. ed.). Washington, DC: Author.

Arntz, A., Tiesema, M., & Kindt, M. (2007). Treatment of PTSD: A comparison of imaginal exposure with and without imagery rescripting. *Journal of Behavioral Therapy and Experimental Psychiatry, 38*, 345–370.

Asukai, N., Saito, A., Tsuruta, N., & Kishimoto, J. (2008). Pilot study on prolonged exposure of Japanese patients with posttraumatic stress disorder due to mixed traumatic events. *Journal of Traumatic Stress, 21*, 340–343.

Baldwin, S. A., Murray, D. M., & Shadish, W. R. (2005). Empirically supported treatments or type I errors? Problems with the analysis of data from group-administered treatments. *Journal of Consulting and Clinical Psychology, 73*, 924–935.

Barrowclough, C., Gregg, L., & Tarrier, N. (2008). Expressed emotion and causal attributions in relatives of posttraumtic stress disorder in patients. *Behaviour Research and Therapy, 46*, 207–218.

Beck, J. G., Coffey, S. F., Foy, D. W., Keane, T. M., & Blanchard, E. B. (2009). Group cognitive behavior therapy for chronic posttraumatic stress disorder: An initial randomized pilot study. *Behavior Therapy, 40*, 82–92.

Becker, C. C., & Zayfert, C. (2001). Integrating DBT-based techniques and concepts to facilitate exposure therapy for PTSD. *Cognitive and Behavioral Practice, 8*, 107–122.

Borkovec, T. D. (1993). Between-group therapy outcome research: Design and methodology. *NIDA Research Monograph, 137*, 249–289.

Bradley, R., Greene, J., Russ, E., Dutra, L, & Westen, D. (2005). A multidimensional meta-analysis of psychotherapy for PTSD. *American Journal of Psychiatry, 162*, 214–227.

Brady, K. T., Back, S. E., & Coffey, S. F. (2004). Substance abuse and posttraumatic stress disorder. *Current Directions in Psychological Science, 13*, 206–209.

Brady, K. T., Dansky, B. S., Back, S. E., Foa, E. B., & Carroll, K. M. (2001). Exposure therapy in the treatment of PTSD among cocaine-dependent individuals: Preliminary findings. *Journal of Substance Abuse Treatment, 21*, 47–54.

Bryant, R. A., Moulds, M. L., Guthrie, R. M., Dang, S. T., Mastrodomenico, J., Nixon, R. D. V., & Creamer, M. C. (2008). A randomized controlled trial of exposure therapy and cognitive restructuring for posttraumatic stress disorder. *Journal of Consulting and Clinical Psychology, 76*, 695–703.

Chilcoat, H. D., & Breslau, N. (1998a). Investigations of causal pathways between PTSD and drug use disorders. *Addictive Behaviors, 23*, 827–840.

Chilcoat, H. D., & Breslau, N. (1998b). Posttraumatic stress disorder and drug disorders: Testing causal pathways. *Archives of General Psychiatry, 55*, 913–917.

Cloitre, M., Stovall-McClough, K. C., Nooner, K., Zorbas, P., Cherry, S., Jackson, C.L., & Petkova E. (2010). Treatment for PTSD related to childhood abuse: A randomized controlled trial. *American Journal of Psychiatry, 167*, 915–924.

Cloitre, M., Koenen, K. C., Cohen, L. R., & Han, H. (2002). Skills training in affective and interpersonal regulation followed by exposure: A phase-based treatment for PTSD related to childhood abuse. *Journal of Consulting and Clinical Psychology, 70*, 1067–1074.

Cloitre, M., Stovall-McClough, C., Miranda, R., & Chemtob, C. M. (2004). Therapeutic alliance, negative mood regulation, and treatment outcome in child abuse-related posttraumatic stress disorder. *Journal of Consulting and Clinical Psychology, 72*, 411–416.

Cook, T. D., & Campbell, D. T. (1979). *Quasi-experimentation: Design & analysis issues for field settings*. Boston: Houghton Mifflin.

Courtois, C. A., Ford, J. D., & Cloitre, M. (2009). Best practices in psychotherapy with adults. In C. A. Courtois & J. D. Ford (Eds.), *Treating complex traumatic stress disorders* (pp. 82–103). New York: Guilford.

Creamer, M., Morris, P., Biddle, D., & Elliot, P. (2004). Treatment outcome in Australian veterans with combat-related posttraumatic stress disorder: A cause for cautious optimism? *Journal of Traumatic Stress, 12*, 554–558.

Crits-Christoph, P., Baranackie, K., Kurcias, J. S., Beck, A. T., Carroll, K., Perry, K., & Zitrin, C. (1991). Meta-analysis of therapist effects in psychotherapy outcome studies. *Psychotherapy Research, 1*, 81–91.

Davidson, P. R., & Parker, K. C. H. (2001). Eye movement desensitization and reprocessing (EMDR): A meta-analysis. *Journal of Consulting and Clinical Psychology, 69*, 305–316.

Donovan, B., Padin-Rivera, E., & Kowaliw, S. (2001). "Transcend": Initial outcomes from a posttraumatic stress disorder/substance abuse treatment program. *Journal of Traumatic Stress, 14*, 757–772.

Ehlers, A., Clark, D. M., Hackmann, A., McManus, F., & Fennell, M. J. V. (2005). Cognitive therapy for post-traumatic stress disorder: Development and evaluation. *Behavioral Research and Therapy, 43*, 413–431.

Ehlers, A., Clark, D. M., Hackmann, A., McManus, F., Fennell, M., Herbert, C., & Mayou, R. (2003). A randomized controlled trial of cognitive therapy, a self-help booklet, and repeated assessments as early interventions for posttraumatic stress disorder. *Archives of General Psychiatry, 60*, 1024–1032.

Foa, E. B., & Cahill, S. P. (2002). Specialized treatment for PTSD: Matching survivors to the appropriate modality. In

R. Yehuda (Ed.), *Treating trauma survivors with PTSD* (pp. 43–62). Washington, DC: American Psychiatric Publishing.
Foa, E. B., Dancu, C. V., Hembree, E. A., Jaycox, L., Meadows, & Street, J. (1999). A comparison of prolonged exposure, stress inoculation, and their combination for reducing posttraumatic stress disorder in female assault victims. *Journal of Consulting and Clinical Psychology, 67*, 194–200.
Foa, E. B., Hembree, E. A., Cahill, E. A., Rauch, S. A. M., Riggs, D. S., Feeny, N. C., & Yadin, E. (2005). Randomized trial of prolonged exposure for posttraumatic stress disorder with and without cognitive restructuring: Outcome at academic and community clinics. *Journal of Consulting and Clinical Psychology, 1073*, 953–964.
Foa, E. B., & Meadows, E. (1997). Psychosocial treatments for posttraumatic stress disorder: A critical review. *Annual Review of Psychology, 48*, 449–480.
Foa, E. B., Keane, T. M., Friedman, M. J., & Cohen, J. (2009). *Effective treatments for PTSD: Practice guidelines from the International Society for Traumatic Stress Studies.* New York: Guilford.
Foa, E. B., Riggs, D. S., Massie, E. D., & Yarczower, M. (1995). The impact of fear activation and anger on the efficacy of exposure treatment for posttraumatic stress disorder. *Behavior Therapy, 26*, 487–499.
Foa, E. B., & Rothbaum, B. O. (1998). *Treating the trauma of rape: Cognitive behavioral therapy for PTSD.* New York: Guilford.
Forbes, D., Creamer, M., Hawthorne, G., Allen, N., & McHugh, T. (2003). Comorbidity as a predictor of symptom change after treatment in combat-related posttraumatic stress disorder. *Journal of Nervous and Mental Disease, 191*, 93–99.
Frueh, B. C., Cusack, K. J., Grubaugh, A. L., Sauvageot, J. A., & Wells, C. (2006). Clinicians' perspectives on cognitive-behavioral treatment for PTSD among persons with severe mental illness. *Psychiatric Services, 57*, 1027–1031.
Glynn, S. M., Eth, S., Randolph, E.T., Foy, D. W., Urbaitis, M., Boxer, L., & Crothers, J. (1999). A test of behavioral family therapy to augment exposure for combat-related posttraumatic stress disorder. *Journal of Consulting and Clinical Psychology, 67*, 243–251.
Greene, C. J., Morland, L. A., Durkalski, V. L., & Frueh, B. C. (2008). Noninferiority and equivalence designs: Issues and implications for mental health research. *Journal of Traumatic Stress, 21*, 433–439.
Hagenaars, M. A., van Minnen, A., & Hoogduin, K. A. L. (2010). The impact of dissociation and depression on the efficacy of prolonged exposure treatment for PTSD. *Behaviour Research and Therapy, 48*, 19–27.
Hembree, E. A., Foa, E. B., Dorfan, N. M., Street, G. P., Kowalski, J., & Tu, X. (2003). Do patients drop out prematurely from exposure therapy for PTSD? *Journal of Traumatic Stress, 16*, 555–562.
Herman, J. L. (1992). Complex PTSD: A syndrome in survivors of prolonged and repeated trauma. *Journal of Traumatic Stress, 5*, 377–391.
Hien, D. A., Cohen, L. R., Miele, G. M., Litt, L. C., & Capstick, C. (2004). Promising treatments for women with comorbid PTSD and substance use disorders. *American Journal of Psychiatry, 161*, 1426–1432.
Institute of Medicine (2008). *Treatment of posttraumatic stress disorder: An assessment of the evidence.* Washington, DC: National Academies Press.
Kessler, R. C., Sonnega, A., Bromet, E., Hughes, M., & Nelson, C. B. (1995). Posttraumatic stress disorder in the National Comorbidity Survey. *Archives of General Psychiatry, 52*, 1048–1060.
Khan, A., Schwartz, K., Redding, N., Kolts, R. L., & Brown, W. A. (2007). Psychiatric diagnosis and clinical trial completion rates: Analysis of the FDA SBA Reports. *Neuropsychopharmacology, 32*, 2422–2430.
Killeen, T., Hien, D., Campbell, A., Brown, C., Hansen, C., Jiang, H., Brigham, G., & Nunes, E. (2008). Adverse events in an integrated trauma-focused intervention for women in community substance abuse treatment. *Journal of Substance Abuse Treatment, 35*, 304–311.
Linehan, M. M. (1993a). *Cognitive-behavioral treatment of borderline personality disorder.* New York: Guilford.
Linehan, M. M. (1993b). *Skills training manual for treating borderline personality disorder.* New York: Guilford.
McGovern, M., Lambert-Harris, C., Acquilano, S., Xie, H., Alterman, A. I., & Weiss, R. D. (2009). A cognitive behavioral therapy for co-occurring substance use and posttraumatic stress disorders. *Addictive Behaviors, 1034*, 892–898.
McIlvain, S., Chard, K., & Bailey, GW. (2011, August). Initial evidence supporting use of CPT-C for veterans with PTSD/TBI. Paper presented at Improving Veteran Mental Health Care Conference in the 21st Century, Baltimore, MD.
Monson, C. M., Schnurr, P. P., Resick, P. A., Friedman, M. J., Young-Xu, Y., & Stevens, S. P. (2006). Cognitive processing therapy for veterans with military-related posttraumatic stress disorder. *Journal of Consulting and Clinical Psychology* (Special Issue: Benefit-Finding), *74*, 898–907.
Morland, L. A., Greene, C. J., Rosen, C., Mauldin, P. D., & Frueh, B. C. (2009). Issues in the design of a randomized noninferiority clinical trial of telemental health psychotherapy for rural combat veterans with PTSD. *Contemporary Clinical Trials, 30*, 513–522.
Mueser, K. T., Bolton, E., Carty, P. C., Bradley, M. J., Ahlgren, K. F., DiStaso, D. R., & Liddell, C. (2007). The trauma recovery group: A cognitive-behavioral program for posttraumatic stress disorder in persons with severe mental illness. *Community Mental Health Journal, 43*, 281–304.
Mueser, K. T., Goodman, L. B., Trumbetta, S. L., Rosenberg, S. D., Osher, F. C., Vidaver, R., & Foy, D. W. (1998). Trauma and posttraumatic stress disorder in severe mental illness. *Journal of Consulting and Clinical Psychology, 66*, 493–499.
Mueser, K. T., Rosenberg, S. D., Goodman, L. A., & Trumbetta, S. L. (2002). Trauma, PTSD, and the course of severe mental illness: An interactive model. *Schizophrenia Research, 53*, 123–143.
Mueser, K.T., Rosenberg, S.D., & Xie, H. (2008). A randomized controlled trial of cognitive-behavioral treatment of posttraumatic stress disorder in severe mental illness. *Journal of Consulting and Clinical Psychology, 76*, 259–271.
Najavits, L. M., Gallop, R. J., & Weiss, R. D. (2006). Seeking Safety therapy for adolescent girls with PTSD and substance use disorder: A randomized controlled trial. *Journal of Behavioral Health Services and Research, 33*, 453–463.
Okie, S. (2006). Traumatic brain injury in the war zone. *New England Journal of Medicine, 352*, 2043–2047.
Olfson, M., Mojtabai, R., Sampson, N. A., Hwang, I., Druss, B., Wang, P., & Kessler, R. C. (2009). Dropout from outpatient mental health care in the United States. *Psychiatric Services, 60*, 898–907.
Ouimette, P., Moos, R. H., & Brown, P. J. (2003). Substance use disorder-posttraumatic stress disorder comorbidity: A survey of treatments and proposed practice guidelines. In P. Ouimette,

& P. J. Brown (Eds.), *Trauma and substance abuse: A survey of treatments and proposed practice guidelines* (pp. 91–110). Washington, DC: American Psychological Association.

Piaggio, G., Elbourne, D. R., Altman, D. G., Pocock, S. J., Evans, S. J.; CONSORT Group. (2006). Reporting of non-inferiority and equivalence randomized trials: An extension of the CONSORT statement. *Journal of the American Medical Association, 295*, 1152–1160.

Rauch, S. A. M., Grunfeld, T. E. E., Yadin, E., Cahill, S. Hembree, E. & Foa, E. (2009). Changes in reported physical health symptoms and social function with prolonged exposure therapy for chronic posttraumatic stress disorder. *Depression and Anxiety, 26*, 732–738.

Rauch, S. A. M., Sripada, R., Tuerk, P., Defever, A. M., Smith, E., Messina, M., & MacPhee, E. (2011, August). Prolonged Exposure in VHA: TBI and treatment response. Paper presented at Improving Veteran Mental Health Care Conference in the 21st Century, Baltimore, MD.

Resick, P. A., Galovski, T. E., Uhlmansiek, M. O., Scher, C. D., Clum, G. A., & Young-Xu, Y. (2008). A randomized clinical trial to dismantle components of cognitive processing therapy for posttraumatic stress disorder in female victims of interpersonal violence. *Journal of Consulting and Clinical Psychology, 76*, 243–258.

Resick, P. A., Nishith, P., Weaver, T. L., Astin, M. C., & Feuer, C. A. (2002). A comparison of cognitive-processing therapy with prolonged exposure and a waiting condition for the treatment of chronic posttraumatic stress disorder in female rape victims. *Journal of Consulting and Clinical Psychology, 70*, 867–879.

Rizvi, S. L., Vogt, D. S., & Resick, P. A. (2009). Cognitive and affective predictors of treatment outcome in cognitive processing therapy and prolonged exposure for posttraumatic stress disorder. *Behavior Research and Therapy, 47*, 737–743.

Rounsaville, B. J., Carroll, K. M., & Onken. L. (2001). A stage model of behavioral therapies research: Getting started and moving on from Stage 1. *Clinical Psychology: Science and Practice, 8*, 133–142.

Ruzek, J. I., Young, B. H., & Walser, R. D. (2003). Group treatment of posttraumatic stress disorder and other trauma-related problems. *Primary Psychiatry, 10*, 53–57.

Schnurr, P.P. (2007). The rocks and hard places in psychotherapy outcome research. *Journal of Traumatic Stress, 20*, 779–792.

Schnurr, P. P. (2010). PTSD 30 years on. *Journal of Traumatic Stress, 23*, 1–2.

Schnurr, P. P., Friedman, M. J., Engel, C. C., Foa, E. B., Shea, M. T., Resick, P.M., & Chow, B. K. (2005). Issues in the design of multisite clinical trials of psychotherapy: CSP #494 as an example. *Contemporary Clinical Trials, 26*, 626–636.

Schnurr, P. P., Friedman, M. J., Engel, C. C., Shea, M. T., Chow, B. K., Resick, P. A., & Bernardy, N. (2007). Cognitive behavioral therapy for posttraumatic stress disorder in women: A randomized controlled trial. *Journal of the American Medical Association, 297*, 820–830.

Schnurr, P. P., Friedman, M. J., Foy, D. W., Shea, M. T., Hsieh, F. Y., Lavori, P. W., Bernardy, N. (2003). A randomized trial of trauma focus group therapy for posttraumatic stress disorder: Results from a Department of Veterans Affairs Cooperative Study. *Archives of General Psychiatry, 60*, 481–489.

Schnurr, P. P., Friedman, M. J., Lavori, P. J., & Hsieh, F. Y. (2001). Design of VA Cooperative Study #420: Group treatment of PTSD. *Controlled Clinical Trials, 22*, 74–88.

Schulz, P. M., Resick, P. A., Huber, L. C., & Griffin, M. G. (2006). The effectiveness of Cognitive Processing Therapy for PTSD with refugees in a community setting. *Cognitive and Behavioral Practice, 13*, 322–331.

Schulz, P. M., Huber, L. C., & Resick, P. A. (2006). Practical adaptations of Cognitive Processing Therapy with Bosnian refugees: Implications for adapting practice to a multicultural clientele. *Cognitive and Behavioral Practice, 13*, 310–321.

Seligman, M. E. P. (1995). The effectiveness of psychotherapy: The consumer reports study. *American Psychologist, 50*, 965–974.

Spates, C. R., Koch, E., Cusack, K., Pagoto, S., & Waller, S. (2009). Eye movement desensitization and reprocessing. In E. B. Foa, T. M. Keane, M. J. Friedman, & J. A. Cohen (Eds.), *Effective treatments for PTSD: Practice guidelines from the international society for traumatic stress studies* (2nd ed., pp. 279–305). New York: Guilford.

Stirman, S. W., DeRubeis, R. J., Crits-Christoph, P., & Rothman, A. (2005). Can the randomized controlled trial literature generalize to nonrandomized patients? *Journal of Consulting and Clinical Psychology, 73*, 127–135.

Tanielian, T. L., & Jaycox, L. H. (2008). *Invisible wounds of war: Psychological and cognitive injuries, their consequences, and services to assist recovery.* Santa Monica, CA: RAND Corporation.

Tarrier, N., & Sommerfield, C. (2004). Treatment of chronic PTSD by cognitive therapy and exposure: 5-year follow-up. *Behavior Therapy, 35*, 231–246.

Tarrier, N., Sommerfield, C., Pilgrim, H., & Faragher, B. (2000). Factors associated with outcome of cognitive-behavioral treatment of chronic posttraumatic stress disorder. *Behaviour Research and Therapy, 38*, 191–202.

Task Force on Promotion and Dissemination of Psychological Procedures. (1998). Update on empirically supported therapies II. *Clinical Psychologist, 51*, 3–16.

Triffleman, E., Carroll, K., & Kellogg, S. (1999). Substance dependent posttraumatic stress disorder therapy. *Journal of Substance Abuse Treatment, 17*, 3–14.

Tunis, S. R., Stryer, D. B., & Clancy, C. M. (2003). Practical clinical trials: Increasing the value of clinical research for decision making in clinical and health policy. *Journal of the American Medical Association, 290*, 1624–1632.

van Etten, M. L., & Taylor, S. (1998). Comparative efficacy of treatments for post-traumatic stress disorder: A meta-analysis. *Clinical Psychology and Psychotherapy, 5*, 126–144.

van Minnen, A., Arntz, A., & Keijsers, G. P. J. (2002). Prolonged exposure in patients with chronic PTSD: Predictors of treatment outcome and dropout. *Behaviour Research and Therapy, 40*, 439–457.

Wagner, A. W., Rizvi, S. L., & Harned, S. L. (2007). Applications of dialectical behavior therapy to the treatment of complex trauma-related problems: When one case formulation does not fit all. *Journal of Traumatic Stress, 20*, 391–400.

Zayfert, C., DeViva, J. C., Becker, C. B., Pike, J. L., Gillock, K. L., & Hayes, S. A. (2005). Exposure utilization and completion of cognitive behavioral therapy for PTSD in a "real world" clinical practice. *Journal of Traumatic Stress, 18*, 637–645.

Zlotnick, C., Johnson, J., & Najavits, L. M. (2009). Randomized controlled pilot study of cognitive-behvaioral therapy in a sample of incarcerated women with substance use disorder and PTSD. *Behavior Therapy, 40*, 325–336.

Zoellner, L. A., Feeny, N. C., Fitzgibbons, L. A., & Foa, E. B. (1999). Response of African American and Caucasian women to cognitive behavioral therapy for PTSD. *Behavior Therapy, 30*, 581–595.

CHAPTER

29 Empirically Supported Psychological Treatments: Prolonged Exposure

Nisha Nayak, Mark B. Powers, *and* Edna B. Foa

Abstract

A large body of evidence supports the efficacy of exposure therapy for the treatment of anxiety disorders, including posttraumatic stress disorder (PTSD). This chapter discusses Prolonged Exposure (PE) therapy, a structured treatment program that uses imaginal and in vivo exposure as the core elements of treatment. It was first applied with survivors of sexual assault but has since been widely applied to survivors of all types of traumas. The chapter provides a description of the treatment program. It also discusses emotional processing theory and proposed underlying mechanisms of the therapy, including fear activation, habituation, and modification of dysfunctional beliefs. The chapter then reviews empirical studies, which have demonstrated the efficacy of PE, and data that support the generalizability of positive outcomes across trauma types, treatment settings, and cultures. Limitations and future directions for research are discussed.

Key Words: Exposure therapy, Prolonged Exposure, PE, posttraumatic stress disorder, PTSD, emotional processing theory

Introduction

Over the past 30 years, research and clinical outcomes have indicated that exposure therapies are highly efficacious in the treatment of anxiety disorders. Consistent with these findings, there is a large body of theoretical and empirical support for the use of exposure for the treatment of posttraumatic stress disorder (Cahill, Rothbaum, Resick, & Follette, 2009). Prolonged Exposure (PE) therapy (Foa, Hembree, & Rothbaum, 2007) is a structured program that uses imaginal and in vivo exposure as the core elements of treatment. It was first applied with survivors of sexual assault, but has since been widely applied to survivors of all types of traumas. This chapter will review PE, beginning with a description of the treatment program. Second, underlying mechanisms of the therapy and empirical support for these proposed mechanisms are explicated. Then, empirical support for efficacy and effectiveness is reviewed. Finally, the chapter concludes by discussing limitations of the treatment and empirical data, and giving suggestions for future directions.

Treatment Description

Prolonged Exposure therapy is a structured treatment program that has been successfully used with patients with PTSD. Like other exposure therapies, the PE treatment program is based on the patient confronting trauma-related cues that continue to evoke excessive or inappropriate fear. It is a form of cognitive-behavioral therapy (CBT), and the duration of treatment is relatively short, typically consisting of 10 to15 ninety-minute sessions. Primary goals of treatment are to reduce the patient's PTSD symptoms and other trauma-related distress and to help return him or her to baseline functioning.

Most trauma survivors show natural recovery within three months and will never need a trauma-focused therapy. Thus, an intake evaluation is an important step prior to initiating treatment. PE may be considered for individuals who have PTSD and related psychopathology or at least clinically significant symptoms after a trauma and who have sufficient memory of the event to describe it in narrative format. Exclusionary criteria for PE are minimal and based on good clinical judgment. They include imminent threat of suicidal or homicidal behavior, serious self-injurious behavior, current psychosis, current high risk of assault (i.e., domestic violence), or lack of clear memory of the traumatic event. Substance abuse or dependence, ongoing risk of danger, severe dissociative symptoms, and comorbid Axis II disorders are not considered categorical reasons for exclusion. Rather, it should be determined whether they are primary or secondary problems relative to PTSD and should be afforded the appropriate clinical attention.

The PE treatment program consists of four elements: psycho-education; training in slow, relaxed breathing; imaginal exposure (i.e., repeated retelling of the traumatic memory); and in vivo exposure. Discussing the rationale for the therapeutic procedures and obtaining buy-in from the patient are important, and various metaphors are used to help the patient understand the value of exposure in overcoming PTSD. Given the structured, short-term nature of treatment, the therapist can develop rapport by discussing the rationale and psycho-education components in an interactive manner. As with most cognitive-behavioral therapies, homework is an essential component of the treatment program, and patients are provided with audio recordings of each session to listen to in between sessions. In this way, learning is consolidated and generalized.

In vivo exposure is one of two main ingredients in the PE treatment program. In vivo exposure involves having the patient confront real-life cues (i.e. places, situations, activities, etc.) that evoke fear responses because of their association with the trauma rather than because of their inherent danger. For example, an individual who was assaulted at night may subsequently avoid leaving the house after dark even if he or she lives in a safe neighborhood. For such an individual, going out at night might be an in vivo exposure exercise. Repeated in vivo exposure is effective by allowing the patient to habituate to feared situations, to learn that these situations are relatively safe, and to learn that he or she can cope with their anxiety. The therapist and the patient collaboratively construct an in vivo exposure hierarchy by making a list of trauma-related situations and activities that elicit avoidance, escape, or fear. For exposure to be effective, it must be prolonged, systematic, and repeated. Thus, the patient is instructed to stay in the situation for 45–60 minutes, or until his or her anxiety decreases by 50% or more, and to repeat the exposure multiple times during the week. Over ensuing weeks, the patient gradually confronts increasingly distressing items on the hierarchy, and in each session the therapist and patient review progress and assignments for the coming week.

Imaginal exposure is the second main ingredient of the PE treatment program. Here, the patient repeatedly imagines and describes the traumatic memory for 45–60 minutes in session, with instructions to return to the beginning of the memory each time that the end is reached. The patient is encouraged to describe the memory as vividly as possible and include sensory details, thoughts, and feelings. The imaginal exposure is followed by 15–20 minutes of discussion between the therapist and patient, allowing further processing of trauma-related thoughts and feelings. This processing can foster shifts in dysfunctional beliefs, such as self-blame. The patient is provided with an audio recording of the imaginal exposure and instructed to listen to it once daily. After its introduction, imaginal exposure and processing consume the majority of session time until the end of treatment.

Proposed Underlying Mechanism and Related Empirical Support

Emotional Processing Theory

The treatment effect of PE therapy can be explained by emotional processing theory (Foa & Kozak, 1986), which was developed to account for how exposure therapy leads to fear reduction. The roots of emotional processing theory derive from Lang's (1977) bioinformational view of fear. Lang (1977, 1984) proposed a framework in which fear functions as a program of action to escape from or avoid danger and consists of stimulus, response, and meaning elements. For example, a fear of crowds, which is common among those with PTSD, would consist of representations of crowds (e.g., voices yelling; people standing nearby), physiological and behavioral fear responses (e.g., rapid heart rate; moving away), and meanings associated with crowds (e.g., "Crowds can lead to a riot and are dangerous.") and with the person's responses (e.g., "Rapid heart rate and moving away mean that I am afraid."). The fear structure exists as an associational network and is activated when information matches some information in the structure and spreads to other representations.

Building on Lang's work, Foa and Kozak (1986) presented a comprehensive theory of emotional processing of fear. According to these authors, pathological fear structures are distinguished by excessive response elements (e.g., avoidance, physiological activity) and resistance to modification. Based on these assumptions, they proposed two conditions that are necessary for emotional processing and associated reduction in fear: (1) activation of the fear structure, and (2) incorporation of corrective information that is incompatible with the pathological elements of the existing fear structure. Foa and Kozak (1986) originally suggested that emotional processing involved modifying the pathological fear structure by replacing old associations with new ones. However, contemporary learning research (Bouton, 2000; Rescorla, 2001) indicates that previous associations persist even after extinction, and that new associations merely compete with old ones (Milad, Rauch, Pitman, & Quirk, 2006). Based on these findings, Foa and McNally (1996) revised the theory by proposing that exposure therapy results in formation of new associations in the fear structure. From a treatment perspective, this theoretical difference highlights the importance of including multiple contexts in the course of therapy to promote generalization (Foa, Huppert, & Cahill, 2006).

Foa and Kozak's theory explicitly distinguished between emotional processing and treatment outcome, which offered the potential for testable hypotheses. Conceptually, emotional processing was described as an ongoing process of change in fear, whereas treatment outcome was viewed as a single time-point measure of a new structure with consideration of both fear symptoms and broader functioning. Using these definitions, the authors proposed three indicators of emotional processing: initial physiological activation, within-session habituation (i.e., reduction in fear during a single exposure session), and across-session habituation (i.e., gradual reduction in fear across multiple exposure sessions). Several studies provide evidence that these indicators change over the course of successful exposure therapy for anxiety disorders in general (Foa & Chambless, 1978; Grayson, Foa, & Steketee, 1982; Lang, Melamed, & Hart, 1970) and thus provide valuable markers of emotional processing. Furthermore, habituation eventually results in the absence of physiological activation in the presence of the target stimulus and thereby provides disconfirming, or corrective, information about the meaning of the stimulus (Foa et al., 2006).

Emotional Processing Theory, PTSD, and Exposure

Foa and Kozak (1986) hypothesized that anxiety disorders, such as PTSD, involve specific pathological features in the fear structure. For a person raped by a man in a park, for example, pathological components may include inaccurate stimulus-stimulus associations (men → gun) and stimulus-response associations (men → racing heart). An even more important element of the pathological fear structure is the inappropriate association of threat meanings with stimuli that, objectively, are relatively safe but remind the person of the trauma. An individual with PTSD related to an assault in a park may perceive parks, or even going outside, as dangerous and therefore exhibit excessive avoidance. Response elements may also be associated with threat or other maladaptive meaning (shortness of breath → fear → beliefs in weakness or inability to cope). When danger meanings are associated with thoughts, memories, and emotions that are related to the trauma, the traumatized individual may exhibit cognitive avoidance. Pathological fear structures also are characterized by exaggerated estimates of the risk and cost of harm, and beliefs about the persistence and negative consequences of anxiety in the absence of avoidance or escape.

According to Foa and Kozak (1986), both in vivo and imaginal exposure promote the emotional processing of fear by activating the fear structure and permitting corrective information to be integrated. Through repeated confrontation of the feared stimulus, or in vivo exposure, fear is experienced in the absence of anticipated negative consequences, which allows for correction of the exaggerated probability estimates of harm. Imaginal exposure is also essential for successful emotional processing because it interrupts the pathological associations between thoughts and memories about the past traumatic event, which cannot be confronted in real life, and threat meanings. Having the individual with PTSD repeatedly revisit the traumatic memory is thought to correct beliefs about the exaggerated cost of feared consequences, for example by helping the trauma survivor learn that initial distress associated with remembering the event does not mean he or she will fall apart or go crazy, or that the distress will persist indefinitely. In addition, imaginal exposure facilitates the distinction between remembering the trauma and being traumatized, so that the memory no longer carries the same threat meaning.

Foa (1997) expanded on emotional processing theory and applied it specifically to explain the effect of exposure therapy on PTSD symptoms. First, emotional engagement was hypothesized as a central ingredient to successful processing pathological fear following a trauma. Emotional engagement corresponds to Foa and Kozak's (1986) condition of activation of the fear structure, but the construct reflects the idea that effective therapy rests not only on presentation of fear-evoking stimuli but also on the patient's willingness to eliminate avoidance and to experience fear. Foa (1997) also proposed that cognitive changes were essential in recovery from PTSD, and stressed the importance of modifying the two most common erroneous beliefs in this disorder (e.g., "The world is extremely dangerous" and "I [the victim] am extremely incompetent.")

Clinical Studies of Emotional Processing Theory

In summary, emotional processing theory posits that fear activation or emotional engagement, habituation, and changing maladaptive beliefs about the self and the world are the central mechanisms underlying the efficacy of PE. Studies supporting these ideas are outlined below.

Several studies support the idea that activation of fear is a necessary condition for successful exposure therapy. For example, heart rate reactivity has been found to be related to successful treatment outcome in exposure-based therapies of phobic patients (Lang et al., 1970), as well as patients with PTSD (Pitman et al., 1996). Because heart rate activation may reflect general arousal rather than fear specifically, Foa, Riggs, Massie, and Yarczower (1995) tested the fear activation hypothesis using a Facial Action Coding System (FACS) measure of emotion. Results indicated that the FACS measure of fear was significantly and positively correlated with percent symptom reduction and that fear activation mediated the effect of pretreatment variables on treatment outcome. The above studies demonstrate that objective measures of fear activation and expression are related to positive outcome in exposure therapy. Jaycox, Foa, and Morral (1998) examined the relation of self-reported emotional engagement and treatment outcome in a group of 37 assault victims who received PE therapy, alone or with stress inoculation training. The study identified three patterns of emotional responding in PE: High Engagers/Habituators (E/H), High Engagers/Non-Habituators (E/NH), and Low Engagers/Non-Habituators (NE/NH). Those with distress ratings that were initially high but that decreased across sessions—the E/H group—had superior treatment outcome and were more likely to achieve "good end-state functioning," a criterion that required improvement in PTSD symptoms, depression, and anxiety, in contrast to those with the other response patterns. Patients with distress ratings that started high and remained relatively high—the E/NH pattern—generally did not achieve good end-state functioning. Taken together, these findings are consistent with the idea that fear activation and emotional engagement are important, but not sufficient, for successful exposure therapy.

Indirect forms of evidence also provide support for the idea that fear activation is an underlying mechanism in PE. That is, if fear activation is a mediator of treatment, then constructs that are negatively related to fear engagement, such as avoidance, would be expected to predict negative outcome. This is indeed the case. For example, anger has been proposed to inhibit fear. Self-reported anger prior to PE was negatively correlated with facial expression of fear and with treatment outcome (Foa et al., 1995). Research on natural recovery from trauma also suggests that emotional engagement promotes healing. In an observational study of female victims of assault, Gilboa-Schechtman and Foa (2001) identified those whose peak symptom levels were delayed, versus immediate, relative to time of assault and proposed that immediate peak reactions reflected greater emotional engagement. Consistent with this hypothesis and the fear activation theory, immediate peak reactors had better outcome at three- and six-month follow-up.

Studies examining the role of habituation generally have indicated that between-session habituation, or reduction in distress across repeated exposure sessions, is more important than within-session habituation, or reduction in distress over the course of a single exposure session. For example, Jaycox et al. (1998) failed to find an association between within-session habituation and end-state functioning. Similarly, other exposure therapy studies failed to indicate that within-session habituation promotes emotional processing (Kozak, Foa, & Steketee, 1988; Riley et al., 1995; van Minnen & Foa, 2006). On the other hand, several studies have provided support that between-session habituation is related to treatment outcome in exposure therapy (e.g., Kozak et al., 1988; Lang et al., 1970; Rauch, Foa, Furr, & Filip, 2004). Indeed, as mentioned previously, between-session habituation, when accompanied by emotional engagement, was associated with superior outcome in patients who received PE (Jaycox et al., 1998). These findings suggest the question of what factors are related to between-session habituation and what steps could be taken to promote it in patients who do not habituate on their own.

Fewer studies have examined change in dysfunctional cognitions about the self and the world during PE. Nonetheless, research findings do provide support for such cognitive changes. Foa and Rauch (2004) reported that significant reductions in negative beliefs about the self and the world occurred over the course of PE and that these reductions correlated with PTSD symptom reduction. Notably, the addition of explicit cognitive restructuring did not produce any greater cognitive change. Results also indicated that change in beliefs about the self, but not beliefs about the world, uniquely predicted change in PTSD symptoms. Thus, cognitive changes related to one's sense of competence and self-efficacy may be particularly significant in recovery from PTSD.

Animal Studies of Fear Extinction

Since most individuals who survive a trauma show PTSD-like symptoms in the immediate aftermath, but only a minority show persistent symptoms (Rothbaum, Foa, Riggs, Murdock, & Walsh, 1992), PTSD may be understood as a failure to extinguish conditioned fear responses. Studies showing that patients with PTSD demonstrate deficiencies in brain areas known to be responsible for extinction support this idea (see Milad, Rauch, Pitman, & Quirk, 2006 for a review). Foa, Zinbarg, and Rothbaum (1992) presented a detailed view of fear conditioning as an animal model of PTSD. The authors discussed how behavioral responses exhibited by animals that have undergone fear conditioning parallel the symptom clusters observed in PTSD. Thus, animal studies of extinction may be used to examine the mechanisms of exposure and the predictions of emotional processing theory.

Animal studies of fear conditioning and extinction follow the principles of basic Pavlovian, or classical, conditioning. During the acquisition phase, a neutral stimulus (e.g., tone or light), which is the conditioned stimulus (CS), is paired with an aversive stimulus, the unconditioned stimulus (US), such as a foot shock. The acquisition phase is akin to the original traumatic experience in the case of PTSD. During extinction training that occurs some time later, the CS is presented repeatedly without the US. During a subsequent test phase, the CS is presented again in the absence of the US. The extinction training and test phases can be viewed as analogous to initial and subsequent exposure sessions.

As previously mentioned, one prediction of emotional processing theory is that fear activation is one of the central mechanisms underlying exposure. Several animal studies support the idea that activation is related to extinction. For example, compared to animals that were not drugged, animals that were given anxiolytic agents, such as barbiturates or benzodiazepines, showed greater fear responses during the test phase, or impaired extinction learning (Barry, Etheredge, & Miller, 1965; Bouton, Kenney, & Rosengard, 1990). Cain, Blouin, and Barad (2004) directly compared the effect of a drug that increases adrenergic activity and anxiety (yohimbine) versus one that decreases adrenergic activity and anxiety (propanolol) on fear-extinction learning. Results from this study indicated that animals that received yohimbine showed enhanced fear extinction during the test phase, whereas animals that received propanolol exhibited impaired extinction. These findings again are consistent with the hypothesis that fear activation during exposure is associated with better treatment outcomes. This finding was replicated with individuals suffering from fear of enclosed places: participants who received yohimbine before two exposure sessions showed significantly less fear at follow-up than those who received placebo (Powers, Smits, Otto, Sanders, & Emmelkamp, 2009). However, the propanolol finding in humans remains to be seen, as a study in humans found no significant effect of propanolol on fear extinction among a group with PTSD (Orr et al., 2006). In addition, there are other findings that are less consistent with the fear-activation hypothesis. For example, Morris and Bouton (2007) showed that yohimbine was associated with less fear expression in animals, as indicated by freezing response, not only during the test phase but also during extinction training. Thus, this study does not provide evidence that greater initial fear activation is responsible for greater extinction learning. Conclusive evidence for the role of pharmacological agents in augmenting activation and thereby enhancing extinction awaits future research.

Another approach that researchers have used is to compare the effects of massed versus spaced presentation of the CS during extinction training on fear responding during extinction and later during recall of extinction—that is, during presentation of the CS without the US some time after the extinction learning. Cain, Blouin, and Barad (2003) showed that massed (versus spaced) presentation of the CS during extinction training, which results in greater within-session fear extinction, also produced lower fear response during the test phase one week later. In other words, within-session habituation was associated with superior extinction learning, which is consistent with the emotional processing theory prediction. Li and Westbrook (2008) reported conflicting results, but differed from the Cain et al. study in its use of longer intertrial intervals and context conditioning rather than presentation of a discrete stimulus. These differences could be responsible for the discrepant outcomes. In summary, although studies examining within-session habituation as an indicator of emotional processing have yielded mixed findings, there is substantial empirical support that fear activation and between-session habituation are mechanisms underlying the effectiveness of PE.

Efficacy and Effectiveness of Prolonged Exposure

As previously described, PE is a structured treatment program that has the components of imaginal and in vivo exposure at its core. Many studies have demonstrated that exposure therapy in general reduces PTSD severity and produces superior outcome compared to wait list and nonspecific control conditions (see Cahill et al., 2009, for a review). Indeed, in a comprehensive 2008 report, the Institute of Medicine found that "the evidence is sufficient to conclude the efficacy of exposure therapies in the treatment of PTSD" (Institute of Medicine, 2008, p. 97) but did not find sufficient evidence to support the efficacy of other pharmacologic treatment or psychotherapies. Variants of imaginal exposure have led to beneficial outcomes among male veterans (Cooper & Clum, 1989; Keane, Fairbank, Caddell, & Zimmering, 1989), mixed gender/mixed-trauma civilian populations (Tarrier et al., 1999; Vaughan et al., 1994), and refugees (Neuner, Schauer, Klaschik, Karunakara, & Elbert, 2004). In a randomized study of earthquake survivors with chronic PTSD, Basoglu and colleagues (Basoglu, Salcioglu, Livanou, Kalender, & Gonul, 2005) demonstrated that just one session of a self-directed form of in vivo exposure produced a significantly greater decrease in PTSD symptoms six weeks later compared to wait list. Similarly, treatments combining imaginal and in vivo exposure, but not using the PE protocol per se, have been found to produce superior outcomes to relaxation therapy (Marks, Lovell, Noshirvani, Livanou, & Thrasher, 1998; Taylor et al., 2003). Although the exposure procedures used in these studies differed somewhat from those used in PE, they nonetheless can provide evidence in support of the efficacy of PE.

The efficacy of PE specifically has been studied in a number of clinical studies. A recent meta-analysis of 13 randomized controlled trials of PE for PTSD (N = 658) demonstrated a large effect for PE versus controls at posttreatment and follow-up (Hedges's g = 1.08 and 0.68, respectively; Powers, Halpern, Ferenschak, Gillihan, & Foa, 2010). Next, we review several well-controlled efficacy studies that meet all or most of the "gold standards" for clinical research (Foa & Meadows, 1997). These features include (1) clearly defined target symptoms; (2) reliable and valid measures; (3) use of evaluators who were unaware of treatment condition; (4) assessor training; (5) manualized, replicable, specific treatment programs; (6) unbiased assignment to treatment; and (7) treatment adherence. These studies are summarized below and presented in table 29.1.

Multiple clinical trials have demonstrated the efficacy of PE relative to a wait list or minimal attention control. A common feature of these studies was the use of all-female civilian samples with index traumas of sexual assault, physical assault, or childhood sexual abuse. In a seminal study, Foa, Rothbaum, Riggs, and Murdock (1991) found that PE was superior to wait-list control with respect to improvement in avoidance and intrusion symptoms of PTSD at posttreatment. Furthermore, PE showed a trend toward further improvement in overall PTSD symptoms from posttreatment to long-term follow-up, unlike groups receiving wait list or stress inoculation training. In a later study, individuals who received PE showed significantly lower levels of posttreatment PTSD, depression, and anxiety symptoms and significantly greater likelihood of good end-state functioning and loss of PTSD diagnosis relative to the wait-list control group (Foa et al., 1999). Subsequent studies have replicated these results, supporting the conclusion

Table 29.1. Selected efficacy studies of Prolonged Exposure (PE) therapy

Study	Sample size	Population	Index trauma	Comparator Treatment(s), Control	Major outcome(s)
Foa et al., 1991	C: 45	Female civilians	Sexual assault	SIT, SC, WL	Avoidance & Intrusion sx: PE & SIT > SC & WL
Foa et al., 1999	ITT: 96 C: 79	Female civilians	Sexual or physical assault	SIT, PE/SIT, WL	PE = SIT = PE/SIT > WL
Resick et al., 2002	ITT: 171 C: 121	Female civilians	Sexual assault	CPT, WL	PE = CPT > WL
Foa et al., 2005	ITT: 179 C: 121	Female civilians	Sexual/physical assault, child sexual abuse	PE/CR, WL	PE = PE/CR > WL
Rothbaum et al., 2005	ITT: 74 C: 60	Female civilians	Sexual assault	EMDR, WL	PE = EMDR > WL
Rothbaum et al., 2006	ITT: 65 C: 58	Mixed gender	Mixed trauma	PE/sertraline vs. sertraline alone	PE/sertraline superior in partial responders
Schnurr et al., 2007	ITT: 284 C: 199	Female military	Sexual trauma, physical assault, war zone	PCT	PE > PCT

Note: Studies meeting "gold standard" for clinical research are listed. C = Completers; ITT = Intent-to-treat; SIT = stress inoculation training; SC = supportive counseling; WL = wait list; PE/SIT = combination PE and SIT; CPT = cognitive processing therapy; PE/CR = combination PE and cognitive restructuring; EMDR = eye movement desensitization and reprocessing; PCT = present-centered therapy.

that PE is efficacious for females with assault-related PTSD (Foa et al., 2005; Resick, Nishith, Weaver, Astin, & Feuer, 2002; Rothbaum, Astin, & Marsteller, 2005).

The efficacy of PE has also been studied relative to other forms of psychotherapy, including both nonspecific and active comparator treatments. Compared to treatments designed to offer only nonspecific therapeutic effects, such as supportive counseling or present-centered therapy, PE produced a significantly greater reduction in symptoms and was more likely to result in loss of PTSD diagnosis or complete remission (Foa et al., 1991; Schnurr et al., 2007). This finding is particularly important because it highlights that PE treatment produced better outcomes not only relative to no treatment, as in the wait-list control studies, but also relative to a credible therapy delivered by competent clinicians. These studies thus demonstrate that the specific elements of exposure therapy offer added value above and beyond therapy in general.

PE also has been studied in comparison to several active treatments—namely, stress inoculation training (SIT), cognitive processing therapy (CPT), and eye movement desensitization and reprocessing therapy (EMDR). In studies that employed both PE and SIT, both treatments were efficacious and comparable at reducing symptoms of PTSD, with no significant differences between the two, although one study showed a trend for PE to show improvement at follow-up compared to SIT (Foa et al., 1991, 1999). Notably, the combination of PE with SIT did not offer any advantage with respect to treatment outcome relative to PE alone (Foa et al., 1999). Resick et al. (2002) reported similar findings, specifically that both PE and CPT were superior to wait list with respect to symptom reduction and change in diagnostic status, but that no significant differences in outcome were observed between the two active treatments. Results of studies comparing PE with EMDR have shown that both treatments led to improvements in PTSD symptoms at the end of treatment, with no significant differences between the two treatments (Lee, Gavriel, Drummond, Richards, & Greenwald, 2002; Rothbaum et al., 2005). Although the Lee et al. study indicated that EMDR produced greater gains at six-month follow-up, this difference may be attributable to their use of a modified protocol that used seven, versus nine, sessions of PE and used half of the session time for SIT-based skills training, thereby reducing the dose of PE. The Rothbaum et al. (2005) study did not reveal any differences in outcome between the two active treatments at follow-up. In summary, for treatment of PTSD, PE consistently has demonstrated superior outcomes to no treatment and nonspecific forms of therapy and comparable outcomes to all other efficacious psychotherapies for PTSD.

Researchers have started to investigate PE in comparison to and in combination with medication for PTSD. Sertraline is currently one of only two medications approved for treatment of PTSD. In a nonrandomized trial that directly compared PE and sertraline for treatment of PTSD, PE produced a significantly greater reduction in PTSD symptoms compared to the medication (Feeny, Zoellner, Mavissakalian, & Roy-Byrne, 2009). In a randomized study using a mixed-gender, mixed-trauma sample who had received 10 weeks of open-label treatment with sertraline, the effect of adding PE during continuation sertraline treatment was investigated (Rothbaum et al., 2006). Those individuals who showed an excellent response to the medication did not receive additional benefit from PE therapy. However, among those who showed only partial response during the initial medication phase, the addition of PE produced a large augmentation effect (Cohen's d = 0.90) on PTSD symptoms. Conversely, relative to placebo, paroxetine did not augment treatment outcome when added to continuation PE among individuals who failed to remit following a standard course of PE treatment (Simon et al., 2008). Thus, although conclusions are tentative given the few studies in this area, initial research findings suggest that PE offers some treatment advantage over medication and that it may augment treatment response among medication nonresponders, but the reverse may not hold true. Another potential advantage of PE relative to medication may be patient preference. When patients were given treatment choice after presentation of videotaped rationales for both treatments, 82% chose PE, whereas only 13% chose sertraline (Feeny et al., 2009).

Most of the large-scale, methodologically rigorous studies of PE have been conducted with female survivors of sexual or physical assault recruited from the community. However, as discussed at the beginning of this section, it has been demonstrated that variants of exposure treatment for PTSD are efficacious across various populations and trauma types, and efficacy results for PE also seem to generalize. For example, several studies have included other types of trauma, including combat/war zone, motor vehicle accidents, and death of a loved one, and other populations, including men and veterans (Nacasch et al., 2011; Rauch et al., 2009; Rothbaum et al., 2006). Another study showed that PE was more effective than time-limited dynamic therapy in a sample of 38 adolescents with PTSD, supporting its use with younger populations (Gilboa-Schechtman et al., 2010). Nor does the efficacy of PE appear restricted to academic medical centers or expert therapists. It has been used successfully in the VA setting (Rauch et al., 2009) and with community counselors in an outreach clinic (Feske, 2008). In both of these settings, therapists were newly trained in PE. Notably, in a large-scale study that included both expert academic clinicians, who were very experienced with PE, and community therapists, treatment outcome did not differ across therapist type (Foa et al., 2005).

Preliminary research findings also indicate that PE therapy is efficacious in other cultures. For example, in a case report study of five Israeli survivors of combat with chronic PTSD, PTSD symptom scores reduced by nearly 50% following PE therapy (Nacasch et al., 2007). Furthermore, in a randomized controlled study conducted with 30 Israeli veterans and survivors of terrorism, there was a significant pre/post treatment reduction in PTSD symptoms in the PE group, but not in the treatment as usual group (Nacasch et al., 2011). The feasibility and acceptability of PE has also been examined in Japan. In a mixed-gender, mixed-trauma sample, 10 patients who completed PE therapy showed significant decreases in symptoms of PTSD and depression, which were maintained at follow-up (Asukai, Saito, Tsuruta, Ogami, & Kishimoto, 2008).

Concerns that exposure therapy is associated with premature dropout or that many patients may not be able to tolerate exposure do not appear supported by empirical evidence. For example, although Tarrier et al. (1999) suggested that imaginal exposure was associated with a "worsening" of symptoms compared to cognitive therapy, Devilly and Foa

(2001) challenged this assertion on several methodological grounds, including the previous authors' failure to base their conclusions on reliable change scores. Moreover, Foa and colleagues (Foa, Zoellner, Feeny, Hembree, & Alvarez-Conrad, 2002) showed that only a minority of PE patients show temporary symptom exacerbation and that these individuals are no different in terms of mean outcome or overall dropout rates. Finally, a review of 25 studies showed that dropout rates were no different for exposure therapy than for other cognitive-behavioral treatments for PTSD (Hembree et al., 2003).

Studies in patients who received PE therapy have revealed few predictors of treatment response or dropout. Emotional engagement does appear related to better outcome (Foa et al, 1995; Jaycox et al., 1998). In addition, in a small study, Doane, Feeny, and Zoellner (2010) reported that sudden treatment gains were associated with significantly greater reductions in PTSD symptoms over the entire course of treatment. Van Minnen, Arntz, and Keijsers (2002) looked at a large number of potential predictors, including demographics, depression, anxiety, personality, trauma characteristics, anger, guilt, shame, and nonspecific variables regarding therapy, as predictors of treatment outcome or dropout across two replication groups. None of these variables consistently predicted treatment response or dropout across both groups. In one sample, alcohol use did predict dropout, but not after controlling for male sex. Anger control predicted positive outcome in one group but not in the other group. Thus, although previous research suggests that high initial anger might produce worse outcome (Foa et al., 1995), this relation is not firmly established. Some clinicians may be hesitant to employ PE with patients who have significant dissociative symptoms. However, in a recent study using a mixed-gender, mixed-trauma sample, dissociative symptoms did not predict dropout or treatment outcome (Hagenaars, van Minnen, & Hoogduin, 2010). Thus, there is no evidence indicating that such symptoms are a contraindication for this form of therapy.

Limitations and Future Directions

One of the advantages of PE is that it does not appear to have many restrictions or contraindications. However, as discussed at the outset of the chapter, one prerequisite is a clear memory of the traumatic event. While the memory may have missing segments, it should have a clear beginning, middle, and end; furthermore, the individual should clearly remember that the event occurred. This criterion suggests that PE may be less appropriate with certain populations. For example, PE is not recommended for use with populations who lack any clear trauma memories, such as those who experienced trauma as very young children. Similarly, individuals who have PTSD and traumatic brain injury (TBI) may not be able to engage in PE in the case of significant amnesia. However, a very similar treatment program, in which in vivo and imaginal exposure were key components, has been used successfully to treat acute stress disorder in patients with mild TBI (Bryant, Moulds, Guthrie, & Nixon, 2003). As such, patients should not be categorically excluded from PE due to TBI.

Gaps in the empirical efficacy data reviewed earlier highlight several potentially fruitful areas for future research. First, although initial studies have been conducted with other trauma types and populations, PE has been studied largely among adult female assault survivors. Thus, additional studies with other trauma types, veterans, men, and younger populations would be useful to provide greater evidence for generalizability. Furthermore, since most research has been done in the United States, studies from other cultures would be useful. Such studies would extend the preliminary studies that have been conducted to date.

Second, identification of predictors of variability in treatment response should be an area for continued research. Although PE results in a mean decline in symptoms, a subset of patients do fail to respond or show partial response as with any treatment. Despite efforts to do so, no clear individual difference factors have emerged that differentiate nonresponders, partial responders, and excellent responders.

Third, an area for future investigations is how PE treatment may be modified or combined with other treatments to increase efficiency or efficacy. For example, such modifications may include changing the spacing of exposure sessions or the procedure used in imaginal exposure. Similarly, the combination of PE with pharmacologic agents, such as those that enhance fear activation, and/or psychotropic medications for PTSD has received limited study.

Finally, given higher rates of PTSD among individuals with certain psychiatric disorders, such as substance use disorders and borderline personality disorder, ways to apply PE among such comorbid populations should be explored. A starting point for this line of research would be to examine the efficacy of treatments that integrate or combine PE for PTSD with evidence-based pharmacologic and/or behavioral treatments for the other co-occurring disorders.

Summary

In conclusion, PE therapy is a structured treatment program that was specifically developed for PTSD. Its key elements include in vivo exposure to avoided or distressing trauma-related situations or activities that are not objectively dangerous and imaginal exposure, which involves repeated revisiting of the traumatic memory. Based on emotional processing theory, the therapy is thought to work through activation of fear, habituation to feared stimuli, and modification of erroneous beliefs about the self, world, and others. Empirical studies in humans and animals are consistent with these hypothesized mechanisms. Rigorous clinical research over the past 20 years provides strong evidence that PE is efficacious for the treatment of PTSD, producing significant symptom reduction, relative to wait-list control and nonspecific forms of psychotherapy. Thus, it is recommended as a first-line form of treatment for patients presenting with PTSD. Future research can provide additional information regarding the precise mechanisms of this therapy, its suitability across diverse patient populations, and how best to apply it in the context of comorbid diagnoses.

References

Asukai, N., Saito, A., Tsuruta, N., Ogami, R., & Kishimoto, J. (2008). Pilot study on prolonged exposure of Japanese patients with posttraumatic stress disorder due to mixed traumatic events. *Journal of Traumatic Stress, 21*, 340–343.

Barry, H., Etheredge, E. E., & Miller, N. E. (1965). Counterconditioning and extinction of fear fail to transfer from amobarbital to nondrug state. *Psychopharmacologia* (Berlin), *8*, 150–156.

Basoglu, M., Salcioglu, E., Livanou, M., Kalender, D., & Gonul, A. (2005). Single-session behavioral treatment of earthquake-related posttraumatic stress disorder: A randomized waiting list controlled trial. *Journal of Traumatic Stress, 18*, 1–11.

Bouton, M. E. (2000). A learning theory perspective on lapse, relapse, and the maintenance of behavior change. *Health Psychology, 19*(1, Suppl.), 57–63.

Bouton, M. E., Kenney, F. A., & Rosengard, C. (1990). State-dependent fear extinction with two benzodiazepine tranquilizers. *Behavioral Neuroscience, 104*, 44–55.

Bryant, R. A., Moulds, M., Guthrie, R., & Nixon, R. D. (2003). Treating acute stress disorder following mild traumatic brain injury. *American Journal of Psychiatry, 160*, 585–587.

Cahill, S. P., Rothbaum, B. O., Resick, P. A., & Follette, V. M. (2009). Cognitive behavioral therapy for adults. In E. B. Foa, T. M. Keane, M. J. Friedman, & J. A. Cohen (Eds.), *Effective treatments for PTSD: Practice guidelines from the International Society for Traumatic Stress Studies* (pp. 139–222). New York: Guilford.

Cain, C. K., Blouin, A. M., & Barad, M. (2003). Temporally massed CS presentations generate more fear extinction than spaced presentations. *Journal of Experimental Psychology: Animal Behavior Processes, 29*, 323–333.

Cain, C. K., Blouin, A. M., & Barad, M. (2004). Adrenergic transmission facilitates extinction of conditional fear in mice. *Learning and Memory, 11*, 179–187.

Cooper, N. A., & Clum, G. A. (1989). Imaginal flooding as a supplementary treatment for PTSD in combat veterans: A controlled study. *Behavior Therapy, 3*, 381–391.

Devilly, G. J., & Foa, E. B. (2001). The investigation of exposure and cognitive therapy: Comment on Tarrier et al. (1999). *Journal of Consulting and Clinical Psychology, 69*, 114–116.

Doane, L. S., Feeny, N. C., & Zoellner, L. A. (2010). A preliminary investigation of sudden gains in exposure therapy for PTSD. *Behaviour Research and Therapy, 48*, 555–560.

Feeny, N. C., Zoellner, L. A., Mavissakalian, M. R., & Roy-Byrne, P. P. (2009). What would you choose? Sertraline or prolonged exposure in community and PTSD treatment seeking women. *Depression and Anxiety, 26*, 724–731.

Feske, U. (2008). Treating low-income and minority women with posttraumatic stress disorder: A pilot study comparing prolonged exposure and treatment as usual conducted by community therapists. *Journal of Interpersonal Violence, 23*, 1027–1040.

Foa, E. B. (1997). Psychological processes related to recovery from a trauma and an effective treatment for PTSD. In R. Yehuda & A. McFarlane (Eds.), *Psychobiology of PTSD* (pp. 410–424). New York, NY: New York Academy of Sciences.

Foa, E. B., & Chambless, D. (1978). Habituation of subjective anxiety during flooding in imagery. *Behavior Research and Therapy, 16*, 391–399.

Foa, E. B., Dancu, C. V., Hembree, E. A., Jaycox, L. H., Meadows, E. A., & Street, G. P. (1999). The efficacy of exposure therapy, stress inoculation training and their combination in ameliorating PTSD for female victims of assault. *Journal of Consulting and Clinical Psychology, 67*, 194–200.

Foa, E. B., Hembree, E. A., Cahill, S. P., Rauch, S. A., Riggs, D. S., Feeny, N. C., et al. (2005). Randomized trial of prolonged exposure for PTSD with and without cognitive restructuring: Outcome at academic and community clinics. *Journal of Consulting and Clinical Psychology, 67*, 194–200.

Foa, E. B., Hembree, E. A., & Rothbaum, B. O. (2007). *Prolonged Exposure for PTSD: Emotional processing of yraumatic experiences.* New York: Oxford University Press.

4Foa, E. B., Huppert, J. D., & Cahill, S. P. (2006). Emotional processing theory: An update. In B. O. Rothbaum (Ed.), *Pathological anxiety: Emotional processing in etiology and treatment* (pp. 3–24). New York: Guilford.

Foa, E. B., & Kozak, M. J. (1986). Emotional processing of fear: Exposure to corrective information. *Psychological Bulletin, 99*, 20–35.

Foa, E. B., & McNally, R. J. (1996). Mechanisms of change in exposure therapy. In R. M. Rapee (Ed.), *Current controversies in the anxiety disorders* (pp. 329–343). New York: Guilford Press.

Foa, E. B., & Meadows, E. A. (1997). Psychosocial treatments for posttraumatic stress disorder: A critical review. In J. Spence, J. M. Darley, & D. J. Foss (Eds.), *Annual review of psychology* (vol. 48, pp. 449–480). Palo Alto, CA: Annual Reviews.

Foa, E. B., & Rauch, S. A. M. (2004). Cognitive changes during prolonged exposure versus prolonged exposure plus cognitive restructuring in female assault survivors with posttraumatic stress disorder. *Journal of Consulting and Clinical Psychology, 72*, 879–884.

Foa, E. B., Riggs, D. S., Massie, E. D., & Yarczower, M. (1995). The impact of fear activation and anger on the efficacy of exposure treatment for posttraumatic stress disorder. *Behavior Therapy, 26*, 487–499.

Foa, E. B., Rothbaum, B. O., Riggs, D. S., & Murdock, T. (1991). Treatment of posttraumatic stress disorder in rape victims: A comparison between cognitive-behavioral procedures and counseling. *Journal of Consulting and Clinical Psychology, 59*, 715–723.

Foa, E. B., Zinbarg, R., & Rothbaum, B. O. (1992). Uncontrollability and unpredictability in post-traumatic stress disorder: An animal model. *Psychological Bulletin, 112*, 218–238.

Foa, E. B., Zoellner, L. A., Feeny, N. C., Hembree, E. A., & Alvarez-Conrad, J. (2002). Does imaginal exposure exacerbate PTSD symptoms? *Journal of Consulting and Clinical Psychology, 70*, 1022–1028.

Gilboa-Schectman, E., & Foa, E. B. (2001). Patterns of recovery from trauma: The use of intraindividual analysis. *Journal of Abnormal Psychology, 110*, 392–400.

Gilboa-Schechtman, E., Foa, E., Shafran, N., Aderka, I. M., Powers, M., Rachamim, L., Rosenbach, L., et al. (2010). Prolonged exposure versus dynamic therapy for adolescent PTSD: A pilot randomized controlled trial. *Journal of the American Academy of Child and Adolescent Psychiatry, 49*, 1034–1042.

Grayson, J. B., Foa, E. B., Steketee, G. (1982). Habituation during exposure treatment: Distraction vs attention-focusing. *Behaviour Research and Therapy, 20*, 323–328.

Hagenaars, M. A., van Minnen, A., & Hoogduin, K. A. L. (2010). The impact of dissociation and depression on the efficacy of exposure treatment for PTSD. *Behaviour Research and Therapy, 48*, 19–27.

Hembree, E. A., Foa, E. B., Dorfan, N. M., Street, G. P., Kowalski, J., & Tu, X. (2003). Do patients drop out prematurely from exposure therapy for PTSD? *Journal of Traumatic Stress, 16*, 555–562.

Institute of Medicine. (2008). *Treatment of posttraumatic stress disorder: An assessment of the evidence*. Washington, DC: National Academies Press.

Jaycox, L. H., Foa, E. B., & Morral, A. (1998). The influence of emotional engagement and habituation on exposure therapy for PTSD. *Journal of Consulting and Clinical Psychology, 66*, 185–192.

Keane, T. M., Fairbank, J. A., Caddell, J. M., & Zimering, R. T. (1989). Implosive (flooding) therapy reduces symptoms of PTSD in Vietnam combat veterans. *Behavior Therapy, 20*, 245–260.

Kozak, M. J., Foa, E. B., & Steketee, G. (1988). Process and outcome of exposure treatment with obsessive-compulsives: Psychophysiological indicators of emotional processing. *Behavior Therapy, 19*, 157–169.

Lang, P. J. (1977). Imagery in therapy: An information processing analysis of fear. *Behavior Therapy, 8*, 862–886.

Lang, P. J. (1984). Cognition in emotion: Concept and action. In C. Izard, J. Kagan, & R. Zajonc (Eds.), *Emotion, cognition, and behavior* (pp. 193–206). New York, NY: Cambridge University Press.

Lang, P. J., Melamed, B. G., & Hart, J. (1970). A psychophysiological analysis of fear modification using an automated desensitization procedure. *Journal of Abnormal Psychology, 76*, 220–234.Lee, C., Gavriel, H., Drummond, P., Richards, J., & Greenwald, R. (2002). Treatment of PTSD: Stress Inoculation with Prolonged Exposure Compared to EMDR. *Journal of Clinical Psychology, 58*, 1071–1089.

Li, S. H., & Westbrook, R. F. (2008). Massed extinction trials produce better short-term but worse long-term loss of context conditioned fear responses than spaced trials. *Journal of Experimental Psychology: Animal Behavior Processes, 34*, 336–351.

Marks, I., Lovell, K., Noshirvani, H., Livanou, M., & Thrasher, S. (1998). Treatment of posttraumatic stress disorder by exposure and/or cognitive restructuring: A controlled study. *Archives of General Psychiatry, 55*, 317–325.

Milad, M. R., Rauch, S. L., Pitman, R. K., & Quirk, G. J. (2006). Fear extinction in rats: Implications for human brain imaging and anxiety disorders. *Biological Psychology, 73*, 61–71.

Morris, R. W., & Bouton, M. E. (2007). The effect of yohimbine on the extinction of conditioned fear: A role for context. *Behavioral Neuroscience, 121*, 501–514.

Nacasch, N., Foa, E. B., Fostick, L., Polliack, M., Dinstein, Y., Tzur, D., et al. (2007). Prolonged exposure therapy for chronic combat-related PTSD: A case report of five veterans. *CNS Spectrums, 12*, 690–695.

Nacasch, N., Foa, E. B., Huppert, J. D., Tzur, D., Fostick, L., Dinstein, Y., et al. (2011). Prolonged exposure therapy for combat- and terror-related posttraumatic stress disorder: A randomized control comparison with treatment as usual. *Journal of Clinical Psychiatry*, 72, 1174–1180.

Neuner, F. Schauer, M., Klaschik, C., Karunakara, U., & Elbert, T. (2004). A comparison of narrative exposure therapy, supportive counseling, and psychoeducation for treating posttraumatic stress disorder in an African refugee settlement. *Journal of Consulting and Clinical Psychology, 72*, 579–587.

Orr, S. P., Milad, M. R., Metzger, L. J., Lasko, N. B., Gilbertson, M. W., & Pitman, R. K. (2006). Effects of beta blockade, PTSD diagnosis, and explicit threat on the extinction and retention of an aversively conditioned response. *Biological Psychiatry, 73*, 262–271.

Pitman, R. K., Orr, S. P., Altman, B., Longpre, R. E., Poiré, R. E., Macklin, M., et al. (1996). Emotional processing and outcome of imaginal flooding therapy in Vietnam veterans with chronic posttraumatic stress disorder. *Comprehensive Psychiatry, 37*, 409–418.

Powers, M. B., Halpern, J. M., Ferenschak, M. P., Gillihan, S. J., & Foa, E. B. (2010). A meta-analytic review of prolonged exposure for posttraumatic stress disorder. *Clinical Psychology Review, 30*, 635–641.

Powers, M. B., Smits, J. A. J., Otto, M. W., Sanders, C., & Emmelkamp, P. M. G. (2009). Facilitation of fear extinction in phobic participants with a novel cognitive enhancer. A randomized controlled trial of yohimbine augmentation. *Journal of Anxiety Disorders, 23*, 350–356.

Rauch, S. A. M., Defever, E., Favorite, T., Duroe, A., Garrity, C., Martis, B., et al. (2009). Prolonged exposure for PTSD in a Veterans Health Administration PTSD clinic. *Journal of Traumatic Stress, 22*, 60–64.

Rauch, S. A. M., Foa, E. B., Furr, J. M., & Filip, J. C. (2004). Imagery vividness and perceived anxious arousal in prolonged exposure treatment for PTSD. *Journal of Traumatic Stress, 17*, 461–465.

Rescorla, R. A. (2001). Experimental extinction. In R. R. Mowrer & S. B. Klein (Eds.), *Handbook of contemporary learning theories* (pp. 119–154). Mahwah, NJ: Lawrence Erlbaum.

Resick, P. A., Nishith, P., Weaver, T. L., Astin, M. C., & Feurer, C. A. (2002). A comparison of cognitive processing therapy with prolonged exposure and a waiting condition for the treatment of chronic posttraumatic stress disorder in female rape victims. *Journal of Consulting and Clinical Psychology, 70*, 867–879.

Riley, W. T., McCormick, M. G. F., Simon, E. M., Stack, K., Pushkin, Y., Overstreet, M. M., et al. (1995). Effects of alprazolam dose on the induction and habituation processes during behavioral panic induction treatment. *Journal of Anxiety Disorders, 9*, 217–227.

Rothbaum, B. O., Astin, M. C., & Marsteller, F. (2005). Prolonged exposure versus eye movement desensitization and reprocessing (EMDR) for PTSD rape victims. *Journal of Traumatic Stress, 18*, 607–616.

Rothbaum, B. O.., Cahill, S. P., Foa, E. B., Davidson, J. R. T., Compton, J., Connor, K. M., et al. (2006). *Journal of Traumatic Stress, 19*, 625–638.

Rothbaum, B. O., Foa, E. B., Riggs, D. S., Murdock, T. & Walsh, W. (1992). A prospective examination of posttraumatic stress disorder in rape victims. *Journal of Traumatic Stress, 5*, 455–475.

Schnurr, P. P., Friedman, M. J., Engel, C. C., Foa, E. B., Shea, M. T., Chow, B. K., et al. (2007). Cogntive behavioral therapy for posttraumatic stress disorder in women: A randomized controlled trial. *Journal of the American Medical Association, 297*, 820–830.

Simon, N. M., Connor, K. M., Lang, A. J., Rauch, S., Krulewicz, S., LeBeau, R. T., et al. (2008). Paroxetine CR augmentation for posttraumatic stress disorder refractory to prolonged exposure therapy. *Journal of Clinical Psychiatry, 69*, 400–405.

Tarrier, N., Pilgrim, H., Sommerfield, C., Faragher, B., Reynolds, M., Graham, E., et al. (1999). A randomized trial of cognitive therapy and imaginal exposure in the treatment of chronic posttraumatic stress disorder. *Journal of Consulting and Clinical Psychology, 67*, 13–18.

Taylor, S., Thordarson, D. S., Maxfield, L., Federoff, I.C., Lovell, K., & Ogrodniczuk, J. (2003). Efficacy, speed, and adverse effects of three PTSD treatments: Exposure therapy, relaxation training, and EMDR. *Journal of Consulting and Clinical Psychology, 71*, 330–338.

van Minnen, A., Arntz, A., & Keijsers, G. P. J. (2002). Prolonged exposure in patients with chronic PTSD: Predictors of treatment outcome and dropout. *Behaviour Research and Therapy, 40*, 439–457.

van Minnen, A., & Foa, E.B. (2006). The effect of imaginal exposure length on outcome of treatment for PTSD. *Journal of Traumatic Stress, 19*, 1–12.

Vaughan, K., Armstrong, M. S., Gold, R., O'Connor, N., Jenneke, W., & Tarrier, N. (1994). A trial of eye movement desensitization compared to image habituation training and applied muscle relaxation in posttraumatic stress disorder. *Journal of Behavior Therapy and Experimental Psychiatry, 25*, 283–291.

CHAPTER

30 Empirically Supported Psychological Treatments: Cognitive Processing Therapy

Kathleen M. Chard, Jennifer L. Schuster, *and* Patricia A. Resick

Abstract

Cognitive Processing Therapy (CPT) has been recognized by the Institute of Medicine (2007) as one of the most effective treatments for PTSD. This chapter provides a brief overview of the CPT session content, the underlying mechanisms of the therapy, a review of the empirically based literature outlining the treatment effectiveness, limitations of the therapy, and areas of future research. In addition, the authors discuss the utility of the various versions of CPT, including cognitive only (CPT-C), group, individual, and combination. Further the research supporting the effectiveness of CPT for treating PTSD related to a variety of traumas, (e.g., combat, child abuse, and rape) and the significant impact CPT can have in areas of mental health related to PTSD (e.g., anger, guilt, social functioning) are described.

Key Words: Cognitive Processing Therapy, cognitive therapy, PTSD, trauma, empirical

Corresponding Author: Kathleen M. Chard, Cincinnati VA Medical Center, PTSD & Anxiety Disorders Clinic, 1000 S. Ft. Thomas Avenue, Ft. Thomas, Kentucky 41075

Phone: 859.572.6208; Fax: 859.572.6748; Email: Kathleen.Chard@va.gov

Author Note: Content of this manuscript does not reflect those of the United States Government or Department of Veterans Affairs.

Description of the Therapy

Cognitive Processing Therapy (CPT: Resick & Schnicke, 1993) is a brief cognitive behavioral treatment, typically lasting 12 sessions, that has been found to be effective for the treatment of posttraumatic stress disorder (PTSD) and other corollary symptoms following traumatic events including rape, assault, sexual abuse, and combat (Chard, 2005; Monson et al., 2006; Resick & Schnicke, 1992; Resick, Nishith, Weaver, Astin, & Feuer, 2002). The therapy can be offered in individual, group, or combined group and individual formats depending on the population being served and resources of the therapy site.

The main goal of CPT is to reduce an individual's psychological distress caused by the symptoms of PTSD and related disorders. To facilitate this change, therapists and clients work together in a "collaborative empiricism" framework in which therapists teach clients the skills they need to achieve maximal improvement. CPT is divided into three phases, including education, processing, and challenging. In the first phase, clients are educated about the symptoms of PTSD, the treatment model, and the connection between thoughts and feelings. In addition, they begin to examine the meaning they have made of the traumatic event and how the traumatic event(s) has affected their beliefs about self, others, and the world. Clients are taught the ways in which people can become derailed in their thinking about traumatic events, and the underlying concepts of assimilation (taking in the new information without changing preexisting beliefs), overaccommodation (changing beliefs about the self and the world to extremes), and accommodation (modifying preexisting beliefs to incorporate new information) are introduced to clients in lay language. A core part of this initial examination of thoughts is the identification of "stuck points," or beliefs that have become extreme or exaggerated. Examples of stuck points include: "I should have been able to prevent it (the trauma) from happening," "I cannot trust anyone," and "The world is always dangerous." Stuck points often lead to strong emotions, such as shame, blame, fear, and anger that do not dissipate quickly and can negatively impact the individual's ability to function effectively and happily in society. Beginning in session two, the A-B-C sheet is introduced to portray the connections between situations, thoughts, and feelings, and is used to begin to identify stuck points. The therapist uses Socratic dialogue to facilitate the clients in uncovering alternative beliefs to their current way of thinking. This in turn teaches the clients the practice of cognitive flexibility that will be enlisted throughout the remainder of the treatment.

In the second phase of treatment, the individual and therapist take a focused look at the traumatic event(s) through written narratives as a way of further identifying where the individual has become stuck in his or her thinking about the event. Although not a true exposure procedure, the written accounts also allow for the natural expression of emotion. Alternatively, the written trauma account may be eliminated and the traumatic event is explored through Socratic dialogue only. In either case, therapists continue to use the A-B-C sheets and Socratic dialogue to help clients generate alternatives to their assimilated beliefs, particularly in the areas of blame, shame, and hindsight bias about the event.

In the third and final phase of treatment, therapists and clients work together to help the clients further examine their stuck points, including those about the trauma, but also beliefs that have overgeneralized from the events (overaccommodated beliefs). The goal of this phase is to generate healthier, and more accurate, beliefs in relation to the event(s), the self, others, and the world. In this phase of therapy, several worksheets that build upon one another are introduced, starting with the Challenging Questions Sheet (CQS). The CQS helps clients challenge their thoughts and interpretations about the trauma by allowing them to weigh the evidence for and against the stuck points, examine the full context of the situation(s) related to the belief, and determine whether the belief is based on facts or feelings. For example, a client may hold a stuck point that the traumatic event (e.g., rape or combat-related death) is "all my fault." Using the CQS, the client can begin to see that the rape or the death of a friend in combat was caused by someone else, and that although the client wishes the outcome were different, there was little the individual could have done to prevent the end result given the situational variables, resources, and knowledge at the time.

The next worksheet is the Patterns of Problematic Thinking, which helps clients identify habitual and frequently unproductive ways in which they tend to respond to situations, such as overgeneralizing from a single incident, mind reading, and emotional reasoning. By reviewing all of their stuck points, and finding their likely patterns of responding, clients can become more aware of their reactions and work to prevent these types of assumptions in their thinking in the future. The Challenging Beliefs Worksheet (CBW) is a culmination of the prior practice assignments, and is typically introduced in session seven. PTSD often causes individuals to think with a narrowed view about the trauma (e.g., "I could have prevented the event from happening"), which can then create further overgeneralized thoughts about the self, others, and the world (e.g., "I always make bad decisions" and "No one in authority can be trusted"). Using the CBW, the therapist and client identify the emotions that are linked to stuck points, challenge the accuracy of the assumptions behind the thoughts, and generate alternative beliefs with related feelings that are more reflective of all variables relevant to the situation. Clients are then able to see how much relief they will likely feel if they look at the situation more realistically instead of through the lens of PTSD. This will typically result in new thoughts, such as "I could not have prevented the trauma," "I did the best I could given the situation," "I am a good person," and "Many people in authority can be trusted."

Along with the CBWs, clients are given a handout for each of the five remaining sessions on a core area typically associated with PTSD: safety, trust, power/control, esteem, and intimacy. These handouts help clients identify stuck points they may have overlooked in these five areas and assist clients in appreciating how PTSD may have impacted their views in a much broader fashion than they previously had realized. Although some clients may resonate more with one of the five areas than others, most clients find that spending time examining all five areas is helpful in ensuring that no overgeneralized stuck points are missed.

For session 12, clients are asked to rewrite their impact statement to reflect what they now believe about the trauma(s), themselves, and the world. Clients and therapists then discuss the differences between the two statements to highlight the ways in which the client has changed his or her thinking. In addition, the final impact statement may be used to generate future areas for work or possible foci for future treatment—for example, couples counseling, vocational rehabilitation, or relapse prevention.

Versions of CPT

Depending on needs of the client, therapists may choose to employ different versions of the CPT manual, including CPT-C, group, individual, or a combination of the two. In a dismantling study to deconstruct CPT into its constituent components, cognitive therapy and narrative writing, compared to the full protocol, Resick and colleagues (2008) found that CPT-C was equally effective and perhaps more efficient than CPT. In another study, Chard (2005) examined a group plus individual format treatment with adult survivors of child sexual abuse and found it to be highly efficacious. This combined individual/group format has since been adopted by residential programs in the VA system and is particularly useful in brief, intensive programs.

In addition to the original rape/assault victim manual (Resick & Schnicke, 1992), there is also a 16–17-week child sexual abuse manual that provides additional focus on the development of trauma related beliefs during childhood (Chard, 2005). Finally, one may choose to use the veteran/military manuals that include example exercises for both combat and military sexual traumas, as well as special sections addressing key issues in working with a military population—for example, how to reconcile religion and events that occurred in combat (Chard, Resick, Monson, & Kattar, 2009; Resick, Monson, & Chard, 2008).

Proposed Underlying Mechanism and Empirical Support

The CPT protocol was developed during a time when there was a convergence of ideas regarding cognition and meaning-making in the wake of trauma. These influences led Resick to focus on cognitive theory and the development of a cognitive therapy for PTSD at a time when most researchers were focusing on applying treatments to PTSD that had been developed for anxiety disorders, such as exposure therapy (Foa, Rothbaum, Riggs, & Murdock, 1991; Keane & Kaloupek, 1982). In one of her first research projects with rape victims, Resick and colleagues (Atkeson, Calhoun, Resick, & Ellis, 1982) conducted a study examining depressive symptoms following rape and noted that trauma responses were frequently accompanied by depressive symptoms. This work also led to the conclusion that PTSD is more than just a fear and anxiety disorder. Other research later confirmed this notion in many epidemiological studies regarding the frequency of comorbid depression, as well as the prevalence of guilt and anger among those with PTSD (e.g., Chemtob, Hamada, Roitblat, & Muraoka, 1994; Kubany, 1994). In her early work on trauma, Resick and colleagues also found that the perception of danger was a more important predictor of later symptoms than was the objective danger of the situation (Girelli, Resick, Marhoefer-Dvorak, & Hutter, 1986). These results suggested that the interpretation of the traumatic event was an important contributor to the traumatic response. As a result, Resick began to explore theories, research, and therapies that were more focused on perceptions and cognitive processing of trauma events.

Around the time that Resick was developing this cognitively based treatment for PTSD, based on the emerging cognitive therapy by Beck (Beck, 1970; Beck & Emery, 1985), others were also examining trauma theory from a cognitive perspective. Horowitz (1975, 1976, 1979) explained PTSD from an information-processing perspective. His model emphasized the impact of trauma on cognitive schemas and the role of control (avoidance) in regulating the processing of information. Cognitive schemas are stable, deeply held sets of beliefs about the self and the world that are used to interpret or make sense of life experiences (Beck, Rush, Shaw, & Emery, 1979). Horowitz proposed that until the traumatic event can be integrated into existing schemas, the trauma memory will be active and intrusive. He proposed a cycling between intrusive memories accompanied by intense affect alternating with numbing and avoidance. From a social psychology perspective, Janoff-Bulman (1979, 1985) focused on how basic assumptions (schemas that the world is meaningful and benevolent, and that the self is worthy) are shattered in the face of trauma. She found that in order to restore a sense of control and predictability over the potential for future negative events, people will engage in self-blame for the trauma rather than sacrifice these core beliefs.

Simultaneously, from a more psychodynamic and developmental perspective, particularly drawn from Piaget's cognitive developmental theory (1971), McCann, Sakheim, and Abrahamson (1988; McCann & Pearlman, 1990) were developing a constructivist self-development theory of trauma in which similar concepts were introduced. Although Janoff-Bulman's theory focused on how positive and self-protective perceptions of the world and self are shattered and reconstructed after trauma, McCann and colleagues (1988) recognized that people may also start with more negative beliefs that may be reinforced by further traumatic events. This model focused on the process by which trauma survivors integrate traumatic events into their overall conceptual systems (e.g., core beliefs, schemas) either by assimilating the information into existing schemas or by altering existing schemas to accommodate the new information.

Assimilation occurs when new information, including information related to traumatic events, is incorporated into prior beliefs about one's self or the world, whether positive or negative. For example, a woman with a history of child sexual abuse may quickly assimilate a later sexual trauma without effort because the information matches her previous schemas (e.g., "I am bad or dirty, therefore bad things happen to me"; Chard, Weaver & Resick, 1997). Assimilation can also occur when individuals' memories or their causal appraisals of the traumatic event are altered to be more congruent with their prior beliefs. For example, if a woman previously believed that no one she knew would rape her and then experienced acquaintance rape, she might conclude that the assault was a misunderstanding or resulted from poor communication on her part. Similarly, if a soldier believes that everyone in the unit will be safe if everyone performs his or her duties correctly, then he may blame himself or others around him if the unit is ambushed. Conversely, when events happen that are schema-discrepant and individuals adjust their schemas to incorporate this new information, this process is termed accommodation. An example of accommodation would be someone who says, "This happened to me but I didn't cause it" or "It happened in spite of my best effort to stop it."

Added to CPT is the concept of overaccommodation (Resick & Schnicke, 1992, 1993), the idea that people can change their thinking about the self and the world to the extreme such that assumptions about the causes of the trauma or conclusions drawn about the trauma overgeneralize to all people, places, concepts, and the like. Overaccommodated beliefs are common consequences of trauma that lead to strong negative affect. Individuals may alter their beliefs about themselves and the world too much and develop rigid beliefs in order to feel safer or more in control (e.g., "I will never trust my judgment again" or "Everybody will try to control me") in an attempt to prevent future victimization (Resick & Schnicke, 1992). Such overaccommodated beliefs can interfere with the processing of natural emotions that originated from the event (e.g., fear, sadness) and increase experiences of emotions secondary to distorted thoughts, which in CPT are referred to as manufactured emotions because they are produced by thoughts and continue to be produced until the thoughts change (e.g., shame, anger). McCann and Pearlman (1992) delineated trauma-related cognitive distortions in five areas: agency, which refers to the attributed cause of a traumatic event; safety; trust; power/control; esteem; and intimacy. Any of the latter five could be self-referent or other-referent disruptions in thinking. Resick included these themes as content areas of CPT.

A growing body of research has explored the relationship between traumatic events and subsequent cognitions. As expected by cognitive theory, trauma survivors often exhibit self-blaming thoughts and guilt about actions that they did or did not engage in during a traumatic incident in order to feel more in control over future events. Research has supported the presence of self-blame and guilt cognitions among those with PTSD (Foa, Ehlers, Clark, Tolin, & Orsillo, 1999; Frazier & Schauben, 1994; Janoff-Bulman & Wortman, 1977; Kubany, 1994; Resick, Nishith, Weaver, Astin, & Feuer, 2002; Resick & Schnicke, 1993; Wenninger & Ehlers, 1998).

In addition to guilt specifically, researchers have explored the link between inaccurate, trauma-related cognitions and symptomatology more generally. Trauma survivors with PTSD often exhibit negative beliefs about self and others (Ali, Dunmore, Clark, & Ehlers, 2002; Janoff-Bulman, 1989; Koss, Figueredo, & Prince, 2002; Newman, Riggs, & Roth, 1997; Owens & Chard, 2001). In both American and German samples of adults who experienced child sexual abuse, correlations (*r*'s 0.46–0.71) have been found between maladaptive beliefs as measured with the Personal Beliefs and Reactions Scale (PBRS; Resick, Schnicke, & Markway, 1991) regarding safety, trust, esteem, intimacy, and severity of PTSD symptoms (Wenninger & Ehlers, 1998). Similarly, Owens and Chard (2001) examined 53 adult survivors of child sexual abuse and found that PTSD severity was correlated with cognitive distortions on all seven subscales of the PBRS.

Following cognitive therapy, one would hypothesize that in addition to a decrease in PTSD and depressive symptoms, one should also see a change in cognitions. Research has supported this hypothesis. Owens, Pike, and Chard (2001) examined the PBRS (Resick et al., 1991), which assesses the cognitive themes that were proposed by McCann and Pearlman (1992), and the World Assumption Scale (Janoff-Bulman, 1989), which assesses the three areas of cognition proposed by Janoff-Bulman (1989, 1992): benevolence of world, meaningfulness, and self as worthy. They found that all of these areas of cognition improved immediately with CPT and were maintained over a year of follow-up. Resick et al. (2002) examined guilt cognitions in their study comparing CPT with prolonged exposure (PE). They found that both groups improved significantly on guilt cognitions. However, CPT improved significantly more on the cognitive scales that reflected guilt over things the trauma victims believed they should or should not have done during the traumatic event and the expectation that they should have known it would happen and prevent it. Even at long-term follow-up 5–10 years later, there were still differences between participants assigned to CPT and participants assigned to PE in terms of guilt cognitions, with CPT outperforming PE on this specific type of cognitive distortion (Resick, 2010). In the dismantling study of CPT, Resick et al. (2008) also found large decreases in both guilt cognitions and on the PBRS over the course of treatment for all three conditions.

Instead of using self-report measures, Sobel, Resick, and Rabalais (2009) conducted a study in which reliable raters coded impact statements that are collected at the beginning and end of CPT. The coding categories were: assimilation, accommodation, overaccommodation, and information. They found that from the beginning to the end of treatment, there were significant increases in accommodated statements and significant decreases in overaccommodated and assimilated statements. The hypothesis that cognitive changes would be related to symptom reduction was partially supported. At pretreatment, the percentage of accommodated statements was inversely related to PTSD symptoms, whereas increases in accommodation and decreases in overaccommodation were associated with improvements in PTSD symptoms. Notably, there were no assimilated statements after treatment on the sample that was studied, so it was not possible to conduct analyses on assimilation at the posttreatment assessment. This suggests that CPT may be particularly effective at modifying assimilated beliefs. Further, in the Monson et al. (2006) study of combat veterans, although the existence of guilt-related cognitions was not significantly different before and after CPT, guilt-related distress was significantly lower in the CPT condition than the WL following treatment. This finding indicates that the nature of the cognitions, if not the presence, may change in veterans who undergo CPT.

Overall, there is a growing literature that beliefs change following trauma and that PTSD is associated with negative beliefs about self, others, and the world. These beliefs are associated with negative emotions such as guilt, anger, and shame, which in turn are associated with PTSD symptoms. Cognitive therapy directly works to correct dysfunctional thinking by helping clients learn to question the factual basis of their thoughts and to replace their faulty assumptions with more balanced statements that will be associated with more healthy emotional responses. What has not been established to date is whether change in PTSD symptoms follows or precedes cognitive change. Because cognitions have not typically been assessed during treatment, there is no research to date that has demonstrated that change in cognition leads to change in symptoms. Future research will need to track both cognitive change, change in emotions, and other PTSD symptoms to determine whether the change in cognitions precedes improvement in PTSD or is a by-product of such improvement.

Empirical Support for Efficacy and Effectiveness of CPT for PTSD

There is a growing amount of empirical support for the efficacy and effectiveness of CPT in a wide range of populations, including extensive research with survivors of interpersonal trauma, individuals who are often considered to be very difficult to treat effectively. The original study of CPT (Resick & Schnicke, 1992) was conducted in a group setting with a small sample of female sexual assault survivors. In this quasi-experimental study, rape victims were compared to a control group of treatment seekers who were on the waiting list for participation for at least 12 weeks before beginning treatment. CPT was found to significantly improve symptoms of PTSD and depression compared to the control group, with moderate effect sizes (Hedges's g = 0.61 for PTSD and 0.36 for depression). Subsequent studies of CPT primarily have been conducted in an individual format. The first large randomized controlled trial (RCT) of CPT compared CPT, PE, and a wait-list (WL) control group in an intent-to-treat (ITT) sample of 171 female rape survivors (Resick et al., 2002). CPT and PE were conducted in individual sessions twice weekly for a total of 13 hours of treatment within six weeks. Following the six-week assessment, WL participants were randomly assigned to one of the two active treatment conditions. Results showed that both the CPT and PE groups demonstrated significant reductions in PTSD symptoms compared to the WL condition, with large effect sizes (Hedges's g = 0.97 and 0.74, respectively, in the ITT sample). The decreases in scores for the CPT and PE groups occurred between pretreatment and posttreatment, and these improvements were sustained at the three-month and nine-month follow-up points. When CPT and PE were compared directly, CPT demonstrated modestly greater symptomatic improvement (small effect size, Hedges's g = 0.10–0.18) at all time points relative to the PE condition.

Resick and colleagues (2008) then conducted a dismantling study of CPT in which the full protocol was compared with its constituent components. An ITT sample of 150 adult women with histories of physical and/or sexual assault was randomized into one of three conditions: the full CPT protocol, a cognitive-only version (CPT-C) that does not include the written account, and a written account-only (WA). Treatment occurred twice weekly for 50 minutes each for six weeks for CPT and CPT-C and after the first week in one weekly two-hour session for the WA condition. Assessments conducted by individuals who were unaware of treatment assignment were conducted prior to treatment, two weeks following the last session, and six months posttreatment. Relative to pretreatment, participants in all three treatment conditions showed significant improvements in PTSD symptoms during treatment and at follow-up, with large effect sizes (Hedges's g = 0.7–1.3). Although the initial hypotheses predicted that the complete CPT protocol would be superior to both the CPT-C and WA conditions, the combination of cognitive therapy and written accounts did not improve upon the results of either component. In fact, when examining PTSD symptoms over the course of treatment, the CPT-C group had significantly lower scores than the WA condition, while the CPT condition did not differ significantly from CPT-C or WA. This finding suggests that cognitive therapy alone may be at least as effective as exposure in the treatment of PTSD. Although the WA component of the CPT protocol is important for some individuals to facilitate the experiencing of previously avoided emotions, CPT-C may be a particularly effective alternative for individuals who have a tendency to dissociate, are reluctant to undergo focused retelling of the event, or have a limited number of sessions to attend treatment (Resick et al., 2008). In addition Chard (2009) found that CPT-C was an effective treatment for PTSD in a pilot study of combat veterans with a comorbid history of mild to severe traumatic brain injury.

Chard (2005) developed an adaptation of CPT (CPT-SA) for survivors of sexual assault and conducted a RCT on this treatment. This study examined the utility of a combined group and individual cognitive-behavioral intervention specifically designed to address issues salient to abuse survivors, such as attachment, communication, sexual intimacy, and social adjustment. Seventy-one women were randomized to active treatment or a minimal attention (MA) wait-list control group. CPT-SA treatment consisted of 17 weeks of group and individual therapy. Assessments were conducted pre- and posttreatment and at three-months and one-year follow-up. The treatment group showed significant improvements from pretreatment to posttreatment compared to the MA group on symptoms of PTSD, depression, and dissociation, with large effect sizes (Hedges's g = 0.98–2.42). Furthermore, there was a significant difference in PTSD symptomatology from posttreatment to the three-month follow-up, suggesting that participants continued to show improvement of PTSD symptoms three months after treatment. For CPT-SA participants, there was no significant difference in PTSD symptom severity between the three-month and one-year follow-up assessments, indicating that the positive effects of treatment remained stable.

Monson and colleagues (2006) conducted a RCT examining CPT in a sample of combat veterans diagnosed with chronic, military-related PTSD. Sixty veterans (54 men, 6 women) were randomized to CPT or a wait-list control condition. Individual CPT was conducted twice weekly for six weeks. Participants were assessed prior to treatment, mid-treatment (or after 3 weeks of waiting), post-treatment (or after 6 weeks of waiting), and one month posttreatment (or after 10 weeks of waiting). Results indicated that participants receiving CPT had a significant reduction in severity of PTSD symptoms over time as compared with the wait-list control group, with large effect size (Hedges's $g = 1.12$). Moreover, although it was hypothesized that veterans receiving compensation for PTSD would have significantly smaller reductions in PTSD symptoms than those not receiving benefits (due to secondary gain issues creating disincentives for treatment improvement), results showed no significant difference in symptom reduction between these two groups. This study was the first to demonstrate the efficacy of CPT in a chronic veteran sample, and provides encouraging results supporting increased use of this treatment for veterans with military-related PTSD.

The RCTs previously described highlight the efficacious use of CPT in a variety of patient populations, including female victims of physical and/or sexual assault, female victims of CSA, and male and female veterans. Although not in a RCT format, CPT has been implemented and investigated in a number of additional diverse groups. For instance, Schulz, Resick, Huber, and Griffin (2006) examined archival data from a service-based community organization that provided treatment to traumatized refugees from Afghanistan and Bosnia-Herzegovina. CPT was administered to 53 refugees (46 women, 7 men) in the client's native language either by a therapist who was a native speaker or through the use of an interpreter. Although treatment requiring an interpreter was significantly longer in duration than treatment without an interpreter (41 vs. 33 hours), participants in both conditions (interpreter or no interpreter) demonstrated a significant decrease in PTSD symptoms at termination of treatment compared to intake. These results provide preliminary evidence that CPT may be relevant to diverse cultural groups who have experienced severe traumas.

A recent program evaluation study by Chard, Schumm, Owens, and Cottingham (2010) provides an exploratory examination comparing a VA hospital outpatient sample of Operation Enduring Freedom (OEF) and Operation Iraqi Freedom (OIF) veterans to Vietnam-era veterans before and after treatment for PTSD using CPT. The sample consisted of 101 veterans (51 OEF/OIF, 50 Vietnam) who were admitted for outpatient treatment and assigned to receive individual CPT. Participants completed assessments prior to and immediately following treatment. Results showed that OEF/OIF veterans attended a significantly lower number of CPT treatment sessions than Vietnam veterans ($M = 10.67$ vs. 13.24, respectively), although they did not significantly differ on the number who dropped out of treatment. There were no significant differences between the two groups on most outcome measures, although there was a trend for OEF/OIF veterans to report lower posttreatment PTSD symptoms. However, multivariate analyses showed lower posttreatment clinician-rated PTSD symptoms for OEF/OIF veterans than Vietnam veterans after controlling for pretreatment PTSD severity and number of sessions attended. This suggests that OEF/OIF veterans may have less severe PTSD symptoms following CPT, and highlights the potential for cohort effects on treatment response when using CPT in a veteran population.

As the previously discussed studies have established the effectiveness of CPT as a treatment for PTSD, additional research has sought to determine what individual differences in pretreatment characteristics may influence treatment outcome. Rizvi, Vogt, and Resick (2009) examined cognitive and affective predictors of CPT and PE treatment outcomes, using the sample from the Resick et al. (2002) study. Cognitive variables of interest included education, intelligence, and age. These factors were proposed to influence openness to new ways of thinking and ability to actively engage in changing beliefs and patterns of thinking, which are key components of CPT. Comorbid affective states including anger, guilt, and depression, which might interfere with emotional and cognitive processing of the trauma memory, were also examined. Consistent with hypotheses, lower intelligence, lower levels of education, and younger age were related to greater likelihood of treatment dropout. However, none of the cognitive variables had a significant effect on treatment efficacy. Conversely, comorbid affective states were not related to treatment dropout. However, depression and guilt appeared to impact treatment efficacy in an unexpected direction. Although higher scores on each of these affective measures were related to higher initial PTSD symptomatology, individuals with higher depression and guilt demonstrated a greater reduction in PTSD over time. This finding highlights that both CPT and PE are shown to be effective for more severe PTSD and for those who have comorbid symptoms. Another interesting finding was a significant interaction for anger and treatment condition, such that higher trait anger was more strongly related to dropout in PE compared to CPT. This suggests the possibility that clients presenting with high trait anger might be better served by CPT than PE. Lastly, it was shown that younger age in CPT and older age in PE were related to the best outcomes. The finding that age interacts with treatment condition underscores the importance of examining different treatments separately when considering potential predictive factors.

Another study examined the effect of borderline personality characteristics (BPC) on outcomes for 131 female rape victims receiving CPT or PE treatment for PTSD (Clarke, Rizvi, & Resick, 2008). Results indicated that although higher BPC scores were related to greater pretreatment PTSD symptom severity, individuals with higher levels of BPC were just as likely to complete treatment and show significant treatment response on outcomes such as PTSD symptom severity, depression, dissociation, and anxious arousal than those with lower levels of BPC. These findings contradict the assumption that individuals with BPC will not benefit from evidence-based treatments for PTSD, and lends support for the inclusion of individuals with borderline personality features in CPT treatment.

Finally, CPT has been shown to have beneficial effects on a wide variety of mental health symptoms (such as affect control, alexthymia, anger, and overall social adjustment) and diagnoses such as depression (Chard, 2005; Monson et al., 2006, Owens et al. 2001; Resick et al., 2002, 2008). In addition, preliminary evidence suggests that CPT may also have a positive effect on physical health outcomes. Galovski, Monson, Bruce, and Resick (2009) compared changes in perceived physical health and sleep quality following CPT and PE within a sample of 108 female sexual assault survivors randomized to one of the two treatment conditions (i.e., PE and CPT). Results showed that participants in both treatments reported lower health-related concerns after treatment and at follow-up nine months later, although there were significantly more improvements for participants in the CPT condition compared to PE, with a moderate effect size difference (partial $r = 0.27$). Participants also reported significant improvements in sleep quality, with no differences between treatments. These findings support the potential for CPT to have beneficial effects on outcomes beyond PTSD symptoms and other mental health factors.

Limitations and Future Directions

The majority of these highlighted studies adhered to the gold standard guidelines for methodologically sound treatment outcome research outlined by Foa and Meadows (1997), including broad inclusion criteria, use of randomized design, and use of assessors who are unaware of treatment condition. However, there are some limitations within these studies that should be noted. Some of the earlier research (e.g., Resick et al., 2002) was conducted before ITT analysis became standard. Therefore, participants who dropped out of treatment were not assessed at the follow-up time points, which created limitations in the analyses of the data. Although strategies such as analyzing data with the last observation carried forward and use of statistical techniques such as random regression modeling were used to address this limitation, it was not possible to determine whether partial therapy provided any benefits to participants. Later studies (e.g., Resick et al., 2008) continued to assess participants even after dropout to obtain a more accurate measure of outcomes.

Another limitation in some of the studies presented is the lack of a control for the nonspecific effects of treatment. Although many studies used a wait-list control condition (e.g., Chard, 2005; Monson et al., 2006; Resick et al., 2002, 2008), the effects of nonspecific factors of psychotherapy (e.g., therapeutic alliance, expectation for change) could not be assessed. Additionally, some studies were limited by small sample sizes (e.g., Monson et al., 2006) or reduced ethnic diversity (e.g., Chard, 2005). The generalizability of the findings of these studies might also be questioned because the studies generally used very specific samples of trauma survivors (e.g., rape victims, OEF/OIF veterans). Finally, only one of the studies published to date has assessed outcomes over the long term. Therefore, it is unknown how long treatment gains are maintained beyond six months to one year, depending on the study.

Current research on CPT seeks to improve the existing treatment for use in a variety of populations, as well as develop adjunctive treatments to enhance CPT. One example is the development of an integrated treatment for veterans with comorbid pain and PTSD (Otis, Keane, Kerns, Monson, & Scioli, 2009). This preliminary descriptive pilot study examined a combined treatment that incorporates components of CPT for PTSD and cognitive behavioral therapy (CBT) for chronic pain management into a 12-session protocol. The small sample reported reductions in pain and PTSD symptomatology and described the treatment favorably. A RCT is currently being conducted to evaluate the efficacy of this treatment approach.

Multiple Channel Exposure Therapy (M-CET) is another example of an integrated treatment, designed to reduce physiological, cognitive, and behavioral symptoms of PTSD and comorbid panic attacks (Falsetti, Resnick, & Davis, 2005, 2008). M-CET includes elements of CPT as well as panic control treatment (a treatment for panic disorder developed by Barlow and Craske, 1988). Treatment is conducted weekly for 12 weeks, and can be delivered individually or in a group. Results of a randomized trial comparing M-CET to a wait-list control condition in a sample of women suffering from PTSD and panic attacks found that treatment was associated with significant decreases in PTSD and panic symptoms at posttreatment. These results were maintained over a six-month period, suggesting that M-CET may be a promising treatment for these comorbid conditions.

Another RCT currently under way is investigating the use of CPT with telemental health technology to provide care in remote areas (Morland, Greene, Rosen, Mauldin, & Frueh, 2009). This prospective randomized study will compare the effectiveness of CPT delivered in person to CPT delivered via video-teleconferencing (VTC). The study is using a noninferiority design to determine if the novel intervention (VTC) is comparable to the standard ("in person") intervention (i.e., are outcomes for participants in the VTC condition as good as those in the in-person condition?). A cost analysis will also be conducted to compare the cost of the two modalities. The findings of studies such as these will have great implications for improving health service delivery across a wide range of settings and will help to promote increased access to care.

Finally, several ongoing funded studies are examining CPT compared to Present Centered Therapy (PCT) to account for the nonspecific elements of psychotherapy, while another study is evaluating CPT to determine if individuals vary in term of the number of sessions needed (i.e., less or more than 12 sessions) to reach a good end-state functioning. With over 12 funded studies occurring at this time, the coming years will provide clinicians and researchers with much more information about how and when to best apply CPT to their traumatized clients.

References

Ali, T., Dunmore, E., Clark, D., & Ehlers, A. (2002). The role of negative beliefs in posttraumatic stress disorder: A comparison of assault victims and non victims. *Behavioural and Cognitive Psychotherapy, 30*, 249–257.

Atkeson, B. M., Calhoun, K. S., Resick, P. A., & Ellis, E. M. (1982). Victims of rape: Repeated assessment of depressive symptoms. *Journal of Consulting and Clinical Psychology, 50*, 96–102.

Barlow, D. H., & Craske, M. G. (1988). *Mastery of your anxiety and panic treatment manual.* Albany, NY: Graywind.

Beck, A. T. (1970). *Depression: Causes and treatment.* Philadelphia: University of Pennsylvania Press.

Beck, A. T., & Emery, G. (1985). *Anxiety disorders and phobias: A cognitive perspective.* New York: Basic Books.

Beck, A. T., Rush, A. J., Shaw, B. F., & Emery, G. (1979). *Cognitive therapy of depression.* New York: Guilford.

Chard, K. M. (2005). An evaluation of cognitive processing therapy for the treatment of posttraumatic stress disorder related to childhood sexual abuse. *Journal of Consulting and Clinical Psychology, 73*, 965–971.

Chard, K. M. (2009, September). *PTSD Treatment II. Using cognitive processing therapy to treat mTBI and PTSD.* Symposium conducted at the Mental Health Research Forum, Kansas City, MO.

Chard, K. M, Resick, P.A., Monson, C. M., & Kattar, K. (2009). *Cognitive Processing Therapy: Veteran/military group manual.* Washington, DC: Department of Veterans Affairs.

Chard, K. M., Schumm, J. A., Owens, G. P., & Cottingham, S. M. (2010). A comparison of OEF and OIF veterans and Vietnam veterans receiving cognitive processing therapy. *Journal of Traumatic Stress, 23*, 25–32.

Chard, K. M., Weaver, T. L., & Resick, P. A. (1997). Adapting cognitive processing therapy for work with survivors of child sexual abuse. *Cognitive and Behavioral Practice, 4*, 31–52.

Chemtob, C. M., Hamada, R. S., Roitblat, H. L., & Muraoka, M. Y. (1994). Anger, impulsivity, and anger control in combat-related posttraumatic stress disorder. *Journal of Consulting and Clinical Psychology, 62*, 827–832.

Clarke, S. B., Rizvi, S. L., & Resick, P. A. (2008). Borderline personality characteristics and treatment outcome in cognitive-behavioral treatments for PTSD in female rape victims. *Behavior Therapy, 39*, 72–78.

Falsetti, S., Resnick, H., & Davis, J. (2005). Multiple Channel Exposure Therapy: Combining cognitive-behavioral therapies for the treatment of posttraumatic stress disorder and panic attacks. *Behavior Modification, 29*(1), 70–94.

Falsetti, S., Resnick, H., & Davis, J. (2008). Multiple Channel Exposure Therapy for women with PTSD and comorbid panic attacks. *Cognitive Behaviour Therapy, 37*(2), 117–130.

Foa, E. B., Ehlers, A., Clark, D. M., Tolin, D. F., & Orsillo, S. M. (1999). The Posttraumatic Cognitions Inventory (PTCI): Development and validation. *Psychological Assessment, 11*, 303–314.

Foa, E.B., & Meadows, E.A. (1997). Psychosocial treatments for posttraumatic stress disorder: A critical review. *Annual Review of Psychology, 48*, 449–480.

Foa, E. B., Rothbaum, B., Riggs, D., & Murdock, T. (1991). Treatment of posttraumatic stress disorder in rape victims: A comparison between cognitive-behavioral procedures and counseling. *Journal of Consulting and Clinical Psychology, 59*, 715–723.

Frazier, P. A., & Schauben, L. J. (1994). Causal attributions and recovery from rape and other stressful life events. *Journal of Social and Clinical Psychology, 13*, 1–14.

Galovski, T., Monson, C., Bruce, S., & Resick, P. (2009). Does cognitive-behavioral therapy for PTSD improve perceived health and sleep impairment? *Journal of Traumatic Stress, 22*, 197–204.

Girelli, S. A., Resick, P. A., Marhoefer-Dvorak, S., & Hutter, C. K. (1986). Subjective distress and violence during rape: Their effects on long-term fear. *Violence and Victims, 1*, 35–46.

Horowitz, M. J. (1975). Intrusive and repetitive thoughts after experimental stress. *Archives of General Psychiatry, 32*, 1457–1463.

Horowitz, M. J. (1976). *Stress response syndromes*. Oxford: Jason Aronson.

Horowitz, M. J. (1979). Psychological response to serious life events. In V. Hamilton & D. M. Warburton (Eds.), *Human stress and cognition: An information-processing approach* (pp. 235–263). New York: John Wiley.

Institute of Medicine. (2007). *Treatment of posttraumatic stress disorder: An assessment of the evidence*. Washington, DC: Academy of the Sciences.

Janoff-Bulman, R. (1979). Characterological versus behavioral self-blame: Inquiries into depression and rape. *Journal of Personality and Social Psychology, 37*, 1798–1809.

Janoff-Bulman, R. (1985). The aftermath of victimization: Rebuilding shattered assumptions. In C. R. Figley (Ed.), *Trauma and its wake: The study and treatment of posttraumatic stress disorder* (pp. 15–35). New York: Brunner/Mazel.

Janoff-Bulman, R. (1989). Assumptive worlds and the stress of traumatic events: Applications of the schema construction. *Social Cognition, 7*, 113–136.

Janoff-Bulman, R. (1992). Shattered assumptions: Towards a new psychology of trauma. New York: Free Press.

Janoff-Bulman, R., & Wortman, C. B. (1977). Attributions of blame and coping in the "real world": Severe accident victims react to their lot. *Journal of Personality and Social Psychology, 35*, 351–363.

Keane, T. M., & Kaloupek, D. G. (1982). Imaginal flooding in the treatment of a posttraumatic stress disorder. *Journal of Consulting and Clinical Psychology, 50*, 138–140.

Koss, M. P., Figueredo, A. J., & Prince, R. J. (2002). Cognitive mediation of rape's mental, physical and social health impact: Tests of four models in cross-sectional data. *Journal of Consulting and Clinical Psychology, 70*, 926–941.

Kubany, E. S. (1994). A cognitive model of guilt typology in combat-related PTSD. *Journal of Traumatic Stress, 7*, 3–19.

McCann, L., & Pearlman, L. A. (1990). *Psychological trauma and the adult survivor: Theory, therapy, and transformation*. New York: Brunner/Mazel.

McCann, I. L., & Pearlman, L. A. (1992). Constructivist self-development theory: A theoretical framework for assessing and treating traumatized college students. *Journal of American College Health, 40*, 189–196.

McCann, I. L., Sakheim, D. K., & Abrahamson, D. J. (1988). Trauma and victimization: A model of psychological adaptation. *Counseling Psychologist, 16*, 531–594.

Monson, C. M., Schnurr, P. P., Resick, P. A., Friedman, M. J., Young-Xu, Y., & Stevens, S. P. (2006). Cognitive processing therapy for veterans with military-related posttraumatic stress disorder. *Journal of Consulting and Clinical Psychology, 74*, 898–907.

Morland, L. A., Greene, C. J., Rosen, C., Mauldin, P. D., & Frueh, B. C. (2009). Issues in the design of a randomized noninferiority clinical trial of telemental health psychotherapy for rural combat veterans with PTSD. *Contemporary Clinical Trials, 30*, 513–522.

Newman, E., Riggs, D. S., & Roth, S. (1997). Thematic resolution, PTSD, and complex PTSD: The relationship between meaning and trauma-related diagnoses. *Journal of Traumatic Stress, 10*, 197–213.

Otis, J. D., Keane, T. M., Kearns, R. D., Monson, C. & Scioli, E. (2009). The development of an integrated treatment for veterans with comorbid chronic pain and posttraumatic stress disorder. *Pain Medicine, 10*, 1300–1311.

Owens, G. P., & Chard, K. M. (2001). Cognitive distortions among women reporting childhood sexual abuse. *Journal of Interpersonal Violence, 16*, 178–191.

Owens, G. P., Pike, J. L., & Chard, K. M. (2001). Treatment effects of cognitive processing therapy on cognitive distortions of female child sexual abuse survivors. *Behavior Therapy, 32*, 413–424.

Piaget, J. (1971). The theory of stages in cognitive development. In D. R. Green, M. P. Ford, & G. B. Flamer (Eds.), *Measurement and Piaget* (pp.1–11). New York: McGraw-Hill.

Resick, P. A. (2010, March). Improvement over the long term: CPT and PE on PTSD, depression, health, and guilt. In M. Powers (Chair), *How do treatments for anxiety disorders benefit patients in the long run?* Symposium conducted at the 30th annual meeting of the Anxiety Disorders Association of America, Baltimore, MD.

Resick, P. A., Galovski, T. E., Uhlmansiek, M. O., Scher, C. D., Clum, G., & Young-Xu, Y. (2008). A randomized clinical trial to dismantle components of cognitive processing therapy for posttraumatic stress disorder in female victims of interpersonal violence. *Journal of Consulting & Clinical Psychology, 76*, 243–258.

Resick, P.A., Monson, C. M., & Chard, K. M. (2008). *Cognitive Processing Therapy: Veteran/military version*. Washington, DC: Department of Veterans Affairs.

Resick, P. A., Nishith, P., Weaver, T. L., Astin, M. C., & Feuer, C. A. (2002). A comparison of cognitive processing therapy, prolonged exposure and a waiting condition for the treatment of posttraumatic stress disorder in female rape victims. *Journal of Consulting and Clinical Psychology, 70*, 867–879.

Resick, P. A., & Schnicke, M. K. (1992). Cognitive processing therapy for sexual assault victims. *Journal of Consulting and Clinical Psychology, 60*, 748–756.

Resick, P. A., & Schnicke, M. K. (1993). *Cognitive processing therapy for rape victims: A treatment manual*. Newbury Park, CA: Sage.

Resick, P. A., Schnicke, M. K., & Markway, B. G. (1991, November). *The relation between cognitive content and PTSD*. Paper presented at the 25th Annual Convention of the Association for the Advancement of Behavioral Therapy, New York.

Rizvi, S. L., Vogt, D., & Resick, P. A. (2009). Cognitive and affective predictors of treatment outcome in cognitive processing therapy and prolonged exposure for posttraumatic stress disorder. *Behaviour Research and Therapy, 47*, 737–473.

Schulz, P. M., Resick, P. A., Huber, L. C., & Griffin, M. G. (2006). The effectiveness of cognitive processing therapy for PTSD with refugees in a community setting. *Cognitive and Behavioral Practice, 13*, 322–331.

Sobel, A. A., Resick, P. A., & Rabalais, A. E. (2009). The effect of cognitive processing therapy on cognitions: Impact Statement Coding. *Journal of Traumatic Stress, 22*, 205–211.

Wenninger, K., & Ehlers, A. (1998). Dysfunctional cognitions and adult psychological functioning in child sexual abuse survivors. *Journal of Traumatic Stress, 11*, 281–300.

CHAPTER

31 Empirically Supported Psychological Treatments: EMDR

C. Richard Spates *and* Sophie Rubin

Abstract

In this chapter we review the empirical foundation for Eye Movement Desensitization and Reprocessing Therapy (EMDR) for posttraumatic stress disorder. We present a brief description of the therapy, critically review recent primary and meta-analytic investigations concerning its efficacy and effectiveness, offer a summary of recent primary investigations that addressed the mechanism of action for EMDR, and based on this overall review, we suggest limitations with recommendations for future research. Recent empirical investigations of the efficacy of EMDR have improved along a number of important dimensions, and these along with the few completed effectiveness trials, position this therapy among evidence-based frontline interventions for PTSD. What is less thoroughly researched, and thus less well understood, are putative models of its theoretical mechanism of action. In addition to continuing specific improvements in research concerning efficacy and effectiveness, we recommend more and higher quality empirical studies of its mechanism of action.

Key Words: Eye Movement Desensitization and Reprocessing, EMDR, posttraumatic stress disorder, PTSD, mechanism of action, meta-analysis, efficacy, effectiveness

Description

Eye Movement Desensitization and Reprocessing (EMDR) was first introduced in 1989 as a treatment for traumatic stress reactions (Shapiro, 1989a, 1989b). Research bearing on EMDR since that time has transitioned from single case studies and quasi-experimental designs (Herbert & Meuser, 1992) to well-controlled experiments and comparative treatment outcome studies (see Spates, Koch, Cusack, Pagoto, & Waller, 2008, for a review). Meta-analytic and qualitative reviews of the empirical literature have determined that EMDR should be regarded as an evidence-based treatment for PTSD (Chambless et al., 1998; Chemtob, Tolin, van der Kolk, & Pitman, 2000; Davidson & Parker, 2001; DeRubeis & Crits-Christoph, 1998; Feske, 1998; van Etten & Taylor, 1998; National Institute for Clinical Excellence [NICE], 2005; Spates et al., 2008). What has been less clear is the mechanism of action that accounts for the efficacy of this procedure. On this basis, a number of critical appraisals (Herbert et al., 2000; Lohr, Hooke, Gist, & Tolin, 2003; Ost & Easton 2006; Rosen & Davidson 2003; Rosen, Lohr, McNally, & Herbert., 1998) have claimed the treatment package to be unscientific (Herbert et al., 2000), or that EMDR received premature recognition as an efficacious intervention (Lohr, Tolin, & Lilienfeld, 1998; Ost & Easton, 2006). Further critical claim has been made, based on dismantling studies, that if selected components do not contribute to successful outcome, then the treatment must be ineffective (Ost & Easton, 2006). Nonetheless, an increasing number of empirical investigations in recent years have sought to address the issues of efficacy, effectiveness, and mechanism of action. The greatest progress has been made with respect to the issue of efficacy and to a much lesser degree, effectiveness of EMDR. Even less progress has been made concerning the issue of its mechanism of action. This latter line of investigation has appealed to a combination of putative mechanisms including facets of memory (Andrade, Kavanagh, & Baddeley, 1997; Dyck, 1993; van den Hout, Muris, Salemink, & Kindt, 2001), dual attention focus (Armstrong & Vaughn, 1996), eye movements (Christman, Garvey, Propper, & Phaneuf, 2003), adaptive information processing (Shapiro & Maxfield, 2002), and more recently neurobiological mechanisms at varying levels of CNS functioning (Lamprecht et al, 2004; Lansing, Amen, Hanks & Rudy, 2005; Levin, Lazrove, & van der Kolk, 1999; Otani, Matsuo, Kasai, Kato, & Kato, 2009; Stickgold, 2002) or their autonomic correlates (Wilson et al., 1996).

In this chapter we provide a brief description of the overall procedure, highlighting its distinctive features, and provide a review of the recent empirical literature addressing the efficacy and effectiveness of EMDR. We summarize recent research that illustrates alternative proposed mechanism(s) of action with a commentary on the quality of that research. Finally, we suggest some limitations and recommend directions for future research. Other recent empirical reviews of EMDR have been thorough in coverage of the treatment outcome literature, but have given less space to putative mechanism(s) of action. Therefore, although we summarize the most recent well-controlled treatment outcome literature, we concentrate more fully on the question surrounding EMDR's mechanism(s) of action. In order to accomplish this goal, we begin with a detailed overview of the procedure and especially its more distinguishing features.

Description of EMDR

EMDR has been summarized as comprising approximately 8 procedural steps that include (a) history taking and treatment planning, (b) preparation and development of a working alliance, (c) trauma assessments and quantification, (d) desensitization and reprocessing proper, (e) installation of positive cognition(s), (f) body scan to identify additional tensions and/or discomforts, (g) closure and the provision of coping techniques, and (h) reevaluation as to whether treatment goals have been met. (See Shapiro, 1995, and Shapiro and Maxfield, 2002, for a thorough description and discussion of protocols).

Although this generic description provides an overview of the approach, the instructional set provided to clients undergoing EMDR treatment more clearly highlights its more distinctive features. These instructions and their presumed impact are pertinent to considerations of the mechanism of action question to be discussed later. In summary these instructions highlight the following distinctive features of the EMDR protocol:

(a) Exposure to trauma-related visual imagery where clients are asked to repeatedly visualize features of a pivotal traumatic experience for a time-limited, therapist-directed period

(b) Exposure to aversive trauma-related negative cognitions associated with the referenced trauma

(c) Rehearsal of adaptive positive cognitions where clients are asked to identify and then rehearse through repeated brief visualizations, adoption of a collaboratively derived positive cognition

(d) Saccadic eye movements where clients are asked to track the therapist's fingers as they move across the field of vision for a period of about 15–20 seconds with

(e) Simultaneous active attention to recalled details of the referenced trauma while the saccadic eye movements take place

(f) Thought and image stopping where clients are repeatedly asked to cease visualizing the referenced trauma material along with cessation of episodes of finger tracking

(g) A period (of up to 90 seconds) of nonjudgmental attentiveness to bodily and other private reactions after trauma visualization while reporting noticed changes in the body and throughout the sensorium

(h) Deep breaths at the end of each set of eye movements where clients are asked to "blank out" the recalled trauma material and to take a deep breath before mindfully attending to private sensations, thoughts and images

These features are contextualized within the broad approach described earlier, and have provided the basis for attempts at explaining EMDR efficacy and proposed qualitative outcomes as distinct from other psychotherapeutic procedures. Although eye movements, as delineated in the title of the technique, are present among these features, clearly other elements are noted as well. The efficacy literature to be reviewed in this chapter speaks to no single feature of this intervention but, rather, to the package that contains all elements. Although dismantling studies have drawn comparisons of the overall protocol with altered protocol versions not containing elements to be evaluated (e.g., eliminating eye movements but holding constant other features of the treatment package), EMDR must be seen as consisting of a number of both familiar and less common intervention elements that go well beyond those implied by its title. Thus interpretations of efficacy, effectiveness, and mechanism are to be understood with these considerations in mind. We next describe the empirical evidence for the efficacy and effectiveness of EMDR.

Empirical Support for Efficacy and Effectiveness

Studies Comparing EMDR to an Exposure-based Intervention

Studies prior to 2000 evaluated EMDR's efficacy relative to wait-list, placebo, or selected active treatments for PTSD. These active treatment comparisons included relaxation and anxiety management but did not include Prolonged Exposure (PE; Chemtob, Tolin, van Der Kolk, & Pitman, 2000). In works completed since 2000, we identified four well-controlled studies that compared EMDR to PE or a primarily exposure-based procedure targeting PTSD for this review. We identified one recent study that compared EMDR to a medication intervention for PTSD diagnosed individuals. We identified one additional efficacy trial that compared EMDR to a wait-list condition with transportation workers suffering from PTSD. Finally, we identified one follow-up investigation of EMDR treatment for PTSD. These works constituted primary investigations and are summarized in table 31.1. In addition we identified seven meta-analytic studies that addressed EMDR for treating PTSD and review those findings. These investigations are summarized in table 31.2.

Review of the Literature

Power et al. (2002) randomly assigned 105 Scottish primary-care patients diagnosed with PTSD to EMDR (n = 39), Exposure plus Cognitive Restructuring (EXP+CR; n = 37), or a wait-list control condition (n = 29). Participants in each treatment condition received up to 10 sessions. Independent evaluators completed assessments at pre- and posttreatment. A follow-up assessment using the Clinician Administered PTSD Scale (CAPS) was conducted by therapists who were aware of treatment conditions at 15 months. Treatment integrity was rated, but no details were provided. Participants assigned to EMDR were treated in an average of 4.2 sessions whereas EXP+CR participants were treated in an average of 6.4 sessions. On the CAPS, both treatment groups improved significantly, compared to those in the wait-list condition. Overall, EMDR and EXP+CR participants did not differ from each other in terms of CAPS outcome. Clinically significant change in PTSD was achieved in 60% of EMDR participants and in 50% of EXP+CR participants.

Although this investigation met many of the established standards for treatment outcome studies (e.g., Foa & Meadows, 1997), by the addition of cognitive restructuring to an exposure protocol it is possible that the effective dose of exposure may have been weakened in this investigation and thus it fails to provide the strongest test of the comparative effectiveness of EMDR and PE.

In another study, Lee, Gavriel, Drummond, Richards, and Greenwald (2002) randomly assigned 24 Australian participants with PTSD to seven sessions of EMDR or Stress Inoculation Training with PE (SIT+PE). The majority of this sample was involved in litigation related to the PTSD index event. Experts in each treatment assessed treatment fidelity and both interventions achieved acceptable ratings. EMDR and SIT+PE were equally efficacious on global measures of PTSD at posttreatment, with 83% of EMDR participants and 75% of SIT+PE participants no longer meeting diagnostic criteria for PTSD. EMDR led to significantly greater reductions in intrusion symptoms at posttreatment and significantly better improvement on two measures (Impact of Event Scale and Structured Interview—Posttraumatic Stress Disorder) at three-month follow-up compared to SIT+PE. There were no differences between treatments on avoidance measures at either posttest or follow-up assessments. Clinically significant improvement was reported in 67% of participants in each treatment condition at posttreatment and 92% of EMDR and 50% of SIT+PE participants at follow-up.

As was noted in the study by Power et al. (2002), this investigation similarly introduced a supplemental feature (SIT) to Prolonged Exposure that may have compromised the degree of exposure delivered to clients, and thus failed to provide a strong test of these two treatments.

In contrast to the two previously reported studies, Taylor et al. (2003) randomly assigned 60 Canadian participants with PTSD to eight weekly sessions of standard EMDR, standard PE, or relaxation.

Table 31.1. EMDR adult treatment studies reviewed between 2000 and 2010

Study	Population	ITT (Comp N)	Main Measure	Between N Group ES Treatment Comparison	ITT	Completer	Results
Hogberg et al. (2007)	Male and female, traumatized public transportation workers	12 (12) 11 (9)	SCID-1 PTSD Dx	EMDR vs WL	*	1.4 GAF	EMDR > WL, $p < .02$
Van der Kolk et al. (2007)	Male and female, mixed trauma	29 (24) 30 (26) 29 (26)	CAPS	EMDR vs. PLA FLU vs. PLA EMDR vs. FLU	0.48 0.04 0.45	0.59 0.06 0.51	EMDR > PLA, $p < .05$[b] FLU > PLA, ns[c] EMDR > FLU, ns[c]
Taylor et al. (2003)[a]	Male and female, mixed traumas	19 (15) 22 (15) 19 (15)	CAPS	EMDR vs. REL PE vs. REL EMDR vs. EXP	0.15 0.37 −0.27	0.04 0.61 −0.67	EMDR > REL, ns[c] EXP > REL, ns[c] EMDR < EXP, ns[c]
Rothbaum et al. (2005)[a]	Female sexual assault	25 (20) 23 (20) 24 (20)	CAPS	EMDR vs. WL PE vs. WL EMDR vs. PE		1.42 2.00 −0.43	EMDR > WL, $p < .001$ PE > WL, $p < .001$ EMDR < PE[d], ns
Power et al. (2002)	Male and female, mixed traumas	39 (27) 37 (21) 29 (24)	IES	EMDR vs. WL EXP + CR vs. WL EMDR vs. EXP + CR		1.66 0.97 0.60	EMDR > WL, $p < .001$ EXP + CR > WL, $p < .05$ EMDR > EXP + CR, ns
Lee et al. (2002)	Male and female, mixed traumas	13 (12) 13 (12)	SI-PTSD	EMDR vs. SIT+PE		0.60	EMDR > SIT + PE, ns
Marcus et al., 2004[a]	Male and female, mixed traumas	67 (44) at 3mos; (36) at 6mos	IES	EMDR vs Standard care at 6 mos	Not available	0.41	EMDR > SC, $p < .01$

Note: ES = effect size, ITT = intent-to-treat. Comp = Completers. Treatment Comparison groups: EMDR = Eye Movement Desensitization and Reprocessing, FLU = Fluoxetine, PLA = pill placebo, PE = Prolonged Exposure, REL = relaxation, WL = wait-list, EXP+CR = exposure plus cognitive restructuring, SIT+PE = Stress Inoculation Training with Prolonged Exposure, EMDR+IVE = EMDR plus in vivo exposure, EXP = exposure. Completer sample values in parentheses. Principal outcome measures: CAPS = Clinician Administered PTSD Scale, IES = Impact of Event Scale, SCID-1 Structured Clinical Interview for *DSM-IV*- Axis 1; SI-PTSD = Structured Interview for PTSD, PSS-SR = PTSD Symptom Scale-Self Report version, IES-R = Impact of Events Scale-Revised. Effect sizes are Hedges's unbiased *g* based on pretreatment and posttreatment comparisons only, except where noted (Cohen's *D* otherwise). Negative effect sizes indicate that the EMDR group was more symptomatic than the comparison group.
Results: treatment comparisons, > equals first treatment has lower mean scores than second treatment and < indicates the opposite. ns = non-significant. [a]Data provided by primary author. [b]Completer group only, but overall ANCOVA was nonsignificant. [c]Results the same for both ITT and completer groups. [d]EMDR group significantly worse on CAPS total at baseline. [e]Three additional treatment sessions offered if needed following the post-treatment assessment. * ITT would have inflated ES.

Forty-five participants, 15 in each group, completed treatment. PE included four imaginal exposure sessions followed by four in vivo exposure sessions. Independent assessments of PTSD diagnosis were conducted at intake using the Structure Clinical Interview for *DSM-IV* (SCID-IV), and independent assessments of PTSD status using the CAPS were conducted at pretreatment, one-month post-treatment, and three-month follow-up. Treatment integrity was rated for 59% of the sessions with 28% also rated by experts in the procedures. They evaluated treatment-specific and treatment-nonspecific elements of the interventions. All three treatments significantly reduced PTSD symptoms, guilt, anger, and depression at posttreatment and follow-up. However, PE produced a significantly greater percentage of participants with clinically significant change and significantly greater reductions in reexperiencing and avoidance symptoms relative to the EMDR and relaxation treatment conditions at posttest and follow-up. PE was reported to achieve significantly more rapid effects on avoidance than either EMDR or relaxation. The treatments did not differ significantly in terms of symptom worsening.

This investigation met all of the gold standards for treatment outcome studies (Foa & Meadows, 1997). There were no additional components added to either intervention that might have altered efficacy. It examined treatment outcome, but also efficiency and tolerability.

In another well-controlled investigation, Rothbaum, Astin, and Marsteller (2005) randomly assigned 74 female rape victims diagnosed with PTSD to EMDR, PE, or a wait-list control (n = 20 completers per group). Treatment sessions consisted of nine sessions conducted two times per week. The EMDR protocol was modified to be more consistent with PE and included information gathering, psycho-education, treatment rationale, and preparation. Independent evaluators conducted assessments at pre- and one-week posttreatment and six-month follow-up. Treatment integrity, adherence, and competence ratings were completed for 25% of the treatment sessions by experts in each condition. Both treatments produced clinically and statistically significant improvements on PTSD symptoms, depression, anxiety, and dissociation. EMDR and PE demonstrated significantly better end-state functioning (based on the CAPS, Beck Depression Inventory–II [BDI-II], and State Trait Anxiety Inventory–State subscale [STAI-S]) compared to the wait-list at posttreatment. Significantly better end-state functioning was demonstrated by PE participants than EMDR at six-month follow-up as measured by a composite index consisting of combined normative scores from CAPS, BDI-II, and STAI-S. EMDR was significantly better than PE at reducing dissociation at posttreatment. This investigation met all gold standards for treatment outcome studies (Foa & Meadows, 1997), and provided a detailed analysis of critical differences between the two active interventions to facilitate future work that might examine treatment components—that is, presence and absence of homework, and differential degree of exposure associated with each intervention, among others.

Comparative Efficacy Study

Van der Kolk et al. (2007) conducted a study that directly compared EMDR and pharmacological treatment for PTSD. Eighty-eight male and female participants with PTSD from diverse traumas were randomly assigned either to EMDR, Fluoxetine, or pill placebo for eight weekly treatment sessions. Seventy-six participants completed treatment, and there were no significant differences in dropout rates between treatment conditions. Reliable and valid measures were administered including the SCID-IV for initial diagnoses, CAPS and BDI-II at pretreatment, posttreatment, and six-month follow-up. Treatment manuals were provided for both active treatment conditions, and fidelity checks on at least 10% of the EMDR sessions were conducted by an expert in the procedure. EMDR was significantly superior to pill placebo for the completer sample at posttreatment, and was significantly better than Fluoxetine at six-month follow-up for PTSD symptoms, percent asymptomatic, and depression for both the completer and intent-to-treat samples. Secondary analyses revealed that individuals with adult-onset traumas treated with EMDR responded significantly better to treatment than those with child-onset trauma events. This was the first reported randomized control trial comparing EMDR to a pharmacological intervention and the study met all of the gold standards for treatment outcome studies proposed by Foa and Meadows (1997).

Follow-up Investigation

In a follow-up to a previously reported comparative effectiveness study, Marcus, Marquis, and Sakai (2004) reported on a three- and six-month evaluation of EMDR compared to standard care in an HMO setting (Marcus, Marquis, & Sakai, 1997). Of 67 participants with PTSD, 44 individuals completed the three-month and 36 finished the six-month follow-up evaluations. Treatment gains were maintained at both follow-ups with EMDR showing significantly superior outcomes compared to standard care on all measures except the STAI-S, which was significant at six months but not at three months. Standardized measures included the IES, Modified PTSD Scale (M-PTSD), BDI, STAI Trait and State subscales (STAI-T, STAI-S), and the Symptom Checklist 90 (SCL-90). Depression and state anxiety also improved significantly from the three- to six-month follow-up for the EMDR group. It was reported, however, that in many instances follow-up assessors were aware of the treatment condition due to participant disclosure. Finally, EMDR treated individuals showed significantly more change within the first three sessions than the Standard Care comparison group, suggesting it may constitute a more efficient intervention than Standard Care.

Primary Efficacy Study

Hogberg et al (2007) conducted a randomized efficacy trial comparing EMDR to a wait list with traumatized Swedish public transportation workers diagnosed with PTSD based on having experienced or witnessed a personal assault at work or "a person under train" accident. Twenty- four participants were randomly assigned to either standard EMDR (n = 13) administered in five 90-minute sessions or a two-month wait-list condition (n = 11). Independent assessments by a trained professional unaware of treatment assignment, established a qualifying diagnosis of full PTSD. Additional assessments included the Global Assessment of Functioning rating (GAF), the Hamilton Anxiety Scale (HAS), the Hamilton Rating Scale for Depression (HRSD), the IES, the Beck Anxiety Inventory (BAI), the Social Desirability Index (SDI), and the World Health Organization Ten Well-being Scale (WHO-10). PTSD status was predefined as the primary outcome variable, and the remaining measured variables, as secondary outcomes of interest. EMDR intervention underwent fidelity ratings by an expert in the treatment, was found acceptable, and the intervention was manualized.

The results revealed that EMDR was superior to the wait-list condition for the primary outcome variable of PTSD status at treatment end. Specifically, 67% of EMDR treated participants failed to fulfill criteria for a PTSD diagnosis at the end of treatment, whereas 11% did not fulfill this criterion in the wait-list condition (p < .05). An analysis of secondary measures revealed that EMDR treated participants showed significant improvement on the GAF, the HAS, the IES, the BAI, and the WHO-10. Among these secondary measures, there were significant differences between groups at posttest (Time 2 assessment) for GAF and HAM-D. It was also noted that there was significant improvement in the IES for wait-list participants from Time 1 to Time 2 assessment.

This study met all of the established gold standards for a treatment outcome study with a novel treatment sample. Drop-outs were particularly low in this study with only one from EMDR treatment and two from the wait-list condition. The 67% remission rate for PTSD reported in this investigation is among the highest of previously reported investigations when drop-outs are taken into account.

Summary of Primary Investigations

In summary, the findings from empirical investigations that compared EMDR with exposure therapy for PTSD revealed efficacy for both treatments and equivalence of measured outcomes in most comparisons. The single medication/EMDR comparative efficacy study revealed that EMDR was superior to standard frontline medication intervention for PTSD. The durability of EMDR was evaluated in one 18-month follow-up investigation during the period of this review, with findings showing that EMDR effects were maintained in a sample of civilian PTSD participants. The single primary investigation examining EMDR compared to a wait list found that, with a novel population, EMDR continued to show efficacy. The quality of the research has steadily improved, with most investigations included in this review achieving full comportment with established gold standards for treatment outcome studies. Nonetheless, future studies should seek to utilize larger sample sizes. Greater attention to research designs that evaluate EMDR and medication interventions should be conducted, utilizing both simultaneous and sequential implementation strategies. This type of research would add to our knowledge of effectiveness in real-world practice. We now review the findings from the meta-analytic investigations.

Meta-Analytic Investigations

We identified seven published meta-analytic studies that addressed EMDR since 1998. Two of the seven studies were meta-analyses of EMDR treatment for PTSD. The remaining five studies were meta-analyses of PTSD treatments that included EMDR. The latter allowed for comparisons of the effects of EMDR to other therapies. The average number of studies reviewed in a meta-analysis was 31 (range 7–61). (See table 31.2.)

Effect of EMDR on PTSD

All studies concluded that EMDR is an effective treatment for PTSD (although the term "effective" was used by the authors in each study's conclusion, it is interpreted here to mean a significant effect size in the comparison of EMDR to a control condi-

Table 31.2. Summary of meta-analyses reviewed between 1998 and 2010

Meta-Analysis	Number of studies included	Selection criteria	Quality assessment	Effect Size	Conclusions
Bisson et al. 2007	38	English; no years; pub'ed and unpub'ed; PTSD main target tx; PTSD diagnosis +3 months; + 70% pts diagnosed; random assignment; pre-and post-tx measures; + 50% of sample at post-tx	Random sequence generation, concealment of allocation, # withdrawals, tolerability, adequate reporting of data, intention-to-treat analysis	PTSD treatment versus wait list control (clinician-rated symptom changes, self-rated symptom change, anxiety, depression) TFCBT d=−1.40, −1.70, −0.99, −1.26 EMDR d=−1.51, −1.13, −1.20, −1.48 Stress management d=−1.14, 0.33, −0.77, −0.73 Other therapies d=−0.43, −0.61, −0.48, −0.25 Group CBT d=−0.72, −0.71, no data, no data EMDR versus TFCBT (clinician-rated symptom changes, self-rated symptom change, anxiety, depression) d=0.02, −0.17, −0.14, −0.32	Trauma-focused psychological treatments (TFCBT or EMDR) are effective for chronic PTSD
Siedler & Wagner, 2006	7	1989–2005; EMDR based on Shapiro's (1995) standard protocol; *DSM-IV* diagnosis of PTSD; random assignment; age 18+; means and sds, percentage improvement rates, or statistical values reported; one or more valid and reliable instrument used	Quality scoring (via gold standards proposed by Foa & Meadows (1997) reported for each study	Global symptoms: Post-post: d=0.28 Follow-up/follow-up: d=0.13 Depression: Post-post: d=0.40 Follow-up/follow-up: d=0.12	No evidence of superiority of one treatment over the other.
Bradley et al., 2005	26	PTSD psychotherapies; Pub'ed 1980-2003; Adult pts, Excluded unpub'ed studies; RCTs, >10 pts/cond; Control or comparison conditions, validated measures, reported in English	None	PTSD symptom changes (pre-post; treatment versus wait list control, treatment versus supportive control) Exposure d=1.57, 1.26,.84 EMDR d=1.43, 1.25,.75	No differential efficacy of exposure and EMDR. Both better than no treatment.
Davidson & Parker, 2001	34	Pub'ed studies; 1997–March 2000; random assignment, sufficient info for effect size calculation; tx condition not confounded with therapist	None	Mean effect sizes for outcome measures EMDR (pre-post) r=.63 EMDR/EMDR without eye movements r=.10	EMDR is effective, no incremental benefit of eye movements.

(*continued*)

Table 31.2. Summary of meta-analyses reviewed between 1998 and 2010 (*continued*)

Meta-Analysis	Number of studies included	Selection criteria	Quality assessment	Effect Size	Conclusions
Sack et al., 2001	17	Pub'ed studies only; EMDR only; 5+ pts treated w/EMDR; follow-up or both; standardized measures; controlled design, follow-up or both; standardized measures;	Quality scoring via Foa & Meadows (1997) gold standards reported for each study and incorporated into analyses	Mean pre-post effect sizes for EMDR Low-quality studies *d*=0.43 medium-quality studies *d*=1.20 high-quality studies *d*=1.76	EMDR is effective. No evidence for differential efficacy from medication and psychotherapy interventions.
Sherman, 1998	17	PTSD psychotherapies; No years; pub'ed and unpub'ed; "clinical trials;" comparison group, inferential stats; objective measures of outcome; threshold PTSD criteria met by pts	None	Overall effect of all exposure-based treatments across measures *d*=0.52 (*r*=.25)	Exposure-based treatments (including EMDR) are effective. No reliable differences across tx modalities.
Van Etten & Taylor, 1998	61	English, 1984–1996; PTSD dx; 5 + pts; pub'ed; sufficient info to calculated effect sizes; outcome on at least 1 of 4 commonly used variables	Studies coded by tx length, controlled vs uncontrolled, and therapist training	Pre-post total severity of symptoms self-report/observer EMDR *d*=1.24 *d*=0.69 Behavior therapy *d*=1.27 *d*=1.89 Drug therapy *d*=0.69 *d*=1.05	Exposure and EMDR are equally effective, and comparable to drugs, but lower drop-out. No differential drop-out for exposure and EMDR.

tion, most often though not exclusively comprising a wait list or usual care. This is technically considered "efficacious" rather than "effective"). The five meta-analyses that reviewed studies comparing EMDR to a control condition found large mean effect sizes ($d \geq .8$; Bisson, Ehlers, Matthews, Richards, & Turner, 2007; Bradley, Greene, Russ, Dutra & Westen, 2005; Davidson & Parker, 2001; Sack, Lempa & Lamprecht, 2001; Van Etten & Taylor, 1998). Sack et al. (2001) showed that studies with higher methodological quality produced the largest effect sizes and that low effect sizes were only evident in studies with serious methodological problems. However, Bisson et al. (2007) concluded that studies with higher quality were conducted more recently and thus time may moderate this interpretation by Sack et al. (1998). Bisson et al. also pointed out that most recent studies included more studies that only involved female participants, and these studies revealed significantly greater responsiveness to treatment than male only studies. One meta-analysis determined that studies with therapists trained at the EMDR Institute did not produce better outcomes than those whose therapists were not trained at the EMDR Institute (Davidson & Parker, 2001). Finally, it was reported that EMDR-treated combat veterans showed less PTSD symptom reduction over that achieved by a wait-list comparison than civilians treated with EMDR (Bisson et al., 2007).

Differential Efficacy for EMDR and Exposure Treatment

Five meta-analyses reviewed studies that compared the efficacy of EMDR to exposure therapies and none found differential efficacy at posttreatment or follow-up. One mixed finding was that exposure therapy was superior to EMDR at posttreatment on observer-rated but not self-report scales (Van Etten & Taylor, 1998); however, that effect was no longer observed at follow-up evaluation.

Added Value of Eye Movements

One meta-analysis addressed whether eye movements or any alternating movement is a necessary component for the EMDR protocol to achieve reported efficacy (Davidson & Parker, 2001). This study concluded that the published data do not support an incremental benefit of eye movements or other alternating movements on single outcome measures or outcome measure composites.

Summary of Meta-Analytic Findings

A review of seven meta-analyses revealed that EMDR is an effective (see above for usage of "effective") treatment for PTSD and equally effective compared to exposure-based therapies. Large effect sizes were reported across all meta-analyses reviewed, suggesting that EMDR is a potent treatment for PTSD. No evidence exists based on these investigations to support the essential use of eye movements or any other alternating movements in EMDR. Thus, EMDR is robust in its effects without the saccadic eye movements or alternating stimulation features for populations studied. Finally, until further primary investigations are completed revealing evidence to the contrary, EMDR may be less efficacious for combat veterans than for civilian populations (Bisson et al, 2007).

Proposed Mechanism(s) of Action and Empirical Support

We now summarize working models of EMDR's mechanism of action. We summarize and critique empirical findings bearing on the putative mechanism(s). We note here, however, that alternative proposed mechanisms are not necessarily antagonistic and may in fact support each other conceptually.

Although much has been written concerning possible mechanisms of action for the efficacy of EMDR, the overwhelming majority of this work is conceptually speculative and often seeks to explain features of the intervention that had not at the time or since been shown empirically to contribute incrementally to efficacy or effectiveness (Armstrong & Vaughn, 1996; Dyck, 1993). From the mid-1990s through 2000, much of the empirical work investigating the process of EMDR centered on the contribution of eye movements to outcome (Andrade, Kavanagh & Baddeley, 1997; Foley & Spates, 1995; Renfrey & Spates, 1994), although many other features of the procedure could still undergo empirical evaluation in an attempt to foster greater understanding. More recent empirical investigations have been conducted along several lines that examine qualitative experiences of EMDR-treated subjects as a function of variations in instructional sets applied in the protocol (Lee, Taylor, & Drummond, 2006; Lee & Drummond, 2008). This work has had a focus on differentiating the phenomenology of EMDR-treated clients from those treated with exposure-based interventions. Other investigations have pursued neurobiological correlates of specific elements of the EMDR procedure (eye movements) or of the entire procedure (Levin, Lazrove & van der Kolk, 1999; Otani et al., 2009). We now summarize two of the leading models that seek to account for the efficacy of EMDR along with a brief critique of illustrative research.

Adaptive Information Processing

Shapiro (Solomon & Shapiro, 2008) presented the Adaptive Information Processing (AIP) model to account for observed effects of EMDR. This view is as much a theory of the origins of PTSD as of EMDR proper. It suggests that PTSD arises when a distressing experience is incompletely processed and this inadequate processing is retained in memory. Its presence in memory leads to maladaptive emotional and behavioral reactions owing to the isolation of this incompletely processed memory. EMDR is believed to unblock or de-isolate this memory, linking it to more adaptive information and greater integration of memory associations. Resolution of PTSD is thought to occur as a result of procedural features that include dual attention focus on (a) the traumatic memory along with (b) some additional source(s) of bilateral stimulation. It is suggested that any of several "dual attention" focusing exercises can substitute for eye movements during the EMDR procedure, such as focusing on sounds (Foley & Spates, 1995) or alternating finger taps (Bauman & Melnyk, 1994).

To date, no well-controlled clinical investigation has provided unequivocal support for the AIP model, although several studies have targeted central concepts. For example, as mentioned, the earliest dismantling work addressed the relevance of eye movements as sources of dual attention to determine if their presence within the protocol led to differential measured effects. The conclusion to date is that evidence at present does not support the incremental contribution to efficacy of eye movements in the protocol (Davidson & Parker, 2001).

Some empirical investigations in nonclinical samples (prior to 2000) in fact revealed measured effects of eye movements on working memory (Andrade et al., 1997). More recently, investigations have revealed measured differences in the quality of clients' subjective experience as a function of dual stimulation combined with differentially administered instructional sets that focus on distancing versus re-experiencing (Lee, Taylor, & Drummonds, 2006). Finally, an innovative investigation of neurobiological correlates of PTSD diagnosed persons treated with EMDR with functional imaging effects measured within the clinical context, showed weak associations with protocol-induced eye movements in the prefrontal cortex of treated individuals (Otani et al., 2009). Specifically functional near infrared spectroscopy (fNIR) findings revealed that decreases in bilateral prefrontal cortical oxygenated hemoglobin during recall were greater with eye movements than without eye movements at both pre- and post-treatment evaluation.

Unfortunately, owing to the nonclinical samples studied in the case of working memory studies, these investigations cannot be said to offer explanatory accounts of EMDR as applied to PTSD diagnosed clinical populations. Although it is understandable from the perspective of research strategy that examining nonclinical populations is both convenient, and can be helpful is establishing proof of concept, owing to important differences in clinical versus nonclinical samples, especially in the memory area concerning PTSD diagnosed persons, further investigation is warranted before relevancy can be established.

The major shortcoming of the studies investigating quality of experiences reported by EMDR-treated individuals is that while seeking qualitative differences between EMDR-treated and exposure-treated persons, they lacked a contrast group of subjects treated with non-EMDR procedures—that is, PE. Instead the investigators relied heavily on presumed theory pertinent to expected effects of exposure-based therapy, rather than utilize a research design that incorporated assignment of such clients to exposure-based treatment. Thus, the relevance of findings is limited to the specific variations of EMDR procedures tested and have little empirical relevance to non-EMDR procedures.

Regarding the investigations of neurobiological correlates, although there have been improvements in mapping in-situation CNS changes before, during, and post EMDR treatment using innovative imaging technology, the research designs employed to date have lacked contrast groups with which to compare observed effects, among other weaknesses. It is, therefore, equivocal as to the relevance of the observed effects for non-EMDR treated patients until such between group comparisons can be made. Furthermore, even when studies have shown a measured effect of eye movements outside the clinical context or with nonclinical samples, these effects may constitute a distinction that does not make a critical difference. Such was the case by analogy, with the role played by relaxation training within the context of systematic desensitization treatment. Although relaxation could be shown to independently impact nonclinical and even clinical populations, its insertion into exposure-based therapy was found none essential for treating anxiety disorders (Marks, 1987), thus demonstrating that relaxation had an effect, but did not make a critical difference in treatment. Clarity on this can best be established by research designs that utilize appropriate contrast interventions with comparable measures of process and outcome. However, the just summarized investigations are welcomed as early attempts to examine the many and various processes associated with this multicomponent treatment package.

Although there is very limited empirical support, it should be noted nonetheless that the Adaptive Information Processing model of EMDR is generally consistent with the work of Lang (1979) and others (Foa and Kozak, 1993) that invoke the notion of perturbations of a fear memory network consisting of stimulus, response, and meaning propositions when distressing events occur. Emotional processing of maladaptive information via complete linkage to all elements of the fear network in the face of new adaptive information is thought to be the critical restorative mechanism. This is believed to consist of more than mere habituation of arousal, as imputed to respondent extinction theory, but in addition, to changes in information and meaning(s) for the client (Foa & Kozak, 1986), which by deduction is assumed not to occur with habituation or extinction models (an assumption that requires empirical examination). It should also be noted that Pitman et al. (1996), based on empirical findings raised doubts about the concept of emotional processing applied to EMDR treated combat veterans diagnosed with PTSD.

Respondent Extinction or Habituation Model

To date, the most plausible competing theoretical account for the observed effects of EMDR based on explicit protocol elements is respondent extinction via dosed exposure with response prevention. Based on the distinctive features of EMDR protocol described earlier in this chapter, clear overlap with empirically established principles (Rosen & Davidson, 2003) and treatments in behavior therapy and cognitive behavior therapy are present—that is, repeated confrontation with distressing imagery and cognitions, establishing adaptive cognitions, response prevention via encouraging mindful attention to distressing arousal without escape, avoidance, or attempts to control. By appeal to the respondent extinction model of emotional arousal to explain the observed outcomes, a reasonably parsimonious accounting can be made without invoking new theory that is unique to EMDR.

The repeated confrontation with distressing visual imagery has been the hallmark of respondent extinction whereby a conditioned stimulus (CS) loses its evocative force after repeated presentation (absent association with an unconditioned stimulus (UCS) that causes aversive arousal). With this in mind, within the EMDR procedure the target imagery (with negative cognitions and associated imagery) comprises the CS. The response to be extinguished (conditioned response or CR) entails the client's distress level or emotional arousal in the presence of the CS, as measured by the SUDs and/or measures of physiological activation. The therapeutic relationship, as well as the therapy surroundings assures the absence of any UCS arising that may provoke a traumatic reaction, and thus provides a safe context in which this exposure process takes place. This conceptualization would account at least in part for reductions in measured arousal by clients undergoing EMDR. However, this procedure resembles exposure therapy administered in a dosed fashion (Pitman et al., 1996; Rothbaum et al., 2005; Renfrey & Spates, 1994; Smyth & Poole, 2002). The dosing is achieved by brief bursts of image confrontation (20–30 seconds) followed by its cessation ("blank it out, take a deep breath"), followed by mindful attention to and verbal report about sensations and arousal, which is in part also characteristic of PE. This step is followed again by reengagement or confrontation with the target imagery and cognitions. The experimental and clinical literature as well as empirically established principles would support the value of this type of intervention when applied either within the standard EMDR protocol with or without eye movements (Carrigan & Levis, 1999; Foley & Spates, 1995; Pitman et al., 1996; Renfrey & Spates, 1994) or outside of that protocol as standalone interventions. The reader is referred to Shipherd and Salters-Pedneault (2008) for a recent review of this literature and a survey of underlying theory.

An examination of the EMDR protocol clearly indicates that its procedures are consistent with targeting anxiety sensitivity among other symptoms of PTSD. Shapiro indicates with respect to phase two, that the avoidant behavior exhibited by some clients with anxiety disorders must be addressed before serious attempts at processing traumatic memories can begin (Shapiro & Maxfield, 2002). Anxiety sensitivity has been found to correlate highly with childhood learning histories of the type referenced in Shapiro's statement (Kashdan, Zvolensky, & McLeish, 2008; Stewart et al., 2001) and with special reference to PTSD (Kilic, Kilic & Yimaz, 2008; Taylor, 2003).

Finally, the EMDR protocol makes contact with another emerging area of empirical psychological knowledge that entails mindful attention to and acceptance of treatment-induced arousal, without attempting to control, avoid, or escape. The instructional set provided to each EMDR client best illustrates this point. The therapist explains "There are no 'supposed to's in this process. So just give as accurate feedback as you can as to what is happening, without judging whether it should be happening or not. Just let whatever happens, happen" (1988, p. 66). Recent literature in cognitive and behavioral therapies point to mindful attentiveness as emerging within treatment protocols for a number of disorders including anxiety (Hayes, Follette, & Linehan, 2004), depression (Segal, Williams, & Teasdale, 2002), and borderline personality disorder (Linehan, 1993). Stein, Ivers-Deliperi, and Thomas (2008) present a review of the psychobiology of mindfulness, and trace its neurobiological impact in greater activation of the prefrontal cortex and greater deactivation of amygdala during affect labeling. EMDR's instruction toward mindful acceptance is emphasized throughout the therapeutic process. Yet, although the instructional set contains this feature, it has not been systematically evaluated as to whether it makes its impact on clients. Such mindfulness impact measures have not been utilized as part of the standard EMDR protocol and this is one area of potentially fruitful dismantling work if implemented in ways that attend to the need for contrasted groups in the research design.

Recapitulation of Limitations and Recommendations for Future Research

The evidence for EMDR as a frontline treatment for PTSD is strong and continues to improve. We note that EMDR is comparatively more efficacious in civilian populations than in combat-related PTSD. Future research could address this by examining the use of supplemental procedures that enhance EMDR's efficacy with this population. The systematic addition of homework to include in vivo exposures might constitute a place to start in this connection, along with additional intervention sessions.

We recommend that EMDR should be investigated with concurrent and sequential use of medications that target PTSD-related symptoms, in view of the widespread utilization of psychotropic agents to treat PTSD. Empirical evaluation of the separate and combined contribution of these interventions would inform practice in an important way.

Continued work addressing the efficiency and comparative tolerability of EMDR versus PE and other empirically supported therapies is recommended, given the concern for relatively high dropouts reported for exposure based therapies.

Future work should also incorporate measures that shed light on meditational factors that bear on explanatory models of EMDR. For example, to determine if imagery vividness, mindful attention instructions, and detachment or distancing experiences are influential in determining outcome, specific measurement of these constructs at time-sensitive periods during treatment would be helpful. It is only by quantifying such possible mediational factors and employing comparative research designs that answers to questions of differences among EMDR, PE, and other interventions can be answered.

References

Andrade, J., Kavanagh, D., and Baddeley, A. (1997). Eye-movements and visual imagery: A working memory approach to the treatment of post-traumatic stress disorder. *British Journal of Clinical Psychology, 36*, 209–223.

Armstrong, M., and Vaughan, K. (1996). An orienting response model of eye movement desensitization, *Journal of Behavior Therapy and Experimental Psychiatry, 27*, 21–32.

Bauman, W., & Melnyk, W. (1994). A controlled comparison of eye movements and finger tapping in the treatment of test anxiety. *Journal of Behavior Therapy and Experimental Psychiatry, 25*(1), 29–33.

Bisson, J., Ehlers, A., Matthews, S., Richards, D., & Turner, S. (2007). Psychological treatments for chronic post-traumatic stress disorder: Systematic review and meta-analysis. *British Journal of Psychiatry, 190*, 97–104.

Bradley, R., Greene, J., Russ, E., Dutra, L., & Westen, D. (2005). A multidimensional meta-analysis of psychotherapy for PTSD. *American Journal of Psychiatry, 162*, 214–227.

Carrigan, M., & Levis, D (1999). The contributions of eye movements to the efficacy of brief exposure treatment for reducing fear of public speaking. *Journal of Anxiety Disorders, 13*, 101–118.

Chambless, D. L., Baker, M., Baucom, D. H., Beutler, L. E., Calhoun, K. S., Crits-Christoph, P., et al. (1998). Update on empirically validated therapies, II. *Clinical Psychologist, 51*, 3–16.

Chemtob, C. M., Tolin, D. F., van der Kolk, B. A., & Pitman, R. K. (2000). Eye movement desensitization and reprocessing. In E. B. Foa, T. M. Keane, & M. J. Friedman (Eds.), *Effective treatments for PTSD: Practice guidelines from the International Society for Traumatic Stress Studies* (pp. 139–154). New York: Guilford.

Christman, S. D., Garvey, K. J., Propper, R. E., & Phaneuf, K. A. (2003). Bilateral eye movements enhance the retrieval of episodic memories. *Neuropsychology, 17*, 221–229.

Davidson, P. R., & Parker, K. C. H. (2001). Eye Movement Desensitization and Reprocessing (EMDR): A meta-analysis. *Journal of Consulting and Clinical Psychology, 69*, 305–316.

DeRubeis, R., & Crits-Christoph, P. (1988). Empirically supported individual and group psychological treatments for adult mental disorders. *Journal of Consulting and Clinical Psychology, 66*, 37–52.

Dyck, M. (1993). A proposal for a conditioning model of eye movement desensitization treatment for posttraumatic stress disorder, *Journal of Behavior Therapy and Experimental Psychiatry, 24*, 201–210.

Feske, U. (1998). Eye movement desensitization and reprocessing treatment for posttraumatic stress disorder. *Clinical Psychology: Science and Practice, 5*, 171–181.

Foa, E., & Kozak, M. (1993). Emotional processing of fears; Exposure to corrective information. *Psychological Bulletin, 99*, 20–35.

Foa, E. B., & Kozak, M. J. (1986). Emotional processing of fear: Exposure to corrective information. *Psychological Bulletin, 99*(1), 20–35

Foa, E. B., & Meadows, E. A. (1997). Psychosocial treatments for posttraumatic stress disorder: A critical review. *Annual Review of Psychology, 48*, 449–480.

Foley, T., & Spates, C. R. (1995). Eye movement desensitization of public-speaking anxiety: A partial dismantling. *Journal of Behavior Therapy & Experimental Psychiatry, 26*, 321–329.

Hayes, S., Follette, V., & Linehan, M. (2004). *Mindfulness and acceptance: Expanding the cognitive-behavioral tradition.* New York: Guilford.

Herbert, J. D., Lilienfeld, S. O., Lohr, J. M., Montgomery, R. W., Donohue, W. T., Rosen, G. M. & Tolin, D. F. (2000). Science and pseudoscience in the development of eye movement desensitization and reprocessing: Implications for clinical psychology. *Clinical Psychology Review, 20*, 945–971.

Herbert, J. D., & Meuser, K. T. (1992). Eye movement desensitization: A critique of the evidence. *Journal of Behavior Therapy and Experimental Psychiatry, 23*, 169–174.
Hogberg, G., Pagani, M., Sundin, O., Soares, J., Aberg-Wistedt, A., Tarnell, B., & Hallstrom, T. (2007). On treatment with eye movement desensitization and reprocessing of chronic post-traumatic stress disorder in public transportation workers: A randomized controlled trial. *Nordic Journal of Psychiatry, 61*, 54–61.
Kashdan, T. B., Zvolensky, M. S., & McLeish, A. C. (2008). Anxiety sensitivity and affect regulatory strategies: Individual and interactive risk factors for anxiety-related symptoms. *Journal of Anxiety Disorders, 22*, 429–440.
Kilic, E., Kilic, C. & Yimaz, S. (2008). Is anxiety sensitivity a predictor of PTSD in children and adolescents? *Journal of Psychosomatic Research, 65*, 81–86.
Lamprecht, F., Kohnke, C., Lempa, W., Sack, M., Matzke, M., & Munte, T. F. (2004). Event-related potentials and EMDR treatment of post-traumatic stress disorder). *Neuroscience Research, 49*, 267–272.
Lang, P. J. (1979). A bio-informational theory of emotional imagery. *Psychophysiology, 16*(6) 495–512.
Lansing, K., Amen, D. G., Hanks, C., & Rudy, L. (2005). High resolution SPECT imaging and eye movement desensitization and reprocessing in police officers with PTSD. *Journal of Neuropsychiatry and Clinical Neuroscience, 17*, 526–532.
Lee, C. W., & Drummond, P. D. (2008). Effects of eye movement versus therapist instructions on the processing of distressing memories. *Journal of Anxiety Disorders, 22*, 801–808.
Lee, C., Gavriel, H., Drummond, P., Richards, J., & Greenwald, R. (2002). Treatment of PTSD: Stress Inoculation Training with Prolonged Exposure compared to EMDR. *Journal of Clinical Psychology, 58*, 1071–1089.
Lee, C., Taylor, G., & Drummond, P. (2006). The active ingredient in EMDR: Is it traditional exposure or dual focus of attention? *Clinical Psychology and Psychotherapy, 13*, 97–107.
Levin, P., Lazrove, S., & van der Kolk, B. (1999).What psychological testing and neuroimaging tell us about the treatment of posttraumatic stress disorder by eye movement desensitization and reprocessing. *Journal of Anxiety Disorders, 13*, 159–172.
Linehan, M. M. (1993). *Cognitive-behavioral treatment for borderline personality disorder*. New York: Guilford.
Lohr, J. M., Hooke, W., Gist, R. & Tolin, D. F. (2003). Novel and controversial treatments for trauma-related stress disorders. In S. O. Lilienfeld, S. J. Lynn & J. M. Lohr (Eds.), *Science and pseudoscience in clinical psychology* (pp. 243–272). New York: Guilford.
Lohr, J. M., Tolin, D. F., & Lilienfeld, S. O. (1998). Efficacy of eye movement desensitization and reprocessing: Implications for behavior therapy. *Behavior Therapy, 29*, 123–156.
Marcus, S. V., Marquis, P., & Sakai, C. (1997). Controlled study of treatment of PTSD using EMDR in an HMO setting. *Psychotherapy: Theory, Research, Practice, Training, 34*, 307–315.
Marcus, S. V., Marquis, P., & Sakai, C. (2004). Three- and 6-month follow-up of EMDR treatment of PTSD in an HMO setting. *International Journal of Stress Management, 11*, 195–208.
Marks, I. (1987). *Fears, phobias and rituals*. Oxford, England: Oxford University Press.
National Institute for Clinical Excellence. (2005). *Post-traumatic stress disorder: The management of PTSD in adults and children in primary and secondary care*. Retrieved May 31, 2005 from http://www.nice.org.uk/pdf/CG026fullguideline.pdf.
Ost, J., & Easton, S. (2006). NICE recommends EMDR for post traumatic stress disorder: Why? *Clinical Psychology Forum, 159*, 23–26.
Otani, T., Matsuo, K., Kasai, K., Kato, T., Kato, N. (2009) Hemodynamic responses of eye movement desensitization and reprocessing in posttraumatic stress disorder. *Neuroscience Research, 65*, 375–383.
Pitman, R., Orr, S., Altman, B., Longpre, R., Poire, R., & Macklin, M. (1996). Emotional processing during Eye Movement Desensitization and Reprocessing Therapy of Vietnam veterans with chronic posttraumatic stress disorder. *Comprehensive Psychiatry, 37*, 419–429.
Power, K., McGoldrick, T., Brown, K., Buchanan, R., Sharp, D., Swanson, V., et al. (2002). A controlled comparison of Eye Movement Desensitization and Reprocessing versus exposure plus cognitive restructuring versus waiting list in the treatment of post-traumatic stress disorder. *Clinical Psychology and Psychotherapy, 9*, 299–318.
Renfrey, G., & Spates, C. R. (1994). Eye movement desensitization: A partial dismantling study. *Journal of Behavior Therapy and Experimental Psychiatry, 25*, 231–239.
Rosen, G., & Davidson, G., (2003). Psychology should list empirically supported principles of change (ESPs) and not credential trademarked therapies or other treatment packages. *Behavior Modification, 27*, 300–312.
Rosen, G. M., Lohr, J. M., McNally, R. J. & Herbert, J. D. (1998). Power therapies, miraculous claims, and the cures that fail. *Behavioral and Cognitive Psychotherapy, 26*, 99–101.
Rothbaum, B. O., Astin, M. C., & Marsteller, F. (2005). Prolonged Exposure versus Eye Movement Desensitization and Reprocessing (EMDR) for PTSD rape victims. *Journal of Traumatic Stress, 18*, 607–616.
Sack, M., Lempa, W., & Lamprecht, F. (2001). Study quality and effect sizes: A meta-analysis of EMDR-treatment for posttraumatic stress disorder. *Psychotherapie Psychosomatik Medizinische Psychologie, 51*(9–10), 350–355.
Segal, Z. V., Williams, J. M. G., & Teasdale, J. D. (2002). *Mindfulness-based cognitive therapy for depression: A new approach to preventing relapse*. New York: Guilford.
Seidler, G. H., & Wagner, F. E. (2006). Comparing the efficacy of EMDR and trauma-focused cognitive behavioral therapy in the treatment of PTSD: A meta-analytic study. *Psychological Medicine, 6*, 1–8.
Shapiro, F. (1989a). Efficacy of the eye movement desensitization procedure in the treatment of traumatic memories. *Journal of Traumatic Stress Studies, 2*, 199–223.
Shapiro, F. (1989b). Eye movement desensitization: A new treatment for post-traumatic stress disorder. *Journal of Behavior Therapy and Experimental Psychiatry, 20*, 211–217.
Shapiro, F. (1988). Efficacy of the multi-saccadic movement desensitization technique in the treatment of post-traumatic stress disorder. Unpublished dissertation, The Professional School of Psychological Studies, San Diego, CA.
Shapiro, F. (1995). *Eye movement desensitization and reprocessing: Basic principles, protocols and procedures*. New York: Guilford.
Shapiro, F., & Maxfield, L. (2002). Eye movement desensitization and reprocessing (EMDR): Information processing in the treatment of trauma. *Journal of Clinical Psychology, 58*, 933–946.

Sherman, J. J. (1998). Effects of psychotherapeutic treatments for PTSD: A meta-analysis of controlled clinical trials. *Journal of Traumatic Stress, 11*, 413–435.

Shipherd, J., & Salters-Pedneault, K. (2008). Attention, memory, intrusive thoughts, and acceptance in PTSD: An update on the empirical literature for clinicians. *Cognitive and Behavioral Practice, 15*(4), 349–363.

Smyth, N., & Poole, D. (2002). EMDR and cognitive-behavior therapy: Exploring convergence and divergence. In F. Shapiro (Eds.), *EMDR as an integrative psychotherapy approach: Experts of diverse orientations explore the paradigm prism* (pp. 151–180).

Solomon, R. M., & Shapiro, F. (2008). EMDR and the adaptive information processing model: Potential mechanisms of change. *Journal of EMDR Practice and Research* (Special Issue: Possible EMDR Mechanisms of Action), *2*, 315–325.

Spates, C., Koch, E., Cusack K., Pagoto, S., & Waller, S. (2008). Eye Movement Desensitization and Reprocessing. In E. Foa, T. Keane, M. Friedman, & J. Cohen (Eds.), *Effective Treatments for PTSD* (2nd ed., pp. 279–305). New York: Guilford.

Stein, D., Ivers-Deliperi, V., & Thomas, K. (2008).Psychobiology of mindfulness: Pearls in clinical neuroscience Placebo, *CNS Spectrums, 13*, 752–756.

Stewart, S., Taylor, S., Jang, K., Cox, B., Watt, M., Federoff, I. & Borger, S. (2001). Causal modeling of relations among learning history, anxiety sensitivity, and panic attacks. *Behaviour Research and Therapy, 39*, 443–456.

Stickgold, R. (2002). EMDR: A putative neurobiological mechanism of action. *Journal of Clinical Psychology, 58*, 61–67.

Taylor, S. (2003). Anxiety sensitivity and its implications for understanding and treating PTSD. *Journal of Cognitive Psychotherapy: An International Quarterly, 17*, 179–186.

Taylor, S., Thordarson, D. S., Maxfield, L., Fedoroff, I. C., Lovell, K., & Ogrodniczuk, J. (2003). Comparative efficacy speed, and adverse effects of three PTSD treatments: Exposure therapy, EMDR, and relaxation training. *Journal of Consulting and Clinical Psychology, 71*, 330–338.

van den Hout, M., Muris, P., Salemink, E., and Kindt, M. (2001). Autobiographical memories become less vivid and emotional after eye movements. *British Journal of Clinical Psychology, 40*, 121–130.

Van Der Kolk, B., Spinazolla, A., Blaustein, J., Hopper, M., Hopper, J., Korn, D., et al. (2007). A randomized clinical trial of eye movement desensitization and reprocessing (EMDR), fluoxetine, and pill placebo in the treatment of posttraumatic stress disorder: Treatment effects and long-term maintenance. *Journal of Clinical Psychiatry, 68*, 37–46.

Van Etten, S., & Taylor, S. (1998). Comparative efficacy of treatments for posttraumatic stress disorder: A meta-analysis. *Clinical Psychology and Psychotherapy, 5*, 126–144.

Wilson, D., Silver, S., Covi, W., Foster, S. (1996). Eye movement desensitization and reprocessing: Effectiveness and autonomic correlates. *Journal of Behavior Therapy and Experimental Psychiatry, 27*(3), 219–229.

CHAPTER

32 Promising Psychological Treatments

Megan C. Kearns *and* Barbara Olasov Rothbaum

Abstract

Exposure to traumatic events is highly prevalent, which has led to the creation of multiple psychosocial and pharmacological treatment approaches for individuals who subsequently develop posttraumatic stress disorder (PTSD). Despite the availability of existing empirically supported treatments for PTSD, research indicates that a significant subset of patients fail to respond to treatment. As a result, there is a great need for the development of novel and innovative treatments that can address the diverse needs of individuals with trauma histories and that can alleviate symptoms of traumatic stress in a greater number of individuals. The following chapter outlines numerous promising treatments, including couple and family-based approaches, technological approaches, emotion-based therapies, pharmacological treatments, and treatments designed to address comorbidity. Although many of these approaches are in preliminary stages of development and require further study, they represent important progress in helping clinicians better serve the many needs of individuals with PTSD.

Key Words: PTSD, treatment, cognitive behavioral therapy, virtual reality, emerging therapies

Introduction

Although effective treatments are available for PTSD, it remains a challenging disorder to treat. A meta-analysis of psychotherapy treatments for PTSD indicated that approximately 67% of patients respond to treatment and no longer meet criteria for PTSD (Bradley, Greene, Russ, Dutra, & Westen, 2005). As a result, novel and innovative treatment approaches are still greatly needed in order to increase our ability to effectively treat a greater number of individuals who have been exposed to traumatic events. The following chapter reviews a number of such treatments that may offer creative ways to address the diverse needs of individuals diagnosed with PTSD. Although many of these treatments are in very preliminary stages of empirical evaluation, they represent promising new avenues of exploration for researchers and clinicians alike, as we attempt to form greater understanding of the best ways to alleviate suffering and impairment caused by PTSD.

Couple and Family-based Approaches to the Treatment of PTSD

Overview

Individuals with PTSD have been noted to have a greater likelihood of reporting marital distress, divorce, parenting problems, difficulties with intimacy and communication, and intimate partner violence (for a review, see Monson & Taft, 2005). Thus, treatments that address relationship functioning in addition to alleviating PTSD symptoms could be extremely beneficial in improving overall quality of life. In a review of the literature, Riggs, Monson,

Glynn, and Canterino (2009) describe two distinct rationales or approaches to using marital and family therapy for treatment of PTSD. The systemic approach targets the distress in family relationships following exposure to trauma and directly attempts to improve family functioning by enhancing communication and reducing conflict. In contrast, the support approach utilizes the trauma survivor's partner and family as additional sources of social support while focusing on alleviating the survivor's symptoms of traumatic stress. Both of these rationales highlight the potential of couple- and family-based approaches to enhance the recovery of individuals exposed to traumatic events.

Cognitive Behavioral Conjoint Therapy (CBCT) for PTSD is advocated (Monson, Fredman, & Adair, 2008) for couples where at least one partner has PTSD. The intervention consists of 15 sessions with both partners that cover three stages: (1) treatment overview, psycho-education, and safety building; (2) behavioral skills for improving relationship satisfaction and communication, and decreasing avoidance; and (3) cognitive strategies aimed at maladaptive thinking patterns that are impacting PTSD symptoms and relationship functioning. Couples are encouraged to discuss the effect of the trauma and associated attributions surrounding the event, although a detailed retelling of the trauma itself is not included in this protocol.

Family systems therapy (FST) has been studied specifically in a veteran population and included one to five family sessions over a two- to eight-week period (Ford et al., 1998). This client-centered treatment involves psycho-education about trauma, cognitive restructuring, exploration of family-of-origin patterns, structural interventions to establish functional family roles and improve communication, strategic interventions to increase a sense of choice and control among family members, and development of a shared family narrative of the trauma experience.

Strategic Approach Therapy (SAT; Sautter, Glynn, Thompson, Franklin, & Han, 2009) is a 10-session manualized behavioral treatment with three phases, including (1) psycho-education and increasing motivation, (2) increasing intimacy and positive emotions, and (3) partner-assisted anxiety reduction, including modified stress inoculation techniques. Although the treatment was designed to specifically target avoidance and emotional numbing symptoms, Sautter and colleagues (2009) suggest that treatment can impact overall PTSD severity as well.

Several other family and couple approaches to treating PTSD have been proposed, but their application and efficacy remain untested. Integrative behavioral couple therapy (IBCT) (Erbes, Polusny, MacDermid, & Compton, 2008) emphasizes the role of experiential avoidance in maintaining PTSD symptoms and negatively impacting relationships, and utilizes both acceptance and change strategies to reduce conflict. They suggest an adapted 12–14 session protocol for veteran populations, with greater emphasis on activity scheduling, motivational interviewing techniques, and psycho-education about trauma.

Emotionally focused marital therapy (Johnson & Williams-Keeler, 1998) is described as a nine-step therapy that aims to access and reprocess emotions and create new interactions between the couple. Critical interaction therapy (Johnson, Feldman, & Lubin, 1995) emphasizes the role of marital conflict in triggering trauma-related distress, and as a result, this approach attempts to identify these behavior patterns and their relationship to trauma memories and work to promote better communication between the couple. Sherman, Zanotti, and Jones (2005) outline appropriate couple interventions for each of the three symptom clusters of PTSD (e.g., behavioral activation for avoidance symptoms, anxiety management for hyper-arousal symptoms, psychoeducation for reexperiencing symptoms). These interventions are presented as part of a conceptual framework for treating PTSD that can be selected based on an individual couple's needs.

Empirical Evidence

Despite the rationale in utilizing couple and family-based approaches in treating PTSD, very little research has investigated the efficacy of these techniques (Riggs et al., 2009), and much of the existing data are limited specifically to survivors of combat trauma (Monson et al., 2008). Data from a pilot study of CBCT applied with Vietnam veterans and their partners indicated significant improvements in PTSD symptoms according to both clinician and partner ratings, and marginally improved relationship satisfaction for partners (Monson, Schnurr, Stevens, & Guthrie, 2004). However, veterans' self-reports of improvement for both PTSD and relationship satisfaction were not statistically significant, although they noted reduced depression and anxiety. Additional research funded by NIMH is currently under way to further test the efficacy of this treatment and improve flexibility in applying this protocol with couples exposed to other types of traumatic events (Monson et al., 2008). A similarly designed study evaluated the efficacy of SAT with six Vietnam veterans and their partners. Although it also represented an uncontrolled study, results indicated that both self-report and clinician-rated scores showed a significant reduction in avoidance, emotional numbing, and overall PTSD severity at posttreatment.

FST has been examined in a quasi-experimental design, with veterans of Operation Desert Storm who requested family therapy versus other veteran comparison groups that did not receive family therapy (Ford et al., 1998). Results indicated that FST participants reported greater reductions in stress and psychiatric symptoms, as well as improved family cohesion and marital satisfaction. However, this study lacked a randomized control group and may not generalize to other populations, so additional replication of these findings is needed.

Currently there are no data to support IBCT as a treatment approach for alleviating symptoms of PTSD, although Erbes and colleagues (2008) outlined a case example to illustrate how this approach may be utilized with veteran populations. Case examples have also been presented for critical interaction therapy (Johnson et al., 1995) and for the conceptual framework described by Sherman et al. (2005), but neither approach has been formally tested. Emotionally focused marital therapy (Johnson & Williams-Keeler, 1998) has not been explicitly evaluated for its effectiveness with couples who are coping with trauma. Thus, further research is needed to test the conceptual frameworks proposed in these various treatment approaches in order to evaluate their efficacy in helping traumatized individuals and their partners and families.

Technological Approaches to the Treatment of PTSD

Internet or Computer-based Treatments

Many barriers to PTSD treatment exist, such as geographical limitations, access to specialized treatment, physical disability, fear of mental health stigma, and the actual symptoms of psychopathology themselves (e.g., avoidance symptoms of PTSD; Reger & Gahm, 2009). One promising new avenue for increasing access to PTSD treatment is the use of Internet-based programs. Amstadter, Broman-Fulks, Zinzow, Ruggiero, and Cercone (2009) outline several benefits to these approaches, including personalization of the presentation format, access to these resources from home in order to avoid stigma and to overcome geographical limitations, and easy revision of information to be consistent with current research. A recent meta-analysis revealed a moderate effect size of $d = 0.75$ for Internet-based approaches to PTSD treatment (compared to no treatment), which suggests some preliminary support (Reger & Gahm, 2009). Also, a survey conducted with a military population indicated that a majority of soldiers were willing to utilize technology-based mental health treatments, and interestingly, 33% of soldiers who were not interested in utilizing in-person treatment reported that they would use a technology-based approach (Wilson, Onorati, Mishkind, Reger, & Gahm, 2008). Thus, innovative technological approaches to treating PTSD may not only increase access but also increase utilization of mental health treatment in general.

Interapy is one such Internet-based approach to PTSD treatment that utilizes an interactive Internet Web site to provide a therapeutic intervention for traumatic stress symptoms. The treatment incorporates three phases, including actualization, cognitive reappraisal, and sharing and farewell (Lange et al., 2003). The actualization phase incorporates psycho-education and structured writing about the traumatic event, and the cognitive reappraisal phase focuses on facilitating new perspectives on the trauma. Finally, the third phase emphasizes the benefits of sharing their story about the traumatic event. The treatment is organized into 10 writing sessions, with therapists providing instructions and feedback within each phase.

Another Internet-based treatment developed for military service members is DE-STRESS (DElivery of Self TRaining and Education for Stressful Situations). This cognitive behavioral program teaches patients how to cope with trauma-related distress, including techniques such as self-monitoring, in vivo exposure, stress-management strategies, and writing sessions regarding the traumatic event (Litz, Engel, Bryant, & Papa, 2007). DE-STRESS is conducted following an initial meeting in person with the therapist to receive psycho-education about PTSD and instructions in utilizing the Web application. Patients received a personal login with unlimited access to online psycho-education, self-assessments, and therapeutic homework assignments.

Another Internet-based format that allows more therapist interaction and guidance is the use of videoconferencing technology. Videoconferencing allows individuals to see and hear each other on computer monitors in real time using cameras. This technology has appeal in that a therapist can observe nonverbal behavior and have more patient contact similar to therapy conducted in the same room. Videoconferencing eliminates many barriers to treatment, such as geographical limits, physical disability, and mental health stigma. Thus far, no protocol has been specifically designed for treating PTSD using videoconferencing technology. However, this approach allows for the use of existing empirically supported treatments for PTSD, although the effectiveness of delivering these treatments via videoconferencing format requires testing.

Empirical Evidence

In an analysis of Interapy, Lange et al. (2000) found significant improvements in PTSD, psychological functioning, and pathological grief over the course of treatment. This study lacked a control group, but results were compared with data from other in person protocols, with Interapy producing greater improvements. The first controlled trial of Interapy utilized a sample of undergraduate trauma survivors (Lange, van de Ven, Schrieken, & Emmelkamp, 2001). Results indicated greater reductions in intrusion and avoidance symptoms following Interapy versus a wait-list control. Lange et al. (2003) extended this research with a large community sample and produced similar findings. A cross-cultural study using a German-speaking population also identified clinically significant improvements in PTSD symptoms for Interapy participants, as well as an association between the therapy alliance and treatment outcomes (Knaevelsrud & Maercker, 2007).

DE-STRESS has been evaluated in a randomized clinical trial in which military service members participated in either DE-STRESS or Internet-based supportive therapy (Litz et al., 2007). Results indicated similar dropout rates to other PTSD treatments and greater improvement in symptoms of traumatic stress, depression, and anxiety compared to the supportive therapy group. However, the study was limited by a small sample size, and more research is needed to research this self-management treatment approach.

Very limited research has evaluated the effectiveness of telepsychiatry, especially for PTSD. Germain, Marchand, Bouchard, Drouin, and Guay (2009) evaluated the effectiveness of cognitive behavioral therapy for PTSD when delivered via videoconferencing versus face-to-face. Results indicated that both delivery methods were equally effective at improving traumatic stress symptoms and overall functioning. However, random assignment was not utilized, and thus, a more stringent randomized clinical trial is needed. Of note, patient perceptions of the technical difficulties inherent in a telepsychiatry approach did not appear to detract from the effectiveness of the treatment. Other research has also shown that therapist competence, including empathy and rapport, was rated equally when a manualized cognitive behavioral treatment for PTSD was administered via videoconferencing technology versus traditional same room delivery of services (Frueh et al., 2007). Although there are several advantages to the use of videoconferencing technology, further evaluation is needed.

Virtual Reality Exposure Therapy

Virtual reality represents another innovative technology involving a computer-simulated reality in which participants can be exposed to multiple sensory stimuli (e.g., olfactory, visual, audio, tactile) through a head-mounted display and can interact with this virtual environment through natural body movements (Gregg & Tarrier, 2007). Virtual reality has been applied in mental health settings to simulate environments that can aid exposure to feared stimuli in the treatment of anxiety disorders. Several advantages of virtual reality have been proposed, including the ability to control stimuli for graded exposures and the ability to expose patients to stimuli that may be otherwise difficult or expensive to recreate in the real world (e.g., flying in an airplane; Rothbaum, 2009). In addition, the sense of presence created by immersion in a virtual environment can potentially enhance engagement and emotional processing, which is seen as essential to effective treatment. Ready, Pollack, Rothbaum, and Alarcon (2006) described a typical VRE session as consisting of therapist assessment and review of progress, followed by 30–45 minutes of exposure using the VR technology. During the exposure, the therapist monitors what the patient is viewing on a separate screen and communicates via microphone to assess distress using subjective units of distress scale (SUDS) ratings. Afterwards, the patient debriefs with the therapist and processes his or her reactions to the exposure. Treatment length is based on response to treatment and terminated when participants can discuss the traumatic memory in detail and be exposed to the virtual stimuli without marked emotional arousal, but are recommended for 9–12 sessions (Rothbaum, Difede, & Rizzo, 2008).

Empirical Evidence

Several empirical studies have examined the use of VRE in the treatment of anxiety disorders, with a recent meta-analysis detecting a large effect size for VRE (Parsons & Rizzo, 2008). However, the applicability of VRE to trauma survivors is limited. Several case studies (Gerardi, Rothbaum, Ressler, Heekin, & Rizzo, 2008; Reger & Gahm, 2008; Rothbaum et al., 1999; Saraiva et al., 2007; Difede & Hoffman, 2002) indicate that VRE produces significant reduction of PTSD symptoms for various types of trauma survivors (e.g., veterans, survivors of motor vehicle accidents and terrorism attacks). Two uncontrolled pilot studies indicated significant and lasting improvement in PTSD (Beck, Palyo, Winer, Schwagler & Ang, 2007; Ready et al., 2006). To date, the only published controlled trial of VRE utilized a wait-list control group to evaluate the efficacy of VRE among survivors of the World Trade Center attacks (Difede et al., 2007). Despite a small sample (N = 21), results indicated significant reductions in PTSD symptoms following VRE. A review by Gregg and Tarrier (2007) concluded that VRE is effective compared to no treatment, but studies with more rigorous designs should be conducted. Given the results of current research and treatment advantages of this approach, VRE represents a promising new method for facilitating recovery from traumatic events.

Emotion-based Approaches to the Treatment of PTSD

DBT

Dialectical Behavior Therapy (DBT) is a treatment approach originally developed for individuals with borderline personality disorder (BPD) that incorporates cognitive behavioral techniques, as well as mindfulness, acceptance, and validation strategies, to reduce emotion regulation deficits and self-harm behavior (Linehan, 1993). Because of the common tendency for individuals with BPD to report trauma histories, Linehan (1993) describes a second stage to DBT, following an initial phase targeting behavioral control, which involves exposure techniques for trauma-related fears and emotions. Alternatively, Becker and Zayfert (2001) proposed that DBT techniques may be utilized to address crises or parasuicidal behavior, and to enhance acceptance of emotions during exposures.

Empirical Evidence

Although multiple randomized controlled trials have demonstrated the effectiveness of DBT for individuals with BPD, as well as binge eating and substance use, no research has evaluated the effectiveness of DBT as a treatment for PTSD symptoms (Wagner & Linehan, 2006). Harned and Linehan (2008) published case studies of two patients treated with a protocol that integrated DBT with exposure therapy for PTSD. Results indicated significant improvement in PTSD symptoms as well as decreases in trauma-related emotions (e.g., fear, shame, guilt). Given that individuals reporting suicidality and other comorbid diagnoses are often excluded from treatment outcome studies for PTSD, Harned and Linehan (2008) emphasize the importance of further research on DBT and its application to PTSD symptoms.

STAIR

The STAIR program (Skills Training in Affective and Interpersonal Regulation) was developed by Cloitre and colleagues (2002) to address problems in emotion regulation and interpersonal relationships, which is common among child abuse survivors and neglected by other existing treatments for PTSD. The treatment was designed to be conducted in two phases for a total of 16 sessions (Levitt & Cloitre, 2005). The first phase involves the development of skills for emotion regulation and interpersonal functioning, while developing a strong alliance with the therapist. Each session in this phase involves psychoeducation, skills practice, and between-session homework to apply skills. The second phase involves a modified form of prolonged exposure where patients utilize the skills from the first phase to emotionally process the traumatic memory. This phase emphasizes identification of emotions and interpersonal schemas generated during the exposure. Although the STAIR treatment utilizes existing cognitive behavioral strategies for PTSD (e.g., imaginal exposure), the authors propose that factors such as poor emotion regulation, dissociation, and interpersonal problems contribute to poorer treatment outcomes (Cloitre, Koenen, Cohen, & Han, 2002). Thus, STAIR may represent a promising treatment approach for PTSD, especially among child abuse survivors.

Empirical Evidence

Only one clinical trial to date has evaluated the efficacy of STAIR-modified PE treatment (Cloitre et al., 2002). Compared to the waitlist control group, participants in the STAIR treatment demonstrated significant reductions in PTSD symptoms, interpersonal problems, and emotion regulation deficits, which were maintained at a 3 and 9-month follow- up assessment. More research is needed to determine whether the addition of the skills acquisition phase augmented the effectiveness of the exposure techniques utilized in this treatment. However, for patients with PTSD who report difficulties with emotion regulation and interpersonal relationships, this treatment may be a useful approach.

Acceptance and Commitment Therapy (ACT)

Another treatment approach that has been proposed and adapted for the treatment of PTSD is acceptance and commitment therapy (ACT). The theoretical basis of ACT emphasizes the role of experiential avoidance and cognitive entanglement in contributing to the development of PTSD (Walser & Hayes, 2006). The goal of ACT is therefore to help patients stop suppressing unwanted feelings or thoughts surrounding the trauma and instead accept their emotional experience and commit to making behavioral changes consistent with their values and goals (Orsillo & Batten, 2005).

Empirical Evidence

Current research is under way to empirically test the effectiveness of ACT as a treatment approach for PTSD, but at present, data to support ACT are limited primarily to case studies (Twohig, 2009; Batten & Hayes, 2005). Although these studies demonstrated improved functioning for PTSD survivors, including a nonresponder to CBT (Twohig, 2009), the application of ACT to individuals with trauma histories requires further study.

Pharmacological Approaches to the Treatment of PTSD

D-Cycloserine

PTSD has often been conceptualized as a form of fear conditioning whereby neutral stimuli are paired with aversive stimuli (i.e., the traumatic event), and to effectively treat PTSD, the fear response must be extinguished (Davis, Myers, Ressler, & Rothbaum, 2005). The extinction process has been linked to an amygdala receptor known as the N-methyl-D-aspartate (NMDA) receptor. D-Cycloserine (DCS) is a partial agonist that enhances the functioning of the NMDA receptor, and in animal research, DCS has been shown to be successful at aiding the extinction process (Davis, Ressler, Rothbaum, & Richardson, 2006). The implications of these findings are relevant in that DCS may be useful as an adjunct to psychotherapy that facilitates learning and extinction of fear during exposure exercises. Because DCS appears to have a time-dependent impact on learning, it is suggested that DCS be taken acutely in conjunction with exposure sessions in order to augment the effects of psychotherapy (Davis et al., 2006). This contrasts with other existing pharmacological treatments for PTSD, and thus appears to be a novel approach with potential to increase psychotherapy benefits through enhanced learning.

EMPIRICAL EVIDENCE

Norberg, Krystal, and Tolin (2008) conducted a meta-analysis of animal and human research studies examining DCS, and confirmed that DCS enhances the outcome of exposure therapy and appears most beneficial when administered immediately prior to extinction training. Although there are currently no published studies specifically examining the efficacy of DCS in treating PTSD, research is already underway (Brunet, 2010). Given the established benefits of treatments for PTSD that aim to extinguish fear and arousal associated with traumatic events, DCS represents a promising approach to augmenting treatment response.

Other Pharmacological Treatments

In addition to DCS, several other pharmacological approaches have potential to treat symptoms of PTSD. In a randomized controlled trial of prazosin, an adrenergic receptor antagonist, results indicated that prazosin produced significant reduction in trauma-related nightmares and improved sleep in a veteran sample (Raskind et al., 2003). Propranolol is a beta-adrenergic blocker that has been shown to counter stress hormones and has been tested both acutely (within six hours of a traumatic event; Pitman et al., 2002) and with individuals with chronic PTSD (Brunet et al., 2008). In both studies, a limited number of propranolol doses produced reductions in physiological responses when participants recalled trauma-related mental imagery. Ketamine, an anesthetic, is an agent linked to PTSD, with some data suggesting lower rates of PTSD in patients who were administered ketamine during surgery (McGhee, Maani, Garza, Gaylord, & Black, 2008). Methylenedioxymethamphetamine (MDMA) is another compound believed to facilitate integration and assist with emotional processing of fear (Doblin, 2002). However, no data on MDMA have been published. Large randomized controlled trials are needed to further explore the potential of these pharmacological agents and their therapeutic application to PTSD.

Approaches to the Treatment of PTSD and Other Comorbid Issues

Overview

One challenge to effectively treating symptoms of traumatic stress is the high rate of comorbidity between PTSD and other mental health disorders, with approximately 88.3% of men and 79% of women with PTSD reporting lifetime comorbid diagnoses (Kessler, Sonnega, Bromet, Hughes, & Nelson, 1995). Research suggests that clinicians find treating comorbid conditions, such as substance abuse and PTSD, more difficult to treat (Back, Waldrop, & Brady, 2009). Thus, novel treatment approaches that can alleviate symptoms of multiple conditions, including PTSD, have great potential to enhance treatment outcome and quality of life for individuals with trauma histories.

Multiple Channel Exposure Therapy

Research suggests that individuals with PTSD often report comorbid panic attacks, which has been theorized to result from chronic hyper-arousal and vigilance toward physiological cues (Falsetti & Resnick, 2000). Multiple Channel Exposure Therapy (M-CET) is a cognitive behavioral approach that was specifically developed to address these commonly co-occurring disorders. Designed as a 12-session protocol implemented in an individual or group format, the treatment consists of psycho-education, interoceptive exposure, in vivo exposure, written narratives about the traumatic event, and cognitive restructuring skills (Falsetti & Resnick, 2000). Falsetti and Resnick (2000) describe this approach as applicable to a variety of traumatic events and also to individuals with multiple trauma histories.

EMPIRICAL EVIDENCE

In a randomized treatment pilot study utilizing a wait-list control group, M-CET was evaluated in women with multiple trauma histories who were diagnosed with PTSD and reported comorbid panic attacks (Falsetti, Resnick, & Davis, 2008). Results indicated that M-CET participants experienced greater reductions in PTSD and panic symptoms, which was maintained over a three- and six-month follow-up. Further research is needed, particularly studies that incorporate male patients and that compare M-CET to other existing PTSD treatments.

Seeking Safety

Substance abuse is another comorbid condition that has a high degree of overlap with PTSD, which often leads to greater impairment and poor treatment response (Najavits, Weiss, Shaw, & Muenz, 1998). Seeking Safety is a manualized cognitive behavioral treatment designed for patients with comorbid PTSD and substance abuse, which has traditionally been treated separately. Although designed as a flexible approach, Seeking Safety is presented as a 24-session treatment conducted in either group or individual format. This treatment is very present-focused, in contrast to some other PTSD treatments, and emphasizes the development of new coping skills. Najavits (2004) outlines a range of topics covered in treatment, including skills for interpersonal relationships, behavioral topics, and cognitive topics. Seeking Safety presents a novel integrative approach that addresses both PTSD symptoms and problematic substance use.

EMPIRICAL EVIDENCE

The first uncontrolled pilot study of Seeking Safety identified decreased substance use and PTSD symptoms at a three-month follow-up, as well as improved social and family functioning and decreased depression and suicide risk (Najavits et al., 1998). Another small, uncontrolled study with predominantly male veterans indicated similar reductions in PTSD and improved quality of life at posttreatment (Cook, Walser, Kane, Ruzek, & Woody, 2006). Preliminary findings comparing Seeking Safety with "treatment as usual" for substance abuse have identified greater improvement among Seeking Safety participants (Najavits, Gallop, & Weiss, 2006), and greater treatment retention (Ghee, Johnson, Burlew, & Bolling, 2009).

However, in a randomized controlled trial comparing Seeking Safety with another manualized CBT treatment approach for substance abuse only, results indicated no significant differences in treatment outcome (Hien, Cohen, Miele, Litt, & Capstick, 2004). Similar findings were documented in a recent large multisite randomized controlled trial that compared Seeking Safety with a health education group (Hein et al., 2009). This calls into question the idea that treatment targeting both PTSD and substance abuse simultaneously produces advantageous benefits. A study on the efficacy of Seeking Safety with incarcerated women also showed no treatment differences at posttreatment, although there was some evidence of continued gains for Seeking Safety participants (Zlotnick, Johnson, & Najavits, 2009). Thus, Seeking Safety appears to be an effective treatment for PTSD and substance use in a number of diverse populations, but may not offer significant benefits above and beyond existing "treatment as usual" approaches for individuals with comorbid substance abuse and trauma histories.

Conclusions and Future Directions

Many of these treatment approaches represent exciting new opportunities to address the diverse needs of individuals with PTSD. Given the often chronic nature of the disorder and the wide-ranging impact on a person's functioning, treatments designed to alleviate comorbid symptoms, relationship distress, and other treatment barriers represent important progress. Family-based approaches target an important presenting problem, but still remain in early stages of evaluation. Similarly, emotion-based treatments may provide important coping skills for individuals undergoing treatment for PTSD, but existing evidence is limited. Pharmacological approaches such as D-cycloserine represent an exciting new avenue of research aimed at enhancing existing empirically supported treatments, but its application to PTSD is still under investigation. Comorbid treatment approaches, such as M-CET and Seeking Safety, are greatly needed for trauma populations, but research has not yet established these approaches to be superior to treatments that target comorbid conditions separately from PTSD. Finally, technological advances have opened up new opportunities to address treatment barriers to PTSD.

However, a great deal of additional work is needed before these approaches can be considered empirically supported or considered first-line treatments relative to more established treatments for PTSD. In particular, much of the existing data for these approaches is based on studies that lacked controlled designs or have yet to be replicated in larger treatment samples. In order to facilitate progress in our ability to effectively treat PTSD, more randomized controlled trials are needed to evaluate these approaches and determine their efficacy. In addition, further attention should be given to the reasons existing treatments fail to produce significant improvement in a subset of individuals. Research on these areas will provide more understanding of the limitations of our existing empirically supported treatments and guide the development of new treatments that can accommodate the diverse needs of individuals with PTSD.

Note

Disclosure Statement: Dr. Rothbaum and Emory University own equity in Virtually Better, Inc., which is developing products related to the VR research described in this chapter. The terms of this arrangement have been reviewed and approved by Emory University in accordance with its conflict-of-interest policies.

References

Amstadter, A. B., Broman-Fulks, J., Zinzow, H., Ruggiero, K. J., & Cercone, J. (2009). Internet-based interventions for traumatic stress-related mental health problems: A review and suggestion for future research. *Clinical Psychology Review, 29*, 410–420.

Back, S. E., Waldrop, A. E., & Brady, K. T. (2009). Treatment challenges associated with comorbid substance use and post-traumatic stress disorder: Clinicians' perspectives. *American Journal on Addictions, 18*, 15–20.

Batten, S. V., & Hayes, S. C. (2005). Acceptance and Commitment Therapy in the treatment of comorbid substance abuse and post-traumatic stress disorder: A case study. *Clinical Case Studies, 4*, 246–262.

Beck, J. G., Palyo, S. A., Winer, E. H., Schwagler, B. E., & Ang, E. J. (2007). Virtual Reality Exposure Therapy for PTSD symptoms after a road accident: An uncontrolled case series. *Behavior Therapy, 38*(1), 39–48

Becker, C. B., & Zayfert, C. (2001). Integrating DBT-based techniques and concepts to facilitate exposure treatment for PTSD. *Cognitive and Behavioral Practice, 8*(2), 107–122.

Bradley, R., Greene, J., Russ, E., Dutra, L., & Westen, D. (2005). A multidimensional meta-analysis of psychotherapy for PTSD.[erratum appears in *American Journal of Psychiatry, 162*(4), p. 832]. *American Journal of Psychiatry, 162*(2), 214–227.

Brunet, A. (Chair). (2010, November). *Facilitating extinction processes with D-cycloserine*. Symposium presented at the 26th annual ISTSS Conference, Montreal, Canada.

Brunet, A., Orr, S. P., Tremblay, J., Robertson, K., Nader, K., & Pitman, R. K. (2008). Effect of post-retrieval propranolol on psychophysiologic responding during subsequent script-driven traumatic imagery in post-traumatic stress disorder. *Journal of Psychiatric Research, 42*(6), 503–506.

Cloitre, M., Koenen, K. C., Cohen, L. R., & Han, H. (2002). Skills training in affective and interpersonal regulation followed by exposure: A phase-based treatment for PTSD related to childhood abuse. *Journal of Consulting and Clinical Psychology, 70*(5), 1067–1074.

Cook, J. M., Walser, R. D., Kane, V., Ruzek, J. I., & Woody, G. (2006). Dissemination and feasibility of a cognitive-behavioral treatment for substance use disorders and post-traumatic stress disorder in the Veterans Administration. *Journal of Psychoactive Drugs, 38*(1), 89–92.

Davis, M., Myers, K. M., Ressler, K. J., & Rothbaum, B. O. (2005). Facilitation of extinction of conditioned fear by d-cycloserine. *Current Directions in Psychological Science, 14*(4), 214–219.

Davis, M., Ressler, K., Rothbaum, B. O., & Richardson, R., (2006). Effects of D-cycloserine on extinction: Translation from preclinical to clinical work. *Biological Psychiatry, 60*(4), 369–375.

Difede, J., & Hoffman, H. G. (2002). Virtual reality exposure therapy for World Trade Center Post-traumatic Stress Disorder: A case report. *Cyberpsychology & Behavior, 5*(6), 529–535.

Difede, J., Cukor, J., Jayasinghe, N., Patt, I., Jedel, S., Spielman, L., et al. (2007). Virtual reality exposure therapy for the treatment of posttraumatic stress disorder following September 11, 2001. *Journal of Clinical Psychiatry, 68*(11), 1639–1647.

Doblin, R. (2002). A clinical plan for MDMA (Ecstasy) in the treatment of posttraumatic stress disorder (PTSD):

Partnering with the FDA. *Journal of Psychoactive Drugs, 34*(2), 185–194.
Erbes, C. R., Polusny, M. A., MacDermid, S. M., & Compton, J. S. (2008). Couple therapy with combat veterans and their partners. *Journal of Clinical Psychology, 64*(8), 972–983.
Falsetti, S. A., & Resnick, H. S. (2000). Cognitive behavioral treatment of PTSD with comorbid panic attacks. *Journal of Contemporary Psychotherapy, 30*(2), 163–179.
Falsetti, S. A., Resnick, H. S., & Davis, J. (2008). Multiple channel exposure therapy for women with PTSD and comorbid panic attacks. *Cognitive Behaviour Therapy, 37*, 117–130.
Foa, E. B., Keane, T. M., Friedman, M. J., & Cohen, J. A. (2009). *Effective treatments for PTSD: Practice guidelines from the International Society for Traumatic Stress Studies* (2nd ed.). New York: Guilford.
Ford, J. D., Chandler, P., Thacker, B. G., Greaves, D., Shaw, D., Sennhauser, S., & Schwartz, L. (1998). Family systems therapy after Operation Desert Storm with European-theater veterans. *Journal of Marital and Family Therapy, 24*(2), 243–250.
Frueh, B. C., Monnier, J., Grubaugh, A. L., Elhai, J. D., Yim, E., & Knapp, R. (2007). Therapist adherence and competence with manualized cognitive-behavioral therapy for PTSD delivered via videoconferencing technology. *Behavior Modification, 31*(6), 856–866.
Gerardi, M., Rothbaum, B. O., Ressler, K., Heekin, M., & Rizzo, A. (2008). Virtual reality exposure therapy using a virtual Iraq: Case report. *Journal of Traumatic Stress, 21*(2), 209–213.
Germain, V., Marchand, A., Bouchard, S., Drouin, M.-S., & Guay, S. (2009). Effectiveness of cognitive behavioural therapy administered by videoconference for posttraumatic stress disorder. *Cognitive Behaviour Therapy, 38*(1), 42–53.
Ghee, A. C., Johnson, C. S., Burlew, A. K., & Bolling, L. C. (2009). Enhancing retention through a condensed trauma-integrated intervention for women with chemical dependence. *North American Journal of Psychology, 11*(1), 157–172.
Gregg, L., & Tarrier, N. (2007). Virtual reality in mental health: A review of the literature. *Social Psychiatry and Psychiatric Epidemiology, 42*, 343–354.
Harned, M. S., & Linehan, M. M. (2008). Integrating dialectical behavior therapy and prolonged exposure to treat co-occurring borderline personality disorder and PTSD: Two case studies. *Cognitive and Behavioral Practice, 15*, 263–276.
Hien, D. A., Cohen, L. R., Miele, G. M., Litt, L. C., & Capstick, C. (2004). Promising treatments for women with comorbid PTSD and substance use disorders. *American Journal of Psychiatry, 161*, 1426–1432.
Hien, D. A., Wells, E. A., Jiang, H., Suarez-Morales, L., Campbell, A. N. C., Cohen, L. R., et al. (2009). Multisite randomized trial of behavioral interventions for women with co-occurring PTSD and substance use disorders. *Journal of Consulting and Clinical Psychology, 77*(4), 607–619.
Johnson, D. R., Feldman, S. C., & Lubin, H. (1995). Critical interaction therapy: Couples therapy in combat-related posttraumatic stress disorder. *Family Process, 34*(4), 401–412.
Johnson, S. M., & Williams-Keeler, L. (1998). Creating healing relationships for couples dealing with trauma: The use of emotionally focused marital therapy. *Journal of Marital and Family Therapy, 24*(1), 25–40.
Kessler, R. C., Sonnega, A., Bromet, E., Hughes, M., & Nelson, C. B. (1995). Posttraumatic stress disorder in the National Comorbidity Survey. *Archives of General Psychiatry, 52*, 1048–1060.
Knaevelsrud, C., & Maercker, A. (2007). Internet-based treatment for PTSD reduces distress and facilitates the development of a strong therapeutic alliance: A randomized controlled clinical trial. *BMC Psychiatry, 7*, 13.
Lange, A., Rietdijk, D., Hudcovicova, M., van de Ven, J. P., Schrieken, B., & Emmelkamp, P. M. G. (2003). Interapy: A controlled randomized trial of the standardized treatment of posttraumatic stress through the Internet. *Journal of Consulting and Clinical Psychology, 71*(5), 901–909.
Lange, A., Schrieken, B., van de Ven, J. P., Bredeweg, B., Emmelkamp, P. M. G., Van der Kolk, J., et al. (2000). "Interapy": The effects of a short protocolled treatment of posttraumatic stress and pathological grief through the Internet. *Behavioural and Cognitive Psychotherapy, 28*(2), 175–192.
Lange, A., van de Ven, J. P., Schrieken, B., & Emmelkamp, P. M. G. (2001). Interapy: Treatment of posttraumatic stress through the Internet: A controlled trial. *Journal of Behavior Therapy and Experimental Psychiatry, 32*, 73–90.
Levitt, J. T., & Cloitre, M. (2005). A clinician's guide to STAIR/MPE: Treatment for PTSD related to childhood abuse. *Cognitive and Behavioral Practice, 12*, 40–52.
Linehan, M. M. (1993). *Cognitive behavioral treatment of borderline personality disorder*. New York: Guilford.
Litz, B. T., Engel, C. C., Bryant, R. A., & Papa, A. (2007). A randomized, controlled proof-of-concept trial of an Internet-based, therapist-assisted self-management treatment for posttraumatic stress disorder. *American Journal of Psychiatry, 164*(11), 1676–1683.
McGhee, L. L., Maani, C. V., Garza, T. H., Gaylord, K. M., & Black, I. H. (2008). The correlation between ketamine and posttraumatic stress disorder in burned service members. *Journal of Trauma-Injury Infection & Critical Care, 64*(2 Suppl.), S195–198; Discussion S197–198.
Monson, C. M., Fredman, S. J., & Adair, K. C. (2008). Cognitive-behavioral conjoint therapy for PTSD: Application to Operation Enduring and Iraqi Freedom service members and veterans. *Journal of Clinical Psychology, 64*(8), 958–971.
Monson, C. M., Schnurr, P. P., Stevens, S. P., & Guthrie, K. A. (2004). Cognitive-behavioral couple's treatment for posttraumatic stress disorder: Initial findings. *Journal of Traumatic Stress, 17*(4), 341–344.
Monson, C. M., & Taft, C. E. (2005). PTSD and intimate relationships. *PTSD Research Quarterly, 16*(4), 1–7.
Najavits, L. M. (2004). Treatment of posttraumatic stress disorder and substance abuse: Clinical guidelines for implementing Seeking Safety therapy. *Alcoholism Treatment Quarterly, 22*(1), 43–62.
Najavits, L. M., Gallop, R. J., & Weiss, R. D. (2006). Seeking Safety therapy for adolescent girls with PTSD and substance use disorder: A randomized controlled trial. *Journal of Behavioral Health Services and Research, 33*(4), 453–463.
Najavits, L. M., Weiss, R. D., Shaw, S. R., & Muenz, L. R. (1998). Seeking Safety: Outcome of a new cognitive-behavioral psychotherapy for women with posttraumatic stress disorder and substance dependence. *Journal of Traumatic Stress, 11*(3), 437–456.
Norberg, M. M., Krystal, J. H., & Tolin, D. F. (2008). A meta-analysis of d-cycloserine and the facilitation of fear extinction and exposure therapy. *Biological Psychiatry, 63*, 1118–1126.

Orsillo, S. M., & Batten, S. V. (2005). Acceptance and commitment therapy in the treatment of posttraumatic stress disorder. *Behavior Modification, 29*(1), 95–129.

Parsons, T. D., & Rizzo, A. A. (2008). Affective outcomes of virtual reality exposure therapy for anxiety and specific phobias: A meta-analysis. *Journal of Behavior Therapy & Experimental Psychiatry, 39*(3), 250–261.

Pitman, R. K., Sanders, K. M., Zusman, R. M., Healy, A. R., Cheema, F., Lasko, N. B., et al. (2002). Pilot study of secondary prevention of posttraumatic stress disorder with propranolol.[see comment]. *Biological Psychiatry, 51*(2), 189–192.

Raskind, M. A., Peskind, E. R., Kanter, E. D., Petrie, E. C., Radant, A., Thompson, C. E., et al. (2003). Reduction of nightmares and other PTSD symptoms in combat Veterans by prazosin: A placebo-controlled study. *American Journal of Psychiatry, 160*(2), 371–373.

Ready, D. J., Pollack, S., Rothbaum, B. O., & Alarcon, R. D. (2006). Virtual reality exposure for veterans with posttraumatic stress disorder. *Journal of Aggression, Maltreatment, and Trauma, 12*, 199–220.

Reger, G. M., & Gahm, G. A. (2008). Virtual reality exposure therapy for active duty soldiers. *Journal of Clinical Psychology, 64*(8), 940–946.

Reger, M. A., & Gahm, G. A. (2009). A meta-analysis of the effects of internet- and computer-based cognitive-behavioral treatments for anxiety. *Journal of Clinical Psychology, 65*(1), 53–75.

Riggs, D. S., Monson, C. M., Glynn, S. M., & Canterino, J. (2009). Couple and family therapy for adults. In E. B. Foa, T. M. Keane, M. J. Friedman, & J. A. Cohen (Eds.), *Effective treatments for PTSD* (pp. 458–478). New York: Guilford.

Rothbaum, B. O. (2009). Using virtual reality to help our patients in the real world. *Depression & Anxiety, 26*(3), 209–211.

Rothbaum, B. O., Difede, J., & Rizzo, A. (2008). *Therapist treatment manual for virtual reality exposure therapy: Posttraumatic stress disorder in Iraq combat veterans.* Unpublished manuscript.

Rothbaum, B. O., Hodges, L., Alarcon, R., Ready, D., Shahar, F., Graap, K., et al. (1999). Virtual reality exposure therapy for PTSD Vietnam Veterans: A case study. *Journal of Traumatic Stress, 12*(2), 263–271.

Saraiva, T., Gamito, P., Oliveira, J., Morais, D., Pombal, M., Gamito, L., et al. (2007). The use of VR exposure in the treatment of motor vehicle PTSD: A case report. *Annual Review of CyberTherapy and Telemedicine, 5*, 199–205.

Sautter, F. J., Glynn, S. M., Thompson, K. E., Franklin, L., & Han, X. (2009). A couple-based approach to the reduction of PTSD avoidance symptoms: Preliminary findings. *Journal of Marital and Family Therapy, 35*(3), 343–349.

Sherman, M. D., Zanotti, D. K., & Jones, D. E. (2005). Key elements in couples therapy with veterans with combat-related posttraumatic stress disorder. *Professional Psychology: Research and Practice, 36*(6), 626–633.

Twohig, M. P. (2009). Acceptance and Commitment Therapy for treatment-resistant posttraumatic stress disorder: A case study. *Cognitive and Behavioral Practice, 16*, 243–252.

Wagner, A. W., & Linehan, M. M. (2006). Applications of Dialectical Behavior Therapy to posttraumatic stress disorder and related problems. In V. M. Follette & I. J. Ruzek (Eds.), *Cognitive-behavioral therapies for trauma* (2nd ed., pp. 117–145). New York: Guilford.

Walser, D. L., & Hayes, S. C. (2006). Acceptance and commitment therapy in the treatment of posttraumatic stress disorder: Theoretical and applied issues. In V. M. Follette & J. I. Ruzek (Eds.), *Cognitive-behavioral therapies for trauma* (2nd ed., pp. 146–172). New York: Guilford.

Wilson, J. A., Onorati, K., Mishkind, M., Reger, M. A., & Gahm, G. A. (2008). Soldier attitudes about technology-based approaches to mental health care. *Cyberpsychology and Behavior, 11*(6), 767–769.

Zlotnick, C., Johnson, J., & Najavits, L. M. (2009). Randomized controlled pilot study of cognitive-behavioral therapy in a sample of incarcerated women with substance use disorder and PTSD. *Behavior Therapy, 40*, 325–336.

CHAPTER

33 Treating Trauma-related Symptoms in Children and Adolescents

Esther Deblinger, Elisabeth Pollio, *and* Felicia Neubauer

Abstract

The significant impact of trauma on children is well documented. This chapter focuses on trauma-specific treatments for children and adolescents that have at least one randomized controlled trial in which one or more standardized outcome measures of trauma symptoms were used. These treatments address varying traumas, including sexual abuse, physical abuse, exposure to violence or loss, medical trauma, and disasters. Many of the treatments demonstrate promising results, but the research is often hampered by methodological limitations. The efficacy of Trauma-Focused Cognitive Behavioral Therapy (TF-CBT) has been documented in over 17 scientific studies, including 10 randomized trials. A more detailed description of TF-CBT is presented in the chapter. Also discussed are future research directions, including specific scientific questions, to advance our knowledge about trauma treatment for children and adolescents.

Key Words: Childhood PTSD, childhood trauma, adolescent trauma, child sexual abuse, child physical abuse, violence exposure, medical trauma, trauma-focused evidence-based treatments, Trauma-Focused Cognitive Behavioral Therapy (TF-CBT)

Introduction

As highlighted in chapter 8, there is little question that a significant percentage of individuals exposed to childhood trauma suffer acute, episodic, and/or chronic symptoms of posttraumatic stress disorder (PTSD), as well as related emotional and behavioral difficulties. Given the potentially highly disruptive effects of these symptoms on children's psychosocial development, as well as adolescent and adult functioning, it is not surprising that many treatments have been developed to prevent and/or ameliorate these symptoms in the aftermath of childhood trauma.

The current chapter describes evidence-based treatments that have been developed to date for this population of children and their families. The chapter begins with a clinical description of Trauma-Focused Cognitive Behavioral Therapy (TF-CBT), an approach that has the strongest empirical base among the therapies designed for children and adolescents experiencing posttraumatic stress. To date, the efficacy of TF-CBT for children and adolescents has been evaluated via 17 scientific studies, which includes ten completed randomized controlled trials. Moreover, several additional experiments are in progress in the United States and abroad. In addition, TF-CBT has earned the highest rating of "well-supported and efficacious" treatment among 24 child-abuse treatments examined through a review funded by the Office for Victims of Crime (Saunders, Berliner, & Hanson, 2004). TF-CBT was similarly highly rated as an effective trauma treatment for children by the California Evidence-Based Clearinghouse for Child Welfare (Rose & Demaree, 2006). Finally, TF-CBT has been named a model program and a best practice by the U.S.

Department of Health and Human Services Substance Abuse and Mental Health Services Administration (SAMHSA) and the Kauffman Best Practices Task Force sponsored by the National Child Traumatic Stress Network, respectively (National Registry of Evidence-based Programs and Practices, 2005; Hensler, Wilson, & Sadler, 2004). Given the depth of the empirical base for this intervention, as well as the first author's role in developing the treatment, we provide a detailed description of this intervention.

The chapter also reviews and highlights research supporting many other promising trauma-focused treatments that have been evaluated via at least one randomized controlled trial in which one or more standardized outcome measures were used. Although the review is not exhaustive, it presents descriptive and empirical information regarding many different therapy approaches that address the needs of children exposed to distinct types of traumas, treatment models from diverse theoretical orientations, treatments that vary in length and formats (i.e., individual vs. group), and interventions provided in different types of settings including outpatient clinics, schools, and other community sites. The review will also offer information on the empirically established efficacy of the interventions, including effect size information when available based on Cohen's criteria of small (0–.29), medium (.30–.79), and large (>.80) effect sizes (Cohen, 1992). The reader is referred to table 33.1 for more details about the treatment studies that are reviewed in this chapter.

Trauma-Focused Cognitive Behavioral Therapy

Clinical Description

Trauma-Focused Cognitive Behavioral Therapy (TF-CBT) shares theoretical underpinnings as well as similar educational, skill building, and gradual exposure components with many other trauma interventions; thus, it serves as a representative model of many of the interventions described later in this chapter. TF-CBT is a structured, short-term treatment that is empirically validated for children who have experienced trauma and their nonoffending parents or caregivers (Cohen, Mannarino, & Deblinger, 2006; Deblinger & Heflin, 1996). This treatment approach has been utilized successfully with children and adolescents who have experienced a single trauma, as well as those who have experienced multiple, chronic, and complex traumas, including sexual abuse, traumatic loss, and exposure to domestic violence (Deblinger, Lippmann & Steer, 1996; Cohen, Deblinger, Mannarino & Steer, 2004; Cohen, Mannarino, & Iyengar, 2011; Lyons, Wiener, & Scheider, 2006). TF-CBT provides psycho-education, skills, and processing exercises that not only help with trauma recovery but also assists parents and children in managing life stressors that may occur in the future. The treatment format includes parallel but separate individual parent and child sessions, as well as conjoint parent-child sessions with the course of treatment ranging from 8 to 20 sessions.

The acronym PRACTICE summarizes the treatment components that build upon each other for both the child and caregiver in terms of providing education, skill building, and therapeutic activities that encourage gradual exposure, mastery, and processing of traumatic memories. *Parenting* skills, including praise, selective attention, active listening, effective communication, and discipline strategies, are taught over the entire course of treatment in order to enhance caregivers' responses to children's emotional and behavioral difficulties. In a parallel format, children and caregivers receive *psycho-education* in terms of providing information about the assessment findings, orienting them to the treatment approach and educating them about the referred trauma, as well as other traumas. *Relaxation* skills are taught and practiced in an age-appropriate and fun manner for children, as well as for the caregivers, to help them manage anxiety and reduce avoidance of innocuous trauma reminders and memories. *Affect* expression and modulation are accomplished through helping clients learn to identify and express a variety of emotions in general and specific to the trauma. Affective regulation skills including problem solving, anger management, thought interruption, positive imagery, and other self-soothing activities are also taught to help clients with emotional dysregulation. *Cognitive* coping skills are the treatment components that emphasize the interrelationships of thoughts, feelings, and behaviors with a primary focus on how changing one's thoughts can dramatically influence one's feelings and behaviors. During this component, both children and caregivers learn to examine the accuracy and helpfulness of their thoughts, first in relation to nontrauma related thoughts and later with respect to trauma-related thoughts and beliefs, with the ultimate goal of replacing dysfunctional thoughts with more accurate and/or helpful thoughts. With children, the processing and replacement of dysfunctional

Table 33.1. Summary of published treatment studies

Study	Target Population	Number of sessions	Treatment/ Control	Major findings
Deblinger, McLeer, & Henry (1990)	Sexually abused U.S. children, ages 3–16 years	12 weekly sessions	19 TF-CBT	TF-CBT led to significant improvement in PTSD symptoms, anxiety symptoms, and behavior problems
Deblinger, Lippmann, & Steer (1996)	Sexually abused U.S. children, ages 8–14 years	12 weekly sessions	22 TF-CBT Parent Only 24 TF-CBT Child Only 22 TF-CBT Parent +Child 22 Community Control	Conditions with the TF-CBT child intervention had significantly greater reduction in PTSD symptoms compared to conditions without child intervention Conditions with the TF-CBT parent intervention had significantly greater improvements in parenting practices and greater reductions in children's externalizing behavior problems and depression compared to conditions without parent intervention Improvements in PTSD, depression, and behavior problems maintained over two-year follow up period (Deblinger, Steer, & Lippmann, 1999)
Cohen & Mannarino (1996)	Sexually abused U.S. children, ages 3-6 years	12 weekly sessions	39 TF-CBT 28 NST	Significantly greater improvement in PTSD symptoms, internalizing symptoms, and sexual behavior problems in TF-CBT condition compared to NST
Cohen & Mannarino (1998)	Sexually abused U.S. children, ages 8–14 years	12 weekly sessions	30 TF-CBT 19 NST	Significantly greater improvement in depression and social competence in TF-CBT condition at post-treatment compared to NST Significantly greater improvement in PTSD and dissociation in TF-CBT condition at 12-onth follow up (Cohen, Mannarino, & Knudsen, 2005)
King et al. (2000)	Sexually abused Australian children, ages 5–17 years	20 weekly sessions	12 TF-CBT Child 12 TF-CBT Family 12 WL	Significantly greater improvements across TF-CBT conditions in PTSD symptoms, fear symptoms, and overall functioning compared to WL condition
Deblinger, Stauffer, & Steer (2001)	Sexually abused U.S. children, ages 2–8 years	11 weekly sessions	21 TF-CBT Group 23 Support Group	Significantly greater reductions in maternal abuse-related intrusive thoughts and negative parental emotions and greater improvement in child-reported knowledge of body safety skills in TF-CBT group compared to support group
Cohen et al. (2004)	Sexually abused, multiply-traumatized U.S. children, ages 8–14 years	12 weekly sessions	89 TF-CBT 91 CCT	Significantly greater reductions in children's PTSD symptoms, depressive symptoms, behavior problems, feelings of shame, and abuse-related attributions, and greater improvements in caregivers' depression, abuse-related distress, parenting practices, and parental support of their child in TF-CBT condition compared to CCT Improvements maintained at 1-year follow-up (Deblinger, et al. 2006)

(*continued*)

Table 33.1. **Summary of published treatment studies (*continued*)**

Study	Target Population	Number of sessions	Treatment/ Control	Major findings
Cohen et al. (2007)	Sexually abused U.S. girls, ages 10-17 years	12 weekly sessions	12 TF-CBT plus sertraline 12 TF-CBT plus placebo	Significant pre/post improvement on PTSD and other symptoms across conditions No significant differences between conditions except on ratings of global functioning, which favored the TF-CBT plus sertraline group
Deblinger et al. (2011)	Sexually abused U.S. children, ages 4–11 years	8 weekly sessions 16 weekly sessions	40 TF-CBT 8 sessions no TN 39 TF-CBT 8 sessions with TN 35 TF-CBT 16 sessions no TN 44 TF-CBT 16 sessions with TN	Significant improvements across conditions on emotional, behavioral, and skill-based outcomes 8 sessions with TN condition was significantly more efficient and effective in helping parents overcome abuse-specific distress and helping children overcome abuse-related fear and general anxiety 16 sessions no TN condition showed significantly greater improvements with respect to parenting practices and children's externalizing behavior problems
Berliner & Saunders (1996)	Sexually abused U.S. children, ages 4–13	10 weekly sessions	32 Abuse-specific group therapy 48 Abuse-specific group therapy plus SIT and gradual exposure	Significant improvements across both conditions No significant differences between groups
Trowell et al. (2002)	Sexually abused girls in London, ages 6–14 years	Individual weekly for up to 30 sessions; Group up to 18 sessions	35 Psychoanalytic individual therapy 36 Psycho-educational group therapy	Significant improvements across both conditions Greater reductions in PTSD symptoms with individual therapy
Jaberghaderi et al. (2004)	Sexually abused Iranian girls, ages 12-13 years	EMDR 4-8 sessions; CBT 10–12 sessions (10 session minimum)	7 EMDR 7 CBT	Significant improvements across both conditions No significant treatment differences in reducing PTSD symptoms and problem school behaviors
Kolko (1996)	Physically maltreated U.S. children, ages 6-13 years	CBT and FT at least 12 sessions within a 16-week period; RCS varying community services	25 CBT 18 FT 12 RCS	Compared to RCS, FT associated with a greater reduction in child-reported parent-to-child violence, and both CBT and FT associated with less parent-reported child-to-parent violence FT and CBT had a greater impact on child abuse potential and individualized problems, children's externalizing behavior, general parental distress, and family cohesion and conflict as compared to RCS
Runyon, Deblinger, & Schroeder (2009)	U.S. children who experienced physical abuse/excessive physical punishment, ages 4-14 years	16 sessions over a 16-20 week period	21 CPC-CBT	Significant improvements in caregiver-reported inconsistent parenting, anger, and internalizing and externalizing behavior problems, and child-reported PTSD symptoms Significant reductions in the use of physical punishment

(*continued*)

Table 33.1. **Summary of published treatment studies** (*continued*)

Study	Target Population	Number of sessions	Treatment/ Control	Major findings
Runyon, Deblinger, & Steer (2010)	U.S. children who experienced physical abuse/excessive physical punishment, ages 7-13 years	16 sessions over a 16-20 week period	24 CPC-CBT 20 Parent-Only CBT	Significant improvements for both conditions in parent and child-reported corporal punishment, total PTSD symptoms, and internalizing symptoms Significantly greater improvements for CPC-CBT condition compared to Parent-Only CBT with regard to children's PTSD symptoms and parent-reported positive parenting Significantly lower scores on the use of physical punishment for Parent-Only CBT
Lieberman, Van Horn, & Ippen (2005)	U.S. children exposed to marital violence, ages 3–5 years	CPP weekly sessions over 50 weeks; Case management at least monthly phone calls plus varying community treatment services	36 CPP 29 Case Management plus Individual Psychotherapy	Significantly greater decreases in children's total behavior problems and trauma stress disorder, and mother's PTSD avoidance symptoms in CPP condition relative to comparison group Significantly fewer child behavior problems and lower maternal global symptom severity for CPP at 6-month follow- up (Lieberman, Ippen, & Van Horn, 2006)
Cohen, Mannarino, & Iyengar (2011)	U.S. children in a women's shelter exposed to domestic violence, ages 7-14 years	8 sessions	64 TF-CBT 60 CCT	Significantly greater improvements for TF-CBT compared with CCT in PTSD symptoms, particularly avoidance and increased arousal, and in other anxiety symptoms Significantly greater adverse events reported in the CCT condition
Cohen, Mannarino, & Staron (2006)	U.S. children who lost a significant other to traumatic causes, ages 6-17	12 weekly sessions	39 CBT-CTG	Significant pre- to post-treatment improvements in children's PTSD, depression, anxiety, traumatic grief and behavioral problems as well as parents' personal PTSD symptoms
Onyut et al. (2005)	Somali children in a refugee settlement, ages 13-17 years	4-6 sessions	6 KIDNET	Significant decreases in symptoms of PTSD and depression
Catani et al. (2009)	Children in a Sri Lankan refugee camp, ages 8-14 years	6 sessions within a two-week period	16 KIDNET 15 MED-RELAX	Significant improvement in PTSD symptoms across both conditions No significant differences between groups
Chapman et al. (2001)	U.S. children admitted to a Level I trauma center, ages 7-17 years	1 session	31 CATTI 27 Standard Hospital Care	No significant differences in symptoms of posttraumatic stress found between groups

(*continued*)

Table 33.1. **Summary of published treatment studies** (*continued*)

Study	Target Population	Number of sessions	Treatment/ Control	Major findings
Kazak et al. (2004)	U.S. adolescent cancer survivors, ages 10-19 years	4 sessions on a single weekend day	76 SCCIP 74 WL	Teens assigned to SCCIP significantly greater decrease in arousal symptoms compared to WL Fathers in the SCCIP condition significantly greater decrease in intrusive symptoms compared to WL
Najavits, Gallop, & Weiss (2006)	Outpatient U.S. adolescent girls with PTSD and SUD, average age 16 years	25 sessions over 3 months	18 SS plus TAU 15 TAU alone	Significant outcomes favoring SS compared with TAU on several variables related to substance use, trauma symptoms, and psychopathology
Smith et al. (2007)	Children in London experiencing a single-incident traumatic event, ages 8–18 years	10 weekly sessions	12 CBT 12 WL	Significantly greater decreases in PTSD symptoms, depression, and anxiety, and significant improvement in functioning in CBT condition compared to WL
Gilboa-Schechtman et al. (2010)	Israeli adolescents who experienced a single-incident trauma, ages 12–18 years	PE-A 12-15 weekly sessions; TLDP-A 15–18 sessions	19 PE-A 19-TLDP-A	Significantly greater improvement in posttraumatic stress, depression, and overall functioning within both groups Significantly greater improvement in posttraumatic stress and overall functioning favoring PE-A compared with TLDP-A No significant differences in treatment expectancy, satisfaction, and therapeutic alliance
Lyons, Weiner, & Scheider (2006)	U.S. children in foster care who experienced a moderate or severe trauma, ages 0–21 years	10 weekly sessions	82 CPP 65 SPARCS 69 TF-CBT 2218 TAU	Significantly greater improvement in child and adolescent needs and strengths domains and greater significant improvement across in placement stability in evidenced based treatments as compared to TAU

Note: TF-CBT, Trauma-Focused Cognitive Behavioral Therapy; PTSD, Posttraumatic Stress Disorder; NST, Nondirective Supportive Therapy; WL, Wait list; CCT, Child Centered Therapy; TN, Trauma Narrative; SIT, Stress Inoculation Training; EMDR, Eye Movement Desensitization and Reprocessing; CBT, Cognitive Behavioral Therapy; FT, Family Therapy; RCS, Routine Community Services; CPC-CBT, Combined Parent-Child Cognitive Behavioral Therapy; CPP, Child-Parent Psychotherapy; CBT-CTG, Cognitive-Behavioral Therapy for Childhood Traumatic Grief; KIDNET, Narrative Exposure Therapy for Children; MED-RELAX, Meditation-Relaxation; CATTI, Chapman Art Therapy Treatment Intervention; SCCIP, Surviving Cancer Competently Intervention Program; SUD, Substance Use Disorder; SS, Seeking Safety; TAU, Treatment as Usual; PE-A, Prolonged Exposure Therapy for Adolescents; TLDP-A, Time-Limited Dynamic Psychotherapy; SPARCS, Structured Psychotherapy for Adolescents Responding to Chronic Stress.

trauma-related thoughts generally occur during and after the exposure and narrative work described below.

The above components set the stage for the next phase of treatment that begins with the *trauma* narrative and processing component. This component involves encouraging the child to acknowledge, share, and process their traumatic memories including thoughts, feelings, and sensations in the context of developing a trauma narrative or other product (e.g., poem, play, song, etc.). In this phase, the therapist provides an opportunity for children and parents to share the myriad emotions they may be experiencing in relation to the trauma(s) endured. The therapist's acknowledgment, review, and acceptance of clients' trauma-related affective and cognitive responses are critically important. Once the children work through a verbal or written narrative of the trauma(s) endured, dysfunctional thoughts may be cognitively and affectively reprocessed to assist with the children's learning to view their trauma history in a less distressing and more helpful manner. During this component, the therapist will elicit children's developing trauma-related thoughts and beliefs about themselves, others, and the world. Thoughts and beliefs that appear to be distressing and/or dysfunctional are identified and challenged by means of education, Socratic questioning, and/or carefully planned "best friend" role plays (Deblinger & Heflin, 1996). *In vivo* exposure may be used as necessary, with a desensitization plan that often involves considerable buy in and involvement of the caregiver in terms of a behavior-management plan to reduce avoidant behavior such as sleep or school refusal in the aftermath of trauma. *Conjoint* sessions are conducted to practice skills, review psycho-education, and enhance open communication related to the trauma between the child and caregiver when clinically indicated. Conjoint sessions are carefully planned and may contain such elements as exchanging mutual praise, playing a game related to psycho-education about trauma, and for many families, the sharing of the child's trauma narrative. When clinically indicated, age-appropriate sex education (e.g., with children with a history of sexual abuse) is provided either by the caregiver with guidance from the therapist or by the therapist with input from the caregiver to give children and adolescents accurate information as well as a positive view of healthy sexuality. Educational activities about healthy sexuality are designed to help children distinguish between acceptable and unacceptable sexual behavior, while also enhancing the parent(s)' and child's comfort and confidence in discussing sex-related issues in order to set the stage for an ongoing parent-child communication about the subject after therapy ends.

The final treatment component, *enhancing* future safety and development, is accomplished through education, skill building exercises, and role plays to assist children with the development or enhancement of real-life skills that can be applied to different personal safety scenarios children may face. Role plays are often individualized to address the most likely situations children may encounter (e.g., bullying, community violence, sibling threats, sexual abuse, etc.). During enhancing the safety component, to minimize the potential for child and/or parental self blame, it is emphasized that children referred for TF-CBT have already engaged in the most important safety skill: the sharing of traumatic experiences with trusted adults who can help. In addition, it is helpful to specifically review and praise clients for effective personal safety steps they may have taken in the past. However, it is important to acknowledge that no child or adult is ever fully prepared to respond to traumatic experiences. Thus, while there is no training that will guarantee protection from future trauma(s), discussing and practicing additional safety skills may help children and their parents feel more prepared to respond to potential dangers in the future. TF-CBT ends with a review of the skills learned, the development of a plan for responding to trauma reminders, and a carefully planned celebration of the family's accomplishments in facing and overcoming the trauma(s) endured.

The dissemination of therapist training in TF-CBT has been greatly advanced by the development of a free Web-based introductory training that can be accessed via http://tfcbt.musc.edu. This Web-based training has been utilized by over 100,000 mental health clinicians from across the United States and around the world (B. Saunders, personal communication, September 19, 2011). Moreover, this introductory training has recently been supplemented with a child traumatic grief web training (www.musc.edu/ctg) and a TF-CBT consultation website (www.musc.edu/tfcbtconsult).

Although the interventions reviewed below will not be described in as much detail as TF-CBT, it is worth noting that there is much overlap across the interventions in terms of the treatment goals and strategies utilized to achieve these goals. Thus, training in one intervention often prepares clinicians for training in other evidence-based practices, especially across those interventions sharing similar theoretical foundations.

Overview of Treatment Outcome Studies for Children/Adolescents by Trauma Type

Research examining the effectiveness of treatments for youth experiencing posttraumatic stress symptoms began to appear in the literature only within the last two decades. Moreover, much of the early work in this area focused on children experiencing PTSD symptoms as a result of child sexual abuse. More recently, treatment outcome studies in this field have begun to address the therapeutic needs of children exposed to other types of traumas, including child physical abuse, exposure to domestic violence, community violence, war/political violence, natural disasters, medical trauma, and multiple traumas. Although work in this area has methodological limitations, there is growing evidence that the dissemination of early, effective trauma-focused interventions may alleviate the symptoms and suffering endured by many survivors of childhood trauma.

Child Sexual Abuse

The earliest studies of PTSD in childhood focused on children who had experienced sexual abuse (e.g., McLeer, Deblinger, Atkins, Foa, & Ralph, 1988; McLeer, Deblinger, Henry, & Orvaschel, 1992). Noting the high prevalence of PTSD symptoms in this population, several researchers began to develop treatments specifically designed to assist children in overcoming PTSD and related difficulties (Cohen & Mannarino, 1998; Deblinger & Heflin, 1996). Deblinger, McLeer, and Henry (1990) conducted an initial within-group design treatment study that demonstrated promising results for a TF-CBT approach that led to significant reductions in PTSD, depression, and behavior problems, but many children remained in the mild depression range at posttreatment. Therefore, this TF-CBT was modified to incorporate cognitive therapy interventions in addition to the original education, skill building, and gradual exposure components. The lack of random assignment and a comparison condition, however, greatly limited the interpretation of the findings of this preliminary study. Thus, a randomized controlled trial was then conducted to examine the effectiveness of the child and parent interventions of TF-CBT as compared to a community referral condition (Deblinger et al., 1996). In this study, 100 children with a history of sexual abuse and at least partial symptoms of PTSD were randomly assigned to one of four treatment conditions, including a child-only TF-CBT condition, a parent-only TF-CBT condition (in which parents were taught to serve as the therapeutic agents for their children), a parent and child TF-CBT treatment (in which parents and children were seen individually and jointly over the course of treatment), and a community treatment condition (in which families were referred by their child protection worker to a therapist in their community). The results of this study documented that the children assigned to the conditions that incorporated the TF-CBT child intervention (i.e., child only and parent/child TF-CBT conditions) demonstrated significantly greater reductions in PTSD symptoms as compared to those who had not been assigned to a condition that included the child TF-CBT intervention (i.e., parent CBT and community referral). On the other hand, participants randomly assigned to the conditions that incorporated the TF-CBT parent intervention (i.e., parent-only CBT and parent/child CBT) exhibited significantly greater improvements with respect to parenting practices and greater reductions with respect to children's externalizing behavior problems and depression. In addition, the results of follow-up assessments of children who participated in this study demonstrated sustained improvements with respect to PTSD, depression, and behavior problems over the course of two-year follow-up period (Deblinger, Steer, & Lippmann, 1999). The community treatment findings of this investigation, however, should be interpreted with caution given the highly diverse experiences of those assigned to the community referral comparison, ranging from receiving minimal to no therapy due to the long community treatment waiting lists to intensive biweekly private therapy experiences.

TF-CBT for child sexual abuse also was evaluated in terms of its implementation in a group format with 44 mothers and their respective children (ages 2 to 8; Deblinger, Stauffer, & Steer, 2001). In this study, participants were randomly assigned to parallel parent and child TF-CBT groups or parallel parent and child support groups. The support groups for the mothers were primarily client centered, but tended to focus on parent-selected topics relating to child sexual abuse, with parents frequently focusing discussions on the investigation and prosecution of the offenders. The children's support groups were also client centered, but the therapists in those groups selected the topics and provided education in a more structured context. The findings demonstrated that, as compared to participants assigned to the support groups, mothers assigned to the TF-CBT groups reported significantly greater reductions in maternal abuse-related intrusive thoughts and abuse-specific distress. Children in the TF-CBT groups reported greater improvement in their body-safety skills knowledge. Within-group effect size changes for the TF-CBT group mothers for intrusive and avoidant symptoms were large and medium, respectively, with only small effect size pre- to posttreatment changes observed with respect to these symptoms for the mothers assigned to the support groups (Cohen et al., 2010).

Simultaneously, Cohen and Mannarino (1996, 1998) developed a very similar TF-CBT approach that shared essentially the same CBT components, but did not incorporate conjoint parent child sessions. Cohen and Mannarino conducted randomized controlled trials that compared the efficacy of individual TF-CBT to a nondirective supportive treatment with both preschool children and school-age children. The results of the preschool study demonstrated that children randomly assigned to TF-CBT showed superior improvements with respect to PTSD, internalizing symptoms, and sexual behavior problems as compared to those assigned to the nondirective supportive treatment (Cohen & Mannarino, 1996). TF-CBT produced large within-group effect sizes and medium between-group effect size differences (Cohen et al., 2010). Similarly, the findings of the study with school-age children (ages 8 to 14) revealed that children assigned to TF-CBT showed significantly greater improvements in depression and social competence at posttreatment (Cohen & Mannarino, 1998) and greater improvements on PTSD and dissociation at a 12-month follow-up assessment (Cohen, Mannarino, & Knudsen, 2005) as compared to those assigned to the nondirective supportive therapy. However, the between-group effect size differences in this study were small (Cohen et al., 2010). King and colleagues (2000) replicated earlier TF-CBT findings in a study examining the efficacy of TF-CBT with children and adolescents (ages 5 to 17) who had experienced child sexual abuse in Australia. Their findings demonstrated that TF-CBT led to significantly greater improvements in children's PTSD, fear symptoms, and overall functioning at posttreatment, with large within-group and between-group effect size differences found as compared to a wait-list condition, but only a small between-group effect size for differences between child versus family TF-CBT (Cohen et al., 2010). Possibly due to study limitations including very small cell sizes (i.e., 12 participants per condition), treatment delivery differences, and lack of measurement sensitivity, the comparison of TF-CBT with or without family/parent participation did not demonstrate significant differences at posttreatment; however, at the three-month follow-up assessment, children assigned to the TF-CBT with the parent intervention reported significantly less abuse-related fear as compared to those who received TF-CBT without the parent intervention.

Given the similarities of their treatment models, Cohen, Mannarino and Deblinger collaborated in refining their TF-CBT approaches for childhood PTSD and conducted the first multisite randomized controlled trial for children with a history of child sexual abuse and symptoms of PTSD (Cohen et al., 2004). In this investigation, 229 children and their respective primary caregivers were randomly assigned to TF-CBT or Child Centered Therapy. Although children and their nonoffending caregivers showed significant improvements pre- to posttreatment across both conditions, the results demonstrated that children assigned to the TF-CBT condition showed significantly greater reductions in terms of PTSD symptoms, depressive symptoms, behavior problems, feelings of shame, and abuse-related attributions as compared to those assigned to the child-centered condition. In addition, this investigation revealed that TF-CBT led to significantly greater improvements with respect to caregivers' levels of depression, abuse-related distress, parenting practices, and parental support of their child. The between-group effect size differences for the child and parent outcome measures cited above ranged from medium to large between the TF-CBT and Child Centered Therapy conditions. Results also documented that children and their caregivers assigned to TF-CBT continued to report significantly less PTSD, feelings of shame, and parental abuse-specific distress as compared to those assigned to the Child Centered Therapy across the one-year follow-up period (Deblinger, Mannarino, Cohen, & Steer, 2006).

TF-CBT alone or in combination with sertraline was recently evaluated for its efficacy in treating childhood PTSD symptoms (Cohen, Mannarino, Perel, & Staron, 2007). Twenty-four 10- to 17-year-old females with sexual abuse-related PTSD symptoms and their nonoffending caregivers were randomly assigned to either TF-CBT with sertraline or TF-CBT with placebo. Participants in both conditions demonstrated significant pre- to posttreatment improvements with respect to PTSD and other clinical outcomes, with medium within-group effect sizes. However, no significant outcome differences were found between the two conditions except on ratings of global functioning, which favored the TF-CBT plus sertraline group. Based on these preliminary findings, the investigators suggested an initial trial of TF-CBT or other evidence-based treatment may be preferable for treating childhood PTSD before adding medication.

Most recently, a multisite study of TF-CBT was conducted to evaluate the impact of the use of a trauma narrative component of TF-CBT, as well as the length of treatment (8 vs. 16 sessions) on child sexual abuse recovery (Deblinger, Mannarino, Cohen, Runyon, & Steer, 2011). Children and their caregivers were randomly assigned to one of four treatment conditions: 8 sessions with a trauma narrative; 8 sessions without a trauma narrative; 16 sessions with a trauma narrative; and 16 sessions without a trauma narrative. One hundred fifty-eight children (ages 4 to 11) completed the posttreatment assessment. The findings demonstrated that children and caregivers exhibited significant improvements that, on average, reflected large within-group effect size differences across all conditions with respect to all 14 emotional, behavioral, and skill-based outcome measures included in the study. The findings also demonstrated, on average, medium between-group effect size differences for specific outcomes relating to both parent and child functioning. The eight-session condition that included the trauma narrative, for example, was significantly more efficient and effective in helping parents overcome abuse-specific distress and helping children overcome abuse-related fear and general anxiety. On the other hand, participants assigned to conditions that focused greater time on parental skill building (e.g., 16 sessions with no trauma narrative) demonstrated significantly greater improvements with respect to parenting practices and children's externalizing behavior problems. Thus, the findings of this investigation support the need to individually tailor TF-CBT based on children's and parents' presenting profiles.

Although the above studies have examined the efficacy of TF-CBT with children who experienced sexual abuse, other studies have recently been conducted that examine the effectiveness of TF-CBT with other types of childhood traumas, including traumatic loss (Cohen, Mannarino, & Staron, 2006), exposure to domestic violence (Cohen et al., 2011), exposure to large-scale disasters (Hoagwood et al., 2007; Jaycox et al., 2010), and traumas resulting in and associated with foster-care placement (Lyons et al., 2006). These recent investigations are described in subsequent sections.

Other randomized controlled trials that have examined the treatment of trauma symptoms in children who have been sexually abused include a comparison of two group approaches, a comparison of a psychoanalytic individual and group therapy approaches, and a comparative evaluation of Eye Movement Desensitization and Reprocessing (EMDR) and a CBT approach.Berliner and Saunders (1996) randomly assigned 80 children (ages 4 to 13) to a sexual abuse-specific treatment group or a similar group treatment with the addition of stress inoculation training and gradual exposure to target the fear and anxiety symptoms commonly experienced by children in the aftermath of sexual abuse. Participants in both groups improved significantly on measures of anxiety, depression, internalizing and externalizing behavior, and sexualized behavior, as well as on an abuse-specific measure of fear. However, no significant between-group differences were found on measures of fear and anxiety. The lack of between-group differences may have been attributable to the majority of children not having significant fear and anxiety symptoms at the pretreatment assessment, the treatments not being meaningfully different owing to overlapping components, or the abuse-specific treatment being sufficient to ameliorate these symptoms without the added treatment components. In an evaluation of psychoanalytic approaches, 71 girls (ages 6 to 14) with a history of child sexual abuse were randomly assigned to individual therapy (i.e., weekly psychoanalytic therapy for up to 30 sessions) or group therapy (with therapeutic and psychoeducational components for up to 18 sessions) with both treatments complemented by supportive work with caregivers (Trowell et al., 2002). The results demonstrated significant improvements for both conditions in terms of levels of functioning and reductions in trauma symptoms. Those assigned to the individual therapy reported significantly greater reductions in PTSD symptoms (medium effect size); however, this finding may be due to the substantially greater number of treatment sessions in the individual therapy condition (i.e., 30 sessions) as compared to the group therapy condition (i.e., 18 sessions).

In a comparison of EMDR and CBT, 14 girls (ages 12 to 13) with a history of child sexual abuse were randomly assigned to the EMDR or CBT intervention condition (Jaberghaderi, Greenwald, Rubin, Zand, & Dolatabadi, 2004). EMDR involves concentrating on trauma memories while performing bilateral eye movements, and it incorporates other components such as coping skills training. The results demonstrated significant improvements for participants assigned to both conditions in terms of reduction of PTSD symptoms (large within-group effect size) and problem school behaviors (medium within-group effect size). However, there were no significant between-group outcome findings. Although EMDR was reported to be more efficient because it was delivered in fewer sessions (4 to 8 sessions versus 10 to 12 sessions, respectively), the study was not designed appropriately to examine treatment efficiency.

Child Physical Abuse

Children who have experienced physical abuse may also be at risk for developing traumatic stress symptoms (e.g., Runyon, Deblinger, Ryan, & Thakkar-Kolar, 2004). Intervention research with this population is particularly important because it may not only ameliorate children's trauma symptoms but also be critical to reduce the potential for future trauma in the form of ongoing child physical abuse. A seminal study conducted by Kolko (1996) examined the efficacy of a CBT approach, a family therapy approach, and routine community services for families at risk for child physical abuse. Fifty-five families were randomly assigned to CBT (n = 25) or family therapy (n = 18) with the remaining 12 families serving as the routine community services comparison. The results of this investigation demonstrated no differences for many of the outcome measures, including the Children's Attributions and Perceptions Scale, a trauma-specific outcome measure. However, as compared to routine community services, family therapy was associated with significantly less child reported parent-to-child violence, and both CBT and family therapy were associated with significantly less parent-reported child to parent violence, as well as significantly greater improvement with respect to child abuse potential, externalizing behaviors, general parental distress, and family cohesion and conflict. Although this investigation was well designed and implemented, it did not focus on childhood PTSD as a primary target or outcome of treatment.

Runyon, Deblinger, and Schroeder (2009), however, did assess and target PTSD symptoms in a pilot investigation of a group therapy approach, Combined Parent-Child Cognitive Behavioral Therapy (CPC-CBT), for children who have experienced physical abuse/excessive physical punishment. In addition to providing psycho-education and CBT skill building to parents and children separately and together, this approach also incorporated innovative components, including a systematic consequence review and motivational procedure to effectively engage this high-risk population (Donohue, Miller, Van Hasselt, & Hersen, 1998), gradual exposure and processing to reduce PTSD symptoms (Deblinger & Heflin, 1996), and the incorporation of the child's abuse narrative into the abuse-clarification process with the parents when appropriate (Lipovsky, Swenson, Ralston, & Saunders, 1998; Kolko & Swenson, 2002). The pilot study demonstrated significant improvements in caregiver-reported inconsistent parenting, anger, and internalizing and externalizing behavior problems, and child-reported PTSD symptoms, as well as significant reductions in the use of physical punishment. Within-group effect sizes were medium to large.

Following up on the promising findings of the Runyon et al. (2009) study, the same group of investigators conducted a randomized controlled trial in which 60 children and their 44 caregivers were randomly assigned to a parent-only group intervention or a combined parent and child group intervention in order to evaluate the benefits of including the child in treatment for parents who had engaged in physical abuse/excessive physical punishment (Runyon, Deblinger, & Steer, 2010). The results of this investigation demonstrated significant pre- to posttreatment improvements for both treatment conditions with respect to parent and child reported corporal punishment, total PTSD symptoms, and child internalizing symptoms. However, significantly greater improvements were found for those assigned to the Combined Parent-Child CBT group intervention relative to those randomly assigned to the parent only CBT group intervention in terms of children's PTSD symptoms and parents' reports of positive parenting. In the combined parent-child condition, there was considerably more time devoted to directly addressing the physically abusive experiences with both the children and parents separately and conjointly through narrative and processing work designed to address abuse-related feelings and dispel dysfunctional abuse-related thoughts. These abuse-specific components may explain the greater reductions in PTSD symptoms in the combined treatment condition relative to the parent-only condition. Interestingly, the parent-only CBT group participants reported greater reductions in the use of the corporal punishment as compared to the combined treatment condition. This surprising finding may be due to the fact that more time was devoted to parenting skills training in the parent-only condition as compared to the combined parent-child condition. The significant between-group treatment differences represented medium effect sizes. Although this study has its strengths, its generalizability is limited due to its group format; however, Combined Parent-Child CBT has been adapted for individual format and plans for a larger scale evaluation are under way.

Exposure to Interpersonal Trauma, Traumatic Loss, War, and/or Other Violence

Recent research also has evaluated the efficacy of treatments designed for children exposed to trauma as a result of interpersonal violence, traumatic loss, crime, war, terrorism, or other political violence. The efficacy of Child Parent Psychotherapy (CPP), a relationship-based intervention designed to address the therapeutic needs of very young children exposed to domestic violence, was evaluated in a randomized controlled trial (Lieberman, Van Horn, & Ippen, 2005). The CPP treatment involves weekly joint parent-child sessions interspersed with individual sessions as indicated, with the goals of minimizing maladaptive child behaviors, supporting healthy parent-child interactions, and guiding a joint trauma narrative process. CPP was evaluated in comparison to case management plus individual treatment that included assessment feedback, at least monthly phone calls, assistance with securing services, crisis intervention, and face-to-face meetings when indicated. Seventy-five children (ages 3 to 5) and their mothers were randomly assigned to either CPP or the case-management condition. The results demonstrated that children assigned to CPP showed significantly greater decreases in total behavior problems and traumatic stress symptoms. Moreover, mothers assigned to CPP showed significantly greater reductions in PTSD avoidance symptoms and a trend toward less global psychiatric distress relative to mothers assigned to the case-management condition. At the six-month follow-up, participants assigned to CPP exhibited significantly fewer child behavior problems and lower maternal global symptom severity as compared to those assigned to the case-management condition, representing medium within-group effect sizes (Lieberman, Ippen, & Van Horn, 2006).

Recently, TF-CBT has also been evaluated for its effectiveness in treating PTSD and related symptoms in children exposed to domestic violence as well as traumatic loss. Cohen et al. (2011) completed a randomized controlled trial of 124 children and adolescents (ages 7 to 14) exposed to domestic violence, conducted in a women's shelter setting. Children and their mothers received eight sessions of either TF-CBT or Child-Centered Therapy (CCT; the usual care in this setting). Children in the TF-CBT condition demonstrated significantly greater improvements in PTSD symptoms, particularly in the avoidance and increased arousal clusters, and in other anxiety symptoms as compared with the CCT condition. In addition, significantly greater adverse events were reported in the CCT group. As this trial demonstrates, TF-CBT appears to be adaptable for demanding real-world settings. TF-CBT has also been adapted for children suffering traumatic grief (Cohen et al., 2006). This adapted treatment model has two phases; the initial phase focuses on the standard TF-CBT components designed to address PTSD and related symptoms, and the second phase addresses traumatic grief. The adapted TF-CBT was utilized with 39 children and adolescents (ages 6 to 17) in a pilot within-group treatment study. The results demonstrated significant pre- to post-treatment improvements (medium to large effect sizes) with respect to children's PTSD, depression, anxiety, traumatic grief, and behavioral problems, as well as parents' personal PTSD symptoms (Cohen et al., 2006). Moreover, findings demonstrated that PTSD improvements occurred primarily in the first phase of treatment, whereas traumatic grief improved both during the initial trauma-focused phase, as well as the grief-focused phase of therapy.

The efficacy of Narrative Exposure Therapy (NET) adapted for child refugees (KIDNET) was also evaluated via a randomized controlled trial. NET is a short-term treatment based on exposure therapy in which clients construct a narrative of their entire lives with a focus on their traumatic experience(s). In a pilot study, six Somali refugee children ages 13 to 17 with PTSD were treated with KIDNET for four to six sessions (Onyut et al., 2005). Significant decreases in PTSD symptoms over time were noted, and at the nine-month follow-up, four out of the six children no longer met PTSD criteria. In addition, at pretreatment, four of the six children presented with significant depressive symptoms but no participant had significant depression at either the posttreatment assessment or the nine-month follow-up. KIDNET was later compared to a meditation-relaxation treatment (MED-RELAX) in a randomized controlled trial design (Catani et al., 2009). Thirty-one children (ages 8 to 14) impacted by civil war and a tsunami in Sri Lanka with a provisional diagnosis of PTSD (the assessments were conducted three weeks after the tsunami, as opposed to the required four weeks for PTSD criteria) received either six sessions of KIDNET or MED-RELAX over a two-week period. Results indicated that children's PTSD symptoms improved significantly from pre- to post-treatment, with large effect sizes for both conditions. Six months after treatment, 81% of the KIDNET participants and 71% of the MED-RELAX participants no longer met criteria for PTSD. Differences between the groups were not significant.

Medical Trauma

Interventions also have been developed to address posttraumatic stress symptoms secondary to medical trauma in children. The Chapman Art Therapy Treatment Intervention (CATTI; Chapman, Morabito, Ladakakos, Schreier, & Knudson, 2001) was designed for incident-specific medical trauma in children. This brief treatment in which children create a drawing and verbal narrative of the event is facilitated at the child's bedside in the hospital. In a prospective, randomized cohort design involving 85 children (ages 7 to 17) admitted to a Level I trauma center, no significant differences in symptoms of posttraumatic stress were found between CATTI and the standard hospital treatment (Chapman et al., 2001).

The Surviving Cancer Competently Intervention Program (SCCIP; Kazak et al., 1999) addresses posttraumatic stress symptoms in adolescent cancer survivors and their families. The treatment, which combines cognitive-behavioral and family systems approaches, is a four-session, one-day manualized intervention. In a randomized clinical trial involving 150 adolescent survivors and their families assigned to either SCCIP or a wait-list condition, findings indicated that the adolescent survivors receiving SCCIP had a significantly greater decrease in arousal symptoms than the adolescent survivors assigned to the wait-list condition (Kazak et al., 2004). In addition, fathers in the SCCIP condition had a significantly greater reduction of intrusive symptoms as compared to fathers in the wait-list condition. No significant changes in posttraumatic stress symptoms were found for mothers or siblings assigned to either SCCIP or wait list, though it should be noted that the sibling sample was very small. There was also a higher dropout rate (i.e., 38%) in the SCCIP condition as compared to the wait-list control (i.e., 7%) and those who dropped out had significantly higher levels of posttraumatic stress symptoms at baseline relative to those who did not drop out. Of note, 79% of those families who dropped out of the intervention condition did so after the initial assessment but before the intervention began.

Multiple Trauma and Mixed Trauma Samples

In a randomized controlled trial of Seeking Safety (SS), a coping skills therapy to address PTSD and substance use disorder, 33 outpatient adolescent girls were randomized to SS plus Treatment As Usual (TAU) or TAU alone (Najavits, Gallop, & Weiss, 2006). SS is a manualized treatment that includes topics relating to cognitive, behavioral, and interpersonal domains. The traumas these teens had experienced were varied, with sexual abuse as the most common category, followed by general disaster/accident, physical abuse, and crime. Significant treatment outcome differences favoring SS over the TAU condition were found on measures of substance use, cognitions related to substance use and posttraumatic stress, some trauma symptoms (sexual concerns and sexual distress subscales), and a range of psychopathology (including symptoms that were not targeted, such as somatic symptoms). Between-group effect sizes for SS were in the medium to large range.

Smith and colleagues (2007) also reported a treatment study assessing the impact of CBT for PTSD that included children with varying trauma histories. The most common traumatic event in this study was motor vehicle accident, followed by assault and witnessing violence. Twenty-four children (ages 8 to 18) with a diagnosis of PTSD were randomly assigned to the CBT or wait-list group after a four-week period of symptom monitoring. The 10-week CBT treatment was manual-based and included individual therapy with the child, meeting with the parents as available, and joint sessions as needed. Results at posttreatment significantly favored the CBT group as compared with the wait-list condition, including significantly greater decreases in PTSD symptoms, depression, and anxiety, as well as significantly better improvement in functioning. The investigators reported that the CBT condition produced large within-group effect sizes and large between-group effect size differences with the wait-list condition for PTSD symptom measures. Posttreatment gains for the CBT condition were maintained at a six-month follow-up.

Gilboa-Schechtman et al. (2010) examined the efficacy of Prolonged Exposure Therapy for Adolescents (PE-A) and Time-Limited Dynamic Psychotherapy (TLDP-A) in a randomized controlled trial of 38 adolescents, ages 12 to 18. All participants had been diagnosed with PTSD secondary to a single-incident trauma, which included motor vehicle accidents and sexual assault. Adolescents in both conditions improved significantly on measures of posttraumatic stress, depression, and overall functioning. Pre-post effect sizes were medium to large for the TLDP-A group and large for the PE-A group. Significant between group differences with medium effect sizes favoring the PE-A condition were found with respect to improvements in posttraumatic stress symptoms and overall functioning. There were no significant between group differences on measures of treatment expectancy, satisfaction, and therapeutic alliance.

Given the complex logistic and ethical issues associated with research involving wards of the state, a quasi-experimental design was chosen to examine the impact of evidence-based treatments as compared to TAU with children in foster care who experienced diverse and numerous traumas prior to their placement (Lyons et al., 2006). This study evaluated the implementation of three treatments—CPP, TF-CBT, and Structured Psychotherapy for Adolescents Responding to Chronic Stress (SPARCS; DeRosa & Pelcovitz, 2009)—in comparison to standard system of care services provided to youth in foster care. SPARCS is a group treatment for trauma-exposed adolescents typically provided over five to six months that incorporates techniques to enhance coping skills, mindfulness, and interpersonal skills (CPP and TF-CBT are described previously). Findings indicated that children assigned to all three treatment conditions improved significantly in terms of all Child and Adolescent Needs and Strengths (CANS) domains (Anderson, Lyons, Giles, Price, & Estle, 2003) with the exception of child strengths for children under five, which may be due to the small sample size of children so young (Lyons et al., 2006). Moreover, the findings demonstrated significantly improved placement stability for the children who received any of the three treatments as compared to those who received the standard system of care. More specifically, children assigned to TF-CBT or CPP were about half as likely to experience a placement disruption as compared to those who received the standard system of care and those assigned to TF-CBT were about one-tenth as likely as other same-age children in the system-of-care to run away from their placement. Similarly, youth who participated in SPARCS were about half as likely to run away from their placement and one-fourth less likely to suffer a placement change as compared to system-of-care children. Although the authors of this study concluded that the evidence-based practices improved outcomes above and beyond the already impressive results of their system-of-care program, they acknowledge that much is needed to be learned about preparing organizations and therapists to utilize evidence-based practices before large-scale dissemination of these interventions could be achieved.

Finally, it should be noted that TF-CBT and other evidence-based interventions have been evaluated and are currently being utilized with children who have been traumatized by natural disasters as well as man-made disasters (i.e., terrorism and war). In the aftermath of 9/11 (Hoagwood et al., 2007) and Hurricane Katrina (Jaycox et al., 2010), dissemination projects were initiated to bring trauma-focused evidence-based practices to children and families affected by these large-scale disasters. Although these investigations were not randomized, controlled trials due to logistical and ethical considerations, the results have demonstrated the feasibility of disseminating TF-CBT and other evidence-based treatments to mental health clinicians and their young clients in the aftermath of these large-scale disasters.

Summary and Conclusions

There is little question that exposure to trauma increases children's risk of developing significant emotional, behavioral, relational, and substance abuse difficulties. Moreover, the accumulation of such exposures and the associated traumatic stress symptoms often have far-reaching effects that can interfere considerably with children's emotional, social, and physical development and long-term well-being (Fellitti et al., 1998). Thus, the increasing focus on the development and evaluation of early, effective treatments designed to ameliorate childhood PTSD and related symptoms in recent decades is encouraging.

As demonstrated by the current review, many creative and practical interventions have been designed and evaluated for their efficacy for children and teens exposed to many different traumas across diverse settings. However, with the exception of TF-CBT, the majority of interventions represented here have been tested with an average of only one randomized controlled trial with this population. Thus, there is much yet to be done in terms of evaluating the benefits of evidence-based practices for this population, while also refining and expanding the current research focus.

Many of the studies cited had small sample sizes and high attrition rates, thereby limiting the power and the generalizability of their findings. Other studies have utilized outcome measures with weak psychometric properties, and some investigators relied on only child self-report or parent-report measures. In addition, very few investigations included long-term follow-up assessments. Finally, the studies almost exclusively focused on outpatient samples, which is unfortunate given the high rates of early trauma exposure among children and adolescents in residential settings. Thus, although there is a great deal of promise among many of the interventions described, there is still much to be evaluated and learned about their effectiveness in real-world settings.

In many respects, the field of childhood trauma remains in its infancy. There are many widely used and creative trauma interventions that have not as yet been rigorously evaluated, including expressive arts (Coulter, 2000; Pifalo, 2007) and systems therapy approaches (Saxe, Ellis, Fogler, Hansen, & Sorkin, 2005). There are also other well-established interventions, such as Parent-Child Interaction Therapy, that have recently been applied to children with a trauma history and outcomes have focused more on behavioral difficulties and abuse risk as opposed to evaluating the treatment's impact on trauma symptoms (Chaffin et al., 2004; Timmer, Urquiza, Zebell, & McGrath, 2005). Taken together, there is much to be learned from further treatment-outcome investigations, both in terms of evaluating widely used but untested interventions and in replicating and building on the limited trauma symptom outcome data available for the interventions examined thus far. Moreover, much needs to be learned about the feasibility of widespread dissemination of well-established, efficacious interventions (Bruns et al., 2008; Cohen & Mannarino, 2008). Given the many statewide efforts currently under way to implement evidence-based practices in child mental health (Bruns & Hoagwood, 2008), as well as the widespread exposure to trauma(s) in childhood (Finkelhor, Turner, & Ormrod 2006), this appears to be an ideal time to further enhance our ability to evaluate the effectiveness of efforts to implement as well as disseminate evidence-based trauma interventions.

Future Directions

There remain many important scientific questions to be addressed to optimize outcomes for children and adolescents exposed to traumatic stress. Research examining the questions outlined below will not only advance the field as a whole but also will help us to individually tailor treatments to most effectively address the specialized needs of children and their families. Given limitations of the available mental health resources, as well as barriers to accessing these resources, it will be important to focus our attention not only on efficacy but also on efficiency, as well as on the cost-effectiveness associated with widespread delivery of evidence-based trauma-focused services. These important future research and policy directions are designed to address both system and therapeutic issues that may help to identify methods for reaching the large numbers of children exposed to trauma in the many severely underserved regions of the United States and the world. Those questions are:

1. What treatment components (e.g., skills, exposure, parenting, etc.) are critical to address which domains of child and adolescent functioning (e.g., behavior, emotion, physiologic, interpersonal, family, academic, etc.)?
2. How can we enhance the efficiency of our treatment delivery methods without undermining the benefits of efficacious trauma-focused services?
3. Which physiological markers best predict positive psychosocial outcomes for traumatized children and adolescents (e.g., cortisol levels, heart rate in response to stressors, etc.)?
4. How does physiological correlates of traumatic stress symptoms inform us about the use of psychopharmacologic agents in treating PTSD and related difficulties in youth?
5. What are the mechanisms of treatment (e.g., therapy process factors, therapist behaviors, client-therapist relationship factors) that are associated with optimal outcomes?
6. What presenting characteristics of the youth, family, and/or trauma predict differential responses to distinct treatment formats? For example, are there some circumstances under which individual therapy would be preferable to group therapy (and vice versa) to optimize outcomes and/or efficient use of resources?
7. What organizational and/or clinician characteristics are associated with better uptake, fidelity and outcomes associated with empirically supported trauma-focused treatments?
8. What training methods produce the most optimal immediate and long-term clinician job satisfaction, treatment fidelity, and treatment outcomes?

9. What organizational change methods result in optimal treatment fidelity, outcomes and maintenance of significant improvements over time?

In sum, although great progress has been made in terms of the development and evaluation of treatments that work to alleviate the suffering of children and adolescents exposed to trauma, the above questions outline the many remaining issues to be addressed. To achieve the goal of ensuring that scientific advances and evidence-based practices reach and benefit as many traumatized youth and their families as possible, there must be an ongoing effort to bridge the gaps that exist between research and clinical professionals. Although the review of studies in this chapter demonstrates that the field has achieved considerable success in this regard, to make significant strides in the future and to enhance the power, generalizability, complexity, and meaningfulness of the studies and analyses conducted, it will be critical to collaborate across professions and institutions to implement larger scale field studies in the future.

References

Anderson, R. L., Lyons, J. S., Giles, D. M., Price, J. A., & Estle, G. (2003). Reliability of the Child and Adolescent Needs and Strengths-Mental Health (CANS-MH) Scale. *Journal of Child and Family Studies, 12*, 279–289.

Berliner, L., & Saunders, B. E. (1996). Treating fear and anxiety in sexually abused children: Results of a controlled 2-year follow-up study. *Child Maltreatment, 1*, 294–309.

Bruns, E. J., Hoagwood, K. E., Rivard, J. C., Wotring, J., Marsenich, L., & Carter, B. (2008). State implementation of evidence-based practice for youths, part II: Recommendations for research and policy. *Journal of the American Academy of Child Psychiatry, 47*, 499–504.

Bruns, E. J., & Hoagwood, K. E. (2008). State implementation of evidence-based practice for youths, part I: Recommendations for research and policy. Journal of the American *Academy of Child Psychiatry, 47*(4), 369–373.

Catani, C., Kohiladevy, M., Ruf, M., Schauer, E., Elbert, T., & Neuner, F. (2009). Treating children traumatized by war and tsunami: A comparison between exposure therapy and meditation-relaxation in North-East Sri Lanka. *BMC Psychiatry, 9*, 22.

Chaffin, M., Silovsky, J. F., Funderburk, B., Valle, L. A., Brestan, E. V., Balachova, T., et al. (2004). Parent-child interaction therapy with physically abusive parents: Efficacy for reducing future abuse reports. *Journal of Consulting & Clinical Psychology, 72*, 500–510.

Chapman, L., Morabito, D., Ladakakos, C., Schreier, H., & Knudson, M. M. (2001). The effectiveness of art therapy interventions in reducing post traumatic stress disorder (PTSD) symptoms in pediatric trauma patients. *Art Therapy, 18*, 100–104.

Cohen, J. (1992). A power primer. *Psychological Bulletin, 112*, 155–159.

Cohen, J. A., Deblinger, E., Mannarino, A. P., & Steer, R. (2004). A multi-site, randomized, controlled trial for children with sex abuse-related PTSD symptoms. *Journal of the American Academy of Child and Adolescent Psychiatry, 43*, 393–402.

Cohen, J. A., & Mannarino, A. P. (1996). A treatment outcome study for sexually abused preschool children: Initial findings. *Journal of the American Academy of Child and Adolescent Psychiatry, 35*, 42–50.

Cohen, J. A., & Mannarino, A. P. (1998). Interventions for sexually abused children: Initial treatment outcome findings. *Child Maltreatment, 3*, 17–26.

Cohen, J. A., & Mannarino, A. P. (2008). Disseminating and implementing trauma-focused CBT in community settings. *Trauma, Violence, & Abuse, 9*, 214–226.

Cohen, J. A., Mannarino, A. P., & Deblinger, E. (2006). *Treating trauma and traumatic grief in children and adolescents.* New York: The Guilford Press.

Cohen, J. A., Mannarino, A. P., & Deblinger, E. (2010). Trauma-Focused Cognitive-Behavioral Therapy for traumatized children. In J. R. Weisz & A. E. Kazdin (Eds.), *Evidence-based psychotherapies for children and adolescents* (2nd ed., pp. 295–311). New York: Guilford.

Cohen, J. A., Mannarino, A. P., & Iyengar, S. (2011). Community treatment of posttraumatic stress disorder in children exposed to intimate partner violence: A randomized controlled trial. *Archives of Pediatrics & Adolescent Medicine, 165*, 16–21.

Cohen, J. A., Mannarino, A. P., & Knudsen, K. (2005). Treating sexually abused children: One year follow-up of a randomized controlled trial. *Child Abuse & Neglect, 29*, 135–145.

Cohen, J. A., Mannarino, A. P., Perel, J. M., & Staron, V. (2007). A pilot randomized controlled trial of combined Trauma-Focused CBT and sertraline for childhood PTSD symptoms. *Journal of the American Academy of Child and Adolescent Psychiatry, 46*, 811–819.

Cohen, J. A., Mannarino, A. P., & Staron, V. R. (2006). A pilot study of modified cognitive-behavioral therapy for childhood traumatic grief (CBT-CTG). *Journal of the American Academy of Child and Adolescent Psychiatry, 45*, 1465–1473.

Coulter, S. J. (2000). Effect of song writing versus recreational music on posttraumatic stress disorder (PTSD) symptoms and abuse attribution in abused children. *Journal of Poetry Therapy, 13*, 189–208.

Deblinger, E., & Heflin, A. H. (1996). *Treating sexually abused children and their nonoffending parents: A cognitive behavioral approach.* Newbury Park, CA: Sage.

Deblinger, E., Lippmann, J., & Steer, R. (1996). Sexually abused children suffering posttraumatic stress symptoms: Initial treatment outcome findings. *Child Maltreatment, 1*, 310–321.

Deblinger, E., Mannarino, A. P., Cohen, J. A., Runyon, M. K., & Steer, R. A. (2011). Trauma-focused cognitive behavioral therapy for children: Impact of the trauma narrative and treatment length. *Depression and Anxiety, 28*, 67–75.

Deblinger, E., Mannarino, A. P., Cohen, J. A., & Steer, R. A. (2006). Follow-up study of a multisite, randomized, controlled trial for children with sexual abuse-related PTSD symptoms: Examining predictors of treatment response. *Journal of the American Academy of Child and Adolescent Psychiatry, 45*, 1474–1484.

Deblinger, E., McLeer, S. V., & Henry, D. E. (1990). Cognitive/behavioral treatment for sexually abused children suffering post-traumatic stress: Preliminary findings. *Journal of the American Academy of Child and Adolescent Psychiatry, 29,* 747–752.

Deblinger, E., Stauffer, L. B., & Steer, R. (2001). Comparative efficacies of supportive and cognitive-behavioral group therapies for young children who have been sexually abused and their non-offending mothers. *Child Maltreatment, 6,* 332–343.

Deblinger, E., Steer, R., & Lippmann, J. (1999). Two-year follow-up study of cognitive behavioral therapy for sexually abused children suffering post-traumatic stress symptoms. *Child Abuse & Neglect, 23,* 1371–1378.

DeRosa, R., & Pelcovitz, D. (2009). Group treatment for chronically traumatized adolescents: Igniting SPARCS of change. In D. Brom, R. Pat-Horenczyk, & J. D. Ford (Eds.), *Treating traumatized children: Risk, resilience and recovery* (pp. 225–239). New York: Routledge/Taylor & Francis Group.

Donohue, B., Miller, E. R., Van Hasselt, V. B., & Hersen, M. (1998). An ecobehavioral approach to child maltreatment. In V. B. Van Hasselt, & M. Hersen (Eds.), *Handbook of psychological treatment protocols for children and adolescents* (pp. 279–356). Mahwah, NJ: Lawrence Erlbaum.

Felitti, V. J., Anda. R. F., Norgenberg, D., Williamson, D. F., Spitz, A. M, Edwards, V., Koss, M. P., & Marks, J. S. (1998). Relationship of childhood abuse and household dysfunction to many of the leading causes of death in adults: The Adverse Childhood Experiences (ACE) Study. *American Journal of Preventive Medicine, 14,* 245–258.

Finkelhor, D., Turner, H. A., & Ormrod, R. K. (2006). Kid's stuff: The nature and impact of peer and sibling violence. *Child Abuse & Neglect, 30,* 1401–1421.

Gilboa-Schechtman, E., Foa, E. B., Shafran, N., Aderka, I. M, Powers, M. B., Rachamim, L., Rosenbach, L., Yadin, E., & Apter, A. (2010). Prolonged exposure versus dynamic therapy for adolescent PTSD: A pilot randomized controlled trial. *Journal of the American Academy of Child and Adolescent Psychiatry, 49,* 1034-1042.

Hensler, D., Wilson, C., & Sadler, B. L. (2004). *Closing the quality chasm in child abuse treatment: Identifying and disseminating best practices. The findings of the Kauffman best practices project to help children heal from child abuse.* Available at: CA: http://www.chadwickcenter.org/Documents/Kaufman%20 Report/ChildHosp-NCTAbrochure.pdf.

Hoagwood, K. E., Vogel, J. M., Levitt, J. M., D'Amico, P. J., Paisner, W. I., & Kaplan S. J. (2007). Implementing an evidence-based trauma treatment in a state system after September 11th: The CATS project. *Journal of the American Academy of Child and Adolescent Psychiatry, 46,* 773–779.

Jaberghaderi, N., Greenwald, R., Rubin, A., Zand, S. O., & Dolatabadi, S. (2004). A comparison of CBT and EMDR for sexually-abused Iranian girls. *Clinical Psychology and Psychotherapy, 11,* 358–368.

Jaycox, L. H., Cohen, J. A., Mannarino, A. P., Walker, D. W., Langely, A. K., Gegenheimer, K. L., Scott, M., & Schonlau, M. (2010). Children's mental health care following Hurricane Katrina: A field trial of trauma-focused psychotherapies. *Journal of Traumatic Stress, 23,* 223–231.

Kazak, A. E., Alderfer, M. A., Streisand, R., Simms, S., Rourker, M. T., Barakat, L. P., Gallagher, P., & Cnaan, A. (2004). Treatment of posttraumatic stress symptoms in adolescent survivors of childhood cancer and their families: A randomized clinical trial. *Journal of Family Psychology, 18,* 493–504.

Kazak, A., Simms, S., Barakat, L., Hobbie, W., Foley, B., Golomb, V., et al. (1999). Surviving Cancer Competently Intervention Program (SCCIP): A cognitive-behavioral and family therapy intervention for adolescent survivors of childhood cancer and their families. *Family Process, 38,* 175–191.

King, N., Tonge, B. J., Mullen, P., Myerson, N., Heyne, D., Rollings, S., et al. (2000). Treating sexually abused children with post-traumatic stress symptoms: A randomized clinical trial. *Journal of the American Academy of Child and Adolescent Psychiatry, 39,* 1347–1355.

Kolko, D. (1996). Individual cognitive behavioral treatment and family therapy for physically abused children and their offending parents: A comparison of clinical outcomes. *Child Maltreatment, 1,* 322–342.

Kolko, D. J., & Swenson, C. (2002). *Assessing and treating physically abused children and their families: A cognitive-behavioral approach.* Thousand Oaks, CA: Sage.

Lieberman, A. F., Ippen, C. G., & Van Horn, P. (2006). Child-parent psychotherapy: 6-month follow-up of a randomized controlled trial. *Journal of the American Academy of Child and Adolescent Psychiatry, 45,* 913–918.

Lieberman, A. F., Van Horn, P., & Ippen, C. G. (2005). Toward evidence-based treatment: Child-Parent psychotherapy with preschoolers exposed to marital violence. *Journal of the American Academy of Child and Adolescent Psychiatry, 44,* 1241–1248.

Lipovsky, J., Swenson, C., Ralston, M., & Saunders, B. (1998). The abuse clarification process in the treatment of intrafamilial child abuse. *Child Abuse & Neglect, 22,* 729–741.

Lyons, J. S., Weiner, D. A., & Scheider, A. (2006). *A field trial of three evidence-based practices for trauma with children in state custody.* Report to the Illinois Department of Children and Family Services. Evanston, IL: Mental Health Resources Services and Policy Program; Northwestern University.

McLeer, S. V., Deblinger, E., Atkins, M., Foa, E., & Ralph, D. (1988). Post-traumatic stress disorder in sexually abused children: A prospective study. *Journal of the American Academy of Child and Adolescent Psychiatry, 27*(5), 650–654.

McLeer, S., Deblinger, E., Henry, D., & Orvaschel, H. (1992). Sexually abused children at high risk for posttraumatic stress disorder. *Journal of the American Academy of Child and Adolescent Psychiatry, 31,* 875–879.

Najavits, L. M., Gallop, R. J., & Weiss, R. D. (2006). Seeking safety therapy for adolescent girls with PTSD and substance use disorder: A randomized controlled trial. *Journal of Behavioral Health Services & Research, 33,* 453–463.

National Registry of Evidence-based Programs and Practices, Substance Abuse and Mental Health Services Administration. (2005). *Cognitive-behavioral therapy for child sexual abuse (CBT-CSA).* Washington, DC: Author. Available online at http://www.nrepp.samhsa.gov/programfulldetails.asp?PROGRAM_ID=217.

Onyut, L. P., Neuner, F., Schauer, E., Ertl, V., Odenwald, M., Schauer, M, & Elbert, T. (2005). Narrative exposure therapy as a treatment for child war survivors with posttraumatic stress disorder: Two case reports and a pilot study in an African refugee settlement. *BMC Psychiatry, 5,* 7.

Pifalo, T. (2007). Jogging the cogs: Trauma-focused art therapy and cognitive behavioral therapy with sexually abused children. *Art Therapy: Journal of the American Art Therapy Association, 24*, 170–175.

Rose, C., & Demaree, J. (2006). *The California Evidence-Based Clearinghouse (CEBC) for child welfare.* The California Department of Social Services. Retrieved from http://www.cebc4cw.org/program/17.

Runyon, M. K., Deblinger, E., & Steer, R. A. (2010). Group cognitive behavioral treatment for parents and children at-risk for physical abuse: An initial study. *Child and Family Behavioral Therapy, 32*, 196–218.

Runyon, M. K., Deblinger, E., & Schroeder, C. M. (2009). Pilot evaluation of outcomes of combined parent-child cognitive-behavioral group therapy for families at-risk for child physical abuse. *Cognitive Behavioral Practice, 16*, 101–118.

Runyon, M. K., Deblinger, E., Ryan, E. E., & Thakkar-Kolar, R. (2004). An overview of child physical abuse: Developing an integrated parent-child cognitive-behavioral treatment approach. *Trauma, Violence, and Abuse, 5*, 65–85.

Saunders, B. E., Berliner, L., & Hanson, R. F. (Eds.). (2004). *Child Physical and Sexual Abuse: Guidelines for Treatment (Revised Report: April 26, 2004).* Charleston, SC: National Crime Victims Research and Treatment Center.

Saxe, G. N., Ellis, B. H., Fogler, J., Hansen, S., & Sorkin, B. (2005). Comprehensive care for traumatized children. *Psychiatric Annals, 35*, 443–448.

Smith, P., Yule, W., Perrin, S., Tranah, T., Dalgeish, T., & Clark, D. M. (2007). Cognitive-behavioral therapy for PTSD in children and adolescents: A preliminary randomized controlled trial. *Journal of the American Academy of Child and Adolescent Psychiatry, 46*, 1051–1061.

Stein, B. D., Jaycox, L. H., Kataoka, S. H., Wong, M., Tu, W., Elliott, M. N., & Fink, A. (2003). A mental health intervention for school children exposed to violence: A randomized controlled trial. *Journal of the American Medical Association, 290*, 603–611.

Timmer, S. G., Urquiza, A. J., Zebell, N. M., & McGrath, J. M. (2005). Parent-Child Interaction Therapy: Application to maltreating parent-child dyads. *Child Abuse & Neglect, 29*, 825–842.

Trowell, J., Kolvin, I., Weeramanthri, T, Sadowski, H, Berelowitz, M., Glasser, D., & Leitch, I. (2002). Psychotherapy for sexually abused girls: Psychopathological outcome findings and patterns of change. *British Journal of Psychiatry, 180*, 234–247.

CHAPTER

34 PTSD at Late Life: Context and Treatment

Lee Hyeri *and* Catherine A. Yeagerii

Abstract

Our knowledge about the role of aging as a moderating or mediating influence on the expression of posttraumatic symptoms, and their remission and resolution, is nascent. This is reflected in the current state of empirically supported psychotherapies for older adults with PTSD. At this time, there are no empirically validated psychotherapeutic or psychopharmacologic treatments for this age group. This chapter highlights general issues and other factors unique to aging, such as changes in cognition, that must be taken into consideration when embarking on PTSD treatment with older adults. We review extant psychotherapy research that has applicability to this cohort: treatment studies on anxiety and depression for older adults, as well as treatment studies for younger adults with PTSD. Next, we describe promising PTSD interventions for older adults that have yet to be tested on large samples or in randomized controlled trials. The chapter culminates in the presentation of a multi-modal psychotherapy intervention designed to address factors unique to aging, and which involves a gentler version of trauma-related therapy that allows exposure to be optional.

Key Words: Posttraumatic stress disorder, aging, psychotherapy research, cognitive behavioral therapy, cognition, memory, exposure therapy, trauma-related therapy

> "The committee found that the available research leaves significant gaps in assessing the efficacy of interventions in important subpopulations of veterans with PTSD, especially those with traumatic brain injury, major depression, other anxiety disorders, or substance abuse, as well as ethnic and cultural minorities, women, and older individuals."
> —*Institute of Medicine, 2008*

The diagnosis, Post Traumatic Stress Disorder (PTSD; American Psychiatric Association, 2000), has been in place for three decades. Much has been learned over this period. As a general rule, the diathesis-stress model of PTSD is commonly accepted: extreme psychological trauma is necessary but not sufficient for PTSD to develop. Also as a rule too, other psychiatric conditions are frequently comorbid with PTSD. PTSD has a kindling effect. Both comorbidities and kindling create special problems for older adults, who may suffer multiple occurrences of posttraumatic symptoms, including depression and anxiety, which in turn increase their susceptibility to repeat episodes. This kindling is often underpinned by internal processes, such as ruminative thinking cycles that are reactivated by minor stresses or dysphoric mood (Ma & Teasdale, 2004).

A spate of studies and meta-analyses on the assessment and treatment of PTSD have appeared in recent years, but the meager data that exist regarding the role of age as a mediating or moderating influence in trauma expression is most often extrapolated from non-trauma research. We also do not yet know if PTSD treatments are efficacious for older adults. Although there is now a great deal of evidence relating to the longer-term sequelae associated with trauma experiences, we are unsure of the mechanisms by which trauma effects persist over the life course. Age, it can be said, interacts with most things "psychiatric," the unfolding of which remains to be clarified. In recent years, the social sciences have addressed trauma and its effects from the clinical perspective, examining the "disorder" of the construct. In fact, we do not yet fully know the importance of a life lived, one's life perspective, and how "the long view" affects reactions to contemporary trauma as well as how past trauma is experienced through the lens of aging.

We can make general statements about long term adaptation to trauma. Older adults with trauma histories tend to adjust reasonably well. They report fewer physiological symptoms of stress and lower rates of PTSD, Major Depressive Disorder (MDD), and Generalized Anxiety Disorder (GAD) than their younger counterparts (Sakauye et al. 2009). This is true regarding anxiety disorders in general, with oldest old having the lowest prevalence of all age groups (Byers, et al., 2010) This was true also of Hurricane Katrina and the September 11th catastrophe – older adults reported fewer trauma-related symptoms than their younger counterparts (Hobfoll, Tracy & Galea, 2006). In addition, we can make reasonable inferences about trauma treatment from recent studies on anxiety and depression for older adults, as well as borrow from data on PTSD treatment studies of younger cohorts. In this context, there are differences in the manifestation of PTSD symptoms in older individuals, especially in the domains of emotion and cognition. We know, for example, that older adults are more vulnerable to source monitoring memory problems and false memory effects (e.g., Roediger & Gereaci, 2007) and are less likely to apply executive functioning strategies to disambiguate source misattributions (Steffens et al., 2006). Developmentally, age-related declines no doubt play an important role in the ongoing processing of trauma, but can these presumed deficits be construed as growth processes as well?

As we finesse the issue of age in the context of PTSD treatment, we have apt models of treatment from other age groups, enough data on anxiety and depression for older adults, and sufficient clinical experience to export empirically supported principles to older adults. We briefly review the prevalence of PTSD in older adults to provide context for treatment considerations. We also highlight variables that are unique to trauma in later life; variables that require careful deliberation when conceptualizing treatment for the elder with PTSD. We then discuss treatment studies related to younger adults with PTSD, studies on depression and anxiety treatments for older adults, and the few treatment studies specific to older adults with PTSD. Finally, we present a model for the treatment of PTSD within the framework of aging.

Background

Older victims tend to be no more vulnerable or reactive to psychological trauma than younger individuals despite high stress rates (Hyer & Sohnle, 2001). Recent studies have confirmed earlier ones (Norris et al., 2002) which show that age is not a problem where a) gender is at issue (Acierno et al., 2001); b), where acute hospital stays are assessed (Zatzick et al., 2007); or c) where primary care is the venue (Frueh et al., 2007). The variable, age, in a word, does not seem to negatively relate to prevalence rates (Creamer & Parslow, 2008).

That said, older adults are prone to developing Acute Stress Disorder (ASD). The most studied acute trauma at late life involves motor vehicle accidents (MVAs) (Norris, 1992). For perspective, estimates of PTSD secondary to MVAs range from 10% to 46% for all ages (Blanchard & Hicking, 1997), in addition to other psychiatric symptoms at one year follow-up (Mayou, Bryant, & Duthie, 1993). Notably, MVAs are the second leading cause of injury in geriatric patients, resulting in the highest crash fatality rate of any age group, with most accidents related to driver error (Newton, 2001). MVAs are associated with increased morbidity and mortality in older drivers as well as older pedestrians due to inability to hear traffic, inability to attain speeds, and poor judgment. When elders are victims, not only may they sustain more serious injuries than other age groups, but also heal more slowly after injury (Brown, et al. 2004). These kinds of vulnerabilities put elders at substantially higher risk of developing ASD/PTSD.

Several other common sources of elder-specific trauma have been reported. For example, the incidence of PTSD following the completion of cancer treatment ranges from 0% to 32% (Kangas, et al., 2005). Other serious health problems, loss of a spouse, and victimization by crime also have been cited as severe stressors at late life. Elder abuse, which refers to many types of maltreatment, including neglect, physical, emotional, financial and sexual abuse, is a major trauma as well (McCartney & Severson, 1997; Newton, 2001). In the primary care clinic, and even in the mental health clinic, these kinds of traumas are often overlooked as producing ASD/PTSD in older adults, thereby preventing or delaying effective intervention.

When trauma is linked to poor health habits or to medical comorbidities, the response to treatment for any psychiatric problem is less robust for older adults than other age groups (Hyer & Sohnle, 2001). Over time, PTSD has been linked to smoking and alcohol abuse, suicidal ideation, high rates of primary care utilization, and behavioral disturbances in long term care (Cook, O'Donnell, Moltzen, Ruzek, & Skeith, 2005; Davidson, Hughes, Blazer, & George, 1991; Frueh et al., 2003; Hyer & Stanger, 1997; Schnurr & Spiro, 1999; Spiro, Schnurr, & Aldwin, 1994). Once established, Kessler et al. (1995) showed that a substantial proportion of adults with PTSD (40%) do not recover even decades later. Several studies have shown that a variety of health problems and physical disability are more common in men and women with PTSD than in their unaffected peers. Sareen et al. (2007) surveyed almost 37,000 community dwelling adults, of which 478 had been diagnosed with PTSD (1%). Despite low prevalence, PTSD was associated with significantly greater odds of chronic illness, including asthma, COPD, chronic fatigue syndrome, arthritis, fibromyalgia, migraines, cardiovascular disease, gastrointestinal disorders, pain disorders, and cancer. These findings underscore the importance of careful screening for PTSD symptoms among older patients presenting with medical problems.

One issue has been debated regarding older adults and trauma: whether or not older adults are more vulnerable or have increased inoculation as a result of a stressor. On the one hand, because of reduced adaptive capacities, coping resources and external resources (e.g., low income, and lack of social supports) and increased exposure to traumatic events through aging (e.g., health-related events or elder abuse), older adults may be more likely than younger people to develop psychiatric disorders, including PTSD, and/or problems with psychosocial functioning. This has been labelled the vulnerability or additive burden hypothesis (Dohrenwend & Dohrenwend, 1981), and more recently, stress proliferation (Pearlin, 2010). The stress inoculation hypothesis, on the other hand, argues that age is protective against the development of PTSD. This occurs particularly when older people have dealt successfully with previous traumas (Gibbs, 1989), or were able to re-experience a trauma with a high degree of voluntary control, or were able to find meaning in the outcome of the trauma, and/or to find social support (Lyons, 1991). Considerable evidence exists for this view (Gleser, Green & Winglet, 1981; Phifer, 1990; Phifer and Norris, 1989). Clearly, the older adult who is resilient in the face of trauma is more likely to respond favourably to psychotherapy (if even needed) or to be a good candidate for "indicated" public health interventions.

Unique Late Life Variables that Effect Treatment

Recent meta-analyses identified the following variables as the best predictors of PTSD: prior trauma, including childhood trauma, prior psychological maladjustment, family history of psychopathology, perceived life threat during trauma, post-trauma poor social supports, peri-traumatic emotional response, and peri-traumatic dissociation (Brewin, Andrews & Valentine, 2000; Ozer, Best, Lipsey, & Weiss, 2003). In addition, neuropsychological deficits occur in PTSD as well as with age (Ehring, Ehlers, & Glucksman, 2008). Certain domains are exceptionally impacted, including: memory (Bremner, Southwick, Johnson, Yehuda, & Charney, 1993; Elzinger & Bremner, 2002; Sutker et al., 1991a; Vasterling, Brailey, Constans, Borges, & Sutker, 1997); attention (Vasterling et al., 2002); executive functioning (Beckham, Crawford, & Feldman, 1998), and global intellect (Sutker, Uddo-Carne, & Allain, 1991b; Vasterling et al., 2002). Older adults are able to generate fewer alternatives than younger adults (Reed, Mikels, & Simon, 2008); they suffer from considerable proactive interference with memories (Emery, Hale, & Meyerson, 2008); they monitor reality less well than younger adults (McDaniel, Lyle, Butler, & Dornburg, 2008); and in general older adults have compromised executive functioning, memory and speed of processing.

In this context, older adults with PTSD have problems retrieving specific autobiographical memories when intentionally attempting to do so, instead recalling categories of repeated events (Williams et al., 2007). This effect is referred to as overgeneral autobiographical memory (OGM). It is currently unclear whether OGM represents a cause, outcome, or risk factor in PTSD. Related, older individuals with PTSD/GAD appear to have brain abnormalities that keep them from spontaneously processing negative emotions (Etkim, et al., 2010). Indications are that these elders initially register negative stimuli normally but show deficits in how they control negative emotions. Over time, these individuals have difficulty returning to baseline emotional functioning. With a positive spin, Carstensen (2003) contends that selective information processing plays a role in well-being at late life: When life expectancy is viewed as finite, older adults shift their goals to regulating emotional states so that mood stays positive and well-being is optimized. This has been labeled a positivity bias, which may decrease cognitive load (Mather & Knight, 2005). Reducing excessive cognitive load in therapy (Mohlman, 2008), as well as fostering a more friendly view of past life (reminiscence), have been applied for the better in therapies for anxiety at late life.

The complexity of the relationship between cognition and PTSD for older adults has yet to be fully understood, but reduced cognitive functioning may be a preexisting risk factor for PTSD as well as a problem in the therapy itself. Using a longitudinal design and large sample, Parslow and Jorm (2007) examined whether such deficits represent a vulnerability factor or consequence of PTSD. Individuals who developed PTSD symptoms showed lower pre-trauma cognitive performance as assessed primarily through verbal measures. This is consistent with a twin study (Kremen et al., 2007) in which lower pre-trauma cognitive ability accounted for 5% of the variance in PTSD. Older adults already grappling with cognitive deficits may therefore be at heightened risk for developing PTSD. Several investigators have suggested that severe or prolonged trauma, or a history of such exposure, places the older adult at increased risk for cognitive decline or dementia (Cook, Ruzek, & Cassedy, 2003).

So, too, can cognitive decline exacerbate PTSD symptoms or cause long dormant symptoms to re-emerge. Grossman et al. (2004) presented a case study of two Holocaust survivors who appeared to have adapted well post-trauma, but later developed severe PTSD symptomatology following the onset of neurologic illness in later life, which weakened executive functioning, attention, and memory. Such case studies demonstrate the need for systematic research to better elucidate the relationship among aging, degenerative disease, and PTSD symptoms in older trauma survivors. In their retrospective study regarding the relationship between PTSD and the risk of dementia among older US veterans receiving care in the Department of Veterans Affairs, Yaffe and colleagues (2010) collected data on 181,093 veterans 55 years or older without dementia from 1997–2000 (53,155 veterans with and 127,938 veterans without PTSD). During the follow-up period between 2000–2007, veterans with PTSD had a 7-year cumulative incident dementia rate of 10.6%, whereas those without PTSD had a rate of 6.6%. Veterans with PTSD were more than twice as likely to develop incident dementia compared with those without the disorder. In older adults, too, neurotransmitter and neuroendocrine systems become altered with repeated activation of the fear response in PTSD (e.g., Cortese & Phan, 2005; Pervanidou, 2008; Strawn & Gercioti, 2008). These neurochemical alterations have known effects on adjustment and treatment response. Findings showing Hypothalamic-Pituitary-Adrenal (HPA) axis dysregulation secondary to chronic PTSD are relatively robust. Given that HPA system function naturally declines in older adults relative to younger ones (Timiras & Gersten, 2007), elders with PTSD may be especially likely to have compromised HPA functioning, further weakening the body's response to stress.

Finally, it needs saying that at late life people are strongly impacted even when experiencing "normal" distress, like illness, divorce, bereavement, or job loss. In fact, older adults who become depressed for the first time have experienced just such a stressor 60% of the time. Older adults develop symptoms to life's vicissitudes at rates similar to those who undergo traumatic stress (Gold et al., 2005). In this sense the impact of a distressing event is similar whether the stressor (trauma) is big or small. This may be particularly true for older adults. Small traumas can appear overtly negligible, but result in a negative perception (of the event) and a stress response (coping). Their expression is epigenetic – a stress sensitization process where a recurrence of the problem is asserted after an exacerbation necessary to trigger the initial episode. Over time, kindling (Post, 1992) occurs, and even minor perturbations become irritating enough to initiate a recurrence of a PTSD-like response (see Monroe & Harkness, 2005). This also applies to more complicated grief reactions, labeled traumatic grief syndrome (Prigerson et al., 1999). In sum, PTSD is not only conceptually richer than the diagnostic criteria listed in the DSM for older adults (e.g., DSM-IV-TR, American Psychiatric Association, 2000; Broman-Fulks, Ruggiero, Green et al. 2006), but problems related to lesser stressors are suitable for the use of PTSD treatments.

Treatments for PTSD

At this time, there are no empirically validated psychotherapeutic or psychopharmacological treatments for older adults with PTSD. That said, several empirically supported psychotherapies do exist for younger adults and these have the potential for successful translation to an older population. Whether young or old, given the engrained nature of trauma memories and the anxiety they cause, effective therapy needs to assist the survivor to tolerate the sensory reminders of the trauma. Victims need to experience efficacy and purpose in response to stimuli that trigger anxiety, helplessness, and feelings of impending calamity. We will thus begin this section with a brief review of empirically supported treatments for anxiety in older adults. Supporting this approach is recent evidence that suggests fear, anxiety (PTSD), and depression share many neuroanatomical and neurochemical substrates (Bryant et al., 2008; Dickie, Brunet & Akerib, 2008; Shin, 2009; Taber & Hurley, 2009). We will then move on to treatment for PTSD in younger adults and end with a PTSD model for older adults and a treatment approach that we believe has merit for this age group.

Empirically Supported Psychotherapies for Older Adults with Anxiety

Generalized Anxiety Disorder has been assessed more than any other type of anxiety condition at late life. Anxiety disorders in older adults are associated with increased disability, diminished wellbeing, and excessive and inappropriate use of medical services (Wetherell, Gatz, & Craske, 2003). Although community prevalence rates for anxiety disorders in elders range from 3.5% - 10%, they are highly prevalent in medical settings and are associated with increased physical disability, decreased quality of life, and increased service use (Wetherell, Lenze, & Stanley, 2005). Ayers et al. (2007) examined empirically supported psychotherapies for older adults with GAD. Cognitive Behavioral Therapy (CBT) and relaxation training had the most consistent support for treatment efficacy, whereas Cognitive Therapy (CT) and supportive therapy showed positive but less robust effects. Other studies, some dating back more than 15 years, support CBT's efficacy with elders suffering from anxiety disorders (Arean, 1993; Scogin, Rickard et al., 1992; Stanley et al., 2003). To this, Macklin and Arean (2008) added reminiscence therapy and brief dynamic therapy, as well as the combination of medication and interpersonal therapy (IPT; Newman, Castonguay, Borkovec, & Molnar, 2004), as candidates for efficacious therapies for anxiety. Mohlman (2008) also investigated an integration of CBT and executive function (EF) training in older adults with anxiety and executive dysfunction. Although preliminary, other studies (e.g., Alexopoulos et al., 2007) suggest that both CBT and EF training are promising for older adults who have anxiety and cognitive decline. Interestingly, Thorp et al. (2009) found that relaxation training was as effective in the treatment of anxiety in older adults as CBT or CBT combined with relaxation.

Other relevant and related therapies, such as Problem Solving Therapy (PST; D'Zurilla & Neu, 2001), metacognitive therapy (Wells, 1997), IPT, intolerance of uncertainty (Ladouceur et al., 2004) and life review (Haight, 2000) have been evaluated in adults with anxiety, but not older adults. Acceptance and Commitment Therapy (ACT) has been applied to older clients with GAD (Wetherell et al., 2008) and results were largely positive. The same conclusion can be applied to mindfulness (Segal et al., 2002), as well as well-being therapy (e.g., Frish, 2006) and positive psychotherapy (Seligman, 2002). In general, however, CBT has not been compared to other psychotherapies in regard to older adults for PTSD.

Interestingly, there have been relatively few randomized controlled trials with combined medication and psychotherapy at later life. Combined medication and CBT or IPT have had some support in the literature for older adults (Gerson et al., 1999; Reynolds et al., 1999; Thompson, Gallagher, Hansen, Gantz, Steffen, 1991). In a meta-analysis, Pinquart and Duberstein (2007) reviewed 32 studies of treatments focused on anxiety disorders in older adults in which subjects received either behavioral interventions or pharmacotherapy. Although more robust effects were found for pharmacotherapy, they concluded that both pharmacotherapy and behavioral interventions are reasonably effective. The use of SSRIs with psychotherapy may be especially beneficial as the efficacy of SSRIs with anxiety and older adults has been proffered (Lenze, Mulsant, Mohlman et al., 2005; Schuurmans et al., 2006).

Empirically Supported Psychotherapies for Younger Adults with PTSD

A number of randomized trials of psychotherapy for PTSD have been conducted on younger adults. Bradley et al. (2005) performed a large meta-analysis of CBT and behavioral therapies for PTSD and showed that 67% of adult clients who completed therapy no longer met criteria for PTSD; whereas 56% of clients who entered, but did not complete treatment, no longer met criteria for PTSD. CBT and behavioral therapies were more effective than wait-list control (ES = 1.11-1.53) or supportive therapy (ES =.83–1.01). Furthermore, Eye Movement Desensitization and Reprocessing (EMDR) was roughly equal to CBT and behavior therapy in this study (Hyer & Sohnle, 2001). EMDR may have special application for older adults with PTSD, as it is client-friendly, can be done at the pace of the client, and performed in short periods of time. The International Society for Traumatic Stress Studies (Foa et al., 2000) endorsed exposure therapy as the best empirically supported intervention, followed by cognitive restructuring and SSRIs. These interventions have not been well studied in older trauma survivors, however.

Many PTSD clients receive pharmacological treatments, either alone or coupled with a psychosocial intervention. In 2004, for example, 80% of PTSD clients treated in US Veteran's Administration settings received psychotropics, the majority of which (89%) were antidepressants. Yet, current data indicate that psychotropic medications are marginally successful for the treatment of PTSD (see Lee & Shubert, 2009; Shalev, 2009). Although a range of medications have been applied to PTSD care, including antidepressants, antipsychotics, anticonvulants, benzodiazepines, and adrenergic modulators, most clients do not achieve full remission, requiring multiple changes in treatment. Although there is optimism for future research with pharmacogenomics, as well as the application of newer drugs treatment of PTSD (e.g., the beta-adrenergic receptor blocker d-cyclocerine), these efforts have limits and have not been examined with older adults.

Empirically Supported Psychotherapies for Older Adults with PTSD

Treatment outcome studies with older adults suffering from PSTD have been few in number and modest in scope (small series or case studies; Boehnlein & Sparr, 1993; Hyer et al, 1990; Lipton & Shaffer, 1986; Molinari & Williams, 1995; Snell & Padin-Rivera, 1997). Cook et al. (2005) applied a CBT to eight older veterans and found changes in clinician-rated measures in severity of PTSD. Their methods reflect those of Hyer et al. (1990) and Boehnlein and Sparr (1993) that use anxiety management, rational thinking, self-reward, mastery, and relaxation, as well as psychoeducation. Absent in all cases was trauma processing via exposure. Thorp (2005), however, applied exposure, adapted for late life to an older group of adults with PTSD. This consisted of 12 sessions of exposure over six weeks and was successful. Other studies or case analyses examining exposure in elders with PTSD also showed generally positive outcomes (Averill & Beck, 2000; Breslau et al., 1991; Cornelius & Kenyon-Jump, 2007; Hidalgo & Davidson, 2000; Markowitz, 2007; Russo, Hersen, and Van Hasselt, 2001; Schnurr et al., 2002; Van Zelst et al., 2003).

Hyer and Sohnle (2001) reported that many older victims find exposure treatments distressing. It is assumed that older patients are not physically or cognitively equipped to benefit from exposure therapy. Issues related to heart condition or hypertension (Morse, Martin, and Moshonov, 1992) or risk factors such as trait anxiety, hostility, anger repression, social isolation, and recent major loss may seem to make exposure therapy difficult to tolerate. However, no empirical evidence indicates that healthy older adults are at increased risk of adverse physical outcomes relating to the experience of acute sympathetic response of the magnitude that is characteristically elicited during prolonged exposure therapy. Additionally, health-related concerns about exposure therapy should be balanced against concerns over the health impact of recurrent episodes of trauma-related anxiety.

There continues to be some interest in life recollection and in loss regarding issues directly or indirectly related to PTSD with older adults. Reminiscence, the act of recollecting a memory of one's past for a variety of purposes, has been used with some efficacy with depressed older adults (Cappeliez & O'Rourke, 2006; Macklin & Arean, 2008). In a recent Cochrane review, Woods and colleagues (2005) highlighted this type of therapy to improve the health and well-being of healthy older adults, but there is no evidence at this time to support its use for the treatment of PTSD.

Weissman and colleagues (2007) modified IPT to target trauma's effects on an individual's current interpersonal perspective and social functioning. The central tenet of IPT for PTSD is that trauma compromises one's ability to use the social environment to process trauma, shattering the perception of safety and destroying relationship trust. Treatment counters perceived helplessness and shame by building interpersonal competence and redirecting the client's attention from a preoccupation with past trauma to coping with current interpersonal relationships. This approach is particularly apt for individuals who cannot tolerate exposure therapies and therefore is a promising candidate intervention with older adults. To date, IPT for PTSD in elders has been described only in case studies or small series (Markowitz, 2007). Robertson, Rushton, Batrim, Moore, and Morris (2007) treated 13 clients with PTSD using IPT in a group format. Average age was 54 years, the oldest participant being 74 years of age. All showed improvements in social functioning, general well being, and in depressive symptoms. Improvements were stable at 3 months.

Proposed Treatment Model for Late Life PTSD

To recap, there are no EBTs for older adults with PTSD. There appears to be no solid evidence that any of the components of CBT work better than others (Arch & Craske, 2009). We therefore borrow from younger age groups as well as from data emanating from treatment studies of older adults with anxiety and depression. With the possible exception of relaxation, there are no differences across cognitive therapy, exposure, or combination thereof for anxiety disorders (Norton & Price, 2007). This is probably accurate for older adults as well. Cognition may be a special concern and requires assessment and consequent planning. What seems appropriate then is a module-based approach with special consideration given to less cognitive approaches (Longmore & Worrell, 2007) and more emphasis to subconscious appraisals, such as mindfulness and acceptance-based therapies (Arch & Craske, 2008).

We now present a multi-modal psychotherapy intervention that may be more applicable to older adults who have intense and continued trauma, which involves a gentler version of trauma-related therapy (Falsetti, Erwin, Resnick, Davis, & Combs-Lane, 2003; Hyer & Sohnle, 2001). Hyer and Sohnle (2001) have argued that four therapies have special merit for the treatment of PTSD symptoms among older adults: (1) anxiety management training (AMT); (2) stress inoculation therapy, representing a coping model; (3) EMDR, providing a dosed exposure that targets state-specific information related to the trauma and has applicability with older victims (Hyer & Kushner, 2007); and (4) cognitive processing therapy, applying gradual and multiple exposures to the trauma and consisting largely of rescripting and altering distortions (Resick, 2003). In this vein, Wetherell and colleagues (2005) have indicated that older adults respond better in therapy to psychotherapy modules (e.g., relaxation, sleep management, etc.). Rygh and Sanderson (2005) outlined a complete package for the treatment of anxiety problems that we believe relates to PTSD. They include a cognitive component (cognitive restructuring, worry exposure, psychoeducation, etc.), a physiologic component (Progressive Muscle Relaxation, self-control, desensitization, etc.), a behavioral intervention (pleasurable activity scheduling, behavioral response prevention, etc.), and ancillary interventions (mindfulness, emotional processing, interpersonal effectiveness, and time management). Notably, Hyer and Sohnle (2001) reported that treatment effects of PTSD are enhanced by a positive treatment alliance and effort at homework by the client. Burns and Spangler (2001) found a similar relationship. Given this, the older adult is more likely to respond positively to an intervention that emphasizes building social relationships and interpersonal skills, as opposed to symptom-based treatments, to promote recovery (Bellack, 2004).

Hyer and Sohnle (2001) provided a six step model of PTSD treatment for older adults (see Table 1). In general, the more the intense the elder's perturbation, the more focus is placed on therapeutic tasks staged at the beginning of the treatment model; the less the individual is impacted by the trauma, the more the therapist can address the latter parts of the model and achieve lasting change.

Table 34.1. Treatment Model

1. Stabilize symptoms → Treat co-morbid disorders or stressors (including health).
2. Relationship Building → Build trust, the ability to confront trauma with a trusted therapist. Apply the client rated Working

Alliance Inventory (WAI; Horvath & Greenberg, 1989).

3. Attend to necessary psychosocial, treatment, and education (normalization) factors → Assure social supports, daily coping, social skills, and treatment compliance.
4. Apply cognitive restructuring (CR) → Teach CR and consider tactics of personality style as therapy-guided treatment.
5. Elicit positive core memories (PCM) → Foster a re-narration of self with core memories that can generalize to current life situations.
6. Decondition trauma memories → Apply AMT.

The rationale for the ordering of these tasks is to keep clients committed, encourage experimentation, and create cognitive change. Note that first task is always to stabilize active symptoms. This includes the treatment of comorbid psychiatric conditions (e.g., alcohol abuse) and current stressors (including health problems). Often the operative tasks of the therapy are basic, however: keeping the client in treatment, being supportive during difficult periods, maintaining appropriate arousal levels, and assuring commitment to the goals of therapy. Second, the therapeutic alliance between client and therapist is critical. For some clients, the relationship is the therapy. The third task is to attend to necessary psychosocial issues, ensure adequate social supports, and reinforce daily coping, social skills, and treatment compliance. The clinician must be assured that the client's lifestyle is reasonably healthy.

Fourth, the therapeutic use of cognitive restructuring (CR) is warranted. CR is influential at enhancing the efficacy of prolonged exposure. Despite some lack of efficacy with older adults, it has merit absent the use of exposure and has been applied in several studies to good effect with trauma (Mueser, 2006). Knowledge of the client's personality can be of assistance. Trauma memories organize themselves by complex schemas that automatically act on and structure incoming information and outgoing responses. Schemas evolve and give rise to personality styles or features. The fifth component involves self-representational stories and positive core memories (PCM). They include: written or taped autobiographies with feedback that may involve listening to tapes, making pilgrimages or reunions, developing a genealogy, doing a scrapbook or photo album, looking at old letters and memorabilia, summarizing one's life work, and exercising the preservation of ethnic identity (Lewis & Butler, 1974). Hyer et al. (1990) applied PCMs alone with older adults to good effect. The application of PCMs involves a simple recounting of a positive event, reinforcing the positive interpretations, re-engaging hope, reframing better world views, and supporting competence (see Hyer & Sohnle, 2001).

The last component of the treatment model involves the trauma memory. We believe that this is best done last. The therapist takes time to assess whether the client is a candidate for this stage of therapy, whether she/he will allow access to the trauma memory, and whether the client has the requisite skills for an unearthing of the traumatic content (see Hyer & Sohnle, 2001). The therapeutic task is to bring the implicit memory (easily triggered by emotional states, interpersonal contexts, external stimuli, and language cues) into awareness as self-as-past, i.e., into language in the form of a narrative. The more the trauma memory is organized, made into a narrative, and placed into explicit memory as disclosed, elaborated, and validated, the more improvement occurs (Foa, 1999; Pennebacker, 1989).

Anxiety management training (AMT) is recommended for this task. This is a "soft" exposure technique that involves a variety of procedures, including biofeedback, relaxation, and cognitive restructuring. The use of exposure in AMT is done empathically and with relaxation as a lead-in (see Hyer & Sohnle, 2001). Procedurally, the sequence of memory work is straightforward. After the therapist has assessed for client skills, willingness, and safety issues, the therapist obtains the facts of the memory - a "clean" rendition of events. Confusion, misattribution, fears, and gaps are highlighted and gently challenged. The objective is not an exacting account of the trauma, as there is little evidence that this helps in therapy. Normalization and education regarding the reasons for unearthing the memory are critical.

Finally, at therapy's end, relapse awareness should be taught, as relapse is the norm. The therapist anticipates the need for continuance of care, discusses issues regarding a change in treatment, and reinforces the importance of booster sessions. The client is taught how to recognize early warning signs, anticipate high risk situations, and develop an emergency plan for relapse. This includes self-help strategies and involves the client's social supports.

Conclusion

Trauma at late life is plentiful but treatable. What data are available from the past three decades of research do not indicate that older adults are at greater risk than younger adults for poor psychosocial outcomes following exposure to trauma. At present, there is simply insufficient evidence to conclude that trauma causes more negative psychosocial consequences in older adults.

In this chapter, we have discussed the myriad issues specific to the treatment of older adults with PTSD. We presented a model of the older traumatized adult with life span implications. And we have argued that ESTs for PTSD designed on younger groups, and ESTs designed for older groups with depression or anxiety, have applicability to older adults with PTSD. In addition, we presented a six step treatment model which incorporates key elements of traditional cognitive and behavioral therapies but also expands them to include a trauma focus. This model is a comprehensive treatment for acute or chronic PTSD, and it addresses the whole person. In this model, trauma memories are modified or transformed directly only as a last step, and only for those individuals who can tolerate it. Throughout, factors related specifically to aging, mourning for losses, giving meaning to experiences, re-establishing self-coherence and self-continuity, and enhancing cultural foundations and social supports, are integrated.

We believe that PTSD is the most severe marker of stress at late life; the final common pathway of one or many losses. Despite lower prevalence rates relative to other age groups, older adults have considerable stress and do respond in problematic ways. Stress is always experienced when there is an inadequate match between the person's coping ability and environmental demands (whether exogenous or endogenous). Loss, cognition, and poorer life circumstances all can tear at a positive coping response. But, as we parse apart the problems of trauma at late life, we do not need to travel down the slippery slope. Trauma-related issues are treatable.

Perhaps there is more. Neria and Litz (2003) hint at the real problem at late life: the symptoms of PTSD alone do not do justice to the unique experiences of those who suffer from living with PTSD, often for years, and with the chronic effects of terrible loss. Clearly, opportunities abound for future research that will increase our understanding of the biology and neuropsychology of PTSD at older ages, as well as for the advancement of evidence-based treatments that take into account the whole person at late life.

Notes

1. Lee Hyer, Professor of Psychiatry, Mercer School of Medicine, 840 Pine St, Suite 880, Macon GA, 31201
2. Catherine A. Yeager, Director, Telehealth Outreach Program, Essex County Hospital Center, Institute for Mental Health Policy, Research, and Treatment, 204 Grove Ave, Cedar Grove, NJ 07009

References

Acierno, R., Gray, M., Best, C., Resnick, H., Kilpatrick, D., Saunders, B., & Brady, K. (2001). Rape and physical violence: Comparison of assault characteristics in older and younger adults in national women's study. *Journal of Traumatic Stress, 14*(4), 685–695.

Alexopoulos, G. S., Murphy, C. F., Gunning-Dixon, F. M., Kalayam, B., Katz, R., Kanellopoulos, D., et al. (2007). Event-related potentials in an emotional go/no-go task and remission of geriatric depression. *Cognitive Neuroscience and Neuropsychology, 18*(3), 217–221.

American Psychiatric Association. (2000). *Diagnostic and Statistical Manual-IV-TR.* Washington, D.C: American Psychiatric Association.

Arean, P. (1993). Cognitive behavioral therapy with older adults. *The Behavior Therapist, 16*, 236–239.

Arch, J. J., & Craske, M. G. (2008). Acceptance and commitment therapy and cognitive behavioral therapy for anxiety disorders: Different treatments, similar mechanisms? *Clinical Psychology: Science and Practice, 15*(4), 263–279.

Arch, J. J., & Craske, M. G. (2009). First-line treatment: A critical appraisal of cognitive behavioral therapy developments and alternatives. *Psychiatric Clinics of North America, 32*(3), 525–547.

Averill, P. M., & Beck, J. G. (2000). Posttraumatic stress disorder in older adults: A conceptual review. *Journal of Anxiety Disorders, 14*(2), 133–156.

Ayers, C. R., Sorrell, J. T., Thorp, S. R., & Wetherell, J. L. (2007). Evidence-based psychological treatments for late-life anxiety. *Psychology and Aging, 22*, 8–17.

Beckham, J. C., Crawford, A. L., & Feldman, M.E. (1998). Trail Making Test performance in Vietnam combat veterans with and without posttraumatic stress disorder. *Journal of Traumatic Stress, 11*, 811–819.

Bellack, A. S. (2004). Skills training for people with severe mental illness. *Psychiatric Rehabilitation Journal, 27*(4), 375–391.

Blanchard, E. B., & Hickling, E. J. (1997). *After the crash: Assessment and treatment of motor vehicle accident survivors.* Washington, D.C: American Psychological Association.

Boehnlein, J. & Sparr, L. (1993).Group therapy with World War II ex-POWs: Longterm adjustment in a geriatric population. *American Journal of Psychotherapy, 47*, 273–282.

Bradley, R., Greene, J., Russ, E., et al. (2005). A multidimensional meta-analysis of psychotherapy for PTSD. *American Journal of Psychiatry*, 162, 214.

Bremner, J. D., Southwick, S. M., Johnson, D. R., Yehuda, R., & Charney, D. S. (1993). Childhood physical abuse and combat-related posttraumatic stress disorder in Vietnam veterans. *American Journal of Psychiatry, 150*(2), 235–239.

Breslau, N., Davis, G. C., Andreski, P., & Peterson, E. (1991). Traumatic events and posttraumatic stress disorder in an urban population of young adults. *Archives of General Psychiatry, 48*(3), 216–222.

Brewin, C. R., Andrews, B., & Valentine, J. D. (2000). Meta-analysis of risk factors for posttraumatic stress disorder in trauma-exposed adults. *Journal of Consulting and Clinical Psychology, 68*(5), 748–766.

Broman-Fulks, J. J., Ruggiero, K. J., Green, B. A., Kilpatrick, D. G., Danielson, C. K., Resnick, H. S., et al. (2006). Taxometric investigation of PTSD: Data from two nationally representative samples. *Behavior Therapy, 37*(4), 364–380.

Brown, A. W., Leibson, C. L., Malec, J. F., Perkins, P. K., Diehl, N. N., & Larson, D. R. (2004). Long-term survival after traumatic brain injury: A population-based population base analysis. *NeuroRehabilitation, 19*(1), 37–43.

Bryant, R. A., Felmingham, K., Whitford, T. J., Kemp, A., Hughes, G., Peduto, A., et al. (2008). Rostral anterior cingulated volume predicts treatment response to cognitive-behavioural therapy for posttraumatic stress disorder. *Journal of Psychiatry and Neuroscience, 33*(2), 142–146.

Burns, D. D., & Spangler, D. L. (2001). Do changes in dysfunctional attitudes mediate changes in depression and anxiety in cognitive behavioral therapy? *Behavior Therapy, 32*(2), 337–369.

Byers, A. L., Yaffe, K., Covinsky, K. E., Friedman, M. B., & Bruce, M. L. (2010). High occurrence of mood and anxiety disorders among older adults: The National Comorbidity Replication. *Archives of General Psychiatry, 67*(5), 489–496.

Cappeliez, P. & O'Rourke, N. (2006). Empirical validation of a model of reminiscence and health at later life. *Journal of Gerontology, 61B*(4), 237–244.

Carstensen, L. L., Fung, H. H., & Charles, S. T. (2003). Socioemotional selectivity theory and the regulation of emotion in the second half of life. *Motivation and Emotion, 27*(2), 103–123.

Cohen, J. A., Mannarino, A. P., & Staron, V. R. (2006). A pilot study of modified cognitive-behavioral therapy for childhood grief (CBT-CTG). *Journal of the American Academy of Child and Adolescent Psychiatry, 45*(12), 1465–1473.

Cook, J., Ruzek, J. I., & Cassidy, E. (2003). Practical geriatrics: Possible association of posttraumatic stress disorder with cognitive impairment among older adults. *Psychiatric Services, 54*, 1223–1225.

Cook, J., O'Donnell, C., Moltzen, J., Ruzek, J., & Sheikh, J. (2005). Clinical observations in the treatment of World War II and Korean War veterans with combat-related PTSD. *Clinical Geropsychologist, 29*(2), 82–94.

Cornelius, T. L., & Kenyon-Jump, R. (2007). Application of cognitive-behavioral treatment for long-standing posttraumatic stress disorder in law enforcement personnel. *Clinical Case Studies, 6*(2), 143–160.

Cortese, B. M., & Phan, K. L. (2005). The role of glutamate in anxiety and related disorders. *CNS Spectrums, 11*(1), 14–15.

Creamer, M., & Parslow, R. (2008). Trauma exposure and posttraumatic stress disorder in the elderly: A community prevalence study. *American Journal of Geriatric Psychiatry, 16*(10), 853–856.

D'Zurilla, T., & Nezu, A. M. (2001). *Problem-solving therapy: A positive approach to clinical intervention.* New York: Springer Publishing.

Davidson, J. R., Hughes, D., Blazer, D. G., & George, L. (1991). PTSD in the community: an epidemiological study. *Psychological Medicine, 21*(3), 713–721.

Dickie, E. W., Brunet, A., Akerib, V., & Armony, J. L. (2008). An fMRI investigation of memory encoding in PTSD: Influence of symptom severity. *Neuropsychologia, 46*(5), 1522–1531.

Dohrenwend, B. S., & Dohrenwend, B. P. (1981). *Stressful life events and their contexts.* New Brunswick, NJ: Rutgers University Press.

Ehring, T., Ehlers, A., & Glucksman, E. (2008). Do cognitive models help in predicting the severity of posttraumatic stress disorder, phobia, and depression after motor vehicle accidents? A prospective longitudinal study. *Journal of Consulting and Clinical Psychology, 76*(2), 219–230.

Elzinger, B. M., & Bremner, J. D. (2002) Are the neural substrates of memory the final common pathway in posttraumatic stress disorder (PTSD)? *Journal of Affective Disorders, 70*, 1–17.

Emery, L., Hale, S., & Myerson, J. (2008). Age differences in proactive interference, working memory, and abstract reasoning. *Psychology and Aging, 23*(3), 634–645.

Etkim, A., Prater, K. E., Hoeft, F., Menon, V., & Schatzberg, A. F. (2010). Failure of Anterior cingulate activation and connectivity with the amygdala during implicit regulation of emotional processing in Generalized Anxiety Disorder. *American Journal of Psychiatry, 167*(5), 545–554.

Falsetti, S. A., Erwin, B. A., Resnick, H. S., Davis, J. & Combs-Lane, A. M. (2003). Multiple channel exposure therapy of PTSD: Impact of treatment on functioning and resources. *Behavior Modification, 29*(1), 70–94.

Foa, E. B., Tolin, D. F., Ehlers, A., Clark, D. M., & Orsillo, S. M. (1999). The Posttraumatic Cognitions Inventory (PTCI): Development and validation. *Psychological Assessment, 11*(3), 303–314.

Foa, EB, Keane, TM, Friedman, MJ, International Society for Traumatic Stress Studies (2000). *Effective treatments for PTSD: Practice guidelines from the International Society for Traumatic Stress Studies.* New York, NY: Guilford Press.

Frish, M. B. (2006). Quality of life therapy and assessment in health care. Clinical Psychology: *Science and Practice, 5*(1), 19–40.

Frueh, C., Elhai, J, Gold, P., Monnier, J., Magruder, K., Keane, T.& Arana, G. (2003). Disability compensation seeking among veterans evaluated for posttraumatic stress disorder. *Psychiatric Services, 54*, 84–91.

Frueh, B. C., Monnier, J., Yim, E., Grubaugh, A. L., Hamner, M. B., & Knapp, R. G. (2007). A randomized trial of telepsychiatry for post-traumatic stress disorder. *Journal of Telemedicine and Telecare, 13*(3), 142–147.

Gerson, S., Belin, T. R., Kaufman, A., Mintz, J., & Jarvik, L. (1999). Pharmacological and psychological treatments for depressed older patients: A meta-analysis and overview of recent findings. *Harvard Review of Psychiatry, 7*(1), 1–28.

Gibbs, M. S. (1989). Factors in the victim that mediate between disaster andpsychopathology: A review. *Journal of Traumatic Stress, 2*(4), 489–514.

Gleser, G. C., Green, B., & Winglet, C. (1981). *Prolonged psychosocial effects of disaster: A study of Buffalo Creek.* New York: Academic Press.

Gold, S. D., Marx, B. P., Soler-Baillo, J. M., & Sloan, D. M. (2005). Is life stress more traumatic than traumatic stress? *Journal of Anxiety Disorders, 19*(6), 687–698.

Grossman, A. B., Levin, B. E., Katzen, H. L., & Lechner, S. (2004). PTSD symptoms and onset of neurologic disease in elderly trauma survivors. *Journal of Clinical & Experimental Neuropsychology, 26*(5), 698–706.

Haight, B. K., Michel, Y., & Hendrix, S. (2000). The extended effects of the life review in nursing home residents. *The International Journal of Aging and Human Development, 50*(2), 151–168.

Hidalgo, R. B., & Davidson, J. R. (2000). Posttraumatic stress disorder: Epidemiology and health-related considerations. *Journal of Clinical Psychiatry, 61*, 5–13.

Hobfoll, S. E., Tracy, M., & Galea, S. (2006). The impact of resource loss and traumatic growth on probable PTSD and depression following terrorist attacks. *Journal of Traumatic Stress, 19*(6), 867–878.

Horvath AO, Greenberg LS (1989). Development and validation of the Working Alliance Inventory. *Journal of Counseling Psychology, 36*, 223–233.

Hyer, L. & Kushner, B. (2007). EMDR: A Review. In P. Lehrer & R. Wolfolk (Eds). *Handbook of stress* (2nd ed.). New York: Guilford Press

Hyer, L., Swanson, G. & Lefkowitz, R. (1990). Cognitive schema model with stress groups at later life. *Clinical Gerontologist. Special Issue: Group Therapy in Nursing Homes, 9*(3), 145–190.

Hyer, L. & Stanger, E. (1997). The interaction of Posttraumatic Stress Disorder and depression among older combat veterans. *Psychological Reports, 80*, 785–786.

Hyer, L. and Sohnle, S (2001). *Trauma among older people: Issues and treatment.* Philadelphia: Brunner-Routledge.

Institute of Medicine (2008). *Treatment of posttraumatic stress disorder: an assessment of the evidence.* Washington, DC: National Academies Press, http://www.nap.edu/catalog/11955.html

Kangas, M., Henry, J. L., & Bryant, R. A. (2005). The course of psyhological disorders in the 1st year after cancer diagnosis. *Journal of Consulting and Clinical Psychology, 73*(4), 763–768.

Kessler, R., Sonnega, A., Bromet, E., Hughes, M.,& Nelson, C. (1995). Posttraumatic stress disorder in the National Comorbidity Survey. *Archives of General Psychiatry*, 52, 1048–1060.

Kremen, W. S.., Koenen, K. C., Boake, C., et al. (2007). Pretrauma cognitive ability and risk for posttraumatic stress disorder. *Archives of General Psychiatry, 64*, 361–368.

Ladouceur, R., Leger, E., Dugas, M., & Freeston, M. H. (2004). Cognitive-behavioral treatment of Generalized Anxiety Disorder (GAD) for older adults. *International Psychogeriatrics, 16*(2), 195–207.

Lee, C. W., & Schubert, S. (2009). Omissions and errors in the Institute of Medicine's report on scientific evidence of treatment for posttraumatic stress disorder. *Journal of EMDR Practice and Research, 3*(1), 32–38.

Lenze, E. H., Mulsant, B. H., Mohlman, J., Shear, M. K., Dew, M. A., Schulz, R., et al. (2005). Generalized anxiety disorder in late life: Lifetime course and comorbidity with major depressive disorder. *American Journal of Geriatric Psychiatry*, 13(1), 77–80.

Lewis, M. I., & Butler, R. N. (1974). Life-review therapy: Putting memories to work in individual and group psychotherapy. *Geriatrics, 29*(11), 165–173.

Lipton, M. & Schaffer, W. (1986). Posttraumatic stress disorder in the older veteran. *Military Medicine, 151*, 522–524.

Longmore, RJ, Worrell, M (2007). Do we need to challenge thoughts in cognitive behavioral therapy? *Clinical Psychology Review, 27*, 173–187.

Lyons, J. A. (1991). Strategies for assessing the potential for positive adjustment following trauma. *Journal of Traumatic Stress, 4*(1), 93–111.

Ma, S. H., & Teasdale, J. D. (2004). Mindfulness-based cognitive therapy for depression: Replication and exploration of differential relapse prevention effects. *Journal of Consulting and Clinical Psychology, 72*(1), 31–40.

Macklin, R. S., & Arean, P. A. (2005). Evidence-based psychotherapeutic interventions for geriatric depression. *Psychiatric Clinics of North America, 28*, 805–820.

Markowitz, J. D. (2007). Post-traumatic stress disorder in an elderly combat veteran: A case report. *Military Medicine, 172*(6), 659–662.

Mather, M., & Knight, M. (2005). Goal-directed memory: the role of cognitive control in older adults' emotional memory. *Psychology and Aging, 20*(4), 554–570.

Mayou, R., Bryant, B., & Duthie, R. (1993). Psychiatric consequences of road traffic accidents. *British Medical Journal, 307*(6905), 647–651.

McCartney, J. R., & Severson, K. (1997). Sexual violence, posttraumatic stress disorder, and dementia. *Journal of the American Geriatrics Society, 45*(1), 76–78.

McDaniel, M. A., Lyle, K. B., Butler, K. M., & Dornburg, C. C. (2008). Age-related deficits in reality monitoring of action memories. *Psychology and Aging, 23*(3), 646–656.

Mohlman, J. (2008). More power to the executive? A preliminary test of CBT plus executive skills training for treatment of late-life GAD. *Cognitive and Behavioral Practice, 15*, 306–316.

Molinari, V. & Williams, W. (1995). An analysis of aging World war II POWs with PTSD: Implication for practice and research. *Journal of Geriatric Psychiatry, 28*, 99–114.

Monroe, S. M., & Harkness, K. L. (2005). Life stress, the "kindling" hypothesis, and the recurrence of depression: Considerations from a life stress perspective. *Psychological Review, 112*(2), 417–445.

Morse, D. R., Martin, J., & Moshonov, J. (1992). Stress induced sudden cardiac death: Can it be prevented? *Stress Medicine, 8*(1), 35–46.

Mueser, K. (2006). Cognitive-Behavioral Treatment of PTSD in Severe Mental Illness: Pilot Study in an Ethnically Diverse Population. NIMH Grant.

Neria, Y., & Litz, B. T. (2004). Bereavement by traumatic means: The complex synergy of trauma and grief. *Journal of Loss and Trauma, 9*(1), 73–87.

Newman, M. G., Castonguay, L. G., Borkovec, T. D., & Molnar, C. (2004). Integrative psychotherapy. In R. G. Heimberg, C. L. Turk, & D. S. Mennin (Eds.), *Generalized anxiety disorder: Advances in research and practice* (pp. 320–350). New York: Guilford Press.

Newton, K. (2001). Geriatric trauma. *Advanced Emergency Nursing Journal, 23*(3), 1–12.

Norris, F. H. (1992). Epidemiology of trauma: frequency and impact of different potentially traumatic events on difficult demographic groups. *Journal of Consulting Clinical Psychology, 60*(3), 409–418.

Norris, F. H., Friedmna, M. J., Watson, P. J., Byrne, C. M., Diaz, E., & Kaniasty, K. (2002). 60,000 disaster victims speak: Part I. An empirical review of the empirical literature, 1981–2001. *Psychiatry: Interpersonal and Biological Processes, 65*(3), 207–239.

Norton, P. J., & Price, E. C. (2007). A meta-analytic review of adult cognitive-behavioral treatment outcome across the anxiety disorders. *The Journal of Nervous and Mental Disease, 195*(6), 521–531.

Ozer, E. J., Best, S. R., Lipsey, T. L., & Weiss, D. S. (2003). Predictors of posttraumatic stress disorder and symptoms in adults: A meta-analysis. *Psychological Bulletin, 129*(1), 52–73.

Parslow, R. A., & Jorm, A. F. (2007). Pre-trauma and post-trauma neurocognitive functioning and PTSD symptoms in a community sample of young adults. *American Journal of Psychiatry, 164*, 509–515.

Pearlin, L. I. (2010). The life course and the stress process: Some conceptual comparisons. *The Journals of Gerontology. Series B, Psychological Sciences and Social Sciences, 65B*(2), 207–215.

Pennebaker, J. W. (1989). Confession, inhibition, and disease. In L. Berkowitz (Ed.), *Advances in experimental social psychology*, Vol. 22 (pp. 211–244). Orlando, F. L.: Academic Press.

Pervanidou, P. (2008). Biology of post-traumatic stress disorder in childhood and adolescence. *Journal of Neuroendocrinology, 20*(5), 632–638.

Phifer, J. F., & Norris, F. H. (1989). Psychological symptoms in older adults followingnatural disaster: Nature, timing, duration, and course. *Journal of Gerontology, 44*(6), S207–217.

Phifer, J. F. (1990). Psychological distress and somatic symptoms after natural disaster: Differential vulnerability among older adults. *Psychology and Aging, 5*, 412–420.

Pinquart, M., & Duberstein, P. R. (2007). Treatment of anxiety disorders in older adults: A meta-analytic comparison of behavioral and pharmacological interventions. *American Journal of Geriatric Psychiatry, 15*(8), 639–651.

Post, R. M. (1992). Transduction of psychosocial stress into the neurobiology of recurrent affective disorder. *American Journal of Psychiatry, 149*, 999–1010.

Prigerson, H. G., Shear, M. K., Jacobs, S. C., Reynolds III, C. F., Maciejewski, P. K., Davidson, J. R., et al. (1999). Consensus criteria for traumatic grief. A preliminary empirical test. *British Journal of Psychiatry, 174*, 67–73.

Reed, A. E., Mikels, J. A., & Simon, K. I. (2008). Older adults prefer less choice than young adults. *Psychology and Aging, 23*(3), 671–675.

Resick, P. A. (2003). Cognitive therapy for posttraumatic stress disorder. *Journal of Cognitive Psychotherapy, 15*(4), 321–330.

Reynolds, C., Miller, M., Pasternak, R. et al. (1999). Treament of bereavement-related major depressive episodes in later life: A controlled study of acute and continuation treatment with nortriptyline and interpersonal psychotherpay. *American Journal of Psychiatry, 156*, 202–208.

Robertson, M., Rushton, P., Batrim, D., Moore, E., & Morris, P. (2007). Open trial of interpersonal psychotherapy for chronic post traumatic stress disorder. *Australasian Psychiatry, 15*(5), 375–379.

Roediger, H.L. & Geraci, L. (2007). Aging and the misinformation effect: A neuropsychological analysis. *Journal of Experimental Psychology: Learning, Memory & Cognition, 33*, 321–334.

Russo, S. A., Hersen, M., & van Hasselt, V. B. (2001). Treatment of reactivated post-traumatic stress disorder: Imaginal exposure in an older adult with multiple traumas. *Behavior Modification, 25*(1), 94–115.

Rygh, J. L., & Sanderson, W. C. (2004). *Treating generalized anxiety disorder: Evidence-based strategies, tools, and techniques.* New York: Guilford Press.

Sakauye, K. M., Streim, J. E., Kennedy, G. J., Kirwin, P. D., Llorente, M. D., Schultz, S. K., Srinivasan, S. (2009). AAGP Position Statement: Disaster Preparedness for Older Americans: Critical Issues for the Preservation of Mental Health. *American Journal of Geriatric Psychiatry, 17*, 916–924.

Sareen, J., Cox, B. J., Stein, M. B., Afifi, T. O., Fleet, C., Asmundson, G.J. (2007). Physical and mental comorbidity, disability, and suicidal behavior associated with posttraumatic stress disorder in a large community sample. *Psychosomatic Medicine, 69*, 242–248.

Schnurr, P., & Spiro, A. (1999). Combat Exposure, Posttraumatic Stress Disorder Symptoms, and Health Behaviors as Predictors of Self-Reported Physical Health in Older Veterans. *Journal of Nervous & Mental Disease, 187*(6), 353–359.

Schnurr, P. P., Friedman, M. J., & Bernardy, N. C. (2002). Research on posttraumatic stress disorder: Epidemiology, pathophysiology, and assessment. *Journal of Clinical Psychology, 58*(8), 877–889.

Schuurmans, J., Comjis, H., Emmelkamp, P. M., Gundy, C. M., Weijnen, I., van den Hout, M., et al. (2006). A randomized, controlled trial of the effectiveness of cognitive-behavioral therapy and sertraline versus a waitlist control group for anxiety disorders in older adults. *American Journal of Geriatric Psychiatry, 14*(3), 255–263.

Scogin, F., Rickard, H.C., Keith, S., Wilson, J., & McElreath, L. (1992). Progressive and imaginal relaxation training for elderly persons with subjective anxiety. *Psychology and Aging, 7*, 419–424.

Segal Z.V., Williams J.M.G., & Teasdale J.D. (2002). *Mindfulness based cognitive behavioral therapy.* New York: Guilford Press.

Seligman, M. E. P. (2002). Positive psychology, positive prevention, and positive therapy. In C. R. Snyder & S. J. Lopez (Eds.): *Handbook of Positive Psychology* (pp. 1–7). New York: Oxford University Press.

Shalev, A. Y. (2009). Posttraumatic stress disorder and stress-related disorders. *Psychiatric Clinics of North America, 32*(3), 687–704.

Shin, L. M., Lasko, N. B., Macklin, M. L., Karpf, R. D., Milad, M. R., Orr, S. P., et al. (2009). Resting metabolic activity in the cingulate cortex and vulnerability to posttraumatic stress disorder. *Archives of Generala Psychiatry, 66*(10), 1099–1107.

Snell, F. I., & Padin-Rivera, E. (1997). Group treatment for older veterans with post-traumatic stress disorder. *Journal of Psychosocial Nursing and Mental Health Services, 35*,10–16.

Spiro, R., Schnurr, P., Aldwin, C. (1994). Combat related post-traumatic stress disorder symptoms in older men. *Psychology and Aging, 9*, 17–26.

Stanley, M., Hopko, D., Diefenbacj, G., Bourland, S., Rodriquez, G., & Wagener, P. (2003). Cognitive behavioral therapy for late life generalized anxiety disorder in primary care: Preliminary findings. *American Journal of Geriatric Psychiatry, 11*, 92–97.

Steffens, D., Otey, E., Alexopoulos, G., et al. (2006). Perspectives on depression, mild cognitive impairment, and cognitive decline. *Archives of General Psychiatry, 63*, 130–136.

Strawn, J. R., & Geracioti, T. D. (2008). Noradrenergic dysfunction and the psychopharmacology of posttraumatic stress disorder. *Depression and Anxiety, 25*(3), 260–271.

Sutker, P. B., Uddo-Carne, M., & Allain, A. N. (1991a). Clinical and research assessment of posttraumatic stress disorder: A conceptual framework. *Psychological Assessment, 3*, 520–530.

Sutker, P. B., Winstead, D. K., Galina, Z. H., & Allain, A. N. (1991b). Cognitive deficits and psychopathology among former prisoners of war and combat veterans of the Korean conflict. *American Journal of Psychiatry, 148*(1), 67–72.

Taber, K. H., & Hurley, R. A. (2009). PTSD and combat-related injuries: Functional neuroanatomy. *The Journal of Neuropsychiatry and Clinical Neurosciences, 21*(1), 1–4.

Thompson, L.W., Gallagher, D., Hanser, S., Gantz, F., & Steffen, A. (1991). Comparison of desipramine and cognitive/behavioral therapy in the treatment of late-life depression. Paper presented at the meeting of Gerontological Society of America, San Francisco.

Thorp, S. R., & Stein, M. B. (2005). Posttraumatic stress disorder and functioning. *PTSD Research Quarterly, 16*, 1–7.

Thorp, S. R., Ayers, C. R., Nuevo, R., Stoddard, J. A., Sorrell, J. T., & Wetherell, J. T. (2009). Meta-analysis comparing different behavioral treatments for late-life nxiety. *American Journal of Geriatric Psychiatry, 17*(2), 105–115.

Timiras, PS, Gersten, O (2007). The adrenals and pituitary – stress, adaptation, and longevity. In: PS Timiras (Ed.), *Physiological Basis of Aging and Geriatrics*, 4th Ed, (pp. 137–158). NY: Informa Healthcare.

Van Zelst, W. H., de Beurs, E., Beekman, A. T., Deeg, D. J., Bramsen, I., & van Dyck, R. (2003). Criterion validity of the self-rating inventory for posttraumatic stress disorder (SRIP) in the community of older adults. *Journal of Affective Disorders, 76*(1–3), 229–235.

Vasterling, J. J., Brailey, K., Constans, J. I., Borges, A., & Sutker, P. B. (1997) Assesment of intellectual resources in Gulf War veterans: Relationship to PTSD. *Assessment, 4*, 51–59.

Vasterling, J. J., Duke, L. M., Brailey, K., Constans, J. I., Allain, A. N., Jr., & Sutker, P. B. (2002). Attention, learning, and memory performances and intellectual resources in Vietnam veterans: PTSD and no disorder comparisons. *Neuropsychology, 16*, 5–14.

Weissman, MM, Markowitz JC, Klerman GL (2007). *Clinician's quick guide to interpersonal psychotherapy*. New York: Oxford University Press

Wells, A. (1997). *Cognitive therapy of anxiety disorders: A practice manual and conceptual guide*. Chichester, UK: Wiley.

Wetherell, J. L., Gatz, M., & Craske, M. G. (2003). Treatment of generalized anxiety disorder in older adults. *Journal of Consulting and Clinical Psychology, 71*(1), 31–40.

Wetherell, J. L., Lenze, E. J., & Stanley, M. A. (2005). Evidence-based treatment ofgeriatric anxiety disorders. *Psychiatric Clinics of North America, 28*(4),871–896.

Wetherell, J. L., & Lenze, E. J. (2008). Bringing the bedside to the bench, and then to the community: A prospectus for intervention research in late-life anxiety disorders. *International Journal of Geriatric Psychiatry, 24*(1), 1–14.

Williams, J. M., Barnhofer, T., Crane, C., Herman, D., Raes, F., Watkins, E., et al. (2007). Autobiographical memory specificity and emotional disorder. *Psychological Bulletin, 133*(1), 122–148.

Woods, B., Spector, A., Jones, C., Orrell, M., & Davies, S. (2005). Reminiscence therapy for dementia. *Cochrane Database of Systematic Reviews, 18*(2), CD001120.

Yaffe, K, Vittinghoff, E, Lindquist, K, Barnes, D, Covinsky, KE; Neylan, T, Kluse, M, Marmar, C (2010). Posttraumatic Stress Disorder and Risk of Dementia Among US Veterans *Archives of General Psychiatry, 67*(6):608–613.

Zatzick, D. F., Rivara, F. P., Nathens, A. B., Jurkovich, G. J., Wang, J., Fan, M. Y., et al. (2007). A nationwide US study of posttraumatic stress after hospitalization for physical injury. *Psychological Medicine, 37*(10), 1469–1480.

CHAPTER

35 Treating Trauma-related Symptoms in Special Populations

Devon E. Hinton *and* Angela Nickerson

Abstract

Though there is much research on the treatment of posttraumatic psychological reactions in survivors of civilian trauma, there is much less empirical evidence to drive interventions with survivors of other kinds of trauma, including persecution, torture, and sexual abuse, particularly in other cultural groups. This chapter illustrates some of the factors that should be taken into consideration when treating such populations. The chapter is divided into sections that address key issues relevant to special populations of trauma survivors: type of trauma, current stressors, comorbidity, anger, cultural issues such as culturally specific interpretations of trauma-related symptoms, and bereavement. We examine the implications for the treatment of refugees and asylum seekers of these issues. As this chapter indicates, the treatment of traumatic distress in special populations warrants more research to ensure that the optimal psychological interventions are available to such highly traumatized groups.

Key Words: Trauma, special populations, refugees, culture, asylum seekers, posttraumatic stress disorder, PTSD

Introduction

Evidence for the treatment of trauma-related symptoms following civilian trauma is well established. Randomized controlled trials undertaken with survivors of motor vehicle accidents (Blanchard, et al., 2003; Fecteau & Nicki, 1999; Holzapfel, Blanchard, Hickling, & Malta, 2005), assault (Bryant, 2000; Resick, et al., 2008), and rape (Foa, Rothbaum, Riggs, & Murdock, 1991; Resick, Nishith, Weaver, Astin, & Feuer, 2002; Resick & Schnicke, 1992) suggest that cognitive behavior therapy is the optimal treatment for posttraumatic stress disorder (PTSD). This consensus is reflected internationally in clinical guidelines for the treatment of PTSD (Australian Centre for Posttraumatic Mental Health, 2007; International Society for Traumatic Stress Studies Treatment Guidelines [ISTSS], 2009; UK National Institute of Clinical Excellence, 2005). Although much research evidence exists to guide the treatment for survivors of discrete civilian trauma, relatively less is known about the factors influencing treatment in other highly traumatized groups. This chapter will outline some of the considerations in treating special populations with PTSD, with a specific emphasis on the treatment of refugees and asylum seekers.

The Type and Degree of Trauma

Exposure to traumatic events is not equally distributed and may differ across societies, countries, cultures, and other groups. Research evidence suggests that, for example, individuals living in wartorn settings are more likely to experience multiple traumatic events than those residing in peaceful contexts (Porter & Haslam, 2005). Other groups who are often exposed to numerous or prolonged traumatic events include emergency service workers (Regehr & Bober, 2005), victims of childhood sexual abuse

(Cloitre, Cohen, & Koenen, 2006), and torture survivors (Basoglu, et al., 1994). With the exception of research with combat veterans, studies have tended to focus on the phenomenology and treatment of the psychological impact of discrete civilian trauma. However, this type of trauma is likely to differ considerably from traumatic events experienced by other groups on a number of dimensions, including frequency, nature, duration, and psychological impact. This variation has significant implications for clinical interventions administered with survivors of different types of traumas, requiring current best-practice treatments to be adapted so as to be optimally beneficial for special populations.

Just as the frequency and duration of traumatic experiences may vary across groups, there also exist qualitative differences in types of traumatic events. For example, "accidental" civilian trauma such as motor vehicle accidents or natural disasters may differ significantly from the repeated, human-instigated trauma that is experienced by torture survivors, prisoners of war, refugees, and victims of childhood sexual abuse. Exposure to this kind of trauma, which is also known as "complex trauma" (Cohen & Hien, 2006; Ford & Courtois, 2009) or "Type II trauma" (Terr, 1991), may give rise to a more complex symptom pattern compared to that seen following other types of traumatic events (Herman, 1992). Diagnostic categories such as Enduring Personality Change After Catastrophic Experience (World Health Organization [WHO], 1992) and the *DSM-IV* construct of Disorders of Extreme Stress Not Otherwise Specified (DESNOS; de Jong, Komproe, Spinazzola, van der Kolk, & van Ommeren, 2005; Roth, Newman, Pelcovitz, van der Kolk, & Mandel, 1997) have been developed to conceptualize the symptom profile often seen among survivors of extreme trauma (Dor-Shav, 1978; Marsella, Friedman, Gerrity, & Scurfield, 1996; Miller, Kulkarni, & Kushner, 2006; Weine, Becker, et al., 1998). Such diagnoses were developed to describe aspects of this symptomatology not adequately addressed by PTSD and commonly seen in individuals who had experienced chronic interpersonal trauma early in life, as well as survivors of repeated or prolonged human-instigated trauma such as torture and concentration camp experiences (Beltran & Silove, 1999; van der Kolk, Roth, Pelcovitz, Sunday, & Spinazzola, 2005).

In these highly traumatized groups, certain symptoms are particularly salient that may not be adequately treated by standard psychological interventions. These symptoms include anger, emotion dysregulation, self-harm, and maladaptive schemata. To give one example of how the clinical presentation of such special populations may impact psychological treatment, exposure therapy—a key component of CBT for PTSD—requires the patient to repeatedly relive the memory of the traumatic event as if it is happening in the present. This treatment strategy is thus initially highly distressing for the trauma survivor and requires adequate emotion regulation skills to manage the associated distress. Exposure therapy may be contra-indicated for patients without such skills (e.g., patients with suicidal behavior or explosive anger) because the patient may be unable to tolerate it, resulting in a worsening rather than an improvement, or in dropout from treatment (Kilpatrick & Best, 1984; Pitman, Orr, Altman, & Longpre, 1991).

In an attempt to overcome these obstacles, phase-based treatment programs have been developed. These initially address emotion regulation difficulties in patients with PTSD, before moving on to exposure-based therapy. The STAIR/MPE (Skills Training in Affect and Interpersonal Relation and Modified Prolonged Exposure) treatment program has applied such a strategy with survivors of childhood sexual abuse, with a randomized controlled trial indicating that it was superior to a wait-list control group in both improving emotion regulation and reducing symptoms of PTSD and anger regulation (Cloitre, Koenen, Cohen, & Han, 2002). Further evidence that emotion dysregulation is related to PTSD treatment outcome can be drawn from a study undertaken with military veterans, which suggested that changes in emotion regulation were associated with decreases in symptoms of PTSD and depression (Price, Monson, Callahan, & Rodriguez, 2006). Findings from a study conducted with Cambodian refugees indicated that improvement in emotion-regulation ability mediated decreases in PTSD following CBT for PTSD and panic disorder (Hinton, Hofmann, Pollack, & Otto, 2009). Thus, preliminary evidence suggests that it may be effective to target emotion dysregulation prior to commencing exposure-based interventions with highly traumatized special populations. If patients are better able to manage the distress associated with trauma-focused therapies, this may reduce treatment attrition and increase tolerance of and participation in treatment strategies. It may also provide patients with a sense of mastery over their own emotions, which is of vital importance following the helplessness often experienced in the context of repeated trauma and complex trauma more generally.

Ongoing Stressors and Threats

Another key factor that requires attention when undertaking therapy with traumatized special populations is the extent to which the individual faces ongoing threat. Current treatments for PTSD assume that the traumatic event is in the past and that the patient is objectively safe in the present. Cognitive behavioral models of traumatic stress support the implementation of exposure and cognitive therapies to alleviate PTSD symptoms following a traumatic event (e.g., Ehlers & Clark, 2000; Foa, Steketee, & Rothbaum, 1989). As a result, CBT interventions focus on the processing of the traumatic memory and the reframing of maladaptive cognitions (often centering on the overestimation of continued threat). Although these techniques have a large evidence base with survivors of civilian trauma, many traumatized populations face the realistic prospect that the trauma will re-occur—for example, asylum seekers who may be repatriated, persons living in wartorn contexts or settings with high-frequency terrorist activity, military and emergency services personnel, and individuals in abusive relationships.

It is, therefore, necessary to consider the utility of standard CBT techniques with the particular patient. For example, treatment is often contraindicated in cases where the patient is in immediate danger (e.g., remaining in an ongoing domestic violence relationship), not least because securing safe circumstances should be prioritized over treating PTSD symptoms. However, recent research suggests that modified CBT may be efficacious when the prospect of future trauma is less immediate or certain—for example, with asylum seekers (Basoglu, Ekblad, Baarnhielm, & Livanou, 2004; Neuner et al., 2009) and individuals residing in refugee camps (Neuner, Schauer, Klaschik, Karunakara, & Elbert, 2004). In some cases, exposure therapy may be adapted to make it more relevant and/or tolerable for the population receiving the treatment. An example of such an adaptation would be to use a narrative approach (e.g., Neuner et al., 2004; Weine, Kulenovic, Pavkovic, & Gibbons, 1998) or emphasize emotion-regulation techniques that are made appropriate for the culture and context of the patient. In the latter instance, trauma exposure would be used as an opportunity to practice those emotion regulation techniques (e.g., Hinton et al., 2004, 2005; Hinton, Hofmann, Rivera, Otto, & Pollack, 2011). Similarly, it is important that cognitive therapists take into consideration the realistic risk in the situation of the particular client. Recent research in the area of relative risk appraisals has highlighted the potential value in helping the patient to be realistic about the threats and generating adaptive appraisals that optimize functioning (Marshall et al., 2007). Such adaptations facilitate the use of evidence-based therapies adjusted for the patient's individual circumstances.

There are other environmental stressors that must be taken into consideration when conducting treatment with traumatized special populations. Refugees and asylum seekers typically face the numerous resettlement stressors associated with undertaking the immigration application process, and finding lodging, employment, and financial support in a new country (Silove, Sinnerbrink, Field, Manicavasagar, & Steel, 1997). Furthermore, the separation from family members who remain in the country of origin or who are elsewhere displaced (Nickerson, Bryant, Steel, Silove, & Brooks, 2010), and the sense of loss of culture associated with fleeing one's homeland (Eisenbruch, 1991; Nickerson, Bryant, Brooks, Steel, & Silove, 2009) may be salient issues. In the case of military, police, and emergency services personnel, there are frequently organizational stressors surrounding traumatic events, especially when posttraumatic stress symptoms impact on the individual's work role or functioning (Carlier, Lamberts, & Gersons, 1997; Pflanz & Ogle, 2006). When there are salient contextual factors that may influence the trauma-related symptoms and treatment, it is important to prioritize the difficulties that are having the greatest impact on the individual. It may be useful to first resolve the most pressing resettlement issues in the case of refugees and asylum seekers prior to commencing psychotherapy (Grey & Young, 2008). Certain contextual factors may also be addressed concurrently with PTSD symptoms in treatment interventions. For example, assisting an emergency services worker to identify ways to manage organizational stress may have a positive impact on the course of treatment for PTSD.

Therapeutic Alliance

A key aspect of the treatment of highly traumatized groups is the development of a trusting therapeutic relationship. Research has suggested that the patient-therapist relationship is of key importance across disorders (Cloitre, Stovall-McClough,

Miranda, & Chemtob, 2004; Macneil, Hasty, Evans, Redich, & Berk, 2009; Norcross, 2002), however, this may be especially vital in the case of individuals who have been subjected to certain types of extreme or human-instigated trauma. Groups such as survivors of childhood sexual abuse, refugees, and prisoners of war may have experienced traumatic events that have significantly impaired their ability to trust others. In the context of a psychological intervention, this may be further exacerbated by the fact that the treating clinician is in a position of authority and may be perceived to be the gatekeeper to various resources, including benefits. Combined, these two factors may well serve as trauma cues for the patient, resulting in fear and possibly anger, and limiting therapeutic gains that may be achieved.

One example of a group with whom the establishment of a strong therapeutic alliance is of key importance is torture survivors. The psychological destruction of the individual is inherent in the goals of torture, with the victim often being forced to withstand unbearable pain, witness unspeakable acts, make impossible choices, or betray others (Silove, 1996). The individual is thus rendered utterly powerless and remains at the mercy of those people inflicting the torture. These experiences and their psychological sequelae have considerable implications for the treatment of torture survivors. The therapeutic environment may serve as a strong reminder of the torture experience—for example, by inadvertently replicating the interrogation process or the setting in which the torture occurred. Sensitivity to this possibility, and the avoidance of factors that are similar to the torture environment (e.g., an interrogative questioning style, a therapy room with no windows, or the presence of psychophysiology equipment) should be avoided as much as possible (McIvor & Turner, 1995). In this case, it is especially important to ensure that a strong, trusting therapeutic alliance is developed, particularly prior to the commencement of trauma-focused interventions such as exposure therapy. In many cases, it is useful to articulate to the patient that the current environment and context (e.g., in which a person is asking them questions) may be a trauma trigger, and to explain how the purpose of this encounter is totally opposite to the associated trauma event. Simple techniques such as asking the patient if he or she has questions or offering a cup of water help to increase the patient's sense of comfort and decrease the triggering of trauma recall. Also, it is important to maintain a gentle manner and to ideally know cultural norms of polite behavior in the cultural group in question.

Cultural Difference

The majority of evidence-based treatments targeting PTSD in trauma survivors have been developed in Western countries. As a large proportion of trauma and violence across the globe occurs outside the West, the Western-centric nature of these interventions may limit their applicability to other cultural groups. Research has suggested that the manner in which trauma-related distress and related symptoms are understood and expressed varies considerably across cultures (e.g., Hinton & Lewis-Fernández, 2010, 2011; Hinton & Otto, 2006). One example of a culturally specific experiencing of traumatic distress is the attribution of trauma-related symptoms—and anxiety symptoms more generally—to khyâl attacks among Cambodian refugees (Hinton, Pich, Marques, Nickerson, & Pollack, 2010). These attacks—and the PTSD symptoms and anxiety symptoms that are considered typical symptoms of the attacks—are thought to be caused by the disturbance of a windlike substance (khyâl), and are greatly feared by Cambodians, as they are believed to cause physiological distress or even death—primarily owing to the surge of khyâl and blood upward in the body. Fear of khyâl attacks results in high rates of panic attacks and panic disorder among traumatized Cambodian refugees. Many PTSD symptoms (e.g., startle responses) and trauma-related arousal symptoms (e.g., somatic symptoms induced by arousal) are catastrophically misinterpreted to indicate that a khyâl attack is occurring, which results in arousal and panic. The arousal and panic then triggers trauma associations. In this way, the cultural syndrome of khyâl attacks worsens PTSD and creates a vicious cycle of symptom escalation.

This example illustrates how the cultural context of the patient is of key importance in informing treatment. It is unlikely that a therapist who is using a standard CBT protocol, and is unaware of the relationship between khyâl attacks and PTSD symptoms, would effectively alleviate the patient's distress. It is therefore vital that interventions take into consideration cultural interpretations and beliefs. Ideally, treating therapists would have some knowledge of the patient's culture, and would work collaboratively with the patient to identify how symptoms are understood within this culture and how this interpretation relates to the patient's individual experience. Failing to do this may result in poor treatment compliance and limited outcomes (Hinton & Lewis-Fernández, 2010). Furthermore, one should be aware of the indigenous methods of healing that are often employed to address such symptoms and syndromes, whether this is through religious practice or types of traditional healing. To ensure that a treatment is relevant and appropriate, adaptation of treatment interventions should be undertaken in close consultation with religious and community leaders.

A related issue is the use of interpreters in treatment when the therapist is unable to meet the client's language needs. Although findings from a recent study have suggested that CBT is equally effective whether delivered in English or via an interpreter (d'Ardenne, Ruaro, Cestari, Fakhoury, & Priebe, 2007), theorists have suggested that the therapeutic relationship is altered by the presence of a third person in the therapy room (Miller, Martell, Pazdirek, Caruth, & Lopez, 2005; Westermeyer, 1990). Care must be taken when working with interpreters to optimize the potential beneficial impact of a member of the patient's language or cultural group on therapy. If the interpreter is from the same cultural background as the patient, he or she may have been exposed to traumatic experiences similar to those of the patient. There exists the possibility that interpreting therapy sessions that involve history taking or techniques such as exposure therapy may elicit strong emotional reactions in the interpreter. It is important for the interpreter to be familiar with the rationale for therapeutic strategies, and to have the opportunity to discuss the session with the therapist privately. Some services achieve this by meeting interpreters before and after each session to prime them regarding the therapeutic techniques and debrief regarding session content. In addition, many refugee communities are small and close-knit, which increases the likelihood of the interpreter's being known to the patient and may generate concerns about confidentiality. The patient may feel uncomfortable disclosing aspects of his or her personal history or engaging in therapeutic strategies in the presence of the interpreter. These concerns may become especially salient if the interpreter is from a different religious or ethnic group, particularly if this group played some role in the persecution or violence experienced by the patient's group. It is important that, during the screening process, the patient is asked about any preferences in terms of gender, religion, or ethnicity of the translator, and if such a translator is not available, the patient should be told that every attempt was made to meet this request. In addition, confidentiality (including its limits) should be explicitly addressed with both the patient and the interpreter prior to the commencement of therapy.

Comorbidity

As with many trauma survivors, comorbid diagnoses are common among refugees and asylum seekers, and concurrent diagnoses may be related to greater functional disability than PTSD alone (Mollica et al., 1999; Momartin, Silove, Manicavasagar, & Steel, 2004a). High rates of worry, generalized anxiety disorder, panic attacks, and panic disorder would be expected (Hinton, Hofmann, et al., 2008), and in those groups with a history of multiple traumas and ongoing threat and insecurity, comorbid anxiety disorders would be expected to be particularly elevated. Depression may also be an important comorbidity (Carlson & Rosser-Hogan, 1991; Gorst-Unsworth & Goldenberg, 1998; Hinton, Rasmussen, Nou, Pollack, & Good, 2009; Mollica et al., 1999; Momartin et al., 2004a).

As discussed above, research suggests that certain cultures may have particularly salient fears of anxiety symptoms that increase anxiety comorbidities (Hinton, Hofmann, et al., 2008). For example, cultural syndromes such as khyâl attacks among Cambodian refugees may lead to catastrophic cognitions about PTSD symptoms such as arousal that then increase anxiety and panic. More generally, highly traumatized refugees may have a tendency to worry, which is a form of hypervigilance, and to be hyperreactive to a wide range of events and mental states, which leads to frequent arousal and panic (Hinton, Rasmussen, et al., 2009). For these reasons, treatment of refugees and minorities should target comorbid anxiety disorders through techniques such as addressing catastrophic cognitions, interoceptive exposure to feared somatic symptoms, and emotion regulation techniques (Hinton, Hofmann, et al., 2011).

Anger

Another clinical issue that is frequently observed in refugees and asylum seekers, but has attracted little empirical research, is anger (Hinton, Hsia, Um, & Otto, 2003; Hinton, Rasmussen, et al., 2009; Momartin, Silove, Manicavasagar, & Steel, 2002; Stepakoff et al., 2006; Zarowsky, 2004). The high prevalence of anger is not surprising considering that injustice is inherent in refugee experiences such as persecution, trauma, torture, and forced displacement. Studies have indicated that anger, hatred, and the desire for revenge are common emotional responses to perceived impunity in groups that have been victim to human rights violations, and may be related to more severe posttraumatic stress reactions (Basoglu et al., 2005; Lopes Cardozo, Kaiser, Gotway, & Agini, 2003; Lopes Cardozo, Vergara, Agini, & Gotway, 2000). Thus, anger may be a salient clinical feature in the presentation of refugees and asylum seekers that must be taken into account in treatment interventions. As mentioned previously, the presence of extreme anger may be a contra-indication for exposure therapy; however, the implementation of a phase-based approach focusing on the regulation of anger responses prior to commencing trauma-focused treatment strategies may be useful. It is clear that there exists the need for much more research investigating the phenomenology and treatment of anger in refugees and asylum seekers.

Bereavement

As a result of the persecution they have endured, as well as the extreme hardship often faced in the country of origin and in refugee camps, many refugees have lost multiple family and friends. These losses may manifest in complicated grief reactions, an underexplored psychological reaction in refugees (Craig, Sossou, Schnak, & Essex, 2008; Momartin, Silove, Manicavasagar, & Steel, 2004b). Inability to perform culturally indicated rituals for the dead, compounded by culturally specific ideas that certain types of death cause the deceased to enter a state of purgatory or even harass the living, exacerbate these processes. When it is thought that the dead may be attacking the living or failing to provide the person with supernatural support, this may cause bereavement reactions to manifest in the form of fear, rather than of sadness (Hagengimana, Hinton, Bird, Pollack, & Pitman, 2003; Hinton, Hinton, et al., 2009). The culturally specific manifestation of grief is of key importance in informing any treatment intervention.

The refugee experience is also associated with multiple losses beyond the deaths of family and friends; for example, refugees may experience the loss of homeland, culture, identity, status, social support, and/or language. The concept of cultural bereavement has been proposed by Eisenbruch (1991) to encapsulate the psychological impact of these many losses on refugees, highlighting the limitations of Western mental health constructs in conceptualizing the refugee experience. It is important to recognize the potential effects of these losses when undertaking psychological treatment with refugees. A refugee who has fled his or her home country may have no stable home base, little financial assistance, no employment, and limited or no ability to communicate in the language of the host country. The refugee may have witnessed the murder of loved ones, be without social support, have suffered a loss of status in the new society, and be disconnected from his or her culture and religion. Treatment of this person is likely to differ significantly from that of a Western assault victim who, while having survived a life-altering trauma, returns to their familiar environment following the event. This analysis suggests various types of bereavement that should be considered in any clinical intervention. We propose the following typology of bereavement, which varies somewhat from that suggested by Eisenbruch (1991):

- Cultural bereavement (the loss of culture, such as ability to be involved in certain rituals or religious rites, the loss of language ability in the next generation)
- Social bereavement (the loss of social connections owing to distance and death)
- Person bereavement (unresolved grief after a death)
- Geographic bereavement (nostalgia for the food, climate, and places of origin)

Conclusion

This chapter has outlined a number of treatment considerations for interventions targeting trauma symptoms in special populations. Clinicians working with trauma survivors should be aware of the potential diversity of traumatic experiences and the variety of ways in which symptoms of traumatic stress can manifest. Although many of the issues discussed above are also applicable to survivors of civilian trauma (e.g., comorbidity, therapeutic alliance, impact of current life stressors, anger), it is especially important to take these into consideration when planning treatment interventions for special populations that bear the psychological scars of extreme trauma.

All the rubrics discussed in this review represent areas of future research. Here we highlight some areas that future research should address:

- To what extent does the construct of PTSD encapsulate the symptom profile of survivors of extreme trauma and how does this impact on treatment?

• How should standard best-practice treatments for PTSD be adapted for special populations such as refugees, asylum seekers, torture survivors, and survivors of childhood sexual abuse?

• Are treatment techniques such as exposure therapy in CBT useful for survivors of extreme trauma, and if so, do such treatments need to be delivered in a different manner (e.g., a phase-type treatment, first teaching emotion regulation techniques, or initially using mild exposure in the context of practicing emotion regulation techniques)?

• How important is therapeutic relationship for special populations compared to survivors of discrete civilian trauma?

• How does culture influence the experiencing, presentation, and treatment of trauma?

References

Australian Centre for Posttraumatic Mental Health (2007). *Australian Guidelines for the Treatment of Adults with Acute Stress Disorder and Posttrauamtic Stress Disorder.* Melbourne: Australian Centre for Posttraumatic Mental Health

Basoglu, M., Ekblad, S., Baarnhielm, S., & Livanou, M. (2004). Cognitive-behavioral treatment of tortured asylum seekers: A case study. *Journal of Anxiety Disorders, 18,* 357–369.

Basoglu, M., Livanou, M., Crnobaric, C., Franciskovic, T., Suljic, E., Duric, D., et al. (2005). Psychiatric and cognitive effects of war in former Yugoslavia: Association of lack of redress for trauma and posttraumatic stress reactions. *Journal of the American Medical Association, 294,* 580–590.

Basoglu, M., Paker, M., Paker, O., Ozmen, E., Marks, I., Incesu, C., et al. (1994). Psychological effects of torture: A comparison of tortured with non-tortured political activists in Turkey. *American Journal of Psychiatry, 151,* 76–81.

Beltran, R. O., & Silove, D. (1999). Expert opinions about the ICD-10 category of Enduring Personality Change After Catstrophic Experience. *Comprehensive Psychiatry, 40,* 396–403.

Blanchard, E. B., Hickling, E. J., Devineni, T., Veazey, C. H., Galovski, T. E., Mundy, E., et al. (2003). A controlled evaluation of cognitive behavioural therapy for posttraumatic stress in motor vehicle accident survivors. *Behavior Research and Therapy, 41,* 79–96.

Bryant, R. A. (2000). Cognitive behavioral therapy of violence-related posttraumatic stress disorder. *Aggression and Violent Behaviour, 5,* 79–97.

Carlier, I. V., Lamberts, R. D., & Gersons, B. P. (1997). Risk factors for posttraumatic stress symptomatology in police officers: A prospective analysis. *Journal of Nervous and Mental Disease, 185,* 498–506.

Carlson, E. B., & Rosser-Hogan, R. (1991). Trauma experiences, posttraumatic stress, dissociation, and depression in Cambodian refugees. *American Journal of Psychiatry, 148,* 1548–1551.

Cloitre, M., Cohen, L. R., & Koenen, K. C. (2006). *Treating survivors of childhood abuse: Psychotherapy for the interrupted life.* New York: Guilford.

Cloitre, M., Koenen, K. C., Cohen, L. R., & Han, H. (2002). Skills training in affective and interpersonal regulation followed by exposure: A phase-based treatment for PTSD related to childhood abuse. *Journal of Consulting and Clinical Psychology, 70,* 1067–1074.

Cloitre, M., Stovall-McClough, K. C., Miranda, R., & Chemtob, C. M. (2004). Therapeutic alliance, negative mood regulation, and treatment outcome in child abuse-related posttraumatic stress disorder. *Journal of Consulting and Clinical Psychology, 72,* 411–416.

Cohen, L. R., & Hien, D. A. (2006). Treatment outcomes for women with substance abuse and PTSD who have experienced complex trauma. *Psychiatric Services, 57,* 100–106.

Craig, C. D., Sossou, M. A., Schnak, M., & Essex, H. (2008). Complicated grief and its relationship to mental health and well-being among Bosnian refugees after resettlement in the United States: Implications for practice, policy and research. *Traumatology, 14,* 103–115.

d'Ardenne, P., Ruaro, L., Cestari, L., Fakhoury, W., & Priebe, S. (2007). Does interpreter-mediated CBT with traumatized refugee people work? A comparison of patient outcomes in East London. *Behavioural and Cognitive Psychotherapy, 35,* 293–301.

de Jong, J. T., Komproe, I. H., Spinazzola, J., van der Kolk, B. A., & van Ommeren, M. H. (2005). DESNOS in three postconflict settings: Assessing cross-cultural construct equivalence. *Journal of Traumatic Stress, 18,* 13–21.

Dor-Shav, N. K. (1978). On the long-range effects of concentration camp internment on Nazi victims: 25 years later. *Journal of Consulting and Clinical Psychology, 46,* 1–11.

Ehlers, A., & Clark, D. M. (2000). A cognitive model of posttraumatic stress disorder. *Behaviour Research and Therapy, 38,* 319–345.

Eisenbruch, M. (1991). From post-traumatic stress disorder to cultural bereavement: Diagnosis of Southeast Asian refugees. *Social Science and Medicine, 33,* 673–680.

Fecteau, G., & Nicki, R. (1999). Cognitive behavioural treatment of post traumatic stress disorder after motor vehicle accident. *Behavioural and Cognitive Psychotherapy, 27,* 201–214.

Foa, E. B., Rothbaum, B. O., Riggs, D. S., & Murdock, T. B. (1991). Treatment of posttraumatic stress disorder in rape victims: A comparison between cognitive-behavioral procedures and counseling. *Journal of Consulting and Clinical Psychology, 59,* 715–723.

Foa, E. B., Steketee, G., & Rothbaum, B. O. (1989). Behavioral/cognitive conceptualizations of post-traumatic stress disorder. *Behavior Therapy, 20,* 155–176.

Ford, J. D., & Courtois, C. A. (2009). Defining and understanding complex trauma and complex traumatic stress disorders. In C. A. Courtois & J. D. Ford (Eds.), *Treating complex traumatic stress disorders: An evidence-based guide* (pp. 13–30). New York: Guilford.

Gorst-Unsworth, C., & Goldenberg, E. (1998). Psychological sequelae of torture and organised violence suffered by refugees from Iraq. Trauma-related factors compared with social factors in exile. *British Journal of Psychiatry, 172,* 90–94.

Grey, N., & Young, K. (2008). Cognitive behaviour therapy with refugees and asylum seekers experiencing traumatic stress symptoms. *Behavioural and Cognitive Psychotherapy, 36,* 3–19.

Hagengimana, A., Hinton, D., Bird, B., Pollack, M., & Pitman, R. K. (2003). Somatic panic-attack equivalents in a community

sample of Rwandan widows who survived the 1994 genocide. *Psychiatry Research, 117*, 1–9.
Hauff, E., & Vaglum, P. (1994). Chronic posttraumatic stress disorder in Vietnamese refugees. A prospective community study of prevalence, course, psychopathology, and stressors. *Journal of Nervous and Mental Disease, 182*, 85–90.
Herman, J. L. (1992). Complex PTSD. *Journal of Traumatic Stress, 5*, 377–391.
Hinton, D. E., Ba, P., Peou, S., & Um, K. (2000). Panic disorder among Cambodian refugees attending a psychiatric clinic. Prevalence and subtypes. *General Hospital Psychiatry, 22*, 437–444.
Hinton, D., Chau, H., Nguyen, L., Nguyen, M., Pham, T., Quinn, S., et al. (2001). Panic disorder among Vietnamese refugees attending a psychiatric clinic: Prevalence and subtypes. *General Hospital Psychiatry, 23*, 337–344.
Hinton, D. E., Chean, D., Pich, V., Safren, S., Hofmann, S., & Pollack, M. (2005). A randomized controlled trial of cognitive-behavior therapy for Cambodian refugees with treatment-resistant PTSD and panic attacks: A cross-over design. *Journal of Traumatic Stress, 18*, 617–629.
Hinton, D. E., Hinton, A. L., Pich, V., Loeum, J. R., & Pollack, M. H. (2009). Nightmares among Cambodian refugees: The breaching of concentric ontological security. *Culture, Medicine and Psychiatry, 33*, 219–265.
Hinton, D. E., Hofmann, S. G., Pitman, R. K., Pollack, M. H., & Barlow, D. H. (2008). The panic attack–posttraumatic stress disorder model: Applicability to orthostatic panic among Cambodian refugees. *Cognitive Behaviour Therapy, 37*, 101–116.
Hinton, D. E., Hofmann, S. G., Pollack, M. H., & Otto, M. W. (2009). Mechanisms of efficacy of CBT for Cambodian refugees with PTSD: Improvement in emotion regulation and orthostatic blood pressure response. *CNS Neuroscience and Therapy, 15*, 255–263.
Hinton, D., Hsia, C., Um, K., & Otto, M. W. (2003). Anger-associated panic attacks in Cambodian refugees with PTSD; a multiple baseline examination of clinical data. *Behaviour Research and Therapy, 41*, 647–654.
Hinton, D. E., & Lewis-Fernández, R. (2010). Idioms of distress among trauma survivors: Subtypes and clinical utility. *Culture, Medicine and Psychiatry, 34*, 209–218.
Hinton D. E., & Lewis-Fernández, R. (2011). The cross-cultural validity of posttraumatic stress disorder: Implications for DSM-5. *Depression and Anxiety, 28*, 783–801
Hinton, D. E., & Otto, M. (2006). Symptom presentation and symptom meaning among traumatized Cambodian refugees: Relevance to a somatically focused cognitive behavior therapy. *Cognitive and Behavioral Practice, 13*, 249–260.
Hinton, D. E., Pham, T., Tran, M., Safren, S., Otto, M., & Pollack, M. (2004). CBT for Vietnamese refugees with treatment-resistant PTSD and panic attacks: A pilot study. *Journal of Traumatic Stress, 17*, 429–433.
Hinton, D. E., Pich, V., Marques, L., Nickerson, A., & Pollack, M. H. (2010). Khyâl attacks: A key idiom of distress among traumatized Cambodian refugees. *Culture, Medicine, and Psychiatry, 34*, 244–278.
Hinton, D. E., Rasmussen, A., Nou, L., Pollack, M., & Good, M. (2009). Anger, PTSD, and the nuclear family: A study of Cambodian refugees. *Social Science and Medicine, 69*, 1387–1394.
Hinton, D. E., Hofmann, S. G., Rivera, E., Otto, M. W., & Pollack, M. H. (2011). Culturally adapted CBT for Latino women with treatment-resistant PTSD: A pilot study comparing CA-CBT to Applied Muscle Relaxation. *Behaviour Research and Therapy, 49*, 275–280.
Holzapfel, S., Blanchard, E. B., Hickling, E. J., & Malta, L. S. (2005). A crossover evaluation of supportive psychotherapy and cognitive behavioral therapy for chronic PTSD in motor vehicle accident survivors. In M. E. Abelian (Ed.), *Focus on psychotherapy research* (pp. 207–218). Hauppauge, NY: Nova Science Publishers.
International Society for Traumatic Stress Studies (ISTSS) (2009). Treatment guidelines for PTSD. In Foa, E. B., Keane, T. M., Friedman, M. K., & Cohen, J. A. (Eds), *Effective treatments for PTSD*. New York: Guilford Press
Kilpatrick, D. G., & Best, C. L. (1984). Some cautionary remarks on treating sexual assault victims with implosion. *Behavior Therapy, 15*, 421–423.
Lopes Cardozo, B., Kaiser, R., Gotway, C. A., & Agini, F. (2003). Mental health, social functioning and feelings of hatred and revenge of Kosovar Albanians one year after the war in Kosovo. *Journal of Traumatic Stress, 16*, 351–360.
Lopes Cardozo, B., Vergara, A., Agini, F., & Gotway, C. A. (2000). Mental health, social functioning and attitudes of Kosovar Albanians following the war in Kosovo. *Journal of the American Medical Association, 284*, 569–577.
Macneil, C. A., Hasty, M. K., Evans, M., Redich, C., & Berk, M. (2009). The therapeutic alliance: Is it necessary or sufficient to engender positive outcomes? *Acta Neuropsychiatrica, 2*, 95–98.
Marsella, A. J., Friedman, M. J., Gerrity, E. T., & Scurfield, R. M. (1996). Ethnocultural aspects of PTSD: Some closing thoughts. In A. J. Marsella, M. J. Friedman, E. T. Gerrity & R. M. Scurfield (Eds.), *Ethnocultural aspects of posttraumatic stress disorder: Issues, research and clinical applications* (pp. 529–538). Washington D.C: American Psychological Association.
Marshall, G. N., Schell, T. L., Elliott, M. N., Berthold, S. M., & Chun, C. A. (2005). Mental health of Cambodian refugees 2 decades after resettlement in the United States. *Journal of the American Medical Association, 294*, 571–579.
Marshall, R. D., Bryant, R. A., Amsel, L., Suh, E. J., Cook, J. M., & Neria, Y. (2007). The psychology of ongoing threat: Relative risk appraisal, the September 11 attacks, and terrorism-related fears. *American Psychologist, 62*, 304–316.
McIvor, R. J., & Turner, S. W. (1995). Assessment and treatment approaches for survivors of torture. *British Journal of Psychiatry, 166*, 705–711.
Miller, K. E., Kulkarni, M., & Kushner, H. (2006). Beyond trauma-focused psychiatric epidemiology: Bridging research and practice with war-affected populations. *American Journal of Orthopsychiatry, 76*, 409–422.
Miller, K. E., Martell, Z. L., Pazdirek, L., Caruth, M., & Lopez, D. (2005). The role of interpreters in psychotherapy with refugees: An exploratory study. *American Journal of Orthopsychiatry, 75*, 27–39.
Mollica, R. F., McInnes, K., Sarajlic, N., Lavelle, J., Sarajlic, I., & Massagli, M. P. (1999). Disability associated with psychiatric comorbidity and health status in Bosnian refugees living in Croatia. *Journal of the American Medical Association, 282*, 433–439.
Momartin, S., Silove, D., Manicavasagar, V., & Steel, Z. (2002). Range and dimensions of trauma experienced by Bosnian refugees resettled in Australia. *Australian Psychologist, 37*, 149–156.

Momartin, S., Silove, D., Manicavasagar, V., & Steel, Z. (2004a). Comorbidity of PTSD and depression: Associations with trauma exposure, symptom severity and functional impairment in Bosnian refugees resettled in Australia. *Journal of Affective Disorders, 80*, 231–238.

Momartin, S., Silove, D., Manicavasagar, V., & Steel, Z. (2004b). Complicated grief in Bosnian refugees: Associations with posttraumatic stress disorder and depression. *Comprehensive Psychiatry, 45*, 475–482.

National Institute of Clinical Excellence (NICE) (2005). *Post-traumatic stress disorder (PTSD): The management of PTSD in adults and children in primary and secondary care*. London: Gaskell & the British Psychological Society.

Neuner, F., Kurreck, S., Ruf, M., Odenwald, M., Elbert, T., & Schauer, M. (2009). Can asylum-seekers with posttraumatic stress disorder be successfully treated? A randomized controlled pilot study. *Cognitive Behaviour Therapy, 39*, 81–91.

Neuner, F., Schauer, M., Klaschik, C., Karunakara, U., & Elbert, T. (2004). A comparison of narrative exposure therapy, supportive counseling, and psycheducation for treating posttraumatic stress disorder in an African refugee settlement. *Journal of Consulting and Clinical Psychology, 72*, 579–587.

Nickerson, A., Bryant, R. A., Brooks, R., Steel, Z., & Silove, D. (2009). Fear of cultural extinction and psychopathology among Mandaean refugees: An exploratory path analysis. *CNS Neuroscience and Therapeutics, 15*, 227–236.

Nickerson, A., Bryant, R. A., Steel, Z., Silove, D., & Brooks, R. (2010). The impact of fear for family on mental health in a resettled Iraqi refugee community. *Journal of Psychiatric Research, 44*, 229–235.

Norcross, J. C. (2002). *Psychotherapy relationships that work: Therapist contributions and responsiveness to patients*. New York: Oxford University Press.

Pflanz, S. E., & Ogle, A. D. (2006). Job stress, depression, work performance, and perceptions of supervisors in military personnel. *Military Medicine, 171*, 861–865.

Pitman, R. K., Orr, S. P., Altman, B., & Longpre, R. E. (1991). Psychiatric complications during flooding therapy for posttraumatic stress disorder. *Journal of Consulting and Clinical Psychology, 52*, 17–20.

Porter, M., & Haslam, N. (2005). Predisplacement and postdisplacement factors associated with mental health of refugees and internally displaced persons: A meta-analysis. *Journal of the American Medical Association, 294*, 602–612.

Price, J. L., Monson, C. M., Callahan, K., & Rodriguez, B. F. (2006). The role of emotional functioning in military-related PTSD and its treatment. *Journal of Anxiety Disorders, 20*, 661–674.

Regehr, C., & Bober, T. (2005). *In the line of fire: Trauma in the emergency services*. New York: Oxford University Press.

Resick, P. A., Galovski, T. E., O'Brien Uhlmansiek, M., Scher, C. D., Clum, G. A., & Young-Xu, Y. (2008). A randomized clinical trial to dismantle components of cognitive processing therapy for posttraumatic stress disorder in female victims of interpersonal violence. *Journal of Consulting and Clinical Psychology, 76*, 243–258.

Resick, P. A., Nishith, P., Weaver, T. L., Astin, M. C., & Feuer, C. A. (2002). A comparison of cognitive-processing therapy with prolonged exposure and a waiting condition for the treatment of chronic posttraumatic stress disorder in female rape victims. *Journal of Consulting and Clinical Psychology, 70*, 867–879.

Resick, P. A., & Schnicke, M. K. (1992). Cognitive processing therapy for sexual assault victims. *Journal of Consulting and Clinical Psychology, 60*, 748–756.

Roth, S., Newman, E., Pelcovitz, D., van der Kolk, B., & Mandel, F. S. (1997). Complex PTSD in victims exposed to sexual and physical abuse: Results from the DSM-IV field trial for posttraumatic stress disorder. *Journal of Traumatic Stress, 10*, 539–555.

Silove, D. (1996). Torture and refugee trauma: Implications for nosology and treatment of posttraumatic syndromes. *International Review of Psychiatry, 2*, 211–232.

Silove, D., Sinnerbrink, I., Field, A., Manicavasagar, V., & Steel, Z. (1997). Anxiety, depression and PTSD in asylum-seekers: Associations with pre-migration trauma and post-migration stressors. *British Journal of Psychiatry, 170*, 351–357.

Stepakoff, S., Hubbard, J., Katoh, M., Falk, E., Mikulu, J-B., Nkhoma, P., & Omagwa, Y. (2006). Trauma healing in refugee camps in Guinea: A psychosocial program for Liberian and Sierra Leonean survivors of torture and war. *American Psychologist, 61*, 921–932.

Terr, L. C. (1991). Childhood traumas: An outline and overview. *American Journal of Psychiatry, 148*, 10–20.

van der Kolk, B. A., Roth, S., Pelcovitz, D., Sunday, S., & Spinazzola, J. (2005). Disorders of extreme stress: The empirical foundation of a complex adaptation to trauma. *Journal of Trauamtic Stress, 18*, 389–399.

Weine, S., Kulenovic, A., Pavkovic, I., & Gibbons, R. (1998). Testimony psychotherapy in Bosnian refugees: A pilot study. *American Journal of Psychiatry, 155*, 1720–1726.

Weine, S. M., Becker, D. F., Vojvoda, D., Hodzic, E., Sawyer, M., Hyman, L., et al. (1998). Individual change after genocide in Bosnian survivors of "ethnic cleansing": Assessing personality dysfunction. *Journal of Traumatic Stress, 11*, 147–153.

Westermeyer, J. (1990). Working with an interpreter in psychiatric assessment and treatment. *Journal of Nervous and Mental Disease, 178*, 745–749.

World Health Organization. (1992). *The ICD-10 Classification of Mental and Behavioural Disorders*. Geneva: World Health Organization.

Zarowsky, C. (2004). Writing trauma: Emotion, ethnography, and the politics of suffering among Somali returnees in Ethiopia. *Culture, Medicine and Psychiatry, 28*, 189–209.

CHAPTER

36 Pharmacotherapy for PTSD

Matthew J. Friedman

Abstract

This chapter reviews the published literature on pharmacotherapy for PTSD with specific attention to randomized clinical trials. Specific agents reviewed include: antidepressants, antiadrenergic agents, glucocorticoids, anticonvulsants, D-cycloserine, benzodiazepines, and antipsychotics. The empirical evidence indicates that selective serotonin reuptake inhibitors and serotonin/norepinephrine reuptake inhibitors can be considered first line medications for PTSD. It also indicates that neither atypical antipsychotic agents nor benzodiazepines can be recommended at this time. Combined approaches are also reviewed in which pharmacotherapy is combined with psychotherapy or other medications. Important gaps in current knowledge are also considered.It is clear that pharmacotherapy remains an important clinical option because medications are effective; they are often useful for treating comorbid depression and other anxiety disorders; they are generally wellaccepted by patients; and, finally the availability of prescribing clinicians is much greater than the availability of qualified psychotherapists.

Key Words: PTSD; pharmacotherapy; Randomized Clinical Trials; antidepressants; anti-adrenergic agents; anticonvulsants/mood stabilizers; benzodiazepines; antipsychotics

Introduction

A number of medications are currently recommended for treatment of posttraumatic stress disorder (PTSD). In most cases, such recommendations are for single medications (e.g., monotherapy) rather than combinations of medications or for combined pharmacotherapy and psychotherapy. In this regard, research has lagged far behind clinical practice, where most patients are receiving treatment with two or more medications or with combinations of medications and psychotherapy. Furthermore, we await future clinical trials on PTSD and comorbid disorders (such as depression, substance use disorder, other anxiety disorders, and traumatic brain injury) since most patients with PTSD are simultaneously afflicted with at least one other co-occurring psychiatric disorder (Kessler, Sonnega, Bromet, Hughes & Nelson, 1995).

In this review we will consider the current evidence concerning pharmacotherapy for PTSD. Effective medications are available (see table 36.1). Two medications, both selective serotonin reuptake inhibitors (SSRIs), sertraline and paroxetine have received approval by the U.S. Food and Drug Administration (FDA) as first-line treatments for PTSD. Other SSRIs, especially fluoxetine, as well as the serotonin norepinephrine reuptake inhibitor (SNRI) venlafaxine, are also highly recommended for PTSD treatment. In addition, other medications, usually antidepressants, have shown efficacy in randomized clinical trials (RCT).

Before beginning a detailed review of the current evidence regarding a variety of pharmacological agents, it is important to state that cognitive behavioral treatment (CBT; especially Prolonged Exposure [PE] and Cognitive Processing Therapy [CPT]), has consistently outperformed pharmacotherapy with regard to efficacy (see Foa, Keane, Friedman, & Cohen, 2009). Despite this, medication remains an important clinical option for a variety of reasons. First, medications are effective.

Table 36.1. Medications For Ptsd: Indications and Contraindications*

Class	Medication	Strength of Evidence	Daily Dose	Indications	Contraindications
Selective Serotonin Reuptake inhibitors (SSRIs)	Paroxetine** Sertraline** Fluoxetine Citalopram Fluvoxamine	A A A F B	10-60mg 50-200mg 20-80mg 20-60mg 50-300mg	• Reduce B, C & D symptoms • Produce Clinical Global Improvement • Effective Treatment for Depression, Panic Disorder, Social Phobia, and Obsessive Compulsive Disorder • Reduce Associated Symptoms (rage, aggression, impulsivity, suicidal thoughts)	• May produce insomnia, restlessness, nausea, decreased appetite, daytime sedation, nervousness, and anxiety • May produce sexual dysfunction, decreased libido, delayed orgasm or anorgasmia • Clinically significant interactions for people prescribed MAOIs • Significant interactions with hepatic enzymes produce other drug interactions
Other Serotonergic Antidepressants	Nefazodone Trazadone	A C	200-600mg 50-600mg	• Superior to placebo in male combat veterans • Effective antidepressants • Trazadone has limited efficacy by itself but is synergistic with SSRIs & may reduce SSRI-induced insomnia	• Reports of hepatotoxicity associated with nefazodone treatment • May be too sedating, rare priapism
Other Serotonergic Agents	Cyprohepta-dine Buspirone	A F	4-24mg 15-60mg	• Not recommended • Make PTSD symptoms worse • Little evidence of efficacy	• Drowsiness, weight gain • Few side effects. Rare dizziness, headache & nausea
Other 2nd Generation Antidepressants	Venlafaxine Mirtazepine Buproprion	A A A	75-225mg 15-45mg 200-450mg	• Effective antidepressants • Efficacy in PTSD has been demonstrated • Efficacy in PTSD has not been shown	• Venlafazine may exacerbate hypertension patients to follow a strict dietary regimen • Mirtazepine may produce somnolence, increased appetite and weight gain • Buproprion may exacerbate seizure disorder
Monoamine Oxidase Inhibitors (MAOIs)	Phenelzine	A	15-90mg	• Reduces B symptoms • Produces Global Improvement • Effective agents for depression, panic and social phobia • Efficacy in PTSD has not been demonstrated for other MAOI's	• Risk of hypertensive crisis makes it necessary for patients to follow a strict dietary regimen • Contraindicated in combination with most other antidepres-sants, CNS stimulants & decongestants • Contraindicated in patients with alcohol/substance abuse/ dependency • May produce insomnia, hypotension, anticholinergic and severe liver toxicity

Tricyclic Antidepressants (TCAs)	Imipramine Amitriptyline Desipramine	A A A	150-300mg 150-300mg 100-300mg	• Reduces B symptoms • Produce Global Improvement • Effective Antidepressant & Antipanic Agents • Imipramine prevented onset of PTSD in pediatric burn patients • Desipramine ineffective in one randomized clinical trial Other TCAs have not been tested in PTSD	• Anticholinergic side effects (dry mouth, rapid pulse, blurred vision, constipation) • May produce ventricular arrhythmias • May produce orthostatic hypotension, sedation, or arousal
Antiadrenergic Agents	Prazosin Propranolol Guanfacine	A B A	6-10mg 40-160mg 1-3mg	• Prazosin has marked efficacy for PTSD nightmares & insomnia • Some effectiveness against B&D symptoms • Reduced physiological reactivity but not PTSD when given acutely • Two RCTs have shown that guanfacine is ineffective	• May be more effective for PTSD in divided doses • May produce hypotension or bradycardia • May produce depressive symptoms, hypotension, bradycardia or bronchospasm • May produce hypotension, bradycardia
Glucocorticoids	Hydrocorti-sone	A	5-30mg	• Prevents later development of PTSD in septic shock and post cardiac surgery patients	• Immunosuppression, osteopenia, hyperglycemia, hypertension
Anticonvulsants	Valproate Tiagabine Carbam-azepine Gabapentin*** Lamotrigine Topiramate***	A A B F A/B B	750-1750mg 4-12mg 400-1600mg 300-3600mg 50-400mg 200-400mg	• Ineffective in large RCT • Effective in Bipolar Affective Disorder • Tiagabine was ineffective in a large randomized trial • Effective on B&D Symptoms • Effective in Bipolar Affective Disorder • Possibly effective in reducing impulsive, aggressive and violent behavior • Small trials suggesting favorable effects for Gabapentin • Lamotrigine-Modestly favorable results in small RCT • Efficacy of topiramate has not been demonstrated in PTSD	• Gastrointestinal problems, sedation, tremor & thrombocytopenia • Valproate is teratogenic and should not be used in pregnancy • Tiagabine-dizziness, somnolence & tremor and seizures • Neurological symptoms, ataxia, drowsiness, low sodium, leukopenia • Gabapentin-sedation & ataxia • Lamotrigine-Stevens-Johnson symdrome, skin rash & fatigue • Topirimate-glaucoma, sedation, dizziness & ataxia

(*continued*)

Table 36.1. **Medications For Ptsd: Indications and Contraindications*** (*continued*)

Class	Medication	Strength of Evidence	Daily Dose	Indications	Contraindications
Glutamatergic Agent (partial NMDA agonist)	D-Cycloserine	F	250-1000mg	• Reduction in PTSD severity when combined with prolonged exposure therapy • Improved cognition • Promising RCTs currently in progress	• Somnolence, headache, tremor, dysarthria, vertigo, confusion, nervousness, irritability, psychotic reactions, hypernerflexia, seizures • Despite above side effects, has been used safely for tuberculosis for many years
Benzodiazepines	Alprazolam Clonazepam	A B	0.5-6mg 1-8mg	• Not recommended • Do not reduce core B&C symptoms • Effective only for general anxiety & insomnia • Other benzodiazepines have not been tested in PTSD	• Sedation, memory impairment, ataxia • Not recommended for patients with past or present alcohol/drug abuse/dependency because of risk for dependence • May exacerbate depressive symptoms • Aprazolam may produce rebound anxiety
Conventional Antipsychotics	Thioridazine Chlorpromazine Haloperidol	F F F	20-800mg 30-800mg 1-20mg	•Not recommended	• Sedation, orthostatic hypotension, anticholinergic, extrapyamidal effects, tardive dyskinesia, neuroleptic malignant syndrome, endocrinopathies, EKG abnormalities, blood dyscrasias, hepatotoxicity
Atypical Antipsychotics	Risperidone Olanzapine Quetiapine	A A B	4-16mg 5-20mg 50-750mg	• Preliminary data suggests effectiveness against PTSD symptom clusters & aggression • May have a role as augmentation treatment for partial responders to other agents	• Weight gain with all agents • Risk of Type II Diabetes with olanzapine

* Modified from Friedman, Davidson, & Stein, 2009
RCT Randomized Clinical Trial
** FDA approval as indicated treatment for PTSD
B Symptoms: intrusive recollections
*** The only data are from small trials and case reports
C Symptoms: avoidant/numbing
D Symptoms: hyper-arousal
* *Strength of Evidence*
Level A - randomized clinical trials
Level B – well-designed clinical studies without randomization or placebo comparison
Level C – service and naturalistic clinical studies, combined with clinical observations which are sufficiently compelling to warrant use of this drug
Level F – a few observations that have not been subjected to clinical or empirical tests

Second, medications are often useful for treating comorbid depression and other anxiety disorders that may accompany PTSD. Indeed, the evidence for efficacy against depression and other anxiety disorders is often stronger than evidence for effectiveness regarding PTSD. Third, medications are generally well accepted by patients. Finally, the availability of prescribing clinicians is much greater than the availability of qualified CBT therapists, since only 10–20% of practicing psychotherapists are qualified to provide such treatment (Rosen et al., 2004), although this percentage is increasing owing to current CBT training initiatives within the U.S. Departments of Veterans Affairs and Defense, as well as in the private sector.

To those familiar with the many alterations in neurocircuitry and neurobiological systems associated with PTSD (Neumeister, Henry, & Krystal, 2007), the superiority of CBT may be surprising. Several explanations are possible. First, all clinical trials, to date, have tested medications that were originally developed to treat other disorders such as depression, cardiovascular illness, seizure disorders, or schizophrenia. It is possible that medications developed specifically for PTSD may prove much more effective in the future. Second, most RCTs have focused on SSRIs that only target the serotonergic system, whereas it is well known that many other psychobiological systems are altered in PTSD (Southwick et al., 2007). These include adrenergic, dopaminergic, GABAergic, glutamatergic, and hypothalamic-pituitary-adrenocortical (HPA) systems, all of which have received relatively little attention by clinical investigators. Given our emerging understanding of the pathophysiology of PTSD, it is entirely possible that medications modulating these systems will eventually prove more effective than SSRIs. Third, it is reasonable to hope that medications currently under development, specifically for PTSD treatment, may prove to have greater efficacy and specificity, especially corticotropin releasing factor (CRF) antagonists and neuropeptide Y (NPY) enhancers. Finally, the best treatment for PTSD may prove to be a combination of CBT and medication. Indeed, one of the most exciting recent developments is the clinical trials in which CBT is augmented with the glutamatergic agent, d-cycloserine (DCS), (see below) or in which medication is augmented with CBT (Rothbaum et al., 2006).

Antidepressants

Selective Serotonin Reuptake Inhibitors (SSRIs)

SSRIs are the medication of choice for PTSD patients. Two SSRIs, sertraline and paroxetine, have received FDA approval for PTSD treatment based on industry-sponsored multisite RCTs (Brady et al., 2000; Davidson, Rothbaum, van der Kolk, Sikes, & Farfel, 2001a; Marshall, Beebe, Oldham & Zaninelli, 2001; Tucker et al., 2001). Furthermore, when sertraline treatment was extended from 12 to 36 weeks, 55% of non- or partial-responding patients converted to medication responders (Londborg et al., 2001). As in treatment for other psychiatric disorders, however, discontinuation of SSRI treatment often results in clinical relapse and return of PTSD symptoms (Davidson, Pearlstein, et al., 2001; Martényi, Brown, Zhang, Prakash, Koke, 2002; Rapaport, Endicott, & Clary, 2002), so it is necessary to keep responsive patients on their medication indefinitely. Clinical trials with other SSRIs have also had positive results, two RCTs with fluoxetine (Martényi, Brown, Zhang, Koke, & Prakash, 2002; van der Kolk et al., 1994) and open-label studies with fluvoxamine and citalopram (see Friedman, Davidson, & Stein, 2009, for references) indicate that SSRIs are an attractive choice of medication because they reduce PTSD re-experiencing, avoidance/numbing and hyper-arousal symptoms; promote rapid improvement in quality of life; and have a relatively benign side-effect profile (Rapaport et al., 2002).

A large negative multisite RCT (sertraline versus placebo) conducted with Vietnam veterans in VA hospital treatment settings had initially caused speculation that PTSD due to combat trauma was less responsive to SSRIs than PTSD due to other causes (Friedman, Marmar, Baker, Sikes, & Farfel, 2007). Other evidence calls this conclusion into question. In the aforementioned successful paroxetine studies (Marshall et al., 2001; Tucker et al., 2001) veterans who had been recruited from the general population (rather than from VA hospital treatment settings) exhibited as much benefit from SSRI treatment as did male and female nonveterans. Furthermore, the successful RCT with fluoxetine (Martényi, Brown, Zhang, Koke, et al., 2002) recruited mostly male veterans of (United Nations and NATO) deployments; indeed, in that trial exposure to combat trauma actually predicted a successful response to fluoxetine. In short, these findings indicate that people with PTSD due to combat trauma appear to be as likely to respond to SSRI treatment as those with PTSD due to other traumatic events. The findings also suggest that male Vietnam veterans in VA settings with chronic and severe PTSD may be an especially refractory cohort who are less likely to benefit either from pharmacotherapy or from psychosocial treatment (Friedman, 1997; Friedman et al., 2007; Schnurr et al., 2003).

Other Serotonergic Antidepressants

Nefazodone and trazodone are two serotonergic antidepressants that combine SSRI action with postsynaptic, 5HT2, blockade. One RCT showed nefazodone to be as effective as sertraline (Saygin, Sungur, Sabol & Çetinkaya, 2002). Similar positive results have been obtained in open-label nefazodone trials (see Friedman et al., 2009, for references). Nefazadone has enjoyed use in PTSD treatment because of its effectiveness and because it is less likely to cause SSRI side effects such as anorgasmia and insomnia. It is important to emphasize that brand-name nefazodone (Serzone) has been withdrawn from the American market because of liver toxicity; however, generic nefazodone is still available but should be used only if liver function is carefully monitored during treatment.

Trazodone has limited efficacy as monotherapy. It is often used in conjunction with SSRIs, especially for patients with insomnia, because of its sedating effects and synergistic serotoninergic action.

Tricyclic Antidepressants (TCAs)

Tricyclics are older antidepressants that variably block presynaptic reuptake of norepinephrine, serotonin, or both. As antidepressants, they are no less effective than SSRIs, but have complicated side-effect profiles that make them more difficult to manage than SSRIs. Such side effects include cardiac arrhythmias, orthostatic hypotension and anticholinergic side effects (e.g. dry mouth, rapid pulse, blurred vision and constipation).With respect to PTSD, RCTs with imipramine (Kosten, Frank, Dan, McDougle & Giller, 1991) and amitriptyline (Davidson et al., 1990), but not desipramine (Reist et al., 1989), have produced symptom reduction in PTSD patients.

It is unlikely that there will be any new RCTs with TCAs because newer agents have more benign side-effect profiles and because pharmaceutical companies are not motivated to fund such studies. TCAs remain an important option for individuals who fail to respond to SSRIs or other medications, although they are most effective in reducing re-experiencing and arousal, but not avoidance/numbing symptoms (Southwick, Yehuda, Giller, & Charney, 1994), whereas SSRIs and SNRIs are effective against all three symptom clusters of PTSD.

A notable TCA study was a prospective RCT comparing imipramine with the hypnotic, chloral hydrate, among children and adolescents hospitalized because of severe burn injuries. Such patients are at very high risk for acute stress disorder and subsequent PTSD. In this study, burn victims randomized to the imipramine group had significantly lower incidence of acute stress disorder than those treated with chloral hydrate (Robert, Blakeney, Villarreal, Rosenberg & Meyer, 1999). Unfortunately, a more recent trial by the same authors failed to replicate these results; fluoxetine was as ineffective as imipramine (Robert et al., 2008).

Monoamine Oxidase Inhibitors (MAOIs)

MAOIs block the intraneuronal metabolic breakdown of monoaminergic neurotransmitters such as serotonin, norepinephrine, and dopamine, thereby making more available for presynaptic release. An RCT with the MAOI, phenelzine, with Vietnam combat veterans was extremely successful in reducing the re-experiencing and arousal symptoms of PTSD (Kosten et al., 1991). Open-label trials have had mixed results (see Friedman & Davidson, 2007) and a small, five-week crossover study with questionable methodology had negative results (Shestatzky, Greenberg, & Lerer, 1988). One open trial with the reversible MAO-A inhibitor, moclobemide, was positive, but it has not been replicated (Neal, Shapland, & Fox, 1997). Clinicians tend to avoid MAOIs because patients must adhere to restricted diets and because the medications have potentially serious side effects, but they can be quite effective and can be managed, if one is careful.

Other Antidepressants

Mirtazapine has both serotoninergic actions (blockade of postsynaptic 5HT-2 and 5HT-3 receptors) and action at presynaptic alpha-2 adrenergic receptors. Mirtazipine has been significantly more effective than placebo in two RCTs (Chung et al., 2004; Davidson et al., 2003) and in an open-label eight-week trial in Korea (Bahk et al., 2002). There is also an interesting report on the usefulness of mirtazapine for traumatic nightmares (or for postawaking memory of such nightmares) among 300 refugees who had previously failed to benefit from other medications (Lewis, 2002). This study should be repeated, since prazosin (see below) is the only medication in current use where a selective action against traumatic nightmares has been emphasized.

Venlafaxine is an SNRI that blocks presynaptic reuptake of norepinephrine and serotonin and has a much less potent effect blocking dopamine reuptake. Two large multicenter trials of venlafaxine-XR have shown superiority relative to placebo, in both a 12-week (Davidson, Rothbaum, et al., 2006), and a six-month RCT in which it was just as effective as sertraline (Davidson, Baldwin, et al., 2006). Furthermore, patients receiving venlafaxine exhibited significantly more resilience, or the ability to deal with daily stress, than placebo patients. Finally, as with SSRIs (Londberg et al, 2001), many patients in the six-month trial did not achieve remission until they had received several months of treatment.

Buproprion blocks presynaptic reuptake of norepinephrine and dopamine, but not serotonin. Although anecdotal evidence and open trials suggest that it may be effective in PTSD (Canive, Clark, Calais, Qualls, & Tuason, 1998), a recent RCT had negative results (Becker et al., 2007).

Anti-Adrenergic Agents

PTSD is associated with excessive adrenergic activity (Southwick et al., 2007), yet despite favorable clinical reports on the efficacy of both propranolol and clonidine 25 years ago (Kolb, Burris, & Griffiths, 1984), there are few studies with antiadrenergic agents. The most exciting findings concern the postsynaptic alpha-1 antagonist prazosin. This research has consistently indicated that prazosin reduces traumatic nightmares. Success against other PTSD symptoms has been inconsistent, possibly because adequate plasma levels of prazosin were not sustained throughout the day. This is because the medication was only prescribed at bedtime rather than in divided doses, which would be needed for 24-hour protection, given prazosin's relatively short half-life (Raskind et al., 2003, 2007). A large-scale multisite trial is currently in progress.

The beta adrenergic antagonist propranolol has previously been shown to reduce enhancement of emotional memories among human volunteers (Cahill & McGaugh, 1996). Propranolol has effectively reduced intrusive recollections and reactivity to traumatic stimuli in a small clinical study with children (Famularo, Kinscherff, & Fenton, 1988), but has not been tested since that time. The most exciting research has indicated that propranolol might be useful as a prophylactic agent for the prevention of PTSD. In acutely traumatized emergency-room patients, treated within 24 hours of their traumatic experiences, propranolol prevented subsequent (e.g., one- and three-month) posttraumatic physiological hyper-reactivity but not overall PTSD symptom severity (Pitman et al., 2002; Taylor & Cahill, 2002; Vaiva et al., 2003). Finally, Brunet et al. (2008) conducted a provocative experiment in which subjects with PTSD were given one day of treatment with propranolol (or placebo) after they had evoked memories of their traumatic experiences. One week later, after re-evocation of the traumatic event, the propranolol group exhibited significantly less physiological arousal than the placebo group. The investigators speculate that propranolol may have interfered with reconsolidation of the traumatic memory. This intriguing finding certainly merits further study.

Alpha-2 adrenergic agonists such as clonidine and guanfacine (which reduce the presynaptic release of norepinephrine) might also be expected to improve PTSD symptom severity. The literature is mixed. Open trials with clonidine are generally favorable (Kinzie & Friedman, 2004; Kolb et al., 1984). In two RCTs with older veterans in a VA hospital setting, however, guanfacine performed no better than placebo (Neylan et al., 2006; Davis et al., 2008).

Anticonvulsant/Mood Stabilizer Agents

Findings with anticonvulsant/mood stabilizer agents have been disappointing. For the most part, they have been sporadically tested in small single-site studies for almost 20 years. Interest in this class of medications was initially prompted by their antikindling actions, since it has been proposed that sensitization/kindling-related alteration of limbic nuclei might contribute to PTSD (Post, Weiss, & Smith, 1995). Detection of abnormalities in glutamatergic and GABAergic systems among PTSD patients has also raised the level of interest in this class of medications (Chambers et al., 1999). Finally, the development of several new anticonvulsant/mood stabilizers in recent years has motivated the pharmaceutical industry to support clinical trials utilizing these agents with PTSD patients. Despite promising open-label studies with several anticonvulsants, three recent large-scale RCTs with tiagabine, valproate, and topiramate have had negative results (Davidson, Brady, Mellman, Stein, & Pollack, 2007; Davis, Davidson, et al., 2008; Tucker et al., 2007). Thus, current evidence does not favor the use of these agents in PTSD, despite significant theoretical interest.

D-Cycloserine (DCS)

DCS is a second-line agent for the treatment of tuberculosis. Its side-effect profile is benign. DCS is also pharmacologically active as a partial agonist at the glutamatergic NMDA receptor (which mediates learning and memory). One of the most exciting developments is the possibility that DCS can accelerate the pace of CBT treatment. To understand this new research with DCS, it is important to consider the Pavlovian fear-conditioning model of PTSD.

The fear-conditioning model proposes that PTSD develops in reaction to a traumatic event (unconditioned stimulus) after which PTSD symptoms are elicited by traumatic reminders (conditioned stimuli). Amelioration of conditioned fear can only be accomplished through extinction. Extinction occurs when new responses to conditioned stimuli are learned so that they no longer elicit PTSD symptoms. This model is the theoretical rationale for exposure therapy, which is, in effect, a clinical paradigm for extinguishing conditioned fear.

Extinction learning is, primarily mediated by NMDA receptors. Since DCS acts at NMDA receptors and since animal research has shown that DCS facilitates extinction of conditioned fear, it has been hypothesized that DCS will enhance the efficacy of exposure therapy and thereby reduce the number of therapeutic sessions needed to achieve clinical remission. Although research with DCS augmentation of exposure therapy for PTSD is currently in progress (Davis, Ressler, Rothbaum, & Richardson 2006), there have been successful RCTs in which DCS accelerated successful exposure therapy for acrophobia (fear of heights) and social phobia (Hofmann et al., 2006; Ressler et al., 2004).

Benzodiazepines

Benzodiazepines are not recommended for PTSD treatment. A RCT with alprazolam did not reduce core re-experiencing or avoidant/numbing symptoms, although it did lead to improvement in insomnia and generalized anxiety (Braun, Greenberg, Dasberg, & Lerer, 1990). Treatment of recently traumatized emergency room patients with clonazepam (Gelpin, Bonne, Peri, Brandes, & Shalev, 1996) or the hypnotic benzodiazepine temazepam (Mellman, Bustamante, David, & Fins, 2002) did not prevent the later development of PTSD. Other open trials with benzodiazepines have also been unsuccessful (see Friedman et al., 2009). Despite these negative findings, practitioners continue to prescribe benzodiazepines for PTSD. In the VA medical system, approximately 26% of PTSD patients are receiving benzodiazepines (Mohamed & Rosenheck, 2008). There are, of course, concerns about the addictive nature of these compounds and the difficulty of discontinuing such medications after they have been started. In addition, evidence from animal research, that benzodiazepines interfere with extinction of fear conditioning (Bouten, Kenney, & Rosengard, 1990), raises additional concerns that benzodiazepines will interfere with exposure therapy. Indeed, it has been shown in one study that benzodiazepines do interfere with Prolonged Exposure (PE); PE patients prescribed benzodiazepines had poorer treatment outcomes than those who did not receive such medication (van Minnen, Arntz & Keijsers, 2002).

It is disappointing that medications acting at GABA-A receptors such as benzodiazepines or the aforementioned ineffective anticonvulsant/mood stabilizers (e.g., tiagabine, valproate, and topiramate) have failed to exhibit efficacy in PTSD treatment. One possible explanation is that any beneficial pharmacological effects are more than offset by benzodiazepine-induced interference with cognitive mechanisms necessary for therapeutic processing of traumatic material. Another possibility is that reduced sensitivity of GABA-A receptors in PTSD nullifies any potential benefit from benzodiazepines or anticonvulsants (Ellen, Olver, Norman, & Burrows, 2008).

Atypical Antipsychotic Medications

In PTSD treatment, atypical antipsychotics have not proved effective as monotherapy for PTSD. Previously, a number of small single-site studies suggested that atypical antipsychotic agents were effective adjunctive treatment for PTSD patients who had poor responses to first-line SSRIs or SNRIs. Most noteworthy, these results were obtained with patient groups that are typically treatment resistant (such as older, chronic American military veteran patients receiving treatment at VA Medical facilities). There are published reports on three antipsychotic medications (risperidone, olanzepine, and quetiapine) as adjuncts to ongoing antidepressant pharmacotherapy. Results from four RCTs (Bartzokis, Lu, Turner, Mintz, & Saunders, 2005; Hammer et al., 2003; Monnelly, Ciraulo, Knapp, & Keane, 2003; Reich, Winternitz, Hennen, Watts, & Stanculescu, 2004) and several case reports using risperidone as adjunctive therapy show reduction in overall PTSD symptom severity in addition to reducing dissociative flashbacks and aggressive behavior. Similar findings were obtained in an RCT with olanzapine (Stein, Kline, & Matloff, 2002) indicating effectiveness as an adjunctive agent in reducing PTSD symptoms among chronic SSRI-refractory patients; however, there is also a negative RCT with olanzapine as adjunctive treatment for PTSD (Butterfield et al., 2001). Positive results have also been obtained with quetiapine as an adjunctive agent in an open-label trial (Hamner et al., 2003), a retrospective medical record review (Sokolski, Denson, Lee, & Reist, 2003) and several case reports.

A recent large-scale multi-site trail of risperidone as adjunct agent for SSRI poor/partial responders showed that there was no benefit for adjunctive use of this agent (Krystal et al., 2011). In comparison with a placebo group, adjunctive risperidone produce no additional benefit in reducing PTSD symptoms. As a result of this finding, the recent VA/DoD PTSD Clinical Practice Guideline recommends against risperidone as an adjunctive agent and concludes that there is insufficient evidence to recommend any other atypical antipsychotic as adjunctive treatment for PTSD.

Combined Psychotherapy and Pharmacotherapy

There are several different strategies for combining pharmacotherapy and psychotherapy, with challenges and advantages to each (Rothbaum, 2008), but there has been little research in this area. Currently, it is unclear whether there are additive and/or interactive effects of simultaneously administered pharmacotherapy and psychotherapy for PTSD. With the possible exception of DCS, the current literature does not suggest any advantage to combining medications with CBT for any anxiety disorder (Gerardi, Ressler, & Rothbaum, in press). Whether one begins with a course of CBT or pharmacotherapy, it makes sense to carry out a full RCT before considering additional treatments. For those patients who have not been treated with an adequate/appropriate dose of CBT for PTSD and who express no strong preference, we recommend starting with CBT. If the antidepressant is the first treatment, we recommend having it on board at least four weeks before commencing the psychotherapy. Patients who achieve complete remission from the medication will need no additional treatment, whereas those with a partial response will probably benefit when CBT is added to pharmacotherapy, as in the Rothbaum et al. (2006) trial described below for PTSD.

After a course of open-label sertraline treatment (up to 200 mg), patients were randomly assigned to receive continuation with sertraline alone or to receive augmentation with PE (including both in vivo and prolonged imaginal exposure; Foa, Hembree, & Rothbaum, 2007). Five additional weeks of treatment with sertraline alone did not result in further improvement on measures of PTSD severity, depression, or general anxiety. In contrast, augmentation with PE significantly reduced PTSD severity among partial responders to medication (Rothbaum et al., 2006). In a recently published trial with almost a mirror design to the Rothbaum et al. (2008) study (Simon et al., 2008), participants first received eight sessions of PE over four to six weeks and then were randomly assigned to receive paroxetine CR plus five additional sessions of PE or placebo plus five additional sessions of PE. The largest reductions of PTSD symptoms occurred following PE, with no significant differences between placebo and paroxetine in the augmentation phase. In other words, PE augmentation of partial responses to SSRI treatment is beneficial, whereas SSRI augmentation of partial responses to PE has no added benefits.

The other promising combined treatment that has been discussed previously is DCS augmentation of CBT treatment. What is unique about this approach is that DCS is only administered prior to a session of CBT and not on a continuous basis as with other approaches. Finally, it should be noted that combining "traditional" psychiatric medications (i.e., antidepressants, benzodiazepines) with CBT for anxiety disorders has not shown any benefit.

Future Directions

It is hoped that newer and more powerful medications can be developed that will target the unique psychobiological alterations in PTSD. Among these are agents that might antagonize corticotrophin-releasing factor (e.g., CRF-antagonists) or that might potentiate the powerful anxiolytic neuropeptide Y (see Friedman, 2002). More effective agents that moderate the human stress response through glutamatergic, GABA-ergic, or other neurotransmitters or neuromodulator sites might also prove very effective in PTSD. Finally, agents that promote neurogenesis in key cerebral sites that have been dysregulated through PTSD-related alterations might also serve as important medications in the future.

A recent finding regarding opioid prophylaxis of PTSD in a war zone has been very exciting. Wounded U.S. naval personnel evacuated to a battalion aid station in Iraq who received opioid treatment for pain within one to three hours of their injuries displayed lower subsequent prevalence of PTSD than wounded and evacuated colleagues who did not receive opioids (Holbrook, Galarneau, Dye, Quinn, & Dougherty, 2010). Whether this result was due to rapid pain reduction and/or inhibition of adrenergic mechanisms (Friedman, 2010) is a very important question that needs to be addressed.

Other populations need to be tested systematically in future clinical trials. These include non-Caucasian subjects, especially refugees from traditional societies (Green et al., 2003).

More research is needed with children and adolescents who suffer from PTSD owing to sexual, physical, or emotional abuse or exposure to accidents. Unfortunately, concerns about increased suicides among children and adolescents treated with SSRIs for depression (Food and Drug Administration, 2004) has slowed the pace of clinical trials with medications for younger people with PTSD.

There is also a need for information on the efficacy of medications for older adults with PTSD.

Concerns about safety, age-related pharmacokinetic capacity, drug-drug interactions, and comorbid medical conditions must always be factored into decisions for treating older individuals. Since PTSD is a risk factor for medical illness (Schnurr & Green, 2003), and since older individuals with PTSD and medical problems frequently present to primary-care clinics, it is important to both identify and treat PTSD in this emerging group of patients.

Summary

1. SSRIs and SNRIs are the best established medications for PTSD.
2. Promising results have been obtained with mirtazapine, and other antidepressants.
3. Prazosin has proved efficacy against traumatic nightmares but its effectiveness for PTSD has not yet to be demonstrated.
4. Augmentation of exposure therapy with d-cycloserine is a very exciting new development, currently under investigation.
5. Augmentation of pharmacotherapy with exposure therapy appears to be effective. However, augmentation of exposure therapy with medication has not proved to be a useful approach.
6. Research on prevention of PTSD with propranolol or amelioration of acute stress disorder with imipramine is inclusive. In a recent military report there were significant reductions in PTSD prevalence following opioid administration within one to three hours of combat injuries.
7. Much more research is needed on pharmacotherapy for non-Caucasians, children, adolescents, and older individuals with PTSD.

References

Bahk, W.-M., Pae, C.-U., Tsoh, J., Chae, J.-H., Jun, T.-Y., Kim, C.-L., et al. (2002). Effects of mirtazapine in patients with post-traumatic stress disorder in Korea: A pilot study. *Human Psychopharmacology, 17*, 341–344.

Bartzokis, G., Lu, P. H., Turner, J., Mintz, J., & Saunders, C. S. (2005). Adjunctive risperidone in the treatment of chronic combat-related posttraumatic stress disorder. *Biological Psychiatry, 57*, 474–479.

Becker, M. E., Hertzberg, M. A., Moore, S. D., Dennis, M. F., Bukenya, D. S., & Beckham, J. C. (2007). A placebo-controlled trial of bupropion SR in the treatment of chronic posttraumatic stress disorder. *Journal of Clinical Psychopharmacology, 27*, 193–197.

Bouton, M. E., Kenney, F. A., & Rosengard, C. (1990). State-dependent fear extinction with two benzodiazepine tranquilizers. *Behavioral Neuroscience, 104*(1), 44–55.

Brady, K., Pearlstein, T., Asnis, G. M., Baker, D., Rothbaum, B., Sikes, C. R., et al. (2000). Efficacy and safety of sertraline treatment of posttraumatic stress disorder: A randomized controlled trial. *Journal of the American Medical Association, 283*, 1837–1844.

Braun, P., Greenberg, D., Dasberg, H., & Lerer, B. (1990). Core symptoms of posttraumatic stress disorder unimproved by alprazolam treatment. *Journal of Clinical Psychiatry, 51*, 236–238.

Brunet, A., Orr, S. P., Tremblay, J., Robertson, K., Nader, K., & Pitman, R. K. (2008). Effect of post-retrieval propranolol on psychophysiologic responding during subsequent script-driven traumatic imagery in post-traumatic stress disorder. *Journal of Psychiatric Research, 42*, 503–506.

Butterfield, M. I., Becker, M. E., Connor, K. M., Sutherland, S. M., Churchill, L. E., & Davidson, J. R. T. (2001). Olanzapine in the treatment of post-traumatic stress disorder: A pilot study. *International Clinical Psychopharmacology, 16*, 197–203.

Cahill, L., & McGaugh, J. L. (1996). Modulation of memory storage. *Current Opinion in Neurobiology, 6*, 237–242.

Canive, J. M., Clark, R. D., Calais, L. A., Qualls, C. R., & Tuason, V. B. (1998). Bupropion treatment in veterans with posttraumatic stress disorder: An open study. *Journal of Clinical Psychopharmacology, 18*, 379–383.

Chambers, R. A., Bremner, J. D., Moghaddam, B., Southwick, S. M., Charney, D. S., & Krystal, J. H. (1999). Glutamate and post-traumatic stress disorder: Toward a psychobiology of dissociation. *Seminars in Clinical Neuropsychiatry, 4*(4), 274–284.

Chung, M. Y., Min, K. H., Jun, Y. J., Kim, S. S., Kim, W. C., & Jun, E. M. (2004). Efficacy and tolerability of mirtazapine and sertraline in Korean veterans with posttraumatic stress disorder: A randomized open label trial. *Human Psychopharmacology, 19*(7), 489–494.

Davidson, J. R. T., Baldwin, D. V., Stein, D. J., Kuper, E., Benattia, I., Ahmed, S., et al. (2006). Treatment of posttraumatic stress disorder with venlafaxine extended release: A 6-month randomized controlled trial. *Archives of General Psychiatry, 63*, 1158–1165.

Davidson, J. R. T., Brady, K. T., Mellman, T. A., Stein, M. B., & Pollack, M. H. (2007). The efficacy and tolerability of tiagabine in adult patients with posttraumatic stress disorder. *Journal of Clinical Psychopharmacology, 27*, 85–88.

Davidson, J. R. T., Kudler, H. S., Smith, R. D., Mahorney, S. L., Lipper, S., Hammett, E. B., et al. (1990). Treatment of posttraumatic stress disorder with amitriptyline and placebo. *Archives of General Psychiatry, 47*, 259–266.

Davidson, J. R. T., Pearlstein, T., Londborg, P. D., Brady, K. T., Rothbaum, B. O., Bell, J., et al. (2001). Efficacy of sertraline in preventing relapse of posttraumatic stress disorder: Results of a 28-week double-blind, placebo-controlled study. *American Journal of Psychiatry, 158*, 1974–1981.

Davidson, J. R. T., Rothbaum, B. O., Tucker, P. M., Asnis, G. M., Benattia, I., & Musgnung, J. J. (2006). Venlafaxine extended release in posttraumatic stress disorder: A sertraline- and placebo-controlled study. *Journal of Clinical Psychopharmacology, 26*, 259–267.

Davidson, J. R. T., Rothbaum, B. O., van der Kolk, B. A., Sikes, C. R., & Farfel, G. M. (2001). Multicenter, double-blind comparison of sertraline and placebo in the treatment of posttraumatic stress disorder. *Archives of General Psychiatry, 58*, 485–492.

Davidson, J. R. T., Weisler, R. H., Butterfield, M. I., Casat, C. D., Connor, K. M., Barnett, S. D., et al. (2003). Mirtzapine vs. placebo in posttraumatic stress disorder: A pilot trial. *Biological Psychiatry, 53*, 188–191.

Davis, L. L., Davidson, J. R. T., Ward, L. C., Bartolucci, A. A., Bowden, C., & Petty, F. (2008). Divalproex in the treatment of posttraumatic stress disorder: A randomized, double-blind, placebo-controlled trial in a veteran population. *Journal of Clinical Psychopharmacology, 28*, 84–88.

Davis, L. L., Ward, C., Rasmusson, A., Newell, J. M., Frazier, E., & Southwick, S. M. (2008). A placebo-controlled trial of guanfacine for the treatment of posttraumatic stress disorder in veterans. *Psychopharmacology Bulletin, 41*(1), 8–18.

Davis, M., Ressler, K., Rothbaum, B. O., & Richardson, R. (2006). Effects of D-cycloserine on extinction: Translation from preclinical to clinical work. *Biological Psychiatry, 60*, 369–375.

Ellen, S., Olver, J., Norman, T. R., & Burrows, G. D. (2008). The neurobiology of benzodiazepine receptors in panic disorder and post-traumatic stress disorder. *Stress and Health, 24*(1), 13–21.

Famularo, R., Kinscherff, R., & Fenton, T. (1988). Propranolol treatment for childhood posttraumatic stress disorder, acute type. *American Journal of Diseases of Children, 142*, 1244–1247.

Foa, E. B., Hembree, E. A., & Rothbaum, B. O. (2007). *Prolonged exposure therapy for PTSD: Emotional processing of traumatic experiences: Therapist guide.* New York: Oxford University Press.

Foa, E. B., Keane, T. M., Friedman, M. J., & Cohen, J.A. (Eds.). (2009). *Effective treatments for PTSD: Practice guidelines from the International Society for Traumatic Stress Studies* (2nd ed.). New York: Guilford.

Food and Drug Administration. (2004). FDA launches a multi-pronged strategy to strengthen safeguards for children treated with antidepressant medications. *FDA News.*

Friedman, M. J. (1997). Drug treatment for PTSD: Answers and questions. *Annals of the New York Academy of Sciences, 821*, 359–371.

Friedman, M. J. (2002). Future pharmacotherapy for post-traumatic stress disorder: Prevention and treatment. *Psychiatric Clinics of North America, 25*(2), 427–441.

Friedman, M. J. (2010). (Editorial) Prevention of psychiatric problems among military personnel and their spouses. *New England Journal of Medicine, 362*, 168–170.

Friedman, M. J., & Davidson, J. R. T. (2007). Pharmacotherapy for PTSD. In M. J. Friedman, T. M. Keane, & P. A. Resick (Eds.), *Handbook of PTSD: Science and practice* (pp. 376–405). New York: Guilford.

Friedman, M. J., Davidson, J. R. T., & Stein, D. J. (2009). Psychopharmacotherapy for Adults. In E. B. Foa, T. M. Keane, M. J. Friedman, & J. A. Cohen (Eds.), *Effective treatments for PTSD: Practice guidelines from the International Society for Traumatic Stress Studies* (2nd ed., pp. 245–268). New York: Guilford.

Friedman, M. J., Marmar, C. R., Baker, D. G., Sikes, C. R., & Farfel, G. M. (2007). Randomized, double-blind comparison of sertraline and placebo for posttraumatic stress disorder in a Department of Veterans Affairs setting. *Journal of Clinical Psychiatry, 68*, 711–720.

Gelpin, E., Bonne, O. B., Peri, T., Brandes, D., & Shalev, A. Y. (1996). Treatment of recent trauma survivors with benzodiazepines: A prospective study. *Journal of Clinical Psychiatry, 57*, 390–394.

Gerardi, M., Ressler, K., & Rothbaum, B. O. (in press). Combined treatment of anxiety disorders. In D. Stein, E. Hollander, and B. O. Rothbaum (Eds.), *Textbook of anxiety disorders* (2nd ed., pp. XX-YY). New York: American Psychiatric Publishing.

Green, B. L., Friedman, M. J., de Jong, J. T. V. M., Solomon, S. D., Keane, T. M., Fairbank, J. A., et al. (2003). *Trauma interventions in war and peace: Prevention, practice, and policy.* New York: Kluwer Academic/Plenum Publishers.

Hamner, M. B., Faldowski, R. A., Ulmer, H. G., Frueh, B. C., Huber, M. G., & Arana, G. W. (2003). Adjunctive risperidone treatment in post-traumatic stress disorder: A preliminary controlled trial of effects on comorbid psychotic symptoms. *International Clinical Psychopharmacology, 18*, 1–8.

Hofmann, S. G., Meuret, A. E., Smits, J. A., Simon, N. M., Pollack, M. H., Eisenmenger, K., et al. (2006). Augmentation of exposure therapy with D-cycloserine for social anxiety disorder. *Archives of General Psychiatry, 63*, 298–304.

Holbrook, T. L., Galarneau, M. R., Dye, J. L., Quinn, K., & Dougherty, A. L. (2010). Morphine use after combat injury in Iraq and post-traumatic stress disorder. *New England Journal of Medicine, 362*(2):110–117.

Kessler, R. C., Sonnega, A., Bromet, E., Hughes, M., & Nelson, C. B. (1995). Posttraumatic stress disorder in the National Comorbidity Survey. *Archives of General Psychiatry, 52*(12), 1048–1060.

Kinzie, J. D., & Friedman, M. J.(2004). Psychopharmacology for refugee and asylum seeker patients. In J. P. Wilson & B. Drozdek (Eds.), *Broken spirits: The treatment of asylum seekers and refugees with PTSD* (pp. 579-600). New York: Brunner-Routledge.

Kolb, L. C., Burris, B. C., & Griffiths, S. (1984). Propranolol and clonidine in the treatment of the chronic post-traumatic stress disorders of war. In B. A. van der Kolk (Ed.), *Post-traumatic stress disorder: Psychological and biological sequelae* (pp. 97–107). Washington, DC: American Psychiatric Press.

Kosten, T. R., Frank, J. B., Dan, E., McDougle, C. J., & Giller, E. L. (1991). Pharmacotherapy for posttraumatic stress disorder using phenelzine or imipramine. *Journal of Nervous and Mental Disease, 179*, 366–370

Krystal, J. H., Rosenheck, R. A., Cramer, J. A. Vessicchio, J. C., Jones, K. M., Vertrees, J. E., . . . Stock, C. (2011). Adjunctive risoeridone treatment for anti-depressant-resistant symptoms of chronic military service-related TSD. *Journal of American Medical Association, 306*(5), 493–502.

Lewis, J. D. (2002). Mirtazapine for PTSD nightmares [letter]. *American Journal of Psychiatry, 159*, 1948–1949.

Londborg, P. D., Hegel, M. T., Goldstein, S., Goldstein, D., Himmelhoch, J. M., Maddock, R., Patterson, W. M., Rausch, J., & Farfel, G. M. (2001). Sertraline treatment of posttraumatic stress disorder: Results of weeks of open-label continuation treatment. *Journal of Clinical Psychiatry, 62*, 325–331.

Marshall, R. D., Beebe, K. L., Oldham, M., & Zaninelli, R. (2001). Efficacy and safety of paroxetine treatment for chronic PTSD: A fixed-dose, placebo-controlled study. *American Journal of Psychiatry, 158*, 1982–1988.

Martényi, F., Brown, E. B., Zhang, H., Koke, S. C., & Prakash, A. (2002). Fluoxetine v. placebo in prevention of relapse in post-traumatic stress disorder. *British Journal of Psychiatry, 181*, 315–320.

Martényi, F., Brown, E. B., Zhang, H., Prakash, A., & Koke, S. C. (2002). Fluoxetine versus placebo in posttraumatic stress disorder. *Journal of Clinical Psychiatry, 63*, 199–206.

Mellman, T. A., Bustamante, V., David, D., & Fins, A. I. (2002). Hypnotic medication in the aftermath of trauma [letter]. *Journal of Clinical Psychiatry, 63*, 1183–1184.

Mohamed, S., & Rosenheck, R. A. (2008). Pharmacotherapy of PTSD in the U.S. Department of Veterans Affairs: Diagnostic- and symptom-guided drug selection. *Journal of Clinical Psychiatry, 69*, 959–965.

Monnelly, E. P., Ciraulo, D. A., Knapp, C., & Keane, T. M. (2003). Low-dose risperidone as adjunctive therapy for irritable aggression in posttraumatic stress disorder. *Journal of Clinical Psychopharmacology, 23*, 193–196.

Neal, L. A., Shapland, W., & Fox, C. (1997). An open trial of moclobemide in the treatment of post-traumatic stress disorder. *International Clinical Psychopharmacology, 12*, 231–237.

Neumeister, A., Henry, S., & Krystal, J. H. (2007). Neurocircuitry and neuroplasticity. In M. J. Friedman, T. M. Keane,

& P. A. Resick (Eds), *Handbook of PTSD: Science and practice* (pp.166–189). New York: Guilford.

Neylan, T. C., Lenoci, M. A., Samuelson, K. W., Metzler, T. J., Henn-Haase, C., Hierholzer, R. W., et al. (2006). No improvement of posttraumatic stress disorder symptoms with guanfacine treatment. *American Journal of Psychiatry, 163*, 2186–2188.

Pitman, R. K., Sanders, K. M., Zusman, R. M., Healy, A. R., Cheema, F., Lasko, N. B., et al. (2002). Pilot study of secondary prevention of posttraumatic stress disorder with propranolol. *Biological Psychiatry, 51*, 189–192.

Post, R. M., Weiss, S. R. B., & Smith, M. A. (1995). Sensitization and kindling: Implications for the evolving neural substrates of post-traumatic stress disorder. In M. J. Friedman, D. S. Charney, & A. Y. Deutch (Eds.), *Neurobiological and clinical consequences of stress: From normal adaptation to post-traumatic stress disorder* (pp. 203–224). Philadelphia: Lippincott-Raven.

Rapaport, M. H., Endicott, J., & Clary, C. M. (2002). Posttraumatic stress disorder and quality of life: Results across 64 weeks of sertraline treatment. *Journal of Clinical Psychiatry, 63*, 59–65.

Raskind, M. A., Peskind, E. R., Hoff, D. J., Hart, K. L., Holmes, H. A., Warren, D., et al. (2007). A parallel group placebo controlled study of prazosin for trauma nightmares and sleep disturbances in combat veterans with post-traumatic stress disorder. *Biological Psychiatry, 61*, 928–934.

Raskind, M. A., Peskind, E. R., Kanter, E. D., Petrie, E. C., Radant, A. D., Thompson, C. E., et al. (2003). Reduction of nightmares and other PTSD symptoms in combat veterans by prazosin: A placebo-controlled study. *American Journal of Psychiatry, 160*, 371–373.

Reich, D. B., Winternitz, S., Hennen, J., Watts, T., & Stanculescu, C. (2004). A preliminary study of risperidone in the treatment of posttraumatic stress disorder related to childhood abuse in women. *Journal of Clinical Psychiatry, 65*, 1601–1606.

Reist, C., Kauffmann, C. D., Haier, R. J., Sangdahl, C., DeMet, E. M., Chicz-DeMet, A., et al. (1989). A controlled trial of desipramine in 18 men with posttraumatic stress disorder. *American Journal of Psychiatry, 146*, 513–516.

Ressler, K. J., Rothbaum, B. O., Tannenbaum, L., Anderson, P., Graap, K., Zimand, E., et al. (2004). Cognitive enhancers as adjuncts to psychotherapy: Use of D-cycloserine in phobic individuals to facilitate extinction of fear. *Archives of General Psychiatry, 61*, 1136–1144.

Robert, R. S., Blakeney, P. E., Villarreal, C., Rosenberg, L., & Meyer, W. J. (1999). Imipramine treatment in pediatric burn patients with symptoms of acute stress disorder: A pilot study. *Journal of the American Academy of Child and Adolescent Psychiatry, 38*, 873–882.

Robert, R., Tcheung, W. J., Rosenberg, L., Rosenberg, M., Mitchell, C., Villarreal, C., et al., (2008). Treating thermally injured children suffering symptoms of acute stress with imipramine and fluoxetine: A randomized, double-blind study. *Burns, 34*(7), 919–928.

Rosen, C. S., Chow, H. C., Finney, J. F., Greenbaum, M. A., Moos, R. H., Sheikh, J. I., et al. (2004). VA practice patterns and practice guidelines for treating posttraumatic stress disorder. *Journal of Traumatic Stress, 17*, 213–222.

Rothbaum, B. O. (2008). Critical parameters for D-cycloserine enhancement of cognitive-behaviorial therapy for obsessive-compulsive disorder. *American Journal of Psychiatry, 165*(3), 293–296.

Rothbaum, B. O., Cahill, S. P., Foa, E. B., Davidson, J. R. T., Compton, J. S., Connor, K. M., et al. (2006). Augmentation of sertraline with prolonged exposure in the treatment of posttraumatic stress disorder. *Journal of Traumatic Stress, 19*, 625–638.

Saygin, M. Z., Sungur, M. Z., Sabol, E. U., & Çetinkaya, P. (2002). Nefazodone versus sertraline in treatment of posttraumatic stress disorder. *Bulletin of Clinical Psychopharmacology, 12*, 1–5.

Schnurr P. P., & Green B. L. (Eds.). (2003) *Trauma and health: Physical health consequences of exposure to extreme stress*. Washington, DC: American Psychological Association.

Schnurr, P. P., Friedman, M. J., Foy, D. W., Shea, M. T., Hsieh, F. Y., Lavori, P. W., et al. (2003). Randomized trial of trauma-focused group therapy for posttraumatic stress disorder. *Archives of General Psychiatry, 60*, 481–489.

Shestatzky, M., Greenberg, D., & Lerer, B. (1988). A controlled trial of phenelzine in posttraumatic stress disorder. *Psychiatry Research, 24*, 149–155.

Simon, N. M., Connor, K. M., Lang, A. J., Rauch, S. A. M., Krulewicz, S., LeBeau, R. T., et al. (2008). Paroxetine CR augmentation for posttraumatic stress disorder refractory to prolonged exposure therapy. *Journal of Clinical Psychiatry, 69*, 400–405.

Sokolski, K. N., Denson, T. F., Lee, R. T., & Reist, C. (2003). Quetiapine for treatment of refractory symptoms of combat-related post-traumatic stress disorder. *Military Medicine, 168*, 486–489.

Southwick, S. M., Davis, L. L., Aikins, D. E., Rassmusson, A, Barron J., & Morgan, C. A. (2007). Neurobiological alterations associated with PTSD. In M. J. Friedman, T. M. Keane, & P. A. Resick (Eds), *Handbook of PTSD: Science and practice* (pp 190–206). New York: Guilford.

Southwick, S. M., Yehuda, R., Giller, E. L., & Charney, D. S. (1994). Use of tricyclics and monoamine oxidase inhibitors in the treatment of PTSD: A quantitative review. In M. M. Murberg (Ed.), *Catecholamine function in posttraumatic stress disorder: Emerging concepts* (pp. 293-305). Washington: American Psychiatric Press.

Stein, M. B., Kline, N. A., & Matloff, J. L. (2002). Adjunctive olanzapine for SSRI-resistant combat-related PTSD: A double-blind, placebo-controlled study. *American Journal of Psychiatry, 159*, 1777–1779.

Taylor, F., & Cahill, L. (2002). Propranolol for reemergent posttraumatic stress disorder following an event of retraumatization: A case study. *Journal of Traumatic Stress, 15*, 433–437.

Tucker, P. M., Trautman, R. P., Wyatt, D. B., Thompson, J., Wu, S.-C., Capece, J. A., et al. (2007). Efficacy and safety of topiramate monotherapy in civilian posttraumatic stress disorder: A randomized, double-blind, placebo-controlled study. *Journal of Clinical Psychiatry, 68*(2), 201–206.

Tucker, P., Zaninelli, R., Yehuda, R., Ruggiero, L., Dillingham, K., & Pitts, C. D. (2001). Paroxetine in the treatment of chronic posttraumatic stress disorder: Results of a placebo-controlled, flexible-dosage trial. *Journal of Clinical Psychiatry, 62*, 860–868.

Vaiva, G., Ducrocq, F., Jezequel, K., Averland, B., Lestavel, P., Brunet, A., et al. (2003). Immediate treatment with propranolol decreases posttraumatic stress disorder two months after trauma. *Biological Psychiatry, 54*, 947–949.

van der Kolk, B. A., Dreyfuss, D., Michaels, M. J., Shera, D., Berkowitz, R., Fisler, R. E., et al. (1994). Fluoxetine in posttraumatic stress disorder. *Journal of Clinical Psychiatry, 55*, 517–522.

van Minnen, A., Arntz, A., & Keijsers, G. P. J. (2002). Prolonged exposure in patients with chronic PTSD: Predictors of treatment outcome and dropout. *Behaviour Research and Therapy, 40*(4), 439–457.

PART 8

Conclusions/Summary

CHAPTER

37 Traumatic Stress Disorders: Looking Back and Moving Forward

Denise M. Sloan *and* J. Gayle Beck

Abstract

This chapter highlights some of the advances in traumatic stress disorders that have been described by contributors of this volume. The chapter also describes areas that will be important for the field to address in the years to come. These areas include advances in the classification of traumatic stress disorders, advances in biological and genetic markers of traumatic stress disorder, advances in assessment measures, especially measures developed for use with children and older adults, and advances in prevention and interventions.

Key Words: Trauma, PTSD, future directions

Although the deleterious effects of trauma have been recognized for some time, the formal diagnosis of posttraumatic stress disorder (PTSD) did not appear in the *Diagnostic and Statistical Manual* until 1980 (American Psychiatric Association, 1980). Given the relatively brief history of the disorder, we have made remarkable progress in our understanding of the epidemiology, etiology, and neurobiology of traumatic stress disorders. We have also made great strides in the development of assessment, prevention, and intervention technologies for trauma survivors. In this chapter, we highlight some of the advances in traumatic stress disorders that have been described by contributors of this volume. We will also describe some of the areas that will important directions for our field in the years to come.

Classification, Epidemiology, and Theories

The classification of traumatic stress disorders has become more precise with progression of work this area. Continued precision will be seen in the upcoming *DSM-5* when revisions to the diagnostic criteria of PTSD and acute stress disorder (ASD) will be made. One substantial proposed change to the PTSD diagnostic disorder in *DSM-5* is to divide the current cluster C criterion based on findings from confirmatory factor analytic studies (American Psychiatric Association [APA], 2011). The proposed revision would retain avoidance symptoms in cluster C (avoidance of internal reminders and avoidance of external reminders), and add a new cluster D criterion that will focus on negative alterations in cognition and mood (e.g., distorted self-blame, diminished interest or participation in activities, inability to experience positive emotions). Another substantial change that is being considered concerns Criterion A2, which currently states that the individual's response to an event must involve fear, helplessness, or horror. Research has suggested that this criterion suffers from poor utility and predictive validity (for a review see Bovin & Marx, 2011). The *DSM-5* committee is considering either dropping Criterion A2 altogether or broadening it to subsume other peritraumatic responses.

Another major change being considered is the addition of a developmental trauma disorder (APA, 2011), which would better capture responses to traumatic stress exposure that have been seen in children. This would be an important addition, as the current PTSD diagnostic criteria do not take into account development factors that influence the expression of symptoms in children (Scheeringa, Zeanah, & Cohen, 2011).

Changes to the diagnostic criteria of ASD are also being considered. As described by Pacella and Delahanty (see part two, chapter 3 of this volume), the initial purpose of the ASD diagnosis was to serve as an early means of identification of individuals who would be at greater risk for developing more chronic problems associated with traumatic stress exposure. However, ASD does not appear to be predictive of PTSD. With increased precision of the diagnostic criteria for both ASD and PTSD in the *DSM-5*, the predictive value of ASD may increase.

In addition to advances in classification, substantial advances have been made in terms of our theoretical understanding of traumatic stress disorders. Much of this progress is the direct result of technological advances in the methods used to assess genetic and other biological risk factors. A recent study by Ressler and colleagues (2011) provides an example of the type of advances that have been made. These investigators found that a protein, known as pituitary adenylate cyclase-activating polypeptide (PACAP), appears to be controlled by estrogen and plays a key role in stress and fear. This finding has important treatment implications, as well as provides a possible explanation for the greater prevalence rate of PTSD in women. Although we have a better understanding of the possible mechanisms through which genes confer vulnerability for development of traumatic stress disorders, there is a great deal of inconsistency in the literature. The inconsistency appears to be the result of the variability in methodology used by investigators. It is also clear that no one gene can account for traumatic stress disorders. Instead, multiple genes are involved in traumatic stress disorders and these genes interact with environmental factors to heighten risk or to facilitate recovery. As the behavioral genetics and molecular genetics field continues to evolve, we can expect continued knowledge of genetics and PTSD.

Assessment

Over the past 20 years, the field has made substantial progress in the development of instruments assessing the presence and severity of traumatic stress disorders. We now have a number of psychometrically strong diagnostic interview and self-report instruments that can be used to assess stressor exposure, ASD, PTSD, and other associated disorders among adults and children. Importantly, brief assessment measures have been developed, which have been useful in mass disaster situations, as well as for screening in primary-care settings.

As noted by contributors in this volume, there are a number of ways in which assessment of traumatic stress disorders can be improved. One area that should be a focus of future work is psychophysiological and biological measures to identify traumatic stress disorders. To date, there are inconsistent findings regarding the utility of biological and psychophysiological measures to identify traumatic stress disorders; yet, physiological responding (e.g., high arousal in response to trauma cues, startle reflex) is considered a core feature of traumatic stress disorders (Pole, 2007). As described by Bovin and Weathers (part five, chapter 16 in this volume), comorbid conditions (e.g., depression) may account for some of the inconsistent findings in the literature. The methods use to assess responses to trauma cues may also contribute to the inconsistent findings.

Another limitation of the currently available assessment instruments concerns the validity of measures adapted for use with children. As described by March and colleagues (part five, chapter 18 in this volume), there are concerns that the PTSD diagnostic criteria that are currently used for both adults and children may not be appropriate for children. Thus, assessment measures currently available for use with children may not be optimal. As previously described, as a result of general concerns of the developmental appropriateness of the PTSD disorder for children, the *DSM-5* work group is considering a separate diagnostic syndrome for use with children, developmental trauma disorder (APA, 2011). If a new diagnostic syndrome is developed for use with children, new measures that are consistent with the new syndrome will be needed. Another general issue with the measures developed for use with children is that these measures do not typically consider the developmental level of the child that is being assessed. The lack of consideration of developmental stage has implications for the validity of the information obtained.

Other areas that will be important directions for assessment of traumatic stress disorders include consideration of comorbid conditions, greater attention to the assessment of older adults, and assessment of functional impairment associated with traumatic stress disorders. Consideration of comorbid traumatic brain injury (TBI) is a particularly pressing issue as this is a comorbid common condition, especially among military servicemen and women. TBI also has substantial symptom overlap with PTSD (e.g., concentration difficulty), which renders assessment of these conditions more complex.

Prevention and Intervention

The last two parts of this volume concerns prevention and intervention. Progress in intervention in traumatic stress disorders has been tremendous in the past 25 years. Nevertheless, substantial gaps remain. One such gap is prevention and early intervention. Preventing the onset of posttraumatic stress symptoms (PSS) and targeting intervention efforts early in the course of PSS are ideal. However, relatively little attention has been focused on prevention and early intervention efforts. We have learned that some of our early interventions efforts, such as critical-incident stress debriefing, are not efficacious and may be deleterious. We have also learned that the most efficacious approaches are cognitive behavioral approaches.

Development of different delivery methods for prevention and early interventions and identifying the best time to intervene following traumatic exposure will be important directions for the field. Although it is clear that the majority of individuals exposed to a traumatic event do not develop PSS, a substantial minority do develop such symptoms. Gaining a better understanding of PSS risk and resilience factors will be critical in targeting early interventions among those individuals who are most in need of such services.

Much progress has been made in understanding risk and resilience factors in recent years. Some of the progress is attributable to advances in longitudinal statistical methods, as described by King and colleagues in this volume (see part six, chapter 22 in this volume). Another reason for the progress is the increase in longitudinal design studies of traumatic exposure. Given the number of longitudinal studies that are currently under way, we will likely know much more about risk and resilience factors associated with traumatic exposure in the years to come.

Another area that needs to be addressed is the treatment of PTSD and comorbid conditions, including substance use disorders and TBI. These comorbid conditions frequently co-occur with PTSD, yet are common exclusion criteria in PTSD clinical trials (Institute of Medicine, 2007). There is a pressing need to examine the efficacy of evidence-based PTSD treatments with individuals who have commonly co-occurring conditions in order to best serve individuals with PTSD. In the wake of veterans returning from Iraq and Afghanistan with PTSD and TBI, the Departments of Defense and Veterans Affairs have funded research to examine these important areas. We can look forward to advances in our field as a result of the studies that are currently under way.

In addition to the gap in knowledge regarding co-occurring conditions, the PTSD clinical trial literature has primarily focused on survivors of interpersonal violence, who are mostly women. The recent Institute of Medicine report of the current PTSD treatment literature (Institute of Medicine, 2007) emphasized the need to include males in PTSD treatment studies, as well as the need to conduct clinical trials that focus on combat-related PTSD individuals. Veterans Administration is the largest PTSD treatment provider in the world, yet there is relatively little available research regarding efficacy of evidence-based treatments for PTSD with combat veterans. Combat-related PTSD presents unique challenges for treatment providers (e.g., chronic PTSD, high prevalence rates of comorbid psychiatric conditions, and physical health conditions) and tends to be predominately males, who are underrepresented in PTSD clinical trials. The large number of returning military servicemen and women who have high rates of PTSD has resulted in increased attention to treating combat-related PTSD and developing early interventions. The high level of research activity currently being conducted should result in a dramatic increase in our knowledge of treatment of combat-related PTSD and early interventions.

The traumatic stress disorders field should also examine mechanism of successful treatment outcome so that we can better understand why treatments work and make existing treatments more efficient by narrowing the treatment protocols to focus on critical mechanisms. An example of this type of work is Resick and colleagues (2008), who conducted a dismantling study of cognitive processing therapy (CPT) and found that the cognitive processing component of CPT was associated with faster treatment gains than the full CPT protocol or a written account only treatment version. As highlighted by Friedman in this volume (part seven, chapter 36), we know little about the efficacy of augmenting psychotherapy with psychotropic medication. In particular, medication augmentation may facilitate psychotherapy treatment progress.

Kearns and Rothbaum (part seven, chapter 32 in this volume) have described emerging evidence that administration of D-cycloserine can facilitate exposure treatment, thereby reducing the number of treatment sessions needed for successful treatment outcome.

Group PTSD treatment is another area that has received surprisingly little attention. Group treatment is frequently used in healthcare settings, including the VA healthcare system. Yet, there is no evidence-based group treatment for PTSD. The cost and complexity of conducting group randomized clinical trials have likely resulted in the group PTSD treatment literature to lag behind the individual treatment literature. Nevertheless, there is a pressing need to identify evidence-based PTSD group treatment.

The use of telehealth methods to deliver treatment is an area that has advanced considerably in recent years and holds much promise as a method to deliver treatment to individuals who might not be able to access services otherwise. Recent research has used videoconferencing to deliver treatment to individuals residing in remote locations (Morland et al., 2010), as well as used the Internet to deliver treatment anonymously to service men and women (Litz, Engel, Bryant, & Papa, 2007). With increasing technological advances and increased availability of this technology, we will likely see increased use of telehealth methods to deliver treatment as well as to conduct assessment (Sloan, Gallagher, Feinstein, Lee, & Pruneau, 2011). The use of telehealth technology will be a critical tool to deliver treatment to large numbers of individuals in situations such as mass disasters and to reach individuals who live in rural areas or regions that do not have expert trauma treatment providers available. The use of smartphones represents another option to deliver treatment rapidly and to large numbers of individuals (Kazdin & Blase, 2011).

In a recent article on improving psychotherapy research, Kazdin and Blase (2011) has described the need to develop alternative methods for delivering treatment in order adequately address the burden of mental illness. Many of the recommendations made by Kazdin and Blase apply to the trauma field. One such recommendation is to include the use of lay people to deliver treatment. An example of this type of application is a program called Combat and Operational Stress First Aid (COSFA; Nash, Krantz, Stein, Westphal, & Litz, 2011). One barrier to seeking mental healthcare services for servicemen and women is confidentiality concerns. Services delivered from a chaplain remain confidential within the military, thus servicemen and women may be more likely to disclosure mental health concerns to chaplains. The COSFA program has trained chaplains to deliver brief interventions to military servicemen and women, and the program appears to be effective in terms of increasing the number of military personnel seeking mental healthcare services. The use of lay people to deliver treatment in the aftermath of mass disasters would represent an ideal method of implementing interventions to a large number of people in a short period of time. Kazdin and Blase (2011) also suggest that self-help interventions should be examined as another alternative method to deliver interventions more quickly and efficiently, and potentially reach individuals who might not present for services otherwise. Self-help interventions might be particularly useful for individuals with more acute and lower distress levels resulting from a traumatic event.

Taken together, we have made remarkable progress in a relatively short amount of time in terms of our understanding of traumatic stress disorders and how best to assess and treat these disorders. Although the field has a number of challenges to face, there is agreement on what these challenges are and how we should be addressing them. Given the plethora of traumatic stress research that is being conducted, we can look forward to significant advances in the field in the years to come.

References

American Psychiatric Association. (1980). *Diagnostic and statistical manual of mental disorders* (3rd ed.). Washington, DC: Author.

American Psychiatric Association. (2011). *American Psychiatric Association DSM-5 development.* Retrieved from http://www.dsm5.org.

Bovin, M. J., & Marx, B. P. (2011). The importance of the peritraumatic experience in defining traumatic stress. *Psychological Bulletin, 137*, 47–67

Institute of Medicine (2007). *Treatment of posttraumatic stress disorder: An assessment of the evidence.* Washington, DC: National Academies Press.

Kazdin, A. E., & Blase, S. L. (2011). Rebooting psychotherapy research and practice to reduce the burden of mental illness. *Perspectives on Psychological Science, 6*, 21–37.

Litz, B., Engel, C., Bryant, R., & Papa, A. (2007). A randomized, controlled proof-of-concept trial of an Internet-based, therapist-assisted self-management treatment for posttraumatic stress disorder. *American Journal of Psychiatry, 164*, 1676–1684.

Morland, L. A., Greene, C. J., Rosen, C. S., Foy, D., Reilly, P., Shore, J., & Frueh, B. C. (2010). Telemedicine for anger management therapy in a rural population of combat veterans with posttraumatic stress disorder: A randomized noninferiority trial. *Journal of Clinical Psychiatry, 71*, 855–863.

Nash, W., Krantz, L., Stein, N., Westphal, R., & Litz, B. T. (2011) Comprehensive soldier fitness, battlemind, and the stress continuum model: Military organizational approaches to prevention. In J. I. Ruzek, P. P. Schnurr, J. J. Vasterling, & M. J. Friedman, (Eds.), *Caring for veterans with deployment-related stress disorders: Iraq, Afghanistan, and beyond* (pp. 193–214). Washington, DC: American Psychological Association.

Pole, N. (2007). The psychophysiology of posttraumatic stress disorder: A meta-analysis. *Psychological Bulletin, 133*, 725–746.

Resick, P. A., Galovski, T. E., Uhlmansiek, M. O., Scher, C. D., Clum, G. A., & Young-Xu, Y. (2008). Randomized clinical trial to dismantle components of cognitive processing therapy for posttraumatic stress disorder in female victims of interpersonal violence. *Journal of Consulting and Clinical Psychology, 76*, 243–258.

Ressler, K. J., Mercer, K. B., Bradley, B., Jovanovic, T., Mahan, A., Kerley, K., & May, V. (2011) Post-traumatic stress disorder is associated with PACAP and PAC1 receptor. *Nature, 470*, 492–497.

Scheeringa, M. S., Zeanah, C. H., & Cohen, J. A. (2011). PTSD in children and adolescents: Toward an empirically based algorithm. *Depression and Anxiety. Early online publication.*

Sloan, D. M. Gallagher, M. W., Feinstein, B. A., Lee, D., & Pruneau, G. (2011). Efficacy of telehealth treatments for posttraumatic stress-related symptoms: A meta-analysis. *Cognitive Behaviour Therapy, 40*, 111–125.

INDEX

Page numbers written in italics denote illustrations.

A

Abrahamson, D.J., 442
acceptance and commitment therapy (ACT), 468
accidents
  risk of PTSD from, 18, 89, 90
  See also motor vehicle accidents (MVAs)
Acierno, R.E., 124, 398, 399
Acute Stress Checklist for Children (ASC-Kids), 273, 277
acute stress disorder (ASD)
  assessment of, 29, 31, 32, 78, 79, 80, 102, 254
  in children and adolescents, 101–04, 113, 273
  classification, 28–29, 528
  as comorbid diagnosis, 77
  cultural considerations in diagnosing, 4, 29, 35
  differentiating from PTSD, 30, 70, 159–60
  distinguishing from normal posttrauma response, 30–31
  early interventions, 35, 70, 371, 373
  epidemiology, 4, 69, 72–75, 78, 79
  etiology of, 55, 159
  memory and cognitive impairments, 103, 202
  in older adults, 120, 121, 125, 492
  as precursor/predictor of PTSD, 29, 31–32, 33–34, 35, 71, 78–80, 102, 104, 159–60, 162, 169, 252, 528
  as predictor of depression, 33
  prevalence in adults, 69, 72–75
  prevalence in children, 101
  research on, 36, 78, 79–80, 103, 104
  risk factors for, 69, 75–77
  in special populations, 129
  subclinical symptoms, 75
  See also diagnostic criteria for ASD (*DSM-IV*)
Acute Stress Disorder Interview (ASDI), 31, 32, 253, 254
Acute Stress Disorder Module of the Diagnostic Interview for Children and Adolescents (DICA-ASD), 273, 277
Acute Stress Disorder Scale (ASDS), 32, 254
acute stress reactions (ASR), 4, 71, 252
  See also acute stress disorder (ASD)
Adams, G.A., 336
ADAPT (Adaptation and Development After Persecution and Trauma), 407
Adenauer, H., 205
adjustment disorders (AD)
  etiology, 55
  first site for ASD symptomatology, 28–29
  proposed changes in *DSM-5,* 57
  subclinical ASD as, 75
Adkins, J.W., 239, 240, 241
Adler, A.B., 354
Adolescent Dissociative Experience Scale (A-DES), 272–73, 277
adolescents. *See* children and adolescents
Adressky, R., 357
Aduriz, M.E., 387
affective disorders, 293
Afghanistan. *See* Iraq/Afghanistan veterans
African Americans
  and Hurricane Katrina, 75
  PTSD risk for, 49, 124–25
  See also Caribbean blacks
age. *See* risk and protective factors for PTSD
aggression. *See* posttraumatic stress responses
aging. *See* older adults
Ahmadzadeh, G., 226
Ahrens, C.E., 354
Alarcon, R.D., 466
alcohol use disorder, 93
  See also substance use disorders
Alden, L.E., 21
Aldwin, C.M., 336
Allen, E.S., 221
Allen, M., 351–52
Allumbaugh, D., 399
Alpert, A., 341
Alvarez, W., 292
American Psychiatric Association, 4
  See also Diagnostic and Statistical Manual of Mental Disorders
Amir, N., 197, 201, 207
amnesia
  complete, 200, 203
  as diagnostic criterion for PTSD, 191, 198
  dissociative, 253
  trauma-induced, 71, 191, 199–200, 203, 250, 253
  See also information processing in PTSD
Amstadter, A.B., 224, 465
Andrews, B., 22, 31
anhedonia, 41
Anthony, J.L., 108
anti-social personality disorder (ASPD), 45
anxiety
  comorbidity with many conditions, 64
  comorbidity with PTSD, 46, 61, 203, 203–07
  and somatoform disorders, 46
  See also anxiety disorders
anxiety disorders
  cognitive biases in, 103
  functional impairments in, 316
  PTSD classified as, 56–57
  screening for, 293
  subclinical ASD as, 75
  treatments for, 427
  See also acute stress disorder (ASD); adjustment disorders (AD); posttraumatic stress disorder (PTSD)
Anxiety Disorders Interview Schedule, Child and Parent Versions (ADIS-C/P), *266,* 268, 277
Arean, P.A., 495

Army Battlemind program, 353–54, 365–66, 370, 374
Arntz, A., 197, 418, 435
Artigas, L., 387
ASD (acute stress disorder). *See* acute stress disorder (ASD)
Asians, and PTSD, 48
Asmundson, G.J.G., 46
assault. *See* child sexual and physical abuse; physical assault; sexual assault
Assaulted Staff Action Program (ASAP), 355
assessment of PTSD
behavioral observations, 5, 245–46, 295
Criterion A issues, 244
detecting malingering, 6, 235, 244–45
future directions, 245–46, 278, 295–96, 312, 357–58, 528
method comparisons, 245
multimodal approach, 245
in multiple traumatic events, 16–17, 23–25, 85, 244
random-event method, 85–86
self-report measures
DSM-correspondent
Davidson Trauma Scale (DTS), 238, 254, 294, 296
Detailed Assessment of Posttraumatic Stress (DAPS), 239, 242
Posttraumatic Stress Diagnostic Scale (PDS), 239, 242, 244, 293, 310
PTSD Checklist (PCL), 238–39, 245, 291–92, *293*
Empirically-derived
PK Scale of MMPI and MMPI-2, 241, 244
Symptom Checklist-90-R (SCL-90-R), 242
Non-DSM-correspondent
Impact of Event Scale (IES), 237, 240–41, 273, *274*, 288–89, *289*
Mississippi Scale for Combat-Related PTSD, 236, 240, *289*, 290
summary and comparisons, 242
structured interviews
Clinician-Administered PTSD Scale (CAPS), 24, 236–37, 238, 244, 245, 267, 310
PTSD Symptom Scale Interview (PSS-I), 237, 238, 310
SCID-I, 236, 237, 238, 244, 284, 285, *286*, 310
Structured Interview for PTSD (SI-PTSD), 237–38, *286*, 288
summary and comparisons, 238
"worst event" method, 16–17, 85–86
See also assessment of traumatic stress symptoms; biological assessments; cultural considerations; non-Western cultures, PTSD assessment in; older adults, assessment methods for; psychophysiological assessments
assessment of traumatic stress symptoms
biological factors, 255–56
cognitive factors, 255
descriptive role of ASD, 252
need for early, 251, 258
Peritraumatic Dissociative Experiences Questionnaire (PDEQ), 32, 254–55, 310
Peritraumatic Distress Scale (PDS), 255
predictive role of ASD, 252
predictive role of peritraumatic dissociation, 34–35, 71–72, 161, 197, 252–53
self-report measures
Acute Stress Disorder Scale (ASDS), 32, 254
Posttraumatic Adjustment Scale (PAS), 254
Stanford Acute Stress Reaction Questionnaire (SASRQ), 32, 253–54
structured clinical interviews
Acute Stress Disorder Interview (ASDI), 31, 32, 253, 254
Structured Clinical Interview for Dissociative Disorders (SCID-D), 253
timing of, 256–57
Trauma Screening Questionnaire (TSQ), 254, 348
See also acute stress disorder (ASD); children and adolescents, trauma assessment in
Astin, M.C., 453
attentional bias. *See* information processing in PTSD
avoidance and numbing
assessments of, 182
as core symptom of PTSD, 133, 136
delay of PTSD onset with, 90
functional impairments from, 221, 316
as response to trauma, 17, 30, 175, 250
See also diagnostic criteria for PTSD
avoidant personality, 45
Axis I and II disorders, 39

B

Bachman, A.W., 148
Baldwin, S.A., 419
Barad, M., 432
Barak, Y., 123
Bar-Haim, Y., 205
Barlow, D.H., 59
Barnes, H.E., 354
Bartels, S., 395
Batrim, D., 497
Battlemind program, 353–54, 365–66, 370, 374
Bayesian hierarchical spatial model, 80
Beaton, R., 341
Beck Anxiety Inventory—Primary Care (BAI-PC), 294
Beck Depression Inventory (BDI), 239
Becker, C.B., 467
Beckford, L.A., 292
Beckham, J.C., 226
Beck, J.G., 204, 208, 222, 241, 289, 419, 441
Behavioral Activation (BA), 368
Behavioral Activation and Therapeutic Exposure (BA-TE), 399
behavioral assessments, for PTSD, 5, 245–46, 295
Bellamy, N.D., 385
benzodiazepines, 375, *516*, 520, 521
bereavement
cultural, 509
further research needed on, 25
See also complicated bereavement
Berger, R., 352
Berliner, L., 482
Bernard-Bonnin, A-C., 107
Berntsen, D., 193, 199
Berry, J.W., 309
Biddle, D., 419
Binder, E.B., 148
bioinformational theory of emotion, 243
biological assessments
in older adults, 294–95, 296
See also biological markers of PTSD
biological markers of PTSD
catecholamines, 161–62
cortisol levels, 162, 163, 164–68, 169, 246, 256, 294
future research needed on, 169, 528
GABA levels, 163, 255, 519, 520
glucocorticoid receptors, 168–69
hippocampal volume, 163–64
HPA axis dysregulation, 94, 148, 152, 168, 169, 256, 294, 494
neuroanatomic predictors, 163–64
predicting PTSD through event response, 161–62
search for, 94, 162–63
See also genetics and genomics of PTSD; learning models of PTSD; psychophysiological assessment
bipolar disorder, 129
Birmes, P.J., 34–35
Bisson, J., 456
blame
and PTSD risk, 21–22, 62, 255, 442
See also risk and protective factors for PTSD
Blanchard, E.B., 21, 22, 195, 245
Blase, S.L., 530
Bliese, P.D., 354
Blouin, A.M., 432
Bluthgen, C., 387
Boals, A., 193
Boehnlein, J., 496
Bohni, M.K., 199
Bolton, P., 311
Bonanno, G.A., 336, 342

Book, S.W., 238
borderline personality disorder (BPD), 45, 129, 421, 446, 467
Borenstein, A.R., 292
Borkovec, T.D., 63
Bouchard, S., 466
Bouton, M.E., 431
Bovin, M., 528
Bowlby, J., 224
BPTSD-12, 296
Bradley, R., 496–97
brain injury. *See* traumatic brain injury (TBI)
Bramsen, I., 123
Bremner, J.D., 205
Breslau, N., 14–15, 16, 18, 22, 58, 61, 85, 91, 164
Brewin, C.R., 22, 30, 31, 62, 63, 193, 197, 198, 202, 335, 348, 383
Briere, J., 310
Brodaty, H., 293
Broman-Fulks, J., 465
Bronfenbrenner, U., 306, 403
Broomhall, L.G.J., 32, 33
Browne, M.W., 339
Brown, L.M., 292
Bruce, S., 446
Brunet, A., 519
Bryant, R.A., 30, 31, 32, 33, 35, 101, 103, 195, 204, 207, 350, 352, 357, 372, 422
Bryk, A.S., 341
Buckley, T.C., 22
Buck, N., 208–09
Buffalo Creek dam collapse, 109, 220
bullying intervention programs, 406
Burgess, A., 56
Burgess, N., 193
Burghardt, K., 242
Burns, D.D., 497
Byrne, C.A., 221

C

Cain, C.K., 432
Cain, N., 209
Calhoun, P.S., 123
Cambodian refugees, 507, 508
Campbell, R., 354, 355
Canterino, J., 464
CAPS (Clinician-Administered PTSD Scale). *See* Clinician-Administered PTSD Scale (CAPS)
Carey, P.D., 107
Caribbean blacks, 125
Carlson, J.G., 192
Carroll, K.M., 416
Carstensen, L.L., 494
Carty, J., 357
Cashman, L., 201
Cassidy, E.L., 292
Castro, C.A., 354
Catastrophizing Interview (CI), 210
catecholamines. *See* biological markers of PTSD
Caucasians, PTSD risk for, 49, 124–25
Cercone, J., 465
Chaffin, M., 405
Chapman Art Therapy Treatment Intervention (CATTI), 485
Chapman, L., 387
Chard, K.M., 441, 443, 444, 445
Charlson, M.E., 123
Chemtob, C., 192
Child and Family Traumatic Stress Intervention (CFTSI), 384
Child Behavior Checklist (CBCL), 267, *269*, 271
Child-Centered Therapy (CCT), 484
Child Development Community Policing program (CD-CP), 384
Child Dissociative Checklist (CDC), 272, 277
Child Parent Psychotherapy (CPP), 484, 486
Child PTSD Reaction Index (CPTSD-RI), *270*, 272, 277
Child PTSD Symptom Scale (CPSS), *270*, 272, 277
children and adolescents, prevention and early intervention, 381–92
  effectiveness of, 384, 386, 387
  key definitions, *382*
  for refugee children, 407–10
  research needs and future directions, 388–90
  types of interventions
    art and massage therapies, 387
    cognitive-behavioral therapy, 386
    community-based early interventions, 352–53, 355, 384–85, 388–89
    debriefing, 387, 389
    Eye Movement Desensitization and Reprocessing (EMDR), 386, 387
    family-centered approaches, 387–88
    individual interventions, 385–88
    Psychological First Aid, 386–87, 389
  See also children and adolescents, PTSD in; children and adolescents, trauma assessment in; children and adolescents, traumatic stress in
children and adolescents, PTSD in
  clinical course, 109–10
    chronic, 106, 107
    comorbid diagnoses, 110
    delayed-onset, 109–10
  definition and diagnostic criteria, 104–05, 108–09, 113
  etiology, 110
  future directions, 111, 112–13
  prevalence, 105–08
    for child abuse and interpersonal violence, 107–08, 109
    for natural disasters and terrorism, 105–06, 109, 111
    for personal injury/accident, 107, 109
  risk factors for, 48, 94, 98–99, 103, 110–12, 382–84
  See also children and adolescents, trauma assessment in; children and adolescents, traumatic stress in
children and adolescents, trauma assessment in
  acute stress disorder measures, 273
  diagnostically-oriented instruments
    chart of, *265–66*
    for school-aged children, 267–68
    for very young children, 264, 267
  diagnostic classification issues, 263, 528
  dissociation measures, 272–73
  future directions, 278, 528
  importance of, 262
  measuring symptoms across ages, 263–64
  psychometric issues, 263
  screening instruments, 273–76
    chart of, 274–75
  self-report questionnaires
    chart of, 269–70
    for school-aged children and adolescents, 271–72
    for very young children, 268, 271
  summary and recommendations, 277
  use of multiple informants, 264
  See also children and adolescents, traumatic stress in
children and adolescents, traumatic stress in
  acute stress disorder, 101–04, 113, 273
  impact of, 48, 99–100, 103, 104, 129, 382
  and parental functioning, 104
  and polyvictimization, 108
  prevalence of, 98, 105, 382
  role of intelligence in response to, 92
  types of exposures, 99–100
  See also children and adolescents, prevention and early intervention; children and adolescents, PTSD in; children and adolescents, trauma assessment in; children and adolescents, treatment therapies; child sexual and physical abuse
children and adolescents, treatment therapies
  chart summarizing, *475–78*
  Child-Centered Therapy (CCT), 484
  Child Parent Psychotherapy (CPP), 484, 486
  for child physical abuse, 483–84
  for child sexual abuse, 441, 480–83, 505, 507
  Combined Parent-Child Cognitive Behavioral Therapy (CPC-CBT), 483–84
  Eye Movement Desensitization and Reprocessing (EMDR), 482–83
  for medical trauma, 485
  MED-RELAX, 484–85
  for multiple or mixed traumas, 485–86

Narrative Exposure Therapy (NET), 484–85
pharmacotherapies, 481–82, 521
Prolonged Exposure Therapy for Adolescents (PE-A), 485–86
Seeking Safety, 420, 469, 470, 485
in situations of extreme trauma, war, violence, 484–85
summary and future directions, 486–88
Time-Limited Dynamic Psychotherapy (TLDP-A), 485–86
Trauma-Focused Cognitive Behavioral Therapy (TF-CBT), 473–74, 478–79, 480–82, 484, 485, 486
Children's PTSD Inventory (CPTSDI), *266*, 268, 277
Children's Revised Impact of Event Scale (CRIES-8), 273, *274*, 277
Children's Revised Impact of Event Scale (CRIES-13), 273, *274*, 276, 277
child sexual and physical abuse
dissociation in, 44
as extreme trauma, 504–05
in incarcerated population, 130, 131
PTSD risk from, 19, 107–08
treatment therapies and concerns, 441, 480–84, 505, 507
Child Stress Disorders Checklist, 102
Child Trauma Screening Questionnaire (CTSQ), *275*, 276, 277
chronic PTSD
comorbid diagnoses, 235
diagnostic criteria, 18, 90
predicting, 41, 206, 207
role of priming in, 196
Chung, I., 341
Civilian Mississippi Scale (CMS), 240, 290
See also Mississippi Scale for Combat-Related PTSD (M-PTSD)
Clapp, J.D., 222
Clark, D.M., 193, 195, 197, 198, 199, 206, 208, 209, 212, 255
classification of PTSD. *See* diagnostic criteria for PTSD
clinical trials
evaluating
attrition and missing data, 417–18
comorbidity accommodation, 420–21, 529
comparison groups, 416–17
controlling for clustering effects, 419–20
efficacy, effectiveness, and practical trials, 415–16
measuring PTSD outcomes, 420
sample size and design choice, 418–19
randomized, 364, 415, 416
See also PTSD treatment research
Clinician-Administered PTSD Scale (CAPS)
cross-cultural use, 310
Life Events Checklist, 236, 285
for PTSD assessment, 24, 236–37, 238, 244, 245, 267, 285–87
use in older adults, *284*, 285–87
Clinician-Administered PTSD Scale for Children and Adolescents (CAPS-CA), *265*, 267–68, 277
Clipp, E.C., 122, 338–39
Cloitre, M., 421, 467
clonidine, 518, 519
Cognitive Behavioral Conjoint Therapy (CBCT), 464
cognitive-behavioral theory, 227–28
cognitive-behavioral therapy (CBT)
as early intervention measure, 35, 251, 367–68, 371–74, 386
as PTSD treatment, 35, 62, 136, 212, 222, 251, 415, 504, 513, 521
training initiatives for, 513
See also Cognitive Behavioral Therapy for Postdisaster Distress (CBT-PD); Cognitive Processing Therapy (CPT); Combined Parent-Child Cognitive Behavioral Therapy (CPC-CBT); Trauma-Focused Cognitive Behavioral Therapy (TF-CBT)
Cognitive Behavioral Therapy for Postdisaster Distress (CBT-PD), 352, 356
Cognitive Processing Therapy (CPT)
description of therapy, 439–41
as early intervention, 375
efficacy with PTSD, 415, 443–46, 529
limitations and future directions, 446–47
underlying mechanism and empirical support, 441–43
Cohen, J.A., 107–08, 481, 484
Coles, M.E., 207
Combat and Operational Stress First Aid (COSFA), 530
Combined Parent-Child Cognitive Behavioral Therapy (CPC-CBT), 483–84
Communal Traumatic Experiences Inventory, 310
community-based early intervention. *See* early interventions, community-based
Community Crisis Response Team (CCRT), 384–85
comorbid diagnoses
clinical trials accommodating, 420–21, 529
See also posttraumatic stress disorder (PTSD); *other disorders*
complex PTSD
diagnostic criteria, 47–48, 49, 57
symptoms, 47, 421
complex trauma, 505
complicated bereavement
in children, 110
in older adults, 399
overlap with PTSD, 25, 39
proposed *DSM-5* category for, 57
symptoms, 43
Composite International Diagnostic Interview (CIDI), 85, *286*, 287–88, 310
Cook, J.M., 291–92
Cortina, L.M., 19
cortisol. *See* biological markers of PTSD
Cottingham, S.M., 445
Creamer, M., 31, 32, 33, 192, 357, 419
Crime-Related PTSD Scale (CR-PTSD), 242
Crisis Counseling and Training Program (CCP), 385
Critical Incident Stress Debriefing (CISD), 35, 365, 369–70, 374, 398, 529
Critical Incident Stress Management (CISM), 365, 370
Crits-Christoph, P., 419
Crow, J.R., 226–27
Crumlish, N., 310
cultural bereavement, 509
cultural considerations
in ASD assessment, 4, 29, 35
in clinical trials, 421–22
cultural bereavement, 509
in older adult trauma survivors, 123–24
in PTSD treatment and assessment, 5–6, 48–49, 305–08, 311–12, 507–08, 509
in PTSD treatment research, 421–22
in trauma experience and expression, 5, 48–49, 84
in treatments for special populations, 305–08, 311–12, 507–08, 509
See also non-Western cultures, PTSD assessment in

D

Dalgleish, T., 101, 193, 207
Dasen, P.R., 309
Davidson, J.R., 226, 237, 238, 288
Davidson Trauma Scale (DTS), 238, 254, 294, 296
Davis, G.C., 16, 91
Davis, M., 30, 176, 178
Davis, M.I., 208
Davison, E.H., 336, 339
Daviss, W.B., 101, 102
d-cycloserine (DCS), 468, 470, 496, *516*, 517, 519–20, 521, 522, 530
death of loved one. *See* risk and protective factors for PTSD
Deblinger, E., 107–08, 481, 483
DeDeyn, J.M., 340
De Jong, J.V.M., 5
De Jong, P.J., 207
Delahanty, D.L., 21–22, 528
delayed-onset PTSD
in adults, 5, 61, 63, 90, 109, 110, 160, 161, 251
in children and adolescents, 109–10

clinical course, 121, 160
in combat veterans, 251, 339
defined, 251
See also late-onset stress symptomatology (LOSS)
demographics
as ASD risk factor, 75
See also risk and protective factors for PTSD
DeMond, M.G., 222
depression
in ASD, 33
assessment measures, 326
cognitive function in, 202
comorbidity with PTSD, 30, 33, 41–42, 61, 93, 110, 207, 222, 325
major, 129
therapies, 368
DeRoon-Cassini, T.A., 342
Detailed Assessment of Posttraumatic Stress (DAPS), 239, 242
Detroit Area Survey, 20, 89
developmental disabilities, 131, 132, 133, 134–35
developmental psychopathology trauma model, 404
developmental trauma disorder, 113, 527–28
Devilly, G.J., 434–35
Diagnostic and Statistical Manual of Mental Disorders (DSM)
first version, 71
on role of culture in diagnostics, 310–11
See also diagnostic criteria for ASD; diagnostic criteria for PTSD
diagnostic criteria for ASD (*DSM-IV*)
conceptualization of, 71–72
Criterion A1 (stressor), 29, 70, 251
Criterion A2 (response), 70, 71
Criterion B (dissociation), 70, 71, 251
Criterion C (re-experiencing), 70, 102, 251
Criterion D (avoidance), 70, 101–02, 208, 251
Criterion E (hyper-arousal), 70, 251
Criterion F (distress or impairment), 70, 251–52
Criterion G (duration), 70, 252
diagnostic criteria overview, 29, 70, 251–52
differentiating from acute stress reactions, 252
dissociation criteria, 31–32, 34–35, 43–44, 70, 71, 79, 101, 102–03, 104
duration criteria, 69, 102, 159, 252
introduction of diagnosis, 5, 28, 29, 71, 251
proposed revisions for *DSM-5*, 29, 34, 35, 36, 57, 72, 75, 79, 252, 528
diagnostic criteria for PTSD (*DSM-III* & *DSM-III-R*)
definition of PTSD, 84
definition of stressor events (Criterion A), 12, 14–15, 85, 87, 90–91, 92, 94
introduction of PTSD in, 3, 39, 40, 56, 59, 71, 84
diagnostic criteria for PTSD (*DSM-IV*)
chart of diagnostic criteria, *40*
chronic PTSD subtype, 18, 41, 90
controversies, 39
Criterion A
controversies, 11–18, 58
etiological questions, 57–58
high stakes in defining, 11–12
history and development, 12–14, 55–57
splitting into A1 and A2, 12–14, 57
Criterion A1 (stressor events)
controversies and proposed changes, 12, 13, 14–16, 57–58, 59, 85
direct exposure criterion, 14, 15–16
multiple traumas, 16–17, 23–25, 85
qualifying stressors, 12, 13, 18–20, 57, 87, 92, 94
Criterion A2 (emotional response)
controversies and proposed changes, 14, 40–41, 58–59, 527
types of emotional responses, 13, 14, 57
Criterion B (re-experiencing), 29, *40*, 41, 55, 62, 191
Criterion C (avoidance and numbing), 29, *40*, 41, 42, 44, 55, 62, 191
Criterion D (hyper-arousal), 29, *40*, 41, 44, 55, 62–63, 191
Criterion E (duration), 63
Criterion F (functional impairment), 63–64, 315, 317–18
definition of PTSD, 55, 84
delayed-onset subtype, 5, 61, 63, 90, 160
dissociation criterion, 29, 43–44
duration criterion, 28, 41, 63, 71, 90
dysphoria factor, 41, 61
functional impairment criterion, 315, 317–18
future directions, 15, 23–25, 43, 49, 64, 527–28
history and development of diagnostic category, 55–57
symptom overlaps with other disorders, 41–47
validity for children and adolescents, 263
diagnostic criteria for PTSD (proposed *DSM-5* changes)
chart of, *60–61*
Criterion A (stressor events), 12, 13, 14, 16, 20, 24, 57–59, 58–59, *60*, 527
Criterion B (reliving of trauma), *60*, 62, 63
Criterion C (avoidance), *60*, 62, 63, 527
Criterion D (cognition and mood), *60*, 62–63, 527
Criterion E (arousal and reactivity), *60*, 63
Criterion F (duration), *61*
Criterion G (functional impairment), *61*, 63–64
proposal for stress-related disorders category, 57, 64
subtypes based on dissociation, 44
three-factor vs. four-factor model, 41, 59–62, 239
Diagnostic Infant Preschool Assessment (DIPA), *265*, 267, 277
Diagnostic Interview Schedule (DIS), *286*, 288
Dialectical Behavior Therapy (DBT), 421, 467
Dijkstra, T., 201
disabilities
developmental, 131, 132, 133, 134–35
physical, 131
disasters/natural disasters
ASD following, 73, 74
early intervention programs for, 351–53, 374, 398, 405, 407
family disruption in, 405
impact on children and adolescents, 105–06, 109, 111
impact on older adults, 394
psychological risks for responders, 73, 76
PTSD screening tools for, 348
risk of PTSD from, 19–20, 21, 58, 89, 105–06, 109, 111
disinhibited social engagement disorder, 57
dismantling studies, 422
dissociation
in ASD, 31–32, 43–44
characteristics of, 335
culturally-related expressions of, 48
as PTSD risk factor, 29, 34–35, 44, 197, 335
risk factors for development of, 44
See also diagnostic criteria for ASD; diagnostic criteria for PTSD; dissociative disorders; peritraumatic dissociation (PD)
dissociative amnesia, 253
See also amnesia
dissociative disorders
DSM-IV description, 43
overlap with PTSD, 43–44
Distressing Event Questionnaire, 296
Doane, L.S., 435
Dohrenwend, B.P., 86, 316–17
domestic violence, 16, 130
See also interpersonal violence
Doron-LaMarca, S., 342
dot-probe task, 204, 205, 207
Drell, M.J., 264
Drost, J., 197
Drouin, M.S., 466
Droždek, B., 307, 308
drug use disorder, 93
See also substance use disorders
Drummond, P., 451
DSM-IV
definition of trauma, 3–4, 99

See also diagnostic criteria for ASD (*DSM-IV*); diagnostic criteria for PTSD (*DSM-IV*)
DSM-5 (proposed revisions)
addition of developmental trauma disorder, 113, 527–28
proposal for traumatic stress disorder category, 57
and WHO classification system, 318
See also diagnostic criteria for PTSD (proposed *DSM-5* changes)
Dubanoski, J., 309
Duberstein, P.R., 495
Duncan, S.C., 341
Duncan, T.E., 341
Dunmore, E., 206
Dutton, M., 242
Dyster-Aas, J., 204–05

E

early intervention. *See* children and adolescents, prevention and early intervention; early interventions, community-based; older adults; prevention and early intervention strategies; special populations
early interventions, community-based, 347–62
for children and adolescents, 352–53, 355, 384–85
for disaster mental health response, 351–53
identification of at-risk survivors, 348–49
for military deployment, 353–54, 365–66, 370, 374
overview, 347–48
program monitoring and evaluation, 356–57
for sexual and physical assault, 354–55
summary and future directions, 357–58
training and supporting providers, 355–56
types of interventions, 349–51
See also prevention and early intervention strategies
ecology of human development, 306–07, 403–04
Ehlers, A., 193, 194, 195, 196, 197, 198–99, 200, 202, 203, 206, 207, 208, 209, 212, 255
Ehring, T., 196, 201, 202, 210
Ehrlich, F., 293
Eisenbruch, M., 509
elder abuse, 123, 394–95, 397, 399
Elder, G., Jr., 122, 338–39
Elhai, J.D., 292
Elizur, A., 123
Elliot, P., 419
Ellis, B.H., 409
Elsesser, K., 195, 204
Elswood, L.S., 210
EMDR. *See* Eye Movement Desensitization and Reprocessing (EMDR)
emotionally-focused marital therapy, 464, 465
emotional processing theory, 428–31
emotional ventilation, 369
Engelhard, I.M., 207
epidemiology of PTSD
future directions, 94–95
See also risk and protective factors for PTSD
Erbes, C.R., 465
ethnicity
as ASD risk factor, 75
and trauma-linked dissociation, 35
See also non-Western cultures, PTSD assessment in; risk and protective factors for PTSD
etiology of PTSD. *See* genetics and genomics of PTSD; posttraumatic stress disorder (PTSD)
European Network for Traumatic Stress (TENTS), 357
Evans, C., 200, 202
Explanatory Model Interview, 311
exposure therapy. *See* Prolonged Exposure (PE) therapy
Eye Movement Desensitization and Reprocessing (EMDR)
description of therapy, 450–51
for early intervention, 386, 387
efficacy with PTSD, 352, 375, 433–34, 454–57
limitations and recommendations, 449–50, 460
proposed mechanisms of action and empirical support, 417, 449–50, 451–54, 457–60
use in children and adolescents, 386, 387, 482–83
use in older adults, 496
Eysenck, H.J., 176, 181

F

Facial Action Coding System (FACS), 430
Fairbank, J.A., 241, 246, 336
Falsetti, S.A., 469
families
disruptions during traumatic events, 405
interventions in support of, 387–88, 405–06, 408, 463–65, 470
See also family models of PTSD; risk and protective factors for PTSD
family models of PTSD
adult attachment, 224
ambiguous loss, 225
caregiver burden, 225
couple adaptation to stress, 219–20, 226–27
effect of close others on trauma recovery and PTSD, 223–24
effect of trauma and PTSD on close others, 224–26
future directions, 223, 228–29
impact of PTSD on couple/family relationships, 219–23
intergenerational transmission of PTSD, 94, 225–26
intimate aggression, 222
reciprocal influences of PTSD and relationship functioning, 226–28
secondary/vicarious traumatization, 224–25
family systems therapy (FST), 464–65
fear
emotional processing of, 429–31
Lang's bioinformational view of, 428–29
as posttraumatic stress response, 43, 295
fear conditioning models. *See* learning models of PTSD
Fear, N.T., 87
Feeny, N.C., 373, 435
FEMA, Crisis Counseling and Training Program (CCP), 385
Feske, U., 204
Field, A.P., 202
Field, T., 387
Figley, C.R., 224
Figueredo, A.J., 342
Fisler, R., 198, 203
5-HTTLPR polymorphism, 111–12, 147, 150, 223–24
FKBP5 polymorphism, 112, 148, 152
Flannery, R.B., 355
Flora, C.M., 5
Flor, H., 195
fluoxetine, *514*, 517
Flynn, B.W., 30
Foa, E.B., 22, 88, 192, 200–201, 204, 206, 207, 237, 239, 293, 355, 369, 373, 429–30, 431, 432, 434–35, 446
FOCUS (Families Over Coming Under Stress), 388
Forbes, D., 352
Ford, J.D., 111
Frankenburg, F.R., 236
Frank, S., 210
Fredman, S.J., 220
Freedman, S., 357
Freeman, J.B., 204
Freeman, T., 149
Frenkiel-Fishman, S., 357
Freshman, M.S., 201
Freud, Sigmund, 191
Friedman, M., 529
Frueh, B.C., 123, 292
Fuchs, N., 210
functional impairment and quality of life, 315–30
assessment concerns, 317–18
current measurement issues, 323–26
future directions, 326–27

importance of accurately measuring, 316–17
measures of, 319–22
PTSD leading to, 5, 315–16, 323, 326
See also diagnostic criteria for PTSD

G

GABA levels, 163, 256, 519, 520
GAD (generalized anxiety disorder). *See* generalized anxiety disorder
Galovski, T., 446
Garner Evans, L., 108
Gavriel, H., 451
Gelkopf, M., 352
gender
as ASD risk factor, 75
See also risk and protective factors for PTSD
generalized anxiety disorder (GAD), 42, 76
genetics and genomics of PTSD, 143–54, 162–63
5-HTTLPR, 111–12, 147, 150, 223–24
alternative neurobiological system candidate gene studies, 144, 146–47, 148–50
analytic considerations, 152–53
candidate gene studies, 143–50
dopaminergic system candidate gene studies, 144–45, 147
epigenetic studies, 150–51
future directions, 94, 153, 154, 528
gene environment interplay, 150
gene expression studies, 151–52
interplay with social support mechanisms, 223–24
overlap with other disorders, 93
race/ethnic influences on, 148
serotonin system candidate gene studies, 144, 145–46, 147–48
suggestion for preexisting vulnerabilities, 143
Gerardi, R.J., 245
Germain, V., 466
Gilbertson, M.W., 92
Gilboa-Schechtman, E., 430, 485
Glancy, G., 334–35
Gleser, G.C., 220
Global Assessment of Functioning (GAF), 317, 318, *319*, 323, 325
Global War on Terror (GWOT), 54
glutamatergic system, 163, 519, 521
See also d-cycloserine (DCS)
Glynn, S.M., 418, 464
Goenjian, A.K., 106, 111
Grant, D.M., 222
Gray, M.J., 201
Green, B.L., 109
Greene, C.J., 419
Greenwald, R., 451
Gregg, L., 467
Gregory, J.D., 193
grief. *See* bereavement; complicated bereavement
Griffin, M.G., 445
Grillon, C., 185
Grinshpoon, A., 123
Grossman, A.B., 494
growth curve modeling, 341
growth, posttraumatic, 70, 333, 337–38, 410
Guay, S., 466
Guthrie, R.M., 195, 202
Guzder, J., 408

H

Hadjez, J., 123
Hahn, K.S., 210
Halle, P., 242
Halligan, S.L., 196, 197, 200, 201, 206, 209
Hamada, R.S., 192
Hamada, W.C., 309
Hamblen, J.L., 204
Hamilton, S., 226–27
Harned, M.S., 467
Harris, M., 136
Hartung, J., 387
Harvard Trauma Questionnaire, 310
Harvey, A.G., 30, 33, 204
Hazan, C., 224
Health and Work Performance Questionnaire (HPQ), *320*, 324
Hearst-Ikeda, D., 373
heart rate
as predictor of ASD symptom severity, 77
as predictor of PTSD, 160, 194–95, 243, 256, 276, 276–77
in response to stress, 77, 160, 194, 243, 256, 276–77
See also psychophysiologic responses to stress
Helzer, J.E., 92
Hickling, E.J., 22
Hill, J., 334–35
Hispanics, and PTSD, 35, 49
Hobfoll, S.E., 404, 410
Hogberg, G., 454
Hoge, C.W., 87, 354
Hohnecker, L., 242
Hollifield, M., 311
Holmes, E.A., 197
Holocaust survivors
cortisol studies, 166, 226
healthcare utilization, 123
intergenerational transmission of PTSD, 162–63, 166, 225–26
suicidality in, 122
Horowitz, M.J., 191, 240–41, 292, 441
Hovens, J.E., 284, 288, 292, 295
Hoyt, W., 399
Hubbard, J., 311
Huber, L.C., 445
Hudson, S.A., 292
Huijding, J., 207
Huntjens, R.J.C., 209
Hurricane Andrew, 105, 106, 108, 109
Hurricane Charley, 106, 109, 112
Hurricane Hugo, 108
Hurricane Katrina
ASD incidence in, 73, 74, 75
early intervention programs, 351–52, 385, 386–87, 405
PTSD incidence in, 19–20, 21, 257
reaction of older adults to, 492
treatment programs for children, 486
See also disasters/natural disasters
Hyer, L., 287, 496, 497, 498
hyper-arousal symptoms
biological causes of, 178, 186
characteristics of, 55
functional impairments from, 316
and intimate aggression, 222
as response to trauma, 30, 175
See also diagnostic criteria for PTSD
hypnosis, 375

I

imipramine, *515*, 518, 522
Impact of Event Scale (IES), 237, 240–41, 273, *274*, 288–89, *289*
Impact of Event Scale-Revised (IES-R), 240, 241, 288, 289, 310
implicit association test (IAT), 207
incarcerated individuals, 130–31, 133, 135–36
information processing in PTSD, 191–218
anxiety, 203–07
attentional bias—experimental findings, 204–05
attentional bias—neuroscience findings, 205–06
attentional bias to threat, 203–04
conclusions, 207
future directions, 207
threatening personal meanings, 206–07
cognitive responses to trauma, 207–10
avoidance, 207–08
conclusions, 210
rumination, 209–10, 211
thought suppression, 208–09, 210
cognitive vulnerabilities predicting PTSD, 210, 255
future directions, 210–12
memory recall, 198–203
conclusions, 203
future directions, 203
intentional recall of trauma memories, 200–202
overgeneral autobiographical memory, 202, 203, 493
poor memory for neutral information, 202
predictions from information processing theories, 198–99
trauma-induced amnesia, 71, 191, 199–200, 203, 250, 253

overview, 191–92
re-experiencing of trauma, 192–98
associative learning in, 194–95, 197
characteristics of, 192
conclusions, 197–98
encoding during trauma, 197, 198
future directions, 197, 198
priming and triggers of, 192, 195–98
theoretical explanations for, 192–93
injury
risk of ASD following, 76
See also motor vehicle accidents (MVAs); physical assault; sexual assault
Institute of Medicine (IOM) Committee on Prevention of Mental Disorders, 364
integrative behavioral couple therapy (IBCT), 464, 465
intelligence
as risk/protective factor in PTSD, 91–92, 94, 210, 334
role in fostering resilience, 92, 210
role in psychiatric disorders, 91–92
International Classification of Diseases, 252
International Family, Adult, and Child Environment Services (FACES), 408
Internet-based programs
for early intervention, 353, 354, 358, 374, 384, 530
for PTSD treatment, 465–66, 470, 530
interpersonal violence
risk of ASD from, 75
risk of PTSD from, 18–19, 39, 107–08, 109, 152–53
See also complex PTSD; physical assault; sexual assault
interventions. *See* early interventions, community-based
intrusive thoughts
differentiating from rumination, 210, 211
as response to trauma, 17, 30, 250
role of rumination in, 209, 210, 211
See also re-experiencing symptoms
Inventory of Psychosocial Functioning (IPF), 325–26
Iraq/Afghanistan veterans
brain injuries in, 87, 421
early interventions for, 95, 354, 357
interpersonal and family impairments, 221, 226
PTSD prevalence, 19, 86–87, 89
PTSD treatments, 445, 521, 529
studies of PTSD in, 54, 204, 207, 223
See also military veterans
Irish, L., 23
Ironson, G., 30
Israel
ASD incidence in, 74, 75, 120
early intervention programs, 352–53, 357, 374, 385
PTSD incidence in children, 106
See also Second Lebanon War
Israeli-Shalev, Y., 357
Isserlin, L., 31
Ivers-Deliperi, V., 459

J
Jackson, S.D., 292
Janet, P., 191
Janoff-Bulman, R., 206, 441–42, 443
Jarero, I., 387
Jaycox, L.H., 316, 430
Jelinek, L., 201, 202
Joffe, C., 293
Johnson, L., 341
Jones, D.E., 464
Jones, D.H., 221, 222
Jones, E., 87
Jones, K., 351–52, 405
Jordan, B.K., 221
Jorm, A.F., 494
Jovanovic, T., 176, 178

K
Kaltreider, N., 292
Kaniasty, K., 223
Kaplan, A., 306
Kassam-Adams, N., 101, 103, 107
Katschnig, H., 317
Katz, S., 404
Kaufman, M.L., 59
Kazak, A.E., 384
Kazdin, A.E., 530
Keane PTSD Scale, 290
Keane, T., 14, 57, 59, 240, 241, 243, 290, 295, 336
Kearns, Megan, 530
Keijsers, G.P.J., 435
Kessler, R.C., 14–15, 19, 58, 493
ketamine, 468
Kiddie Schedule for Affective Disorders and Schizophrenia for School-Aged Children - Parent and Lifetime Version (K-SADS-PL), *266*, 268, 277
Kilpatrick, D.G., 19, 58, 110, 112, 223–24
Kimble, M.O., 59, 207
Kindt, M., 197, 202, 208–09, 418
King, D.W., 222, 240, 336, 340, 342, 343
King, L.A., 222, 240, 336, 338, 340, 342, 343, 529
Kirk, M., 31
Kirmayer, L.J., 305, 308
Kläsener, I., 210
Kleim, B., 196, 202
Kleiner, J.S., 202
Kleinman, A., 306
Knapp, R.G., 292
Knopfler, C., 387
Knudson, M., 387
Kolb, L.C., 245
Kolko, D., 483
Korean War veterans, 121–22, 339
Koss, M.P., 342
Kozak, M.J., 204, 429–30
Kraemer, H.C., 343
Krause, N., 122
Krystal, J.H., 468
Kudler, H., 226, 237
Kühn, M., 77
Kulka, R.A., 236, 240, 284, 290

L
Lachs, M.S., 123
Lacker, J.M., 204
Ladakakos, C., 387
La Greca, A.M., 105, 106, 109–10
Landolt, M.A., 107
Lange, A., 466
Lang, P.M., 192, 243, 428, 458
Laor, N., 245, 385
Laposa, J.M., 21
Larrieu, J.A., 264
latent difference score analysis, 342
late-onset PTSD. *See* delayed-onset PTSD
late-onset stress symptomatology (LOSS), 121, 339
Lauterbach, D., 240
Layne, C.M., 408–09
learning models of PTSD, 175–90
associative fear conditioning, 175, 176–78, 180–83, 255–56, 519
associative-learning deficits and anxiety, 177, 181, 187, 294
failure to inhibit fear, 178, 181, 187
overgeneralization of fear, 177–78, 182–83, 187, 195
in re-experiencing of trauma, 194–95
resistance to extinction, 176–77, 180–81, 187, 195
two-stage learning, 177, 182
future directions, 182, 186–87
introduction, 175–76
nonassociative fear conditioning, 175, 178–79, 183–85
habituation, 178, 183, 187
sensitization, 178–79, 184–85, 187
research limitations, 186
toward integrated understandings, 185
Lee, C., 451
Lee, H.J., 153
Lee, K.A., 121
Lenze, E.J., 284
Levav, I., 123
Levenson, M.R., 336
Lichty, L.F., 355
Liebowitz Self-Rated Disability Scale (LSRDS), *321*, 324
Li, F., 341
Life Events Checklist, 236, 285
See also Clinician-Administered PTSD Scale (CAPS)
lifespan developmental perspectives, 338–39
Life Stressor Checklist-Revised (LSC-R), 244

Linehan, M.M., 467
Lin, M.K., 305
Lipton, M., 193
Li, S.H., 432
Litz, B.T., 63, 499
Lombardo, T.W., 201
Longitudinal Aging Study Amsterdam (LASA), 288, 292
Lucia, V.C., 16
Lunney, C.A., 315
Luscombe, G., 293

M

M-3 Checklist, 293
Macklin, R.S., 495
Magruder, K.M., 292
Mainous, A.G., 125
major depressive disorder (MDD), 41–42
Malekian, A., 226
Malik, M.A., 237
malingering
  defined, 6, 235, 244–45
  See also assessment of PTSD
Malloy, P.F., 241
Mancini, A.D., 342
Mannarino, A.P., 107–08, 481
Mansfield, A.J., 228–29
Mapother, E., 6
Marchand, A., 466
March, S., 528
Marcus, S.V., 453
Markman, H.J., 221
Markowitsch, H.J., 199
Marmar, C.R., 240, 241
Marquis, P., 453
Marsella, A.J., 305–06, 309
Marshall, G.N., 315–16
Marshall, R.D., 33
Marsteller, F., 453
Massie, E.D., 430
Masten, A.S., 336
Mastrodomenica, J., 35
McArdle, J.J., 342
McCann, L., 228, 442, 443
McCarthy, P.R., 204
McEwen, B.S., 166
McFall, M.E., 240
McGurk, D., 354
McManus, F., 207
McNally, R.J., 58, 92, 161, 198, 199, 370, 429
Meadows, E.A., 369, 446
Medical Outcomes Study Short Form (SF-36), 317, 318, *319*, 323, 324, 325
medical trauma
  ASD from, 73, 74
  in children, 485
meditation-relaxation treatment (MED-RELAX), 484–85
Meehl, P.E., 284
Meiser-Stedman, T., 101
memory disorganization
  in ASD, 103, 202
  overgeneral autobiographical memory, 202, 203, 493
  in PTSD, 41, 191, 198–203, 250, 294, 295
  See also amnesia; information processing in PTSD; memory elaboration
memory elaboration, 199, 203
Mendoza, R., 305
mental illness. *See* severe mental illness
methylene-dioxymethamphetamine (MDMA), 468
Mezey, G., 200
Michael, T., 195, 196, 209
mild traumatic brain injury. *See* traumatic brain injury (TBI)
military veterans
  Army Battlemind program, 353–54, 365–66, 370, 374
  ASD rates, 74
  early intervention programs for, 353–54, 357–58, 365–66, 387–88
  family relationships, 220–21, 226, 387–88
  healthcare utilization by, 123
  late-onset stress symptomatology (LOSS), 121, 339
  lifespan developmental analysis of, 338–39
  potential PTEs in, 17
  PTSD in, 19, 21, 89, 121, 235, 251, 287, 339, 349
  PTSD treatments for, 208, 441, 445, 446–47, 456–57, 464–66, 520, 529, 530
  See also Iraq/Afghanistan veterans; Korean War veterans; Vietnam War veterans; World War II veterans; World War I veterans
Miller, C., 351–52
Miller, K.E., 311
Miller, M.W., 57
Milliken, C.S., 221
Minnesota Multiphasic Personality Inventory-PTSD (MMPI-PTSD), *289*, 290
mirtazapine, 518, 522
Mississippi Scale for Combat-Related PTSD (M-PTSD), 236, 240, *289*, 290
  See also Civilian Mississippi Scale (CMS)
Miterany, D., 222
Miyake Island volcano eruption, 123
mnestic block syndrome, 199
Moffitt, T.E., 17, 150
Mohlman, J., 495
Molnar, C., 200–201
Monson, C.M., 220, 227, 245, 417, 443, 444, 446, 463–64
Moore, E., 497
Morabito, D., 387
Morel Emotional Numbing Test for PTSD-Revised (MENT-R), 244–45
Morral, A., 430
Morris, P., 419, 497
Morris, R.W., 431
Morse, H., 309
mortality, and trauma stress, 123
Mortimer, J.A., 292
motor vehicle accidents (MVAs)
  and ASD, 72, 74, 76, 77, 78, 207
  and cortisol levels, 165–66
  and dissociation, 31
  and PTSD, 195, 196, 251, 334
  therapeutic interventions, 372
Mueser, K.T., 134, 136, 421
Multi-dimensional Scale of Perceived Social Support (MSPSS), 77
Multiple Channel Exposure Therapy (M-CET), 447, 469, 470
multiple traumas
  assessment strategies for, 16–17, 23–25, 85, 244
  See also risk and protective factors for PTSD
Muñoz, M., 120
Murdock, T.B., 204, 432
Murphy, C.M., 340
Murphy, S.A., 341
Musser, P.H., 340
Mustapic, M., 149
mutual maintenance model, 46

N

Najavits, L.M., 469
Narrative Exposure Therapy (NET), 484–85
National Center for PTSD (NCPTSD), 238, 352, 354, 386
National Comorbidity Survey (NCS), 17, 22, 70
National Comorbidity Survey-Replication (NCS-R), 120
National Epidemiological Survey on Alcohol and Related Conditions, 22, 120
National Institute of Mental Health-Diagnostic Interview Schedule (NIMH-DIS), 85
National Stressful Events Survey (NSES), 24
National Survey of Adolescents, 108, 111
National Vietnam Veterans Readjustment Study (NVVRS), 19, 22, 86, 221, 222, 240, 284, 316–17
National Women's Study (NWS), 24, 394
natural disasters. *See* disasters/natural disasters
Neal, L.A., 288
Nehmy, T., 209
Nelson Goff, B.S., 221, 226–27
Neria, Y., 499
Nesselroade, J.R., 339
neuroanatomic predictors of PTSD, 163–64
neuroticism, 210

Nevid, J.S., 404
Nicholas, J.S., 292
9/11 attacks. *See* September 11 terrorist attacks
Nixon, R.D.V., 209
nonspecific adjustment disorder, 28–29
non-Western cultures, PTSD assessment in, 302–14
  contextual model of assessment, 306–07, 312
  cultural-sensitivity required for, 307–08
  development of culturally-grounded measures, 311–12
  diagnostic instruments, 309–11
  empirically-based studies, 304
  future directions, 312
  general considerations and questions, 302–04
  potential complications, 309
  PTSD as psychiatric category or spectrum, 305
  role of culture in, 302–03, 305–06
  toward new paradigm, 306
  use of interpreters in, 308
Norberg, M.M., 468
Normative Aging Study, 290
Norris, F.H., 223, 351–52, 356, 385, 394
Norwood, A.E., 30
Novikov, I., 123
numbing. *See* avoidance and numbing

O

O'Brien, S., 123
obsessive-compulsive personality disorder, 45
O'Donnell, M.L., 18, 357
Oehler-Stinnett, J., 108
Olatunji, B.O., 210
older adults
  acute stress disorder in, 120, 121, 125, 492
  anxiety disorders in, 495
  cognitive difficulties, 283, 397, 493–94, 497
  early interventions
    adaptation for elders, 397–98
    behavioral approaches and exposure, 399
    community-level preventions, 395–97, 400
    for complicated bereavement, 399
    for disasters, 398
    for elder abuse, 397, 399
    identifying at-risk persons, 396–97, 400
    providing access to care, 395–96, 400
    psychoeducation, 398
    psychological first aid, 398
    in sexual and physical assault, 398
    social support and ADL management, 399, 400
  functional impairment, 122, 125
  healthcare utilization, 122–23, 125
  longitudinal studies, 121–22, 529
  PTSD
    late-onset, 121
    prevalence of, 120–21, 125, 282–83, 493
  research literature and future directions, 119–20, 125
  risk and resiliency factors
    coping style, 492
    cultural factors, 123–24, 125
    demographics, 124–25, 282
    in disasters, 394
    in elder abuse, 394–95
    general, 282, 393–95, 399–400
    in sexual and physical assault, 394
  severe stressors for, 492–93
  somatic illnesses, 283
  suicide risk, 122, 125
  treatment modalities
    late life variables, 493–94
    for older adults with anxiety, 495
    for older adults with PTSD, 496–97
    pharmacotherapies, 521–22
    treatment model for late-life PTSD, 497–98, 499
    for younger adults with PTSD, 495–96
  vulnerability to trauma, 492–93
  See also older adults, assessment methods for
older adults, assessment methods for, 282–301
  behavioral assessments, 295
  diagnostically-oriented instruments
    Clinician-Administered PTSD Scale, 285–87
    Composite International Diagnostic Interview (CIDI), *286*, 287–88
    structured clinical interview, 284–85
    Structured Interview for PTSD, *286*, 288
  future directions, 295–96
  general considerations, 282–84
  psychophysiological and biological measures, 294–95
  screening instruments
    advantages of, 291
    closely following *DSM*, 292–93
    other, 293–94
    PTSD Checklist (PCL), 291–92, *293*
    Self Rating Inventory for PTSD (SRIP), *291*, 292
  self-report instruments
    Impact of Event Scale (IES), 288–89, *289*
    Minnesota Multiphasic Personality Inventory (MMPI-PTSD), *289*, 290
    Mississippi Scale (M-PTSD), *289*, 290
olfactory identification deficits, 294
Olweus Bullying Prevention Program (OBPP), 406
Onken, L., 416
opiod prophylaxis of PTSD, 521, 522
Orcutt, H.K., 222
O'Rourke, K., 310
Orr, S.P., 245, 294
Orsillo, S.M., 63
Osterman, J.E., 5
overgeneral autobiographical memory, 202, 203, 493
Owens, G.P., 443, 445
Ozer, E.J., 91, 335, 336

P

Pacella, M., 528
pain
  as risk factor for ASD, 76
  See also risk and protective factors for PTSD
Palestinians, 106
Palyo, S.A., 222
panic attacks, 161
paranoia, 45
Parent-Child Interaction Therapy (PCIT), 405
parents
  influence on child functioning, 104
  underestimates of children's PTSD symptoms, 102, 105, 111
  See also families
paroxetine, 513, 517, 521
Parslow, R.A., 494
Patterson, D., 355
PCL (PTSD Checklist). *See* PTSD Checklist (PCL)
Pearlman, L.A., 228, 443
Pearson, N., 311
Pediatric Emotional Distress Scale (PEDS), 271
Penn Inventory, 296
peritraumatic dissociation (PD)
  defined, 44
  predictive of PTSD, 34–35, 71–72, 161, 197, 252–53
Peritraumatic Dissociative Experiences Questionnaire (PDEQ), 32, 254–55, 310
Peritraumatic Distress Scale (PDS), 255
peritraumatic panic, 161
Perry, K.J., 373
Personal Beliefs and Reactions Scale (PBRs), 206
personality disorders
  anti-social personality disorder, 45
  comorbidity with PTSD, 44–45, 93–94, 222
  disability from, 129
Peterson, E.L., 16
PFA Field Operations Guide, 386

pharmacotherapy for PTSD
anti-andrenergic agents, *515*, 518–19
anticonvulsant/mood stabilizer agents, *515*, 519
antidepressants
monoamine oxidase inhibitors (MAOIs), *514*, 518
other antidepressants, *514*, 518
other serotonergic antidepressants, *514*, 517
selective serotonin reuptake inhibitors (SSRIs), 513, *514*, 517, 521
tricyclic antidepressants (TCAs), *515*, 518
atypical antipsychotic medications, 520
benzodiazepines, 375, *516*, 520, 521
combining with psychotherapy, 431–32, 496, 520–21, 529–30
d-cycloserine (DCS), 468, 470, 496, *516*, 517, 519–20, 521, 522, 530
efficacy in comorbid diagnoses, 513
future directions, 496, 521–22
glutamatergic agents, *516*
imipramine, *515*, 518, 522
opiod prophylaxis, 521, 522
prazosin, 468, *515*, 518, 519, 522
propranolol, 162, 375, 468, *515*, 518, 519, 522
sertraline, 434, 481, 513, *514*, 517, 521
table summarizing, *514–16*
usefulness of, 513
Philpot, M.P., 292
physical assault
impact on older adults, 394
risk of ASD from, 72, 76, 77, 78–79
risk of PTSD from, 18–19, 21, 89, 93, 94, 251
See also sexual assault
Piacentini, J.C., 404
Pike, J.L., 443
Pillemer, K.A., 123
Pimlott-Kubiak, S., 19
Pine, D.S., 205
Pinquart, M., 495
Pitman, R.K., 176, 245, 294, 459
PK Scale of MMPI and MMPI-2, 241, 244
Poisson, L.M., 16
Pole, N., 194
Pollack, S., 466
Ponizovsky, A., 123
Poortinga, Y.H., 309
postconcussive symptoms (PCS), 33, 76
Posttraumatic Adjustment Scale (PAS), 254
Posttraumatic Cognitions Inventory (PTCI), 206
posttraumatic growth, 70, 333, 337–38, 410
Posttraumatic Stress Diagnostic Scale (PDS), 239, 242, 244, 293, 310
posttraumatic stress disorder (PTSD)
acute, 41
chronic
diagnostic criteria, 18, 90
predicting, 41, 206, 207
role of priming in, 196
comorbid diagnoses
chronic pain, 46–47
depression, 30, 33, 41–42, 61, 93, 110, 207, 222, 325, 528
GAD, 42
other psychiatric disorders, 93–94, 235, 325
personality disorders, 44–45, 93–94, 222, 325
rates of, 420
severe mental illness, 129–30, 134–35, 421
somatoform disorders, 46
substance use disorders, 55, 130, 131, 222, 325, 420, 469, 529
traumatic brain injury, 46, 87, 421, 529
complex
diagnostic criteria, 47–48, 49, 57
symptoms, 47, 421
delayed-onset
in adults, 5, 61, 63, 90, 109, 110, 160, 161, 251
in children and adolescents, 109–10
clinical course, 121, 160
in combat veterans, 251, 339
defined, 251
differentiating from ASD, 30, 70, 159–60
etiology, 55, 56–58, 59, 84, 159, 179
public health impact, 55
symptom overlap with other disorders, 42–47, 49, 203
See also children and adolescents, PTSD in; diagnostic criteria for PTSD; older adults; posttraumatic stress responses; prevalence of PTSD; recovery from PTSD; risk and protective factors for PTSD
Posttraumatic Stress Disorder Semi-structured Interview and Observational Record for Infants and Young Children (PTSD-SSIORIYC), *265*, 267, 277
Post-Traumatic Stress Management (PTSM) program, 385
posttraumatic stress responses
acute vs. chronic trajectories, 160–61
aggression, 42, 55, 63, 71, 221, 222, 283, 294, 295
amnesia, 71, 191, 199–200, 203, 250, 253
anxiety, 203–07
avoidance and numbing, 17, 30, 207–08, 250
cognitive and memory difficulties, 41, 191, 198–203, 250, 294, 295
common, 3, 4, 30–31, 44–45, 55, 56, 70–71, 250–51
depression, 30, 33, 41–42, 61, 93, 110, 207, 222, 325
fear, 43, 295
function (*See* functional impairment)
insomnia, 250
intrusive thoughts, 17, 30, 250, 295
irritability, 251
multiple possible trajectories, 160–61, 251, 257
negative thoughts (rumination), 4, 202, 207, 209–10, 211, 442–43
normal vs. pathological, 4, 30–31, 159–61, 169
panic attacks, 161
peritraumatic dissociation (PD), 34–35, 71–72, 161, 197
psychological disorders, 325
reduced quality of life (*See* functional impairment)
re-experiencing of trauma, 175, 192–98
shame, 295
substance use/abuse, 90, 93, 130, 131, 134, 222, 325
thought suppression, 208–09, 210
See also acute stress disorder (ASD); assessment of traumatic stress symptoms; diagnostic criteria for PTSD; information processing in PTSD; posttraumatic stress disorder (PTSD)
Posttraumatic Symptom Scale (PSS), 293
potentially traumatic events (PTE), 11
Potts, M.K., 293
Power, K., 451
prazosin, 468, *515*, 518, 519, 522
Preschool Age Psychiatric Assessment (PAPA), *265*, 267, 277
prevalence of PTSD
in United States (lifetime), 14–15, 87, 88, 94, 129, 143, 159, 235
worldwide, 87, 88, 129
prevention and early intervention strategies
future directions, 373–76
goals of early intervention, 6, 251, 255
identifying those at risk, 348–49, 364, 376
methodological challenges, 368–69, 376
models of intervention, 364–65, 403–04
in special populations, 407–10
timing of interventions, 364, 376
types of interventions
anxiety management, 368, 372
Behavioral Activation (BA), 368, 372
cognitive behavioral therapy (CBT), 35, 251, 367–68, 371–74, 386
cognitive restructuring, 35, 367, 368, 372, 422
Critical Incident Stress Debriefing (CISD), 35, 365, 369–70, 374, 398, 529

Eye Movement Desensitization (EMDR), 352, 375, 386, 387, 417
hypnosis, 375
Internet and telephone, 353, 354, 358, 374–75, 384, 530
pharmacotherapy, 162, 375, 386
prolonged exposure (PE), 35, 367, 368, 372
psychoeducation, 367, 368, 370–71, 374, 386
psychological debriefing (PD), 35, 365–66, 369–70, 374
Psychological First Aid (PFA), 70, 350, 354, 356, 366–67, 370, 374, 386–87, 389, 398
self-help methods, 347, 350, 353, 374–75
See also children and adolescents, prevention and early intervention; early interventions, community-based; older adults; special populations
Prideaux, F., 6
Primary Care PTSD screen, 348–49
priming, 195–97
Project SHIFA, 409–10
Prolonged Exposure (PE) therapy
clinical support for, 430–32
clinician training for, 355
description of treatment, 427–28, 436
with dissociative symptoms, 44, 435
efficacy with PTSD, 35, 415, 427, 429–30, 432–35, 436, 521
future directions, 435–36
limitations of, 435
pharmacological adjuncts to, 468, 519–20
underlying theory, 428–30, 519
prolonged grief disorder. *See* complicated bereavement
propranolol, 162, 375, 468, *515*, 518, 519, 522
protective factors for PTSD. *See* risk and protective factors for PTSD
Psychological First Aid (PFA), 70, 350, 354, 356, 366–67, 370, 374, 386–87, 389, 398
psychological treatments for PTSD
combining with pharmacotherapy, 431–32, 496, 520–21, 529
comorbid treatment approaches, 468–69, 470
couple and family-based approaches, 463–65, 470
emotion-based approaches, 467–68, 470
future directions, 470, 530
Multiple Channel Exposure Therapy (M-CET), 447, 469, 470
technological approaches, 465–66, 470, 530
virtual reality exposure therapy, 466–67
See also cognitive-behavioral therapy (CBT); pharmacotherapy for PTSD; Prolonged Exposure (PE) therapy; Psychological First Aid (PFA)
Psychopathic Personality Inventory-Short Form (PPI-SF), 326
psychophysiological assessments
in adults, 5, 235, 242–44, 294–95, 296
in children, 276–77
compared with other methods, 245
future directions, 528
in older adults, 294–95, 296
psychophysiologic responses to stress
accelerated aging, 294
blood pressure, 294
heart rate, 77, 160, 194, 243, 256, 276–77
measuring reactivity to, 5, 235, 242–44, 276–77
startle reflex, 175, 178, 179, 184, 235, 243, 507, 528
PTSD-AA (for children), 263
PTSD Checklist (PCL), 238–39, 245, 291–92, *293*
PTSD-Reaction Index, 106
PTSD-Scale (based on *DSM-III-R* criteria), 292–93
PTSD Symptom Scale Interview (PSS-I), 237, 238, 310
PTSD Symptom Scale-Self Report Version (PSS-SR), 239, 254
PTSD treatment research
comorbid diagnoses and associated features, 420–21
cultural considerations, 421–22
evaluating clinical trials
attrition and missing data, 417–18
comparison groups, 416–17
controlling for clustering effects, 419–20
efficacy, effectiveness, and practical trials, 415–16
measuring PTSD outcomes, 420
sample size and design choice, 418–19
optimizing treatment delivery, 422–23
recommendations for future, 423–24, 529
Pynoos, R.S., 404

Q

quality of life. *See* functional impairment and quality of life
Quality of Life Inventory (QOLI), 317, 318, *322*, 323, 324, 325
Quality of Well-Being Scale (QWB), *322*, 324

R

Rabalais, A.E., 443
race
as PTSD risk factor, 90, 124–25, 148, 334
See also African Americans; Asians; Caucasians
Ramchand, R., 315–16
random-event method, 85–86
randomized clinical trials (RCTs), 364, 415, 416
See also clinical trials
Range of Impaired Functioning Tool (LIFE-RIFT), *320*, 324
Rapaport, M.H., 316
rape
early intervention programs, 349, 354–55, 371, 372
PTSD risk from, 58, 89, 94, 251, 363
Rauch, S.A.M., 431
Raudenbush, S.W., 341
Rayner, R., 177, 182, 187
reactive attachment disorder, 57
Ready, D.J., 466
reckless behavior, 63
recovery from PTSD
biological predictors for, 162–63, 166
cultural considerations in, 305
defined, 336
estimates of, 41
See also resilience
re-experiencing symptoms
characteristics of, 192
functional impairments from, 316
as response to trauma and PTSD, 175, 192
role of dissociation in, 197
triggers, 192, 198
See also diagnostic criteria for PTSD; information processing in PTSD
refugees
definition of, 407
early intervention strategies for, 407–10
extreme trauma faced by, 306, 307, 405, 407, 505
PTSD risk in, 48–49
treatment therapies and concerns, 505, 506, 507, 508–09
See also Cambodian refugees; cultural considerations; non-Western cultures, PTSD assessment in; Somali refugees
Regambal, M.J., 21
Regehr, C., 334–35
Reisbig, A.M.J., 226–27
Renshaw, K.D., 221, 222
Resick, P.A., 57, 206, 417, 422, 423, 433, 441, 442, 443, 444, 445, 446, 529
resilience
defined, 57, 334, 336, *382*
factors promoting, 337
as response to trauma, 4, 70, 336
role of intelligence in, 92, 210
role of social support in, 229, 337
See also recovery from PTSD; risk and protective factors for PTSD

Resnick, H.S., 342, 355, 371, 469
response bias, 235
Ressler, K.J., 176, 178, 528
RGS2 polymorphism, 224
Rhoades, G.K., 221
Richards, J., 451
Riggs, D.S., 206, 221, 430, 432, 463–64
risk and protective factors for PTSD
  analyzing
    definitions, 333–34
    directions for future research, 343
    lifespan development perspectives, 334, 338–39, 343
    methodological tools, 339–42
    understanding resilience and growth, 336–38
  individual risk factors
    age, 22, 90, 103, 110–11, 153, 334, 337, 393
    anxiety, 41, 46, 210
    biological/genetic markers, 111–12, 143, 153–54, 162–63, 255–56
    childhood trauma, 48, 94, 336–37
    cognitive and coping styles, 210, 255, 335–36, 337, 383
    death of loved one (unexpected), 20, 89, 90, 130, 382
    demographics, 22–23, 124–25, 282
    dissociation, 29, 34–35, 44, 197, 335
    ethnicity, 22–23, 49, 90, 111, 124–25, 334, 337
    family functioning, 112, 162, 335, 337, 383
    family history of psychiatric disorders, 90, 91, 93, 94, 335
    gender, 22, 33, 87–89, 90, 103, 111, 124, 129, 134, 153, 334, 337, 382–83, 393, 528
    historical context, 339
    intelligence, 91–92, 94, 210, 334
    mild traumatic brain injury, 33, 59, 87, 258
    negative thoughts (rumination), 41, 63, 202, 207, 209–10, 255, 336, 442–43
    pain and ongoing stressors, 21, 41, 46–47
    perceived threat, 20–21, 335
    preexisting psychiatric disorders, 90, 91, 93–94, 112, 210, 335, 382, 383
    prior trauma exposure, 23–25, 90, 91, 92–93, 111, 152, 153, 179, 185, 334, 336, 383, 394, 404
    race, 90, 124–25, 148, 334
    self-blame, 21–22, 62, 255, 442
    self-perception, 337
    severity of trauma, 21, 89–90, 91, 92–93, 335, 382
    social support factors, 41, 91, 94, 112, 123, 223–24, 336, 337, 351, 382, 383, 393, 394
    socioeconomic status, 23, 49, 90, 337, 393, 394
    witnessed violence, 20, 90
Rizvi, S.L., 445
Roberts, N.P., 373
Robertson, M., 497
Rodrigues, C.S., 221, 222
Roediger, H.L., 198
Roelofs, K., 201
Roemer, L., 63
Roitblat, H.L., 192
Rosenberger, S.R., 240
Rosenberg, S.D., 421
Rosenblum, J., 123
Rosen, J.B., 179
Rose, S., 31
Rothbaum, B.O., 30, 431, 432, 434, 453, 466, 521, 530
Rounsaville, B.J., 416, 423
Rousseau, C., 408, 409
Rubin, D.C., 193, 199, 201
Ruggiero, K.J., 465
rumination, 209–10, 211
Runyon, M.K., 483
Rusch, M.D., 342
Rushton, P., 497
Rwandan genocide, 149
Ryan, R., 131
Rygh, J.L., 497

S

Sack, M., 456
Saigh, P.A., 246
Sakai, C., 453
Sakheim, D.K., 442
Sanderson, W.C., 497
Sareen, J., 493
Sartory, G., 195
Saunders, B.E., 19, 482
Sautter, F.J., 464
Savarese, V.W., 222
Saxe, G., 104
Sayers, S.L., 221
Scafidi, F., 387
Schaffrick, C., 210
Schanberg, S., 387
Scheeringa, M.S., 263, 264
Schelling, G., 166
Schell, T.L., 315–16
Schinka, J.A., 292
schizoaffective disorder, 129
schizophrenia, 129, 134
schizotypal personality disorder, 129
Schlenger, W.E., 236, 290
Schnicke, M.K., 217
Schnurr, P.P., 58, 315, 415–20
Schreier, H., 387
Schroeder, C.M., 483
Schultz, L.R., 16
Schulz, P.M., 445
Schumm, J.A., 445
Schwartzberg, S., 410
SCID (Structured Clinical Interview for *DSM-IV*), 284, *286*, 310
SCID-D (Structured Clinical Interview for Dissociative Disorders), 253
SCID-I (Structured Clinical Interview, Axis 1), 236, 237, 244, 284, 285, *286*
Screen for Posttraumatic Stress Symptoms (SPTSS), 293
Screening Tool for Early Predictors of PTSD (STEPP), *275*, 276
screening tools for trauma assessment
  for children and adolescents, 273–76
  for older adults, 291–94
  See also specific questionnaires
Second Lebanon War, 74–75, 120
Seeking Safety, 420, 469, 470, 485
Seeman, T., 166
Sefl, T., 354
Segall, M.H., 309
selective serotonin reuptake inhibitors (SSRIs), 513, *514*, 517, 521
self-blame. *See* blame
Self Rating Inventory for PTSD (SRIP), 288, *291*, 292
self-report measures
  in assessing functional impairment, 324
  compared to other methods, 245
  reliability of, 317
  See also assessment of traumatic stress symptoms
Seligman, M.E.P., 416
Seligman, S., 387
Sense of Coherence (SOC) scale, 310
separation anxiety, in children posttrauma, 102
September 11 terrorist attacks
  ASD following, 75, 76, 77, 79, 120
  delayed-onset PTSD following, 110
  PTSD following, 79, 105–06, 160, 161, 251, 394
serotonin norepinephrine reuptake inhibitors (SNRIs), 513, 517, 521
sertraline, 434, 481, 513, *514*, 517, 521
severe mental illness
  comorbidity with PTSD, 129–30, 134–35, 421
  treatment of PTSD in, 135–36
sexual assault
  early intervention programs, 354–55, 371, 373, 374, 375
  gender differences in, 88–89
  in incarcerated individuals, 130
  reporting by older vs. younger women, 124
  response of older adults to, 124, 394
  risk of ASD from, 72, 77
  risk of PTSD from, 18–19, 22, 89, 93, 94, 124, 334
  self-blame in, 22

treatments for, 444
See also rape
Sexual Assault Nurse Examiner (SANE) programs, 349, 355
Seymour, M., 209
SF-36 (Medical Outcomes Study Short Form), 317, 318, *319*, 323, 324, 325
Shalev, A.Y., 30, 342, 357
Shapinsky, A.C., 241
Shapiro, F., 457, 459
Sharkansky, E., 335
Shaver, P.R., 224
Shaw, J.A., 106
Sheehan Disability Scale (SDS), *319*, *320*, 324, 325
"shell shock," 4, 6, 56, 87
See also military veterans
Shephard, B., 4
Sherman, M.D., 464, 465
Shin, L.M., 205
Shipherd, J.C., 204
Short Posttraumatic Stress Disorder Rating Interview (SPRINT), 296
Sijbrandij, M., 372
Silverman, W., 110
SIP. *See* Structured Interview for PTSD (SI-PTSD)
Skills for Psychological Recovery (SPR), 352, 356, 386–87
Smith, D.W., 19
Smith, K., 103
Smith, M., 305
Smith, P., 276, 485
Smith, R., 226, 237
Sobel, A.A., 443
Social Adjustment Scale-Self-Report (SAS-SR), *321*, 324
Social and Occupational Functioning Assessment Scale (SOFAS), 318, *319*
Social Attainment Scale (SAS), *321*, 324
Social Functioning Questionnaire (SFQ), *321*, 324
social support
impact on resilience, 229, 337
importance for older adults, 123, 399, 400
as risk factor for PTSD, 91, 94, 112, 123
role in trauma recovery and PTSD, 223–24, 229
socioeconomic status
and ASD risk, 75
See also risk and protective factors for PTSD
Sohnle, S., 496, 497
Solomon, Z., 220, 224
Somali refugees, 404, 409–10, 484
somatoform disorders, 46
Southwick, S.M., 163
SPAN, 293–94
Spangler, D.L., 497
Sparr, L., 496
Specialized Crisis Counseling Services (SCCS), 405
special populations
acute stress disorder in, 129
assessing trauma and PTSD in, 132–34, 135
defined, 128–29
developmental disabilities, 131, 132, 133, 135
extreme and multiple traumas faced by, 504–06
future research areas, 135–36, 410
prevention and early intervention strategies
across larger community, 406–07, 409–10
addressing immediate needs, 404–05, 408
bolstering family support, 405–06, 408
case example: refugee children, 407–10
future directions, 410
microsystem focus, 403–04
school settings, 406, 408–09
severe mental illness, 129–30, 132, 133, 134–35
substance use disorders in, 130, 133
treatments for trauma and PTSD, 133, 135–36
attention to emotion regulation in, 505–06
attention to ongoing stressors and threats, 506
cognitive and exposure therapies for, 505, 506
comorbid diagnoses in, 508
cultural considerations, 507–08
feelings of anger, 508–09
feelings of bereavement, 509
future research directions, 509–10
issues of trust in, 506–07
use of interpreters in, 508
See also children and adolescents; incarcerated individuals; non-Western cultures, PTSD assessment in; older adults; refugees
Speed, N., 122
Spinazzola, J., 310
Spirman, S., 385
Spiro, A., 336
Stafford, J., 201
STAIR (Skills Training in Affective and Interpersonal Regulation), 467–68, 505
Stallard, P., 107, 387
Stamm, B.H., 310
Stanford Acute Stress Reaction Questionnaire (SASRQ), 32, 253–54
Stanley, S.M., 221
startle. *See* psychophysiologic responses to stress
Steer, R.A., 107–08
Steil, R., 208
Stein, B.D., 355
Steinberg, A.M., 404
Stein, D., 459
Stoddard, F.J., 104
Strategic Approach Therapy (SAT), 464
stress inoculation training, 422
Stroop methodology, 204, 205, 207, 222
Structured Clinical Interview for *DSM-IV* (SCID). *See* SCID
structured diagnostic interviews
in assessing functional impairment, 323
compared with other methods, 245
as gold standard, 245
See also assessment of PTSD; assessment of traumatic stress symptoms; SCID; *specific structured interviews*
Structured Interview for PTSD (SI-PTSD, SIP), 237–38, *286*, 288
Structured Interview of Reported Symptoms (SIRS), 244–45
Strycker, L.A., 341
Suarez, E., 306
substance use/abuse
in ASD, 77
in incarcerated individuals, 130, 131
PTSD as contributor to, 90, 93, 134, 420
See also substance use disorders
substance use disorders
alcohol use disorder, 93
comorbidity with PTSD, 55, 130, 131, 222, 325, 420, 469
drug use disorder, 93
genetics of, 93
risk factors for, 130
treatment of PTSD in, 133, 135–36, 420, 469
suicidality
in BPD, 45
in older adults with PTSD, 122
in PTSD, 43, 94
Summerfield, D., 304, 305, 306
Sundin, E.C., 240–41
Surviving Cancer Competently Intervention Program (SCCIP), 485
Sutherland, K., 202
Suvak, M.K., 222
Sveen, J., 204–05
Symptom Checklist-90-R (SCL-90-R), 242
Szeimies, A.K., 210
Szor, H., 123

T

Tackenberg, A., 195
Taft, C.T., 222, 340
Tang, A., 311
Tang, C., 309, 310
Tarrier, N., 434, 467

Taylor, A.E., 22
Taylor, S., 46, 451–53
Tel Aviv Model, 385
Terno, P., 123
terrorist attacks. *See* September 11 terrorist attacks
Thomas, K., 459
Thompson, C., 293
Thorp, S.R., 495, 496
Tiesema, M., 418
Tolin, D.F., 22, 88, 468
torture survivors, 505, 507
Trauma-Focused Cognitive Behavioral Therapy (TF-CBT), 473–74, 478–79, 480–82, 484, 485, 486
Trauma Recovery and Empowerment model, 136
Trauma Screening Questionnaire (TSQ), 254, 348
  See also Child Trauma Screening Questionnaire (CTSQ)
Trauma Symptom Checklist (TSCC), 271, 294
Trauma Symptom Checklist for Children (TSCC), *269*, 271–72, 277
Trauma Symptom Checklist for Young Children (TSCYC), *269*, 271, 277
traumatic brain injury (TBI)
  comorbidity with PTSD, 46, 87, 421, 529
  depression associated with, 87, 421
  dissociation associated with, 33, 257
  in Iraq combatants, 87, 421
  as risk factor for ASD, 33, 76, 257–58
  as risk factor for PTSD, 33, 59, 87, 258
  symptom overlap with ASD, 257
  symptoms of, 76, 87, 257
Traumatic Events Questionnaire (TEQ), 244
traumatic grief. *See* complicated bereavement
traumatic stress disorders
  as new diagnostic category, 57, 64
  See also acute stress disorder (ASD); *DSM-5* (proposed revisions); posttraumatic stress disorder (PTSD)
trauma/traumatic events
  direct vs. indirect exposures, 15–16
  DSM-IV definition of, 3–4, 99
  future directions, 79–80
  lifetime risk of exposure to, 70, 94, 143, 363
  loss of resources in, 351, 404
  variables in type and classification, 99
  See also acute stress disorder (ASD); posttraumatic stress disorder (PTSD); posttraumatic stress responses; risk and protective factors for PTSD
treatment for PTSD
  future directions, 423–24, 470, 486–88, 509–10, 521–22, 529, 530
  group vs. individual, 419, 530
  overview, 6–7
  See also children and adolescents, treatment therapies; cognitive-behavioral therapy (CBT); Cognitive Processing Therapy (CPT); older adults; pharmacotherapy for PTSD; Prolonged Exposure (PE) therapy; psychological treatments; PTSD treatment research; special populations
Triandis, H.C., 305
triple vulnerability model, 46
Tucker, P.M., 294
Twentyman, C.T., 192
Type II trauma, 505

U
UCLA PTSD Index for *DSM-IV* (UPID), *270*, 272, 277
Uddin, M., 150

V
Valentine, J.D., 22
Van den Hout, M., 197, 202, 207, 208–09
Van der Kolk, B.A., 198, 203, 453
Van der Ploeg, H.M., 123
Van Minnen, A., 201, 203, 435
Van Zelst, W.H., 123
Vasterling, J.J., 202, 340
venlafaxine, 513
Verwoerd, J.R.L., 209
veterans. *See* military veterans
Vickers, K., 336
victimization
  polyvictimization, 108
  in severe mental illness, 129
Vietnam War veterans
  ASD studies, 71
  depression in, 92
  PTSD prevalence in, 19, 86, 89, 91, 92, 93, 94, 316–17
  PTSD studies in, 163, 168, 196, 204, 517
  readjustment difficulties, 339
  role of intelligence in response to adversity, 92
  startle responses in, 163
  treatments for PTSD, 517, 518
  See also National Vietnam Veterans Readjustment Study (NVVRS)
Vila, G., 220
violence. *See* physical assault; sexual assault
virtual reality exposure therapy, 466–67
Vogt, D., 343, 445
Vrana, S., 240

W
Wagner, A.W., 372
Wallot, F., 202
Walsh, F., 387
Warda, G., 207
"war neurosis," 4
War-Zone-Related PTSD Scale (WZ-PTSD), 242
Wasco, S.M., 354
Watson, J.B., 177, 182, 187
Weathers, F., 14, 59, 238, 242, 291, 295, 528
Wegner, D.M., 208
Weine, S., 408
Weiss, D.S., 240, 241
Weissman, M.M., 496
Wells, A., 208
Wessa, M., 195
Wessel, I., 201, 209
Wessely, S., 87
Westbrook, R.F., 432
Wetherell, J.L., 497
White, M., 207
WHO-Composite International Diagnostic Interview (WHO-CIDI), 85, *286*, 287–88, 310
WHO-Disability Assessment Scale-II (WHODAS-II), 310, 318, *319*, 323, 324, 325
WHO International Family of Classifications, 318
WHO-Quality of Life (WHO-QOL), 310
Widom, C.S., 109
Wiener, Z., 385
Willebrand, M., 204–05
Williams, C.S., 123
Williams, N.L., 210
Williams, R.H., 340
Wilner, N., 292
Wilson, J.P., 307, 308, 309, 310
Winston, F.K., 101, 103, 107
Witteveen, A.B., 288
Wolmer, L., 385
Woods, B., 496
Work Limitation Questionnaire (WLQ), *320*, 324
Work Productivity and Activity Impairment (WPAI), *320*, 324
World Assumption Scale, 206
World Health Organization. *See* WHO
World War I veterans, 56, 87
World War II veterans, 6, 56, 121–22, 338–39
"worst event" assessment method, 16–17, 85–86
Wright, M.O., 336

X
Xie, H., 421
Xie, P., 153

Y
Yamada, A.M., 306
Yarczower, M., 430
Yeager, D.E., 292
Yehuda, R., 152, 167–68
Young, E.A., 164

Z
Zanarini, M.C., 236
Zanotti, D.K., 464
Zatzick, D.F., 18
Zayfert, C., 420, 467
Zeanah, C.H., 264
Zimmerman, D.W., 340
Zinbarg, R., 431
Zinzow, H., 465
Zoellner, L.A., 373, 435